2

ENCYCLOPEDIA OF
TELEVISION SHOWS,
1925 THROUGH 2010

Second Edition / Three Volumes

ENCYCLOPEDIA OF TELEVISION SHOWS, 1925 THROUGH 2010

Second Edition

Vincent Terrace

VOLUME 2
Entries 3883–7597 (He–Q)

McFarland & Company, Inc., Publishers
Jefferson, North Carolina, and London

Volume 2

LIBRARY OF CONGRESS CATALOGUING-IN-PUBLICATION DATA

Terrace, Vincent, 1948–
Encyclopedia of television shows, 1925
through 2010 / Vincent Terrace. — 2nd ed.
p.   cm.
Includes index.

3 volume set —
ISBN 978-0-7864-6477-7
softcover : 50# alkaline paper ∞

1. Television programs — United States — Catalogs.   I. Title.
PN1992.3.U5T463 2011   791.45'750973 — dc23   2011030517

BRITISH LIBRARY CATALOGUING DATA ARE AVAILABLE

Front cover image © 2011 Shutterstock.

Manufactured in the United States of America

*McFarland & Company, Inc., Publishers
Box 611, Jefferson, North Carolina 28640
www.mcfarlandpub.com*

Table of Contents

3883   *He and She.* (Series; Comedy; CBS; 1967–1968). Richard Hollister is a cartoonist and the creator of the comic strip turned television series *Jetman*. Paula is his beautiful wife, an employee for the Manhattan Tourist Aid Society (she has a heart of gold and can't resist helping people in trouble). They live in an apartment at 365 East 84th Street in Manhattan. Their side living room window faces the side of the local firehouse (station number 26). Fireman Harry Zarakardos has placed a plank from their window to the fire station window to provide easy access to both buildings.

Oscar North is the egotistical star of *Jetman* (a superhero with a jet-shaped helmet and two jets on the back of his vest for flying). Andrew Humble is the not-so-handy apartment house handyman. Stories follow events in Richard and Paula's life, especially those in which she involves herself in the problems of others. Jerry Fielding composed the "He and She" theme.

Cast: Richard Benjamin *(Richard Hollister)*; Paula Prentiss *(Paula Hollister)*; Jack Cassidy *(Oscar North)*; Hamilton Camp *(Andrew Humble)*; Kenneth Mars *(Harry Zarakardos)*; Harold Gould *(Norman Nugent)*; Alan Oppenheimer *(Murray Mouse)*.

3884   *He-Man and the Masters of the Universe.* (Series; Cartoon; Syn; 1983). He-Man is the protector of the Castle Grayskull. He is in reality Prince Adam, the son of King Randor and Queen Marlena, the rulers of the planet Eternia. Adam has a twin sister, Adora, who battles the evils of the Horde (see *She-Ra: Princess of Power*). The Sorceress of Castle Grayskull has given Adam special powers and his weapon, the Sword of Grayskull, to defend the castle from the evil Skeletor. When Adam holds the sword and says, "By the power of Grayskull, I have the power," he is transformed into He-Man (his tiger, whom he rides, Cringer, becomes the mighty Battle Cat). Castle Grayskull resembles a large skull and is the source of He-Man's powers. Skeletor, an evil sorcerer "from another dimension," has blue skin with a skull for a head. He operates from Snake Mountain and the Havoc Staff is his weapon of choice. Stories relate He-Man's battles against the evil Skeletor, who seeks the powers of Castle Grayskull. See also the following title and *The New Adventures of He-Man*. Two versions appeared.

Voice Cast: John Erwin *(He-Man)*; Alan Oppenheimer *(Skeletor)*; Linda Gary *(Teela/Queen Marlena/Sorceress)*; Lou Scheimer *(Modulok)*; Alan Oppenheimer *(Buzz-Off/Mer-Man/Roboto)*.

3885   *He-Man and the Masters of the Universe.* (Series; Cartoon; Cartoon Network; 2002). A revised version of the prior title that finds Prince Adam, the son of King Randor and Queen Marlena, secretly defending the Castle Grayskull from the evil Skeletor as He-Man, a mighty warrior. Skeletor is seeking the repository of universal knowledge that is hidden deep within the recesses of Castle Grayskull. He-Man and his assistants, the Masters of the Universe, risk their lives to protect the castle and their home planet, Eternia, from Skeletor's evil warriors. See also *The New Adventures of He-Man*.

Voice Cast: Cam Clarke *(He-Man)*; Lisa Ann Beley *(Teela)*; Kathleen Barr *(Evil-Lyn)*; Michael Donovan *(King Randor)*; Nicole Oliver *(Queen Marlena)*; Nicole Oliver *(Castle Grayskull Sorceress)*; Paul Dobson *(Man-E-Faces)*; Paul Dobson *(Snake Face)*; Paul Dobson *(Trap Jaw)*; Paul Dobson *(Tri-Klops)*; Scott McNeil *(Beast Man)*; Scott McNeil *(Mer0Man)*; Scott McNeil *(Ram Man)*; Scott McNeil *(Kobra)*.

3886   *He Said, She Said.* (Series; Game; Syn.; 1969). Four celebrity couples compete, playing for selected members of the studio audience. The husbands are on camera and the wives are isolated backstage in a soundproof room. The husbands have to state a personal association that will hopefully trigger a response from the in-dividual's wife, to recognize it as what "He Said." The wives are aired and seen through four monitors that are built into the set and placed before their mates. The topic is stated and one answer is revealed. The first wife to sound a buzzer signal receives a chance to answer. If she matches the response her husband gave, she receives points. Round two is played in the same manner; rounds three and four are played in reverse (he has to recognize what "She Said"). The highest scoring team wins $250 and a seven-day vacation at a Holiday Inn.

Program Open: "This is Tin Pan Alley's Dick Clark and his wife Loretta Clark. This is show business star Peter Lind Hayes and his wife, who glows by her own light, Mary Healy. This is tuneful Peter Duchin and his wife Cheri Duchin. This is TV's best cross-examiner, Bill Cullen and his wife, Anne Cullen. These four celebrity couples are here top play *He Said, She Said*. And now here is the star of *He Said, She Said*, Joe Garagiola."

Host: Joe Garagiola. **Announcer:** Johnny Olson.

3887   *The Head.* (Series; Cartoon; MTV; 1997). Gork is an evil extraterrestrial who plans to conquer the Earth. A good alien (the blue-skinned Roy) wants to stop Gork, but his life form is not adaptable (in its present state) to life on Earth. To solve his problem, Roy takes up residence in the head of Jim, a student whose head suddenly grows to an enormous size. A week later Roy emerges from Jim's head; he is now able to breathe on Earth (although he still must use Jim's head to live). Roy explains why he has chosen Jim and the two become partners in a quest to stop Gork. However, they are not able to battle the enemy alone and recruit others to help. They are: Madelyn, Jim's girlfriend; Jim's doctor, Richard Axe (both of whom have aliens residing in their heads); and aliens Mona (who has a tail); Ivan (has a mouth in his chest); Raquel (has the nose of a rat); Chin (former freak show performer); Earl (has a fishbowl in his mouth) and Shane Blackman, the only member of the group with a normal head.

Voices: Maia Danziger, Dick Rodstein, Eric Fogel, Chris Johnston, Melanie Holtzman, Tad Hills, Mike Judge, Jason Candler, Patricia Bibby.

3888   *Head Case.* (Series; Comedy; Starz; 2008). Spoof of psychiatry-based television shows in which Dr. Elizabeth Goode, a therapist who dispenses judgmental advice to her patients — actual Hollywood celebrities (who appear with scripted problems).

Cast: Alexandra Wentworth *(Dr. Elizabeth Goode)*; Sally Kirkland *(Elizabeth's mother)*; Sam McMurray *(Elizabeth's father)*; Michelle Arthur *(Lola Buckingham)*; Steve Landesberg *(Dr. Myron Finkelstein)*; Rob Benedict *(Jeremy Berger)*.

3889   *Head Cases.* (Series; Crime Drama; Fox; 2005). Jason Payne is a brilliant criminal attorney with a prestigious law firm whose cases finally get the best of him and he suffers a nervous breakdown. Russell Shultz is a somewhat unorthodox lawyer (an ambulance chaser) with an anger management problem. Fate unites the two men when Russell is assigned to be Jason's outpatient buddy. Jason, who is unable to face the pressures of a corporate law firm, begins his own practice with Russell as his assistant. Jason feels his breakdown and his being institutionalized in a mental hospital has given him a great gift — the ability to get into the mind of a criminal. Stories relate the rather unusual methods Jason and Russell use to defend clients.

Cast: Chris O'Donnell *(Jason Payne)*; Adam Goldberg *(Russell Shultz)*; Richard Kind *(Lou Albertini)*; Krista Allen *(Laurie Payne)*; Rhea Seehorn *(Nicole Walker)*; Rockmond Dunbar *(Dr. Robinson)*; Jake Cherry *(Ryan Payne)*.

3890 *Head Games.* (Series; Game; Science Channel; 2009). Questions based on scientific principals are posed to contestants, who range from genius to ordinary people interested in science. The program is billed as "the Science Channel's first ever trivia series" and combines humor with fascinating facts to challenge the intellect of the players and enlighten viewers with facts about science.

Host: Greg Proops. **Voice Overs:** Christopher Magnum.

3891 *Head of the Class.* (Pilot; Game; NBC; June 24, 1960). Four contestants compete. Each correct answer to a question moves a player one space on a large board. When a player reaches the finish line he attempts to keep his position as head of the class by answering questions based on comedy sketches or musical numbers. An incorrect response defeats a player and he loses his position as head of the class.

Host: Gene Rayburn. **Regulars:** Marilyn Lovell, The Noteworthies. **Music:** Elliot Lawrence.

3892 *Head of the Class.* (Series; Comedy; ABC; 1986–1991). Life at New York's Fillmore High School as seen through the eyes of I.H.P. (Individual Honors Program) history teachers Charles ("Charlie") Moore (1986–90) and William ("Billy") MacGregor (1990-91).

Charlie was born in Idaho and attended Weesur High School and Idaho State College. Before becoming a teacher, Charlie came to New York to direct Broadway, but it never happened. He began as a substitute teacher at Fillmore and became a faculty member when the previous I.H.P. teacher left. Charlie appeared in television commercials as "The King of Discount Appliances" for Veemer Appliances and left Fillmore to become an actor when he accepted the lead in the road company production of *Death of a Salesman*.

Billy is from Glasgow, Scotland, and attended Oxford University in England and has a second job at the Mother Hubbard Day Care Center. He has a comical approach to teaching and interweaves his life experiences with his lessons. See *Billy*, the spin off series.

Bernadette Meara is the attractive vice principal. She is from North Carolina and came to New York in 1974 to take the job she now has. Dr. Harold Samuels is the principal. He proposed the I.H.P. to the school board as a means of letting students monitor their own studies.

Simone Foster is the prettiest girl in the Honors Program. She is sweet, shy and very sensitive and has been a straight "A" student all her life. Her greatest gift is her romantic vision of life. Simone's specialty is English, and her spare time is occupied by charity work. Darlene Merriman is from a wealthy family and lives on Park Avenue. Her specialty is speech and debate, and she believes she is extremely attractive to men: "I represent the physical and intellectual ideals men want." She is also editor of the school newspaper, the Fillmore *Spartan*.

Sarah Nevins is president of the Student Council and works after school at City General Hospital. Maria Borges is dedicated to learning. If she gets a B, she grounds herself ("It's the only way I can learn"). Her greatest gift is her understanding of the human condition. She left after three years to further her singing career at the High School of the Performing Arts.

Arvid Engen is a math major and has a perfect attendance record. He has not missed one day of school since he first started — nothing has stopped him—"not subway strikes, blizzards, hurricanes or illness." Dennis Clarence Blunden is the practical joker of the group. He is skilled in chemistry and physics and has been sent to the principal's office more times than any other student. Eric Mardian is the son of an alcoholic father. When he was four, his father read *Treasure Island* aloud to him; one year later, Eric read it back to him. Janice Lazarotto is gifted in all areas of study and has a photographic memory. She is a child genius and left the I.H.P. after three years to attend Harvard.

Alan Pinkard is a member of the Young Americans for Freedom and has set his goal as that of becoming president of the United States. He is gifted in the natural sciences. Viki Amory is adopted and has a knack for falling in love with her teachers: "It's something I can't control. It comes, poof; it goes, poof." Jawaharlal Choudhury is gifted in the political sciences (he left after three years when his family moved to California to take advantage of a business opportunity). T.J. Jones calls Billy "Mr. Bill" and has a beautiful singing voice. Jasper Quincy speaks five languages. Aristotle MacKenzie and Alex Torres are the remaining students.

Cast: Howard Hesseman (*Charlie Moore*); Billy Connolly (*Billy MacGregor*); Jeannetta Arnette (*Bernadette Meara*); William G. Schilling (*Harold Samuels*); Khrystyne Haje (*Simone Foster*); Robin Givens (*Darlene Merriman*); Kimberly Russell (*Sarah Nevins*); Leslie Bega (*Maria Borges*); Dan Frischman (*Arvid Engen*); Dan Schneider (*Dennis Blunden*); Brian Robbins (*Eric Mardian*); Tannis Vallely (*Janice Lazarotto*); Tony O'Dell (*Alan Pinkard*); Lara Piper (*Viki Amory*); Jory Husain (*Jawaharlal Choudhury*) De'voreaux White (*Aristotle*); Michael DeLorenzo (*Alex*).

3893 *Head of the Family.* (Pilot; Comedy; CBS; July 19, 1960). The life of television writer Rob Petrie. Rob, Sally Rogers and Buddy Sorrell write the variety series *The Alan Sturdy Show*. Laura, Rob's wife, plays baseball with their six-year-old son, Richie, on Sundays because Rob doesn't have the time — it is the day on which his show airs live. With a new title, a total change in cast and a struggling first season, the premise went on to become the now classic *Dick Van Dyke Show*.

Cast: Carl Reiner (*Rob Petrie*); Barbara Britton (*Laura Petrie*); Gary Morgan (*Richie Petrie*); Morty Gunty (*Buddy Sorrell*); Sylvia Miles (*Sally Rogers*); Jack Wakefield (*Alan Sturdy*).

3894 *Head Over Heels.* (Series; Comedy; UPN; 1997-1998). Head Over Heels is a Miami-based dating service owned by brothers Jack and Warren Baldwin. As a kid Warren watched *The Dating Game* (Jim Lange, the host, was his hero) and because of that show, he went into the dating business. His dream is to become a TV game show host. Warren and Jack attended Lincoln High School. Warren is straight laced and all business; he hopes to find true love for his clients. Jack, the footloose younger brother, is a playboy and sees the agency as a means by which to meet beautiful women. Jack, an Elvis fan, has a VIP card at his favorite strip club, the Booty Bar, and has a crush on Carmen Montalvo, the agency's pretty office manager. Carmen, who likes picnics and mambo music, is studying to become a psychologist. She detests Jack's advances and longs for Warren to notice her. Valentina, the receptionist, was a former stripper at the Booty Bar. Her favorite pastime is shopping at the South Beach Fashion Mall. Jack and Warren have drinks at the Banana Bar.

Cast: Peter Dobson (*Jack Baldwin*); Mitchell Whitfield (*Warren Baldwin*); Cindy Ambuehl (*Valentina*); Eva LaRue (*Carmen Montalvo*).

3895 *Headline Chasers.* (Series; Game; Syn.; 1985-1986). Two couples are situated in a set that resembles a newspaper's city room. A newspaper headline is revealed with most of its letters missing. The headline is worth $500 but decreases in value with each letter that is revealed to complete the headline. The first couple to identify the headline wins the money value at the time. Round two increases the money value — which begins at $1,000 and decreases to a minimum of $200.

Host: Wink Martindale. **Announcer:** Johnny Gilbert.

3896 *Headliners with David Frost.* (Series; Interview; NBC; 1978). Live and videotaped interviews with "people who are making the news."

Host: David Frost. **Regulars:** Kelly Garrett, Liz Smith. **Music:** Elliot Lawrence.

3897   *Headmaster.* (Series; Comedy-Drama; CBS; 1971). A tender portrayal of student-teacher relationships and their problems, both scholastic and personal, as seen through the eyes of Andy Thompson, the caring, sensitive headmaster of Concord, a small, private coeducational school in California. Margaret Thompson is Andy's wife; Jerry Brownell is the coach; Mr. Purdy is the custodian; Judy is Andy's student helper. Linda Ronstadt performs the theme, "He's Only a Man."
  Cast: Andy Griffith *(Andy Thompson)*; Claudette Nevins *(Margaret Thompson)*; Lani O'Grady *(Judy)*; Jerry Van Dyke *(Jerry Brownell)*; Parker Fennelly *(Mr. Purdy)*.

3898   *The Healers.* (Pilot; Drama; NBC; May 22, 1974). The work of Dr. Robert Kier, the director of the Institute for Medical Research in California. Other regulars are Joe Tate, the financial director; Laura, Robert's ex-wife; Nikki and Vince, Robert's children; Barbara, Robert's secretary; and Claire, a doctor.
  Cast: John Forsythe *(Robert Kier)*; Pat Harrington, Jr. *(Joe Tate)*; Kate Woodville *(Claire)*; Beverly Garland *(Laura Kier)*; Shelly Juttner *(Nikki Kier)*; Christian Juttner *(Vince Kier)*; Ellen Weston *(Barbara)*.

3899   *Hear No Evil.* (Pilot; Crime Drama; CBS; Nov. 10, 1982). Fearing that Bill Dragon, a detective with the San Francisco Police Department, is coming too close to uncovering their illegal drug dealing operations, members of the Bay Riders (a motorcycle gang) rig Dragon's car with explosives. The ensuing explosion injures Dragon and disables him when he loses his hearing. With the aid of a speech therapist (Meg) and a "hearing dog" (Bozo), Bill adjusts and the proposed series was to relate the cases of a deaf police detective. Other regulars are Inspector Monday, Bill's partner; Lieutenant Lew Haley, their superior.
  Cast: Gil Gerard *(Bill Dragon)*; Bernie Casey *(Inspector Monday)*; Mimi Rogers *(Meg)*; Ron Karabatsos *(Lew Haley)*.

3900   *Heart and Soul.* (Pilot; Comedy; NBC; July 21, 1988). A comical look at the recording industry as seen through the misadventures of Curtis and Richard, young executives with Unisound Records. Other regulars are Jeff, the mailroom boy; Dawnelle, a recording artist; and Helen, the secretary. Morris Day performs the theme. "Are You Ready?"
  Cast: Morris Day *(Curtis Rousseau)*; Clark Johnson *(Richard Bradley)*; Tisha Campbell *(Jamie Sinclair)*; Barry Sobel *(Jeff)*; Arnetia Walker *(Dawnelle Washington)*; Marge Redmond *(Helen Dewey)*; James Avery *(Harlan Sinclair)*.

3901   *Heart and Soul.* (Pilot; Comedy; ABC; April 30, 1989). Philadelphia in 1961 is the setting for a proposal about Brenda Kincaid and Wesley Harris, aspiring singer-songwriters who are also lovers. Other regulars are Brenda's parents, Jean and Cecil; Wesley's mother, Tonia; and Wesley's brother, Buzzy.
  Cast: Renee Jones *(Brenda Kincaid)*; B'Nard Lewis *(Wesley Harris)*; Denise Nicholas *(Jean Kincaid)*; Jason Bernard *(Cecil Kincaid)*; Loretta Devine *(Tonia Harris)*; Shavar Ross *(Buzzy Harris)*.

3902   *Heart Beat.* (Pilot; Drama; NBC; Aug. 14, 1985). Carla, a tough New York–born street dancer; Erin, a free spirit and the insecure Monica (a friend from Kansas City) are dancers determined to pursue their dreams of show business careers. The program combines music and video sequences to relate their struggles. Antonia is Carla's sister; Kevin is their manager.

Cast: Karen Kopins *(Erin)*; Whitney Kershaw *(Monica)*; Christine Langer *(Carla)*; Michael Sabatino *(Kevin)*; Bernice Massi *(Antonia)*.

3903   *Heart Beat.* (Series; Drama; ABC; 1988-1989). The personal and professional lives of the doctors of the Women's Medical Arts Center, a progressive practice that treats the patient as well as the disease. The series is later set (1989) at Bay General Hospital.
  1988 Cast: Kate Mulgrew *(Dr. Joanne Springsteen)*; Laura Johnson *(Dr. Eve Autry)*; Lynn Whitfield *(Dr. Cory Banks)*; Gail Strickland *(Dr. Marilyn McGrath)*; Ben Morris *(Dr. Leo Rosetti)*; Ray Baker *(Dr. Stan Gorshalk)*; Darrell Larson *(Dr. Paul Jared)*; Claudette Sutherland *(Nurse Robin Flowers)*; Hallie Todd *(Allison, Marilyn's daughter)*; Gina Hecht *(Patty, Marilyn's lover)*; Julie Cobb *(Beverly Rosetti, Leo's wife)*; Michael Faustino *(Nicky Rosetti, Leo's son)*.
  1989 Cast: Kate Mulgrew *(Dr. Joanne Halloran)*; Laura Johnson *(Dr. Eve Calvert)*; Lynn Whitfield *(Dr. Cory Banks)*; Julie Ronnie *(Nurse Alice Swanson)*; Carmen Argenziano *(Dr. Nathan Solt)*; Robert Gossett *(Dixon Banks, Cory's husband)*; Amy Moore Davis *(Donna Calvert, Eve's niece)*.

3904   *Heart of the City.* (Series; Crime Drama; ABC; 1986-1987). Wes Kennedy is a detective with the Los Angeles Police Department. He is a widower and the father of two children, Robin and Kevin. Wes solves 24 percent of his case load, which is 10 percent higher than the rate of other cops in the precinct. He became a cop "To get the animals off the streets. It's what I do, it's what has to be done." Wes has a photographic memory and an impressive arrest record but too many shootings. He lives at 5503 Pacific Way and is dating Kathy Priester, a waitress at a diner called Trio's Grill.
  Robin, 16 years old, and Kevin, 15, attend West Hollywood High School. Robin changed from a sweet and innocent girl to a radical girl with an attitude when she felt she needed to change her girl next door image. Kevin is studious and confused by girls (he doesn't know what to make of them and thinks they prefer muscles, not brains).
  Ed Van Duzer is Wes's superior, the watch commander. Sergeant Halui is the Hawaiian-by-birth cop who calls everyone Brother. Stories follow Wes as he struggles to do his job and be a father to Robin and Kevin.
  Cast: Robert Desiderio *(Wes Kennedy)*; Christina Applegate *(Robin Kennedy)*; Jonathan Ward *(Kevin Kennedy)*; Dick Anthony Williams *(Ed Van Duzer)*; Branscombe Richmond *(Sgt. Halui)*.

3905   *Heartland.* (Series; Comedy; CBS; 1989). The McCutcheon Ranch is a 350-acre farm in Pritchard, Nebraska. B.L. McCutcheon owns the ranch and runs it with his son, Tom, Tom's wife, Cassandra, and their children, Kim, Johnny and Gus. B.L. is "a cantankerous old coot" who is set in his ways and has an opinion about everything. He is a widower and had three dogs: Chester, General Patton and Silky. His favorite recording artist is Elmo Tanner, the World's Greatest Whistler; he enjoys relaxing in the chair on the front porch of his home.
  Tom and Cassandra, whom Tom calls "Casey," have been married for 15 years. Johnny and Gus are their biological children; Kim is adopted. The kids attend Pritchard High School; Kim is a talented violinist who hopes one day to play with the New York Philharmonic Orchestra; Johnny longs for a life away from the farm in a big city; Gus is content with farm life and has a pet pig named Dolly. Dion sings the theme, "Heartland."
  Cast: Brian Keith *(B.L. McCutcheon)*; Richard Gilliland *(Tom McCutcheon)*; Kathleen Layman *(Cassandra McCutcheon)*; Daisy Keith *(Kim McCutcheon)*; Jason Kristopher *(Johnny McCutcheon)*.

3906   *Heartland.* (Series; Drama; TNT; 2007). Nathaniel Grant is a lung and heart transplant surgeon at the St. Jude Regional Transplant Center in Pittsburgh. He is television's first such doctor and he has also been given an extra special gift — the ability to see the donor (who sometimes speaks) as he prepares to operate on the organ recipient. Kate Armstrong, Nathaniel's ex-wife, works with him as the organ donor coordinator; they have a teenage daughter named Thea. Nathaniel is a workaholic and appears to have a hobby (collecting baseball cards) and would also like a cigarette on occasion, but someone always prevents him from lighting up. Nathaniel rarely has time for himself, is rather pushy and seems to work well with Kate. Stories relate Nathaniel's experiences with the people in need of transplants — as well as those who died to save others. Mary Singletary is the head ICU nurse; Jessica Kivala is a surgical nurse; Chris William Martin is a transplant surgeon; Bart Jacobs is Nathaniel's boss.

Cast: Treat Williams (*Dr. Nathaniel Grant*); Kari Matchett (*Kate Armstrong*); Gage Golightly (*Thea Grant*); Simon Griffith (*Dr. Chris William Martin*); Danielle Nicolet (*Nurse Mary Singletary*); Morena Baccarin (*Nurse Jessica Kivala*); Rockmond Dunbar (*Dr. Thomas Jonas*); Dabney Coleman (*Bart Jacobs*).

3907   *Hearts Afire.* (Series; Comedy; CBS; 1992–1994). Georgie Ann Lahti is a liberal journalist. She wrote questions for *Jeopardy* and an episode of *Rhoda*. She worked for the *Chicago Tribune* then the *Chicago Post*. She left the *Post* to write the book *My Year with Fidel* (she had an affair with Castro and thought it should be told). When that failed, she went to work as "a cultural liaison in Paris" ("I worked at Euro Disney helping people on and off the teacup ride"). She then moved to Georgetown and found a job as speechwriter for Strobe Smithers, a senile, conservative senator. When John Hartman, Strobe's senatorial aide, learns that Georgie is broke, he offers to let her stay at his spacious home (1184 Arlington Drive). John is divorced (from Diandra, who left him for another woman) and the father of Ben and Eliot.

Georgie has done outrageous things ("I ran around the Trevi Fountain in Rome in my bra and panties") and when she took the SAT test, she was singled out for writing the longest answers ever given on a multiple choice test ("I wasn't satisfied with E — none of the above").

As stories followed John and Georgie's working relationship in the political arena, love developed as did a marriage. The story line also changed: they moved to Clay County, John's hometown, to find a better family life. Here, John, Georgie and their friend, Billy Bob Davis, take over the weekly newspaper, the *Courier* with John as the editor, Georgie the reporter, and Billy Bob, the society editor. Madeline Sossinger, a psychologist who rents space in the paper's building, writes the advice column, "Dear Madeline."

In final-season episodes, the paper's name is changed to the *Daily Beacon*. At this time, Georgie gives birth to a girl she and John name Amelia Rose.

Strobe has been married to Mary Fran for 30 years. She was born in Sparta, Georgia, and took the beauty pageant route to get out of town. She won the Miss Tennessee and the Miss USA crown. Strobe met her when he was a beauty contest judge. She sang "As Time Goes By" and he could see no one but her. Mary Fran wants Strobe to retire so she can take his seat in the Senate ("It's my turn now after putting up with him for 30 years"). If Strobe doesn't quit, Mary Fran is threatening to air their dirty laundry in public. Dee Dee Star is the office receptionist and carries on a secret affair with Strobe. She believes other women feel threatened by her good looks. To show them that she is as intelligent as she is beautiful, she began a business called "Mail Order Bikini Bra and Panties." Mavis Davis, the office secretary, is married to Billy Bob (John's assistant). She believes Dee Dee is "the last bimbo on the hill" and left Billy Bob (when the series switched locales) to get her Masters Degree at NYU. Their daughter, Carson Lee lives with Billy Bob. Miss Lula has cared for Georgie since she was three years old (her mother died shortly after her birth).

Georgie's father, George Lahti, is a disbarred attorney. He is staying with John and works as the housekeeper (first season episodes). To pay for her father's legal fees, Georgie wrote several romance novels: *Flamingo Summer*, *Naked Spring* and *Lust Beyond Tomorrow* (all under the pen name Dusty Silver).

Cast: Markie Post (*Georgie Ann Lahti*); John Ritter (*John Hartman*); George Gaynes (*Strobe Smithers*); Mary Ann Mobley (*Mary Fran Smithers*); Billy Bob Thornton (*Billy Bob Davis*); Beth Broderick (*Dee Dee Star*); Wendie Jo Sperber (*Mavis Davis*); Beah Richards (*Miss Lula*); Edward Asner (*George Lahti*); Justin Burnette (*Ben Hartman*); Clark Duke (*Eliot Hartman*).

3908   *Hearts Are Wild.* (Series; Drama; CBS; 1992). Rooms start at $90 a day and businesses pay an average of $7,000 a month rent. The place is Caesar's Palace Hotel and Casino in Las Vegas and the efforts of 36-year-old Jack Thorpe to run it is the focal point of stories. Kyle is the head of guest relations; Pepe is Jack's right hand man; and Caroline is Jack's mother.

Cast: David Beecroft (*Jack Thorpe*); Catherine Mary Stewart (*Kyle Hubbard*); Jon Polito (*Leon "Pepe" Pepperman*); Barbara Rush (*Caroline Thorpe*).

3909   *Heart's Island.* (Pilot; Comedy; NBC; Aug. 31, 1985). Shreveport, Louisiana, in 1952 is the setting. Johnnie Baylor is a hard-working single mother (a widow) with many problems who lives at 411 Leo Drive in the Town of Heart's Island. She works as a cocktail waitress at the Blue Moon Cafe and runs a dressmaking business with her best friend, Mattie (who lives with her and helps her care for her children, Tammy Jean and Buster). The proposal was to relate Johnnie's struggles as she attempts to provide a decent life for her children, especially Tammy Jean, who has polio. Other regulars are Clay, Johnnie's boarder; Sarge, the Blue Moon bartender; and Patsy, a waitress at the Blue Moon. Rosemary June performs the theme, "Everything We Need Is Here."

Cast: Dorothy Lyman (*Johnnie Baylor*); Sydney Penny (*Tammy Jean Baylor*); Christopher Burton (*Buster Baylor*); Clarice Taylor (*Mattie*); Gary Sandy (*Clay Tanner*); Court Miller (*Sarge*); Donna Bullock (*Patsy*).

3910   *Hearts of Steel.* (Pilot; Comedy; ABC; June 13, 1986). When Annie's partner backs out of a deal to turn her bar into a restaurant, a group of her patrons, laid-off steel workers (Eddie, Tom, Jake and Granville), pool their resources to help her open a restaurant in Pennsylvania. The proposal was to relate the group's efforts to make a success of the business. Michelle is their chef.

Cast: Annie Potts (*Annie*); Tracy Nelson (*Michelle*); Matt Craven (*Eddie*); Gregory Salata (*Tom*); Kevin Scannell (*Jake*); Harold Sylvester (*Granville*).

3911   *The Heat.* (Pilot; Crime Drama; CBS; Aug. 8, 1989). Charley Wayne, Rafe Morea, Emory Hacker, Whip St. John and Eli Saxon are federal marshals known as "The Heat." The proposal was to relate their investigations into extremely volatile situations.

Cast: William Campbell (*Charley Wayne*); David Ciminello (*Rafe Morea*); Bobby Hosea (*Emory Hacker*); Scott Kraft (*Whip St. John*); Stephen Shellen (*Eli Saxon*).

3912   *Heat of Anger.* (Pilot; Crime Drama; CBS; Mar. 3, 1972). Jessica Fitzgerald is a prominent Los Angeles attorney. Gus Pride is her young, ambitious, eager to battle injustice associate. Together they operate Fitzgerald and Pride, Attorneys-at-Law and the proposal was to relate their case investigations. Barbara Stanwyck was originally cast as Jessica but was replaced due to illness at the time.

Cast: Susan Hayward (*Jessica Fitzgerald*); James Stacy (*Gus Pride*).

3913   The Heathcliff and Dingbat Show. (Series; Cartoon; ABC; 1980-1981). The overall title for two cartoon segments. The first segment, *Heathcliff*, relates the antics of a very mischievous cat who delights in annoying others. *Dingbat and the Creeps*, the second segment, tells of Dingbat, a vampire dog, Bone Head, a skeleton, and Nobody, a pumpkin, as they attempt to help people in trouble.

Voices: Mel Blanc (*Heathcliff*); Frank Welker (*Dingbat*), Julie McWhirter, Marilyn Schreffler, Michael Bell, Melendy Britt, Rachel Blake, Henry Corden, Joan Van Ark, Joe Baker, Alan Oppenheimer, Shep Menkin.

3914   The Heathcliff and Marmaduke Show. (Series; Cartoon; ABC; 1981-1982). The overall title for two cartoon series: *Heathcliff* and *Marmaduke*. The *Heathcliff* segment follows the misadventures of a very mischievous alley cat. *Marmaduke* relates the antics of a loveable but mischievous Great Dane.

Voice Cast: Mel Blanc (*Heathcliff*); Marilyn Schreffler (*Sonia; his girlfriend*); Mel Blanc (*Spike, the Bulldog*); Don Messick (*Marmaduke*); Paul Winchell (*Father; Marmaduke's owner*); Russi Taylor (*Mother*); Marilyn Schreffler (*Barbie, their daughter*).

3915   Heave Ho Harrigan. (Pilot; Comedy; NBC; Sept. 22, 1961). "Heave Ho" Harrigan is a Navy flagman stationed on an aircraft carrier. The proposal follows Harrigan's antics as he attempts to carry out special assignments for his captain (Towers). Ensign Smithers is his friend.

Cast: Myron McCormick (*Heave Ho Harrigan*); Allyn Joslyn (*Captain Towers*); Darryl Hickman (*Ensign Smithers*).

3916   Heaven for Betsy. (Series; Comedy; CBS; 1952). "Being married to Peter is heaven for Betsy" says an unidentified announcer after an episode's opening teaser. Betsy is a former secretary who is now married to Peter Bell, "an underpaid, underappreciated, overworked cog in the Willmot Department Store." Peter is timid and shy and easily taken advantage of; Betsy is strong and forceful and gives Peter the courage he needs to face obstacles.

Peter and Betsy are newlyweds and reside at 136 Oak Tree Lane in New York. Peter earns $42.50 a week as an apprentice executive to Mr. Willmot, but "do you realize the services I've been performing that are not even part of my job? I'm a combination salesman, floor walker, buyer, accountant, working store detective, complaint bureau and errand boy." Peter's haphazard attempts to make his boss, Alonzo Willmot, realize his worth paid off in one episode when Peter received a ten dollar raise.

Program Open: "*Heaven for Betsy* stars Jack Lemmon and Cynthia Stone and is brought to you by Pepsodent toothpaste. And now *Heaven for Betsy*."

Cast: Jack Lemmon (*Peter Bell*); Cynthia Stone (*Betsy Bell*); Cliff Hall (*Alonzo Willmot*).

3917   Heaven Help Us. (Pilot; Comedy; CBS; Aug. 14, 1967). Dick Cameron is a magazine editor whose life is complicated not only by his work, but by the spirit of his late wife, Marge, who has come back to earth to find him a new mate. The proposed series was to relate Dick's misadventures as Marge plays matchmaker. Other regulars are Mildred, Dick's housekeeper; and Mr. Walker, Dick's publisher.

Cast: Barry Nelson (*Dick Cameron*); Joanna Moore (*Marge Cameron*); Mary Grace Canfield (*Mildred*); Bert Freed (*Mr. Walker*).

3918   Heaven Help Us. (Series; Drama; Syn.; 1994-1995). Doug Monroe, a baseball player, and Lexy Kitteridge, the daughter of rich parents, marry. While en-route to their honeymoon hideaway, the plane Doug is flying, develops engine trouble and crashes into a skyscraper.

When first seen by viewers Doug and Lexy appear fine and are in a large room. Here they meet a mysterious man named Mr. Shepherd (an angel) who tells them they were killed in that plane crash but are in a state of limbo — "We are not sure which way you are going yet." They are then transported to the nerve center of Greenwich Meantime where all time is kept — "It starts here and ends here. It was decided to add a second to the clock this year (1994). Something to do with a change in the Earth's orbit." It was precisely at that change that Doug and Lexy's plane crashed (they weren't covered and slipped through the cracks). Doug and Lexy were flying from Houston to Scotsdale — but "the Seers goofed" and nobody was watching them. Because of Mr. Shepherd's inability to assign them to Heaven or Hell, he gives them a choice to make their own destiny by seeing how well they help people in trouble. Doug and Lexy are assigned an apartment in the non-existent 13th floor of the Marriott Hotel in which they crashed (the floor exists only for them). Doug and Lexy remain invisible if they remain pure of heart; if they get angry, they can be seen by others. Stories follow Doug and Lexy as they try to remain pure of heart and invisible as they help people to earn their wings.

Cast: Ricardo Montalban (*Mr. Shepherd*); John Schneider (*Doug Monroe*); Melinda Clarke (*Lexy Monroe*); Efrem Zimbalist, Jr. (*Martin Kitteridge, Lexy's father*); Shirley Jones (*Amy Kitteridge, Lexy's mother*).

3919   Heaven on Earth. (Pilot; Comedy; NBC; June 28, 1979). Roxy and Karen are two beautiful girls whose lives are claimed in a fatal car accident. When it is learned that a celestial error caused the girls to be called before their time, Roxy and Karen are returned to their earthly status. The proposal was to focus on their efforts to repay the kindness by performing good deeds. Sebastian Parnell is the celestial messenger.

Cast: Carol Wayne (*Roxy*); Donna Ponterotto (*Karen*); William Daniels (*Sebastian Parnell*).

3920   Heaven on Earth. (Pilot; Comedy; NBC; April 12, 1981). Katie Fredericks, a former actress; former ad agency executive Jerry Davidson; and former gang member Luis Padia are fledgling angels on the W.T.R. (Wings Through Rehabilitation) Program — the Almighty's way of allowing deserving souls entry into Heaven by performing good deeds. The proposal was to relate Katie, Jerry and Luis's efforts to make up for their past misgivings by helping people on earth. Repeated on July 5, 1981 as *Heaven Sent*.

Cast: Jack Gilford (*The Almighty's Representative*); Ilene Graff (*Katie Fredericks*); Douglas Sheehan (*Jerry Davidson*); Ron Contreras (*Luis Padia*).

3921   Heavens to Betsy. (Series; Comedy; NBC; 1949). Elizabeth "Betsy" Cote and Mary Best are young actresses seeking their big break on the Great White Way. Their struggles are made even more difficult by the fact that they are talented, but they are unknowns and most producers are not willing to take a chance on them. Stories follow their efforts to disprove their is a broken heart for every light on Broadway.

Cast: Elizabeth Cote (*Betsy Cote*); Mary Best (*Mary Best*); Nick Dennis (*Their Landlord*); Russell Nype (*Their friend, a cab driver*).

3922   Heavens to Betsy. (Pilot; Comedy; Unaired; Produced for CBS in 1994). An unfortunate accident claims the life of Betsy Baxter, a gorgeous singer, before her time. When celestial authorities realize that Betsy has potential to enter Heaven, they allow her to return to earth to help deserving people. The proposal was to follow

Betsy as she helps where needed, seeking to earn her way through the Pearly Gates.

Cast: Dolly Parton *(Betsy Baxter)*.

3923   *Hec Ramsey.* (Series; Western; NBC; 1972–1974). New Prospect, Oklahoma, in 1901 is the setting. It is here that Hector "Hec" Ramsey, an ex-gunfighter turned law enforcer has taken up residence. Hec represents the new breed of law enforcer: a man who encompasses a thinking that science and technology can play an important role in solving crimes. People like Amos Coogan, the town doctor and barber, and Oliver Stump, the town sheriff, are skeptical, while Hec's romantic interest, Norma Muldoon, believes as Hec does. Stories follow Hec as he sets out to prove his theories and solve crimes through science that might have otherwise remained unsolved. Andy is Norma's son (Norma is a widow).

Cast: Richard Boone *(Hec Ramsey)*; Rick Lenz *(Oliver Stamp)*; Harry Morgan *(Amos Coogan)*; Sharon Acker *(Norma Muldoon)*; Brian Dewey *(Andy Muldoon)*. **Narrator:** Harry Morgan.

3924   *The Heckle and Jeckle Show.* (Series; Cartoon; Syn.; CBS; NBC; 1955–1971). Antics of the very mischievous, talking magpies (birds), Heckle and Jeckle, as they create mischief wherever and however they can. Aired in syndication (1955-56), on CBS (1957–1966) and NBC (1969–71).

Voice Cast: Paul Frees *(Heckle)*; Paul Frees *(Jeckle)*.

3925   *Heck's Angels.* (Pilot; Comedy; CBS; Aug. 31, 1976). France in 1917 is the setting for a proposal about Colonel Gregory Heck and his Aero Squadron 35, a group of inferior aviators who battle the Huns during World War I. Other regulars are Lieutenants David Webb, Eddie Almont, Billy Bowling and George McIntosh; Odette, the German spy; Pierre Ritz, the squadron's cook; and Ludwig, the squadron's P.O.W.

Cast: William Windom *(Gregory Heck)*; Joe Barrett *(David Webb)*; Christopher Allport *(Billy Bowling)*; Jillian Kesner *(George McIntosh)*; Susan Silo *(Odette)*; Henry Polic II *(Pierre Ritz)*; Chip Zien *(Eddie Almont)*; Abraham Soboloff *(Ludwig von Stratter)*.

3926   *The Hector Heathcote Show.* (Series; Cartoon; NBC; 1963–1965). Hector Heathcote is a brilliant scientist who has invented a means by which to travel back in time through history. Stories relate his intervention into the major events that have shaped the world.

Voice Cast: John Myhers *(Hector Heathcote)*.

3927   *Hee Haw.* (Series; Variety; CBS, 1969–1971; Syn., 1971). Kornfield Kounty is the setting for performances by country and western artists coupled with short skits and running gags played against the Nashville sound.

Host: Roy Clark, Buck Owens. **Regulars:** Slim Pickens, Barbi Benton, Misty Rowe, Kathie Lee Johnson, Linda Johnson, Gailard Sartain, Gunilla Hutton, Cathy Baker, Roni Stoneman, Grady Nutt, Grandpa Jones, Don Harron, John Henry Faulk, Archie Campbell, Sheb Wooley, Gordie Tapp, Jeannine Riley, Susan Raye, Jennifer Bishop, Lulu Roman, Zella Lehr, Minnie Pearl, Alvin "Junior" Samples, Claude Phelps, Jimmy Riddle, Don Rich, Ann Randall, Mary Ann Gordon, Kenny Price, Don Gibson, George Lindsey, Jimmy Little, Lisa Todd, Nancy Traylor, The Hagers, The Buckaroos, The Inspiration, The Nashville Addition. **Orchestra:** George Richey, Charlie McCoy.

3928   *The Hee Haw Honeys.* (Pilot; Comedy; Syn.; June 1978). Chrissy, Lee Anne and Toby are three beautiful singers who appear in bit parts on the television series *Hee Haw*. The girls are unhappy

and yearn to become big-time singers. The proposed series was to follow their struggles as they strike out on their own as a singing group they call The Hee Haw Honeys.

Cast: Kathie Lee Johnson *(Chrissy)*; Catherine Hickland *(Toby)*; Muffy Durham *(Lee Anne)*; Kenny Price *(Kenny; their manager)*.

3929   *The Hee Haw Honeys.* (Series; Comedy; Syn.; 1978). *Hee Haw* spin off about the Honey family, the owner-operators of a country music nightclub in Nashville, Tennessee. Kenny and Lulu are the parents; Kathie Lee, Misty and Willy Billy are their children and stories relate the mishaps that befall the family as they host country and western entertainers.

Cast: Kenny Price *(Kenny Honey)*; Lulu Roman *(Lulu Honey)*; Kathie Lee Johnson *(Kathie Lee Honey)*; Misty Rowe *(Misty Honey)*; Gailard Sartain *(Willy Billy Honey)*.

3930   *Heist.* (Series; Crime Drama; NBC; 2006). "Every episode gets you closer to the greatest heist in history. They are about to hit an entire city" says an announcer in promotional spots for the intriguing, but totally fanciful program. It actually asks: can five highly skilled thieves pull off an extremely complex, if not impossible, series of robberies without getting caught?

The slick and always-cool Mickey O'Neil heads the robbery team. He is assisted by the ultra sexy but bitchy, Lola (hates to be called "Babe"), his best friend, James, the elderly Robert (called Pops) and the youngest gang member, James Johnson.

Rodeo Drive in Beverly Hills has the three most expensive blocks of real estate in the world — "Anything worth stealing can be found here," says Mickey. "They also have the three most expensive jewelry stores in the world." Mickey's plan is to rob each of these stores at the same time and net one half billion dollars.

The L.A.P.D. is unaware of their plan but the brilliant detective, Amy Sykes, believes something is up but can't quite put her finger on it. She detests sloppy police work and wants only the best from her detectives (Tyrese Evans and Billy O'Brien are the featured officers)

Each episode brings the viewer closer to the heist. The intricate planning as well as numerous practice runs is also shown. Amy's suspicions are first aroused when a practice run nets only the theft of an $8000 item; later, when a clever bank heist is pulled (to help finance their plan) she feels the worst is about to happen.

Cast: Dougray Scott *(Mickey O'Neil)*; Michele Hicks *(Amy Sykes)*; Mariska Dominczyk *(Lola)*; Steve Harris *(James Johnson)*; Reno Wilson *(Tyrese Evans)*; Seymour Cassel *(Pops)*; Billy Gardell *(Billy O'Brien)*; David Walton *(Rick Watman)*; K Callan *(Helen; Pops' wife)*.

3931   *The Helen O'Connell Show.* (Series; Variety; NBC; 1957). Singer Helen O'Connell hosts a summer program of music and songs.

Host: Helen O'Connell. **Orchestra:** David Rose.

3932   *The Helen Reddy Show.* (Series; Variety; NBC; 1973). Summer program of music and songs with singer Helen Reddy as the host.

Program Open: "Flip Wilson presents *The Helen Reddy Show.* Tonight Helen's guests are Albert Brooks, B.B. King, the legendary Modern Jazz Quartet and the New Seekers."

Host: Helen Reddy. **Regulars:** The Jaime Rogers Dancers. **Orchestra:** Nelson Riddle.

3933   *Hell Date.* (Series; Reality; BET; 2007). What happens when two people are set up for a date and one turns out to be a nightmare from hell? That is the premise behind *Hell Date.* An unsuspecting subject is matched with a date (an actor) that defies all the etiquette of dating (for example, a handsome young man is set up with a gorgeous girl whom he later discovers is a foul-mouthed alcoholic). Cameras capture the reactions of the poor soul who wound up with the date from hell. Peter M. Cohen is the producer.

3934   Hell Girl. (Series; Cartoon; IFC; 2009). Hell Correspondence is a very unusual web site. By logging on at Midnight one can submit a grievance. Ai Enma, a beautiful young lady who is also known as Hell Girl, delivers the vengeance that has been requested.

Ai Enma is a mysterious girl who has been damned to Hell and lives in a world of perpetual twilight (where her only companions are her faceless grandmother, the Silent Spider and a computer). Ai's fate began 400 years ago when she instituted an act of vengeance against the people of her village when they chose her for a sacrificial death. Her punishment for burning her village to the ground was to fulfill other people's vengeance and ferry souls to Hell. Following her act of vengeance, the Lord of Hell appeared to Ai. In order to prevent her loved ones forever wandering in Hell, Ai accepted his deal to become his messenger.

Ai is assisted by Wanyudo, Ren Ichimoku and Hone Onna. Wanyudo, who most often appears as an old man, is Ai's coach to help her claim souls. Ren, who takes the form of a young man, helps Ai with his ability to see through building walls. Hone is "a devastatingly beautiful woman" who investigates the people who submit the grievance and the ones to whom the grievance is directed. Hone Onna (translated as "bone woman") has the ability to expose her body's bones to scare the victims Ai is seeking.

Ai's Faceless Grandmother is seen only in shadows and occasionally informs Ai of new clients (she mostly spends her time in her room spinning thread). The Silent Spider appears to be Ai's superior. He holds the soul's of Ai's parents hostage to ensure Ai carries out her duties (if Ai should refuse, the Spider will condemn her parents to wander in darkness for all eternity). Produced in Japan in 2005 (to 2006).

Voice Cast: Brina Palencia *(Ai Enma)*; R. Bruce Elliott *(Wanyudo)*; Todd Haberkjorn *(Ren Ichimoku)*; Jennifer Seman *(Hone Onna)*; Juli Erickson *(Ai's Grandmother)*; John Swasey *(Spider)*.

3935   Hell on Earth. (Pilot; Comedy; Unaired; Produced for the WB in 2007). Amber is a young woman with a nasty attitude who grew up in the lap of luxury. She looked down upon those of lower social class and believed she was head and shoulders above everyone else. One day, while crossing the street, Amber is hit and killed by a bus. Celestial powers believe Amber needs to be taught a lesson and reincarnate her as Jessie, a normal girl who struggled to get what she has. The proposal was to follow Amber, now as Jessie, as she learns to live a life she has never known before.

Cast: Dawnn Lewis *(Amber/Jessie)*; Kyla Pratt *(Keri)*; Kim Coles *(Sera)*; Brian Palermo *(Luc)*; Kenni Anderson *(Kathie)*.

3936   Hell Town. (Series; Crime Drama; NBC; 1985-1986). St. Dominick's is a Catholic church in a crime-ridden section of Los Angeles called Hell Town. Father Noah Rivers is a compassionate priest at the church who is called "The Guardian Angel of the Streets." Noah is also an embittered ex-con who, while serving time, was called "Hardstep." While the bitterness has not totally left Father Noah, he is dedicated to protecting the people of his poor parish. Stories follow his work with the church (and its adjoining orphanage) as he goes beyond the call of duty (with rough tactics when necessary) to spread the faith. Mother Mary Margaret ("Maggie Jiggs") is the nun who runs St. Dominick's Orphanage and school; One Ball is Noah's friend, a pool hustler; Brandy Wine is the hostess at Roy Bean's the local bar (owned by Roy Bean); Sister Anastasia, called

"Angel Cakes," and Sister Indigo assist Maggie Jiggs. Sammy Davis, Jr., sings the Theme, "Hell Town."

Cast: Robert Blake *(Father Noah Rivers)*; Natalie Core *(Mother Maggie Jiggs)*; Whitman Mayo *(One Ball Tremayne)*; Vonetta McGee *(Sister Indigo)*; Isabel Grandin *(Sister Angel Cakes)*; Tracy Morgan *(Brandy Wine)*; Warren Vanders *(Roy Bean)*; Rhonda Dotson *(Sister Daisy)*; Guy Stockwell *(Matthew the Cop)*; Jeff Corey *(Lawyer Sam)*; Eddie Quillan *(Poko Loco)*; Zitto Kazann *(Crazy Horse)*.

3937   The Hellcats. (Pilot; Adventure; ABC; Nov. 24, 1967). Lee Ragdon is an aerial daredevil who performs stunts in a World War I biplane. Bugs Middle and Rippy Sloane are somewhat inexperienced student fliers who assist him. The proposal, filmed in 1964 and broadcast on *Off to See the Wizard* was to relate their adventures as they help people in trouble.

Cast: George Hamilton *(Lee Ragdon)*; John Craig *(Buggs Middle)*; Warren Berlinger *(Rippy Sloane)*.

3938   Hellcats. (Series; Drama; CW; 2010-2011). Marti Perkins is a first year law student at Lancer University in Memphis, Tennessee. She lives with her mother, Wanda, and her dream is to become a lawyer and start life anew elsewhere. All is progressing well for Marti until her mother, an alcoholic, neglects to tell Marti that her scholarship has been canceled and she will be losing her financial aid. Marti finds, however, that not all is lost. She can remain in school if she applies for and is successful at another scholarship choice. With few options available, she finds one that suits her — cheerleading; but she must first make the team. Marti, a competitive gymnast in high school, auditions and quickly acquires a position on the football team's cheerleading squad, the Hellcats. With the first step now successfully taken, Marti is on her way to acquiring the means by which to continue her schooling. Stories follow Marti as she and her team practice, cheer, and seek the ultimate goal — winning the state's cheerleading championship. Alice is the head cheerleader; Savannah is a team member and Marti's roommate; Vanessa, a former Hellcat, is the coach; Lewis is Alice's ex-boyfriend; Dan is Matt's friend.

Cast: Aly Michalka *(Marti Perkins)*; Ashley Tisdale *(Savannah Monroe)*; Heather Hemmens *(Alice Verdura)*; Sharon Leal *(Vanessa Lodge)*; Gail O'Grady *(Wanda Perkins)*; Robbie Jones *(Lewis Flynn)*; Matt Barr *(Dan Patch)*.

3939   Hellinger's Law. (Pilot; Crime Drama; CBS; Mar. 10, 1981). Nick Hellinger is a lawyer with the Philadelphia-based firm of Carroll & Hellinger. Nick is also somewhat unorthodox and the proposal was to relate his and his legman's Andy Clay, case investigations. Dottie is the office secretary; Judge Carroll is Nick's partner.

Cast: Telly Savalas *(Nick Hellinger)*; Ja'net DuBois *(Dottie Singer)*; Morgan Stevens *(Andy Clay)*; Roy Poole *(Judge Carroll)*.

3940   Hello Dere. (Pilot; Comedy; CBS; Aug. 9, 1965). Marty and Steve are television reporters who try to present an honest look at the day's news. The proposal was to relate their antics as they go to outrageous lengths to provide their viewers with breaking news. Vincent J. Vincent is the station manager; Miss Malone is his secretary.

Cast: Marty Allen *(Marty)*; Steve Rossi *(Steve)*; Roland Winters *(Vincent J. Vincent)*; Nina Shipman *(Miss Malone)*.

3941   Hello Kitty's Furry Tale Theater. (Series; Cartoon; CBS; 1987). Fairy tale adventures with a feline twist as Hello Kitty, the program's host, is transported to fairytale worlds each week to become the main characters in stories.

Voice Cast: Tara Strong *(Hello Kitty)*; Elizabeth Hanna *(Grandma*

Kitty); Elizabeth Hanna (*Mama Kitty*); Len Carlson (*Papa Kitty*); Carl Banas (*Grandpa Kitty*).

3942 Hello, Larry. (Series; Comedy; NBC; 1979–1981). Larry Alder and his daughters, Ruthie and Diane live at 46 Lafayette Street in Los Angeles. Larry is divorced from Marion and works for radio station KTCS as the host of a call-in talk program called *The Larry Alder Show*. When the opportunity arises for Larry to begin a new life for himself and his daughters, he accepts a job at radio station KLOW-AM in Portland, Oregon. There he hosts a call-in program called first *Hello, Larry*, then *The Larry Alder Show*. The station is owned by Trans-Allied, Inc.

Ruthie and Diane are very pretty teenage girls who attend Portland High School. While both girls respect their father, Diane is a bit wilder and will tempt fate (punishment) by breaking house rules. Morgan Winslow is Larry's attractive producer; Henry Alder is Larry's father (who resides with them in second season episodes). Wendell the Drunk is the president of the Larry Alder Fan Club. When the series first began, the main characters had the last name of Adler. Earl is Larry's engineer; Ruth, Rita and Rita's son, Tommy are Larry's neighbors; Meadowlark is the sports store owner; Lionel Barton I is the radio station owner; Lionel Barton II is his grandson.

Cast: McLean Stevenson (*Larry Alder*); Kim Richards (*Ruthie Alder*); Donna Wilkes (*Diane Alder*); Krista Errickson (*Diane Alder; later*); Joanna Gleason (*Morgan Winslow*); George Memmoli (*Earl*); Ruth Brown (*Leona Wilson*); Meadowlark Lemon (*Himself*); Fred Stuthman (*Henry Alder*); Shelley Fabares (*Marion Alder*); Don Chastain (*Scott Thomas; Marion's boyfriend*); John Femia (*Tommy Roscini*); Rita Taggart (*Marie Roscini*); Parley Baer (*Lionel Barton I*); David Landesberg (*Lionel Barton II*); Will Hunt (*Wendell*).

3943 Hell's Kitchen. (Series; Reality; Fox; 2005–). Hell's Kitchen is a Hollywood based restaurant owned by Gordon Ramsay, a world-renowned chef who is noted for wanting perfection from his staff. He is also very temperamental and foul-mouthed. The program has 12 aspiring young chefs (each of whom has either graduated from cooking school or has worked in a restaurant) competing for the top prize: head chef at one of Gordon's restaurants. But getting that honor is an extremely difficult task. Each of the contestants are placed in very trying meal preparation tests where, due to time restrictions and perfectionist standards Gordon places on them, leads to much yelling and foul (bleeped for broadcast) language. Each episode ends with Gordon shattering the dreams of a hopeful chef by eliminating him (or her) due to his poor performance. The one chef who meets Ramsay's expectations is the winner.

Host: Gordon Ramsay. **Narrator:** Jason Thompson.

3944 Hellzapoppin. (Pilot; Variety; ABC; Mar. 1, 1972). A revue based on Ole Olsen and Chick Johnson's 1938 Broadway hit (and 1941 movie) of the same title that blends vaudeville and burlesque: zany one-liners, sight gags, walk-ons and variety acts.

Host: Jack Cassidy, Ronnie Schell. **Guests:** The Jackson Five, Lynn Redgrave, Rex Reed, The Volantes, Bob Williams and his dog Louie. **Cameos:** Ruth Buzzi, Peter Lupus, Lyle Waggoner. **Orchestra:** Nick Perito.

3945 The Help. (Series; Comedy; WB; 2004). The Help refers to a group of servants who work for the wealthy Ridgeway family in Florida.

Arlene Ridgeway heads the eccentric family (her husband is not seen as he is constantly away on business "working on his latest hostile takeover"). Adam is her eldest son, a slacker who spends most of his days drinking beer by the pool and chasing women. Veronica is a teen pop star who rocketed to stardom with her hit song "Who Does Your Nails?" She relishes in this but doesn't realize she will only be a hit wonder. Cassandra, Arlene's older daughter, is a neurotic plastic surgeon with a violent temper and is feared by everyone in the house. Douglas, Arlene's youngest child, is constantly ignored by the family but finds an attraction to older women (and he is only 14 years old).

Helping the Ridgeway family cope with life are their servants: Anna, Maggie, Maria, Ollie, Dwayne and Molly. Anna is the sexy nanny on whom Douglas has a crush. Maggie is the cook who keeps the help in line. She does fear losing her job — "Who's gonna pay me this kind of money for mediocre cooking of standard American food?" Maria is the maid. She believes she is exceptionally beautiful and hopes to one day open her own salon — "to make the world beautiful except for blondes. I hate blondes." Molly is a gorgeous blonde who works as the dog walker for Arlene's three pampered pooches — Pookie, Priscilla and Cinnamon. Ollie is the chauffeur who puts in extra hours as a personal stud for Veronica. Dwayne is the personal trainer for Arlene and her daughters. He is superficial and self-absorbed.

Cast: Brenda Strong (*Arlene Ridgeway*); David Faustino (*Adam Ridgeway*); Keri Lynn Pratt (*Veronica Ridgeway*); Megan Fox (*Cassandra Ridgeway*); Graham Murdoch (*Douglas Ridgeway*); Jack Axelrod (*Grandpa Eddie Ridgeway*); Mindy Cohn (*Maggie*); Mariska Dominczyk (*Anna*); Tori Spelling (*Molly*); Camille Guaty (*Maria*); Al Santos (*Ollie*); Antonio Sabato, Jr. (*Dwayne*).

3946 H.E.L.P. (Series; Drama; ABC; 1990). The Harlem Eastside Lifesaver Program, H.E.L.P. for short, is an experimental New York City emergency unit that combines paramedics, cops and fire fighters. Stories detail the work of its battalion chief, Patrick Meacham and his crew: Firemen Jimmy Ryan and E. Jean Ballentry; Paramedics Mike Pappas and Danny Tran; and Patrolmen Lou Barton, Frank Sordoni, Larry Alba and Suki Rodriquez. Kathleen is Patrick's wife; Maureen is his daughter. Originally titled *911*.

Cast: John Mahoney (*Patrick Meacham*); Tom Breznahan (*Jimmy Ryan*); Wesley Snipes (*Lou Barton*); David Caruso (*Frank Sordoni*); Lance Edwards (*Mike Pappas*); Kay Tong Lim (*Danny Tran*); Marjorie Monaghan (*E. Jean Ballentry*); Joe Urla (*Larry Alby*); Kim Flowers (*Suki Rodriquez*); Fionnula Flanagan (*Kathleen Meacham*); Danielle Marcot (*Maureen Meacham*).

3947 Help! It's the Hair Bear Bunch. (Series; Cartoon; CBS; 1971-1972). Hair, Square and Bubi are three bears that call themselves the Hair Bear Bunch. They live in Cave Block Number 9 of the Wonderland Zoo and stories relate their efforts to improve their living conditions against the wishes of Mr. Peevley, the zoo keeper and his fumbling assistant, Botch.

Voice Cast: Daws Butler (*Hair Bear*); Paul Winchell (*Bubi Bear*); Bill Calloway (*Square Bear*); John Stephenson (*Mr. Peevley*); Joe E. Ross (*Botch*).

3948 Help Me, Help You. (Series; Comedy; ABC; 2006). Dr. Bill Hoffman is a therapist with a successful practice in Manhattan. He is also the author of several books on psychology and is well regarded by his fellow therapists. Bill and his wife, Anne have just separated after 15 years of marriage and his daughter, Sasha, is a college student who is dating a much older man — her psychology professor.

Bill says he has twelve degrees "and I know what I am doing." However, at times he flies off the handle when situations become difficult and it appears he needs a therapist. Bill has several patients and it is his efforts to help these people that comprises the main focus of stories. Dave is the newest member of Bill's therapy group. He is suicidal. Jonathan is a metro sexual who is in serious denial that he might possibly be gay. Inger, at age 25, is a self-made millionaire (now retired) who lacks social skills. Darlene has numerous psychological problems (including an obsession with Bill). Michael has serious anger issues.

Cast: Ted Danson (*Dr. Bill Hoffman*); Jane Kaczmarek (*Anne Hoffman*); Lindsay Sloane (*Sasha Hoffman*); Suzy Nakamura (*Inger*); Charlie Finn (*Dave*); Jim Rash (*Jonathan*); Darlene Hunt (*Darlene*); Jere Burns (*Michael*).

3949 *Hench at Home.* (Pilot; Comedy; Unaired; Produced for ABC in 2003). After years in the spotlight, famed hockey player Terry Hench retires and become the husband and father he never was during his game career. The proposal, created by Michael J. Fox, was to follow Terry as he tries to become the family man he never was. Kay, a psychologist, is his wife; Ally and Jake are their children.

Cast: Craig Bierko (*Terry Hench*); Tracy Pollan (*Kay Hench*); Molly Ephraim (*Ally Hench*); Michael Charles Roman (*Jake Hench*).

3950 *Hennessey.* (Series; Comedy; CBS; 1959–1962). Lieutenant Charles J. Hennessey, called "Chick," is a doctor with the U.S. Navy who has been assigned to the San Diego Naval Base in California. Stories follow his misadventures as he attempts to do his job but becomes involved in the antics of the enlisted men who are now a part of his life. Nurse Martha Hale is Chick's romantic interest; William Hale is Martha's stern father; Harvey Spencer Blair III is the base dentist; Max Bronsky is the chief corpsman; other personnel are listed in the cast.

Cast: Jackie Cooper (*Charles J. Hennessey*); Abby Dalton (*Martha Hale*); Harry Holcombe (*William Hale*); James Komack (*Harvey Spencer Blair III*); Henry Kulky (*Max Bronsky*); Herb Ellis (*Lt. Dan Wagner*); Roscoe Karns (*Captain Shafer*); Steve Roberts (*Commander Wilker*); Robert Gist (*Dr. King*); Ted Fish (*Chief Branman*); Frank Gorshin (*Seaman Pulaski*); Arte Johnson (*Seaman Shatz*).

3951 *Henny and Rocky.* (Series; Variety; ABC; 1955). A filler series of music and comedy with comedian Henny Youngman and former prize fighter Rocky Graziano that is presented following the ABC network's presentation of boxing.

Host: Henny Youngman, Rocky Graziano. **Vocalist:** Marion Colby. **Music:** The Jazz Combo of Bobby Hackett.

3952 *Henry Fonda Presents the Star and the Story.* (Series; Anthology; Syn.; 1955). Actor Henry Fonda hosts a program of dramas based on stories selected by guests.

3953 *Henry Morgan's Great Talent Hunt.* (Series; Variety; NBC; 1951). Performances by unusual talent acts (which are interspersed with comedy skits and songs).

Host: Henry Morgan. **Regulars:** Arnold Stang, Dorothy Claire, Art Carney, Kaye Ballard, Pert Kelton.

3954 *Herb Shriner Time.* (Series; Variety; ABC; 1951-1952). Music and comedy featuring the homespun philosophy of comedian Herb Shriner.

Host: Herb Shriner. **Regulars:** Peggy Allenby, Lenka Peterson, Biff McGuire, Eda Heinemann, Joseph Sweeney, Paul Hurber. **Music:** Milton DeLugg, Bernard Green.

3955 *Herbert Hoover Telecast.* (Experimental; Speech; April 7, 1927). The earliest known attempt to broadcast a radio and TV program at the same time. This occurred on April 7, 1927, by a group of people at Bell Telephone labs at 463 West Street in Manhattan. Then Secretary of Commerce Herbert Hoover was seen in a speech broadcast from Washington, D.C. (over wire for video; via radio networks for audio). It actually marked two firsts: the complete transmission of sound and picture and of long distance video broadcasting.

3956 *Herbie, the Love Bug.* (Series; Comedy; CBS; 1982). Jim Douglas, a former race car driver, has retired from the circuit and is now the owner of the Famous Driving School in California. In his heyday, Jim won dirt track races with the help of Herbie, a magical Volkswagen that has a mind of its own. While the origin of Herbie is not stated, it is revealed that when Jim sought to buy a car, Herbie found him compatible and attached itself to him. Herbie, license plate OFP 857, has the racing number 53 and now "assists" Jim as he attempts to run his business.

Susan is a pretty widow and Jim's romantic interest. She has three children (Julie, Martin and Robbie) and a jealous ex-boyfriend (Rodney) who blames Jim for stealing Susan away from him (it was actually Herbie's matchmaking attempts that brought Jim and Susan together). Rodney is now determined to win Susan back. Bo is Jim's assistant; Mrs. Bigelow, Robbie's mother, owns the Valley Basin Savings Bank. Based on the feature film *The Love Bug*. Dean Jones performs the theme, "Herbie, My Best Friend."

Cast: Dean Jones (*Jim Douglas*); Patricia Harty (*Susan McLane*); Claudia Wells (*Julie McLane*); Nicky Katt (*Martin McLane*); Douglas Emerson (*Robbie McLane*); Larry Linville (*Rodney Bigelow*); Natalie Cole (*Mrs. Bigelow*); Richard Paul (*Bo Phillips*).

3957 *Hercule Poirot.* (Pilot; Crime Drama; CBS; April 1, 1962). Hercule Poirot is a master Belgian detective. He uses his sheer wit to solve crimes and the proposal, based on the character created by Agatha Christie, was to follow Poirot as he solves cases of the most deadly nature—murder. Broadcast as a segment of *G.E. Theater*.

Cast: Martin Gabel (*Hercule Poirot*).

3958 *Hercules.* (Pilot; Adventure; ABC; Sept. 12, 1965). Hercules, the mythical Greek hero who is half god (son of Zeus) and half human (mortal mother) is brought to television for the first time in a proposal that was to follow his efforts to help people threatened by evil.

Cast: Gordon Scott (*Hercules*); Paul Stevens (*Diogenes*); Mart Hulswit (*Ulysses*); Diana Hyland (*Diana*). **Narrator:** Everett Sloane.

3959 *Hercules: The Animated Series.* (Series; Cartoon; ABC; 1998-1999). A spin off from the 1997 Disney film *Hercules*. Hercules, the half-mortal son of the god Zeus and a mortal woman (changed to Zeus and Hera for the series) is portrayed as a teenager and being trained for his future greatness by Philoctetes, the hero trainer on the Isle of Idra. Pegasus is the winged horse created by Zeus from the clouds to be a pet for his son; Icarus is Hercules's friend, the son of Daedalus, a teacher at the Hero Academy; Cassandra is the girl with the ability to see the future.

Voice Cast: Tate Donovan (*Hercules*); French Stewart (*Icarus*); Robert Costanzo (*Philoctetes*); Sandra Bernhard (*Cassandra*); David Hyde White (*Daedalus*); Frank Welker (*Pegasus*).

3960 *Hercules: The Legendary Journeys.* (Series; Adventure; Syn.; 1994–2000). Hercules, the legendary hero of ancient Greece, is a half-god (the son of the god Zeus and a mortal woman named Alcmene), who uses his mighty strength to help those the gods have turned away. He is assisted by Iolaus, his friend and traveling companion.

Zeus (Anthony Quinn, Peter Vere-Jones, Charles Keating) is King of the Gods. He rules from Mount Olympus and is married to

Hera, the all-powerful Queen of the Gods. Based on the ancient Greek myth (which was adapted to TV), Zeus was unfaithful and had an affair with Alcmeme (Jennifer Ludlam, Elizabeth Hawthorne, Liddy Holloway), a beautiful mortal woman. The tryst resulted in a half mortal son (Hercules) and angered Hera who frowned on infidelity and set her goal to kill Hercules, a constant reminder of Zeus's infidelity. When Hera attempts to kill Hercules with a fireball but misses and destroys his home, killing his wife, Deianeira and his three children, Hercules begins a quest to avenge their deaths by destroying Hera (Hera is only seen in human form in the last episode, "Full Circle." She is played by Meg Foster and was previously only heard and usually represented by an animated pair of all-seeing eyes).

Hercules has chosen to live among mortals and has a certain knack for arriving just as a crisis erupts and, being of kind heart, feels honor bound to resolve the conflict.

Being a half-god means Hercules is also related to full gods. His half-brother, the devilishly evil Ares (Mark Newham, Kevin Smith), the God of War, is his most troublesome relative (Ares seeks only to create havoc; Hercules despises Ares for this and risks his life to stop him and restore the peace).

Iolaus considers himself to be a great comedian (he tells jokes and is often the only one who laughs at them). He is two years older than Hercules and was a thief (as a child he would steal donuts from villagers). It was Hercules who turned his life around. Iolaus is the son of Skouros, a professional soldier who spent little time at home and was later killed in a battle. Although Iolaus does not possess the strength of Hercules, he often becomes offended when Hercules thinks he cannot defend himself and steps in to help. Iolaus believes he and Hercules find trouble without looking for it (Iolaus is a mortal and must use his skills and wits to survive).

Salmoneus (Robert Trebor) is the fast-talking toga salesman who befriends Hercules and Iolaus and involves them in his various get-rich quick schemes (that always seem to fail). Autolycus (Bruce Campbell) is the self-proclaimed "King of Thieves," a master cat burglar whose crimes often mean trouble for Hercules. Aphrodite (Alexandra Tydings) is the beautiful Goddess of Love (in one episode she called Hercules her brother, although in mythology they are not related). She is very protective of her shrines and often causes trouble when her love spells backfire. Callistro (Hudson Leick) is an evil warrior condemned to the hell of Tartarus (the underworld's place of punishment). She is used by Hera in plans to kill Hercules. Xena (Lucy Lawless) is the evil and ruthless warrior princess reformed by Hercules to use her skills to help people besieged by evil. See also *Xena: Warrior Princess*.

Five 1994 TV movies preceded the series: *Hercules and the Amazon Women*, *Hercules and the Lost Kingdom*, *Hercules and the Circle of Fire*, *Hercules in the Underworld* and *Hercules and the Maze of the Minotaur*.

Program Open: "This is the story of a time long ago. A time of myth and legend when the ancient gods were petty and cruel and they plagued mankind with suffering. Only one man dared to challenge their power — Hercules. He possessed a strength the world had never seen; a strength that was surpassed only by the power of his heart. He journeyed the earth battling the minions of his wicked stepmother, Hera, the all-powerful Queen of the Gods. But wherever there was evil, wherever an innocent would suffer, there would be Hercules."

Cast: Kevin Sorbo *(Hercules)*; Michael Hurst *(Iolaus)*.

3961   *The Herculoids.* (Series; Cartoon; CBS; 1967–1969). The Herculoids, animals as strong as they are invincible, risk their lives to protect their king, Zandor, and the inhabitants of their peaceful and utopian planet from evil creatures from other galaxies.

Voice Cast: Mike Road *(Zandor/Igoo/Zok)*; Virginia Gregg *(Tarra)*; Teddy Eccles *(Dorno)*; Don Messick *(Gloop/Gleep)*.

3962   *Here and Now.* (Series; Comedy; NBC; 1992-1993). Alexander James, better known as A.J., is a graduate student at Columbia University in New York City who works at the Manhattan Youth Center. He wants to make a difference in the lives of children who may be heading down the wrong path. A.J. works closely with Danielle Harrison, a graduate of Columbia University. Kalilla, Tanya, Malik, Randall and William are the featured kids at the center. Stories follow A.J.'s mishaps as he attempts to provide a bright future for kids with no direction.

Other Regulars: Sal, Danielle's uncle, a doorman (who calls her "Sugar Plum"); Amy, a counselor; Hubert, called "T," A.J.'s friend; Curtis Freeman, Randall's older brother; and Claudia St. Marth, A.J.'s supervisor.

Cast: Malcolm-Jamal Warner *(Alexander James)*; Rachel Crawford *(Danielle Harrison)*; Charles Brown *(Sid Harrison)*; Daryl "Chill" Mitchell *(T)*; Essence Atkins *(Kalilla)*; Natalie Harris *(Tanya)*; S. Epatha Merkerson *(Claudia St. Marth)*; Jessica Stone *(Amy)*; Pee Wee Love *(Randall Freeman)*; Omar Epps *(Curtis Freeman)*; Alexander Jackson *(Malik)*; Shaun Weiss *(William)*.

3963   *Here Come the Brides.* (Series; Adventure; ABC; 1968–1970). Seattle, Washington, in 1870 is the setting. Jason, Joshua and Jeremy Bolt are brothers who run a logging camp (Bridal Veil Mountain Logging) on Bridal Veil Mountain, the legacy left to them by their parents. There are few women in town and their woman-starved loggers are seeking companionship and threatening to quit. Strapped for money, but with a plan to transport 100 marriageable women from New Bedford, Massachusetts, Jason approaches Aaron Stemple, the sawmill owner (Stemple's Mill), for a loan. The condition: he must keep the women in Seattle for one year or forfeit the mountain. (Jason gave each of the brides one acre of land as a dowry.) Stories follow the Bolt's as they not only struggle to maintain their camp, but live up to the conditions of the loan agreement.

Carlotta "Lottie" Hatfield is the owner of Lottie's Saloon (sometimes seen as just Lottie's); Candy Pruitt is Jeremy's love interest; Roland Francis Clancey is the ship captain (of *The Seamus O'Flynn*); Molly Pruitt is Candy's sister; Christopher Pruitt is Candy's brother; Ben Perkins is the featured Bolt camp logger; Uncle Duncan is the head of the Bolt clan; Essie Halliday is the schoolteacher; Corky Sam McGee is the camp foreman; Mr. Gaddings is the reverend; and the featured brides (who reside in The Dormitory) are Biddie Cloom, Amanda, Peggy, Lulu, Ann, Franny, Maude, Polly, Beth, Mary Ellen and Sally; Julia is Aaron's sister; Ben Perkins is the shopkeeper. Miss Essie and logger Big Swede later married. The New Establishment perform the theme, "Seattle."

Cast: Robert Brown *(Jason Bolt)*; David Soul *(Joshua Bolt)*; Bobby Sherman *(Jeremy Bolt)*; Joan Blondell *(Lottie Hatfield)*; Bridget Hanley *(Candy Pruitt)*; Mark Lenard *(Aaron Stemple)*; Henry Beckman *(Roland Clancey)*; Hoke Howell *(Ben Perkins)*; Patti Cohoon *(Molly Pruitt)*; Eric Chase *(Christopher Pruitt)*; Susan Tolsky *(Biddie Cloom)*; Mitzi Hoag *(Essie Halliday)*; Bo Svenson *(Olaf "Big Swede" Gufferston)*; Robert Biheller *(Corky Sam McGee)*; William Schallert *(the Rev. Mr. Gaddings)*; Lindsay Workman *(the Reverend; later)*; Kristina Holland *(Amanda)*; Mary Jo Kennedy *(Peggy)*; Stefani Warren *(Lulu)*; Cynthia Hull *(Ann)*; Carole Shelyne *(Franny)*; Myra De Groot *(Maude)*; Loretta Laversee *(Polly)*; Susannah Darrow *(Beth)*; Karen Carlson *(Mary Ellen)*; Diane Sayer *(Sally)*; Denver Pyle *(Uncle Duncan)*; Katherine Crawford *(Julia)*.

3964   *Here Come the Double Deckers.* (Series; Comedy; ABC; 1970–1972). Scooper, Spring, Billie, Brains, Doughnut, Sticks and Tiger are pre-teen children who call themselves the Double Deckers (named after their clubhouse — an old double decker British bus that is parked in a London junkyard). The Double Deckers believe they are quite independent and stories follow their attempts to solve problems without help from the adult world. Albert is their adult friend.

Cast: Peter Firth (*Scooper*); Brinsley Forde (*Spring*); Gillian Bailey (*Billie*); Michael Anderson (*Brains*); Douglas Simmonds (*Doughnut*); Bruce Clark (*Sticks*); Debbie Russ (*Tiger*); Melvyn Hayes (*Albert*).

3965 *Here Come the Newlyweds.* (Series; Reality; ABC; 2008). Seven newlywed couples appear. Each couple was chosen for a specific reason (for example, together since high school; Barbie and Ken clones) and the program, a more athletic version of *The Newlywed Game*, puts trust to the test. In addition to the question-and-answer sessions, each of the couples is required to participate in stunts that seek to find the most compatible couple. The challenges are quite ridiculous (for example, a blindfolded husband seeking to determine which of the kisses he receives is that of his wife; a wife giving directions to her husband who is driving a car blindfolded). The laughs are provided by the trouble the couples face while performing their assigned tasks. The couple who are judged the most compatible (best at completing the weekly challenges) receives a cash prize. Pat Bullard hosts.

3966 *Here Come the Stars.* (Series; Variety; Syn.; 1968). Testimonial dinners that honor special guests. George Jessel, "The Toastmaster General of the United States" serves as the host.

Program Open: "A glittering celebrity night at the nation's smartest show place — George Jessel's *Here Come the Stars*, a formal dinner party in tribute to guest of honor Rod Serling and special guest stars Joey Adams, Jean Pierre Aumont, Carol Burnett, Rory Calhoun, Dan Dailey, Billy Daniels, Marty Ingels, Rich Little, Ralph Nelson, Pamela Paul, Mickey Shaughnessy. Produced by Ernest D. Glucksman. In a moment, *Here Come the Stars*."

3967 *Here Comes Melinda.* (Pilot; Comedy; Unaired; Produced in 1960). Melinda Gray is an elderly baby-sitter for the Westwood Baby Sitters Service in California. While in her seventies, Melinda is young at heart and capable (almost) of handling any situation. The proposal was to follow Melissa on her various baby sitting assignments. Other regulars are Paula, the agency director; and Ann, Melinda's niece.

Cast: Spring Byington (*Melinda Gray*); Alice Backes (*Paula Trowbridge*); Toby Michaels (*Ann Gray*).

3968 *Here Comes the Grump.* (Series; Cartoon; NBC; 1969–1971). As a magic fantasyland is put under the Curse of Gloom by the evil Grump, Terry Dexter, a young American boy, and his dog, Bib, are magically transported to the affected kingdom. There, Terry meets Princess Dawn, the only citizen who has not been affected by the curse. From the Princess, Terry learns about the Land of a Thousand Caves. In the Cave of the Whispering Orchids, the Grump has hidden the Crystal Key, which, if found, will lift the dreaded curse. Stories relate Terry and Dawn's efforts to find the Crystal Key; and the Grumps attempts, assisted by his fumbling Jolly Green Dragon, to keep secret the location of the Cave of Whispering Orchids.

Voice Cast: Stefanianna Christopher (*Princess Dawn*); Jay North (*Terry Dexter*); Rip Taylor (*The Grump*).

3969 *Here Comes Tobor.* (Pilot; Adventure; Unaired; Produced in 1955). A proposed spin off from *Captain Video and His Video Rangers* that was to use the evil (but now reformed) robot, Tobor, as a U.S. government secret weapon against crime. Tobor (robot spelled backwards) is now owned by Bruce Adams, a professor at the Adams Research Center (exactly how Tobor came to be in Bruce's possession is not explained; nor is it explained how Tobor, who came from the 22nd century on *Captain Video* is suddenly in the 20th century). Assisting the professor is his nephew, Tommy, a boy who was born with one of the highest ESP quotients ever known. Tobor has built-in Extra-Sensory Perception. Tommy has been cleared for top-secret material and because of his gift, controls Tobor through thought transferences. Together they work with Professor Adams to thwart evil. The screen credit for Tobor reads, "Tobor played by Tobor."

Cast: Arthur Space (*Bruce Adams*); Tommy Terrell (*Tommy Adams*).

3970 *Here We Go Again.* (Series; Comedy; ABC; 1973). Living at 1450 North Valley Lane in Encino, California, are Richard Evans, an architect (owner of Evans Architecture, Inc.), and his new wife, Susan. One block away, at 1490 North Valley Lane, lives Jerry Standish, Susan's ex-husband, a former Los Angeles Rams quarterback, who now owns the Polynesia Paradise Café. Half a mile away is 361 Oak Tree Drive, the address of Richard's ex-wife, Judy Evans, the editor of *Screen World* magazine. Jan and Cindy, Jerry and Susan's preteen children, now reside with Susan and Richard (Jerry maintains a bachelor pad), and Richard and Judy's son, Jeff, now lives with his father (Richard) and stepmother, Susan.

Richard and Susan's struggles to find serenity in a neighborhood where they are plagued by the constant intrusion of their former spouses constitute the focal point of stories.

Richard and Judy were married for 17 years before their marriage ended. Richard just couldn't take Judy's bossiness and left. Jerry and Susan met in college, fell in love, married and hoped for a storybook life together. What they found was a divorce after ten years of marriage. While Judy is bossy, formidable and efficient, Susan is sweet, tender and very trusting. While Richard is easygoing and trusting, Jerry is a playboy and unfaithful. Jerry's philandering cost him his marriage. Shortly after divorcing Jerry, Susan, a representative of the Better Boys Foundation (an organization that provides facilities for underprivileged boys), meets Richard when she hires him to design a new center.

Program Open: "Richard Evans, previously married. Susan Standish, previously married. I now pronounce you man and wife."

Cast: Larry Hagman (*Richard Evans*); Diane Baker (*Susan Evans*); Nita Talbot (*Judy Evans*); Dick Gautier (*Jerry Standish*); Kim Richards (*Jan*); Chris Beaumont (*Jeff*); Leslie Graves (*Cindy*).

3971 *Hereafter.* (Pilot; Comedy; NBC; Nov. 27, 1975). Nathan, Cliff and Lionel are three forgotten singers who make a pact with the Devil's youngest son (Rick) to sell their souls in return for a year at the top of the music world. The unsold series was to chart their new lease on life as a successful rock group. Served as the basis for *A Year at the Top*.

Cast: Josh Mostel (*Nathan*); Greg Evigan (*Cliff*); Paul Shaffer (*Lionel*); Don Scardino (*Rick*); Vivian Blaine (*Lillian*); Robert Donley (*Frank*); Phil Leeds (*Lou*).

3972 *Here's Barbara.* (Series; Interview; Syn.; 1969). The program's opening best describes the premise: "*Here's Barbara* with fashion, politics and people; an insiders look at Washington and the world with your hostess Barbara Coleman And now *Here's Barbara*."

3973 *Here's Boomer.* (Series; Anthology; NBC; 1980–1982). Boomer is an un-owned, roving shaggy dog that helps people in distress (he sort of crosses their paths, senses a troublesome situation and hangs around just long to receive a temporary home and use his canine smarts to help them overcome their problems). Tom Moore provides the voice of Boomer's thoughts; the pilot film, *A Christmas for Boomer*, aired on Dec. 6, 1979.

3974   *Here's Click.* (Experimental; Variety; DuMont; April 5, 1944). Following in the footsteps of *Mademoiselle* magazine (see *What's New with Mademoiselle*), the variety magazine *Click* attempted to transform its May 1944 issue to the video screen. Acts included ballroom dancing by the team of Maye and Harger (with the piano backing of Sam Medoff), interviews with Anabella, Jack Dempsey and Mickey Walker; a novelty act with the girls of the Stratosphere Club; pop songs from Kay Carroll and Naomi Stevens; a "Barber of Seville" excerpt from Met opera star Gerhard Peschner; and an interview with Max Weinberg, a Brooklyn bartender who sells $18.75 war bonds for a dollar off.

Host: Danton Walker. **Performers:** Anabella, Kay Carroll, Jack Dempsey, Gerhard Peschner, Maye and Harger, Naomi Stevens, Mickey Walker, Max Weinberg.

3975   *Here's Edie.* (Series; Variety; ABC; 1963-1964). Singer-actress Edie Adams hosts a program of music and songs with the music of Peter Matz and his orchestra. Also known as *The Edie Adams Show*.

3976   *Here's Hollywood.* (Series; Interview; NBC; 1960–1962). Intimate aspects of celebrities' lives are revealed through in-person interviews. Dean Miller and Joanne Jordan host.

3977   *Here's Lucy.* (Series; Comedy; CBS; 1968–1974). Lucille Carter is a widow who works as secretary to her brother-in-law, Harrison Otis Carter, the owner of the Unique Employment Agency ("Unusual Jobs for Unusual People"). Lucy lives at 4863 Valley Lawn Drive in Encino, California (in the San Fernando Valley) with her teenage children, Kim and Craig. Kim and Craig attend Los Angeles High School and stories follow Lucy's attempts to do a good job for Harrison; unfortunately, her good intentions always backfire, causing untold mishaps for Harrison (who must resolve the situations she causes). Mary Jane Lewis is Lucy's friend.

Cast: Lucille Ball *(Lucille Carter)*; Gale Gordon *(Harrison Otis Carter)*; Lucie Arnaz *(Kim Carter)*; Desi Arnaz, Jr. *(Craig Carter)*; Mary Jane Croft *(Mary Jane Lewis)*.

3978   *Here's Morgan.* (Pilot; Variety; ABC; June 6, 1946). A proposal based on the routines of radio comedian Henry Morgan. Basically, the pilot was just 15 minutes of Henry Morgan performing his material—from lampooning his sponsor (Adler Shoes) to complaining about the terrible conditions under which actors on TV must perform (referring to the heat generated from the overhead lights; heat so intense that it can melt vinyl records).

Host: Henry Morgan.

3979   *Here's Richard.* (Series; Variety; Syn.; 1982). Health guru Richard Simmons hosts a program that combines comedy sketches, celebrity guests, interviews health advice and cooking tips to help people get in shape and exercise. The pilot film aired in April of 1982 (the actual series began in October of 1982) and featured guests Judy Landers and Erma Bombeck.

Host: Richard Simmons. **Music:** Louis A. McLean.

3980   *Here's the Show.* (Series; Comedy; NBC; 1955). A weekly program of music and comedy with comedians Jonathan Winters and Ransom Sherman.

Host: Jonathan Winters, Ransom Sherman. **Regulars:** Kay O'Grady, Stephanie Antie, Tommy Knox, The Ted Carpenter Singers, The Double Daters. **Music:** John Scott Trotter.

3981   *Herman's Head.* (Series; Comedy; Fox; 1991–1993). Herman Brooks is a magazine fact checker and researcher for the Waterton Publishing Company in Manhattan. He lives at 564 West 58th Street, Apartment 3C, and hopes one day to become a writer. Viewers see not only this side of Herman but also "inside" Herman's head as characters representing his sensitivity, intellect, lust and anxiety battle over his actions.

Angel is Herman's sensitivity ("Without me he wouldn't feel tenderness, honesty or love — the good things in life"). Animal represents Herman's lust ("Without me he'd miss out on all the good stuff— you know, fun, food, babes"). Wimp is Herman's anxiety ("I keep him out of trouble. And believe me, there is trouble everywhere"). Genius is Herman's intellect ("Without me he couldn't hold a job, pay his rent or tie his shoes").

Paul Bracken is Herman's boss. He is an editor and "knows facts about everything." Heddy Newman is a researcher and Herman's beautiful colleague. Louise Fitzer is the office assistant. She is very sweet and trusting and looking to find a husband. Jay Nichols is Herman's lecherous, womanizing friend and co-worker; Jim Crawford is the senior editor (he calls Herman "Sherman"). Originally called *It's All in Your Head*.

Cast: William Ragsdale *(Herman Brooks)*; Jane Sibbett *(Heddy Newman)*; Yeardley Smith *(Louise Fitzer)*; Jason Bernard *(Paul Bracken)*; Hank Azaria *(Jay Nichols)*; Edward Winter *(Jim Crawford)*.

3982   *Hernandez, Houston P.D.* (Pilot; Crime Drama; NBC; Jan. 16, 1973). A proposal about Juan Hernandez, a Mexican-American detective with the Houston, Texas, Police Department. Other regulars are his mother, Mamacita Hernandez; and his partner, Sergeant Lukas.

Cast: Henry Darrow *(Juan Hernandez)*; Desmond Dhooge *(Sergeant Lukas)*; Amapola Del Vando *(Mamacita)*.

3983   *Herndon and Me.* (Pilot; Comedy; ABC; Aug. 26, 1983). Herndon P. Pool is a clumsy computer genius for the Judicto Computer Company in the Silicone Valley in San Jose, California. Jeff Shackelson is his friend and executive assistant and the proposed series was to follow their mishaps as Herndon, who is trying to prove he is not a nerd, finds his life being run by Jeff. Hilary is Judicto's P.R. lady; Miss Helter is the office secretary.

Cast: Michael Richards *(Dr. Herndon P. Pool)*; Ted McGinley *(Jeff Shackelson)*; Randi Brooks *(Hilary Swanson)*; Ann Ramsey *(Miss Helter)*.

3984   *The Hero.* (Series; Comedy; NBC; 1966-1967). Sam Garrett is an actor. He is married to Ruth and is the father of Paul. Sam lives in Los Angeles and is the star of the television series *Jed Clayton, U.S. Marshal*. In real life Sam is a bumbling klutz; on TV he plays a fearless and dauntless law enforcer. Stories follow Sam's home and working life and in particular his efforts to conceal his real life from his adoring fans. Other regulars are Fred and Adele Gilman, Sam's neighbors; Burton, Fred and Adele's son; Marilyn, Sam's niece. The Gilman's dog is named Brownie.

Cast: Richard Mulligan *(Sam Garrett)*; Mariette Hartley *(Ruth Garrett)*; Bobby Horan *(Paul Garrett)*; Victor French *(Fred Gilman)*; Maureen Arthur *(Adele Gilman)*; Joey Baio *(Burton Gilman)*; Laurel Goodwin *(Marilyn)*; Norman Palmer *("Jed Clayton" Show Director)*; Jack Perkins, John Harmon *(Bartender in "Jed Clayton")*. **Announcer:** Dick Tufeld.

3985 *Hero 108.* (Series; Cartoon; Cartoon Network; 2010). In a mythical world called the Hidden Lands (also called the Hidden Kingdom), humans and animals live together in peace — until an evil being, High Roller, learned the language of the animals and convinced them to revolt against humans. Soon afterward, High Roller created his Animal Army and they in turn forced humans to flee from their homes and live as refugees. High Roller had his dream: to rule the land until an alliance of humans, called the Big Green (named after the abandoned shell of a giant tortoise) was formed to oppose High Roller. Stories follow the Big Green as they as they attempt to defeat High Roller and restore the harmony between humans and animals. Mr. No Hands is the leader of the First Squad, the elite fighting team of the Big Green. Lin Chung, who possesses Panther Vision (ability to see great distances), is the unit's most skilled warrior. Mystique is a tough, seasoned warrior; Jumpy Ghostface (a.k.a. Rabbit King) is a warrior who fears nothing; Mighty Ray is the brute force of the team; Ape Trully is the leader of the peace making aspect of Big Green.

Voices: Tabitha St. Germain, James Corbett, Brian Drummond, Andrew Francis, Kelly Sheridan, Adrian Petriw, Elias Eliot.

3986 *The Hero Factory.* (Series; Cartoon; Nick; 2010–). The Hero Factory, located in Makuhero City, is a futuristic defense organization that dispatches factory-built robots to battle evil throughout the galaxy. Mr. Makuro is the founder of the Hero Factory and stories focus on the activities of two groups: The Alpha Team (Stormer, Bulk and Stringer) and the Rookie Team (Furno, Breeze and Surge) as they struggle to prove themselves worthy heroes while fighting for justice.

Voice Cast: Christopher B. Duncan *(Bulk)*; Jean Louisa Kelly *(Breeze)*; John Schneider *(Stormer)*; Stephen Stanton *(Stringer)*; Bryton James *(Surge)*; Eric Christopher Olsen *(Furno)*.

3987 *Heroes.* (Series; Science Fiction; NBC; 2006–2009). Following an eclipse, several people are endowed with special powers. Brothers Peter and Nathan (ability to fly); Claire (ability to heal herself), Hiro (bend the time continuum); Niki (incredible strength); Matt (mind reading); Eden (telepath); Ellen (derives power from electricity); Daphne (supersonic speed) and Monica (acquires powers from what she sees on TV). Isaac, an artist, has no powers, but has future perception — what he paints happens. His latest painting is that of world destruction. The complex series attempts to unite the heroes in an effort to save the world before Isaac's painting becomes a reality.

Cast: Jack Coleman *(Noah Bennet)*; Hayden Panettiere *(Claire Bennet)*; Milo Ventimiglia *(Peter Petrelli)*; Masi Oka *(Hiro Nakamura)*; Adrian Pasdar *(Nathan Petrelli)*; Sendhil Ramamurthy *(Mohinder Suresh)*; James Kyson Lee *(Ando Masahashi)*; Greg Grunberg *(Matt Parkman)*; Ali Larter *(Niki Sanders)*; Ashley Crow *(Sandra Bennet)*; Zachary Quinto *(Sylar)*; Cristine Rose *(Angela Petrelli)*; Kristen Bell *(Ellen Bishop)*; Jimmy Jean-Louis *(The Haitian)*; Noah Gray-Cabey *(Micah Sanders)*; Randall Bentley *(Lyle Bennet)*; Santiago Cabrera *(Isaac Mendez)*; Leonard Roberts *(D.L. Hawkins)*; Brea Grant *(Daphne Millbrook)*; Adair Tishler *(Molly Walker)*; Dania Ramirez *(Maya Herrera)*; Elizabeth Lackey *(Janice Parkman)*; Tawny Cypress *(Simone Deveaux)*; David Anders *(Adam Monroe)*; Zelijko Ivanek *(Emile Danko)*; Thomas Dekker *(Zach)*; George Takei *(Kaito Nakamura)*; Nora Zehetner *(Eden McCain)*; Dana Davis *(Monica)*; Brea Grant *(Daphne)*; Moira Kelly *(Abby Collins)*.

3988 *He's a Lady.* (Series; Reality; TBS; 2004). Eleven men compete for $250,000 by learning what it is like to be a lady. The participants are given feminine makeovers and compete in challenges that involve living like a lady and bonding in female activities. The final episode is a beauty pageant that determines the winner. Tony Frassrand hosts; Morgan Fairchild, John Salley and Debbie Matenopoulos are the judges.

3989 *He's the Mayor.* (Series; Comedy; ABC; 1986). Carl Burke is a 25-year-old college graduate who is fed up with the conditions of his (unidentified) city. On a whim he decides to run for mayor on a platform of improving the quality of life. Unexpectedly he is elected. Carl lacks political savvy but he does possess charisma, honesty, resourcefulness and a lot of help from his friends. Stories follow Mayor Burke as he struggles to solve the problems that befall his crisis-ridden community.

Other regulars are Alvin Burke, Carl's father, the City Hall janitor; Paula Hendricks, Carl's secretary (later replaced by Kelly Enright); Walter Padgett, the police chief; Harlan Nash, a councilman; Wardell Halsey, Carl's chauffeur; Penny, a waitress at the local diner; and Ivan Bronski, Alvin's friend.

Cast: Kevin Hooks *(Carl Burke)*; Al Fann *(Alvin Burke)*; Mari Gorman *(Paula Hendricks)*; Margot Rose *(Kelly Enright)*; David Graf *(Harlan Nash)*; Wesley Thompson *(Wardell Halsey)*; Pat Corley *(Walter Padgett)*; Shuko Akune *(Penny)*; Stanley Brock *(Ivan Bronski)*.

3990 *Hex.* (Series; Drama; BBC America; 2006). Cassie Hughes is a young woman who is new to a British boarding school called Mendenham Hall. Cassie is a plain girl who delights in her study of art and literature. Life changes for her when she begins exploring a long forgotten room at the school and discovers an ancient vase that endows her with visions and the ability to not only see ghosts, but a fallen angel named Azazeal, a demon that has tormented young women, including Cassie's mother, over the centuries; it has now set its sights on acquiring Cassie's soul. The school's past might explain what has happened: the school was, at one time, a stately home when the daughter of its owner dabbled in voodoo and conjured up evil — evil that eventually killed her when she was unable to control it. Stories follow Cassie as she battles Azazeal — not always winning and, at times, becoming evil herself. Thelma is Cassie's roommate (although she is later killed and becomes a lesbian ghost); and Troy, Roxanne and Leon are Cassie's friends. Produced in England in 2004 (to 2005).

Cast: Christina Cole *(Cassandra "Cassie" Hughes)*; Jemima Rooper *(Thelma Bates)*; Joseph Morgan *(Troy)*; Amber Sainsbury *(Roxanne Davenport)*; Jamie Davis *(Leon Tyler)*; Anna Wilson-Jones *(Jo Watkins)*; Samuel Collings *(Tom)*; David Tyler *(Colin Salmon)*; Michael Fassbender *(Azazeal)*; Jemima Abey *(Alex)*; Joseph Beattic *(Malachi)*; Laura Pyper *(Ella Dee)*.

3991 *Hey Arnold!* (Series; Cartoon; Nick; 1994–2005). Arnold is a nine-year-old boy (with a football shaped head for which he received the nickname "Football Head") who lives in a boarding house with his grandparents. He loves to daydream and jazz and football are his favorite pastimes. Arnold hangs out with his best friend, Gerald and stories follow his misadventures as he faces the daily pressures of life at school, with his friends and at home. Arnold's main problem is that he feels obligated to help others — a situation that becomes all too complicated when he starts minding other people's business. Helga, the meanest girl in school, has a crush on Arnold (although Arnold is not aware of it); Phoebe is the brainy kid; Harold is the school's overweight bully; Rhonda is the school's rich girl; Phil and Pookie are Arnold's grandparents (his parent's absence is explained as their being "out in the wild saving people's lives"). Stinky, Sid and Eugene are other classmates. Oskar, his wife Susie and construction worker Ernie are residents of the boarding house.

Voice Cast: Phillip Glen Van Dyke, Alex D. Linz, Spencer Klein (*Arnold*); Jamil Walker Smith (*Gerald*); Francesca Smith (*Helga*); Justin Shenkarow (*Harold*); Anndi McAfee (*Phoebe*); Olivia Hack (*Rhonda*); Dan Castellaneta (*Grandpa Phil*); Tress MacNeille (*Grandma Pookie*); Christopher P. Walberg (*Stinky*); Sam Gifaldi (*Sid*); Benjamin Diskin (*Eugene*); Jarrett Lennon (*Eugene*); Steven Viksten (*Oskar*); Mary Scheer (*Susie*); Dom Irrera (*Ernie*).

3992 Hey Dude. (Series; Comedy; Nick; 1989–1991). The Bar None is a dude ranch in Tucson, Arizona. It is owned by Benjamin Ernst, an over enthusiastic man who often goes out of his way to make sure his guests receive the best service possible; unfortunately, his scheming employee, Ted, causes more problems than solutions as he goes out of his way to do what is best for Ted. Other employees of the Bar None are Lucy, Ernst's assistant; Melody, the lifeguard; Brad, the horse instructor; Sam, the ranch cook; and Buddy, Benjamin's young son; Jake is Ernst's mischievous nephew.

Cast: David Brisbin (*Benjamin Ernst*); Christine Taylor (*Melody Hanson*); Deborah Kalman (*Lucy*); David Lascher (*Ted McGriff*); Kelly Brown (*Brad Taylor*); Josh Tygiel (*Benjamin "Buddy" Ernst, Jr.*); Joe Torres (*Kyle Chandler*); Jonathan Galkin (*Jake Decker*); Roger B. Ramsden (*Sam*).

3993 Hey, Jeannie! (Series; Comedy; CBS; 1956–1958). Jeannie MacLennan is a young Scottish woman who resides at 132 24th Street in Brooklyn, New York. But it wasn't always so. Jeannie, the daughter of Rory, a deep sea fisherman, and Janet MacLennan, was born in Dumfernline, Scotland, in 1932. Her parents were born in Ireland but moved to Scotland "because the kippers were running." As she grew, Jeannie became fascinated by America and dreamed of living in Pittsburgh where her hero, Andrew Carnegie (born in her home town) made his fortune. After her father is killed in a job-related accident, her mother arranges for Jeannie to live her dream. It is arranged that Jeannie will stay with a friend of the family (David Forrester) in New York City before moving to Pittsburgh. Jeannie arrives in New York at Pier 23 and clears customs. However, when she goes to David's home she finds that he has moved (explained that he "was on relief" [welfare] and no longer able to afford his home). With no place to go, Al Murray, the cabbie who drove Jeannie to David's address, takes her under his wing and arranges for her to become a border in the home he shares with his sister, Liz in Brooklyn.

Jeannie becomes fascinated by America and decides to remain in Manhattan. Stories relate her various mishaps as she explores new avenues seeking to find her calling in life.

Second season episodes (1958) drop the characters of Al and Liz and place Jeannie in an occupation as an airline stewardess. Charlie O'Connell becomes her landlord; Herbert is her friend, an airline pilot; Mabel is Jeannie's boss. The program also features a song by Jeannie Carson in virtually every episode. Also known as *The Jeannie Carson Show: Hey Jeannie!*

Cast: Jeannie Carson (*Jeannie MacLennan*); Allen Jenkins (*Al Murray*); Jane Dulo (*Liz Murray*); Barbara Jo Allen (*Mabel*); William Schallert (*Herbert*); Jack Kirkwood (*Charlie O'Connell*).

3994 Hey, Landlord! (Series; Comedy; NBC; 1966–1967). At 140 West 41st Street in Manhattan stands an old brownstone that has been converted into a ten room apartment house by its youthful owner, Woodrow ("Woody") Banner, an aspiring writer who inherited the building from his late uncle. Woody shares his ground-floor apartment with his friend Charles ("Chuck") Hookstratten, a brash city boy who aspires to be a comedian. Pursuing girls is uppermost in their minds, and they take whatever jobs they can find while waiting for their big breaks.

Woody grew up on a farm in Ohio. He was a Boy Scout and attended Fillmore High School in Toledo. Chuck was born and raised in New York City. He was, as he says, "a rotten kid." He wrote on the school walls, stuck chewing gum under the seats in the auditorium and once tried to burn down the school. He somehow managed to graduate and attended Ohio State University — where he met Woody. The two became quick friends. After graduation, they decided to pursue their career goals in New York City.

"Why did I move into this building? They said the rent would be lower. But what about my medical bills — who else buys pills by the gross?" Such is one of the many complaints from upstairs tenant Jack Ellenhorn, an ulcer-ridden, easily exasperated commercial photographer who feels that the antics of "the Boy Landlord" (Woody) and "Chuckula" (Chuck) are tied with the aggravation of his job to see who can kill him first. Other tenants are Timmie Morgan and Kyoko Mitsui, two gorgeous girls who share an upstairs apartment; and Mrs. Henderson, another complaining tenant. Quincy Jones composed the theme.

Cast: Will Hutchins (*Woody Banner*); Sandy Baron (*Chuck Hookstratten*); Michael Constantine (*Jack Ellenhorn*); Pamela Rodgers (*Timmie Morgan*); Jayne Massey (*Gayle*); Miko Mayama (*Kyoko Mitsui*); Ann Morgan Guilbert (*Mrs. Henderson*).

3995 Hey Mack. (Pilot; Comedy; CBS; April 26, 1957). Conal F. McConnell is an easy-going widower with a teenage daughter (Sharon). Together they run the Fisherman's Bend Hotel and Sportsman's Lodge in Northern California and the proposed series was to relate the problems they encounter.

Cast: Gary Merrill (*Conal F. McConnell*); Sue George (*Sharon McConnell*).

3996 Hey, Mulligan. (Series; Comedy; NBC; 1954-1955). Michael "Mickey" Mulligan is a page (official title: Guest Relations Staff) at the Los Angeles Bureau of the New York–based I.B.C. (International Broadcasting Company). Mickey earns $47.62 a week take-home pay and believes he is meant for bigger and better things; his only problem is, what are those bigger and better things?

Mickey, who considers himself "the tallest short man you'll ever meet," feels that his five-foot height is preventing him from going places at the network. He has enrolled in the Academy of Dramatic Arts (figuring acting may be his goal), but he also seizes upon every opportunity to find his actual goal in life and stories also focus on those outside careers Mickey feels will be the future he is looking for.

Patricia "Pat" Harding is Mickey's romantic interest, the secretary to Charles Brown, the program director at I.B.C. Freddie Devlin is Mickey's friend, a page also; J.L. Patterson is the head of the network.

Mickey's father, Joseph "Joe" Mulligan is a police officer (with the 23rd Precinct of the L.A.P.D.), and his mother, Nell Mulligan, is a former vaudeville actress. Also known as *The Mickey Rooney Show.*

Cast: Mickey Rooney (*Mickey Mulligan*); Carla Balenda (*Pat Harding*); Joey Forman (*Freddie Devlin*); John Hoyt (*J.L. Patterson*); John Hubbard (*Charles Brown*); Hillary Brooke (*Alice Brown, Charles' wife*); Regis Toomey (*Joe Mulligan*); Claire Carleton (*Nell Mulligan*).

3997 Hey Paula. (Series; Reality; Bravo; 2007). Singer and *American Idol* judge Paula Abdul is profiled. The program reveals a side of Paula that is not known by the public — her expertise as a businesswoman (for example, developing her own fragrance; confrontations with home shopping QVC network executives). Her public life experiences as well as a playful side (playing jokes on her assistants) are also "exposed."

Star: Paula Abdul.

3998 *Hey Teacher.* (Pilot; Comedy; CBS; June 15, 1964). The teaching profession is spoofed as Joe Hannon becomes the only male teacher in an elementary school dominated by females. Mrs. Foley is the principal; Lester is the custodian.

    Cast: Dwayne Hickman (*Joe Hannon*); Reta Shaw (*Mrs. Foley*); Wallace Ford (*Lester Tinney*).

3999 *Hey Vern, It's Ernest.* (Series; Comedy; CBS; 1988–1989). Various offbeat comedy sketches that features the humor of Jim Varney as Ernest P. Worrel, the wacky character who plagues the never-seen Vern, a man who wishes Ernest would just go away and leave him alone. Jim, as well as the other show regulars, play several different characters.

    Cast: Jim Varney (*Ernest P. Worrel/Baby Ernest/Sergeant Glory/Dr. Otto/Auntie Nelda*); Gailard Sartain (*Lonnie Don/Chuck/Matt Finish*); Bruce Arnston (*Mike the Clown/Existo*); Jackie Welch (*Mrs. Simon Simmons/Daniel Butler/Willie the Robot/Earl the Barber*).

4000 *Hi Honey, I'm Home.* (Series; Comedy; ABC; 1991). In September 1952, *Hi Honey, I'm Home* premiered at 8:00 P.M. following *Dragnet.* It was a typical sitcom about the Nielsens, a squeaky clean American family: parents Honey and Lloyd and their children, Babs and Chuckie. They lived in the town of Springfield. Honey was the problem-solving housewife, and Lloyd, "the idiot father"; he was a businessman, "but darned if I know what kind." Babs was the high school beauty queen, and Chuckie, the youngest, a Boy Scout. Then it happened — their show was canceled; but it was picked up for syndication and ran for many more years in reruns. As the years passed, stations began to drop the series. When the last station on which the series was running decided to pull the plug, the S.R.P. (Sitcom Relocation Program) stepped in and relocated the black and white characters to 178 Morgan Road in New Jersey (all characters from canceled television shows are sent to different cities across the country).

It is 1991 and the S.R.P. places them next door to the Duffs, a single mother (Elaine) and her two children (Mike and Sidney), who are the direct opposite of the Nielsens. Lloyd doesn't like the 1990s Honey — she has ideas and thinks. Honey looks like a Barbie doll. She is starched and ironed and cheerfully goes about her wifely household duties. Honey has a naturally sunny disposition; when something goes wrong she says, "Oh pooh." She is the only one who can grasp the reality of life in the 1990s. Lloyd is impervious to what is going on. He is a wimp — but a hero in Honey's eyes. He first worked for Mr. Mooney (Gale Gordon) in an unnamed position; then as a salesman for the Bijou Furniture Company, as a broker for a savings and loan company, and finally as a golf ball salesman at Mr. G's World-O-Golf.

Barbara ("Babs") is rather well developed and loves to wear tight, cleavage-revealing sweaters. Elaine has a tendency to call her "Boobs" (the 1950s Babs doesn't realize what Elaine means and just smiles). Babs says, "I'm not only beautiful on the outside, I'm beautiful on the inside too." Charles ("Chuckie") Nielsen is a Boy Scout (Nest 14).

Elaine Duff is a hard working single mother struggling to raise two kids. While she never mentioned a job, she was seen wearing a phone company tool belt, and she seems to be either a line "man" or an in-home installer. Elaine can't believe a woman like Honey exists and is determined to make a 1990s woman out of her. Elaine mentioned that her husband, Ted, deserted her and the family.

Mike Duffy is Elaine's oldest son. He uses TV to escape from reality and *Hi Honey, I'm Home* is his favorite daily TV show (when it was replaced by *Joanie Loves Chachi* the Nielsen's appeared next door). The show made Mike laugh and feel happy. When he visits his new neighbors, he realizes they are the TV Nielsens, and he agrees

to help them keep their secret (if the truth were known about the Nielsens, they would never get picked up for reruns again and would have to remain in the real world forever).

    Cast: Charlotte Booker (*Honey Nielsen*); Stephen Bradbury (*Lloyd Nielsen*); Julie Benz (*Babs Nielsen*); Danny Gura (*Chuckie Nielsen*); Susan Cella (*Elaine Duff*); Peter Benson (*Mike Duff*); Eric Kushnick (*Sidney Duff*).

4001 *Hi Mom.* (Series; Information; NBC; 1957–1959). The program, hosted by ventriloquist Shari Lewis (and her hand puppets Lamb Chop, Hush Puppy and Charlie Horse) presents advice and information geared to young mothers.

    Host: Shari Lewis. **Assistant:** Johnny Andrews. **Regulars:** Paul Ritts, Mary Ritts, Josephine McCarthy, Jane Paler.

4002 *Hi Mom.* (Pilot; Variety; Unaired; Produced for NBC in 1960). A live closed-circuit audition program for a daily series (9–10 A.M.) of entertainment geared to young mothers and their children. The program contains chatter between the hosts, Paul and Mary Ritts; songs and drawings by Mary; an interview with a five-year-old girl (Terry Kenney) by Paul; and the antics of the Ritts Puppets: Magnolia the Ostrich (voiced by Mary) and Sir Geoffrey the Giraffe, Calvin the Crow and Albert the Squirrel (all voiced by Paul).

4003 *Hickey vs. Anybody.* (Pilot; Comedy; NBC; Sept. 19, 1976). If it sounds a bit fishy; if it's unethical; if there is a buck to be made — it's Julius V. Hickey, attorney-at-law who will take the case. He is assisted by Phyllis Avedon, a pretty law student who believes in helping people for the sake of helping, not for profit. Other regulars are Netty, Hickey's secretary; and Willie, a colleague.

    Cast: Jack Weston (*Julius V. Hickey*); Liberty Williams (*Phyllis Avedon*); Beverly Sanders (*Netty*); Malcolm Atterbury (*Willie*).

4004 *Hidden Agenda.* (Series; Game; GSN; 2010). Couples are the subjects. Each partner secretly sets the other up to perform a chore — something that he or she wouldn't normally do. Actors, posing as ordinary people, enter the scene to complicate the tasks that are being performed. The chaotic results are captured on hidden cameras and the couples win cash prizes based on how many tasks they are able to successfully complete.

    Host: Debi Gutierrez.

4005 *Hidden Faces.* (Series; Drama; NBC; 1968-1969). Daily program about Arthur Adams, a lawyer in a small Mid-Western town. His only case: defending Katherine Logan, a physician accused of causing a patient's death.

    Cast: Conrad Fowkes (*Arthur Adams*); Gretchen Walther (*Katherine Logan*); Linda Blair (*Allyn Jaffe*); Ludi Claire (*Grace Ensley*); Betsy Durkin (*Jeannet Sloan*); Joseph Daly (*Robert Jaffe*); Rita Gam (*Mimi Jaffe*); Stephen Joyce (*Mark Utley*); John Karlen (*Sharkey Primrose*); Tony Lo Bianco (*Nick Capello Turner*); Nat Polen (*Earl Harriman*); Louise Shaffer (*Martha Logan*); John Towey (*Wilbur Ensley*).

4006 *Hidden Hills.* (Series; Comedy; NBC; 2002-2003). Hidden Hills is a seemingly quiet suburban community in Southern California. It is here that two couples live side by side — Doug and Janine Barber and their neighbors Zack and Sarah Timmerman. Doug, the owner of The Barber Building Construction Company, is married to Janine (a doctor) and they are the parents of Emily and Derek. Zack works for Doug and his wife, Sarah is a sports columnist. Stories follow the friends as they seek, but seldom find a life of bliss in a community that is filled with hidden secrets and sexual escapades.

Belinda Slypich is their neighbor, a very sexy softball mother with her own website.

Cast: Justin Louis *(Doug Barber)*; Paula Marshall *(Dr. Janine Barber)*; Dondre T. Whitfield *(Zack Timmerman)*; Tamara Taylor *(Sarah Timmerman)*; Kristin Bauer *(Belinda Slypich)*; Alexa Nikolas *(Emily Barber)*; Sean Marquette *(Derek Barber)*.

4007 *Hidden Palms.* (Series; Drama; CW; 2007). Johnny Miller appears to be a normal teenager. Everything also appears to be going well for him. Then, unexpectedly, his father (for unexplained reasons) commits suicide (gun to head) in front of him. The incident traumatizes Johnny in a way that he turns to drugs and alcohol. His grades go from *A* to *F* and he eventually drops out of his junior year in high school. The situation becomes so bad that his mother sends him to a rehab center. One year later (when the series actually begins), Johnny and his mother Karen (and her new husband, Bob) move from Seattle, Washington, to Palm Springs, California, where Karen, and especially Johnny, hope to put the past behind them. Johnny is interested in photography and appears to have recovered from the ordeal of the past year (he has also been enrolled in school and is repeating his junior year). Serial-like stories follow Johnny's efforts to start a new life with new friends as he faces all the problems that teenagers face in any city or town.

Cast: Taylor Handley *(Johnny Miller)*; Gail O'Grady *(Karen Hardy)*; D.W. Moffett *(Bob Hardy)*; Amber Heard *(Greta)*; Michael Cassidy *(Cliff Wiatt)*; Ellary Portefield *(Liza Witter)*; Tessa Thompson *(Nikki)*; Sharon Lawrence *(Tess Wiatt)*; Kyle Secor *(Alan" Skip" Matthews)*; J.R. Cacia *(Travis Dean)*; Valerie Cruz *(Nina Carter)*; Leslie Jordan *(Jesse Jo)*.

4008 *The Hidden Room.* (Series; Anthology; Lifetime; 1991). Dramas that focus primarily on women and the problems they face when unexpected (and often unnatural) incidents occur (for example, a woman who sees the life she could have had if she chose a different path; a woman seeing her romance novel hero come to life; a woman seeing the baby she never had).

Host: Mimi Kuzak.

4009 *Hidden Treasure.* (Series; Game; Syn.; 1957). The object calls for contestants to piece together clues in musical numbers to distinguish between similar words (for example, "padded" or "added," "sitter" or "setter"). Players with the most correct answers are the winners.

Host: Robert Q. Lewis. **Vocalists:** Russell Arms, Judy Johnson, Richard Hayes, Eve DeLuca. **Music:** Ray Bloch. **Trumpet Soloist:** Bobby Hackett.

4010 *Higglytown Heroes.* (Series; Cartoon; Disney; 2004–). A computer animated program, aimed at preschoolers, that celebrates everyday heroes — from police officers to mailmen as seen through the experiences of Kip, Twinkle, Wayne, Eubie and their friend, Fran, the talking squirrel.

Voice Cast: Rory Thost *(Kip)*; Liliana Mumy *(Twinkle)*; Taylor Masamitsu *(Eubie)*; Edie McClurg *(Fran)*; Frankie Ryan Manriquez *(Wayne)*; Dee Bradley Baker *(Uncle Zooter)*; Kevin Michael Richardson *(Uncle Lemmo)*; Rachel York *(Bitty)*.

4011 *High.* (Pilot; Drama; Unaired; Produced for CBS in 1990). Life at Ray Kroc High, a suburban middle-class school where social classes, ethnic groups and generations collide in the pursuit of education.

Cast: Craig Ferguson *(Declan Connelly)*; Zach Braff *(Brad Bryant)*; Rodney Eastman *(Palmer Bryant)*.

4012 *High Bar.* (Pilot; Drama; Unaired; Produced for ABC in 2006). Wilson, Porter & Knox is a prestigious law firm where a young attorney (Caroline) is hoping to become a partner despite the situations that constantly try her patience and test her abilities. Marcia is the office vixen; Pamela, a lesbian, is the voice of reason in the office; Lauren is a working mother struggling to divide her time between the office and home.

Cast: Paige Turko *(Caroline Fordham)*; Kelli Williams *(Pamela)*; Gracelle Beauvais *(Marcia)*; Regina King *(Lauren)*; Xander Berkeley *(Campbell Knox)*; Julie Warner *(Mary Porter)*; Jill Ritchie *(Kristin)*.

4013 *The High Chaparral.* (Series; Western; NBC; 1967–1971). Tucson, Arizona, in the 1870s is the setting for the saga of the Cannon family as they struggle to maintain and operate the High Chaparral Ranch in an era of violence and lawlessness. John Cannon is the ranch owner; he is married to Victoria de Montoya. Buck Cannon is John's brother and Billy Blue Cannon is John's son from a prior marriage. Don Sebastian de Montoya is Victoria's father, the owner of the Montoya Ranch. Manolito de Montoya is Sebastian's son. Anna Lee is John's first wife (flashbacks); Sam Butler is the Chaparral Ranch foreman; Ira is the wrangler; and ranch hands are Ted, Pedro, Wind, Joe and Vaquero.

Cast: Leif Erickson *(John Cannon)*; Cameron Mitchell *(Buck Cannon)*; Linda Cristal *(Victoria de Montoya Cannon)*; Mark Slade *(Billy Blue Cannon)*; Frank Silvera *(Don Sebastian de Montoya)*; Henry Darrow *(Manolito de Montoya)*; Don Collier *(Sam Butler)*; Jerry Summers *(Ira)*; Joan Caulfield *(Anna Lee Cannon)*; James Almonza *(Soldado)*; Ted Markland *(Ted Reno)*; Roberto Contreras *(Pedro)*; Rudy Ramos *(Wind)*; Bob Hoy *(Joe)*; Rodolfo Acosta *(Vaquero)*.

4014 *High Feather.* (Series; Comedy; PBS; 1980). A group of children attending the High Feather Summer Camp are profiled as they learn about animals, the wilderness and how to care for themselves when dealing with Mother Nature.

Cast: Jacqueline Allen *(Leslie)*; Brian Goldberg *(Stan)*; Virgil Hayes *(Leo)*; Richard Levey *(Tom)*; Cindy O'Neill *(Suzanne)*; Emily Wagner *(Cathy)*; Taisha Washington *(Ann Campbell)*; Tino Zaldivar *(Domingo)*; Robert Y.R. Chung *(Kim)*; Barbara Brown *(Mrs. Riggs; counselor)*; Ernesto Gonzalez *(Chef)*; Mrs. Rodriquez *(Nurse)*.

4015 *High Finance.* (Series; Game; CBS; 1956). Contestants, selected from various cities across the country, are quizzed on news items that appear in their local papers. Question-and-answer rounds, consisting of three levels, are played one per week. The winner of the first round, the highest cash scorer, receives the choice of either keeping his earnings or returning to increase his money by tackling level two. If the player decides to continue and attempts the third level, he can win his secret desire (up to $35,000) but he stands to lose everything he has won up to this point if he fails.

Host: Dennis James. **Announcer:** Jay Sims, Jack Gregson.

4016 *High Five.* (Pilot; Comedy; NBC; July 22, 1982). KBHX, Channel 55, is an all-black television station located in the Watts section of Los Angeles. Because of its high ranking on the UHF dial, it has been nicknamed the "High Five." The proposal was to relate the antics of its staff as they try to run the station. Al Cook is the station manager; Wilson Porter and Velma Williams are the news co-anchors; Stacey is the receptionist; Calvin, the station owner; and Jamal, an employee.

Cast: Harrison Page *(Al Cook)*; Franklyn Seales *(Wilson Porter)*; Clarice Taylor *(Velma Williams)*; Cindy Herron *(Stacey)*; Ted Ross *(Calvin T. Washburn)*; Clinton Derricks Carroll *(Jamal)*.

4017 ***High Hopes.*** (Series; Drama; Syn.; 1978). The dramatic story of Dr. Neal Chapman, counselor in the fictional town of Cambridge, Canada.

Cast: Bruce Gray (*Dr. Neal Chapman*); Marianne McIsaac (*Jessie Chapman*); Nuala Fitzgerald (*Paula Myles*); Barbara Kyle (*Trudy Bowen*); Colin Fox (*Walter Telford*); Doris Petrie (*Meg Chapman*); Gena Dick (*Amy Sperry*); Jayne Eastwood (*Louise Bates*); Michael Tait (*Michael Stewart, Sr.*); Gordon Thompson (*Michael Stewart, Jr.*); Gerry Salsberg (*Georgia Morgan*); Dorothy Malone (*Carol Tauss*); Nehemiah Persoff (*Victor Tauss*); Jan Muszynski (*Dr. Dan Gerard*).

4018 ***High Incident.*** (Series; Crime Drama; ABC; 1996–1997). A true-to-life depiction of police work in action as seen through the assignments of Jim Marsh, a sergeant with the El Camino Police Department, as he and his fellow officers risk their lives battling street crime.

Cast: David Keith (*Sgt. Jim Marsh*); Catherine Kellner (*Off. Gayle Van Camp*); Blair Underwood (*Off. Michael Rhoades*); Matt Beck (*Officer Terry Hagar*); Aunjanue Ellis (*Off. Leslie Joyner*); Cole Hauser (*Off. Randy Willitz*); Matt Craven (*Off. Len Gaye*); Lisa Vidal (*Off. Jessica Helgado*); Lindsay Frost (*Sgt. Helen Sullivan*); Wendy Davis (*Off. Lynette White*); Julio Oscar Mechoso (*Off. Richie Fernandez*); Louis Mustillo (*Off. Russell Topps*).

4019 ***The High Life.*** (Pilot; Comedy; ABC; Aug. 3, 1990). Teresa "Tracy" Peters is a beautiful Manhattan fashion model whose life suddenly changes when she is made guardian of Paul, Frank and Dion, her three orphaned nephews when their parents are killed in a car accident. The proposal was to relate Tracy's efforts to change her lifestyle and care for three mischievous orphans. J. Mason Lowell is Tracy's friend, a lawyer. Tracy Scoggins is listed as Francesca Peters on ABC's press release (Tracy is her screen name).

Cast: Tracy Scoggins (*Tracy Peters*); Raye Birk (*J. Mason Lowell*); Danny Nucci (*Paul Minetti*); Michael Miceli (*Frank Minetti*); Matthew Lawrence (*Dion Minetti*).

4020 ***High Low.*** (Series; Game; NBC; 1957). The object calls for a contestant to challenge a panel of three experts by offering to answer one or more parts of questions containing several segments. A player has to match the panelist claiming to have the most answers (High) or the one with the fewest (Low). If the player matches the High expert, he receives $1500; if he matches the Low expert he wins $1000. Failure to match either High or Low results in the loss of everything and a new challenger is introduced.

Host: Jack Barry. **Panelists:** Burl Ives, Walter Slezak, Patricia Medina. **Announcer:** Don Pardo.

4021 ***High Mountain Rangers.*** (Series; Adventure; CBS; 1988). High Mountain Rangers is a rescue organization based in the Sierra Nevadas near Lake Tahoe. It was founded by Jesse Hawkes as an attempt to rescue people who become trapped in perilous situations while in the mountains. His sons, Matt and Cody, assist him. "Frostbite" is headquarters code for the rangers; Yamaha snowmobiles are used. Jesse's sled is Top Gun; Cody's is White Eagle; Ranger T.J. Cousins rides a sled called Black Magic; and Snow Babe is the sled of Ranger Robin Carstairs. Jesse has a dog named Ding, and a girl named Jackie appears to be Jesse's romantic interest (it is not made clear whether Jesse is a widower or divorced). Lee Greenwood performs the "High Mountain Rangers" theme. See also *Jesse Hawkes*, the spin off series.

Cast: Robert Conrad (*Jesse Hawkes*); Christian Conrad (*Matt Hawkes*); Shane Conrad (*Cody Hawkes*); Toni Towles (*T.J. Cousins*); P.A. Christian (*Robin Carstairs*); Robyn Peterson (*Jackie*).

4022 ***High Performance.*** (Series; Adventure; ABC; 1983). High Performance is an elite protection agency that undertakes hazardous assignments for $5,000 a day plus expenses. Kate Flannery, a martial-arts expert; Blue Stratton, an ex-military intelligence officer; and Shane Adams, a former stunt car driver, are its top operatives. Stories relate their case assignments and the rather unorthodox methods they use to achieve results. Brennan, Kate's father is the head of High Performance; Fletch is Brennan's mechanical design genius.

Cast: Lisa Hartman (*Kate Flannery*); Jack Scalia (*Blue Stratton*); Rick Edwards (*Shane Adams*); Mitchell Ryan (*Brennan Flannery*); Jason Bernard (*O.T. "Fletch" Fletcher*).

4023 ***High Risk.*** (Pilot; Adventure; ABC; May 15, 1976). Sebastian, Sandra, Guthrie, Daisy, Walter T. and Eric are ex-circus performers who use their expert skills as thieves to help the U.S. government solve complex cases.

Cast: Victor Buono (*Sebastian*); JoAnna Cameron (*Sandra*); Joseph Sirola (*Guthrie*); Ronne Troup (*Daisy*); Don Stroud (*Walter T*); Wolf Roth (*Eric*).

4024 ***High Rollers.*** (Series; Game; NBC/Syn.; 1974–1988). A question is read to two competing players. The first player to correctly answer receives the chance to roll two large dice. When the dice are rolled, the player uses the numbers that appear to deduct that number from a large board of nine numbers. Each of the three columns of numbers (which appear in a tic tac toe like board) contains a prize. Players try to eliminate the numbers in the columns to win their prizes. If, however, a player rolls an inactive number, he is defeated (for example, if a player rolls a six and six has already been eliminated, he loses his turn and a new question is read). The first player to win two games is the winner and receives what prizes he has uncovered.

1974 Program Open: "Now a game of high stakes where every decision is a gamble and every move can be your last—*High Rollers*. Now, here the man with the action, Alex Trebek." Four versions appeared:

1. High Rollers (NBC, 1974–76). **Host:** Alex Trebek. **Assistant/Dice Roller:** Ruta Lee. **Announcer:** Kenny Williams.

2. High Rollers (NBC, 1978–80). **Host:** Alex Trebek. **Assistants:** Becky Price, Lauren Firestone. **Announcer:** Kenny Williams.

3. High Rollers (Syn., 1975–76). **Host:** Alex Trebek. **Assistant:** Elaine Stewart. **Announcer:** Kenny Williams.

4. High Rollers (Syn., 1987–88). **Host:** Wink Martindale. **Assistant:** K.C. Winkler, Crystal Owens. **Announcer:** Dean Goss.

4025 ***High School Musical: Get in the Picture.*** (Series; Reality; ABC; 2008). An audition to find a teenager to star in a music video that will be shown during the closing credits of the fall 2008 feature film *High School Musical 3: Senior Year*. Twelve teenagers compete in music and dance challenges for the music video and a contract with ABC and Disney Records. The teens are guided by a professional faculty to hone their acting, singing, dancing and performing skills.

Host: Nick Lachey. **Faculty:** Tiana Brown (*dancer*); Regina Williams (*actress*); Rob Adler (*actor*); Chris Prinzo (*Broadway star*).

4026 ***High School Reunion.*** (Series; Reality; WB; 2003–2005). Graduates from various high schools are reunited ten years later to share experiences about their lives. Since scandal is needed for a reality show to work, the fourteen chosen subjects range from the class player to the class bitch to the class nerd. Have they changed? How do they interact with each other now when they are all placed in a house together? The good, the bad and the ugly of the situation is highlighted as *High School Reunion* sets out to show how each has progressed and what each seeks to gain. First season episodes (Cycle 1) focus on the graduates of Oak Park Forest High School (class of 1992); Cycle 2 reunites the class of 1993 from Round Rock High School; students from Cardinal Gibbons High School, class of 1994, are reunited in Cycle 3. Mike Richards and Ananda Lewis host.

TV land revised the concept in 2008 with a look at 16 former high school students from J.J. Pearcde High School in Richardson, Texas.

4027   *High School, U.S.A.* (Pilot; Comedy; NBC; Oct. 16, 1983). Life at mythical Excelsior Union High School in Indiana. A second pilot aired on May 26, 1984.

Faculty Cast Pilot 1: Tony Dow (*Principal Peter Kinney*); Dwayne Hickman (*Mr. Plaza*); Angela Cartwright (*Miss D'Angelo*); Steve Franken (*Dr. Fritz Hauptmann*); Dawn Wells (*Miss Lori Lee*); Barry Livingston (*Mr. Sirota*); David Nelson (*Mr. Krinksy*).

Students Cast Pilot 1: Nancy McKeon (*Beth Franklin*); Dana Plato (*Cara Ames*); Cathy Silvers (*Peggy*); Lauri Hendler (*Nadene*); Michael J. Fox (*Jay Jay Manners*); Anthony Edwards (*Beau Middleton*); Crystal Bernard (*Ann Marie Conklin*); Todd Bridges (*Otto Lipton*); Michael Zorek (*Chuckie Dipple*); Crispin Glover (*Archie Feld*); Tom Villard (*Leo Bandini*).

Faculty Cast Pilot 2: Rick Nelson (*Principal Peter Kinney*); Henry Gibson (*Vice Principal Roman Ing*); Harriet Nelson (*Mrs. Crosley*); Melody Anderson (*Cindy Franklin*); Jerry Mathers (*Mr. Sirota*); Ken Osmond (*The Biology teacher*); Paul Petersen (*The Coach*).

Students Cast Pilot 2: Crystal Bernard (*Ann Marie Conklin*); Anne-Marie Johnson (*Beth Franklin*); Ben Marley (*Jay Jay Manners*); Michael Zorek (*Chuckie*); Crispin Glover (*Bo Middleton*); Jonathan Gries (*Leo Bandini*); Jo Ann Willett (*Nadene*).

4028   *High Sierra Search and Rescue.* (Series; Adventure; NBC; 1995). The Bear Valley Search and Rescue Team is a volunteer mountain rescue team based in the town of Bear Valley in California's Sierra Nevada Mountains. Episodes, based on true life incidents, follow the team as they risk their lives to save people trapped in perilous situations. *The Team:* Griffin "Tooter" Campbell, a helicopter pilot for hire (he gets his nickname from playing the bagpipes); Morgan Duffy, owner of the Bear Valley General Store; Kaja Wilson, her clerk; Lisa Peterson, a service station owner; Enrique Cruz, the town's only school teacher; Ty Cooper, a deputy sheriff; and Flynn Norstedt, a ski instructor. Based on the TV movie *Search and Rescue* (NBC, Mar. 27, 1994).

Cast: Robert Conrad (*Tooter Campbell*); Dee Wallace Stone (*Morgan Duffy*); Brittney Powell (*Kaja Wilson*); Lavelda Fann (*Lisa Peterson*); Alistair MacDougall (*Ty Cooper*); Ramon Franco (*Enrique Cruz*); Jason Lewis (*Flynn Norstedt*).

4029   *High Society.* (Series; Comedy; CBS; 1995-1996). Eleanor "Ellie" Walker, a New York socialite and novelist (known for her trashy love stories), lives at 511 Sutton Place in Manhattan. Ellie, whose real name is Eleanor Antoinette Worshorsky, was born in Pittsburgh. She is sassy, chases men and drinks a bit too much. In fourth and fifth grades Ellie was voted "best French kisser" and had a dog named Goochie. She frequents restaurants but doesn't like corner tables "because no one can see me." Ellie has written the following books: *Swedish Meat Boys, Hermaphrodite, High Sierra Streetwalker, Hung Jury, Pool Boys Plunge, Stiletto Summer, Submissive Samurai* and *The Naked and the Deadline.*

Dorothy "Dot" Emerson owns Emerson Publishing, the company that produces Ellie's books. Dot's company is number one in travel and leisure books. Valerie "Val" Brumberg is the bland, uninteresting,

non-wealthy friend. Val was hostess at Le Petit Burger (fired for arguing with the chef over the size of a burger) and was born in New Jersey. Ellie, Dot and Val are also friends and stories relate the events that spark their lives.

Cast: Jean Smart (*Ellie Walker*); Mary McDonnell (*Dot Emerson*); Faith Prince (*Val Brumberg*).

4030   *High Society.* (Series; Reality; CW; 2010). An intimate look at the privileged, close knit inhabitants of Manhattan's Upper East Side as seen through the experiences of Tinsley Mortimer, a socialite ("The most talked-about Park Avenue Princess") as she and her society friends "circulate through New York's black tie affairs...."

4031   *High Stakes Poker.* (Series; Reality GSN; 2006–). High stakes poker players compete in tournaments wherein wagers range from $100 to $1 million. Daniel Alaei, Gabe Kaplan, A.J. Benza, Kara Scott and Norm McDonald host; Danette Morway is the dealer.

4032   *High Tide.* (Series; Adventure; Syn.; 1994-1995). Mick Barrett and his younger brother, Joey, run a surf shop on the boardwalk off the beach in Los Angeles. Mick is an ex cop; Joey is an ex surfer. The surf shop, however, doesn't pay the bills. A man named Gordon is a former CIA agent with a mission to stop crime. He hires the brothers to be his legmen to investigate crimes and bring criminals to justice. Stories follow Mick and Joey as the plunge head first into dangerous situations to get the job done. Fritz, a gorgeous girl, assists Gordon and Anne runs the local gift shop.

Cast: Rick Springfield (*Mick Barrett*); Yannick Bisson (*Joey Barrett*); George Segal (*Gordon*); Julie Cialini (*Annie*); Cay Helmich (*Fritz Boller; 1994*); Diane Frank (*Fritz Boller; 1994-1995*).

4033   *Highcliffe Manor.* (Series; Comedy; NBC; 1979). The Blacke Foundation is a scientific institute located in Highcliffe Manor on a desolate island. Helen Blacke, a beautiful but mysterious woman, runs the foundation and stories present a look at the eccentric residents of the manor: Frances Cascan, a scientist obsessed with creating life; Wendy Sparks, Helen's sexy secretary; Rebecca, the housekeeper; Bram Shelley, the bionic man Frances is building; Dr. Felix Morger, the man seeking to seduce Helen; the Reverend Mr. Ian Glenville; Smythe, Ian's valet; Cheng, Frances's assistant; and Doctors Sanchez and Knootz.

Cast: Shelley Fabares (*Helen Blacke*); Eugenie Ross-Leming (*Frances Cascan*); Audrey Landers (*Wendy Sparks*); Jenny O'Hara (*Rebecca*); Christian Marlowe (*Bram Shelley*); Gerald Gordon (*Dr. Felix Morger*); Stephen McHattie (*Ian Glenville*); Ernie Hudson (*Smythe*); Harold Sakata (*Cheng*); Luis Avalos (*Dr. Sanchez*); Marty Zagon (*Dr. Knootz*). **Narrator:** Peter Lawford.

4034   *Higher and Higher, Attorneys at Law.* (Pilot; Crime Drama; CBS; Sept. 9, 1968). Liz and John Higher are a husband-and-wife law team who operate the firm of Higher and Higher. Liz and John have basically the same approach to tackling cases although Liz often believes her feminine intuition is a plus when it comes to uncovering facts. The proposal was to relate their case investigations into murders.

Cast: Sally Kellerman (*Liz Higher*); John McMartin (*John Higher*).

4035   *Higher Ground.* (Pilot; Adventure; Unaired; Produced for CBS in 1988). Jim Clayton is an FBI agent who has a dream of becoming a bush pilot in Alaska. One day, after 20 years on the job, Jim quits over a questionable assignment. Rick Loden, Jim's ex-partner, urges him to come to Alaska and fulfill his dream by becoming a partner in his company, the Annakin Air Charter Service. Shortly after, Rick is killed in a drug related incident. Jim teams with Rick's widow, Ginny, and her young son, Tommy, in an effort to keep the fledgling air service from bankruptcy. The proposal was to relate their adventures. Other regulars are Linc Holmes, an Indian trapper who helps them; and Lieutenant Smight, a no-nonsense cop Jim aids from time to time.

Cast: John Denver (*Jim Clayton*); Meg Wittner (*Ginny Loden*); Brandon Marsh (*Tommy Loden*); John Rhys-Davies (*Lieutenant Smight*); David Renan (*Linc Holmes*).

4036 *Highlander.* (Series; Adventure; Syn.; 1992–1998). Duncan MacLeod and Tessa Noel are co-owners of a business called The Antique Shop. Tessa and Duncan are also lovers and Tessa is one of the two people who know Duncan's secret: he is an Immortal.

Although he looks to be 35, Duncan was born in the Scottish Highlands 400 years ago. He knows only that he was brought to his father as an infant by a midwife when the baby that was born to his mother died at birth. It was not until Duncan was a young man that he learned he was an Immortal. During a battle with a rival clan Duncan was mortally wounded. Duncan's father praised him as a brave warrior; but when Duncan's wounds healed and he returned to life, his father condemned him, saying he was in league with the devil. Although cast out by his parents, Duncan kept the only name he knew. Now, as a representative of the Clan MacLeod, Duncan is seeking to become the last Immortal and acquire the power of all Immortals to rule the world for good. Legend states that all knowledge is contained by the Immortals. When one Immortal encounters another, the Gathering is held. This is followed by the Quickening (combat by sword) to acquire additional strength. An Immortal can only be killed by beheading. When this happens, the surviving Immortal acquires the other's knowledge and strength. If a virtuous Immortal delivers the final blow, goodness triumphs; if the last surviving Immortal is evil, darkness will reign forever. "In the end there can be only one." There is no information given as to where the Immortals come from or how they came to be. As Duncan seeks to fulfill his destiny, he helps people who have become victims of crime and dispenses justice with his ornamental Japanese sword (he also seeks to prevent evil Immortals from harming people and has become a vigilante of sorts).

Duncan and Tessa live in a loft over the antique store. Before her career as a sculptress proved financially sound, Tessa worked as a tour guide on a sightseeing boat. It is here that she met Duncan when he boarded at the last moment. Duncan's assistant, Richie Ryan is a young hoodlum Duncan reformed and the only other person who knows Duncan's secret.

In the episode of Oct. 23, 1993, "The Darkness," Tessa and Richie become involved in a struggle with car thieves and are shot; Tessa is killed and Richie seriously wounded. Richie miraculously recovers and learns from Duncan that he is an Immortal. Richie, however, has no recollection of his past. The following episode, "An Eye for an Eye," finds Duncan selling what is now called The Art Gallery and purchasing controlling interest in DeSalvo's, a gym run by Charlie DeSalvo. Duncan remains basically behind the scenes; Charlie and Richie conduct the daily operations. The following episode, "The Watcher," introduces an additional regular — Joe Dawson, the owner of Joe's Bookstore at 27 North Jay Street. Joe is a member of the Watchers, a secret society of mortals who observe and record the deeds of Immortals. Joe also helps Duncan in his quest (which has been changed somewhat to destroy the evil Immortals).

First season episodes also feature Randi McFarland, a television reporter for KLCA, Channel 8 News, who covers the incidents that just happen to involve Duncan. Amanda is a beautiful Immortal who is not only Duncan's romantic interest (after Tessa) but a cunning thief who is drawn to the good things in life (see *Highlander: The Raven*). Queen performs the theme, "I Am Immortal." Based on the 1985 feature film of the same title.

Cast: Adrian Paul (*Duncan MacLeod*); Alexandra Vandernoot (*Tessa Noel*); Stan Kirsch (*Richie Ryan*); Philip Akin (*Charles DeSalvo*); Jim Byrnes (*Joe Dawson*); Amanda Wyss (*Randi McFarland*).

4037 *Highlander: The Animated Series.* (Series; Cartoon; USA; 1994). An animated adaptation of the live action theatrical film (and television series) *Highlander*. In a futuristic time a great catastrophe has befallen the Earth. A meteorite has destroyed virtually everything mankind has built. An evil Immortal named Kortan has risen from the ashes to rule from the fortress city of Mogonda. Immortals are a race of beings that have been battling each other for centuries to become the last remaining Immortal to gain enormous power. But now the knowledge lost to humanity must be saved. The Immortals put their differences aside and join together to pass on knowledge. The Immortals are awaiting the arrival of Quentin MacLeod, the last member of the Clan MacLeod, who has been proclaimed the one to battle Kortan and set the human race free of his rule. The wait has been long. After 700 years Quentin arrives and meets with Ramirez, the oldest and wisest of the Immortals. It is Ramirez's job to train and guide Quentin for the ultimate confrontation. Stories follow Quentin as he defends survivors of the Great Catastrophe from Kortan.

Voice Cast: Miklos Perlus (*Quentin MacLeod*); Lawrence Bayne (*Kortan*); Ben Campbell (*Ramirez*); Stuart Stone, Tracey Moore.

4038 *Highlander: The Raven.* (Series; Adventure; Syn.; 1998-1999). There is a mysterious Eskimo legend about a raven who stole the sun, the moon and the stars to protect them from an evil thief who wanted to rob them and plunge the world into darkness. When the evil was defeated, the raven returned light and goodness to the world.

A mysterious, modern-day woman named Amanda is the human incarnation of that raven. She is an Immortal and, like the raven, a creature of the night who steals only the most fabulous treasures — "from jewels to paintings to fine cigars."

Amanda (called Amanda Montrouse in the pilot) is a "Princess of Thieves." She targets only the rich and famous. She never kills "I only steal." Amanda cannot die, except by beheading (which is her ultimate death. Other methods can kill her, but she will be reborn again). Like Duncan MacLeod (of the series *Highlander*; see title), Amanda fights injustice with a Samurai sword. Amanda, said to be 1200 years old in dialogue (but 1000 years old in the theme), has lived for centuries as a roguish beauty who is attracted to the good things in life. She is never malicious and not without scruples. Like Duncan, Amanda's history is a mystery; there is no explanation given as to who she really is or where she actually came from. Amanda says only that she belongs to a privileged class called the Immortals. She has lived and died many times and recalled her first birth as a young peasant girl in Normandy in A.D. 850. This life was cut short when she was killed for stealing a loaf of bread. She was reborn that same day, but was unaware of her destiny. She was found and taken in by a mysterious woman named Rebecca Horne. It was Rebecca, who is assumed to be a good Immortal, who cared for Amanda until she became a young woman. At this time, Amanda was taught the martial arts and the art of swordplay. She was also told that she was an Immortal and that to survive, she must defeat the evil Immortals who seek to plunge the world into darkness (when a good Immortal meets her evil counterpart, the Quickening is held — a fight to the death by sword. The Immortal who is victorious acquires the strength and powers of the defeated Immortal). Amanda has been a duchess, a slave and a woman of nobility (what she has mentioned).

Nick Wolfe is a detective with the South Police Precinct, 52nd Division. He is a dedicated, skilled investigator who believes in what he is doing. He also believes Amanda is a thief but can't prove it. When Amanda is framed by a dishonest cop for a crime she didn't commit, Nick and his partner begin an investigation. The case turns sour when Nick confronts the real culprit but his partner is killed protecting Amanda. Amanda cannot forget what Nick's partner did for her. She is suddenly developing something she has never known before—a sense of responsibility. Nick, on the other hand, brought down a crooked cop, something he thought was good for the department—until he finds his superiors unwilling to admit that one of their own was a killer. Now, feeling betrayed, he begins to question his definition of right. When he is offered a promotion to lieutenant to forget about the incident, he quits. Nick, however, cannot abandon his right "to protect and serve." While working outside the law to solve crimes and defend people, Nick finds unexpected help from Amanda—her way of trying to pay back Nick for what he has done for her. Rather than work as separate entities, they join forces to return light to the world by waging a private war against evil and injustice. Some episodes are set in Europe and find Amanda and Nick becoming detectives to return stolen art objects for a percentage of their value. Joe Dawson (Jim Byrnes), the Watcher from the prior series, appears only once in the third episode.

Cast: Elizabeth Gracen (*Amanda*); Paul Johansson (*Nick Wolfe*).

4039 *Highway Honeys.* (Pilot; Comedy; NBC; Jan. 3, 1983). Carol Lee and Datona Shepherd are a sister-and-brother team of clean-living tow truckers whose father, Cannonball Shepherd, runs the Good Shepherds Towing Service in Sierra Madre, Texas. The proposed series was to relate their adventures as they attempt to run an honest business. Originally titled *Towheads* (the nickname for tow truckers). Other regulars are Sheriff Wilbur T. Mossburgh; Draggin' Lady, a trucker for the corrupt Apocalypse Towing Service; Wolfe Crawley, the owner of Apocalypse; Conchita Valdez, Wilbur's deputy; and Amigo, Tattoo and Pig Long, Wolfe's other truckers.

Cast: Mary Davis Duncan (*Carol Lee Shepherd*); Will Bledsoe (*Datona Shepherd*); Don Collier (*Cannonball Shepherd*); Glen Ash (*Wilbur T. Mossburgh*); Kirstie Alley (*Draggin' Lady*); Matt Clark (*Wolfe Crawley*); Tina Gail Hernandez (*Conchita Valdez*); Miguel Rodriquez (*Amigo*); Keenan Ivory Wayans (*Tattoo Calhoune*); Michael Weston Crabtree (*Pig Long*).

4040 *Highway Patrol.* (Series; Crime Drama; Syn.; 1956). Dramatizations based on the experiences of Highway Patrol officers in all 48 states (at the time of filming). Dan Matthews, a Highway Patrol Chief, is representative of such officers who serve to patrol and protect as members of the Highway Patrol.

Program Open: "Whenever the laws of any state are broken, a duly authorized organization swings into action. It may be called the State Police, State Troopers, Militia, the Rangers or the Highway Patrol. These are the stories of the men whose training, skill and courage have enforced and preserved our state laws."

Cast: Broderick Crawford (*Dan Matthews*); William Boyett (*Sergeant Williams*). **Narrator:** Art Gilmore.

4041 *Highway to Heaven.* (Series; Drama; NBC; 1984–1989). Arthur Morton was born in 1917 and worked as an honest lawyer all his life. He died in 1948. He was married to Jane (Dorothy McGuire) and was the father of a daughter named Mandy (Joan Welles). Sometime after his death, Arthur became an apprentice angel and was given an assignment in order to gain his wings: to help people on earth. He was given the new name of Jonathan Smith and worked alone until he met Mark Gordon, a cynical ex-cop. When Jonathan restored Mark's faith in his fellow man and revealed himself to be an angel, Mark asked to let him help. Mark attended Lathrop High School and had the nickname of "Stick." He was with the Oakland Police Department for 15 years. Mark wears a California A's baseball cap and drives a Ford sedan. Jonathan calls God "The Boss" (Mark blames "The Boss" for all the little misadventures he encounters). Bob Hope made a rare dramatic appearance as Symcopop, the Assignment Angel. David Rose composed the theme, "Highway to Heaven."

Cast: Michael Landon (*Jonathan Smith*); Victor French (*Mark Gordon*); John McLiam (*Carl Fred Sims; Mark's grandfather*); Sean de Veritch (*Mark as a child; flashbacks*).

4042 *The Highwayman.* (Pilot; Adventure; NBC; Aug. 17, 1958). England in 1750 is the setting for a proposal about James McDonald, a man of leisure who is actually a highwayman (thief) who helps people in trouble.

Cast: Louis Hayward (*James McDonald*).

4043 *The Highwayman.* (Series; Adventure; NBC; 1988). In an effort to battle crime and corruption in areas where laws often terminate (at county lines on long stretches of highway), the Justice Department institutes a test program called the Stealth Project and creates a new breed of lawmen called Highwaymen who work in secret. Our mysterious Highwayman is known only as "Highway" or "Highwayman." He uses a high tech 12-ton black Mack truck and an awesome handgun (capable of firing grenades like bullets) to battle crime in those legal blackouts. His field code is "Highway One" and although the opening theme narration tells us that "Highwaymen work in secret and alone," Jetto, an Australian-bred Highwayman, assists our hero. A girl known only as Dawn was Highway's original contact (she was a government agent who posed as a disc jockey; she hosted *The Dawn Patrol* on an unnamed 50,000 watt clear channel station—"The Mighty 690 from New Orleans"). She was replaced by Tanya Winthrop, an agent who met with Highway in the field (as opposed to over the airwaves). Highway's superior is Admiral Conte, who supervises operations for the Control Center as Master Key.

Highway has no other name. If someone asks "Who are you?" he responds with "Someone who may be able to help." We are told the Highwayman is a legend: "They say his mother was born of fire and his father was born of wind—you hear a lot of legends told when you ride the long hard slab. Some who say the man is good and some who say he is bad; but all agree who try to play a cheatin' hand, you only get one chance to draw against the Highwayman." William Conrad narrates. The pilot aired on Sept. 20, 1987.

Cast: Sam J. Jones (*Highwayman*); Claudia Christian (*Dawn*); Jane Badler (*Tanya Winthrop*); Jack Ging (*Admiral Conte*); Jacko (*Jetto*).

4044 *The Hilarious House of Frightenstein.* (Series; Variety; Syn.; 1975). The castle of Frightenstein in Transylvania is the setting for a spooky program of comedy sketches, songs, blackouts and music that revolve around Count Frightenstein, his servant Igor, and their attempts to bring to life Bruce, an "out of order" Frankenstein-style monster.

Cast: Vincent Price (*Host*); Billy Van (*Count Frightenstein*); Rais Fishka (*Igor*); **Regulars:** Prof. Julius Sumner Miller, Joe Torby, Guy Big.

4045 *Hildegard Withers.* (Pilot; Mystery; ABC; Mar. 4, 1972). Hildegard Withers is a school teacher who, throughout her years of teaching, became fascinated by crime and read criminology books at every opportunity. Now retired, and with time on her hands,

Hildegard feels she is talented enough to investigate crimes. While not a registered sleuth, she pokes her nose into police business and attaches herself to Oscar Piper, a police inspector who grudgingly accepts her help but later appreciates it when her instincts help him bring criminals to justice. Al is the young man who assists Hildegard.

Cast: Eve Arden (*Hildegard Withers*); Dennis Rucker (*Al Fisher*); James Gregory (*Oscar Piper*).

4046 *The Hill.* (Pilot; Drama; Unaired; Produced for ABC in 2006). While it is widely believed that the government is run by elder statesmen, the majority of people who work in Congress are of the average age of 25. Matt O'Brien and Maggie Rogers are two such people and the proposal was to follow their activities in Washington, D.C. Matt, a Democratic congressional staffer with presidential aspirations, works for Bryce Lowell, an ambitious female Senator. Maggie, a Republican, is 18 years old and works as a congressional page in Bryce's office.

Cast: Eric Christian Olsen (*Matt O'Brien*); Michelle Trachtenberg (*Maggie Rogers*); Mark Moses (*Senator Rogers*); Smith Cho (*Cheyenne*).

4047 *Hill Street Blues.* (Series; Crime Drama; NBC; 1981–1987). A realistic look at the everyday lives of the men and women attached to an inner city police precinct. The program, created by Steven Bochco and Michael Kozoll, was actually the first series since ABC's *Naked City* in 1958 to go beyond crime solving and realistically focus on the personal and professional problems law enforcers face in their everyday lives. Mike Post composed the "Hill Street Blues" theme.

Cast: Daniel J. Travanti (*Capt. Frank Furillo*); Barbara Bosson (*Fay Furillo*); Charles Haid (*Officer Andy Renko*); Veronica Hamel (*Joyce Davenport*); Michael Conrad (*Sgt. Phil Esterhaus*); James B. Sikking (*Lt. Howard Hunter*); Betty Thomas (*Sgt. Lucy Bates*); Michael Warren (*Officer Bobby Hill*); Bruce Weitz (*Sgt. Mick Belker*); Barbara Babcock (*Grace Gardner*); Gerry Black (*Det. Alf Chesley*); Taurean Blacque (*Det. Neal Washington*); Robert Clohessy (*Officer Patrick Flaherty*); Lindsay Crouse (*Kate McBride*); Pat Corley (*Coroner Wally Nydorf*); Kiel Martin (*Officer J.D. LaRue*); Lynne Moody (*Martha Nichols*); Ken Olin (*Sgt. Stan Jablonski*); Megan Gallagher (*Officer Tina Russo*); Dennis Franz (*Det. Sal Benedetto, 1983*); Dennis Franz (*Lt. Norman Buntz, 1985–87*); Jon Cypher (*Chief Fletcher Daniels*); Rene Enriquez (*Lt. Ray Calletano*); Robert Hirschfeld (*Officer Leo Schnitz*); Peter Jurasik (*Sid, the snitch*); Vincent Lucchesi (*Capt. Jerry Fuchs*); Ed Marinaro (*Officer Joe Coffey*); Ken Olin (*Det. Harry Garibaldi*); Robert Prosky (*Sgt. Stan Kablonski*); Trinidad Silva (*Jesus Martinez*); Joe Spano (*Det. Henry Goldblume*); Lisa Sutton (*Officer Robin Tataglia*); Jeffrey Tambor (*Judge Alan Wachtel*).

4048 *Hiller and Diller.* (Series; Comedy; ABC; 1997). Ted Hiller and Neil Diller are friends who write the TV series *The Katie Show* (they previously wrote a series called *Captain Al's Circus*).

Ted is a normal, sensible family man. He is married to Jeanne and is the father of Alice, Lizzie and Josh. Neil is a slick and sarcastic. He is divorced (from Sherry) and the father of Brooke and Zane. Stories follow events in the lives of Ted and Neil as they struggle to cope with life at home and at work with an overbearing boss (Gordon Schermerhorn), the producer of *The Katie Show*. Ted lives at 422 West Grove Street; his kids attend the Meadowland School; their family dog is Nathan.

Cast: Kevin Nealon (*Ted Hiller*); Jordan Baker (*Jeanne Hiller*); Richard Lewis (*Neil Diller*); Jill Bernard (*Allison Hiller*); Faryn Einhorn (*Lizzie Hiller*); Jonathan Osser (*Josh Hiller*); Allison Mack (*Brooke Diller*); Kyle Sabihy (*Zane Diller*); Eugene Levy (*Gordon Schermerhorn*).

4049 *The Hills.* (Series; Reality; MTV; 2006). *Laguna Beach* spin off that follows Lauren Conrad as she moves to Los Angeles to attend the Fashion Institute of Design and Merchandising (while also interning for *Teen Vogue* magazine). Lauren, called "L.C.," is from a wealthy family and has decided to do something constructive with her life. That struggle is profiled as she proves she is not a spoiled rich girl. Also appearing are Whitney Port, Heidi Montag, Lisa Love, Jordan Eubanks and Brian Drolet.

4050 *Him & Us.* (Pilot; Comedy; Unaired; Produced for ABC in 2004). For over 25 years British pop star Max Flash has been burning up the charts with hit after hit. Max is flamboyant, adored by fans and everybody seems to want a piece of him. Max relishes in the glory, but it is Freddie Lazarus, his long-suffering manager, who manages to keep him under control and out of trouble. The proposal was to follow their mishaps as they perform concerts with as little controversy as possible.

Cast: Kim Cattrall (*Freddie Lazarus*); Anthony Head (*Max Flash*).

4051 *Hip Hop Harry.* (Series; Children; TLC; 2006). Hip Hop Harry is a large friendly bear (actor in costume) blessed with the ability to dance and entertain children. Harry lives in a classroom like setting and is surrounded by a group of children who come to his "clubhouse" to sing, dance, play games and learn various aspects of life through the songs and dances Hip Hop Harry teaches them.

Cast: David Joyner, Kelfa Hare (*Hip Hop Harry in Costume*); Ali Alimi (*Hip Hop Harry Voice*); Valerie Sheppard (*Letter Carrier Carla*); Ben Blair (*Dr. Vinnie*). **The Children:** Elizabeth Small, Veronica Miller, Davide Schiavone, Scott Thomas, Sophina DeJesus, Jay Jay Harris, Hayden Harrah, Meagan Woo, Savannah DeJesus, Kelli Berglund, Kiana Contreras.

4052 *Hippodrome.* (Series; Variety; CBS; 1966). A summer program, hosted by a guest of the week, that showcases European circus variety acts.

Program Open: "From London, *Hippodrome* ... with this week's host Bill Dana ... Guest stars, the Everly Brothers ... Starring Dusty Springfield, and the world's top variety circus performers with Peter Knight and his orchestra."

Guest Hosts: Woody Allen, Bill Dana, Allan Sherman, Merv Griffin, Eddie Albert, Tony Randall. **Orchestra:** Peter Knight.

4053 *The His and Her of It.* (Series; Discussion; Syn.; 1969). A topical-issues program that is designed to reveal the male and female points of view (the His and Her of it) with appropriate guests representing both sides of the issue.

Program Open: "From the ABC television center in Hollywood, it's *The His and Her of It* starring Suzanne and Geoff Edwards."

Host: Geoff Edwards, Suzanne Edwards.

4054 *His and Hers.* (Pilot; Comedy; CBS; May 15, 1984). Jimmy McCabe is a syndicated newspaper columnist and playboy who marries a pretty widow (Barbara) with two children (Kelly and Stacy) when he believes she is the girl of his dreams. The proposal, set in New York City, was to relate Jimmy's attempts to end his playboy life and adjust to marriage. Other regulars are Sharon, the owner of Jimmy's watering hole, Sharon's Place; and Larry and Pete, Jimmy's friends.

Cast: Richard Kline (*Jimmy McCabe*); Shelley Fabares (*Barbara McCabe*); Dana Kimmell (*Kelly McCabe*); Shannen Doherty (*Stacy McCabe*); Leslie Estabrook (*Sharon*); Richard Forongy (*Larry*); Terrence McGovern (*Pete*).

4055 *His and Hers.* (Series; Comedy; CBS; 1990). Douglas

("Doug") Lambert is divorced and the father of two children, Mandy and Noah. Regina ("Reggie") Hewitt is a divorcée with no children. They are also marriage counselors — and married to each other. They live at 960 North Eagle Lane in Los Angeles and have a pet cat named Fluffy. Doug and Reggie share adjoining offices in a high-rise building in downtown Los Angeles. They also co-host *Marriage Talk*, a call-in radio program on station KRTM.

Doug was born in Muncie, Indiana. He is a Capricorn, and banana pancakes are his favorite breakfast. He collects Civil War cigar bands as a hobby and estimates that he saved 84 marriages. Reggie is a Taurus and was born in Los Angeles. She was voted "the psychologist you'd most like to share a couch with" in grad school. Her mentor (not seen) is Dr. Emile Ludwig.

Other regulars are Jeff Spencer, Doug's friend; Debbie, Reggie and Doug's receptionist; Lynn, Doug's ex-wife; Marian Hewitt, Reggie's mother; Ben Hewitt, Reggie's father; Belle Lambert, Doug's mother.

Cast: Martin Mull *(Doug Lambert)*; Stephanie Faracy *(Reggie Lambert)*; Lisa Picotte *(Mandy Lambert)*; Blake Soper *(Noah Lambert)*; Richard Kline *(Jeff Spencer)*; Blair Tefkin *(Debbie)*; Randee Heller *(Lynn Lambert)*; Peggy McKay *(Marian Hewitt)*; Barbara Barrie *(Belle Lambert)*; William Windom *(Bill Lambert)*.

4056 *His Honor, Homer Bell.* (Series; Comedy; Syn.; 1955). Homer Bell is a respected judge in the small town of Spring City. He is also an understanding man and always strives to be fair in his courtroom. At home, Homer cares for his orphaned niece, Cassandra (called Casey), a mischievous girl who doesn't mean to, but often causes problems for her uncle with her tomboyish ways. Stories follow the events that spark the lives of Judge Bell, Casey and their housekeeper, Maude.

Cast: Gene Lockhart *(Judge Homer Bell)*; Mary Lee Dearing *(Cassandra Bell)*; Jane Moutrie *(Maude)*.

4057 *His Model Wife.* (Pilot; Comedy; CBS; Sept. 4, 1962). Events in the lives of the Laurens: Jean, a former model turned housewife; John, her husband, a magazine publisher; and their children, Benjy and Chris. Miss Bickle is their housekeeper.

Cast: Jeanne Crain *(Jean Lauren)*; John Vivyan *(John Lauren)*; Jimmy Gaines *(Benjy Lauren)*; Jerry Barclay *(Chris Lauren)*; Alice Frost *(Miss Bickle)*.

4058 *Histeria.* (Series; Cartoon; WB Kids; 1998). Animation is coupled with comedy to present history lessons to children. The program has many characters, most notably Pepper Mills and Father Time, but the format just didn't work as just too much was squeezed into each program, limiting the lessons to focus on the comedy of the featured historical characters.

Voice Cast: Tress McNeille *(Pepper Mills)*; Frank Welker *(Father Time)*; Laraine Newman *(Miss Information)*; Rob Paulsen *(General Custer)*; Cody Ruegger *(Loud Kiddington)*; Cree Summer *(Alka Pella)*. **Announcer:** Dick Tufeld.

4059 *The History Detectives.* (Series; Reality; PBS; 2003–). Items, which may be of historic interest and owned by ordinary people, are thoroughly investigated for their authenticity by a team of experts. The most often pain staking research needed to uncover the facts are relayed as well as the findings and the reactions of the objects' owners. The experts are Elyse Luray-Marx (Appraiser), C. Wesley Cowan (Appraiser), Tukufu Zuberi (Sociology professor), Gwen Wright (Architecture professor).

4060 *Hit Man.* (Series; Game; NBC; 1983). Three contestants compete. A story (for example, "The Making of the Wizard of Oz")

is read and illustrated with photographs. When it is completed, questions based on the story are asked. Behind each player is a vertical row of six spaces. When a player gives a correct response an animated Hit Man moves up one of those spaces; an incorrect response eliminates a player from the next question. The first two players to correctly answer six questions (scoring six Hit Men) receive $300 and continue into round two; the third place player is eliminated. In Round Two, the two players are pitted against the previous champion. The champion receives seven Hit Men; the first-place winner four Hit Men; and the second place winner three Hit Men. Another story is read and the champion must defeat the challengers while the challengers try to defeat the champion. A series of questions based on the story are asked. If the champion answers correctly, one of the Challengers Hit Men is eliminated; if one of the Challengers answers correctly, one of the Champion's Hit Men is eliminated. The first player to eliminate the others' Hit Men is the winner.

Host: Peter Tomarken. **Announcer:** Rod Roddy.

4061 *Hit Man.* (Pilot; Adventure; ABC; June 29, 1991). Roger Woods is a motion picture producer-director who uses his writers, stunt coordinator, special effects men, make-up artists, actors and crew to create elaborate stings to help people in trouble. Sara, Spider, Jerry, Billy and Vigo are the team who assist Roger.

Cast: Dennis Boutsikaris *(Roger Woods)*; Gail O'Grady *(Sara Gibson)*; Daryl Anderson *(Spider)*; Tim Dunigan *(Jerry Wilson)*; Eagle Eye Cherry *(Billy)*; Ferdinand Mayne *(Vigo Bonifont)*.

4062 *Hit Me Baby, One More Time.* (Series; Reality; NBC; 2005). Veteran singers perform the songs that made them famous then compete in various musical challenges, performing new songs, with the object being to return to the spotlight. Home viewer votes determine the winner. Vernon Kay hosts.

4063 *Hit Squad.* (Pilot; Comedy; Syn.; Jan. 11, 1988). Hidden cameras record the reactions of ordinary people caught in elaborate practical jokes set up by the show's staff. Also featured are outtakes from movies and TV shows.

Host: Kelly Monteith.

4064 *Hit Video, USA.* (Series; Variety; Syn.; 1988). Music videos featuring the industries top recording artists.

Host: Jacqueline Black. **Interviewer:** Ricky Marks. **Music:** Bill Bowen.

4065 *Hitched.* (Pilot; Drama; Unaired; Produced by Fox in 2005). Activities that abound at a 24-hour wedding emporium in the heart of the glitz and glamour of Las Vegas.

Cast: Leslie Bibb *(Emily)*; Mark-Paul Gosselaar *(Michael)*; Megalyn Echikunwoke *(Christina)*.

4066 *Hitched.* (Pilot; Comedy; Unaired; Produced for CBS in 2009). Brett Applebaum, the son of Jerry Applebaum (a widower), and Rachel Reynolds, the daughter of Judy and Wally Reynolds, meet, fall in love and marry. They rent an apartment and the proposal was to relate their mishaps as they navigate a new life together — a life made a bit more complicated by the intrusion of their parents.

Cast: Jack Carpenter *(Brett Applebaum)*; Sara Fletcher *(Judy Reynolds)*; Sharon Lawrence *(Judy Reynolds)*; Kurtwood Smith *(Wally Reynolds)*; Eugene Levy *(Jerry Applebaum)*.

4067 *Hitched or Ditched.* (Series; Reality; CW; 2009). Couples who are planning to marry but have not yet taken the big step are the subjects. Each couple is offered an all expenses paid TV wedding and given one week to decide if this is the right choice for them. During that week, cameras follow the couple as they contemplate whether or not to marry or stay a couple without the commitments of marriage. Friends and family of both subjects are also interviewed and express opinions as to whether or not the couple should marry. The wedding is featured if the couple decides to marry. Tanya McQueen hosts.

4068   The Hitchhiker. (Series; Anthology; HBO; 1983). A seemingly innocent hitchhiker stands by the side of the road seeking a ride to an unknown destination. He can also be in any town or in any city. People who cross his path are revealed to have evil intentions. Stories relate what happens when such people are led to encounter the terrors of the unknown. Contains nudity, adult situations and strong language.

Cast: Nicholas Campbell, Page Fletcher (*The Hitchhiker*).

4069   The Hitchhiker's Guide to the Galaxy. (Series; Science Fiction; PBS; 1982). Seconds before the Earth is destroyed, Ford Prefect, an alien being from the galaxy Betelgeuse and a filed researcher for *The Hitchhiker's Guide*, rescues Arthur Dent, an Englishman, from the impending doom. As the Earth is destroyed by a Vogon construction fleet (to make way for a new hyperspace bypass) Ford and Arthur are transported to one of the cabins of the Vogon ship. Soon they are ejected from the Vogon ship — and thus begin a series of intergalactic adventures as they become hitchhikers in space.

Other regulars are Trillian, the beautiful alien; Marvin, Trillian's robot; Eddie, Trillian's computer; Marvin, the paranoid android; Zaphod Beeblebrox, the alien with two heads and three arms; Deep Thought, the greatest computer in the universe. Produced in England.

Cast: David Dixon (*Ford Prefect*); Simon Jones (*Arthur Dent*); Saundra Dickinson (*Trillian*); Peter Jones (*Voice of the Book*); David Lerner (*Marvin*); David Tate (*Voice of Eddie*); Stephen Moore (*Voice of Marvin*); Mark Wing-Davey (*Zaphod Beeblebrox*); Martin Benson (*Vogon Captain*); Valentine Dyall (*Voice of Deep Thought*).

4070   Hitz. (Series; Comedy; UPN; 1997). Busby Evans and Robert Moore are artist representatives for Hi Tower Records, a struggling record company run by the obnoxious Jimmy Esposito. Equally "bad" is Jimmy's promotional head, Tommy Stans, "the most pathetic, slimy weasel in the promo game" (and those are his good points). Angela is the company's lawyer; April is the publicist; and Rif's Bar is the local watering hole. Stories follow Busby and Robert's antics as they struggle to do their job against numerous obstacles. A Hi Tower C.D. sells for $15.95.

Cast: Andrew Dice Clay (*Jimmy Esposito*); Claude Brooks (*Busby Evans*); Rick Gomez (*Robert Moore*); Rosa Blasi (*April Beane*); Kristin Dattilo (*Angela*); Spencer Garrett (*Tommy Stans*).

4071   Hizzoner. (Series; Comedy; NBC; 1979). Michael Cooper is the mayor of a typical American city (although not identified by a particular name). He is jovial, kind-hearted and dedicated to carrying out the promises he made in his campaign speeches: make his city a better place to live and assisting people in need. Although a good premise for a dramatic series, *Hizzoner* is a comedy and stories follow Michael's efforts to do what he promised — only to meet with calamity along the way.

Michael is a widower and he is also struggling to raise two children, Annie and James (he is assisted here by his butler, Nails). Melanie is Michael's heart-of-gold secretary; Timmons is his chief of staff.

Cast: David Huddleston (*Michael Cooper*); Diana Muldaur (*Ginny Linden*); Kathy Cronkite (*Annie Cooper*); Will Selzer (*James Cooper*); Gina Hecht (*Melanie*); Mickey Deems (*Nails Doyle*); Don Galloway (*Timmons*).

4072   H.M.S. Pinafore. (Experimental; Opera; DuMont; Aug. 13, 1944). The first known television adaptation of the Gilbert and Sullivan opera about Sir Joseph Porter, Lord of the British Admiralty.

Cast: Cecil Carol, Joseph DeStefano, Ione DiCaron, Andrew Duvries, Charles Kingsley, Josephine Lombardo, The Light Opera Theater Chorus.

4073   Hobby Lobby. (Series; Human Interest; ABC; 1959-1960). People and their usual and often unusual hobbies are showcased. Celebrity guests appear to lobby their hobbies.

Host: Cliff Arquette as Mount Idy Hillbilly Charley Weaver. **Announcer:** Tom Reddy. **Music:** John Gart.

4074   The Hogan Family. (Series; Comedy; NBC, 1986–1989; CBS, 1990-1991). Valerie Angela Hogan, the manager of Forman-Lydell Antiques (a.k.a. the Forman-Lydell Auction House), is married to Michael, an airline pilot, and the mother of three sons (David, Willie and Mark). The Hogans live on Crescent Drive in Oak Park, Illinois, and the family dog is named Murray. Valerie and Michael have been married for 17 years when the series begins and stories follow Valerie as she struggles to run a household.

When a contract dispute between Valerie Harper and the show's producers could not be resolved, Valerie Hogan was written out (killed in a car crash). Michael, who is unable to raise his sons alone, asks his sister, Sandy, to come and live with him and help in their upbringing.

Sandy was first a guidance counselor, then the vice principal of Colfax High School.

David, the eldest son, first attended Colfax, then Northwestern University. Twins Willie and Mark attended Lincoln Junior High, Oak Park Junior High and finally Colfax High.

"Hi-dee-ho" is the shrill cry the Hogans and viewers hear when next door neighbor Patricia ("Patty") Poole drops by for a visit. Mrs. Poole (as she is called) is happily married to Peter Poole, whom she calls "The Mister." Patty has a dog named Casey and a parrot she calls Tweeters.

Lloyd Hogan is Sandy and Michael's father. He is rather bossy, set in his ways and came to live with his children in last season episodes (he previously lived in California). Originally titled *Valerie*. Cara is Mark's girlfriend; Brenda is Willie's girlfriend; Burt Weems is David's friend; Annie was the Hogans neighbor before Mrs. Poole; Rebecca is her daughter. Roberta Flack sings the theme, "Together Through the Years."

Cast: Valerie Harper (*Valerie Hogan*); Sandy Duncan (*Sandy Hogan*); Josh Taylor (*Michael Hogan*); Jason Bateman (*David Hogan*); Danny Ponce (*Willie Hogan*); Jeremy Licht (*Mark Hogan*); Edie McClurg (*Patty Poole*); John Hillerman (*Lloyd Hogan*); Willard Scott (*Peter Poole*); Josie Bissett (*Cara Eisenberg*); Angela Lee (*Brenda*); Steve Witting (*Burt Weems*); Judith Kahan (*Annie*); Paula Hoffman (*Rebecca*); Kathleen Freeman (*Patty's Mother-in-Law Poole*).

4075   Hogan Knows Best. (Series; Reality; Spike TV; 2005–2007). Terry "Hulk" Hogan, a World Wrestling Federation wrestler, is married to Linda and is the father of Brooke and Nick. Cameras follow Hulk and his family as they go about their daily lives to allow the viewer to see, for the most part, a side of Hulk that does not reflect his life as a superstar wrestler.

4076   Hogan's Heroes. (Series; Comedy; CBS; 1965–1971). Robert Hogan, a U.S. Army Air Corps Colonel (with the 504th Bomber Squadron), is a World War II prisoner of war. His plane was shot down and he is now confined to Stalag 13, a camp outside Hammelburg, Germany, commanded by Colonel Wilhelm Klink and his bumbling assistant, Sergeant Hans Schultz. Also residing with Hogan in Barracks 2 are Captain Peter Newkirk, Corporal Louis LeBeau, Sergeant Andrew Carter and Sergeant James Kinchloe, Allied prisoners who have banded together to help fellow prisoners escape the Nazi high command and secure German secrets for their superiors. (In last-season episodes, Kinchloe was replaced by Sergeant Richard Baker.) Hogan plots to outwit his captors and leads his squadron of four "heroes" on various missions to achieve his goals. They have a secret radio receiver (disguised as a coffee pot), a series of tunnels (entrances are under the guard dog doghouse in the kennel, the tree stump in the woods outside the camp, a lower bunk in the barracks, and under the stove in Klink's quarters), a hidden microphone (behind the picture of Hitler in Klink's office), and a submarine (code-named Mama Bear). Hogan's first code name was Goldilocks and Papa Bear was the code for London. Later, Papa Bear became Hogan's code name while Mama Bear (and sometimes Goldilocks) became the code for London. Peter Newkirk, the British prisoner, is actually a master pickpocket with a talent for impersonation. Andrew Carter ran a drugstore in Muncie, Indiana, and hopes to become a pharmacist when he returns home. In the pilot, Carter is a lieutenant and escapes from Stalag 13; for the series he is returned as a sergeant.

Louis LeBeau, the French POW, is a jack-of-all-trades — from cooking to sewing. LeBeau's weekly assignment is to visit Wilhelmina, the underground contact, a beautiful woman he loved but described as "a mean old lady" to his fellow prisoners. James Kinchloe (later called Ivan Kinchloe) was nicknamed "Kinch" and was a former Golden *Gloves* boxer. He and Baker ran the underground communications center; Kinch was also a radio and electronics expert.

Colonel Klink and Sergeant Schultz are members of the Luftwaffe (the German Air Force). They opposed Hitler and hated the war. They performed as soldiers because it was their job (their fear of the Gestapo and combat duty led Hogan to manipulate them for his own benefit). Klink was born in Leipzig and received military training in Potsdam. Hogan's men have nicknamed him "Klink the Fink" (the "Fink" standing for "Firm Impartial Nazi Kommandant"). Schultz was the owner of a toy company before the war. He is a bumbling klutz and rather naive and easily manipulated by Hogan. He wants only to come home from the war alive and often looks the other way when he feels Hogan is up to something. His catchphrase became "I know nothing, I see nothing."

Bruno, Hans, Heidi and Wolfgang are the guard dogs at Stalag 13. Helga was Klink's first secretary; she was replaced by Hilda. Marya is the beautiful Russian spy who helped Hogan (and was fond of him). The real villains were General Albert Burkhalter and Major Wolfgang Hochstetter. Burkhalter, Klink's superior, was a stern Gestapo agent with a weakness for pretty women. Hochstetter was devoted to Hitler's cause and intent on destroying the enemy. He constantly threatened to send Klink to the Russian front if he didn't do his job. Jerry Fielding composed the *Hogan's Heroes* theme.

Cast: Bob Crane *(Robert Hogan)*; Werner Klemperer *(Wilhelm Klink)*; John Banner *(Sgt. Schultz)*; Richard Dawson *(Peter Newkirk)*; Robert Clary *(Louis LeBeau)*; Larry Hovis *(Andrew Carter)*; Ivan Dixon *(James Kinchloe)*; Kenneth Washington *(Richard Baker)*; Cynthia Lewis *(Helga)*; Bernard Fox *(Colonel Crittendon)*; Howard Caine *(Major Hockstedder)*; Leon Askin *(Gen. Alfred Burkhalter)*; Nita Talbot *(Marya)*; Sigrid Valdis *(Hilda)*; Kathleen Freeman *(Gertrude Linkmier)*; Jon Cedar *(Corporal Langenscheid)*.

4077   Hold 'Er Newt. (Series; Children; ABC; 1950). Marionettes are incorporated to tell the tale of Newton Figg, the proprietor of a general store in the town of Figg Center.

Cast: Don Tennant *(Newton Figg)*.

4078   Hold It Please. (Series; Game; CBS; 1949). A telephone call is placed at random to a viewer. If the viewer is able to correctly answer a question, he is awarded a prize and receives a chance to win the jackpot, which consists of valuable merchandise prizes. To win, the caller must identify the portrait of a celebrity that is shown on a spinning wheel.

Host: Gil Fates. **Regulars:** Cloris Leachman, Bill McGraw, Mort Marshall, Evelyn Ward.

4079   Hold That Camera. (Series; Game; DuMont; 1950). Two players compete: a studio contestant and a home viewer. The viewer, whose voice is amplified over the telephone, directs the studio player through a series of shenanigans. The time needed to complete the stunts is recorded. Another set of players competes in the same manner. The team that performs the stunts in the least amount of time is the winner and both the home viewer and the studio player receive prizes.

Host: Jimmy Blaine, Kyle MacDonnell. **Music:** Ving Merlin.

4080   Hold That Note. (Series; Game; NBC; 1957). The object calls for players to identify song titles as fast as possible and in as few notes as possible. The first player to identify three tunes wins a round and money. The player with the most wins is the overall champion and keeps what money he has accumulated.

Host: Bert Parks. **Announcer:** Johnny Olson.

4081   Holding the Baby. (Series; Comedy; Fox; 1998). Gordon Stiles is an enterprising businessman. He is married and the father of an infant son. Life changes suddenly for George when his wife walks out on him and leaves him the responsibility of raising their son (Dan). Stories follow Gordon as he struggles to cope with an overbearing boss at work (Stan) and raise Dan — with the help of Kelly, a grad student he has befriended, and Jimmy, his off-center brother, who offers little help as he pursues an elusive acting career.

Cast: Jon Patrick Walker *(Gordon Stiles)*; Jennifer Westfeldt *(Kelly O'Malley)*; Eddie McClintock *(Jimmy Stiles)*; Ron Leibman *(Stan Peterson)*; Carter and Jordon Kemp *(Dan Stiles)*.

4082   Hole in the Wall. (Series; Game; Fox; 2008-2009). Two three member teams compete in a silly game wherein they must make themselves into the right shape to fit through a shape cut out in a Styrofoam wall. Round one has each individual member of each team face the wall. As the wall approaches, the player must position himself and run toward the wall and pass through the cutout. Success earns one point; failure results in a dip in the water under the wall. Round two has two players, working as a team, attempting to jump through cutouts; round three encompasses all three members and a wall with three cutouts. The team with the highest score wins $25,000.

Hosts: Brooke Burns, Mark Thompson. **Lifeguard:** Laila Odom, Matt Clifton.

4083   Holidate. (Series; Reality; Soap Net; 2009). Two women, living in different parts of the country, exchange places to date men selected by the other lady. Each woman first explores her new surroundings then embarks on three dates with the object being to spark a romance. At the end of the dating cycle, the man each woman finds most compatible is invited by the woman to visit her hometown. It is his choice to continue the romance or end the relationship. Jack Rodgers is the producer.

4084   Holiday Hotel. (Series; Variety; ABC; 1950-1951). Entertainment performances set against the background of the Pelican Room of the fashionable but fictitious Holiday Hotel on Park Avenue in New York City.

Hotel Manager: Edward Everett Horton, Don Ameche. **Regulars:** Betty Brewer, Dorothy Greener, Leonore Longergan, Don Sadler, The June Graham Dancers, Bob Dixon, Bill Harrington. **Orchestra:** Bernard Green.

4085   *Holiday Lodge.* (Series; Comedy; CBS; 1961). Johnny Miller and Frank Boone are the social directors of the plush Holiday Lodge Hotel in Upper New York State. Their efforts to provide interesting entertainment despite an encounter with ever-present obstacles are the focal point of stories. J.W. Harrington is the hotel manager; Dorothy Johnson is the receptionist; Woodrow is the bellboy/handyman.

Cast: Johnny Wayne (*Johnny Miller*); Frank Shuster (*Frank Boone*); Justice Watson (*J. W. Harrington*); Maureen Arthur (*Dorothy Johnson*); Charles Smith (*Woodrow*).

4086   *Hollis & Rae.* (Pilot; Crime Drama; Unaired; Produced for ABC in 2005). Hollis Chandler and Rae Devereaux are friends who grew up together in a small southern city. Rae has become a police detective while Hollis has become a prosecuting attorney with the D.A.'s office. The girls do not always see eye-to-eye on cases. Rae refuses to bend the rules even if it means a criminal could beat the system; Hollis believes that you have to be as underhanded as the enemy in order for justice to prevail. The proposal was to relate Hollis's courtroom prosecutions of the cases that Rae investigates.

Cast: Jaime Ray Newman (*Hollis Chandler*); Laura Harris (*Rae Devereaux*); Harold Sylvester (*Lt. Dupree*).

4087   *Holloway's Daughters.* (Pilot; Crime Drama; NBC; May 11, 1966). When Nick Holloway, a private investigator and the owner of the Holloway Detective Agency, retires, he turns over the business to his son, George. George, who dislikes the way his father ran the company (by instinct), changes it to a by-the-books operation. The change not only angers Nick, who decides to remain active and run the company as he feels it should, but his two beautiful granddaughters, Fleming and Casey, amateur sleuths who side with their grandfather. The proposed series was to focus on the investigations of Nick, Fleming and Casey as they attempt to solve crimes. Martha is George's wife; Miss Purdy is the agency secretary. Aired a s a segment of *The Bob Hope Chrysler Theater.*

Cast: Robert Young (*Nick Holloway*); David Wayne (*George Holloway*); Marion Ross (*Martha Holloway*); Brooke Bundy (*Fleming Holloway*); Barbara Hershey (*Casey Holloway*); Ellen Corby (*Miss Purdy*).

4088   *Holly Golightly.* (Pilot; Comedy; Unaired; Produced for ABC in 1969). Events in the life of Holly Golightly, a New York playgirl who enjoys standing outside of Tiffany's (a jewelry store) at dawn, nibbling on a bun, sipping coffee and gazing at the precious gems in the elegant store window. She was married, at age 15, to a goodhearted Texan named Doc Golightly, but had the marriage annulled and now supports herself (as an escort) and lives in a partially furnished apartment on Manhattan's East Side. The visits to Tiffany's keep Holly from becoming depressed. Based on the feature film *Breakfast at Tiffany's.*

Cast: Stefanie Powers (*Holly Golightly*), Jean Pierre Aumont, George Furth, Jack Kruschen.

4089   *Holly's World.* (Series; Reality; E!; 2010). A spin off from *The Girls Next Door* in which series regular Holly Madison departs Los Angeles for greener pastures in Las Vegas. The gorgeous blonde quickly makes a name for herself as the sexy lead in the film *Peepshow* and episodes follow Holly as she makes new friends and takes on the town — tackling everything from local politics to issues on the famous

Las Vegas Strip. Angel is Holly's personal assistant; Josh, a musical comedy star, is Holly's "boy BFF"; Laura is Holly's party girl roommate.

4090   *Hollywood.* (Series; Documentary; Syn.; 1980). A British-produced program that traces the history of the Hollywood silent film via film clips and interviews with guests from the era.

Narrator: James Mason.

4091   *Hollywood a Go Go.* (Series; Variety; Syn.; 1965). Sam Riddle hosts a program of performances by rock personalities. The Sinners and The Gazzarri Dancers are the regulars.

4092   *Hollywood and the Stars.* (Series; Documentary; NBC; 1963-1964). The behind-the-scenes story of Hollywood — its stars and its celluloid accomplishments.

Host-Narrator: Joseph Cotten.

4093   *Hollywood Backstage.* (Series; Magazine; Syn.; 1965). A behind-the-scenes report on Hollywood, showcasing the people, the parties and the premieres.

Program Open: "Let's go — *Hollywood Backstage! Hollywood Backstage,* exciting stars, premieres, glamorous parties, exclusive interviews — all in color. The fascinating world of Hollywood and its people; let's go *Hollywood Backstage.* This is John Willis at Sunset and Vine in the heart of Hollywood, ready to take you behind the scenes to *Hollywood Backstage,* the magic kingdom whose personalities are the royalty of entertainment. On this program, another glittering lineup of stars and the glamour in which they live; you are about to have an intimate look at these and other well-known celebrities and their glamorous world called Hollywood. After this short message, we'll go *Hollywood Backstage.*"

Host: John Willis.

4094   *Hollywood Beat.* (Series; Crime Drama; ABC; 1985). Nick McCarren and Jack Rado are undercover police officers with the Los Angeles Police Department. They are masters of disguises and use that talent to help apprehend criminals. They have such street contacts as Lady Di, a bag lady, and at times receive help from Norman, a man who believes he is Captain Crusader and on a mission to right wrongs. Billy Night Eyes is a Blackfoot Indian who runs the local newsstand; George Grinsley is the bar tender at their favorite watering hole, Lita's (owned by Lita Delaware). Nick and Jack's superiors are Captain Milton Treadwell and Captain Wes Biddle. Natalie Cole sings the theme, "Hollywood Beat."

Cast: Jack Scalia (*Nick McCarren*); Jay Acavone (*Jack Rado*); Ann Turkel (*Lita Delaware*); Edward Winter (*Wes Biddle*); Lane Smith (*Milton Treadwell*); Robert Englund (*Norman/Captain Crusader*); Michael Horse (*Billy Night Eyes*); Barbara Cason (*Lady Di*); John Matuszak (*George Grinsley*).

4095   *The Hollywood Connection.* (Series; Game; Syn.; 1977). Six celebrity guests appear, divided into two three-member teams. Two non-celebrity contestants are the players. A question is read that involves one team in a hypothetical situation. One player has to predict how each member of that team responded to the question. Each correct prediction awards the player one point. The remaining player competes in the same manner (although a different question is used). The player with the highest score is the winner and receives merchandise prizes.

Host: Jim Lange. **Announcer:** Jay Stewart.

4096   *Hollywood Division.* (Pilot; Crime Drama; Unaired; Produced for Fox in 2003). *21 Jump Street*-like proposal wherein youthful detectives with the Hollywood Division of the L.A.P.D. go undercover in high schools and clubs frequented by young people to ferret out criminal activities.

Cast: Geoff Stults *(George Booth)*; Leighton Meester *(Michelle Nichols)*; Nathan Fillion *(Tommy Garrett)*; D.J. Cotrona *(Cody Walker)*; Moon Bloodgood *(Morales)*; Tsianina Joelson *(Cassidy)*.

4097 *Hollywood Dog.* (Pilot; Comedy; Fox; July 25, 1990). Hoping to make his mark in the world of rock and roll music, Bodine Frank leaves his home in Nebraska and heads for Hollywood. At the bus depot he meets Dog, an animated toon with an attitude, who takes him under his "paw." Dog, a con artist, invites Bodine to share his room (2-B) at the Hollywood Bahama Lounge Hotel until such time as he can become a big performer. The proposal, which combines live action and animation, was to follow the escapades of Dog and Bodine as they struggle to make ends meet. Other regulars are Louise, the landlady; Dwayne, her son; Rhonda, Bodine's friend; and Tyler, Rhonda's son.

Cast: Hank Azaria *(Voice of Dog)*; Tim Ryan *(Bodine Frank)*; Conchata Ferrell *(Louise)*; Raymond O'Connor *(Dwayne)*; Lenora May *(Rhonda)*; Matthew Brooks *(Tyler)*.

4098 *The Hollywood Freeway.* (Pilot; Variety; Syn.; Nov. 18, 1974). An attempt to combine talk and entertainment in a weekly syndicated series. The pilot was more talk than variety with only a brief amount of time allotted for singers Barbara McNair, Melissa Manchester and Jose Felicinao.

Host: Charles Ashman. **Guests:** Melvin Belli, Ernest Borgnine, Nate Branch, Minnesota Fats, Marty Feldman, Jose Feliciano, Barbara McNair, Melissa Manchester, George C. Scott, Trish Van Devere. **Orchestra:** Jack Elliott.

4099 *The Hollywood Game.* (Series; Game; CBS; 1992). Two teams compete. Each of the letters of the word *Hollywood* represent a category topic. One player (flip of coin) receives a chance to select a category. Three questions are asked, earning the teams $100 per correct response. Round Two is played in the same manner with values increasing: $200 for one correct answer; $400 for two; $800 for three correct answers (all questions are accompanied by clips of movies and TV shows). Round Three doubles the money—$500, $1,000 and $1,500. Round Four is the Double Feature Round. A category is stated. The teams can bet half, all or none of the money they have thus far won. The question is read. Players write down their answers. The team with the correct and best bet (to earn the most money) wins the game. Peter Allen hosted the 1991 unaired pilot.

Host: Bob Goren.

4100 *Hollywood Heat.* (Series; Reality; TruTV; 2007). A look at the crime and the pursuit of justice within the entertainment industry.

Hosts: Lynne White, Ashleigh Banfield.

4101 *Hollywood High.* (Pilot; Comedy; NBC; July 21, 1977). Hollywood High is a not-so-typical school in Los Angeles. It is here that the antics of a group of students are depicted in two attempts (broadcast back-to-back on July 21, 1977) that failed to produce a series. The first, *Hollywood High*, features students Phoebe, Dawn, Wheeler, Bill, Icky and Dr. Bad. The second, *Hollywood High II* showcases students Paula, Eugene, Allison, Judith, Janet and Stu.

First Pilot Cast: Annie Potts *(Phoebe)*; Kim Lankford *(Dawn)*; Chris Pina *(Wheeler)*; Rory Stevens *(Bill)*; John Megna *(Icky)*; Sam Kwassman *(Dr. Bad)*.

Second Pilot Cast: Annie Potts *(Paula Lindell)*; Darren O'Connor *(Eugene Langley)*; Roberta Wallach *(Allison)*; Beverly Sanders *(Judith)*; Janet Wood *(Janet)*; John Guerrasio *(Stu)*.

4102 *The Hollywood Hounds.* (Pilot; Cartoon; Fox; Nov. 25, 1994). Dude, a talented dog with a good singing voice, believes he was meant for the big time. He leaves his home in Nashville and moves to Hollywood where the proposal was to chart his mishaps as he seeks to become the next big recording star.

Voices: Jeff G. Bennett, Theodore Borders, Christopher Broughton, Candi Milo, Frank Welker.

4103 *Hollywood Junior Circus.* (Series; Variety; NBC; ABC; 1951-1952). Hollywood Candy sponsored program of circus variety acts set against the backdrop of a circus tent. Aired on NBC (Mar. 25 to July 1, 1951) and ABC (Sept. 8, 1951 to Jan. 19, 1952).

Host: Art Jacobson, Paul Barnes. **Clown:** Carl Marx. **Regulars:** Marie Louise, George Cesar, Bill Hughes, The Hanneford Family. **Commercial Spokesman:** Max Bronstein *(as Zero)*. **Orchestra:** Brad Chase.

4104 *Hollywood Lives.* (Series; Reality; Disney; 1995). An early cable reality program that follows the lives of a group of young Hollywood hopefuls as they attempt to make it in the world of show business.

Hopefuls: Brandy Norwood, Bianca Lawson, Jamie Kennedy, Joe Loera, Devin Oatway, Tamara Ruth, Brian Gross, Poppi Monroe.

4105 *Hollywood Offbeat.* (Series; Crime Drama; Syn.; 1952-1953). "Steve Randall, Investigator" is the sign on the door at 6103 Gentry Avenue in Hollywood, California. "Trouble is his business," and he charges $25 a day for his services. Steve Randall has one weakness: "insatiable curiosity." He is "allergic to being detained when a lady is screaming for help," and bitter—determined to regain his right to practice law by finding those who are responsible for a frame that got him disbarred. He became a private detective to gain the legal authority to find those who framed him.

"This is Hollywood," Melvyn Douglas would say over a scene of Steve driving his car. "It is a town like any other town.... There may be a few more pretty girls because of the pull of the motion picture studios, but otherwise just another American town.... And there is Steve Randall, who knows Hollywood like the palm of his hand. Steve Randall is in his own way a composite of Hollywood. He's seen everything a man can see anywhere and has been disillusioned by most of it. And he belongs in Hollywood, for its fame and so-called glamour are magnets for the money-hungry riffraff of the outside world.... They bring their greed to Steve Randall's town, and greed's companion is trouble. And that's fine for Steve Randall because trouble is his business." Filmed, despite its Hollywood locale, at the Parsonnet Studios on Long Island.

Cast: Melvyn Douglas *(Steve Randall)*.

4106 *Hollywood Opening Night.* (Series; Anthology; CBS; NBC; 1951–1953). Filmed (CBS) and live (NBC) productions from the West Coast (the first anthology series to originate in Hollywood). Aired on CBS from July 20, 1951 to Mar. 28, 1952; and on NBC from Oct. 6, 1952 to Mar. 23, 1953. William Corrigan is the producer.

4107 *The Hollywood Palace.* (Series; Variety; ABC; 1964–1970). Lavish program of variety acts broadcast from the Hollywood Palace Theater. Weekly Guests host and a virtually unknown at the time Raquel Welch appears as the Card Holder (appears on stage to introduce the acts).

Program Open: "From Hollywood, the heart of the entertainment world, *The Hollywood Palace*, with your host, Don Knotts. Tonight starring Charo ... Bobby Goldsboro ... Joey Heatherton ... We'll return to *The Hollywood Palace* after a word from one of our sponsors."

Card Holder: Raquel Welch. **Regulars:** The Ray Charles Singers, The Buddy Schwab Dancers. **Announcer:** Bill Ewing *(first episode)*; Dick Tufeld. **Orchestra:** Mitchell Ayres.

4108 *Hollywood Reporter.* (Pilot; Magazine; Syn.; Dec. 1985). An attempt at a daily series of show business gossip with reports on current movies and TV programs.

Host: Peter Torkayan. **Reporters:** David Kriet, Meredith MacRae.

4109 *Hollywood Residential.* (Series; Comedy; Starz; 2008). A spoof of home repair programs that spotlights an accident-prone celebrity home makeover expert. Tony King is the "expert" and stories follow Tony as he and his crew attempt to wreck as little havoc as possible while remodeling the homes of celebrities (like Paula Abdul, Carmen Electra, Jamie Kennedy, Beverly D'Angelo and Cheryl Hines). Lila is Tony's assistant; Don, Pete and Carrie are his crew.

Cast: Adam Paul *(Tony King)*; Lindsey Stoddart *(Lila Mann)*; David Ramsey *(Don Merritt)*; Eric Allan Kramer *(Pete)*; Carrie Clifford *(Carrie)*.

4110 *Hollywood Screen Test.* (Series; Anthology; ABC; 1948–1953). Dramatic productions in which young hopefuls appear with established stars.

Host: Bert Lytell, Neil Hamilton, Hurd Hatfield, Betty Furness. **Assistant:** Martha Wayne, Robert Quarry. **Announcer:** Ted Campbell.

4111 *Hollywood Sexcapades.* (Series; Anthology; Cinemax; 2004-2005). Candi Hicks, Cooper Snow and Olivia Hartley are three gorgeous women who run a Las Vegas based dating service. Anthology-like stories (different supporting casts each week) relate incidents in the lives of the people matched by the women.

Cast: Beverly Lynne *(Candi Hicks)*; Tiffany Bolton *(Cooper Snow)*; Amy Lindsay *(Olivia Hartley)*.

4112 *Hollywood Showcase.* (Series; Anthology; Syn.; 1966). The 1966 syndicated title (with June Allyson as the host) for repeats of the 1961 NBC series *The Dick Powell Show.*

4113 *Hollywood Showdown.* (Series; Game; PAX; 2001). Six players compete for the entire week. A box office cash amount is established at $10,000. Each of the players possesses a ticket-shaped stub that contains several cards with money amounts printed on them. An on-stage player selects one of the seated players as an opponent. The opponent removes one of the cards from his ticket stub and the amount of money printed on it is added to the box office. The two players then compete in a round wherein they must answer questions based on pop culture. The first player to answer three questions correctly becomes the champion and selects another player as an opponent. If the reigning champion is defeated, he joins the seated players. The player who answers the most questions correctly over the course of five episodes claims the box office jackpot.

Host: Todd Newton. **Announcer:** Randy West.

4114 *The Hollywood Squares.* (Series; Game; NBC; Syn.; 1966–2004). An elaborate game of tic tac toe that involves two players (Player "X" and Player "O") and nine celebrity guests (each occupying one square on a large board). A celebrity, chosen by a player, is asked a question. The player agrees or disagrees with the celebrity's answer. A correct guess wins the player the square; an incorrect guess awards

the square to the opponent. The first player to acquire three squares in a row — up, down, or diagonally — is the winner and receives a cash prize (varied over the years).

Program Open: "Rob Reiner ... Joan Rivers ... Marty Allen ... Arthur Godfrey ... William Conrad ... Connie Stevens ... George Gobel ... Charo ... Paul Lynde ... All in *The Hollywood Squares*. And here's the master of *The Hollywood Squares*, Peter Marshall." Five versions appeared:

1. The Hollywood Squares (NBC Daytime, 1966–80; Primetime, 1968; Syn., 1971–81). **Host:** Peter Marshall. **Regulars:** Cliff Arquette (as Charley Weaver), Wally Cox, George Gobel, Paul Lynde, Rose Marie, Karen Valentine, Abby Dalton. **Announcer:** Kenny Williams.

2. The Storybook Squares (NBC, 1969). **Host:** Peter Marshall. **Announcer:** Kenny Williams. See entry.

3. The Match Game-Hollywood Squares Hour (NBC, 1983–84). **Host:** Jon Bauman. **Announcer:** Gene Wood. See entry.

4. Hollywood Squares (Syn., 1986–89). **Host:** John Davidson. **Announcer:** Shadoe Stevens.

5. Hollywood Squares (Syn., 1998–2004). **Host:** Tom Bergeron. **Announcer:** Shadoe Stevens (1998–2002), Jeffrey Tambor (2002-03), John Moschitta (2003-04). **Regulars:** Whoopi Goldberg (1998–02), Bruce Vilanch (1998–02), Martin Mull (2003-04).

4115 *Hollywood Starr.* (Pilot; Crime Drama; ABC; Feb. 23, 1985). Dani Starr is a female detective with the Los Angeles Police Department, Hollywood Station. Dani, a gorgeous girl with street-smart knowledge, has been assigned to the Vice Squad division and the proposal was to relate her investigations into cases ranging from prostitute deaths to sleazy adult film producers taking advantage of naïve young girls. A proposed spin off from *T.J. Hooker*. Paulette McWilliams performs the theme, "Hollywood Starr."

Cast: Sharon Stone *(Dani Starr)*.

4116 *Hollywood Talent Scouts.* (Series; Variety; CBS; 1962–1966). The talent discoveries of Hollywood celebrities are profiled (who appear with their protégés to introduce them and hopefully lead the on the road to stardom).

Host: Jim Backus *(1962)*; Merv Griffin *(1963)*; Art Linkletter *(1965)*. **Orchestra:** Harry Sosnik, Harry Zimmerman.

4117 *Hollywood Teen.* (Series; Variety; Syn.; 1978). Interviews with and performances by young Hollywood personalities.

Host: James Vincent McNichol.

4118 *Hollywood Theater Time.* (Series; Anthology; NBC; 1950-1951). Early West Coast program of dramatic stories produced by George M. Cahan and Thomas Sarnoff. Notable performers include Gale Storm, Don DeFore, Marjorie Reynolds, Shirley Mitchell, Gil Lamb.

4119 *Hollywood Treasure.* (Series; Reality; Syfy; 2010). Erin Gray, Ardala on *Buck Rogers in the 25th Century* has what she believes is one the space ship models used on the program. Dawn Wells, Mary Ann on *Gilligan's Island*, has an extensive collection of items used on that show. Ordinary people also have items they claim to be authentic movie and TV props. These are the items that interest Joe Maddalena, a Hollywood film and TV collector who roams the globe seeking iconic objects. Through his travels, the viewer is shown the treasures Hollywood has created that have now fallen into private hands.

4120 *Hollywood's Most Sensational Mysteries.* (Pilot; Documentary; NBC; Feb. 4, 1984). Film clips, interviews and dramatizations that recall the headline-making stories of Hollywood celebrities (for example, in the pilot: John Belushi, Sal Mineo, Marilyn Monroe, Freddie Prinze and Lana Turner).

Host: Ben Gazzara. **Re-enactment Performers:** Patti Blankinship, Angus Duncan, Biff Elliott, Troy Evans, Lois Hamilton, Marcia Mae Jones, Claudia Lamb, Leslie Landon, Kathy Maisnik, Shirley Mitchell, Aarika Wells.

4121   *Hollywood's Talking.* (Series; Game; CBS; 1973). A video tape, divided into three cash amounts ($150, $100 and $50) is played, showing celebrities expressing their opinions on people, places or things. Each of the three contestants who compete have to determine exactly what is being talked about. A player receives money according to the segment at which he correctly guesses the topic of discussion. The first player to score $250 is the winner.

Program Open: "From Television City in Hollywood, CBS presents ... Mary Tyler Moore ... Ross Martin ... Pearl Bailey ... Milton Berle ... Sally Struthers ... Rich Little ... Lloyd Haynes ... John Forsythe ... Fess Parker ... Judy Carne ... Jo Anne Worley ... Doc Severenson ... Dean Jones ... Joan Rivers ... Sebastian Cabot ... Red Buttons ... and David Janssen — all revealing their thoughts and opinions about people, places and things on *Hollywood's Talking.* And now here's the host of our show, Geoff Edwards."

Host: Geoff Edwards. **Announcer:** Johnny Jacobs.

4122   *Holmes and Yoyo.* (Series; Comedy; ABC; 1976-1977). Alexander Holmes is a not-too-bright police officer with the Los Angeles Police Department. Gregory Yoyonovich, called Yoyo, is a not-yet-perfected computer robot designed to combat crime. For reasons that do not quite make sense, it is decided to team Alexander with Yoyo in the hope that Alexander can help fine tune Yoyo's crime fighting abilities. Stories follow the unlikely pair as Yoyo tries to act human and Alexander tries to become the cop the department can be proud of. Other regulars are Harry Sedford, their captain; Officer Maxine Moon; Dwight Buchanan, the police chief; Dr. Bancock, Yoyo's creator; and Mimi. Dwight's wife.

Cast: Richard B. Shull (*Sgt. Alexander Holmes*); John Schuck (*Sgt. Gregory Yoyonovich*); Bruce Kirby (*Capt. Harry Sedford*); Andrea Howard (*Off. Maxine Moon*); Ben Hammer (*Chief Dwight Buchanan*); Larry Hovis (*Dr. Babcock*); Fritzi Burr (*Mimi Buchanan*); G. Wood (*Police Commissioner*).

4123   *Home.* (Series; Women; NBC; 1954–1957). A daily program of information geared to the female members of the audience that is presented in a series of segments corresponding to a magazine.

Cast: Arlene Francis (*Host/Leisure Activities Editor/Shopping Guide Expert*); June Lockhart (*Substitute Hostess*); Eve Hunter (*Women's Interest/Fashion and Beauty Editor*); Sydney Smith (*Decorating Editor*); Poppy Cannon (*Food Editor*); Will Peiglebeck (*Fix-It-Shop/Home Gardening Editor*); Rose Frangblau (*Children's Problem Editor*); Estelle Parsons (*Special Projects Editor*); Johnny Johnston (*Vocalist*); The Norman Paris Trio (*Music Editors*). **Announcer:** Hugh Downs.

4124   *Home.* (Pilot; Drama; ABC; Mar. 6, 1987). The Costigans are a family of five living in Chicago. Will, a construction worker, is married to Maggie. They are the parents of Kelly, Susan and Brian (who attend Hillcrest High School) and the proposal was to relate events in their lives as they struggle to retain their strong family values.

Cast: Max Gail (*Will Costigan*); Anne Twomey (*Maggie Costigan*); Tracy Nelson (*Susan Costigan*); Michael Sharrett (*Kelly Costigan*); Jody Lambert (*Brian Costigan*).

4125   *Home Again.* (Pilot; Comedy; ABC; July 2, 1988). Following the death of their mother, two sisters (Maureen and Estelle) inherit Ma's Place, a small restaurant in a rural Ohio town. The proposal was to relate Maureen and Estelle's efforts to run the restaurant despite the fact that are not particularly fond of each other. Other regulars are Angela, Maureen's daughter; Duke, the chef; Derek, the waiter; and Brian, the busboy.

Cast: Betty Thomas (*Maureen DeFranco*); Deborah Rush (*Estelle Parker*); Pamela Segall (*Angela DeFranco*); Henry Gibson (*Duke Coleman*); Joe Guzaldo (*Derek Baker*); Bo Dremann (*Brian Thompson*).

4126   *Home Cookin'.* (Pilot; Comedy; ABC; July 11, 1975). Ernie's Truck Stop is a roadside diner that is run by a married couple (Ernie and Adelle) and offers home-cooked meals to the weary traveler. The proposed series was to focus on the interactions between the owners and their customers. Dinette is the waitress; Jammer and Bevo are regular customers.

Cast: Wynn Irwin (*Ernie*); Fannie Flagg (*Adelle*); Nancy Fox (*Dinette*); Burton Gilliam (*Jammer*); Frank McRay (*Bevo*).

4127   *The Home Court.* (Series; Comedy; NBC; 1995). Sydney J. Solomon is a family court judge who lives at 22 West Oak Street in Chicago, Illinois. She is divorced from Jeffrey and is raising four children alone: Neal, Marshall, Ellis and Mike. Stories relate the events in Sydney's life as she struggles to balance her duties in the courtroom with her responsibilities at home.

Other regulars are Judge Gil Fitzpatrick, Sydney's friend; and Greer Stanton, Sydney's sister.

Cast: Pamela Reed (*Sydney Solomon*); Meghann Haldeman (*Neal Solomon*); Robert Gorman (*Marshall Solomon*); Breckin Meyer (*Mike Solomon*); Philip Van Dyke (*Ellis Solomon*); Charles Rocket (*Gil Fitzpatrick*); Meagen Fay (*Greer Stanton*); Stephen Tobolowsky (*Jeffrey Solomon*).

4128   *Home Delivery.* (Series; Reality; Syn.; 2004). A daily program that attempts to help people improve their lives (mostly through makeovers). People with compelling stories (submitted to the show) are surprised at their homes by a crew who attempt to give them what they requested. The subjects are interviewed and cameras record all the details as wishes are granted. Egypt, Sukanya Krishnan, Stephanie Lydecker, John Senico are the hosts.

4129   *Home Fires.* (Series; Comedy; NBC; 1992). Ted and Anne Kramer have been married for 21 years. They are the parents of two children, Libby and Jesse, and are in good shape. "We have enough money, the roof stopped leaking and the kids are healthy," says Ted. "I don't think our family has one large problem, just a lot of little pieces that need fine tuning." Helping the family "fine tune" those little pieces is Dr. Frederic Marcus, a therapist who appears to be having a difficult time understanding and helping the family — each of whom has his or her own unique outlook on life.

Ted is old-fashioned and has traditional values. Anne also says "he is opinionated" and despite the complaints, Anne loves Ted: "I do, it's just that we grew up in very different homes. In his, the more flawed, the more flawed the reason, the louder the volume. In mine, a little decorum went a long way."

Libby is a beautiful 18-year-old girl whom Ted would like to see remain a little girl ("Life was a lot easier before children were given their rights," says Ted). "The idea that I am a product of them is terrifying," says Libby. "My father thinks he is clever and insightful. He's not; he's annoying and irrational. My mother sees the world in an angle undiscovered in any geometry textbook. This dimension of Dad's for me to change is another thing. I swear there must be some correlation between breast development and parental psychic degeneration. I always wished I was in another family."

Jesse is 14 years old and is obsessed with driving. He wants a Saab—"The only trouble is, my parents want me to get a driver's license for it." He generally accepts his family members for what they are.

Anne believes her incompatible family is about to go the way of the elephant and the crocodile—endangered species on the brink of extinction. Ted fights with Libby; Libby argues with Jesse; and Anne is constantly at odds with her mother, Nana. Nana is a widow and goes through everything. She has no concept of privacy and says whatever is on her mind without taking into consideration Anne's feelings (one of the reasons why Anne feels Nana embarrasses her). Libby believes that Nana is the only cultured member of the family. Also living with the family are two dogs named Nick and Nora.

Cast: Michael Brandon (*Ted Kramer*); Kate Burton (*Anne Kramer*); Nicole Eggert (*Libby Kramer*); Jarrod Paul (*Jesse Kramer*); Norman Lloyd (*Dr. Fredric Marcus*); Alice Hirson (*Nana*).

4130   *Home Free.* (Pilot; Drama; NBC; July 13, 1988). Hoping to help problem youngsters from broken homes, Michael Davis establishes his large residence in Long Beach, California, as a foster home under the supervision of the juvenile court. The proposal was to relate Michael's efforts to care for the kids put in his charge. Other regulars are Ms. Tracy, the social worker; Eddie, the live-in cook; Barry, Michael's business partner; and the kids: Jerome, Douglas, Dennis, Willie and Vladimir.

Cast: Michael Warren (*Michael Davis*); Lonetta McKee (*Ms. Tracy*); Trinidad Silva (*Eddie*); Charles Levin (*Barry*); Teddy Abner (*Jerome*); Donnie Jeffcoat (*Douglas*); Danny Nucci (*Dennis*); Ben Hoag (*Willie*); Jonathan Brandis (*Vladimir*).

4131   *Home Free.* (Series; Comedy; ABC; 1993). Vanessa Bailey is the divorced mother of two children (Abby and Lucas) who, at age 37, is starting law school. She lives with her brother, Matthew Bailey and her mother Grace Bailey at 1273 Ashbury Drive in Ocean View, California. Vanessa won "The Miss Penmanship Award of 1967" and for her sixteenth birthday, her father hired the Rolling Stones to follow her around "so I could have music wherever I go." Her favorite punishment for Abby and Lucas is potato peeling. Abby practices kissing on her pillow while Lucas, afraid of the dark, sleeps with a Tinkerbell night light. Matt is a reporter for the *Beach Cities News Advertisers*, a local newspaper.

Matt tried television by becoming the weekend Lifestyle Reporter for Channel 6 News ("If It's Important to You, It's News to Us"). He quit when they would not allow him to do hard news stories (only fluffy news). Matt also writes "Chat with Matt" for his elementary school newsletter and covers stories like the new scorpion at the Insect Museum.

Other regulars are Laura, the photographer (she is from a wealthy family and wants to make it on her own); and Ben, the paper's editor.

Cast: Diana Canova (*Vanessa Bailey*); Matthew Perry (*Matthew Bailey*); Marian Mercer (*Grace Bailey*); Anndi McAfee (*Abby*); Scott McAfee (*Lucas*); Brooke Theiss (*Laura Peters*); Alan Oppenheimer (*Ben Brookstone*).

4132   *Home Improvement.* (Series; Comedy; ABC; 1991–1999). Tim Taylor, nicknamed "The Tool Man," is the host of *Tool Time*, a comical Detroit cable TV home improvement show. Tim is married to Jill and is the father of Randy, Mark and Brad. They live at 508 Glenview Road. Tim worked as a salesman for Binford Tools when owner John Binford selected him to host *Tool Time*. Tim appears to be a master of any project on TV, but is a klutz at home when it comes to fixing things. The motto of Binford Tools is "If it doesn't say Binford on it, somebody else makes it." A claw hammer was the first tool manufactured by Binford.

Tim's hobby is restoring classic cars and won the "Car Guy of the Year Award" for his devotion to classic automobiles. His sacred, "no women allowed" area at home is the garage, where he maintains a workshop. When Jill gets angry at Tim, she slams the workshop door; the vibration knocks his Binford tools off their pegboard hooks.

As a teenager, Jill had a dog named Puddles, wore Tinker Bell perfume, and was called "Jilly Dilly" by her father. She was an army brat, attended Adams High School and met Tim in college. Jill, a song expert, considers herself "The High Priestess of Pop Songs." Jill was a researcher for *Inside Detroit* magazine; when she was laid off, she went back to school to get her master's degree in psychology. Jill later mentions she attended the Huntley School for Girls and the Hockaday School for Girls.

Al Borland assists Tim on *Tool Time*. He was a Navy man and spent a year as a heavy crane operator before joining Tim. Al, constantly teased by Tim for wearing flannel shirts, invented the "Tool Time" board game and made a video called "How to Assemble Your Tool Box." Al's superior knowledge of tools and construction actually saves the show when Tim's antics foul up projects. Al and Tim hang out at Harry's Hardware Store (originally called Kelly's Hardware Store; Al later owns 20 percent of the store, located at 3rd and Main in Royal Oak).

"Hi-dee-ho, Neighbor" is the greeting Tim gets from his neighbor, Wilson Wilson, Jr. Wilson lives at 510 Glenview Road and his face is never fully seen (always obstructed by something, usually the picket fence that divides their property). Wilson gives Tim advice on how to solve his problems and calls him "Good Neighbor." Wilson celebrates unusual "holidays" (like the end of the Punic Wars), has had dinner with Albert Einstein, knows world leaders and can talk brilliantly about anything. He greets Jill with "Hi ho, neighborette." His father, a scientist, was Wilson Wilson, Sr.

Lisa was the first "Tool Time Girl" (announces the show, shows a bit of cleavage and leg, brings in needed props). Heidi replaced her when Lisa left to attend medical school (later becoming a paramedic at Detroit Hospital). Heidi opens each show with "Does everybody know what time it is?" (The audience responds with "Tool Time").

Cast: Tim Allen (*Tim Taylor*); Patricia Richardson (*Jill Taylor*); Richard Karn (*Al Borland*); Earl Hindman (*Wilson Wilson, Jr.*); Jonathan Taylor Thomas (*Randy Taylor*); Taran Noah Smith (*Mark Taylor*); Zachery Ty Bryan (*Brad Taylor*); Pamela Anderson (*Lisa*); Debbe Duning (*Heidi*).

4133   *Home Life of a Buffalo.* (Experimental; Drama; NBC; July 21, 1946). Original TV drama about incidents in the lives of an old time vaudeville family (Eddie, his wife, June, and their son, Joey).

Cast: John McQuade (*Eddie*); Virginia Smith (*June*); Mickey Carroll (*Joey*); Percy Helton (*Performer*); Enid Markey (*Performer*).

4134   *Home Made Millionaires.* (Series; Reality; TLC; 2010). Five women, who feel they have invented what it takes to become rich, appear as contestants. Kelly Ripa assists them as they prepare to pitch their inventions the Home Shopping Network executives and a panel of guest judges. The women who best impress the judges are given the opportunity to sell their products on HSN.

Host: Kelly Ripa.

4135   *Home Movies.* (Series; Cartoon; UPN, 1999). Brendon Small is an 18-year-old boy whose parents are divorced. He lives with his mother (Paula) and his best friends are Melissa and Jason. Stories follow Brendon's life at school and at home—where he has taped over one thousand home movies of his family and where, with Melissa and Jason, he continues to produce them (and showcase them for viewers).

Voice Cast: Brendon Small (*Brendon Small*); Paula Poundstone, Janine Ditullio (*Paula Small*); Melissa Bardin Galsky (*Melissa Robbins*); H. Jon Benjamin (*Jason Penopolis*); Ron Lynch (*Ronald Lynch*); Sam Seder (*Fenton Mulley*).

4136   *Home on the Range.* (Pilot; Cooking; NBC; April 12, 1948). An unusual attempt at a cooking show that used actors to prepare meals for the home audience. Comedian Hiram Sherman and budding actress Gloria Stroock prepared (without much success) sauce, crepes and pancakes. Broadway restaurant owner Vincent Sarde appears to comment on the menu.

Host: Hiram Sherman, Gloria Stroock. **Guest:** Vincent Sardi.

4137   *Home Room.* (Pilot; Comedy; ABC; Aug. 10, 1981). Karen Chase and her brother Craig are newly enrolled students at Hancock High School. The proposal was to relate their adventures as freshmen with a group of outrageous friends (Annette, Elvis Clone, Billy Coe, Ron and "Crazy" Willie). Steve is the school bully; Steve Thomas is the guidance counselor; Mr. Melish is the biology teacher.

Cast: Ally Sheedy (*Karen Chase*); Michael Spound (*Craig Chase*); Irene Arranga (*Annette Savinski*); Lee Lucan (*Elvis Clone*); Donald Fullilove (*Billy Coe*); Eddie Deezen (*Ron Carp*); Antony Alda ("*Crazy*" *Willie*); Andrew Levant (*Steve*); Nicholas Pryor (*Steve Thomas*); Severn Darden (*Mr. Melish*).

4138   *Home Team with Terry Bradshaw.* (Series; Talk; Syn.; 1997). Former football star and sportscaster Terry Bradshaw hosts an informal daily talk show that features celebrity interviews and how-to segments as well as segments devoted to children who are interviewed for their unpredictable responses to the questions asked of them.

Host: Terry Bradshaw.

4139   *Homeboys in Outer Space.* (Series; Comedy; UPN; 1996-1997). Ty and Morris are 23rd century slackers who earn a living by tackling whatever odd jobs come their way. They are hoping to find "that big one" that will give them an easy life and easy money. Ty and Morris are a also bit dense and do not realize this will never happen. They travel through the universe in their space ship, the *Space Booty*, and stories relate their endless mishaps as they seek that easy life.

Loquatia, a gorgeous female android, guides their ship; Carl is their competent but somewhat clueless mechanic; Vashti is Ty's brother-in-law, the owner of the Jupiter Too, a bar that is also the "office" for Ty and Morris (Vashti is a humanoid who enjoys cigars and eating humans).

Cast: Flex Alexander (*Ty Walker*); Darryl M. Bell (*Morris Clay*); Rhona Bennett (*Loquatia*); Kevin Michael Richardson (*Vashti*); John Webber (*Carl*); Paulette Braxton (*Amma*); Michael K. Colyar (*Silky Jay/Milky Way*).

4140   *Homefront.* (Pilot; Drama; CBS; Oct. 9, 1980). Shelter Cove, Massachusetts, during World War II is the setting for a proposal about John Travis, a shipyard owner, his wife, Enid, and the problems they and their friends and family face during wartime. Other regulars are Kate, Christopher, Cynthia and Jack, their children; Helen, John's secretary; Leona, their neighbor; Angela, Leona's daughter; and Rocco, Leona's son.

Cast: Craig Stevens (*John Travis*); Jean Simmons (*Enid Travis*); Martina Deignan (*Kate Travis*); Dane Witherspoon (*Christopher Travis*); Mayo McCaslin (*Cynthia Travis*); Nicholas Hammond (*Jack Travis*); Christine DeLisle (*Helen Maddox*); Eunice Christopher

(*Leona Spinelli*); Delta Burke (*Angela Spinelli*); Joe Penny (*Rocco Spinelli*); Janice Carroll (*John's housekeeper*).

4141   *Homefront.* (Series; Drama; ABC; 1991–1993). River Run, Ohio, right after World War II provides the backdrop for a look at a group of army veterans and their families as they attempt to adjust to the post war world: Jeff and Hank Metcalf, who are both in love with the same woman (Sarah Brewer); Robert Davis, a young black veteran who is having a difficult time readjusting due to the discrimination that existed at the time; Mike and Ruth Sloan, parents of a slain soldier (Mike Jr.) who left behind a pregnant Italian wife (Gina); Charlie Hanley, a vet who promised to marry his girlfriend, Ginger Szabo, when he returned but instead married a woman (Caroline) he fell in love with in England; Judy Owen is a war widow who works at the local bar.

Cast: Kyle Chandler (*Jeff Metcalf*); Wendy Phillips (*Anne Metcalf*); Jessica Steen (*Linda Metcalf*); David Newsom (*Hank Metcalf*); Giuliana Santani (*Gina Sloan*); Tammy Lauren (*Ginger Szabo*); Mimi Kennedy (*Ruth Sloan*); Sammi Davis (*Caroline Hailey*); Harry O'Reilly (*Charlie Hailey*); Dick Anthony Williams (*Abe Davis*); Hattie Winston (*Gloria Davis*); Ken Jenkins (*Mike Sloan, Sr.*); John Slattery (*Al Kahn*); Sterling Macer, Jr. (*Robert Davis*); Kelly Rutherford (*Judy Owen*); John DiSanti (*Sam Schenkkan*); Montrose Hagins (*Grandmother Davis*); Alexandra Wilson (*Sarah Brewer*).

4142   *Homeland Security.* (Series; Reality; ABC; 2009). A look at the dangerous work the men and women of the Department of Homeland Security endure as they patrol and protect more than 100,000 miles of America's borders (including seaports, airports, cyberspace, land borders and airports). Based on the Australian series of the same title. Phillip Crowley narrates.

4143   *Homemaker's Exchange.* (Series; Women; CBS; 1949–1952). Louise Leslie hosts a program of cooking, decorating, household tips and shopping advice.

4144   *Homicide: Life on the Street.* (Series; Crime Drama; NBC; 1993–1999). A gritty, realistic look at the work of the Homicide Division of the Baltimore, Maryland, Police Department. Filmed on location in the Fells Point Community of Baltimore, Maryland; Based on the book *Homicide: A Year on the Killing Streets* by David Simon. While *Homicide: Life on the Street* is a crime drama, it differs from series like *Law and Order* in the fact that the focus is on case closure—finding the culprit—as opposed to showing the act of the crime. Hand-held cameras are used to follow the detectives assigned to the case as the investigation that eventually leads to an arrest and a "case closed."

Cast: Ned Beatty (*Det. Stanley Bolander*); Yaphet Kotto (*Lt. Al Giardello*); Richard Belzer (*Det. John Munch*); Daniel Baldwin (*Det. Beau Felton*); Andre Braugher (*Det. Frank Pembleton*); Melissa Leo (*Det. Kay Howard*); Clark Johnson (*Det. Frank Lewis*); Jon Polito (*Det. Steve Crosetti*); Michelle Forbes (*Dr. Julianna Cox*); Callie Tjorne (*Det. Laura Ballard*); Michael Michele (*Dr. Carol Blyth*); Kyle Secor (*Det. Tim Bayliss*); Toni Lewis (*Det. Terri Stivers*); Jon Seda (*Det. Paul Falsone*); Isabella Hofmann (*Det. Meagn Russert*); Zelijko Ivanek (*Det. Ed Fanvers*).

4145   *Homicide Squad.* (Series; Crime Drama; Syn.; 1955). The syndicated title for *Mark Saber*. See this title for information.

4146   *Hondo.* (Series; Western; ABC; 1967). The Arizona Territory during the late 1860s is the setting for a look at Hondo Lane, a United States Army troubleshooter, as he attempts to resolve the bloodthirsty conflict between settlers and the Apache Indians over the possession of land. Hondo travels with his dog, Sam. Buffalo Baker is Hondo's partner; Angie Dow is a settler Hondo befriends (a widow); Johnny Dow is Angie's son; Vittoro is the Apache Chief; Captain Richards is Hondo's superior. Based on the feature film of the same title.

Cast: Ralph Taeger (*Hondo Lane*); Noah Beery, Jr. (*Buffalo Baker*); Kathie Brown (*Angie Dow*); Buddy Foster (*Johnny Dow*); Michael Pate (*Chief Vittoro*); Gary Clarke (*Captain Richards*).

4147   *Honest Al's A-OK Used Car and Trailer Rental Tigers.* (Pilot; Comedy; Syn.; Jan. 1978). When the Tigers, a youth league football team lose their sponsor, "Honest" Al, the owner of Honest Al's Used Cars and Trailer Rentals, becomes the team's new sponsor. The proposed series was to relate Al's misadventures as he tries to run a business and manage a group of kids. Other regulars are Franklin, his mechanic; Ethel, Franklin's aunt; and the kids: Moody, Doc and Chicago.

Cast: Herb Edelman (*Honest Al*); Danny Bonaduce (*Franklin*); Zoey Wilson (*Aunt Ethel*); Kyra Stempel (*Moody*); Marc Jason (*Doc*); J.R. Miller (*Chicago*).

4148   *Honestly, Celeste.* (Series; Comedy; CBS; 1954). Celeste Anders is a young woman who teaches journalism at a college in Minnesota. Celeste wants to bring more to her students than what is written in textbooks. She wants to bring them real-life experiences. She begins by moving to New York and, although not really qualified to be a reporter, her book-knowledge experience of journalism, gets her a job as a cub reporter on a newspaper called *The New York Express*. Stories follow Celeste as she struggles to acquire real journalism experience. Mr. Wallace is the paper's editor; Bob Wallace, his son, is Celeste's romantic interest; Marty Gordon is Celeste's friend, a cab driver; Mary is Mr. Wallace's secretary.

Cast: Celeste Holm (*Celeste Anders*); Geoffrey Lumb (*Mr. Wallace*); Scott McKay (*Bob Wallace*); Mike Kellin (*Marty Gordon*); Mary Finney (*Mary*); Henry Jones (*The Obit Editor*).

4149   *Honey, I Shrunk the Kids: The TV Series.* (Series; Comedy; Syn.; 1997–2000). Matheson is a small town in Colorado that is also the home of Wayne Szlinski, an ingenious inventor whose creations often backfire. Wayne is married to Diane and is the father of Amy and Nicholas. They live at 6808 Bonnie Meadow Court and have a dog named Quark.

Wayne works as a research scientist for Jen Tech West Labs, a company whose motto is "Exceptional Living Through Expensive Technology." While Wayne enjoys the scientific challenges of his job, he finds pure satisfaction at home in his private attic lab where he has invented such devices as the Shrink Ray, the Time Hopper (for travel through time) and the Igloo of Health (a plastic isolation bubble). Matheson appears to be a peaceful town. However, when crime threatens its citizens, Wayne comes to the rescue, using one of his inventions to secretly help the police apprehend the bad guys. It was when Wayne was in college that his life changed. He was exploring a cave as part of a science project when he discovered a strange, glowing metal. After experimenting with the metal, Wayne determined that it was alien in nature as it produced extraordinary power. He called his find "Szlinskism" and it enabled him to invent items no one else could. Diane is a successful lawyer with Coleman and Associates who often becomes the "victim" of one of Wayne's inventions when it backfires (for example, becoming a gorgeous but evil Egyptian queen; reverting back to a 16-year-old girl; aging far beyond her years; speaking in rhymes). Diane is also president of the Matheson School Board.

Amy, called "Ames" by Wayne, is a pretty 16-year-old girl who attends Matheson High School (where she is a member of the Spartans'

basketball team). Amy worries that her father's wacky inventions are ruining her reputation. When Amy tinkered with Wayne's Neuron Nudger (a device to improve mental power) she acquired amazing powers and sought to become Mistress of the Universe. Amy also became a victim of Wayne's Suntan Block (made from fish oils) that slowly turned her into a mermaid.

Nicholas, called Nick and "The Nick Meister" by Wayne, attends Matheson Elementary School. He is very smart and seems to be following in Wayne's footsteps (as he understands the logic behind what his father invents). He is a member of the Science Club at school and if he doesn't get an *A* on a test, he feels he will be living in disgrace.

Jake McKenna is the police chief; H. Gordon Jennings is Wayne's boss. Based on the theatrical feature *Honey I Shrunk the Kids*.

Cast: Peter Scolari (*Wayne Szlinski*); Barbara Alyn Woods (*Diane Szlinski*); Hillary Tuck (*Amy Szlinski*); Thomas Dekker (*Nicholas Szlinski*); George Buza (*Chief Jake McKenna*); Bruce Jarchow (*H. Gordon Jennings*).

4150   *Honey Vicarro.* (Pilot; Comedy; Unaired; Produced for Fox in 2001). Honey Vicarro is a gorgeous, voluptuous actress of the 1960s whose TV series, a sexier version of *Honey West*, is cancelled for being too risqué. Rather than wallow in self pity, Honey decides to use her experiences as a TV detective in real life. The proposal was to follow Honey as she incorporates her knowledge of criminals as an amateur sleuth to help people in trouble.

Cast: Jenny McCarthy (*Honey Vicarro*).

4151   *Honey West.* (Series; Crime Drama; ABC; 1965–1966). H. West and Company is a Los Angeles–based private detective organization owned by Honey West, a shapely (36-24-34) blonde who inherited the company and her partner, Sam Bolt, from her late father. Honey had assisted her father and Sam and has now become a much sought after detective.

Honey operates out of her luxurious apartment at 6033 Del Mar Vista in Los Angeles. She is shrewd, uncanny and capable of defending herself. Although she possesses a black belt in karate, she does take an occasional beating. Honey uses the latest in scientific equipment and incorporates a mobile base of operations disguised as a TV repair truck (H. West TV Repairing). Honey has a pet ocelot named Bruce and the living room wall displaying various vases in Honey's apartment is actually the secret entrance to her lab. Honey carries a gun — and uses it. Her earrings also double as miniature gas bombs when thrown and broken. Honey is not always successful and does let clients down. She often risks her life by going undercover to solve a case such as a society woman or wealthy playgirl. She and Sam try to cooperate with the police but Honey can't promise they will always go by the book.

Sam is always there for Honey although he does sometimes arrive too late to save Honey from being roughed up. He thinks Honey is a born cynic as she believes every case is connected to a murder. Sam also feels Honey is not as effective as her father when he ran the company. Honey has a tendency to let cases pile up and becomes too focused on a case when it gets the best of her. Sam also does undercover work, usually posing as a chauffeur or playboy to fool confidence men. The innocent looking ball point pen Honey gives to certain clients is actually a miniature transmitter she uses for tracking purposes.

The pilot episode, "Honey West: Who Killed the Jackpot," aired on *Burke's Law* on April 12, 1965.

Cast: Anne Francis (*Honey West*); John Ericson (*Sam Bolt*); Irene Hervey (*Meg West; Honey's aunt*).

4152   *Honeymoon Hotel.* (Series; Comedy; Syn.; 1987). The alternate title for *Isabel Sanford's Honeymoon Hotel*. See this title for information.

4153   *The Honeymoon Race.* (Series; Game; ABC; 1967-1968). Three newlywed couples compete in a scavenger hunt. The couples are situated in the Hollywood Mall Shopping Center in Florida. The players are each given a series of clues and have to find the items they represent. The couples who find the most items are the winners and receive the articles as their prizes.

Host: Bill Malone.

4154   *Honeymoon Suite.* (Pilot; Comedy; ABC; Jan. 30, 1973). Vignettes that depict brief incidents in the lives of couples that check into Room 300 of the plush Honeymoon Suite of the Beverly Hills Hotel. Maggie is the maid; Charlie, the bellboy; and Duncan, the hotel manager. Two ABC pilots were produced: *Honeymoon Suite* (Jan. 30, 1973) and *Honeymoon Suite II* (Oct. 23, 1973).

Cast: Rose Marie (*Maggie*); Morey Amsterdam (*Charlie; first pilot*); Henry Gibson (*Charlie; second pilot*); Richard Deacon (*Duncan*).

4155   *The Honeymooners.* (Series; Comedy; CBS; 1955-1956). The apartment house at 728 Chauncey Street in Bensonhurst, Brooklyn, New York, is home to Ralph and Alice Kramden and their upstairs neighbors Ed and Trixie Norton. The address is also given as 328 and 358 Chauncey Street.

Ralph attended P.S. 73 grammar school and at age 14 worked as a newspaper delivery boy. He had high hopes of playing the cornet in a band but couldn't afford the price of lessons. Ralph took his future wife, Alice Gibson, dancing at the Hotel New Yorker on their first date, but three versions were given as to how he met her. It is first said that Ralph noticed Alice in a diner when she yelled to the waiter "Hey Mac, a hot frank and a small orange drink." Next, it is a snowy winter day when Ralph, assigned by the WPA to shovel snow, meets Alice, a WPA employee who is handing out the shovels. Finally, Ralph mentions that he met Alice in a restaurant called Angie's when they both ordered spaghetti and meatballs. A marriage took place in 1941 and the newlywed Kramdens moved in with Alice's mother (whom Ralph calls "Blabbermouth"). They rented their first (and only) apartment when Ralph became a bus driver for the Gotham Bus Company. He drives bus number 247 (also given as 2969) along Madison Avenue in Manhattan. Alice was also said to have worked in a Laundromat before meeting Ralph.

Edward L. Norton works as an "Engineer in Subterranean Sanitation" (a sewer worker for the department of sanitation). He says the *L* in his name stands for Lilywhite (his mother's maiden name) and that he majored in arithmetic at vocational school (in another episode he mentions attending P.S. 31 in Oyster Bay, Brooklyn). As a kid Ed had a dog named Lulu (although in another episode he is allergic to dogs) and did a hitch in the Navy (he later took up typing on the G.I. Bill). He found that he couldn't stand being cooped up in an office, so he took the job in the sewer (which he started in 1938).

Ed calls Ralph "Ralphie Boy" and it is mentioned that when Ed came down to invite Ralph and Alice to dinner they became instant friends. Ralph and Ed are members of the Raccoon Lodge (also called the International Order of the Friendly Sons of Raccoons and the International Loyal Order of Friendly Raccoons). Ralph is the treasurer; Alice and Trixie are members of the Ladies' Auxiliary of the lodge.

Ralph has a dream of making it big. He ventured into a number of moneymaking schemes that all failed, the most famous being paying 10 cents each for 2,000 Handy Housewife Helpers (a combination peeler, can opener and apple corer) that he and Ed tried to sell for one dollar each in a "Chef of the Future" commercial (during

the third break in a Charlie Chan movie). Ralph got stage fright and ruined the commercial. Ralph also started the Ralph Kramden Corporation (where, for $20, Ed got 35 percent of everything Ralph made above his salary, which was first $42.50, then $60 and $62 a week). Jackie Gleason and Bill Templeton composed the theme, "You're My Greatest Love."

Program Open: "Jackie Gleason ... *The Honeymooners* ... with the stars Art Carney ... Audrey Meadows ... and Joyce Randolph."

Cast: Jackie Gleason (*Ralph Kramden*); Audrey Meadows (*Alice Kramden*); Art Carney (*Ed Norton*); Joyce Randolph (*Trixie Norton*). **Various Roles:** George O. Petrie, Frank Marth. **Announcer:** Gaylord Avery, Jack Lescoulie.

Origins: Jackie Gleason first played Ralph Kramden on DuMont's *Cavalcade of Stars* from 1950 to 1952. Art Carney was Ed Norton, Pert Kelton, Alice Kramden, and Elaine Stritch, Trixie Norton. A series of "Honeymooners" segments appeared on *The Jackie Gleason Show* (CBS, 1952–1955) featuring the same cast as the 1955 series. The same cast returned to a new *Jackie Gleason Show* (CBS, 1956–1961) wherein additional "Honeymooners" segments were produced.

Updates: On *Jackie Gleason and His American Scene Magazine* (CBS, 1962–1966), Jackie Gleason and Art Carney reprised their roles as Ralph and Ed with Sue Ane Langdon and Patricia Wilson as Alice and Trixie in short "Honeymooners" segments. Jackie and Art reprised their roles of Ralph and Ed with Sheila MacRae and Jane Kean as Alice and Trixie in short and then full-hour episodes of "The Honeymooners" on *The Jackie Gleason Show* (CBS, 1966–1970). This cast repeated their roles on two *Jackie Gleason Specials* (CBS, Dec. 12, 1970 and Nov. 11, 1973).

Four additional ABC specials aired with Jackie Gleason, Art Carney, Sheila MacRae and Jane Kean reprising their roles:

1. The Honeymooners Second Honeymoon (Feb. 2, 1976). Ed and Trixie join Ralph and Alice as they celebrate their 25th wedding anniversary.

2. The Honeymooners Christmas (Nov. 28, 1977). Ralph directs the play *A Christmas Carol* for the Raccoon Lodge.

3. The Honeymooners Valentine Special (Feb. 13, 1978). Alice attempts to surprise Ralph with a new suit for Valentine's Day.

4. The Honeymooners Christmas Special (Dec. 10, 1978). Ralph and Ed attempt to win a million dollars by investing in lottery tickets.

4156   *Hong Kong.* (Series; Adventure; ABC; 1960-1961). Glen Evans is a foreign correspondent based in Hong Kong. He works for the World Wide News Service and lives at 24 Peak Road. Stories relate his story gathering assignments. Neil Campbell is the police chief; Tully is the owner of Glen's favorite watering hole, Tully's Bar; and Ching Mei is a waitress at the Golden Dragon Café. Fong then Ling are Glen's houseboys.

Cast: Rod Taylor (*Glenn Evans*); Lloyd Bochner (*Neil Campbell*); Jack Kruschen (*Tully*); Mai Tai Sing (*Ching Mei*); Harold Fong (*Fong*); Gerald Jann (*Ling*); Maria McClay (*Glenn's secretary*).

4157   *Hong Kong Phooey.* (Series; Cartoon; NBC; 1974–1978). Henry is a meek police station janitor who can transform himself into Hong Kong Phooey, "America's secret weapon against crime." Hong Kong is also accident prone and stories relate his fumbling attempts to solve crimes.

Voice Cast: Scatman Crothers (*Henry/Hong Kong Phooey*); Joe E. Ross (*Police Sgt. Flint*); Kathi Gori (*Rosemary; telephone operator*); Don Messick (*Spot; Henry's cat*).

4158   *The Hoofer.* (Pilot; Comedy; CBS; Aug. 15, 1966). Donald Dugan and Freddy Brady are a struggling vaudeville comedy team trying to make a name for themselves. It is the 1920s and the proposal was to relate their endless efforts to find work.

Cast: Donald O'Connor *(Donald Dugan)*; Soupy Sales *(Freddy Brady)*; Jerome Cowan *(Brainsley Gordon, their agent)*.

4159   *Hookers Saved.* (Series; Reality; Investigation Discovery; 2010). Annie Lobert, a former high class Las Vegas call girl, has reformed and begun a mission to help girls who were once in her position called Hookers for Jesus. Annie has also established a Christian Safe House (Destiny House) as a place of refuge where prostitutes can hide from their pimps, retrain for legitimate work and most importantly, learn how to reclaim their lives. Stories follow Annie and her efforts to help the young girls who have fallen into the dangerous world of prostitution.

4160   *Hooperman.* (Series; Comedy; ABC; 1987–1989). Harry Hooperman is an inspector with the San Francisco Police Department. He is single and lives with his vicious little dog, Bijoux. Harry is also a landlord and owns an apartment building at 633 Columbus Street. Harry is dating a girl named Alex and for relaxation he plays saxophone at a club owned by Max on Tuesday nights. Stories relate the hectic events in his life as he struggles to be a cop, landlord and normal guy just seeking a little peace and quiet from life.

Other regulars are Celeste Stern, the police captain; Officer Betty Bushkin, the police dispatcher; Susan Smith, Harry's building manager; Gail Minkoff, the seedy lawyer; T.J., the cabbie; Police Officers Boris "Bobo" Pritzger, Maureen "Mo" DeMott, Clarence McNeal and Rick Silardi; Lou, Celeste's husband; Rudy, Harry's complaining tenant; and Susan's mother.

Cast: John Ritter *(Insp. Harry Hooperman)*; Barbara Bosson *(Capt. Celeste Stern)*; Debrah Farentino *(Susan Smith)*; Daphne Ashbrook *(Alex)*; Sydney Walsh *(Off. Betty Bashkin)*; Clarence Felder *(Det. Boris Pritzger)*; Felton Perry *(Det. Clarence McNeal)*; Joseph Gain *(Off. Rick Silardi)*; Jim Haynie *(Max)*; Andrew Divoff *(Rudy)*; Dan Lauria *(Lou Stern)*; Lee Garlington *(Gail Minkoff)*; Rod Gist *(T.J.)*.

4161   *Hooray for Hollywood.* (Pilot; Comedy; CBS; June 22, 1964). World Goliath Studios was a famous but mythical movie studio of the 1920s. The proposal is an attempt to recapture its glory via the experiences of its head, Jerome P. Baggley. Other regulars are Vanda Renee, his celebrated but brainless leading lady; Albert P. Leviathan, the rival studio head; Miss Zilke, Baggley's secretary; and Ruby, Albert's secretary.

Cast: Herschel Bernardi *(Jerome P. Baggley)*; Joyce Jameson *(Vanda Renee)*; Joan Blondell *(Miss Zilke)*; John Litel *(Albert P. Leviathan)*; Ruby Keeler *(Ruby)*.

4162   *Hooray for Love.* (Pilot; Comedy; CBS; Sept. 9, 1963). Schuyler Young, called Sky, is a college student pursuing a Ph. D. He is married to Abby, the daughter of Gillie and Clara Boone. Sky works part time for Gillie and the proposed series was to relate their struggles as newlyweds. Otis is Sky's friend.

Cast: Darryl Hickman *(Sky Young)*; Yvonne Craig *(Abby Young)*; Beverly Willis *(Clara Boone)*; Don Edmonds *(Gillie Boone)*; Alvy Moore *(Otis Platt)*.

4163   *Hootenanny.* (Series; Variety; ABC; 1963). Performances by folk music artists who are filmed performing at various college campuses.

Host: Jack Linkletter. **Regular:** Glenn Yarbrough. **Music:** The Chad Mitchell Trio.

4164   *Hopalong Cassidy.* (Series; Western; Syn., 1948; NBC, 1949–1953). Hopalong Cassidy is a rancher (the owner of the Bar 20 Ranch) and a daring defender of range justice in the Old West. Stories relate Hopalong's adventures as he and his partner, Red Connors, help people who are unable to help themselves (protecting them from outlaws).

In 1935 producer Harry Sherman bought the screen rights to Clarence E. Mulford's *Hopalong Cassidy* stories. Offered a chance to star in the first film, William Boyd accepted, but refused to play the part of the ranch foreman. His persistence awarded him the role of Cassidy. As written, Cassidy was originally an illiterate, "tobacco-chewin', hard drinkin', able-swearin' son of the Old West who got his nickname because of a limp." However, when the first feature film, *Hop-a-Long Cassidy* was released by Paramount, Boyd dropped everything that the original literary character had possessed, including the limp, with an explanation in the second film that the wound had healed (although the nickname stuck). Between 1935 and 1948, sixty-six *Hopalong Cassidy* films were made. A television series appeared in 1948; a radio series, also starring William Boyd, appeared on Mutual in 1949. Hopalong rides a horse named Topper.

Cast: William Boyd *(Hopalong Cassidy)*; Edgar Buchanan *(Red Connors)*.

4165   *Hope and Faith.* (Series; Comedy; ABC; 2003–2006). Hope Shanoski is a 35-year-old housewife who lives at 22 Cherry Lane in Glen Falls, Ohio. She is married to Charlie, a dentist, and is the mother of Sydney, Hayley and Justin.

Faith Fairfield is Hope's sister, a once famous TV soap opera star (10 years on *The Sacred and the Sinful*) who lost her job (written out) and has returned to her childhood town of Glen Falls to live with Hope and her family (she claims to have no money and no prospects for a job other than in show business).

Faith lives in the glory of her past and hopes to one day return to New York (where her soap was taped) and once again make her mark on the world. In the meantime she is struggling to adjust to a much simpler life — and in doing so causes numerous problems for the family, especially for Hope, who always becomes the innocent victim in her harebrained schemes to make money. Charlie also feels his life is plagued by Faith as he is always the one who has to step in and get the girls out of trouble (often involving himself in their silliness).

Sydney is the eldest child, a sophomore in high school. She is very pretty and totally devoted to looking the best she can. While smart, she is not addicted to school work and believes she can get by on her physical assets. Younger sister Hayley is pretty and very smart. Her life revolves around her ability to improve her mind and while she could be very attractive, she doesn't dress to impress boys. Justin, the youngest, is smart but not as intellectual as Hayley. He is easily impressed by others and often takes on their persona to impress people (for example, several episodes portray him as imitating Frank Sinatra).

In the original unaired pilot film, Josh Stamberg played Charlie; Brie Larson was Sydney and Slade Pearce was Justin.

Cast: Faith Ford *(Hope Shanoski)*; Kelly Ripa *(Faith Fairfield)*; Ted McGinley *(Charlie Shanoski)*; Nicole Paggi *(Sydney Shanoski, 2003-04)*; Megan Fox *(Sydney Shanoski, 2004–06)*; Macey Cruthird *(Hayley Shanoski)*; Paul Litowsky *(Justin Shanoski)*.

4166   *Hope and Gloria.* (Series; Comedy; NBC; 1995). Hope Davidson and Gloria Utz are friends who share adjoining apartments in Philadelphia. Hope is divorced after ten years of marriage and works as the producer for *The Dennis Dupree Show* (airs on WPNN, Channel 5). Gloria is also divorced and the mother of five-year-old Sonny. She works as a hair stylist at Cookie's Salon; her ex-husband, Louis, works for Bud Green's Carpetorium.

Hope is a bit wild and unpredictable and always looking for a good time; Gloria is shy, sweet and vulnerable and feels comfortable in her own environment (Hope calls her a "Gushy Gush" and is trying to make her more aggressive). Stories relate events in their lives. Dennis began his career with Regis Philbin as co-host of the mythical *Morning Zoo Program* twenty-five years ago. His mentor was Merv Griffin, who called him "The Kid."

Cast: Cynthia Stevenson (*Hope Davidson*); Jessica Lundy (*Gloria Utz*); Alan Thicke (*Dennis Dupree*); Robert Garrova (*Sonny Utz*).

4167 *Hope Division*. (Pilot; Crime Drama; ABC; Aug. 17, 1987). Anne Russell (white) and James Reynolds (black) are homicide detectives with the Hope Division of the L.A.P.D. James and Anne are an experimental male-female team and each has their own views on pursuing justice. The proposal was to relate their case assignments. James is married to Lilah and is the father of Melissa and Louis. Anne is divorced and the mother of Jenny.

Cast: Mimi Kuzak (*Anne Russell*); Dorian Harewood (*James Reynolds*); H. Richard Green (*Bruce Thorpe*); Hattie Winston (*Lilah Reynolds*); Saban Shawel (*Melissa Reynolds*); Cliffy Magee (*Louis Reynolds*); Hayley Carr (*Jenny Russell*).

4168 *Hope Island*. (Series; Drama; PAX; 1999-2000). The Community Church is a neglected house of worship on Hope Island. Daniel Cooper is a reverend who has come to the island to reopen the church and reintroduce religion to the colorful and somewhat eccentric residents. Stories follow Daniel's experiences and his relationship with Alex Stone, a widow who runs the local tavern (Widow's Walk) and her son, Dylan.

Cast: Cameron Daddo (*Daniel Cooper*); Suki Kaiser (*Alex Stone*); Max Peters (*Dylan Stone*); Duncan Fraser (*Brian Brewster*); Beverley Elliott (*Bonita Vasquez*); Allison Hossack (*Molly Brewster*); Veena Sood (*Callie Pender*); Gina Stockdale (*Ruby Vasquez*).

4169 *Hoppity Hopper*. (Series; Cartoon; Syn.; 1962). The shortened *TV Guide* title for *The Adventures of Hoppity Hopper from Foggy Bogg*. See this title for information.

4170 *The Horace Heidt Show*. (Series; Variety; CBS; 1950-1951). Performances by undiscovered, promising talent.

Host: Horace Heidt. **Announcer:** Clayton "Bud" Collyer. **Orchestra:** Horace Heidt.

4171 *Hornblower*. (Pilot; Adventure; ABC; Feb. 28, 1963). Horatio Hornblower is captain of the *HMS Firedrake* a British warship during the early 1800s. It is also a time when England was at war with France and the proposal was to follow Horatio's assignments on behalf of the Crown. Based on the stories by C.S. Forester.

Cast: David Buck (*Capt. Horatio Hornblower*); Terence Longdon (*Lieutenant Bush*); Peter Arne (*Nathaniel Sweet*); Sean Kelly (*Lieutenant Carlon*); Jeremy Bulloch (*Midshipman Bowser*).

4172 *Horseland*. (Series; Cartoon; CBS; 2005). The area in and around a stable called Horseland is the setting. Here, beside a group of humans, also live a dog (Shep) a cat (Angora), and a pig (Teeny). Through the observations of these animals (as they speak only among themselves), the activities of five close girlfriends, Alma Rodriquez, Chloe Stilton, Zoe Stilton (Chloe's sister), Molly Washington and Sarah Whitney are depicted as they interact with each other and their love of horses. Alma's horse is Button; Chloe's horse is Chili; Zoe's horse is Pepper; Sarah's horse is Scarlet; Molly's horse is Calypso. Will is the stableman (his parents own Horseland) and has a horse named Jimber.

Voices: Dana Donlan, Emily Hernandez, Bianca Heyward, David Kalis, Jerry Longe, Vincent Michael, Marissa Shea, Aleyah Smith, Michelle Zacharia.

4173 *Hot*. (Pilot; Reality; Unaired; Produced in 2010). Tammy Murdock is what guys (even girls) would call "hot." She has blonde hair, blue eyes, long legs, a slim waist and, as she says, "an ample bosom." But, can a girl with Tammy's looks actually get men to do what she wants? The proposal was to put that theory to the test as Tammy approaches men and asks them to perform a task that is too difficult for her to accomplish on her own.

4174 *Hot Babes Doing Stuff Naked*. (Series; Reality; Playboy; 2007). Gorgeous girls, naked or scantily clad, perform non sexual "stuff" as requested by viewers from a survey conducted by the Playboy Channel. Requested activities include roller skating, deep sea fishing, chicken farming, shooting guns and washing a truck. The girls, connected with *Playboy* magazine or the Playboy mansion, are identified by first names only (for example, Amber, Brooke, Andrea and Zoe).

4175 *Hot City Disco*. (Series; Music; Syn.; 1978). Shadoe Stevens and David Jones host a program of performances by disco artists. The Jeff Kutect Dancers are regulars.

4176 *Hot Country Nights*. (Series; Variety; NBC; 1991-1992). A Sunday evening program that spotlights country and western entertainers. Guests host and the program also features country comedians and a segment called "Hot New Hit Maker" that showcases a promising singer. Dick Clark is the producer.

4177 *Hot Dog*. (Series; Children; NBC; 1970-1971). An interesting program, aimed at children that explores in a humorous light the mysteries that surround the making of everyday items.

Regulars: Woody Allen, Jonathan Winters, Jo Anne Worley. **Music:** The Youngbloods.

4178 *Hot Footage*. (Pilot; Comedy; CBS; May 15, 1960). Jonathan Love is a TV news cameraman, and Hank Wahr is also a cameraman, but for a rival news service. The proposal was to relate their efforts to beat each other to stories for their news service. Aired as a segment of *G.E. Theater*.

Cast: Richard Greene (*Jonathan Love*); Robert Strauss (*Hank Wahr*).

4179 *Hot Gay Comics*. (Series; Comedy; Here; 2008–). Performances by established as well as up-and-coming gay and lesbian standup comics.

Host: Dave Rubin. **Comics Include:** Anne Neczypor, Mike Singer, Shawn Hollenbach, Jackie Monahan, Paul Case, Danny Leary, Poppi Kramer, David Hadorowski, Ben Lerman, Chantal Larrere. Amy Beckerman, Michael Brill, Joanne Fillan.

4180 *Hot Girls in Scary Places*. (Pilot; Reality; E!; 2009). Three gorgeous and "hot" girls are challenged to spend a night in a supposedly haunted location for a chance to win $10,000. In the pilot presentation, three University of Southern California cheerleaders (friends who are members of the Song Girls) agree to spend the night in an abandoned hospital that is reputed to be haunted. Unknown to the girls, scary situations have been set up as challenges they must face and overcome. The girls are "armed" with the latest in paranormal detecting equipment and must investigate the situations that are posed to them ("and look fabulous doing it"). The one girl brave enough to complete all tasks assigned to her wins the money. Lindsey Grubbs, Adrianna Kourafas, Shelley La Rue are the girls.

4181 *Hot Hero Sandwich*. (Series; Variety; NBC; 1979–1982).

A potpourri of celebrity interviews, music and comedy aimed at young people.

Regulars: Vicky Dawson, Paul O'Keefe, Matt McCoy, Denny Dillon, Nan-Lynn Nelson, Jarrett Smithwrick, L. Michael Craig, Andy Breckman, Andrew Duncan, Frankie Faison, Saundra McClain, Adam Ross, Claudette Sutherland. **Music Director:** Felix Pappalardi. **Theme Music:** "Hot Hero Sandwich" by Bruce Hart, Stephen Lawrence.

4182　*Hot Hot Los Angeles.* (Series; Comedy; Internet; 2008-2009). A spoof of network TV's prime time soap operas (for example, *Gossip Girl*, *One Tree Hill* and *90210*) that focuses on a Los Angeles society where money is power and beautiful girls are held in the highest esteem.

Cast: Olivia Hardt *(Skylar)*; Randy Wayne *(Victor Papsworth)*; Scott Spenser *(Pip Coburn)*; Kodi Kitchen *(Claudia)*; Christian Monzon *(Pepe)*; Alyshia Ochse *(Roxy)*; Jayson Blair *(Ty)*; Spencer Hill *(Rafe)*; Marnie Alton *(Karen Yamamoto)*.

4183　*Hot House.* (Series; Drama; ABC; 1998). The Garrison Center, a psychiatric clinic, is the setting for a look at the personal and professional lives of its doctors and staff.

Cast: Michael Learned *(Dr. Marie Teller)*; Art Malik *(Dr. Ved Lahari)*; Josef Sommer *(Dr. Sam Garrison)*; Alexis Smith *(Dr. Lily Garrison-Shannon)*; Michael Jeter *(Dr. Art Makter)*; Tony Soper *(Matt Garrison)*; Maureen Moore *(Lucy Cox)*; Louise Latham *(Louise Dougherty)*; Katherine Borowitz *(Issy Garrison Schrader)*; Susan Diol *(Claudia)*.

4184　*Hot in Cleveland.* (Series; Comedy; TV Land; 2010-). Melanie, a recently divorced author; Victoria, a former soap opera star (of *The Edge of Tomorrow*); and Joy, a cynic and high-end eyebrow specialist, are best friends who decide to leave the hustle and bustle of Los Angeles for a vacation in Paris to celebrate the publication of Melanie's new book. En-route, the plane on which they are traveling malfunctions, causing it to land in Cleveland. Immediately, the women feel out of place until they, each over the age of 40, are hit upon by local men of the same age. Instantly, and what could only happen in a sitcom, the women feel they are desirable and decide to stay. Melanie rents a home and invites Joy and Victoria to become her roommates. As they settle in, they discover another resident of the home — nearly 90-year-old Elka, the home's cantankerous caretaker. Melanie, Joy and Victoria are now "Hot in Cleveland" and stories not only relate their efforts to live together but adjust to a whole new way of life — a life made more comical by Elka's outrageous observations of her new tenant's way of doing things. A recurring storyline is Victoria's continual observations of her rival, Susan Lucci (of *All My Children*) whom she feels takes all the glamour and prestige she should receive.

Cast: Valerie Bertinelli *(Melanie Moretti)*; Wendie Malick *(Victoria Chase)*; Jane Leeves *(Joy Scroggs)*; Betty White *(Elka Ostrovsky)*.

4185　*Hot L Baltimore.* (Series; Comedy; ABC; 1975). Life in the seedy Hotel Baltimore (the title reflects the fact that the *E* in the neon sign has burned out) as seen through the activities of the eleven people who live like a family in the decaying Maryland establishment. Based on the Broadway play of the same title.

Bill Lewis is the desk clerk; Clifford Ainsley is the hotel manager; Suzy and April are prostitutes who reside at the hotel; Winthrop Morse is the cantankerous old man; Charles Bingham is the philosopher; Jackie is the young, unemployed girl; Millie is the waitress; Esmee Belotti is the mother of the never-seen psychotic younger, Moose; George and Gordon are homosexuals.

Cast: James Cromwell *(Bill Lewis)*; Richard Masur *(Clifford Ains-*

ley*)*; Jeannie Linero *(Suzy Marta Rocket)*; Conchata Ferrell *(April Green)*; Stan Gottlieb *(Winthrop Morse)*; Al Freeman, Jr. *(Charles Bingham)*; Robin Wilson *(Jackie)*; Gloria LeRoy *(Millie)*; Charlotte Rae *(Esmee Belotti)*; Lee Bergere *(George)*; Henry Calvert *(Gordon)*.

4186　*Hot Line.* (Series; Discussion; Syn.; 1964). Discussions on topical issues with appropriate guests.

Host: Gore Vidal. **Panelists:** Dorothy Kilgallen, David Susskind.

4187　*Hot Line.* (Series; Erotica; Cinemax; 1994–1996). A beautiful, sexy-voiced woman named Rebecca hosts a late night call-in radio program that is devoted to answering listener's questions regarding sex. As Rebecca takes a call and offers advice to those who call 555-KISS, a story is shown that illustrates the sexual fantasy (which contains nudity).

Cast: Shannon Tweed *(Rebecca, 1994)*; Tanya Roberts *(Rebecca, 1994–96)*.

4188　*Hot Metal.* (Series; Comedy; Syn.; 1988). A British produced program that takes a lighthearted look at England's Fleet Street Journalists as seen through the experiences of Howard Stringer, executive editor of *The Daily Crucible*, a struggling newspaper. Terrence Rathbone is the paper's owner; Russell Spam is Howard's assistant, and Greg Kettler is a reporter.

Cast: Geoffrey Palmer *(Howard Stringer)*; Robert Hardy *(Terrence Rathbone/Russell Spam)*; John Gordon Sinclair *(Greg Kettler)*.

4189　*Hot Momma.* (Pilot; Comedy; Unaired; Produced for ABC in 2003). Holly is sexy, flirtatious and confident. She is also a single mother (of Ashley) whose husband she claims is "missing in action." Ashley, a teenager is pretty, conservative and shy. The proposal was to follow a grown up girl and immature mother who are best friends and share each other's interests.

Cast: Gina Gershon *(Holly Ryan)*; Elizabeth Lundberg *(Ashley Ryan)*.

4190　*Hot Music.* (Series; Music; Syn.; 1984). A daily countdown of the week's top thirty music videos (as determined by a viewer poll).

Host: Claud Mann *(series)*; **Host:** Michael Binder *(pilot)*. **Announcer:** Tom Pino.

4191　*Hot Off the Wire.* (Series; Comedy; Syn.; 1960). The shortened title for *The Jim Backus Show: Hot Off the Wire*. See this title for information.

4192　*Hot Potato.* (Series; Game; NBC; 1984). Two three-member teams compete. A question containing seven possible answers is read. The returning champions receive the first opportunity to answer the question. They can answer it themselves or pass it to their opponents. If they choose to answer it themselves and are correct they score one point; if the player who answers (each takes a turn) is incorrect, he is disqualified from that round and the opponents can score the point if a correct answer is given. A seven-point round is played and the team with the highest score (in a two-out-of-three game match) is the winner. The champions then receive the opportunity to win $5,000 by answering a series of questions that begin at $300 and increase with difficulty to $5,000.

Host: Bill Cullen. **Announcer:** Charlie O'Donnell.

4193　*Hot Properties.* (Series; Comedy; ABC; 2005). Ava Summerlin, Chloe Reid, Emerson Ives and Lola Hernandez are four beautiful women who work for Summerlin and Associates Realty Company in Manhattan. Ava started the company in 1995 with the philosophy "We are not only real estate agents, we're matchmakers for people and homes." Chloe constantly puts herself down. She feels she is pretty, yearns for bigger breasts and feels she doesn't make a lasting impression on people.

Lola is the sexiest of the women and feels she is only attracted to gay men but doesn't know it at first sight. She was married to a gay man for 10 years before he left her when he discovered he was gay. Ava is somewhat self-centered and is an expert on makeup. She is from a rich family and has a tendency to wear blouses whose buttons don't always stay buttoned (she feels the sexy bras she wears help sell properties).

Other regulars are Mary, the agency receptionist; and doctors Charlie Thorpe and Sellers Boyd, friends of the women. Charlie is a plastic surgeon; Sellers, a psychologist.

Cast: Gail O'Grady *(Ava Summerlin)*; Nicole Sullivan *(Chloe Reid)*; Sofia Vergara *(Lola Hernandez)*; Christina Moore *(Emerson Ives)*; Stephen Dunham *(Dr. Charlie Thorpe)*; Evan Handler *(Dr. Sellers Boyd)*; Amy Hill *(Mary)*.

4194   Hot Prospects. (Pilot; Comedy; CBS; July 31, 1989). Silverberg, California, a small gold mining town in 1902, is the setting for an unsold series about Ben Braddock, a former prospector who opens a restaurant in a train depot. Other regulars are Ben's waitresses, Lorelei and Molly; Goldie, the brothel owner; Franklin Roosevelt, Ben's cook; and Blackie, the town banker.

Cast: George Clooney *(Ben Braddock)*; Crystal Bernard *(Lorelei LaRue)*; Leann Hunley *(Goldie)*; Cathy Ladman *(Molly Singer)*; James Watkins *(Franklin Roosevelt)*; Steve Tobolowsky *(Blackie)*.

4195   Hot Pursuit. (Series; Adventure; NBC; 1984). In an attempt to stop her husband from squandering company money to develop a car she feels will be a disaster, Estelle Modrian arranges for his murder. When Estelle learns that her husband, Victor, has promised a share of the profits to Kate Wyler, the designer of the car, she decides to use Kate in her plan.

On the pretext that one of their horses is sick, Estelle phones Kate's husband, Jim, a veterinarian. While Jim is at the Modrian home, Victor is shot — and a woman fitting Kate's description is seen fleeing from the scene. Kate, who has no alibi, is arrested and later charged with murder when a gun with her fingerprints is found.

Sometime later, while in a bar, Jim spots the dead ringer but is unable to capture her after she spots him and escapes. When Jim tries to convince authorities that Kate was set up, no one will believe him. Jim devises a plan. He ambushes the car that is carrying Kate to prison and the two escape. Stories relate their adventures as Kate and Jim become the pursued and the pursuer — on the run from the law and the real killers — and searching for the only hope they have of clearing themselves — the impersonator.

Other regulars are Alex Shaw, Estelle's henchman; Edward Wyler, Jim's father; Stephanie Josephson, Jim's sister; and Jody, Stephanie's daughter.

Cast: Teri Keane *(Kate Wyler)*; Eric Pierpoint *(Jim Wyler)*; Dina Merrill *(Estelle Modrian)*; Mitchell Ryan *(Edward Wyler)*; Deidre Hall *(Stephanie Josephson)*; Deborah Foreman *(Jody Josephson)*; Bradford Dillman *(Victor Modrian; first episode)*.

4196   Hot Seat. (Series; Game; ABC; 1976). Two husband-and-wife teams play, but compete one at a time. One member is placed in the Hot Seat, a skin response machine that measures emotional reactions. The sound is turned off in the booth and the other member is asked a question that requires a specific answer. The player chooses the answer that he feels will register highest on the machine when his mate is asked the same question. Correct predictions award players points. The highest scoring couple is the winner and receives merchandise prizes.

Host: Jim Peck. **Announcer:** Kenny Williams. **Music:** Stan Worth.

4197   Hot Shots. (Series; Crime Drama; CBS; 1986). Amanda Reed and Jason West are reporters for *Crime World*, a national magazine devoted to reporting the facts behind crimes. Amanda is a carefree young woman who believes in taking chances and risking her life if it means getting the facts (and solving crimes). Jason, on the other hand, is a bit more conservative and believes in caution while investigating a case. Jason, however, is rarely able to convince Amanda of his beliefs and always winds up protecting her while risking his life to gather the facts. Nicholas Broderick is their editor.

Cast: Dorothy Parke *(Amanda Reed)*; Booth Savage *(Jason West)*; Paul Burke *(Nicholas Broderick)*.

4198   Hot Springs Hotel. (Series; Comedy; Cinemax; 1998-1999). Hot Springs Hotel is a resort owned by Kat Matthus, a responsible businesswoman, and her irresponsible, female-chasing brother, Randy. Kat and Randy inherited the hotel, which is in financial difficulty, from their late aunt and stories follow their efforts to deal with the erotic antics of their staff and guests. Lacey is Kat's friend; Theo is Randy's friend.

Cast: Samantha Phillips *(Katherine "Kat" Matthus)*; Robert Abrams *(Randy Matthus)*; Glori Gold *(Lacey)*; Marc Revivo *(Theo)*; C.C. Costigan *(Marina)*; Vickie Vogel *(Donna)*; Sabrina Allen *(Vicky)*; Sondra St. Cyr *(Minnie)*; Avalon Anders *(Cory)*.

4199   Hot W.A.C.S. (Pilot; Comedy; ABC; June 1, 1981). Privates Pamela Jordan, Kitty Trumpp and Leslie Bates are U.S. Army W.A.C.S. stationed at Fort Ord in Monterey, California. The proposal was to relate their misadventures as they attempt to adjust to military life.

Cast: Ellen Regan *(Pamela Jordan)*; Dana Vance *(Kitty Trumpp)*; Damita Jo Freeman *(Leslie Bates)*; Julie Payne *(Major Janet Morehead)*; Susan Duvall *(Private Charlene Kellogg)*; Rebecca Holden *(Private Heather Cassidy)*; Richard Jaeckel *(Major Philip Seabrook)*.

4200   Hot Wheels. (Series; Cartoon; ABC; 1969–1971). The experiences of a group of responsible young teenage drivers who are members of Hot Wheels, an automobile racing club in Metro City. The program, aimed at teenagers, is designed to advocate automotive safety. Jack Wheeler is the club organizer; Janet Martin is Jack's girlfriend; Ardeth Pratt is the tomboy; Mother O'Hara is the owner of the local café hangout; Dexter Carter is the reckless driver; Doc Warren is the school's driving teacher; Mike Wheeler is Jack's father; and club members are Kip, Mickey Barnes and Tank Mallory. Mike Curb and the Curbstones perform the theme, "Hot Wheels."

Voice Cast: Bob Arbogast *(Jack Wheeler)*; Melinda Casey *(Janet Martin)*; Albert Brooks *(Mickey Barnes/Kip)*; Susan Davis *(Ardeth Pratt)*; Casey Kasem *(Tank Mallory/Dexter Carter)*; Nora Marlowe *(Mother O'Hara)*; Michael Rye *(Mike Wheeler)*; Bob Arbogast *(Doc Warren)*.

4201   Hot Wheels: Battle Force 5. (Series; Cartoon; Cartoon Network; 2009). During a long distance car race, Vert Wheeler is engulfed by a mysterious storm and transported to another dimension where he becomes involved in a conflict between its citizens and inter dimensional aliens. Vert, being the do-gooder he is, rescues a powerful girl (Sage) and learns that the aliens are planning to conquer the universe with Earth being their next target. To repay Vert for his kindness, Sage transports him (and herself) back to Earth. Here Sage transforms his car into an indestructible fighting machine. Vert recruits a team (Battle Force 5) and with Sage's help, battles to protect earth from the inter dimensional aliens.

Voice Cast: Mark Hildreth (*Vert Wheeler*); Kira Tozer (*Sage*); Michael Dobson (*Zemerik*); Kathleen Barr (*Aqura/Hatch*); Gabe Khouth (*Spinner*); Noel Johansen (*Standford*); Colin Murdock, Alessandro Juliani, Brian Drummond.

4202   *Hotel.* (Series; Drama; ABC; 1983–1988). Brief incidents in the lives of the guests who check in at the posh St. Gregory Hotel in San Francisco. The hotel is owned by Laura Trent and is overseen by Victoria Cabot. Peter McDermott is the manager. He is assisted by Christine Francis (she later becomes the manager when Peter inherits the hotel after Victoria's death). Billy Griffin provides the hotel's security; Julie Gillette is the reservations clerk (later the Director of Guest Relations). Megan Kendall is the desk clerk and her husband, Dave is the bellhop. Cheryl Dolan and Ryan Thomas are the receptionists in later episodes. Drew Hayward is the Director of Operations; and Eric Lloyd is the bellman.

Cast: James Brolin (*Peter McDermott*); Bette Davis (*Laura Trent*); Anne Baxter (*Victoria Cabot*); Connie Sellecca (*Christine Francis*); Nathan Cook (*Billy Griffin*); Shari Belafonte (*Julie Gillette*); Heidi Bohay (*Megan Kendall*); Michael Spound (*Dave Kendall*); Valerie Landsburg (*Cheryl Dolan*); Susan Walters (*Ryan Thomas*).

4203   *Hotel Babylon.* (Series; Drama; BBC America; 2007). A British version of *Hotel* that relates incidents in the lives of guests who check into the elegant Hotel Babylon in England. Rebecca Mitchell is the hotel director; Charlie Edwards is her assistant. Jackie Clunes is the head of housekeeping; Tony Casemore is the concierge; Anna Thornton-Wilton is the lobby receptionist. Like the American series, stories also focus on the efforts of the hotel staff to help patrons overcome their problems.

Cast: Tamzin Outhwaite (*Rebecca Mitchell*); Emma Pierson (*Anna Thornton-Wilton*); Max Beesley (*Charlie Edwards*); Dexter Fletcher (*Tony Casemore*); Natalie Mendoza (*Jackie Clunes*).

4204   *Hotel Broadway.* (Series; Variety; DuMont; 1949). Music, songs and comedy set against the background of the fictitious Manhattan-based Hotel Broadway, an establishment that spotlights both established and new talent discoveries.

Host: Jerri Blanchard. **Regulars:** Avon Long, Rose and Rana, The Striders. **Music:** The Harry Ranch Sextet.

4205   *Hotel Cosmopolitan.* (Series; Drama; CBS; 1957-1958). Dramatizations based on incidents in the lives of the people who frequent the Hotel Cosmopolitan as seen through the eyes of television actor Donald Woods.

Cast: Donald Woods (*Himself*); Henderson Forsythe (*House Detective*).

4206   *Hotel De Paree.* (Series; Western; CBS; 1959-1960). "There is no law in Georgetown, Colorado (1870s)—only what a man makes for himself," says a man known only as Sundance, an ex-gunfighter turned law enforcer. Sundance was born in Tombstone, Arizona, and is now half owner of Georgetown's Hotel De Paree, "One of the West's most colorful gathering places." Sundance is partners with a French woman named Annette Devereaux and her niece, Monique.

Sundance, also called "The Sundance Kid," has a very special trademark: a black Stetson with a hatband of ten small mirrors (its reflection in the sun blinds opponents). He has a dog named Useless and carries a Colt .45, which he will only use (or wear) when there is a need. Sundance also has a knack for whittling. While the Hotel De Paree has a bar and gambling hall, there is another watering hole in town called simply "The Saloon." Aaron Donager runs Donager's General Store and is sweet on "Miss Annette" (who enjoys playing checkers with him). Dimitri Tiomkin composed the theme, "Sundance."

Cast: Earl Holliman (*Sundance*); Jeanette Nolan (*Annette Devereaux*); Judi Meredith (*Monique Devereaux*); Strother Martin (*Aaron Donager*).

4207   *The Hotel Inspector.* (Series; Reality; BBC America; 2009). British bed and breakfasts are inspected and evaluated with the object being to correct their faults and upgrade them to a five star quality business.

Host: Ruth Watson.

4208   *Hotel Malibu.* (Series; Drama; CBS; 1994). On Malibu Beach in Southern California stands the Hotel Malibu, a fashionable establishment that is owned by the Mayfield family (Ellie, the widowed owner; her career-minded daughter, Stevie; and her scheming son, Jack). Incidents in their lives and the lives of their guests are dramatized. **Other Regulars:** Nancy, a maid; Harry, the bartender; and Sal Lopez, a parole officer who is Ellie's romantic interest; Melinda is Sal's daughter, the assistant bartender at the hotel; Mark Whitsett is Stevie's former fiancé.

Cast: Joanna Cassidy (*Ellie Mayfield*); Cheryl Pollak (*Stephanie "Stevie" Mayfield*); John Dye (*Jack Mayfield*); Romy Walthall (*Nancy*); Harry O'Reilly (*Harry*); Pepe Serna (*Sal Lopez*); Jennifer Lopez (*Melinda Lopez*); Paul Satterfield (*Mark Whitsett*).

4209   *Hound Town.* (Pilot; Cartoon; NBC; Sept. 1, 1989). A view of suburban life as seen through the eyes of Rusty, the shy dog of the Anderson family (parents John and Betty and their daughter, Susie).

Voice Cast: Michael Manasseri (*Rusty*); Christopher Rich (*John Anderson*); Jennifer Darling (*Betty Anderson*); Jeannie Elias (*Susie Anderson*).

4210   *The Houndcats.* (Series; Cartoon; NBC; 1972-1973). The cases of the Houndcats, a group of fumbling U.S. government dog and cat agents organized to combat evil. They drive a car they call Sparkplug and the program is a takeoff on *Mission: Impossible*. Studs is the leader; Muscle Mutt is the strong dog; Rhubarb is the inventor; Puddy Puss is the cat of a thousand faces; Ding Dog is the daredevil.

Voice Cast: Daws Butler (*Studs*); Aldo Ray (*Muscle Mutt*); Arte Johnson (*Rhubarb*); Joe Besser (*Puddy Puss*); Stu Gilliam (*Ding Dog*).

4211   *Hour Glass.* (Series; Variety; NBC; 1946-1947). Helen Parrish and Eddie Mayehoff host a program that features performances by the top name entertainers of the day. Evelyn Eaton hosted the first episode.

4212   *The Hour Glass.* (Series; Anthology; ABC; 1952–1956). The plight of people confronted with sudden, unexpected situations.

4213   *Hour Magazine.* (Series; Magazine; Syn.; 1980). A daily program of celebrity interviews and discussions on various topical issues that affect people in their daily lives.

Host: Gary Collins, Pat Mitchell, Bonnie Strauss.

4214   *Hour of Stars.* (Series; Anthology; Syn.; 1958). Rebroadcasts of filmed episodes that originally played on *The 20th Century–Fox Hour*. John Conte hosts.

4215   *House.* (Series; Drama; Fox; 2004–). Press release information states "Every week a new mystery and every week a new baffling case that only one team can solve." The mysteries are baffling medical diseases and the team are doctors stationed at the Princeton-Plainsboro Teaching Hospital in New Jersey.

Gregory House, a maverick, anti-social doctor, heads the team (he is assisted by Allison Cameron, Eric Foreman, Robert Chase, Thirteen Hadley, Lawrence Kutner, James Wilson and Martha Masters). Gregory is an expert in infectious diseases and his philosophy is "We treat. If the patient gets better we're right. If not, we learn something else." Gregory does not believe in pretense and says what he thinks. He rarely talks to a patient (only when he becomes intrigued) and balks at having to work the common cases in the hospital's clinic. While Gregory appears to solve every medical mystery by himself, it is only accomplished with the investigative work of his specialized team. Lisa Cuddy is Gregory's superior. The series has the screen title *House, M.D.*

Cast: Hugh Laurie (*Gregory House*); Jennifer Morrison (*Allison Cameron*); Omar Epps (*Eric Foreman*); Jesse Spencer (*Robert Chase*); Lisa Edelstein (*Lisa Cuddy*); Kal Penn (*Lawrence Kutner*); Peter Jacobson (*Chris Taub*); Olivia Wilder (*Thirteen Hadley*); Robert Sean Leonard (*James Wilson*); Amber Tamblyn (*Martha Masters*); Stephanie Venditto (*Nurse Brenda Previn*); Anne Dudek (*Amber Volakis*).

4216 *House Calls.* (Series; Comedy; CBS; 1979–1982). Adaptation of the motion picture that relates the escapades of the staff of the fictional Kensington General Hospital in Los Angeles. Charley Michaels is the playboy surgeon; Ann Anderson, the administrator (later replaced by Jane Jeffreys); other doctors and nurses are listed in the cast. Louella Grady is Charlie's girlfriend; Conrad Peckler is Ann's superior; Mrs. Phipps is a hospital volunteer.

Cast: Wayne Rogers (*Dr. Charley Michaels*); Lynn Redgrave (*Ann Anderson*); Sharon Gless (*Jane Jeffreys*); David Wayne (*Dr. Amos Weatherly*); Ray Buktenica (*Dr. Norman Solomon*); Aneta Corsaut (*Head Nurse Bradley*); Sharon DeBord (*Admissions Nurse*); Roger Bowen (*Dr. Floyd Beiderbeck*); Deedy Peters (*Mrs. Phipps*); Candice Azzara (*Louella Grady*); Mark L. Taylor (*Conrad Peckler*); Dick Martin (*Dr. Shineberg*); Beth Jacobs (*Nurse Nancy McMillan*); Richard Stahl (*Dr. Albert*); Vince Howard (*Anesthesiologist*); Peggy Frees (*Nurse*); Terri Berland (*Nurse*); Georgia Jeffries (*Nurse*); Linda Dangcil (*Nurse's Aide*); Bob Larkin (*Orderly*); Christopher Blanc (*Orderly*).

4217 *House Husbands of Hollywood.* (Series; Reality; Fox Reality Channel; 2009). A male version of Bravo's *Real Housewives* franchise that focuses on five stay-at-home men who run the house and care for the children while their wives work ("and do it without worrying about chipping a nail"). The participants are Billy Ashley (former L.A. Dodger), Danny Barclay (actor), Darryl M. Bell (married to actress Tempestt Bledsoe), Charles Mattera (actor), Grant Reynolds (married to *Good Day L.A.* anchor Jillian Reynolds).

4218 *House of Buggin'.* (Series; Comedy; Fox; 1995). Latin-themed skits that satirize television, movies and everyday life.

Host: John Leguizamo. **Regulars:** Jorge Luis Abreu, Tammi Cubilette, Luis Guzman, David Herman, Yolba Osorio, Gina Torres. **Announcer:** Harry Pritchard. **Music:** Stephen M. Gold.

4219 *House of Clues.* (Series; Reality; Court TV; 2004). Two amateur sleuths (per episode) are given free reign in a real person's home to uncover clues to make a profile of who the home owners are. At the end of their investigation, the sleuths and home owners meet face-to-face to determine the accuracy of their profiles. Reef Karim hosts.

4220 *House of Dreams.* (Series; Reality; A&E; 2004). Sixteen contestants (called "Dream Builders") and having some knowledge of architecture or construction, are brought to Harmony, Florida, to not only build a home, but win it. Construction engineer Joe Buckey oversees and supervises the construction challenges and the Dream Builders who do not meet expectations are eliminated. The one participant who shows the greatest potential wins the house (here a Dream Builder named Viveca). Losing participants receive a gift card from the show's sponsors (J.C. Penney and Lending Tree.com).

Host: George Wendt.

4221 *House of Jazmin.* (Series; Reality; MTV; 2009). Li Cari is a fledgling fashion line created by Jazmin Whitley, a 20-year-old woman who is struggling to make her line a success. Cameras chart her progress—from sketching and pulling fabrics to selecting the models she feels will bring her designs to life. Susan Costa is Jazmin's mother and her financial backer; Morgan Weirich is Jazmin's best friend and partner.

4222 *House of Mouse.* (Series; Cartoon; Disney; 2001-2002). The House of Mouse is a dinner club located on Main Street in Toon Town. It is run by Mickey Mouse and his girlfriend, Minnie Mouse and stories follow their efforts to run the club (and perform in floor shows) while attending patrons and solving the problems associated with running the establishment. Donald Duck is the assistant manager; Daisy Duck, Donald's girlfriend, is the reservations clerk; Goofy is the head waiter; Pluto is Mickey's pet dog.

Voice Cast: Wayne Allwine (*Mickey Mouse*); Russi Taylor (*Minnie Mouse*); Bill Farmer (*Goofy*); Tony Anselmo (*Donald Duck*); Tress MacNeille (*Daisy Duck*); April Winchell (*Clarabell Cow*); Kevin Schon (*Timon*); Ernie Sabella (*Pumbaa*); Jonathan Freeman (*Jafar*).

4223 *House of Payne.* (Series; Comedy; Syn./TBS; 2006–). The lives of three generations of one family living under the same roof. Curtis and Ella Payne are a couple who have been married for thirty-one years. Curtis is a firefighter (a lieutenant) and they are the parents of C.J. (a firefighter also). C.J. is married to Janine and they are the parents of Jasi and Malik. Janine is not the best role model for her children. She loves her children but is addicted to drugs. She uses the money C.J. gives her to pay the bills to buy drugs. In a desperate effort to cover this up, Janine sets fire to their house. When an investigation discovers that arson was to blame and the finger points to Janine, she regrettably leaves her children "until things cool off." Now, without a place to live (and no insurance money as Janine never paid the premium), C.J. and his children move in with his parents. Miss Cloretha is Ella's righteous, church-going friend.

When the series returned in 2007 to TBS after its run in syndication, Curtis and Ella are the parents of Calvin, a college student with a knack for pulling off schemes. Curtis is now a fire chief (of Engine Company 5 in Atlanta, Georgia); C.J. is now Curtis's nephew. Janine, his wife, is now responsible and they are the parents of Jazmine and Malik. Here, when C.J.'s house catches fire, C.J. and his family move in with Calvin. Stories follow the same basic format with three generations of one family living under the same roof. Angel, Bart and Keenan are the firefighters who work with Curtis. Also known as *Tyler Perry's House of Payne.*

Cast: LaVan Davis (*Curtis Payne*); Cassi Davis (*Ella Payne*); Allen Payne (*C.J. Payne*); Demetria McKinney (*Janine Payne*); China Anne McClain (*Jazmine "Jasi" Payne*); Larramie "Doc" Shaw (*Malik Payne*); Lance Gross (*Calvin Payne*); Denise Burse (*Cloretha Jenkins*); Palmer Williams, Jr. (*Floyd*); Bobbi Baker (*Kiki*); Bart Hansard (*Bart*); Joyce Giraud (*Angel*); Jason Dirden (*Delante*); Susie Castillo (*Mercedes Herandez*); J.R. Ramirez (*Diego Herandez*); Keshia Knight Pulliam, Marlene Forte (*Miranda*); Robinne Lee (*Nicole Jameson*); Cedric Pendleton (*Keenan*).

4224 *House of Style.* (Series; Reality; MTV; 1989–2000). The program alerts viewers to the latest news on fashion, models and shopping. Interviews with models, designers and other people associated with the fashion industry are also presented.

Host: Cindy Crawford *(1989–95)*; Amber Valletta and Sharon Harlow *(1996-97)*; Daisy Fuentes *(1997-98)*; Rebecca Romijn *(1998–2000)*; Molly Simms *(2000)*.

4225 *The House on High Street.* (Series; Drama; NBC; 1959-1960). Dramatizations of actual records from the Domestic Relations Court as presented through the investigations of John Collier, a Los Angeles defense counselor. Stories are episodic, running from three to five installments.

Cast: Philip Abbott *(John Collier)*; James Gehrig *(Judge James Gehrig)*; Harris B. Peck *(Dr. Harris B. Peck)*.

4226 *House Party.* (Series; Variety; CBS; 1952–1959). The shortened title for *Art Linkletter's House Party.* See this title for information.

4227 *House Party.* (Series; Magazine; NBC; 1990). Steve Dooey hosts a daily program of entertainment and information. Dan Ingram is the announcer.

4228 *House Rules.* (Pilot; Drama; Unaired; Produced for CBS in 2009). The freshmen class of elected representatives are followed as they learn the ins and outs of the Washington, D.C., political system.

Cast: Anna Chulmsky *(Scotty Fisher)*; Kristin Bauer *(Kathy McAdams)*; Eion Bailey *(Alan Levi)*; Denzel Whitaker *(Peter Chiba)*; Zoe McLellan *(Julia Bryce)*.

4229 *Houston Knights.* (Series; Crime Drama; CBS; 1987-1988). Joey LaFiamma and Levon Lundy are sergeants with the Houston, Texas, Police Department. Sherina McLaren (then Joanna Beaumont) is a lieutenant with the Major Crime Unit of the Houston Police Department. Joey, Levon and Sherina (Joanna) join forces and stories relate their efforts to solve complex murder cases.

Other regulars are Captain Scully; Detectives Lipscombe and McCandless; Annie, the wheelchair bound cop; Chicken, the owner of the Alamo Bar (the local hangout); Legs, Chicken's waitress; and Sara Kelsay, Annie's niece.

Cast: Michael Pare *(Sgt. Joey LaFiamma)*; Michael Beck *(Sgt. Levon Lundy)*; Robyn Douglass *(Lt. Joanne Beaumont)*; Leigh Taylor-Young *(Lt. Sherina McLaren)*; John Hancock *(Chicken)*; Madlyn Rhue *(Annie Kelsay)*; James Hampton *(Captain Scully)*; Bill McKinney *(Det. Lipscomb)*; James Crittenden *(Det. McCandless)*; Nancy Everhard *(Legs)*.

4230 *How Do You Rate?* (Series; Game; CBS; 1958). Selected members of the studio audience compete in a program designed to test hidden aptitudes. The players compete in a series of tests that are designed to test their intelligence and reasoning power. The first player who successfully completes the problems (for example, mathematics, observation, logic, mechanics, etc.) is the winner and receives merchandise prizes.

Host: Tom Reddy. **Announcer:** Jack Clark.

4231 *How Do You Solve a Problem Like Maria?* (Series; Reality; BBC America; 2009). Fifty hopeful women compete for the opportunity to become the next Maria in Andrew Lloyd Webber's British stage production of *The Sound of Music.* The women attend "Maria School" where each is put through a series of acting, singing, dancing and personality challenges. The women are judged by a panel of three (producer David Ian; actor John Barrowman; vocal coach Zoe Tyler) who eliminate those they feel are not right for the role. The one woman who possesses all the attributes associated with the Maria character wins the role. Produced by the BBC. Graham Norton hosts; John Barrowman, David Ian and Zoe Tyler are the judges; contestant Connie Fisher won.

4232 *How I Met Your Mother.* (Series; Comedy; CBS; 2005–). Ted and Robin, a happily married couple living in New York City, are the parents of two teenage children (a boy and a girl who are seen as teenagers in 2030; names not given). But how did Ted and Robin meet, fall in love and eventually marry? Flashback sequences are used to tell that story. It began with Ted, an architecture student (later a college professor at NYU) and Robin, a reporter (of fluff stories) for Metro News (she also hosts the early morning TV series *Come On, Get Up, New York*; she later works for World Wide News) meeting by chance and falling in love. Their rough road to marriage is charted as are the ups and downs of their close friends: Marshall, a student at Columbia School of Law (later a lawyer with GNB [Goliath National Bank]), his girlfriend, Lily, a kindergarten teacher, and Barney, a swinging bachelor who originally works as an executive for Altrucel (a company that makes "the fuzzy yellow stuff on the surface of tennis balls"; he is later with GNB). Robin, born in Canada, was known as Robin Sparkles when she broke into show business. At that time she and her girlfriend, Jessica Glitter, starred in a TV series called *Space Teens:* (about outer space crime fighters). McClarren's Bar is the local hangout.

Cast: Josh Radnor *(Ted Mosby)*; Cobie Smulders *(Robin Scherbatsky)*; Alyson Hannigan *(Lily Aldrin)*; Neil Patrick Harris *(Barney Stinson)*; Jason Segel *(Marshall Eriksen)*; Lyndsy Fonseca *(Daughter)*; David Henrie *(Son)*; Bob Saget *(Narrator/Older Ted Mosby)*; Michael Gross *(Albert Mosby, Ted's father)*; Piper Mackenzie Harris *(Lily at age 11)*; Nicole Scherzinger *(Jessica Glitter)*.

4233 *How It's Made.* (Series; Reality; Discovery Channel; 2001–2010). Canadian produced program that explores how everyday items are made — from bubble gum to straws to car radiators. Brooks T. Moore, Mark Tewksbury and Tony Hirst narrate.

4234 *How Much Is Enough?* (Series; Game; GSN; 2008). Four contestants compete. A money clock is set at zero and progresses to $1,000 (in round one). Players have to secretly lock in a money amount (trying not to be the greediest). The player who locks in the most money loses the round (as does the person who is the most cautious and chooses very low money amounts). Round three ($3,000) and Round five ($5,000) play in the same manner. Round two ($2,000) and Round four ($4,000) have the clock set at the round rate but begin counting down from the amount. The player who is not too greedy or too cautious and who banks the most money wins.

Host: Corbin Bernsen.

4235 *How the West Was Won.* (Series; Western; ABC; 1977–1979). The saga of the Macahans, a Virginia homesteading family, as they attempt to establish a new life on the Great Plains during the mid–1860s. The pilot film, *The Macahans* aired on Jan. 19, 1976.

Cast: James Arness *(Zeb Macahan)*; Eva Marie Saint *(Kate Macahan)*; Richard Kiley *(Timothy Macahan)*; Bruce Boxleitner *(Seth Macahan)*; Kathryn Holcomb *(Laura Macahan)*; William Kirby Cullen *(Jeb Macahan)*; Vicki Schreck *(Jessie Macahan)*. **Narrator:** William Conrad.

4236 *How To.* (Series; Discussion; CBS; 1951). A person with a problem is brought on stage. The host and three regular panelists then attempt to resolve his or her problem. If the subject takes the advice, he or she returns at a later to date to explain how the advice helped or hindered the situation.

Host: Roger Price. **Panelists:** Anita Martell, Leonard Stern, Stanley Adams. **Announcer:** Bob Lemond.

4237 *How to Be a Better American.* (Pilot; Comedy; Unaired; Produced for ABC in 2010). Hugh Pell had redeeming qualities. He was sweet and romantic but over time he has become bitter and rude. He is married to Katie, the father of Lola and Martin and more interested in his big screen TV than he is in the welfare of his family. Suddenly, it dawns on Hugh that he is not the man he once was, the man Katie fell in love with and married. The years have taken their toll on Hugh but now he is determined to change for the better if he can. The proposal was to follow Hugh as he attempts to become the man he once was. Chad is Hugh's slacker brother.

Cast: Jason Jones *(Hugh Pell)*; Missi Pyle *(Katie Pell)*; Emily Rose Everhard *(Lola Pell)*; Dylan Matzke *(Martin Pell)*; Johnny Sneed *(Chad Pell)*.

4238 *How to Get the Guy.* (Series; Reality; ABC; 2006). Four very attractive women appear to find the man of their dreams. Two "love coaches" guide the women, all from San Francisco, as cameras follow their every move (including embarrassing themselves) to find Mr. Right. The girls, identified by a first name only, are Anne, a girl next door type; Alissa, a massage therapist; Kris, a party girl (in her own words) and Michelle, a career girl. Each girl faces a series of interviews (which appear to be scripted and rehearsed) but their attempts to follow the advice of the love coaches and impress men appears to be real (although a review in the New York *Post* reported "a ridiculous, condescending, wrong-headed reality show about four desperate women willing to humiliate and demean themselves — including being coached by two certified blockheads — just to get a man, any man") Teresa Strasser and J.D. Roberto are the love coaches.

4239 *How to Look Good Naked.* (Series; Reality; Lifetime; 2008–). Women with poor self-esteem and poor body image are the subjects — to help them realize there is potential for improvement without the need for plastic surgery. The basic premise has the host working with one such woman and her transformation over a five day period is showcased (there is no nudity). There are also no operations, no diet to follow and no psychiatrists to see. When the transformation is complete (wardrobe and makeup) never before (or seldom heard) compliments from strangers indicate that the program succeeded. Based on the British series of the same title. Carson Kressley hosts.

4240 *How to Make It in America.* (Series; Comedy; HBO; 2010). Ben Epstein and his best friend and partner Cam Calderon are young men determined to achieve their version of the American Dream — make a name for themselves in the competitive world of the New York fashion scene. Ben is a graduate of the Fashion Institute of Technology and now works as a jeans folder at Barneys in Manhattan. With Cam, he has started a floundering retro 1970s jeans business. Stories relate their antics as they use their less-than-reputable connections and street knowledge to achieve success. Rachel is Ben's ex-girlfriend (whom he hopes to win back), an interior designer; Edie is Rachel's boss, a self-made interior designer; Gingy is Ben and Cam's friend, an artist who owns his own gallery; Rene is Cam's cousin, an ex-con with an idea for instant wealth — a new soft drink called Rasta Monsta. Domingo is Ben's friend, a lawyer; David is a former high school classmate of Ben's who now manages a hedge fund; Darren is Rachel's new boyfriend. Aloe Blace performs the theme, "I Need a Dollar."

Cast: Bryan Greenberg *(Ben Epstein)*; Victor Rasuk *(Cameron "Cam" Calderon)*; Lake Bell *(Rachel Chapman)*; Shannyn Sossamon *(Gingy Wu)*; Martha Plimpton *(Edie Weitz)*; Scott "Kid Cudi" Mescudi *(Domingo)*; Luis Guzman *(Rene)*; Jason Pendergraft *(Darren Hall)*; Eddie Kay Thomas *(David "Kappo" Kaplan)*.

4241 *How to Marry a Millionaire.* (Series; Comedy; Syn.; 1958–1960). Penthouse G on the 22nd floor of the Tower Apartment House on Park Avenue in New York City is home to Michele "Mike" McCall, Loco Jones and Greta Hanson, three beautiful girls seeking millionaire husbands. The girls have taken a pledge ("On my honor I promise to do my best to help one of us marry a millionaire. So help me, Fort Knox").

Mike, Loco and Greta were each renting a small apartment on Amsterdam Avenue before Mike convinced them to pool their resources ("You gotta spend money to make money") and rent a swank penthouse ("We have something to sell — ourselves — and we have to surround ourselves in the best possible surroundings").

Mike, the schemer of the group, works as an analyst for the Wall Street firm of Hammersmith, Cavanaugh and Hammersmith. She believes that "the only way for a girl to be smart is to be dumb."

Greta is a hostess on the TV game show *Go for Broke*, a takeoff of *The $64,000 Question*. She reads *Who's Who in America* (her research material) and hopes that if there is a millionaire out there for her that "he comes along before he has to whisper sweet nothings in my ear trumpet."

Loco (her given name) was born in North Platte, Nebraska, on February 25. She was voted "The one most likely to go further with less than anyone" at North Platte High School. She is a bit naive when it comes to current events but has acquired encyclopedic knowledge of comic strips by reading *Super Comics* magazine. Loco is nearsighted and needs to wear eyeglasses but feels men will not find her attractive if she does. The resulting chaos often costs the girls a prospective husband ("Loco has cost us more millionaires than the 1929 stock crash" says Greta). Loco, a fashion model for the Travis (later Talbot) Modeling Agency, is called "a fabulous blonde with an hourglass figure."

At the start of the second season it is learned that Greta married and moved to California ("Greta wanted to marry an oil man," said Mike, "but she married a man who owns a gas station"). Mike and Loco acquire new roommate Gwen Kirby when she responds to their *Journal News* newspaper ad. Gwen, born in Illinois, was a girl scout and had been working on a small magazine before coming to New York. She now works as an editor for *Manhattan Magazine*.

In the original, unaired 1957 pilot, Greta Lindquist (Lori Nelson), Loco Jones (Charlotte Austin) and Mike Page (Doe Avedon) are the women seeking millionaire husbands (they share a 13th floor Manhattan penthouse apartment). Loco is a brunette (not blonde) but just as vain about wearing her glasses. She mentions that her real name is Rita Marlene Gloria Claudette Jones and that Loco is her nickname. She is a model but no agency name is given. Greta, a blonde who majored in psychology at college, is hostess on the TV game show *The Dunlap Quiz Show*. Mike is a stockbroker for the firm of Hammersmith, Cavanaugh and Hammersmith. Both versions are based on the feature film of the same title.

Cast: Merry Anders *(Mike McCall)*; Barbara Eden *(Loco Jones)*; Lori Nelson *(Greta Hanson)*; Lisa Gaye *(Gwen Kirby)*.

4242 *How to Succeed in Business Without Really Trying.* (Pilot; Comedy; ABC; June 27, 1975). J. Piermont Finch is a young man determined to make it in the business world — even if it means starting at the bottom. The proposal was to chart his progress — beginning with his first step: quitting his job as a window washer and joining the ranks of the World Wide Wicket Company as a mailroom boy. Based on the feature film of the same title.

Cast: Alan Bursky (*J. Piermont Finch*); Susan Blanchard (*Rosemary*); Larry Haines (*Bratt*); Jim Jansen (*Frump*); Marcella Lowery (*Smitty*); Steve Roland (*Gatch*); Max Showalter (*J.B. Biggey*); Polly Rowles (*Miss Jones*); Sam Smith (*Twimble*).

4243   *How to Survive a Horror Movie: All the Skills to Dodge the Kills.* (Series; Comedy; Internet; 2007). A spoof of horror films (reminiscent of the feature film *Scream*) that offers short tips on how to survive the pitfalls characters encounter in horror movies. Tips include "Seven Things to Never, Ever, Ever Put in a Child's Room," "How to Defeat a Killer Doll" and "How to tell if Your House Is Haunted." The horrifically campy webisodes are based on the book of the same title.

4244   *How to Survive a Marriage.* (Series; Drama; NBC; 1974-1975). The problems of marriage, divorce and separation as depicted through the lives of the people of Lakeview, a suburb of Chicago.

Cast: Rosemary Prinz (*Dr. Julie Franklin*); Joan Copeland (*Monica Courtland*); Lynn Lowry (*Sandra Henderson*); Jennifer Harmon (*Chris Kirby*); Elissa Leeds (*Rachel Bachman*); Allan Miller (*David Bachman*); Fran Brill (*Fran Bachman*); Tricia O'Neil (*Joan Willis*); Suzanne Davidson (*Lori Ann Kirby*); Cathy Greene, Lori Lowe (*Lori Ann Kirby*); Peter Brandon (*Terry Courtland*); Michael Landrum (*Larry Kirby*).

4245   *How'd You Get So Rich?* (Series; Reality; TV Land; 2009). Comedienne Joan Rivers' quest to discover how once ordinary people became millionaires. To do so, she travels around the country and interviews people whose ideas made them rich (Joan even "ambushes" people she sees on the street driving luxury cars or shopping in exclusive shops to ask how they acquired their fortune — and how they spend it).

Star: Joan Rivers.

4246   *Howdy.* (Pilot; Variety; NBC; Aug. 8, 1969). Music and comedy sketches set against the background of a fictional town called Mildew, Arkansas.

Host: Ferlin Husky. **Regulars:** Sidney Blackmer, Chanin Hale, Bob Hastings, Gene Sheldon, William Sylvester, Lyle Talbot. **Guests:** Eddie Albert, Pat Buttram, Jimmy Durante, Barbara Eden, Nanette Fabray, Henry Fonda, Glenn Ford, Eva Gabor, Jack Jones, Terry-Thomas. **Orchestra:** Alan Copeland.

4247   *Howdy Doody.* (Series; Children; NBC; 1947–1960). On December 27, 1941, in the town of Doodyville, Texas, twin boys were born to the wife of a ranch hand named Doody. The boys, named Howdy and Double, grew quickly and enjoyed life on the ranch where their parents earned a living by doing chores for the owner. At the age of six, the boys learn that their rich Uncle Doody has died and bequeathed them a small parcel of land in New York City (that would later become 30 Rockefeller Plaza — NBC's headquarters). When NBC offered to purchase the land to construct a television studio, Mr. Doody arranged it so that Howdy, who yearned to run a circus, could have his dream come true. NBC built a circus grounds, surrounded it with cameras and appointed Buffalo Bob Smith as Howdy's guardian. The program is set against the background of Doodyville and surrounded by the Peanut Gallery (children). Stories follow a circus troupe's efforts to perform against numerous obstacles, in particular those of Phineas T. Bluster, a mean old man who is opposed to people having fun. Clarabelle Hornblow is the circus clown (he does not speak but responds to questions by honking a "yes' or "no" horn; he spoke only once — on the last episodes to say goodbye).

Puppet characters are Howdy and Double Doody, Phineas T. Bluster, the Flubadub (the main circus attraction) and Dilly Dally (the confused boy). Live characters are Buffalo Bob Smith; Clarabelle Hornblow; The Story Princess; Chief Thunderthud; Tim Tremble (the nervous chap); Princess Summerfall Winterspring; Bison Bill (Buffalo Bob's temporary replacement during his illness in 1954). George "Gabby" Hayes, playing himself (also served as a temporary host); Ugly Sam (the wrestler); Lowell Thomas, Jr., the traveling lecturer.

Cast: Bob Smith (*Buffalo Bob Smith*); Bob Keeshan, Henry McLaughlin, Bob Nicholson, Lew Anderson (*Clarabelle Hornblow*); Arlene Dalton (*Story Princess*); Bill Lecornec (*Chief Thunderthud*); Don Knotts (*Tim Tremble*); Judy Tyler, Linda Marsh (*Princess Summerfall Winterspring*); Ted Brown (*Bison Bill*); George "Gabby" Hayes (*Himself*); Bob Smith (*Voice of Howdy Doody*); Allen Swift (*Voice of Howdy Doody in 1954*); Dayton Allen (*Voice of Phineas T. Bluster*); Bob Smith (*Voice of Double Doody*); Bill Lecornec (*Voice of Dilly Dally*); Dayton Allen (*Voice of the Flubadub*); Lowell Thomas, Jr. (*Lowell Thomas, Jr.*).

4248   *Howie.* (Series; Comedy; CBS; 1992). Comedy sketches that spotlight the talents of comedian Howie Mandel. Clarence Clemons provides the music.

4249   *Howie and Rose.* (Pilot; Comedy; ABC; Aug. 2, 1991). Howie Neumann is an easy going, carefree young bachelor who co-hosts a radio talk show on WCRY in New York City with his friend, Lawrence Fine. Shortly after his sister and her husband are sent to prison for bookmaking, Howie is given custody of Rose, their daughter, a pretty 11-year-old girl with an attitude, street smarts and a hood-like personality (she drinks coffee and smokes cigarettes). Rita is Lawrence's ex-wife and the proposal was to relate Howie's efforts to care for (and reform) Rose.

Cast: Howie Mandel (*Howie Neumann*); Shanelle Workman (*Rose Haber*); Stephen Furst (*Lawrence Fine*); Dee Dee Rescher (*Rita Fine*).

4250   *Howie Do It.* (Series; Reality; NBC; 2009). Hidden camera program that catches the reactions of people caught in sometimes bizarre pre-arranged situations. Like *Candid Camera*, the series that started it all in 1947, *Howie Do It* plays the previously recorded prank to a live studio audience (as opposed to seeing it happen live) for their laugh responses. And, like *Candid Camera*, wherein host Allen Funt participated in the stunts, so does show host Howie Mandel.

4251   *How's Your Mother-in-Law?* (Series; Game; ABC; 1967-1968). The object calls for three guest celebrities, acting as lawyers for the defense, to judge (through a series of question-and-answer probe rounds) which of three contestants is the best mother-in-law. The decision of the judges determines the winner (who receives merchandise prizes).

Program Open: "From Hollywood, USA, *How's Your Mother-in-Law?* And now here's your host and the star of *How's Your Mother-in-Law?*, Wink Martindale."

Host: Wink Martindale. **Music:** Milton DeLugg.

4252   *The Hoyt Axton Show.* (Pilot; Drama; NBC; Sept. 28, 1981). Following the death of his wife, Del Parsons, a constantly-on-the-road country and western singer-musician, is forced to settle down and raise his three estranged children (Jenny, Norma Sue and Dean). He begins by converting his barn into a recording studio for aspiring performers and the proposal was to chart his experiences. Carol Dean is Del's neighbor. Hoyt Axton performs the theme, "Honeysuckle Rose."

Cast: Hoyt Axton (*Del Parsons*); Tonja Walker (*Jenny Parsons*); Tonya Crowe (*Norma Sue Parsons*); John Shepherd (*Dean Parsons*); Joy Garrett (*Carol Dean*).

4253 *H.R. Pufnstuf.* (Series; Adventure; NBC; 1969–1973). While playing near the edge of a river, Jimmy and his talking gold flute, Freddie, board a boat that beckons to them. As it drifts out to sea, the evil Miss Witchiepoo, seeking Freddie for her collection, casts a spell and the boat vanishes. Swimming to the shore of Living Island, Jimmy is rescued by its mayor, H.R. Pufnstuf, who has vowed to help Jimmy. Stories follow Jimmy's efforts to protect Freddie and defeat Miss Witchiepoo to find the secret of the way home. Characters, with the exception of Jimmy and Miss Witchiepoo, are Sid and Marty Krofft puppets.

Cast: Jack Wild (*Jimmy*); Billie Hayes (*Miss Witchiepoo*), Joan Gerber, Felix Silla, Jerry Landon, John Linton, Angelo Rosetti, Hommy Stewart, Buddy Douglas.

4254 *The Huckleberry Hound Show.* (Series; Cartoon; Syn.; 1958). The overall title for four animated segments:

1. Huckleberry Hound. Huckleberry Hound, a slow talking (and thinking) dog tackles various occupations to discover his goal in life.

2. Pixie and Dixie. A cat (Mr. Jinks) plagued by two mischievous mice (Pixie and Dixie).

3. Hokey Wolf. Antics of a conniving wolf named Hokey.

4. Yogi Bear. Yogi Bear, a resident of Jellystone National Park, and his buddy, Boo Boo Bear, scheme to acquire picnickers' lunch baskets against the wishes of the park ranger, John Smith.

Voice Cast: Daws Butler (*Huckleberry Hound/Yogi Bear/Mr. Jinks/Dixie/Hokey Wolf*); Don Messick (*Boo Boo Bear/Pixie/Ranger Smith*).

4255 *The Hudson Brothers Show.* (Series; Variety; CBS; 1974–1977). Music, songs and sketches hosted by the Hudson Brothers that are designed to convey value-related messages to children.

Program Open: "It's *The Hudson Brothers Razzle Dazzle Show* starring Bill, Mark and Brett ... the Hudson brothers ... with Ted Zeigler, Billy Van and Peter Cullen ... Murray Langston and Freeman King ... and Rod Hull and his extraordinary Australian Emu ... and sets, lights and all sorts of fun things on *The Hudson Brothers Razzle Dazzle Show.*" Two versions appeared:

1. The Hudson Brothers Show (CBS, 1974). *Hosts:* Bill, Brett and Mark Hudson. *Regulars:* Stephanie Edwards, Ronny Graham, Rod Hull, The Jaime Rogers Dancers, Katee McClure, Gary Owens. *Orchestra:* Jack Eskew.

2. The Hudson Brothers Razzle Dazzle Show (CBS, 1974–77). *Host:* Bill, Brett and Mark Hudson. *Regulars:* Billy Van, Peter Cullen, Ted Zeigler, Rod Hull, Murray Langston, Scott Fisher, Freeman King. *Announcer:* Peter Cullen. *Orchestra:* Jimmy Dale.

4256 *Hudson Street.* (Series; Comedy; ABC; 1995). Precinct Number 7 on Hudson Street in Hoboken, New Jersey, is home to Tony Canetti, a conservative homicide detective. He is divorced from Lucy and the father of Mickey. Tony was born in New Jersey and attended Hoboken High School. His late father owned a shoe store, Canetti's Discount Shoes; it was here that Tony worked after school and on weekends. A botched robbery attempt cost Tony's father, Victor, his life, but made Tony realize he had to do something about it — become a cop. He graduated from rookie school and became a beat cop. He upheld the law and he made people feel safe. He made friends and acquired snitches he could trust — and who could trust him.

Melanie Clifford is a young woman who dreams of becoming a reporter for the *New York Times.* She was born in New Jersey and lives with her parents at 11 Wilson Street. She is liberal and works as the obituary editor for the *Hoboken Reporter.* After several years on the job she receives a promotion to the Metro Desk (police reporter) and finds a new hangout — the press room of Precinct 7. A short time earlier, Melanie and Tony met on a blind date. They were opposites who were attracted to each other but barely able to stand each other. They agreed not to see each other again. Circumstances place them together again and their bickering love-hate relationship is the actual focal point of stories.

Kirby McIntire is the gorgeous police detective who works with Tony. She is well endowed and when someone says "Nice bust," she takes it the wrong way, believing they are referring to her breasts. Kirby is the precinct's Jill of all trades. She always manages to get the cases nobody else wants — for example, catching a lingerie thief — and the work nobody else will do — for example, filing, filling out reports, making coffee.

Jennifer Bassey and Steven Gilborn played Melanie's parents, Betsy and Nelson Clifford.

Cast: Tony Danza (*Tony Canetti*); Shareen Mitchell (*Lucy Canetti*); Lori Loughlin (*Melanie Clifford*); Frankie J. Galasso (*Mickey Canetti*); Christine Dunford (*Kirby McIntire*).

4257 *Hudson's Bay.* (Series; Adventure; Syn.; 1959). Canada during the 1800s provides the backdrop for the saga of Jonathan Banner, an agent for the Hudson's Bay Fur Company, and his partner, Pierre Falcone, as they safeguard the trading company from unscrupulous characters. Produced in Canada.

Program Open: "Hudson's Bay, the saga of the great Hudson's Bay Fur Company and of the brave men who traveled the untracked wilderness. From Labrador to California; from Minnesota to Alaska. Starring Barry Nelson as Jonathan Banner, Hudson Bay's man; with George Tobias as Pierre Falcone."

Cast: Barry Nelson (*Jonathan Banner*); George Tobias (*Pierre Falcone*).

4258 *Huff.* (Series; Comedy; Showtime; 2005). Dr. Craig Huffstodt is a Los Angeles based psychiatrist who devotes all his energies to helping his patients. Huff, as he is called, is suddenly faced with a crisis when a 15-year-old patient commits suicide in his office and his life is thrown into turmoil. Huff is now re-evaluating his life and stories follow Huff as he struggles to get through the events that affect his daily life (some of which are seen as outburst of delusions by viewers).

Other regulars are Beth, Huff's loving and empathetic wife (she helps him overcome his meltdowns); Izzy, Huff's tough and manipulative mother (she lives in the apartment over the garage); Russell Tupper, Huff's longtime friend, a not so moral attorney; Byrd, Huff's 14-year-old son; Teddy, Huff's younger, mentally unstable brother, who has been confined to a mental institution; Paula Dellahouse, Huff's office manager; Maggie Del Rosario, Russell's assistant; and Kelly Knipper, Russell's romantic interest, a TV sales representative.

Cast: Hank Azaria (*Dr. Craig Huffstodt*); Paget Brewster (*Beth Huffstodt*); Blythe Danner (*Izzy*); Anton Telchin (*Byrd Huffstodt*); Oliver Platt (*Russell Tupper*); Andy Comeau (*Teddy Hoffstodt*); Kimberly Brooks (*Paula Dellahouse*); Liza LaPira (*Maggie Del Rosario*); Faith Prince (*Kelly Knippers*).

4259 *Huge.* (Series; Drama; ABC Family; 2010–). Camp Victory is a summer camp for overweight teenagers. It is here that Dr. Dorothy Rand, the camp administrator, believes in a strict program of exercise and food to help her charges lose weight and live a happier, healthier life. Stories, which focus on the efforts of a group of teens to slim down, also relate incidents in the lives of the camp staff: George, the fitness coach and Chef, the camp cook. The featured teens are Amber, a beautiful girl who is thinner than most of the other campers (she posts pictures of super models as her "thinspiration"); Willamina, who prefers to be called Will, a rebellious girl who objects to the idea of such camps as she feels it singles out overweight kids everywhere; Alistair, an insecure teen who hides his faults with humor; Ian, Alistair's bunkmate, loves music and openly accepts the fact that he is overweight; and Chloe, a girl who is burdened by overprotective parents.

Cast: Gina Torres (*Dr. Dorothy Rand*); Hayley Hasselhoff (*Amber*); Nikki Blonsky (*Willamina Rader*); Zander Eckhouse (*George*); Harvey Guillen (*Alistair*); Ashley Holliday (*Chloe Delgado*); Ari Stedham (*Ian Schonfeld*); Raven Goodwin (*Becca*); Stefan Van Ray (*Trent*); Paul Dooley (*Chef*).

4260   *The Huggie Bunch.* (Pilot; Children; Syn.; July 1985). Huggins and Hugsy are two adorable creatures (puppets) that spread love and joy. They live on the other side of mirrors and the proposal was to relate their adventures as they help humans find happiness.

Voice Cast: Terry Castillo (*Huggins*); Tony Urbano (*Hugsy*).

4261   *Huggy Bear and the Turkey.* (Pilot; Crime Drama; ABC; Feb. 19, 1977). Huggy Bear, the snitch who helps Starsky and Hutch (on the series *Starsky and Hutch*) and his honest friend, J.D. Turquet, called Turkey, pool their resources and open a private detective agency. The proposal was to relate their haphazard efforts to solve crimes with Huggy using his rather devious connections and Turkey trying to look the other way and do things as close to the book as possible.

Cast: Antonio Fargas (*Huggy Bear*); Dale Robinette (*J.D. Turquet*).

4262   *The Hugh Herbert Show.* (Pilot; Comedy; ABC; Nov. 1, 1950). A proposed series of comedy skits that feature the talents (and antics) of stage and movie comedian Hugh Herbert ("Mr. Woowoo"). The program involved Hugh in three skits: a soft-hearted judge; the patsy for a love-starved maid; and a man who finds misadventure in a department store.

Host: Hugh Herbert. **Regulars:** Frank Scannell, Charlie Williams, Gloria Wood.

4263   *The Hughleys.* (Series; Comedy; ABC, 1998-1999; UPN, 1999–2002). Darryl Hughley and his wife, Yvonne, own the home at 317 Crestview in the West Hills section of Los Angeles. They are the parents of Sydney and Michael and are attempting to adjust to a mostly all white neighborhood having previously lived in a Los Angeles all-black community ("from the hood to the burbs," says Darryl).

Darryl grew up in a poor family and managed to become a success by starting a business called the Hughley Vending Machine Company with his childhood friend Milsap Morris (they previously worked as vending machine repairmen before starting their own company). Milsap, the vice president of the company is one of 14 children and also from a poor family. It was Yvonne, however, who sought a better life for her children, who persuaded Darryl to relocate. Unlike Darryl, Yvonne hails from a rich family. She has a master's degree in business and later works in marketing at the Staples Sports Center. Darryl likes to insult people (make jokes) and hates to admit that he is wrong. He is afraid of no one — except Yvonne, whom he fears.

Sydney is ten years old and Michael is nine when the series begins. Sydney and Michael attend West Hills Middle School. Sydney is a very pretty girl and smart (enrolled in the accelerated class at school)

while Michael is having a difficult time due to dyslexia (Coral Mills is Michael's tutor).

Sally and Dave Rogers are the Hughley's neighbors. Sally is a professional therapist and Dave owns a store called Dave's Extreme Sports. They are the parents of Otto and infant Gretchen. Otto is rarely seen and has many problems (like imaginary friends — one of whom beat him up). Sally wrote a book called *Coping with Sally Rogers* (also the name of her TV call-in show on KMDE, Channel 87).

Cast: D.L. Hughley (*Darryl Hughley*); Elise Neal (*Yvonne Hughley*); Ashley Monique Clark (*Sydney Hughley*); Dee Jay Daniels (*Michael Hughley*); John Henton (*Milsap Morris*); Marietta DePrima (*Sally Rogers*); Eric Kramer (*Dave Rogers*); Alex Meneses (*Coral Mills*); Conrad Mathews, Ian Meltzer (*Otto Rogers*).

4264   *Hulk Hogan's Celebrity Championship Wrestling.* (Series; Reality; CMT; 2008). Ten celebrities are brought together and trained in the art of wrestling to compete in challenges and eventually master the ring to become professional-quality wrestlers.

Host: Hulk Hogan. **Judges:** Hulk Hogan, Eric Bischoff, Jimmy Hart. **Celebrities:** Danny Bonaduce, Todd Bridges, ButterBean, Trishelle Cannatella, Dustin Diamond, Erin Murphy, Dennis Rodman, Frank Stallone, Nikki Ziering, Tiffany Ziering. **Ring Announcer:** Todd Keneley. **Referee:** Anthony Rosas.

4265   *Hulk Hogan's Rock 'n' Wrestling.* (Series; Cartoon; CBS; 1985–1987). Live action is combined with animation to detail the adventures of wrestler Hulk Hogan: in the ring in live action matches; outside the ring (in animation) battling evil wherever he finds it.

Cast: Hulk Hogan (*Hulk Hogan*); Gene Oakland (*Announcer*). **Voices:** Charles Allen, Lewis Arquette, Jodi Carlisle, George DiCenzo, Neilson Ross, Pat Fraley, Ernest Harada.

4266   *Hull High.* (Series; Comedy-Drama; NBC; 1990). Life at Cordell Hull High, a large, full service middle-class suburban school to which many of the minority kids are bused (by the Whitmarsh Bus Lines). Originally titled *Be True to Your School*.

Camilla Croft is the new student on campus. She originally lived in Philadelphia, where she attended Rush High School. She now lives in a mobile home in King's Trailer Park at 34 Cove Road. Camilla is older than the other girls in her sophomore class (she started school late), and rumors began to spread that she was a narc.

Student D.J. Cameron is a gorgeous red-head who knows she is very sexy, and she strives to drive the boys wild. D.J. also has a reputation for doing the outrageous (for example, inciting a riot "to protest the revolting cafeteria food," joining the men's wrestling team to prove that a woman is equal to a man). Cody Rome is another new student and has a mysterious past; and 16-year-old Mark Fuller is a lovesick student with a crush on Camilla. Although she wants nothing to do with him, he takes desperate measures to impress her.

Principal teachers are Donna Breedlove and John Deerborn. Donna is 23 years old and lives in an apartment at Farrington Place. She is considered so beautiful that the students in her English class tend to watch her rather than listen to what she is saying. She dresses in short skirts and tight blouses, and moves in such sexy ways that her students are mesmerized. John Deerborn is a history teacher who taught previously at All City High School.

Jennifer Blang and April Dawn are billed as the "Hull High Bulletin Announcers," and Trey Parker, Philip DeMarks, Carl Anthony Payne and Lawrence Edwards are credited as the "Hull High Rappers" (also called "Hull High Devils"). In the original pilot, Mark Ballou played Mark Pastorelli. Kenny Ortega is the choreographer, and Stanley Clarke composed the theme and musical score.

Cast: Cheryl Pollak *(Camilla Croft)*; Kristin Dattilo *(D.J. Cameron)*; Harold Pruett *(Cody Rome)*; Nancy Valen *(Donna Breedlove)*; Will Lyman *(John Deerborn)*.

4267   *Hullabaloo*. (Series; Variety; NBC; 1965-1966). Guests host a weekly program that features performances by the top names in rock and roll music.
Regulars: Lada Edmonds, Jr., Sheila Forbes, The Hullabaloo Dancers, The David Winters Dancers. **Orchestra:** Peter Matz.

4268   *The Human Adventure*. (Experimental; Human Interest; NBC; Aug. 15, 1939). A program of science fact and fiction with dramatizations to illustrate specific principles.
Host: Frank Gallop. **Cast:** Ted DeCorsia, Kenny Delmar, John Gibson, Neal O'Malley, Vicki Vola, Dwight Weist, Ruth Yorks.

4269   *The Human Comedy*. (Pilot; Comedy; CBS; Sept. 19, 1964). A 13-year-old boy's experiences as the man of the house following his father's death is the premise of an unsold series set in Ithaca, New York. Alice is Homer's mother; Ulysses is his brother.
Cast: Timmy Rooney *(Homer Macauley)*; Phyllis Avery *(Alice Macauley)*; Jimmy Honer *(Ulysses Macauley)*.

4270   *The Human Factor*. (Series; Drama; CBS; 1992). Dr. Alec McMurty is a physician at an "inner city hospital" who also teaches a course called "The Human Factor." Alec has constructed the course to make hopeful doctors more humane. Alec, himself, is married (to Joan) but rather unorthodox as he likes to do things his way. He has also forsaken wealth to treat people who are seriously ill and stories relate his efforts to implant that philosophy on his students as well as other doctors in the hospital.
Cast: John Mahoney *(Dr. Alec McMurty)*; Jan Lucas *(Joan McMurty)*; Kurt Deutsch *(Dr. Matt Robbins)*; Eriq La Salle *(Dr. Michael Stoven)*; Matthew Ryan *(Dr. Joe Murphy)*; Melinda McGraw *(Rebecca Travis)*; Allan Miller *(Dr. Walter Burke)*.

4271   *Human Feelings*. (Pilot; Comedy; NBC; Oct. 16, 1978). Angry at the crime, the divorce rate and the general sleaziness of the world, God decides to give the earth one chance to redeem itself before She destroys it. Myles Gordon, an angel, is dispatched to find righteous people that will show Her that the world is worth saving. The proposal was to follow Myles as he seeks to fulfill God's mission. Verna Gold is the human who befriends and helps Myles; Lester is God's secretary.
Cast: Nancy Walker *(God)*; Billy Crystal *(Myles Gordon)*; Pamela Sue Martin *(Verna Gold)*; John Fiedler *(Lester)*.

4272   *Human Giant*. (Series; Comedy; MTV; 2007). Paul Scheer, Jason Woliner, Aziz Ansari and Rob Huebel are a sketch comedy team known as Human Giant, They are known for edgy, reckless comedy and their style of humor is spotlighted in a weekly session.

4273   *The Human Jungle*. (Series; Drama; Syn.; 1964). The work of Dr. Roger Corder, a London-based psychiatrist, as he attempts to help people overcome by the turmoil of human emotion.
Cast: Herbert Lom *(Dr. Roger Corder)*; Michael Johnson *(Davis; his assistant)*.

4274   *Human Target*. (Series; Adventure; ABC; 1992). The *Wing*, a huge, highly technical black plane that resembles the wings of an airliner, is the mobile headquarters of Christopher Chase, a man who steps into the lives of people marked for murder to become a human target until he can restore that person's safety. It was an incident from Chris's past that led him to become a human target.

During the Vietnam War, Chase was in charge of a special unit that went into villages to destroy them. During one such raid Chris was captured by the Vietcong and placed in a tiger cage. Chris spent ten days in the cage before he was rescued. When he was discharged from the service, he realized what he had done and it all came crashing in on him; so much so that he spent 19 months in the psychiatric ward of the Walter Reed Hospital. When he was released he knew the only way to keep sane was to somehow balance it all out and right wrongs through his unique abilities. He begins by commissioning construction of the *Wing* (although it is not made clear, Chris is apparently wealthy). He then hires three highly skilled people to assist him: Libby Page, Philo Marsden and Jeff Carlyle. Chris has an amazing ability to impersonate voices and through the use of highly advanced computer makeup (masks) Chris becomes the person he is seeking to protect. The fee varies depending on the job (usually ten percent of a client's yearly income) and the client remains in safety on the *Wing* until Chris completes the job.

Libby previously worked for the Company, a secret U.S. government organization, in a top level security position. When the project she was working on collapsed, she found employment with Chris, who required her expertise to operate his high tech telecommunications equipment.

Philo is a movie special effects makeup expert who impressed Chris with his computer-generated masks for the film *Zombies on Holiday*. Philo now incorporates his computer skills to make the target masks for Chris (which combine Chris's general features with special features of a target's face).

Jeff served with Chris in Vietnam; he now pilots the *Wing*. The team also assists in the field if necessary. When a woman is marked as a target, Chris goes undercover as the male closest to her. An unaired pilot version exists with Frances Fisher as Libby and Clarence Clemmons as Jeff. Based on the D.C. comic book character.
Cast: Rick Springfield *(Christopher Chase)*; Signy Coleman *(Libby Page)*; Kirk Baltz *(Philo Marsden)*; Sami Chester *(Jeff Carlyle)*.

4275   *Human Target*. (Series; Adventure; Fox; 2010-2011). Christopher Chance is a man of mystery, a man who will risk his life to save the lives of others. Chance works as a bodyguard and his compulsion to put his life on the line hints at a dark incident in his past or even a death wish (details regarding Chance's past are not immediately given; he says only "I hated my old job. I thought I had more potential"). Chance works with Laverne Winston, his partner in a private security company, and Guerrero, an elusive and shady computer genius who appears to be a former bad guy (professional assassin/hired gun/computer hacker) who uses his abilities and past experience (and contacts) to help Chance.

Chance, who has a dog named Carmine, is well versed in the martial arts, computers, math and an array of other fields, and becomes a human target to protect people (and find the culprit) when their lives are threatened. Chance assures his clients "I can eliminate the threat, trust me" and can resolve the matter safer and faster than the police. Once Chance (and Winston, a former police detective) accept a case, Chance completely immerses himself in his client's life and takes all the risks (setting himself up as the target) until he resolves the situation. Emma Barnes is the FBI agent who occasionally assists Chance (and vice versa). Layla is the computer hacker who assists Guerrero; Ilsa Pucci is the sophisticated, rich widow who becomes a silent partner in Chance's firm after he helps her solve the murder of her husband (she names the company The Ilsa Pucci Foundation); Ames is a chameleon-like thief Winston hires to not only help her straighten out her life, but help Chance solve cases.

In the episode of April 14, 2010 ("Christopher Chance"), it is revealed that the man who calls himself Christopher Chance was a hit man for "The Old Man." Chance, who used various aliases, performed well for "The Old Man." Six years earlier, however, life changed for Chance. A case involving waterfront corruption brings Chance in contact with Laverne Winston, a police detective who is investigating the case, and Catherine Walters (Amy Acker), an innocent girl who unknowingly holds the key to a mysterious book that can expose high officials. Chance, posing as U.S. Attorney General Conrad Hill, has been ordered to kill Catherine. But he can't bring himself to do it and breaks from the "family." Despite his best efforts to protect Catherine, he fails when a "family" hit man, Baptiste, does the job Chance was hired to do.

A team is formed when Winston, who resigned when he too was unable to protect Catherine, tells Chance, "We couldn't save Catherine but we can save the next one." Winston, who is aware that Chance is using the alias Conrad Hill, then asks, "Who are you?" Chance pauses, then replies, "Christopher Chance" (He chose this name to honor a former friend who died saving him and called himself Christopher Chance—"The guy you go to when no one else can help"). Guerrero also worked for "The Old Man" as a hit man and resigned when Chance prevented him from carrying out his assignment—killing Catherine. The dog, Carmine, belonged to Catherine and is the only solid remembrance Chance has of a girl he loved but lost.

Based on the D.C. comic, the idea was originally adapted to TV in 1991 as an unaired pilot (with Rick Springfield as Chance) and a short lived 1992 ABC series (again with Rick Springfield as Chance). See the prior *Human Target* title for information.

Cast: Mark Valley *(Christopher Chance)*; Chi McBride *(Laverne Winston)*; Jackie Earle Haley *(Guerrero)*; Emmanuelle Vaugier *(Emma Barnes)*; Autumn Reeser *(Layla)*; Lenny James *(Baptiste)*; Indira Varma *(Ilsa Pucci)*; Janet Montgomery *(Ames)*.

4276   Hung. (Series; Comedy; HBO; 2009). Ray Drecker is an underpaid and uninsured high school teacher and basketball coach in Detroit. He is married to Jessica and the father of twins Darby and Damon. While Ray's life is not all he hoped for (he was popular and athletic and destined for success in high school) he puts up with what the hand of fate has dealt. Life changes drastically for Ray when, after 20 years of marriage, Jessica leaves him for (and latter marries) her dermatologist (Dr. Ronnie Haxon). The final blow occurs when the twins move in with Jessica and the house he inherited from his parents is damaged by fire. It appears Ray has little to look forward to. Feeling he is at his wit's end, Ray enrolls in a get rich quick seminar and meets a former love, Tanya, a struggling poet. The encounter leads to a one night stand and a new way for Ray and Tanya to make money (and where the show's title comes into play). Ray is well endowed in the love making department and Tanya sort of becomes his pimp, setting themselves up as "happiness consultants" (an exclusive escort service for higher class women looking for sex without commitment). Stories relate events in Ray's life as he begins life as a professional gigolo in what appears to be an effort on his part to recapture his life—the one that seemed possible but some how slipped away from him.

Cast: Thomas Jane *(Ray Drecker)*; Jane Adams *(Tanya Skagle)*; Anne Heche *(Jessica Haxon)*; Siamoa Smit-McPhee *(Darby Drecker)*; Charlie Saxon *(Damon Drecker)*; Eddie Jemison *(Dr. Ronnie Haxon)*.

4277   The Hunter. (Series; Adventure; CBS, 1952; Syn., 1952–1954). Bartholomew "Bart" Hunter is a mysterious United States undercover agent who is known as "The Hunter." Adopting the guise of a wealthy American playboy, he attempts to corrupt the forces of Communism in the Western world. Stories are spiced with light humor as it depicts Bart's somewhat unorthodox methods (usually in a variety of disguises) to accomplish his missions. Liz is Bart's friend in Prague; Janet Wood is the American reporter based in Eu-

rope; Rita is Bart's friend in Copenhagen; Ruby Ellis is Bart's old flame (1954 episodes).

Cast: Barry Nelson *(Bart Adams, 1952–1954)*; Keith Larsen *(Bart Adams, 1954)*; Anna Minot *(Liz)*; Lisa Howard *(Janet Wood)*; Barbara Bolton *(Rita)*; Susanna TaFel *(Ruby Ellis)*.

4278   Hunter. (Series; Adventure; Syn.; 1968). COSMIC, the Commonwealth Office of Security and Military Intelligence Co-ordination, is a branch of the Australian government that has been established to combat the evils of CUCW (the Council for the Unification of the Communist World). John Hunter is COSMIC's top operative attached to Division SCU-3, which works behind a front organization called Independent Surveys. Hunter, a veteran of the Korean War, combines the elements of commando, spy and detective. He works above the law and knows the law offers him no protection "and no exemption. If necessary, his country will deny his existence." Eve Halliday is an undercover agent and Hunter's partner on assignments. Her cover is a stenographer for Independent Surveys. Blake is the stern Security Chief and head of SCU-3.

A man called Mr. Smith is the scheming local representative of CUCW. It is his job to disrupt the inner workings of COSMIC and pick the targets his agents must destroy or sabotage around Australia and South East Asia. Kragg is Smith's chief operative, an expert killer with no conscience. Produced in Australia.

Cast: Tony Ward *(John Hunter)*; Fernande Glyn *(Eve Halliday)*; Nigel Lovell *(Blake)*; Ronald Morse *(Mr. Smith)*; Gerard Kennedy *(Kragg)*.

4279   Hunter. (Series; Adventure; CBS; 1977). James Hunter and Marty Shaw are U.S. Government Special Intelligence agents who cover the world of contemporary espionage. James and Marty, however, have other jobs. In his free time, James operates a bookshop in Santa Barbara, California; Marty is a high fashion model. Harold Baker is their superior and stories chart their exploits as they tackle dangerous assignments for the government.

Cast: James Franciscus *(James Hunter)*; Linda Evans *(Marty Shaw)*; Ralph Bellamy *(Harold Baker)*.

4280   Hunter. (Series; Crime Drama; NBC; 1984–1991). Rick Hunter is a detective sergeant with the Los Angeles Police Department, Division 122. The department is also called Central Division, the Parker Division, the Parker Center Police Station and Metro Division. Rick is an honest but tough cop who has a skeleton in his closet: he is the son of a mobster but has rejected a life of crime to uphold the law.

Hunter resides at 5405 Ocean Front Drive and over the course of the series he was partnered with three women: Dee Dee McCall, Joann Molinski and Christine Novak. Dee Dee, a detective sergeant, was teamed with Rick from 1984–90. Like Rick, she was tough and honest and those qualities earned her the nickname "The Brass Cupcake." Dee Dee, a widow, had been married to Steve McCall (Franc Luz), a sergeant killed in the line of duty. In the episode "Street Wise" (May 7, 1990), Dee Dee accepts the marriage proposal of her old flame, Dr. Alex Turner (Robert Conner Newman), a college professor. In part two of the episode (May 14), Dee Dee leaves the force to marry Alex. The episode of Sept. 19, 1990, "Deadly Encounters," teams Rick with a tough rookie cop, Officer Joann Molinski. Joann is written out in the episode of Jan. 9, 1991 ("Fatal Obsession") when she is killed (shot three times) by a psychotic woman named Loreen Arness (Ellen Wheeler). Rick remains without a steady partner until Sept. 9, 1991, when he is teamed with Christine Novak, a sergeant who prefers to be called Chris. Chris is the mother of a young daughter named Allie (Courtney Barilla) and is divorced from Al Novak (Robin Thomas), Allie's now estranged father.

Rick's superiors also varied throughout the series. Lester Cain was the first captain. He was replaced by Captain Dolan; Dolan by Captain Wyler; and Wyler by Chief Charles Devane. Sporty James, owner of the somewhat shady Sporty James Enterprises, is Rick's information man (snitch). See also *Hunter* (next title) for the series revival.

Cast: Fred Dryer *(Rick Hunter)*; Stepfanie Kramer *(Dee Dee McCall)*; Darlanne Fluegel *(Joann Molinski)*; Lauren Lane *(Christine Novak)*; Michael Cavanaugh, Arthur Rosenberg *(Lester Cain)*; John Amos *(Capt. Dolan)*; Bruce Davison *(Capt. Wyler)*; Charles Hallahan *(Charles Devane)*; Garrett Morris *(Sporty James)*.

Note: NBC presented two TV movie updates:

1. The Return of Hunter (TV Movie; April 30, 1995). Rick Hunter (Fred Dryer) is now a lieutenant with the Parker Division of the L.A.P.D. He is as tough as ever but now works alone. He is engaged to Vickie Sherry (Beth Toussant) and Charlie Devane (Charles Hallahan) is still his superior. The TV movie, subtitled "Everyone Walks in L.A.," finds Hunter taking on a personal vendetta: finding Jack Valko (Miguel Ferrer), a madman who killed Vickie and now taunts Hunter to catch him.

2. Hunter: Return to Justice (TV Movie; Nov. 16, 2002). Rick Hunter (Fred Dryer) is a lieutenant with the L.A.P.D. Dee Dee McCall (Stepfanie Kramer) is now a sergeant with the Juvenile Division of the San Diego Police Department. Dee Dee was not a part of the prior TV movie. Dee Dee is engaged to Roger Prescott (Sam Hennings), a wealthy drug company owner who is running for mayor. The story, also promoted by NBC as *Hunter: The Movie*, reunites Rick and Dee Dee when Dee Dee invites Hunter to her engagement party. Trouble begins when Roger's past is uncovered — a Russian KGB agent and traitor to the U.S. — and Dee Dee is kidnapped by members of the Russian Mafia seeking to trade her for secret lists of former KGB agents possessed by Roger. Rick intervenes and in a violent confrontation with the mafia, rescues Dee Dee but is unable to save Roger's life. The program ends with Rick and Dee Dee parting company. "Don't be a stranger" are Dee Dee's final words as the story ends. No mention is made of what happened to Alex, the man Dee Dee left the force to marry in 1990.

4281   *Hunter.* (Series; Crime Drama; NBC; 2003). An update of the 1984 series that finds Rick Hunter leaving Los Angeles after the shooting death of his partner for a position with the Robbery-Homicide Division of the San Diego Police Department. Here, he is partnered with Dee Dee McCall, formally with the Juvenile Division of the San Diego, P.D., and his former partner from the original series (Dee Dee left the force in 1990 to marry a man named Alex, who is not a part of the program). Captain Gallardo is their superior and stories follow Rick and Dee Dee as they continue their rather violent crusade against crime.

Cast: Fred Dryer *(Rick Hunter)*; Stepfanie Kramer *(Dee Dee McCall)*; Mike Gomez *(Captain Gallardo)*.

4282   *The Hunters.* (Pilot; Drama; Unaired; Produced for Lifetime in 2005). Assignments of a family of U.S. government undercover agents overseen by Quinn Hunter, the devious matriarch.

Cast: Callum Keith Rennie *(Quinn Hunter)*; Hillary Tuck *(Cat Hunter)*; Kelly Lynch *(Joan Hunter)*; Neal Andrew Bledsoe *(Troy Hunter)*.

4283   *Hunter's Moon.* (Pilot; Adventure; CBS; Dec. 1, 1979). Fayette Randall and his family are sheepherders in Wyoming (late 1860s). When a feud between cattlemen and sheepherders erupts over grazing land, Fayette's father and two brothers are killed in an ensuing conflict. To avenge their deaths, Fayette becomes a mysterious figure for justice, a man who appears from out of nowhere to help people threatened by evil. He is assisted by his friend, Isham Hart.

Cast: Cliff DeYoung *(Fayette Randall)*; Robert DoQui *(Isham Hart)*.

4284   *Huntic: Secret and Seekers.* (Series; Cartoon; CW Kids; 2009). Lok is a college student in Venice, Italy. He dreams of uncovering ancient artifacts and is called "Indy" (after Indiana Jones) by his classmates. One day, while in his dorm room being tutored by his friend, Sophie, Sophie notices a strange looking vase that, when she grabs, slips from her hands, falls to the floor and breaks. In the rubble, Lok finds a journal (of treasure maps from his father) and an amulet. Suddenly, mysterious creatures appear, seeking the journal. With Sophie's help, Lok escapes and finds unexpected help from a man named Dante Vale, a professor of ancient history who defeats the creatures and saves Lok's life. Lok learns that Dante and Sophie are members of the Huntic Foundation, a group of special people seeking to stop the Organization, an evil entity headed by DeFoe, that controls evil spirit beings called Titans. The Organization wants to control the world and can only do so by acquiring Lok's journals (which apparently contain ancient secrets). Lok learns that his father was a member of Huntic and now, with the amulet, he is also a member. Like the Organization, members of Huntic, called Seekers, can control Titans (by their strong wills) but for good. Stories follow Lok, Sophie and Dante as they use their special powers as Seekers to bring down the Organization.

Voice Cast: Yuri Lowenthal *(Lok)*; Rebecca Soler *(Sophie Casterwill)*; Marc Thompson *(Dante Vale)*; Mark Thornton *(DeFoe)*; Karen Strassman *(Zarilla)*.

4285   *The Huntress.* (Series; Crime Drama; USA; 2000–2001). Dottie Thorson is a unique woman. She is a mother (of Brandi) and was a housewife but is now a bounty hunter who earns a living by tracking down wanted men and women. Dottie was married to Ralph Thorson, a legendary bounty hunter. When Ralph was killed in the line of duty, financial necessity forced Dottie to take over her husband's business and become one of the rare breed — a beautiful woman who is a bounty hunter. Joining Dottie is her equally beautiful daughter, Brandi, an 18-year-old who often goes undercover to help bring a wanted felon to justice. Stories follow the mother-daughter team as they risk their lives to earn a living.

Other regulars are Ricky Guzman, the bail bondsman Dottie works for; and Tiny Bellows, Dottie's love interest, a criminal she once put behind bars.

Cast: Annette O'Toole *(Dottie Thorson)*; Aleska Palladino *(Brandi Thorson; pilot)*; Jordana Spiro *(Brandi Thorson; series)*; James Remar *(Tiny Bellows)*; Paulie Dortmunder *(Ricky Guzman; pilot)*; Luis Antonio Ramos *(Ricky Guzman; series)*.

4286   *Hurdy Gurdy.* (Series; Variety; Syn.; 1967). The music, song and dance of the Gay 1890s era.

Host: Pete Lofthouse. **Regulars:** Barbara Kelly, The Sportsmen, The Hurdy Gurdy Dancers. **Music:** The Second Story Men.

4287   *Hurricane Sam.* (Pilot; Comedy; CBS; July 25, 1990). Jeannie and Bob Kelvin are a typical mother and father of a not-so-typical son — a mischievous whirlwind of energy with a high I.Q. they nickname "Hurricane" Sam (a student at Bronson Elementary School). The efforts of Sam's parents to keep him under control were the focal point of the proposal. Other regulars are Trisha, Sam's sister; Ed, Bob's father; Renee, their neighbor; and Neil, Renee's son.

Cast: Karen Valentine *(Jeannie Kelvin)*; Tim Stack *(Bob Kelvin)*; Ben Savage *(Sam Kelvin)*; Kiersten Warren *(Trisha Kelvin)*; Ray Walston *(Ed Kelvin)*; Fran Drescher *(Renee)*; Christopher Castile *(Neil)*.

4288 Hurricanes. (Series; Cartoon; Syn.; 1993–1997). The Hurricanes are a soccer team owned by Amanda Carey and coached by Jock Stone. Stories follow the team as they compete against other teams (most notably the Gorgons) for the championship.

Voice Cast: Stuart Hepburn (*Jock Stone*); Andrew Airlie (*Andy Stone*); Chiara Zanni (*Amanda Carey*); Lesley Fitzsimmons (*Sheila Stone*).

4289 Husbands, Wives and Lovers. (Series; Comedy; CBS; 1978). The hassles, foibles and frivolities of five suburban couples living in the San Fernando Valley.

Murray and Paula Zuckerman are a couple whose marriage is full of ups and downs due to Murray, a pharmaceutical salesman, who is frequently out of town.

Harry Bellini is a gruff, self-educated garbage truck tycoon whose cute, blonde and innocent second wife, Joy, is young enough to be his daughter.

Lennie Bellini is Harry's younger, unmarried brother. He lives with Rita DeLatorre, a woman who is several years his senior. Dr. Ron Wilson is a dentist who is separated from his wife, Helene. They are splitting up in order to attain new heights in personal growth and fulfillment. They retain their friendship with the rest of the group.

Dixon Carter Fielding is a corporate lawyer and Ron's oldest friend (Dixon is representing Helene in Ron's separation proceedings). Dixon's wife, Courtney, is a woman with one goal in life: to find ways to spend her husband's money.

Harry is the owner of the Bellini Waste Removal Service; Lennie and Rita run a trendy boutique called Rita's (which specializes in denim "with more zippers than anyone could use"); Dixon is a lawyer with the firm of Lindquist, Provost and Fielding.

In the original pilot film (CBS, July 18, 1977), titled *Husbands and Wives,* the couples were Murray and Paula Zuckerman (Alex Rocco, Cynthia Harris); Harry and Joy Bell (Ed Barth, Suzanne Zenor); Lennie Bell (Mark Lonow) and his wife, Rita Bell (Randee Heller); Ron and Helen Cutler (Ron Rifkin, Linda Miller); and Dixon and Courtney Fielding (Charles Siebert, Claudette Nevins).

Cast: Stephen Pearlman (*Murray Zuckerman*); Cynthia Harris (*Paula Zuckerman*); Eddie Barth (*Harry Bellini*); Lynne Marie Stewart (*Joy Bellini*); Mark Lonow (*Lennie Bellini*); Randee Heller (*Rita DeLatorre*); Ron Rifkin (*Ron Wilson*); Jesse Welles (*Helene Wilson*); Charles Siebert (*Dixon Fielding*); Claudette Nevins (*Courtney Fielding*).

4290 Hustle. (Series; Crime Drama; AMC; 2006). Albert Stroller is a very distinguished gentleman one would never suspect of being a thief. He is, though, a brilliant veteran con artist who has assembled a team of expert thieves and together they steal what they want from whomever they want. Albert is based in London, England and chooses the victims; Mickey Stone devises the plans; Stacie Monroe is the distraction specialist; Ash Morgan manages the team's specialized equipment; and Danny Blue is the young amateur with high potential Mickey has taken under his wing. Following in the steps of *Mission: Impossible,* episodes relate the team's experiences as they pull off very complicated scams that always offer them unexpected twists and turns.

Cast: Robert Vaughn (*Albert Stroller*); Marc Warren (*Danny Blue*); Jaime Murray (*Stacie Monroe*); Robert Glenister (*Ash Morgan*); Adrian Lester (*Mickey Stone*).

4291 The Hustler. (Series; Drama; Internet; 2009). Well produced (television-like production values) program about a man, known only as the Hustler, who seeks revenge against the family of a man (Danny Goldman) who changed the course of his life when he cheated him out of a college football scholarship.

Cast: Mark Feuerstein (*The Hustler*); Chris Fernandez Lizardi (*Danny Goldman*); Lindsay Smith-Sands (*Anna Goldman*); Al Brown (*Bernie Goldman*); Angela McEwain (*Ethel Goldman*); Zack Cumer (*Joe Maddox*).

4292 Hyperion Bay. (Series; Drama; WB; 1998-1999). Dennis Sweeney is the son of Frank and Amy Sweeney and has an older brother named Nick. Dennis was somewhat of a loner and grew up in the shadow of Nick. After graduating from college, Dennis left the town of Hyperion Bay to seek fame and fortune. After achieving success with a computer company (Muse Prime), Dennis returns to Hyperion Bay to open a branch of the company and bring the modern world to the small town. Dennis is accompanied by his girlfriend, Jennifer Worth, and together they face the problems of small town life as Dennis suddenly captures the spotlight and Nick becomes overshadowed by Dennis's success.

Cast: Mark-Paul Gosselaar (*Dennis Sweeney*); Sydney Penny (*Jennifer Worth*); Dylan Neal (*Nick Sweeney*); Raymond J. Barry (*Frank Sweeney*); Christina Moore (*Amy Sweeney*); Cassidy Rae (*Trudy Tucker*); Bart Johnson (*Nelson Tucker*); Carmen Electra (*Sarah Hicks*); Cindy Pickett (*Marjorie Sweeney*).

4293 I (Almost) Got Away with It. (Series; Reality; Investigation Discovery; 2010). Recreations of true crime stories in which the culprit almost got away with it.

Reenactment Performers: Goldie Chan, Eric Anderson, Michael Abt, Diana Gregg, Cole Alexander Smith, Diana Tenes, Carl Marino.

4294 I Am the Greatest: The Adventures of Muhammad Ali. (Series; Cartoon; NBC; 1977-1978). Muhammad Ali is a heavyweight boxing champion who feels that today's young people need a hero to whom they can relate. Adopting the philosophy of the legendary Robin Hood, Muhammad becomes a crusader of sorts, using the abilities he learned in the ring to help good defeat evil. Nicky, his niece, and Damon, his nephew, assist him.

Voice Cast: Muhammad Ali (*Himself*); Patrice Carmichael (*Nicky*); Casey Carmichael (*Damon*).

4295 I Am Weasel. (Series; Cartoon; Cartoon Network; 1997–1999). I.M. Weasel and I.R. Baboon are friends who are as different as night and day. Weasel is young, handsome and gifted. He is famous, is admired by everyone but never lets his celebrity status go to his head. Baboon is extremely jealous of Weasel's success and will do his best to top him whenever he can. Baboon, however, is dim-witted and his efforts to outshine Weasel always backfire. Stories follow the problems that occur as Weasel and Baboon struggle to get along despite their differences. Loulabelle is Weasel's assistant.

Voice Cast: Michael Dorn (*Weasel*); Charlie Adler (*Baboon*); Susan Blakeslee, Teresa Ganzel (*Loulabelle*); Dee Bradley Baker (*Jolly Roger*); Jess Harnell and Michael Gough (*Admiral Bullets*).

4296 I and Claudie. (Pilot; Comedy; CBS; July 2, 1964). Clint Hightower and Claudie Hughes are con artists who devise unique schemes to make a living. The proposal was to chart their adventures as they travel across the country and prey on the unsuspecting.

Cast: Jerry Lanning (*Clint Hightower*); Ross Martin (*Claudie Hughes*).

4297 I Can't Believe I'm Still Single. (Series; Comedy; Showtime; 2008). Eric Schaeffer is 35 years old and single. He thought, as a teenager, that when the time was right, he could easily find a girl with whom to settle down. Unfortunately, as he grew older, he found this to be a myth. He has searched and searched but to no avail. Stories follow Eric as he goes to extremes — from hookers to internet dating — to find that one elusive girl.

Star: Eric Schaeffer.

4298   *I Can't Believe You Said That!* (Series; Game; Fox Family; 1998). Two families compete. A specific statement, made by one family member about another, is revealed. The family at play must determine who revealed the family secret or fact. Points are scored for each correct identification; the family with the most points wins.

Host: John Salley. **Announcer:** Marc Summers.

4299   *I Carly.* (Series; Comedy; Nick; 2007–). *I Carly* is a web show hosted by 13-year-old Carly Shay and her girlfriend, Samantha (called Sam). Their friend, Freddie is the show's "tech guy." Carly lives at the Bushwell Apartments in Seattle, Washington, with her 26-year-old eccentric would-be artist brother, Spencer (their father, a widower, is on assignment for the military). Carly wanted to make a difference and came up with the idea; Sam liked the concept and joined her "as your amusing little side kick." Carly has converted her loft into a studio and each week *I Carly* presents "a show about everything — something different each week." Stories follow Carly, Sam and Freddie as they produce their weekly show. Carly's web site is real (www.icarly.com) and viewers can log onto it to express their opinions and share messages with Carly. Mr. Franklin is the principal of Carly's school (Ridgeway Junior High School); Francine Briggs is the stern vice principal; Lewbert is the hyper building doorman; Nevel Pepperman is the boy seeking to take over Carly's website; Mandy is the annoying girl who is Carly's biggest fan; Marissa is Freddie's mother; Pam is Sam's outrageous mother; T-Bo is the owner of the hangout, The Smoothy Groovy. Miranda Cosgrove and Drake Bell perform the theme, "Leave It All to Me."

Cast: Miranda Cosgrove *(Carly Shay)*; Jennette McCurdy *(Sam Puckett)*; Jerry Trainor *(Spencer Shay)*; Nathan Kress *(Freddie Benson)*; Tim Russ *(Principal Franklin)*; Mindy Sterling *(Francine Briggs)*; Jeremy Rowley *(Lewbert)*; Mary Scheer *(Marissa Benson)*; Reed Alexander *(Nevel Pepperman)*; Aria Wallace *(Amanda "Mandy" Valdez)*; Jane Lynch *(Pam Puckett)*; Bobby "Boogie" Bowman *(T-Bo)*.

4300   *I-Caught.* (Series; Reality; ABC; 2007). An unusual program that goes behind the scenes to explore the stories associated with the video images that are generated by surveillance cameras, computer up loads and down loads, cell phone images and web cameras. The people involved in producing these images are also featured. Bill Weir hosts.

4301   *I Cover Times Square.* (Series; Crime Drama; ABC; 1950-1951). Johnny Warren is a crusading Broadway newspaper columnist whose beat is the out-of-town newsstand on Seventh Avenue in Times Square (New York City). Stories relate Johnny's relaxed, easy-going attitude as he covers stories for his paper. The pilot episode, titled *I Cover Times Square*, aired on *Chevrolet Tele-Theater* on December 26, 1949.

Cast: Harold Huber *(Johnny Warren)*.

4302   *I Dare You: The Ultimate Challenge.* (Series; Reality; UPN; 2000). Daredevils, like Evel Kneivel, put their reputations on line to perform death-defying challenges that are presented to them.

Studio Host: Lee Reherman. **Field Host:** Tyler Harcort, Tracy Melchoir.

4303   *I Do, I Don't.* (Pilot; Comedy; ABC; Sept. 2, 1983). Shelley Hewitt is married to Earl and stepmother to his children, Lisa and Zack. Earl is a widower; Shelley is divorced and was previ-

ously married to Ivan. The proposal was to relate Shelley's misadventures as Ivan constantly plagues her life in his fruitless attempts to win her back.

Cast: Linda Purl *(Shelley Hewitt)*; Bo Svenson *(Earl Hewitt)*; Martha Byrne *(Lisa Hewitt)*; Scott Schutzman *(Zack Hewitt)*; Charles Rocket *(Ivan)*.

4304   *I Dream of Jeannie.* (Series; Comedy; NBC; 1965–1970). The home at 1030 Palm Drive in Cocoa Beach, Florida, is owned by Captain (later Major) Anthony Nelson, an astronaut with the NASA Space Center at Cape Kennedy. Also living with him is Jeannie, a beautiful genie he found after a rocket he was testing malfunctioned and crash-landed on a deserted island in the South Pacific.

Jeannie was born in Baghdad on April 1, 64 B.C. When she became of age, the Blue Djin, the most powerful and most feared of all genies, asked for her hand in marriage. When she refused, he turned her into a genie, placed her in a bottle and sentenced her to a life of loneliness on a deserted island. Centuries later Anthony, called Tony by Jeannie, found her green bottle (while making an S.O.S. signal), opened it, set her free and became her master.

Jeannie wears a pink harem costume; she crosses her hands over her chest and blinks her eyes to invoke her powers and appears and disappears in a pink smoke.

Tony was born on July 15 in Fowlers Corners, Ohio, and attended Fowlers Corners High School (where he was called "Bunky Nelson"). He has piloted *Apollo 14* and *Apollo 15*, *Stardust I* (the ship that misfired in the pilot), the *X-14*, the *Trail Blazer* and the *T-38*.

Tony's main goal is to keep Jeannie's presence a secret — especially from NASA officials (he fears the Air Force will discharge him for having a genie). Tony has forbidden Jeannie to use her powers. She rarely listens and Tony often winds up in trouble.

Captain (then Major) Roger Healey is Tony's best friend and the only other person who knows about Jeannie. Dr. Alfred Bellows is the base psychiatrist who, after meeting Tony, has set two goals for himself: to prove to someone else that something strange is going on, and to figure out what it is (Dr. Bellows most often experiences the after effects of Jeannie's magic). Dr. Bellows is married to Amanda and she becomes Jeannie's close friend in later episodes but is unaware of Jeannie's true identity.

A recurring aspect of the series is the efforts of Jeannie's evil sister, Jeannie II, to steal Tony away from Jeannie and marry him. This failed when Tony and Jeannie wed in 1969. Jeannie II wears a green harem outfit and has been married 47 times.

Gin Gin is Jeannie's genie dog (she was mistreated by palace guards as a puppy and hates uniforms — thus she wreaks havoc at NASA). General Martin Peterson and General Winfield Schaefer are the base commanders.

Program Open: "Once upon a time in a mythical place called Cape Kennedy, an astronaut named Tony Nelson went up on a space mission. The missile went up but something went wrong and they had to bring it down. Captain Nelson landed on an island in the South Pacific where he found a bottle — at least it looked like a bottle, but it didn't act like a bottle (visual follows with Tony opening the bottle; Jeannie popping out; Tony wishing to be rescued; helicopter appearing). Captain Nelson was so grateful he set Jeannie free — only she didn't want to be free — you know how it is when you've been cooped up in a bottle for 2,000 years; she wanted to have fun and she wanted to have it with Captain Nelson. So she followed him back to Cocoa Beach, a mythical town in a mythical state called Florida. And there, in this house, the girl in the bottle play spin the astronaut."

Cast: Barbara Eden *(Jeannie/Jeannie II)*; Larry Hagman *(Tony Nelson)*; Bill Daily *(Roger Healy)*; Hayden Rorke *(Dr. Alfred Bellows)*; Emmaline Henry *(Amanda Bellows)*; Barton MacLane *(Gen. Martin*

Peterson); Vinton Hayworth *(Gen. Winfield Schaefer)*; Abraham Sofaer *(Hadji; master of all genies)*; Ted Cassidy *(Habib; Jeannie's sister's master)*; Florence Sundstrom, Lurene Tuttle *(Jeannie's mother)*; Michael Ansara *(The Blue Djin)*.

NBC TV Movie Updates:

1. I Dream of Jeannie: 15 Years Later (Oct. 20, 1985). Jeannie (Barbara Eden) and Tony (Wayne Rogers), now a colonel, have a teenage son, T.J. (for Tony Jr.) (Mackenzie Astin). Major Roger Healey (Bill Daily) and Dr. Alfred Bellows (Hayden Rorke) have retired. The locale has changed to Houston, Texas. The story finds Jeannie II (Barbara Eden) attempting to make the content-as-a-housewife Jeannie independent when Tony decides to forsake retirement and continue with the space program.

2. I Still Dream of Jeannie (Oct. 20, 1991). The setting is the Lyndon B. Johnson Space Center in Houston, Texas. Jeannie (Barbara Eden) is still married to Tony (not seen) and the mother of Tony Nelson, Jr. (Christopher Bolton). Jeannie's past was also changed. She was born in Mesopotamia 4,233 years ago and attended genie school to learn her craft. She was said to have had many masters over the centuries. Roger (Bill Daily) is now a colonel and Jeannie II (Barbara Eden) was said to have never had a master; hence she is bound to remain in Mesopotamia forever (she can only leave for a period of 24 hours at a time and has to return to maintain her beauty and powers). Tony is away on a top secret mission and Jeannie cannot remain in Houston without a master (she will be exiled to Mesopotamia forever if Tony does not return in three months). The story finds Jeannie choosing high school guidance counselor Bob Simpson (Ken Kercheval) as a temporary master until Tony returns (who is left in unknown space as the movie-pilot ends).

4305   *I Gave at the Office.* (Pilot; Comedy; NBC; Aug. 15, 1984). The Brinker Advertising Agency is a small company based in Denver and owned by Larry Brinker. His staff includes Michael, Julie, Janet and Jimbo (copywriters); Yvonne, his secretary; and K.C., the receptionist. The proposal was to focus on their antics as they attempt to run the company.

Cast: Michael Lerner *(Larry Brinker)*; Matt de Ganon *(Michael Boatwright)*; Candy Clark *(Julie)*; Janet Carroll *(Janet Holloway)*; Max Wright *(Jimbo)*; Kathleen York *(K.C. Conklin)*; Jill Jacobson *(Yvonne)*.

4306   *I Had Three Wives.* (Series; Crime Drama; CBS; 1985). "Just about every client I ever had wants to kill me," says Jackson Beaudine, a three times divorced private detective who owns Jackson Beaudine Investigations at 1163 Vandover Street in Los Angeles.

While Jackson does investigate cases and tries to help people in trouble, he has a knack for asking the wrong questions of the wrong people and constantly puts his life in jeopardy. "I need all the help I can get," he says, and he relies on the assistance of this three ex-wives — Liz Bailey, Samantha Collins and Mary Parker. Liz, Samantha and Mary are career women. Jackson claims each of the marriages failed "because we got in the way of each other's career and stopped each other's personal growth." Elizabeth is a reporter for the Los Angeles *Chronicle*. She lives at 6 Preston Drive. Samantha, called Sam by Jackson, is an aspiring actress. Her claim to fame is the starring role in the horror film *Hatchet Honeymoon*. She lives in an apartment at the Roxbury Apartment Complex. Mary is a lawyer with the firm of Maxwell, Cooper and Associates. She is the mother of their son, Andrew and they live at 12718 Kenmore Road in Brentwood.

Cast: Victor Garber *(Jackson Beaudine)*; Shanna Reed *(Elizabeth Bailey)*; Teri Copley *(Samantha Collins)*; Maggie Cooper *(Mary Parker)*; David Faustino *(Andrew Beaudine)*.

4307   *I Hate My 30s.* (Series; Comedy; VH-1; 2007). A coming of age comedy about a group of office workers who have or are about to reach the age of thirty. While there are a number of characters, most with nothing more to do than brood about the prospect, particular focus is on Carol, a 29-year-old who is rapidly approaching the most dreaded day of her life — her next birthday. Carol is in a panic as she has no boyfriend, her biological clock is ticking and she needs to be married to have a child. Chad has turned that "horrible" corner and is struggling to accept the fact that he is no longer a young man in his twenties but a man in his thirties. Carol is secretly in love with Chad but fears approaching him as they have a great working relationship and an office romance may upset the bond they have. Mandy is a beautiful, self-absorbed woman who constantly worries about what thirty may do to her looks. She is vain, and is also looking to settle down, but can't seem to find anyone (besides dreading wrinkles, Mandy worries about becoming another bridesmaid but never a bride). Kyle is the office assistant who is smitten with every girl he sees but is a patsy — especially in the hands of Mandy who constantly takes advantage of him. Stories are narrated by a so-called expert on such matters, Dr. Rod (somewhat in the style of Rod Serling on *The Twilight Zone*) and are actually a look at leaving one's twenties and assuming a greater responsibility in life as one grows older.

Cast: Megahn Perry *(Carol)*; David Fickas *(Chad)*; Jill Ritchie *(Mandy)*; Liam Sullivan *(Kyle)*; Michele Specht *(Katie)*; James Mathis III *(Bruce)*; Rachael Lawrence *(Vicki)*; Mark Kelly *(Travis)*; Brice Beckham *(Corey)*; Ric Barbera *(Dr. Rod)*.

4308   *I Know My Kid's a Star.* (Series; Reality; VH-1; 2008). Former child star Danny Bonaduce *(The Partridge Family)* hosts a program that seeks to find the next child star. The children appear with their parents and must compete in a series of weekly challenges (like voicing a cartoon character) with the weakest performers facing elimination. The one child left standing wins the competition and the opportunity to star on a television series.

4309   *I Led Three Lives.* (Series; Drama; Syn.; 1953–1956). Herbert Philbrick is a man who has led three lives: private citizen, undercover agent, and FBI counterspy. His life as a counterspy and his efforts to infiltrate the American Communist Party and inform the U.S. government officials of the Red military movement are the focal point of stories. Eva Philbrick is Herbert's wife; Constance is their daughter; Steve Daniels and Joe Carney are FBI agents.

Program Open: "This is a true story, the fantastically true story of Herbert L. Philbrick who, for nine frightening years did lead three lives — private citizen, bi-level member of the Communist Party and counterspy for the Federal Bureau of Investigation. For obvious reasons, the names, dates and places have been changed, but the story is based on fact. It's the job of a counterspy to help find the enemies of the United States. This week's story concerns a secret Communist cell meeting and the search for such an enemy."

Cast: Richard Carlson *(Herbert Philbrick)*; Virginia Stefan *(Eva Philbrick)*; Patricia Morrow *(Constance Philbrick)*; John Beradino *(Steve Daniels)*; Charles Maxwell *(Joe Carney)*.

4310   *I Love a Mystery.* (Pilot; Mystery; NBC; Feb. 27, 1973). A television adaptation of the radio series of the same title about Doc Long, Jack Packard and Reggie York, private detectives who roam the world solving crimes. Filmed in 1966.

Cast: David Hartman *(Doc Long)*; Les Crane *(Jack Packard)*; Hagan Beggs *(Reggie York)*.

4311   *I Love Her Anyway!* (Pilot; Comedy; ABC; Aug. 3, 1981). Laurie Martin is a pretty but scatterbrained woman. She is married to Jerry, a level-headed man who loves her despite the crazy things she does. Jerry is aware of a viewing audience and talks directly to them as he sets up a simple situation that will involve Laurie, how she manages to complicate it and how he has to come to the rescue to resolve it. Fred, Jerry's free-loading brother, and his wife, Mona, also live with them in their California home. Willie Winslow is their neighbor.

Cast: Dean Jones (*Jerry Martin*); Diane Stilwell (*Laurie Martin*); Charles Levin (*Fred Martin*); Jane Daly (*Mona Martin*); Peter Boyden (*Willie Winslow*).

4312   *I Love Lucy.* (Series; Comedy; CBS; 1951–1957). The converted Brownstone at 623 East 68th Street in Manhattan is owned by Fred and Ethel Mertz. Lucy and Ricky Ricardo are tenants who occupy Apartment 3B (later 3D). They pay $125 a month in rent and moved into the building on August 6, 1948 (at which time they lived on the fourth floor).

Lucille "Lucy" Esmerelda McGilicuddy was born in Jamestown, New York, on August 6, 1921 (another episode claims she was born in West Jamestown in May 1921). She has been juggling her age for so long "that I kinda lost track of how old I am." Lucy met Ricky Ricardo Alberto Fernando Acha (a.k.a Ricky Alberto Ricardo IV) in New York City in 1941 when her friend Marian Strong arranged a blind date for her with Ricky. They fell in love and Ricky proposed to Lucy at the Byrum River Beagle Club in Connecticut.

Ricky, a Cuban drummer who later has his own rumba band, performs at the Tropicana Club in Manhattan. In 1956 Ricky buys a controlling interest in the Tropicana and renames it the Club Babalu, after his favorite song (the club is also called the Ricky Ricardo Babalu Club and the Babalu Club). Ricky made a TV pilot for an unrealized musical series called *Tropical Rhythms* and traveled to Hollywood to star in a movie called *Don Juan.* The movie is shelved and the film that Ricky eventually makes is never revealed. Lucy gets the hiccups when she cries ("It's happened since I was a little girl") and is famous for her "spider noise" ("Eeeuuuuu") when something doesn't go her way. Many episodes relate Lucy's efforts to defy Ricky and break into show business.

Lucy has a hard time managing the family budget, appeared on the TV game show *Females Are Fabulous* ("Any woman is idiotic enough to win a prize") and did the infamous Vitameatavegamin TV commercial on *Your Saturday Night Variety Show* (the vitamin product contained meat, vegetables, minerals and 23 percent alcohol; Lucy became intoxicated during rehearsals). In 1953 Lucy and Ricky become parents with the birth of Ricky Ricardo, Jr., better known as Little Ricky.

Ethel was born in Albuquerque, New Mexico, and has been married to cheapskate Fred Mertz for 18 years (in 1951; in 1952, they mention they have been married for 25 years). Fred, born in Steubenville, Ohio, met Ethel (both of them were performers) in vaudeville.

In the European-based episodes (Dec. 1955 through June 1956), Fred becomes Ricky's band manager and the quartet books passage on the ocean liner *SS Constitution.* While visiting friends in Connecticut, Lucy falls in love with an Early American–style house for sale. She convinces Ricky to move. When they find the cost of living higher than expected, they decide to raise chickens and take on boarders — Fred and Ethel Mertz. These particular episodes are also known as *Lucy in Connecticut.* Betty Ramsey and her husband, Ralph, become their neighbors.

The series is based on the 1948–51 radio series *My Favorite Husband.* Lucille Ball played Liz Cooper and Richard Denning her husband, George. A TV pilot, called *I Love Lucy,* was produced in 1951 (it aired in 1990 after being lost for 39 years) that cast Lucille Ball and Desi Arnaz as Lucy and Ricky Ricardo (not Lucy and Larry Lopez as reported in *TV Guide*). Here, Lucy and Ricky live in a seventh-floor Manhattan apartment. Fred and Ethel are not a part

of the concept (although Lucy's efforts to break into show business are).

Cast: Lucille Ball (*Lucy Ricardo*); Desi Arnaz (*Ricky Ricardo*); William Frawley (*Fred Mertz*); Vivian Vance (*Ethel Mertz*); Richard Keith (*Little Ricky*); Jerry Hausner (*Jerry; Ricky's agent*); Kathryn Card (*Mrs. Magilicuddy; Lucy's mother*); Mary Jane Croft (*Betty Ramsey*); Frank Nelson (*Ralph Ramsey*).

4313   *I Love Money.* (Series; Reality; VH-1; 2008-2009). Contestants from former VH-1 series (*Flavor of Love, I Love New York* and *Rock of Love*) are brought together on Huachuca Beach in Mexico to compete against each other in a series of challenges wherein the best performer wins $250,000. Craig Jackson hosts.

4314   *I Love My Doctor.* (Pilot; Comedy; CBS; Aug. 14, 1962). Jim Barkley is a doctor with a large city practice who relocates to a small suburban community to help its people. The proposal was to relate his experiences. Connie is Jim's wife; Liz and Albert are their children.

Cast: Don Porter (*Dr. Jim Barkley*); Phyllis Avery (*Connie Barkley*); Terry Burnham (*Liz Barkley*); Ricky Kelman (*Albert Barkley*).

4315   *I Love New York.* (Series; Reality; VH-1; 2007). A spin off from *Flavor of Love.* The title refers to Tiffany Pollard, the girl known as New York (given the name by rapper Flavor Flav because she is from upstate New York) not the city. The simplistic format has twenty "hunks" competing for New York's affections and become the one she chooses as her own. After a number of challenges that narrows down the field (contestants eliminated) New York chooses the one man she feels will love her (New York claims to have the ability "to look into a man's soul and see if he is sincere"). Patrick "Tango" Hunter was chosen by New York "as the one who will love me the most." It looked like a good match, but Hunter later dumped New York.

4316   *I-Man.* (Pilot; Fantasy; ABC; April 6, 1986). After several years in space, the *Galaxy I* U.S. Space probe returns to Earth with a sample of alien atmosphere. Shortly after, while en-route to a NASA research lab, a truck carrying the alien sample is involved in an accident. While attempting to help the truck driver, cabby Jeffrey Wilder is exposed to a canister of the leaking alien atmosphere. The alien gas reacts with his molecular structure and renders him indestructible. Immediately, he is recruited by the International Security Agency to become an agent for the U.S. government. The proposal was to relate Jeffrey's exploits as he uses his amazing abilities to benefit mankind. Other regulars are Karen McCorder and Harry Murphy, Jeffrey's assistants; Art Bogosian, their supervisor; Eric Wilder, Jeffrey's son.

Cast: Scott Bakula (*Jeffrey Wilder*); Ellen Bry (*Karen McCorder*); Herschel Bernardi (*Art Bogosian*); Joey Cramer (*Eric Wilder*); John Bloom (*Harry Murphy*).

4317   *I Married a Dog.* (Pilot; Comedy; NBC; Aug. 4, 1961). Peter Chance and Joyce Nicoll are a newlywed couple with an unusual problem: Jonah, Joyce's extremely jealous French poodle, has taken a dislike to Peter and growls when he gets too close to her. The proposal was to relate Peter's efforts to win over Jonah and have normal life with Joyce. In the actual program, the dog is called Jonah; in *TV Guide* the dog is called Noah.

Cast: Hal March (*Peter Chance*); Marcia Henderson (*Joyce Nicoll-Chance*).

4318   *I Married a Princess.* (Series; Reality; Lifetime; 2005). The personal lives of marrieds Catherine Oxenberg (from TV's *Dy-*

nasty) and Casper Van Dien (from the theatrical film *Starship Troopers*) and their blended family of five children. India is Catherine's daughter; Gracie and Cappy are Casper's children from his first marriage; Maya and Celeste are their children together.

4319 *I Married Dora.* (Series; Comedy; ABC; 1987-1988). Peter Farrell, an architect with the firm of Hughes Whitney Lennox, lives at 46 LaPaloma Drive in Los Angeles with his children Kate and Will. When his wife leaves him, Peter hires Dora Calderon, a young woman from El Salvador, as his housekeeper. Several months later, when Dora's visa is about to expire, Peter marries her to keep her in the country and with his family. Stories relate Dora's efforts to care for and resolve the problems that affect her new family.

Peter claims he and Dora are not really married and are free agents when it comes to dating. Dora agrees that they have a marriage of convenience (although she secretly loves him) and asks simply "If our marriage is going to work you can't sneak around with other women. You have to bring them home to meet your wife and children." Dora calls Peter "Mr. Peter" and functions only as his housekeeper (had the series been renewed, the focus would have changed to Peter and Dora falling in love with each other, based on the last episode).

Kate, Peter's 13-year-old daughter, considers her best assets to be her gorgeous thick hair and her love of the Beastie Boys' music. She is beautiful, a bit dense and believes going around the world "is like going from here to the mall a lot of times." She also claims to possess the three P's to be popular: "positive, pretty and perky." When Kate and her friends dress in short skirts and tight blouses and "feel sexy," they go to the mall "so other people can see how hot we are." Other than being there when he is needed, no information is given about Will, Peter's younger and smarter child. Kate calls him a jerk "but he's a nice jerk." His only interest appears to be snooping in Kate's room when she is not home. Hughes Whitney Lennox is Peter's boss; Dolf is his co-worker.

Cast: Daniel Hugh-Kelly (*Peter Farrell*); Elizabeth Pena (*Dora Calderon*); Juliette Lewis (*Kate Farrell*); Jason Horst (*Will Farrell*); Henry Jones (*Hughes Whitney Lennox*); Sanford Jensen (*Dolf Mennenger*).

4320 *I Married Joan.* (Series; Comedy; NBC; 1952–1955). Joan Stevens is a woman who walks hand in hand with calamity. She doesn't go looking for trouble, but trouble just seems to find her. She is married to Bradley Stevens, a domestic relations court judge and they live at 133 Stone Street (also given as 345 Laurel Drive) in Los Angeles.

Joan means well, but all her good intentions inevitably backfire (even her fortune cookie fortunes are against her — "When you opened this cookie, you read the fortune we put in it. But when you opened your mouth, you just stuck your foot in it"). She is president of the local Women's Club and a member of the Women's Welfare League. Joan considers herself to be very popular ("When you have a wife as popular as I am, you have to make a date five weeks in advance") and can't resist a bargain (salesmen call her "one of those yo-yo dames"). Joan is also a whiz at maneuvering the household funds "to balance the books." Brad, on the other hand, is level-headed, patient, understanding and deeply in love with Joan. No matter what she does to complicate his life, he always forgives her. Brad loves hunting and golf and, according to Joan, likes to hear most, "Dinner is ready." When Brad runs for re-election, his campaign posters read "Re-elect Judge Bradley Stevens. Honest Brad, Always Keeps His Promises." Janet and her husband, Dan Tobin are the Stevens' neighbors; Beverly is Joan's sister (real life too); Alan is her husband in later episodes. The series' official screen title is *The Joan Davis Show:*

I Married Joan. The Roger Wagner Chorale performs the "I Married Joan" theme.

Program Open: "*The Joan Davis Show — I Married Joan*, America's favorite comedy show starring America's Queen of Comedy, Joan Davis as Mrs. Joan Stevens ... and featuring Jim Backus as Judge Bradley Stevens."

Cast: Joan Davis (*Joan Stevens*); Jim Backus (*Bradley Stevens*); Sheila Bromley (*Janet Tobin*); Dan Tobin (*Dan Tobin*); Geraldine Carr (*Mabel*); Hal Smith (*Charlie*); Sandra Gould (*Mildred Webster*); Beverly Wills (*Beverly Grossman*); Alan Grossman (*Alan Grossman*).

4321 *I Married Sofia.* (Pilot; Comedy; Unaired; Produced for ABC in 2004). Sofia is a gorgeous soap opera star in Colombia who travels to New York City hoping become a star on American TV. Unfortunately, she is unable to find work and her visa is about to expire. Tony Wilson is an ex-stockbroker with money problems. By chance, Sofia and Tony meet and when each learns of the other's problems, they agree to marry. Sofia will be allowed to stay in New York to pursue her career; Tony will get the money he needs as a green card marriage nets $5,000 up front. The only problem: they have to stay married for three years and the proposal was to follow Sofia and Tony as they plan their futures — which also include Sofia's seven-year-old son (Carlos) and foul-mouthed parrot; and Tony's girlfriend, Victoria.

Cast: Sofia Vergara (*Sofia*); Joey Lawrence (*Tony*); Victoria Jackson (*Victoria*); Lil Maxso (*Carlos*).

4322 *I Pity the Fool.* (Series; Reality; TV Land; 2006). "I Pity the Fool" is a catchphrase used by Mr. T in the movie *Rocky III* and on the TV series *The A-Team*. Taking that concept, Mr. T travels around the country to offer advice (or help) to people he feels need all the help they can get.

4323 *I Remember Caviar.* (Pilot; Comedy; NBC; May 11, 1959). Margaret "Maggie" Randall is a debutante who lives with her aunt, Caroline, and her brother, Eric. The Randalls come from a once wealthy family who lost their money through bad investments. The family must now learn to live with poverty and their efforts to do just that was the focal point of the unsold series. Broadcast as a segment of *Goodyear Theater*; see also *All in the Family*, the 1960 sequel pilot film.

Cast: Patricia Crowley (*Maggie Randall*); Lurene Tuttle (*Caroline Randall*); Elliott Reid (*Eric Randall*).

4324 *I Spy.* (Series; Anthology; Syn.; 1956). Tales of intrigue and espionage that span time from the sixteenth to the twentieth centuries. Anton, the Spy Master, relates stories.

Host: Raymond Massey (*as Anton*).

4325 *I Spy.* (Series; Adventure; NBC; 1965–1968). Kelly Robinson and Alexander Scott are U.S. government undercover agents who pose as a tennis pro (Kelly) and his trainer/masseur (Scott, called Scotty). Their exact affiliation is not mentioned by name; they call their "boss" "our people," "our superiors" or "Washington." Kelly, called Kel by Scotty, is a graduate of Princeton University. He is skilled in karate but still manages to take a beating from the enemy. He loves fishing, golfing and duck hunting and has a bad habit of repeating what the person he is speaking to says. Kelly calls himself a "tennis bum" and has won two Davis Cup trophies (when asked why he chose such a life, he responds with "It's better than digging ditches"). Although he travels around the world to compete, he doesn't always win (for example, he lost in five sets at Forest Hills).

Scotty is a Rhodes Scholar and can speak eight languages. He was born in Philadelphia and mentioned he would have become a basketball coach at Allentown High School had he not become a spy (he also mentioned, when under the influence of truth serum, that his name was Fat Albert, referring to Cosby's real life friend in South Philly). Scotty, a black belt in the martial arts, has the instincts of an alley cat and is an explosives expert. He has training as a chemist and can make a bomb out of almost anything (for example, dry ice, ammonia, fertilizer and a cigarette). Scott will also shoot to kill and while they work well as a team, they constantly argue — mostly about how a case should progress and who saves who the most.

Cast: Robert Culp (*Kelly Robinson*); Bill Cosby (*Alexander Scott*).

4326   *I Survived a Japanese Game Show.* (Series; Game; ABC; 2008). Ten Americans are sent to Japan to compete against each other in outrageous (as well as hilarious) stunt challenges. The ten players live together in a large residence for the duration of the contest. The weakest performers are eliminated on a weekly basis. The one player left standing not only wins the grand prize ($250,000) but receives the opportunity to exclaim, "I Survived a Japanese Game Show."

Host: Tony Sano. **Master of Ceremonies:** Rome Kanda.

4327   *I Want a Famous Face.* (Series; Reality; MTV; 2004). There are celebrity impersonators and people who resemble celebrities. Then there are people who idolize celebrities but do not resemble them. That is the subject of *I Want a Famous Face*, a reality series not for the faint of heart, as plastic surgery scenes are quite graphic. The program attempts to provide such people with their dreams of celebrity status. It should be noted that MTV offers no incentive to the subjects being profiled. They do not pay for the surgeries nor do they hold any open auditions to acquire candidates for the purposes of a reality show. Jessica Chesler narrates.

4328   *I Want to Be a Hilton.* (Series; Reality; NBC; 2005). Fourteen contestants vie for the opportunity to win a $200,000 trust fund, an apartment, wardrobe and live for a year like a Hilton. Kathy Hilton, the mother of Paris Hilton, instructs each of the players on how to become a part of high society. Those Kathy feels are unsuitable are disqualified. The one player who best emulates Kathy wins.

4329   *I Want to Be a Soap Star.* (Series; Reality; Soap Net; 2006). A group of ordinary people compete for the opportunity for a role on a network soap opera. Each contestant is placed in single acting chores as well as in group sessions. A panel of judges determines which candidate is worthy of the role. Cameron Mathison hosts; Debbi Morgan and Michael Bruno are the judges.

4330   *I Want to Work for Diddy.* (Series; Reality; VH-1; 2008). *Apprentice*-like program in which hip hop mogul Sean "P. Diddy" Combs seeks an assistant by putting 13 young hopefuls through a series of challenges. The weakest performers are eliminated on a weekly basis with the best performer receiving the job as Sean's business assistant. A second cycle, *I Want to Work for Diddy 2* appeared in 2009 with Sean again seeking assistants.

Host: Sean "P. Diddy" Combs.

4331   *I Was a Bloodhound.* (Pilot; Comedy; CBS; Feb. 15, 1959). Barney Colby is a private detective with an uncanny sense of smell — a gift he uses to solve baffling crimes. Eunice is Barney's wife; and Jennie is Barney's secretary.

Cast: Ernie Kovacs (*Barney Colby*); Yvonne White (*Eunice Colby*); Shirley Mitchell (*Jennie*).

4332   *I Witness.* (Pilot; Mystery; Unaired; Produced for NBC in 1991). An interactive program that follows an investigative reporter (Jack Barnett) whose detective work is seen through the lens of his video camera operator (Mike) but whose face is never seen. The idea was to end each mystery with the solution unrevealed. Viewers could then call a special 900 number to guess the identity of the culprit. At the beginning of the next episode, the culprit and the prize winner were to be revealed.

Cast: Robert Firth (*Jack Barnett*); Larry Hankin (*Mike*); Walter Addison (*Lt. Stanislaus Wisniewski*).

4333   *I Witness Video.* (Series; Reality; NBC; 1992–1994). Videos of natural disasters, crime scene investigations, car chases and other such happenings as caught on videotape by both amateur and professional photographers.

Hosts: Patrick Van Horn (*1992-93*); John Forsythe (*1993-94*).

4334   *The Ian Tyson Show.* (Series; Variety; Syn.; 1970). Performances by U.S. and Canadian folk and country and western artists.

Host: Ian Tyson, Sylvia Tyson. **Music:** The Great Speckled Bird.

4335   *The Ice Palace.* (Series; Variety; CBS; 1971). Entertainment acts set against the background of a mythical ice palace.

Program Open: "Tonight, Carol Lawrence at *The Ice Palace* ... with Godfrey Cambridge and skating star Gisela Head ... the Bob Turk Ice Dancers ... and now starring at *The Ice Palace*, Miss Carol Lawrence."

Guest Hosts: Vikki Carr, Dean Jones, Carol Lawrence, The Lennon Sisters, Roger Miller, Leslie Uggams, Jack Jones, Johnny Mathis, John Davidson. **Regulars** (Ice Skating Personalities): Tim Wood, Linda Carbonetto, Billy Chappell, Gisela Head, Don Knight, Tim Noyers, Roy Powers, Sandy Parker, The Bob Turk Ice Dancers. **Orchestra:** Alan Copeland.

4336   *Ice-T's Rap School.* (Series; Reality; VH-1; 2006). Tracy Morrow, better known as actor-rapper Ice-T, appears in an experiment that attempts to teach prep school students (mostly white) how be rappers. York Prep School in Manhattan is the setting. Here Ice-T is presented with a group of eight students and through musical exercises, trains them to become rappers for a public performance. While they will not become real rappers, the purpose of the program is to make the public more aware of the genre.

4337   *Ichabod and Me.* (Series; Comedy; CBS; 1961-1962). Bob Major, a widower with a young son named Benjie, quits his job as an editor for the *New York Times* and moves to Phippsboro, a small town in New Hampshire. There, he purchases the *Phippsboro Bulletin*, the town newspaper, from its owner, Ichabod Adams. Ichabod, a widower with a daughter named Abigail ("Abby"), is the town's mayor, traffic commissioner and overall problem solver. Bob lived at 720 Madison Avenue in New York City; he now resides at 432 Maple Lane; Ichabod and Abby (who becomes Bob's romantic interest) live at R.F.D. number 6.

When Bob sets his mind to get a story, he doesn't give up until he gets it (he uses "the famous Major charm" to get what he wants). Bob's housekeeper, Ichabod's aunt, Lavinia Perkins, receives $35 a month and room and board. Jonathan assists Bob at the paper.

In the original pilot, *Adams Apples* (broadcast on *G.E. Theater* on April 24, 1960), Fred Beir played Terry Major, an advertising executive who gives up his job "to emancipate himself and become a gentleman farmer." Ichabod (George Chandler) and his daughter Abby (Christine White) own an unnamed lodge (where, a year before, Terry vacationed; when Terry returned to New York and found he missed the peaceful life of Phippsboro, he arranged to rent an apple farm from Ichabod for $125 a month). Dorothy Neuman played Terry's housekeeper, Aunt Lavinia; Terry had a dog named Fownes (after his former boss, Herbert Fownes [Leon Ames]) and was never married (Abby became his romantic interest).

Cast: Robert Sterling (*Bob Major*); Jimmy Mathers (*Benji Major*); George Chandler (*Ichabod Adams*); Christine White (*Abigail Adams*); Reta Shaw (*Aunt Livinia*); Jimmy Hawkins (*Jonathan*).

4338 *I'd Do Anything.* (Series; Reality; BBC America; 2010). A talent search to find promising unknown performers to star in a London production of the musical *Oliver*. The judges are Andrew Lloyd Webber, Graham Norton, Cameron Mackintosh, Denise Van Outen, Barry Humphries, John Barowman.

4339 *I'd Like to See.* (Series; Documentary; NBC; 1948). Ray Morgan hosts a filmed program of highlights of past historic events.

4340 *I'd Rather Be Calm.* (Pilot; Comedy; CBS; Aug. 24, 1982). The lives, loves and relationships of a group of singles who gather in a swinging singles restaurant-bar in Cleveland, Ohio. The regulars are Katherine, a department store buyer; Julie, a school teacher; Sissy, a dizzy beauty contest winner; Herbie, a lawyer; Leslie, the seductive widow suspected of killing Herbie's father; Wally, Katherine's boyfriend; Michael, a seminary school drop-out; Jack, the bar owner; and Seymour, the waiter. Carol Connors performs the theme, "I'd Rather Be Calm."

Cast: Susan Spilker (*Katherine Lange*); Melissa Steinberg (*Julie Williams*); Trisha Hilka (*Sissy Shaefer*); Gregg Berger (*Herbie Weinstein*); Fran Drescher (*Leslie Harper Weinstein*); Charles Levin (*Wally*); Buddy Powell (*Michael Riley*); Paul Stolarsky (*Jack Minkus*); Justin Lord (*Seymour*).

4341 *The Ida Lupino Theater.* (Series; Anthology; Syn.; 1956). Actress Ida Lupino hosts a program of dramatic presentations from Hollywood.

4342 *Ideal.* (Series; Comedy; IFC; 2009). British produced (in 2005) program that revolves around Moz, an obese, small time drug dealer living in a filthy, rat infested flat in Salford (Manchester, England). Moz is stoned most of the time and sells only the various varieties of marijuana (he sees himself as "providing a crucial service to the community"). Stories, which relate the rather unsavory life of Moz, are hindered (for U.S. audiences) by the thick, hard to understand accents of the actors. Nikki (later Jenny) are Moz's girlfriends; PC is Moz's friend and chief drug supplier (he is a Police Constable and acquires weed from seized drug raids); Troy is Moz's brother; Cartoon Head (always wears a mask) and "Psycho" Phil Nevin are rival drug dealers who work for Stemroach. Judith, Moz's across-the-hall neighbor, is a necrophilia (has sex with dead bodies) who experiments with drugs and disgusts Moz; Brian, a homosexual, is an old friend of Moz's; China and Derrick are customers of Moz; Dawn is Jenny's mother; Keith is Moz's estranged step father; Colin is the petty criminal; Tania is Colin's sister.

Cast: Johnny Vegas (*Moz*); Nichola Reynolds (*Nikki*); Sinead Matthews (*Jenny*); Tom Goodman-Hall (*PC*); Tony Burgess (*Troy*); James Foster (*Cartoon Head*); Ryan Pope ("*Psycho" Phil Nevin*); David Bradley (*Stemroach*); Joanna Neary (*Judith*); Graham Duff (*Brian*); Natalie Gumede (*China*); Julia Davis (*Dawn*); Mick Miller (*Keith*); Ben Crompton (*Colin*); Emma Fryer (*Tania*); Alfie Joey (*Derrick*).

4343 *Identity.* (Series; Game; NBC; 2007). One player stands before twelve strangers. A board with twelve occupations is displayed. Based on looks, the player must match the stranger with the occupation. The player chooses one occupation from the board and the stranger he believes it matches. If he is correct he wins $1,000 and a choice: quit and leave with his money or continue playing (the player is allowed one mistaken identity; the chance to ask a panel of experts for help; or a narrow down to three possibilities). Money increases with each additional challenge and if he identifies all twelve strangers, he wins $500,000. The pilot presentation aired from December 18 to December 22, 2006.

Host: Penn Jillette. **Panel of Experts:** Mark Edgar Stevens (*body language expert*); Stacy Kaiser (*psycho therapist*); Bill Stanton (*private detective*).

4344 *If I Had a Chance.* (Pilot; Variety; NBC; Aug. 14, 1947). What career would a celebrity have chosen if he or she were given a second chance? That was the idea behind a proposal where celebrities appeared to tell you what might have been had they not chosen show business. Here, model Carol Brooks said she by-passed a nursing career to become a night club singer; actress Jessica Dragonette would have become a museum curator; Russ Case (RCA Records music director) had plans to become a car designer; and commentator Ben Grauer would have become a singer.

Host: Robert P. Lieb. **Announcer:** Roger Bowman.

4345 *If I Had a Million.* (Pilot; Anthology; NBC; Dec. 31, 1973). An unknown, wealthy young man randomly selects a name from a phone book. That person anonymously receives a check for one million dollars and the proposed series was to relate how the money helps or hinders the recipient.

Cast: Peter Kastner (*The Millionaire*).

4346 *If I Love You, Am I Trapped Forever?* (Pilot; Comedy; CBS; Mar. 22, 1974). The trials and tribulations of a group of close-knit high school friends: twins Leah and Sophie Pennington; the non-conformist Alan Bennett; the always gloomy Doomed; and the wealthy Carleton Penner. Other regular are Alice, Alan's mother; Alan's grandfather; Gwen, a student; and Lucius, the coach.

Cast: Tannis G. Montgomery (*Leah Pennington*); Denise Nickerson (*Sophie Pennington*); Teddy Eccles (*Alan Bennett*); Rod Berger (*Doomed*); Paul Clemens (*Carleton Penner*); Elinor Donahue (*Alice Bennett*); Liam Dunn (*Grandfather Bennett*); Vicky Huxtable (*Gwen Graney*); Joe DiReda (*Lucius Luther*).

4347 *If Not for You.* (Series; Comedy; CBS; 1995). Jessie Kent is an audio book producer. She is engaged to Elliott Borden, an architect. Craig Schaeffer is a producer at Gopher Records, a recording studio in Minneapolis. He is engaged to Melanie, a dull woman who happens to be a psychologist.

A chance meeting at a restaurant brings Jessie and Craig together and it is a love at first sight. Craig and Jessie find they have a lot in common and want to be with each other. Unfortunately, they are each engaged to someone else. The short lived (four episode) program really didn't have a chance to establish what would actually happen, but in its brief presentation, Jessie and Craig carry on a secret romance with each other hoping to build up the courage to break off their other relationships. Other regulars are Cal, Craig's audio engineer, and Eileen, a voice actor and gopher.

Cast: Elizabeth McGovern (*Jessie Kent*); Hank Azaria (*Craig Schaffer*); Debra Jo Rupp (*Eileen Mott*); Jane Sibbett (*Melanie*); Peter Krause (*Elliott Borden*); Reno Wilson (*Bobby*); Jim Turner (*Cal*).

4348 *If You Knew Tomorrow.* (Pilot; Drama; NBC; Oct. 7, 1958). Ned Carver is a newscaster with a very unusual teletype machine — it reports news that will happen instead of what has happened. Ned's attempts to help the people whose lives are affected by the future were to be the focal point of the proposal.

Cast: Bruce Gordon (*Ned Carver*).

4349 *If You Lived Here, You'd Be Home by Now.* (Pilot; Comedy; Unaired; Produced for Fox in 2006). A corporate, less-than-desirable housing complex is the setting for a proposal about a group of young friends struggling to make ends meet.

Cast: Boris Kodjoe *(Brad)*; Cameron Richardson *(Amy)*; Zac Efron *(Cody)*; Brendan Hines *(Scott)*; Jennifer Coolidge *(Sherry)*; Reg Rogers *(Curtis)*.

4350 *The Igor Cassini Show.* (Series; Interview; DuMont; 1953–1954). Newspaper columnist Igor Cassini oversees a program of celerity interviews.

4351 *I'll Bet.* (Series; Game; NBC; 1965). Two married couples compete. A question is asked of one mate via a telephone (to prevent the other player from hearing it). The telephoned player then silently bets points (from 25 to 100) as to whether or not his mate can or can't answer it. The question is read aloud and the mate's answers determine the score. The team with the highest score is the winner and receives merchandise prizes.

Host: Jack Narz.

4352 *I'll Buy That.* (Series; Game; CBS; 1953–1954). An object, submitted by a home viewer, is put up for sale. A celebrity panel then questions the host regarding the article's identity. Each question raises the purchase price from five dollars to a limit of one hundred dollars. Contestants, chosen from the studio audience, then receive the opportunity to identify the article. A correct guess awards the player the purchase price of the article and the opportunity to triple his money by answering three questions. If the player takes the challenge, he must answer all three questions correctly. Failure to so costs him his money and his prize becomes the article he identified.

Host: Mike Wallace. **Panelists:** Hans Conried, Vanessa Brown, Robin Chandler, Albert Mooreland, Audrey Meadows. **Commercial Spokeswoman:** Robin Chandler.

4353 *I'll Fly Away.* (Series; Drama; NBC; 1991–1993). A social awareness program that is set in the South during the fledging Civil Rights movement of the late 1950s. Here Forrest Bedford is a liberal prosecuting attorney who is basically satisfied with his life. He is a widower and the father of three children: John Morgan, Francie and Nathan. Lilly Harper, an African-American woman, cares for them (their housekeeper). Stories follow Forrest as he slowly becomes involved with civil rights issues through his cases; his children's efforts to adjust to a new situation; and Lilly's personal involvement with the movement.

Cast: Sam Waterson *(Forrest Bedford)*; Regina Taylor *(Lilly Harper)*; Jeremy London *(Nathaniel "Nathan" Bedford)*; Ashlee Levitch *(Francie Bedford)*; John Aaron Bennett *(John Morgan Bedford)*; Kathryn Harrold *(Christina LeKatzis)*; Michael Genevie *(Winset Carter)*.

4354 *I'll Never Forget What's Her Name.* (Pilot; Comedy; ABC; Mar. 29, 1976). Rosa Dolores is a New York girl who dreams of becoming a star in Hollywood. Her adventures with her girlfriend (Lillian) and her ex-con boyfriend (Howie) as she struggles to make a name for herself was the focal point of the unsold series.

Cast: Rita Moreno *(Rosa Dolores)*; Yvonne Wilder *(Lillian)*; Hamilton Camp *(Howie Weston)*.

4355 *Illeana.* (Pilot; Comedy; Unaired; Produced by E! in 2005). Illeana Douglas is an actress who, after becoming fed up with the glitz and glamour of show business, quits the Hollywood acting scene for a job as a grocery store clerk. The proposal was to follow Illena as she attempts to adjust to a new life style — a life style she finds is hampered by her celebrity status.

Cast: Illeana Douglas *(Herself)*.

4356 *The Ilona Massey Show.* (Series; Variety; DuMont; 1954–1955). Music and songs set against the background of a Continental supper club.

Host: Ilona Massey. **Music:** The Irving Fields Trio.

4357 *I'm a Big Girl Now.* (Series; Comedy; ABC; 1980–1981). The original format, episodes 1 through 17, relates the story of Diana Cassidy, a divorcee with a young daughter (Rebecca) and her father, Benjamin Douglas, just divorced after 34 years of marriage, as they attempt to share an apartment and help each other through the difficult times. Diana's efforts to prove to her intrusive and acerbic father, who still treats her like a child, that she is a big girl now is the actual focal point of stories. Without explanation, the remaining episodes (18 through 20) changes the format of the program to depict Diana, employed by the Kramer Research and Testing Company (a think tank in Washington, D.C.) in the above episodes, as a columnist for a newspaper called *The Arlington Dispatch* in Washington. Edie McKendrick, her employer in the first 17 episodes, is now the paper's editor, and her previous co-workers, Karen Hawks and Neal Stryker, are now reporters for the paper. The program ended its first run production after producing three of the newer episodes. Benjamin is a dentist; Walter is Diana's brother; and Preston Kramer is the research company owner. Diana Canova performs the theme, "I'm a Big Girl Now."

Cast: Diana Canova *(Diana Cassidy)*; Danny Thomas *(Benjamin Douglas)*; Sheree North *(Edie McKendrick)*; Rori King *(Rebecca Cassidy)*; Michael Durrell *(Walter Douglas)*; Deborah Baltzell *(Karen Hawks)*; Martin Short *(Neal Stryker)*; Joan Wells *(Polly Douglas)*; Richard McKenzie *(Preston Kramer)*.

4358 *I'm a Celebrity: Get Me Out of Here!* (Series; Reality; ABC; 2003). Ten celebrities of varying notoriety are brought together and placed in the rather inhospitable Australian rain forest. Here, removed from their comfortable lifestyle, the celebrities must learn how to survive on limited rations and primitive living conditions. They are presented with survival tasks and compete for a large cash prize (to be donated to charity) and the title "King (or Queen) of the Jungle." Toll free numbers are offered to viewers to vote for their favorite celebrities and keep them in the outpost camp; celebrities who receive the least amount of votes are eliminated from the competition. John Lehr hosts. Melissa Rivers, Alana Stewart, Robin Leach, Maria Conchita Alonso, Nikki Schieler Ziering, Tyson Beckford, Dowtown Julie Brown, Bruce Jenner, John Melendez and Chris Judd are the celebrities.

A revised version appeared in 2009 with Mayleene Klass and Damien Fahey as the hosts. The celebrities, stranded in the Costa Rican jungle were Stephen Baldwin, Janice Dickinson, Lou Diamond Phillips, Sanjaya Malakar, Spencer Pratt, Heidi Montag, John Salley, Frances Callier, Angela Shelton, Torrie Wilson and Patti Blogojevich (wife of former Illinois Governor, Rod Blogojevich).

4359 *I'm Dickens ... He's Fenster.* (Series; Comedy; ABC; 1962–1963). Harold ("Harry") Dickens and Archibald ("Arch") Fenster have been friends for ten years. They are carpenters and work for the Bannister Construction Company in Los Angeles. Harry is married and henpecked; Arch is a swinging young bachelor with more girls than he can handle.

Harry married Katherine ("Kate") Conway in 1953. Harry, the shop foreman at Bannister, is a bit of a klutz and not very handy when it comes to making repairs around the house (for example, he has "this thing about magnets" and always uses ones that are too powerful for the job at hand). Kate, a stunning blonde, dyed her hair black when she and Harry were dating; she became a natural blonde after she married.

Arch, famous for "his little black book" (a 300-page, six-by-nine-inch soft cover), is more competent than Harry and can usually repair the damage Harry's bungling has caused.

Melvin ("Mel") Warshaw, a fellow carpenter, has 11 kids, two dogs and three cats; his never-seen wife is named Isabel. Robert ("Bob") Mulligan is also a carpenter and constantly teases Harry about his foul-ups. Bob calls Arch "Lover Boy" and has a never-seen wife named Eloise. Joe Bentley is a fellow carpenter; Myron Bannister is the owner of the company and, strange as it may seem, the carpenters do not use power tools.

Program Open: "*I'm Dickens ... He's Fenster ...* Starring Marty Ingels and John Astin ... with Emmaline Henry. Created and produced by Leonard Stern."

Cast: John Astin (*Harry Dickens*); Marty Ingels (*Arch Fenster*); Emmaline Henry (*Kate Dickens*); Dave Ketchum (*Mel Warshaw*); Henry Beckman (*Bob Mulligan*); Frank DeVol (*Myron Bannister*).

4360   *I'm Home.* (Pilot; Comedy; Fox; Aug. 8, 1990). Events in the lives of the Singers (parents Charlene and Ronald and their grown daughters, Carrie and Jennifer) a wealthy Beverly Hills family. Sarah is their housekeeper. Franne Gold performs the theme, "Are You Going My Way."

Cast: Andrea Martin (*Charlene Singer*); Tom Sharp (*Ronald Singer*); Stacy Galina (*Carrie Singer*); Laurel Morgan (*Jennifer Singer*); Shelley Morrison (*Sarah Santos*); Rae Allen (*Charlene's mother*).

4361   *I'm in Hell.* (Pilot; Comedy; Unaired; Produced for CBS in 2007). Scott Pengarten is a man who has it all—until, while driving and using his cell phone, he crashes, is killed and sent back to earth by celestial powers to experience life without all the privileges. The proposal was to follow Scott, now stripped of his former fabulous life, as he tries to live as the common man.

Cast: David Cross (*Scott Pengarten*); Erika Christensen (*Jennifer*); Jason Biggs (*Nick*); Timm Sharp (*Fisher*).

4362   *I'm in the Band.* (Series; Comedy; Disney XD; 2009–). Tripp Campbell is a talented 15-year-old musician (guitarist) who dreams of becoming part of a rock band. With a hope to further that dream, Tripp enters a radio contest and, to his surprise, he wins an audition and dinner with his favorite band, Iron Weasel. Tripp's Jimmi Hendrix–like skills impress the band and he is asked to become their lead guitar. Tripp's mother, Beth, however, has doubts, feeling he is too young to play with a band made up of three middle-aged stooges. Tripp convinces his divorced mother that the band members will be good role models for him and help him through his high school years with the ultimate goal of turning him into a real rock star. Stories relate the mishaps that occur as Tripp, mentored by three morons, seeks his dream. Derek Jupiter is the band's lead singer; Burger Pitt is the always cheerful bassist; Ash is the simple-minded drummer. Izzy is Tripp's friend, an aspiring singer who shares his mishaps with the band.

Cast: Logan Miller (*Tripp Campbell*); Steve Valentine (*Derek Jupiter*); Greg Baker (*Burger Pitt*); Stephen Full (*Ash*); Caitlyn Taylor Love (*Isabella "Izzy" Fuentes*); Beth Littleford (*Beth Campbell*).

4363   *I'm Paige Wilson.* (Pilot; Drama; Unaired; Produced for the WB in 2006). The experiences of Paige Wilson, a pretty, bright 27-year-old congressional aide in Washington, D.C.

Cast: Jaime Ray Newman (*Paige Wilson*); Mary Page Keller (*Nicole*

Shelton); Merle Dandridge (*Gloria*); Reggie Austin (*Larry Gearman*); Will Lyman (*Ben Foxworthy*); Neal Bledsoe (*Michael McGinty*).

4364   *I'm Telling.* (Series; Game; NBC; 1987-1988). A variation on *The Newlywed Game.* Three two-member teams compete, each composed of an actual brother and sister. In round one, the brothers are isolated offstage and their sisters are asked three questions regarding their relationship. Their answers are recorded. The brothers are brought on stage. The brothers are asked the same questions. If they match their sister's answers they score points. Round two reverses round one. The highest scoring team wins a $1000 savings bond.

Host: Laurie Faso. **Announcer:** Dean Goss.

4365   *I'm the Law.* (Series; Crime Drama; Syn.; 1953). George Kirby is a tough, no-nonsense plainclothes police detective with the N.Y.P.D. His not so orthodox investigations as he deals his own brand of justice but always keeping within the limits of the law are the focal point of stories. Also known as *The George Raft Casebook.*

Cast: George Raft (*Lt. George Kirby*).

4366   *I'm with Busey.* (Series; Comedy; Comedy Central; 2003). Adam de la Pena is a young writer fascinated by actor Gary Busey. He has idolized him since childhood and, by chance, the two meet and become friends. Gary takes Adam under his wing and, in what is made to look like an unscripted documentary, Gary helps Adam with his writings about the world based on his own warped view of life.

Stars: Gary Busey, Adam de la Pena.

4367   *I'm with Her.* (Series; Comedy; ABC; 2003-2004). Patrick Owen teaches English literature at Center High School in West Hollywood. He is dating Alexis Young, better known as Alex, a beloved movie actress (called "America's Sweetheart"). Patrick and Alex met by accident—her dog bit him and he and Alex found an instant attraction to each other.

Alex is 31 years old and has been in show business for 12 years. She made her debut in a movie called *Cause for Alarm* (playing Hooker Number 3). She made 20 additional films and received an Oscar nomination for *September Song.* Alex's real name is Alexis Baldzikowski. She was born in Tennessee and raised by her mother, Suzanne, an actress who gave up her career to raise her and her sister, Cherie. Suzanne drank, smoked and was a bit wacky (she lived in a tree for three years; cooked food in pickle juice) and always embarrassed Alex (for example, at Alex's high school graduation, Suzanne's blouse just happened to pop open and expose her breasts). Suzanne had her one success as the female lead in a production of *The Music Man.*

Alex is with the William Morris Agency and Cherie works by her side as her hairdresser, publicist, makeup artist and wardrobe girl (she lives with Alex in her Beverly Hills mansion). Cherie is 29 years old and is hoping to become a fashion designer. She has a fascination with fire and loves to roller blade in hot pants. She had breast implants and can be seen naked on the Internet (at www.gunsandbuns.net).

Patrick attended Harvard Law School but dropped out after two years when he felt it was not the right career choice for him. He returned to his hometown of Connecticut and enrolled in State University to acquire his teaching degree.

Stevie Hanson is Danny's friend, a substitute teacher. Stories follow not only Alex and Patrick's work lives but their efforts to establish and enjoy a relationship away from the glitter of Hollywood.

Cast: Teri Polo (*Alex Young*); David Sutcliffe (*Patrick Owen*); Rhea Seehorn (*Cheri Baldzikowski*); Danny Comden (*Stevie Hanson*); Cybill Shepherd (*Suzanne Baldzikowski*); Alexandra Deberry (*Young Alex; flashbacks*); Kennedy Noel (*Young Cherie; flashbacks*).

4368 *I'm with Stupid.* (Pilot; Comedy; Unaired; Produced for NBC in 2008). Paul has the weight of the world on his shoulders. He lives in his own apartment but is wheelchair bound and desperate for attention. Sheldon is broke, homeless and the only friend Paul seems to have. In order to have the companionship he is seeking, Paul invites Sheldon to move in with him. The proposal was to relate their Odd Couple–like mishaps. Leah, a sexy calendar girl; Sid, a cool and charismatic dude, and Graham, who speaks through a voice box, are their neighbors.

Cast: Christopher Thornton *(Paul)*; Kevin Daniels *(Sheldon)*; Teal Sherer *(Leah)*; Darryl "Chill" Mitchell *(Sid)*; Bryan Dilbeck *(Graham)*.

4369 *I'm with the Band.* (Pilot; Comedy; Unaired; Produced for HBO in 2010). It is the 1960s and Pamela Des Barres is a young woman obsessed with the various rock bands that are appearing on the scene. The proposal was to follow Pamela as she attaches herself to members of various rock bands.

Cast: Zooey Deschanel *(Pamela Des Barres)*.

4370 *Imagination Movers.* (Series; Children; Disney; 2008). Imagination Movers, a New Orleans based music group, oversees a program that encourages children to utilize their creative skills to solve everyday problems.

Wendy Calio, Frank Crim, David Poche comprise the group.

4371 *Imagine That.* (Series; Comedy; NBC; 2002). Josh Miller and Kenny Fleck are friends who work as comedy writers for the TV sketch show *Barb Thompson's Imagine That.* Barb Thompson, the star of the show, is also their boss, the head writer, a flaky woman with her mind on everything but comedy writing. She is also stern and Josh is a doormat; he let's Barb take total advantage of him. The short-lived program (two episodes) follows the events in Josh and Kenny's lives as they try to provide comedy material for a weekly show.

Josh is married to Wendy, a lawyer, and uses aspects of their married life as a basis for comedy skits. Tabitha, Rina and Koozman are fellow staff writers for the show. When Josh gets upset he goes to Hardy's, a fast food store, to have a Hardy Burger.

Cast: Hank Azaria *(Josh Miller)*; Jayne Brook *(Wendy Miller)*; Katey Sagal *(Barb Thompson)*; Joshua Malina *(Kenny Fleck)*; Suzy Nakamura *(Rina Oh)*; Julia Schultz *(Tabitha)*; David Pressman *(Koozman)*.

4372 *The Immortal.* (Series; Adventure; ABC; 1970-1971). Jordan Braddock is a billionaire and the owner of Braddock Industries. He is also quite elderly, suffering from a heart condition and doctors believe nothing can save him. In an attempt to give Jordan a little more time, he is given a transfusion of Type O Negative blood that was donated earlier by Ben Richards, a Braddock Industries employee (in the automotive division. Ben is 43 years old and has never been sick a day in his life). Within hours Jordan miraculously recovers, looking and feeling younger. Matthew Pearce, Jordan's doctor, conducts tests and discovers that Ben's blood is quite unusual. It possesses rare factors that make him immune to old age and disease. Further tests reveal that Jordan's rejuvenation is only temporary; to sustain it, periodic transfusions are necessary. To insure the supply of life-saving blood, Jordan has Ben imprisoned, then begins a search to find Jason Richards, Ben's long-lost brother (separated as infants) who may also possess the same blood antibodies. Jordan's plan is thwarted, however, when Ben escapes and begins his own search to find Jason. Episodes follow Ben's search for Jason—and his efforts to escape capture by Fletcher, the henchman Jordan has ordered to find and bring back Ben. Janet Braddock is Jordan's younger wife; Sylvia Cartwright is Ben's girlfriend.

Program Open: "This man [Ben Richards] has a single advantage over other men. He is immune to every known disease, including old age. Periodic transfusions of his blood can give other men a second or third lifetime, perhaps more. [Ben:] "I didn't ask for this. I was a test driver. I liked the job. The doctor told me I had a kind of special blood. But I know this. Everything they're offering I don't want. I gotta live free."

Cast: Christopher George *(Ben Richards)*; Barry Sullivan *(Jordan Braddock)*; Don Knight *(Fletcher)*; Michael Strong *(Jason Richards)*; Jessica Walter *(Janet Braddock)*; Ralph Bellamy *(Dr. Matthew Pearce)*; Carol Lynley *(Sylvia Cartwright)*.

4373 *The Immortal.* (Series; Adventure; Syn.; 2000-2001). Rafael "Rafe" Caine is an Immortal, a man who has sworn an oath of vengeance to send demons back to hell. It was while on a trip to Japan in the year 1638 to acquire silk and spices for his father, an importer, that destiny would change young Rafe's life. A severe storm sinks the ship on which Rafe is traveling. Rafe manages to swim to shore and after three days of wandering, meets a man named Yashiro (Robert Ito). Yashiro welcomes Rafe into his home. Rafe remained and eventually married Yashiro's daughter, Mikko (Grace Park). They built a home near a small stream and were blessed with a child. One day, in 1643, evil demons named Mallos (Keith Martin Corday) and Vashista (Kira Clavell) kill Mikko and steal Rafe's child. An enraged Rafe burns his house to the ground, forges a sword of revenge and swears an oath: "I'll hunt them forever and never rest until they're dead. With this sword I seek an oath of vengeance. The evil ones will know my name and fear it. I will send them back to hell with this blade and never stop until it's done." "Me too," says the man who is at his side, Rafe's companion, who is known only as Goodwin. Rafael is the Chosen One and Goodwin his Squire.

It is not until the year 2000 that Rafael and Goodwin acquire a companion—Dr. Sarah Beckman, a paranormal physicist who specializes in psychokinetic exploration (Sarah was threatened by a demon when Rafe came to her rescue. When Sarah saw Rafe dispose of the demon by using his sword to behead it and send it back to hell, she became intrigued and attached herself to Rafe and Goodwin in the hope of acquiring material on demons for her studies).

Rafael can smell demons when they are near and has a plan for everything ("We make it up as we go along"). Demons call Rafe "The Vengeful One." Rafe can be killed, but Yashiro taught him how to survive. "If the demons win," says Rafe, "the world would be plunged into darkness."

"Goodwin," Rafe says "is a good companion but don't turn to him for help in a fight—he's a coward." Goodwin contends "I'm not a coward, I'm practical."

Sarah rides with Rafe and Goodwin in a mobile home. She has invented the Sonic Transponder to study subjects believed to be suffering from demonic possession (they react to the ultrasonic stimulus; Rafe calls it "a dog whistle for demons"). Sarah thinks she, Rafe and Goodwin make an excellent team ("With your experience and my research, we're going to kick some serious demon butt").

While Rafe seeks to destroy evil and find his daughter, he must also contend with Randall (Bret Harte), a demon hunter known as "The Collector." Randall comes from the fifth level of Hell hunting. He is relentless and his mission is to find demons that have strayed from the darkness of evil to the goodness of light and return them to evil by beheading them.

Program Open: "An oath sworn is an oath answered. An oath of vengeance for a life taken, a past destroyed, a future threatened. Enemy of darkness, eternal, he walks the earth relentless. His mission is to hunt the messengers and drive them back to hell. Now the light of earth depends on the Immortal."

Cast: Lorenzo Lamas *(Rafe Caine)*; Steve Braun *(Goodwin)*; April Telek *(Dr. Sandra Beckman)*.

4374   *The Imogene Coca Show.* (Series; Variety; NBC; 1954-1955). Actress-comedienne Imogene Coca hosts a program of comedy sketches coupled with songs by her musical guests.

Host: Imogene Coca. **Regulars:** Billy DeWolfe, Ruth Donnelly, Hal March, David Burns, Bibi Osterwald. **Orchestra:** George Bassman.

4375   *The Imperial Grand Band.* (Pilot; Comedy; ABC; Feb. 22, 1975). Following the death of her parents, Sue Barton inherits their hotel, the Imperial Grand, which is badly in need of repair. The proposal was to depict her efforts to restore the hotel and make it profitable once again. The title refers to her brother, Dick's band, who perform at the hotel. Other regulars are Skip and Marvin, band members; Albert, the eccentric hotel manager; and Margaret, Albert's wife.

Cast: Libby Stevens *(Sue Barton)*; Jaro Dick *(Dick Barton)*; Shimmy Piener *(Skip Jenkins)*; Martin Short *(Marvin Baxter)*; Jack Creley *(Albert Flynn)*; Kay Hawtrey *(Margaret Flynn)*.

4376   *Important Things with Demetri Martin.* (Series; Comedy; Comedy Central; 2009). An "important topic" is established for each episode (for example, "power," "timing"). Comedian Demetri Martin then proceeds to explore the topic via monologues, music skits, animated images and brief interactions with the studio audience.

Host: Demetri Martin. **Regulars:** Natalie Gold, H. Jon Benjamin, Meghan Rafferty, Damian Schilles, Becky Ann Baker, Tom Kanes, Jon Kohler, Chazz Mendez, Dan Ziskie.

4377   *The Imposter.* (Pilot; Adventure; NBC; Mar. 18, 1975). Joe Tyler is a former Army intelligence officer who possesses a unique talent for impersonation. He now works as an off-Broadway actor to cover his real activities as a troubleshooter for hire. The unsold series was to relate his hazardous assignments as he impersonates other people to solve crimes.

Cast: Paul Hecht *(Joe Tyler)*.

4378   *Improv Tonight.* (Series; Comedy; Syn.; 1988). A weekly showcase for stand-up comedians. Acts are performed in front of a live audience and presented as if the viewer were part of an improv club audience.

Host: Budd Friedman.

4379   *In a Heartbeat.* (Series; Drama; Disney; 2000-2001). Val Lanier, Tyler Connell and Hank Beecham are teenagers attending high school and working as Emergency Medical Technicians under the supervision of Alex Freeman, the man who runs the local EMT station. Val is a cheerleader; Tyler and Hank are members of the football team. Jamie Waite, the fourth member of the team, has been arrested for stealing but is out on parole and assigned to community service with the EMT. Brooke is Val's 12-year-old sister (and Alex's assistant, a genius at organization); Caitie Roth is Val's friend and stories follow Val, Tyler and Hank as they deal with the pressures of school and work while at the same time trying to live the lives of normal teenagers.

Cast: Reagan Pasternak *(Val Lanier)*; Danso Gordon *(Hank Beecham)*; Christopher Ralph *(Jamie Waite)*; Shawn Ashmore *(Tyler Connell)*; Lauren Collins *(Brooke Lanier)*; Kevin Hicks *(Alex Freeman)*; Jackie Rosenbaum *(Caitie Roth)*.

4380   *In Case of Emergency.* (Series; Comedy; ABC; 2007).

Harry Kennison, Kelly Lee, Jason Ventress and Sherman Yablonsky are graduates of Westwood South High School, Class of 1987. Today, they each have nobody (except each other, as they are still friends) but no one else to put down in case of emergency.

Harry is divorced, the father of a young son (Dylan) and a greeting card writer. Kelly, a Korean girl with a promising future, is a masseuse at Korean Massage. Jason is an investment broker who performs shady deals (he later works as a volunteer nurse at Westside Hospital and begins a relationship with Dr. Joanna Lupone). Sherman, once overweight, has become a diet guru and the author of the book *Eating for Mama — Confessions of a Mother's Best Eater.* Unfortunately, he has a sweet tooth and his efforts to acquire snacks often destroys his public image. Stories follow the ups and downs (but mostly downs) of the four friends as they struggle to cope with life.

In case of emergency, the four have the following phone numbers: Harry (310-555-0135); Kelly (213-555-0169); Jason (310-555-0127) and Sherman (818-555-0156).

Cast: Jonathan Silverman *(Harry Kennison)*; Kelly Hu *(Kelly Lee)*; David Arquette *(Jason Ventress)*; Greg Germann *(Sherman Yablonsky)*; Jackson Bond *(Dylan Kennison)*; Lori Loughlin *(Dr. Joanna Lupone)*; Arbell Field *(Stephanie; Sherman's ex wife)*; Jane Seymour *(Donna Ventress; Jason's mother)*.

4381   *In Common.* (Series; Game; CBS; 1954). Three specially selected contestants who have never met, but who each have something in common, compete. Each player has three minutes to question the other and determine the common dominator. Players receive merchandise prizes for participating.

Host: Ralph Story.

4382   *In Gayle We Trust.* (Series; Comedy; Internet; 2009). Maple Grove is a small town populated by a host of colorful characters, a number of whom need professional counseling to help them deal with their problems. Gayle Evans is an insurance agent who finds herself saddled with a second job — helping those characters with their endless problems. Gayle's sound advice and pleasant disposition have made her a much sought after healer and stories follow Gayle as she involves herself in other people's problems. Mike is Gayle's husband; Charlie is their son.

Cast: Elisa Donovan *(Gayle Evans)*; Brian Palermo *(Mike Evans)*; Shane Cambria *(Charlie Evans)*; Jennifer Chang *(Anna)*; Jack Donner *(Lloyd Adams)*; Eric George *(Mark Bronson)*; Kirk Fox *(Jack the Plumber)*; Ginger Gonzaga *(Kim)*.

4383   *The In-Laws.* (Series; Comedy; NBC; 2002). Matt and Alexandra (called Alex) are a happily married couple with one big problem — a lack of money to buy their own home (Matt is currently in cooking school). To solve their problem, Matt and Alex move in with her parents, Victor and Marlene Pellet.

Victor is overly protective of his daughter; Marlene has traded cooking and cleaning for a job in real estate, leaving Matt to deal with Victor while Alex tends to the household chores. Matt naturally clashes with Victor and stories relate the problems that befall the newlyweds, especially Matt, as he attempts to live with his in-laws.

Victor ran an armored car service called Pellet Armored. He drives a classic Cadillac Fleetwood car that is a gas-guzzler (8 miles per gallon highway; 4 miles city). Alex knows Victor believes she is perfect — "And I'm not going to burst that bubble" when she does something wrong and tries to hide it from him. Alex and Matt are hoping to open a restaurant when Matt graduates.

Cast: Elon Gold *(Matt Landis)*; Bonnie Somerville *(Alex Landis)*; Dennis Farina *(Victor Pellet)*; Jean Smart *(Marlene Pellet)*.

4384   *In Like Flynn.* (Pilot; Adventure; ABC; Sept. 14, 1985). Terri MacLaine is a female novelist who writes *In Like Flynn* adventure novels under the pen name of Darryl F. Raymond. She poses as Darryl's researcher and the proposal was to relate her escapades as she gathers story material. Other regulars are Mr. Fulton, Terri's publisher (Action Novels); and Beattie Woodstock, the freelance photographer who helps Terri.

Cast: Jenny Seagrove *(Terri MacLaine)*; Murray Cruchley *(Mr. Fulton)*; William Gray Espy *(Beattie Woodstock)*.

4385   *In Living Color.* (Series; Comedy; Fox; 1990–1994). A series of risqué (for the time) skits that spoof everything—from products to TV shows to movies to the everyday man and woman and the challenging situations they face. While a majority of the cast was African-American, the program saw no ethnic barriers—as it poked fun at all races. The program featured many skits, several of which became very popular; among them were *Fire Marshal Bill* (Jim Carrey as a fireman whose demonstrations on fire safety found him becoming a victim of what he was trying to prevent); *Handi-Man* (Marlon Wayans as a handicapped super hero); *Men on Film* (Damon Wayans and David Alan Grier as gay film reviewers); *Homey D. Clown* (Damon Wayans as an ex con who works as a nasty clown).

Regulars: Damon Wayans, Keenan Ivory Wayans, Kim Wayans, Marlon Wayans, Shawn Wayans, Jim Carrey, David Alan Grier, Tommy Davidson, Keymah Crystal T'Keyah, Carrie Ann Inaba, Kelly Coffield Park, Alexandra Wentworth, Kim Coles, Jamie Fox, Steve Park, Anne-Marie Johnson, Marc Wilmore, Reggie McFadden. **Dancers (Fly Girls):** Jennifer Lopez, Lisa Joann Thompson, Lisa Marie Todd, Deidre Lang, Lauree-Ann Gibson, Michelle Whitney-Morrison, Cari French, Masako Willis, Jossie Thacker. **Music:** Tom Rizzo, David Aguirre.

4386   *In Person with Maureen O'Boyle.* (Series; Talk; Syn.; 1996). Newswoman Maureen O'Boyle tackles current (and sometimes controversial) topics with appropriate guests discussing both side of the issue.

4387   *In Plain Sight.* (Series; Crime Drama; USA; 2008). Mary Shannon is a U.S. Marshal attached to WITSEC (the Federal Witness Protection Program). She is based in Albuquerque, New Mexico and is partners with Marshall Mann. Mary's job is to protect and manage relocated federal witnesses (people who are relocated to the Southwest to begin a new life under a new name for helping authorities collar criminals). Stories follow Mary and Marshall as they risk their lives to keep federally protected witness safe.

Mary, who must keep the true nature of her job secret, lives with her mother, Jinx, and her younger sister, Brandi. To help the people she is assigned to protect, Mary (and Marshall) must often pretend to be somebody else (from marriage counselor to mother) to help witnesses make an easy transition into their new lives.

Jinx adores her daughters, but has never really been a supportive mother. She appears to be adverse to work but loves to drink and has had many romantic interludes. Brandi is a bit more ambitious than her mother but has a tendency to use drugs and fall for the worst possible men.

Stan McQueen is Mary's superior, a chief inspector for WITSEC; Raphael is Mary's on-and-off again boyfriend.

Cast: Mary McCormack *(Mary Shannon)*; Frederick Weller *(Marshall Mann)*; Lesley Ann Warren *(Jinx Shannon)*; Nichole Hiltz *(Brandi Shannon)*; Paul Ben-Victor *(Stan McQueen)*; Cristian DeLa Fuente *(Raphael Ramirez)*.

4388   *In Record Time.* (Series; Game; NBC; 1951). The Alternate title for *The Art Ford Show.* See this title for information.

4389   *In Search Of....* (Series; Documentary; Syn.; 1976–1982). An attempt to offer possible explanations for some of the mysteries that surround us in our everyday lives (for example ghosts, myths, psychic happenings).

Host/Narrator: Leonard Nimoy.

4390   *In Search of the Partridge Family.* (Series; Reality; VH-1; 2004). An attempt to recreate the 1970s ABC series *The Partridge Family* with a new cast of singers that resemble Keith, Shirley, Laurie, Danny, Tracy and Chris. After selecting look-alike finalists from open auditions around the country, the finalists are brought to Los Angeles to be coached by their real life counterparts (Shirley Jones, David Cassidy and Danny Bonaduce) and compete in various singing and acting competitions. Toll free phone numbers allow viewers to vote for their favorites. The ultimate prize was to star in a pilot for an update (but now unsold) version of the original *Partridge Family.*

Talent Agents Cast: Adam Baldwin *(Danny Love)*; Jay Harrington *(Paul Ryan)*; Peter Coyote *(Virgil Webster)*; Katie Finneran *(Melody Sin)*; Rachel Nichols *(Rebecca Locke)*. **Winners:** Suzanne Sole *(Shirley Partridge)*; Leland Grant *(Keith Partridge)*; Emily Stone *(Laurie Partridge)*; Spencer Tuskowski *(Danny Partridge)*; Hannah Leigh Dworken *(Tracy Partridge)*; Anthony Skillman *(Chris Partridge)*.

4391   *In Security.* (Pilot; Comedy; CBS; July 7, 1982). Mayfield's is a large department store in Philadelphia. Eldon Radford is the head of security and his officers are Annie, Doris, Rudy and Henry. The proposal was to relate their mishaps as they attempt to protect the store. Other regulars are Garrett, Annie's neighbor; and Jennie, Garrett's daughter.

Cast: John Randolph *(Eldon Radford)*; Annie Potts *(Annie Leighton)*; Cara Williams *(Doris Gleen)*; James Keane *(Rudy DeMayo)*; Peter Jurasik *(Henry)*; James Murtaugh *(Garrett Lloyd)*; Kari Ann Patterson *(Jennie Lloyd)*.

4392   *In Security.* (Pilot; Comedy; Unaired; Produced for NBC in 1992). The after hours activities of a group of security guards in a New York high-rise office building.

Cast: Trevor Eve *(Riddle)*; Cathy Lind Hayes *(Cooper)*; Kris Kamm *(Pete Johnson)*; Richard Schiff *(Hasselhoff)*; Eric Allan Kramer *(DuPont)*.

4393   *In Security.* (Pilot; Drama; Unaired; Produced for TBS in 2010). Meg and Nikki are sisters who head a private security firm whose clients include the super elite. The proposal was to relate their case assignments and efforts to deal with personal and family issues.

Cast: Constance Zimmer *(Meg)*; Kat Foster *(Nikki)*; Hal Linden *(Meg and Niiki's father)*; Tina Majorino *(Cricket)*; Kevin Michael Richardson *(Ben)*; Amir Arison *(Eton)*.

4394   *In the Beginning.* (Series; Comedy; CBS; 1978). Father Dan Cleary is an uptight, conservative priest; Sister Agnes is a free-spirited, streetwise nun. Bickering ensues when the two join forces and open a mission at 122 15th Street amid the hookers, drunks, teenage gangs and runaways. Their inability to agree on issues concerning the welfare of the mission and its people is the focal point of stories.

Other regulars are Monsignor Frank Barlow, Dan's superior; Sister Lillian, Agnes's superior; and the neighborhood kids: Willie, Jerome, Tony, Bad Lincoln and Frank.

Cast: McLean Stevenson *(Father Dan Cleary)*; Priscilla Lopez *(Sister Agnes)*; Priscilla Morrill *(Sister Lillian)*; Jack Dodson *(Monsignor Frank Barlow)*; Olivia Barash *(Willie)*; Bobby Ellerbee *(Jerome Rock-*

efeller); Cosie Costa *(Tony)*; Michael Anthony *(Bad Lincoln)*; Fred Lehne *(Frank)*.

4395 *In the Dark.* (Series; Game; WB; 1998). Couples compete for prizes in a game played in total darkness (special infrared cameras allow the action to be seen by the home audience). Based on the concepts of *Beat the Clock* and *Truth or Consequences*, each of the couples that compete must perform a stunt in the dark. The show is not so much for the game aspect, but for the comical mishaps that occur as the players try to accomplish a task without being able to see what they are doing.

Host: Julian Clary.

4396 *In the Dead of Night.* (Pilot; Thriller; ABC; Aug. 30, 1969). Jonathan Fletcher is a ghost hunter who believes the paranormal exists but also knows there are people who use spirits to perpetrate frauds. He is assisted by Sajeed Rau and the proposal was to follow Jonathan as he investigates cases of residences supposedly haunted by evil spirits.

Cast: Kerwin Matthews *(Jonathan Fletcher)*; Cal Bellini *(Sajeed Rau)*.

4397 *In the Doghouse.* (Pilot; Comedy; ABC; Aug. 14, 1950). The family dog is named Rover. The master of the house (the husband here) spends much time with Rover after a fight with the wife. Opening and closing sequences are set in the doghouse where hubby's conversations with the canine set up and conclude the episode. The unsold series was to depict the marital spats of a typical American husband and wife.

Cast: George O'Hanlon *(Husband)*; Joan Dolan *(Wife)*; George Clark *(Neighbor)*.

4398 *In the Game.* (Pilot; Comedy; Unaired; Produced for ABC in 2004). Riley Reid, the daughter of a football coach, grew up with sports and, inspired by the NFL cheerleaders she saw at games, decided that she too wanted to become one. Her moves become noticed and she is plucked from the sidelines to become an on-air camera spokes girl to become "the voice of the fan." The proposal follows Riley as she interviews the fans at games to find out what they have to say. Michael is her six-year-old son.

Cast: Jennifer Love Hewitt *(Riley Reid)*; Ed O'Neill *(Buzz)*; Anthony Tavera *(Michael Riley)*; James Patrick Stuart *(T.J.)*; Josie Davis *(Brandee)*.

4399 *In the Heat of the Night.* (Series; Crime Drama; NBC, 1988–1992; CBS, 1992–1994). Sparta, Mississippi, is a small southern town with a considerable amount of crime. William O. Gillespie is the town's white police chief and Virgil Tibbs is his black chief of detectives.

William, called Bill, was born in Mississippi. He resides at 11 Vanover and has a hunting dog named Roscoe. Bill first mentions he was married to a woman named Anna Caterina but never had any children. Anna died in childbirth. "I lost him when I lost her." Later, Bill mentions he was married to a woman named Georgia Farren, who deserted him shortly after the birth of their daughter, Lana (played as an adult by Christine Elise). In 1988, Bill dated JoAnn St. John, a cashier at his favorite eatery, the Magnolia Cafe. Ten years earlier, JoAnn was a $100 a night call girl known as Kelly Kaye. Their romance ended a short time later. In 1991, Bill began a romance with Harriet DeLong, a younger woman who was also a black city councilwoman.

Virgil was born in Philadelphia and was a member of the state police department before relocating to Sparta. He tends to go by the book and often objects to Bill's sometimes unorthodox investigative procedures. Bill feels you have to think like a criminal to catch a criminal. Virgil is married to Althea, a teacher at Sparta Community High School. They are later the parents of a son they name William Calvin Tibbs.

In 1989, when Carroll O'Connor entered the hospital for by-pass surgery, the former police chief, Captain Thomas Dugan was brought out of retirement to replace him. Bill's absence was explained as the Chief attending a month-long symposium on domestic terrorism in Washington, D.C., as the representative from Mississippi. Another change occurred in 1994 when the City Council objects to Bill's relationship with Harriet and declines to renew his contract. As Bill steps down to become the county sheriff, Hamilton Forbes, a former police inspector from Memphis, Tennessee, is brought in as Sparta's new police chief. It is at this time that Virgil also leaves to complete school and become a lawyer. The series ended shortly after.

Other officers working under Bill are Parker Williams, Bubba Skinner, Wilson Sweet, Chris Rankin and Lu Ann Corbin. Based on the 1967 feature film of the same title. Bill Champlin performs the theme, "In the Heat of the Night."

Cast: Carroll O'Connor *(William Gillespie)*; Howard Rollins *(Virgil Tibbs)*; Lois Nettleton *(JoAnn St. John)*; Denise Nicholas *(Harriet DeLong)*; Anne-Marie Johnson *(Althea Tibbs)*; Joe Don Baker *(Thomas Dugan)*; David Hart *(Parker Williams)*; Alan Autry *(Bubba Skinner)*; Geoffrey Thorne *(Wilson Sweet)*; Sheryl Lynn Piland *(Chris Rankin)*; Crystal Fox *(Lu Ann Corbin)*; Carl Weathers *(Hamilton Forbes)*.

4400 *In the House.* (Pilot; Comedy; NBC; July 1, 1991). Derek Brantley is a college graduate who returns to his Detroit neighborhood to start a business and help its people. His father, Ike, is a successful businessman who frowns on his son's intentions, yearning for him to join him in the corporate world. Derek refuses and thus the proposed premise: the comical conflict between a father and his son. Originally titled *Homeboy*. Other regulars are Charlotte, Derek's aunt; Roxy, Derek's high school sweetheart; Daphne, Roxy's sister; and Dave, Derek's friend.

Cast: Bruce A. Young *(Ike Brantley)*; Don Cheadle *(Derek Brantley)*; Loretta Devine *(Aunt Charlotte)*; Vivica A. Fox *(Roxy)*; Liliani Fields *(Daphne)*; Troy Burgess *(Dave Collins)*.

4401 *In the House.* (Series; Comedy; NBC; 1995–1999). Jackie Warren is the mother of two children (Tiffany and Austin), who, after her divorce, enters the work force to make ends meet. She acquires a secretarial position at a law firm (Comstock, Nathan and Smythe) and a place to live — in the home of Marion Hill, an injured NFL star, at $200 a month rent. Marion played with the Raiders and injured himself when he ran into a goal post; he is now hoping for a comeback (he too is in need of money and lives in a room over the garage to meet expenses). Episodes follow the misadventures that occur as Jackie goes to work and Marion becomes a nanny of sorts. Marion later runs a sports health clinic with Tonia Harris, an unpredictable physical therapist. James Todd Smith uses his better known alias, rapper LL Cool J as his screen credit.

Cast: Debbie Allen *(Jackie Warren)*; L.L. Cool J *(Marion Hill)*; Maia Campbell *(Tiffany Warren)*; Jeffrey Wood *(Austin Warren)*; Kim Wayans *(Tonia Harris)*; John Amos *(Coach Sam Wilson)*; Chris Browning *(Clayton)*; Lisa Arrindell Anderson *(Heather Comstock)*; Dee Jay Daniels *(Rodney)*.

4402 *In the Kelvinator Kitchen.* (Series; Women; NBC; 1947-1948). A program of cooking advice and instruction sponsored by Kelvinator Kitchen Appliances.

Hostess: Alma Kitchell. Announcer: Ray Forrest.

4403   *In the Lion's Den.* (Pilot; Comedy; CBS; Sept. 4, 1987). Hoping to further her career in TV, Dana Woodrow, the associate producer of a New York game show (*Target Practice*) moves to San Antonio, Texas, where she becomes the producer of *In the Lion's Den*, a puppet show on KPLP-TV (a PBS station). The proposal was to relate Dana's experiences. Other regulars are Keith Warfield, the star of the show (the voice of the puppet lion Maynard), Stan, the writer; Newton, the station's fundraiser; and Kim, an employee at the station.

Cast: Wendy Crewson *(Dana Woodrow)*; Dennis Boutsikaris *(Keith Warfield)*; Marsha Gay Harden *(Kim Fellows)*; Brian Backer *(Stan Timmerton)*; Fred Applegate *(Newton Gorse)*.

4404   *In the Morgan Manner.* (Series; Variety; ABC; 1950). Singer-bandleader Russ Morgan hosts a program of music and songs that features the Russ Morgan Orchestra.

4405   *In the Motherhood.* (Series; Comedy; Internet 2007-2008). True life situations faced by mothers and their children. The six-to-eight minute episodes are written by real life mothers (submitted to the website created by Suave and Sprint) but portrayed by a professional cast. Kim, Kelly and Heather are the featured mothers. Kelly and Heather (divorced) are sisters; Ashley is Kim's daughter; Joyce is Kim and Heather's mother.

Cast: Leah Remini *(Kim)*; Jenny McCarthy *(Kelly)*; Chelsea Handler *(Heather)*; Alina Foley *(Ashley)*; Lainie Kazan, Jane Curtin *(Joyce)*; Kylee Anderson *(Kelly, age 6)*; Brian Norris *(Jonas)*; Eileen Galindo *(Maria)*.

4406   *In the Motherhood.* (Series; Comedy; ABC; 2009). Rosemary, Jane and Emily are women who are also mothers (and supposedly representative "of mothers we all know"). Rosemary has been married several times and is the mother of a teenage son (Luke). She appears to live by her own rules, enjoys the company of men but laments that being 50 years old, she will miss the perks of pregnancy (for her: getting things for free and being treated like a queen). Jane is divorced and the mother of Annie (a pre-teen, and infant Sophie). Jane works for 9 Yellow Architects and, having just returned to the office after a maternity leave, is struggling to balance her personal and business life. Emily, Jane's younger sister, is a stay-at-home mother. She is married to Jason and Esther and Bill are her children. Stories, "inspired by real life experiences of real life mothers," relate brief incidents in the daily lives of three very different women who are there for each other in the good as well as bad times. Based on the prior Internet series title. Horatio is Jane's "manny" (a male nanny).

Cast: Megan Mullally *(Rosemary)*; Cheryl Hines *(Jane)*; Jessica St. Clair *(Emily)*; RonReaco Lee *(Jason)*; Horatio Sanz *(Horatio)*; Matt Prokop *(Luke)*; Sayeed Shahid *(Bill)*; Yari Shahidi *(Esther)*; Charlotte Foley *(Annie)*.

4407   *In the Weeds.* (Pilot; Drama; Unaired; Produced for Fox in 2005). "A cool, hip" Los Angeles restaurant is the backdrop for a look at the lives of a group of people who work at the establishment.

Cast: Elizabeth Hendrickson *(Becky)*; Greg Cromer *(Adam)*; Taylor Stanley *(Martha)*; Jeremy Fonicello *(Marlon)*.

4408   *In Town Today.* (Pilot; Human Interest; NBC; Aug. 15 and 22, 1946). Two proposed ideas that have a very simple format: to take the TV camera to a specific location and interview people on the street. In the first outing, the camera caught people on Times Square in New York City. A Manhattan restaurant called the 21 Club was the setting for the second telecast where the host moved from table to table for informal chatter with the celebrities who just hap-

pened to be present: Danton Walker, Sonja Henie, Arthur William Brown, Patrice Munsel, Ray Bolger and John Loder.

Host: Ben Grauer.

4409   *In Treatment.* (Series; Drama; HBO; 2008–). The meeting between a psychiatrist (Paul Weston) and his patients are presented as a weeknight therapy session. Each night is devoted to a different patient: Laura (Monday), Alex (Tuesday), Sophie (Wednesday), Jake and Amy Bickerson (Thursday), and Paul (Friday), who meets with his therapist (Gina) to deal with his own problems (including a troubled marriage and "losing patience with my patients"). Paul is a man in his fifties who conducts his practice from his home. He is married to Kate. Gina, a retired therapist, has just turned 60 and is writing a book based on her experiences.

Second season episodes change the format somewhat. Instead of a daily dose, the five episodes have been reworked to air two half-hour episodes each Sunday with the remaining three airing back-to-back on Monday. Paul (now divorced) still meets with a different patient in four half-hour programs with the fifth devoted to his own session with his therapist (Gina). Paul's new patients are Walter; Oliver; April and Mia. Third season episodes find Paul with a new therapist (Adele) and three new patients: Sunil, Jesse and Frances.

Cast: Gabriel Byrne *(Paul Weston)*; Michelle Forbes *(Kate Weston)*; Dianne Wiest *(Gina Toll)*; Melissa George *(Laura)*; Blair Underwood *(Alex)*; Mia Wasikowska *(Sophie)*; Josh Charles *(Jake Bickerson)*; Embeth Davidtz *(Amy)*; Hope Davis *(Mia)*; John Mahoney *(Walter)*; Alison Pill *(April)*; Aaron Show *(Oliver)*; Debra Winger *(Frances)*; Amy Ryan *(Adele)*; Irrfa Khan *(Sunil)*.

4410   *In Trouble.* (Pilot; Comedy; ABC; Aug. 24, 1981). "We're in trouble again" is a common exclamation from Ivy Miller, a pretty but prankish high school student, who, with her two best friends, Annie and Janey, are always in hot water. The proposal was to relate Ivy, Annie and Janey's encounters with innocent situations that somehow manage to become big trouble. Other regulars are Irma DeGroot, the principal; Mr. Zerneck, Janey's father; students Abenauer and Elaine; and Mr. Damrush, the school custodian. Leslie Briscusse performs the theme, "In Trouble."

Cast: Lisa Freeman *(Ivy Miller)*; Nancy Cartwright *(Annie Monahan)*; Deena Freeman *(Janey Zerneck)*; Doris Roberts *(Irma DeGroot)*; Tim Thomerson *(Mr. Damrush)*; Charles Bloom *(Abenauer)*; Cathy Cutler *(Elaine)*; Peter Michael Getz *(Mr. Zerneck)*.

4411   *In Turn.* (Series; Reality; Internet; 2006–2008). Ten hopeful actors must live together and compete in various acting challenges for a 13 week contract role on the CBS soap opera *As the World Turns*. Airs exclusively on CBS.com. Richard Mansing is the producer.

4412   *The Ina Ray Hutton Show.* (Series; Variety; NBC; 1956). Performances by female guests coupled by a bevy of beautiful regulars (the program has a no-men allowed policy) and the music of the all-girl Ina Ray Hutton Orchestra.

Host: Ina Ray Hutton. **Regulars:** Dee Dee Ball, Helen Smith, Margaret Rinker, Janice Davis, Harriet Blackburn, Judy Var Buer, Mickey Anderson, Evie Howeth, Helen Wooley, Lois Cronen, Peggy Fairbanks, Helen Hammond, Zoe Ann Willy. **Announcer:** Diane Brewster. **Music:** The All-Girl Ina Ray Hutton Orchestra.

4413   *The Inbetweeners.* (Series; Comedy; BBC America; 2010). Coming-of-age tale about a group of teenage friends struggling to fit into a world they find awkward and confusing. Will, Simon, Jay and Neil attend a public school in London and their experiences at school, at home, with girls and life itself in suburbia is the focal point of the program. Will is the new kid, a transfer from a private school;

Simon is a romantic who has a terrible time impressing girls; Jay is a know-it-all whose boasts are tall tales; Neil is the nerd, "a near moron" who believes ignorance is bliss; Carli is the attractive girl on whom Simon has a secret crush; Charlotte is the class beauty (and sexually active); Mark is the school bully; Mr. Gilbert is a teacher.

Cast: Simon Bird *(Will MacKenzie)*; Joe Thomas *(Simon Cooper)*; James Buckley *(Jay Cartwright)*; Blake Harrison *(Neil Sutherland)*; Emily Head *(Carli D'Amato)*; Emily Atack *(Charlotte Hinchcliffe)*; Henry Lloyd-Hughes *(Mark Donovan)*; Grey Davies *(Mr. Gilbert)*; Belinda Stewart-Wilson *(Polly MacKenzie)*; Alex Macqueen *(Kevin Sutherland)*.

4414 *Inch High, Private Eye.* (Series; Cartoon; NBC; 1973-1974). Inch High, the world's smallest man, is a master detective employed by the Finkerton Organization. He is assisted by his niece, Laurie, and her dog, Bravehart and stories follow their mishaps as Inch High attempts to solve baffling and dangerous crimes.

Voice Cast: Lennie Weinrib *(Inch High)*; Kathi Gori *(Laurie)*; Don Messick *(Bravehart)*; John Stephenson *(Mr. Finkerton)*; Jean VanderPyl *(Mrs. Finkerton)*.

4415 *Inconceivable.* (Series; Drama; NBC; 2005). The Family Options Clinic is the setting for a drama that revolves around the couples who are desperate to have children but unable and seek alternative methods. Dr. Malcolm Bowers is the head of the clinic; Drs. Rachel Lu and Nora Campbell assist him. Other regulars are Nurse Patrice Locicero, psychologist Lydia Crawford, attorney Scott Garcia and office manager Marissa Jaffee.

Cast: Ming-Na *(Rachel Lu)*; Jonathan Cake *(Malcolm Bowers)*; Alfre Woodard *(Lydia Crawford)*; Mary Catherine Garrison *(Marissa Jaffee)*; Angie Harmon *(Nora Campbell)*; David Norona *(Scott Garcia)*; Joelle Carter *(Patrice Locicero)*.

4416 *The Increasingly Poor Decisions of Todd Margaret.* (Series; Comedy; IFC; 2010). Todd Margaret is an office temp at Thunder Muscle, a company that manufacturers a North Korean energy drink of questionable ingredients. When Todd exaggerates his importance, hoping for a better job position, he is mistakenly sent to England to run the company's newly established office. Todd is totally incapable of doing the job and stories relate his mishaps as he makes increasingly poor decisions regarding the British culture and selling the product. Dave is Todd's less-than-ambitious helper; Alice is the café owner on whom Todd has a crush; Brent is Todd's psychotic boss.

Cast: David Cross *(Todd Margaret)*; Sharon Horgan *(Alice)*; Russell Tovey *(Dave)*; Will Arnett *(Brent Wilty)*.

4417 *The Incredible Crash Dummies.* (Pilot; Cartoon; Fox; May 1, 1993). Slick and Spin are car crash dummies who work for Dr. Zub at an automotive test center. Their job is not only to test the safety of cars by crashing them but stop Junkman, an evil robot that was accidentally activated with an experimental Torso 900 Body Suit and now wants to control the world (he wants to end the reign of the crash dummies and safety). Produced in computer animation and based on the buckle your seat belt TV commercials.

Voice Cast: James Rankin *(Slick)*; Michael Caruana *(Spin)*; John Stocker *(Dr. Zub)*; Dan Hennessey *(Junkman)*; Richard Bineley *(Spare Tire)*; Lee MacDougall *(Ted)*; Susan Roman *(Test Center computer voice)*.

4418 *The Incredible Hulk.* (Series; Adventure; CBS; 1978-1982). During an experiment to discover how certain people can tap hidden resources of strength under stress situations, Dr. David Bruce Banner, a research scientist, is exposed to an extreme overdose of gamma radiation. The exposure causes a change in his DNA chemistry: whenever he becomes angry or enraged, his mild nature is transformed into a green creature of incredible strength. When he relaxes, the metamorphous is reversed and David again becomes himself. David's secret is exposed however, when, during one such transformation, he is seen (as the Hulk) by Jack McGee, a reporter for a newspaper called *The National Register*. Jack's curiosity is aroused and he has made it his goal to track down and expose the creature he saw. Jack's persistence causes serious problems for David. While in a lab with his partner, Elaina Marks, a fire starts and David, in an attempt to battle the flames, transforms into the Hulk. The Hulk manages to rescue Elaina, but she dies shortly after. Jack, witnessing the Hulk carrying Elaina out of the building falsely assumes he killed her. There is also no trace of David and he is assumed to be dead, a victim of the fire. David, now believed to be dead, wanders across the country, seeking a way to control the Hulk and find a means by which to reverse the process. Jack, who has vowed to bring the creature to justice, hinders his efforts. (Though the Hulk is innocent, Jack's so-called eyewitness description to the police has made him a fugitive. David cannot prove the Hulk is innocent as he has little or no recollection of his actions as the Hulk). The actual focus of each episode is David's efforts to help the people with whom he comes in contact. The pilot film, which aired on November 4, 1977 as a two-hour TV movie, has been re-edited and syndicated as the first two episodes of the series.

Program Open: "Dr. Daniel Banner, physician, scientist, searching for a way to tap into the hidden strengths that all humans have. Then an accidental overdose of gamma radiation alters his body chemistry. And now when David Banner grows angry or outraged, a startling metamorphous occurs [scene of David becoming the Hulk]. The creature is driven by rage ... the creature is wanted for a murder he did not commit. David Banner is believed to be dead. And he must let the world think that he is dead until he can find a way to control the raging spirit that dwells within him."

Cast: Bill Bixby *(Dr. David Banner)*; Lou Ferrigno *(The Hulk)*; Jack Colvin *(Jack McGee)*; Ric Drasin *(The Demi Hulk; transformation from Hulk to human)*; Susan Sullivan *(Elaina Marks; pilot episode)*.

4419 *The Incredible Hulk.* (Series; Cartoon; NBC; 1982-1984). An animated adaptation of the comic book that more closely follows the comic's story that the prior live action CBS series, *The Incredible Hulk.* Here Dr. Bruce Banner is a scientist at Gamma Base, a military research center under the command of General Ross. Bruce suffered an accident (the after effects of a gamma bomb explosion) that altered his DNA and under stress, transforms him into a green creature called the Hulk — a creature Banner uses to help good defeat evil while at the same time trying to reverse the gamma ray accident that causes the transformations. Betty Ross is a scientist and David's fiancée (and the General's daughter); Major Ned Talbot, the General's aide, is seeking to capture he mysterious Hulk; Rio and his daughter, Rita, are the owners of the local restaurant; and Rick Jones, is the teenager who helps David (responsible for David becoming exposed to the gamma radiation when David saved him, but not himself, from the bomb when Rick wandered onto the test site).

Voice Cast: Michael Bell *(Dr. Bruce Banner)*; Bob Holt *(The Incredible Hulk)*; Robert Ridgely *(General Thaddeus "Thunderbolt" Ross)*; B.J. Ward *(Betty Ross)*; Michael Horton *(Rick Jones)*; Roberto Cruz *(Rio)*; June Foray *(Rita)*; Pat Fraley *(Major Ned Talbot)*; Stan Lee *(Narrator)*.

4420 *The Incredible Hulk.* (Series; Cartoon; UPN; 1996-1999). A second animated adaptation of the comic book (see prior title) about Dr. Bruce Banner, a scientist who develops a gamma bomb for the military but who is accidentally exposed to its rays and suffers a startling metamorphosis — whenever he becomes angered Bruce becomes a green creature called the Hulk (which he uses to help good defeat evil). General Ross, Bruce's former boss, becomes his mortal enemy (determined to capture the Hulk). His daughter, Betty Ross, opposes her father and is attempting to help Bruce find a means by which to end the transformations. Also assisting them is Rick Jones, the teenager whose recklessness caused Bruce to become exposed to the gamma radiation (driving near the bomb test site and saved by Bruce, but Bruce didn't have enough time to get to shelter himself). In later episodes, a She-Hulk is introduced in the person of Jennifer Walters, a scientist who suffered a similar exposure to gamma radiation, and with Bruce, battles evil (save the world) for Gabriel Jones, an agent for SHIELD, an organization that experiments with Gamma Power.

Voice Cast: Neal McDonough (*Bruce Banner*); Lou Ferrigno (*The Hulk*); Genie Francis, Philece Sampler (*Betty Ross*); Cree Summer (*Jennifer Walters/She Hulk*); John Vernon (*Gen. Thaddeus "Thunderbolt" Ross*); Luke Perry (*Rick Jones*); Thom Berry (*Gabriel Jones*); Kevin Schon (*Maj. Glenn Talbot*); Michael Donovan (*Gray Hulk*); Matt Frewer (*The Leader*).

4421   *The Incredible Ida Early.* (Pilot; Comedy; NBC; May 29, 1987). Following his wife's sudden death, Chicopee Falls school principal Paul Sutton finds unexpected help in caring for his four mischievous children (Ellen, Randall, Clay and Dewey) when Ida Early, an outlandishly attired magical woman appears and becomes his housekeeper. The proposal was to follow Ida's efforts to run the Sutton household.

Cast: Jackee Harry (*Ida Early*); Ed Begley, Jr. (*Paul Sutton*); Missy Crider (*Ellen Sutton*); Huckleberry Fox (*Randall Sutton*); Artie DeCheser (*Clay Sutton*); Allen DeCheser (*Dewey Sutton*).

4422   *Incredible Kids and Company.* (Pilot; Reality; Syn.; Aug 8, 1981). Bobby Day and Mickey Dougherty host a program that encourages children to pursue their talents by showcasing talented youngsters.

4423   *Indemnity.* (Pilot; Crime Drama; NBC; Aug. 10, 1958). A proposed series about Paul Scott, an insurance company investigator.

Cast: Richard Kiley (*Paul Scott*); Chuck Webster (*Lt. Mike Kappell*).

4424   *Independence.* (Pilot; Western; NBC; Mar. 29,1987). Sam Hatch is the sheriff of Independence, Missouri, a somewhat peaceable town of the 1880s. He is married to Bridie (his second wife) and is the father of four children (Chastity, Prudence, Keela and Fitz). His efforts to maintain law and order were the focal point of the proposed series.

Cast: John Bennett Perry (*Sam Hatch*); Isabella Hofmann (*Bridie Hatch*); Stephanie Dunnam (*Prudence Hatch*); Vanessa Vallez (*Keela Hatch*); Amanda Wyss (*Chastity Hatch*); Joshua Julian (*Fitz Hatch*); Macon McCalman (*Mayor Angus Thurston*).

4425   *Infatuation.* (Series; Game; Syn.; 1992). A single person appears on stage and talks to the host about the person he or she is infatuated with. That person is then brought out and the host interviews the two. The two people then talk to each other — either to make a date or reject each other based on their questions.

Host: Bob Eubanks.

4426   *The Infiltrator.* (Pilot; Adventure; CBS; Aug. 14,1987). During an experiment in tele-transportation, Dr. Paul Sanderson of the Stuart Institute of Technology, accidentally links his cells and atoms to Infiltrator, an experimental space probe being tested in another part of the lab by Dr. Kerry Langdon. The probe's power is absorbed by Paul's molecules; now, when he becomes angered or enraged, a startling metamorphosis takes place and he becomes the Infiltrator, a metal, robot-like defense mechanism that the U.S. government uses for its most hazardous assignments. Stewart is their supervisor.

Cast: Scott Bakula (*Dr. Paul Sanderson*); Deborah Mullowney (*Dr. Kerry Langdon*); Charles Keating (*John J. Stewart*).

4427   *Information Please.* (Series; Game; CBS; 1952). A television version of the long-running radio series that features the "Brain Panel" attempting to answer questions submitted by home viewers.

Host: Clifton Fadiman. **Panelists:** Oscar Levant, Franklin P. Adams, John Kiernan.

4428   *The Informer.* (Series; Crime Drama; Syn.; 1966-1967). British produced program about Alexander Lambert, a disbarred British barrister who works with New Scotland Yard (in London) as a police informer — infiltrating criminal organizations to supply information for authorities. Helen is Alexander's wife; Sylvia is his department contact.

Cast: Ian Hendry (*Alexander Lambert*); Jean Marsh (*Sylvia Parrish*); Heather Sears (*Helen Lambert*); Neil Hullett (*Det. Sgt. Piper*).

4429   *The Inhumanoids.* (Series; Cartoon; Syn.; 1986). In a future era, a deadly breed of creatures called the Inhumanoids arise and threaten to destroy all living creatures. Stories relate the efforts of Earth Core, a specialized unit of humans, to defeat their deadly enemies.

Voice Cast: Michael Bell (*Auger/Eddie Aggutter/Blackthorn*); Susan Silo (*Sandra Shore/Cypher*); John Stephenson (*General Granetary/Dr. Herman/Mangler/Nightcrawler/Liquidator/Jonathan Slattery*); Dick Gautier (*Magnakor/Crygen/Pyre*); Edward Gilbert (*Senator Masterson/Meltar*); Chris Latta (*Tendril/D'Compose*); Neil Ross (*Herc Armstrong*); Richard Sanders (*Dr. Derek Bright*).

4430   *Injustice.* (Series; Crime Drama; ABC; 2006). A disclaimer appears on the screen before an episode begins: "The following program is not intended to reflect any actual person or event." A crime is established after the disclaimer. When the police investigation goes wrong (things just don't add up) and an individual feels a wrong has been done, the case is turned over to the National Justice Project, a group of lawyers who tackle the cases of people with no where else to turn. The lawyers investigate the facts and try to make sense of what makes no sense in a crime. As the team tackles a case, flashbacks are used to highlight the crimes as the investigators check into the facts. David Swayne heads the group. Charles Conti, Brianna Brown and Sonya Quintano assist him.

Cast: Kyle MacLachlan (*David Swayne*); Jason O'Mara (*Charles Conti*); Constance Zimmer (*Brianna Brown*); Marisol Nichols (*Sonya Quintano*).

4431   *Ink.* (Series; Comedy; CBS; 1996-1997). Kate Montgomery and Mike Logan are journalists. They met at a presidential conference on the lawn of the White House and married three months later. The marriage broke up after 15 years (they are the parents of a daughter named Abby) and each continued in their respective fields.

Mike is a reporter for the New York *Sun* while Kate has just become its first female managing editor — and Mike's boss (due in part to her impressive and hard-nosed reporting). Stories follow the minor problems that arise as the formally divorced couple find themselves together again — as employer and employee.

Other regulars are Ernie Trainor, the no-nonsense reporter; Alan Mesnick, the neurotic financial reporter; Belinda Carhardt, author of the column "On the Town"; and Donna French, the editorial assistant.

Cast: Ted Danson *(Mike Logan)*; Mary Steenburgen *(Kate Montgomery)*; Alana Austin *(Abby Logan)*; Christine Ebersole *(Belinda Carhardt)*; Charles Robinson *(Ernie Trainor)*; Saul Rubinek *(Alan Mesnick)*; Jenica Bergere *(Donna French)*.

4432   *The Inner Sanctum.* (Series; Anthology; Syn.; 1954). Raymond, the unseen narrator, relates stories of people confronted with sudden, perilous situations. Adapted from the radio program of the same title.

Narrator: Paul McGrath as Raymond.

4433   *Innocent Jones.* (Pilot; Comedy; NBC; Aug. 11, 1961). Innocent Jones is a free-lance, footloose magazine reporter whose assignments often lead to misadventure when he becomes personally involved in his subjects' problems. The proposal was to follow Innocent as he struggles to extricate himself from the awkward situations he manages to find.

Cast: Chris Warfield *(Innocent Jones)*.

4434   *Insatiable.* (Pilot; Comedy; Unaired; Produced for Showtime in 2006). Small town America is spoofed as cameras spotlight the lives of its citizens—where everyone seemingly has some sort of addiction.

Cast: Andie MacDowell *(JoAnn Chervinac)*; Andrea Martin *(Marla)*; Lara Flynn Boyle *(Lonna)*; Kyle Gallner *(Dickie Cherninac)*; Lance Barber *(Jerry)*; Beth Riesgraf).

4435   *Inseparable.* (Pilot; Comedy; Produced for Fox in 2007). Melinda and Len are a young married couple with a problem: Melinda's family, who feel they must be a constant part of their lives. Alan and Barbara are her parents and Brian and Steph are her siblings and the proposal was to relate Melinda and Len's efforts to cope with the constant intrusion in their lives.

Cast: Krysten Ritter *(Melinda)*; Chip Zien *(Len)*; Ed O'Neill *(Alan)*; Christine Baranski *(Barbara)*; Coby Ryan McLaughlin *(Brian)*; Rachel Boston *(Steph)*.

4436   *Inseparable.* (Pilot; Drama; Unaired; Produced for Fox in 2008). Dr. Jekyll and Mr. Hyde type proposal about Justin Lambreaux, a man with two personalities: forensic psychiatrist (Justin), who is married to Emily and helps the police solve crimes, and (Clyde), who is involved with a single woman (Mason Wicks) who knows and keeps his secret.

Cast: Lloyd Owen *(Justin/Clyde)*; Tricia Helfer *(Mason Wicks)*; Malik Yoba *(Lt. Curtis Corrales)*; Morgan Turner *(Emily Lambreaux)*; Warren Kole *(Ryan Farber)*.

4437   *Inside America.* (Series; Magazine; ABC; 1982). Provocative and informative features that explore various aspects of American life.

Host: Dick Clark. **Correspondents:** Anson Williams, Rex Reed, Lynn Shawn, Shawn Weatherly.

4438   *Inside Detective.* (Series; Crime Drama; DuMont; 1950–1954). The alternate title for *Rocky King, Inside Detective.* See this title for information.

4439   *Inside Edition.* (Series; Magazine; Syn.; 1989). A daily program of hard-hitting investigative reports, celebrity profiles and human-interest stories.

Host: David Frost, Bill O'Reilly. **Reporters:** Marguerite Bardone, Bill O'Reilly, Jeff Cole, Rich Kirkham. **Music:** Ed Kalehoff.

4440   *Inside Jokes.* (Pilot; Comedy; Unaired; Produced for Fox in 2009). Skits coupled with rapid-fire one liners delivered by a cast of improve actors.

Host: Cameron Bender. **Regulars:** Carrie Wiita, Jay Phillips, Lauren Rose Lewis, Mary Scheer, Paul Schackman.

4441   *Inside O.U.T.* (Pilot; Comedy; NBC; Mar. 22, 2971). The Office of Unusual Tactics (O.U.T.) is a semi-official U.S. government organization that handles the cases nobody else wants. Ron Hart is the director of O.U.T. and his agents, who have normal jobs on the side, are Pat Bouillon (a museum tour guide), Chuck Dandy (a moving man) and Edgar Winston (an airline pilot). The proposal was to take viewers inside O.U.T. to detail their case assignments.

Cast: Bill Daily *(Ron Hart)*; Farrah Fawcett *(Pat Bouillon)*; Alan Oppenheimer *(Edgar Winston)*; Mike Henry *(Chuck Dandy)*.

4442   *Inside Schwartz.* (Series; Comedy; NBC; 2001-2002). Adam Schwartz is a young man obsessed with sports. His passion has enabled him to become a sportscaster (for a minor league ball team) but his obsession has also presented him with another problem—his inner thoughts and fantasies are revealed through conversations with sports personalities. Stories relate Adam's efforts to deal with the personal issues in his life while at the same time trying not to let the sports side control his actions. Eve is his ex-girlfriend; Julie is the new girl in his life; David and Emily are his married friends; Gene is Adam's father, the owner of St. Pita's, a pita sandwich shop (where Adam is vice president of operations).

Cast: Breckin Meyer *(Adam Schwartz)*; Maggie Lawson *(Eve Baker)*; Miriam Shor *(Julie Hermann)*; Bryan Callen *(David Cobert)*; Jennifer Irwin *(Emily Cobert)*; Richard Kline *(Gene Schwartz)*; Dondre T. Whitefield *(William Morris)*.

4443   *Inside the Actor's Studio.* (Series; Interview; Bravo; 1994–). In-depth interviews with top actors, writers and directors. Students and Actor's Studio alumni comprise the studio audience.

Host: James Lipton.

4444   *Inside the Box.* (Series; Game; Syn.; 2008). Three players compete. One is placed inside "the box"; two remain outside. The box player has a series of questions relating to a television show, character or actor. The outside players have only one image of the subject two whom the questions refer. Two minutes is placed on a clock and the box players ask indirect questions of the outside players, one at a time. The box players can stop the clock and attempt to guess the subject at any time. The amount of time left on the clock when an identification is made becomes the player's score. If an outside player gives an incorrect response to a question, he receives a five second penalty (which is deducted from his two minutes box time). Each player receives a chance inside the box with the highest scoring time player at the end of two rounds being declared the winner. This player then competes against the host in a similar game wherein the player questions the host. Each five seconds that pass before the player makes an identification deducts $500 from a $10,000 jackpot, Cash is awarded based on the point at which the player identified the subject.

Host: Sam Kalilieh.

4445   *Inside the Box.* (Pilot; Drama; Unaired; Produced for ABC in 2009). The competitive and cutthroat world of television news reporting is explored through the actions of the staff of the CNS network in Washington, D.C. Kenneth Donnegan is the shallow bureau chief; Catherine Powell is a top investigator; Jake Fisher is her right-hand man; Samantha Hathaway is a brutally ambitious reporter; Kyle Chisholm is the White House correspondent.

Cast: Indira Varma *(Catherine Powell)*; Kim Raver *(Samantha Hathaway)*; Lloyd Owen *(Kenneth Donnegan)*; Jennifer Finnigan *(Lauren Thomas)*; Jason George *(Kyle Chisholm)*; Martin Henderson *(Jake Fisher)*; Sarah Drew *(Molly)*.

4446 *Inside the Jury Room.* (Pilot; Reality; Unaired; Produced for ABC in 1992). Condensed versions of actual trials. Each episode was to begin with a compressed version of a trial then switch to the jury room for the deliberations and verdict using the actual people and no recreations.

Host: Jason Robards.

4447 *Inside U.S.A. with Chevrolet.* (Series; Variety; NBC; 1949–1950). Chevrolet sponsored program of music and songs with singers Peter Lind Hayes and Mary Healy.

Hosts: Peter Lind Hayes, Mary Healy. **Regulars:** Sheila Bond, Marion Colby. **Orchestra:** Jay Blackton.

4448 *The Insider.* (Pilot; Drama; Unaired; Produced in 1962). A proposal about Dan Castle, a Hollywood press agent who becomes personally involved with the problems of his clients.

Cast: David Janssen *(Dan Castle)*.

4449 *The Insider.* (Series; Magazine; Syn.; 2004–). A daily program dedicated to reporting the stories behind the Hollywood stories — from celebrities, the movies, TV shows and other entertainment related fields where gossip can be found.

Hosts: Pat O'Brien, Ananda Lewis, Victoria Recano, Lara Spencer, David Caplan.

4450 *The Insiders.* (Series; Crime Drama; ABC; 1985–1986). Nick Fox is an investigative reporter for *Newspoint*, a national magazine whose editor, Alice West, wants her reporters to go beyond the norm and find the little known facts that can blow a case wide open and lead to an eventual conclusion. James Mackay is a street-wise ex con who has gone straight (almost) hired by Alice to use his expertise as a thief, con artist and schemer to assist Nick in getting stories. Episodes relate Nick and James' efforts to acquire stories by becoming a part of them.

Other regulars are Melissa, Alice's secretary; Roxanne, Nick's cousin; and Louise, Alice's mother.

Cast: Nicholas Campbell *(Nick Fox)*; Stoney Jackson *(James Mackay)*; Gail Strickland *(Alice West)*; Kelly Ann Conn *(Melissa)*; Jeannie Elias *(Roxanne)*; Jane Greer *(Louise Browning)*.

4451 *The Inspector.* (Pilot; Crime Drama; UPN; Mar. 7, 1995). Ted Harrison is a former Chief Inspector with Scotland Yard who, after 33 years on the job, retires to buy a sheep ranch in Australia. He's had enough of police work and wants to experience new horizons. Before moving to Australia, Ted decides to visit his daughter, Cecilia, in New York City. Cecilia is engaged to Detective Sergeant Frank Jeffries, a media public relations liaison for the N.Y.P.D. It is when Frank takes Ted to see an old friend, now his boss, Police Deputy Chief O'Connor, that Ted becomes interested in a case involving a serial killer whose victims frequented a bar called the Shamrock. After helping the police solve the case, Ted is offered a position as a consultant to the N.Y.P.D. and the proposal was to relate his case assignments.

Cast: Edward Woodward *(Edward "Ted" Harrison)*; Elizabeth Hurley *(Cecilia Harrison)*; Jeffrey Nordling *(Frank Jeffries)*; Al Waxman *(Chief O'Connor)*.

4452 *Inspector Fabian of Scotland Yard.* (Series; Crime Drama; Syn.; 1955). Inspector Robert Fabian is the superintendent of Detectives of New Scotland Yard in London, England. He believes in scientific evaluation and modern techniques and stories relate his efforts to solve crimes based on his principals.

Cast: Bruce Seton *(Insp. Robert Fabian)*.

4453 *Inspector Gadget.* (Series; Cartoon; Syn.; 1983). Inspector Gadget is a unique crime fighter. He is half human and "half contraption" and the savior of Metro City. Inspector Gadget is assisted by his niece, Penny, and his dog, Brain and stories follow the somewhat misadventure-prone Inspector as he incorporates his unique abilities (over 13,000 mechanical devices) to battle crime and corruption. Chief Quimby is his superior; Dr. Claw is his nemesis and Madcat is Claw's pet cat.

Voice Cast: Don Adams *(Inspector Gadget)*; Mona Marshall *(Penny)*; Jesse White *(Chief Quimby)*; Frank Welker *(Dr. Claw/Madcat/Brain)*.

4454 *Inspector Mom.* (Series; Crime Drama; Lifetime; 2006). Madeline (called Maddie) Monroe is a former journalist (investigative reporter) turned housewife and mother. She is married to Craig and they are the parents of Tara and Nate. While Maddie appears to be living the life of an average American housewife, she longs for the excitement her former life gave her. She receives partial fulfillment when she acquires a part time job as a reporter. Maddie is curious (and her curiosity could get her killed); wherever she goes she always manages to find something that intrigues her (most often a murder she stumbles upon). Stories follow Maddie as she detaches herself from the kids and housework and puts her investigative genius to work to solve crimes. Maddie likes to know what makes people tick. She's a smart problem solver and quick with her wits. These attributes help her solve the complex mysteries she encounters. *Inspector Mom* is a unique series. It began as a two-hour television movie on the Lifetime Movie Network (LMN). Eight episodes then aired as "webisodes" on the Internet (www.LMN.tv) followed by an additional television movie.

Cast: Danica McKellar *(Maddie Monroe)*; Drew Waters *(Craig Monroe)*; Ashlan Cunningham *(Tara Monroe)*; Nate Bell *(Nate Monroe)*.

4455 *Inspector Perez.* (Pilot; Crime Drama; NBC; Jan. 8, 1983). Shortly after the death of his wife, Antonio Perez, a detective with the N.Y.P.D., decides to begin a new life in California and transfers to the Homicide Division of the San Francisco Police Department. He moves in with his widowed mother and the proposal was to relate his and his partner, Sergeant Richard's case investigations.

Cast: Jose Perez *(Antonio Perez)*; Dana Elcar *(Captain R.C. Hodges)*; Michael Corneilson *(Sergeant Richards)*; Betty Carvalho *(Mama Perez)*.

4456 *Instant Beauty Pageant.* (Series; Reality; Style; 2006). Five ordinary (but very attractive) women are selected at random in a mall and participate in an instant beauty pageant. The competition begins with the women allowed to shop for clothes then use what they just selected in contests of style, fashion, swimwear and evening gown competitions. The best performer is crowned "Ms. Instant Beauty" and receives the clothing she selected and a tiara. Debbie Matenopoulos and Rossi Morreale host.

4457 *Instant Family.* (Pilot; Comedy; NBC; July 28, 1977). In an attempt to cut expenses, Clifford Beane and Frank Boyle, two single fathers, pool their resources and rent an apartment. The proposal was to relate the efforts of both families to live together. Other regulars are Lisa and Robbie, Frank's children; and Kevin, Ernie and Alexander, Clifford's offspring.

Cast: William Daniels *(Clifford Beane)*; Lou Criscuolo *(Frank Boyle)*; Wendy Fredericks *(Lisa Boyle)*; Brad Wilkin *(Robbie Boyle)*; Jeff Harlan *(Kevin Beane)*; Robbie Rist *(Ernie Beane)*; Sparky Marcus *(Alexander Beane)*.

4458   *Instant Recall.* (Series; Game; GSN; 2010). A subject (in some cases multiple subjects) are tricked into attending a specific function. Actors play specific parts in the charade and what they wear and do are vital (although the subject does not know this). Hidden cameras capture the action and after several minutes (of edited for broadcast footage) the host appears and reveals to the subject that he (or they) are on a game show. A crew immediately turns the scene into the show's set and the subjects are tested on their ability to recall what happened. Players receive $500 "for just showing up" and additional cash (up to $3,000) for each instance they can correctly recall (usually linked to two or three questions).

Host: Wink Martindale. **Assistant:** Angela Daun. **Actors:** Nicole Neuman, Michael McCusker, David Imani, Jefandi Cato, Derek Baynham, Shannon Freyer, Dan Lawler.

4459   *Instant Star.* (Series; Drama; The N; 2004–2008). Jude Harrison is an amateur singer-songwriter who suddenly finds her life changing, for what she thinks is the better, when she enters a song writing contest and wins a contract with G-Major Records. Jude is in seventh heaven until she learns that company representatives will be making all her decisions — from what to sing to what to wear. Jude desperately wants a singing career and reluctantly accepts what is being dealt, but upsets her family and friends who feel she may not be making a wise choice. Stories focus on Jude as she struggles to cope with the pressures of a promising career and deal with the normal problems that a high school girl faces at home and at school. Produced in Canada.

Cast: Alex Johnson *(Jude Harrison)*; Laura Vandervoort *(Sadie Harrison)*, Kristopher Turner *(Jamie Andrews)*; Tim Rozon *(Tommy Quincy)*; Wes Williams *(Darius Mills)*; Simon Reynolds *(Stuart Harrison)*; Ian Blackwood *(Kyle)*; Jane Sowerby *(Victoria Harrison)*; Miku Graham *(Portia Quincy)*.

4460   *Institute for Revenge.* (Pilot; Adventure; NBC; Jan. 22, 1979). The Wyatt Foundation for Human Rights is a Palm Springs–based organization run by the IFR 700 Computer and nicknamed the Institute for Revenge (it is dedicated to righting nonviolent wrongs). John Schroeder is its chief agent and the proposal was to relate his case assignments for the institute. Other regulars are Lilah, John's assistant; Mr. Wellington, the head of the foundation; and agents JoAnn and T.J. (Terence James).

Cast: Sam Groom *(John Schroeder)*; Lauren Hutton *(Lilah Simms)*; Robert Coote *(Mr. Wellington)*; Lane Binkley *(JoAnn Newcombe)*; T.J. McCavitt *(T.J. Bradley)*; John Hillerman *(Voice of IFR 700)*.

4461   *Interceptor — The Game of High Adventure.* (Pilot; Game; Syn.; April, 1989). Two teams compete, each composed of one celebrity and one non-celebrity contestant. Each team member is fitted with a back pack that contains valuable prizes and an infra-red sensitive target mounted on the pack. Each team has to make its way through a rugged outdoor survival course and seek banners that award prizes — but also avoid the Interceptor, their enemy who possesses an infra-red gun. The Interceptor's mission is to track the teams and seal their back packs by hitting a concealed target on the pack. After an exhausting five-mile run and endless attempts to avoid the Interceptor, the teams are brought together at headquarters at Studio

6 in University City Studios. Here the host attempts to open the back packs. Those that were hit by the Interceptor are locked and no prizes are awarded: however, each banner that was retrieved during the game awards various prizes.

Host: Erik Estrada. **Guests:** Barbi Benton, Bruce Boxleitner. **The Interceptor:** Gary Davis. **Off-Screen Interceptor Voice:** Bill Ratner.

4462   *Intercourse with Whitney Cummings.* (Pilot; Comedy; Unaired; Produced for Comedy Central in 2010). Narrative, scripted proposal (made to look like a reality series) that presents comedienne Whitney Cummings view on sex, dating and marriage.

Cast: Whitney Cummings *(Herself)*.

4463   *Interesting People.* (Experimental; Reality; NBC; Mar. 22, 1944). A sponsored program (by Ben Pulitzer Neckwear) that featured performances by show business people (here, actor Guy Kibbee did a comical monologue; Madelyn Balaban, the daughter of the director of the Roxy Theater in New York, sang; and Anne Bracken, a teenager who appeared in the Broadway production of *Lady in the Dark*, performed a skit).

Performers: Madelyn Balaban, Anne Bracken, Dick Bradley, Marie Howard, Guy Kibbee.

4464   *International Airport.* (Pilot; Drama; ABC; May 25, 1985). The problems of running an airport as seen through the eyes of David Montgomery, the manager of International Airport. Other regulars are Beverly, David's secretary; Kathy, his assistant; Marjorie, the information desk girl; Jack, the head of security; and Pepe, the shoeshine boy.

Cast: Gil Gerard *(David Montgomery)*; Patricia Crowley *(Beverly Gerber)*; Berlinda Tolbert *(Kathy Henderson)*; Kitty Moffat *(Marjorie Lucas)*; Cliff Potts *(Jack Marshall)*; Danny Ponce *(Pepe)*.

4465   *The International Animation Festival.* (Series; Cartoon; PBS; 1975). Actress Jean Marsh hosts a series of award-winning cartoons from around the world.

4466   *International Detective.* (Series; Crime Drama; Syn.; 1959). Ken Franklin is a highly trained former police detective turned chief investigator for the William J. Burns Detective Agency. No case is considered too small or too insignificant for the agency to handle and stories follow Ken's world-wide investigations as he attempts to solve the problems of his clients.

Cast: Arthur Fleming *(Ken Franklin)*.

4467   *The International Sexy Ladies Show.* (Series; Comedy; G-4; 2009). Clips, culled from various sources from around the world, that showcase beautiful women (some scantily clothed) in comical and provocative situations. A group of comedians provide commentary.

Narrator: Phil Nichol. **Comedians:** Doug Benson, Steve Byrne, John Caparulo, Mitch Fatel, Amber James, Jo Koy, Dani O'Neal, Sherrod Small, Alex Zane.

4468   *International Showtime.* (Series; Variety; NBC; 1961–1965). Highlights of various European circus variety acts with actor Don Ameche as the host.

4469   *The Interns.* (Series; Drama; CBS; 1970-1971). The personal and professional lives of Gregg Pettit, Lydia Thorpe, Pooch Hardin, Sam March and Cal Barrin, interns, supervised by Dr. Peter Goldstone, at New North Hospital in Los Angeles. Bobbie is Sam's wife.

Cast: Broderick Crawford (*Peter Goldstone*); Christopher Stone (*Pooch Hardin*); Sandra Smith (*Lydia Thorpe*); Mike Farrell (*Sam Marsh*); Stephen Brooks (*Greg Pettit*); Hal Frederick (*Cal Barrin*); Elaine Giftos (*Bobbie Marsh*); Skip Homeier (*Dr. Jacoby*); Edward Faulkner (*Dr. Lansing*); Jenny Blackton (*Nurse*); David Sachs (*Dr. Cherry*).

4470 *Interpol Calling*. (Series; Crime Drama; Syn.; 1960). Interpol, the International Police Force, is made up of sixty-three member nations and is the most complex and powerful law enforcement agency in the world. Cases undertaken by Interpol are seen through the experiences of Paul Duval, a chief inspector.
Cast: Charles Korvin (*Insp. Paul Duval*); Edwin Richfield (*Police Inspector*).

4471 *Intertect*. (Pilot; Crime Drama; ABC; Mar. 11, 1973). John McKennon is a former FBI agent who runs Intertect, an international investigative agency. The proposal was to relate John's case assignments.
Cast: Stuart Whitman (*John McKennon*).

4472 *Intimate Sessions*. (Series; Anthology; Cinemax; 1998). Stories based on the discussions a group of women have when they gather once a week to talk to each other about their most erotic fantasies. As a woman describes her fantasy it is seen in a reenactment (that contains female nudity). Casts change from episode to episode. Marilyn Vance is the producer.

4473 *Into the Unknown*. (Pilot; Reality; Syn.; Aug. 1986). The program explores then attempts to answer the mysteries of paranormal phenomena (for example, faith healing, UFO's, psychokinetic metal bending).
Host: Kevin Sanders. **Narrator:** Ron McKuen.

4474 *Intrigue*. (Pilot; Adventure; CBS; Sept. 11, 1988). Alexander Crawford was born in Chicago and attended Princeton University. He now works as an American undercover intelligence agent who poses as a cultural attaché based at the U.S. Embassy in Brussels. The proposal was to relate Crawford's exploits as he relies more on brains and wits than guns to solve cases.
Cast: Scott Glenn (*Alexander Crawford*).

4475 *Introducing Lennie Rose*. (Pilot; Comedy; Unaired; Produced for ABC in 2005). Lennie Rose is a young woman with extremely high hopes. She lives in Manhattan and, at 26 years of age, has set her goal to become someone extraordinary. The proposal was to follow Lennie as she seeks her seemingly impossible goal. Jackson is a former Olympic champion who is also seeking a dream; Harper is a novelist who sees Lennie as his ultimate heroine. The three work together in a busy restaurant with Stella, a sexy, aspiring actress; and Tess, an adorable but clumsy law student.
Cast: Abigail Spencer (*Lennie Rose*); Warren Christie (*Jackson*); Keir O'Donnell (*Harper*); Aya Sumika (*Stella*); Sasha Barrese (*Tess*).

4476 *Invader ZIM*. (Series; Cartoon; Nick; 2001–2006). ZIM is an alien soldier who desires to be an invader but he is terribly accident-prone and a big disappointment to his superiors, the Almighty Tallest Red and Purple, the leaders of the planet Irk. The Irkin Empire is slowly taking over the universe but ZIM is a thorn in their side. In order to get rid of him, they assign him a bogus secret mission: explore a worthless planet called Earth. ZIM accepts the assignment and establishes himself as a schoolboy on the planet. His guise is uncovered, however, by Dib Membrane, an absent-minded ten-year-old paranormal researcher who has taken it upon himself to stop

ZIM. Dib is as fumbling as ZIM and stories follow Dib's endless efforts to foil ZIM's attempts to destroy the planet (in order to prove himself to his superiors. On Irk tallness determines status. ZIM is short and thus considered quite worthless). ZIM is assisted by GIR, a badly programmed (deranged) robot that hinders ZIM's efforts.
Voice Cast: Richard Steven Horvitz (*ZIM*); Andy Berman (*Dib*); Rosearik Rikki Simons (*GIR*); Jhonen Vasquez (*Computer voice*); Rodger Bumpass (*Professor Membrane*); Lucille Bliss (*Ms. Bitters*); Melissa Fahn (*Gaz*); Mo Collins (*Zita*); Kevin McDonald (*Almighty Tallest Purple*); Wally Wingert (*Almighty Tallest Red*).

4477 *The Invaders*. (Series; Science Fiction; ABC; 1967-1968). Landers and Vincent is an architectural firm at 3006 Willow Street in Santa Barbara, California. David Vincent, a graduate of State College, is the eager, young partner; Alan Landers (James Daly), the senior partner, has been an architect for 30 years.
David is returning home from a business trip one night when he decides to take a shortcut. He exits Highway 166 and soon finds himself on a dark and desolate country road. He passes a closed and deserted café (Bud's Diner) and decides to stop. The time is 4:20 A.M. and David has been driving for 20 hours. David is suddenly startled by a loud, strange noise. He sees a bright light and witnesses the landing of a spacecraft from another galaxy. David reports the incident later that morning, but an investigation by the sheriff's department fails to uncover any evidence of what David saw. Unable to accept the explanation that he had gone too long without sleep and just imagined what he saw, David begins an investigation on his own. In the town of Kinney, he uncovers proof of what he saw: in an abandoned hydroelectric plant, aliens from a dying planet (unnamed) have established a base of operations as the beginning of an invasion to make the Earth their home. Before he is able to show others his proof, the Invaders vanish (a series problem for David). Stories relate David's efforts "to convince a disbelieving world that the nightmare has already begun."
The Invaders take human form, and their plan is to assimilate into society. David knows their one flaw—"Some of them have mutated hands: a crooked fourth finger"—and he knows that where an invasion has begun, there must also be a recharging base for them (to maintain their human forms, the aliens must use their glass tube-like regeneration chambers. These tubes are also a device by which the aliens kill humans—by producing an untraceable heart attack or cerebral hemorrhage). Failure to rejuvenate in time causes an alien's death (disintegration in a glowing light).
The Invaders are emotionless and appear to be horrifying and indistinguishable in their natural form. Police departments have David listed as "a kook who believes aliens are trying to take over the Earth." As David gathers evidence to prove his story, he makes contact with several powerful people who have seen what David has seen and who know the aliens must be stopped. The group becomes known as the Believers. (Corporate head Edgar Scoville is the only Believer with a recurring role). "You can't stop it, it's going to happen. Don't fight us," the aliens tell David. But for as long as it takes, David will fight, "for they must be stopped, they must be exposed. If David Vincent doesn't do it, who will?"
Program Open: "The Invaders, alien beings from a dying planet. Their destination: the Earth. Their purpose—to make it their world. David Vincent has seen them. For him it began one lost night on a lonely country road looking for a shortcut that he never found. It began with a closed, deserted diner and a man too long without sleep to continue his journey. It began with the landing of a craft from another galaxy. Now David Vincent knows the Invaders are here, that they have taken human form. Somehow he must convince a disbelieving world that the nightmare has already begun."
Cast: Roy Thinnes (*David Vincent*); Kent Smith (*Edgar Scoville*).

4478 *Invasion.* (Series; Science Fiction; ABC; 2005-2006). Are natural disasters (such as hurricanes) created by outer space aliens as smoke screens for their landings on Earth or for something more ominous?

It all begins in Homestead, a small town in Florida, following a fierce hurricane. Have aliens landed in the lake? Bizarre incidents begin occurring and signs indicate that unearthly forces are controlling life in Homestead. Stories explore this concept through Russell Varon, the park ranger; his second wife, Larkin Groves, the local TV reporter; Dave Groves, Larkin's wayward brother; Rose, Russell's daughter from a previous marriage (she claims to have seen hundreds of lights floating toward the water during the storm); Dr. Mariel Underlay, Russell's ex wife (now married to Tom Underlay, the sheriff); Jesse, Russell's 15-year-old son; Kira, Tom's 16-year-old daughter; and Mona, the assistant park ranger.

Cast: Eddie Cibrian *(Russell Varon)*; William Fichtner *(Tom Underlay)*; Kari Matchett *(Mariel Underlay)*; Lisa Sheridan *(Larkin Groves)*; Tyler Labine *(Dave Groves)*; Alexis Dziena *(Kira Underlay)*; Aisha Hinds *(Mona Gomez)*; Ariel Gade *(Rose Varon)*; Evan Peters *(Jesse Varon)*.

4479 *Invasion Earth.* (Series; Cartoon; WB; 1998). It is the early 1980s when a group of humanoid aliens from the dying planet Tyrus begin their invasion of Earth to capture its resources. Cale-Oosha, the ruler of Tyrus, opposes his uncle, the Dragit, who believes invading Earth is their only salvation. As a civil war breaks out, Cale and his bodyguard Rafe, escape to Earth where, disguised as humans, they blend in with society. As time passes, Cale meets Rita Carter, a human girl, and they eventually marry. When Cale believes it is time for him to return to Tyrus, he leaves Rita and their son, David, with Rafe. On Tyrus, Cale attempts to strengthen his forces, the Ooshati. Meanwhile, the Dragit has found Cale's family and is now determined to kill them. David becomes a warrior of sorts when his mother is killed battling the Dragit and he learns his true calling: the future ruler of Tyrus. Stories follow David as he battles Dragit to avenge his mother's death.

Voice Cast: Mikey Kelley *(David Carter)*; Edward Albert *(Rafe)*; Kath Soucie *(Rita Carter)*; Lorenzo Lamas *(Cale Oosha)*; Tony Jay *(Dragit)*.

4480 *Invasion of the Hidden Cameras.* (Series; Reality; Fox; 2002). Hidden cameras capture the reactions of ordinary people caught in outrageous pranks. Doug Stanhope hosts.

4481 *The Investigator.* (Series; Crime Drama; NBC; 1958). Jeff Prior is a private detective working out of New York City. He is young and eager and as tough as nails when he has to be. Lloyd Prior, his father, is also his assistant. Lloyd, however, is not as headstrong as his son, and prefers a laid-back approach when it comes to investigating cases. Stories relate their case investigations and the clash that ensues as each tries to do what is best for their clients.

Cast: Lonny Chapman *(Jeff Prior)*; Howard St. John *(Lloyd Prior)*.

4482 *The Investigators.* (Series; Crime Drama; CBS; 1961). Russ Andrews and Steve Banks are highly skilled insurance investigators based in New York City. While Russ and Steve normally adhere to a strict interpretation of the law, they often find that, when dealing with truly unscrupulous criminals, being just as underhanded often results in a successful conclusion to the case on which they are working. Maggie Peters and Bill Davis assist them in the field; Polly is their office secretary.

Cast: James Philbrook *(Steve Banks)*; James Franciscus *(Russ Andrews)*; Mary Murphy *(Maggie Peters)*; Al Austin *(Bill Davis)*; June Kenny *(Polly Walters)*.

4483 *The Investigators.* (Series; Comedy; HBO; 1984). A spoof of news programs as seen through the outrageous reports of Truman Knuman and Peter Quest, two "Crusading Reporters on the Air." Angry Arnie is the consumer reporter.

Cast: Charles Rocket *(Truman Knuman)*; Mark King *(Peter Quest)*; Bill Kirchenbauer *(Angry Arnie)*.

4484 *The Invisible Avenger.* (Pilot; Adventure; Unaired; Produced in 1960). A proposed TV series based on the radio program *The Shadow.* Many years ago in the Orient, Lamont Cranston learned the mysterious power to cloud men's minds so they cannot see him from a mystic named Jogendra (when Lamont concentrates he sends a powerful image into the minds of others. The affected person does not see Lamont — only his image in a shadow). Lamont poses as a wealthy man-about-town and is said to be a friend of the Shadow and the only man who knows how to contact him. Like the radio program, Lamont helps people in trouble; however, his "lovely traveling companion, Margot Lane," has been replaced by Jogendra (who uses the power of hypnosis to help Lamont) for TV.

Cast: Richard Derr *(Lamont Cranston)*; Mark Davids *(Jogendra)*.

4485 *The Invisible Man.* (Series; Adventure; Syn.; 1958–1960). During an experiment he is conducting on the refraction of light, Peter Brady, a research scientist for the Castle Hill Research Lab in England, is sprayed with a gas when one of the reactors leaks.

His body absorbs the gas and it renders him invisible. Peter, however, lacks the knowledge to become visible. (He wears facial bandages, sunglasses and gloves to be seen). Before Peter can do anything, he is put under lock and key by the Ministry (they fear panic will result if it is known an invisible man exists). Peter escapes and retreats to the home of his sister, Diane Wilson. There he explains to Diane and her daughter, Sally, what has happened. He concludes with, "It's quite simple. Take a jellyfish, put it in water and you can't see it. That's happened to me. My reflective index has been lowered to that of theirs."

The situation changes drastically when a rival experimenter learns what has happened and attempts to steal Brady's formula for invisibility. The Ministry reverses its decision about Peter and allows him to continue his research: to find the key to becoming visible again. In the meantime, Peter uses his great advantage of invisibility to assist the British government in its battle against crime. In later episodes, Peter's invisibility is known to the general public.

The identity of the actor portraying the lead (Peter Brady) had been (and still is) a closely guarded secret. (The cast for each episode, including the regulars, is listed only during the end credits. While the lead is listed first, he is credited only as "The Invisible Man"; the remainder of the cast follows, each with a character name.) It has been rumored that series producer Ralph Smart played Brady (Smart did the same anonymous casting for *The Iron Mask* series) or that actor Tim Turner, who appeared in the episode "Man in Disguise," was actually the uncredited actor behind the bandages. The actor's identity was concealed not only from the public, but also from the cast and crew. (The actor wore bandages on the set; his voice was dubbed in after the episodes were shot. In some episodes he sounds American; in others there is a slight British accent.) Sir Charles is the British Cabinet Minister (Peter's boss).

A dramatically different version of the H.G. Wells story was produced in early 1958 but was scrapped and never aired. In it, Peter Brady is conducting an experiment in optical density on a guinea pig (which disappears, then reappears) when a reactor begins leaking. Peter's system absorbs too much of the gas, and he is rendered invisible; his clothes, however, do not become invisible. Peter is free to leave the lab; in fact, it is known that Peter Brady has become invisible (as television and newspaper reporters constantly annoy him). In this version he lives with his widowed sister Jane Wilson (Lisa Daniely) and her daughter Sally (Deborah Watling).

It is difficult to predict how this version of the series would have progressed, since there was only one episode. Based on the storyline — Brady using his invisibility to rescue Sally from kidnappers — it appeared that he would either become a detective and use his invisibility to help solve crimes; or would follow the aired format and work with the British government — which would give him the greatest chance of discovering the formula for visibility. There is no real ending explaining what Brady would do next.

Cast: ? *(The Invisible Man)*; Lisa Daniely *(Diane Wilson)*; Deborah Watling *(Sally Wilson)*; Ernest Clark, Ewen MacDuff *(Sir Charles)*.

4486   The Invisible Man. (Series; Adventure; NBC; 1975–1976). Believing that it is possible to transfer objects from one place to another with laser beams, Daniel Wilson, a scientist for the Los Angeles–based KLAE Corporation, receives the authority to prove his theory via his Tele-Transportation Project. Eight months later, and after having spent $1.5 million in research money, Daniel reaches the point where he believes he can make a man invisible. Although the project is still experimental, Daniel is able to make himself invisible (by standing between two laser beams) and bring himself back to visibility (by injecting himself with a special serum he developed).

Although excited about his discovery, Daniel is soon dismayed when he learns from his superior, Walter Carlson, that his invention can be used as the ultimate military weapon. Opposed to a military use of his weapon, Daniel takes matters into his own hands and destroys the Tele-Transporter. In order to escape from the building, Daniel makes himself invisible. Later, when Daniel injects himself with the visibility serum, it fails to work; he discovers that he is permanently invisible.

Daniel seeks help from his friend, Nick Maggio, a brilliant plastic surgeon who has been experimenting with a plastic lifelike substance he calls Derma Pleque (which can reconstruct a patient's face). To help Daniel, Nick modifies the process to what he calls Derma Plex, a rubbery liquid plastic that he uses to reconstruct Daniel's face and hands (for his eyes, Nick develops a special set of contact lenses; caps are used for his teeth; a wig becomes his hair — hence Daniel appears as he did before).

When Daniel realizes that KLAE Corporation's research center is his only way of finding the means to become visible, he becomes their chief investigator, using his invisibility to tackle dangerous national and international assignments.

Daniel and his wife, Kate, live at 40137 Hazelton Road in Los Angeles; the KLAE Corporation is a highly specialized research center that undertakes government contracts. In the 90 minute NBC pilot film (May 6, 1975), Jackie Cooper played Walter Carlson.

Cast: David McCallum *(Daniel Weston)*; Melinda Fee *(Kate Weston)*; Craig Stevens *(Walter Carlson)*; Henry Darrow *(Nick Maggio)*; Ted Gehring, Paul Kent *(KLAE Security Chief)*.

4487   The Invisible Man. (Series; Adventure; Syfy; 2000). When petty thief Darien Fawkes is caught in the act of robbery, it becomes his third strike and he is sentenced to life without parole in the Bakersfield State Penitentiary. While awaiting transfer to the prison, Darien is approached by his brother, Kevin, a government scientist with the Agency, who feels that he got a raw deal. Kevin offers Darien an option: to become the subject of a secret experiment in lieu of spending his life behind bars. Kevin's experiments on invisibility have been successful on rats; he now needs a human guinea pig.

An artificial gland called Quick Silver is implanted in Darien's brain. When fear is induced, the Quick Silver seals the skin (like Saran Wrap) and makes the subject invisible (the Quick Silver bends light instead of reflecting it). When the subject relaxes, the Quick Silver dissolves and the subject returns to visibility again. The government wants to use Darien to make a difference — to fight for right. This version of the H.G. Wells story adds a drawback to becoming invisible: the procedure drives Darien violently insane and he must be injected with a counteragent every week (which is also how the government continues to get him to do what they want).

Bobby Hobbes is Darien's partner, a government agent who will break the rules to accomplish his assignments. A woman, known only as "The Keeper" is a mysterious figure who represents rationality, control and the established order. She has an uneasy alliance with Darien and is the one who administers the special Quick Silver counteragent that preserves Darien's sanity and keeps his violent temper in check. Alexandra "Alex" Monroe is the Agency's highest ranking agent. She is an expert in weapons, seduction, surveillance and infiltration. While Alex does help Darien, she has instituted her own personal mission: to destroy Chrysalis, the Agency's arch rival organization. Alex wanted a child without the hassles of a marriage. She used artificial insemination to conceive a child but the fertility clinic that performed the procedure was owned by Chrysalis (they implanted her with a genetically engineered fetus and abducted her son shortly after birth). Alex is now determined to find her son — and destroy Chrysalis for what they did to her.

The Agency is headed by a man called The Official. He is a typical bureaucrat and appears to have many hidden secrets. The Official controls all top secret experiments (like the one performed on Darien). He gets others to do what he wants by wielding red tape and paperwork like a Samurai wields a sword. Albert Eberts is the Official's right hand man. Eberts is a computer genius and a master of the double ledger (his job is to keep the Agency's paperwork organized and secure); he is also responsible for trying to keep the Agency's meager budget under control despite Fawkes' and Hobbes' tendency to destroy property and cars.

Cast: Vincent Ventresca *(Darien Fawkes)*; Paul Ben-Victor *(Bobby Hobbes)*; Shannon Kenny *(The Keeper)*; Brandy Ledford *(Alex Monroe)*; Eddie Jones *(The Official)*; Michael McCafferty *(Albert Eberts)*.

4488   The Invisible Woman. (Pilot; Comedy; NBC; Feb. 13, 1983). Hoping to get a scoop from her biochemist uncle (Dudley Plunkett), Sandy Martinson, a cub reporter for the Washington, D.C., *Daily Express*, touches a spilled chemical solution (mixed and spilled by Dudley's lab chimp, Chuck) that renders her invisible. When Sandy learns that Dudley is unable to reduplicate the formula to make her visible again, she makes the best of the situation and uses her misfortune to investigate stories. By using makeup, contact lenses, caps, a wig and clothes, Sandy appears as a normal girl. The proposal was to relate Sandy's adventures as she uses her invisibility to investigate and solve crimes. Other regulars are Neil, Sandy's editor; Dan Williams, Sandy's boyfriend, a police lieutenant; and Spike, the sportswriter for the paper. David Frank performs the theme, "She Must Be Around Here Someplace."

Cast: Alexa Hamilton *(Sandy Martinson)*; Bob Denver *(Dudley Plunkett)*; David Doyle *(Neil Gilmore)*; Jacques Tate *(Dan Williams)*; Ron Palillo *(Spike Mitchell)*.

4489   Invitation Only. (Series; Variety; CMT; 2009). Reba McEntire, Keith Urban and Darius Rucker are among the country and western entertainers who perform songs before an intimate gathering in Studio A at Nashville's Grand Ole Opry House. The featured performer of each episode also serves as the host.

4490   Ireene Wicker Sings. (Experimental; Variety; NBC; July

28, 1939). Radio star Ireene Wicker ("The Singing Lady") performs some of the top hits of the day in her first television appearance.
Host: Ireene Wicker.

4491   *Ireene Wicker Story Time.* (Series; Children; ABC; 1948). The alternate title for *The Singing Lady*. See this title for information.

4492   *Irene.* (Pilot; Comedy; NBC; Aug. 19, 1981). Irene Cannon is a hopeful singer who leaves her home in Omaha to pursue a career in New York City. She begins by acquiring a job as a waitress at Dotty Bushmill's Talent Hutch and the unsold series was to chart her rocky climb up the ladder of success. Other regulars are Dede and Lois, Irene's roommates; Lloyd, Irene's uncle; Dotty, the club owner; and Michael, a waiter at the club.
Cast: Irene Cara (*Irene Cannon*); Dee Dee Rescher (*Dede Thomas*); Julia Duffy (*Lois Swenson*); Theodore Wilson (*Lloyd Cannon*); Kaye Ballard (*Dotty Bushmill*); Michael Winslow (*Michael*).

4493   *Iron Chef America.* (Series; Reality; Food Network; 2004–). Chefs compete in various cooking and camera skill challenges for the opportunity to star on a four-to-six episode Food Network program.
Host: Marc Summers, Bobby Flay. **Judges:** Bob Tuschman, Susie Fogelson, Bobby Flay, Gordon Elliott. **Commentator:** Alton Brown. **Floor Reporter:** Kevin Brauck.

4494   *Iron Horse.* (Series; Western; ABC; 1966–1968). Wyoming during the 1870s is the setting. In a poker game in Kansas City, Benjamin P. Calhoun wins the Buffalo Pass, Scalplock and Defiance Railroad — a railroad that is not only penniless but deeply in debt. Ben is a man who will gamble on anything. He believes the future is the railroad and that once his line is built and connects with the Union Pacific Railroad, it will open up the 16 million acres of land to settlers and make him rich.

People say Ben is arrogant; he says "I'm lucky" (but he's also a con artist, a schemer, a fighter and a cheat — he will do what it takes to get what he wants).

Ben begins his take over by adding a luxurious sleeping coach (the La Bonne Chance) to his engine (Number 3), coal car and baggage/passenger coach. Stories relate Ben's efforts to overcome the numerous difficulties he encounters in making the BPS&D Railroad profitable and build his empire. Dave is Ben's construction engineer (they have to lay track through each town as they head west to California); Barnabas is Ben's assistant; Nils is Ben's logger (acquires the wood for the track ties); Julie is the freight line operator. Hannibal is Ben's horse; Ulysses is Barnaby's raccoon.
Cast: Dale Robertson (*Ben Calhoun*); Gary Collins (*Dave Tarrant*); Bob Rando (*Barnabas Rogers*); Roger Torrey (*Nils Torvald*); Ellen McRae (*Julie Parsons*).

4495   *Iron Man.* (Series; Cartoon; Syn.; 1994-1995). Tony Stark is a billionaire industrialist who heads Stark Enterprises. He is also Iron Man, a mysterious armor-clad super hero who battles evil wherever he finds it. Tony has created armor that is unique: it adapts to different environments and becomes whatever Tony needs to protect him. Tony's principal enemy is Mandarin, a villain with the power of his ten deadly rings, who is seeking to take over Tony's company; Justin Hammer is another villain Tony battles. Stories relate Tony's efforts to defeat the evils that plaque his city. Based on the comic book of the same name.
Voice Cast: Robert Hays (*Tony Stark*); Ed Gilbert, Tony Ito (*Mandarin*); Tony Steedman, Efrem Zimbalist, Jr. (*Justin Hammer*); John Reilly (*Clint Barton*); Linda Holdahl (*Hypnotia*); Casey Defranco,

Jennifer Hale (*Julia Carpenter*); Jennifer Darling (*Scarlet Witch*); Jim Cummings (*Modak*).

4496   *Iron Man: Armored Adventures.* (Series; Cartoon; Nick; 2009). As originally conceived, Anthony Edward "Tony" Stark was the highly intellectual son of Howard and Maria Stark. At the age of 15, Tony enrolled in M.I.T. as an undergraduate in electrical engineering. Six years later he inherited his father's company, Stark Enterprises, when his parents were killed in a car accident. Sometime later, while inspecting a company plant in East Asia, Tony is injured in a lab explosion and captured by Wong Chu, an evil war lord who has also captured a noted physicist (Ho Yinsen). Together, they are forced to develop weapons for him. A small piece of shrapnel from the lab explosion had entered Tony's body and begins to affect his health. It is slowly moving toward his heart and can kill him. Tony and Ho create an iron suit to keep Tony alive. The suit also enables Tony to escape, but in the process, Ho is killed. It is at this time that Tony meets Jim Rhodes, a helicopter pilot who helps him return to America (Jim eventually becomes Tony's personal bodyguard). With improvements made to the iron suit, Tony would use it to battle evil as Iron Man.

The modernized version has Tony as a 16-year-old computer whiz whose father founded a company called Stark International (produces technology to help mankind). The evil Obadiah Stane, Tony's father's deputy, hopes to one day use the company's technology to build weapons. When a mysterious accident kills Tony's father (the plane on which he is traveling explodes), Obadiah becomes the new head of Stark International (until Tony turns 18). As Obadiah begins to implement his plans to build weapons, Tony establishes a secret lab and develops a suit of armor that endows him with incredible powers to battle evil and find the truth about his father's death. Pepper Potts and Jim "Rhodey" Rhodes are Tony's teenage friends. Based on the Marvel comic.
Voice Cast: Adrian Petriw (*Tony Stark/Iron Man*); Daniel Bacon (*Jim Rhodes*); Anna Cummer (*Pepper Potts*); Mackenzie Gray (*Obadiah Stane*); Catherine Haggquist (*Roberta Rhodes*); Vincent Tong (*Gene Khan/Mandarin*).

4497   *The Iron Mask.* (Pilot; Adventure; Unaired; Produced in 1958). Seventeenth century France is the setting for a proposal about Philippe, an escaped political prisoner who is secretly the Iron Mask, a daring crusader who defends the people against the soldiers of King Louis XIV. The identity of the actor portraying the lead was never revealed.
Cast: ? (*Philippe*); Lynn Roberts (*Louise*); Dorothy Patrick (*Constance*); Carl Esmond (*Chief of Police*).

4498   *Ironside.* (Series; Crime Drama; NBC; 1967–1975). While vacationing, Robert T. Ironside, a no-nonsense, dedicated Chief of Detectives of the San Francisco Police Department, is shot by an assassin and crippled when the bullet shatters his spinal column. Determined not to let his handicap stop him, Ironside continues with his work, now as Special Consultant to the department. He is given a specially furnished room (48) of police headquarters. Sergeant Ed Brown and Officer Eve Whitfield are assigned to work with him, Marc Sanger, a reformed criminal, becomes Ironside's personal helper (lives with him, pushes his wheelchair and drives his special police van). Ironside has very strict principals and sticks to them. He likes to have a free hand and do what he thinks will conclude a case. He takes pure delight when his plans come together and an arrest is made. Ironside believes in concealing evidence if it will help catch a killer. He incorporates trickery — and if it's a bit irregular, but legal he will do it. Ed usually does the legwork on a case; Eve is also serves as an undercover agent when needed.

Cast: Raymond Burr (*Robert T. Ironside*); Barbara Anderson (*Eve Whitfield*); Don Galloway (*Ed Brown*); Elizabeth Bauer (*Sgt. Fran Belding*); Don Mitchell (*Marc Sanger*); Jane Pringle (*Diana Sanger; Marc's wife*); Gene Lyons (*Police Commissioner Randall*); Jessie Royce Landis (*Robert's Aunt Victoria*).

4499 Is She Really Going Out with Him? (Series; Reality; MTV; 2009). Why do beautiful young women fall for self-absorbed, overly tanned and overly tattooed men? That is the question the program attempts to answer as it explores one such couple on each episode. Dave Cox is the narrator.

4500 Is There a Doctor in the House? (Pilot; Comedy; NBC; Mar. 22, 1971). Wendell Falls is a small, conservative New England town. Timothy Newly is its kindly physician and Michael Griffin, a recent medical school graduate is his female assistant. Newly hired Michael sight unseen because he thought she was a man and the unsold series was to relate Michael's efforts to prove herself to him and to the townspeople — who are distrustful of women doctors — even if she has a man's first name. Emma is Newly's housekeeper.

Cast: William Windom (*Dr. Timothy Newly*); Rosemary Forsyth (*Dr. Michael Griffin*); Margaret Hamilton (*Emma Procter*).

4501 Isabel Sanford's Honeymoon Hotel. (Pilot; Comedy; Syn.; Jan. 1987). Isabel Scott is the divorced (from K.C.) manager of Isabel's Honeymoon Hotel. The hotel, once a prestigious establishment has fallen on hard times and is now in serious debt. The proposal was to follow Isabel and her staff as they attempt to return to the hotel to its glorious past. Carlton and Martha assist Isabel; Mel is the hotel bartender; Agnes is the chambermaid; Jolie is Isabel's niece; Rooster is Jolie's friend.

Cast: Isabel Sanford (*Isabel Scott*); John Lawlor (*Carlton*); Rhonda Bates (*Martha*); Earl Boen (*Mel*); Renee Jones (*Jolie Scott*); Lana Schwab (*Agnes*); Ernie Banks (*K.C. Scott*); Miguel Nuez (*Rooster*).
Announcer: Casey Kasem.

4502 Isis. (Series; Adventure; CBS; 1975–1978). While on an expedition in Egypt, high school science teacher Andrea Thomas uncovers a magic amulet that is possessed of unique abilities that endows its possessor with the powers of Isis, the Egyptian goddess of fertility. Later, when Andrea is at home in California, she decides to use the powers of the amulet to help good defeat evil. Andrea, a teacher at Larkspur High School, is now "The dedicated foe of evil, defender of the weak and champion of truth and justice." Andrea wears the amulet as her necklace. When she holds it and says "O Mighty Isis," she becomes Isis (the skies darken around her, the symbol of Isis is seen and Andrea is magically transformed into the goddess. She is able to soar, has power over animals and the ability to control the elements of earth, sea and sky). As Isis, Andrea wears a white tunic with a short skirt and a tiara that allows her to see beyond her normal vision. Her hair also increases in length — from Andrea's mid-back length to hip length for Isis. Little effort is made to hide JoAnna Cameron's beauty as Andrea. Conservative dress, glasses and a ponytail are the "disguises" Andrea uses to conceal her secret identity.

Cindy Lee is Andrea's teaching assistant for the first two seasons. Renee Carroll replaced her in the final season. Rick Mason is Andrea's friend, a fellow teacher; Dr. Barnes is the science department head. Last season episodes were broadcast as *The Secrets of Isis*. When broadcast back-to-back with the series *Shazam!* (see entry), it was titled *The Shazam!/Isis Hour*.

Program Open: "O, My Queen," said the Royal Sorceress to Hashipseth, "With this amulet you and your descendants are endowed by the goddess Isis. With the powers of the animals and the elements,

you will soar as the falcon soars; run with the speed of gazelles; and command the elements of sky and earth." Three thousand years later, a young science teacher dug up this lost treasure and found she was heir to the secrets of Isis. And so, unknown to her closets friends, Rick Mason and Cindy Lee, she becomes a dual person — Andrea Thomas, teacher — and Isis, dedicated foe of evil, defender of the weak, champion of truth and Justice."

Cast: JoAnna Cameron (*Andrea Thomas/Isis*); Joanna Pang (*Cindy Lee*); Ronalda Douglas (*Renee Carroll*); Brian Cutler (*Rick Mason*); Albert Reed (*Dr. Barnes*).

4503 Island Son. (Series; Drama; CBS; 1989-1990). The title refers to Daniel Kulani, a Caucasian doctor at the Kamehameha Medical Center in Honolulu, who was adopted as an infant by Hawaiian parents (Tuti and Nana). Daniel has a native brother, James, an ex-wife (Janine) and a son, Sam. Daniel is a graduate of Stamford University and returned to Hawaii to help the people of his adopted state. Stories follow events in the private and professional life of Daniel as he treats patients with dignity and respect. In addition to the doctors listed in the cast, other regulars are Emma, a nurse and Laura, Kenji's wife.

Cast: Richard Chamberlain (*Dr. Daniel Kulani*); Carol Huston (*Dr. Caitlin McGrath*); Timothy Carhart (*Dr. Anthony Metzger*); Leslie Bevis (*Dr. Veronica Redfield*); Kwan Hi Lim (*Tutu Kulani*); Betty Carvalho (*Nana Kulani*); Brynn Thayer (*Dr. Margaret Judd*); Clyde Kusatsu (*Dr. Kenji Fushida*); Carmela Barut (*Emma*); Christine Ebersole (*Janine Willis*); William McNamara (*Sam Kulani*); Ray Bumatai (*James Kulani*); Roxanne Hart (*Laura Fushida*).

4504 Island Sons. (Pilot; Adventure; ABC; May 15, 1987). When their wealthy father disappears under mysterious circumstances, his four estranged sons, Tim (the owner of a charter boat service), Sam (an assistant D.A. in Honolulu), and Joe (a hotel owner) join forces with Ben to preserve their family dynasty — the Farraday Cattle Ranch (which is run by Ben) in Hawaii. The proposal was to relate their efforts to become a family again and help each other in time of need.

Cast: Timothy Bottoms (*Tim Farraday*); Joseph Bottoms (*Joe Farraday*); Samuel Bottoms (*Sam Farraday*); Benjamin Bottoms (*Ben Farraday*); Clare Kirkconnell (*Abby Farraday*).

4505 The Islander. (Pilot; Drama; CBS; Sept. 16, 1978). Following his retirement from the law profession, Gabe McQueen moves to Hawaii and purchases the Queen Kulani, a Honolulu hotel fraught with problems. The proposal was to depict Gabe's attempts to run the hotel and his involvement with and attempts to help people in trouble. Other regulars are Shauna, the hotel manager; and Kimo and Al, who work for Gabe. Shelby Flint performs the theme, "My Islander."

Cast: Dennis Weaver (*Gabe McQueen*); Sharon Gless (*Shauna Cooke*); Ed Kaahea (*Kimo*); Dick Jenson (*Al Kahala*).

4506 The Islanders. (Series; Adventure; ABC; 1960-1961). Latitude 4 south, longitude 128 east in the East Indies is the location of Ambowina, a small island off the coast of Sumatra, whose "chief natural resources are beautiful native girls." The tropical paradise is also the base for Lato Airlines, a Grumman Goose seaplane that is owned by Sandor ("Sandy") Wade and Zachary ("Zack") Malloy, two argumentative partners who share billing as president of the company on alternate months. They paid $35,000 for the plane and have another partner, a beautiful but scheming woman named Wilhelmina ("Willie") Vandeveer, who manages the business ("I'll be your treasurer") for 15 percent of the profits.

Jim ("Shipwreck") Callahan runs Shipwreck Callahan's American

Bar on Ambowina. He served on the destroyer USS Houston during World War II, and his favorite drink to serve is a Bamboo Bomb. Naja is a gorgeous 20-year-old Balinese girl who works in the American Bar as a dancer. She previously worked as a switchboard operator at Macaser Imports in Singapore. Naja looks more European than Balinese ("My father was Portuguese but more of an Islander than my mother") and loves to dance.

Sandy was born in Cincinnati, and he and Zack served in Korea together during the war. Willie was born in Holland, and the Vandeveer family is one of the biggest plantation owners in the Dutch East Indies. Islanders call her "Steamboat Willie" because after a con "she always catches the next steamboat out."

Program Open: "*The Islanders* starring Bill Reynolds ... James Philbrook ... Diane Brewster ... with Gordon Jones and Daria Massey ... an M-G-M television production."

Cast: William Reynolds (*Sandy Wade*); James Philbrook (*Zack Malloy*); Diane Brewster (*Willie Vandeveer*); Gordon Jones (*Shipwreck Callahan*); Daria Massey (*Naja*).

4507   *It Could Be You.* (Series; Game; NBC; 1956–1961). Contestants selected from the studio audience compete by performing stunts. Winners receive a prize they have always wanted (which is stated before the game begins) but could never afford to purchase. The series ran in prime time from July 2 to Sept. 17, 1958 (and Dec. 11, 1958 to Mar. 12, 1959) and on NBC daytime from June 4, 1956 to Dec. 29, 1961.

Program Open: "*It Could Be You.* It's America's show of surprises brought to you by new Liquid Prell, the shampoo that's extra rich to leave your hair looking radiantly alive, and by Ivory Soap, recommended by more doctors for baby's skin and yours. And now here is your master of surprises, Bill Leyden."

Host: Bill Leyden. **Announcer:** Wendell Niles,.

4508   *It Could Happen to You.* (Series; Game; ABC; 1951-1952). Three married couples are involved in a game wherein each must reenact a personal situation that was brought about as the result of a popular song. Prizes are awarded for participating. Also known as *The Bill Gwinn Show* and *This Could Be You*.

Host: Bill Gwinn.

4509   *The IT Crowd.* (Pilot; Comedy; Unaired; Produced for NBC in 2006). Roy and Moss are tech geniuses who can fix any computer but when it comes to making friends they are losers. They do have each other and the proposal was to present a look at the unseen people who repair the equipment that keeps the office running. Denholm is their boss, the head of the IT Department of a company that regulates them to the basement; Jen is a fellow employee.

Cast: Joel McHale (*Roy*); Richard Ayoade (*Moss*); Rocky Carroll (*Denholm*); Jessica St. Clair (*Jen*).

4510   *The IT Crowd.* (Series; Comedy; IFC; 2008). Reynholm Industries is a large corporation in England. While the company employs many people, the entire focus is on three workers in the computer division: Jen, Roy and Moss, three young people who lack not only social skills and, for Jen, the ability to actually use a computer for business. Jen lied about her qualifications and has to pretend to know what she is doing. Roy is an Irishman who thinks he's a ladies' man; Moss is a genius who is also a goof off. Produced in England.

Cast: Katherine Parkinson (*Jen Barber*); Chris O'Dowd (*Roy*); Richard Ayoade (*Moss*).

4511   *It Had to Be You.* (Pilot; Comedy; Unaired; Produced in 1987). The original pilot film for *Just in Time*. Metropol Press is a publisher of literary books that has not had a successful title in over three years. Joanna Farrell and Harry Stadlin are its chief editors and are forever seeking authors, especially Carlie Hightower, who has penned three successful novels. The proposal was to relate Joanna and Harry's efforts to keep the press alive and on the romantic relationship that develops between them. Isabel is their flaky Girl Friday.

Cast: Annette Bening (*Joanna Farrell*); Tim Matheson (*Harry Stadlin*); Ronnie Claire Edwards (*Carlie Hightower*); Nada Despotovich (*Isabel*).

4512   *It Had to Be You.* (Series; Comedy; CBS; 1993). Laura Scofield is a glamorous woman who owns the posh Scofield Publications in Boston. She lives on Beacon Hill at 204 Chandler and has been married twice, but never had time for husbands and divorced.

Mitch Quinn is a widowed carpenter with three children, David, Christopher and Sebastian. David, the oldest, sort of runs the house—he cooks, cleans, does the laundry and takes his younger brothers to school. He works at the Eager Beaver Car Wash. Sebastian has "an old" football injury—"he fell off the couch while watching the Super Bowl." When Mitch was 14 years old he worked in his father's hardware store. He began by sweeping the floors and worked his way up to sorting screws.

One day Laura decides to put shelves in her office and goes to the Yellow Pages seeking a carpenter. She sees an ad, placed by Mitch, of a smiling screwdriver, and calls him. It's a virtual love at first sight and the short lived (4 episode) program follows their unlikely courtship (and possible eventual marriage) as a woman who is afraid of marriage struggles to change her ways and possibly find what she has been looking for all her life (Laura and Mitch have their first date in the second episode). Other regulars are Eve, Laura's assistant; and Mary Lou Maloney, the girl with a crush on Mitch's son, Chris.

Cast: Faye Dunaway (*Laura Scofield*); Robert Urich (*Mitch Quinn*); Justin Whalen (*David Quinn*); Will Estes (*Chris Quinn*); Justin Jon Ross (*Sebastian Quinn*); Robin Bartlett (*Eve*); Melody King (*Mary Lou Maloney*).

4513   *It Happenes in Spain.* (Series; Crime Drama; Syn.; 1958). Joseph Jones, called Joe, is an American private detective operating out of Spain. He has established a small office and his only assistant is his secretary, Tina. Stories relate his case assignments, which generally involve helping distressed American tourists.

Cast: Scott McKay (*Joe Jones*); Elena Barra (*Tina*).

4514   *It Only Hurts When I Laugh.* (Series; Reality; TruTV; 2009). A clip program that showcases "people caught in the craziest predicaments. It is a half-hour of the zaniest stunts and dumbest situations ever caught on tape." Thom Kirlot narrates.

4515   *It Only Hurts When You Laugh.* (Pilot; Comedy; NBC; Jan. 4, 1983). Skits that take a comical look at life's everyday frustrations.

Host: Robert Guillaume. **Regulars:** Lewis Arquette, Hank Bradford, Marvin Braverman, Sid Caesar, Bob Elliott, Ray Goulding, Doug Hale, Renny Temple, Martin Rudy. **Orchestra:** Peter Matz.

4516   *It Pays to Be Ignorant.* (Series; Game; CBS; NBC; 1949–1951). Two players compete. Each player, in turn, picks a question from the Dunce Cap and reads it aloud (for example, "What color was George Washington's White Horse?"). Three regular panelists are supposed to answer it but evade giving the correct response. The object is for the contestant, if at all possible, to get a word in and extract the right answer. Prizes are awarded accordingly—basically for attempting to face the panel. Based on the long-running radio series of the same title. Aired on CBS (June 6 to Sept. 19, 1949) and NBC (July 5, to Sept. 27, 1951).

Host: Tom Howard. **Panelists:** Harry McNaughton, George Shelton, Lulu McConnell. **Vocalists:** The Townsmen Quartet. **Announcer:** Dick Stark. **Organist:** Ray Morgan.

4517   *It Pays to Be Married.* (Series; Game; NBC; 1955). Married couples first converse with the host and relate their marital difficulties and how they overcame them. The couples then compete in a general knowledge question-and-answer round with the highest scoring players receiving $350.

Host: Bill Goodwin. **Announcer:** Jay Stewart.

4518   *It Takes a Thief.* (Series; Adventure; ABC; 1968–1970). Alexander Mundy is a cunning cat burglar who is captured in the act but granted a pardon (from the San Jobel Prison) in exchange for performing acts of thievery for Noah Bain, a U.S. government S.I.A. Chief. Alexander poses as an international playboy as a cover for his assignments (which include highly dangerous feats of thievery to acquire information the government needs). He is a master pickpocket, escape artist, explosives expert and skilled at posing as someone else. Alexander can recognize style in a thief and "I can spot a pickpocket in the middle of St. Petersburg Square on Easter Sunday."

Charlotte Brown, nicknamed "Chuck," is the beautiful but "kooky" thief who complicates Al's assignments. Alistair is Alexander's father; Wally Powers replaced Noah as Alexander's superior in last season episodes.

Cast: Robert Wagner (*Alexander Mundy*); Malachi Thorne (*Noah Bain*); Fred Astaire (*Alistair Mundy*); John Russell (*SIA Agent Dover*); Edward Binns (*Wally Powers*); Susan Saint James (*Charlotte "Chuck" Brown*).

4519   *It Takes a Village.* (Pilot; Comedy; Unaired; Produced for ABC in 2010). Karen and Howard appear to be a normal, happily married couple. They have a 15-year-old son (George) and all is progressing well until Howard announces that he is gay. A divorce follows and Howard, who wants to be an active part of his son's life, moves across the street from Karen. To further complicate life for all concerned, especially George, Howard invites his boyfriend, Scott, to move in with him. The proposal was to follow the situations that occur, especially to George, who had been raised in a protective bubble and now must face the reality of life.

Cast: Leah Remini (*Karen Keener*); Christopher Sieber (*Howard Keener*); Zach Mills (*George Keener*); Cheyenne Jackson (*Scott*).

4520   *It Takes Two.* (Series; Comedy; ABC; 1982-1983). Molly and Sam Quinn are a busy professional couple. They live in Manhattan and are the parents of Lisa and Andy. Also living with them is Molly's elderly and somewhat senile mother, Anna (who is fondly called "Mama"). Molly works as an Assistant District Attorney; Sam is the chief of surgery at the Rush-Thornton Medical Center. Stories follow Molly and Sam as they struggle to divide their time between work, home and time for each other. Molly is a woman who gives of herself to help others. She believes that everyone is entitled to a fair trial — even those who break the law and she must prosecute. However, if she feels uneasy about a case and personally believes a wrong was done, she sort of turns defense lawyer and digs deeper into the facts. On occasion, she sides with the defense. While Sam is a chief surgeon, the medical applications associated with such a position are not seen (they are only referenced when Sam and Molly are together). Sam is seen at the office and with patients but not in an operating room. Lisa is a high school student and works part time as a waitress as the Pizza Palace. Like her mother, she is devoted to helping others (she is also a member of the save the environment organization No

Nukes). Crystal Gayle and Paul Williams sing the theme, "Where Love Spends the Night."

Cast: Patty Duke (*Molly Quinn*); Richard Crenna (*Sam Quinn*); Helen Hunt (*Lisa Quinn*); Anthony Edwards (*Andy Quinn*); Billie Bird (*Anna*); Richard MacKenzie (*Dr. Walter Chenkins*); Della Reese (*Judge Caroline Phillips*); Gale Gordon (*Judge in Program Opening*); Charles Levin (*Jeffrey Maixes; state's attorney*); Jerry Houser (*Jeremy Fenton; state's attorney*).

4521   *It Takes Two.* (Series; Game; NBC, 1969-1970; Family Channel, 1997). Three celebrity couples compete and are each asked a question that must be answered in numbers (which are written on a card and the totals automatically calculated). The announcer, stationed in the studio audience, selects a player who chooses the couple he feels has come closest to the correct answer. The correct answer is revealed and the player receives a merchandise gift if he chooses the right couple.

Host: Vin Scully (*1969-70*); Dick Clark (*1997*). **Announcer:** John Harlan (*1969-70*); Burton Richardson (*1997*).

4522   *It Takes Two.* (Pilot; Comedy; ABC; Aug. 2, 1985). Kate Weston and her husband, Elliot are psychiatrists with differing points of view who share the same office and often the same patients. The proposal was to relate the problems of such a relationship when their mix of business often overflows into their personal lives.

Cast: Beth Howland (*Kate Weston*); Geoffrey Bowes (*Elliot Weston*).

4523   *It Was a Very Good Year.* (Series; Variety; ABC; 1971). The music, fads, sports, politics, and the sensational and tragic moments of the years 1918 through 1968 are recalled through film clips. Mel Torme hosts and performs the theme, "It Was a Very Good Year."

4524   *The Item of the Scarlet Ace.* (Experimental; Adventure; NBC; Nov. 29, 1941). A television adaptation of the radio series *The Bishop and the Gargoyle*. The Bishop is a crime fighter who once served on the parole board of Sing Sing Prison; the Gargoyle is a convict the Bishop befriended and, upon his release, became the Bishop's sidekick, the one who provides the physical force when it comes to battling criminals. Richard Gordon and Ken Lynch, the radio stars, appeared in this TV version of an episode wherein they try to nab an elusive criminal known as the Scarlet Ace.

Cast: Richard Gordon (*The Bishop*); Ken Lynch (*The Gargoyle*).

4525   *It's a Business.* (Series; Variety; DuMont; 1952). It is the early 1900s and a time when singers visited the publisher to find material to perform. The New York–based Broadway Music Publishing Company is one such music producer and Bob and Leo are the composers seeking performers. With help of Dorothy, their secretary, music and songs are presented as Bob and Leo test the material they are presented.

Cast: Bob Haymes (*Bob*); Leo DeLyon (*Leo*); Dorothy Loudon (*Dorothy*).

4526   *It's a Gift.* (Series; Game; CBS; 1946). John Reed King hosts a very early television game that features contestants competing in question-and-answer sessions in return for prizes. The series ran from Jan.29, 1946 to July 6, 1946.

4527   *It's a Great Life.* (Series; Comedy; NBC; 1954–1956). Denny David and Steve Connors are ex–GI's struggling to better their position in life. They live in Hollywood, California, in the Morgan Boarding House and stories follow their misadventures as they tackle various jobs in an effort to find their place in life. Amy Morgan is the owner of the boarding house; Uncle Earl is Amy's conniving brother; Katy Morgan is Amy's daughter. Also known as *The Bachelors*.

Cast: Michael O'Shea (*Denny David*); William Bishop (*Steve Connors*); Frances Bavier (*Amy Morgan*); James Dunn (*Uncle Earl*); Barbara Bales (*Katy Morgan*).

4528   *It's a Great Life*. (Series; Magazine; Syn.; 1983). A program of celebrity interviews, visits to exotic locales and lifestyle magazine segments.

Hosts: Robert Stack, Rosemarie Stack.

4529   *It's a Hit*. (Series; Game; ABC; 1957). Two teams of children, aged seven to fourteen, compete in a series of question-and-answer rounds based on subjects the contestants are studying in school. Points are scored for each correct answer and prizes are awarded to the highest scoring teams.

Host: Happy Felton. **Regulars:** Jack Norwine, Al Chotin, George Able.

4530   *It's a Living*. (Series; Comedy; ABC, 1980–1982; Syn., 1985–1989). Lois, Jan, Cassie, Dot, Vickie, Maggie, Amy and Ginger are waitresses who work at Above the Top, a posh thirtieth floor Los Angeles restaurant that features "Sky High Dining" (Above the Top is owned by Pacific Continental Properties). Nancy is the hostess; Sonny is the lounge singer; and Howard is the chef.

Lois Adams is the most sophisticated of the waitresses. She is married to the never-seen Bill and is struggling to raise two children (Amy and Joey). Maggie McBirney is a widow and has become shy and unsure of herself since the death of her husband, Joseph (a salesman for Kitchen Help dishwashers). Katie Lou ("Cassie") Cranston is the sexiest and most beautiful of the group. She was born in Kansas, is man-crazy and looking to marry money. Jan Hoffmeyer is divorced, the mother of a young girl (Ellen) and is attending night classes at North Los Angeles Law School. She later marries Richard Grey.

Dorothy ("Dot") Higgins, born in Detroit, majored in theater at Baxter College and is a hopeful actress. Victoria ("Vickie") Allen, born in Pocatello, Idaho, is best friends with Dot and the most sensitive of the women. Amy Tompkins was born in Snyder, Texas, and now lives in the Carrie Nation Hotel for Women in Los Angeles. She is a member of A.G.O.A. (American Gun Owners Association). Amy owns a chrome-plated .357 Magnum with a six inch barrel that her father gave her (with these words: "Keep you chin up and your skirt down"). Virginia ("Ginger") St. James was born in Buffalo, New York, and has a flair for fashion designing. She is the only black waitress employed by Above the Top.

Nancy Beebee, the snobbish hostess, was a ballerina for 15 years, then a waitress at Above the Top before acquiring her current position; she was born in South Philadelphia and married Howard Miller, the restaurant's chef. Sonny Mann, the restaurant's one-man entertainment center, has aspirations of becoming a singer.

Cast: Susan Sullivan (*Lois Adams*); Barrie Youngfellow (*Jan Hoffmeyer*); Ann Jillian (*Cassie Cranston*); Wendy Schaal (*Vickie Allen*); Crystal Bernard (*Amy Tompkins*); Sheryl Lee Ralph (*Ginger St. James*); Louise Lasser (*Maggie McBirney*); Gail Edwards (*Dot Higgins*); Marian Mercer (*Nancy Beebee*); Paul Kreppel (*Sonny Mann*); Richard Stahl (*Howard Miller*); Richard Kline (*Richard Grey*); Bert Remsen (*Mario; the chef*); Keith Mitchell (*Joey Adams*); Tricia Cast (*Amy Adams*); Lili Haydn, Virginia Keehne (*Ellen Hoffmeyer*).

4531   *It's a Man's World*. (Series; Comedy-Drama; NBC; 1962-1963). Moored at Stott's Landing in the Ohio River town of

Cordella is the *Elephant*, a houseboat owned by Wesley ("Wes") Macauley, Thomas A. ("Tom Tom") DeWitt and Vernon ("Vern") Hodges, three friends who are also students at Cordella College. Also residing with them is Howard ("Howie") Macauley, Wes's younger (14-year-old) brother (Wes, 22, became Howie's guardian after their parents were killed in an automobile accident).

Wes pumps gas for Houghton Stott, the owner of Stott's Landing and Stott's Service Station. Houghton is a former river barge pilot who was forced to retire after 50 years and is bitter about losing his job; he never had the time to raise a family and looks upon Howie as the son he never had. Tom Tom is the lazy one of the group — "he'll sleep his life away if he could," says Wes. He is a kid at heart and is fascinated by everything. Tom Tom enjoys every moment of life, but is in a dither most of the time and unreliable. Vern, from the South, is quiet, and loves to play the guitar. He works at Dobson's Market. Howie, who attends Cordella High School, has a paper route for the Cordella *Gazette* and works part time at Stott's Service Station.

Irene Hoff is Wes's girlfriend and is also a student at Cordella College. Nora Fitzgerald is Tom's friend, a kindred free spirit and aspiring artist. She attends Cordella College, rarely wears shoes or socks (even in the winter), dresses in jeans and sweatshirts and, as Tom says, "Can't even tell you're a girl." She was born in Westchester County and does her studying in the cemetery near the headstone of Priscilla Butler, who died in 1802.

Cast: Glenn Corbett (*Wes Macauley*); Ted Bessell (*Tom Tom DeWitt*); Randy Boone (*Verne Hodges*); Michael Burns (*Howie Macauley*); Ann Schuyler (*Nora Fitzgerald*); Jan Norris (*Irene Hoff*); Harry Harvey (*Houghton Scott*); Kate Murtaugh (*Iona Dobson*); Jeannie Cashell (*Alma Jean Dobson*); Mary Adams (*Mrs. Meredith*); Dawn Wells (*Molly*); Joyce Bulifant (*Lois*); Scott White (*Virgil Dobson*); James Bonnet (*Jeff*); Diane Sayer (*Jeri*); Sally Mills (*Helen*); Cathy Birch (*Sue*).

4532   *It's a Miracle*. (Series; Anthology; PAX; 1999). Heartwarming stories about people whose lives have been touched by miracles. In reenactments based on true incidents, people are seen facing an insurmountable obstacle; then, from out of nowhere, the strength to overcome it occurs — by Divine intervention when pleas for help are answered by total strangers who, for one reason or another, found themselves in a position to help.

Hosts: Richard Thomas, Roma Downey, Nia Peeples.

4533   *It's a Small World*. (Pilot; Comedy; Syn.; April 1957). The pilot film for *Leave It to Beaver* about Wally and Beaver Cleaver, two young brothers, and their experiences growing up in a small American town. Despite reviewers' objections that *It's a Small World* was "horribly juvenile," it did go on to launch the now classic *Beaver* series. Originally titled *Wally and the Beaver*. Broadcast as a segment of *Studio '57* and Other regulars are Ward and June, the boys' parents; Mr. Baxter, Ward's boss; and Frankie, Wally's friend.

Cast: Barbara Billingsley (*June Cleaver*); Casey Adams (*Ward Cleaver*); Jerry Mathers (*Beaver Cleaver*); Paul Sullivan (*Wally Cleaver*); Richard Deacon (*Mr. Baxter*); Harry Shearer (*Frankie*).

4534   *It's a Wacky World*. (Pilot; Comedy; NBC; Sept. 13, 1971). Skits, blackouts and songs performed by weekly guest stars.

Pilot Guests: John Cleese, Tony Curtis, Lulu, The New Seekers, Elke Sommer, Jacques Tati.

4535   *It's a Wonderful World*. (Series; Reality Syn.; 1963). Films that depict the customs and lifestyles of various countries throughout the world.

Host-Narrator: John Cameron Swayze.

4536   It's About Time. (Series; Game; ABC; 1954). Selected members of the studio audience compete in a game wherein they must identify incidents from the past through a series of clues (verbal, scrambled newspaper headlines, dramatic vignettes, etc.). Players with the highest score receive merchandise prizes.

Host: Dr. Bergen Evans. **Panelist:** Sherl Stern, Robert Pollack, Ruth Duskin.

4537   It's About Time. (Series; Comedy; CBS; 1966-1967). The U.S. spaceship *Scorpio* is completing a NASA mission and about to land. The capsule sets down in a remote jungle area that its astronauts, Captain Mac MacKenzie and Lieutenant Hector ("Hec") Canfield find has the same gravity as Earth, but no electron field or radiation. Believing they are on another planet, they begin to explore their surroundings. When they spot a cave family and then a dinosaur (a Tyrannosaurus rex), Mac theorizes that when they blacked out at 60,000 miles a second, they broke the time barrier and are now in the year 1 million B.C.

Just then, Mac and Hec hear a cry for help. They rush to a cliff and see a young cave boy (Breer) clinging to a branch. Breer, who grabbed the branch to escape from the rex, is rescued by Mac and Hec. Breer, beginning his test of manhood (to survive one day in the jungle) runs away. As Mac and Hec head back to their capsule, they are surrounded by a group of cavemen. Because of their dress, the Cave Boss believes they are evil spirits and orders Clon, his dim-witted aide, to kill them. Just then, Breer appears and saves the astronauts by telling the Cave Boss that they saved his life. Later, Mac and Hec befriend Breer's family — his father, Gronk; mother, Shad; and teenage sister Mlor.

Later, after a thorough examination of the *Scorpio*, the astronauts discover that the condenser points have been damaged, and without crystal and carbon it is impossible to fix and they cannot return to their time (in another episode, Mac mentions that they need copper to replace the filament of the solenoid transistor block, which controls liftoff). Stories relate Mac and Hec's efforts to survive and find the minerals they need to repair their craft and return home.

The astronauts are believed to be evil spirits by the other cave people and to have come from a forbidden area called "The Other Side of the Hill." Shad calls Gronk "Gronkie." Mlor, a teenage beauty, is a fabulous cook and famous for her mastodon stew. Several months later, Gronk realizes what minerals Mac and Hec are seeking and takes a diamond from the eye of his tribal idol. Hec is able to repair the condenser points; Mac reverses the flight information from their last trip and programs it into the computer. Just as they are about to blast off, Gronk, Shad, Mlor and Breer run to Mac and Hec for help (the Cave Boss now considers Gronk and his family traitors for helping evil spirits). Mac and Hec take the cave family aboard the capsule and blast off. Soon it is traveling faster than the speed of light and touches down outside of Los Angeles. Realizing that the cave family would become like animals in a zoo if the government knew about them, Mac and Hec decide to conceal their presence; they hide them in the three room apartment they share. Stories relate Mac and Hec's efforts to educate the cave family and keep not only the government but also their apartment house manager, Howard Tyler, from finding out who the cave family really are (the cave family believes that Los Angeles is "The Other Side of the Hill").

Cast: Frank Aletter *(Mac MacKenzie)*; Jack Mullaney *(Hector Canfield)*; Joe E. Ross *(Gronk)*; Imogene Coca *(Shad)*; Mary Grace *(Mlor)*; Pat Cardi *(Breer)*; Cliff Norton *(Cave Boss)*; Mike Mazurki *(Clon)*; Kathleen Freeman *(Mrs. Boss)*; Frank Wilcox *(General Morley)*; Alan DeWitt *(Howard Tyler)*; Jan Arvan *(Dr. Hamilton)*.

4538   It's All Relative. (Series; Comedy; ABC; 2003-2004).
Mace O'Neill and his wife Audrey, the owners of O'Neill's, a pub in Boston, are also the parents of Bobby and Maddie.

Simon Banks and Philip Stoddard are gays who live with Liz, a girl they are raising (Liz's mother died when she was just a baby. Simon and Philip were best friends with Liz's mother and when the biological father could not be found, Simon and Philip adopted Liz). Philip is a perfectionist and owns an art gallery; Simon is a third grade school teacher.

Fate brings Liz and Bobby together when they meet at a ski lodge in Vermont. Liz is a student at Harvard. Bobby works as a bartender in his parent's pub. Liz and Bobby fall in love and plan to marry — much to the delight of all but Mace when he finds out that Liz's fathers are gay — "If you marry a girl you marry their family" (and Mace appears to have an issue with gays as he is uncomfortable around them). Stories follow the efforts to the parents of both families to get along with each other as they are soon to become related by marriage.

Philip, an excellent cook, is proud and very protective of his kitchen. Simon is somewhat untidy. Audrey performs in the church choir and playwright Eugene O'Neill is Mace's great uncle. Maddie spent two years in the third grade and has nothing in common with smart people. She dates what she calls drunks and losers; she hopes to marry someone dumber than her. She loves showing cleavage and is in a band called Jail Bait.

Cast: Lenny Clarke *(Mace O'Neill)*; Harriet Sansom Harris *(Audrey O'Neill)*; Maggie Lawson *(Liz)*; John Benjamin Hickey *(Philip Stoddard)*; Christopher Sieber *(Simon Banks)*; Paige Moss *(Maddie O'Neill)*; Reid Scott *(Bobby O'Neill)*.

4539   It's Always Jan. (Series; Comedy; CBS; 1955-1956). The Harry Cooper Talent Agency represents Janis ("Jan") Stewart, a talented but relatively unknown singer who is hoping to make the big time. Jan is a widow and the mother of ten-year-old Josie. Jan and Josie share an apartment at 46 East 50th Street in Manhattan with Valerie Marlowe, a shapely blonde model, and Patricia Murphy, a secretary with a heart of gold.

Jan currently works as a nightclub entertainer who performs regularly at Tony's Cellar, a small supper club in New York's Greenwich Village. She dreams of starring on Broadway and singing at the prestigious Sky Room of the Sherry-Waldorf Hotel. Sid Melton plays Jan's agent, Harry Cooper.

Program Open: "Janis Paige ... *It's Always Jan* ... Created by Arthur Stander ... Presented by Dash, great new detergent for automatic washers and Drene, today's Drene shampoo with hairspring formula."

Cast: Janis Paige *(Janis Stewart)*; Merry Anders *(Valerie Malone)*; Patricia Bright *(Patricia Murphy)*; Jeri Lou James *(Josie Stewart)*; Arch Johnson *(Stanley Schrieber)*; Sid Melton *(Harry Cooper)*.

4540   It's Always Sunday. (Pilot; Comedy; NBC; Jan. 11, 1956). Charles Parker is a minister in a small town. He is married to Mary and they are the parents of Nancy and Danny. Charles is dedicated to his profession, but he is also a soft touch and the proposal was to relate the problems that arise when people begin to take advantage of him (something Mary is determined to stop from happening). Broadcast as a segment of *Screen Director's Playhouse*.

Cast: Dennis O'Keefe *(Charles Parker)*; Fay Wray *(Mary Parker)*; Eileen Janssen *(Nancy Parker)*; Terry Rangno *(Danny Parker)*.

4541   It's Always Sunny in Philadelphia. (Series; Comedy; FX; 2005–). Paddy's Irish Pub is a bar in Philadelphia that is owned by four slackers: Mac, Kelly, Dennis and Dee (Charlie and Dee are brother and sister; Frank is their wealthy but blustery father). Stories follow the argumentative group's efforts to run the bar despite both personal and financial problems. Charlie and Dee are graduates of St. Vincent's Elementary School and Penn State University (where Dee majored in psychology).

Cast: Charlie Day *(Charlie Kelly)*; Kaitlin Olson *(Deandra "Dee" Kelly)*; Rob McElhenney *(Mac)*; Glenn Howerton *(Dennis Reynolds)*; Danny DeVito *(Frank Reynolds)*; Anne Archer *(Barbara Reynolds, Frank's wife)*.

4542   *It's Back to School.* (Pilot; Children; Syn.; Aug. 1987). Michael Young hosts a program of information geared to and about children.

4543   *It's Garry Shandling's Show.* (Series; Comedy; Showtime; 1986–1990). Garry Shandling is a comedian who lives at the Happy Pilgrim Estates. He has a girlfriend (Phoebe) and a best friend, Pete Schumaker. Garry also has one other thing: An open life as the events that befall him unfold before a home and studio audience.

As a boy Garry's mother, Ruth, called him Bubba. (Ruth owns a pet shop called Ruth's Pet Corral). Nancy, who works for the Going Places Travel Agency, is Garry's friend from childhood; Pete, whose middle name is Horatio, is married to Jackie and they are the parents of Grant. Louis and Leonard are Garry's friends.

Cast: Garry Shandling *(Himself)*; Jessica Harper *(Phoebe)*; Molly Cheek *(Nancy)*; Michael Tucci *(Pete Schumaker)*; Bernadette Birkett *(Jackie Schumaker)*; Paul Willson *(Leonard Smith)*; Geoffrey Blake *(Louis)*; Scott Sherk *(Young Garry; flashbacks)*; Melanie Gaffin *(Young Nancy; flashbacks)*; Barbara Cason *(Ruth Shandling)*; Amzie Strickland *(Pete's mother)*; Marty Zagon *(Pete's father)*.

4544   *It's Happening.* (Series; Variety; ABC; 1968). Amateur band contests, performances by guest rock stars, comedy skits and other entertainment geared to teenagers.

Host: Mark Lindsay. **Regulars:** Allison Keith, Freddie Welles. **Music:** Paul Revere and the Raiders, Tommy Boyce, Bobby Hart.

4545   *It's Like, You Know.* (Series; Comedy; ABC; 1989). Arthur Garment is a New York writer who has a vision of Los Angeles as a place "populated with vapid, neurotic, self-absorbed, flaky airheads." Determined to write about the City of Angels, Arthur relocates, acquires accommodations with a former college friend (Robbie) and sets out to find out what Los Angeles is all about. Stories present a look at Los Angeles as seen through the eyes of a New Yorker. Robbie made a fortune with a TV scam called "Pay Per Jew" (a site where one can celebrate the Jewish Holy Days in the comfort of their homes). Jennifer Grey is their neighbor, an actress; Lauren is their friend, a masseuse who earns extra money as a process server.

Cast: Chris Eigeman *(Arthur Garment)*; Steven Eckholdt *(Robbie Graham)*; Jennifer Grey *(Herself)*; A.J. Langer *(Lauren Woods)*; Evan Handler *(Shrug)*.

4546   *It's Magic.* (Series; Children; CBS; 1955). Paul Tripp oversees a program of performances by guest magicians. Hank Sylvern supplies the music.

4547   *It's News to Me.* (Series; Game; CBS; 1951–1954). A celebrity panel is presented with a prop or picture that is related to a news event. Three of the panelists relate the wrong events; one tells the truth. Each of the two competing players has to determine which panelist gave the correct news event. Players begin with thirty dollars and increase their winnings by ten dollars with each correct guess.

Host: John Daly, Walter Cronkite, Quincy Howe.
Panelist: Anna Lee, Nina Foch, Quentin Reynolds, Constance Bennett, John Henry Faulk. **Regular:** Frank Wayne.

4548   *It's Not Easy.* (Series; Comedy; ABC; 1983). Jack Long is a divorced sporting goods store owner and the father of two children, Carol and Johnny. His mother, Ruth also lives with them. Living across the street is Sharon Townsend, Jack's ex-wife, who has recently married, and her second husband, Neal. Focal point of stories are the efforts of Jack and Sharon to live their own individual lives while sharing custody of their children. Other regulars are Sherry Gabler, Jack's girlfriend, and Matthew, Neal's son.

Cast: Ken Howard *(Jack Long)*; Carlene Watkins *(Sharon Townsend)*; Bert Convy *(Neal Townsend)*; Jayne Meadows *(Ruth Long)*; Rachel Jacobs *(Carol Long)*; Evan Cohen *(Johnny Long)*; Billy Jacoby *(Matthew Townsend)*; Christine Belford *(Sherry Gabler)*.

4549   *It's on with Alexa Chung.* (Series; Talk; MTV; 2009). Celebrity interviews, musical performances from mainstream and independent artists, viral video stars and the latest pop culture news.

Host: Alexa Chung. **Music:** Jon Murray.

4550   *It's Only Human.* (Pilot; Reality; NBC; Nov. 13, 1981). Taped interviews with ordinary people who speak their minds on subjects that concern them.

Host: Allen Funt. **Guests:** Barbara Eden, Reggie Jackson.

4551   *It's Polka Time.* (Series; Variety; ABC; 1956-1957). Bruno "Junior" Zienlisnki hosts a program of polka music and songs with the music of Stan Wolowic and polka performers Carolyn DeZurik, The Polka Chips and the Konal Siodmy Dancers.

4552   *It's Rock and Roll.* (Pilot; Game; Syn.; Jan. 1983). A proposed game show based on the 30-year history of rock and roll music. Two teams compete, the Blue and the Gold, each composed of one contestant and two performers associated with rock and roll music. An opening to a song is played. The first team to sound their buzzer receives a chance to answer. While no points are scored, the team does receive the first opportunity to select a category from a board of six topics. The team is then asked three questions, each of which is worth five points. The opposing team then selects a topic and is asked three questions. Two such rounds are played. The team with the highest score is the winner and receives a cash prize. While somewhat amateurish in production values, the program is entertaining for its use of rarely or never before seen clips of rock stars.

Host: Mike Egan.

4553   *It's Rod Hull and Emu.* (Series; Children; Syn.; 1973). The antics of Emu, the large puppet bird of ventriloquist Rod Hull, as he relates his adventures traveling from Australia to England (where the program is taped).

Host: Rod Hull.

4554   *It's Sunny Again.* (Pilot; Comedy; ABC; July 3, 1956). Sunny is a popular singer struggling to find her place in the entertainment world. Julie is her theatrical agent, a man who can't seem to find her work. The proposal was to relate Julie's efforts to find Sunny work and make her a star.

Cast: Vivian Blaine *(Sunny)*; Jules Munshin *(Julie)*; Casey Adams *(Stanley)*; Shirley Mitchell *(Dottie)*; Ray Walker *(Dottie's husband)*.

4555   *It's Time for Ernie.* (Series; Comedy; NBC; 1951). Satirical skits featuring the comic genius of Ernie Kovacs.

Host: Ernie Kovacs. **Regulars:** Edie Adams, Hugh Price. **Music:** Harry Sosnik.

4556   *It's Your Bet.* (Series; Game; Syn.; 1969). Two celebrity couples play for selected members of the studio audience. A small, movable wall is placed between each player. One partner is asked a question via a telephone to prevent the others from hearing it. The player then bets points (25 to 100) as to whether or not his partner can or cannot answer it. The question is then read aloud. Points are added or deducted from the couples' scores based on the verbal replies by the other partner of the team. The first team to score 300 points is the winner and their studio audience members receive merchandise prizes.

Host: Hal March, Tom Kennedy, Dick Gautier, Lyle Waggoner. **Announcer:** John Harlan.

4557   *It's Your Chance of a Lifetime.* (Series; Game; Fox; 2000). Contestants, who compete one at a time, vie for $1,000,000 by correctly answering ten questions in a row. The first round question, worth $10,000 is called "The Credit Card Question" and if the player answers it correctly, his credit card bill is paid off. The second question is worth $5,000 and becomes the money in his bank if he answers it correctly. The following eight questions are based on categories players choose from ten subjects. The player bets a portion (or all) of his winnings and if he correctly answers the question, the money is added to the bank. A player can continue or quit at any time. An incorrect answer costs the player the game and what money he has won up to that point. Based on the Australian series *The $1,000,000 Chance of a Lifetime* hosted by Frank Warrick and Sandy Roberts.

Host: Gordon Elliott. **Announcer:** Mark Thompson.

4558   *It's Your Move.* (Series; Game; Syn.; 1967). Two teams compete, each composed of two members. One team member acts out a charade; the other member must guess it within a specific time limit. The amount of time is determined through bidding. The team that bids the lowest amount of time receives it and must act it out and solve it within that bid amount of time. Prizes are awarded to successful players.

Host: Jim Perry.

4559   *It's Your Move.* (Series; Comedy; NBC; 1984-1985). Eileen Burton is a beautiful legal secretary for a never-seen private practice lawyer named Mr. Clayburn. She is a widow and lives with her two teenage children, Julie and Matt, at 46 Wilshire Boulevard (Apartment 407) in Van Nuys, California. Sixteen-year-old Julie, and Matt, who is 14, attend Van Buren High School.

Julie is a cheerleader and captain of the Pom Pom Team. "Hell Hound" is but one of the many terms of endearment Julie uses to describe Matt, a juvenile wheeler-dealer. Matt enjoys "torturing" Julie at every opportunity and he has a scam for any occasion to make money. When Matt does use a scam to acquire money, his intentions are good — to supplement Eileen's income (Eileen appears to be a bit confused when it comes to money; Matt sneaks the money into her purse; and Eileen is always amazed to find extra money — but she has no idea where it came from).

Dialing the telephone number "Zoo Life" will get you Mort Stumplerutt, the rich but boring owner of the Stumplerutt Lumber Mills. Matt believes Mort is right for his mother, the man who can give her the life of luxury she deserves. Matt's efforts to spark a romance between the two is hampered when Norman Lamb, a former insurance salesman from Chicago turned freelance writer, moves into the apartment (406) across the hall. Norman is always in need of money and is not the man Matt wants for Eileen. Fate brings Eileen and Norman together (a chance meeting in the hallway); Mort becomes a thing of the past. (Matt is concerned about Eileen's future and feels it is his obligation to find her the right man.) Matt's antics were curtailed halfway through the series when Eileen caught him red-handed in a scam. He was put on probation, and the original

series concept was lost. Norman, who became an English teacher at Van Buren, and Eileen were now the focal point (the series declined and soon went off the air).

Eli is Matt's "cohort in crime"; Lou Donatelli is the apartment building super; and Dwight Ellis is the principal of Van Buren.

Cast: Caren Kaye *(Eileen Burton)*; Tricia Cast *(Julie Burton)*; Jason Bateman *(Matt Burton)*; David Garrison *(Norman Lamb)*; Adam Sadowsky *(Eli)*; Ernie Sabella *(Lou Donatelli)*; Garrett Morris *(Dwight Ellis)*.

4560   *The Itsy Bitsy Spider.* (Series; Cartoon; USA; 1994). A simple program about a young spider named Itsy and his efforts to avoid the exterminator, a somewhat off-center "bug killer" who is determined to rid his life of the defiant itsy bitsy spider.

Voice Cast: Frank Welker *(Itsy)*; Matt Frewer *(Exterminator)*.

4561   *Ivan the Terrible.* (Series; Comedy; CBS; 1976). Ivan Petrovsky is the head waiter at the Hotel Metropole in Moscow, Russia, and the head of a family of nine who live in a three-and-a-half room apartment. Stories focus on Ivan's endless attempts to solve family problems. **Other Regulars:** Olga, his wife; Sonia, Sascha and Nikolai, his children; Svetlana, Nikolai's wife; Vladimir, Olga's ex-husband; Tationa, Olga's mother; Raoul, the Cuban exchange student; Federov, the government official; and Mr. Yoshanka Ivan's boss. Also living with Ivan is his dog, Rasputin.

Cast: Lou Jacobi *(Ivan Petrovsky)*; Maria Karnilova *(Olga Petrovsky)*; Caroline Kava *(Sonia Petrovsky)*; Matthew Barry *(Sascha Petrovsky)*; Nan Tucker *(Sventlana Petrovsky)*; Phil Leeds *(Vladimir)*; Despo *(Tationa)*; Manuel Martinez *(Raoul Sanches)*; Christopher Hewell *(Federov)*; Joseph Leon *(Mr. Yoshanka)*.

4562   *Ivanhoe.* (Series; Adventure; Syn.; 1957). England during the 1190s is the setting for tales of Ivanhoe, a young Saxon knight, as he battles the forces of injustice. Based on the characters created by Sir Walter Scott.

Cast: Roger Moore *(Ivanhoe)*; Robert Brown *(The Monk)*; Bruce Seton *(King Richard)*; Paul Whitsun *(Sir Maverick)*; John Pike *(Bart)*.

4563   *I've Got a Secret.* (Series; Game; CBS; Syn.; Oxygen, GSN; 1952–2008). The object calls for a celebrity panel of four to guess (through a series of indirect question-and-answer probe rounds) the secret of a guest contestant. Players receive both cash and merchandise prizes. Five versions appeared:

1. I've Got a Secret (CBS 1952–67). **Host:** Garry Moore (1952–64), Steve Allen (1964–67). **Announcer:** John Cannon, Johnny Olson. **Panelists:** Bess Myerson, Bill Cullen, Jayne Meadows, Henry Morgan, Betsy Palmer, Faye Emerson.

2. I've Got a Secret (Syn., 1972-73). **Host:** Steve Allen. **Announcer:** John Cannon. **Panelists:** Pat Carroll, Richard Dawson, Nanette Fabray, Gene Rayburn, Jayne Meadows, Henry Morgan, Anita Gillette.

3. I've Got a Secret (CBS, 1976). **Host:** Bill Cullen. **Announcer:** Johnny Olson, Richard Hayes. **Panelists:** Henry Morgan, Elaine Joyce, Phyllis George, Richard Dawson, Pat Collins.

4. I've Got a Secret (Oxygen; 2000–02). **Host:** Stephanie Miller.

5. I've Got a Secret (GSN, 2006–08). **Host:** Bill Dwyer. **Panelists:** Suzanne Westenhoefer, Jermaine Taylor, Frank DeCaro, Billy Bean.

4564   *I've Got News for You.* (Series; Game; NBC; 1952). The alternate title for *Up to Paar.* See this title for information.

4565   *Ivonna Cadaver's Macabre Theater.* (Series; Horror; Syn.; 2000–2007). Ivonna Cadaver is a gorgeous "timeless ghoul who has chosen to reinvent herself in the 21st century as the new diva of darkness" (replacing, but not completely, Elvira, Mistress of the Darkness). Ivonna is situated in a spooky dungeon where she hosts "classic" horror films of the past. In addition to her comical commentary, the sexy hostess (adorned in provocative, cleavage-revealing black attire similar to Elvira's), presents movie trivia, CD and DVD picks of the week and "The Ghoul Shopping Network," a macabre look at new products. Butch Patrick appears on occasion as Eddie Munster (the character her played on *The Munsters* in the 1960s).

Cast: Natalie Popovich *(Ivonna Cadaver)*; Butch Patrick *(Eddie Munster)*.

4566 *Ivy League.* (Pilot; Comedy; NBC; Mar. 13, 1959). Bull Mitchell, a former Marine sergeant, enrolls in college to get the education that was denied him earlier in life. The proposal was to depict his efforts to adjust to nonmilitary life. Other regulars are Timmy, Bull's son; Mamie, Bull's landlady; and the college dean.

Cast: William Bendix *(Bull Mitchell)*; Tim Hovey *(Timmy Mitchell)*; Florence MacMichael *(Mamie Parker)*; Bartlett Robinson *(Dean)*. **Also:** Arte Johnson, Doug McClure and Mary Tyler Moore *(Students)*; and Sheila Bromley and Kathleen Warren *(Teachers)*.

4567 *Jabberjaw.* (Series; Cartoon; ABC; 1976–1978). A futuristic undersea world is the setting where teenagers Biff, Shelley, Bubbles and Clam Head have formed The Neptunes, a rock group whose drummer is Jabberjaw, a 15-foot pet white shark. The teens (and Jabberjaw) are also detectives and their efforts to solve baffling crimes are the focal point of stories.

Voice Cast: Frank Welker *(Jabberjaw)*; Julie McWhirter *(Bubbles)*; Pat Paris *(Shelley)*; Tommy Cook *(Biff)*; Barry Gordon *(Clam Head)*.

4568 *Jack and Bobby.* (Series; Drama; WB; 2004-2005). What does it take to become the president of the United States? *Jack and Bobby* attempts to answer that question by looking at the lives of two brothers — Jack and Bobby McCallister, the children of a single mother (Grace) growing up in the fictional town of Hart, Missouri.

Stories are set in present times and follows the events in the lives of the brothers and the people who will (and do) shape their personalities and give them values.

Grace is a brilliant (but eccentric) college professor (she is unaware that she is raising a future president). Jack is the older, wiser brother, a natural born leader and the perfect role model for Bobby (who is smart, but not as outgoing as Jack).

Peter Benedict is the newly appointed president of Hart College. Peter appears to be a brilliant businessman but his character is questionable. Nonetheless, Grace falls for him and a romance blossoms for them. Peter, a widower, is the father of Courtney, a beautiful girl with a troubled past, who becomes attracted to Jack and forms a sister-like friendship with Bobby. Marcus Ride is Jack's best friend, the son of the owner of J.R.'s, the neighborhood gathering spot.

In addition to exploring the present day lives of Jack and Bobby, glimpses of the future are seen as Jack becomes president (nicknamed "The Great Believer").

Cast: Christine Lahti *(Grace McCallister)*; Matt Long *(Jack McCallister)*; Logan Lerman *(Bobby McCallister)*; Jessica Pare *(Courtney Benedict)*; John Stanley *(Peter Benedict)*; Edward Hodge *(Marcus Ride)*.

4569 *Jack and Jill.* (Series; Comedy-Drama; WB; 1999). Events in the hectic lives of Jacqueline Barrett (called "Jack" by her friends) and David Jillefsky (called "Jill" by his friends). Remembering that Jack is the girl and Jill is the boy, viewers first meet Jack as she is about to be married — but walks out of the service when she feels guilty about being unfaithful (sleeping with the groom). She immediately leaves town and heads for New York City, where she feels she

can begin a new life. Jill has a girlfriend (Elisa) and is contemplating moving in with her — until he meets Jack, who has rented an apartment in his building. Jack also meets Elisa and the two become friends. Elisa finds Jack a job at the TV station where she — and Jill work. Voice overs are used to convey the problems Jack and Jill encounter as they begin to date and try to make their relationship work.

Cast: Amanda Peet *(Jacqueline "Jack" Barrett)*; Ivan Sergei *(David "Jill" Jillefsky)*; Sarah Paulson *(Elisa Cronkie)*; Jaime Pressly *(Audrey Griffin)*; Justin Kirk *(Bartholomew "Barto" Zane)*; Simon Rex *(Michael "Mikey" Russo)*; Gary Marks *(Eddie Naiman)*; Chad Willett *(Jonathan Appel)*; Josh Hopkins *(Matt Prophet)*; Lindsay Price *(Emily Cantor)*; Ed Quince *(Peter McCray)*.

4570 *Jack and Mike.* (Series; Drama; ABC; 1986-1987). Jackie Shea is a beautiful columnist ("Our Kind of Town") for the Chicago *Mirror*; Mike Brennan is her husband, a hip restaurateur (owner of the 1935 Café). Jacqueline, who prefers to be called Jackie, is a sophisticated woman who dresses so elegantly that most people mistake her for a high fashion model. She is also very feminine and softspoken and mingles with people of all types (something that worries Mike) for her column. Mike is not the kind of guy most people would suspect of being married to a girl like Jackie. He is a bit rough around the edges and more outgoing than Jackie. Despite their different lifestyles, they love each other and are determined to make their marriage work. Kathleen is Mike's sister; Mary and John are his parents.

Cast: Shelley Hack *(Jackie Shea)*; Tom Mason *(Mike Brennan)*; Carol Rossen *(Charlotte Branigan)*; Jacqueline Brookes *(Nora Adler)*; Holly Fulger *(Carol Greene)*; Kevin Dunn *(Anthony Kubecek)*; Noelle Bou-sliman *(Belinda)*; Vincent Baggetta *(Rick Scotti)*; Carol Potter *(Kathleen)*; Beatrice Straight *(Mary)*; James Green *(John)*.

4571 *Jack and the Beanstalk.* (Experimental Series; Children; CBS; July 1941). A daily program that tells in serial form the story of "Jack and the Beanstalk." A young girl kneels down by her mother's chair and is told the story. As she listens, an artist draws pictures that fit the narration. The camera switches back and forth between mother, child and the ever-expanding panel of drawings.

Cast: Lydia Perera *(Mother)*; Anne Francis *(Girl)*; John Rupe *(Artist)*.

4572 *The Jack Benny Program.* (Series; Comedy; CBS, 1950–1964; NBC, 1964-1965). Jack Benny is an entertainer who stands five feet, 11 inches tall and weighs 158 pounds. He was born in Waukegan, Illinois, and claims to be only 39 years old ("I've been 39 for so long I've forgotten how old I really am"). Jack felt he was born with show business in his blood but before he could test that theory, he joined the Navy. After his discharge in 1921, he broke into vaudeville. Audiences seemed to despise him, but Jack pushed on and teamed with a comedian named George Burns when they met in Philadelphia. They formed their own comedy team (Benny and Burns) but with Jack as the foil and George as the straight man, the act bombed and broke up. George teamed with a girl named Gracie Allen (forming "Burns and Allen") and Jack became famous when he went into radio and began his own show, *The Jack Benny Program*. When television began to take hold, Jack transformed his radio program into a visual treat for his audience.

Like his radio program, Jack's TV series is a glimpse into his life at home and at the studio. Jack lives at 366 North Camden Drive in Beverly Hills, California. Eddie "Rochester" Anderson, his ever-faithful valet, lives with him (he calls Jack "Boss" or "Mr. Benny"). Jack has an image for being cheap; he blames this on his writers, who thought making him stingy would be funny. Although Jack has an account at the California Bank, he rarely withdraws money; he enjoys visiting it. When he decides to make a withdrawal, people fear the economy is in trouble and rush to withdraw their money. While Jack trusts banks, he feels safer storing most of his money in a large vault in the dungeon beneath his home.

Professor Pierre LeBlanc is Jack's long-suffering violin teacher. Mary Livingston is Jack's girlfriend, a salesgirl at the May Company department store. Dennis Day is Jack's vocalist. Don Wilson is Jack's overweight announcer; Lois is Don's wife; Harlow (whom Don is grooming to become a TV announcer) is their overweight son. Don lives at 4946 West End in Beverly Hills and it was mentioned that when Jack first hired Don, he paid him $5 a week plus meals. Fred is Jack's director; Miss Gordon (then Miss Adrian) is Jack's secretary; Joe is Jack's agent; Sam is Jack's writer; Mr. Kitzel is the Jewish foil.

Cast: Jack Benny (*Himself*); Mary Livingston (*Herself*); Dennis Day (*Himself*); Don Wilson (*Himself*); Eddie "Rochester" Anderson (*Himself*); Lois Corbett (*Lois Wilson*); Dale White (*Harlow Wilson*); Mel Blanc (*Professor LaBlanc*); Maudie Prickett (*Miss Gordon*); Iris Adrian (*Miss Adrian*); Fred DeCordova (*Fred*); Russ Conway (*Joe*); Herb Vigran (*Sam; Jack's writer*); Artie Auerbach (*Mr. Kitzel*); Mel Blanc (*Si, the Mexican*); Frank Nelson (*Yes Man*).

4573 *The Jack Carson Show.* (Series; Variety; NBC; 1954–1955). Comedian Jack Carson oversees a program of music, songs and comedy sketches.

Host: Jack Carson. **Regulars:** Constance Towers, Don Ameche, Kitty Kallen, Donald Richards, Peggy Ryan, Ray McDonald, The Asia Boys. **Announcer:** Ed Peck, Bud Heistand. **Orchestra:** Harry Sosnik, Vic Schoen.

4574 *Jack Carter and Company.* (Series; Variety; ABC; 1949–1951). Sketches, music and songs with comedian Jack Carter as the host. Also known as *The Jack Carter Show.*

Host: Jack Carter. **Regulars:** Elaine Stritch, Jack Albertson, Sonny King, Bill Callahan, Don Richards, Paul Castle. **Orchestra:** Lou Breese, Harry Sosnik.

4575 *The Jack Cole Dancers.* (Experimental; Variety; NBC; June 16, 1939). A program of East Indian music with Jack Cole and two unidentified female dancers who performed two routines.

4576 *The Jack LaLanne Show.* (Series; Health; Syn.; 1951–1970). The benefits of daily systematic exercise coupled with nutritional guidance with health and fitness expert Jack LaLanne and the assistance of his wife, Elaine.

Host: Jack LaLanne. **Assistant:** Elaine LaLanne.

4577 *Jack of All Trades.* (Series; Adventure; Syn.; 2000–2001). The time is 18081. Pulau Pulau is a small island in the East Indies that is ruled by Governor Croque, the wimpy brother of Napoleon Bonaparte, the emperor of France. Pulau Pulau is also the home of Jack Stiles and Emilia Smythe Rothschild, secret agents who have been ordered to thwart the French expansion and save Pulau Pulau from French rule.

Emilia works on behalf of the British government and Jack on orders from U.S. President Thomas Jefferson. Emilia is a brilliant scientist and has a secret laboratory in the basement of her home. She has the cover of an exporter and Jack poses as her attaché. To protect himself, as well as Emilia, Jack adopts the alias of the Daring Dragoon, a local folk hero who helps good defeat evil (mostly the devious plans of Croque as he sets out to prove to his brother that he is capable of ruling a country). Although Croque fears the Dragoon, he is more fearful of his wife, Camille, a buxom woman who is seeking to become the ruler of Pulau Pulau.

Jack, as the Daring Dragoon, wears a black mask and hat and a red cape. He rides a horse named Nutcracker and fights for the people — "I am an enemy of all crime." Jack hangs out at a pub called The Drunken Pig and jokes endlessly about everything. Emilia believes that God is a woman and tries to impose her beliefs that Britain is better than America on Jack (Jack tries to prove just the opposite). Emilia takes a daily break for tea time and has invented such military weapons as knock-out gas, ginger spray, bullet-proof clothing (using titanium thread) and a submarine. Emilia is a graduate of Oxford; Jack attended West Point. Jean Claude (voice of Shemp Wooley) is the secret courier, a parrot that delivers messages from the Resistance.

Governor Croque is fond of wealth and fancy clothes (that portray him as a "sissy") and secretly runs the Bonaparte family vineyards on the island. Croque carries a cow hand puppet with him at all times that he calls Mr. Nippers and is quite fearful of his brother, Napoleon, the diminutive (literally here) ruler of France. Napoleon believes Croque is a wimp and will never follow in his footsteps. Napoleon despises the Daring Dragoon and beats on a Daring Dragoon doll to control his rage.

Cast: Bruce Campbell (*Jack Stiles*); Angela Dotchin (*Emilia Smythe Rothschild*); Stuart Devine (*Governor Croque*); Ingrid Parke (*Camille Croque*); Verne Troyer (*Napoleon*).

4578 *The Jack Paar Show.* (Series; Variety; CBS; NBC; ABC; 1953–1973). Humorist Jack Paar oversees programs of talk, variety performances and light comedy. See also *Up to Paar.* Three versions appeared:

1. The Jack Paar Show (CBS, 1953–56). **Host:** Jack Paar. **Regulars:** Edie Adams, Richard Hayes, Martha Wright, Betty Clooney, Johnny Desmond, Jose Melis, Jack Haskell. **Announcer:** Hal Simms. **Music:** Ivan Ditmars, Pupi Campo, Jose Melis.

2. The Jack Paar Show (NBC, 1962–65). **Host:** Jack Paar. **Music:** Jose Melis.

3. Jack Paar Tonight (ABC, 1973). **Host:** Jack Paar. **Co-Host-Announcer:** Peggy Cass. **Music:** Charles Randolph Grean.

4579 *Jack the Ripper.* (Series; Mystery; Syn.; 1974). A recreation of three terrifying months in British history: August 31 to November 9, 1888 — a time when five women met death in Whitechapel, London, at the hands of the mysterious Jack the Ripper. Through modern-day investigations of Scotland Yard detectives Barlow and Witt, new evidence is presented in an attempt to uncover the identity of history's most notorious criminal.

Cast: Sebastian Cabot (*Host*); Stratford Johns (*Det. Jack Barlow*); Frank Windsor (*Detective Witt*). **Music:** Bill Southgate.

4580 *Jackass.* (Series; Reality; MTV; 2000–2002). Laughs are acquired by showcasing sheer stupidity. Professional stuntmen and women are seen performing not only stupid but dangerous stunts that send the wrong message to children (who have a tendency to copy what they see). The stunt performers are Bam Margera, Johnny Knoxville, Steve-O, Ehren McGhehey, Preston Lacy, Chris Ponticus, Trip Taylor, Rick Kosick, Ryan Dunn, Jeff Tremaine, Dave England, Jess Margera, Jason Acuna, Dimitry Elyashkevich.

4581 *Jackee.* (Pilot; Comedy; NBC; May 11, 1989). Hoping to make her mark in New York City, Sandra Clark leaves her home in Washington and moves to Manhattan where she plans to become a fashion designer for Midway Productions. When she discovers that Midway produces pornographic films, she quits but later acquires a job as the assistant manager of the Sensations Health and Fitness Club. The proposal, a spin off from *227* was to follow Sandra as she attempts to run the club. Stephanie, Nathan, Zoltan, Margaret and Sven are club members.

Cast: Jackee Harry (*Sandra Clark*); Deborah Stricklin (*Stephanie Potter*); John Karlen (*Nathan Pollock*); B'nard Lewis (*Zoltan*); Margaret Kemp (*Margaret*); Dan Blom (*Sven*).

4582 *Jackie and Darlene.* (Pilot; Comedy; ABC; July 8, 1978). Jackie Clifton and Darlene Shilton are roommates and police officers with the West Valley Precinct in California. Jackie is a street officer and Darlene is a radio dispatcher and the proposal was to relate their adventures with Jackie working the street beat and Darlene guiding her from the inside.

Cast: Sarina Grant (*Jackie Clifton*); Anna L. Pagan (*Darlene Shilton*); Lou Frizzell (*Sergeant Guthrie*).

4583 *Jackie Bison.* (Pilot; Cartoon; NBC; July 2, 1990). Jacob Bisonowitz is a bison who, after leaving the army and journeying to Hollywood, becomes a big star when he changes his name to Jackie Bison. He also becomes the first animal to ever host his own TV show — *The Jackie Bison Show* from television city in Wyoming. Jackie's show is patterned after *The Jack Benny Program* and features a comical look at his home and working life.

Voice Cast: Stan Freberg (*Jackie Bison*); Richard Karron (*Larry Lizard*); Rose Marie (*Doris*); Jayne Meadows (*Jill St. Fawn*); Pat Paulsen (*Franklin*).

4584 *Jackie Chan Adventures.* (Series; Cartoon; Kids WB; 2000–2005). Martial arts expert Jackie Chan is depicted here in animation as an amateur archeologist who is also a member of Section 13, a secret law enforcement organization that is battling the Dark Hand, an evil society ruled by Valmont and guarded by a spirit called Shendu. Jackie is assisted by his niece, Jade, and his Uncle and stories relate their battle against the Dark Hand (seasons one and two); Dalong Wong and the Dark Chi Warriors (Finn, Chow, Ratso and Hak Foo) in the third season; Tarakudo the Shadowkhan King (fourth season); and the Demon Sorcerers in the final fifth season.

Voice Cast: Jackie Chan (*Jackie Chan*); Stacie Chan (*Jade*); James Sie (*Chow*); Sab Shimono (*Uncle*); Clancy Brown (*Ratso*); Noah Nelson (*Tohru*); Adam Baldwin (*Finn*); James Hong (*Dalong Wong*); John Di Maggio (*Hak Foo*); Michael Rosenbaum (*Drago*); Susan Eisenberg (*Viper*); Miguel Ferrer (*Shadowkhan King*); Frank Welker (*Dai Gui*); Miguel Sandoval (*El Toro Fuerte*); Noah Nelson (*Tohru*).

4585 *Jackie Gleason and His American Scene Magazine.* (Series; Variety; CBS; 1962–1966). Music, songs and comedy sketches culled from the mythical *American Scene Magazine*. Host Jackie Gleason plays a number of characters, including Joe the Bartender (where he converses with Crazy Goggenheim and the never-seen Mr. Donnehy), the Poor Soul and Reginald Van Gleason III. Also featured is a comedy segment called *It Pays to Be Ignorant* (a panel trying to evade answering simple questions like "From what state do we get Hawaiian canned pineapple?") and a reprisal of *The Honeymooners* with Jackie recreating his role as bus driver Ralph Kramden.

Program Open: "From the sun and fun capitol of the world, Miami Beach, we bring you *The Jackie Gleason Show* starring Jackie Gleason, Art Carney." [Girl] "With special guest star Milton Berle, The June Taylor Dancers and Sammy Spear and His Orchestra. And away we Go!"

Cast: Jackie Gleason (*Host*); Frank Fontaine (*Crazy Goggenheim*); Elizabeth Allen (*The Away We Go Girl*); Barbara Heller (*Segment Introductions*). **Regulars:** Sid Fields, Sue Ane Langdon, Phil Bruns, Jan Crockett, Patricia Wilson, Rip Taylor, Barney Martin, Stan Ross, Jerry Berger, Helen Curtis, Lucille Patton, Frank Marth, Charley Bolender, Stormy Berg, Pat Dahl, The June Taylor Dancers, The Glea Girls. **It Pays to Be Innocent Cast:** Jayne Mansfield, Frank Fontaine, Professor Irwin Corey. **Honeymooners Cast:** Jackie Gleason (*Ralph Kramden*); Art Carney (*Ed Norton*); Sue Ane Langdon (*Alice Kramden*); Patricia Wilson (*Trixie Norton*). **Announcer:** Johnny Olson. **Orchestra:** Sammy Spear.

4586 *The Jackie Gleason Show.* (Series; Variety; CBS; 1952–1961). Music, songs and comedy sketches that also feature *Honeymooners* skits with Jackie Gleason as Ralph Kramden, Art Carney as Ed Norton, Audrey Meadows as Alice Kramden and Joyce Randolph as Trixie Norton. These skits originally aired from 1952 to 1955. In 1955-1956, the skits were spun off into the now classic *Honeymooners* series (CBS, 1955-1956). When the series failed to make it past the first season, Jackie returned to his variety series format, where additional *Honeymooners* segments were produced. Many of these segments were first seen on the Showtime cable network as *The Honeymooners: The Lost Episodes.* After the cable run, they were syndicated as part of the original *Honeymooners* package. Other characters played by Jackie, called "The Great One," are Reginald Van Gleason III, Rudy the Repairman, Joe the Bartender, Fenwick Babbitt, the Poor Soul and Charlie Babbitt, the loud mouth (with Art Carney as his foil, Clem Finch).

Host: Jackie Gleason. **Regulars:** Art Carney, Audrey Meadows, Joyce Randolph, George O. Petrie, Frank Marth, Buddy Hackett, The Gleason Girls, The June Taylor Dancers. **Announcer:** Jack Lescoulie. **Orchestra:** Ray Bloch.

4587 *The Jackie Gleason Show.* (Series; Variety; CBS; 1966–1970). Music, songs and comedy sketches, including a reprisal of *The Honeymooners* both in vignettes and full hour episodes (Jackie Gleason played bus driver Ralph Kramden with Audrey Meadows as his wife, Alice; Art Carney as sewer worker Ed Norton and Sheila MacRae as Ed's wife, Trixie Norton).

Host: Jackie Gleason. **Regulars:** Art Carney, Audrey Meadows, Sheila MacRae, Lanita Kent, Jami Henderson, Andrea Duda, Carlos Bas, The June Taylor Dancers, The Glea Girls. **Announcer:** Johnny Olson. **Orchestra:** Sammy Spear.

4588 *The Jackie Thomas Show.* (Series; Comedy; ABC; 1992-1993). The mythical *Jackie Thomas Show* is America's top-rated comedy series. It is about a wacky father (Jackie), his wife, Helen, and their teenage son, Timmy. Its star, Jackie Thomas, is conceited, demanding, obnoxious and overbearing; his mere presence strikes fear in the hearts of his writing staff, co-stars and network executives. The series presents a behind-the-scenes look at the making of a weekly television show as Jackie attempts the impossible — to deliver a funny show without bloodshed.

Jackie is from Iowa and previously worked in a slaughterhouse. He wants the show to himself and gets very upset when a co-star gets too popular, too much fan mail or too much airtime. Jackie can't act and think at the same time, and he is quite naive when it comes to world affairs.

Jerry Harper is the new head writer (previously wrote for *Barney Miller, Cheers* and *Taxi*). Laura Miller is Jerry's assistant; she says simply, "Jackie is insane. I'm not talking wacky, funny insane; I'm talking clinical, dangerously insane." Laura longs to be a writer. Nancy Mincher is a staff writer and previously wrote for *The Brady Bunch* and *Who's the Boss?* Grant Watson and Bobby Wynn are the remaining members of Jerry's writing team. Bobby is Jackie's drinking buddy from Iowa. He performs standup comedy at various clubs, and Jackie keeps him around as the writers' joke man.

Doug Talbot is the network's flunkie. He was a vice president at NBC and worked there at the same time as Jerry (when he wrote for *Cheers*). Doug was fired for trying to cancel *Cheers.*

The co-stars of *The Jackie Thomas Show* are Sophia Ford, who plays Jackie's television wife, Helen, and Chas Walker, who plays their son, Timmy. Jackie plays a butcher; Sophia dreads the thought of having to kiss Jackie on the show and does so only to keep her job.

Cast: Tom Arnold (*Jackie Thomas*); Alison LaPlaca (*Laura Miller*); Dennis Boutsikaris (*Jerry Harper*); Maryedith Burrell (*Nancy Mincher*); Paul Feig (*Bobby Wynn*); Martin Mull (*Doug Talbot*); Michael Boatman (*Grant Watson*); Jeanetta Arnette (*Sophia Ford*); Breckin Meyer (*Chas Walker*); Chris Farley (*Chris Thomas*).

4589   *Jackpot*. (Series; Game; NBC; Syn.; 1974–1989). Sixteen players compete. One is made the "expert"; the others become the players. The expert pushes a button to establish a money amount and begins the game by calling on a player. When called, the player states the value of a riddle he possesses (placed on board) and reads it. If the expert solves it, he keeps his place and calls on another player; if he fails to answer it, he trades places with the player who stumped him. Each riddle that is solved increases the money on the board which can only be won by the player who matches or surpasses the previously established amount. The sixteen players compete for five days. Four versions appeared:

1. Jackpot (NBC, 1974-75). **Host:** Geoff Edwards. **Announcer:** Don Pardo.

2. Jackpot (Unaired Pilot, 1984). **Host:** Nipsey Russell. **Announcer:** Johnny Gilbert.

3. Jackpot (USA, 1985–88). **Host:** Mike Darrow. **Announcer:** Ken Ryan.

4. Jackpot (Syn. 1989). **Host:** Geoff Edwards. **Announcer:** John Harlan.

4590   *Jack's House*. (Pilot; Comedy; Unaired; Produced for Fox in 2003). Jack is a mid-twenties slacker who has come to realize that he must start taking control of his life. He uses his savings to buy and house and must now grow up. His efforts to do just that, despite the bad advice from friends, are the focal point of the proposal.

Cast: Will Friedle (*Jack*); Kathleen Rose Perkins (*Sophie*); Heath Hyche (*Wes*); Patrick Fabian (*Lyle*).

4591   *Jack's Place*. (Series; Drama; ABC; 1992). Jack's Place is actually Jack's Bar and Restaurant. It is world famous for its chocolate fudge cake, and customers are not obligated to pay for a meal if they do not like it. Jack Evans is the charming proprietor, a former jazz musician during the 1960s. The only information revealed about Jack is that he was on the road a lot as a musician and felt it would be best for his wife and daughter if he left them to lead his own life. Chelsea Duffy is the waitress and Greg Toback is the bartender. Susan Sullivan is Jack's estranged daughter.

Cast: Hal Linden (*Jack Evans*); Finola Hughes (*Chelsea Duffy*); John Dye (*Greg Tobuck*); Michele Green (*Susan Sullivan*).

4592   *The Jackson 5*. (Pilot; Variety; CBS; Nov. 4, 1972). Songs by the Motown group The Jackson Five; comedy from Johnny Brown and Jo Anne Worley (it was considered as a replacement for *Anna and the King* but, despite good reviews, it was not picked up).

Hosts: The Jackson Five (*Jackie, Marlon, Michael, Randy and Tito Jackson*). **Regulars:** Johnny Brown, Jo Anne Worley.

4593   *Jackson and Jill*. (Series; Comedy; Syn.; 1949–1953). Jackson and Jill Jones are a married couple who live in a one-room apartment (1A) at 167 Oak Street in Manhattan. Jackson is an accountant for the Gimmling Company; Jill is a beautiful housewife who believes she is "mean, suspicious and narrow-minded" (Jackson says she isn't — "You're sweet, lovely and wonderful"). Jackson served with the Marines during World War II and believes you can tell a man's character by the coat he wears. Jill believes Jackson is forgetful "because he has something else on his mind" and always asks Jackson

"if he prefers a girl with looks or a girl with brains." Jackson's answer, "Neither one darling, I prefer you," causes Jill to give a puzzled look to the camera. Jill does have a suspicious mind and constantly believes Jackson is seeing other women (each episode finds Jill threatening to leave Jackson). She ultimately learns she has jumped to the wrong conclusions. Each episode opens and closes with Jill writing an entry about the day's events in her diary (which is presented as a flashback).

Cast: Todd Karns (*Jackson Jones*); Helen Chapman (*Jill Jones*).

4594   *The Jackson Five*. (Series; Cartoon; ABC; 1971–1973). Michael Jackson and his brothers, Randy, Jackie, Tito and Marlon appear in animated form as the famous Motown rock group; here encountering misadventures at home and on tour.

Voice Cast: Michael Jackson (*Michael Jackson*); Randy Jackson (*Randy Jackson*); Jackie Jackson (*Jackie Jackson*); Tito Jackson (*Tito Jackson*); Marlon Jackson (*Marlon Jackson*), Paul Frees, Edmund Silvers, Joel Cooper, Mike Martinez, Craig Grandy.

4595   *The Jacksons*. (Series; Variety; CBS; 1976-1977). Music, songs and light comedy with the Jackson family.

Cast: Michael Jackson, Marlon Jackson, Randy Jackson, Janet Jackson, Jackie Jackson, Maureen Jackson, La Toya Jackson, Tito Jackson. **Regulars:** Marty Cohen, Jim Samuels. **Orchestra:** Rick Wilkens.

4596   *The Jacksons: A Family Dynasty*. (Series; Reality; A&E; 2009-2010). Jackie, Marlon, Tito and Jermaine Jackson are the surviving members of the pop singing group The Jackson Five (Michael Jackson, the fifth member, died June 25, 2009). The first episode was filmed six days before Michael's death and the future of the series looked doubtful (even though Michael does not appear in the episode). After a time of mourning, the brothers decided to continue the series as a tribute to Michael. The program relates events in the daily lives of the brothers as they cut a new album and prepare for a performance to commemorate the 40th anniversary of the founding of The Jackson Five.

4597   *Jacob Two-Two*. (Series; Cartoon; NBC; 2003–2007). Jacob is a young boy who earned the nickname "two-two" for his habit of repeating certain words (for example, "Let's go Renee, let's go" or "good luck Renee, good luck"). This habit occurred as Jacob, the youngest member of his family, had to repeat himself to be heard. Jacob is a best friend with Renee, a girl with a French accent, and stories follow their adventures as they face the daily challenges of being kids (situations are made more complex because of Jacob — called a double talker in some episodes) when he speaks before he thinks and then says, "My big mouth gets me into trouble all the time."

Voice Cast: Billy Rosenberg (*Jacob*); Julie Lemieux (*Renee*); Janet-Lanie Green (*Florence*); Harvey Atkin (*Morty*); Kaitlin Howell (*Emma*); Marc McMulkin (*Noah*); Kristopher Clarke (*Beauford Pew*); Duane Hill (*I.M. Greedyguts*); Fiona Reed (*Sour Pickles*).

4598   *The Jacqueline Susann Show*. (Series; Women; DuMont; 1951). Author Jacqueline Susann oversees a program of fashion previews, guests and celebrity interviews. Also known as *Jacqueline Susann's Open Door*.

4599   *Jacques Fray's Music Room*. (Series; Variety; ABC; 1949). Music by Jacques Fray coupled with performances by aspiring talent.

Host: Jacques Fray. **Regulars:** Bess Myerson, Jeri Nagle, Bob Calder, Joan Francis, Russell and Aura. **Orchestra:** Charles Stark.

4600 *The Jacquie Brown Diaries.* (Series; Comedy; Logo; 2010). Jacquie Brown is a somewhat insecure reporter for TV-3 in England. She reports stories on *McHuntly at 7* but is not satisfied being a relief reporter and yearns to become TV-3's number one correspondent. Stories, produced in England in 2009, chart Jacquie's often misguided efforts to do what it takes to achieve her goal. Kim Sharee is TV-3's stunning publicist; Serita Singh is a stunning woman hired as a reporter for TV-3 to appeal to the channel's multi-ethnic viewers. Ian McHuntly is the anchor of *McHuntly at 7*. Elena is the controlling producer of Ian's show; Tom is Jacquie's friend, a struggling comic, artist and writer.

Second season episodes (2010) find Jacquie losing her job when she tried to get Serita (whom she felt was a threat to replacing her) fired. Now, down on her luck, Jacquie and her equally impoverished roommate (Tom) leave their decent home at Cox's Bay for a less desirable, low rent apartment on K Road. Jacquie had achieved a semi-celebrity status at TV-3 and now uses that notoriety to pay the bills. As time goes by, Jacquie finds herself less in demand and takes a job as the co-host of a mid-day radio talk show with only one goal in mid — make her way back up the media ladder.

Cast: Jacquie Brown (*Herself*); Hannah Banks (*Serita Singh*); Jonathan Brugh (*Ian McHunly*); Geeling Ng (*Elena*); Ryan Lampp (*Tom*).

4601 *JAG.* (Series; Drama; NBC, 1995-1996; CBS, 1996–2005). Commander Harmon Rabb, Jr., and Lieutenant Colonel Sarah MacKenzie are lawyers attached to the Judge Advocate General's office (JAG for short), the legal department of the U.S. Navy.

Harmon was a fighter pilot who became a Navy lawyer after he and his co-pilot were involved in accident. He and his team investigate and litigate crimes involving marine and navy personnel. Harmon and his team are not lawyers who sit back and let others do the legwork. They personally involve themselves in their investigations and risk their lives to see that justice is served. See also *N.C.I.S.*, the spin off series.

Program Open: "Following in his father's footsteps as a naval aviator, Lieutenant Commander Harmon Rabb, Jr., suffered a crash while landing his Tomcat on a storm-tossed carrier at sea. Diagnosed with night blindness, Harmon transferred to the Navy's Judge Advocate General's core, which investigates, defends and prosecutes the law of the sea. There with fellow JAG lawyer Major Sarah MacKenzie, he now fights in and out of the courtroom with the same daring tonicity that made him a top gun in the air."

Cast: David James Elliott (*Cmdr. Harmon "Harm" Rabb, Jr.*); Catherine Bell (*Lt. Col. Sarah "Mac" MacKenzie*); Patrick Labyorteaux (*Lt. Cmdr. Bud Roberts, Jr.*); John M. Jackson (*Adm. Albert Jethro "A.J." Chegwidden*); Karri Turner (*Lt. Harriet Sims*); Zoe McLellan (*P.O. Jennifer Coates*); Chuck Carrington (*P.O. Jason Tiner*); Scott Lawrence (*Cmdr. Sturgis Turner*); Randy Vasquez (*Sgt. Victor "Gunny" Galindez*); Nanci Chambers (*Lt. Loren Singer*); Steven Culp (*Agent Clayton Webb*); Paul Collins (*Naval Sec. Alexander Nelson*); Michael Bellisario (*Midshipman Mike Roberts*); Harrison Page (*Rear Adm. Stiles Morris*); Jennifer Savidge (*Cmdr. Amy Helfman*); Tracey Needham (*Lt. J.G. Meg Austin*); David Andrews (*Maj. Gen. Gordon Creswell*); Anne-Marie Johnson (*Rep. Bobbi Latham*); Isabella Hoffman (*Meredith Cavanaugh*); Cindy Ambuehl (*Rene Peterson*); Dean Stockwell (*Naval Sec. Edward Sheffield*); Sibel Erhener (*Lt. Elizabeth "Skates" Hawkes*); Susan Haskell (*Lt. Cmdr. Jordan "Jordi" Parker*).

4602 *Jake and the Fatman.* (Series; Crime Drama; CBS; 1987–1992). Jason Lochinvar McCabe, called J.L. for short, was born in Atlanta, Georgia, where he became a lawyer then a prosecutor for the D.A.'s office (1987-88). He next became a prosecuting attorney for the Honolulu Police Department (1988–90), then the D.A. of Costa Del Mar, a small city in California. Jake Styles is the stylish investigator who assists him in all locales. He was joined in 1991 by Neely Capshaw, an investigator for the Costa Del Mar D.A.'s office. Dixie's Bar, owned by Dixie, is their favorite watering hole.

J.L. is somewhat overweight and has earned the nickname Fatman. He is a tough prosecutor and will use every means at his disposal to convict a felon. J.L. has also been called "Buster" and he has a somewhat lazy (appears to always be sleeping) dog named Max.

Jake was born in California and as a kid had the nickname Butchie. His childhood hero was Tom Cody, star of the mythical TV series *Sky Hawk*. Neely lives at 5440 Canyon Drive with her daughter, Sarah (who attends the Folger Park Grammar School). Each episode is titled after a song; for example, "It Had to Be You," "The Tender Trap," and this song is played over the episode's after-theme opening credits.

Cast: William Conrad (*J.L. McCabe*); Joe Penny (*Jake Styles*); Melody Anderson (*Neely Capshaw*); Anne Francis (*Dixie*); Taylor Fry (*Sarah Capshaw*).

4603 *Jake in Progress.* (Series; Comedy; ABC; 2005-2006). Jake Phillips is a publicist for the Magnum Public Relations Firm in New York City. Women say, "he's charming and handsome but he doesn't know it." Jake is a smooth-as-silk fast-talking publicist who is totally devoted to work — and dating the ladies although he has no time for a commitment. He feels his life is a work in progress and stories follow his seemingly carefree life style as he uses his suave and sophisticated moves to deal with an assortment of temperamental clients to his private life where he is determined (as soon as he gets a chance) to find the one perfect girl to settle down with and raise a family.

Naomi Clark is Jake's boss, a single woman who is struggling through the mood swings of her first pregnancy. She is a lady of class but even though she deals with people she hates dealing with people and uses Jake as the go between on deals. Adrian is Jake's married friend, a dentist who lives in the suburbs and wishes he had a life like Jake's. Patrick is Jake's friend, an out-of-work magician who is seeking to break a record and become famous. Brooke is a temp worker at the office who Jake feels an attraction to — but she always rejects his advances, knowing the type of non-committal person he really is.

Cast: John Stamos (*Jake Phillips*); Wendie Malick (*Naomi Clark*); Ian Gomez (*Adrian Grossman*); Rick Hoffman (*Patrick Van Dorn*); Julie Bowen (*Brooke*).

4604 *Jake Lassiter: Justice on the Bayou.* (Pilot; Crime Drama; NBC; Jan. 9, 1995). Jake Lassiter is a pro football player whose career comes to an end when he injures his knee. He takes up the study of law and becomes an attorney with the public defender's office in New Orleans. Years later, when he gets tired of seeing sleazy criminals get off, he quits and joins the law firm of Harmon and Fox. The proposed series was to relate Jake's somewhat controversial defenses of clients the conservative firm would not like him to handle. Cindy is Jake's assistant, a free spirit who lives in a trailer with her dog Arnold.

Cast: Gerald McRaney (*Jake Lassiter*); Poppy Montgomery (*Cindy*).

4605 *Jake 2.0.* (Series; Science Fiction; UPN; 2003). Jake Foley is a tech support worker for the NSA (National Security Agency) in Washington, D.C. While attempting to fix a computer glitch, Jake finds himself in the middle of a hostage situation when a renegade scientist attempts to steal a top-secret computer file. Just as Jake thought it was the end, security guards appear. In the ensuing gun battle, a bullet strikes a computer and shatters debris — some of which strike Jake. The scientist is brought down and all appears to be fine for Jake. Later, however, he finds he has changed. The wound inflicted by the debris on his arm has healed and he now has a personal connection with computers (he can wave his hand and command them). He has encompassed the nano technology program of the molecular computer that struck him (which was a Department of Defense experiment for soldiers in combat that would enable them to repair damaged tissue. The nanites are now part of Jake's system and they cannot be removed).

Jake suddenly finds himself as an agent for the NSA — and the head of a special operations team. Stories follow Jake's adventures as he uses his new found abilities, including increased hearing and incredible strength to battle the enemies of the U.S. (the NSA is the largest intelligence agency in the world — 46,000 people who work to keep the U.S. safe).

Other regulars are Louise Beckett, called Lou, the Deputy Director of the NSA; Diana Hughes-Keegan, the NSA doctor who takes a personal interest in Jake (she is hoping to get a Nobel Peace Prize — and a medal, fame and money — for her work with Jake); Agents Sara Heywood and Kyle Durante; and Jerry, Jake's brother.

Program Open: "Jake Foley was an ordinary guy until a freak accident transformed him into the world's first computer enhanced man. Millions of microscopic computers interfaced with his biochemistry and made him stronger and faster; able to see and hear farther than normal men. They give him the power to control technology with his brain, Jake Foley — America's secret weapon; he takes on missions no ordinary agent can perform. He is the ultimate human upgrade."

Cast: Christopher Gorham (*Jake Foley*); Judith Scott (*Louise Beckett*); Marina Black (*Sara Heywood*); Philip Anthony Rodriquez (*Kyle Durante*); Connor Tracy (*Diana Hughes-Keegan*); Drew Tyler Bell (*Jerry Foley*).

4606 *Jakers: The Adventures of Piggley Winks.* (Series; Children; PBS; 2003–2007). A computer animated program that is set in Ireland in the 1930s (flashback sequences). Piggley Winks is a young pig that lives on a farm with his parents (Elly and Padrig) and his sister Molly. Dannan the duck and Fernando the cow are Piggley's friends and stories follow the learning experiences they encounter at home and at school.

Each episode opens with Grandpa Piggley (who now lives in North America) relating a story about his youth to his grandchildren. A flashback is used to show his life in 1930s Ireland. Each episode concludes with a live action segment with host Codi Jones recapping the lessons presented in the story.

Cast: Cody Jones (*Host*); Peadar Lamb (*Grandpa Piggley*); Maile Flanagan (*Young Piggley Winks*); Tara Strong (*Molly Winks*); Tara Strong (*Dannan*); Charlie Adler (*Padrig Winks*); Russi Taylor (*Elly Winks/Fernando*); Mel Brooks (*Wiley the Sheep*); Joan Rivers (*Shirley the Sheep*); Pamela Adlon (*Hector MacBadger*); Nika Futterman (*Sean*).

4607 *Jake's Journey.* (Pilot; Fantasy; Unaired; Produced in 1988.). Shortly after Mike and Jean Finley and their children, Jake and Sarah move from the U.S. to England, Jake discovers he has the ability to travel to an amazing fantasy world of different medieval time periods. Here, he becomes the squire to Sir George, an unpredictable, cranky old Knight. The unsold series was to relate incidents in Jake's normal and boring life and his escapades with Sir George in strange fantasy lands.

Cast: Lane Smith (*Mike Finley*); Nancy Lenehan (*Jean Finley*); Chris T. Young (*Jake Finley*); Fay Masterson (*Sarah Finley*); Graham Chapman (*Sir George*).

4608 *Jake's M.O.* (Pilot; Crime Drama; NBC; July 30, 1987). Jake Tekulve is a veteran crime reporter who now works for CNS (Country New Service), a group of radio and television stations that air Jake's stories. The proposal was to relate Jake's exploits as he uses his keen instincts and memories of the good old days of police work to solve crimes. Other regulars are Tab, his assistant; Flo, a reporter for International Wire Service; Sigourney, Jake's boss; and Police Detective Abel Barnes.

Cast: Fred Gwynne (*Jake Tekulve*); Jeff McCracken (*Tab Hoberman*); Caroline McWilliams (*Flo Duffy*); Claudette Nevins (*Sigourney Tompkins*); James Avery (*Abel Barnes*).

4609 *Jake's Way.* (Pilot; Crime Drama; CBS; June 26, 1980). Jake Rudd is sheriff of Fox County, a rural town near San Antonio, Texas. Fox County is a growing community and, as the county grows, so does the crime rate. The proposal was to relate Jake's efforts, assisted by his deputies Sam, Daniel and Steve, to protect and serve. Christina is the radio dispatcher.

Cast: Robert Fuller (*Jake Rudd*); Slim Pickens (*Sam Hargis*); Steve McNaughton (*Daniel Doggett*); Ben Lemon (*Steve Cantwell*); Lisa LeMole (*Christina O'Toole*).

4610 *Jambo.* (Series; Anthology; NBC; 1969–1971). Wildlife stories filmed in Africa and geared toward children. (Jambo is African for Hello).

Host-Storyteller: Marshall Thompson.

4611 *Jamboree.* (Series; Variety; DuMont; 1950). A summer program of music, songs and comedy.

Hostess: Gloria Van. **Regulars:** Jane Brokeman, Jimmy McPartland, Dick Edwards, Danny O'Neill, Bud Tygett, Paula Raye, John Dolie, "Woo Woo" Stevens. **Music:** Julian Stockdale.

4612 *James at 15.* (Series; Drama; NBC; 1977-1978). A realistic approach to the problems faced by today's teenagers as depicted through the experiences of James Hunter, a student at Bunker Hill High School in Boston. After ten episodes, the title changed to *James at 16.* Paul and Joan Hunter are James's parents (called Alan and Meg in the pilot); Sandy and Kathy Hunter are James's sisters; Marlene and Sly are James's friends. Lee Montgomery performs the theme, "James."

Cast: Lance Kerwin (*James Hunter*); Linden Chiles (*Paul Hunter*); Lynn Carlin (*Joan Hunter*); Kim Richards (*Sandy Hunter*); Deirdre Berthrong (*Kathy Hunter*); Susan Myers (*Marlene Mahoney*); David Hubbard (*Ludwig "Sly" Hazeltine*).

4613 *James at 16.* (Series; Drama; NBC; 1978). The revised series title for *James at 15* (when the title character, James Hunter, turned 16 years of age). See *James at 15* for information.

4614 *James Bond, Jr.* (Series; Cartoon; Syn.; 1991). Wakefield is a spy prep school based in England. James Bond, the famous international spy known as 007, is a graduate. His nephew, James Bond, Jr., yearns to be just like his uncle. He has been enrolled in the school and is studying to be a spy. Although he is only a student, he has already acquired the skills of his uncle — skills that enable him to battle the evils of S.C.U.M. (Saboteurs and Criminals United in Mayhem), a cartel of mad scientists seeking to take over the world. With the help of his schoolmates I.Q. and Gordo, James Jr. fights to keep the word safe from S.C.U.M.

Voice Cast: Corey Burton (*James Bond, Jr.*); Jeff Bennett (*Horace "I.Q." Boothroys*); Julian Holloway (*Gordo*); Jan Rabson (*Goldfinger*); Sheryl Bernstein (*Princess Yasmine*); Jennifer Darling (*Phoebe Farragut*).

4615   The James Boys. (Pilot; Comedy; NBC; June 25, 1982). William "Willie" James is a divorced construction worker (for the Heinwell Construction Company). He has custody of his young son, Sam, but is having a difficult time raising him. Sam's efforts to do what is best for Sam — and Sam's efforts to look out for the welfare of his father is the focal point of the proposed series. Other regulars are Kate, the owner of Kate's Kitchen, a diner; Emily, Kate's daughter; Jake, Willie's friend; Dan, Willie's boss; and Kathy, Dan's secretary.

Cast: Brian Kerwin (*Willie James*); Eric Coplan (*Sam James*); Kelly Harmon (*Kate Allgood*); Viveka Davis (*Emily Allgood*); Edward Edwards (*Jake*); Arthur Rosenberg (*Dan Felix*); Patricia Cobert (*Kathy*).

4616   Jamie. (Series; Comedy; ABC; 1953-1954). Jamison John Francis McHummer, Jamie for short, is a young boy who comes to live with his grandfather, Frank M. Dimmer, Frank's daughter, Laurie, and Laurie's daughter, Liz, after the death of his parents. Jamie has an allowance of 50 cents a week and earns $3 a week as a bicycle delivery boy for Briggs Hardware Store. If there are chores to be done, Jamie takes his time coming home from school. Frank, called "Grandpa," owns Dimmer's Drug Store. Laurie earns money through a catering business she runs with her friend Annie. Eva Marie Saint played Liz in the pilot episode.

Program Open: "It's Time for *Jamie* starring Brandon DeWilde with Ernest Truex, Polly Rowles and Kathy Nolan. Brought to you by Sunsweet Prune Juice, the juice that gives you something extra."

Cast: Brandon DeWilde (*Jamie McHummer*); Ernest Truex (*Frank Dimmer*); Polly Rowles (*Laurie*); Kathy Nolan (*Liz*); Alice Pearce (*Annie Moakum*).

4617   The Jamie Foxx Show. (Series; Comedy; WB; 1996–2002). The King's Tower is a Los Angeles hotel run by Junior King and his wife, Helen. Jamie King, their nephew, is a hopeful actor who has just left his home in Texas to pursue his dream. Until that time comes he is residing (and working) at his aunt and uncle's hotel. Stories follow the events in Jamie's life as he deals with staff and hotel patrons while at the same time trying to find his niche in show business.

Francesca Monroe, called Fancy, is the drop dead gorgeous desk clerk (a future romantic interest for Jamie); Braxton P. Hartnabrig is the stuffy perfectionist accountant who also has eyes for Fancy.

Cast: Jamie Foxx (*Jamie King*); Gracelle Beauvais (*Francesca "Fancy" Monroe*); Garrett Morris (*Uncle Junior King*); Ellia English (*Aunt Helen King*); Christopher B. Duncan (*Braxton P. Hartnabrig*).

4618   The Jamie Kennedy Experiment. (Series; Comedy; WB; 2002–2004). A *Candid Camera* type of program that plays pranks on unsuspecting people but expands the idea to have it done as part of a skit in front of a studio audience (who are in on the gag). Unsuspecting people are brought to the studio on a pretext. Actor/comedian Jamie Kennedy plays a wide variety of characters in an attempt to pull off the prank. Cameras capture the unsuspected "marks" reactions to the situation as it unfolds. When the skit appears to have run its course, Jamie drops the disguise and turns to the mark to say "You've been X-ed."

Host: Jamie Kennedy. **Regulars:** Nick Swardson, Joannah Portman, Chris Tallman, Mighty Rasta, Lisa Deanne Young, Ivar Brogger, Masi Oka, Carrie Reeves, Larry Milburn.

4619   The Jan Murray Show. (Series; Variety; NBC; 1955). Comedian Jan Murray oversees a program of music, song and comedy.

Host: Jan Murray. **Regulars:** Tina Louise, Fletcher Peck, The Novelettes. **Music:** Milton DeLugg.

4620   Jana of the Jungle. (Series; Cartoon; NBC; 1981-1982). A young girl (Jana), traveling on the Amazon River with her father, is separated from him when their boat hits a rock and sinks. Jana is found and rescued by Montaro, a noble descendant of a lost warrior tribe. Jana has only the necklace her father gave her before the disaster as a remembrance. She is taught the ways of the jungle by Montaro and grows up to become a daring defender of the jungle and its creatures. Jana, assisted by Montaro and her jaguar, Ghost, battles evil while at the same searching for her father, whom she believes is still alive. Jana's weapon is the Mystic Staff of Power.

Program Open: "The last thing I remember was traveling up the Great River with my father. He had just given me my special necklace when [boat hitting rocks and capsizing]. I was rescued by Montaro, the noble descendant of a lost warrior tribe. Endlessly searching for my lost father, Montaro, Keiko and my jaguar, Ghost, help me guard the jungle from those who dwell within it. I grew up by the laws of nature and the animals became my friends, I am ... Jana of the Jungle."

Voice Cast: B.J. Ward (*Jana*); Ted Cassidy (*Montaro*); Ross Martin (*Various Voices*).

4621   Jane. (Series; Adventure; Syn.; 1989). Jane is a beautiful undercover agent for the British government during World War II. Her mission is to battle the enemies of freedom and protect people who are important to the war effort. Jane is not a superhero; she has no amazing powers and she is not impervious to harm. Her sexuality is her only "weapon" (it appears that the enemy has never encountered a woman as sensuous as Jane and their bedazzlement becomes their downfall). While Jane can fly an enemy plane by instinct, fire complicated weapons accurately by chance, she does have one serious problem: keeping on her clothes. Jane wears only dresses and losing that dress to reveal her sexy lingerie is not her fault: things just happen (for example, snagging the dress on a nail while climbing over a wall; being stranded on a raft and needing a sail). To add further spice for the viewer, Jane often manages to lose her bra (while split second nudity is seen, Jane is most often depicted from the back, side or in a silhouette). Finding outerwear becomes Jane's number one priority. In addition to Jane's lack of wardrobe, the program is unique in its presentation: that of a comic strip come to life. The series is based on the World War II *Daily Mirror* British newspaper comic strip *Jane*. Each scene is a panel and all backgrounds and props (such as cars, trucks and planes) are drawings. Through special effects, the live actors are convincingly placed in comic book–like situations.

All of Jane's serial-like adventures involve her faithful companion, her dog, Fritz, a Dachshund whose thoughts are seen in balloons (the cloud-like areas used for comic book characters' speeches).

Colonel Birdie Ewell is Jane's superior, a Royal Navy commander who often joins Jane on assignments. He is cared for by Tombs, his ever-faithful butler. Jane and her boyfriend, Georgie, are very much in love and would like to marry but circumstances will not allow it: "There is a war on, man." Georgie, an undercover British army agent, has been assigned to capture Lola and Pola Pagola, deadly spies who are more of a threat to the Allies' success than Hitler. The seductive twins feel that Jane is a threat to their missions and killing her has become their top priority. Bob Danvers Walker does the narrating; Neil Innes sings the theme.

Cast: Glynis Barber (*Jane*); Robin Bailey (*Col. Birdie Ewell*); Max Wall (*Tombs*); John Bird (*Georgie*); Suzanne Danielle (*Lola and Pola Pagola*).

4622   Jane and the Dragon. (Series; Cartoon; NBC; 2006–). Jane Turnkey is a young girl in medieval times who is being trained as a Lady-in-Waiting (like her mother, Adeline). Jane, however, refuses to accept this and would like to become a Knight. But, being a female, she cannot be taken seriously. Determined to prove everyone is wrong, Jane trains in secret (how to wield a sword) to prove her worthiness by slaying a dragon. As she trains, a playful dragon snatches the Royal Prince. Believing this is the opportunity she has been waiting for, Jane sets out to find and slay the dragon. Jane finds the dragon's cave but discovers something she didn't expect — a friendly dragon. The dragon befriends Jane and allows her to "rescue" the prince. Upon returning to the castle, the King bestows upon Jane the title of Knight Apprentice. "Jane and the Dragon are best friends now," as the theme explains and stories follow Jane as she trains to become a Knight and the antics of the dragon (whom Jane calls Dragon) to impress Jane and help her achieve her dream.

King Carodoc and his wife, the Queen Gwendolyn, rule the land (Lavinia and Cuthbert are their children). Sir Theodore is the head knight; Pepper, the cook; Rake, the gardener; Smitty the blacksmith; Gunther is a knight-in-training; Sir Ivon, a knight; Jester, the court jester; Magnus Breech is the dishonest merchant. Tajja Isen performs the theme, "Jane and the Dragon."

Voice Cast: Tajja Isen (*Jane*); Adrian Truss (*Dragon*); Aron Tager (*Sir Theodore*); Noah Reid (*Gunther*); Sunday Muse (*Pepper*); Alex Belcourt (*Queen Gwendolyn*); Jill Frappier (*Adeline Turnkey*); Ben Campbell (*Sir Ivon*); Mark Rendell (*Jester*); Will Seatle Bowers (*Rake*); Alex House (*Smitty*); Clive Walton (*Magnus*); Cameron Ansell (*Prince Cuthbert*); Isabel de Carteret (*Princess Lavinia*).

4623 Jane Doe. (Series; Crime Drama; Hallmark Channel; 2005). Cathy Davis is a suburban mother who works part time designing children's puzzle games. Before her marriage, Cathy worked as a spy for a government organization called CSA (Central Security Agency). However, unknown to her family and friends, Cathy still works for the CSA under the code name Jane Doe (Cathy's mother, Polly, was also a CSA agent). Stories, which are reminiscent of Amanda King on *Scarecrow and Mrs. King*, follow Cathy as she secretly performs missions for the CSA (usually those involving threats to the national security). Cathy is married to Jack; Susan is her daughter; Frank Darnell is her CSA partner in the field.

Cast: Lea Thompson (*Cathy Davis*); William R. Moses (*Jack Davis*); Jessy Schram (*Susan Davis*); Joe Penny (*Frank Darnell*); Donna Mills (*Polly*); Nick Davis (*Zack Shada*).

4624 Jane Eyre. (Experimental; Drama; NBC; Oct. 12, 1939). A television adaptation of the 1847 novel by Charlotte Bronte that tells of Jane Eyre, an orphan girl, educated at Mr. Brocklehurst's Lowood School, who becomes the governess to Adele, the ward of Edward Rochester, the gruff owner of Thornfield Hall in Mikote, England.

Cast: Flora Campbell (*Jane Eyre*); Dennis Hoey (*Edward Rochester*); Eleanor Pitts (*Adele*); Effie Shannon (*Mrs. Fairfax*); Ruth Matteson (*Blanche Ingrams*); Naomi Campbell (*Leah*); Daisy Belmore (*Grace Poole*); Philip Tonge (*Mason*).

4625 Jane Eyre. (Series; Drama; PBS; July 1982). Adaptation of the Charlotte Bronte novel about Jane Eyre, a governess hoping to find love and romance in a 19th century class-ridden society in Thornfield (Yorkshire) (England).

Cast: Sorcha Cusack (*Jane Eyre*); Juliet Waley (*Jane Eyre; as a child*); Michael Jayston (*Edward Rochester*); Isabel Rosin (*Adele*); John Phillips (*Mr. Brocklehurst*); Megs Jenkins (*Mrs. Fairfax*); Zara Jaber (*Grace Poole*); Hazel Clyne (*Leah*); Anna Korwin (*Sophie*); Jean Hervey (*Mrs. Reed*).

4626 Jane Froman's U.S.A. Canteen. (Series; Variety; CBS; 1952-1953). A serviceman's canteen (recreation facility) provides the backdrop for performances by the men and women of the U.S. armed

services. It aired as *Jane Froman's U.S.A. Canteen* from Oct. 18, 1952 to July 2, 1953; and as *The Jane Froman Show* from Sept. 1, 1953 to June 23, 1955.

Host: Jane Froman. **Regulars:** The Peter Birch Dancers. **Announcer:** Allyn Edwards. **Orchestra:** Alfredo Antonini.

4627 The Jane Pauley Show. (Series; Variety; NBC; 2004). Daily program of celebrity interviews coupled with discussions on topical issues with NBC newswoman Jane Pauley as the host.

4628 The Jane Pickens Show. (Series; Variety; ABC; 1954). Singer Jane Pickens hosts a program of music and songs.

Host: Jane Pickens. **Regulars:** The Vikings. **Music:** Milton De-Lugg.

4629 Jane Wyman Presents the Fireside Theater. (Series; Anthology; NBC; 1955–1958). A continuation of *Fireside Theater* under a new title (and host, actress Jane Wyman) that encompasses tense, highly dramatic stories.

Host: Jane Wyman. **Announcer:** Joel Crager.

4630 Jane Wyman's Summer Playhouse. (Series; Anthology; CBS; 1957). Rebroadcasts of dramas that originally aired on *Fireside Theater* with actress Jane Wyman as the host.

4631 Janet Dean, Registered Nurse. (Series; Drama; Syn.; 1954). Janet Dean, a private duty nurse in New York City, is young, pretty and dedicated to helping people who cannot help themselves. She believes that some patients' problems are psychosomatic and that by incorporating applied psychology, she can resolve a problem by uncovering the cause of the problem. Stories follow Janet's efforts to treat her patients while at the same time, struggling to prove her theories.

Cast: Ella Raines (*Janet Dean*).

4632 Janice and Abbey. (Series; Reality; Oxygen; 2008). Abbey Clancy is a potential model who became the runner up on the British TV series *Britain's Next Top Model*. Supermodel Janice Dickinson sees potential in Abbey and sets out to train her. Episodes follow Abbey as she travels to Los Angeles to begin the regime of modeling chores with the hope of becoming a super model.

Stars: Janice Dickinson, Abbey Clancy.

4633 The Janice Dickinson Modeling Agency. (Series; Reality; Oxygen; 2006). A cable version of the UPN (then the CW) broadcast network series *America's Next Top Model* (which puts a dozen potential models through a series of real life modeling situations to find one girl who qualifies to be a top model). Here super model Janice Dickinson, who appeared on *America's Top Model*, opens her own agency and grooms potential models.

Host: Janice Dickinson.

4634 Jarrett. (Pilot; Crime Drama; NBC; Aug. 11, 1973). Sam Jarrett is an ex-prize fighter turned private detective who specializes in solving crimes associated with the fine arts. His major nemesis is Bassett Cosgrove, an international art thief, while his stumbling block is his niece, Luluwa, a somewhat spacey girl who works as a snake dancer.

Cast: Glenn Ford (*Sam Jarrett*); Yvonne Craig (*Luluwa*); Anthony Quayle (*Bassett Cosgrove*).

4635 Jason King. (Series; Crime Drama; Syn.; 1971-1972). A spin-off from *Department S* that takes Jason King (writer of Mark Caine Mystery novels) away from crime solving for the Paris-based Department S (a unit of Interpol) to solve crimes on his own.

After an audit it is discovered that the flamboyant Jason King overlooked paying taxes. To help solve his financial burden, Jason agrees to help the British government solve crimes (and acquire stories for his books). Although Jason works alone, he is just as extravagant as he was in the prior program with an interest in fast cars, travel, wine and beautiful women. Other regulars are Sir Brian, Jason's government supervisor; Ryland, Sir Brian's assistant; and Nicola Harvester, Jason's publisher.

Cast: Peter Wyngarde (*Jason King*); Dennis Price (*Sir Brian*); Ronald Lacey (*Ryland*); Ann Sharp (*Nicola Harvester*).

4636   Jason of Star Command. (Series; Science Fiction; CBS; 1979–1981). Star Command is a futuristic interplanetary police station that is supervised first by Commander Carnarvin then by Commander Stone. Jason, the unit's chief pilot, captains the ship *Starfire* and he is assisted by Cadets Nicole and Samantha. E.J. Parsafoot is the weapon's chief and Peepo is the unit's robot. Stories follow Jason as he and his cadets battle the evils of Dragos, a being bent on controlling the universe.

Cast: Craig Littler (*Jason*); James Doohan (*Commander Carnarvin*); John Russell (*Commander Stone*); Susan O'Hanlon (*Cadet Nicole*); Charlie Dell (*Professor E.J. Parsafoot*); Tamara Dobson (*Cadet Samantha*); Sid Haig (*The Evil Dragos*).

4637   The Jay Leno Show. (Series; Variety; NBC; 2009-2010). A nightly prime time program of celebrity interviews, monologues and light comedy. NBC's big gamble, dropping scripted dramas in favor of what is essentially a talk show on a nightly basis and in prime time (10 P.M.). Jerry Seinfeld was the premiere guest. The program scored an 18.4 rating on its first telecast (dropped off by 40 percent the following night) and mostly unfavorable reviews. NBC had been heavily promoting the series and, as *Variety* summed it up: "NBC would be strongly advised to keep those 'King of 10 O'clock' press releases under wraps for a while."

In January of 2010, dismal ratings, loss of ad revenue and threats by local NBC affiliates to abandon Leno's show (which was a poor lead-in for their local newscasts), forced NBC to drop "The biggest blunder in TV history" after five months (despite its earlier statement that no matter what happens, they will stick with the show for a year). *The Jay Leno Show* ended on February 11, 2010 as NBC began its coverage of the 2010 Winter Olympics. Original dramatic programming replaced Leno (who returned to his former late night spot as host of *The Tonight Show with Jay Leno*).

Host: Jay Leno. **Correspondents:** Jim Norton, Dan Finnerty. **Music:** Kevin Eubanks.

4638   The Jaye P. Morgan Show. (Series; Variety; ABC; 1956). Singer Jaye P. Morgan hosts a lively summer program of music and songs that also features performances by her brothers, Dick, Charlie and Duke.

Hostess: Jaye P. Morgan. **Regulars:** Dick Morgan, Charlie Morgan, Duke Morgan. **Orchestra:** Joel Herron.

4639   Jazmin's Touch. (Series; Erotica; Playboy Channel; 2010–). "For centuries," Playboy's press release states, "people have hunted for that one magic love potion that can attract fantasy lovers and turn a shy wall flower into a raging bedroom goddess." That aphrodisiac is not chocolate, perfume or even vivid imagery, it is Jazmin (appearing as herself), a gorgeous Latina woman whose mere touch can release sexual desires, especially in beautiful women, Jazmin's choice for a sex partner. Situated in an exotic Argentinean villa, Jazmin seduces "burned out" women and introduces them to a whole new world of sexual pleasures.

4640   TV Funhouse. (Series; Comedy; Comedy Central; 2000-2001). Doug, the host, appears before the camera to announce a theme for the day's program (for example, Shopping Day, Party Day). He then assigns his Aniplas (animal puppets Hojo, Fogey, Chickie, Hank and Larry) the task of performing skits that correspond to the day's theme. The puppets do anything but and the chaos they cause Doug is the focal point of the program. The program also features re-edited (for laughs) educational films and short cartoons by Robert Smigel.

Cast: Doug Dale (*Doug*); Jon Glaser (*Hojo*); Robert Smigel (*Fogey*); Dino Stamatopoulos (*Chickie*); Tommy Blacha (*Hank*); David Juskow (*Larry*).

4641   The Jean Arthur Show. (Series; Comedy; CBS; 1966). Marshall and Marshall, Attorneys at Law, is a prestigious law firm located at 100 West Beverly Boulevard in Beverly Hills, California. Patricia Marshall is an attractive widow (in her fifties) who founded the firm with her late husband. She is now partners with her 30-year-old son, Paul Marshall. Patricia, who attended Harvard Law School, lives at 367 South Oak Street. She has a brilliant record of corporate litigation wins, but is known for helping the underdog and taking cases that no other high-class firm would handle (for example, defending a boy's pet rooster, who is accused of crowing and disturbing a neighborhood; or defending a two-bit hood). Her favorite pastime is going to the beach and hunting for sea shells.

Paul, who also attended Harvard, lives in an apartment at 360 Etchfield Road. Unlike his mother (who will go to extremes), Paul is a by-the-books, laid-back attorney who will never tackle the cases she does (he seems to represent only corporate clients). Paul is a young man with spunk, Patricia makes things happen, and together they form a team that clients seem to want. Morton is Patricia's chauffeur, and Sally is the Marshalls' receptionist; Richie Wells is the reformed hood. Johnny Keating, Richard Quine and Richard Kennedy composed the theme, "Merry-Go-Round."

Cast: Jean Arthur (*Patricia Marshall*); Ron Harper (*Paul Marshall*); Richard Conte (*Richie Wells*); Leonard J. Stone (*Morton*); Sue Taylor (*Sally*).

4642   The Jean Carroll Show. (Pilot; Variety; CBS; April 26, 1951). Comedy sketches with former night club and vaudeville comic Jean Carroll. Other than dancer Bill Callahan (who assisted Jean in skits) additional regulars are not known: the live show ran longer than planned and the closing credits were cut.

Host: Jean Carroll. **Regular:** Bill Callahan. **Orchestra:** Ray Bloch.

4643   The Jean Carroll Show. (Series; Comedy; ABC; 1953-1954). Jean Carroll is a comedienne through whom incidents in the life of a typical American housewife are depicted. Jean is married to Alan and they are the parents of a young daughter (Lynn). They live in New York City (the borough of the Bronx or Brooklyn is suggested as the setting, although this is not specifically stated) and stories, based on actual incidents in Jean's life, follow Jean as she assumes the role of housewife, mother and all around problem solver. Also known as *Take It from Me*.

Cast: Jean Carroll (*Housewife*); Alan Carney (*Husband*); Lynn Loring (*Daughter*); Alice Pearce (*Neighbor*).

4644   Jean Shepherd's America. (Series; Documentary; PBS; 1971-1972). Perspectives on American life as seen through the eyes of humorist Jean Shepherd.

4645   Jeannie. (Series; Cartoon; CBS; 1973-1975). While surfing, Corey Anders, a Center High School student, is overcome by a wave that washes him ashore and uncovers a bottle that had been buried in the sand. Upon opening the bottle, a beautiful young genie, named Jeannie, and her friend, an inept apprentice genie named Babu, emerge and become his slaves. Stories depict Corey's attempts to conceal their presence and live the normal life of a teenager, and Jeannie and Babu's efforts to adjust to life in the 1970s. A take-off on *I Dream of Jeannie.*

Voice Cast: Julie McWhirter (*Jeannie*); Mark Hamill (*Corey Anders*); Joe Besser (*Babu*); Bob Hastings (*Henry Glopp; Corey's friend*).

4646 *The Jeff Dunham Show.* (Series; Comedy; Comedy Central; 2009). Jeff Dunham is a talented ventriloquist known basically for his dummy Walter, a sour-faced older gentleman who gripes about everything. Jeff's other alter egos include Peanut, Bubba J (the redneck with a drinking problem) and Achmed the Dead Terrorist (a skeleton with anger issues). The program, based on Jeff's Las Vegas stage show, spotlights Jeff's antics with his characters — live before the studio audience and in location pieces where his characters interact with real people.

Star: Jeff Dunham.

4647 *The Jeff Foxworthy Show.* (Series; Comedy; ABC, 1995-1996; NBC, 1996-1997). Foxworthy Heating and Air is an air conditioning and heating company in Indiana, It is owned by Jeff Foxworthy, a likeable, easy-going man who is married to Karen, a nurse at Bloomington General Hospital. Jeff and Karen are the parents of Matt, a gifted child who attends the genius program for gifted kids at school. Stories relate the events that befall the family of three.

Other regulars are Russ and Walt, Jeff's employees (their favorite hangout is Hagen's Bar; they also eat at Earl's Diner). Elliot and Lois are Karen's parents (who appear to look down on Jeff as they feel their daughter could have done better); Craig, Jeff's neighbor; Big Jim, Jeff's father; and Sandy, Karen's friend.

When the series switched to NBC, the locale switched to Georgia and Jeff and Karen suddenly had another child, Justin. Karen's parents were dropped and Jeff's father, Big Jim, was brought on, as was Bill Pelton, a best friend for Jeff.

Cast: Jeff Foxworthy (*Himself*); Anita Barone (*Karen Foxworthy; 1995-96*); Ann Cusack (*Karen Foxworthy; 1996-97*); Haley Joel Osment (*Matt Foxworthy*); Jonathan Lipnicki (*Justin Foxworthy*); Bibi Besch (*Lois*); Dakin Matthews (*Elliott*); Matt Clark (*Walt Bacon*); Matt Borlenghi (*Big Jim Foxworthy*); Sue Murphy (*Sandy*); Steve Hytner (*Craig*); Bill Engvall (*Bill Pelton*).

4648 *Jefferson Drum.* (Series; Western; NBC; 1958-1959). Jubilee is a lawless gold-mining town of the 1850s. It is here that Jefferson Drum, a widower and the father of a young son (Joey) has sworn to establish peace through the power of the press. Jefferson, a newspaper editor, lost his wife in a senseless shooting and believes that fighting violence with violence will not achieve results. Lucius Coin is his typesetter; Big Ed and Hickey are his friends. Also known as *The Pen and the Quill.*

Cast: Jeff Richards (*Jefferson Drum*); Eugene Martin (*Joey Drum*); Cyril Delevanti (*Lucius Coin*); Robert J. Stevenson (*Big Ed*); Hal Smith (*Hickey*).

4649 *The Jeffersons.* (Series; Comedy; CBS; 1975-1985). A spin off from *All in the Family.* George, Louise and Lionel Jefferson, Archie Bunker's neighbors, have moved from Queens, New York, to a high rise apartment in Manhattan after George's business begins to expand (Jefferson Cleaners) and he decides it is high time for him to live the good life. Stories follow the Jefferson family, in particular the somewhat snobbish George, as they adjust to their new status.

Prior their home in Queens, George and Louise lived in Harlem; it was when he moved to Queens that he opened his first dry cleaning shop. George was born in Georgia and served time in the Navy as a galley cook. He is always thought of as cheap as he grew up in poverty and treasured every cent he could earn.

Louise, called "Weezie" and "Weez" by George, and George have been married for 25 years and the reason the marriage works, says Louise, is that she is the one who puts up with all of George's faults ("his nonsense," as she calls it).

Tom and Helen Willis, their upstairs neighbors (on the fourteenth floor), are television's first interracial couple. Tom (who is white) is an editor for the Pelham Publishing Company. He has been married to Helen (who is black) for 23 years. They have a beautiful daughter, Jenny, who is engaged to George and Louise's son, Lionel. Lionel and Jenny later marry and become the parents of a girl they name Jessica.

Harry Bentley is George's across-the-hall neighbor (Apartment 12E). He was born in England, attended Oxford University and now works as an interpreter at the UN. Florence Johnston is George's sassy maid (who also puts up with all of George's antics). The Florence character was spun off into the series *Checking In* (which see). Olivia is George's mother.

Cast: Sherman Hemsley (*George Jefferson*); Isabel Sanford (*Louise Jefferson*); Mike Evans, Damon Evans (*Lionel Jefferson*); Franklin Cover (*Tom Willis*); Roxie Roker (*Helen Willis*); Berlinda Tolbert (*Jenny Willis*); Ebonie Smith (*Jessica Jefferson*); Paul Benedict (*Harry Bentley*); Marla Gibbs (*Florence Johnston*); Zara Cully (*Olivia Jefferson*).

4650 *Jeffrey and Cole Casserole.* (Series; Comedy; Logo; 2009). Wacky and sometimes bizarre skits geared to the gay and lesbian community and hosted by the self-professed VGL (very good looking) Internet stars Jeffrey and Cole.

Host: Jeffrey Self, Cole Escola.

4651 *Jeff's Collie.* (Series; Drama; CBS; 1954–1957). "To Jeff Miller I leave the best thing I've got, my dog, Lassie." With these words, read at the will of his neighbor, Homer Carey, ten-year-old Jeffrey ("Jeff") Miller inherits a beautiful and intelligent collie named Lassie. Jeff lives with his widowed mother, Ellen Miller, and his grandfather, George Miller, on a farm on Route 4 in Calverton, a small town about 30 miles from Capital City.

George, affectionately called "Gramps," owns the farm — "I was born on the land, married on the land and raised a family on the land." Ellen was married to George's son, Johnny. (In episode nine, Gramps tells Jeff that he got Johnny a rifle when he was 12 years old and put that "gun away ten years ago when we heard about your father." In episode 81, it is mentioned that Johnny lost his life attempting to save 20 men in his squadron, in 1944, during World War II.). Ellen refers to herself as "George Miller's daughter" (although she is actually his daughter-in-law). Gramps is a volunteer fireman and he calls anyone who irritates him a "pusillanimous polecat."

Jeff attends Calverton Elementary School and is planning to become a veterinarian. Sylvester ("Porky") Brockway is Jeff's best friend (his dog is named Pokey and has the official name of Pokerman III). Stories relate the adventures Jeff and Lassie encounter in and around the Miller farm.

Jenny is the telephone operator; Matt is Porky's father; Berdie is his mother; Dr. Peter Wilson was the original vet (replaced by Dr. Frank Weaver); Clay Horton was the original sheriff; he was replaced by Sheriff Jim Billings; Clay now runs a garage.

Program Open: [Jeff calling: "Lassie, Lassie"]. Announcer: "Starring Tommy Rettig as Jeff Miller ... Jan Clayton as his mother, Ellen ... George Cleveland as Gramps ... and of course, Lassie."

Cast: Jan Clayton (*Helen Miller*); George Cleveland (*Gramps*); Tommy Rettig (*Jeff Miller*); Donald Keeler (*Sylvester "Porky" Brock-*

way); Paul Maxey (*Matt Brockway*); Richard Garland (*Sheriff Clay Horton*); Arthur Space (*Dr. Peter Wilson/Dr. Frank Weaver*); Dayton Loomis (*Dr. Stuart*); Florence Lake (*Jenny*).

4652 *Jekyll*. (Series; Drama; BBC America; 2008). A modern adaptation of the Robert Louis Stevenson novel, *Dr. Jekyll and Mr. Hyde*. It is the present (2007) when Tom Jackman learns that he is the only known living descendant of the 19th century physician, Dr. Henry Jekyll, the man who was plagued by an evil alter ego named Edward Hyde. Henry's medical experiments cursed him to become two people living in the same body. Like his ancestor, Tom has inherited a dark side — his own alter ego, Mr. Hyde. While the two share the same body, Mr. Hyde is unaware that Tom has a family (a wife, Claire, and two children, Harry and Eddie). Through the use of modern technology, Tom has found a way to keep Mr. Hyde from overtaking him; Mr. Hyde, however, grows stronger each day and seeks to get out and becomes increasingly persistent. Stories follow Tom as he struggles to suppress his evil side and avoid capture by a secret, ancient organization that seeks to harness Mr. Hyde for their own sinister purposes. Produced in England.

Cast: James Nesbitt (*Tom Jackman/Mr. Hyde*); Gina Bellman (*Claire Jackman*); Christopher Day (*Harry Jackman*); Andrew Byrne (*Eddie Jackman*); Meera Syal (*Miranda*); Michelle Ryan (*Nurse Katherine Reemer*); Paterson Joseph (*Benjamin*); Fenella Woolgar (*Min*); Denis Lawson (*Peter Syme*).

4653 *Jellabies*. (Series; Cartoon; Fox; 1999). Jolly Jelly World is a land at the end of the rainbow that is inhabited by the Jellabies, people made of jelly, who live to make rainbows. They monitor weather conditions and create the needed rainbows via their Jellyscope, a computer that is also a rainbow generator. Stories, which relate aspects of life to children, focus on six Jellabies, each representing a color of the rainbow: Strum (purple), Bouncey (yellow), Denny (blue), Pepper (red), twins Amber (orange) and Amber (pink) and Duffy, a green Dragon. Also known as *Jellikins* (the European title).

Narrator: Rik Mayall.

4654 *Jem*. (Series; Cartoon; ABC; 1985–1988). In an effort to help his daughter, Jerrica Benton, run the Starlight Orphanage for Girls, Professor Emmett Benton creates Synergy, a sophisticated computerized holographic device. Through the abilities of Synergy (and the star-shaped earrings Jerrica wears), Jerrica is able to transform herself into Jem, a beautiful singer who is the leader of the Holograms (Kimber, Jetta, Aja and Shana), a stunning all-female group. Stories relate Jerrica's adventures as she uses the power of her holographic image to help others — and to battle the evils of Pizzazz, the leader of the Misfits rock group (Flasher, Roxie and Stormer) who seeks to dethrone Jem and the Holograms to become queen of the rock world.

Jerrica grew up around music and technicians and is now, after her father's death, the C.E.O. of the Starlight Music Company. When Jerrica touches her earrings and says, "Showtime, Synergy," her holographic image is created (by saying, "Show's over, Synergy," her image disappears). The Holograms are aware that Jerrica and Jem are the same person. Kimber is Jerrica's younger sister, co-owner of the company. While Jerrica is the lead singer, Kimber writes songs and plays keyboard. Aja Leith and Shana Elmsford were the first two girls adopted by Jerrica's parents (Emmett and Jacqui). Aja plays guitar; Shana (later replaced by Raya Alonso) is the drummer. Jetta (real name Sheila Burns) plays saxophone (she was formally with a group called the Tinkerbellies). Rio Pacheco is the group's road manager.

Pizzazz (real name Phyllis Gabor) is the daughter of rich parents and wants something her father can't give her — a position on top of the music world (she plays guitar). Roxy Pelligrini plays guitar (as

does Stormer) and gets what she wants by lying and cheating. Stormer, a girl with a conscience who tries to do what is right, is the Misfits song writer. Eric is the manager of the Misfits. Clash (real name Constance Montgomery) is a big fan of the Misfits and desperately wants to become a part of the group. Another rock group, the Stingers was introduced in later episodes to cause further friction between the Holograms and the Misfits. This group consisted of Riot (lead singer), Rapture (lead guitar) and Minx (keyboards). The pilot episode, *Jem: Truly Outrageous*, aired as a five-part miniseries in syndication in April of 1985.

Voice Cast: Samantha Newkirk (*Jerrica Benton/Jem; speaking voice*); Britta Phillips (*Jem; singing voice*); Catherine Blore (*Kimber Benton*); Cindy McGee (*Shana Elmsford*); Patricia Albrecht (*Pizzazz; speaking voice*); Eden Bernfield (*Pizzazz; singing voice*); Susan Blu (*Stormer*); Ellen Gerstell (*Rapture*); Louise Dorsey (*Jetta*); Linda Dangcil (*Raya Alonso*); Bobbie Block (*Roxie*); Michael Sheehan (*Rio Pacheco*); Kath Soucie (*Minx*); Charlie Adler (*Eric Raymond*); Marlene Aragon (*Synergy*); Ford Kinder (*Riot*).

4655 *Jenna's American Sex Star*. (Series; Reality; Playboy; 2005-2006). Sexual reality competition wherein four gorgeous women (per episode) compete in adult film oriented sexual challenges for a contract with adult film star Jenna Jameson's film studio, Club Jenna. The girls are judged by industry performers but viewers (via the Internet at Playboy.com) determine who goes and who stays. The weekly winners appear for a final judging with the most qualified girl receiving the contract. Brea Bennett was the season one winner; Roxy Jezel, the second season winner. Andrea Lowell is the Envelope Presenter (delivers the good or bad news regarding eliminations to the girls).

Host: Jenna Jameson. **Season One Judges:** Christy Canyon, Ron Jeremy, Jim Powers. **Season Two Judges:** Jenna Lewis, Jim Powers, Jay Gradina.

4656 *Jennie: Lady Randolph Churchill*. (Series; Biography; PBS; 1975). The life of Lady Randolph Churchill (nee Jennie Jerome, 1845–1921), the American-born mother of England's Sir Winston Churchill.

Cast: Lee Remick (*Jennie Jerome*); Ronald Pickup (*Randolph Churchill*); Dan O'Herlihy (*Mr. Jerome*); Helen Horton (*Mrs. Jerome*); Barbara Parkins (*Leonie*); Linda Liles (*Clara*); Cyril Luckham (*Duke of Marlborough*); Rachel Kempson (*Duchess of Marlbrough*); Thorley Walters (*Prince of Wales*).

4657 *Jennifer Slept Here*. (Series; Comedy; NBC; 1982-1983). Jennifer Farrell is a young girl with a dream of becoming a movie star. At age 17 she defies her mother (who wants her to become a beautician) and leaves her home in Illinois to pursue her dream in Hollywood. She made her television debut as a costumed banana in the audience of *Let's Make a Deal*, and several months later, in 1966, when Jennifer was 18 years old, hungry and flat broke, she posed nude for a calendar. Jennifer landed a small role in the movie *Desire*, but it was her outstanding singing and dancing performance in her next film, *Stairway to Paradise*, that brought her overnight stardom. Jennifer soon became one of America's most glamorous and beloved stars.

Jennifer's untimely death in 1978 saddened the world. Five years later, New York lawyer George Elliot, his wife, Susan, and their children, Joey and Marilyn, move into Jennifer's fabulous mansion at 32 Rexford Drive in Beverly Hills. Shortly after, while settling into his room, Joey is startled to see the ghost of Jennifer Farrell — who appears and speaks only to him (she feels he needs help and has decided to guide his life). Joey attends Beverly Hills High School. A school for Marilyn is not given, nor is a company name for George.

Stories follow the mishaps that occur as Joey struggles to deal with the antics of a ghost whose well-intentioned efforts often backfire. Alice is Jennifer's mother, a ghost also; Marc is Joey's friend.

Cast: Ann Jillian (*Jennifer Farrell*); Georgia Engel (*Susan Elliot*); Brandon Maggart (*George Elliot*); John P. Navin, Jr. (*Joey Elliot*); Mya Akerling (*Marilyn Elliot*); Glenn Scarpelli (*Marc*); Debbie Reynolds (*Alice Farrell*).

4658   *Jenny.* (Series; Comedy; NBC; 1997-1998). "We were obnoxious little brats. We cut classes, broke curfew and snuck into 'R' rated movies," says Margaret "Maggie" Marino about her and her best friend, Jennifer "Jenny" McMillan. "But now we're poised, composed and no longer kids as we start a new beginning." Maggie is referring to their move from Utica, New York, to the Playpen, a mansion in the Hollywood Hills that was owned by Jenny's late father, movie star Guy Hathaway. (While filming *It Happened in Paris* in Utica, Guy met Jenny's mother. They had an affair and he left after the wrap party. A year later Jenny was born but Guy distanced himself. He never forgot Jenny and willed her his mansion.)

Guy was a "big" star whose glory years were 1970-1971. He made a disco album (*Me, Myself and Guy*), an exercise tape ("Guy-Zercise") and a six-episode TV series called *The Adventures of Dickie* (about a father and his young son).

Jenny and Maggie work at Inky Pete's High Speed Copying and Offset Printing and sell Skin So Nice skin care products on the side. In Utica, Jenny and Maggie worked at Chubby Boy Burger. "We may have our quarrels, we may go our separate ways, but we'll be there for each other. We're friends," says Maggie. Cooper and Max are their friends.

Cast: Jenny McCarthy (*Jenny McMillan*); Heather Paige Kent (*Maggie Marino*); George Hamilton (*Guy Hamilton*); Dale Godboldo (*Cooper*); Roger Weigel (*Max*); Kevin Ruf (*Ted Tucker*); Carolyn Hennesy (*Chase Gardner*).

4659   *The Jenny Jones Show.* (Series; Talk; Syn.; 1991–2003). A daily program that features discussions with appropriate guests on sensational topics. The gimmick was to bring an unexpected guest who would appear during a discussion to hype the excitement (and ratings). Jenny, standing in the middle of her studio audience, conducted the stage happenings and often asked audience members for their reactions (or if they had any questions for the guests).

Host: Jenny Jones.

4660   *The Jenny McCarthy Show.* (Series; Comedy; MTV; 1997-1998). Gorgeous former Playboy Playmate (and Bunny) Jenny McCarthy headlines a skit program that spotlights her comedic talents (playing most often, as she still does, a ditzy blonde). Jenny is backed by an ensemble group of comedians and anything that can be spoofed gets the royal treatment.

Hostess: Jenny McCarthy. **Regulars:** Paul Greenberg, H. Jon Benjamin, Michael Loprete, Jack Plotnick, Lou Thornton, Brian Michael Tracy.

4661   *Jeopardy.* (Series; Game; NBC; Syn.; 1964–1975; 1984–). Three players compete in a game wherein they must supply answers to questions. A category board containing six subjects, each with five concealed answers and each worth a varying amount of money, is revealed. A player selects a subject and a money amount and must supply the question for the answer that is given. If he gives the correct question, he wins the money and continues to play. An incorrect response ends his turn. One of the remaining players must give the correct question to gain control of the board. The player with the highest score is the winner. See also *Jep!* and *Rock 'n' Roll Jeopardy*. Two versions appeared:

1. *Jeopardy* (NBC, 1964–75). **Host:** Art Fleming. **Announcer:** Don Pardo, John Harlan.
2. *Jeopardy* (Syn. 1984–). **Host:** Alex Trebek. **Announcer:** Johnny Gilbert.

4662   *Jep!* (Series; Game; GSN; 1998–2000). A children's version of *Jeopardy* that is basically played in the same manner with contestants having to give the questions to answers. Three children, aged ten to thirteen, compete. A board with five category topics is revealed (each has four questions worth from 100–500 points; not cash as in the adult version). One player chooses a category topic then pushes a plunger to determine the point value. The host reads the answer. If the player responds with the right question, he scores the points. If he gives an incorrect question or fails to answer within the ten second time limit, the points are deducted from his score and the other players (through a buzzer signal) receive a chance to answer. The player with the last correct response is in charge of the board. Round two, called "Hyper Jep" ("Double Jeopardy" in the adult version) adds two spaces that allows players to double their points if the question if answered correctly. "Super Jep" ("Final Jeopardy" on the parent show) allows all three players to bet all or a portion of their points on their ability to answer one final question. The person who scores the highest wins.

Host: Bob Bergen.

4663   *Jeremiah.* (Series; Science Fiction; Showtime; 2002–2004). It is the year 2006 and a virus called "The Big Death" has been unleashed on the earth. The virus strikes virtually everyone over the age of puberty and nearly destroys what is left of mankind. It is the year 2021 when the series begins and the children who survived the virus are now grown, Jeremiah being one of them, and facing a decision: work to rebuild what once was or scavenge off what remains.

Jeremiah, the son of a viral researcher, is a loner who believes his father, who disappeared in the confusion, may still be alive and safe in a place called Valhalla Sector. With that belief, Jeremiah begins a trek to find the mysterious Valhalla Sector. Along the way, he meets Kurdy, a lone traveler, who involves him with Thunder Mountain, a group of people dedicated to rebuilding society, led by the former child prodigy Markus Alexander. First season episodes focus on Jeremiah and Kurdy as they become a part of Thunder Mountain and battle its enemies, in particular, what Jeremiah had been seeking — Valhalla Sector, a heavily armored complex in West Virginia that seeks to rebuild the world as an authoritarian society. The second season begins with the defeat of Valhalla Sector but also introduces a new enemy: an army, led by the profit Daniel, that seeks to control what remains of the world. Erin is Markus's second-in-command; Mister Smith is the man who claims to be a messenger from God; Byron is the Thunder Mountain security chief; Meaghan is a "Big Death" survivor who carries the plague (she is housed in a containment room in Thunder Mountain); Ezekiel is the mysterious man who protects Jeremiah; Theodora is the ruthless warlord; Elizabeth is a resident of Thunder Mountain; Devon is Jeremiah's father; Liberty is Devon's assistant at Valhalla Sector.

Cast: Luke Perry (*Jeremiah*); Malcolm-Jamal Warner (*Kurdy Malloy*); Peter Stebbings (*Markus Alexander*); Ingrid Kavelaars (*Erin*); Sean Aston (*Mister Smith*); Lee Chen (*Byron Lawson*); Suzy Joachim (*Meaghan Lee Rose*); Alex Zahara (*Ezekiel*); Kim Hawthorne (*Theodora Coleridge*); Kandyse McClure (*Elizabeth Munroe*); Robert Wisdom (*Devon*); Joanne Kelly (*Liberty Kaufman*).

4664   *Jeremiah of Jacob's Neck.* (Pilot; Comedy; CBS; Aug. 13, 1976). The house at 960 Post Road in the small New England town of Jacob's Neck, is now owned by Tom Rankin, the police chief, and his family (his wife, Anne, and their children Tracy and Clay). The quaint little beach house has one other resident — the spirit of Jeremiah Starbuck, an eighteenth-century ghost who refuses to depart from his once earthly dwelling. The efforts of both the family and the ghost to adjust to each other are the focal point of the proposed series. Wilbur is Tom's deputy.

Cast: Keenan Wynn (*Jeremiah Starbuck*); Ron Masak (*Tom Rankin*); Arlene Golonka (*Anne Rankin*); Quinn Cummings (*Tracy Rankin*); Brandon Cruz (*Clay Rankin*); Elliott Street (*Wilbur Swift*).

4665   *Jericho*. (Pilot; Western; CBS; May 18, 1961). A man, known only as Jericho, is an undercover agent for the Attorney General. It is the 1860s and the proposed series, a spin off from *Zane Grey Theater* was to follow Jericho as he helps people wrongly accused of crimes.

Cast: Guy Madison (*Jericho*); Les Tremayne (*Attorney General*).

4666   *Jericho*. (Series; Adventure; CBS; 1966). Europe during World War II is the setting. It is here that a group of Allied agents, Franklin Shepard (American), Nicholas Gage (British) and Jean-Gatson Andre (French) have established a secret base and operate under the code name Jericho. With orders to infiltrate enemy lines, stories follow their efforts to discredit German operations. Also known as *Code Name Jericho*.

Cast: Don Francks (*Franklin Sheppard*); John Leyton (*Nicholas Gage*); Marino Mase (*Jean-Gatson Andre*).

4667   *Jericho*. (Series; Drama; CBS; 2006–2008). Jericho is a small town typical of any such town or small city in the U.S. It is also a town that is concerned with a new threat to the world — global vengeance (which, according to news reports, is on the rise). But, by fate, Jericho becomes unlike any town or city. It is a town that is spared destruction when an apparent nuclear bomb is detonated in what is said to be Denver, Colorado (and another in Atlanta). All communication is cut off and the people of Jericho are left wondering what happened and are they the only survivors? Was the explosion an accident? Or an attack? While the series focuses on the incidents that have propelled the town into panic and their desperate efforts to contact other survivors, it pays particular attention to the Green family and their various problems as they attempt to keep the calm.

Jonathan Green is the town's mayor. He is married to Gail and they are the parents of Jake and Eric (the Deputy Mayor). Jake had just returned after a five-year absence to claim his inheritance (from his grandfather) when he became trapped in Jericho right before he was to leave. Jonathan seems to have the needed leadership to keep the citizens under control; Gail is the typical loving mother, totally dedicated to her family. Eric is the all too perfect son who seems to do no wrong. Emily Sullivan is the local high school teacher; other characters are Robert Hawkins, Heather Lisinksi, Gray Anderson, Dale, Bonnie and Stanley.

Cast: Skeet Ulrich (*Jake Green*); Gerald McRaney (*Jonathan Green*); Pamela Reed (*Gail Green*); Kenneth Mitchell (*Eric Green*); Ashley Scott (*Emily Sullivan*); Sprague Grayden (*Heather Lisinksi*); Shoshannah Stern (*Bonnie*); Erik Knudsen (*Dale Turner*); Michael Gaston (*Gray Anderson*); Brad Beyer (*Stanley*); Lennie James (*Robert Hawkins*); Darby Stanchfield (*April*); Christopher Wiehl (*Roger Hammond*); Siena Goines (*Sarah*).

4668   *The Jerk, Too*. (Pilot; Comedy; NBC; Jan. 6, 1984). A proposed series based on the 1979 feature film, *The Jerk*, about Navin Johnson, the naive, adopted white son of a black farm family (the Johnsons), the owners of a farm in Hendersonville, Georgia. Mama and Papa Johnson found the baby in their mailbox and raised him as one of their own. He grew up with the Johnson children, Damon,

Harold, Carmen and Cheetah, but never really managed to mature. His misguided efforts to adjust to life as an adult were to be the focal point of stories. John B. Sebastian performs the theme, "Navin's Theme."

Cast: Mark Blankfield (*Navin Johnson*); Mabel King (*Mama Johnson*); Al Fann (*Papa Johnson*); Todd Hollowell (*Damon Johnson*); Larry B. Scott (*Harold Johnson*); Stacy Harris (*Carmen Johnson*); Linda Raymond (*Cheetah Johnson*); Helen Martin (*Grandma Johnson*).

4669   *Jerry*. (Pilot; Comedy; CBS; May 16, 1974). Jerry Edwards is a 30-year-old bachelor who works in a bank. He yearns for an exciting romance and the unsold series was to follow his misadventures as he tries to find the girl of his dreams. He is helped by Nina Pope, a not-so-gay divorcee; Morree Wu, his friend, a lady killer; and his neighbors, Frank and Gloria Fuller. Winston Barlow is Jerry's boss.

Cast: Robert Walden (*Jerry Edwards*); Linda Lavin (*Nina Pope*); Keone Young (*Morree Wu*); Bob Hastings (*Frank Fuller*); Beatrice Colen (*Gloria Fuller*); Norman Alden (*Winston Barlow*).

4670   *The Jerry Colonna Show*. (Series; Variety; ABC; 1951). Comedian Jerry Colonna oversees a program of music, songs and comedy skits.

Host: Jerry Colonna. **Regulars:** Barbara Ruick, Gordon Polk, Frankie Laine, Arthur Duncan, Isabel Randolph, Louis Colonna. **Announcer:** Del Sharbutt. **Music:** The Cookie Fairchild Band.

4671   *The Jerry Lee Lewis Show*. (Pilot; Variety; Unaired; Produced in 1971). Country and western songs by singer Jerry Lee Lewis and his sister, Linda Gail Lewis coupled with performances by guest stars.

Hosts: Jerry Lee Lewis, Linda Gail Lewis. **Guests:** Kenneth Lovelace, Carl Perkins, Bill Strom, Jackie Wilson, The Memphis Beats, The Nashville Sound Quartet, The Russ College Quintet, The Sound Generation. **Orchestra:** Bill Walker.

4672   *The Jerry Lester Show*. (Series; Variety; ABC; 1953–1954). Music, songs and comedy sketches hosted by comedian Jerry Lester.

Host: Jerry Lester. **Regulars:** Nancy Walker, Betty George, Bobby Sherwood, Lorenzo Fuller, Kathy Collin, Eddie Russell, Leon Belasco. **Orchestra:** Buddy Weed. **Announcer:** Don Pardo.

4673   *The Jerry Lewis Show*. (Series; Variety; ABC; NBC; Syn; 1963; 1967; 1984). Entertainment acts coupled with talk and celebrity interviews with comedian Jerry Lewis as the host. Three versions appeared:

1. The Jerry Lewis Show (ABC, 1963). **Host:** Jerry Lewis. **Announcer:** Del Moore. **Orchestra:** Lou Brown.

2. The Jerry Lewis Show (NBC, 1967–69). **Host:** Jerry Lewis. **Orchestra:** Lou Brown.

3. The Jerry Lewis Show (Pilot; Syn., June 1984). **Host:** Jerry Lewis. **Announcer:** Charlie Callas.

4674   *Jerry Mahoney's Club House*. (Series; Children; NBC; 1954–1956). A Saturday morning program of comedy and games for children with ventriloquist Paul Winchell and the antics of his wooden friends, Jerry Mahoney and Knucklehead Smiff.

Host: Paul Winchell. **Regulars:** Dorothy Claire, Hilda Vaughn, Sid Raymond, Jimmy Blaine. **Music:** John Gart.

4675   *The Jerry Reed When You're Hot, You're Hot Hour*. (Series; Variety; CBS; 1972). Singer Jerry Reed hosts a summer program of music, songs and comedy sketches.

Host: Jerry Reed. **Regulars:** Carl Wilson, Spencer Quinn, Merie

Earle, John Twomey, Norman Alexander, The Lou Regas Dancers. **Announcer:** Bill Thompson. **Orchestra:** George Wyle.

4676   *The Jerry Springer Show.* (Series; Talk; Syn.; 1991–). A sensationalized daily program that has gone where no other talk show has: nudity (although blurred for broadcast), foul language (bleeped) and fights between guests (prevented from becoming violent by on stage security guards). The show exposes secrets between family and friends and, although overseen by host Jerry Springer, the situations are allowed to get explosive and thus produce the rage and violence that follows.

Host: Jerry Springer. **Security Guards:** Steve Wilkos, Mimi Madrigal, Katie Darwin, Mari Flores.

4677   *Jerry Visits.* (Series; Interview; Syn.; 1971). Hollywood celebrities open their homes to television cameras and reveal their dreams, ambitions, and aspects of their public and private lives.

Host: Jerry Dunphy.

4678   *The Jersey.* (Series; Comedy; Disney; 1999–2004). Nick Lighter, Coleman Galloway and Elliot Rifkin are kids who have discovered the secret to achieving success in sports: a magical jersey that transforms ordinary children into sports athletes. Stories, based on the Monday Night Football Club books by Gordon Korman, follows the path of the jersey and its affect on the children who possess it.

Cast: Michael Galeota (*Nick Lighter*); Theo Greenly (*Elliot Rifkin*); Jermaine Williams (*Coleman Galloway*); Courtnee Draper (*Morgan Hudson*); Brianne Prather (*Hilary Lighter*); Kathleen Bailey (*April Hudson*).

4679   *Jersey Shore.* (Series; Reality; MTV; 2009–). A look at the activities of a group of young Italian Americans who enjoy beer and going to the Jersey Shore for some fun in the sun: Nicole "Snookie" Polizzi, Mike "The Situation" Sorrentino, Paul "Pauly" Del Vecchio, Jenni "JWOWW" Farley, Ronnie Ortiz-Margo, Vinny GuaDagnino, Sammi Giancola, Angelina Pivarnick and Deena Nicole Cortese.

4680   *Jesse.* (Series; Comedy; NBC; 1998–2000). Jesse Warner is a young woman trying to reorganize her life following her divorce from Roy (whom she caught in bed "with that chick" from the video store. "And what's worse," Jesse says, "that shank still charges me if I don't rewind"). Jesse is the mother of "Little" John and works as a waitress at her father's pub, Der Biergarten, in Buffalo, New York.

Jesse lives at 346 McCord Avenue with her father, John Warner and brothers Darren and John Junior. Jesse and her brothers attended Fledgemore High School. Although she dropped out of school to get married, Jesse has now returned to get her diploma and become a nurse (she later receives a scholarship to the Rochester Nursing School). Jesse becomes manager of the pub whenever her father leaves town or there is something unpleasant to be done.

Junior worked as a gas station attendant, then stopped talking for a time; he now washes dishes at the pub. Darren is a hopeful actor whose only credit appears to be a TV commercial as pitchman for Freddie's Electronics Store. John Sr. is divorced from Susan. Jesse is dating Diego Vasquez, her next door neighbor, a college art teacher and hopeful artist. Linda and Carrie are the pub's waitresses.

Second-season episodes changed the premise somewhat. The bar, Jesse's brothers and father are gone (as if they never existed). Jesse, a single mother, attends nursing school and works part time at the Student Health Center. Carrie is now a keeper at the Buffalo Zoological Society; Linda, who lives next door to Jesse in Diego's house, is a bartender (later a security officer) at the Buffalo Airport.

Cast: Christina Applegate (*Jesse Warner*); George Dzundza (*John Warner*); David DeLuise (*Darren Warner*); John Lehr (*John Warner, Jr.*); Liza Snyder (*Linda*); Bruno Campos (*Diego Vasquez*); Jennifer Milmore (*Carrie*).

4681   *Jesse Hawkes.* (Series; Crime Drama; CBS; 1989). A spin off from *High Mountain Rangers*. Jesse Hawkes is the head of the High Mountain Rangers, a rescue unit based in the Sierra Nevada Mountains near Lake Tahoe. When drug smugglers invade Jesse's territory and his son, Matt is injured, Jesse travels to San Francisco to track them down. Later, with the help of his sons Matt and Cody, Jesse accomplishes his goal. Rather than return to the mountain, Jesse, Matt and Cody decide to become modern-day bounty hunters and help people who have nowhere else to turn. Stories relate their adventures. David Cummings performs the theme, "Edge of the Sky."

Cast: Robert Conrad (*Jesse Hawkes*); Christian Conrad (*Matt Hawkes*); Shane Conrad (*Cody Hawkes*).

4682   *Jesse James Is a Dead Man.* (Series; Reality; Spike TV; 2009). The title refers to West Coast Choppers, a bike shop owned by Jesse James, not the Old West outlaw. Jesse is a thrill seeker with a death wish. He tackles extremely dangerous stunts with a motorcycle simply because it's a challenge (he is an extreme version of legendary daredevil Evel Knievel). The program glamorizes the hazardous stunts Jesse attempts (although most of the program is devoted to the stunt's preparation and the only action occurs in the last minutes of each episode). Jesse has no logical scientific reason for being so reckless; it appears he just likes to tempt fate to see if he can survive horrific accidents.

4683   *Jesse Stone.* (Pilot; Crime Drama; CBS; 2005–2011). Paradise is a mid-size Massachusetts town where Jesse Stone, a former police detective with the L.A.P.D. has come to serve as its police chief (when the former chief retires). Jesse is somewhat of a loner, enjoys scotch and women and finds his training as a big city cop beneficial to upholding the law. Rose Gammon and Luther Simpson are his deputies. Six TV movies were produced, but failed to generate a series: *Stonecold* (2005), *Jesse Stone: Night Passage* (2006), *Jesse Stone: Death in Paradise* (2006), *Jesse Stone: Sea of Change* (2007), *Jesse Stone: Thin Ice* (2009) and *Jesse Stone: Innocents Lost* (2011).

Cast: Tom Selleck (*Jesse Stone*); Kathy Baker (*Rose Gammon*); Kohl Sudduth (*Luther Simpson*); Stephen McHattie (*Captain Healy*).

4684   *Jessica.* (Pilot; Comedy; Unaired; Produced for ABC in 2003). Singer and reality show star Jessica Simpson is blonde, beautiful and buxom and most people believe she is just a beautiful dumb blonde and hasn't an intelligent thought in her head. Jessica was born in Texas, is quite intelligent and, despite the fact that she is a pop culture icon, she decides to show the world she is more than just a pretty face. It begins when Jessica applies for and receives a job on a TV newsmagazine that her life begins to change. Although a bit rough around the edges, she proves to have the ability to deliver the goods and the proposal was to follow Jessica as she embarks on a new career to prove she is not an airhead.

Cast: Jessica Simpson (*Herself*); Ali Hills (*Holly*); Aimee Garcia (*Amanda*); Brad Rowe (*Mike*); Bryan Callen (*Dan*).

4685   *Jessica Novak.* (Series; Crime Drama; CBS; 1981). Jessica Novak is the on-the-air reporter for *Close-Up News* on KLA-TV, Channel 6, in Los Angeles. She is not just content with reporting stories; she has to be in the field to get the facts and interview the people involved. She sometimes finds herself becoming a detective as she needs to uncover the information that helps the police make an arrest and bring the story to a successful conclusion. Phil Bonelli is her field cameraman, and Ricky Duran is her field soundman; Audrey Styles is the videotape editor; Jackson Gage is the co-anchor; Vince Halloran is the public defender; Katie is Jessica's friend; and Richie is an employee of KLA-TV. Fred Karlin composed "The Theme from Jessica Novak."

Cast: Helen Shaver (*Jessica Novak*); David Spielberg (*Max Kenyon*); Andrew Rubin (*Phil Bonelli*); Nina Wilcox (*Audrey Styles*); Eric Kilpatrick (*Ricky Duran*); Michael D. Roberts (*Jackson Gage*); Kenneth Gilman (*Vince Halloran*); Lara Parker (*Katie Robbins*); Scott Thompson (*Richie*); Frank Taylor (*KLA Dispatcher*).

4686   *Jessie*. (Series; Drama; ABC; 1984). Jessica "Jessie" Hayden is a woman of principal. She is a psychologist and rejected a "big bucks" hospital job to work with the Behavioral Science Department of the San Francisco Police Department, Metro Division. She also rejected the idea of opening her own practice as she feels she is best able to put her skills to use by compiling profiles and helping the police put criminals behind bars. Jessie refuses to carry a gun ("A doctor's duty is to preserve human life, not destroy it"). She doesn't drink coffee, likes Mexican food and is a loner (she "lives in a little shack in the hills"). Jessie is the daughter of a wealthy family and grew up on Winterhaven Street, where her widowed mother, Molly Hayden, still lives. Alex Ascoli is a lieutenant who has been taken off street duty and reassigned as Jessie's liaison — "to interface her with the department." Mac McClellan is the police captain; Ellie is Mac's secretary.

Cast: Lindsay Wagner (*Dr. Jessie Hayden*); Tony Lo Bianco (*Alex Ascoli*); William Lucking (*Capt. Mac McClellan*); Tom Nolan (*Off. Hub Hubbell*); Renee Jones (*Ellie*).

4687   *Jet Fighter*. (Pilot; Adventure; ABC; June 28, 1953). A proposed series about Chuck Powers, a captain with the U.S. Air Force. Filmed at the McGuire Air Force Base.

Cast: John Granger (*Chuck Powers*); Tige Andrews (*Gunner Maddigan*); Ben Hammer (*Colonel Warner*); Jackson Beck (*Narrator*).

4688   *Jet Jackson, Flying Commando*. (Series; Adventure; Syn.; 1956). The 1956 title for *Captain Midnight* (which see for information) when Ovaltine, the original sponsor of the series, retained its right to the original name and the series was reworked and renamed for syndication after its run on CBS.

4689   *The Jetsons*. (Series; Cartoon; ABC; 1962-1963). A futuristic view of life in the twenty-first century as seen through the experiences of the Jetson family: George, his wife, Jane and their children, Judy and Elroy.

George is employed by Cosmo G. Spacely, the owner of Spacely Space Sprockets. George and Jane live at the Sky Pad Apartments, and Jane appears content being a housewife and mother. Fifteen-year-old Judy attends Orbit High School and has a talking diary she calls Di Di. Elroy, eight years old, attends the Little Dipper School and has a pet dog named Astro. Rosie, the Jetsons' robot maid, is a model XB-500 service robot they acquired from "U-Rent-a-Maid." Henry Orbit is the apartment house janitor. Mr. Spacely and his wife, Stella, reside at 175 Snerdville Drive.

Voice Cast: George O'Hanlon (*George Jetson*); Penny Singleton (*Jane Jetson*); Janet Waldo (*Judy Jetson*); Daws Butler (*Elroy Jetson*); Jean VanderPyl (*Rosie*); Mel Blanc (*Cosmo G. Spacely*); Howard Morris (*Henry Orbit*); Daws Butler (*Mr. Cogswell*); Selma Diamond (*Di Di*). **Announcer:** Dick Tufeld.

4690   *Jigsaw*. (Series; Crime Drama; ABC; 1972-1973). Frank Dain is a detective with the Sacramento State Bureau of Missing Persons. He has a genius for solving complicated, clueless mysteries (taking what little evidence he has, envisioning them as a jigsaw puzzle then filling in the missing pieces until the mystery is solved). Stories follow Frank as he uses his expertise to solve missing persons cases. Broadcast as a segment of *The Men*.

Cast: James Wainwright (*Lt. Frank Dain*).

4691   *Jigsaw John*. (Series; Crime Drama; NBC; 1976). John St. John is a detective with the Robbery-Homicide Division of the L.A.P.D. His talent for figuring out people and solving complex crimes has earned him the nickname "Jigsaw John." He has a record of crime solution and criminal conviction that is the highest in the nation. John likes Chinese food for breakfast but has to take pills for his stomach — "worries related to the job." Maggie Hearn is his girlfriend, and Detective Sam Donner is his partner. In the television movie pilot, *They Only Come Out at Night* (NBC, April 29, 1975), John was married to a woman named Helen (Madeleine Sherwood) and was said to "take bits and scraps, find patterns and solve cases" — hence the name "Jigsaw John."

Cast: Jack Warden (*Det. John St. John*); Pippa Scott (*Maggie Hearn*); Alan Feinstein (*Det. Sam Donner*).

4692   *Jim and Judy in Teleland*. (Series; Cartoon; Syn.; 1953). Various adventures in the lives of two children, Jim and Judy.

Voice Cast: Merrill Jolls (*Jim*); Honey McKenzie (*Judy*).

4693   *The Jim Backus Show — Hot Off the Wire*. (Series; Comedy; Syn.; 1960-1961). The Headline Press Service is a New York City based news gathering organization that is run by John Michael "Mike" O'Toole, a publisher who was banned in his hometown of Boston and now seeks to turn a faltering service into a profitable one. While O'Toole fancies himself an editor, he finds that he must resort to his former skills as a reporter to get the stories he wants ("If you want a story done right, you have to do it yourself. I can't trust my reporters to do anything right").

Dora Miles, Mike's glamorous secretary, is also his reporting assistant. She constantly complains about the money Mike owes her, claims she has only two outfits for work (one dress and one tight skirt) and will not date loafers — burglars are okay, "as long as they are working."

Sidney is Mike's combination office boy, photographer and reporter. He believes he has a nose for news but rarely has a chance to put it to the test. Fingers Larkin, Mike's information man, has a business card that reads "Fingers Larkin, Thief Extraordinaire. Holdups, second story jobs, muggings and safes cracked while you wait. 24-hour service; day work double time."

Bob's Alterations and Tailoring is the office across the hall from the paper; Mike uses the services of the New York *Globe* for research material and publication of stories. David Rose composed the theme, "Hot Off the Wire."

Cast: Jim Backus (*John O'Toole*); Nita Talbot (*Dora Miles*); Bobs Watson (*Sidney*); Lewis Charles (*Fingers Larkin*).

4694   *Jim Bowie*. (Series; Adventure; ABC; 1956–1958). The shortened title for *The Adventures of Jim Bowie*. See this title for information.

4695   *The Jim Henson Hour*. (Series; Anthology; NBC; 1989-1990). The overall title for *Muppet Central* and *The Storyteller*. The first segment revolves around Kermit the Frog as he struggles to operate a television station with a group of misadventure-prone Muppets as his staff. Shows presented by *Muppet Central* are *Dog City* (see entry for information), *Lighthouse Island* (tale of a young man and a mermaid); *The Monster Maker* (about a young boy's eagerness to work in a creature special effects shop); *Secrets of the Muppets* (a behind-the-scenes look at the making of the Muppets with creator Jim Henson); *Living with Dinosaurs* (a boy with a talking dinosaur toy); and *Song of the Cloud Forest* (a tree frog seeks to stop his own extinction). *The Storyteller* segment features a well-versed old man telling stories based on traditional folktales to his dog.

Host: Jim Henson. **Storyteller:** John Hurt. **Muppet Voices:** Frank Oz, Rickey Boyd, Kevin Clash, Richard Hunt, Rick Lyon, Rob Mills, Bob Stutt, Gord Robertson.

4696   *Jim Henson Presents Mother Goose Stories.* (Series; Anthology; Fox; 1997-1998). Stylish adaptations of fairy tales adapted from the book *Mother Goose in Prose* by L. Frank Baum (creator of *The Wizard of Oz*) as well as original stories written in the style of the book (these included *Queen of Hearts, The Woman Who Lived in a Shoe, Mother Hubbard, Jack and Jill, Mary's Little Lamb* and *Twinkle, Twinkle Little Star*).

Cast: Nicholle Tom, Scott McAfee, Jodie Sweetin, James Conway, Michelle Weston, Simon Bright, Ethan Glazer, Ilan Ostrove, John Christian Graas.

4697   *Jim Henson's Animal Show with Stinky and Jake.* (Series; Children; Fox; 1994–1997). A daily morning program that, aimed at children two to five years of age, incorporates wildlife footage, videos and Jim Henson's Muppet characters to familiarize children with nature and the environment. Muppets Stinky and Jake host the program.

Muppet Voices: Dave Goelz, Frank Oz, Katherine Smee, Steve Whitmire, Karen Prell, Mike Quinn, David Grenaway, Louise Gold, John Eccleston.

4698   *Jim Henson's Muppet Babies.* (Series; Cartoon; CBS; 1984-1985). Jim Henson's fanciful creations, the Muppets, are seen as babies (before they became stars on *Sesame Street*) as they enjoy life and wreck havoc for the nursemaid (called Nanny).

Voice Cast: Frank Welker (*Kermit the Frog/Beaker*); Laurie O'Brien (*Piggie*); Greg Berg (*Fozzie/Scooter*); Katie Lee (*Rowlf*); Howie Mandel (*Skeeter*); Russi Taylor (*Gonzo*); Howie Mandel (*Animal/Bunsen*); Barbara Billingsley (*Nanny*).

4699   *The Jim Nabors Show.* (Series; Variety; CBS; Syn.; 1969; 1978). Comedian Jim Nabors hosts a program of music, songs and comedy sketches.

Program Open: "From television city in Hollywood, it's ... *The Jim Nabors Hour* ... starring Jim Nabors and Frank Sutton ... with Ronnie Schell, The Nabors Kids, The Tony Mordente Dancers, Paul Weston and his orchestra and special guest, Miss Kate Smith." Two versions appeared:

1. The Jim Nabors Hour (CBS, 1969–71). **Host:** Jim Nabors. **Regulars:** Frank Sutton, Ronnie Schell, Karen Morrow, The Tony Mordente Dancers, The Nabors Kids. **Orchestra:** Paul Weston.

2. The Jim Nabors Show (Syn., 1978). **Host:** Jim Nabors. **Regulars:** Susan Ford, Ronnie Schell. **Orchestra:** Fred Werner.

4700   *The Jim Stafford Show.* (Series; Variety; ABC; 1975). Music, songs, dances and comedy sketches hosted by Jim Stafford.

Host: Jim Stafford. **Regulars:** Valerie Curtin, Richard Stahl, Philip Charles MacKenzie, Debbie Allen, Jeannie Sheffield, Tom Biener, Gallagher, Lyndi Wood, The Carl Jablonski Dancers. **Music:** Eddie Karam.

4701   *Jiminy Glick.* (Series; Comedy; Comedy Central; 2001–2003). See *Primetime Glick* for information.

4702   *The Jimmie Rodgers Show.* (Series; Variety; NBC; CBS;

1959; 1969). Singer Jimmie Rodgers hosts a program of music and songs. Two versions appeared:

1. The Jimmie Rodgers Show (NBC, 1959). **Host:** Jimmie Rodgers. **Regulars:** Connie Francis, The Kirby Stone Four, The Clay Warnick Singers. **Orchestra:** Byron Morrow.

2. The Jimmie Rodgers Show (CBS, 1969). **Host:** Jimmie Rodgers. **Regulars:** Vicki Lawrence, Lyle Waggoner, Nancy Austin, Don Crichton, Bill Fanning, The Burgundy Street Singers, **Announcer:** Lyle Waggoner. **Orchestra:** Harry Zimmerman, Frank Comstock.

4703   *The Jimmy Dean Show.* (Series; Variety; CBS; ABC; 1957; 1963). Singer Jimmy Dean oversees a program of country and western music, songs and comedy. Two versions appeared:

1. The Jimmy Dean Show (CBS, 1957-58). **Host:** Jimmy Dean. **Regulars:** Jo Davis, Herbie Jones, Jeri Miyazaki, Mary Klick, Jan Crockett, The Double Daters. The Country Lads, The Noteworthies, Alec Houston's Wildcats. **Orchestra:** Joel Herron.

2. The Jimmy Dean (ABC, 1963–66). **Host:** Jimmy Dean. **Regulars:** Molly Bee, The Grass Roots Band, The Doerr-Hutchinson Dancers, The Chuck Cassey Singers, Rowlf (the hound dog Muppet). **Orchestra:** Peter Matz, Al Pellegrini, Don Sebesky.

4704   *Jimmy Durante Presents the Lennon Sisters Hour.* (Series; Variety; ABC; 1969-1970). A lively program that features the lovely and talented Lennon Sisters and comedian Jimmy Durante in various songs, dances and comedy sketches.

Program Open: "You're watching *Jimmy Durante Presents the Lennon Sisters Hour* with tonight's guests Buddy Ebsen, Bobby Goldsboro and special guest star Martha Raye."

Host: Jimmy Durante. **Stars:** Dianne Lennon, Peggy Lennon, Kathy Lennon, Janet Lennon. **Regulars:** Edna O'Dell, Bernie Kukoff. **Announcer:** Charlie O'Donnell. **Orchestra:** George Wyle.

4705   *The Jimmy Durante Show.* (Series; Variety; CBS; 1957). A summer program of music and comedy with comedian Jimmy Durante that also features kinescoped highlights of Jimmy's prior series, *Texaco Star Theater*.

Host: Jimmy Durante. **Regulars:** Eddie Jackson, Jack Roth, Jules Buffano. **Orchestra:** Roy Bargy.

4706   *The Jimmy Durante Show.* (Pilot; Comedy; CBS; July 18, 1964). Jimmy Banister is a famous entertainer who would like his son, Eddie, to follow in his footsteps. Eddie has no interest in show business and Jimmy's efforts to convince his son otherwise were the focal point of the unsold series. Rose is Jimmy's sister.

Cast: Jimmy Durante (*Jimmy Banister*); Eddie Hodges (*Eddie Banister*); Audrey Christie (*Rose Banister*).

4707   *Jimmy Hughes, Rookie Cop.* (Series; Crime Drama; DuMont; 1953). When he returns to his home in New York City after serving in Korea, Jimmy Hughes learns that his father, a policeman, has been killed in the line of duty. After Jimmy learns that the case is still unsolved, he joins the force in an attempt to find his father's killers. Later, after accomplishing his goal, he learns to serve for reasons other than revenge and that teamwork and concern for others is more important than individual action and motivation. He is also presented with is father's badge and stories concern the life and problems faced by Jimmy Hughes, a rookie cop with the N.Y.P.D.

Cast: Billy Redfield, Conrad Janis (*Billy Hughes*); Rusty Lane (*Inspector Ferguson*); Wendy Drew (*Jimmy's sister*).

4708   *Jimmy Kimmel Live.* (Series; Talk; ABC; 2002–). A late night talk show (12:05 A.M. to 1:05 A.M.) that goes beyond the celebrity interview formula to include one-on-one interviews with athletes, political figures and regular people of interest. The program also features comedy skits and the humorous monologues from host Jimmy Kimmel.

Host: Jimmy Kimmel. **Regulars:** Sal Iacono *(as Cousin Sal)*; Frank Potenzo *(as Uncle Frank)*; Guillermo Diaz *(Security guard)*. **Music:** The Jimmy Kimmel Band. **Announcer:** Dicky Barrett.

4709 *The Jimmy Stewart Show.* (Series; Comedy; NBC; 1971-1972). James K. Howard is an anthropology professor at Josiah Kessel College in Easy Valley, California. He is married to Martha and they are the parents of P.J. and Teddy (they live at 35 Hillview Drive). P.J. is married to Wendy and he and Wendy are the parents of Jake. Stories follow the simple pleasures and trying time of James as he attempts to cope with life at work and at home. Luther Quince is James's friend, the chemistry professor.

Cast: Jimmy Stewart *(James K. Howard)*; Julie Adams *(Martha Howard)*; Jonathan Daly *(P.J. Howard)*; Ellen Geer *(Wendy Howard)*; Dennis Larson *(Teddy Howard)*; Kirby Furlong *(Jake Howard)*; John McGiver *(Luther Quince)*; Will Geer *(Uncle Everett)*; Mary Wickes *(Jo Ballard)*; Jack Soo *(Woody Yamada)*; Roy Applegate *(Garvey Hike)*.

4710 *Jimmy Two-Shoes.* (Series; Cartoon; Disney XD; 2009). Miseryville is, like its name implies, a miserable town occupied by demons and monsters that is ruled by Lucius Heinous VII, a tyrant who enjoys misery. Upsetting Lucius's cherished lifestyle is Jimmy Two-Shoes, an optimistic, happy-go-lucky 14-year-old boy who sees only the goodness in others. Stories follow Jimmy as he sets out to change Miseryvillle by making it fun and exciting. Beezy is Lucius's idiotic son — and Jimmy's best friend (he would rather help Jimmy than obey his father); Heloise is Lucius's brilliant daughter who enjoys spreading chaos on her father's behalf.

Voice Cast: Cory Doran *(Jimmy)*; Brian Froud *(Beezy)*; Tabitha St. Germain *(Heloise)*; Sean Cullen *(Lucius)*.

4711 *Jingles.* (Pilot; Reality; Unaired; Produced for CBS in 2007). Commercials are the backbone of the television industry and some people believe they could have come up with a better ad campaign for the products they see. Such people are the participants and are challenged to pick a product and devise a campaign for it. The proposal was to chart their progress with a panel of judges determining the winner.

Host: Kimberly Caldwell. **Judges:** Gene Simmons, Julie Roehm, Linda Kaplan Thaler.

4712 *J.J. Starbuck.* (Series; Crime Drama; NBC; 1987-1988). J.J. Starbuck is an eccentric Texas billionaire who meddles in other people's business in the name of justice. J.J. (Jerome Jeremiah) lives on the Starbuck Ranch in San Antonio. He owns a Beverly Hills company called Marklee Industries and drives a 1964 Lincoln Continental with the license plate TX BRONCO. His niece, Jill, often assists him in his case investigations as does con-artist E.L. "Tenspeed" Turner (from the series *Tenspeed and Brown Show*). Ronnie Milsap performs the theme, "Gone Again."

Cast: Dale Robertson *(J.J. Starbuck)*; Shawn Weatherly *(Jill Starbuck)*; Ben Vereen *(E.L. "Tenspeed" Turner)*.

4713 *Jo Jo's Circus.* (Series; Cartoon; Disney; 2003). An entertaining program for the small fry that revolves around Jo Jo, an adorable clown who lives in a clown town and presents games and learning lessons to children.

Voice Cast: Madeleine Martin *(Jo Jo)*; Robert Smith *(Goliath)*; Marnie McPhail *(Peaches)*; Tajja Isen *(Trina)*; Jayne Eastwood *(Ms. Kersplatski)*; Diana Peressini *(Croaky)*; Austin DiIulio *(Skeebo)*; Noah Weisberg *(Mr. Tickle)*; Kathryn Greenwood *(Dr. Seltzer)*.

4714 *The Jo Stafford Show.* (Series; Variety; CBS; 1954-1955). Singer Jo Stafford hosts a program of music and songs.

Host: Jo Stafford. **Vocalists:** The Starlighters. **Music:** Paul Weston.

4715 *The Joan Edwards Show.* (Series; Variety; DuMont; 1950). A twice-weekly program of music and songs with singer-pianist Joan Edwards as the host.

4716 *Joan of Arcadia.* (Series; Drama; CBS; 2003–2005). Joan Girardi, a very pretty 16-year-old girl, lives in the town of Arcadia, Maryland. She was born on November 24, 1987, and is the daughter of Will and Helen Girardi. She has two siblings, Kevin and Luke, and attends Arcadia High School. Joan is also a very special girl. She has been chosen by God to perform small miracles for him.

God appears to Joan in various disguises (from janitor to old man to school girl) and tells Joan what to do. Joan is never quite sure why God asks her to do what he asks, but she does it (sometimes reluctantly) and it is only by following through does Joan not only help others, but helps herself better understand life. Stories follow Joan as she performs small miracles for God.

Will is the town's police chief; Helen teaches art at Arcadia High School; Luke is the smartest of the children; Kevin is crippled due to an automobile accident. Although he is bound to a wheelchair, he is hopeful that he will one day walk again. Adam Rove and Grace Polk are Joan's closest friends.

Cast: Amber Tamblyn *(Joan Girardi)*; Joe Mantegna *(Will Girardi)*; Mary Steenburgen *(Helen Girardi)*; Jason Ritter *(Kevin Girardi)*; Michael Welsh *(Luke Girardi)*; Becky Wahlstrom *(Grace Polk)*; Chris Marquette *(Adam Rove)*; Mageina Tovah *(Glynis Figliola)*; April Grace *(Sgt. Toni Williams)*; Annie Potts *(Lt. Lucy Preston)*; Constance Zimmer *(Sister Lilly Watters)*; Sprague Grayden *(Judith Montgomery)*; Morocco Omari *(Principal Stephen Chadwick)*; John Getz *(D.A. Gabe Fellowes)*.

4717 *Joan of Arkansas.* (Pilot; Comedy; Unaired; Produced in 1958). When the U.S. space program requires an ordinary person to become the first human in space, the Saraback Computer chooses Joan Jones, a dental technician from Hot Springs, Arkansas. The proposal was to follow Joan's mishaps as she trains to become an astronaut. Dr. John Dolan is head of the space program; Professor Henry Newkirk assists him.

Cast: Joan Davis *(Joan Jones)*; John Emery *(Dr. John Dolan)*; Wilton Graff *(Henry Newkirk)*.

4718 *The Joan Rivers Show.* (Series; Talk; Syn.; 1989). A daytime program that goes slightly beyond the norm (celebrity interviews) to present interviews with interesting, ordinary people as well as people who are a bit out of the ordinary.

Host: Joan Rivers.

4719 *Joanie Loves Chachi.* (Series; Comedy; ABC; 1982-1983). A spin off from *Happy Days*. In the pilot episode ("Love and Marriage," broadcast on *Happy Days* on Mar. 23, 1982), Al Delvecchio (co-owner of the local hamburger hangout, Arnold's Drive-In), proposes to Louisa Arcola, Chachi's widowed mother. Louisa accepts his proposal and Al, Louisa and Chachi move from Milwaukee to Chicago, where Al begins a new business, Delvecchio's Family Restaurant. Shortly after, Al meets Louisa's Uncle Rocco, a con artist who talks him into hiring his motley music group for his restaurant. When Chachi joins the group as a singer, he asks the girl he left behind, Joanie Cunningham, to come to Chicago and join him in the act. Joanie agrees (after getting permission from her parents, Howard and Marion). Soon Joanie and Chachi are a success as a singing duo.

Stories depict their struggle as they decide to become professionals and make a name for themselves in the music business. Other regulars are Mario, Bing and Annette, other band members; and Suky, Joanie's roommate.

Cast: Erin Moran *(Joanie Cunningham)*; Scott Baio *(Chachi Arcola)*; Ellen Travolta *(Louisa Delvecchio)*; Al Molinaro *(Al Delvecchio)*; Art Metrano *(Uncle Ricco)*; Derrel Maury *(Mario)*; Robert Peirce *(Bingo)*; Winifred Freedman *(Annette)*; Chris McDermott *(Suky)*. **Theme Vocal:** "You Look at Me" by Erin Moran, Scott Baio.

4720 *Joanna.* (Pilot; Comedy; ABC; April 30, 1985). When Joanna Weston, a Los Angeles girl, moves to Brooklyn, New York, to be with her boyfriend, Charles, she learns that he has run off with another woman. With no other choice but to begin a new life, Joanna applies for and acquires the position of executive director of the Rosebud Trucking Company. Her misadventures as she attempts to run the company are the focal point of the unsold series. Other regulars are Michael, Joanna's neighbor; Elvis, the dispatcher; Rosenthal, the company manager; Napoleon Flipper, "the resident loon"; the truckers: Little Joe, Paulie, Sigourney, Petey and Dean; and Mrs. Benson, Joanna's landlady.

Cast: Cindy Williams *(Joanna Weston)*; Reni Santoni *(Michael Braxton)*; Ron Karabatsos *(Elvis Valentine)*; Lou Jacobi *(Rosenthal)*; Florence Halop *(Mrs. Benson)*; Larry Hankin *(Little Joe)*; John DelRegno *(Paulie)*; Julie Payne *(Sigourney Schultz)*; Danny Mora *(Petey Flowers)*; Larry Joshua *(Dean)*; W.H. Macy *(Napoleon Flipper)*.

4721 *Joanne Carson's V.I.P.'s.* (Series; Interview; Syn.; 1972). Celebrity interviews with Joanne Carson (the wife of TV talk show host Johnny Carson). Hugh Douger is the announcer.

4722 *The Job.* (Series; Comedy; ABC; 2001–2002). Mike McNeil is a detective with the 21st Precinct of the N.Y.P.D. in Manhattan. He is Irish and "The only thing I like is being a cop." He breaks the rules, or, as he says, "bends them," to solve a case. Mike lives in the suburbs and works in the city. He smokes, drinks, and is totally unfaithful to his wife, Karen.

Mike is a womanizer and is secretly dating a woman named Toni. While Toni knows about Karen, Karen is unaware of Toni. Karen eventually discovered Mike's mistress, but the series ended without any resolutions. Mike takes pain killers even though he has no pain. He is not very friendly, sometimes looks the other way instead of arresting a suspect and believes he is unlucky, not only at gambling but with women. Mike works with Frank Harrigan, Jan Hendrix and Terrence Phillips.

Terrence is nicknamed Pip and is mystified as to why he has that nickname. Jan is the only regular female cop in the squad room. She was born in the Bronx and attended Cardinal Spellman High School where she was called Duck — "because I had a voice like a duck." Jan is single and looking for Mr. Right but feels the pressures of her job will never make that happen. Frank is the overweight cop who appears to be the only person in the precinct who can stand being Mike's patrol car partner. He enjoys eating — at home, in the squad room, in the car, on the street — wherever and whenever a free moment allows him to indulge in his favorite activity. Before becoming a cop, Frank felt he had a calling to become a priest — "But the celibacy thing got me. I couldn't imagine giving up sex." Stories follow Mike's day-to-day activities.

Cast: Denis Leary *(Mike McNeil)*; Wendy McKenna *(Karen McNeil)*; Karyn Parsons *(Toni)*; Lenny Clarke *(Frank Harrigan)*; Bill Nunn *(Terrence Phillips)*; Diane Farr *(Jan Hendrix)*.

4723 *Joe and Mabel.* (Series; Comedy; CBS; 1955–1956). A blind date brought Mabel Spooner and Joe Sparton together. Mabel

is beautiful, stubborn, a bit wacky and ready for marriage. Joe is hard working, level headed and not ready to tie the knot; he is a long range planner and looks ahead. Joe feels Mabel is the prettiest girl in his crowd — "She loves me no matter how stupid I am; she laughs at all my old jokes and knows how to fix my eggs. I say every guy ought to have a girl like Mabel, even if she sometimes inspires you to do crazy things." Mabel is dead set on convincing Joe that she is the perfect wife for him. She does her best to impress him (although her plans most often backfire) and has already planned on a house and three kids (Joe Jr., Adele and Stanley).

Mabel lives with her mother, Adele Spooner, and her brother, Sherman Spooner, at 2314 Bushwick Avenue (Apartment 3H) in Brooklyn, New York. Mabel works as a manicurist at the Westside Beauty Shop in Manhattan.

Joe lives at 764 Chauncey Street in Brooklyn and is an independent cab driver. Each episode begins with Joe driving his cab and relating an incident about himself and Mabel. A flashback is used to relate the tale. Joe returns right before the closing theme to give a final remark and tell the audience about next week's episode. Joe's hangout is Mac's Coffee Shop ("the Waldorf Astoria of the coffee shops"). While "Mac's Coffee Shop" is seen on the front door, it is called Harry's Coffee Shop in dialogue. Mike is Joe's friend, a cabbie also.

Cast: Nita Talbot *(Mabel Spooner)*; Larry Blyden *(Joe Sparton)*; Luella Gear *(Adele Spooner)*; Michael Mann *(Sherman Spooner)*; Norman Fell *(Mike)*.

4724 *Joe and Sons.* (Series; Comedy; CBS; 1975–1976). Joe Vitale is a widowed sheet metal worker living in Hoboken, New Jersey. He is the father of two teenage sons, Mark and Nick, and stories relate his efforts as he struggles to raise Mark and Nick on the straight and narrow. Other regulars are Estelle, Joe's neighbor; Josephine Molonaire, Joe's married sister; Mo, Josephine's husband; Gus Duzik, Joe's friend; and Charlie, Joe's uncle. In the pilot episode (Mar. 5, 1975), Joe resides in Pennsylvania. Mitch Brown played Nick Vitale; Maureen Arthur played Estelle as Joe's sister (not neighbor).

Cast: Richard S. Castellano *(Joe Vitale)*; Barry Miller *(Mark Vitalie)*; Jimmy Baio *(Nick Vitalie)*; Bobbi Jordan *(Estelle)*; Florence Stanley *(Josephine Molonaire)*; Jerry Stiller *(Gus Duzik)*; Harold J. Stone *(Charlie)*.

4725 *J.O.E. and the Colonel.* (Pilot; Adventure; ABC; Sept. 11, 1985). Seeking to develop the perfect soldier, U.S. government scientists develop J.O.E., a product of DNA experiments they hope will become the ultimate terminator. However, when J.O.E., a Project Omega creation, is ordered to kill, he shows a fatal flaw when he disobeys the command. J.O.E. is considered a failure and ordered destroyed. Before action can be taken, Michael Roarke, one of J.O.E.'s creators, flees with J.O.E. and begins programming him as a human being. Shortly after, they move to an obscure town (Touchstone) and begin a business called Special Services, Incorporated (through which they tackle very hazardous jobs for a price). During one mission, Michael is killed and Colonel H.C. Fleming, the government agent assigned to destroy J.O.E. resigns. Fleming had given his own cells to help create J.O.E. and teams with J.O.E., who now calls himself Joe Smith, to continue where Michael left off. The unsold series was to relate Joe and Fleming's adventures as they tackle dangerous assignments and attempt to avoid the government agents who are still seeking to destroy J.O.E. (whom they feel contains vital information that may fall into the wrong hands).

Cast: Gary Kasper *(Joe Smith)*; William Lucking *(H.C. Fleming)*; Aimee Eccles *(Miss Kai; their secretary)*.

4726 *Joe and Valerie.* (Series; Comedy; NBC; 1978–1979). Joe Pizo is a young man who works as a plumber and lives with his widowed father, Vincent. Valerie Sweetzer is a young woman who works as a cosmetics sales girl and lives with her widowed mother, Stella. Joe and Valerie are dating and contemplating marriage but both feel that are not ready to take that big step. Stories for the first four episodes (April 14 to May 10, 1978) relate events in their lives as they plan their futures; the remaining three episodes (Jan. 5 to Jan. 19, 1979) relate the proposal, marriage and Joe and Valerie's efforts to begin a married life together. In these episodes, Valerie now works as a clothing sales girl. Frank and Paulie are Joe's friends; Thelma (later called Rita) is Valerie's friend.

Cast: Paul Regina *(Joe Pizo)*; Char Fontane *(Valerie Sweetzer)*; Robert Costanzo *(Vincent Pizo)*; Pat Benson *(Stella Sweetzer; 1978)*; Arlene Golonka *(Stella Sweetzer, 1979)*; Donna Ponterotto *(Thelma Medina/Rita Medina)*; Bill Beyers *(Frank Berganski)*; David Elliott *(Paulie Barone)*.

4727   Joe Bash. (Series; Comedy; ABC; 1986). Joe Bash and Willie Smith, police officers with the 33rd Precinct in New York City, patrol a ghetto section of the city at night. Joe, a veteran, is nearing retirement; Willie is young and eager to learn from Joe. Stories focus in particular on Joe as he attempts to put in his remaining time quietly and collect his pension — something his young partner can't understand.

Cast: Peter Boyle *(Officer Joe Bash)*; Andrew Rubin *(Officer Willie Smith)*; Val Bisoglio *(Sergeant Carmine DiSalvo)*; Michael Cavanaugh *(Lieutenant Pendleton)*.

4728   Joe Dancer. (Pilot; Crime Drama; NBC; 1981–1983). "I handle the garbage — and get paid for it," says Joe Dancer, a tough Los Angeles–based private detective who takes the cases of people who are unable to turn to the police for help. He is assisted by his secretary, Charlie. Three TV movie pilots aired:

1. The Big Black Pill (Jan. 29, 1981). Joe attempts to solve a murder that was cleverly set up to frame him.

2. The Monkey Mission (Mar. 23, 1981. Joe uses a trained monkey to help him steal a priceless European vase from a tightly guarded museum.

3. Joe Dancer: Murder One, Dancer 0 (June 5, 1983). Joe attempts to clear himself of a false murder charge: that of running down a 17-year-old boy with his car.

Cast: Robert Blake *(Joe Dancer)*; Sondra Blake *(Charlie)*.

4729   The Joe DiMaggio Show. (Series; Children; NBC; 1950). Baseball star Joe DiMaggio chats with youngsters, answers their questions and interviews guest stars.

Host: Joe DiMaggio. **Assistant:** Jack Barry. **Announcer:** Ted Brown.

4730   Joe Forrester. (Series; Crime Drama; NBC; 1975-1976). Joe Forrester is a veteran police office who, after years of faithful service, is offered a desk job. Joe, who loves to walk a beat, feels he can accomplish more on the street than sitting in an office. He rejects the offer and stories follow Joe as he continues to walk his old beat as a uniformed cop. Sergeant Bernie Vincent is his superior; Georgia Cameron is Joe's romantic interest; Jolene Jackson is Joe's informant.

Cast: Lloyd Bridges *(Off. Joe Forrester)*; Eddie Egan *(Sgt. Bernie Vincent)*; Patricia Crowley *(Georgia Cameron)*; Dwan Smith *(Jolene Jackson)*; Michael Warren *(Detective Marshall)*; Lynn Redding *(Sergeant Storm)*; Andra Akers *(Assistant D.A. Johnson)*; Dale Tarter *(Polygraph Operator)*; Taylor Lacher *(Det. Will Carson)*.

4731   Joe Millionaire. (Series; Reality; Fox; 2003). Twenty single women are flown to France to meet Joe Millionaire, a man each of the women believe is worth over $50 million. In reality (and unknown to the women), Joe is a construction worker with an annual income of $19,000. The women each hope to win Joe's affection and become the one he chooses to possibly become his wife. Joe romances each of the women (using the show's bank account and hoping not to expose the fact that he is a fraud). At the end of a month, he must choose the one he feels is right for him (the one who will not be spoiled by riches). Also, at that time, he must reveal his true identity and true financial status.

Cast: Alex McLeod *(Hostess, Cycle 1)*; Samantha Harris *(Hostess, Cycle 2)*; Evan Marriott *(Joe Millionaire, Cycle 1)*; David Smith *(Joe Millionaire, Cycle 2)*; Paul Hogan *(Joe's Butler, Cycles 1 and 2)*; Mark Thompson *(Narrator)*.

4732   The Joe Namath Show. (Series; Interview; Syn.; 1969). A program of interviews with sports figures and show business personalities with former football star Joe Namath.

Host: Joe Namath. **Co-Host:** Dick Schaap. **Announcer-Assistant:** Louisa Moritz.

4733   The Joe Palooka Story. (Series; Comedy-Drama; Syn.; 1954). The fictitious story of heavyweight boxer Joe Palooka, a clean living, moral champ who is ignorant of gambling, fixed fights, blonde sirens and nightclubs. Ann Howe is Joe's romantic interest; Knobby Walsh is Joe's manager; Humphrey Pennyworth is Joe's trainer. Based on characters created by Ham Fisher.

Cast: Joe Kirkwood, Jr. *(Joe Palooka)*; Cathy Downs *(Ann Howe)*; Luis Van Rooten *(Knobby Walsh)*; Maxie Rosenbloom *(Humphrey Pennyworth)*.

4734   The Joe Piscopo Show. (Pilot; Variety; Unaired; Produced in 1988.). The many characters comedian Joe Piscopo created on *Saturday Night Live* were to be featured on a weekly basis.

Host: Joe Piscopo.

4735   The Joe Pyne Show. (Series; Discussion; Syn.; 1966). Joe Pyne hosts a weekly discussion program on topical issues with appropriate guests.

4736   Joe's Life. (Series; Comedy; ABC; 1993). Joe Gennaro is a house husband living in Manhattan. When the Cold War ended, his job at an aircraft manufacturing plant was terminated. His wife, Sandy, has found employment at Temp Jobs and Joe, able to work nights as a chef at Gennaro's Restaurant (owned by his brother Stan), cares for their children, Amy, Paulie and Scotty. Stories relate events in the family's lives. Joe, a N.Y. Giants football fan, hates to shop (on his twelfth birthday, he was given ten dollars by an uncle. He went to Macy's passed up footballs, basketballs and baseballs and bought a Susie Q Easy Bake Oven).

Amy, 14, hangs out at the Pizza Place after school. Her dream car is a white K-80 convertible. Twelve-year-old Paulie is interested in astronomy. When he was five, Amy dared him to eat the Yellow Pages. He was up to "air conditioning" when his parents walked in and stopped him. Scotty, five years old, has three plush animals: Petey (the talking dinosaur), Quacky Duck and Puff Puff.

Cast: Peter Onorati *(Joe Gennaro)*; Mary Page Keller *(Sandy)*; Morgan Nagler *(Amy Gennaro)*; Robert Gorman *(Paulie Gennaro)*; Spencer Klein *(Scotty Gennaro)*.

4737   Joe's World. (Series; Comedy; NBC; 1980). Joe Wabash is a union painter living in Detroit, Michigan. He is married to Katie and they are the parents of Maggie, Steve, Jimmy, Linda and Rick. Joe enjoys a relaxing drink at the Hangout Bar and stories follow Joe as he attempts to cope with life at home and at work (where he does not have the most intelligent crew in the world. They are Rick, Judy and Bard). Tessie is the owner of the bar.

Cast: Ramon Bieri (*Joe Wabash*); K Callan (*Katie Wabash*); Melissa Sherman (*Maggie Wabash*); Christopher Knight (*Steve Wabash*); Michael Sharrett (*Jimmy Wabash*); Missy Francis (*Linda Wabash*); Ari Zeltzer (*Rick Wabash*); Misty Rowe (*Judy Wilson*); Russ Banham (*Brad Hopkins*); Frank Coppola (*Andy*); Joan Shawlee (*Tessie*).

4738   *Joey*. (Series; Comedy; NBC; 2004–2006). A spin off from *Friends* that transplants Joey Tribbiani from New York City to Los Angeles to further his acting career (he gave up his role on *Days of Our Lives* to make the move). His sister, Gina, gets him an apartment and his 20-year-old nephew, Michael (Gina's son) moves in with him (when Joey suggests Michael spread his wings and move out of his mother's apartment). Joey then acquires an agent (Bobbie Morganstern), a new neighbor, Alexis "Alex" Garrett (a divorced lawyer who has eyes for Joey, but Joey is too blind to see it), an assistant, Zach, and very few jobs until he landed the lead on a prime time series called *Deep Powder*. The series is suddenly pushed aside when Joey acquires a role in a major motion picture called *Captured*.

Gina was originally a hairdresser, then the neurotic Bobbie's assistant. She loves to wear low cut blouses and show cleavage. She is outspoken and not afraid to say what is one her mind. Michael is quite intelligent and is attending college. He idolizes Joey and hopes to do just as well in the girl department. Stories follow events in Joey's life at home and at work — more often than not getting himself in all kinds of mishaps as he struggles to make his mark in Hollywood.

Cast: Matt LeBlanc (*Joey Tribbiani*); Drea de Matteo (*Gina Tribbiani*); Andrea Anders (*Alex Garrett*); Paulo Costanzo (*Michael Tribbiani*); Jennifer Coolidge (*Bobbie Morganstern*); Miguel A. Nunez, Jr. (*Zach*).

4739   *Joey and Dad*. (Series; Variety; CBS; 1975). Singer-actress Joey Heatherton and her father, Ray Heatherton team for a lively hour of music, songs and light comedy.

Hosts: Joey Heatherton, Ray Heatherton. **Regulars:** Bob Einstein, Dorothy Meyers, Nick Nicholas, Pat Paulsen, Pat Proft, Gene Taylor, Henny Youngman. **Announcers:** Peter Cullen, David Black. **Orchestra:** Lex DeAvezedo.

4740   *The Joey Bishop Show*. (Series; Comedy; NBC; 1961-1962). Joey Barnes is a public relations man for the Los Angeles firm of Wellington, Willoughby, Cleary and Jones (originally called the J.P. Willoughby Company). He is a bit trouble prone and tries to do everything right, but everything usually goes wrong. He lives with his widowed mother, his sister, Stella and his younger brother, Larry. He also finds himself supporting his married sister, Betty Grafton, and her adverse-to-work husband, Frank. Stella is studying to become an actress; Larry is attending medical school and Frank impresses people by telling them he doesn't need a job (Joey says he should impress people by telling people he needs a job). Barbara Simpson is Joey's girlfriend and secretary; J.P. Willoughby is Joey's boss; Peggy is J.P.'s secretary. The original pilot version of the series aired on *The Danny Thomas Show* (CBS, Mar. 27, 1961) as "Everything Happens to Me." In it, Joey Bishop played Joey Mason, a Hollywood press agent. Billy Gilbert and Madge Blake played his parents, "Pop" and "Mom" Mason; Marlo Thomas was his sister, Stella Mason; Joe Flynn was his boss, J.P. Willoughby.

Cast: Joey Bishop (*Joey Barnes*); Marlo Thomas (*Stella Barnes*); Warren Berlinger (*Larry Barnes*); Joe Flynn (*Frank Grafton*); Virginia Vincent (*Betty Grafton*); Madge Blake (*Mrs. Barnes*); John Briggs (*J.P. Willoughby*); Jackie Russell (*Peggy*); Nancy Hadley (*Barbara Simpson*).

4741   *The Joey Bishop Show*. (Series; Comedy; NBC, 1962–1964; CBS, 1964-1965). A revised version of the 1961 black and white NBC series *The Joey Bishop Show* that is now in color (but reverts to black and white when it switches to CBS). Joey Barnes is now a former nightclub comedian who gave up the circuit in 1960 to host *The Joey Barnes Show*, an evening talk-variety series broadcast from Studio 5-H at 30 Rockefeller Plaza. He is married to Ellie and, a year later, becomes the father of a young son, Joey Barnes, Jr. (born at Mid-Town Hospital). They live in the Carlton Arms Apartments (Apt. 711) in New York City. (Last season episodes are set in Los Angeles.)

Larry Corbett is Joey's writer (Joey often files his stale jokes by crumbling them and tossing them into the waste basket). Joey first met Larry in 1953 when he was a struggling young writer. (Prior to his role as Larry, Corbett Monica played Johnny Edwards, a comedian at the Purple Pussycat Club, who substituted for Joey when he went on vacation.) Freddie is Joey's agent; they have known each other since childhood. Jillson is the building's overweight superintendent. Hilda is Joey's maid who also doubles as the baby's nurse. Joey and Hilda rarely get along and are always insulting each other; Jillson is henpecked and fears his wife (who is only heard) Tantalia. Ellie, born in Texas, is called "Texas" by Joey. Stories focus on Joey's home and working life, with a behind-the-scenes look at the preparations that go into putting on a variety show.

Program Open: [Chorus:] "Joey, Joey, Joey." [Joey:] "Son of a gun." [Announcer:] *The Joey Bishop Show* ... Starring Joey Bishop ... with Abby Dalton as his wife ... Corbett Monica, Joe Besser and Mary Treen."

Cast: Joey Bishop (*Joey Barnes*); Abby Dalton (*Ellie Barnes*); Corbett Monica (*Larry Corbett*); Guy Marks (*Freddie*); Joe Besser (*Jillson*); Mary Treen (*Hilda*); Matthew David Smith (*Joey Barnes, Jr.*); Joey Forman (*Sam Nolan*); Maxine Semon (*Tantalia*). **Announcer:** Eddie King.

4742   *The Joey Bishop Show*. (Series; Variety; ABC; 1967–1969). Comedian Joey Bishop oversees a late night program of light comedy and celebrity interviews.

Program Open: "From Hollywood, *The Joey Bishop Show*. Joey's guests tonight are Rod McKuen, Zsa Zsa Gabor and Paul Winchell. But first these messages."

Host: Joey Bishop. **Announcer:** Regis Philbin. **Orchestra:** Johnny Mann.

4743   *Joey Faye's Frolics*. (Series; Comedy; CBS; 1950). A two-week experimental series (April 5 to April 12, 1950) that spotlights the talents of comedian Joey Faye.

Host: Joey Faye. **Regulars:** Audrey Christie, Mandy Kaye, Danny Dayton, Joe Silver.

4744   *The John Byner Comedy Hour*. (Series; Variety; CBS; 1972). Music, songs and comedy skits hosted by comedian John Byner.

Program Open: "*The John Byner Comedy Hour* with tonight's guests Frankie Avalon and Annette Funicello. Ladies and gentlemen, John Byner."

Host: John Byner. **Regulars:** Patti Deutsch, R.G. Brown, Linda Sublette, Gary Miller, Dennis Flannigan, The Lori Regas Dancers. **Announcer:** Bill Thompson. **Orchestra:** Ray Charles.

4745   *John Conte's Little Show*. (Series; Variety; NBC; ABC; 1950–1953). Actor John Conte hosts a program of music and songs that, under the sponsorship of Stokey-Van Camp Foods, is also known as *Van Camp's Little Show* It aired on NBC (June 27, 1950 to Nov. 22, 1951) and ABC (April 3 to June 19, 1953).

Host: John Conte. **Regulars:** Marguerite Hamilton, The Three Beaus and a Peep, The Jesse Bradley Trio. **Music:** The Tony Mottola Trio.

4746   *The John Davidson Show.* (Series; Variety; ABC; NBC; Syn.; 1969; 1976; 1980). Music, songs and comedy with singer John Davidson as the host. See also *The Kraft Summer Music Hall.*

1969 Program Open: "Good evening ladies and gentlemen and welcome to the show. I'm John Davidson. Hope you enjoy the evening because you are going to be hearing a whole lot from Mirielle Mathieu, Rich Little, Amy McDonald. Our special guest, Paul Anka." Three versions appeared:

1. The John Davidson Show (ABC, 1969). **Host:** John Davidson. **Regulars:** Rich Little, Mirielle Mathieu, Amy McDonald. **Orchestra:** Jack Parnell.

2. The John Davidson Show (NBC, 1976). **Host:** John Davidson. **Announcer:** Pete Barbutti. **Orchestra:** Lenny Stack.

3. The John Davidson Show (Syn., 1980–82). **Host:** John Davidson. **Announcer:** Jerry Bishop. **Music:** John Toben.

4747   *John Doe.* (Series; Drama; Fox; 2002). Who am I? And where did I come from?" says John Doe, a man of mystery who knows everything about everything — except who he is. Life for John Doe, as he knows it, began when he awoke on the deserted Horseshoe Island. With no apparent means of escape, he dove into the ocean possibly hoping to swim to a mainland. This failed and he attached himself to some floating driftwood and let the tides guide him. He was found by Asian fishermen and rescued. He was put ashore in Seattle, taken to a hospital and given the name John Doe.

The first episode reveals two clues to John's possible identity. The first is a symbol on his right shoulder — " a circle in a K," as John calls it. The symbol of ancient Egyptian hieroglyph from 29 BC shows slight similarities. It is also the symbol of a defunct Asian publishing house's logo — is it a birthmark or a branding? The second clue comes at the end of the episode when it shows John standing on a pier. A ferry is passing and a woman is seen looking toward the pier. She apparently recognizes John Doe and calls out the name Tommy. John turns and looks, but doesn't recognize the woman. He attempts to find her but is unable when the ferry docks. Is Tommy his name? Does someone finally recognize him? John's search for the mysterious woman is a continuing aspect of the series.

John is not only unaware of who he is, but he is color blind. He sees everything in black and white as does the viewer when a scene is shown through his eyes. However, when something he sees is related to his life (a clue) he can see in color as what happened with the girl on the ferry. And "did I mention I know everything from the contents of a box of Applejacks to the mating habits of the zebra to everything in between?" However, John is not a psychic; "I can't predict things" and "for a guy who has all the answers, I don't have the one that means the most."

To help him find out who he is, John begins his life by acquiring money. He has an amazing ability to calculate odds and wins a great deal at a race track; he later acquires money by investing in the stock market. John next finds an apartment and to make the best use of his abilities, establishes himself as a consultant to help the police solve crimes or, as he says, "I'm a privately funded think tank." He next hangs posters on telephone poles reading "Have You Seen Me? I'm Missing." He has also contacted 150 police precincts across the country reporting himself missing. He hires a homeless teenage girl named Karen Kalwalski as his secretary and office organizer. John lives above a bar, The Sea, and plays piano in its lounge. A character named Digger is the apparent bar owner. About his name he says, "Don't even ask."

Frank Hayes is the Seattle police detective John helps; Lt. Jamie Avery is Frank's superior (she is skeptical of John and reluctant to work with him — but John has the unique ability to find clues even the best forensic scientists overlook and Frank sees this as beneficial to the department). Frank is married and the father of two children. Karen is currently studying art, but she is a foster child and has been in trouble with the law. She also works two days a week as a tour guide at the Art Museum.

Before the series ended without revealing who or what John Doe is, he found one other clue to his identity — the plastic figure of a Phoenix. He saw this in red and a Phoenix is the ancient Greek symbol of rebirth.

Cast: Dominic Purcell *(John Doe)*; Sprague Grayden *(Karen Kalwalski)*; William Forsythe *(Digger)*; John Marshall Jones *(Det. Frank Hayes)*; Jayne Brook *(Lt. Jamie Avery)*.

4748   *John Edwards Cross Country.* (Series; Reality; WE; 2006). Psychic John Edwards takes to the road to help families reconnect with loved ones who have passed on.

4749   *The John Forsythe Show.* (Series; Comedy; NBC; 1965-1966). The original format tells the story of John Foster, a former U.S. Air Force major who inherits the Foster School for Girls in California from his late aunt (his misadventures as he assumes the position of headmaster and attempts to run the school is the focal point of stories). After several months the format changed to depict John's adventures as a world-traveling secret agent when the government recalls him to active duty. Sergeant Edward Robbins is John's assistant; Margaret Culver is the school's principal; Miss Wilson is the physical education teacher; Jeannie Hayes is a teacher; and the featured students are Joanna, Marcia, Kathy, Pamela, Janice, Susan, Norma Jean and Connie.

Cast: John Forsythe *(John Foster)*; Guy Marks *(Edward Robbins)*; Elsa Lanchester *(Margaret Culver)*; Ann B. Davis *(Miss Wilson)*; Peggy Lipton *(Joanna)*; Page Forsythe *(Marcia)*; Darleen Carr *(Kathy)*; Pamelyn Ferdin *(Pamela)*; Sara Ballantine *(Janice)*; Tracy Strafford *(Susan)*; Brooke Forsythe *(Norma Jean)*; Celia Kaye *(Connie Stewart)*; Lisa Gaye *(Jeannie Hayes)*.

4750   *John from Cincinnati.* (Series; Drama; HBO; 2007). Imperial Beach, California, is called "The last surf break before Tijuana, where the U.S. meets Mexico and water meets land." It is here, on Imperial Beach, that a family of surfing legends, the Yosts, live: Mitch, his estranged wife, Cissy, their son, Butchie, and Shaun, Butchie's 13-year-old son. Mitch, somewhat of a derelict, is bitter, having to give up surfing when he blew out his knee; Butchie, a legend like his father, ruined his career when he turned to drugs; and Shaun, a surfer, is being groomed by Cissy to become the next great surfer. It is also Cissy who keeps the family together as the owner of the local surf shop. Life changes for the Yosts when John, a mysterious man comes into their lives. Is John magical? Is he a profit? Is he a demon? Whatever (it is not made clear) his presence begins to change the destinies of those with whom he comes in contact. Stories follow the events that affect the Yosts and the situations that result from John's presence. Bill is an eccentric ex-cop who lives in a houseful of birds; Ramon owns the rundown hotel in which Butchie lives; Meyer Dickstein is a local lawyer; Barry Cunningham is a businessman; Linc is the surfer agent seeking to represent Shaun.

Cast: Rebecca De Morney *(Cissy Yost)*; Bruce Greenwood *(Mitch Yost)*; Brian Van Holt *(Butchie Yost)*; Greyson Fletcher *(Shaun Yost)*; Austin Nichols *(John)*; Ed O'Neill *(Bill)*; Willie Garson *(Meyer Dickstein)*; Luis Guzman *(Ramon)*.

4751   *The John Gary Show.* (Series; Variety; CBS; Syn.; 1966; 1968). Singer John Gary hosts a program of music and songs.

Program Open: "Welcome to *The John Gary Show* with John's guests Tim Conway, Susan Barrett and special guest Liberace; with Mitchell Ayres and his orchestra." Two versions appeared:

1. The John Gary Show (CBS, 1966). **Host:** John Gary. **Regulars:** The Jimmy Joyce Singers, The Jack Regas Dancers. **Orchestra:** Mitchell Ayres.

2. The John Gary Show (Syn., 1968). **Host:** John Gary. **Orchestra:** Sammy Spear.

4752   *The John Larroquette Show.* (Series; Comedy; NBC; 1993–1994). The Crossroads Bus Terminal in St. Louis, Missouri, provides the setting. John Hemingway, the manager, is an alcoholic who is trying to quit "but everybody keeps offering me a drink." He has a master's degree in English lit and got the bus-terminal job because he was the only one who applied for it. He has a sign in his office that reads, "This Is a Dark Ride" (which he found in an amusement park as a kid) and frequents the Raincheck Room Bar (where he typically orders a club soda). John, who says, "I've been a drunk for 20 years," lives in Apartment 3 of a building with the number 1138 on it (when John lived in Chicago, Clancy's Bar was his hangout). When John moves into a new apartment (2B, second season), he acquires a romantic interest — Catherine Merrick, a nurse at the County General Emergency Room, who lives in Apartment 2C.

Mahalia Sanchez is John's assistant. Her husband ran off with a 17-year-old girl and left her to raise their four children. Carlie Watkins is a gorgeous prostitute who charges $300 a night. She has a pet crow (Phoenix) and gave up her profession to buy the Rainbow Room Bar. Dexter Wilson is a tough black youth who runs the food counter in the terminal.

Cast: John Larroquette (*John Hemingway*); Liz Torres (*Mahalia Sanchez*); Gigi Rice (*Carlie Watkins*); Daryl "Chill" Mitchell (*Dexter Wilson*).

4753   *John Oliver's New York Stand-Up Show.* (Series; Comedy; Comedy Central; 2010). John Oliver, host of *The Daily Show*, presents a showcase for established and up-and-coming comedians.

Host: John Oliver. **Comics:** Marian Bamford, Matt Braunger, Hannibal Burress, Eugene Mirman, Janeane Garofalo, Greg Fitzsimmons, Chris Hardwick, Pete Holmer, Hari Kondabolu, Marc Maron, Matt McCarthy, Brian Posehn, Mary Lynn Rajskub, Kristen Schaal, Amy Schumer, Paul Tompkins.

4754   *Johnny and the Sprites.* (Series; Children; Disney; 2006–2007). Johnny T. is a musician (guitarist) who often needs to find time away from the world of music. One day, to find some solitude (and inspiration) Johnny retreats to a wooded area where he encounters a group of sprites (Muppet-like characters) who instantly become his friends. Each program is composed of two stories — each of which is presented like a mini Broadway musical and designed to relay messages and learning aspects to young children. The songs and musical numbers, written by name Broadway composers, are linked to the show's daily theme. The program premiered as a five-minute filler series in 2006; it became a half-hour series in 2007.

Cast: John Tartaglia (*Johnny T.*); Leslie Carrara (*Ginger*); James T. Kroupa (*Seymour the Schmole*); Tim Lagasse (*Basil*).

4755   *Johnny Bago.* (Series; Drama; CBS; 1993). John Francis Tenuti is in a restaurant when a beautiful girl walks in and kills a mobster (Chico Roselli) who is sitting opposite him. The girl casually walks by Johnny and drops the gun in his food. Johnny picks up the gun and yells, "The bimbo did it," but the girl is nowhere to be found. Fearing the worst, Johnny runs and is now sought by the police, the

mob (who want revenge) and his ex-wife Beverly Florio, his parole officer (Johnny is out on parole after serving five years for driving the getaway car for mobster Vincent Roselli). Shortly after, Johnny befriends an old-timer named Hick Benson (Dub Taylor) who owns a 31-foot Winnebago. When Hick asks the stranger his name, Johnny sees the word "bago" on the dashboard and says Johnny Bago. The following day, Heck dies and Johnny takes control of the Winnebago. He is now a fugitive and travels the back roads of America — hoping to keep out of sight and find the real killer to clear himself. Jimmy Buffett performs the theme, "Johnny Bago."

Cast: Peter Dobson (*Johnny Bago*); Rose Abdoo (*Beverly Florio*); Richard Romanus (*Vincent Roselli*).

4756   *Johnny Blue.* (Pilot; Mystery; CBS; Sept. 4, 1983). Johnny Blue is a New Orleans–based detective who also runs a restaurant called Johnny Blue's. The proposal was to relate his efforts to help the police solve baffling crimes. Other regulars are Deputy Police Chief "Mitch" Mitchell; and Saffron, Johnny's chef.

Cast: Gil Gerard (*Johnny Blue*); Eugene Roche (*"Mitch" Mitchell*); George Kee Cheung (*Saffron*).

4757   *Johnny Bravo.* (Series; Cartoon; Cartoon Network; 1997–2004). Johnny Bravo is a dim-witted, muscular young man who sports an Elvis Presley like voice and a pompadour hairstyle. Johnny believes he is irresistible to women and stories relate his misguided efforts to get the women he becomes infatuated with to fall in love with him; unfortunately for Johnny, he is not only beaten up by the boyfriends of his desire, but always dumped in the end. Bunny is Johnny's mother; Little Suzy is Johnny's 12-year-old neighbor, a girl who has a crush on Johnny; Carl is a nerd who considers Johnny to be his best friend (Johnny finds him annoying); Pops is the owner of the local diner; Master Hamma is the martial arts master who is trying to teach Johnny how to defend himself (with little success); Jungle Boy is the rescued youth who lived with animals.

Voice Cast: Jeff Bennett (*Johnny Bravo*); Brenda Vaccaro (*Bunny Bravo*); Mae Whitman (*Little Suzy*); Tom Kenny (*Carl Chryniszzswics*); Larry Drake (*Pops*); Brian Tochi (*Master Hamma*); Mark Hamill (*King Raymond*); Cody Dorkin (*Jungle Boy*).

4758   *The Johnny Carson Show.* (Series; Variety; CBS; 1955–1956). A program of music, songs, interviews and comedy sketches with comedian Johnny Carson as the host. Prior to this network series, Johnny had starred in three local series: *The Squirrel's Nest* (in Omaha, Nebraska), *Carson's Cellar* and *Carson's Corner* (both in Los Angeles in 1953).

Host: Johnny Carson. **Regulars:** Virginia Gibson, Barbara Ruick, Glenn Turnbull, Laurie Carroll, Peter Hanley, Hank Simms, Jill Corey. **Music:** Lud Gluskin, Cal Gooden.

4759   *Johnny Cash and Friends.* (Series; Variety; CBS; 1976). Country-western singer Johnny Cash heads the festivities of a program that features music, songs and comedy from a cast of regulars.

Host: Johnny Cash. **Regulars:** June Carter Cash, Steve Martin, Jim Varney, Howard Mann. **Orchestra:** Bill Walker.

4760   *The Johnny Cash Show.* (Series; Variety; CBS; 1969–1971). Music, songs and light comedy with a country and western accent.

Host: Johnny Cash. **Regulars:** June Carter Cash, The Carter Family, Carl Perkins, The Statler Brothers, The Tennessee Three. **Announcer:** Mike Lawrence. **Orchestra:** Bill Walker.

4761   *Johnny Come Lately.* (Pilot; Comedy; CBS; Aug. 8,

1960). Johnny Martin is a TV newscaster who will go to any lengths to get a story. The proposal was to relate the mishaps he encounters while trying to get firsthand information on the stories he reports. Angela Talbot is the station owner. Filmed in 1956.

Cast: Jack Carson (*Johnny Martin*); Marie Windsor (*Angela Talbot*).

4762   *The Johnny Dugan Show.* (Series; Variety; NBC; 1952). Daily summer program of music and songs from Hollywood with singer Johnny Dugan.

Host: Johnny Dugan. **Regulars:** Barbara Logan, Arch Presby.

4763   *Johnny Garage.* (Pilot; Comedy; CBS; April 13, 1983). A financially troubled garage (called simply Garage) in Queens, New York, and the story of the man who owns it, Johnny Antonizzio (nicknamed "Johnny Garage") was the focal point of a proposal that was to also focus on his endless attempts to get out of debt. Other regulars are Frankie Parker, his mechanic; Mike, Frankie's assistant; and Harriet, Johnny's landlady.

Cast: Ron Carey (*Johnny Antonizzio*); Val Bisoglio (*Frankie Parker*); Timothy Van Patten (*Mike*); Carlin Glynn (*Harriet Garfield*).

4764   *Johnny Guitar.* (Pilot; Western; CBS; July 31, 1959). A singing cowboy (Johnny Guitar) who roams throughout the West and helps people in trouble is the focal point of the proposed series

Cast: William Joyce (*Johnny Guitar*).

4765   *The Johnny Johnston Show.* (Series; Variety; CBS; 1951). Singer Johnny Johnston hosts a daily program of music and songs.

Host: Johnny Johnston. **Regular:** Rosemary Clooney.

4766   *Johnny Jupiter.* (Series; Comedy; DuMont, 1953; ABC, 1953-1954). Ernest P. Duckweather is a mild mannered clerk at the Frisby General Store in the town of Clayville. Horatio Frisby owns the store; Katherine Frisby is Horatio's daughter and Ernest's girlfriend.

Ernest earns $15 a week and is a jack-of-all-trades. He accidentally discovered interplanetary television when he fooled around with a television set and contacted the inhabitants of Jupiter. The Jupiterians we see are puppets Johnny Jupiter, Major Domo (the head robot) and Reject, "the factory rejected robot." Stories relate Ernest's misadventures as he seeks the Jupiterians' help in solving his earthly problems. When Ernest contacts Johnny, he turns several dials on a large television and says, "Duckweather on Earth, calling the planet Jupiter." Through some primitive but effective special effects, Jupiter comes into view. Ernest can see and speak to Johnny and vice versa.

If Ernest requires extraordinary help, Johnny sends Reject the Robot to Earth. To accomplish this, Johnny touches the puppet Reject and says, "Super Jelly Bean Power." Reject is sent through space and appears to Ernest (the only one who can see him). During the trip from Jupiter to Earth, the puppet becomes life-sized.

Reta Shaw (as Mrs. Clandish, a townsperson) and Florenz Ames (as Mr. Latham, Horatio's nemesis) were semi-regulars in this version of the series (ABC owned and operated stations; syndicated elsewhere).

An earlier version aired on DuMont. In this format, Ernest P. Duckweather is a television station janitor who dreams of becoming a producer. One night he sneaks into the control room and begins playing producer. While fiddling with the various controls, he accidentally discovers interplanetary television when he contacts the people of Jupiter (puppets Johnny Jupiter; Major Domo, "the head robot"; Reject, "the factory rejected robot"; and Johnny's pal, B-12). It appears that the DuMont version, which was broadcast live, had

only two actors: Vaughn Taylor as Ernest and Gilbert Mack doubling as Ernest's boss at the television station and as the puppet voices. Stories revolved around Johnny and Ernest assessing the values of their respective planets (which differed greatly; what was commonplace on Earth was usually just the opposite on Jupiter).

Cast: Wright King (*Ernest P. Duckweather*); Vaughn Taylor, Cliff Hall (*Horatio Frisby*); Patricia Peardon (*Katherine Frisby*); Gilbert Mack (*Voice of Johnny Jupiter/Reject the Robot*).

4767   *Johnny Mann's Stand Up and Cheer.* (Series; Variety; Syn.; 1971). America in a musical revue with bandleader Johnny Mann as the host. Also known as *Stand Up and Cheer.*

Program Open: Chevrolet presents *Stand Up and Cheer* starring Johnny Mann and featuring the Johnny Mann Singers with special guest star Edie Adams. *Stand Up and Cheer* brought to you by Chevrolet, building a better way to see the U.S.A."

Host: Johnny Mann. **Regulars:** The Johnny Mann Singers. **Orchestra:** Johnny Mann.

4768   *Johnny Midnight.* (Series; Crime Drama; Syn.; 1960). Johnny Midnight is a former actor turned private detective who says, "Broadway is the world of make-believe, but I found out that the curtain never comes down on the real things that happen on the Street of Dreams. That's why I gave up acting to become a private investigator." Johnny lives in a penthouse on West 41st Street and Broadway; "My favorite street in my favorite town—New York City." Johnny owns his own theater, The Midnight Theater, and still frequents the actors' hangout, Lindy's Bar, where he likes to eat and keep in touch with his show business friends. Cost doesn't matter much when it comes to his clients. If he sees that a person is in real trouble, the money becomes secondary. Johnny also works on behalf of the Mutual Insurance Company and uses his skills as a former actor to help him solve cases. His favorite disguise is Gearhart Houtsman, the Old German.

Aki is Johnny's houseboy; he calls Johnny "Mr. Johnny Midnight." Lupo Olivera is Johnny's police department contact, a sergeant with the Homicide Division of the N.Y.P.D.

A jazz adaptation of the song "The Lullaby of Broadway," played by Joe Bushkin, is the show's theme song.

Cast: Edmond O'Brien (*Johnny Midnight*); Yuki Shimoda (*Aki*); Arthur Batanides (*Lupo Olivera*); Barney Phillips (*Lieutenant Geller*).

4769   *Johnny Moccasin.* (Pilot; Western; Unaired; Produced in 1955). Johnny Moccasin is a white teenage boy who has been raised by an Indian tribe after his parents were killed in a wagon train massacre. Johnny is learned in the ways of the Indian and Johnny appears to be a wanderer. His adventures as he helps the people he finds in trouble is the focal point of the proposed series.

Cast: Jody McCrea (*Johnny Moccasin*).

4770   *Johnny Nighthawk.* (Pilot; Adventure; CBS; Sept. 1, 1959). Johnny Nighthawk and Matt Brent are the owners of a one-plane airline that handles both passengers and cargo. Johnny and Matt are adventurers and the proposal was to relate their assignments, more often than not, risking their lives to help people in trouble.

Cast: Scott Brady (*Johnny Nighthawk*); Richard Erdman (*Matt Brent*).

4771   *Johnny Olson's Rumpus Room.* (Series; Variety; DuMont; 1949–1952). Music, songs and comedy coupled with a game segment wherein selected members of the studio audience compete in stunt contests for prizes.

Host: Johnny Olson. **Regulars:** Kay Armen, Gene Kirby, Hal McIntyre. **Music:** Buddy Weed, Hank D'Amico.

4772   Johnny Ringo. (Series; Western; CBS; 1959-1960). Velardi, Arizona, is a growing town in the 1870s; there is a lot of traffic; the railroad has started laying track going east and there is also a lot of trouble — from outlaws who find the town an easy mark. To stop the growing crime rate, Mayor Hartford hires Johnny Ringo, an ex-gunfighter, as the town's sheriff. Johnny, a right-handed gunfighter, receives $200 a month and has to prove he is as fast as his reputation — "Velardi didn't hire me, they hired my guns. I know that and got to live with it. Maybe someday it will be different."

Johnny doesn't know much about the law — he puts things on a personal basis. He philosophizes, and people say he sounds more like a preacher than a gunfighter. He sometimes poses as a wanted man and calls on his reputation as a gunfighter to apprehend criminals. Johnny never killed a man for money. He relinquished his gun fighting career to become a lawman. Johnny's gun is a variation on the French firearm, the Le Met Special. It was designed by Cason ("Case") Thomas, Johnny's original deputy, "to even up the odds." Cason calls it "a seven shooter." It looks like a regular Colt .45 and fires the normal six bullets. But there is a separate barrel for an extra shell — a .410 shotgun shell. William Charles, Jr., better known as Cully, is Johnny's young deputy. Cully's father was a trick shot and taught him how to use a gun when he was five years old. Four years later Cully's father was killed, and Cully went to work as a roustabout in a carnival. He practiced shooting every day and eventually became a traveling show attraction called "Kid Adonis, the Fastest Gun in the World." When the show came to Velardi and the Kid found Johnny was a split second faster than he was, he decided to settle down and lead a normal life. When Cason tells Cully that he is getting too old for the job, Cully steps into his shoes and becomes Johnny's deputy. Cason buys the general store (which he runs with his daughter and Johnny's romantic interest, Laura Thomas). The original pilot film, titled "Man Alone," aired on *Zane Grey Theater* (CBS) on Mar. 5, 1959. Don Durant played Johnny Ringo, Thomas Mitchell was Cason Thomas and Marilyn Erskine was Laura Thomas (Cully did not appear; the reworked pilot, titled "Arrival" for *Johnny Ringo* is a word-for-word remake of "Man Alone." The proposed series title at the time was *The Loner*). Don Durant sings the theme, "Johnny Ringo."

Cast: Don Durant (*Johnny Ringo*); Mark Goddard (*Cully*); Karen Sharpe (*Laura Thomas*); Terrence DeMarney (*Cason Thomas*).

4773   Johnny Risk. (Pilot; Adventure; NBC; June 16, 1958). Alaska, 1896, is the setting for a proposal about Johnny Risk, a gambling boat entrepreneur who helps people in trouble. Broadcast as a segment of *Alcoa Theater*.

Cast: Michael Landon (*Johnny Risk*).

4774   Johnny Sokko and His Flying Robot. (Series; Science Fiction; Syn.; 1968). Shortly after a group of aliens secretly land on Earth (in Japan), they kidnap Dr. Lucas Gardion, a brilliant scientist, and force him to construct Giant Robot, an indestructible mechanical machine that they plan to use to destroy Earth. As the doctor completes the robot, a prehistoric type of creature brought to Earth by the aliens escapes and attacks a Japanese ship. Two people, Johnny Sokko (a young boy) and Jerry Mono (Agent 43), an agent for Unicorn (an international defense organization) survive and wash up on a nearby uncharted island — the alien's base. There, they meet Dr. Gardion, who tells them about the robot and what the aliens plan to do. They also learn that the robot will obey the first voice it hears and that it is complete except for an atomic charge to activate its circuits. Just then, as the aliens attack the lab. Dr. Gardion detonates the atomic bomb he planted in the robot to destroy it. However, instead of destroying the robot, the bomb supplies the necessary power to activate it. Amid the ensuing confusion, Johnny finds the wrist watch-

type control and speaks to the robot. He becomes its master. With the help of Giant Robot (as Johnny calls it), Johnny and Jerry return to Tokyo (where the series is set) and where Johnny becomes a member of Unicorn (Agent 7) and Giant Robot becomes Earth's most valuable defense weapon. Stories depict Unicorn's battle against sinister alien invaders. Produced in Japan and dubbed in English.

Cast: Mitsundbu Kaneko (*Johnny Sokko*); Akjo Ito (*Jerry Mono*).

4775   Johnny Staccato. (Series; Crime Drama; NBC; 1959-1960). Johnny Staccato is a former jazz musician (the Staccato Combo) turned private detective who operates out of New York City. Johnny, who was born in Manhattan (he now lives at 860 West 40th Street), says, "I'm a native, but I still ask questions, especially of pretty girls, to get around." He also knows a lot — "It's all from odd bits of information I picked up here and there." Johnny's hangout is Waldo's, a mid–Manhattan bar owned by his friend Waldo, an Old World Italian who likes opera but puts up with jazz. It's here where Johnny seems to find his only means of relaxation when he plays piano in the jazz band that supplies the bar's music. Also known as *Staccato*. Elmer Bernstein composed "Staccato's Theme."

Cast: John Cassavetes (*Johnny Staccato*); Eduardo Ciannelli (*Waldo*).

4776   Johnny Test. (Series; Cartoon; Kids WB; 2005). Johnny Test is not your typical 11-year-old boy. He is the brother of Susan and Mary, twin, scientific genius girls who constantly use him as a guinea pig for their experiments. But as Johnny says, "It's just another day in the life of a boy." Johnny also has a dog, Dukie, who was given the ability to speak by his sisters when they created a DNA program for him. Mary and Susan often use their genius to create items to help mankind and so impress the government that they (and Johnny and Dukie) are sworn in as secret agents for SSGA (located in an area called 51.1). Stories follow Johnny as he helps out where he can — with the enhanced help of Susan and Mary's experiments (which do not always go as planned and complicate matters even further. But, as they say to Johnny, "You have to trust us, Johnny, we're family").

Voice Cast: James Arnold Taylor (*Johnny Test*); Brittney Wilson (*Susan and Mary Test*); Jeff Woodlock (*Dukie*); Kathleen Barr (*Johnny's mother*); Ian James Corlett (*Johnny's father*).

4777   Johnnytime. (Series; Children; USA; 1997). An educational program for children that addresses the various problems they face as seen through the eyes of John Kassir, an imaginative actor who plays numerous characters in skits designed to show a problem and how to deal with it.

Host: John Kassir. **Music:** Garry Stockdale.

4778   The Johnsons Are Home. (Pilot; Comedy; CBS; July 19, 1988). A slightly off-beat view of domestic life as seen through the experiences of the Johnsons, a not-so-typical American family: parents Andrew and Ora, their children, Mary and Andrew ("Andy") Jr., and Ora's Aunt Lunar.

Cast: Geoffrey Lewis (*Andrew Johnson*); Lynn Milgrim (*Ora Johnson*); Hannah Cutrona (*Mary Johnson*); John Zarchen (*Andy Johnson*); Audrey Meadows (*Aunt Lunar*).

4779   Joint Custody. (Pilot; Comedy; Unaired; Produced for ABC in 2005). Joel is a 22-year-old "child" of divorce. His parents, Mike and Roz have just divorced and Joel now lives in two homes — weekdays with Roz and weekends with Mike. Joel lives in New Jersey, has a part-time job in Manhattan, likes to hang out with former high school buds and the proposal was to follow Joel as he struggles to cope with the problems of his new lifestyle.

Cast: Nicholas D'Agosto *(Joel)*; Will McCormack *(Mike)*; Marilu Henner *(Roz)*; Whitney Sloan *(Lisa)*; Kurt Fuller *(Charlie)*.

4780 *Jokebook.* (Series; Cartoon; NBC; 1982). Animated characters such as Treeman, the Nerd and Eve and Adam host short cartoon segments that are culled from cartoon classics, foreign and student films.

Voices: Bob Hastings, Henry Corden, Joyce Jameson, Joan Gerber, Don Messick, Sidney Miller, Frank Welker, Lennie Weinrib, Janet Waldo, Ronnie Schell, Marilyn Schreffler.

4781 *Joker! Joker!! Joker!!!* (Series; Game; Syn.; 1980). A children's version of the *The Joker's Wild.* Two contestants compete. One player pulls a lever to activate a large slot-like mechanism that contains five category topics. The machine pinpoints three question categories, one of which the player chooses. If the contestant answers correctly, he wins money and continues to play; if he is wrong, he loses his turn and his opponent receives the opportunity to win points. The winner is the first player to score 500 points (he wins a savings bond). Contained within the categories are jokers, as in a deck of playing cards, which sometime appear with a subject and allow a player to double his points (if one appears with two identical categories) or triple his score (if two jokers appear with one category). If three jokers appear during one spin, the player automatically wins the game and the savings bond.

Host: Jack Barry. **Announcer:** Jay Stewart.

4782 *The Joker's Wild.* (Series; Game; CBS, 1972–1974; Syn., 1977–1991). Two contestants compete. One player pulls a lever to activate a large slot-like mechanism that contains five category topics. The machine pinpoints three question categories, one of which the player chooses. If the contestant answers correctly, he wins money and continues to play; if he is wrong, he loses his turn and his opponent receives the opportunity to win money. The winner is the first player to score $500. Contained within the categories are jokers, as in a deck of playing cards, which sometime appear with a subject and allow a player to double his cash (if one appears with two identical categories) or triple his cash (if two jokers appear with one category). If three jokers appear during one spin, the player automatically wins the game and $500. The pilot film, with Allen Ludden as the host, was taped in 1969.

Host: Jack Barry *(1972–74, network; 1977–84, Syn.)*; Jim Peck *(1984 substitute host)*; Bill Cullen *(1984–86, Syn.)*; Pat Finn *(1990-91, Syn.)*. **Announcer:** Johnny Jacobs, Jay Stewart, Charlie O'Donnell.

4783 *The Joke's On You.* (Pilot; Comedy; Unaired; Produced for CBS in 2006). Ordinary people are recruited to play practical jokes on friends and family without realizing the marks are aware of what is going to happen and play the joke on them.

Host: Wayne Brady.

4784 *Jon and Kate Plus 8.* (Series; Reality; TLC; 2007–2009). Incidents in the lives of the Gosselin family — parents Jon and Kate and their eight children, six of whom are sextuplets; two of whom are twins.

The 2009 season has made more headlines than any other reality show of its type. While the series started off as a look at the lives of Jon and Kate and their children, it has progressed into a sensationalized nightmare for the children (who have balked at cameras following their every move) and scandal as hubby Jon has become unfaithful (allegedly with 23-year-old school teacher Deanna Hummel; later his girlfriend is Hailey Glasman). The scandal has caused a series rift (Jon and Kate appear to have separated with the children remaining with Kate). Cameras have been rolling and all the tension that now exists is shamelessly presented — all to the delight of TLC and a ratings boost. The episode of June 22, 2009 revealed that Jon and Kate's marriage is over and divorce papers have been filed in a Pennsylvania court (where the series is filmed). With the return of the series on August 3, 2009, Jon and Kate have separated. Jon has moved to a "two-room bachelor pad" at the Alexandra, a luxury apartment building on the Upper West Side; Kate has relocated to Rockville, Maryland, where she purchased a condo a block from her bodyguard, Steve Neild (with whom she is rumored to have had an affair). Although the children still resent the cameras and on-line sources report that people have gotten tired of Jon and Kate, TLC's cameras continue to capture and report on the drama in their lives (sequences with the children are filmed separately with each parent).The continuing disruption of the family has lead to a drastic drop in the ratings but, being TLC's most popular show, a decision was made to keep running it.

On October 26, 2009, TLC aired the last first-run episode of *Jon and Kate Plus 8.* Repeats aired until November 23, 2009. On November 2, 2009, *Jon and Kate* was pre-empted by the special *Kate: Her Own Story.* Here Kate, interviewed by NBC newswoman Natalie Morales, revealed intimate details about her life, children and her series. The following three weeks consisted of repeats. On November 11, 2009, TLC made it official: November 23, 2009 will be the final episode of *Jon and Kate Plus 8* (the episode featured Jon and Kate reflecting on the recent events in their lives and events and what the future holds).

4785 *The Jon Dore Television Show.* (Series; Comedy; IFC; 2009). "It's a heartwarming adventure for the whole family — assuming your family is somewhat insane and finds repulsive nudity heartwarming" is the tagline for a program that sort of borrows its format from *My Name Is Earl* to focus on a man (Jon Dore) who sets out to correct his faults and make all wrongs right (these include getting beat up by children, painfully removing body hair, seeing a hypnotist to stop smoking and hiring an army drill sergeant to whip him into shape). Stories also feature a flashback sequence wherein Little Jon Dore (as a 10-year-old with a full beard like his elder self) shows how he grew up to become a dysfunctional adult. Philip is Jon's friend; Allison is his sister.

Cast: Jon Dore *(Himself)*; Ricardo Hoyos *(Little Jon Dore)*; Steve Patterson *(Philip)*; Allison Dore *(Allison)*.

4786 *The Jon Stewart Show.* (Series; Talk; MTV; 1993–1995). MTV's first comedy-accented talk-interview show with Jon Stewart interviewing celebrities and presenting comedy bits.

Host: Jon Stewart. **Assistant:** Howard Feller.

4787 *Jonas.* (Series; Comedy; Disney; 2008–). The Lucas Brothers (Joe, Kevin and Nick) are singer-musicians who live with their father, Tom (also their manager) in a converted firehouse on Jonas Street and attend Horace Mantis High School. By day the brothers are ordinary teens facing the problems teenagers face. By night and on weekends they are rock stars — the Jonas Brothers and the heartthrobs of "tween girls." Stories follow the brothers as they try to lead a normal life despite their careers as rock stars. Macy is their friend; Stella is their stylist.

Second season episodes, titled *Jonas Brothers: Living the Dream* continues to follow the lives of the brothers as rock stars. *Jonas L.A.,* third season episodes, find Joe, Kevin and Nick navigating new territory in Los Angeles as they move up the entertainment ladder. Here, Joe befriends Vanessa Page, a free-spirited actress who is helping him pursue an acting career. Kevin becomes part of the scene when Joe is cast in Vanessa's movie and Kevin receives the opportunity to learn how to direct a feature film. Nick's life changes also. Instead of writing songs for the group, he sets out to prove he is more than just a rock star. Third season episodes also feature Lisa, Stella's aunt; Big Man, the brothers' security chief; and D.Z., their neighbor.

The program was actually conceived as J.O.N.A.S. (Junior Operatives Networking As Spies) with the Jonas brothers as rock band who are secretly spies for the U.S. government. The program was shelved due to the 2007-08 writers strike and retooled as stated above.

Cast: Joe Jonas *(Joe Lucas)*; Kevin Jonas *(Kevin Lucas)*; Nick Jonas *(Nick Lucas)*; John Ducey *(Tom Lucas)*; Nicole Anderson *(Macy Misa)*; Chelsea Staub *(Stella Malone)*; Abby Pivaronas, Beth Crosby *(Aunt Lisa)*; Adam Hicks *(D.Z.)*; Rob Feggans *(Big Man)*; Debi Mazar *(Mona Klein)*.

4788   *The Jonathan Winters Show.* (Series; Comedy; NBC; 1956-1957). An interlude program of songs and comedy sketches with comedian Jonathan Winters as the host.

Host: Jonathan Winters. **Vocalists:** The Platters. **Music:** Eddie Shfronski.

4789   *The Jonathan Winters Show.* (Series; Variety; CBS; 1967–1969). Comedian Jonathan Winters oversees a program of music, songs and comedy sketches that features his wide array of characters and his ability to improvise on the spot.

Host: Jonathan Winters. **Regulars:** Paul Lynde, Alice Ghostley, Cliff Arquette, Dick Curtis, Abby Dalton, Pamela Rodgers, Debi Storm, Diane Davis, Georgene Barnes, Jerry Renneau, The Establishment, The Wisa D'Orso Dancers, The Andre Tayer Dancers. **Announcer:** Bern Bennett. **Music:** Paul Weston.

4790   *Jones and Jury.* (Series; Reality; Syn.; 1994-1995). Real people with a pending small claims court case appear before Star Jones, a former Brooklyn senior assistant district attorney and NBC's legal correspondent, to present their sides of the case. When the evidence on both sides has been presented, Star instructs the studio audience on the legal issues involved in the case they just heard. The audience then votes to determine the winner. No matter which side wins (the defendant or the plaintiff) the audience's decision is legal and binding and cannot be appealed in another court.

Host: Star Jones.

4791   *The Jones Boys.* (Pilot; Comedy; CBS; Aug. 21, 1967). Moose, Nick and Dixie are the Jones boys, the employees of Oliver Jones, the owner of the Jones Maintenance Company. Oliver's efforts to run a company beset with problems was the focal point of the unsold series. Other regulars are Mary, Oliver's wife; and Betty, his secretary.

Cast: Mickey Shaughnessy *(Oliver Jones)*; Jeanne Arnold *(Mary Jones)*; Barbara Stuart *(Betty Kelly)*; Bob Dishy *(Moose)*; Dick Gautier *(Nick Matero)*; Norman Grabowski *(Dixie)*.

4792   *Jonny Quest.* (Series; Cartoon; ABC; 1964-1965). The shortened title for *The Adventures of Jonny Quest.* See this title for information.

4793   *Jonny Zero.* (Series; Crime Drama; Fox; 2004). Jonny Calvo is a bouncer at a nightclub called Club Club in Manhattan (he previously worked at Club Ecstasy). One night, during a confrontation with a drug dealer, Jonny accidentally kills him. Jonny is arrested, charged with manslaughter and sentenced to eight years in Sing Sing Prison. He is released from prison after four years for good behavior.

Jonny is not the most positive role model on TV. He is a low life thug with a nasty temper and a drug habit. He knows all the unde-

sirables and he knows the underworld. He is called Jonny Zero because his life is nothing. When first released Jonny found work at Captain Jack's, a sleazy diner. He next worked in a gym (Jethro's Boxing Ring) as a sparring partner and janitor. Although Jonny knows the bad guys, he's a good guy compared to those bad guys (criminals). As Jonny seeks to change his life, he befriends Random, a wannabe hip-hop Renaissance Man, and Danni Styles, a troubled ex-stripper.

Jonny's life changes somewhat for the better when an FBI agent blackmails him into going undercover as an informant to use his criminal knowledge to infiltrate the New York club scenes to help people and solve crimes. With the help of Random and Danni, who call themselves "Alternative Detectives," Jonny helps those who are unable to help themselves. Jonny comes up with the worst possible plans for a job that always puts him in danger (and often a beating).

Cast: Franky G *(Jonny Zero)*; GQ *(Random)*; Brennan Hesser *(Danielle "Danni" Styles)*.

4794   *The Jordan Chance.* (Pilot; Crime Drama; CBS; Dec. 12, 1978). Frank Jordan is an attorney who was once wrongly imprisoned for murder. When he was released he made a vow to help others who have been falsely convicted of a crime. The unsold series was to relate the detective work of Frank's legmen (Brian, Karen and Jimmy) as they uncover the evidence Frank needs to defend his clients and give them that Jordan chance at freedom.

Cast: Raymond Burr *(Frank Jordan)*; Ted Shackelford *(Brian Klosky)*; Jeannie Fitzsimmons *(Karen Wagner)*; James Canning *(Jimmy Foster)*.

4795   *Jo's Cousins.* (Pilot; Comedy; NBC; April 14, 1982). A proposed spin off from *The Facts of Life* about the Largos, a family of four who operate a gas station–garage in Weehawken, New Jersey. (The Largos, Sal, a widower, and his children, Terry, Pauli and Bud, are the cousins of *Facts* regular Jo Polniaszek.) Tony is a friend of the family.

Cast: Donnelly Rhodes *(Sal Largo)*; Megan Follows *(Terry Largo)*; John Mengatti *(Pauli Largo)*; D.W. Brown *(Bud Largo)*; Grant Cramer *(Tony Valente)*; Nancy McKeon *(Jo Polniaszek)*.

4796   *The Joseph Cotten Show.* (Series; Anthology; CBS; 1956-1957). The alternate title for *On Trial.* See this title for information.

4797   *Joseph Schildkraut Presents.* (Series; Anthology; DuMont; 1953-1954). Author Joseph Schildkraut hosts a series of filmed dramas produced by Ray Benson.

4798   *Josephine Little.* (Pilot; Drama; NBC; 1960-1961). Josephine Little, called "Little Jo," is the beautiful owner of an import-export business in Hong Kong. She is a legendary adventuress who knows everyone and who has been all over the world. Josephine deals in everything from emeralds to elephants and gambles with everything but her American passport. Her life is rarely as simple as operating a business as she often finds herself bucking horns with the unscrupulous characters that come with the territory. Ah Sing is her assistant. Josephine's adventures were chronicled in three pilot films (broadcast on *The Barbara Stanwyck Show*):

1. The Miraculous Journey of Tadpole Chan (Nov. 14, 1960). Josephine tries to help Tadpole Chan (Dick Kay Hong), a little boy who wants to see America.

2. Dragon by the Tail (Jan. 30, 1961). Josephine teams with a U.S. intelligence agent to track down a dangerous spy.

3. Adventures in Happiness (Mar. 20, 1961). Josephine risks her life to help Dr. Paul Harris (Lew Ayres) get much needed medical supplies.

Cast: Barbara Stanwyck *(Josephine Little)*; Anna May Wong *(Ah Sing)*.

4799   *Joshua's World*. (Pilot; Drama; CBS; Aug. 21, 1980). Dr. Joshua Torrance is a widower with two children, Thorpe and James. He lives in the small town of Strawee, Arkansas, during the 1930s. The town is torn by racial strife and Joshua's practice is jeopardized by his opposition to racism. His attempts to treat all people as equals were the focal point of the unsold series. Other regulars are Donie, his housekeeper; Caroline, the school teacher; and Dawn and Josie, friends of Thorpe and James.
   Cast: Richard Crenna *(Dr. Joshua Torrance)*; Tonya Crowe *(Thorpe Torrance)*; Randy Gray *(James Torrance)*; Mary Alice *(Donie)*; Carol Vogel *(Caroline Morgan)*; Alexandra Pauley *(Dawn Starr)*; LaShana Dendy *(Josie)*.

4800   *Josie and the Pussycats*. (Series; Cartoon; CBS; 1970–1972). Josie, the group leader and head singer, and Melody and Valerie compose the rock group Josie and the Pussycats (Melody also plays the drums; Valerie is the guitarist). Alan is the group's manager; Alexander is his assistant; Alexandra is Alexander's sister; and Sebastian is the group's pet cat. Stories follow the group as they become involved with and attempt to solve mysteries during their tours. See also the spin off series *Josie and the Pussycats in Outer Space*.
   Voice Cast: Janet Waldo *(Josie)*; Cathy Douglas *(Josie; singing voice)*; Jackie Joseph *(Melody)*; Cheryl Ladd *(Melody; singing voice)*; Barbara Pariot *(Valerie)*; Patricia Holloway *(Valerie, singing voice)*; Jerry Dexter *(Alan)*; Casey Kasem *(Alexander)*; Sherry Alberoni *(Alexandra)*; Don Messick *(Sebastian)*.

4801   *Josie and the Pussycats in Outer Space*. (Series; Cartoon; CBS; 1972–1974). A spin off from *Josie and the Pussycats*. The rock group Josie and the Pussycats is posing for publicity pictures near a spaceship at NASA when Alexandra, a member of the group, moves forward and accidentally knocks the others off balance. As they fall backward into the open capsule hatch, the blast-off mechanism is activated, sending the craft and its passengers into the far regions of space. Stories detail the group's adventures as they seek a way to return to Earth. Josie is the group leader, a singer; Melody (a drummer and singer) and Valerie (guitarist and singer) are the Pussycats. Alan is the group's manager; Alexander is his assistant; Alexandra is Alexander's sister; Sebastian is the group's pet cat; and Bleep is the space creature Melody befriends on the planet Zelcor.
   Voice Cast: Janet Waldo *(Josie)*; Cathy Douglas *(Josie, singing voice)*; Jackie Joseph *(Melody)*; Cheryl Ladd *(Melody, singing voice)*; Barbara Pariot *(Valerie)*; Patricia Holloway *(Valerie, singing voice)*; Jerry Dexter *(Alan)*; Sherry Alberoni *(Alexandra)*; Casey Kasem *(Alexander)*; Don Messick *(Sebastian and Bleep)*.

4802   *The Journey of Allen Strange*. (Series; Comedy; Nick; 1997–2000). Allen Strange is an alien (from the planet Xela) who is now stranded on Earth (Allen stowed away on an intergalactic transport vessel. It landed on Earth to refuel; Allen wandered off and was left behind when the ship blasted off). He is found wandering by Robbie and Josh Stevenson, a sister and brother who befriend him and agree to keep his secret when they learn he is an alien. Robbie and Josh become Allen's guide as he learns about life on Earth and seeks a way to return to his home planet.
   Cast: Arjay Smith *(Allen Strange)*; Erin J. Dean *(Robbie Stevenson)*; Jack Tate *(Ken Stevenson)*; Robert Crow *(Manfred Strange)*; Evan Scott *(Erika Roman)*; Steve Sobel *(Prince Alazar)*; Sean Babb *(Moose)*; Ethan Glazer *(Hamilton Gerrigan)*; Jaquita Ta'le *(La Tanya)*; Reggie Lee *(Zero)*.

4803   *Journey to the Center of the Earth*. (Series; Cartoon; ABC; 1967–1969). When Professor Oliver Lindenbrook uncovers the long lost trail of Arnie Saccnuson, a lone explorer who made a descent to the earth's center but died with its secret when he broke his leg, he organizes an expedition to follow Arnie's trail. Accompanied by his niece, Cindy; student Alec Hewit; Lars, a guide, and his pet duck Gertrude, Professor Lindenbrook begins a journey to the center of the earth. Unknown to them, the evil Count Saccnuson, the last living descendant of the once noble family, follows them. Possessing a power-mad scheme to claim the earth's core for his own sinister purposes, he instructs his servant Torg to kill the Lindenbrook expedition. A dynamite explosion set off by Torg instead seals off the entrance, trapping them all. Stories relate their adventures as they struggle to find the secret of the way back to the earth's service. Based on the novel by Jules Verne.
   Voice Cast: Ted Knight *(Oliver Lindenbrook/Count Saccnuson)*; Jane Webb *(Cindy Lindenbrook)*; Pat Harrington, Jr. *(Alec Hewit/Lars/Torg)*.

4804   *Journey to the Center of the Earth*. (Pilot; Science Fiction; NBC; Feb. 28, 1993). Chris Turner is a geophysicist who believes that by penetrating the interior wall of an erupting volcano it is possible to access a fascinating and unexplored subterranean "inner world." Chris receives backing from Hiram Wentworth, a ruthless billionaire who is seeking the mythical *Book of Knowledge*, which is supposed to exist at the earth's center. Chris then assembles a crew: Dr. Margo Peterson, Wentworth's representative; Dr. Tessue Itsukawa, the medical officer; Sandra Miller, a master caver; Dr. Cecil Chalmers, an expert on mystic inner worlds who possesses what he believes is a piece of the Book of Knowledge; Tony Estrella, a young jet pilot; and Joe Briggs, an ex–Navy Seal who is head of security. Wentworth then begins construction on the *Venture*, a 182-foot long craft designed by Chris that will enable them to journey to the center of the earth. The volcano in Mount Oliver is chosen as the point at which to begin the journey. Each member is paid one million dollars and the journey is expected to last six months. But the voyagers encounter an unforeseen problem: the underworld is in a constant state of flux. The *Venture* is hurled down through the darkness and lost in the labyrinth of ever-shifting tunnels. Soon, they are cut off from the surface and trapped in a dangerous and startling world. Their one hope for rescue lies in finding the *Book of Knowledge*, which Cecil believes is the only way back to the surface. Complicating matters is an unknown being called the Evil One who senses Chalmers has the one piece he needs to complete the puzzle to the *Book of Knowledge* and gain immense power to rule the world. Devin is the *Venture*'s female computer (she controls the craft); and Dallas, an abominable snowman–like creature they befriend and who becomes a part of the crew. Based on the novel by Jules Verne.
   Cast: Jeffrey Nordling *(Chris Turner)*; Farrah Forke *(Dr. Margo Peterson)*; John Neville *(Dr. Cecil Chalmers)*; Kim Miyori *(Dr. Tessue Itsukawa)*; Fabiana Udenio *(Sandra Miller)*; Tim Russ *(Joe Briggs)*; David Dundara *(Tony Estrella)*; Justina Vail *(Devin)*; Carel Struycken *(Dallas)*.

4805   *Journey to the Unknown*. (Series; Anthology; ABC; 1968-1969). British-produced mystery and suspense stories that depict the plight of people caught between the world of nightmare and reality. An established American performer appears with British supporting actors. American performers include Carol Lynley, Barbara Bel Geddes, Vera Miles, Patty Duke and Michael Callan.

4806   *Journeyman*. (Series; Drama; NBC; 2007). Dan Vasser appears to be a normal guy. He works as a reporter for the San Francisco *Register* and is married to Katie, a former reporter for Channel

6 news (under the name Katherine Barron). Dan is also the father of Zack and possesses a very unique gift: the ability to travel back in time (although he cannot explain how he acquired the ability).

Dan cannot control what happens to him. He suddenly disappears (seen in a flash of light) when something in the past needs to be changed before it becomes history. He appears to pass out at the moment of his journey and awakens to find himself in another time period. He cannot predict (or cause it to happen) and he has no idea whom he is to help until some sort of altercation brings him in contact with the person he needs to save (to affect some future good). The people Dan helps he has never known and he is not always sure why he was chosen to help someone (it is only when he completes his task and returns to the present that he discovers what he has accomplished). Stories follow Dan as he struggles to cope with life in the present day world and solve the problems he encounters in a past time.

Jack Vasser is Jack's brother, a detective with the S.F.P.D.; Hugh is Dan's editor; Olivia is a girl who possesses the same ability as Dan. Olivia and Dan were engaged but Olivia was thought to have been killed in a plane crash. She escaped the crash (journeyed back in time) and now appears to be a part of the past — and a guide Dan uses for help on his missions. Olivia too, is unaware as to why she was chosen or how she acquired her ability.

Cast: Kevin McKidd *(Dan Vasser)*; Gretchen Egolf *(Katie Vasser)*; Reed Diamond *(Jack Vasser)*; Moon Bloodgood *(Olivia)*; Charles Henry Wyson *(Zac Vasser)*; Brian Howe *(Hugh Skillen)*.

4807   Joyce and Barbara: For Adults Only. (Series; Discussion; Syn.; 1970). Topical issue discussions conducted by Joyce Susskind and Barbara Howar and produced by David Susskind.

4808   The Joyce Davidson Show. (Series; Interview; Syn.; 1975). Joyce Davidson oversees a program of topical issues discussions as well as interviews with celebrity and non-celebrity guests.

4809   The Joyce Jillson Show. (Series; Variety; Syn.; 1978). Astrology coupled with celebrity interviews with astrologist Joyce Jillson. Charlie Tuna is the host.

4810   The Joyce Matthews Show. (Series; Interview; CBS; 1950). Celebrity interview with actress Joyce Matthews as the host.

4811   Juarez. (Pilot; Crime Drama; ABC; May 28, 1988). Rosendo Juarez is a Mexican-American sergeant with the El Paso, Texas, Sheriff's Office. The proposal was to follow Juarez as he tackles criminal elements with a combination of fierce resolve and a unique perspective of two cultures. Other regulars are Marielena, Rosendo's wife; Sergeant Quintana, his superior; Bobby Carillo, Rosendo's neighbor and fellow lawman; Miguel Rodriquez, the empire-building local gangster; Vincente Juarez, Rosendo's brother; and Lieutenant C.P. Hardin.

Cast: Benjamin Bratt *(Rosendo Juarez)*; Ada Maris *(Marielena Juarez)*; Ramon Bieri *(C.P. Hardin)*; Ismael Carlo *(Sergeant Quintana)*; Charles Martinez *(Bobby Carillo)*; Gregory Cruz *(Vincente Juarez)*.

4812   Jubilee U.S.A. (Series; Variety; ABC; 1955–1960). Country and western entertainers perform in a program that is also known as *Ozark Jubilee*.

Host: Red Foley. **Regulars:** Wanda Jackson, Marvin Rainwater, Suzi Arden, Chuck Bowers, Norma Jean, Smiley Burnette, Shug Fisher, Pete Stamper, Bobby Lord and His Timber Jack Trio, Uncle Cyp and Aunt Sap Brasfield, Slim Wilson and His Jubilee Band, The Promenaders, The Marksmen, Bill Wimberly and His Country Rhythm Boys.

4813   The Jud Strunk Show. (Pilot; Variety; ABC; Aug. 17, 1972). Music, songs and comedy with Jud Strunk, a comic singer from Maine.

Host: Jud Strunk. **Guests:** Jack Burns, Tina Cole, Alice Ghostley, Andy Griffith, Louis Nye, The Lovin' Spoonful, The Carrabassett Grange Hall Talent Contest Winning Band.

4814   Judd, for the Defense. (Series; Drama; ABC; 1967–1969). Clinton Judd is a defense attorney based in Texas. He is a man of principal and will not give into pressure to compromise his beliefs. He is set in his ways and will almost always go by the book; he will, on occasion, bend the rules (just slightly) to accomplish a goal. Ben Caldwell, Clinton's younger partner, is a firm believer in doing what it takes to gather the evidence to defend a client. While they really do not bicker over their views, Ben's sometimes unorthodox methods do produce results and give Clinton the necessary ammunition to bring a case to a successful conclusion.

Cast: Carl Betz *(Clinton Judd)*; Stephen Young *(Ben Caldwell)*.

4815   The Judge. (Pilot; Drama; NBC; Feb. 5, 1963). A proposed spin off from *The Dick Powell Show* about Daniel Zachary, a newly appointed Supreme Court judge. Other regulars are Chief Justice Caleb Cooke; and Karen Holm, Daniel's secretary.

Cast: Richard Basehart *(Daniel Zachary)*; Otto Kruger *(Caleb Cooke)*; Mary Murphy *(Karen Holm)*.

4816   The Judge. (Series; Drama; Syn.; 1986). Courtroom dramas based on actual cases involving family disputes

Cast: Robert F. Shield *(Judge Robert J. Franklin)*.

4817   Judge Alex. (Series; Drama; Syn.; 2005–). Actual small claims court cases presided over by Alex Ferrer, a former police officer turned judge (one of the more relaxed judges on TV).

Judge: Alex Ferrer. **Bailiff:** Victor Scott.

4818   The Judge and Jake Wyler. (Pilot; Crime Drama; NBC; Dec. 2, 1972). Judge Meredith is a retired, hypochondriac lady magistrate. Jake Wyler is a charming ex-con serving his probation with her. With time on her hands and a need to pursue justice, the Judge and Jake open a private detective agency. The proposal was to relate their efforts to help people in deep trouble.

Cast: Bette Davis *(Judge Meredith)*; Doug McClure *(Jake Wyler)*.

4819   Judge David Young. (Series; Reality; Syn.; 2007–2009). Real small claims cases presided over by David Young, an openly admitted gay judge (and television's first such star of a syndicated court series). That aspect aside, the program follows the format of other such programs with the plaintiffs and defendants presenting their own cases before the judge (whose final decision is binding and cannot be appealed elsewhere).

Judge: David Young. **Bailiff:** Antonia Young.

4820   Judge Dee. (Pilot; Mystery; ABC; Dec. 29, 1974). Seventeenth century China is the setting for a proposal about Judge Dee, a Chinese magistrate who roams the country solving crimes (usually murder) and dispensing justice where needed.

Cast: Khigh Dhiegh *(Judge Dee)*.

4821   Judge for Yourself. (Series; Game; NBC; 1953-1954). Performances by promising new talent acts. Three studio audience members and three guest judges rate performances. In a later format, a panel rated the merit of new songs performed by Kitty Kallen, Bob Carroll and The Skylarks.

Host: Fred Allen, Dennis James. **Vocalists:** Kitty Kallen, Bob Carroll, Judy Johnson, The Skylarks. **Announcer:** Dennis James, Don Pardo. **Music Director:** Milton DeLugg.

4822   *Judge for Yourself.* (Series; Drama; Syn.; 1995). An actual court case is reenacted with twelve studio audience members serving as the jury. Following the deliberations, the case is discussed with the audience and the jury's verdict is revealed at the end of the program. Home viewers could also cast a guilty or not guilty vote through 900 telephone numbers.
   Narrator: Bill Handel.

4823   *Judge Hatchett.* (Series; Drama; Syn.; 2000). Actual small claims court cases presided over by Judge Glenda Hatchett.
   Judge: Glenda Hatchett. **Bailiff:** Tom O'Riordan.

4824   *Judge Jeanine Pirro.* (Series; Reality; CW, 2008-2009; Syn., 2009–). Former Westchester County (New York) district attorney and judge, Jeanine Pirro, presides over real small claims cases.
   Judge: Jeanine Pirro.

4825   *Judge Joe Brown.* (Series; Drama; Syn.; 1997–). Actual small claims courtroom cases presided over by Judge Joe Brown.
   Program Open: "He's a real judge. In his courtroom everyone has the right to a fair trial. But if they are proven wrong, he has the right to make them pay. *Judge Joe Brown.*"
   Judge: Joe Brown. **Bailiff:** Holly Evans. **Commentator:** Jacque Kessler, Jeanne Zelesko. **Announcer:** Ben Patrick Johnson, Rolonda Watts.

4826   *Judge Judy.* (Series; Drama; Syn.; 1996). A daily program of actual small claims court cases presided over by America's most famous judge, Judith Sheindlin.
   Program Open: "You are about to enter the courtroom of Judge Judith Sheindlin. The people are real, The cases are real. The rulings are final. This is *Judge Judy.*"
   Judge: Judith Sheindlin. **Bailiff:** Petri Hawkins-Byrd. **Announcer:** Jerry Bishop. **Music:** Bill Bodine.

4827   *Judge Karen.* (Series; Reality; Syn.; 2008-2009). Daily program of actual small claims cases presided over by Judge Karen Mills-Francis. In 2009 after one season, *Judge Karen* was canceled and replaced by *Street Court.* When the replacement failed to generate ratings, it was replaced by *Judge Karen's Court* in 2010 with Karen Mills-Francis overseeing small claims cases in much the same way she did on the original series.
   Judge: Karen Mills-Francis. **Bailiff:** Christopher Gallo.

4828   *Judge Maria Lopez.* (Series; Drama; Syn.; 2006). Actual small claims court cases presided over by Judge Maria Lopez. The program opens with Maria's words: "There's only one person who decides the truth—I do. I tell it like it is. I was a judge for 15 years. I've seen it all. I came to this country as a little girl from Cuba. Talk about the American Dream. I am the American Dream."
   Judge: Maria Lopez. **Bailiff:** Pete Rodriquez.

4829   *Judge Mathis.* (Series; Drama; Syn.; 1999). A daily program of actual small claims court cases presided over by Judge Greg Mathis. Judge Mathis opens the program: "Troubled kids? I was one. Gangs, jail—I was there. Second chances. I got one. I went to law school, became a lawyer and then a judge. Now I get to give second chances. In my courtroom the disputes are real. The cases are real. It's time for hard decisions and tough love. That's what I'm about."

Judge: *Greg Mathis.* **Bailiff:** Doyle Deveraux, Kevin Lingle, Brendan Morgan.

4830   *Judge Mills Lane.* (Series; Drama; Syn.; 1998). Actual small claims court cases presided over by Mills Lane, a very strict, no-nonsense judge—you obey his rules (like no talking when he is talking, or when the opposing litigant is talking) or are thrown out of the courtroom and lose the case.
   Program Open: "He grew up in the country and in the corps. He was a boxer, a lawyer, a prosecutor and a referee. In the ring and in the courtroom he's fair and he's firm. A fighter and a family man, He's Mills Lane, America's judge."
   Judge: Mills Lane. **Bailiff:** Jasper Cole, Ron Smith. **Court Reporter:** Kym Adams.

4831   *Judge Roy Bean.* (Series; Western; Syn.; 1955-1956). Roy Bean, the self-appointed judge of Langtry, Texas (1870s), is also the town's sheriff and owner of Roy Bean's General Store. He is a bit on the heavy side, nearsighted without his glasses, older than the typical Wild West lawman and fond of apple pie. He is not quick on the draw, nor does he carry a fancy gun. He does possess a genius for figuring out the criminal mind and conning the con man. The judge does take an active part in apprehending outlaws; the rough work falls on the shoulders of his deputy, Jeff Taggard, a young man who is fast on the draw and quick with his fists.
   Assisting Roy in the store is his niece, Letty Bean, who came to live with him after the death of her parents. She is beautiful, extremely feminine and dynamite with a gun (her dress conceals a gun strapped to her ankle). While Jeff does court her, he calls her "a big tomboy" and admires her ability to handle a gun—"You shoot just like a man." Letty is forever getting angry when Jeff thinks of her as a man and remarks, "Can't you think of me as a woman just once?" He tries—at least for the remainder of that particular episode.
   Carson City is the neighboring town; Salt Lake City is the community north of Langtry; and the Southern Pacific Railroad services the area.
   Program Open: "During the 1870s, as the railroads pushed their way west, they attracted the most vicious characters in the country. Soon, the desolate region west of the Pecos River became known as the wildest spot in the United States. It was said that civilization and law stopped at the east bank of the Pecos. It took the courage of one man, a lone storekeeper who was sick of the lawlessness, to change all this. His name was Judge Roy Bean."
   Cast: Edgar Buchanan (*Judge Roy Bean*); Jean Lewis, Jackie Loughery (*Letty Bean*); Jack Beutel (*Jeff Taggard*); Russell Hayden (*Steve; a Texas Ranger*).

4832   *Judging Amy.* (Series; Drama; CBS; 1999–2005). Amy Gray is a corporate lawyer in New York City. She is married to Michael and is the mother of Lauren. Shortly after Lauren's fifth birthday, Michael wanted out of the marriage but wasn't brave enough to say it so Amy said it for him. A month later he was with someone else and Amy moved back to her hometown of Hartford, Connecticut, where she and Lauren take up residence with her mother, Maxine Gray, a former lawyer turned social worker.
   Life is now progressing well for Amy, especially when she becomes a Juvenile Court judge (also said to be a Family Court judge). Lauren, however, doesn't like "the judge thing" and wants a normal family life. Amy can't promise her that, but assures her "that raising you is the best job I'll ever have." Stories follow Amy as she struggles to be a single parent despite the demands of her career. Lauren attends Jefferson Elementary School; Maxine, who not only helps raise Lauren, but helps Amy with her career, has a dog named Socrates.
   Cast: Amy Brenneman (*Amy Gray*); Tyne Daly (*Maxine Gray*);

Karle Warren (*Lauren Cassidy*); Dan Futterman (*Vincent Gray*); Jessica Tuck (*Gillian Gray*); Marcus Giamatti (*Peter Gray*); Jillian Armenate (*Donna Kozlowski*); Timothy Omundson (*Sean Potter*); Richard T. Jones (*Bruce Van Exel*); Columbus Short (*Thomas McNab*); Alice Dodd (*Kimberly Fallon*); Richard Crenna (*Jared Duff*); Sarah Danielle Madison (*Heather Labonte*); Sara Mornell (*Carole Tobey*); Reed Diamond (*Stuart Collins*); Cheech Marin (*Ignacio Messina*); Kristin Lehman (*Dr. Lily Reddicker*); Inny Clemons (*Robert Clifton*); Adrian Pasdar (*David McClaren*); Kevin Rahm (*Kyle McCarty*).

4833   *Judgment Day.* (Pilot; Drama; NBC; Dec. 6, 1981). An unusual proposal that is set in a celestial courtroom where a deceased is sent to be judged for either Heaven or Hell. The in-limbo soul, seated before the Judge, is placed on trial and Mr. Heavener (representing Heaven) and Mr. Heller (representing Hell) present the good and bad aspects of that person's life (seen in flashbacks). The Judge views these aspects to determine whether the forces of good or evil acquire the soul.

Cast: Barry Sullivan (*The Judge*); Victor Buono (*Mr. Heavener*); Roddy McDowall (*Mr. Heller*).

4834   *The Judy Garland Show.* (Series; Variety; CBS; 1963-1964). Actress Judy Garland's only television series, a weekly program that teams Judy with a guest star for songs, dances and light comedy.

Host: Judy Garland. **Regular:** Jerry Van Dyke. **Orchestra:** Mort Lindsey. **Special Musical Material:** Mel Torme.

4835   *The Judy Lynn Show.* (Series; Variety; Syn.; 1969). Singer-musician Judy Lynn oversees a program of performances by country and western entertainers.

4836   *Judy Splinters.* (Series; Children; NBC; 1949-1950). Judy Splinters is the female dummy of ventriloquist Shirley Dinsdale. Judy is quite mischievous and while stories relate her antics, it focuses in particular on Judy's endless matchmaking attempts as she tries to find a husband for Shirley.

Hostess: Shirley Dinsdale.

4837   *Judy's Got a Gun.* (Pilot; Crime Drama; Unaired; Produced for ABC in 2007). After a five-year hiatus, Judy Lemen, a single mother (of seven-year-old Brenna) returns to her job as a police officer with the San Carlos, California P.D. Despite being a small city, San Carlos is crime ridden and Judy, a street cop, has set her sights on becoming a detective. The proposal was to follow Judy as she tackles the two toughest jobs in America — motherhood and crime fighting.

Cast: Louise Lombard (*Judy Lemen*); Bailee Madison (*Brenna Lemen*); Colm Feore (*Captain Ruttgauer*); Margo Harshman (*Maya Spektor*); Michael Michele (*Pamela Coates*); Keith Powell (*Brad Wilkes*).

4838   *Julia.* (Series; Comedy; NBC; 1968–1971). Julia Baker is a registered nurse with the Inner Aero-Space Center, an industrial health office in Los Angeles. She is a recent widow (her husband, an Air Force captain, was killed in Viet Nam) and the mother of a young son (Corey). Stories follow Julia's life at work and at home and her efforts to raise her son as a single mother.

Other regulars are Dr. Morton Chegley, Julia's employer; Hannah Yarby, the head nurse; Carol Deering, Julia's part-time mother's helper; Ted Neumann, Julia's romantic interest (later replaced by Paul Carter, then Steve Bruce); Melba Chegley, Morton's wife; Earl J. Waggedorn, Corey's friend; Marie and Len, Earl's parents; Sol Cooper, Julia's landlord; Mrs. Deering, Carol's mother; Roberta,

Corey's babysitter; Lou, Julia's uncle; and Mrs. Bennett, a tenant in Julia's building.

Cast: Diahann Carroll (*Julia Baker*); Lloyd Nolan (*Dr. Morton Chegley*); Marc Copage (*Corey Baker*); Michael Link (*Earl J. Waggedorn*); Betty Beaird (*Marie Waggedorn*); Hank Brandt (*Len Waggedorn*); Lurene Tuttle (*Hannah Yarby*); Alison Mills (*Carol Deering*); Ned Glass (*Sol Cooper*); Virginia Capers (*Mrs. Deering*); Don Marshall (*Ted Neumann*); Chuck Wood, Paul Winfield (*Paul Carter*); Fred Williamson (*Steve Bruce*); Janear Hines (*Roberta*); Eugene Jackson (*Lou*); Mary Wickes (*Melba Chegley*); Jeff Donnell (*Mrs. Bennett*).

4839   *Julie.* (Series; Comedy; ABC; 1992). *The Julie Carlisle Show* is a top rated variety program produced in Hollywood. When star Julie Carlisle decides to marry Dr. Sam McGuire, a veterinarian with a practice in Sioux City, she also decides to move her show to Iowa — to make her marriage work (Julie's first marriage ended in divorce when "my career got in the way. I'm not going to let it happen again"). Her program is now taped at KCDM-TV, Channel 10, in Sioux City.

Julie sings in the key of C, and her first job was that of understudy to an actress named Minerva Philbert. Sam calls Julie "Jules," and she hates the song "Feelings."

Sam is a widower and the father of two children: 14-year-old Allie and 12-year-old Adam.

Sam runs the animal clinic and teaches at Iowa State University. Allie takes singing and dancing lessons and has a dog named Dog; Sam coaches the Tigers Little League team.

I.F. ("Wooley") Wollstein is Julie's always complaining, easily upset producer; and Clem is Sam's gorgeous assistant (a situation that seems not to upset Julie). Originally titled *Millie* and starred Julie Andrews as Millie Cramer (storyline and supporting characters are the same).

Henry Mancini composed the theme, "Julie" (which, surprisingly, has no vocal by Julie Andrews).

Cast: Julie Andrews (*Julie Carlisle*); James Farentino (*Dr. Sam McGuire*); Hayley Tyrie (*Allie McGuire*); Rider Strong (*Adam McGuire*); Eugene Roche (*I.F. Wollstein*); Alicia Brandt (*Clem*).

4840   *The Julie Andrews Hour.* (Series; Variety; ABC; 1972-1973). Music, songs, dances and comedy with singer-actress Julie Andrews as the host.

Host: Julie Andrews. **Regulars:** Rich Little, Alice Ghostley, The Tony Charmoli Dancers, The Dick Williams Singers. **Announcer:** Dick Tufeld. **Orchestra:** Nelson Riddle.

4841   *The Julie Brown Show.* (Pilot; Comedy; NBC; July 28, 1991). As a young girl, Julie Robbins kidnapped herself to raise the ransom to buy a Barbie Dream House. She sold cosmetics, did a commercial for a bug killer and now works as the celebrity reporter for *Inside Scoop*, a TV show that looks behind the news stories. The proposal was to follow Julie's misadventures as she hits the streets to get the scoops. Other regulars are Debra, the host of *Inside Scoop* (she worked for Greenpeace, danced in the New York Ballet for three years, speaks five languages and was second runner-up as Miss Ohio in the Miss America Pageant); Cheryl, Julie's roommate (she has show business contacts — "I know everyone at the Home Shopping Network by their first names"); Tony, the show's producer; and Janet, Julie's mother. Julie Brown performs the theme, "I Know Who I Am."

Cast: Julie Brown (*Julie Robbins*); DeLane Matthews (*Debra Deacon*); Susan Messing (*Cheryl*); Kevin O'Rourke (*Tony Barnell*); Marian Mercer (*Janet Robbins*).

4842   *Julie Brown: The Show.* (Pilot; Comedy; CBS; Sept. 4,

1989). *Julie Brown: The Show* is a fictional CBS TV talk program hosted by bubbly actress Julie Brown. The proposal was to relate her misadventures on and off the set. Other regulars are Grant, her co-host; Candace, the producer; Jeff, the director; Michelle, the secretary; and Rhonda, the make-up lady. Julie Brown performs the theme, "The Art of Being Fabulous."

Cast: Julie Brown *(Herself)*; Larry Poindexter *(Grant)*; Marcia Strassman *(Candace)*; Adam Arkin *(Jeff Goldner)*; Nada Despotovich *(Michelle)*; Luisa Leschin *(Rhonda)*.

4843 Julie Farr, M.D. (Series; Drama; ABC; 1978-1979). Julie Farr, an obstetrician with a private practice at 13471 East La Brea, is also on call at City Memorial Hospital in Los Angeles. Julie, originally in residence at Riverside Hospital, is proud of her work. It has taken her a long time to build her practice and she has put off marrying and raising a family of her own to help women she feels are dependent upon her. Dr. Blake Simmons works with Julie at City Memorial Hospital, and Kelly Williams is Julie's receptionist (Alice Hirson, as Mimi, was Julie's original receptionist). The series, which deals with the joys and traumas of childbirth, was originally titled *Having Babies* (see title for information on the pilot film). Marilyn McCoo sings the theme, "There Will Be Love."

Cast: Susan Sullivan *(Julie Farr)*; Mitchell Ryan *(Blake Simmons)*; Beverly Todd *(Kelly Williams)*; Dennis Howard *(Rod Danvers)*.

4844 Julie Reno, Bounty Hunter. (Series; Unaired; Comedy; Produced for Fox in 2007). Julie Reno is a young, single mother (of Eileen), lives in Reno, Nevada, and works as a bounty hunter. Julie is tough and not afraid of confrontation. She does what she has to get the job done. Stories were set to follow her exploits — made more complicated by her jealous (of her abilities) partner T-Bone, as she tracks down the most dangerous bail jumpers in the state.

Cast: Erin Daniels *(Julie Reno)*; Brooke MacKenzie *(Eileen Reno)*; Vincent Ventresca *(T-Bone)*; Cindy Cheung *(Li Ming)*; Windell Middlebrooks *(Windell)*; Spencer Hill *(Freddy)*.

4845 Julius Caesar. (Experimental; Drama; NBC; Mar. 15, 1940). The first known television adaptation of William Shakespeare's classic story about the life and times of the Roman emperor, Julius Caesar.

Cast: Judson Laire *(Julius Caesar)*; Muriel Hutchinson *(Portia)*; Patrick Ludlow *(Cassius)*; Eric Mansfield *(Casca)*; Evelyn Allen *(Calpurnia)*; Richard Coogan *(Decius)*; Douglas Gilmore *(Antonius)*; Grant Gordon *(Cinna)*; Arthur Alexander *(Lucius)*.

4846 The Julius LaRosa Show. (Series; Variety; NBC; 1955; 1956; 1957). Singer Julius LaRosa hosts a program of music and songs. Three versions appeared:

1. The Julius LaRosa Show (NBC, 1955). **Host:** Julius LaRosa. **Regulars:** Sherry Ostrus, Connie Desmond, Bix Brent, Irene Carroll. **Orchestra:** Russ Case.

2. The Julius LaRosa Show (NBC, 1956). **Host:** Julius LaRosa. **Regulars:** George DeWitt, The Mariners, The Spellbinders, The Evans Dancers. **Orchestra:** Mitchell Ayres.

3. Perry Como Presents the Julius LaRosa Show (NBC, 1957). **Host:** Julius LaRosa. **Regulars:** Steve Ashton, Lou Cosler, The Artie Malvin Chorus, The Louis Da Pron Dancers. **Orchestra:** Mitchell Ayres.

4847 Jumanji. (Series; Cartoon; UPN; 1996-1997). An animated adaptation of the feature film of the same title. Many years ago a man named Alan Parrish found a board game called Jumanji (which has a life of its own). He opened the box, laid out the board and rolled the dice. A rhyming message appeared and he was sucked into the game, apparently trapped there forever. In 1996 Peter and Judy

Shepherd, an orphaned brother and sister, come to live with their Aunt Nora. While exploring the house they come across the cursed board game Jumanji. Curiosity gets the best of them and they begin playing the game. The dice are rolled, a rhyming clue appears and they too are transported to the strange jungle-like world of Jumanji. Here, they meet and befriend Alan and the three join forces to solve the mystery of the riddles and return to their own world. Thwarting their attempts is Van Pelt, an English hunter (who is seeking Alan as prey), his foil Oafel, and a mad inventor named Master Builder.

Voice Cast: Bill Fagerbakke *(Alan Parrish)*; Debi Derryberry *(Judy Shepherd)*; Ashley Johnson *(Peter Shepherd)*; Melanie Chartoff *(Nora Shepherd)*; Sherman Howard *(Van Pelt)*; Dabney Coleman *(Ashton Phillips)*; Richard Allen *(Officer Bentley)*; Tim Curry *(Trader Slick)*.

4848 Jump! (Pilot; Variety; NBC; May 31, 1984). Eight dancers perform video-style vignettes that sketch the moods of the songs they perform. A second pilot, *Jump II*, aired on Jan. 16, 1985.

Dancers: Chelsea Field, Peggy Holmes, Brad Jeffries, Kenneth Jezek, Lynda Baines Johnson, Vincent Paterson, Kimmy Smith, Peter Tramm. **Music:** Gary Scott. **Choreography:** Kenny Ortega.

4849 Jumpin' Joe. (Pilot; Drama; ABC; July 9, 1992). Joe Dugan is a widower and the father of two youngsters (Beth and Joey). Joe was a former ball player whose promising career was ended when he was hit by a pitched ball and injured. The proposal was to relate Joe's efforts to find work (he lives from check to check) and provide a decent life for Beth and Joey. Other regulars are Irene, Joe's mother; Patsy, Joe's friend; and Christine, Joe's wife (seen in flashbacks).

Cast: Ron Eldard *(Joe Dugan)*; Amy Reedman *(Beth Dugan)*; Gregory Smith *(Joey Dugan)*; Caroline Kava *(Irene Dugan)*; Kehli O'Byrne *(Christine Dugan)*; Paul Ben-Victor *(Patsy)*.

4850 The June Allyson Show. (Series; Anthology; CBS; 1959–1961). Original dramatic presentations, including those written especially for host Jane Allyson, are presented by producer Dick Powell. Also known as *The DuPont Show with June Allyson*. Notable performers are Dick Powell, June Allyson, Gerald Mohr, Rossano Brazzi, Joseph Cotton, Russell Johnson, Maxine Stuart, Henry Beckman, Chester Stratton, Alan Reed, Jr., David White, Celia Lovsky.

Host: June Allyson. **Announcer:** Donald Rickles.

4851 The June Havoc Show. (Series; Interview; Syn.; 1964). Actress June Havoc oversees a daily program of celebrity interviews.

4852 Jungle Boy. (Series; Adventure; Syn.; 1957). The shortened title for *The Adventures of a Jungle Boy*. See this title for information.

4853 Jungle Cubs. (Series; Cartoon; ABC; 1996). A prequel to the Disney movie *The Jungle Book* that presents younger versions of the film's main characters as they struggle to survive in the wild: Baloo the Bear, Hathi the Panther, Shere Kahn the Tiger; Prince Louie the Ape and Kaa the Snake.

Voice Cast: Charles Adler *(Ned)*; Pamela Adlon *(Baloo the Bear)*; Jason Marsden, Cree Summer *(Louie the Ape)*; Jason Marsden *(Shere)*; Jim Cummings *(Kaa)*; Kath Soucie *(Winifred)*; Rob Paulsen *(Akela the Wolf)*; Tress MacNeille *(Martha)*; Stephen Furst *(Hathi)*; Jim Cummings *(Fred)*; Dee Bradley Baker *(Bagheera)*.

4854 Jungle Jim. (Series; Adventure; Syn.; 1955). A man known and respected as Jungle Jim is an African Safari guide. He is a widower and lives with his son, Skipper, in Nairobi, Africa. While Jim earns his living as a guide, he also finds himself becoming a defender of his domain when he battles the unscrupulous characters who seek to harm the animals or cause problems among the native tribes. Skipper assists Jim on the guide tours as does Kaseem, their Hindu servant. They also receive help from Trader, Skipper's dog and Tamba, Jim's chimpanzee. Based on characters created by Alex Raymond.

Cast: Johnny Weissmuller (*Jungle Jim*); Martin Huston (*Skipper*); Norman Fredric (*Kaseem*); Peggy (*Tamba*).

4855   *Jungle of Fear.* (Pilot; Drama; NBC; April 22, 1965). Panama in 1850 is the setting for a proposal about a casino owner known only as O'Rourke who helps people in trouble. Broadcast on *Kraft Suspense Theater.*

Cast: Robert Fuller (*O'Rourke*).

4856   *Junior Almost Anything Goes.* (Series; Game; ABC; 1976-1977). A children's version of *Almost Anything Goes* that features three four-member teams competing in outrageous outdoor games for prizes.

Host: Soupy Sales. **Commentator:** Eddie Alexander. **Music:** The Junior High School Band.

4857   *Junior High Jinks.* (Series; Game; CBS; 1952). The antics of Willie the Worm, the puppet of ventriloquist Warren Wright (who also showcases comedy shorts from the 1920s and 1930s).

Host: Warren Wright.

4858   *Junior Miss.* (Pilot; Comedy; CBS; Dec. 30, 1957). Judy and Lois are the teenage daughters of Harry and Grace Graves. Lois is a college girl with her two feet planted firmly on the ground. Judy, an imaginative high school girl, is overly concerned about the problems of others. The proposal was to relate the situations that arise when Judy feels the need to help people—whether they want her help or not. Fuffy is Judy's friend; Willis is Judy's uncle; J.B. is Harry's employer; Ellen is J.B.'s daughter.

Cast: Carol Lynley (*Judy Graves*); Don Ameche (*Harry Graves*); Joan Bennett (*Grace Graves*); Jill St. John (*Lois Graves*); Susanne Sidney (*Fuffy Adams*); David Wayne (*Willis Reynolds*); Paul Ford (*J.B. Curtis*); Diana Linn (*Ellen Curtis*).

4859   *Junior Rodeo.* (Series; Children; ABC; 1952). A program of games, music and songs geared to children. Bob Atcher hosts and is assisted by Valerie Alberts.

4860   *The Jury.* (Series; Drama; Fox; 2004). A failed attempt to present a twist on typical lawyer programs. Instead of focusing on the actual court case, the program goes behind the scenes to look at what transpires in the jury deliberation room. While the jury ponders the facts in a capital case, flashbacks are used to reveal the particulars of the case in question. After the jury reaches its decision and the verdict is revealed, the concluding aspects of the actual case is shown.

Cast: Billy Burke (*John Ranguso*); Adam Busch (*Steve Dixon*); Cote de Pablo (*Marguerite Cisneros*); Anna Friel (*Megan Delaney*); Shalom Harlow (*Melissa Greenfield*); Jeffrey Hephner (*Keenan O'Brien*).

4861   *Jury Duty.* (Series; Reality; Syn.; 2007). Real life small claims cases are brought before a real judge but in a twist on the traditional judge programs, a panel of three celebrity jurors are allowed to question the plaintiff and defendant then deliberate before offering a verdict.

Judge: Bruce Cutler. **Rotating Jurors:** Charlene Tilton, Todd Bridges, Ed Begley, Jr., Phyllis Diller, Scott Hamilton, Kevin Sorbo, Shadoe Stevens, Dick Van Patten, Bruce Vilanch, Paula Poundstone, Vicki Roberts.

4862   *Just a Coupla Guys.* (Pilot; Comedy; NBC; Dec. 14, 1979). Eugene and Mickey are klutzy New Jersey punks desperately trying to break into the rackets. The proposal, broadcast on *The Rockford Files* was to relate their misguided efforts to achieve that goal.

Cast: Greg Antonacci (*Eugene*); Gene Davis (*Mickey*).

4863   *Just a Phase.* (Pilot; Comedy; Unaired; Produced for ABC Family in 2004). Simon is a teenage boy with a problem: he appears to like girls, but he is also attracted to boys. The proposal was to follow Simon as he attempts to come to terms with his sexual identity.

Cast: Mitchel David Federan (*Simon*); Andrea Brooks (*Jennifer*); Brett Kelly (*Jackson*); Carly McKillip (*Suzie*); James Michael McCauley (*Butch*); Kristin Kowalski (*Gail*).

4864   *Just Cause.* (Series; Crime Drama; PAX; 2002-2003). Alexandra DeMonaco is a young woman seeking to begin a new life. She has just been released from prison after serving three years of a five year sentence for insurance fraud. During her time at the Mendocino Women's Prison, Alexandra, called Alex, studied law via Bay City College's internet program. Although Alex acquired her degree, she is a felon and is thus unable to practice law. Alex was framed but she can't prove it. She was working as the office manager for her husband, Jason, a lawyer. Unknown to Alex, her husband was working with unethical doctors to defraud insurance companies. When an investigation into her husband's business affairs showed that Alex had manipulated the books, she was arrested and her husband disappeared, taking their daughter, Mia, with him. She chose to use her time in prison to become a lawyer to help people.

Burdick, Whitney and Morgan is a prestigious San Francisco law firm. It is here that Alex hopes to find a job and get her name cleared by a pardon from the governor. Her meeting with senior partner Hamilton Whitney III nets her a job as his researcher when he becomes impressed by her enthusiasm.

Alex is not your typical researcher or paralegal. She is a bright and determined woman with the mind of a detective. Her enthusiasm and sleuthing skills immediately change Whitney's way of thinking when Alex proves two cases of corporate suicide were actually murder. Whitney changes the focus of the law firm from civil litigation to criminal defense.

Alex was a model prisoner and has been released on parole. She was born in East Los Angeles and attended Roosevelt High School. In prison she worked kitchen detail and says, "I developed a talent for reading people." Although she is not supposed to associate with felons, Alex does break parole by visiting her prison friends for help in solving crimes. She likes to do her own detective work but becomes too emotionally involved in cases.

Alex, called Miss DeMonaco by Whitney, believes her boss is rich and stuck up as he appears to be all work and no play. Whitney, a graduate of Harvard Law School, has an undergraduate degree in Asiatic languages. Whitney comes from a family of professionals: his father was a surgeon; his uncle, the author of a book called *Just Cause,* was a criminal lawyer. Whitney will not violate a court order ("I have a code of ethics"). He loves San Francisco and hates to see it dragged through the mud. He says of Alex, "She's a bully. She won't listen. She irritates the hell out of me."

Whitney has been married three times and maintains a working relationship with his third wife, Rebecca, an FBI agent whom he met when she interrogated him during a case.

Cast: Elizabeth Lackey (*Alexandra DeMonaco*); Richard Thomas (*Hamilton Whitney III*); Shaun Heller (*Shaun Benson*); Roger R. Cross (*C.J. Leon*); Khairia Ledeyo (*Peggy Tran*); Mark Hildreth (*Ted Kasselbaum*).

4865 *Just Deal.* (Series; Drama; NBC; 2000–2002). The fictional town of Beachwood, Washington, is the setting for a dramatic look at the events that spark the lives of three teenage friends — Dylan Roberts, Ashley Gordon (called Ash) and Jermaine Green.

Just Deal premiered on September 23, 2000 and became part of NBC's Saturday morning teen block of shows called T-NBC (which included *Saved by the Bell, One World, Hang Time* and *All About Us*). With the exception of *Skate*, which mixed comedy with light drama, *Just Deal* was all drama and departed from the T-NBC style. Surprisingly, it became a hit but by the fall of 2002, when NBC dropped its T-NBC (in favor of Discover Kids on NBC) *Just Deal* was also cancelled.

Other regulars are Mike and Colleen Roberts, Dylan's parents; Mike Jr., Dylan's older brother; Mandy, Mike Jr.'s girlfriend; and Naomi, Hunter and Kim, other friends of Ashley.

Cast: Brian T. Skala (*Dylan Roberts*); Erika Thormahlen (*Ashley Gordon*); Shedrack Anderson III (*Jermaine Green*); Fiona Scott (*Naomi Esterbrook*); Kandyse McClure (*Kim*); Eileen Pedde (*Colleen Roberts*); Eric Keenleyside (*Mike Roberts, Sr.*); William Sanderson (*Mike Roberts, Jr.*); John L. Adams (*Andre Peno*).

4866 *Just Deserts.* (Pilot; Drama; ABC; Aug. 15, 1992). Whisper Mountain is a mysterious retreat where evil doers find their just deserts. Michael Price is the director, a mysterious man who runs the resort with a woman named Amy. Michael appears as various people — the manager, the bellboy, caretaker, reservations clerk — whoever is needed he becomes to see that the evil are punished (for example, allowing an unscrupulous person to face the consequences of what he is doing; permitting a murdered woman to return to life to catch her killer). The proposal was to present anthology-like tales of evil people who get what they deserve.

Cast: Joel Grey (*Michael Price*); Jane Leeves (*Amy*).

4867 *Just for Laughs.* (Series; Comedy; ABC; 2007). An extreme version of *Candid Camera* that pulls very elaborate practical jokes on unsuspecting people. Their reactions, caught by hidden cameras, is the focal point of the program. The program addresses itself as "The biggest hidden camera show. "We've hidden cameras where you least expect them — just for laughs."

Host: Rick Miller.

4868 *Just in Time.* (Series; Comedy; ABC; 1988). *The West Coast Review*, "California's Monthly Magazine," was established in 1967 and is based in a skyscraper at 133 Wilshire Boulevard. When its rival, *California Magazine*, begins to show an increase in circulation (to 350,000 copies) and Review's numbers begin to fall drastically, management hires Harry Stadlin, the editor of Chicago Magazine, to turn their publication around. His assignment (which he has six months to accomplish): make the revamped *West Coast*, "California's Weekly Magazine," a success. Stories follow his efforts and his romantic relationship with Joanna Gail Farrell, the magazine's beautiful, vibrant and free spirited columnist-reporter.

Isabel Miller is the art department director, and Carlie Hightower is the magazine's gossip columnist. The La Crosse is the local bar-restaurant hangout. See also *It Had to Be You* for information on the pilot film.

Cast: Tim Matheson (*Harry Stadlin*); Patricia Kalember (*Joanna Farrell*); Nada Despotovich (*Isabel Miller*); Ronnie Claire Edwards (*Carlie Hightower*).

4869 *Just Jordan.* (Series; Comedy; Nick; 2007). Justin Lewis is a 16-year-old from Little Rock, Arkansas, who must readjust to life when his single mother, Pamela, relocates the family to California, to live with her father, Grant. Stories follow Jordan as he encounters the everyday 1950s–like television kid adventures (wholesome and clean) with his friends Joaquin and Tony. Monica is Jordan's sister; Tangie is Jordan's cousin; Tamika is the girl on whom Jordan has a crush but is too shy to do anything but keep it a personal secret. Jordan works part time at the diner (Papa Grant's Fresh 'n Grill) owned by his grandfather.

Cast: James "Lil' JJ" Lewis (*Jordan Lewis*); Shana Accius (*Pamela Lewis*); Kristen Combs (*Monica Lewis*); Beau Billingslea (*Grant Cunningham*); Raven Goodwin (*Tangie*); Eddy Martin (*Joaquin*); Justin Chon (*Tony Park*); Chelsea Harris (*Tamika Newsome*).

4870 *Just Legal.* (Series; Crime Drama; WB; 2005-2006). Grant Cooper is a down on his luck criminal defense attorney with a drinking problem. He is cynical but once he gets involved in a case he does what it takes to win. David Ross, called Skip (for skipping grades in school) is an 18-year-old prodigy and lawyer who, because of his age, is unable to acquire a job with a law firm (they find he is too young). Skip feels his age is a plus because it gives him the time to become what he wants — possibly a trial lawyer "because every great cause in this country was fought by trial lawyers."

Skip is a graduate of U.C.L.A. and is first seen as a caddy for Grant (exactly how they know each other is not really explained). When Grant learns of Skip's dilemma he takes him on as a partner to give him a taste of the legal profession. The two become an odd couple–like team and stories follow their cases as they defend clients with little money and nowhere else to turn.

Grant seeks press for his cases but he can never seem to get it (he hopes the publicity will put him on the map). Grant was a great trial lawyer with a big ego. During a cop beating case, Grant was accused of bribing a witness — a false fact he couldn't disprove and it cost him his career. Skip is, as he says, "an up with people guy." He likes to do things by the book — something he can't always do because Grant believes that to win a case you sometimes have to make bad deals. Working with Grant contradicts everything Skip learned in law school. Dulcinea Real (called Dee) assists Grant and Skip in their one flight up office in California.

Cast: Don Johnson (*Grant Cooper*); Jay Baruchel (*David "Skip" Ross*); Jamie Lee Kirchner (*Dulcinea "Dee" Real*).

4871 *Just Life.* (Pilot; Crime Drama; ABC; July 26, 1990). Claire Moreno is divorced (from Joe), the mother of a young girl (Lulu) and a former police officer turned investigator for the Los Angeles District Attorney's Office. The proposal was to relate Claire's case investigations. David Robbins is the D.A.

Cast: Victoria Principal (*Claire Moreno*); Alanna Ubach (*Lulu Moreno*); Nicholas Surovy (*David Robbins*); Joe Cortese (*Joe Moreno*).

4872 *Just Married.* (Pilot; Comedy; ABC; May 10, 1985). Shortly after Linda Shaughnessy and Michael "Mikey" Altobello marry, they find a glitch in their happiness via Linda's father, Jake, who believes that Mikey, a construction worker, is not worthy of his little girl. The proposal was to relate the newlyweds' struggles to make their marriage work despite Jake's constant interference. Doreen and Buddy are Linda's neighbors.

Cast: Gail Edwards (*Linda Altobello*); Paul Reiser (*Mikey Altobello*); Barton Heyman (*Jake Shaughnessy*); Kathleen Wilhoite (*Doreen Banasack*); Matt Craven (*Buddy Banasack*).

4873 *Just Men.* (Series; Game; NBC; 1983). Two female contestants compete; seven male celebrities appear. The object calls for the contestants to predict, with a yes or no answer, how the celebrities will respond to specific questions asked of them (for example, "Are you a grouch in the morning?"). A player chooses a celebrity and is permitted to indirectly interview him. After 60 seconds she must give her prediction. The celebrity reveals his "yes" or "no" card. If the contestant is correct, she receives a set of car keys possessed by that celebrity. The player with the most sets of car keys is the winner and receives the opportunity to win a new car. The player selects one of the sets of car keys that she has won and uses it to start a car that appears on stage. If the car starts, she wins the car; if not, she returns to compete again.

Hostess: Betty White. **Music:** Stormy Stacks.

4874 *Just One of the Girls*. (Pilot; Comedy; Unaired; Produced for CBS in 1992). When a financial setback threatens to close the Crawford Academy, an expensive private school for girls, headmistress Dorothy Loomis changes the enrollment to allow boys. Claire meets opposition from the uptight Coach Dezell, who feels a coed school will not work. After much discussion, Dezell agrees to a test program — to allow one boy to enroll. Rob McGuire becomes the test subject and the unsold series was to focus on Rob as he becomes "one of the girls" and struggles to follow all the rules (one violation will cause his dismissal). Other regulars called "little hoodlums" by Coach Dezell are Allison, the prettiest girl at the school ("America's perfect sitcom daughter"); Didi, a tough-talking, street-wise Italian-American whose father is in the witness protection program; and Patti, an insecure innocent who desperately wants to be liked.

Cast: Tiffani-Amber Thiessen (*Allison Morgan*); Leah Remini (*Didi DiConcini*); T.C. Warner (*Patti Hale*); Michael Landes (*Rob McGuire*); Caroline McWilliams (*Dorothy Loomis*); Diane Delano (*Margaret Dezell*).

4875 *Just Our Luck*. (Series; Comedy; ABC; 1983-1984). While jogging on the beach of Venice, California, Keith Barrow, a weatherman (later roving reporter) for the KPOX-TV, Channel 6 news program, bumps into a souvenir stand and cracks an odd-looking green bottle, which he is forced to buy ("You break it — you pay for it"). Later, at his home, Keith's pet cat knocks the bottle off the table and breaks it. From the debris there emerges Shabu, a genie who becomes Keith's slave — and is able to grant him any wish. Stories relate Shabu's adventures, having spent 196 years in the bottle, in the 1980s as he struggles to please his new master.

Other regulars are Meagan Huxley, the KPOX-TV program director; Nelson Marriott, the station manager; Professor Bob, the weatherman; Chuck, Shabu's friend; Jim Dexter, the newscaster; The Bag Lady (in program open who sells Keith the bottle).

Cast: T.K. Carter (*Shabu*); Richard Gilliland (*Keith Barrow*); Ellen Maxted (*Meagan Huxley*); Rod McCary (*Nelson Marriott*); Hamilton Camp (*Professor Bob*); Richard Schaal (*Chuck*); Leonard Simon (*Jim Dexter*); Connie Sawyer (*Bag Lady*).

4876 *Just Plain Folks*. (Pilot; Comedy; NBC; July 5, 1956). The "Just Plain Folks" are Cy Howard, a successful Hollywood writer who is married to a beautiful Hungarian actress named Zsa Zsa. The proposal was to relate events in their home and show business lives.

Cast: Cy Howard (*Cy*); Zsa Zsa Gabor (*Zsa Zsa*); Nelson Case (*Host-Narrator*).

4877 *Just Say Julie*. (Series; Comedy; MTV; 1989–1992). A potpourri program created, written, co-produced and starring comedienne Julie Brown. There is no real storyline to speak of; the format has Julie displaying her comedic genius (on her theme shows, like "The Julie Awards" and "How to Be Cool"), introducing music videos (it is MTV), interviewing celebrities or music artists (also poking fun at them) and her recurring commentary envisioning singer Bon Jovi is her fiancé.

Host: Julie Brown. **Regulars:** Paul Brown, Stacy Harris, Charlie Coffey, Larry Poindexter.

4878 *Just Shoot Me*. (Series; Comedy; NBC; 1997–2003). Jack Gallo is the owner of *Blush*, a fashion magazine based in Manhattan. Jack claims *Blush* was the first magazine to encourage women to express their sexuality; to encourage them to "drop their mops and pick up a briefcase" and the first magazine to give a voice to female politicians. Most women, however, believe *Blush* treats women like trophies.

Jack began *Blush* in 1967 and runs it like his blood type — B-positive. He is married to Allie, a woman 30 years his junior, and is the father of Hannah (neither are seen). He is divorced from Eve (his first wife), the mother of his daughter, Maya.

Maya is the articles editor for *Blush* (she previously worked as a writer for Channel 8 news). She tutors children in her spare time, finds video games exciting and believes people see her as "a straight-laced, uptight school teacher." "But I'm not," she says, "I like to have fun."

Assisting Jack is Dennis Finch, a schemer who sees his job as an opportunity to meet beautiful models. Jack sees his magazine as his castle and Dennis as his gargoyle. Dennis writes the advice column "Dear Miss Pretty," believes he works hard, gets little pay, and is given no respect.

Nina Van Horn is the fashion editor for *Blush*. Her real name is Claire Noodleman and she was a top model of the 1970s and '80s (her big break came when she was discovered modeling hats in Boston). Nina, voted Model of the Year in 1974, bases her entire life on her looks (which she fears losing) and believes casual wear is ruining society ("adults should wear sophisticated clothes").

Elliott DeMoreau is the head photographer for *Blush*. He attended Hawthorne High School in New Jersey and was working as a street photographer when Jack hired him. He and Nina are constantly at odds and seem to have only one thing in common — an old blues singer named Cholera Joe Hopper (who had such hits as "A Pebble in My One Good Shoe," "Chin Hair Mama" and "Swollen Glands").

Cast: George Segal (*Jack Gallo*); Laura San Giacomo (*Maya Gallo*); David Spade (*Dennis Finch*); Wendie Malick (*Nina Van Horn*); Enrico Colantoni (*Elliott DeMoreau*); Brian Posehn (*Kevin Liotta*); Rena Sofer (*Vicki Costa*).

4879 *Just the Ten of Us*. (Series; Comedy; ABC; 1988–1990). A spin off from *Growing Pains*. Graham Lubbock, the former coach at Dewey High School on Long Island (New York), is now the athletic director and coach of the Hippos football team at Saint Augustine's, a Catholic high school for boys in Eureka, California. Graham is married to Elizabeth and is the father of eight children (Marie, Cindy, Wendy, Connie, Sherry, J.R. and twins Harvey and Michelle). They have a dog named Hooter and a milk cow named Diane.

Elizabeth, a deeply religious Catholic, met Graham at a C.Y.O. (Catholic Youth Organization) mixer, and they fell in love at first sight. They married in 1970. Marie, Wendy, Cindy and Connie formed a sexy singing group called the Lubbock Babes (who perform regularly at Danny's Pizza Parlor). Graham is overweight and constantly nagged by Elizabeth to go on a diet. Elizabeth does volunteer work at the food bank, and, for a short time, Graham held a second job as a counter boy at Burger Barn.

Marie is 18 years old and very religious (she is hoping to become a nun). She is also very attractive and boy-shy and hides her obvious beauty behind glasses and loose fitting clothes. In one episode, Marie began her career as a nun by taking a two-week seminar at Saint Bartholomew's Convent.

Wendy, 17, the most beautiful of the Lubbock girls, is boy-crazy and appears totally self-absorbed (although she'll secretly help one of her sisters in a crisis). Although she acts like a bimbo — her ploy to attract the opposite sex — she is deeply hurt when called one. Cindy, 16, the beautiful but not too bright Lubbock Babe, is as boy-crazy as Wendy — but is also constantly in a dither about everything else. Cindy has a slight weight problem and is a member of the Diet Control Clinic. She had her own radio show (over KHPO, "The Voice of Saint Augie's") called *What's Happening, Saint Augie's* and her first job was as the receptionist at the Eureka Fitness Center.

Fifteen-year-old Constance, nicknamed Connie, is pretty, very intelligent and the most sensitive of the girls. While not as boy-shy as Marie, she is quite intimidated by Wendy and Cindy, feels because of her small breasts, that she will never attract "hunks" as do Cindy and Wendy. Connie, who hopes to become a journalist, is a writer for the school newspaper, Saint Augie's *Herald-Gazette*; her first job was sweeping animal entrails at the MacGregor slaughterhouse.

Sherry, the youngest of the girls before Michelle's birth, is 11 years old and the most intelligent of the girls. She strives for excellent grades, and although she should be in grammar school she is seen attending Saint Augustine's (an exception to the all-boy rule was made to allow the Lubbock girls to attend). Sherry is constantly amazed by the antics of her sisters and has trouble believing Cindy and Wendy are related to her.

J.R. (Graham Lubbock, Jr.) is the older male child. He attends Saint Augustine's and loves playing practical jokes on his sisters. Father Robert Hargis is the priest in charge of Saint Augustine's, and Janitor Bob is the strange ex-con custodian at school. Bill Medley sings the theme, "Doin' It the Best I Can."

Cast: Bill Kirchenbauer *(Graham Lubbock)*; Deborah Harmon *(Elizabeth Lubbock)*; Heather Langenkamp *(Marie Lubbock)*; Jamie Luner *(Cindy Lubbock)*; Brooke Theiss *(Wendy Lubbock)*; Jo Ann Willett *(Connie Lubbock)*; Heidi Zeigler *(Sherry Lubbock)*; Matt Shakman *(J.R. Lubbock)*; Frank Bonner *(Father Robert Hargis)*; Lou Richards *(Father Bud)*; Maxine Elliott Hicks *(Sister Ethel)*; Sid Haig *(Janitor Bob)*.

4880 *Justice*. (Pilot; Anthology; ABC; April 12, 1953). A proposal, slated to use a different cast each week, based on the files of the Legal Aid Society. In the pilot episode, an impoverished wife seeks the society's help when she learns that her husband is being blackmailed.

Cast: John Lehine *(Judge)*; Lee Grant *(Wife)*; Paul Douglas *(Husband)*. **Commentator:** Judge Leonard Hand.

4881 *Justice*. (Series; Drama; NBC; 1954–1956). "The official records of poor people who are in need of help" provides the basis for stories based on the files of the Legal Aid Society and seen through the investigations of attorneys Richard Adams and Jason Tyler.

Cast: Dane Clark, William Prince *(Richard Adams)*; Gary Merrill *(Jason Tyler)*. **Narrator:** Westbrook Van Voorhis. **Announcer:** Bill Lazar.

4882 *Justice*. (Series; Crime Drama; Fox; 2006). Trott, Nicholson, Tuller and Graves is a prestigious Los Angeles law firm that specializes in high profile crime cases especially those that garner much media attention. Ron Trott is a senior, media-seeking partner; Tom Nicholson is the partner called "The Face of the Not Guilty" (he sincerely believes all the firm's clients are innocent); Luther Graves is the African-American member of the team, the man who appears to keep Ron and Tom in line; Alden Tucker, the only female partner, is a no nonsense girl who is totally dedicated to uncovering the truth — even if it means their clients are actually guilty.

Ron, who appears to be the man puling all the strings, and his team are brilliant trial lawyers. Ron feels the media attention not only makes them look good, but also adds to the power of the firm. Ron and his team know what works — and how to work it. They also push the limits of the law — to stay within the law while not actually breaking it to help a client.

Unlike other lawyer programs that have been broadcast, *Justice* is more like a behind-the-scenes look at the cases and follows the defense attorneys from jury selection to the media spin. The trial prep is shown, the meticulous document search work that is done; how mock juries are conducted; and how computer graphics are also used to help the team recreate the crime. The program begins with a crime; the last few minutes of each episode shows the viewer what the jury never saw — what really happened (and whether the firm defended a guilty or not guilty client).

Ron, as previously mentioned, likes media attention — and he gets it most often from Suzanne Fulcrum, the anchor of a cable show called *American Crime*, a live newscast that thoroughly covers the cases of the firm of TNT&G.

Cast: Victor Garber *(Ron Trott)*; Rebecca Mader *(Alden Tuller)*; Eamonn Walker *(Luther Graves)*; Kerr Smith *(Tom Nicholson)*; Katherine LaNasa *(Suzanne Fulcrum)*.

4883 *Justice of the Peace*. (Pilot; Drama; NBC; June 30, 1959). A proposed spin off from *The David Niven Theater* about Mark Johnston, a small town justice of the peace.

Cast: Dan Duryea *(Mark Johnston)*; Dorothy Green *(Ellen Johnston; Mark's wife)*.

4884 *Justified*. (Series; Crime Drama; FX; 2010–). Raylan Givens is a modern day Deputy U.S. Marshal with the Marshal Services in Miami, Florida. In the spirit of the cowboys of the Old West, he sports a white Stetson, cowboy boots and a hip holstered gun. He also embraces a violent form of 19th century justice that places a target on his back and puts him at odds with his superiors, who disapprove of his Chuck Norris–like *Walker, Texas Ranger* approach to fighting crime. Raylan will only draw his gun when he feels the need — and will shoot to kill (which he believes is the purpose of a gun). His one goal is to become the best marshal he can despite what liberties he takes to uphold the law. Life changes for Raylan when he kills a criminal who deserved to be shot (Raylan provokes the bad guys to draw first, thus justifying his actions). The incident ignites and uproar in the department and the seemingly out-of-control Raylan is transferred to the Lexington, Kentucky branch. Raylan was born in the backwoods-like town of Harlan, Kentucky, and worked the coal mines when he was a teenager. Now, back to where he started, Raylan, and fellow deputies Rachel Brooks and Tim Gutterson, chase fugitives, protect witnesses and transport prisoners.

Art Muller is the Chief Deputy of the Lexington office; Winona is Raylan's ex-wife; Arlo is Raylan's career criminal father; Ava is Raylan's former high school sweetheart; Boyd is Ava's brother, once Raylan's friend, now his enemy (a nasty white supremacist). Helen is Raylan's aunt; Mags Bennett is the pot growing, moonshine selling schemer who always manages to stay one step ahead of the law; Loretta is the young girl Mags has taken in and grooming to follow in her footsteps; Doyle, Dickie and Coover are Mags deceitful sons.

Cast: Timothy Olyphant *(Raylan Givens)*; Erica Tazel *(Rachel Brooks)*; Jacob Pitts *(Tim Gutterson)*; Nick Searcy *(Art Muller)*; Natalie Zea *(Winona Hawkins)*; Joelle Carter *(Ava Crowder)*; Walton Goggins *(Boyd Crowder)*; Raymond Barry *(Arlo Givens)*; Margo Martindale *(Mags Bennett)*; Linda Gehringer *(Helen)*; Kaitlyn Dever *(Loretta)*; Joseph Lyle Taylor *(Doyle Bennett)*; Jeremy Davies *(Dickie Bennett)*; Bruce William Henke *(Coover Bennett)*; William Ragsdale *(Gary Hawkins)*.

4885 *Justin Case*. (Pilot; Comedy; ABC; May 15, 1988). When Jennifer Spalding, an unemployed actress, applies for a secretarial position with private detective Justin Case, she discovers his body on the floor and promptly meets his ghost, who has only one question on his mind — who killed him? With Jennifer's help, Justin finds his killer and decides to remain on earth as a ghostly detective. The proposal was to relate Jennifer's adventures as the partner of a ghost who appears and speaks only to her.

Cast: George Carlin *(Justin Case)*; Molly Hagan *(Jennifer Spalding)*.

4886 *Juvenile Jury.* (Series; Children; NBC; CBS; 1947–1955). A panel of five children answer questions or give their opinions on questions or problems submitted by home viewers or presented by studio audience members. Based on the radio program of the same title. Aired on NBC (April 3, 1947 to Oct. 3, 1953) and CBS (Oct. 11, 1953 to Sept. 14, 1954; and Jan. 2 to Mar. 27, 1955).

Host: Jack Barry. **Music:** Joe Diamond.

4887 *K-9.* (Pilot; Crime Drama; ABC; July 6, 1991). After Jack Bergen, an officer with the L.A.P.D. loses a collar, he is given a partner—a German Shepherd named Jerry Lee. The proposal was to relate Jake and the dog's efforts to ferret out criminals. Other regulars are Lieutenant Emmett Broussard, Jack's superior; and Margaret Slate, Jack's neighbor, a pastry chef at a restaurant called Le Petit Giraffe.

Cast: Robert Carradine *(Jack Bergen)*; Jason Bernard *(Emmett Broussard)*; Lisa Darr *(Margaret Slate)*.

4888 *K-9 and Company.* (Pilot; Science Fiction; Syn.; Aug. 1985). A proposed spin off from *Doctor Who* that teams Sarah Jane Smith, one of the Doctor's beautiful assistants, with K-9, the Doctor's mechanical dog. Shortly after Sarah Jane and the Doctor part company, Sarah Jane returns to work as a journalist. Some time later, when Sarah Jane visits her Aunt Lavinia, she learns that a large crate has been waiting for her. Upon opening it, she discovers the contents to be K-9, a present from the Doctor. The proposal was to relate their experiences as they team to solve crimes.

Cast: Elisabeth Sladen *(Sarah Jane Smith)*; John Leeson *(Voice of K-9)*; Mary Wimbush *(Aunt Lavinia)*.

4889 *K-9000.* (Pilot; Crime Drama; Unaired; Produced for Fox in 1989). In an attempt to battle crime, the L.A.P.D. commissions Aja, a beautiful British scientist to create Niner, a cloned German Shepherd with a computer-enhanced brain. Niner and Aja are assigned to Detective Eddie Monroe and the proposal was to relate their battle against crime.

Cast: Catherine Oxenberg *(Aja)*; Chris Mulkey *(Eddie Monroe)*.

4890 *K Street.* (Series; Reality; HBO; 2003). Promoted as "a combination reality and semi-improvised comedy-drama that takes viewers behind the scenes" to detail the lives of the political consultants with the firm of Bergstrom and Lowell on K Street in Washington, D.C. The main characters are James Carville and Mary Matalin, image specialists who interact with actual political figures (who appear in fictional stories). Tommy Flannigan is James's aide; Fran Cisco Dupre is the firm's newest "oddball" employee; Bergstrom is the reclusive employee who attaches himself to Caville; Maggie Morris is Mary's assistant.

Cast: James Carville *(Himself)*; Mary Matalin *(Herself)*; Roger Guenveur *(Francisco Dupre)*; Mary McCormack *(Maggie Morris)*; Elliott Gould *(Bergstrom)*; Jennice Fuentes *(Woman in Red)*; John Slattery *(Tommy Flanegan)*.

4891 *K-Ville.* (Series; Crime Drama; Fox; 2007). A real disaster (Hurricane Katrina) and real incidents (the rising crime rate in a city ripped apart by the storm) are the basis for stories. It is now two years after Katrina and New Orleans is still a city in chaos. The work of determined and dedicated police officers as they struggle to uphold the law and help rebuild their inner city are depicted.

Marlin Boulet is a member of the department's Felony Action Squad, a specialized unit that targets the worst offenders. Marlin is totally dedicated to his job. In the face of the hurricane he stood his ground, doing all he could to help where he could. Trevor Cobb, a former soldier (deployed to Afghanistan) is Marlin's partner (an unlikely pair as Trevor is still troubled by the fighting he experienced and is now seeking redemption). Marlin has his own methods of dealing with criminals but Trevor cannot always accept his gung ho tactics. Malcolm is married to Anaya and is the father of a young daughter (Tawni). He believes New Orleans (now called K-Ville; short for Katrinaville) can rebound and he is determined to see that it does.

Also part of the team is Ginger "Love Tap" Le Beau, Jeff "Glue Boy" Gooden and James Embry, their captain. Filmed on location.

Cast: Anthony Anderson *(Marlin Boulet)*; Cole Hauser *(Trevor Cobb)*; Tawny Cypress *(Ginger LeBeau)*; Blake Shields *(Jeff Gooden)*; John Carroll Lynch *(James Embry)*; Elise Neal *(Anaya Boulet)*; Jiya Fowler *(Tawni Boulet)*.

4892 *Kablam!* (Series; Cartoon; Nick; 1996–2000). An animated anthology program hosted by characters Henry and June. While various cartoon shorts comprise the bulk of the series, several segments became regular features. These are *Prometheus and Bob* (an alien's efforts to educate a caveman); *Life with Loopy* (a teenager who tells tall tales); *Sniz and Fondue* (antics of two wombats); and *Action League Now!* (action figure toys come to life to battle evil via stop motion photography).

Voice Cast: Julia McIlvaine *(June)*; Noah Segan *(Henry)*; Burt Pence *(Announcer)*.

4893 *The Kaiser Aluminum Hour.* (Series; Anthology; NBC; 1956-1957). Kaiser Aluminum-sponsored program of dramatic presentations that feature both well known and lesser-known personalities. Alternates with *The Armstrong Circle Theater*, *The 20th Century–Fox Hour* and *Playwrights '56*. Notable performers include Natalie Wood, Claude Rains, Eli Wallach, Roland Winters, June Lockhart, Jan Sterling, Nanette Fabray, Kim Hunter, Jacqueline Scott, Henry Hull and Franchot Tone.

4894 *The Kallikaks.* (Series; Comedy; NBC; 1977). In an attempt to find a better life, Jasper T. Kallikak, Sr., his wife, Venus, and their children, Bobbi Lou and Jasper Jr., leave their home in Appalachia and migrate to Nowhere, California, to become the new owners of a run-down two-pump gas station. Their efforts to run the gas station is the focal point of stories. Oscar is Jasper's mechanic. Roy Clark performs the theme, "Beat the System."

Cast: David Huddleston *(Jasper T. Kallikak, Sr.)*; Edie McClurg *(Venus Kallikak)*; Bonnie Ebsen *(Bobbi Lou Kallikak)*; Patrick J. Petersen *(Jasper T. Kallikak, Jr.)*; Peter Palmer *(Oscar Heinz)*.

4895 *Kama Sutra.* (Series; Anthology; Cinemax; 2002). Dalia is a gorgeous woman who operates a mysterious house of prostitution. It is here that people can realize their sexual fantasies and stories, which are adult in nature, present Dalia's efforts to satisfy those desires. Produced by adult film actress Rebecca Lord.

Cast: Tamara Landry *(Dalia)*.

4896 *Kamen Rider: Dragon Knight.* (Series; Adventure; CW Kids; 2009-2010). Kit Taylor is an orphan, just turned 18, who is living with a foster family. His mother died when he was young and his father (Frank) mysteriously disappeared ten years earlier. Kit believes his father was kidnapped by General Xaviax, a renegade warlord who is holding him hostage (Xaviax rules in a world opposite ours called Ventra, a mirror world that is able to be entered through glass and reflective surfaces). Kit has only one object from his father—a deck of advent cards (magical playing–like cards that give him the ability to bond with a dragon and transform into a Kamen Rider, a being endowed by the Power of the Dragon). Kit rides a motorcycle (that can do things that defy the laws of physics) and, when seen in costume, is called "The Masked Vigilante." Stories follow Kit as he joins with other Kamen Riders to battle General Xaviax and his evil army in the hope to one day find and rescue his father.

Len, a Wing Knight, is the leader of the Kamen Riders; Maya is a bookstore employee (at her aunt's store, Grace's Books in California) who hopes to become an investigative reporter. She writes for the paranormal website www.wayabovesecret.com. She also becomes involved in Kit's plight when Kit saves her from Xaviax's attempts to kidnap her (Xaviax, who poses as the Earth businessman Connor, kidnaps people to help him rebuild his world—something the Kamen Riders must stop). Michelle is the reporter Maya assists; Lacey is Maya's friend.

Cast: Stephen Lunsford (*Kit Taylor*); Matt Mullins (*Len*); Aria Alistar (*Maya Young*); Victoria Jackson (*Grace Kiefer*); Jeff Davis (*Frank Taylor*); Kathleen Gati (*Kit's foster mother*); William O'Leary (*Xaviax*); Marisa Lauren (*Lacey*); Kathy Christopherson (*Michelle Walsh*).

4897　Kane's Sex Chronicles. (Series; Anthology; Cinemax; 2008). Erotic adaptations of African-American short stories penned by Zane, a *New York Times* best-selling author. Adult stories feature strong sexual situations and female nudity. Suzanne De Passe, Zane Madison Jones are the producers.

4898　Kangaroos in the Kitchen. (Pilot; Comedy; NBC; July 25, 1982). The apartment at 140 Cambridge Street in New York City is home to Ginny Provost, an animal talent scout, and her array of pets: Dagmar (Great Dane), Mickey (chimpanzee), Dolly (llama), Sidney (kangaroo) and Ramone (parrot). The proposal was to relate Ginny's misadventures as she tries to find the right animals for the right show business jobs. Based on the book *Kangaroos in the Kitchen: The Story of Animal Talent Scouts* by Lorraine D'Essen. Richard is Ginny's husband, a lawyer; Lila is Ginny's assistant.

Cast: Lauralee Bruce (*Ginny Provost*); Sam Freed (*Richard Provost*); Peggy Pope (*Lila*).

4899　The Karate Kid. (Series; Cartoon; NBC; 1989-1990). An animated adaptation of the feature film of the same title. Here a karate master (Miyagi Yakuga) and his students (Daniel and Taki) travel around the world to battle injustice through the use of their martial arts skills.

Voice Cast: Robert Ito (*Miyagi Yakuga*); Joey Dedio (*Daniel*); Janice Kawaye (*Taki*).

4900　Karen. (Series; Comedy; NBC; 1964-1965). Karen Scott is a beautiful 16-year-old girl with an uncontrollable penchant for mischief (she doesn't go looking for it but it seems that no matter what she does, something always goes wrong and she winds up in hot water). She first lives at 90 Bristol Court (in Southern California) then at 437 Maple Lane in Los Angeles with her parents (Steve and Barbara) and younger sister Mimi. Karen is very bright although her grades sometimes suffer because she does not apply herself. She likes boys but does not go "gaa gaa" over them. Karen has aspirations to become an actress and, despite the crazy things she does, the parents of her friends feel she is wholesome and are glad their children are friends with her (it's one less thing for them to worry about). Karen attends Beverly High School and is best friends with Candy, Janis, Spider and David. Candy and Janis believe "Karen has a natural beauty that attracts boys" (which she does but she is not always comfortable meeting boys who are only attracted to her because of her

looks). Steve is a lawyer and he and Barbara do punish Karen for her hi jinks—"It's only fair," Steve says. Mimi, who is not as unpredictable as Karen, often sides with Karen when she does something wrong and calls her parent's punishing her "being mean to her." Mimi attends Beverly Junior High and is more of a homebody than Karen. Mrs. Rowe is the Scott's housekeeper; Cliff Murdock is the handyman. The Beach Boys sing the theme, "Karen."

Originally aired as a segment of *90 Bristol Court* (Oct. 5, 1964 to Jan. 4, 1965) and as a series of its own from Jan. 11, 1965 to Sept. 6, 1965.

Cast: Debbie Watson (*Karen Scott*); Richard Denning (*Steve Scott*); Mary LaRoche (*Barbara Scott*); Gina Gillespie (*Mimi Scott*); Grace Albertson (*Mrs. Rowe*); Guy Raymond (*Cliff Murdock*); Trudi Ames (*Candy*); Bernadette Winters (*Janis*); Murray MacLeod (*Spider*); Richard Dreyfuss (*David*).

4901　Karen. (Series; Comedy; ABC; 1975). Karen Angelo is a young woman with a deep determination to help other people. It started when she was a child (although the most she could ever do was help her mother around the house) but the feeling stayed with her through her grammar school and high school years. When Karen attended college (Berkeley) she joined every committee that was involved with helping others. She even protested for what she thought was wrong (and was even taken into custody for doing so). This, however, did not discourage her. After graduating, she applied for a position with Open America, a citizens lobby in Washington, D.C. While not the ideal job (she is hired as a staff worker) she feels that it is one step in the right direction—a direction that she hopes will lead her to make a significant change in the world. Stories follow Karen as she attempts to meet the political needs of the people of her community.

Dale W. Bush is the stern, no-nonsense founder of Open America (he demands results when his people go out and lobby). Karen lives at 1460 Cambridge Street. Cissy Peterson is Karen's roommate; Dena Madison and Adam Coopersmith are staff workers as Open America; Jerry Siegel is a tenant in Karen's rooming house; Cheryl is Jerry's wife; Senator Bob Hartford is Karen's friend; Ernie is another friend of Karen's.

Cast: Karen Valentine (*Karen Angelo*); Denver Pyle (*Dale W. Bush; pilot*); Charles Lane (*Dale W. Bush; series*); Dena Dietrich (*Dena Madison*); Aldine King (*Cissy Peterson*); Will Selzer (*Adam Cooperman*); Oliver Clark (*Jerry Siegel*); Alix Elias (*Cheryl Siegel*); Edward Winter (*Bob Hartford*); Joseph Stone (*Ernie*); Liam Dunn (*Captain Pike*).

4902　Karen Sisco. (Series; Crime Drama; ABC; 2003). Karen Sisco is a beautiful, tough and seductive Miami-based U.S. Marshal. Karen is stubborn and would like to do things her way—but she has to work with warrants (she can't legally do anything without one). That technicality doesn't always stop her. She does act on her own. She steals evidence from crime scenes—and she worries about the consequences—three to five years if she is caught.

Karen's superior is Captain Amos Andrews and she sometimes seeks the help of her father, Marshall Sisco, a private detective who charges $5,000 per case with ten percent up front for expenses. Karen enjoys meals at Angelo's Pizza Parlor and is an expert at poker. She is a graduate of North Central High School and stories follow Karen as she risks her life to bring criminals to justice.

Cast: Carla Gugino (*Karen Sisco*); Robert Forster (*Marshall Sisco*); Bill Duke (*Amos Andrews*).

4903　The Karen Valentine Show. (Pilot; Comedy; ABC; May 21, 1973). Karen Scott is a beautiful Girl Friday to Buddy Loudon, the zany owner of the Buddy Loudon Public Relations Firm in New York City. The proposal was to relate Karen's misadventures as she seeks ways to publicize the clients Buddy acquires — uninteresting people no other PR firm wants.

Cast: Karen Valentine *(Karen Scott)*; Charles Nelson Reilly *(Buddy Loudon)*.

4904   *Karen's Song*. (Series; Comedy; Fox; 1987). Karen Matthews is a 40-year-old publishing executive for the Dexter Publishing Company. She is divorced from Zach and is the mother of Laura. Steve Foreman is 28 years old and single. He is the owner of a catering company (A Tasteful Affair) and is dating the older Karen Matthews. Stories present an honest approach to the problems of an older woman-younger man relationship as Karen and Steve struggle to enjoy each other's company despite the objections of family and friends who oppose their relationship. Other regulars are Claire, Karen's friend; and Michael, Karen's former lover (after Zach). Suzanne Pleshette was originally cast in the role of Karen when CBS had the project.

Cast: Patty Duke *(Karen Matthews)*; Louis Smith *(Steve Foreman)*; Teri Hatcher *(Laura Matthews)*; Lainie Kazan *(Claire Steiner)*; Granville Van Dusen *(Zach Matthews)*; Charles Levin *(Michael Brand)*.

4905   *The Karenskys*. (Pilot; Comedy; Unaired; Produced for CBS in 2009). Events in the lives of a large, ethnic family headed by Pearl and Max Karensky. Anne-Marie, Bill, "Little Max" and married daughter Bernadette are their children; Emily is Bernadette's daughter and their efforts to put up with each other's faults is the focal point of the proposal.

Cast: Annie Potts *(Pearl Karensky)*; Jack Thompson *(Max Karensky)*; Desi Lydic *(Bernadette Atwood)*; Sasha Alexander *(Emily Atwood)*; Tinsley Grimes *(Anne-Marie Karensky)*; Mather Zickel *(Bill Karensky)*; Todd Stashwick *("Little" Max Karensky)*.

4906   *Kat Plus One*. (Pilot; Drama; Unaired; Produced for ABC in 2003). Kat Montgomery has it all. She is a highly paid publicist for a top New York firm and has the ability to make things happen. Then, suddenly, her life changes when her sister and brother-in-law are killed in a car accident and she receives custody of their five-year-old son, A.J. Now with new responsibilities, Kat struggles to adjust to a job she is totally unprepared for: becoming a parent.

Cast: Marisa Coughlan *(Kat Montgomery)*; Jimmie Bennett *(A.J.)*; Heather Burns *(Violet)*; Michael Urie *(Roger)*.

4907   *Kate and Allie*. (Series; Comedy; CBS; 1984–1989). Katherine ("Kate") Elizabeth Ann McArdle is the divorced mother of Emma. Kate was married to Max, an actor who now lives in California. Allison ("Allie") Julie Charlotte Adams Lowell is the divorced mother of two children, Jennie and Chip. Allie was married to Charles, a doctor who now resides in Connecticut with his second wife, Claire. Kate and Allie are longtime friends (they met as kids at the orthodontist's office) who now share an apartment in New York's Greenwich Village to save on expenses. Kate works as an agent for the Sloane Travel Agency. Allie loves to cook and cares for the kids while Kate works. She attends night classes at Washington Square College and held several part time jobs: bookstore salesclerk, box office cashier at the 9th Street Cinema and volunteer at Channel G, a Manhattan cable station run by a woman named Eddie Gordon (Andrea Martin). In 1986 Kate and Allie formed their own company, Kate and Allie Caterers, which they operate from their home. In the episode of December 11, 1987 Allie marries former football player Robert ("Bob") Barsky, a sportscaster for WNTD-TV, Channel 10, in Washington, D.C. (He commutes between New York and Washington and does the 11 O'clock Sports Update.) Allie and Chip move to a new apartment (21C) on West 55th Street; Kate remains for a short time at their old apartment and later moves in with Allie.

Jennie, Allie's daughter, had an after school job as a waitress at Le Bon Croissant, a French diner. While a high school for Jennie is not given, she attends Columbia University in 1987 and lives in dorm room 512. Emma, Kate's daughter, attended the same unnamed high school as Jennie and moved to California in 1987 to attend UCLA. John Lefler sings the theme, "Along Comes a Friend."

Cast: Susan Saint James *(Kate McArdle)*; Jane Curtin *(Allie Lowell)*; Ari Meyers *(Emma McArdle)*; Allison Smith *(Jennie Lowell)*; Frederick Koehler *(Chip Lowell)*; Sam Freed *(Bob Barsky)*; John Herd *(Max McArdle)*; Paul Hecht *(Dr. Charles Lowell)*; Wendie Malick *(Claire Lowell)*.

4908   *Kate Bliss*. (Pilot; Comedy; ABC; May 26, 1978). Kate Bliss is beautiful woman one would suspect of being an actress or woman of social standing. Kate, however, is neither. She is a private detective at a time when women simply did not occupy such positions. It is the early 20th century and the proposed series was to relate Kate's lighthearted misadventures as she begins her travels west to help people in need. Also known as *Kate Bliss and the Ticker Tape Kid* (the pilot title wherein Kate seeks to capture a Wall Street businessman turned outlaw).

Cast: Suzanne Pleshette *(Kate Bliss)*.

4909   *Kate Brasher*. (Series; Drama; CBS; 2001). Kate Brasher is 34 years old. She is the single mother of two teenage boys, Daniel and Elvis, and is working two jobs to make ends meet — cleaning woman and waitress at the Club Café in Santa Monica (although the series setting is said to be Los Angeles). One day, when her employer stiffs her, Kate seeks legal advice from Brother's Keeper, a Legal Aid Society run by Joe DeMatta. When Kate helps with a case (accidentally becoming involved when a speechless woman seeks her help) Joe finds she is a natural and offers her a job as a case worker at $500 a week. Stories follow Kate as she begins a new career helping people and learning about the harsh realities of life. Also working with Kate is Abbe Schaffer, a lawyer who was formally Joe's secretary (she spent seven years in law school and it took her two years to pass the bar exam). Kate's sons attend Westside High School. Kate believes the Bible has the answers to her problems. She opens the book, flips through the pages and lets he finger stop on a page. What she picks usually solves her problem.

Cast: Mary Stuart Masterson *(Kate Brasher)*; Hector Elizondo *(Joe DeMatta)*; Rhea Perlman *(Abbe Schaffer)*; Gregory Smith *(Daniel Brasher)*; Mason Gamble *(Elvis Brasher)*.

4910   *Kate Loves a Mystery*. (Series; Crime Drama; NBC; 1979). Kate Columbo is the wife of the famed homicide detective, Lieutenant Columbo of the L.A.P.D. On the series *Columbo* Kate was never seen or mentioned by a first name; she was either "The Wife" or "Mrs. Columbo." Kate was never much of a detective on the *Columbo* series. Columbo would remark that when he and the Mrs. would go to the movies, she would always pick the wrong person as the killer. Kate suddenly inherited her husband's sleuthing abilities in two short lived series: *Mrs. Columbo* (Feb. 26 to Mar. 24, 1979) and *Kate Loves a Mystery* (Oct. 18 to Dec. 6, 1979). In *Mrs. Columbo*, Kate lives at 728 Valley Lane in San Fernando, California, with her daughter, Jenny. "My husband" or "The Lieutenant," as Kate referred to her husband, is never seen; he is always on a case or away on business. Kate works as a writer for the *Weekly Advertiser*, a "throwaway" newspaper published by Josh Alden. Jenny attends the Valley Elementary School. While hubby is away, Kate cares for Fang, the lazy basset hound who was also called Dog in the *Columbo* series. Kate studied journalism in college and worked at it for a time before she gave it up for marriage and a family. Six months ago she woke up and asked herself where she was. It was then that she decided she needed to get back in the work force.

Although Kate is supposed to cover events like pet shows and garden clubs, she always manages to stumble upon and solve crimes. When *Kate Loves a Mystery* premiered, Kate was now divorced and used her maiden name. Kate Columbo was now Kate Callahan and Lili Haydn her daughter, Jenny Callahan. They lived in the same house, had the same dog and Jenny attended the same school. Kate still worked for Josh Alden but at a different paper, the *Weekly Advocate*, in the San Fernando Valley. Kate still managed to stumble upon crimes, but solved them with the help of her friend, Mike Varrick, a sergeant with the Valley Municipal Police Department.

Cast: Kate Mulgrew (*Kate Columbo*); Lili Haydn (*Jenny Columbo*); Henry Jones (*Josh Alden*); Don Stroud (*Mike Varrick*).

4911   *Kate McShane.* (Series; Crime Drama; CBS; 1975). Kate McShane is an uninhibited and unorthodox Irish-American lawyer working out of Los Angeles. She is also fiercely dedicated to her clients and will do what it takes (just pushing the limits of the law) to get satisfaction (not only for her clients but for herself). Stories follow Kate as she not only defends people but takes an active part in the investigation. Pat McShane, her father, is also her investigator; Ed McShane is Kate's brother, a Jesuit priest; and Julie is Kate's secretary. In the pilot episode, Marian Seldes played Eileen, Kate's secretary.

Cast: Anne Meara (*Kate McShane*); Sean McClory (*Pat McShane*); Charles Haid (*Ed McShane*); Rachel Malkin (*Julie*).

4912   *Kate Plus 8.* (Series; Reality; TLC; 2009). The relaunched title for *Jon and Kate Plus 8* (which see for information) that focuses on Kate Gosselin after her divorce from Jon as she cares for her eight children.

4913   *The Kate Smith Evening Hour.* (Series; Variety; NBC; 1951-1952). A prime-time version of the daytime series, *The Kate Smith Hour* that features music, songs, comedy, fashion advice and interviews with and performances by guest celebrities.

Host: Kate Smith. **Regulars:** Ted Collins, Paul Lukas, Susan Douglas, Ann Thomas, The Williams Brothers, The Stuart Morgan Dancers, The John Butler Dancers, The Jack Allison Singers. **Announcer:** Bob Warren. **Orchestra:** Harry Sosnik.

4914   *The Kate Smith Hour.* (Series; Variety; CBS; 1950–1954). Singer Kate Smith hosts a program of music, song and comedy. Featured segments include *Ethel and Alert* (a domestic comedy with Peg Lynch and Alan Bunce. The segment was spun off into its own series; see *Ethel and Albert*); *The World of Mister Sweeney* (a comedy with Charlie Ruggles and Glenn Walker that also became a series; see *The World of Mister Sweeney*); *House in the Garden* (a vignette about small town life); and *The Talent Showcase* (performances by aspiring newcomers).

Host: Kate Smith. **Regulars:** Peggy Ryan, Jeff Clark, Jimmy Nelson, Ray MacDonald, Evelyn Tyner, Richard Stuart, Flora Stuart, Fran Barber, Billy Mills, Robert Maxwell, Claire Frin, Virginia McCurdy, Diane Carol, Peg Lynch, Alan Bunce, Charlie Ruggles, Glenn Walker, Hal LeRoy, Adolph Dehm, Barry Wood, Dorothy Day, Lauren Gilbert, Monica Lovett, Mimi Strongin, James Vickery, Arlene Dalton, The McGuire Sisters, The Showtimers, The John Butler Ballet Group, The Jack Allison Singers. **Announcer:** Andre Baruch. **Orchestra:** Jack Miller.

4915   *The Kate Smith Show.* (Series; Variety; CBS; 1960). Music, songs and light comedy with singer Kate Smith as the host.

Host: Kate Smith. **Regulars:** The Harry Simeone Chorale. **Orchestra:** Neil Hefti, Bill Stegmeyer.

4916   *Kath and Kim.* (Series; Comedy; NBC; 2008-2009). Kimberly "Kim" Day is a beautiful young woman who believes she was meant for the finest things life has to offer. She is the daughter of Kathleen "Kath" Day, a single mother who has just found romance with Phil Knight, the owner of a fast food store (Phil's Sandwich Island) in the mall. All appears to be progressing well until Kim leaves her husband of six weeks (Craig) and moves back home to live with Kath. Kim became disillusioned living with Craig ("I didn't sign up for cooking or caring about how anybody's day was. I'm a trophy wife") and is now seeking to find herself but also putting a damper on Kath's new romance.

Kath is shallow and self-absorbed and admits that she is a high maintenance girl. Kim is a self-obsessed woman-child (a spoiled brat who wants things her way or no way at all). Craig, an electronics store employee at Circuit Surplus, loves Kim and is trying to make the marriage work, but he can never seem to say what Kim wants to hear. Stories follow Kath as she tries to begin a new life and Kim as she wallows in self-pity with no apparent ambition but to find someone to treat her like she believes she should be. Based on the Australian series of the same title (see next title).

Cast: Selma Blair (*Kim Day*); Molly Shannon (*Kath Day*); John Michael Higgins (*Phil Knight*); Mikey Day (*Craig Baker*).

4917   *Kath and Kim.* (Series; Comedy; Sundance; 2010). The 2002–2007 Australian series on which NBC based its 2008-2009 series of the same title. Kath Day-Knight and Kim Craig are a mother and daughter who live together in Fountain Lakes, a fictional suburb in Melbourne, Australia. Kath is a 50-year-old divorcee who is currently dating the uptight Kel Knight (whom she later marries). Kim is a young woman (twenty-something) who believes she was meant for the finer things in life. She is spoiled, estranged from her husband (Brett Craig) and the mother of their baby Epponnea. Stories follow the two women as they attempt to cope with each other as well as the men in their lives.

Cast: Jane Turner (*Kath Day-Knight*); Gina Riley (*Kim Craig*); Glenn Robbins (*Kel Knight*); Peter Rowsthorn (*Brett Craig*); Zara Harrington, Emma Le Boeuf, Makayla Berkers (*Epponnea-Rae Craig*); Magda Szubanski (*Sharon Strezlecki; Kim's friend*).

4918   *Kathy Griffin: My Life on the D-List.* (Series; Reality; Bravo; 2005–). A profile of actress-stand up comedienne Kathy Griffin as she not only performs her comedy club routines but goes about living her daily life; friends and family members are also featured.

Star: Kathy Griffin.

4919   *Katie and Orbie.* (Series; Cartoon; PBS; 1995-1996). Story book (or cartoon panel)–like stills are used to relate the learning adventures of Orbie, a creature from the planet Orbie, who now lives on Earth with a young girl (Katie) and her parents.

Narrator: Leslie Nielsen.

4920   *Katie Joplin.* (Series; Comedy; WB; 1999). *The Katie Joplin Show* is a call-in radio program on WLBP-FM (87.5) in Philadelphia. Katie Joplin, a sassy single mother hosts the show. Katie was born in Knoxville, Tennessee. She is separated from her husband, Jerry and is the mother of a teenage son (Greg)

When Katie got fed up with her life in Knoxville (working 16 hours a day in a bottling plant), she chose to begin a new life in Philadelphia. She first worked at the Crescent Corset Company, then at Car City. It was here that Glen, the manager of WLBP became aware of Katie (she was attempting to sell him a car and he became impressed by her outspoken ways and offered her the six hour overnight show). Stories follow the events in Katie's life as she struggles to balance her life between her work and her son.

Other regulars are Tiger French, Katie's engineer; Mitchell, the program director; and Liz, Katie's niece. Greg attends Franklin High School; Seventeen years ago Glen was a night disc jockey at a Cleveland radio station. Jockey Shorts was the first big time sponsor to buy time on Katie's show.

Cast: Park Overall (*Katie Joplin*); Jay Thomas (*Glen*); Jesse Head (*Greg Joplin*); Jim Rash (*Mitchell Tuitt*); Simon Max (*Tiger French*); Ana Reeder (*Liz*).

4921 Katie Ka-Boom. (Pilot; Cartoon; WB; April 30, 1994). Katie is a teenage girl who lives with her mother and father on Oak Tree Lane. Katie, however, is not quite your typical teenage girl: when she gets upset she goes "Ka-Boom" and turns into a hideous monster that wrecks havoc until she gets what she wants, then she returns to her normal pretty self. Aired on *The Animaniacs*.

Voice Cast: Laura Mooney (*Katie*); Rob Paulsen (*Katie's father*); Mary Gross (*Katie's mother*).

4922 Kay Kyser's Kollege of Musical Knowledge. (Series; Game; NBC; 1949–1954). Musical numbers are interspersed with a quiz segment situated against a college format. Players compete in tests of musical questions divided into midterms and final exams. The Professor (host) leads the orchestra in a selection that the player must identify. If he is correct, a cash prize is awarded; if he is unable to answer it, the song title is relayed by the studio audience (students).

Host: Kay Kyser (*1949–54*), Tennessee Ernie Ford (*1954*). **Regulars:** Mike Douglas, Sylvia Michaels, Diana Sinclair, Liza Palmer, Sue Bennett, Merwyn Bogue, Ken Spaulding, Donna Brown, Maureen Cassidy, Spring Mitchell, The Honeydreamers. **Announcer:** Jack Narz, Verne Smith.

4923 Kay O'Brien. (Series; Drama; CBS; 1986). The victories and defeats of Kay O'Brien, a second year surgical resident at Manhattan General Hospital in New York City. Kay was born in Manhattan and is the daughter of Jack and Lucille O'Brien. Dr. Josef Wallach is her superior and she is best friends with Rosa Villanueva, a nurse. Rosa is married to Lee and is the mother of Allison and Danny. Other doctors at the hospital are Robert Moffitt, Mark Doyle, Cliff Margolis and Michael Kwan. Kay's real name is Katherine and she also has the nickname "Kayo." Originally titled *Kay O'Brien, Surgeon*.

Cast: Patricia Kalember (*Kay O'Brien*); Jan Rubes (*Joseph Wallach*); Priscilla Lopez (*Rosa Villanueva*); Lane Smith (*Robert Moffitt*); Brian Benben (*Mark Doyle*); Keone Young (*Michael Kwan*); Tony Soper (*Cliff Margolis*); John McMartin (*Jack O'Brien*); Scotty Bloch (*Lucille O'Brien*); Walter Boone (*Lee Villanueva*); Lisa Jakub (*Alison Villanueva*); Stuart Stone (*Danny Villanueva*).

4924 The Kay Starr Show. (Series; Variety; Syn.; 1957). Singer Kay Starr hosts a weekly program of music and song. Pete King and his orchestra supply the music.

4925 Kaya. (Series; Drama; MTV; 2007). A music oriented teen drama that focuses on Kaya, the lead singer in a rock band (Crossing Coldwater) as she and her friends struggle up the rocky road to music stardom. Particular focus is on Kaya when, after the band goes from obscurity to stardom, she suddenly finds herself in a world she is not prepared for — producers, lavish parties and male admirers while at the same time attempting to remain the same girl she was before success went to her head.

Cast: Danielle Savre (*Kaya*); Mike Dopud (*Don*); Joe McLeod (*Manny*); Justin Wilczynski (*Taylor*); Cory Monteith (*Gunnar*); Jessica Parker Kennedy (*Natalee*); Eric Benet (*T. Davis*); Alexia Fast (*Kristin*);

Paul Anthony (*Marc*); Lynda Boyd (*Ellie*); Ari Cohen (*Trip Thayer*); Christy Carlson Romano (*Kat*); Jana Mitsoula (*Victoria*); Robert Moloney (*Rossi*).

4926 Kaz. (Series; Crime Drama; CBS; 1978-1979). Martin Kazinski, called "Kaz," is an ex-cop turned attorney who studied for the bar while serving a six-year prison term for grand theft auto. He is now working as an attorney for the Los Angeles firm of Bennett, Reinhart and Colcourt and stories follow his sincere efforts to help people in deep trouble with the law. Mary Parnell is the owner of the Starting Gate Nightclub (over which Kaz lives; Mary is replaced in later episodes by a man named Malloy); Katie McKenna is Kaz's girlfriend, a court reporter for the *Herald*; Samuel Bennett is the senior partner; Peter Colcourt is Bennett's partner; Ilsa Fogel is Bennett's secretary; and Frank Revko is the District Attorney.

Cast: Ron Leibman (*Martin Kazinski*); Patrick O'Neal (*Samuel Bennett*); Gloria LeRoy (*Mary Parnell*); Dick O'Neill (*Malloy*); Linda Carlson (*Katie McKenna*); Mark Withers (*Peter Colcourt*); Edith Atwater (*Ilsa Fogel*); George Wyner (*Frank Revko*).

4927 The Keane Brothers Show. (Series; Variety; CBS; 1977). Brothers John and Tom Keane oversee a program of music, songs and comedy.

Host: John Keane, Tom Keane. **Regulars:** Jimmy Caesar, The Anita Mann Dancers. **Orchestra:** Alan Copeland.

4928 The Keefe Brasselle Show. (Series; Variety; CBS; 1963). Summer program of music, songs and comedy with singer Keefe Brasselle as the host.

Host: Keefe Brasselle. **Regulars:** Ann B. Davis, Rocky Graziano, Noelle Adam, John Style, Deanne Style, Deanda Style, The Buddy Foster Dancers. **Music:** Charles Sanford.

4929 Keen Eddie. (Series; Crime Drama; Fox; 2003). Eddie Arlette is a maverick cop with the 8th Precinct of the N.Y.P.D. A case to bust a drug ring brings Eddie to England where his rather unusual tactics impress Superintendent Nathan Johnson of New Scotland Yard. Eddie is invited to stay and help the local authorities. After receiving permission, Eddie is teamed with Monty Pippin, a by-the-books inspector, and stories follow Eddie as he uses his keen instincts to help solve crimes for New Scotland Yard. Other regulars are Fiona, Eddie's roommate. She has a pet cat named Duchess while Eddie has a dog named Pete (who has his own TV remote control and starred in a TV commercial for Snoot Snacks Dog Biscuits for D.F. and Company Advertising).

Cast: Mark Valley (*Eddie Arlette*); Sienna Miller (*Fiona*); Julian Rhind-Tutt (*Monty Pippin*); Colin Salmon (*Nathan Johnson*).

4930 The Keenan Ivory Wayans Show. (Series; Talk; Syn.; 1997-1998). Promoted as "Late night talk the Wayans way," the program features comedian Keenan Ivory Wayans interviewing celebrities (as well as lesser known personalities), performing comedy monologues and exchanging small talk with his announcer, Angelique Perrin. Vassal Benford provides the music.

4931 Keep It in the Family. (Pilot; Comedy; NBC; May 27, 1954). The pilot film for *Father Knows Best* about events in the lives of an American family of five: parents Tom and Grace, and their children, Peggy, Jeff and Patty. Aired as a segment of *Ford Theater*.

Cast: Robert Young (*Tom*); Ellen Drew (*Grace*); Sally Fraser (*Peggy*); Gordon Gebert (*Jeff*); Tina Thompson (*Patty*).

4932 Keep It in the Family. (Series; Game; ABC; 1957-1958). Two families, each composed of five members (the mother, father and three children) compete. General knowledge questions are asked of each member of the family, beginning with the youngest. Each correct response earns points. The winners, the highest point scorers, receive merchandise prizes. Singer Keefe Brasselle was slated to host the show but never did (he was replaced by Bill Nimmo but press information with Keefe as the host was sent out and appears in publications like *TV Guide*).

Host: Bill Nimmo. **Announcer:** Johnny Olson.

4933 *Keep on Crusin'.* (Series; Variety; CBS; 1987). Music and comedy acts from Los Angeles are showcased with hosts Stephen Bishop and comedian Sinbad.

4934 *Keep on Truckin'.* (Series; Comedy; ABC; 1975). A potpourri of broad comedy sketches, freewheeling spoofs and blackouts.

Cast: Franklyn Ajaye, Rhonda Bates, Katherine Baumann, Jeannine Burnier, Didi Conn, Charles Fleischer, Wayland Flowers, Richard Lee Sung, Larry Ragland, Marion Ramsey, Jack Riley, Fred Travalena. **Music:** Marvin Laird.

4935 *Keep Talking.* (Series; Game; CBS; ABC; 1958–1960). Two teams compete, each composed of two celebrities. One member of each team receives a secret phrase that he must work into an ad-libbed conversation. At the end of the time, the player's teammate must identify the concealed phrase. Each correct guess awards the team points, The team with the highest score is the winner and prizes are awarded to the home and studio audience players being represented by the celebrities. Aired on CBS (July 15, 1958 to Sept. 2, 1959) on ABC (Oct. 29, 1959 to May 3, 1960).

Host: Monty Hall *(1958)*, Carl Reiner *(1958-59)*, Merv Griffin *(1959)*. **Panelists:** Elaine May, Ilka Chase, Joey Bishop, Morey Amsterdam, Audrey Meadows, Orson Bean, Paul Winchell, Pat Carroll, Peggy Cass, Danny Dayton.

4936 *Keep the Faith.* (Pilot; Comedy; CBS; April 14, 1972). Rabbi Mossman is old and set in his ways. Rabbi Miller is young and somewhat opposed to Mossman's archaic thinking. The proposal was to relate the clash that erupts when Miller attempts to modernize the temple with his progressive ideas. Hosentha is the ill-tempered caretaker.

Cast: Howard Da Silva *(Rabbi Mossman)*; Bert Convy *(Rabbi Miller)*; Henry Corden *(Hosentha)*.

4937 *Keeper of the Wild.* (Pilot; Drama; Syn.; Jan. 1977). Jim Donaldson, Holly James and Paul Limkula are the owner-operators of an animal preserve in Africa. The proposal was to relate the various problems they encounter protecting animals from unscrupulous characters.

Cast: Denny Miller *(Jim Donaldson)*; Pamela Susan Shoop *(Holly James)*; James Reynolds *(Paul Limkula)*.

4938 *Keeping an Eye on Denise.* (Pilot; Comedy; CBS; June 19, 1973). A proposed series about a happy-go-lucky single (Jackie Cooper) who is suddenly saddled with the care of Denise (Lynne Frederick), an uninhibited teenage daughter he never knew he had from a Korean War romance. A second, unaired version exists wherein Jackie Cooper agrees to care for Denise (Lynne Frederick), the 18-year-old daughter of a friend (Richard Dawson) he met during the Koran War when she leaves England to visit America.

4939 *Keeping Up with the Joneses.* (Pilot; Comedy; NBC; April 24, 1972). The Brownstone at 15 East 46th Street in New York City is shared by two couples who have the same last name of Jones but who are not related: Ernie, a white construction worker, and his wife, Pat; and Walt, a black police officer, and his wife, Liz. The proposal was to relate the misadventures the two couples, who are best friends, encounter.

Cast: Warren Berlinger *(Ernie Jones)*; Pat Finley *(Pat Jones)*; John Amos *(Walt Jones)*; Teresa Graves *(Liz Jones)*.

4940 *Keeping Up with the Kardashians.* (Series; Reality; E!; 2007–). A real life portrait of Kim Kardashian (daughter of lawyer Robert Kardashian), "a tinsel town babe" hoping to make her mark in show business. Kim is gorgeous and cameras manage to capture every inch of her, especially in low cut blouses. Kim is managed by her mother, Kris Jenner (now married to Olympic decathlon champion Bruce Jenner) and she is seen with her equally gorgeous sisters, Khloe and Kourtney. The events that befall Kim and her family are shared with the viewing audience.

4941 *Kell on Earth.* (Series; Reality; Bravo; 2010). A look at the hectic world of fashion publicist Kelly "Kell" Cutrone (owner of the PR firm People's Revolution) as she and her staff race against time to mount ten prestigious New York Fashion Week presentations. Called "another pithy title in search of a series" by *Variety*, *Kell on Earth* focuses more on the foul-mouthed (even in front of her seven-year-old child) Kell as she dos what it takes to make herself a success — from outrageous demands from her staff, hobnobbing with the echelon of the fashion industry to kissing the butt of fashion designers.

4942 *Kelly Monteith.* (Series; Comedy; The Entertainment Channel; 1982-1983). British produced Program of comedy skits about life with American comedian Kelly Monteith.

Host: Kelly Monteith. **Regulars:** Gabrielle Drake, Nicholas McArdle, Louise Mansi, Michael Stainton. **Music:** Ronnie Hazelhurst.

4943 *The Kelly Monteith Show.* (Series; Comedy; CBS; 1976). Sketches that present comedian Kelly Monteith's unique view of contemporary life.

Host: Kelly Monteith. **Regulars:** Nellie Bellflower, Henry Corden. **Music:** Dick DeBenedictis.

4944 *Kelly's Kids.* (Pilot; Comedy; ABC; Jan. 4, 1974). Ken and Kathy Kelly are childless couple who adopt three children of different ethnic backgrounds: Matt (white), Steve (oriental) and Dwayne (black). The proposal, broadcast as a segment of *The Brady Bunch* was to relate the incidents that arise in the newly formed family. Mrs. Payne is their neighbor.

Cast: Ken Berry *(Ken Kelly)*; Brooke Bundy *(Kathy Kelly)*; Todd Lookinland *(Matt)*; Carey Wong *(Steve)*; William Attmore *(Dwayne)*; Molly Dodd *(Mrs. Payne)*.

4945 *Kelsey Grammer Presents the Sketch Show.* (Series; Comedy; Fox; 2005). Skit program that spoofs various aspects of life.

Host: Kelsey Grammer. **Regulars:** Kaitlin Ilson, Lee Mack, Malcolm Barrett, Mary Lynn Rajskub.

4946 *The Ken Berry Wow Show.* (Series; Variety; ABC; 1972). A nostalgic look at the 1930s to 1960s through music, song, dance and comedy.

Program Open: "Wow is excitement. Wow is laughter. Wow is Fun. Wow is now. ABC proudly presents *Ken Berry's Wow Show* with Laara Lacey, Billy Sands, Teri Garr, Steve Martin, Don Wayne, Cheryl Stopplemore, Carl Gottlieb, the New Seekers, Barbara Joyce ... and starring Ken Berry."

Host: Ken Berry. **Regulars:** Cheryl Ladd (under her real name, Cheryl Stopplemore), Steve Martin, Billy Van, Carl Gottlieb, Teri Garr, Barbara Joyce, Don Ray, The New Seekers, The Jaime Rogers Dancers. **Orchestra:** Jimmy Dale.

4947   *The Ken Murray Show.* (Series; Variety; CBS; 1950–1953). Songs, blackouts, dramatic vignettes, comedy sketches and novelty acts.

Host: Ken Murray. **Regulars:** Darla Jean Hood, Joe Besser, Laurie Anders, Jack Mulhall, Betty Lou Walters, Art Lund, Pat Conway, Annie Shelton, Jack Marshall, Richard Webb, Johnny Johnston, Anita Gordon, Joan Shea, Herbert Marshall, Lillian Farmer, Cathy Hild, Tommy Labriola, The Ken Murray Chorus, The Ken Murray Dancers, The Glamour Lovelies. **Announcer:** Nelson Case. **Orchestra:** David Broekman, Jane Bergmeler.

4948   *Kenan and Kel.* (Series; Comedy; Nick; 1996–2000). Kenan Rockmore and Kel Kimble are teens and best friends who seek fun wherever they can find it. Particular focus, however, is on Kenan and his experiences at school, his job (clerk at Rigby's Grocery Store) and at home (where he lives with his parents, Roger and Sheryl, and his sister, Kyra). Chris Potter is Kenan's boss at Rigby's; Sharla Morrison (introduced in 1998) works with Kenan at Rigby's.

Cast: Kenan Thompson (*Kenan Rockmore*); Kel Mitchell (*Kel Kimble*); Ken Foree (*Roger Rockmore*); Teal Marchande (*Sheryl Rockmore*); Vanessa Baden (*Kyra Rockmore*); Dan Frischman (*Chris Potter*); Alexis Fields (*Sharla Morrison*); Biago Messina (*Marc Cramm*).

4949   *Kendra.* (Series; Reality; E!; 2009). A spin off from *The Girls Next Door* wherein Kendra Wilkinson, the busty blonde bombshell who was one of Hugh Hefner's favorite girls, leaves him and her pampered life at the Playboy Mansion to live on her own for the first time. Kendra is engaged (then married) to Hank Bassett (Philadelphia Eagles wide receiver) and cameras follow Kendra (with Hank by her side) as she becomes accustomed to doing things ordinary people do (including housewife and mother after the birth of her son, Hank Jr.).

4950   *The Kenny Everett Video Show.* (Series; Variety; Syn.; 1981). Imaginative program that incorporates visual and audio effects to present comedy sketches, music and songs. Produced in England.

Host: Kenny Everett. **Regulars:** Kay Bush, Katie Boyle, Arlene Phillips, Hot Gossip.

4951   *Kenny the Shark.* (Series; Cartoon; Discovery Kids; 2003). A young girl named Kat is very special (at least she thinks so; others disagree). She has a pet eight-foot 1500-pound pet Tiger Shark named Kenny. Kenny, however, is not your typical house pet: he craves food and is also very mischievous (causing numerous problems for Kat whose parents have vowed to return Kenny to the sea if he does not behave himself). Kat can speak shark and can control Kenny (and most of the time talking him out of eating Oscar, her younger brother, and anything else that looks good to him; he does get "Imitation Seal Flakes" for breakfast, though). Stories relate Kat's efforts to keep Kenny in line — and with her, despite Kenny's efforts to want to eat everything in sight.

Voice Cast: Kelli Rabke (*Kat*); Jim Conroy (*Kenny*); Russell Horton (*Dad*); Karen Culp (*Mom*); Alexander King (*Oscar*).

4952   *Kenny vs. Spinney.* (Series; Reality; Comedy Central; 2007). Canadian series about two childhood friends (Kenny Hotz, Spencer "Spenney" Rice) who live together in Toronto in a house wired for video and sound. Each week the two dysfunctional friends challenge each other to bizarre competitions with the loser getting the raw end of the deal: perform a humiliating stunt decreed by the winner (comedy also stems from the devious Kenny as he tries to put one over on the ethical Spenney).

4953   *Kentucky Jones.* (Series; Drama; NBC; 1964-1965). Several weeks after the death of his wife, Kenneth ("Kentucky") Jones, a professional horse trainer turned veterinarian, receives notice of the arrival of the Chinese orphan he and his wife had planned to adopt. Feeling that he is no longer qualified to raise the child, he attempts but fails to stop the adoption. Stories relate the efforts of Kentucky Jones (owner of the 40-acre Jones Ranch in California) to raise his ten-year-old adopted son, Dwight Eisenhower Wong (called Ike). Seldom Jackson is Kentucky's partner (called Seldom because he seldom won a horse race), Annie Ng is Ike's friend; Tommy Wong is Kentucky's friend; Miss Thorncroft is Ike's teacher; Mr. Ng is Annie's father.

Cast: Dennis Weaver (*Kentucky Jones*); Harry Morgan (*Seldom Jackson*); Ricky Der (*Dwight Eisenhower Wong*); Cherylene Lee (*Annie Ng*); Keye Luke (*Thomas Wong*); Nancy Rennick (*Miss Thorncroft*); Arthur Wong (*Mr. Ng*).

4954   *Kenya.* (Pilot; Drama; Unaired; Produced in 1988). Following the death of her husband, Jennifer Yates elects to remain in Kenya, East Africa, to continue managing the wild game ranch they own and raise her two children, Chelsea and Terry. The proposal was to relate Jennifer's efforts to carve out a life for herself and her children — with a little help from her father, Will.

Cast: Lisa Eichhorn (*Jennifer Yates*); Kimber Shoop (*Terry Yates*); Mary Griffin (*Chelsea Yates*); David Huddleston (*Will*).

4955   *Kevin Hill.* (Series; Drama; UPN; 2004-2005). Kevin Hill is a swinging young bachelor and top-notch attorney with the Manhattan law firm of Davis, Dugan and Kelly. He and his close friend Dame Ruiz enjoy attention in the courtroom and hitting the hottest nightspots in New York City. Life suddenly changes for Kevin when he becomes the guardian of Sarah, the 10-month-old daughter of his cousin (who was electrocuted trying to steal cable. His cousin's cocaine-addicted wife ran off and left him to care for Sarah when she was only six days old. When no other relative could be found, the courts elected Kevin as Sarah's guardian).

With his life now in complete turmoil, Kevin makes some changes: he quits his high-pressured job for a more relaxed position at Grey and Associates, a law firm owned and staffed by women.

Stories follow Kevin as he attempts to care for Sarah, curtail his nightlife and adjust to a work situation dominated by females. Other regulars are Jessica Grey, the senior partner; Nicolette Raye, an attorney; George , Kevin's gay nanny; and Veronica Carter, a lawyer who finds it difficult working with Kevin.

Cast: Taye Diggs (*Kevin Hill*); Michael Michele (*Jessica Grey*); Jon Seda (*Damian "Dame" Ruiz*); Christina Hendricks (*Nicolette Raye*); Kate Levering (*Veronica Carter*); Patrick Breen (*George Weiss*).

4956   *Key Club Playhouse.* (Series; Anthology; ABC; 1957). Rebroadcasts of dramas that originally aired on *Ford Theater*. See this title for information.

4957   *Key Tortuga.* (Pilot; Adventure; CBS; Sept. 11, 1981). John Jack Tyree is a widower and the father of two children (Laura and Matt) who runs a combination fishing charter and salvage service in Key Tortuga, Florida (the *Hemingston* is his charter boat; the *Henry Morgan* his salvage boat). The proposal was to relate Jack, Laura and Matt's adventures as they attempt to run their business. Cyclone Williams is Jack's friend.

Cast: Scott Thomas (*John Jack Tyree*); Janet Julian (*Laura Tyree*); Brett Cullen (*Matt Tyree*); Paul Winfield (*Cyclone Williams*).

4958 Key West. (Pilot; Adventure; NBC; Dec. 10, 1973). Key West, Florida, is the setting for a proposal about Steve Cutler, a retired C.I.A. agent who helps people in trouble. Other regulars are Candy, Steve's sidekick; Brandi, Steve's girlfriend; Sam, Steve's friend; and Police Chief Jim Miller.

Cast: Stephen Boyd (*Steve Cutler*); Woody Strode (*Candy*); Sheree North (*Brandi*); George Fisher (*Sam*); Don Collier (*Jim Miller*).

4959 Key West. (Series; Drama; Fox; 1993). Seamus O'Neill is a New Jersey factory worker who yearns to become a writer like his idol, Ernest Hemingway. One day Seamus buys a quick pick lotto ticket. The following morning when he checks the newspaper and finds he is the winner of a one million dollar prize, Seamus quits his job and moves to Key West, Florida, to follow in the footsteps of Hemingway. He begins by getting a job as a reporter with *The Meteor* (where Hemingway once worked). Stories follow Seamus's efforts to fulfill a dream.

King Cole is the blind editor of the paper; Paul Bouseleaux, called Gumbo is the owner of Gumbo's Bar and Grill; Savannah is a high class prostitute (charges $100 an hour and is proud to do so — "It was a lifelong dream of mine since childhood"); Rikki Clark is a doctor conducting experiments with dolphins for the Atlantic Dolphin Research Center; Chauncey Caldwell is the deputy mayor; and Tickled Pink is Gumbo's pet alligator (he wears a pink bow on his head and "dreams of devouring beautiful native girls").

Seamus has always dreamed of living in Key West where all the artists come. King Cole calls Seamus "Newshound." "They call me King," he says, "because I've been king of this paper [*The Meteor*] before you [Seamus] were born. Gumbo's bar and Grill features scantily clad dancing girls. Savannah is one of Gumbo's prostitutes.

Chauncey is an alcoholic. Although she is the deputy mayor, she doesn't care about the environment, animal rights or anything else — except progress no matter what it costs. Sheriff Cody is the local law enforcer. He claims to be a direct descendant of Wyatt Earp and the Lone Ranger. He worked previously as a clown in a circus. Cocoa assists King Cole, whom he calls "My eyes" and "Cocoanut."

Cast: Fisher Stevens (*Seamus O'Neill*); Denise Crosby (*Chauncey Caldwell*); Lara Piper (*Dr. Rikki Clark*); Jennifer Tilly (*Savannah Sumner*); Ivory Ocean ("*King*" *Roosevelt Cole*); Leland Crooke (*Gumbo*); Brian Thompson (*Sheriff Cody Jeremiah Jefferson*); Sandra Domepower (*Cocoa*); Nicholas Surovy (*Mayor Penbrooke*); T.C. Carson (*Jo Jo Nobulee*).

4960 Keyshawn Johnson: Tackling Design. (Series; Reality; A&E; 2009). Former New York Jets football star Keyshawn Johnson has a dream: to become an interior designer. A&E gives him that chance as Keyshawn and his design team help families make changes to their home while staying within the budget the family has set for remolding.

4961 Keyshia Cole: The Way It Is. (Series; Reality; BET; 2008). Keyshia Cole is a young woman who struggles to make her mark in the music world (a singer with A&M Records). She yearns to be an inspiration for young people, especially those growing up "in the hood" as Keyshia herself had a difficult childhood and struggled to become a success. Keyshia believes everyone has goals to realize and through her series she attempts to relate the problems she had and does encounter with family, friends and business associates. The title, "The Way It Is," reflects her first album for A&M Records.

4962 Khan! (Series; Crime Drama; CBS; 1975). The apartment above the Canton Bazaar in San Francisco's Chinatown is home to Annie Khan, her brother, Kim and their father (who only goes by his last name) Khan, a Chinese private detective. Khan helps people who have no other place to turn. While he is an expert in the martial arts and is opposed to violence, he often finds himself in situations where talking does not work and he must resort to physical skills to achieve a goal. While Khan does enlist the help of the police (in particular Lieutenant Gubbins), he also finds help from Annie and Kim, who turn amateur detective to help their father solve a case. Stories follow Khan as he takes on cases that are not only dangerous but puzzling as well. *Khan* is the only series in which the star refused screen billing.

Cast: Khigh Dhiegh (*Khan*); Irene Yah-Ling Sun (*Anna Khan*); Evan Kim (*Kim Khan*); Vic Tayback (*Lieutenant Gubbins*).

4963 Kibbee Hates Fitch. (Pilot; Comedy; CBS; Aug. 2, 1965). Russell Kibbee and Arthur Fitch are best friends who are also firemen with the New York City Fire Department. One day Kibbee is promoted to captain of Hook and Ladder Company Number 23. Fitch, a lieutenant who was also up for the promotion, becomes jealous and decides he now hates Kibbee for taking his job. The proposal was to relate the bickering that occurs between two friends who now hate each other, but who must work together. Other regulars are Selena, Russell's wife; Kevin, their son; Marcia, Arthur's wife; Nancy, their daughter; Captain O'Brien; and firemen Callahan and Walsh. See also *Kibbee Hates Fitch, Fitch Hates Kibbee*.

Cast: Don Rickles (*Russell Kibbee*); Lou Jacobi (*Arthur Fitch*); Nancy Andrews (*Selena Kibbee*); William Ade (*Kevin Kibbee*); Pert Kelton (*Marcia Fitch*); Karleen Wiese (*Nancy Fitch*); Ralph Dunne (*Captain O'Brien*); Herb Edelman (*Callahan*); Bob Kaliban (*Walsh*).

4964 Kibbee Hates Fitch, Fitch Hates Kibbee. (Pilot; Comedy; Unaired; Produced in 1974). A remake of *Kibbe Hates Fitch* about two sisters (Kate and Peg) who marry two bickering firemen (Kibbee and Fitch) and the complications that ensue when they attempt to work together as well as live next door to each other. The pilot episode relates how the bickering begins when Russell Kibbee is promoted to captain and his best friend, Arthur Fitch, becomes jealous.

Cast: Michael Bell (*Russell Kibbee*); Chuck McCann (*Arthur Fitch*); Lynnette Mettey (*Kate Kibbee*); Bonnie Boland (*Peg Fitch*); Alan Oppenheimer (*Captain Fox*).

4965 Kick Buttowski: Suburban Daredevil. (Series; Cartoon; Disney XD; 2010–). Clarence "Kick" Buttowski is a young boy who is determined to become the world's greatest daredevil. He is opposed to the ordinary and has made it his goal to make every moment a bit more awesome. Inspired by his idol, stuntman Billy Stumps, Kick sets out by devising daring physical feats and stories relate his adventures as he attempts to achieve a dream. Gunther is Kick's friend and staunchest supporter; Wade is the slacker who works as a convenience store clerk; Mr. Vickle is Kick's neighbor, whom Kick turns to for encouragement.

Voice Cast: Charlie Schlatter (*Clarence "Kick" Buttowski*); Matt L. Jones (*Gunther*); Danny Cooksey (*Brad*); John DiMaggio (*Mr. Vickle*); Eric Christian Olsen (*Wade*).

4966 Kicks. (Series; Music; Syn.; 1979). Jeff Kutash hosts a weekly program of performances by disco personalities.

4967 The Kid-A-Littles. (Pilot; Children; Syn.; Sept. 1984). The office of a newspaper called *The Daily Typo* is the setting for a proposal that was to teach learning experiences to children through the antics of the puppet characters who work for the editor-in-chief, Clipper (the only live character on the program).

Cast: John Wheeler (*Chief Clipper*).

4968 *Kid Gloves.* (Series; Children; CBS; 1951). Two children compete in a series of three thirty-second boxing bouts that follow the rules of the professionals. Between rounds, John DaGroza, the Pennsylvania Boxing Commissioner, conducts a question-and answer session with the studio audience.

Commentator: Bill Sears. **Referee:** Frank Goodman. **Ring Announcer:** Barry Cassel.

4969 *Kid Knievel.* (Series; Cartoon; Disney XD; 2009–). Francis Little is a 12-year-old boy with a big dream: to become the world's greatest daredevil (even bigger than his idol, Robbie Knievel, the son of famed daredevil Evel Kinevel). Francis, however, is short in stature but big in heart, and he must overcome great obstacles to achieve his dream. With the help of his friends Brad and Gunther, Francis tackles the seemingly impossible for one so young—from riding a super powered kayak down a raging river to riding a unicycle blindfolded.

Voice Cast: Chris Edgerly *(Francis Little)*; Matt Jones *(Gunther)*; Danny Cooksey *(Brad)*.

4970 *Kid 'n' Play.* (Series; Cartoon; NBC; 1990). Christopher Reid (Kid) and Christopher Martin (Play), the rap duo from the film *House Party*, appear as aspiring rappers living in New York City. Their misadventures as they seek their goal are seen in animation while their introductions and closing segments are live action—all of which is designed to relay positive lessons to children.

Cast: Christopher Reid *(Kid)*; Christopher Martin *(Play)*.

4971 *Kid Nation.* (Series; Reality; CBS; 2007). The format, borrowed from the book *Lord of the Flies*, follows 40 children as they attempt to build a society for themselves without help from adults. Bonanza City, New Mexico, a real Old West ghost town, is the site where the kids (aged 8–15) spend one month attempting to do what their forefathers were not able to accomplish—build a town that works. The kids must prepare their own meals, run the town businesses (for example, the saloon, where root beer is served) and uphold the law. Unlike other reality shows, there are no elimination rounds. A child can leave at any time if things become too difficult. The object is to show adults that kids have a better vision of what needs to be done in the real world. Jonathan Karsh hosts.

4972 *Kid Notorious.* (Series; Comedy; Comedy Central; 2003). Robert Evans, alias Kid Notorious, is the legendary bad boy and ladies' man extraordinaire. He is an actor and producer with many hit films and just as many ex-wives. Whatever Kid does and wherever he goes he makes headlines. Stories, which parody Hollywood, follow Kid as he goes about proving his prowess—whether it be climbing the highest mountain or driving the world's fastest car.

Cast: Robert Evans *(Kid Notorious)*; Alan Selka *(English)*; Niecy Nash *(Tollie Mae Wilson)*; Jeannie Elias *(Sharon Stone)*; Billy West *(Donald Rumsfeld)*.

4973 *Kid Power.* (Series; Cartoon; ABC; 1972–1974). The story of a group of children, all members of the Rainbow Club, who are struggling to save the environment and improve the world in which they live. The object of the program is to show kids of different ethnic backgrounds sharing thoughts on prejudice, teamwork and responsibility.

Voice Cast: Charles Kennedy, Jr. *(Wellington)*; Jay Silverheels, Jr. *(Oliver)*; John Gardiner *(Nipper)*; Allan Melvin *(Jerry)*; Carey Wong *(Connie)*; Gary Shapiro *(Ralph)*; Michele Johnson *(Sybil)*; Jeff Thomas *(Diz)*; Greg Thomas *(Albert)*.

4974 *The Kid Super Power Hour with Shazam.* (Series; Cartoon; NBC; 1981-1982). Animated programs *Hero High* and *Shazam* are interspersed with live action segments that revolve around the music and joke telling of the rock group Hero High (who also appear in *Hero High*, about the students who attend a training school for super heroes: Captain California, Glorious Gal, Dirty Trixie, Misty Magic, Rex Ruthless, Weatherman and Punk Rock; teachers are Mr. Sampson and Miss Grim). *Shazam* relates the adventures of super heroes Billy Batson (alias Shazam), Mary Freeman (alias Mary Marvel) and Freddy Freeman (alias Captain Marvel) as they battle the sinister forces of evil.

Voice Cast: Christopher Hensel *(Captain California)*; Becky Perle *(Glorious Gal)*; Mayo McCaslin *(Dirty Trixie)*; Jere Fields *(Misty Magic)*; John Berwick *(Rex Ruthless)*; John Greenleaf *(Weatherman)*; John Venocour *(Punk Rock)*; Alan Oppenheimer *(Mr. Sampson)*; Erica Scheimer *(Miss Grim)*; Erica Scheimer *(Mary Freeman/Mary Marvel)*; Burr Middleton *(Billy Batson/Shazam)*; Barry Gordon *(Freddy Freeman/Captain Marvel)*. **Announcer:** Casey Kasem.

4975 *Kid Talk.* (Series; Children; Syn.; 1972). Two guest celebrities (per show) discuss topical issues with four children.

Host: Bill Adler. **Panelists:** Mona Tera, Andy Yamamoto, Nellie Henderson, Alan Winston.

Announcer: Johnny Olson.

4976 *Kid vs. Kat.* (Series; Cartoon; Disney XD; 2009–). Coop Burtonburger is a ten-year-old boy who had a normal life until his younger sister, Millie, found and adopted a stray kitten (whom she named Mr. Kat) that changed the course of Coop's life. Mr. Kat resembles a hairless Sphinx and Coop has discovered that the feline is actually an alien that is stranded on Earth. Stories relate the chaos that ensues when Coop tries to convince people that Mr. Kat is an alien but finds that nobody will believe him (except for his friend, Dennis, who also becomes involved in the situations that develop as Mr. Kat outsmarts them to keep his true identity a secret).

Voice Cast: Erin Matthews *(Coop)*; Kathleen Barr *(Mr. Kat/Millie)*; Cathy Weseluck *(Dennis)*; Trevor Devall *(Dad Burtonburger)*; Linda Sorenson *(Old Lady Munson)*.

4977 *The Kid with the Broken Halo.* (Pilot; Comedy; NBC; April 15, 1982). The live action pilot film for the animated series *The Gary Coleman Show* (NBC, 1982-83) about Andy LeBeau, a prankish angel who is sent to Earth to perform good deeds to prove himself worthy of entering Heaven. Other regulars are Blake, Andy's guardian angel; and God, who appears as Michael, their superior.

Cast: Gary Coleman *(Andy LeBeau)*; Robert Guillaume *(Blake)*; Ray Walston *(God)*.

4978 *Kidd Video.* (Series; Children; NBC; 1984-1985). While rehearsing a song, the rock group Kidd Video is transported to an animated flip side of reality—a world of rock and roll—by the Master Blaster, an evil wizard. Their experiences as they escape from Master Blaster and set out to find their way back to reality is the focal point of stories. The program, which also relates their efforts to free rock stars kidnapped by the Master Blaster, features music videos. Kidd Video, Carla, Whiz and Ash are members of Kidd Video; Glitter is their friend; Fat Cat and Cool Kitty are Master Blaster's aides.

Cast: Bryan Scott *(Kidd Video)*; Gabrielle Bennett *(Carla)*; Robbie Rist *(Whiz)*; Steve Alterman *(Ash)*; Cathy Cavadini *(Glitter)*; Peter Renaday *(Master Blaster)*; Marshall Efrom *(Fat Cat)*; Robert Towers *(Cool Kitty)*.

4979 *Kideo TV.* (Series; Cartoon; Syn.; 1986). The actual title for a block of three syndicated half-hour cartoons: *Popples, Rainbow Brite* and *Ulysses 31*. See these individual titles for information.

4980   *Kidnapped.* (Series; Drama; NBC; 2006). Conrad and Ellie Cain are an apparently happily married couple with three children: Aubrey (attending college, Brown University), Alice and Leopold. The Cain's are wealthy and their children lead rather sheltered lives. They have a nanny (Maria) and a bodyguard (Virgil Hayes) for Alice and Leopold. All appears to be normal for the family until one morning when Virgil is driving Leopold to school, that Leopold is kidnapped in a well-executed traffic maneuver.

Shortly after, the Cain's receive a note telling them not to call the police or FBI. Conrad abides by the note, but calls a mysterious man named Knapp, a specialist in recovering kidnap victims. A woman named Turner assists him and Knapp cares about retrieval—everything else is a distraction. His fee is not negotiable and payable on the safe return of the victim. All is going according to plan until word about the kidnapping leaks out and the FBI gets wind of it—just at the same time veteran agent Latimer King is about to retire. Kidnappings are cases King cannot resist and he puts off his retirement to investigate the Cain kidnapping—something Knapp doesn't want (as he feels FBI involvement will endanger the chances of a safe retrieval). Agent Andrea "Andy" Archer assists King. The series, which is actually a mystery, relates the independent efforts to Knapp and the FBI to find Leopold and uncover the people responsible for his abduction and the reason why. Unfortunately, low ratings ended the series and no conclusion was shown.

Cast: Jeremy Sisto (*Knapp*); Timothy Hutton (*Conrad Cain*); Dana Delany (*Ellie Cain*); Lydia Jordan (*Alice Cain*); Will Denton (*Leopold Cain*); Olivia Thirlby (*Aubrey Cain*); Delroy Lindo (*Latimer King*); Carmen Ejogo (*Turner*); Linus Roache (*Andy Archer*); Mykelti Williamson (*Virgil Hayes*); Doug Hutchinson (*Schroeder*); Michael Mosley (*FBI Agent Atkins*); Otto Sanchez (*Otto*); Lisa Dawnell James (*FBI Agent*); Michael McLaughlin (*Leopold as a child*); Susan Kelechi Watson (*Ella King*); Robert Clohessy (*Caller*).

4981   *Kids and Company.* (Series; Variety; DuMont; 1951-1952). "Red Goose Shoes presents *Kids and Company*, starring the kids of America" opened a program that presented performances by aspiring child performers as well as honoring children who performed outstanding deeds. Acts were determined by applause and the winner was crowned "Kid of the Week." The program's announcer is Mona, the Little Red Goose (the shoe product's logo).

Host: Johnny Olson. **Assistant:** Ham Fisher. **Music:** Al Greiner, Bill Wirges.

4982   *Kids Are People Too.* (Series; Children; ABC; 1980–1982). Celebrity interviews, music, information, cartoons and related entertainment geared to show kids that they are people too.

Host: Bob McAllister, Michael Young. **Regulars:** Joy Behar, Ellie Dylan, Randy Hamilton.

4983   *Kids' Biz.* (Pilot; Magazine; Syn.; Nov. 1986). Music, fashion, advice, and other information and entertainment geared to children.

Host: Stacy Scott, Suzy Stone.

4984   *Kids' Court.* (Series; Children; Nick; 1985). Courtroom proceedings coupled with an understanding of how the law works to familiarize children with the judicial system. A simulated case is presented with children portraying the principals of a courtroom (lawyers, defendants, plaintiff, judge and jury). The case is presented as if it was real and the jury (via applause) determines the guilt or innocence of accused parties.

Host: Paul Provenza.

4985   *The Kids from C.A.P.E.R.* (Series; Comedy; NBC; 1976-1977). C.A.P.E.R. is short for the Civilian Authority for the Protection of Everybody, Regardless. It is a unit of the 927th Police Precinct in a town called Northeast Southwestern. Its top (and apparently only) operatives are P.T., Bugs, Doomsday and Doc, four somewhat fearless teenagers who do their best to right wrongs. Mr. Clintsinger is the newspaper reporter who follows "the kids" and stories relate the case investigations of the kids from C.A.P.E.R.

Cast: Steve Bonino (*P.T.*); Cosie Costa (*Bugs*); Biff Warren (*Doomsday*); John Lansing (*Doc*); Robert Lussier (*Mr. Clintsinger*).

4986   *Kids in the Hall.* (Series; Comedy; HBO; 1988–1995). A sketch comedy featuring the all male group the Kids in the Hall portraying virtually every character needed (including women) for their spoof of anything, everything and anybody.

Kids in the Hall: Dave Foley, Bruce McCulloch, Kevin McDonald, Mark McKinney, Scott Thompson. **Semi-Regulars:** Tamara Gorski, Nicole deBoer, Paul Bellini. **Music:** Shadowy Men on a Shadowy Planet.

4987   *Kids Incorporated.* (Series; Comedy; Syn.; 1985). P*lace is a teen club where the group, Kids Incorporated, play. Robin, Gloria, Stacy, Kid, Ryan and Renee are the young adults who comprise the group and stories relate their efforts to make a success of their group.

Cast: Jennifer Love Hewitt (*Robin*); Martika Marrero (*Gloria*); Stacy Ferguson (*Stacy*); Renee Sands (*Renee*); Ryan Lambert (*Ryan*); Rashaan Patterson (*Kid*); Moosie Drier (*Riley*); Devyn Pyett (*Devyn*); Richie Shoff (*Richie*); Kenny Ford, Jr. (*Kenny*); Haylie Johnson (*Haylie*); Eric Balfour (*Eric*); Anastasia Horne (*Anastasia*); Kimberly Duncan (*Kim*); Joseph Conrad (*Joe*); Tiffany Robbins (*Tiffany*); Cory Tyler (*Cory*); Leilani Lagamy (*Leilani*); Connie Lew (*Connie*); Sean O'Riordan (*P*lace Club Owner*).

4988   *Kids Say the Darndest Things.* (Series; Comedy; CBS; 1996–2000). During the 1950s on *Art Linkletter's House Party*, host Art Linkletter devoted a segment of each program to interviewing children for their humorous reactions to the questions he asked. When *House Party* ended in 1969, so did the child interview concept. After an absence of almost 30 years, CBS adapted the *House Party* segment into the series *Kids Say the Darndest Things* with an adult (Bill Cosby) interviewing children for their funny (if not unpredictable) answers to questions asked of them.

Host: Bill Cosby. **Co-Host:** Art Linkletter. **Music:** Bruce Miller.

4989   *Kids 2 Kids.* (Pilot; Children; Syn.; Aug. 18, 1981). An informative idea that explores the world of children—who they are and what they are doing.

Hosts: Kirk Brennan, Lynette Paradise.

4990   *The Kidsong TV Show.* (Series; Children; Syn.; 1987). When a group of children discover an abandoned TV studio, they make it their clubhouse. Soon they learn how to operate the equipment and set up their own station—Kidsongs. Borrowing its format from *Your Hit Parade*, the series presents songs for children sung by children (the Kidsong Kids).

Hosts: Tristen Potter, Chris Lytton. **The Kidsong Kids:** Todd Alyn Durboraw, David Chan, Julie Ann Gourson, Hillary Hollingsworth, Tiffany Johnson, Nicole Mandich, Robby Rosellen, Scott Trent.

4991   *Kiernan's Kaleidoscope.* (Series; Children; Syn.; 1949). John Kiernan hosts and narrates a program geared to children that explores the wonders of nature and science.

4992   ***Kiki's American Adventure.*** (Series; Erotica; Playboy; 2010). Kiki (as she is known) is a gorgeous Australian stripper with one great ambition: becoming an adult film actress like her idols Sasha Grey, Jenna Jameson and Savanna Samson, current American "porn queens." With the necessary assets, and encouragement from her peers, Kiki leaves Australia and heads for the San Fernando Valley, the adult film capital of the world, to fulfill her dream. While taking on the aspects of a reality series (Kiki's exploration of America) it also becomes adult only when Kiki experiences the world of pornography, including its sexy stars, sleazy producers, "horny bisexuals, shady managers and, night benders ... and a lot of new naked mates." The press release also states "If you want to know how your favorite adult actresses REALLY got started, don't miss a minute of *Kiki's American Adventure.*"

4993   ***The Kilborn File.*** (Pilot; Talk; Fox; June 28 to Aug. 2, 1010). A six week experiment, broadcast on select Fox stations in New York, Los Angeles, Philadelphia, Boston, Phoenix, Austin and Detroit that presents a humorous look at pop culture and current events.

     Host: Craig Kilborn.

4994   ***Killer Instinct.*** (Series; Crime Drama; Fox; 2005). Jack Hale and Danielle Carter are members of the Deviant Squad of the San Francisco Police Department who investigate gruesome murders. Stories detail Jack and Danielle's investigations into cases most seasoned officers would find upsetting.

     Cast: Johnny Messner (*Det. Jack Hale*); Kristin Lehman (*Det. Danielle Carter*); Chi McBride (*Lt. Matt Cavanaugh*); Jessica Steen (*Dr. Francine Kleep*); Ramone DeOcamo (*Harry Oka*); Rukiya Bernard (*Eden Cavanaugh*).

4995   ***Kim.*** (Pilot; Comedy; CBS; 1972). Kim Carter, the daughter of Lucy Carter (from *Here's Lucy*) leaves the family nest and sets out on her own after acquiring a job with a PR firm. She finds an apartment at the Marina overlooking San Francisco Bay in a building owned by Lucy's brother, Herb Hinkley, a would-be song writer. The proposal was to relate Kim's misadventures as she attempts to live her own life away from her interfering mother. Sue Anne is Kim's neighbor, a tour guide at the Museum of History.

     Cast: Lucie Arnaz (*Kim Carter*); Alan Oppenheimer (*Herb Hinkley*); Susan Tolsky (*Sue Anne Ditenner*).

4996   ***Kim Possible.*** (Series; Cartoon; Disney; 2002–2007). Kim Possible is a beautiful high school cheerleader. She is the daughter of brilliant parents and has twin mischievous brothers, Jim and Tim. Kim is also a girl who can do anything, including battling evil with her amazing powers and an array of gadgets. She is assisted by Ron Stoppable, her classmate and partner in crime fighting; Rufus, Ron's pet rat; and Wade Load, her computer contact.

     Dr. Drakken, a not-too-bright super villain seeking to take over the world, is assisted by Shego, a sharp-minded arch villain who is actually the one Kim should fear (as she makes up for the Doctor's mistakes). Shego wants to rule the world, as do the villains Senor Senior, Sr., and his son Senor Senior, Jr. Bonnie Rockwaller is Kim's high school rival. Stories follow Kim as she tries to be a normal school girl while at the same time protecting the world from evil.

     Voice Cast: Christy Carlson Romano (*Kim Possible*); Will Friedle (*Ron Stoppable*); Nancy Cartwright (*Rufus*); Tahj Mowry (*Wade Load*); Jean Smart (*Kim's mother*); Gary Cole (*Kim's father*); Shaun Fleming (*Jim and Tim Possible*); Nicole Sullivan (*Shego*); John DiMaggio (*Dr. Drakken*); Earl Boen (*Senor Senior, Sr.*); Nestor Carbonell (*Senor Senior, Jr.*); Kirsten Storms (*Bonnie Rockwaller*).

4997   ***Kimba, the White Lion.*** (Series; Cartoon; Syn.; 1966).

"Who lives down in deepest, darkest Africa? Who's the one who brought the jungle fame? Who believes in doing good and doing right? Kimba the white lion is his name...." In Egypt four thousand years ago, a spendthrift pharaoh, King Tut Tut, caused the country to lose its prosperity. In an attempt to save his country, Fradies, the king's minister, develops a special wisdom formula that he feeds to his rare, pet white lion. The lion is sent into the village and the people, who believe it is the spirit of the Sphinx, follow its leadership. The lion teaches them economy and the development of strong bodies and minds. As Egypt prospers once again, the king extends good will to all its neighboring African tribes. He selects one tribe in particular, the Kickapeels, to receive a special gift — the white lion.

     The lion teaches, the tribe prospers and in return, the lion is made king. Thus, generation after generation, a white lion has ruled Africa. In 1966, Caesar, the aging, current lion ruler, bestows upon his son, Kimba, the title of king.

     A second history has Caesar, the African animal king, married to the lioness Snowene. Caesar's rule has all animals living free. When hunter's invade Africa and begin capturing animals, Caesar foils them by setting the animals free. Caesar is killed during one mission and Snowene (who is pregnant) is captured. Aboard a ship bound for England, Snowene gives birth to Kimba, who learns from his mother the good work his father tried to do.

     Kimba, through his mother's urging, escapes from the ship and manages to make his way back to Africa. He establishes himself as a ruler with one purpose: develop an understanding between humans and animals.

     Kimba is young but wise beyond his years. Stories follow Kimba as he struggles to safeguard his homeland from evil. Dan'l Baboon, Sampson, Pauley Cracker, Tadpole, Roger Ranger, Kitty and King Speckle Rex are Kimba's friends; Claw his enemy.

     A revised version of the Japanese series aired in 1994 with the voices of Kathleen Barr, Lisa Ann Beley, Michael Dobson, Venus Terzo and Richard Newman.

     Voice Cast: Billie Lou Watt (*Kimba*); Gilbert Mack (*Pauley Cracker*); Ray Owens (*Dan'l*); Hal Studer (*Roger Ranger*).

4998   ***Kimbar of the Jungle.*** (Pilot; Adventure; Unaired; Produced in 1958). Africa is the setting for a proposed serial about Kimbar, a white "Lord of the Jungle," and his pet chimpanzee, Tamba, as they help people in trouble (information regarding Kimbar's background is not given).

     Cast: Steve Reeves (*Kimbar*).

4999   ***Kimora: Life in the Fab Lane.*** (Series; Reality; Style; 2007–2010). Cameras follow fashion superstar Kimora Lee, surrounded by stylists, managers and publicists, as she goes about her daily activities (which include shopping and visiting friends and establishing a global fashion line).

5000   ***Kincaid.*** (Pilot; Drama; ABC; April 22, 1963). A proposed spin off from *Stoney Burke* about Andy Kincaid, a sergeant with the juvenile division of a large metropolitan police department.

     Cast: Dick Clark (*Andy Kincaid*).

5001   ***Kindred: The Embraced.*** (Series; Drama; Fox; 1996). The Haven is a seemingly innocent San Francisco nightclub owned by Lillie Langtry. It is, beneath the surface, a gathering place for modern-day vampires. San Francisco appears to be infested by a number of disparate (kindred) vampire clans. Julian Luna is a prince of several of these clans and his efforts to keep the peace among the clans is the focal point of stories (here, humans are not bitten to become vampire members of the clans; for a vampire to bite a human means death to that vampire. Humans volunteer for transformation into a clan).

Cast: Mark Frankel (*Julian Luna*); Stacy Haiduk (*Lillie Langtry*); Patrick Bauchau (*Archon Raine*); Brigid Brannagh (*Sasha*); C. Thomas Howell (*Frank Kohanek*); Erik King (*Sonny Toussaint*); Jeff Kober (*Daedalus*); Brian Thompson (*Eddie Fiori*); Kelly Rutherford (*Caitlin Byrne*); Channon Poe (*Cash*).

5002 King Arthur. (Series; Adventure; Syn.; 1987). Medieval England is the setting for tales about King Arthur and his Knights of the Round Table as they set about dispensing justice and helping people who are unable to defend themselves from the evils that surround them.

Cast: Richard Austin, Andrew Burt (*King Arthur*); Robert Eddison (*Merlin the Magician*); Maureen O'Brien (*Morgan Le Fay*); Martin Chamberlain (*Sir Kay*); David Robb (*Sir Lancelot*); Felicity Dean (*Queen Guinevere*).

5003 King Arthur and the Knights of Justice. (Series; Cartoon; Syn.; 1992). Medieval England is the setting. With a plan to take over Camelot, the evil witch Morgana casts a spell that captures her enemy, King Arthur (and his Knights of Justice) and imprisons them in a tomb of ice. Merlin, Arthur's faithful magician, casts a spell that transports a modern day American football team, the Knights (lead by quarterback Arthur King) to his time to battle Morgana and help free Camelot's rightful king. Stories follow the football team as they become real Knights and set out to rescue their king and stop Morgana from becoming ruler.

Voice Cast: Andrew Kavadas (*Arthur King*); Jim Byrnes (*Merlin*); Kathleen Bar (*Queen Guinevere*); Lee Jeffrey (*Sir Breeze*); Mark Hildreth (*Sir Gallop*); Michael Donovan (*Sir Darren*); Scott McNeil (*Sir Lancelot*); Venus Terzo (*Lady Elaine*); Gary Chalk (*Lord Viper*).

5004 The King Family Show. (Series; Variety; ABC; 1965-1966; 1969). Members of the King family, a large family of talented singers and musicians, share the spotlight in a program of music and songs. The family, at the time, features: William King, Karlton King, Alyce King, Louise King Rey, Donna King Conklin, Maxine Thomas, Yvonne King Birch, Marilyn King Larsen, William King, Phyllis King, Steve King, Della King, Jonathan King, Barbara King, Tammy Kong, Todd King, Don King, Cheryl King, Don King, Jr., Ray King, Bob Clark, Lex Clark, Linda Clark, Julie Clark, Carrie Clark, Cameron Clark, Alvino Rey, Lisa Rey, Robi Rey, James Conklin, Candice Wilson, Robert Wilson, Kristen Wilson, Alexander Wilson, La Varn Thomas, Donna Thomas, Carolyn Thomas, Bill Brennan, Bill Birch, Tina Cole, Volney Howard IV, Cathy Birch Green, Jim Greene, Kent Larsen, Jennifer Larsen, Susannah Larsen, Lloyd Larsen.

5005 King Features Trilogy. (Series; Cartoon; Syn.; 1963). The overall title for an adaptation of three King Features comic strips.

1. Barney Google. Hillbilly hustler Barney Google and his friend Snuffy Smith's antics.

2. Beetle Bailey. Army private Beetle Bailey's efforts to adjust to military life at Camp Swampy. Sergeant Snorkel is his superior.

3. Krazy Kat. A lovesick cat plagued by the mischievous Ignatz Mouse.

Voice Cast: Allan Melvin (*Barney Google/Sgt. Snorkel*); Howard Morris (*Snuffy Smith/Beetle Bailey*); Penny Phillips (*Krazy Cat*); Paul Frees (*Ignatz Mouse*).

5006 The King Kong Show. (Series; Cartoon; ABC; 1966–1969). After Professor Bond, an American scientist establishes a base on Mondo Island in the Java Sea, his young son, Bobby, discovers and befriends the sixty-foot-tall gorilla, King Kong, a creature the Professor believes is intelligent and an important clue in the study of anthropology. Stories relate the struggles of the Professor, his children Bobby and Susan, and King Kong, as they struggle to battle the influences of Dr. Who, a power-mad scientist who seeks Kong for his own diabolical plan to control the world. Very loosely based on the 1933 feature film *King Kong*.

The second segment, *Tom of T.H.U.M.B.*, relates the adventures of six-inches tall Tom and his Oriental sidekick, Swinging Jack, as agents for Tiny Humans Underground Military Bureau, a secret U.S. government spy organization.

Voice Cast: Carl Banas (*Professor Bond*); Billie Mae Richards (*Bobby Bond*); Susan Conway (*Susan Bond*).

5007 King Leonardo and His Short Subjects. (Series; Cartoon; NBC; 1960–1963). The overall title for a trio of short animated segments. Also known as *The King and Odie*.

1. King Leonardo. The African kingdom of Bongoland is the setting as its ruler, King Leonardo, and his assistant, Odie Cologne battle the evil influences of Itchy Brother and Biggy Rat.

2. The Hunter. A beagle detective's attempts to apprehend the cunning Fox.

3. Tutor the Turtle. A turtle becomes whatever he wishes through the magic of Mr. Wizard, the Lizard.

Voice Cast: Jackson Beck (*King Leonardo*); Allen Swift (*Odie Cologne*); Jackson Beck (*Biggy Rat*); Allen Swift (*Itchy Brother*); Kenny Delmar (*The Hunter*); Ben Stone (*The Fox*); Allen Swift (*Tutor the Turtle*); Frank Milano (*Mr. Wizard*).

5008 King of Clubs: The Palomino. (Series; Reality; Playboy Channel; 2009). A behind-the-scenes look at the Palomino, a legendary adult entertainment club in Las Vegas. In addition to spotlighting the gorgeous girls who perform in the club's dance shows, the people who run the club are also profiled, in particular Dominic Gentile, the owner; his ex-wife, Michelle, the bookkeeper; and their son, Adam, the manager.

5009 King of Diamonds. (Series; Drama; Syn.; 1961-1962). Continental Diamond Industries is a New York based company that is responsible for protecting gems and industrial diamonds from the time they come out of the ground until they reach their final destination. John King is the company's security chief. Along with his partner, Casey "Case" O'Brien, John investigates crimes associated with the diamond district. Continental Diamond Industries is located on West 47th Street in Manhattan in the heart of the diamond industry. John, who wears a white trench coat (making him look more like a shady character than the hero) lives at 146 East 36th Street; he refers to diamonds as "ice."

Cast: Broderick Crawford (*John King*); Ray Hamilton (*Casey O'Brien*).

5010 King of Kensington. (Series; Comedy; Syn.; 1981). Events in the lives of the Kings, a family of three living in the city of Kensington near Toronto, Canada. Larry King, the husband, is the owner of King's Variety Store; he is married to Cathy. Larry's mother, Gladys King, also lives with them. Duke, Nestor and Max are Larry's friends and stories relate the incidents befall Larry at home and at work. Produced in Canada. Bob Francis performs the theme, "The King of Kensington."

Cast: Al Waxman (*Larry King*); Fiona Reid (*Cathy King*); Helene Winston (*Gladys King*); Ardon Bess (*Nestor Best*); Bob Vinci (*Duke Zaro*); John J. Dee (*Max*); Vivian Reis (*Rosa Zaro; Duke's wife*).

5011 The King of Queens. (Series; Comedy; CBS; 1998–

2006). Doug and Carrie Heffernan are an argumentative but happily married couple who live at 3121 Alberdine Avenue in Rego Park, Queens, New York. Also living with them is Arthur Spooner, Carrie's sarcastic father.

Doug works as a driver for IPS (International Parcel Service). Carrie first worked as a legal secretary for the Mid-Manhattan firm of Haskell and Associates (later called Kaplan, Hornstein and Stickler). She later works for a real estate company called The Dugan Group (also known as Dugan Properties).

Carrie is grouchy and bitchy. She is not a happy person by nature and enjoys seeing other people miserable. Doug is her complete opposite and most often takes verbal abuse from Carrie just to avoid arguments. Food is an important factor in Doug's life and he has the uncanny ability to make a delicious sandwich (he hopes to one day open a sandwich shop). Arthur is a hot head who often loses his temper (he threatens people with his catch phrase "Do you want a piece of me?").

Stories follow the daily incidents that spark romance, mistrust and arguments in the Heffernan household.

Arthur is 75 years old (first season episodes) and came to live with Doug and Carrie after his wife, Teresa, died and he burned his house down by accident. He now lives in the basement. Doug has Route 8 (the boonies) with IPS (he has been working there eight years when the series begins). Other regulars are Deacon Palmer, Spencer Olchin, Danny Heffernan, Richie Iannucci, Holly Shumpert and Lou Ferrigno.

Deacon, Spencer and Richie are Doug's friends. Deacon works with Doug and is separated from his wife, Kelly; they are the parents of Kirby and Major. Spencer is a subway toll booth operator (at the Queens Plaza Station). He is single (shares an apartment with Richie). Danny, Doug's cousin, is a not-so-great landscape artist and runs a company called The Garden of Weedin'.

Holly is a dog walker whom Carrie hired to "walk" Arthur so he could get his daily exercise. Lou Ferrigno is a former TV actor, best known for *The Incredible Hulk*, who is Doug and Carrie's neighbor. Janet and Joe are Doug's parents; Veronica is Spencer's mother; Patrick O'Boyle is the IPS dispatcher.

In the last episode Doug and Carrie adopt a baby Chinese girl (Ling Mai) at the same time Carrie (who was told she could not have children) becomes pregnant. Doug had quit his job with IPS (now works as a salesman for Finelli Home Furnishings) and in a flash forward sequence (one year in the future), Doug and Carrie are seen as the parents of two children. Arthur in the meantime, has married Spencer's mother, Veronica.

Cast: Kevin James (*Doug Heffernan*); Leah Remini (*Carrie Heffernan*); Jerry Stiller (*Arthur Spooner*); Victor Williams (*Deacon Palmer*); Patton Oswalt (*Spencer Olchin*); Larry Romano (*Richie Iannucci*); Nicole Sullivan (*Holly Shumpert*); Gary Valentine (*Danny Heffernan*); Merrin Dungey (*Kelly Palmer*); Omari Lyles (*Kirby Palmer*); Desmond Roberts (*Major Palmer*); Lou Ferrigno (*Himself*); Jenny O'Hara (*Janet Heffernan*); Dakin Matthews (*Joe Heffernan*); Anne Meara (*Veronica Olchin*); Tyler Hendrickson (*Young Doug; flashbacks*); Shelly Berman (*Arthur's brother, Skitch*); Sam McMurray (*Patrick O'Boyle*).

5012   *King of the Building.* (Pilot; Comedy; CBS; July 31, 1987). Joey (no last name given) is the doorman at 731 Park Avenue, a posh hotel in New York City. His attempts to manipulate the building and its employees for his own benefit — as well as helping tenants in need — was the focal point of the unsold series. Other regulars are Hector, the plumber; Leon, the janitor; Eddie, the bellhop; and Mr. Jamison, the manager.

Cast: Richard Lewis (*Joey*); Jose Perez (*Hector*); Tiger Haynes (*Leon*); Bobby Slayton (*Eddie*); Simon Jones (*Mr. Jamison*).

5013   *King of the Crown.* (Series; Reality; TLC; 2009). Before most girls can compete in contests such as Miss America, Miss Teen USA and Miss Universe, they require pageant coaching. Cyrus Frakes is such a coach and with his staff at Gowns and Crowns (in Queens, New York) episodes focus on girls who are new to the pageant world and need all the help they can get as they prepare for their big events. Cyrus is assisted by Shane Mason, the interview coach; Kyle Taylor, the fashion coordinator; and Amanda Pennekamp, "the true story girl" (an ugly duckling Cy transformed into a winner and who now shares her experiences with those girls who feel they have no chance).

5014   *King of the Hill.* (Series; Cartoon; Fox; 1997–2009). Hank Hill is an old-fashioned family man who works for Strickland Propane in Arlen, Texas. He is married to Peggy and is the father of a young son, Bobby. They live at 123 Ramsey Street. Hank's dog is Lady Bird.

Hank works hard, enjoys his job (he is hoping Bobby will follow in his footsteps) and relaxes by drinking beer with his friends, Bill Dauterive, Dale Gribble and Boomhauer. Also living with Hank is Luanne Platter, his sexy niece, who is hoping to become a beautician.

Peggy is opinionated. She works as a substitute Spanish teacher (also seen as a reporter for the *Arlington Bystander* and a realtor with Seizemore Realty) and Hank often obeys her every command (although he believes his strong sense of morality makes him "King of the Hill" household). Bobby is somewhat of a disappointment to Hank as he seems to be interested in everything but propane. Bill is a divorced military barber; Dale, owner of Dale's Dead Bug Exterminating, is paranoid (he believes the government is out to get him); and Boomhauer speaks gibberish that only Hank seems to understand.

Other regulars are Joseph Gribble, Dale's son; Buck Strickland, Hank's boss; Kahn and Minh Souphanousinphone, Hank's neighbors; John Redcorn, Hank's neighbor; Nancy Gribble, Dale's wife; Connie, Kahn and Minh's daughter. In later episodes Luanne marries the lazy Lucky and they become the parents of Gracie. Luanne also becomes famous as Luanne and the Manger Babies (entertains children with hand puppets).

Voice Cast: Mike Judge (*Hank Hill/Boomhauer*); Kathy Najimy (*Peggy Hill*); Pamela Segall (*Bobby Hill*); Brittany Murphy (*Luanne Platter*); Brittany Murphy, Breckin Meyer (*Joseph Gribble*); Johnny Hardwicke (*Dale Gribble*); Stephen Root (*Bill Dauterive/Buck Strickland*); Ashley Gardner (*Nancy Gribble*); Toby Hill (*Kahn*); Lauren Tom (*Minh/Connie*); Tom Petty (*Lucky*).

5015   *King of the Road.* (Pilot; Comedy; CBS; May 10, 1978). Cotton Grimes is a semi-retired country and western singer who runs a motel in Muscle Shoals, Alabama. The proposal was to relate Cotton's efforts to run the hotel and spotlight the performances of guest artists. Other regulars are Maureen, his girlfriend; Sam, his partner; Mildred, Sam's wife; and motel employees Bille Dee and Rick.

Cast: Roger Miller (*Cotton Grimes*); Lee Crawford (*Maureen Kenney*); Larry Haines (*Sam Braffman*); Marian Mercer (*Mildred Braffman*); R.G. Brown (*Billy Dee Huff*); Ric Carrott (*Rick*).

5016   *The Kingdom Chums.* (Pilot; Children; ABC; Nov. 28, 1986). When an unusual pattern of stars appears in the sky, a young boy (Peter), his sister (Mary Ann) and their friend (Sauli) are magically transported by a stream of light to an animated world where they become cartoon characters and meet the Kingdom Chums (Christopher Lion, Magical Moz and Little David) — animals who allow them to witness stories from the Bible (the unsold series format).

Cast: Jenna Von Oy *(Mary Ann)*; Christopher Fitzgerald *(Peter)*; Andrew Cassese *(Sauli)*.

5017 *Kingdom Hospital.* (Series; Drama; ABC; 2004). Kingdom Hospital in Maine is anything but a normal medical facility. Strange things occur (like patients mysteriously dying — or miraculously cured). The hospital has been built over an ancient cemetery, is earthquake plagued and is haunted (psychic Sally Druce is seeking to discover why the ghost of a young girl — who may hold the secret about the hauntings — has not passed over). Stories play out like a book with each episode (12 aired) like a chapter and leading into the next episode (a fancy way of producers saying a serialized story). Created by Stephen King (but based on a Danish miniseries called *The Kingdom*).

Cast: Ed Begley, Jr. *(Dr. Jesse James)*; Diane Ladd *(Sally Druce)*; Bruce Stegman *(Dr. Stegman)*; Andrew McCarthy *(Dr. Hook)*; William Wise *(Dr. Louis Traff)*; Suki Kaiser *(Natalie Rickman)*; Jack Coleman *(Peter Rickman)*; Meagen Fay *(Brendan Abelson)*; Lena Georgas *(Nurse Carrie Von Trier)*; Allison Hossack *(Dr. Christina Draper)*; Sherry Miller *(Dr. Lona Massingale)*; Jamie Harrold *(Dr. Elmer Traff)*; Jennifer Cunningham *(Christa)*.

5018 *Kingpin.* (Series; Drama; NBC; 2003). The activities of the Cadena family, a powerful Mexican drug trafficking family as they seek to keep their illegal enterprise going despite the D.E.A.'s (Drug Enforcement Agency) efforts to stop them. Miguel Cadena, educated at Sanford University, is head of the family; Marlene is Miguel's wife, an American lawyer who protects the business from government intervention; Joey is their eight-year-old son. Chato is Miguel's ambitious brother; Della Flores is the D.E.A. agent seeking to put Miguel behind bars; Heywood Klein is a plastic surgeon that heads the Cadenas' North American operations; Junie Gatling assists him.

Cast: Yancey Arias *(Miguel Cadena)*; Sheryl Lee *(Marlene Cadena)*; Ruben Carbajel *(Joey Cadena)*; Bobby Cannavale *(Chato Cadena)*; Angela Alvarado Rosa *(Della Flores)*; Brian Benben *(Dr. Heywood Klein)*; Shay Roundtree *(Junie Gatling)*.

5019 *Kingpins.* (Pilot; Comedy; CBS; Sept. 18, 1987). Kingpins is an Akron, Ohio, bowling alley owned by Hank Whittaker and managed by his daughter, Lindsay. Hank has an easy-going attitude and lets his friends ring up large tabs; Lindsay is a business-minded young woman who disagrees with her father's way of doing business. The proposal was to relate Hank's efforts to run the alley his way despite Lindsay's attempts to change his methods. Other regulars are Sonny, Hank's brother; and the alley regulars: Deter, Vern, Spud, Milt and Duncan.

Cast: Dorian Harewood *(Hank Whittaker)*; Marie-Alise Recasner *(Lindsay Whittaker)*; Ji-Tu Cumbuka *(Sonny Whittaker)*; David Alan Grier *(Deter Philbin)*; Jason Bernard *(Vern Puckett)*; Leonard Garner *(Spud Bunsen)*; Tommy Hicks *(Milt Simmons)*; Eric Flecks *(Duncan Moss)*.

5020 *Kings.* (Series; Drama; NBC; 2009). Gilboa is a mythical nation in a world parallel to Earth. In its capitol, Shiloh (a digitally enhanced version of New York City), a wicked and charismatic king (Silas Benjamin) rules from his palace in the Apthrop Building (Silas claims he rules by divine right: a swarm of butterflies nested on his head and formed the shape of a crown). Rose is Silas's queen, a distant but supportive wife; Michelle is their intelligent and outspoken daughter; Jack is their son, a soldier in the king's army; Linus Abner is Silas's general (of his armies); William Cross is Rose's brother; David Shepherd is a young soldier who finds a place in Silas's court when he saves Jack's life (Gilboa is at war with neighboring Goth;

David is used as a pawn by Silas to represent the common man — which appears to be quite invisible in Gilboa); Revered Ephraim Samuels is the king's religious advisor.

Serialized stories, reminiscent of *Dallas* and *Dynasty* relate events in the lives of the people close to King Silas (as he is called) as he attempts to run his kingdom as he believes it should be run.

Cast: Ian McShane *(King Silas Benjamin)*; Susanna Thompson *(Queen Rose Benjamin)*; Allison Miller *(Michelle Benjamin)*; Chris Egan *(David Shepherd)*; Dylan Baker *(William Cross)*; Wes Studi *(Gen. Linus Abner)*; Eamonn Walker *(the Rev. Ephraim Samuels)*.

5021 *King's Crossing.* (Series; Drama; ABC; 1982). The lives of the Hollisters, a close-knit American family who move from Chicago to King's Crossing, a small California village, to rebuild their shattered lives. The regulars are Paul (a writer) and Nan Hollister, the parents; Carey and Lauren, their daughters; Louisa, Nan's wealthy aunt; Billy, the stable hand; Jillian, Paul's cousin; Willa, the maid; Jonathan, the orchestra conductor; Carol, Jonathan's wife; Sam, Louisa's former lover, a horse breeder; and Robert, Sam's son.

Cast: Bradford Dillman *(Paul Hollister)*; Mary Frann *(Nan Hollister)*; Marilyn Jones *(Carey Hollister)*; Linda Hamilton *(Lauren Hollister)*; Beatrice Straight *(Louisa Beauchamp)*; Daniel Zippi *(Billy McCall)*; Doran Clark *(Jillian)*; Jean LeBouvier, Dorothy Meyer *(Willa)*; Michael Zaslow *(Jonathan Hardari)*; Stephanie Braxton *(Carol Hardari)*; Mitchell Ryan *(Sam Garrett)*; Brian Patrick Clarke *(Robert Garrett)*.

5022 *King's Crossroads.* (Series; Anthology; ABC; 1951-1952). Carl King oversees screenings of theatrical shorts from the 1930s and 1940s.

5023 *King's Party Line.* (Series; Variety; CBS; 1946). John Reed King oversees a live program of music, audience participation, games, stunts and quizzes.

5024 *King's Record Shop.* (Pilot; Game; ABC; Oct. 25, 1945). A record is played by the host. Viewers call in and attempt to identify either the song or its singer. The program also features a stunt segment that places a married couple and a sailor in an isolation booth. The wife is blindfolded and has to detect which man is making advances toward her. The program is unscripted and relies mostly on the host's ability to ad lib.

Host: John Reed King.

5025 *King's Row.* (Series; Drama; ABC; 1955-1956). The town of King's Row at the turn of the century is the setting for a look at the life of Dr. Parris Mitchell, a psychiatrist, as he attempts to begin a practice in his hometown. Based on the feature film of the same title and broadcast as seven segments of *Warner Bros. Presents*.

Cast: Jack Kelly *(Parris Mitchell)*; Nan Leslie *(Randy Monaghan)*; Peggy Webber *(Elsie Sandor)*; Robert Horton *(Drake McHugh)*; Victor Jory *(Dr. Alexander Tower)*; Lillian Bronson *(Grandma)*; Robert Burton *(Dr. Gordon)*.

5026 *Kingston: Confidential.* (Series; Crime Drama; NBC; 1977). R.B. Kingston is the editor-in-chief of the Frazier News Group, an influential organization of newspapers and television stations in California. R.B. is also not a man to sit around and let others do the work when an important story breaks. He was an investigative reporter who worked his way up to the top, but he never forgot his roots. Stories follow R.B. as he takes an active part in covering crime stories. Jessica Frazier is the head of the organization; Beth Kelly and Tony Marino are reporters who assist R.B. In the pilot film, *Kingston:*

The Power Play (NBC, Sept. 15, 1976), Lenka Peterson played Laura Frazier, the head of the organization.

Cast: Raymond Burr (*R.B. Kingston*); Pamela Hensley (*Beth Kelly*); Art Hindle (*Tony Marino*); Nancy Olson (*Jessica Frazier*); Milt Kogan (*Police Lt. Vokeman*).

5027 *Kirk.* (Series; Comedy; WB; 1995–1997). When his parents are killed in a car accident, Kirk Hartman, a recent college graduate who has just entered the work force, finds himself with the added responsibility of caring for his younger siblings (Phoebe, Corey and Russell). The family now resides in a small Manhattan apartment and stories follow Kirk as he struggles to divide time between work and caring for his sister and brothers. Kirk is a talented artist and dreams of creating his own comic book character. He first worked as a graphic artist for Graphics, a billboard company then as an artist for Wham Comics. He is finally the vice president of creative affairs for Shotz Comics (where he revises an old comic, *Mercury Man* and creates his own character, *Magno Man*, a super hero endowed with Earth's magnetic forces). Last season episodes find Kirk marrying his neighbor, Elizabeth Waters, a nurse at St. Bernard's Hospital (the newly formed family also moves into a larger apartment).

Phoebe has just become a teenager and is having a difficult time facing the fact that she is becoming a young woman. Corey is the wild one and unpredictable. Russell, the youngest (seven) is the only one who listens to Kirk and presents little or no problems for him. Eddie is Kirk's best friend, a clown at the local car wash (later a valet at the Parker Health Club).

Cast: Kirk Cameron (*Kirk Hamilton*); Taylor Fry (*Phoebe Hartman*); Will Estes (*Corey Hartman*); Courtland Mead (*Russell Hartman*); Chelsea Noble (*Elizabeth Waters*); Louis Vanaria (*Eddie Verducci*).

5028 *Kirstie Alley's Big Life.* (Series; Reality; A&E; 2010). Actress Kirstie Alley first attracted attention as a regular on the series *Cheers*. In the years that followed she became the star of her own comedy series (*Veronica's Closet*) and faced a daily battle with weight gain. She became obsessed with shedding pounds and became a spokesperson for Jenny Craig. Despite the unflattering tabloid photos, Kirstie has risen above this and has proven, time and time gain, that she is not only charming, but a funny lady. In her new series, Kirstie continues her battle to lose weight, but also invites viewers to experience events in her daily life (which she also narrates with amusing tidbits as she faces all the challenges that are presented to her).

Star: Kirstie Alley.

5029 *Kiss and Tell: The Do's and Don'ts of Dating.* (Series; Reality; MTV; 2010). "Kiss and Tell Experts" help insecure high school boys become more confident when it comes to girls. Teenage girls are also interviewed and relate what they are looking for in a boyfriend. Bob Kusbit and Francis Lyons are the producers.

5030 *Kiss Me ... Kill Me.* (Pilot; Crime Drama; ABC; May 8, 1976). Stella Stafford is a former police woman turned investigator for Edward Fuller of the Los Angeles District Attorney's Office. The proposal was to relate Stella's exploits as she risks her life to solve crimes.

Cast: Stella Stevens (*Stella Stafford*); Robert Vaughn (*Edward Fuller*); Dabney Coleman (*Police Captain Logan*).

5031 *Kissyfur.* (Series; Cartoon; NBC; 1985). Dissatisfied with life in the circus, a young bear cub (Kissyfur) and his father (Gus) leave the big top to begin life elsewhere. Stories relate their adventures as they attempt to enjoy their new lives in a swampland kingdom.

Voice Cast: R.J. Williams (*Kissyfur*); Ed Gilbert (*Gus*); Frank Welker (*Claudette/Uncle Shelby*); Lennie Weinrib (*Charles/Lenny*); Russi Taylor (*Beehonie/Bessie/Cackle Sister/Miss Emmy Lou/Toot*); Neilson Ross (*Duane*); Stu Rosen (*Floyd/Stuckey*); Doug Parker (*Jolene*).

5032 *Kit Carson.* (Series; Western; Syn.; 1951). The shortened title for *The Adventures of Kit Carson*. See this title for information.

5033 *Kitchen Confidential.* (Series; Comedy; Fox; 2005). From the age of eight years, Jack Bourdain knew exactly what he wanted to do — become a chef. At the age of 12 he would dress in a chef's outfit and prepared the family's Thanksgiving dinner. Twelve years later he appeared on the cover of the *New Yorker* magazine with the headline "Raw Ambition: Jack Bourdain creates a Feeding Frenzy."

Jack worked as the head chef at the Icaru Restaurant in Manhattan but smoking pot and accidentally setting the restaurant on fire got him fired and busted. Four years later (2005) he was released from prison and acquired a job at the Nolita, a top Manhattan restaurant. Stories revolve around Jack as he attempts to prepare meals and deal with a mixed bag of outrageous employees.

Other regulars are Seth, the pastry chef; Teddy, the seafood chef; Steve, the kitchen manager; Mimi, the daughter of the restaurant owner; and kitchen workers Jim and Tanya.

Cast: Bradley Cooper (*Jack Bourdain*); Nicholas Brendon (*Seth Klein*); Bonnie Somerville (*Mimi*); John Cho (*Teddy Wong*); Jamie King (*Tanya*); John Francis Daley (*Jim*); Owain Yeoman (*Steven*).

5034 *Kitchen Nightmares.* (Series; Reality; Fox; 2007–). A spin off from *Hell's Kitchen* (wherein Chef Gordon Ramsay put potential chefs through hell seeking one to run his restaurant). Rather than be chained to the kitchen, Chef Ramsay takes to the road to solve the kitchen nightmares of restaurants across the country. Nothing gets Chef Ramsay more angered than an untidy restaurant's kitchen (or staff members who do not seem to know what they are doing). Chef Ramsay is sort of the 911 of the restaurant world and episodes relate his efforts to solve the problems restaurants are encountering. Based on the British series of the same title.

Host: Gordon Ramsay. **Narrator:** J.V. Martin.

5035 *Kitty Foyle.* (Series; Drama; NBC; 1958). Events in the life of Kitty Foyle, a teenage girl "just discovering life."

Cast: Kathleen Murray (*Kitty Foyle*); Bob Hastings (*Edward Foyle*); Ralph Dunn (*Pop Foyle*); Judy Lewis (*Molly Scharf*); Patty Duke (*Molly; flashbacks as a girl*); Billy Redfield (*Wyn Stafford*); Jan Merlin (*Kenneth*); Les Damon (*Rosie Rittenhouse*); Valerie Cassert (*Olivia Stafford*); Marie Worsham (*Stacylea*).

5036 *The Kitty Wells/Johnny Wright Family Show.* (Series; Variety; Syn.; 1969). Singers Kitty Wells and Johnny Wright oversee a program of performances by country and western entertainers.

Hosts: Kitty Wells, Johnny Wright. **Regulars:** Carol Sue Wright, Bobby Wright, Bill Phillips, Rudy Wright.

5037 *Klein Time.* (Pilot; Comedy; CBS; Aug. 2, 1977). Skits with comedian Robert Klein (who is assisted by a group of regulars and guest stars).

Host: Robert Klein. **Regulars:** Hilary Jean Bean, Michael Keaton, Kres Mersky, Gailard Sartain. **Guests:** Peter Boyle, Madeline Kahn.

5038 *Kleo the Misfit Unicorn.* (Series; Cartoon; Nick; 1998). ZaZma is a magical land where Kleo, the only existing winged unicorn lives. Kleo has also been charged with a one hundred year mission: travel to Misfit Land, an island of misfit animals, to help them enjoy their stay on the island or help them find their way back into their animal society. The residents of Misfit Land are Slim, the stripped hippo; Henry, the walking fish; Wannabee, a shape shifting bee; Lyle, the timid dragon; and Jazz Cat, the color-changing cat.

Voice Cast: Saffron Henderson *(Kleo)*; David Kaye *(Slim)*; Mickey Rooney *(Talbut)*.

5039 *Klondike.* (Series; Adventure; NBC; 1960-1961). The muddy gold mining camps of Skagway, Alaska, in 1898 are the setting for a look that at the lives of four people: Michael ("Mike") Halliday, an adventurer who has come to Skagway to find his fortune; Katherine ("Kathy") O'Hara, the daughter of a sea captain, who is struggling to operate the Golden Nugget Hotel and maintain an honest operation in a lawless territory; and Jeff Durain and Goldie, an ingenious con artist and his beautiful assistant, who seek to become rich on the fortunes of others. Mike resides in Room 2 of the hotel; the town saloon is the Monte Carlo Gambling Hall; and the *Circuit Queen* is the riverboat that services the area.

Cast: Mari Blanchard *(Kathy O'Hara)*; Ralph Taeger *(Mike Halliday)*; James Coburn *(Jeff Durain)*; Joi Lansing *(Goldie)*; J. Pat O'Malley *(Kathy's Uncle Jonah)*; L.Q. Jones *(Joe Teel)*.

5040 *The Knife and Gun Club.* (Pilot; Drama; ABC; July 30, 1990). A medical drama set in the emergency room of Osler General Hospital in Los Angeles. During the week it is an emergency room, but from Friday Midnight to dawn on Monday it is referred to as "The Knife and Gun Club" due to the hospital's location in an area riddled with drugs, crime, accidents and sudden illnesses. The proposal was to relate the work of Drs. Matt Haley and Jack Ducette and nurses Nancy Denison and Mary Faulk. Ginny is Jack's wife.

Cast: Perry King *(Matt Haley)*; Dorian Harewood *(Jack Ducette)*; Cynthia Bain *(Nancy Denison)*; Fran Bennett *(Mary Faulk)*; Suzanne Douglas *(Ginny Ducette)*.

5041 *Knight and Daye.* (Series; Comedy; NBC; 1989). When Hank Knight and Everett Daye, the hosts of a morning radio talk show of the 1940s called *Knight and Daye* (over New York station WLMM) have a dispute over a woman, they dissolve the program and go their separate ways. Thirty years later (1989) KLOP radio station manager Janet Glickman arranges a reunion between the two men in hopes of getting them to do a show for her station. The meeting brings about what Janet had hoped for when Hank and Everett agree to do *The Knight and Daye Show* for the San Diego area. Stories relate their misadventures as they form a new friendship and attempt to do a daily radio program. **Other Regulars:** Gloria, Everett's wife; Ellie, Everett's married daughter; Cito, Ellie's husband, and Chris, Amy and Laurie, Ellie's children.

Cast: Jack Warden *(Hank Knight)*; Mason Adams *(Everett Daye)*; Hope Lange *(Gloria Daye)*; Julia Campbell *(Janet Glickman)*; Lela Ivey *(Ellie Escobar)*; Joe Lala *(Cito Escobar)*; Emily Schulman *(Chris Escobar)*; Shiri Appleby *(Amy Escobar)*; Brittany Thornton *(Laurie Escobar)*.

5042 *Knight of the Realm.* (Pilot; Comedy; Unaired; Produced in 1992). A proposal, set in medieval times, that tells of Dennis St. Dennis, a knight-at-arms and owner of a village (which he won during a joust) as he struggles to protect its eccentric citizens from the evil Black Knight, who is fiercely guarding his province.

Cast: Clayton Rohner *(Dennis St. Dennis)*; Christine Dunford *(Anne Hanover)*; Paul Benedict *(Bob)*; Bobcat Goldthwait *(Navy Blue Knight)*; Phil Buckman *(Francis)*; Michael Talbot *(Grizelda)*; Cameron Thor *(Percy)*; Tony Jay *(Narrator)*.

5043 *Knight Rider.* (Series; Adventure; NBC; 1982–1986).

KITT is a Knight Industries Two Thousand black Trans Am car that was created for the Foundation for Law and Government as a means to battle crime. It is made of a molecular bonded shell and has the serial number Alpha Delta 227529. The car is able to talk via its ultra sophisticated and elaborate micro circuitry. Microprocessors make it the world's safest car and it has been programmed with a chip to protect human life. Engineers April Curtis and Bonnie Barstow developed many of KITT's unique abilities. KITT's driver is Michael Knight, a former police officer with the 11th Precinct of the L.A.P.D. At this time Michael was known as Michael Long. While on an undercover assignment, Long was shot in the face during a bust that went wrong. Although not expected to survive, he is saved by Wilton Knight, a dying billionaire and owner of Knight Industries, who provides life-saving surgery, a new face (patterned after his own when he was young), a new identity, and a mission: apprehend criminals who are above the law.

Michael now works for Devon Miles, the head of the Foundation for Law and Government. Michael calls KITT "Buddy." The foundation also has a portable lab that assists Michael in the field: the Roving Knight Industries black with gold trim 18-wheel truck.

KITT's prototype was KARR (Knight Automated Roving Robot), an evil car that Wilton designed as the car of the future; he neglected, however, to program it with a respect for human life. KITT's enemy is Goliath, an indestructible truck owned by Wilton's evil son, Garthe. Garthe seeks to kill Michael because he feels he is a living and breathing insult to his likeness.

Program Open: "Knight Rider, a shadowy flight into the world of a man who does not exist. Michael Knight, a young loner on a crusade to change the cause of the innocent, the helpless, the powerless in a world where criminals operate above the law."

Cast: David Hasselhoff *(Michael Knight)*; William Daniels *(Voice of KITT)*; Edward Mulhare *(Devon Miles)*; Rebecca Holden *(April Curtis)*; Patricia McPherson *(Bonnie Bristow)*; David Hasselhoff *(Garthe Knight)*; Peter Cullen *(Voice of KARR)*; Richard Basehart *(Wilton Knight)*.

5044 *Knight Rider.* (Series; Adventure; NBC; 2008-2009). An updated version of the prior title (about Michael Knight, a lone crusader who battled crime with the help of KITT, a Knight Industries 2000 car). It is the present time and a new KITT (Knight Industries 3000) has been developed. It has many improvements, including the ability to change shape and color, artificial intelligence and a super computer capable of hacking virtually any system.

In the original series, Wilton Knight created KITT. Here, scientist Charles Graiman makes the improvements needed to bring KITT into the 21st century. His daughter, Sarah, a Ph D. candidate at Stanford University, is following in his footsteps. Mike Tracer, a 23-year-old ex–Army Ranger (and childhood friend of Sarah's) is chosen to drive KITT. Carrie Rivai is the FBI agent Knight Industries helps (and vice versa) to bring criminals to justice. Stories follow Michael and Sarah as they use KITT's unique abilities to solve complex criminal situations. Michael later takes the name of Michael Knight when the FBI arranges his "death" to keep Michael's past a secret.

In the episode of January 21, 2009, the format changed. Charles is killed in a plane crash. Michael, Sarah, Zoe and Billy become the new team, doing what Wilton Knight had originally intended for FLAG (the Foundation for Law and Government)—apprehend criminals who believe they are above the law. The pilot film aired on NBC on February 17, 2008.

Cast: Justin Bruening *(Mike Tracer/Michael Knight)*; Deanna Russo *(Sarah Graiman)*; Sydney Tamiia Poitier *(Carrie Rivai)*; Bruce Davison *(Charles Graiman)*; Val Kilmer *(Voice of KITT)*; Smith Cho *(Zoe Chase)*; Paul Campbell *(Billy Morgan)*; Yancey Arias *(Alex Torres)*.

5045 *Knight Rider 2000.* (Pilot; Adventure; NBC; May 19, 1991). A proposed update of the 1982 *Knight Rider* series. The Foundation for Law and Government and Knight Industries have been combined to form the Knight Foundation, an independent corporation that is concerned with law enforcement and seeks to help various police departments enforce the law. It is the year 2000, and the foundation's ultimate weapon against crime is the Knight Rider 4000 car, a highly upgraded model of the Knight Industries 2000 (KITT) from the series *Knight Rider*.

Although the red Knight Rider 4000 is still in the experimental stage, Devon Miles, the head of the foundation, decides to recruit Michael Knight, KITT's former driver, to come back to the foundation and help them launch the new car. Michael left the foundation in 1990 to open a bass charter service.

Michael is reluctant at first and becomes bitter when he learns that KITT has been dismantled and his parts sold off. Devon orders the repurchase of KITT's parts; all but one memory chip is recovered. Meanwhile, Officer Shawn McCormick of the Metropolitan Police Department is shot in the head during a case investigation. To save her life, Shawn is given a memory chip transplant to replace the part of her brain that was lost. The chip used is KITT's missing chip, which was sold to a trauma hospital. When Shawn finds that she has lost all memory of what happened to her and will be assigned to desk duty, she quits. She applies for a position at the Knight Foundation — and is hired when Russell ("Russ") Maddock, Devon's assistant and the designer of the Knight 4000, discovers that she carries KITT's memory chip in her brain. She is teamed with Michael and, had the series sold, it would have followed Michael and Shawn's assignments for Devon.

Cast: David Hasselhoff *(Michael Knight)*; Susan Norman *(Shawn McCormick)*; Carmen Argenziano *(Russ Maddock)*; Edward Mulhare *(Devon Miles)*; William Daniels *(Voice of KITT)*.

5046 *Knight Rider 2010.* (Pilot; Adventure; Syn.; Feb. 4, 1994). A proposed series, though *not* based on *Knight Rider*, about Jake McQueen, an outlaw turned law enforcer who uses a high tech car to battle crime. The story is set in the year 2010. Jake was a smuggler (brought aliens into the U.S. from Mexico) and was apprehended by his brother, Will, a U.S. marshal. Shortly after Jake's girlfriend, Hannah Tyree, arranges for his bail, Jake's father, Zeke McQueen, is killed by thugs. Zeke, an automotive genius, ran a garage and left Jake a special engine he designed. With the help of his friend, Junkyard Dean, Jake places the engine in a 1969 Ford Mustang and equips the car with weapons and a special coating that protects it from bullets and fire. As Jake and Will team to find their father's killers, Hannah, a virtual reality video game designer for the Crybalis Corporation, discovers that the company owner (Jarod) is involved in illegal medical experiments (to cure Lou Gehrig's Disease). To keep his secret, Jarod has Hannah killed. Hannah, however, does not actually die. Before she dies, she transforms her life force into a special crystal prism she developed. Jake discovers the prism and attaches it to a special unit in his car. Hannah now composed of electrons, has unlimited power, can speak to Jake and appear to him via a holographic image she projects. Hannah "lives" in the car and assists Jake as he and Will attempt to uphold the law (Will is unaware that Hannah is part of Jake's car).

Cast: Richard Joseph Paul *(Jake McQueen)*; Michael Beach *(Will McQueen)*; Heidi Leigh *(Hannah Tyree)*; Don McManus *(Junkyard Dean)*.

5047 *Knight Watch.* (Series; Crime Drama; ABC; 1988-1989). Father Tim is a Catholic priest with a most unusual sideline — he presides over the Knights of the City, an inner-city community group that protects people from the criminal elements of an unidentified city. Tony, Calvin, Casey, Burn and Condo are the principal members of the Knights of the City. Their gang is based in the basement of Father Tim's church and although the Knights engage in some violent confrontations with evildoers, Father Tim stresses (but knows it cannot be) non violent confrontations. Stories follow Tony and the Knights as they seek to keep the bad elements out of their community.

Cast: Tom Bower *(Father Tim)*; Benjamin Bratt *(Tony Malonado)*; Don Franklin *(Calvin Garvey)*; Ava Haddad *(Casey Mitchell)*; Calvin Levels *(Mark "Burn" Johnson)*; Joshua Cadman *(John "Condo" Snyder)*; Paris Vaughn *(Leslie)*; Samantha Mathis *(Jake)*; Harley Jane Kozak *(Babs)*; Gail Mayron *(Baldwin)*; John O'Neill *(Tracey)*.

5048 *Knight's Gambit.* (Pilot; Drama; NBC; Mar. 26, 1964). A proposed spin off from *Kraft Suspense Theater* about Anthony Griswold Knight, a reporter who uses unorthodox methods to acquire stories.

Cast: Roger Smith *(Anthony Knight)*.

5049 *The Knights of Prosperity.* (Series; Comedy; ABC; 2006-2007). Eugene Gurkin is a janitor with a dream — own his own bar in his Queens, New York neighborhood. Problem is he doesn't have the money (only $89 in the bank and he can't get a bank loan). One night while watching *E-News* Eugene sees a story in which singer Mick Jagger flaunts his wealth. Suddenly an idea dawns on him — rob Mick Jagger to make his dream become a reality.

Eugene knows a lot of people who are in the same situation and he recruits five of them to help him achieve not only his dream, but those of his fellow thieves: Squatch (a janitor), Esperanza (a beautiful waitress at Ruby's, the bar hangout), Gary (a cabbie), Rockefeller (a security guard; real name Reginald Von Hoogstratten) and Louis Plunkin ("the intern" college student). Once Eugene forms his group, he exclaims "We henceforth have a criminal organization — the Knights of Prosperity." The group also acquires a meeting place (their headquarters) — Glickman's Jewish Supplies (a warehouse). The Knights are quite inexperienced and their comical attempts to plot, plan and execute the heist is the focal point of the series (which was originally titled *Let's Rob Mick Jagger*. The pilot episode features Mick flaunting his wealth before each commercial break). When the caper to rob Mick Jagger fails (someone beat them and were caught), the Knights first choose Kelly Ripa as their next target ("Let's Rob Kelly Ripa"). However, by the end of the episode (of Feb. 28, 2007), the Knights change their mind and choose comedian Ray Romano as the one to rob.

Cast: Donal Logue *(Eugene Gurkin)*; Lenny Ventio *(Squatch)*; Sofia Vergara *(Esperanza)*; Maz Jobrani *(Gary)*; Kevin Michael Richardson *(Rockefeller)*; Josh Grisetti *(Louis Plunkin)*.

5050 *Knockout.* (Series; Game; NBC; 1977-1978). Three contestants compete in a game wherein they have to spell the word "knockout." Four items appear on a board (for example, peach, apple, mustard and pizza) and the first player to identify the out-of-place item (mustard in the above example) wins one letter of the word "knockout." The player can win a second letter by naming the common denominator for all these items (pies in the example). The first player to spell the word "knockout" is the winner and receives merchandise prizes.

Host: Arte Johnson. **Announcer:** Jay Stewart.

5051 *Knots Landing.* (Series; Drama; CBS; 1979–1993). A spin off from *Dallas* that is set in fictional Knots Landing, California. Serial-like episodes follow the lives of Valene and Gary Ewing, the outcast members of the oil-rich Ewing family of Dallas, as well as members of the Sumner, Fairgate, Avery and Ward families.

Cast: Joan Van Ark (*Valene Ewing*); Ted Shackelford (*Gary Ewing*); Michele Lee (*Karen Fairgate*); Don Murray (*Sid Fairgate*); Kim Lankford (*Ginger Ward*); James Houghton (*Kenny Ward*); Constance McCashin (*Laura Avery*); John Pleshette (*Richard Avery*); Donna Mills (*Abby Cunningham*); Julie Harris (*Lilimae Clements*); Claudia Lonow (*Diana Fairgate*); Kevin Dobson (*Mack MacKenzie*); William Devane (*Greg Sumner*); Ava Gardner (*Ruth Sumner*); Danielle Brisebois (*Mary Sumner*); Lisa Hartman (*Ciji Dunn/Cathy Geary*); Teri Austin (*Jillian Meredith*); Stephen Macht (*Joe Cooper*); Karen Allen (*Annie Fairgate*); Pat Peterson (*Michael Fairgate*); Tonya Crowe (*Olivia Cunningham*); Justin Dana, Danny Gellis, Danny Ponce (*Jason Avery*); Claudette Nevins (*Susan Philby*); Bobby Jacoby (*Brian Cunningham*); Barry Jenner (*Jeff Cunningham*); Douglas Sheehan (*Ben Gibson*); Joanna Pettet (*Det. Janet Raines*); Michael Sabatino (*Chip Roberts*); Howard Duff (*Paul Galveston*); Carol Bruce (*Annette Cunningham*); Ruth Roman (*Sylvia Lean*); Hunt Block (*Peter Hollister*); Steve Shaw (*Eric Fairgate*); Nicollette Sheridan (*Paige*); Michelle Phillips (*Anne Winston*).

5052   *Koala Brothers*. (Series; Cartoon; Disney; 2003). Frank and Buster Koala are brothers who live in the Australian outback. They own a two-seat airplane and stories follow their adventures as they set out on missions to help others. The series is a puppet-animated program and each of the stories is meant to relay a message (like responsibility, caring, sharing) to children. Ned, a wombat, is Frank and Buster's mechanic; Mitzi, a possum, is Frank and Buster's know-it-all neighbor; Alice, a platypus, is the absent-minded messenger; George, a slow-moving tortoise, is the mailman; Sammy, an echidna, is the owner of the town's general store; Josie, a kangaroo, works the gas pump at Sammy's.

Voice Cast: Keith Wickham (*Buster/Frank/Archie/Sammy*); Jonathan Coleman (*Narrator*).

5053   *Kobb's Corner*. (Series; Variety; CBS; 1948-1949). A program of music, song and comedy set against the background of the Shufflebottom General Store, a southern business establishment that sponsors a musical-comedy get-together on Wednesday evenings. Maw Shufflebottom is the store owner (and host); Josie Belle is her daughter (and assistant).

Cast: Hope Emerson (*Maw*); Jo Hurt (*Josie Belle*). **Regulars:** Stan Fritz, Jimmy Allen, Eddie Grosso, Howard McElroy, Marty Gold, Nels Laakso, Charles Koenig, Joan Nobles. The Korn Kobblers.

5054   *Kodak Request Performance*. (Series; Anthology; NBC; 1955). Jack Clark hosts a Kodak sponsored program of dramas that originally aired on other filmed anthology programs.

5055   *Kodiak*. (Series; Crime Drama; ABC; 1974). Cal McKay is a rugged member of the Alaska State Police Patrol. He has been nicknamed "Kodiak" (after the great bear that roams the area by the natives) for his relentless pursuit of justice. Stories follow Cal, and his assistant, Abraham Lincoln Imhook, as they risk their lives to protect the people of Alaska.

Mandy is their police radio dispatcher.

Cast: Clint Walker (*Cal "Kodiak" McKay*); Abner Biberman (*Abraham Lincoln Imhook*); Maggie Blye (*Mandy*).

5056   *Kojak*. (Series; Crime Drama; CBS, 1973–1978; ABC, 1989-1990). The Manhattan South Precinct of the N.Y.P.D. is an old building that is cold in the winter and hot in the summer. The detectives work long hours and overtime is a necessary part of the job. The coffee is one step ahead of suicide and the squad room detectives joke all the time — "They have to. These guys don't know what they'll find out there. It could be a killer with a .351 Magnum or a body

chopped into pieces. They gotta get their laughs when they can," says Theo Kojak, a dedicated, hard-working detective whose beat is lower Manhattan.

Kojak was previously an officer with the 26th Precinct. He works on hunches which often pay off, and when he personally becomes involved in a case, he becomes fixated and doesn't care what it takes to solve it. He lives at 215 River Street, smokes pencil-thin cigars, but is famous for being the only cop on the force who loves lollipops — the round Tootsie Roll Pops. Theo is abrasive and has to be to deal with the gory cases he investigates. Because of the nature of cases, there are no female detectives in Theo's unit. Stella's is Theo's favorite restaurant and Irene Van Patten is his romantic interest. Theo is Greek and his catchphrase is "Who loves ya, baby."

Frank McNeil is the chief of detectives, and Theo most often works with detectives Crocker, Stavros, Rizzo and Saperstein.

In the ABC version Kojak is a police inspector with the 74th Precinct in Manhattan and his assistant is Detective Warren Blake (Andre Braugher). Kevin Dobson reprised his role in the episode of Feb. 3, 1990, "It's Always Something." He is now assistant D.A. Robert Crocker. Kojak's lollipops have also been changed from Tootsie Roll Pops to an unknown sugar-free brand.

Telly Savalas also played Theo Kojak in three CBS TV Movies: *The Marcus-Nelson Murders* (Mar. 8, 1973), *Kojak: The Belarus File* (Feb. 16, 1985) and *Kojak: The Price of Justice* (Feb. 21, 1987).

Cast: Telly Savalas (*Lt. Theo Kojak*); Dan Frazer (*Chief Frank McNeil*); Kevin Dobson (*Lt. Bobby Crocker*); George Savalas (*Detective Stavros*); Vince Conti (*Detective Rizzo*); Mark Russell (*Detective Saperstein*); Carole Cook (*Marie Stella; restaurant owner*); Diane Baker (*Irene Van Patten*); Darrell Zivering (*Detective Agajanian*); Borah Silver (*Detective Prince*).

5057   *Kojak*. (Series; Crime Drama; USA; 2005). A remake of the 1973–1978 CBS series of the same title in which Telly Savalas played Detective Theo Kojak, a bald, Greek, lollipop-loving crime fighter for the N.Y.P.D. For the new series, Theo Kojak is black and bald but he uses lollipops to help him kick his smoking habit (the original Kojak did smoke — pencil thin cigars).

The 1970s Kojak would not allow a woman to become a part of his team because he felt the gruesome aspects of the crimes he handles were too much for a woman to handle. The new Kojak has a female member of the team — Emily Patterson — a woman who can handle anything her male counterparts can handle. Bobby Crocker, Theo's partner, and Frank McNeil, their captain, have also been resurrected from the original program. New to the series are Detective Henry Messina and Carmen Warrick, the Assistant District Attorney. Stories follow Theo's intensive case investigations as he and his team seek to solve disturbing crimes.

Cast: Ving Rhames (*Lt. Theo Kojak*); Chazz Palminteri (*Capt. Frank McNeil*); Michael Kelly (*Det. Bobby Crocker*); Sybil Temtchine (*Det. Emily Patterson*); Chuck Shamata (*Det. Henry Messina*); Roselyn Sanchez (*Carmen Warrick*).

5058   *Kolchak: The Night Stalker*. (Series; Thriller; ABC; 1974-1975). When first introduced in the television movie *The Night Stalker* (ABC, Jan. 11, 1972), Carl Kolchak is a down-on-his-luck reporter for the Las Vegas *Daily News*. He has been a reporter for 22 years, and he apparently first becomes involved with the supernatural when he attempts to prove that Janos Skorzeny (Barry Atwater) is a modern-day vampire and responsible for the deaths of several showgirls. Although he does prove it (and kills Janos by driving a stake through his heart), Carl is prevented by the police from printing his story; he is charged with murder (but not jailed) and ordered to leave town.

Carl, who wears a white suit and hat, next turns up in Seattle as a reporter for the Washington, D.C., *Daily Chronicle* (in the television movie, *The Night Strangler*, ABC, Jan. 16, 1973). Here, Carl tries to solve the bizarre murders of young women: beginning in 1889, and every 21 years thereafter (during an 18 day period from March 29 through April 16), six women have been murdered — found with crushed necks and partially drained of blood. Carl discovers that the crimes were committed by Dr. Richard Malcolm (Richard Anderson), a doctor who had found a means of gaining immortality which requires human blood.

When the series begins, Carl is a reporter for the INS (Independent News Service) in Chicago. His easily exasperated editor, Anthony ("Tony") Vincenzo, has assigned him to investigate stories of general interest, not the bizarre (which Carl manages to stumble upon week after week). Episodes relate the constant bickering between the two men as Carl defies Tony and seeks stories involving supernatural creatures.

Emily Cowles is the INS advice columnist ("Dear Emily"); Ron Updyke and Monique Marmelstein are INS reporters; and Gordon ("Gordie the Ghoul") Spangler is Carl's contact at the morgue. Simon Oakland also played Carl's editor, Tony Vincenzo, in both television movies; Darren McGavin also narrates each episode.

Cast: Darren McGavin *(Carl Kolchak)*; Simon Oakland *(Tony Vincenzo)*; Jack Grinnage *(Ron Updyke)*; Carol Ann Susi *(Monique Marmelstein)*; John Fielder *(Gordon Spangler)*; Ruth McDevitt *(Emily Cowles)*.

5059 *Komedy Tonite.* (Pilot; Variety; NBC; May 9, 1978). A program of music, songs and comedy sketches featuring an African American cast.

Regulars: Cleavon Little, Paula Kelly, Marion Ramsey, Shon Vaughn, Charles Valentino. **Guests:** Todd Bridges, Lawrence Hilton-Jacobs, Paul Lynde, Danielle Spencer. **Orchestra:** H.B. Barnum.

5060 *Kong: The Animated Series*. (Series; Cartoon; ABC Family; 2000). A very loosely based adaptation of the 1933 feature film *King Kong*. When the feature film ended, King Kong, the giant gorilla, fell from the Empire State Building. For the series, there was apparently a scientist named Lorna Jenkins who was present at the scene and was somehow able to get some of Kong's DNA. She used the sample to clone Kong and later took him back to his home on Skull Island so he could be protected from the world. Some time later, Lorna's grandson, Jason and his friend, Tan, bring their teacher to the island to show him King Kong. The teacher, Ramon De La Porta, however, has other plans (to steal the island's rare and valuable Primal Stones, which control the balance of the island). After accomplishing his plan and disappearing with the stones, Jason, Tan and a Shaman island girl, Lua, team with Kong and begin a worldwide journey to capture Ramon and return the stones to the island. Stories relate their efforts.

Voice Cast: Kirby Morrow *(Jason Jenkins)*; Scott McNeil *(Eric "Tan" Tannenbaum)*; Daphne Goldrich *(Dr. Lorna Jenkins)*; Saffron Henderson *(Lua)*; David Kaye *(Ramon De La Porta)*; Ron Halder *(Andre)*; Paul Dobson *(Chyros)*; Nicole Oliver *(Tiger Lucy)*; Pauline Newstone *(Harpy)*; Richard Newman *(Howling Jack Crockett)*.

5061 *The Kopycats.* (Series; Variety; ABC; 1972). Show business personalities are lampooned by a group of talented impressionists called the Kopycats.

The Kopycats: Rich Little, Marilyn Michaels, Frank Gorshin, George Kirby, Charlie Callas, Joe Baker, Fred Travalena. **Regulars:** The Norman Maen Dancers. **Orchestra:** Jack Parnell.

5062 *Korg: 70,000 B.C.* (Series; Adventure; ABC; 1974-1975). Earth in the year 70,000 B.C. is the setting for a depiction of the struggle for survival of a Neanderthal family. Based on assumptions and theories drawn from artifacts.

Cast: Jim Malinda *(Korg)*; Bill Ewing *(Bok)*; Naomi Pollack *(Mara)*; Christopher Man *(Tane)*; Charles Morted *(Tor)*; Janelle Pransky *(Ree)*; Burgess Meredith *(Narrator)*.

5063 *Koska and His Family.* (Pilot; Comedy; NBC; Dec. 31, 1973). When he is unable to find work in his chosen field (an aerospace engineer), Herbert Koska decides to work at home and invent the things people need but haven't been invented yet. His efforts to do so, despite constant interruptions from his slightly off-the-wall family (wife, Isabel; children, Gina, Jimmy and Al; and senile grandfather) was to be the focal point of the unsold series.

Cast: Herb Edelman *(Herbert Koska)*; Barbara Barrie *(Isabel Koska)*; Ellen Sherman *(Gina Koska)*; Jack David Walker *(Jimmy Koska)*; Albert Anderson *(Al Koska)*; Liam Dunn *(Grandpa Koska)*.

5064 *Kourtney and Khloe Take Miami.* (Series; Reality; E!; 2009–2011). Kourtney and Khloe Kardashian, the sisters of Kim Kardashian (*Keeping Up with the Kardashians*) embark on their own series to open a Dash Boutique in Miami. Cameras capture their efforts as well as exploring their adventures "through South Beach's sexy, simmering scene." Also featured are Lily Abel, the manager of the Calabasas Dash Boutique, who volunteered to help Khloe and Kourtney establish their business. Erica Mena and Carrie Ann Stutz are the sisters' shop girls; Terrence J. is a friend and mentor to Khloe. A sequel Series, *Kourtney and Kim Take New York* aired on E! in 2011 wherein the Kourtney and Khloe are joined by sister Kim as they struggle to make their Dash Boutique a success in New York City.

Stars: Khloe Kardashian, Kourtney Kardashian, Kim Kardashian.

5065 *Kovacs on the Corner.* (Series; Comedy; NBC; 1951-1952). Sketches and blackouts that satirize everyday life.

Host: Ernie Kovacs. **Regulars:** Edie Adams, Joe Behar. **Music:** The Dave Appel Trio.

5066 *Kovacs Unlimited.* (Series; Comedy; CBS; 1952–1954). Split second blackouts and sketches that satirize everyday life.

Host: Ernie Kovacs. **Regulars:** Edie Adams, Andy McKay, Trig Lund, Peter Hanley. **Music:** Eddie Hatrak.

5067 *The Kowboys.* (Pilot; Comedy; NBC; July 13, 1970). A musical spoof of the Old West as seen through the adventures of four flower children (Matthew, Smitty, Zak and Sweetwater) as they travel from town to town helping people in trouble.

Cast: Boomer Castleman *(Matthew)*; Joy Bang *(Smitty)*; Michael Martin Murphy *(Zak)*; Jamie Carr *(Sweetwater)*.

5068 *The Kraft Music Hall.* (Series; Variety; NBC; 1958; 1967). Kraft Foods sponsored program of music, songs and comedy sketches. Two versions appeared:

1. The Kraft Music Hall (NBC, 1958–62). **Host:** Milton Berle, Perry Como, Dave King. **Regulars:** Ken Carpenter, The Bill Foster Dancers, The Jerry Packer Singers. **Announcer:** Ed Herlihy. **Orchestra:** Billy May, Mitchell Ayres.

2. The Kraft Music Hall (NBC, 1967–71; weekly guests host). **Regulars:** The Peter Gennero Dancers, The Michael Bennett Dancers. **Announcer:** Ed Herlihy. **Orchestra:** Peter Matz.

5069 *The Kraft Music Hall Presents Sandler and Young.* (Series; Variety; NBC; 1969). The 1969 summer replacement for *The Kraft Music Hall* that, taped in London, England and sponsored by the Kraft Foods Company, features music, songs and the comedy of Tony Sandler and Ralph Young.

Hosts: Tony Sandler, Ralph Young. **Regulars:** Judy Carne, The Paddy Stone Dancers. **Show Announcer:** Paul Griffith. **Kraft Announcer:** Ed Herlihy. **Orchestra:** Jack Parnell.

5070 *The Kraft Music Hall Presents the Dave King Show.* (Series; Variety; NBC; 1959). Dave King, a singer who has been called "The British version of Perry Como," hosts the summer 1959 replacement for *The Kraft Music Hall*, a Kraft Foods sponsored program of music and songs.

Host: Dave King. **Regulars:** The Jerry Packer Singers, The Bill Foster Dancers. **Announcer:** Ed Herlihy. **Orchestra:** Vic Schoen.

5071 *The Kraft Mystery Theater.* (Series; Anthology; NBC; 1961–1963). Kraft Foods sponsored program of original British mystery and suspense dramas coupled with repeats of dramas that aired on other filmed anthology programs. Notable performers include Jayne Mansfield, Honor Blackman, Whitney Blake, David Janssen, John Forsythe, Antoinette Bower, Beverly Garland, Glynis Johns, Denver Pyle, John Ericson and Lola Albright.

5072 *The Kraft Summer Music Hall.* (Series; Variety; NBC; 1966). The 1966 summer replacement of music and songs for *The Kraft Music Hall*.

Program Open: "Hi ya, hi ya, hi ya, I'm John Davidson and welcome to *The Kraft Summer Music Hall*. Boy, have we got some wonderful guests for tonight. Of course the whole gang is right here, so let's meet them once more: George Carlin, Jackie and Gayle, the Lively Set, the Four King Cousins. Our guests, Flip Wilson and our special guests Chad and Jeremy. All brought to you by Kraft. Kraft for good food and good food ideas."

Host: John Davidson. **Regulars:** George Carlin, Richard Pryor, The Four King Cousins, Jackie and Gayle, The Lively Set. **Announcer:** Ed Herlihy. **Orchestra:** Jimmie Haskell.

5073 *The Kraft Suspense Theater.* (Series; Anthology; NBC; 1963–1965). Mystery and suspense presentations sponsored by the Kraft Foods Company. Notable performers include Katharine Ross, Anne Francis, Leslie Nielsen, Barbara Nichols, Pippa Scott, Jack Klugman, Tippi Hedren, Tina Louise, Gloria Swanson, Telly Savalas, Lee Marvin, Edie Albert, Pat O'Brien, Ronald Reagan, Dina Merrill and Ethel Merman. Johnny Williams composed "The Theme from the Kraft Suspense Theater."

5074 *The Kraft Television Theater.* (Series; Anthology; NBC; ABC; 1947–1955). Dramatic and comedic productions featuring Broadway veterans, well known and lesser-known actors. The program, sponsored by Kraft Dairy Foods, was the first hour-long anthology series to be broadcast to the Midwest by the coaxial cable (1949). It ran on NBC from May 7, 1947 to Oct. 1, 1958; and ABC from Oct. 15, 1953 to Jan. 6, 1955. Notable performers include Tammy Grimes, Lee Remick, Farley Granger, Sylvia Sidney, Peggy Ann Garner, Cliff Robinson, Sal Mineo, Nancy Malone, Betsy Palmer, Shelley Winters, Rudy Vallee, William Shatner, Fay Wray, Pat O'Brien, Milton Berle, Joanne Woodward, Basil Rathbone, Hope Lange, Elizabeth Montgomery, James Whitmore and Patrick Macnee.

Announcer: Ed Herlihy, Charles Stark.

5075 *Kristin.* (Series; Comedy; NBC; 2001). Kristin Yancey was born in Tulsa, Oklahoma and attended Broken Arrow High School. She is a talented singer and dancer and yearns to become a Broadway star. Kristin begins by moving to New York. Although she managed to get roles in two off-Broadway plays (*Peter Pan* in Schenectady, and *A Kiss Before Midnight* in Brooklyn) she finds disappointment when she auditions for a role in *42nd Street* and is turned down. With a need for money she applies for the position of personal assistant to Tommy Ballantine, the wealthy owner of Ballantine Enterprises, a real estate development company.

Tommy made a lot of money really fast "and darn it if it hasn't spoiled me rotten," he says. He is so successful that he is called "New York's Playboy Developer." When he wants to eat dinner he makes reservations at his three favorite restaurants (Baltazar's, Crescent and Moomba) because he is never sure at which one he wants to eat.

Stories follow Kristin as she continues to audition for Broadway shows and make her dream come true. Other regulars are Aldo, Tommy's best friend and right hand man; Santa, a sales agent for Tommy who insists she be called San-ta not Santa; and Tyree, the bike messenger.

Kristin Chenoweth sings the theme, "Hold on to Who You Are."

Cast: Kristin Chenoweth (*Kristin Yancey*); Jon Tenney (*Tommy Ballantine*); Larry Romano (*Aldo Bonadonna*); Ana Ortiz (*San-Ta*); Dale Godboldo (*Tyree*).

5076 *Krod Mandoon and the Flaming Sword of Fire.* (Series; Comedy; Comedy Central; 2009). In an ancient fantasy realm, the evil chancellor Dongalor rules with an iron fist. To combat Dongalor and protect the people of the realm, a hero (Krod Mandoon) steps out of the shadows and begins a quest to save his kingdom (with the aid of his sword, which bursts into flames). Krod is not the most efficient swordsman there ever was and his band of followers are just as ineffectual: Aneka, a beautiful Pagan warrior whose greatest weapon is her sexuality (but to be fair, she has skill with many other weapons); Zezelryck, a second rate stage magician who masquerades as a powerful wizard; Loquasto, a member of a race of pig-like creatures called Grobbles (he is also quite dense); and Bruce, a young gay, who was the lover of Krod's late mentor, General Arcodius. Stories follow their somewhat misguided efforts to overcome the numerous obstacles they encounter while struggling to defeat the evil they encounter.

Cast: Sean Maquire (*Krod Mandoon*); India de Beaufort (*Aneka*); Kevin Hart (*Zezelryck*); Steve Spears (*Loquasto*); Marques Ray (*Bruce*); Matt Lucas (*Chancellor Dongalor*); John Rhys-Davies (*Grimshank*); Emma Clifford (*Mara*); Janine Duvitski (*Agnes Grimshank*).

5077 *The Krofft Komedy Hour.* (Pilot; Variety; ABC; July 29, 1978). Comedy sketches coupled with performances by guest artists under the supervision of producers Sid and Marty Krofft.

Hosts: Patty Harrison, Robin Tyler. **Regulars:** Bart Braverman, Gino Conforti, Kaptain Kool and the Kongs, Deborah Malone, Sheryl Lee Ralph. **Guests:** Redd Foxx, Sha Na Na.

5078 *The Krofft Super Show.* (Series; Children; ABC; 1976-1977). The overall title for *Dr. Shrinker, Electra Woman and Dyna Girl* and *Wonderbug*. See individual titles for information. The program itself is hosted by the rock group Kaptain Kool and the Kongs and features their songs and antics.

Cast: Michael Lembeck (*Kaptain Kool*); Debra Clinger (*Super Chick*); Louise Duart (*Nashville*); Micky McMeel (*Turkey*).

5079 *The Krofft Super Show II.* (Series; Children; ABC; 1977-1978). A revised version of *The Krofft Super Show* that presents the music and antics of the rock group Kaptain Kool and the Kongs and three short series: *Big Foot and Wild Boy, Magic Mongo* and *Wonderbug* (see individual titles for information).

Cast: Michael Lembeck (*Kaptain Kool*); Debra Clinger (*Super Chick*); Louise Duart (*Nashville*); Micky McMeel (*Turkey*).

5080 *Krypto the Superdog.* (Series; Cartoon; WB/CW; 2005). Krypto, Superman's white dog with super powers, lives with a young boy named Kevin and battles evil with the help of Streaky, a super cat. Mechanikat, a devious cat with a plan to conquer the universe, is their nemesis. Assisting him are Snooky Wookums, a kitten, and Delilah, a cat woman (and her cat, Isis). Also coming to the aid of Krypto are the Dog Patrol, a group of super hero dogs (Bull Dog, Mammoth Mutt, Brainy Barker, Tail Terrier, Paw Pooch and Tusky Husky).

Voice Cast: Sam Vincent *(Krypto)*; Alberto Ghisi *(Kevin Whitney)*; Michael Dangerfield *(Superman)*; Brian Dobson *(Lex Luther)*; Nicole Oliver *(Kevin's mother)*; Dale Wilson *(Paw Pooch)*; Kelly Sheridan *(Mammoth Mutt)*; Scott McNeal *(Bathound)*; Terry Klassen *(Tusky Husky)*; Ellen Kennedy *(Brainy Barker)*; Peter Kelamis *(Tail Terrier)*; Nicole Bouma *(Snooky Wookums)*.

5081   *The Krypton Factor.* (Series; Game; ABC; 1981). Four players compete in what is perhaps television's most challenging game at the time: to match wits in various mental and physical contests. The title refers to the ultimate test of mental and physical ability and the program's attempt to find one player who possesses the ultimate combination of intelligence and physical ability. The one player who scores the most points wins the game and $5000 in gold. Winners from the first four programs return to compete in the fifth program for $50,000 in gold.

Host: Dick Clark. **Announcer:** Dick Tufeld.

5082   *Kuda Bux, Hindu Mystic.* (Series; Variety; CBS; 1950). Feats of magic, illusions and mind reading by Kuda Bux, a Hindu mystic.

Host: Kuda Bux. **Asssitant:** Janet Tyler. **Announcer:** Rex Marshall.

5083   *Kudzu.* (Pilot; Comedy; CBS; Aug. 13, 1983). Odell "Kudzu" DuBose is a teenage boy who dreams of becoming a writer. He lives in the small town of Bypass, North Carolina, and the proposal was to follow Odell as he seeks to make that dream a reality. Other regulars are Mavis, Kudzu's mother; Dub, Kudzu's uncle, the owner of an antique store called Dub's Pineywoods One Stop; Betty Jane, Dub's salesgirl; and Kudzu's friends, Maurice and Veranda.

Cast: Tony Becker *(Odell "Kudzu" DuBose)*; Linda Kaye Henning *(Mavis DuBose)*; James Hampton *(Dub Dennible)*; Mallie Jackson *(Betty Jane)*; Larry B. Scott *(Maurice)*; Teri Landrum *(Veranda)*.

5084   *Kukla, Fran and Ollie.* (Series; Children; NBC; ABC; 1947–1957). The Kuklapolitan Theater is home to the Kuklapolitans, a group of puppets created by Burr Tillstrom: Kukla, the bald-headed, round-nosed little man; Ollie, his friend, a scatterbrained dragon; Beulah Witch; Madam Ooglepuss; Colonel Crockie; Cecil Bill; Dolores Dragon; and Mercedes Rabbit. Fran Allison is a lovely young woman who appears in each episode to converse with, become involved in and solve the various problems they present her with. Aired locally in Chicago (1947–49), on NBC (1949–54) and ABC (1954–57).

Program Open: "Here comes the fun, it's time for *Kukla, Fran and Ollie.* Martin Tossi presents Burr Tillstrom, creator of Kukla and Ollie and all the Kuklapolitan players, with Fran Allison in *Kukla, Fran and Ollie.*"

Host: Fran Allison. **Puppeteer-Voices:** Burr Tillstrom. **Regulars:** Carolyn Gilbert, Cesar Giovannini. **Announcer:** Hugh Downs. **Music:** Jack Fascinato, Billy Goldenberg, Cesar Giovannini.

5085   *Kung Fu.* (Series; Drama; ABC; 1972–1975). Kwai Chang Caine is a fugitive Shaolin priest who wanders across the American frontier of the 1870s seeking an unknown brother (Danny Caine). His travels bring him in contact with people in trouble and through Caine's efforts to help these people, the viewer learns of his past and upbringing through flashbacks.

Caine was born in China in the 1850s to a Chinese mother and an American father. He was orphaned shortly after but found a home at the Temple at Whonon when he was accepted by the priests to learn the art of Kung Fu, the medieval Chinese science of disciplined combat developed by Buddhist and Taoist monks. It is here that he befriends Master Po, the blind Shaolin priest who becomes his mentor and nicknames him "Grasshopper." Caine later learns of Master Po's great desire to make a pilgrimage to the Forbidden City.

The years pass and Caine, now a young man, completes his training. He approaches a cauldron of burning coals and places his arms around the sides. The symbol of a tiger and a dragon are branded onto Caine's arms — the final step to his becoming a Shaolin priest. Caine leaves the temple with the final words of Master Teh: "Remember, the wise man walks always with his head bowed, humble like the dust."

At an unspecified time thereafter, Caine meets Master Po on the road to the Temple of Heaven (which leads to the Forbidden City). As they journey to celebrate Master Po's desire, they encounter the bodyguards of the Royal Nephew. The guards are shoving people aside to allow passage of the Royal Nephew when one is tripped by Master Po. A ruckus ensues and Master Po is shot by one of the guards. At the request of his master, Caine takes a spear from a guard and kills the Royal Nephew of the Imperial House. Before he dies, Master Po warns Caine to leave China and begin a new life elsewhere. The emperor dispatches men to find Caine; the Chinese Legation circulates posters: "Wanted for Murder: Kwai Chang Caine. $10,000 Alive. $5,000 Dead." As Caine battles the injustice of the American West, he encounters situations that parallel those of his past. Flashbacks show Caine's strict training and the wisdom of his masters as he disciplines himself to face circumstances as a respected Shaolin priest (although Caine is seen killing in the pilot, the series depicts him as humble, just and wise, with a profound respect for human life).

Cast: David Carradine *(Kwai Chang Caine)*; Keye Luke *(Master Po)*; Radames Pera *(Young Caine)*; Philip Ahn *(Master Kan)*; John Leoning *(Master Teh)*; Stephen Manley *(Caine, age 6)*; Season Hubley *(Margit McLean; Caine's cousin)*; Tim McIntire *(Danny Caine)*.

Note: On Feb. 1, 1986 ABC presented *Kun Fu: The Movie,* an attempt to update the series. It is 1885 and the proposal continues to depict events in the life of Kwai Chang Caine (David Carradine) as he roams the American West seeking an unknown brother.

5086   *Kung Fu: The Legend Continues.* (Series; Crime Drama; Syn.; 1993). "I am Caine. I will help you" are the comforting words heard by people in trouble when they find Kwai Chang Caine, a Shaolin priest and a master of the martial arts who uses his skill to defeat evil. He is also the grandson of his namesake, Kwai Chang Caine, the Shaolin priest of the 1870s who roamed the West helping people in trouble (see *Kung Fu*).

The 1993 Caine is the father of Peter Caine, a detective with the 101st Precinct of the Metro Division of the San Francisco Police Department and operates Master Caine's Kung Fu Academy. To find Caine, one needs only to ask for him by name and like his grandfather, Kwai Chang cannot stand by and do nothing. Caine enjoys eating at the Golden Dragon Cafe and hates to be called "Pop" by Peter. Stories follow Caine as uses the wisdom of his Chinese ancestors to help Peter solve crimes. The Ancient provides guidance to the people of Chinatown; Paul Blaisdell is the police captain (married to Annie) Peter and Caine help.

Cast: David Carradine *(Kwai Chang Caine)*; Chris Potter *(Peter Caine)*; Robert Lansing *(Paul Blaisdell)*; Janet-Lanie Green *(Annie Blaisdell)*; Ernest Abuda *(The Ancient)*.

5087 ***Kung Fu: The Next Generation.*** (Pilot; Crime Drama; CBS; June 19, 1987). A modern-day update of *Kung Fu*. After years of wandering and helping people in trouble, Kwai Chang Caine marries and begins a family. Caine passes the wisdom of his training as a Shaolin priest to his son, who in turn passes it onto his son (Kwai Chang, the Kung Fu of the title), a 1980s father who has a rebellious son named Johnny (it is when Kwai Chang deters Johnny from a life of street crime that Johnny sees the wisdom of his father and joins with him to help battle injustice). Lois Poole is a Lieutenant with the L.A.P.D. whom Caine helps.

Cast: David Darlow (*Kwai Chang Caine*); Brandon Lee (*Johnny Caine*); Paula Kelly (*Lois Poole*).

5088 ***Kwick Witz.*** (Series; Game; Syn.; 1996). Two teams of improve comedians compete. Each team performs a skit (although not improvised as they were told what it would be). Audience applause determines the winners (the funniest performers). The losing team presents their opponents with a prize of their choosing — usually a comedic gift. Andi Matheny hosts.

5089 ***The Kwicky Koala Show.*** (Series; Cartoon; CBS; 1981-1982). The overall title for four animated segments.

1. Kwicky Koala. Kwicky Koala, a fast moving but laid back Australian Koala Bear, seeks to avoid Wilfred Wolf, an ornery critter who plagues Kwicky with his various get-rich schemes.

2. Dirty Dawg. Dirty Dawg, a down-on-his-luck dog, and his equally ragged pal, Ratso (a rat), attempt various cons to survive.

3. Crazy Claws. Crazy Claws, a quick-witted wildcat, struggles to outwit Rawhide, a hunter who seeks his hide.

4. The Bungle Brothers. Antics of George and Joey, two trouble-plagued dogs.

Voice Cast: Robert Allen Ogle (*Kwicky Koala*); John Stephenson (*Wilfred Wolf*); Frank Welker (*Dirty Dog*); Marshall Efrom (*Ratso*); Jim MacGeorge (*Crazy Claws*); Robert Allen Ogle (*Rawhide*); Peter Cullen (*Bristeltooth*); Michael Bell (*Ranger Rangerfield/George*); Allan Melvin (*Joey*).

5090 ***The Kyle MacDonnell Show.*** (Series; Variety; NBC; 1948). The alternate title for *Girl About Town*. See this title for information.

5091 ***Kyle XY.*** (Series; Science Fiction; ABC Family; 2006-2009). A 16-year-old boy, who is unaware of who he is or where he came from, is found wandering in a Seattle, Washington, town and sent to a juvenile holding center. Here psychologist Nicole Trager takes an interest in him (he has no navel, appears to be very intelligent but he is like an infant and needs to learn). Nicole names him Kyle and, to help him, takes him home (where he now lives with Nicole's husband, Stephen and her children Lori and Josh). Kyle learns by watching and listening. Stories follow Nicole's efforts to solve the puzzle of who Kyle is and where he came from. Other regulars are Amanda, the girl next door on whom Kyle has a crush; Heather, Lori's friend; Declan, Lori's boyfriend; and Tom Foss, the mysterious man who appears to know what Kyle is all about.

Second season episodes explain that Kyle was an experiment (XY) based on Einstein's theory that the longer an embryo stays in the womb the smarter it will be. A man named Adam was the only survivor of the first such experiment (at this time, the surrogate mothers, who carried the child for 13 months, died in childbirth; the infants died shortly after). Adam knew his past and wanted to create a world of geniuses. He experimented and created a birth chamber with a pink fluid that could sustain life until the embryo reached an adult stage. Kyle was such an experiment — the first since Adam to survive. But Kyle is not alone. A second experiment, conducted by the vi-

sionaries of a organization called Madacorp, produced a female — XX. This experiment escapes (like Kyle did) when an explosion destroys the lab. A bounty hunter (Emily Hollander) is hired by Madacorp to find her. The girl is nude, covered in pink "goo" (from the birth tank) and like Kyle, has no navel. She is captured by Emily and brought to Madacorp. Here she is programmed to be Jessica Hollander, Emily's sister. Madacorp's plan is to use Jesse (as Jessica is called) to befriend Kyle and monitor him for Madacorp's ultimate goal — reclaim both XY and XX. But unknown to Madacorp, Kyle has a protector, Brian Taylor, the late Adam's faithful servant, who now watches over Kyle and helps him to understand his developing abilities (Adam was shot by persons and for reasons unknown).

Cast: Matt Dallas (*Kyle*); Marguerite MacIntyre (*Nicole Trager*); Bruce Thomas (*Stephen Trager*); April Matson (*Lori Trager*); Jean-Luc Bilodeau (*Josh Trager*); Kirsten Prout (*Amanda Bloom*); Chelan Simmons (*Heather*); Nicholas Lea (*Tom Foss*); Chris Olivero (*Declan*); Leah Cairns (*Emily Hollander*); Jaimie Alexander (*Jesse Hollander*).

5092 ***The L Word.*** (Series; Drama; SHO; 2004–2009). The intimate lives and loves of a group of lesbians living in Los Angeles: Bette, an art curator and Dean of the CU School of the Arts; Helena, the director of her family's foundation; Kit, a professional jazz singer; Niki, an actress; Tasha, a former military police officer (Army National Guard); Tina, a producer at Shaylyn Studios (currently producing the play *Les Girls*) and co-host of the TV show *The Look*; Jenny, a writer (formally a waitress, then a stripper); Shane, a former prostitute and lingerie model turned hairdresser; Grace, a dancer; Jodi, a sculptor and art professor; Maria, the owner of The Planet, the local coffee shop; Dana, a tennis pro; and Alice, a magazine writer.

Cast: Mia Kirshner (*Jenny Schecter*); Jennifer Beals (*Bette Porter*); Erin Daniels (*Dana Fairbanks*); Leisha Hailey (*Alice Pieszecki*); Laurel Holloman (*Tina Kennard*); Katherine Moennig (*Shane McCutcheon*); Pam Grier (*Kit Porter*); Karina Lombard (*Marina Ferrer*); Eric Mabius (*Tim Haspel*); Rachel Shelley (*Helena Peabody*); Eric Lively (*Mark Wayland*); Sarah Shahi (*Carmen de la Pica Morales*); Janina Gavankar (*Papi*); Cybill Shepherd (*Phyllis Kroll*); Marlee Matlin (*Jodi Lerner*); Jessica Capshaw (*Nadia*); Dallas Roberts (*Angus Partridge*); Daniela Sea (*Max Sweeney*); Lauren Lee Smith (*Lara Perkins*); Kate French (*Niki Stevens*); Laurel Holloman (*Tina*); Rose Rollins (*Tasha Williams*).

5093 ***L.A. Confidential.*** (Pilot; Drama; Unaired; Produced for Fox in 2001). Adaptation of the feature film that, set in the 1950s, follows the lives of a group of tough cops with the L.A.P.D.

Cast: Kiefer Sutherland (*Jack Vincennes*); David Conrad (*Ed Exley*); Eric Roberts (*Pierce Patchett*); Josh Hopkins (*Bud White*); Melissa George (*Lynn Bracken*); Tom Nowicki (*Capt. Smith*).

5094 ***L.A. Doctors.*** (Series; Drama; CBS; 1998-1999). Roger Cattan, Tim Lonner, Sarah Church and Evan Newman are doctors with a small, upscale medical firm in Los Angeles. Although NBC dominated the airwaves with its medical drama *ER*, CBS tried to ride on its heels with *L.A. Doctors*; unfortunately, it couldn't and the series was cancelled within a year.

L.A. Doctors tried to do what *ER* didn't — focus more on the patient rather than the doctor and set the action away from a large bustling hospital to a small, far less hectic clinic. The patients on *L.A. Doctors* were there for one episode only; on *ER* they often appeared in arc stories lasting several weeks.

Cast: Ken Olin (*Dr. Roger Cattan*); Matt Craven (*Dr. Tim Lonner*); Sheryl Lee Ralph (*Dr. Sarah Church*); Rick Roberts (*Dr. Evan Newman*); Coby Bell (*Patrick Owen*); Rebecca Rigg (*Kelly Newman*); Joseph Ashton (*Nathan Newman*); Adam Wild (*Jesse Cattan*);

Brian Wild *(Sammy Cattan)*; Talia Balsam *(Julie Lonner)*; Erica Jiminez-Alvarado *(Eva Lonner)*; Vanessa Jiminez-Alvarado *(Christine Lonner)*.

5095   *La Femme Nikita*. (Series; USA; 1997; CW; 2010). Adaptation of the French film of the same title. For the USA version see *La Femme Nikita* (under letter F — *Femme Nikita*) and *Nikita* for the CW version.

5096   *L.A. Firefighters*. (Series; Drama; Fox; 1996). A look at the lives (both personal and professional) of the firefighters of Los Angeles County Fire Company 132. Jack Malloy is the Captain; Erin Coffey, a firefighter, is also Battalion Chief Dick Coffey's daughter. Bernie Ramirez is the arson investigator; Laura is Jack's wife. Other firefighters are Jed Neal, R.K. Martin, Mike Durning, Kay Rizzo, Ray Grimes, J.B. Baker and Lenny Rose.
   Cast: Jarrod Emick *(Jack Malloy)*; Christine Elise *(Erin Coffey)*; Miguel Sandoval *(Bernie Ramirez)*; Carlton Wilborn *(Ray Grimes)*; Alexandra Hedison *(Kay Rizzo)*; John Bradley *(Mike Durning)*; Michael Gallagher *(Lenny Rose)*; Brian Leckner *(J.B. Baker)*; Elizabeth Mitchell *(Laura Malloy)*; Brian Smiar *(Dick Coffey)*; Rob Youngblood *(Jed Neal)*.

5097   *L.A. Heat*. (Series; Crime Drama; TNT; 1999). August Brooks and Chester "Chase" McDonald are detectives with the Robbery Homicide Division of the Los Angeles Police Department. August, a seasoned veteran (with the force for 16 years), likes to take things slow and easy (and go by the books). Chase has been with the department for seven years and lives for the action the job gives him (or rather, the action his impulsiveness makes on the job). August had hoped to become a professional boxer but when he was forced to take a dive on his first outing, he quit the ring and opted to uphold the law as a cop. Still enthused about the sport, August runs the Hoover Street Boxing Center for troubled youths. Chase believes in taking risks to achieve a goal and it is only through August's guidance that Chance gets to see another day. He lives in Malibu with his girlfriend, Jodi Miller (an art gallery manager who left Chase in later episodes for a job in Texas).
   Kendra Brooks is August's wife (and a counselor at the boxing center); Captain Jensen is August and Chase's superior.
   Cast: Steven Williams *(August Brooks)*; Wolf Larson *(Chase McDonald)*; Renee Tenison *(Kendra Brooks)*; Kenneth Tigar *(Captain Jensen)*; Clay Banks *(Det. Sam Richardson)*; Dawn Eason *(Jodi Miller)*.

5098   *L.A. Ink*. (Series; Reality; TLC; 2007–2009). Katherine von Drachenberg, better known as Kat Van D, is a tattoo artist who made a name for herself in Miami. She has given up that business and returned to her hometown of Los Angeles to open her own tattoo parlor. Cycle One (July 7, 2007 to April 3, 2008) follows Kat as she begins her own business as well as the people and events that surround her in her personal life. Cycle Two (July 9 to Oct. 1, 2009) follows Kat as she attempts to establish herself as a celebrity tattoo artist and begin her own makeup line.

5099   *La La Land*. (Series; Comedy; Showtime; 2010). Crude series in which British comedian Marc Wootton portrays three obnoxious characters seeking fame and fortune in Los Angeles: Brendon Allen, Shirley Ghostman and Gary Garner.
   Brendon is a rather untalented documentary filmmaker who longs to produce a film that changes the world and prove to his estranged son (Jack) that he is not the loser critics call him. Brendon is in the midst of a messy divorce from his wife (Susie) but is hoping to redeem himself and win her back by proving himself a success. He has come to Hollywood because he believes that is where the money is and will

be able to convince a producer to back his harebrained ideas. Veteran actress Ruta Lee becomes his mentor.
   Shirley Ghostman (a man) is a psychic with the unique ability to contact deceased celebrities. He lies, cheats and steals and came to Los Angeles to prove his abilities and become America's next psychic superstar. Gary Garner is an East End taxi cab driver who yearns to become an action star like his heroes Vinnie Jones and Jason Statham. Gary's late mother, a porn star, left him some money and he has journeyed to Los Angeles to fulfill that dream.
   Cast: Marc Wootton *(Brendon/Shirley/Gary)*; Ruta Lee *(Herself)*.

5100   *La La's Full Court Wedding*. (Series; Reality; VH-1; 2010). Cameras follow TV host La La Vazquez and NBA superstar Carmelo Anthony as they become engaged (after dating for seven years) and prepare for their wedding.

5101   *L.A. Law*. (Series; Drama; NBC; 1986–1994). The private and personal lives of the attorneys attached to Los Angeles–based law firm of McKenzie, Brackman, Chaney and Kuzak. Members of the prestigious, high-priced law firm tackle cases of all types, most often tempting the bounds of the legal system to achieve their goal.
   Cast: Richard Dysart *(Leland McKenzie)*; Alan Rachins *(Douglas Brackman)*; Harry Hamlin *(Michael Kuzak)*; Susan Dey *(Grace Van Owen)*; Jill Eikenberry *(Ann Kelsey)*; Jimmy Smits *(Victor Sifuentes)*; Michael Tucker *(Stuart Markowitz)*; Corbin Bernsen *(Arnie Becker)*; Michele Greene *(Abby Perkins)*; Susan Ruttan *(Roxanne Melman)*; Amanda Donohoe *(Cara Jean "C.J." Lamb)*; Larry Drake *(Benny Stulwicz)*; Blair Underwood *(Jonathan Rollins)*; Cecil Hoffman *(Zoey Clemmons)*; John Spencer *(Tommy Mullaney)*.

5102   *Lacy and the Mississippi Queen*. (Pilot; Comedy-Western; NBC; May 17, 1978). Kate Lacy and her half-sister, Queenie, are ranchers who moonlight as detectives for the Union Pacific Railroad during the 1880s. Kate is pretty, level-headed and takes a careful approach to each case they handle. Queenie is more of a tomboy. She is a sharpshooter, enjoys a good game of poker and rushes into dangerous situations without really thinking first. The proposal was to relate their efforts to solve crimes in ways that their differing outlooks work together and pay off in arrests.
   Cast: Kathleen Lloyd *(Kate Lacy)*; Debra Feuer *(Queenie Lacy)*.

5103   *Ladette to Lady*. (Series; Reality; Sundance; 2009). British produced series (2005–2008) that attempts to turn Ladettes (uncouth and unpleasant women who curse, drink, smoke and are sexually promiscuous) into refined young ladies. Ten (later eight) such women are given a five week course on behavior and etiquette and assigned to live together at Eggleston Hall, a finishing school in Teesdale, England. Here, the women must attend classes designed to change their wild ways and make them acceptable to society. The Ladettes who fail to live up to their teacher's expectations are expelled. The one girl who shows the most improvement is the winner and receives an Eggleston Hall diploma. Jean Broke-Smith, Gill Harbord, Rosemary Shrager, Liz Brewer are the teachers.

5104   *The Ladies*. (Pilot; Comedy; NBC; June 22, 1987). When her marriage of 24 years comes to an abrupt end, Darlene Patten, a neurotic, chain-smoking mother, moves in with her divorced daughter (Linda Taylor), a plant-loving young woman who cherishes her privacy. The proposal was to relate the misadventures of a mother and daughter struggling to cope with being single in the 1980s. The pilot was filmed in 1983. Other regulars are Jerry, Darlene's ex-husband; Stephen, Linda's ex-husband; and Sachiko, Linda's friend.
   Cast: Talia Balsam *(Linda Taylor)*; Patricia Elliott *(Darlene Patten)*;

Robert Webber *(Jerry Patten)*; Steven Peterman *(Stephen Taylor)*; Jeanne Mori *(Sachiko)*.

5105 *Ladies Be Seated.* (Experimental Series; Game; DuMont; Feb. 25 to Mar. 24, 1945). A five-week experiment, adapted from the radio series of the same title. The basic format involves female members of the studio audience participating in a series of stunts for prizes. Interviews, guests and sing-a-longs were also a part of the program.

Hosts: Johnny Olson, Penny Olson. **Announcer:** Helen Rhodes.

5106 *Ladies Be Seated.* (Pilot; Game; ABC; May 16, 1946). A slapstick show that features female members of the studio audience competing in outrageous stunts for prizes. The idea would sell three years later with Tom Moore as the host.

Host: Johnny Olson.

5107 *Ladies Be Seated.* (Series; Game; ABC; 1949). Female members of the studio audience compete in various contests (game, stunt, quiz) for merchandise prizes. Winners are those best at performing their segments.

Host: Tom Moore. **Assistant:** Phil Patton. **Announcer:** George Ansbro. **Music:** The Buddy Weed Trio.

5108 *Ladies Before Gentlemen.* (Series; Discussion; DuMont; 1951). The program encompasses the format of a game show (without prizes) in which a female guest must defend the woman's point of view on a topical issue (against a panel of six men) to maintain her position on a pedestal. If she should fail, she loses her position and the argument is scored in favor of the men; should she successfully defend it, the argument is scored in the favor of women.

Host: Ken Roberts. **Panelists:** Harvey Stone, Dick Joseph, Fred Robbins, Robert Sylvester, John Kullers. **Premiere Female Guest:** Cara Williams.

5109 *Ladies' Choice.* (Series; Variety; NBC; 1953). The program showcases undiscovered aspiring talent that is presented by female talent scouts. The quiz segment begins when an unrecognizable photograph is flashed on the screen, accompanied by a hint or jingle. A telephone call is then placed to a home viewer (post card selection). If the viewer identifies the photograph, he wins a merchandise prize; If he fails to do so, a wristwatch is awarded. The program also features guests selected by various women's clubs.

Host: Johnny Dugan.

5110 *Ladies First.* (Pilot; Comedy; Unaired; Produced for ABC in 1992). Dana and Monie are best friends who live together and work together as check out girls at Smitty's Market. The proposal was to relate their experiences as they tackle life head on.

Cast: Queen Latifah *(Dana)*; Mother Love *(Monie)*.

5111 *Ladies in Blue.* (Pilot; Crime Drama; ABC; Mar. 19, 1980). Casey Hunt and Britt Blackwell are beautiful police women with the San Francisco Police Department. Casey is from a wealthy family; Britt is from a working class middle family. Casey is the prim and proper girl; Britt, the girl with street smarts. Together, their differing values work well to bring cases to a successful conclusion. Aired as a segment of *Vegas.* Other regulars are Captain Turner; Sergeant Culley; and Mrs. Hunt, Casey's mother.

Cast: Michelle Phillips *(Casey Hunt)*; Tanya Roberts *(Britt Blackwell)*; Peter Haskell *(Captain Turner)*; Bruce Kirby *(Sergeant Culley)*; Natalie Schafer *(Mrs. Hunt)*.

5112 *Ladies' Man.* (Series; Comedy; CBS; 1980). Alan Thackeray is the token male writer for *Women's Life,* a New York–based monthly magazine that is staffed by a bevy of gorgeous women. Elaine S. Holstein is the managing editor; Andrea Gibbons, Gretchen and Susan Watson are the featured writers.

"The publisher," says Elaine, "wants a man's point of view. I don't," and hence, Alan got the job. Alan is divorced and the father of a pretty 10-year-old girl named Amy; Betty Brill, Alan's neighbor, believes she is the world's best problem solver (she has a master's degree in clinical psychology).

Elaine runs the magazine like a finely tuned engine, is fashion conscious and dedicated to seeing that *Women's Life* remains a publication with a women's point of view. Gretchen has a dry wit, lousy moods and once posed as a centerfold for the girlie magazine *Body* ("I was a senior in college and it was a political statement"). The sign on her desk reads "researcHer."

Susan was on the varsity swim team in high school and ran track in college. Andrea, who is from Kansas, is the most naive of the group. She has a degree in journalism from Kansas State College and hopes one day to become a top notch reporter. Sheila Thackeray, is Alan's ex-wife; Reggie is the magazine's accountant.

Cast: Lawrence Pressman *(Alan Thackery)*; Louise Sorel *(Elaine Holstein)*; Betty Kennedy *(Andrea Gibbons)*; Simone Griffeth *(Gretchen)*; Allison Argo *(Susan Watson)*; Natasha Ryan *(Amy Thackery)*; Karen Morrow *(Betty Brill)*; Herb Edelman *(Reggie)*; Julie Cobb *(Sheila Thackery)*.

5113 *Ladies' Man.* (Series; Comedy; CBS; 1999-2000). Jimmy Styles is married to Donna, divorced from Claire, and the father of Bonnie and Wendy (who live with him and Donna).

Jimmy resides in Van Nys, California, and earns a living as a carpenter (his specialty is making furniture; in later episodes he becomes a contractor and his first job was for TV game show host Alex Trebek. His partner in the business is Sabrina).

Jimmy lives in a house full of females: "I love women," he says, but of the women in his household he says, "Jimmy hates women." The reason for such a remark: Jimmy has a difficult time coping with all the mood swings he experiences, including those of his ex-wife, his mother (Mitzi), and Peaches, Donna's mother — all of whom have opinions to express (and Jimmy is seldom right about anything). Stories follow Jimmy as he attempts to cope with life — and find some serenity in a house full of women.

Claire works as a cocktail waitress ("I work for tips and I'm rude") and sells Debbie Dean Cosmetics on the side. Bonnie, Jimmy's oldest daughter (16) likes to hang out at the mall (and spend her father's money); Wendy, the youngest (9) attends the Buddy Ebsen Elementary School. She is a smart alec and Jimmy calls her "not a girl but a miniature woman." Jimmy and Donna have been married ten years and Jimmy's e-mail address is lumpybottom@yahoo.com. Donna's maiden name is DeVille; Mitzi's maiden name is Phister (in her youth she and her sister Louise were in a show business act called the Phister Sisters).

Cast: Alfred Molina *(Jimmy Styles)*; Sharon Lawrence *(Donna Styles)*; Alexa Vega *(Bonnie Styles)*; Kaley Cuoco *(Wendy Styles)*; Park Overall *(Claire Styles)*; Dixie Carter *(Peaches DeVille)*; Betty White *(Mitzi Styles)*; Elizabeth Beckwith *(Sabrina)*; Rue McClanahan *(Louise)*.

5114 *Ladies on Sweet Street.* (Pilot; Crime Drama; ABC; Aug. 16, 1990). Ruth Egan, a former school teacher from Chicago, and Bea Morina, a former New Jersey butcher, are senior citizens who live in a retirement village on Sweet Street. With time on their hands they indulge in their favorite pastime — amateur sleuthing, and the unsold series was to relate their efforts to help the police solve crimes. Other regulars are Anne, Bea's daughter; Patrick, Ruth's son; Lieutenant Spicer; and Sergeant Polsky.

Cast: Gloria DeHaven (*Ruth Egan*); Doris Roberts (*Bea Morina*); Gina Hecht (*Anne Morina*); Mark Shera (*Patrick Egan*); Robert Pine (*Lieutenant Spicer*); Robert Katims (*Sergeant Polsky*).

5115   Lady Blue. (Series; Crime Drama; ABC; 1985-1986). Katy Mahoney is a detective with the Violent Crimes Division of the 39th Street Station of the Chicago Metro Police Department. Katy, the daughter of a cop, is street smart, street tough, and an expert when it comes to using her guns. She is young, beautiful and mean — a female version of Clint Eastwood's Dirty Harry film character. Katy is called ABC's Dirty Harriet in press information. Katy plays by her own rules. While she respects the law and has sworn to uphold it, she bends it to accomplish her goals and keep the streets of her hometown free of thugs. Her superior, Lieutenant Terry McNichols says, "Katy can read a crime scene in progress like most guys read the sports page," although he does complain about her violent approaches and too frequent use of her gun. Katy lives at 1107 West Brandis Place and her badge number is 28668 (688 in the pilot episode). Arnetia Walker sings the theme "Lady Blue."

Cast: Jamie Rose (*Det. Katy Mahoney*); Danny Aiello (*Lt. Terry Michaels*); Bruce A. Young (*Officer Cassidy*); Ron Dean (*Det. Gino Gianelli*); Diane Dorsey (*Rose Gianelli; Gino's wife*); Nan Woods (*Willow; Terry's niece*); Ricardo Gutierrez (*Harvey; Katy's snitch*).

5116   Lady Chatterly's Stories. (Series; Anthology; Showtime; 2000-2001). Constance Chatterly is, by day, a real estate broker; by night she is known as Lady Chatterly, a sexual psychiatrist who operates from her secluded mansion. As Lady Chatterly consults with her patients, sexually-based stories, geared to the female perspective, unfold to depict the problem, its solutions and possible consequences.

Cast: Shauna O'Brien (*Constance Chatterly*).

5117   Lady Lovelylocks and the Pixietales. (Series; Cartoon; Syn.; 1987). The Grand Duchess Raven Hair is an evil woman who is seeking to take over the kingdom of Lovelylocks. When an attempt fails and she destroys herself, a young farmer's daughter is suddenly endowed with rainbow streaks in her blonde hair — a symbol that she is the ruler of the land. Now, as Lady Lovelylocks, and with the help of her two friends, Maiden Fair Hair and Lady Curly Crown, Lady Lovelylocks seeks to restore the kingdom and assume the throne. As she begins, she befriends a group of magical creatures called Pixietales who offer their help. However, seeking to gain control of the kingdom is Raven Waves, Raven Hair's vain and evil daughter who believes she is the rightful heir. She also believes that the rainbow streaks in Lady Lovelylocks hair will give her the power she needs to become the ruler and control the Pixietales. Stories follow Lady Lovelylocks as she begins her quest — and Raven Waves efforts to cut the rainbow streaks from Lady Lovelylocks hair and acquire the power she needs to rule. Also assisting Lady Lovelylocks is Shining Glory, the Wizard and Prince, an enchanted dog who is actually a young man named Strong Heart.

Voice Cast: Jeannie Elias (*Lady Lovelylocks*); Jeannie Elias (*Maiden Fair Hair*); Louise Vallance (*Raven Waves*); Louise Vallance (*Lady Curly Crown*).

5118   Lady Luck. (Pilot; Comedy; NBC; Feb. 12, 1973). She is beautiful and mysterious and magically appears to help people who are in trouble. She is not a witch but she seems to possess supernatural powers. She uses the earth name Laura and the unsold series was to relate her slightly misguided efforts to help people in need of a little Lady Luck.

Cast: Valerie Perrine (*Lady Luck*).

5119   The Lady Next Door. (Series; Children; NBC; 1949). Stories for children as read by Madge Tucker.

5120   Laguna Beach. (Series; Reality; MTV; 2004). Laguna Beach is a wealthy community of Orange County, California. Cameras follow eight high school seniors who are ready to graduate and begin the next chapter in their lives. Each of the teens is rich and lives the privileged life. What they do — day and night for six months is taped and edited highlights of their activities — living the rich life are seen. Also known as *Laguna Beach: The Real Orange County*. See also *The Hills*, the spin off series. The teens are Kristin Cavallari, Lauren Conrad, Taylor Cole, Alex Murrel, Jessica Smith, Raquel Donatelli, Kyndra Mayo, Lauren Bosworth, Morgan Olsen, Christina Schuller, Tessa Keller, Breanna Conrad, Cami Edwards, Stephanie Moreau, Curtis Dean Harrier, Christopher Bland, Lexi Contursi, Trey Phillips, Chase Johnson, Alex Atkinson, Kelan Hurley, Dieter Schmitz, Jason Wahler, Talan Torriero, Stephen Colletti.

5121   The Lair. (Series; Drama; Here!; 2007–). The Lair is a mysterious club established for a specific clientele: attractive (hunky) gay vampires — vampires who feed on equally attractive gay men (in some rather graphic and bloody violent scenes; there is also male nudity and love scenes). The specialized series (broadcast on the gay channel Here!) follows a journalist (Thom) as he attempts to uncover the vampire clan (and solve a series of mysterious murders whose victims have been drained of blood) when his boyfriend (Jonathan) becomes a victim of the clan leader (Damian).

Cast: David Moretti (*Thom*); Peter Stickles (*Damian*); Beverly Lynne (*Laura*); Dylan Vox (*Colin*); Jesse Cutlip (*Jonathan*); Brian Nolan (*Frankie*); Colton Ford (*Sheriff Trout*); Michael Von Steele (*Eric*); Ted Newsom (*Dr. Cooper*); Evan Stone (*Jimmy*); Arthur Roberts (*Dr. Belmont*).

5122   The Lake. (Series; Drama; Internet; 2009). A look at the lives of a group of young adults who retreat to Lake Eleanor during the summer to escape the pressures of their daily lives.

Cast: Erica Dasher (*Madison*); Heather Ann Davis (*Olivia*); Devin Crittenden (*Drew*); Meredith Dilg (*Shelby*); Elisa Donovan (*Leslie*); Mim Drew (*Claire*); Amy Stewart (*Sondra*); Robb Derringer (*Jack*); Nick Thurston (*Luke*); Mark Totty (*Dennis*); Drew Van Acker (*Ryan*).

5123   Lamb Chop's Play-Along. (Series; Children; PBS; 1992). A potpourri of stories, games and songs for children hosted by Lamb Chop, the hand puppet of ventriloquist Shari Lewis. Her other hand puppets, Charlie Horse and Hush Puppy assist her and Lamb Chop.

Star: Shari Lewis. **Music:** John Rodby.

5124   The Lambs Gambol. (Series; Variety; NBC; 1949). Performances by members of the all-male Lambs Club, a fraternal order of show business people.

Host: Bert Lytell. **Music:** Johnny McManus.

5125   Lance White. (Pilot; Crime Drama; NBC; Nov. 16, 1979). Lance White is a handsome, rich and elegant private detective who seems to do everything wrong but still gets the glory for solving crimes. The proposal, a spin off from *The Rockford Files*, was to follow the smooth operating Lance as he uses his charm and wit to help him solve cases for his clients. Fred Beamer is his friend and assistant.

Cast: Tom Selleck (*Lance White*); James Whitmore, Jr. (*Fred Beamer*).

5126 *Lancelot Link, Secret Chimp.* (Series; Comedy; ABC; 1970–1972). Lancelot Link is a fumbling counter-espionage agent for A.P.E. (the Agency to Prevent Evil), an international organization dedicated to fighting C.H.U.M.P. (Criminal Headquarters for Underground Master Plan) and its goal of world domination. Stories relate Lancelot's efforts to safeguard the world from C.H.U.M.P. Characters are enacted by chimpanzees with voice-over dubbing. Commander Darwin is the head of A.P.E.; Marti Hari is Lancelot's assistant; Baron Von Butcher is the commander of C.H.U.M.P.; Creator is Butcher's assistant.

Voice Cast: Dayton Allen (*Lancelot Link*); Joan Gerber (*Marta Hari*); Malachi Thorne (*Narrator*), Mel Blanc, Bernie Kopell, Steve Hoffman.

5127 *Lancer.* (Series; Western; CBS; 1968–1971). With a dream to begin a new life in America, Murdoch Lancer leaves his homeland (Scotland, 1840s) and arrives in Boston. It is here that he meets, falls in love with and marries Catherine Garrett. With a hope of establishing a ranch in California, Murdoch and Catherine begin a long and hazardous trek to the San Joaquin Valley and, over time, forge the beginnings of an empire. Shortly after, Catherine presents Murdoch with a son (Scott) but dies during childbirth. Catherine's grandfather, Harlan Grant, feels Scott can not be properly raised by Murdoch and petitions the court (and receives) custody of Scott. As Murdoch builds his ranch (into a 100,000 acre cattle and timberland ranch) he marries a Mexican woman named Maria Madrid. She blesses him with a son (Johnny) but is unfaithful and deserts Murdoch, taking Johnny with her (to be with a gambler with whom she fell in love with). It is the 1870s and Murdoch finds that he is unable to maintain his empire in a era of lawlessness. He needs his sons by his side and hires the Pinkerton Detective Agency to find them. Scott is a Boston bred scholar; Johnny has become a gunfighter and drifter. Scott and Johnny meet for the first time when they arrive at the ranch and are offered one-third ownership in the Lancer Ranch. Although born of different mothers, and opposite as day and night, the brothers agree to Murdoch's proposal. Stories relate their efforts to become a family and protect their ranch from the unscrupulous characters that threaten its livelihood. Teresa O'Brien is Murdoch's ward (the daughter of his ranch foreman, Paul O'Brien, who had been killed by land pirates); Jelly Hoskins is the ranch foreman; Chad Lancer is from the Kentucky side of the family, a hillbilly who took up residence on the ranch in last season episodes.

Cast: Andrew Duggan (*Murdoch Lancer*); Wayne Maunder (*Scott Lancer*); James Stacy (*Johnny Madrid Lancer*); Elizabeth Baur (*Teresa O'Brien*); Paul Brinegar (*Jelly Hoskins*); John Beck (*Chad Lancer*).

5128 *The Land Before Time.* (Series; Cartoon; Cartoon Network; 2007). A television adaptation of the 1988 feature film of the same title that follows the adventures of a group of lovable dinosaurs as they explore the Great Valley (a lush place where dinosaurs thrive and live in peace) and a world called the Mysterious Beyond.

Voice Cast: Cody Arens (*Littlefoot*); Aria Noelle Curzan (*Ducky*); Rob Paulsen (*Spike*); Anndi McAfee (*Cera*); Jeff Bennett (*Petrie*); Max Burkholder (*Chomper*); Peter Sepenuk (*Saro*); Meghan Strange (*Ruby*).

5129 *Land of Hope.* (Pilot; Drama; CBS; May 13, 1976). The struggles of four immigrant families (the Barskys, Gottschalks, Dwyers and Giannis) living on New York's Lower East Side during the early 1900s.

Cast: Marian Winters (*Reva Barsky*); Phil Fisher (*Isaac Barsky*); Roberta Wallach (*Devvie Barsky*); Richard Liberman (*Herschel Barsky*); Joseph Miller (*Benji Barsky*); Ariane Munker (*Gerda Gottschalk*); Roy Poole (*Gustav Gottschalk*); Donald Warfield (*Ernst Gottschalk*); Robin Rose (*Rose Dwyer*); Colin Duffy (*Kevin Dwyer*); Maria Tucci (*Lea Gianni*); John Dunn (*Angelo Gianni*).

5130 *Land of the Giants.* (Series; Adventure; ABC; 1968–1970). On June 12, 1983, as the *Spinthrift,*, suborbital flight 612, approaches London (departure was from New York), Captain Steve Burton and his co-pilot, Dan Erickson, find they have lost all communication with the London control tower. Suddenly, the ship hits an area of solar turbulence and is pulled into a large glowing green cloud. All control of the ship is lost until they exit the cloud. With only partial reserve power remaining, Burton spots what he believes are airport lights and lands the craft. A thick fog makes visibility zero. Steve and Dan venture outside the craft to investigate. They are walking on a paved road when an enormous car passes over them. They then hear footsteps and rush back to the ship. Betty Hamilton, the stewardess, prepares the passengers for an emergency takeoff. As Steve fires up the engines, they are picked up by "a giant boy." As the giant looks at the ship, Steve manages to escape his grasp. At 5,000 feet they are still passing buildings. With the reserve power virtually exhausted, Steve makes an emergency landing in a dense forest. In addition to crew members Steve, Don and Betty, the passengers are Valerie Scott, a beautiful but rich and spoiled heiress; Mark Wilson, an engineer who is also a wealthy business tycoon; Commander Alexander Fitzhugh, a master thief who is being pursued by authorities for stealing one million dollars (which he is carrying with him in a briefcase); and Barry Lockridge, an orphan with a dog (Clipper), who is to live with cousins in England.

Shortly after, when they realize they have crashed on a strange planet, the *Spinthrift* is attacked by a giant cat. The ship is damaged and the seven earthlings are now marooned. Stories follow their adventures as they struggle for survival and seek the material they need to repair the craft and find a way to reverse the time warp.

The Land of the Giants, as this world is called, appears to be parallel to Earth. English is spoken, the alphabet is the same and all devices used by these people are identical to what is used on Earth — only bigger. As their presence becomes known, they are branded "The Little People" (they are only about six inches tall in this world), and a reward has been offered for their capture; death is the penalty for assisting them. The giant Kobic is the SIB inspector seeking them.

Cast: Gary Conway (*Steve Burton*); Don Marshall (*Dan Erickson*); Heather Young (*Betty Hamilton*); Deanna Lund (*Valerie Scott*); Don Matheson (*Mark Wilson*); Kurt Kasznar (*Alexander Fitzhugh*); Stefan Arngrim (*Barry Lockridge*); Kevin Hagen (*SIB Inspector Kobic*).

5131 *Land of the Lost.* (Series; Adventure; NBC; 1974–1977). Forest ranger Rick Marshall and his children, Holly and Will, are exploring the Colorado River on a raft when they are caught in a time vortex and transported to a closed universe they call the Land of the Lost, a prehistoric world from which there is no escape. They make a home in a cave they call High Bluff and discover that two other races inhabit the land: the simple, simian Palcus, and the saurian Sleestak. Through Enik, an intelligent Sleestak who fell through a time doorway and is now in his future, the Marshalls learn that their world is controlled by a series of pyramid-shaped triangles called Pylons. Each Pylon contains a series of colored crystals; escape can only be made by finding the right series of crystals that will open a time doorway. However, the crystals control the delicate balance of life; it is extremely dangerous to disturb them.

It is also learned that, although Enik is friendly, the other Sleestak (who hunt with bow and arrow) are not; they pose a constant threat to the Marshalls' survival. Enik's mission is to find the doorway and return to his time, and prevent his people from becoming savages.

Ron Harper joined the cast in 1976 as Rick's brother, Jack. (While experimenting with the crystals, Rick finds the time doorway, but he is swept away before he can get Holly and Will. Since this is a closed universe, for each being that leaves it, one must take his place or her place to maintain the harmony. As Rick is freed, Jack becomes his replacement.) Chaka is the Palcu boy, Chaka; Sa is the Palcu girl.

Cast: Spencer Milligan *(Rick Marshall)*; Kathy Coleman *(Holly Marshall)*; Wesley Eure *(Will Marshall)*; Ron Harper *(Jack Marshall)*; Walker Edmiston *(Enik)*; Philip Paley *(Chaka)*; Sharon Baird *(Sa)*; Scott Fullerton *(Ta; the Palcus leader)*; Richard Kiel *(Malak; an enemy)*; Jon Locke *(Sleestak Leader; before Enik)*.

5132   Land of the Lost. (Series; Adventure; ABC; 1991–1993). A revised version of the 1974 NBC series. While riding in their camper, Tom Porter and his children, Annie and Kevin, "fall into a time warp" when an earthquake opens a time doorway and transports them to a world of prehistoric creatures called the Land of the Lost. The Porters, who were on a camping trip at the time, quickly adjust to their new home when they feel there is no escape. They establish a new home in a large tree ("The Compound") and quickly make friends with Christa, a beautiful but mysterious jungle girl, and her companion, Stink, a simian creature who is a member of the Palcu tribe. Their enemies are the Sleestak, intelligent saurian creatures led by Shung. Shung and his bungling assistants, Nim and Keeg, are based in an old temple in a cave. (The Sleestak were forced underground by pollution; Shung, Nim and Keeg are criminals who were banished to the surface. Shung uses a power crystal as his main weapon and believes everything in the Land of the Lost is his — including the humans.)

Tom is convinced that there is a tunnel or a canyon concealing a time doorway that will take them back to their world. He believes that the camper is their ticket home.

Christa, whom Shung calls "Long Hair," is apparently an American who was engulfed by the Land of the Lost at an early age. She understands English, but cannot speak it well. She has a language all her own and has control over the dinosaurs via a Tarzan-like yell; she rides a triceratops with a broken left horn she calls Princess. Christa lives in a cave and has a Giants baseball cap and a picture of herself as a child — but she doesn't remember who she is or where she came from. Stink is intelligent and can understand and speak English once he grasps it.

Cast: Timothy Bottoms *(Tom Porter)*; Jennifer Drugan *(Annie Porter)*; Robert Gavin *(Kevin Porter)*; Shannon Day *(Christa)*; Bobby Porter *(Stink)*; R.C. Tass *(Nim)*; Brian Williams *(Keeg)*.

5133   Landon, Landon & Landon. (Pilot; Comical Mystery; CBS; June 14, 1980). While investigating a case, private detective Ben Landon, owner of the Hollywood-based Landon Private Detective Agency, is murdered. When his children, Holly and Nick, take over the agency, Ben returns to Earth as a ghost to become the father he never was to his children and help them run the newly formed Landon, Landon & Landon Agency. Other regulars are Judith, Holly and Nick's secretary; and police inspector Ulysses Barnes.

Cast: William Windom *(Ben Landon)*; Nancy Dolman *(Holly Landon)*; Daren Kelly *(Nick Landon)*; Millie Slavin *(Judith Saperstein)*; Richard O'Brien *(Ulysses Barnes)*.

5134   Land's End. (Series; Crime Drama; Syn.; 1997-1998). Mike Land is a detective with the L.A.P.D. He has been on the force for 23 years but when a bribe attempt destroys his investigation into the murder of his wife, he quits the force and retreats to Cabo San Lucas, Mexico, to help an old friend (Willis) out of a jam. After accomplishing his goal, Willis convinces Mike to join him and his friend, Dave "Thunder" Thornton, in the private detective agency they started. Stories follow Mike's case investigations as he uses his skills as a former cop to help him solve crimes. Courtney Sanders is the manager of the Westin Regina, the resort hotel where Mike now lives.

Cast: Fred Dryer *(Mike Land)*; Tim Thomerson *(Dave Thornton)*; Pamela Bowen *(Courtney Sanders)*; Geoffrey Lewis *(Willis P. Dunlevy)*; William Marquez *(Police Chief Ruiz)*.

5135   Lanigan's Rabbi. (Series; Crime Drama; NBC; 1977). The partially clothed body of a young girl named Arlette is found on the grounds of the Temple Beth Hallel Synagogue in Cameron, California. While investigating the case, Paul Lanigan, the Irish police chief, meets David Small, a rabbi with the mind of a detective, who has begun his own investigation. The two form an unlikely alliance and solve the homicide (proving it was the least thought-of suspect — the cop on the beat). They remain a team and stories relate their efforts to solve crimes. Paul has been a cop for 22 years and lives with his wife, Kate, at 3601 Sycamore Lane. Paul doesn't make arrests that don't stick, he doesn't speculate about murder cases, and he strives not to let innocent people get hurt; he also drinks a special blend of coffee he calls Turkish coffee. David and his wife, Miriam, live at 171 Circle Drive. Bobbi Whittaker is the reporter; Hanna Price is a temple member. In the pilot film, *The Rabbi Slept Late* (NBC, June 17, 1976), Stuart Margolin played Rabbi David Small.

Cast: Art Carney *(Paul Lanigan)*; Janis Paige *(Kate Lanigan)*; Bruce Solomon *(Rabbi David Small)*; Janet Margolin *(Janet Small)*; Robert Doyle *(Lt. Osgood)*; Barbara Carney *(Bobbi Whittaker)*; Reva Rose *(Hannah Price)*.

5136   Lanny and Isabelle. (Pilot; Comedy; Unaired; Produced for ABC in 1988). A proposal about a mismatched pair of Manhattan roommates: Isabelle, a mid-thirties woman who is struggling to overcome the traumas of a broken marriage; and her 18-year-old niece, Lanny, a hopeful writer who believes there is a rainbow around each corner and all the good things she wants are just there for the taking.

Cast: Andrea Martin *(Isabelle)*; Louanne Ponce *(Lanny)*.

5137   The Lanny Ross Show. (Series; Variety; NBC; 1948-1949). Singer Lanny Ross hosts a program of music and songs.

Host: Lanny Ross. **Regulars:** Martha Logan, Sandra Gahle. **Orchestra:** Harry Simone.

5138   L.A.P.D.: Life on the Beat. (Series; Reality; Syn.; 1995). Los Angeles police officers are followed by camera crews as they respond to calls to show how they deal with the various situations they encounter. A copy of Fox's *Cops* that uses narration and added music to intensify the action that is seen. Andy Geller narrates.

5139   Laramie. (Series; Western; NBC; 1959–1963). Events in the shaping of Wyoming during the 1880s as seen through the eyes of the Sherman brothers, Slim and Andy, and their friend Jess Harper, the operators of a swing station (a combination of a ranch and stage depot) in Laramie for the Overland Mail Stage Lines. After the death of their father, Matt Sherman during the Civil War, and their mother, Mary, shortly after, Slim, the oldest child, finds that he has not only become responsible for maintaining the Sherman Ranch and Relay Station but caring for his younger brother, Andy. He receives help from Jonesy, a family friend who worked for Matt, and Jess Harper, a reformed Texas gunfighter who first began working as a ranch hand and eventually became his partner.

At the beginning of the second season, Jonesy and Andy are written out (explained as Jonesy accompanying Andy to St. Louis to watch over him as he attends school). A widow, Daisy Cooper is brought on as a housekeeper for Slim and Jess; and Mike Williams, a youngster orphaned by an Indian attack and rescued by Slim, comes to live at the ranch.

Cast: John Smith *(Slim Sherman)*; Robert Fuller *(Jess Harper)*; Hoagy Carmichael *(Jonesy)*; Robert Crawford, Jr. *(Andy Sherman)*; Dennis Holmes *(Mike Williams)*; Spring Byington *(Daisy Cooper)*; Stuart Randall *(Sheriff Mort Corey)*; Roy Barcroft *(Sheriff Douglas)*.

5140 Laredo. (Series; Western; NBC; 1965–1967). Reese Bennett, Joe Riley and Chad Cooper are Texas Rangers with Company B in Laredo, Texas. Reese, Joe and Chad are a bit unorthodox and do what it takes to get the job done. They are also set in their ways and each likes to do things his way. This is not always possible as they must make comprises. They dress in attire that is not typical of a Texas Ranger and some people believe they are saddle tramps.

Reese is the not-to-bright ranger. He is easily manipulated (especially by Chad) and is always seeking to do his job and bring honor to the Rangers (but rubbing Reese the wrong way makes him angry and always takes the fall when something goes wrong). Chad, the ladies' man, constantly schemes to avoid the less desirable jobs (most often by making it seem appealing to Reese). Joe, an expert tracker, is the laid back member. He often agrees with Chad and enjoys tricking Reese. Cotton Buckmeister, the new recruit is honest and tries, but almost always fails to get Reese, Chad and Joe to do what is right (go by the code of the Texas Rangers. However, they are anything but ethical and do what it takes to get the job done). The Rangers earn $10 a week, enjoy drinks at the Silver Slipper Saloon and, despite the constant bickering, manage to capture criminals and make their superior, Captain Parmalee, proud.

Cast: Neville Brand *(Reese Bennett)*; Peter Brown *(Chad Cooper)*; William Smith *(Joe Riley)*; Philip Carey *(Edward Parmalee)*; Claude Akins *(Cotton Buckmeister)*.

5141 Larry Boy Stories. (Series; Cartoon; NBC; 2006). Larry the Cucumber works as a janitor for the *Daily Bumbler*, a newspaper in the town of Bumblyburg (where vegetables live like humans). When evil strikes Larry becomes Larry Boy, an heroic crime fighter who risks his life to save innocent people. Larry is based at the Larry Cave and is assisted by Archie, his mentor. Bob the Tomato is the paper's editor; Vickie is a reporter; Awful Alvin is the chief villain, who is seeking to take over the town and rid his life of Larry Boy. Awful Alvin is also a bit daft as his assistant is Lampie, a lamp with a face painted on the shade that Alvin believes is alive.

Voices: Shari Belgeau, Marc Graue, Lee Marshall, Mike Nawrocki, Lisa Vischer, Phil Vischer, Larry D. Whitaker, Jr.

5142 The Larry Kane Show. (Series; Variety; Syn.; 1971). Larry Kane hosts of program of performances by and interviews with rock personalities.

5143 The Larry Sanders Show. (Series; Comedy; HBO; 1992–1998). A parody of late night talk shows that focuses on Larry Sanders, the paranoid host of *The Larry Sanders Show*, a popular (but mythical) late night talk show. Larry, who is also very insecure, is assisted by Hank Kingsley, his announcer and sidekick. The series also takes viewers behind the scenes for a glimpse at the preparations that go into presenting such a show. Arthur (called Artie) is Larry's over protective producer and name celebrities (portraying themselves) appear as guests on Larry's show.

Cast: Garry Shandling *(Larry Sanders)*; Jeffrey Tambor *(Hank Kingsley)*; Rip Torn *(Arthur)*; Wallace Langham *(Phil)*; Penny Johnson *(Beverly Barnes)*; Janeane Garofalo *(Paula)*; Scott Thompson *(Brian)*; Linda Doucett *(Darlene Chapinni)*; Mary Lynn Rajskub *(Mary Lou Collins)*.

5144 The Larry Storch Show. (Series; Variety; NBC; 1953). Comedian Larry Storch oversees a program of music, songs and comedy sketches.

Host: Larry Storch. **Regulars:** Georgann Johnson, Milton Frome, Mildred Hughes, Tomi Romer, Russell Hicks, Ethel Owen, The June Taylor Dancers, The June Taylor Singers. **Announcer:** Jack Lescoulie. **Orchestra:** Sammy Spear, Ray Bloch.

5145 Las Vegas. (Series; Drama; NBC; 2003–2008). The Montecito Resort and Casino in Las Vegas is the setting for a behind-the-scenes look at the inner workings of a gambling hall. Principal focus is on an elite surveillance team charged with maintaining the security of the casino.

Ed Deline heads the team. Danny McCoy is his protégé, a former U.S. Marine. Monica Mancuso is the owner of the Montecito. Mike Cannon is the valet and assistant to Danny when needed; Delinda is Ed's seductive daughter; Mary Connell, Samantha Marquez and Nessa Holt (called "The Ice Princess") are casino hostesses and Ed's eyes on the floor.

Ed monitors casino activities from a large surveillance room and stories reveal the methods people use to cheat (or try to) despite the high tech equipment that is watching their every move.

In the episode of September 28, 2007, A.J. Cooper (who likes to be called Cooper) purchases the debt-ridden Montecito Hotel and Casino for $241 million. Cooper, worth $2 billion, runs the largest cattle ranch in Wyoming — and he plans to make the Montecito profitable once again.

Cast: James Caan *(Ed Deline)*; Josh Duhamel *(Danny McCoy)*; Nikki Cox *(Mary Connell)*; Vanessa Marci *(Samantha Marquez)*; James Lesure *(Mike Cannon)*; Molly Simms *(Delinda Deline)*; Marsha Thompson *(Nessa Holt)*; Lara Flynn Boyle *(Monica Mancuso)*; Cheryl Ladd *(Jillian Deline, Ed's ex-wife)*; Tom Selleck *(A.J. Cooper)*; Camille Guaty *(Piper)*.

5146 Las Vegas Beat. (Pilot; Crime Drama; Unaired; Produced for NBC in 1964). Bill Ballin is a former police officer turned highly respected private detective who works for the Las Vegas Casino Owners Association but who also helps the police (especially Lieutenant Bernard McFeety) solve crimes related to his beat. Bill has a girlfriend (Cynthia) and is assisted by a newspaper reporter (R.G.) and a wisecracking friend (Gopher).

Cast: Peter Graves *(Bill Ballin)*; Jamie Farr *(Gopher)*; Dick Bakalyan *(Bernard McFeety)*; Diana Millay *(Cynthia Raine)*; William Bryant *(R.G. Joseph)*.

5147 Las Vegas Gambit. (Series; Game; NBC; 1980-1981). Two teams, each composed of two members, compete in a card game based on blackjack ("21"). The first card, from an oversized deck of 52 playing cards, is revealed. A general knowledge question is read and the first team to correctly answer it receives the opportunity to either keep or pass the card to their opponents. A two-out-of-three match game is played. If twenty-one is not scored, the couple who comes closest but does not surpass twenty-one is the winner of that particular game and receives $200. $1000 is awarded if a couple scores an exact 21. Taped in Las Vegas, Nevada.

Host: Wink Martindale. **Card Dealer:** Beverly Malden. Lee Menning. **Announcer:** Kenny Williams.

5148 The Las Vegas Show. (Series; Variety; United Network; 1967). Entertainment performances set against the background of various Las Vegas nightclubs. *The Las Vegas Show* was the first (and only) series to be produced by a proposed network called the United Network. After one month, the idea collapsed when money could not be raised to meet the next month's expenses.

Program Open: "From the Hacienda Hotel in Las Vegas, Nevada, the United Network presents *The Las Vegas Show* starring Bill Dana, with tonight's guests Robert Loggia, Sergio Mendez and Brazil '66, Paula Wayne, Stan Fisher, Dave Madden and Pete Barbutti, Ann Elder, Dick Curtis, Bernie Kukoff, Danny Meehan, Cully Richards, Jack Sheldon and Jo Anne Worley. And now, here's your host and the star of the show, Bill Dana."

Host: Bill Dana. **Regulars:** Ann Elder, Pete Barbutti, Jo Anne Worley, Cully Richards, Danny Meehan. **Music:** Jack Sheldon.

5149   *Lash of the West.* (Series; Children; Syn., 1951; ABC, 1953). A western-accented-program in which western film star Lash LaRue demonstrated his cowboy skills (particularly his ability with a whip) and presented re-edited versions of his western theatrical films (wherein he played Marshal Lash LaRue and, in others, Marshal Cheyenne Davis).

Host: Al "Lash" LaRue. **Assistant:** Al "Fuzzy" St. John *(Syn. version)*; John Martin *(as Deputy Tom Stratton, ABC)*; Cliff Taylor *(Flapjack, ABC)*.

5150   *Lassie.* (Series; Drama; CBS; 1964–1968). A continuation of the *Lassie* series from where *Timmy and Lassie* leaves off. The need for American farmers overseas prompts Paul Martin to sell his farm and move to Australia with his wife, Ruth, and son, Timmy. Timmy, who is unable to take his dog, Lassie with him due to quarantine laws, leaves her in the custody of his friend, the elderly Cully Wilson. A short time later, when Cully suffers a heart attack and is no longer able to care for Lassie, he gives her to his friend, Corey Stuart, the local forest ranger. Stories relate Lassie's adventures as she assists Ranger Corey Stuart. See also *Jeff's Collie* and *The New Lassie*.

Cast: Robert Bray *(Ranger Corey Stuart)*; Jed Allan *(Ranger Scott Turner)*; Jack DeMave *(Ranger Bob Erickson)*; John Archer *(Ranger Kirby Newman)*.

5151   *Lassie.* (Series; Drama; CBS; 1968–1971). The last network version of *Lassie* that drops the format of the 1964 (to 1968) version (wherein Lassie was the assistant to forest ranger Corey Stuart) to present Lassie as a dog who is no longer bound to a human master and now a wanderer who roams and assists those she finds in trouble — both human and animal.

5152   *Lassie.* (Series; Drama; Syn.; 1972). The first syndicated version of *Lassie* that ends Lassie's days of wandering (as depicted in the 1968 CBS version of the series) to focus on Lassie's adventures when she finds a temporary home at the California ranch of Keith Holden. Keith is a widower and the father of Ron and Mike. Dale Mitchell is his assistant; Lucy Baker is Ron and Mike's friend; Sue Lambert is the veterinarian.

Cast: Larry Pennell *(Keith Holden)*; Larry Wilcox *(Dale Mitchell)*; Skip Burton *(Ron Holden)*; Joshua Albee *(Mike Holden)*; Sherry Boucher *(Sue Lambert)*; Pamelyn Ferdin *(Lucy Baker)*.

5153   *Lassie.* (Series; Drama; Animal Planet; 1997-1998). The town of Hudson Falls, Vermont is the setting. It is here that Karen Cabot, a widow, runs a veterinary clinic. She is also the mother of young Timmy Cabot. One day Timmy finds an injured Collie (mistreated by her owner) he names Lassie. Karen helps nurse the dog back to health and she and Timmy bond. Stories follow the adventures shared by a young boy and his dog as they help people — and animals — in trouble.

Cast: Susan Almgren *(Dr. Karen Cabot)*; Corey Sevier *(Timmy Cabot)*; Walter Massey *(Dr. Donald Stewart)*; Tom Post *(Ethan Bennett)*; Nathalie Vansier *(Natalie)*; Tod Fennell *(Jeff MacKenzie)*; Al Vandeeruys *(Jay MacKenzie)*.

5154   *Lassie: The New Beginning.* (Pilot; Drama; ABC; Sept. 17 and 24, 1978). Samantha and Chip Stratton, orphans who live with their uncle, Stuart Stratton in Lake Pines, California, are the new owners of Lassie. The proposal was to relate the adventures Samantha and Chip share with Lassie. Stuart is the editor of *The Lake Pines Journal*; Kathy is Stuart's friend; Buzz is Kathy's son; J.D. Marsh is the sheriff; and Amos Rheams is the doctor.

Cast: John Reilly *(Stuart Stratton)*; Sally Boyden *(Samantha Stratton)*; Shane Sinutko *(Chip Stratton)*; Lee Bryant *(Kathy McKendrick)*; David Wayne *(Dr. Amos Rheams)*; Gene Evans *(J.D. Marsh)*; Jeff Harlan *(Buzz McKendrick)*.

5155   *Lassie's Rescue Rangers.* (Series; Cartoon; ABC; 1973–1975). Lassie, the beautiful Collie that starred in several theatrical films and television series, has found a new home with Ben Turner, his wife, Laurie, and their children Jackie and Susan, the operators of a Rocky Mountain rescue service. Lassie has become the leader of the Rescue Force, animals that assist the Turners, and stories follow the efforts of humans and animals to work as a team to help people in distress. Ranger Jean Fox assists them.

Voice Cast: Ted Knight *(Ben Turner)*; Jane Webb *(Laura Turner)*; Lane Scheimer *(Jackie Turner)*; Erica Scheimer *(Susan Turner)*; Ted Knight *(Jean Fox)*.

5156   *Lassiter.* (Pilot; Crime Drama; CBS; July 8, 1968). Pete Lassiter is a tough investigative reporter for *Contrast* magazine. Pete is not one for sitting around and getting his information from the police. He is restless and has to be where the crime occurred and do his own investigating to put his spin on the case at hand. Stories were to relate those case investigations.

Cast: Burt Reynolds *(Pete Lassiter)*.

5157   *The Last Chance Cafe.* (Pilot; Comedy-Drama; ABC; Feb. 28, 1986). The Last Chance Cafe is situated in the middle of nowhere and allows weary travelers to partake of a meal before continuing their journey. It is run by a mysterious old man named Virgil who allows troubled customers to "see" crucial moments from their pasts with themselves as they were many years ago. The proposal, a broadcast on *The New Love, American Style*, was to relate what happens when the past is relived.

Cast: Henry Jones *(Virgil)*.

5158   *Last Comic Standing.* (Series; Reality; NBC; 2003–2010). Professional as well as up-and-coming stand-up comedians compete for an exclusive contract with NBC. Ten finalists, selected from open auditions across the country, are brought to Los Angeles and placed in a large residence (where they live together during the competition). While cameras follow their preparations for a show (and how they get along with each other), it is the club audience that judge the material and vote their least favorite off the stage (must leave). The last comic standing is the winner. Jay Mohr, Bill Bellamy and Craig Robinson host.

5159   *The Last Days of Russell.* (Pilot; Drama; ABC; July 22, 1995). Russell Angel is a 13-year-old boy who feels that if something bad will happen it will happen to him. When his 14-year-old cousin Russell (after whom he is named) dies, Russell fears he too will die at 14. He decides to live life to the fullest. The proposal was to follow Russell as he struggles to live a normal life despite the fact that he feels he is cursed. Walter and Darlene are his parents; Sanfus and Meatloaf are his friends.

Cast: Yohance Serrant *(Russell Angel)*; Wendell Pierce *(Walter Angel)*; Vernee Watson *(Darlene Angel)*; Johnta Austin *(Sanfus)*; Charles Duke *(Meatloaf)*.

5160   *The Last Frontier.* (Series; Drama; Fox; 1996). Andy, an Air Force officer; Billy, an architect, Reed, the owner of an outdoor adventure company are bachelors who share their home in Alaska with Kate, an executive for a hotel conglomerate. Kate is also single and stories relate their experiences working and living on the Last Frontier. Matt, Reed's brother, runs the local bar.

Cast: Jessica Tuck (*Kate*); John Terlesky (*Reed Garfield*); Anthony Starke (*Billy McPherson*); Patrick Labyorteaux (*Andy*); Leigh-Allyn Baker (*Joy*); Meredith Salinger (*Tina Adamson*); David Kriegel (*Matt Garfield*).

5161   *The Last Ninja.* (Pilot; Adventure; ABC; July 7, 1983). On a rainy evening in California in 1951, a Japanese-American family, the Sakuras, find an abandoned baby on their doorstep — a Caucasian boy they adopt and name Ken. The father, Mantaro, trains Ken in the art of the Ninja — the ability to use disguise and illusion to battle evil. Thirty-two years later Ken begins a double life — as an antique dealer, and the mysterious Ninja, who battles crime and corruption. (The title refers to Ken being the last of his adopted family line to become a Ninja). Other regulars are Noriko, Ken's sister; and Mr. Cosmo, the U.S. government agent for whom Ken works.

Cast: Michael Beck (*Ken Sakura*); Nancy Kwan (*Noriko Sakura*); Mako (*Mantaro Sakura*); John McMartin (*Mr. Cosmo*).

5162   *Last of the Ninth.* (Pilot; Crime Drama; Unaired; Produced by HBO in 2008). New York City in the 1970s is the setting for a hard-hitting proposal that was to look not only at the scandalous crime within the police department, but how authorities handled the counter cultural rabble rousers of the era.

Cast: Michael Gaston (*Lt. John White*); Lily Rabe (*Mary Byrne*); Jonah Lotan (*Joe Dalton*); Michael Raymond-James (*Tommy Leone*); Ray Winstone (*John Giglio*).

5163   *Last of the Private Eyes.* (Pilot; Comedy; NBC; April 30, 1963). J.F. Kelly considers himself to be the last of a dying breed — a 1940s style private detective who puts his nose to the grindstone to solve cases. The proposal was to relate Kelly's efforts to solve crimes — which he does quite by accident. Aired as a segment of *The Dick Powell Show.*

Cast: Bob Cummings (*J.F. Kelly*).

5164   *The Last Precinct.* (Series; Comedy; NBC; 1986). Precinct 56 is a former county morgue turned funeral parlor turned police station that city officials use as a dumping ground for what it calls odd-ball officers — psychologically challenged cops who are part of the force but just not stable enough for regular precinct duties and assignments. They handle non-violent crimes but always manage to stumble upon real crimes that require their unique brand of justice to solve.

Rob Wright is the laid back, indecisive captain of Precinct 56. Rob feels he must do what is right because his last name is Wright and "I stand for right." His inability to command a regular precinct was the reason for his transfer. The officers under his command are Melba Brubaker, Tremayne Lane, Martha Haggerty, Butch Briscoe, Sundance, Alphabet and the King.

Melba is blonde, beautiful and tough. You would never guess it by looking at her, but Melba, who likes to be called Mel, was formerly a man — Melvin Brubaker. Mel tried living the life of a man, was a star ballplayer, but felt he was meant to be a woman and underwent a sex change operation. Mel's toughness makes her a loner.

Tremayne is nicknamed Night Train for his love of working the night shift. Martha is from a military family and assists Rob as his second in command. She runs the precinct like an army base and is too aggressive which is the reason for her transfer. Alphabet is the nickname for Officer Shivoramanbhai Poonchwalla, an exchange officer from Calcutta who has little knowledge of American police procedures and is hoping to learn from his fellow officers and bring this knowledge back to his homeland.

The King, who has no other name, is a former Elvis impersonator who "overdosed" and now believes he is the reincarnation of Elvis Presley. William, the overweight officer, is nicknamed Raid for his habit of raiding the refrigerator. Butch and Sundance are elderly officers who work as a team and prefer to be called Butch and Sundance after their Old West heroes, Butch Cassidy and the Sundance Kid. Felony is the lazy precinct dog.

Stacey is the waitress at the Honey Bunns Drive-In, the local eatery; Arnold Bludhorn is the frustrated police chief who oversees Precinct 56 and is seeking a way to disband it and its officers.

Cast: Adam West (*Rob Wright*); Randi Brooks (*Mel Brubaker*); Ernie Hudson (*Tremayne Lane*); Yana Narvanna (*Martha Haggerty*); Keenan Wynn (*Butch Briscoe*); Hank Rolike (*Sundance*); Vijay Amritaj (*Alphabet*); Nicollette Sheridan (*Stacey*); James Cromwell (*Arnold Bludhorn*).

5165   *The Last Resort.* (Series; Comedy; CBS; 1979-1980). Michael Lerner, Duane Kaminski, Zack Comstock and Jeffrey Barron are four college students who decide to work as waiters at a resort during their summer vacation. Stories relate their antics as they turn a genteel mountain hotel into a madhouse. Other regulars are Gail Collins, the pastry chef; Kevin, the cook; Murray, the maitre d'; and Mrs. Trilling, the overbearing hotel guest.

Cast: Larry Breeding (*Michael Lerner*); Stephanie Faracy (*Gail Collins*); Zane Lasky (*Duane Kaminski*); Walter Olkewicz (*Zack Comstock*); Ray Underwood (*Jeffrey Barron*); John Fujioka (*Kevin*); Robert Costanzo (*Murray*); Dorothy Konrad (*Mrs. Trilling*).

5166   *Last Restaurant Standing.* (Series; Reality; BBC America; 2009). Nine couples compete for the opportunity to open their own restaurant for the world-renowned chef Raymond Blanc. Each of the couples competes in various challenges to determine if they have what it takes to not only prepare meals but operate a restaurant (each couple is given an empty restaurant and must make it their own with the principal object being to open it to the public within one week. Their decisions, arguments and mistakes are shared with the viewer). The weakest performing couples are eliminated with the one couple proving their ability receiving the financial and personal backing of Raymond as they start their own restaurant. Raymond Blanc hosts; Raymond Blanc, Sarah Willingham and David Moore are the judges.

5167   *The Last Word.* (Series; Discussion; CBS; 1957-1959). The program features discussion on the vagaries of the English language.

Host: Dr. Bergen Evans. **Panelists:** June Havoc, Arthur Knight, John Mason Brown.

5168   *The Last Word.* (Pilot; Comedy; NBC; May 10, 1986). The Last Word is a restaurant for the young-at-heart in California. It is run by Nicky and Tyler and the proposal, a spin off from *Gimme a Break* was to relate their misadventures. Other regulars are Stefan Popalardo, the owner (Nicky's father); Sherry, the cashier; and Gloria, the waitress.

Cast: Harry Basil (*Nicky Popalardo*); Brian Backer (*Tyler McVey*); Reuven Bar-Yotam (*Stefan Popalardo*); Melody Hamilton (*Sherry*); Shari Ballard (*Gloria*).

5169   *The Last Word.* (Series; Game; Syn.; 1989-1990). Two teams compete, each composed of a celebrity captain and a non-celebrity player. A board with three unknown words (indicated by blank spaces) is shown. One player from each team competes. One player begins by asking for a letter. If it is contained in the word it appears in its appropriate place on the board. The object is for players to guess each word (which are related to each other). The first player to identify the last word of the three words that are shown wins the round for his team. The team with the most correct identifications wins the game and merchandise prizes.

Host: Wink Martindale. **Assistant:** Jennifer Lyall.

5170 *Late Bloomer.* (Pilot; Comedy; CBS; Jan. 19, 1987). Hoping to find more meaning to life, actress Julia Peterson relinquishes her career and enrolls in Washington Square College in New York City where she hopes to become a psychologist. The proposal, a spin off from *Kate and Allie* was to relate Julia's activities at school (where she also teaches drama) and at home in Brooklyn Heights, where she teaches cooking. Other regulars are Ann and Henry, Julia's parents; Millie, her friend; Keith, her ex-husband; and Sandy, a student of Julia's.

Cast: Lindsay Wagner (*Julia Peterson*); Barbara Barrie (*Ann*); Roger Bowen (*Henry*); Mercedes Reuhl (*Millie*); Sam Freed (*Keith*); Kelly Wolfe (*Sandy*).

5171 *Late Date with Sari.* (Series; Talk; Lifetime; 1995-1996). Sari Locker, the author of the book *Mind-Blowing Sex in the Real World*, hosts a program about sex and relationships as seen from the woman's point of view. Ordinary people are seen discussing (quite frankly) intimate details of their lives — in group sessions and in on-the-street interviews.

5172 *The Late Fall, Early Summer Bert Convy Hour.* (Series; Variety; CBS; 1976). Bert Convy hosts a program of music, songs and comedy that aired for four weeks in the late summer and early fall of 1976 (Aug. 25 to Sept. 15).

Host: Bert Convy. **Regulars:** Sallie Janes, Donna Ponterotto, Marty Barris, Lennie Schultz, Susie Guest, Shirley Kirkes, Judy Pierce, Darcell Wynne. **Announcer:** Donna Ponterotto. **Orchestra:** Perry Botkin, Jr.

5173 *The Late Late Show with Craig Ferguson.* (Series; Talk; CBS; 2005–). Middle-of-the-night talk show hosted by actor-comedian Craig Ferguson, perhaps best known as Mr. Wick on *The Drew Carey Show*.

Host: Craig Ferguson. **Regulars:** Shadoe Stevens, Richard Malmos.

5174 *Late Line.* (Series; Drama; NBC; 1998-1999). *Late Line* is a late night news program based in the nation's capitol. Al Freundlich is the anchor and stories offer a behind-the-scene look at the operations of a news program.

Cast: Al Franken (*Al Freundlich*); Catherine Lloyd Burns (*Mona Megyn Price*); Robert Foxworth (*Pearce McKenzie*); Sanaa Lathan (*Briana Daryll*); Miguel Ferrer (*Vic Karp*); Montse Viader (*Luisa Sandoval*); Ajay Nardu (*Raji*).

5175 *Late Night Liars.* (Series; Comedy; GSN; 2010). A late night (11:00 P.M.) program that features five Jim Henson Muppets (Shelley Oceans, William A. Mummy, Cashmere Ramada, Sir Sebastian Simian and the Weasel). Two contestants appear opposite a panel of the four Muppets who are not only half-sauced but also outrageous. Adapting the format of the 1969 game show *The Liar's Club*, the contestants must determine which Muppet is relating the truth about a question or fact posed to them. The Muppets adult-oriented stories provide the comedy and the first contestant to determine which panelist is telling the truth wins a cash prize.

Shelley, once the world's greatest insult comic, has now become a permanent game show panelist. William, called "Mr. Double Entendre," is a confirmed bachelor (although he has been married and divorced twice from Shelley and just can't seem to find the right woman). Cashmere is a dimwitted tabloid target who had a series of naughty video tapes that have become hits on the Internet. Sir Sebastian is an entrepreneur who believes he is the smartest person on the panel. Weasel is a rodent who also doubles as the show's announcer and score keeper.

Host: Larry Miller. **Voices:** Victor Yerrid (*Weasel*); Donna Kimball (*Shelley Oceans*); Brian Patrick Clarke (*William Mummy*); Colleen Smith (*Cashmere Ramada*); Tyler Bunch (*Sir Sebastian Simian*) .**Music:** The Elements.

5176 *Late Night with Conan O'Brien.* (Series; Variety; NBC; 1993–2009). A late night talk show of celebrity interviews, musical numbers and a feature that spotlights off-the-wall characters.

Host: Conan O'Brien **Announcer:** Joel Godard. **Semi-Regulars:** Andy Richter, Darrell Hammond, Al Franken, Jim Gaffigan, Will Ferrell, Dave Chappelle, Jerry Vivino, Jimmy Vivino. **Band Leader:** Max Weinberg.

5177 *Late Night with David Letterman.* (Series; Variety; NBC; 1982). Late night program of celebrity (and non-celebrity) interviews and off-beat satirical sketches.

Host: David Letterman. **Regular:** Larry "Bud" Melman. **Announcer:** Bill Wendell, Alan Kalder. **Music:** Paul Shaffer.

5178 *Late Night with Jimmy Fallon.* (Series; Variety; NBC; 2009–). The replacement for *Late Night with Conan O'Brien* that continues the same basic format with late night (12:30 A.M. to 1:30 A.M.) celebrity interviews, music and comedy.

Host: Jimmy Fallon. **Announcer:** Steve Higgins. **Music:** The Roots.

5179 *The Late Show Starring Joan Rivers.* (Series; Variety; Fox; 1986-1987). A live, nightly program of talk, music and interviews. The premiere program of the new Fox Broadcasting Company, a fourth broadcast network. After eight months on the air, Joan Rivers was relieved of her duties as host (from Oct. 9, 1986 to May 15, 1987). On May 22, 1987, the program became *The Late Show* and featured daily guest hosts in an attempt to boost its less-than-desirable ratings.

Host: Joan Rivers. **Announcer:** Clint Holmes. **Music:** Mark Hudson and the Party Boys Plus the Tramp.

5180 *The Late Show with Craig Kilborn.* (Series; Talk; CBS; 1994–2004). A middle-of-the-night talk show that features celebrity interviews and short comedy skits.

Host: Craig Kilborn.

5181 *The Late Show with David Letterman.* (Series; Variety; CBS; 1993–). Comedy bits, celebrity interviews and musical numbers that became CBS's first late night talk program (David replaced the network's program of movies and series repeats that aired under the umbrella title of *The CBS Late Movie*).

Host: David Letterman. **Regular:** Larry "Bud" Melman. **Band Leader:** Paul Shaffer.

5182 *Laugh-In.* (Series; Comedy; NBC; 1977-1978). A cast of virtual unknowns (at the time) in comedic nonsense satirizing everyday life.

Regulars: Nancy Bleiwess, Ed Bluestone, Kim Braden, Claire

Faulkonbridge, Antionette Attell, Robin Williams, Wayland Flowers, June Gable, Jim Giovanni, Ben Powers, Bill Rafferty, Michael Sklar, Lennie Schultz, April Tatro. **Music:** Tommy Oliver.

5183   *Laugh Line.* (Series; Game; NBC; 1959). The object calls for a celebrity panel to supply comic captions that are presented in tableau form. The winners are determined by studio audience applause and contestants, represented by the celebrities, receive prizes accordingly.
   Host: Dick Van Dyke. **Panelists:** Dorothy Loudon, Mike Nichols, Elaine May, Orson Bean.

5184   *Laugh Trax.* (Series; Variety; Syn.; Sept. 1982). Comedy Skits coupled with performances by guest rock personalities. The pilot presentation, *Rock Comedy*, aired in syndication in May of 1982.
   Host: Jim Staahl. **Regulars:** Gail Matthius, Lucy Webb, Frank Welker, Howie Mandel, Jim Fisher. **Theme Music:** "Laugh Trax" by Bob Summers.

5185   *Laughs for Sale.* (Series; Comedy; ABC; 1963). Guest comics perform material (sketches, routines, monologues) that is submitted by fledging comedy writers. After the performance, the material is evaluated and offered for sale. Interested parties can purchase the material by contacting the show's producers.
   Host: Hal March. **Announcer:** Mike Lawrence.

5186   *Laughter in Paris.* (Experimental; Drama; NBC; Feb. 17, 1946). An unusual experiment: submitting an original story to motion picture executives through the use of television. NBC issued special invitations to film producers and story editors to watch the program in the network's viewing room. The play, written by the head of NBC's script department, told the tale of two brothers (Lawrence Dobkin, Oliver Thorndike) who are driven apart by a fight and of one of the brother's torment in his old age when his supposedly dead brother comes back to haunt him.
   Cast: Charles Avery, Bill Beach, Haskell Coffin, Lawrence Dobkin, Don Gillette, John Graham, Alan Hayes, Eda Heinemann, Eva Langbord, Larry Parke, Michael Rosenberg, Arnold Stang, Oliver Thorndike, Graham Velsey.

5187   *Laughtime.* (Experimental; Comedy; CBS; Oct. 16, 1945). A program of burlesque-like acts with Buddy Hackett in his first TV appearance (discovered by producer Bud Gamble in a G.I. entertainment unit). "The cast tried hard," Variety said, "but never had a chance. Hackett's mugging and timing were creditable and the youngster should go places with better material."
   Performers: Paul Brilliant, Herbert Graham, Buddy Hackett, Hildegarde Holliday, Marcella Markham.

5188   *Launch My Line.* (Series; Reality; Bravo; 2009). Ten expert fashion designers are paired with one of ten "established professionals" who have sought but failed to establish their own clothing line. The contestants work with their professional partners to bring their vision of fashion to life. The designs are then judged in a runway walk by a panel of fashion experts. The least plausible fashion design costs its creator a chance at that dream. The one contestant whose designs prove to be the best by the end of the competition wins $50,000 and the launch of his or her clothing line. Dan Caten hosts. Stephanie Greenfield and Lisa Klein are the judges.

5189   *Laurel and Hardy Laughtoons.* (Series; Comedy; Syn.; 1979). Edited versions of silent Laurel and Hardy shorts of the 1920s. Stan Laurel and Oliver Hardy are the featured stars. Music (by George

Korngold) and sound effects have been added to the original films produced by Hal Roach.

5190   *The Laurel and Hardy Show.* (Series; Comedy; Syn.; 1986). A collection of Stan Laurel and Oliver Hardy theatrical shorts and feature films from the 1930s and 1940s. The series incorporates new prints made directly from the original negatives.

5191   *Lauren Hutton And....* (Series; Talk; Syn.; 1995). Model-actress Lauren Hutton hosts a one-on-one celebrity interview program wherein she tries to get her guests "to be honest because real human information is the sexiest thing there is."

5192   *Laurie Hill.* (Series; Comedy; ABC; 1992). Laurie Hill is a mid-thirties woman struggling to balance her roles as housewife, mother and doctor. She is married to Jeff, a freelance journalist and eternal kid at heart, and is the mother of five-year-old Leo (who attends the Davis Preschool and has a plush dog named Floppy Dog).
   Laurie has a B.A. from Cornell University, an M.D. from the University of Michigan and ten years of clinical experience. She now works at (and is partners in) the Weisman, Kramer and Hill Family Medical Clinic. Laurie listens to radio station KOLD (91.3 FM) and is on emergency call at Saint John's Hospital.
   Laurie's business partners are Dr. Walter Weisman, a grandfatherly physician with one eye on retirement; and Dr. Spencer Kramer, a family practitioner with an aversion to people who attended the Crittendon Academy for Boys. Nancy MacIntire is an office doctor, and Beverly Fiedler is the office receptionist.
   Cast: DeLane Matthews (*Laurie Hill*); Robert Clohessy (*Jeff Hill*); Eric Lloyd (*Leo Hill*); Joseph Maher (*Dr. Walter Weisman*); Kurt Fuller (*Dr. Spencer Kramer*); Ellen DeGeneres (*Nancy MacIntire*); Doris Belack (*Beverly Fiedler*).

5193   *Laverne and Shirley.* (Series; Comedy; ABC; 1976–1983). A spin off from *Happy Days*. Laverne DeFazio and Shirley Feeney are friends who live in Milwaukee, Wisconsin, during the 1960s (at 730 Knapp Street, Apartment A; also given as 730 Hampton Street). They work in the beer bottle-capping division of the Shotz Brewery.
   The series changed locales beginning with the episode of October 31, 1981 when Laverne and Shirley move to California to begin new lives. They acquire an apartment at 113½ Laurel Vista Drive in Los Angeles and find employment in the gift wrapping department of Bardwell's Department Store. One year later, Shirley marries her fiancé, Dr. Walter Meeney; Laverne works for the Ajax Aerospace Company.
   Laverne, an Italian Catholic, suffers from a fear of small places. She loves milk and Pepsi (her favorite drink), Scooter Pies (favorite snack), and peanut butter and sauerkraut on raisin bread is her favorite sandwich. She wears a large capital L on all her clothes, including her lingerie.
   Shirley, an Irish Protestant, is famous for the Shirley Feeney scarf dance, has a plush cat named Boo Boo Kitty, and uses the Feeney family traditional greetings "Hi-Yooo" (for hello) and "Bye-Yooo" (for goodbye).
   Andrew ("Squiggy") Squigman and Leonard ("Lenny") Kosnoski are friends of Laverne and Shirley and work as beer truck drivers for the Shotz Brewery. In California episodes, they are co-owners of the Squignoski Talent Agency of Burbank, and ice cream vendors with a truck called Squignoski's Ice Cream. Their favorite food is Bosco (which they put on everything).
   Frank DeFazio, Laverne's father, first owns the Pizza Bowl (a pizzeria and bowling alley); then, after he and Edna Babish marry and

move to Burbank, Cowboy Bill's Western Grub (a fast food chain with the slogan "Stuff your face Western style"). Carmine Ragusa, Shirley's original boyfriend (who calls her "Angel Face"), is nicknamed "The Big Ragu," and works as a singing messenger. Rhonda Lee, an actress, is Laverne and Shirley's neighbor (California episodes); Rosie Greenbaum is Laverne's nemesis; Mary is the Pizza Bowl waitress; Sonny St. James is the apartment house manager (California); Harvey Hilderbrand is the manager of Bardwell's; Alvina P. Plout is the sergeant (when Laverne and Shirley served a hitch in the army); Amy is Edna's daughter; Bill Ajax owns Ajax Aerospace (managed by "G. Bullets" Klein); Squendelyn is Squiggy's sister. Cyndi Grecco sings the theme, "Making Our Dreams Come True."

Cast: Penny Marshall (*Laverne DeFazio*); Cindy Williams (*Shirley Feeney*); Michael McKean (*Lenny Kosnoski*); David L. Lander (*Andrew "Squiggy" Squigman*); Eddie Mekka (*Carmine Raguso*); Phil Foster (*Frank DeFazio*); Betty Garrett (*Edna Babish*); Carol Ita White (*Rosie Greenbaum*); Frances Peach (*Mary*); Ed Marinaro (*Sonny St. James*); Norman Bartold (*Harvey Hilderbrand*); Vicki Lawrence (*Sgt. Alvinia P. Plout*); Raleigh Bond (*Bill Ajax*); Robert Hogan ("*G Bullets" Klein*); David L. Lander (*Squendelyn Squigman*); Linda Gillin (*Amy Babish*).

5194   *Laverne and Shirley in the Army.* (Series; Cartoon; ABC; 1981–1982). An extension series based on the live action comedy *Laverne and Shirley*. The antics of Laverne DeFazio and Shirley Feeney as privates with the U.S. Army at Camp Fillmore. Their superior is Sergeant Squeely, a talking pig; Sergeant Turnbuckle is Squeely's superior.

Voice Cast: Penny Marshall (*Pvt. Laverne DeFazio*); Cindy Williams (*Pvt. Shirley Feeney*); Ron Palillo (*Sgt. Squeely*); Ken Mars (*Sgt. Turnbuckle*).

5195   *Laverne and Shirley with the Fonz.* (Series; Cartoon; ABC; 1982–1983). An animated Fonzie (from *Happy Days*) becomes an army private assigned to the motor pool at Camp Fillmore. Laverne and Shirley (from the above title) are also privates here and stories follow their efforts to adjust to a military life. They are supervised by Sergeant Squeely — the U.S. Army's only talking pig. Mr. Cool is Fonzie's dog; and Sergeant Turnbuckle is Squeely's superior.

Voice Cast: Julie McWhirter (*Pvt. Laverne DeFazio*); Lynne Stewart (*Pvt. Shirley Feeney*); Henry Winkler (*Pvt. Fonzie*); Ron Palillo (*Sgt. Squeely*); Frank Welker (*Mr. Cool*); Ken Mars (*Sgt. Turnbuckle*).

5196   *The Law.* (Pilot; Comedy; Unaired; Produced for ABC in 2009). Cedric Battiste spends his weekdays tending to the gardening store he owns. On Saturdays and Sundays, he becomes a weekend warrior — a member of the Deputy Reserve Unit of the L.A. County Sheriff's Department. But Cedric is not alone: Dan, a high-strung orthodontist; Michael, a graphic artist; and Liz, a bored housewife are the reservist deputies he oversees. The proposal was to follow Cedric and his team as they often fumble their way around solving petty crimes.

Cast: Cedric the Entertainer (*Cedric Battiste*); Donald Faison (*Dan*); John Amos (*Charles*); Larry Joe Campbell (*Carl Tucker*); Mercedes Masohn (*Theresa Ramirez*); Ryan Devlin (*Michael*); Madchen Amick (*Liz*).

5197   *The Law and Harry McGraw.* (Series; Crime Drama; CBS; 1987–1988). Harlan H. McGraw III, better known as Harry McGraw, is the owner-operator of Harry McGraw Private Investigations in Boston. Harry is tough, disorganized and irritable. He is reluctant to tell the whole truth, or "The Straight Skinny" as he calls it. He believes he attracts the worst clients; he considers them missions of mercy clients. Harry rarely hands out a business card — "I'd give you a card but I'm fresh out. I'm in the book." He has a gambling

problem and especially likes to play the horses ("I never forget a nag I lose on"). He rarely uses a gun and relies on his fists ("Okay, I get busted up a bit, but at least I get a case solved"). He claims that murder cases have a way of bringing out the worst in people and that if you need a lot of protection, he's the guy that can give it to you.

Harry lives in an untidy apartment on Melrose. He has a police record — arrested by the Boston Police for suspicion of murder and burglary — and had his private investigator's license suspended four times in three years. Once on a case, Harry's seedy and abrasive side appears. He becomes relentless and a determined fact finder despite the dangerous obstacles he might encounter. He is also a master of disguise and uses such deception to trick suspects into revealing information.

Harry uses the resources of the local paper, the *Morning Bulletin*, and hangs out at a bar called Gilhooley's.

Ellie Maginnis, a criminal attorney with the firm of Maginnis and Maginnis, has the office opposite Harry's agency. The program is a spin off from *Murder, She Wrote*, wherein the character of Harry McGraw appeared several times.

Cast: Jerry Orbach (*Harry McGraw*); Barbara Babcock (*Ellie Maginnis*).

5198   *The Law and Mr. Jones.* (Series; Drama; ABC; 1960–1962). Abraham Lincoln Jones is a tough but honest criminal attorney working out New York City. Named after the 16th President of the United States, Abraham believes in everything his namesake stood for; he will not comprise his beliefs and firmly believes that honesty from his clients is his best defense. Stores follow Abraham as he struggles to defend people falsely accused of serious crimes. Marsha Spear is Abraham's secretary; C.E. Carruthers is his law clerk; Thomas Jones is Abraham's father.

Cast: James Whitmore (*Abraham Lincoln Jones*); Janet DeGore (*Marsha Spear*); Conlan Carter (*C.E. Carruthers*); Russ Brown (*Thomas Jones*). **Theme Song Adaptation:** "When the Saints Go Marching In" by Hans Salter.

5199   *Law and Order.* (Series; Crime Drama; NBC; 1990–2009). A crime is established at the beginning of each episode. The first half of the program relates the investigations of the N.Y.P.D. detectives assigned to that case. The episode concludes with the D.A.'s prosecution of the suspects charged with the crime (usually murder). See also: *Law and Order: Criminal Intent, Law and Order: Special Victims Unit, Law and Order: Trial by Jury* and *Law and Order: Los Angeles*.

Program Open: "In the criminal justice system the people are represented by two separate yet equally important groups — the police who investigate crimes and the district attorneys who prosecute the offenders. These are their stories."

Cast: Jerry Orbach (*Det. Lenny Briscoe*); Steven Hill (*D.A. Adam Schiff*); Jesse L. Martin (*Det. Ed Green*); S. Epatha Merkerson (*Lt. Anita Van Buren*); Chris Noth (*Det. Mike Logan*); Leslie Hendrix (*Dr. Elizabeth Rodgers*); Fred Dalton Thompson (*D.A. Arthur Branch*); Benjamin Bratt (*Det. Ray Curtis*); Michael Moriarty (*A.D.A. Ben Stone*); Elisabeth Rohm (*A.D.A. Serena Southerlyn*); Angie Harmon (*A.D.A. Abbie Carmichael*); Dann Florek (*Capt. Donald Cragen*); Richard Brooks (*A.D.A. Paul Robinette*); Jill Hennessy (*A.D.A. Claire Kincaid*); Carolyn McCormick (*Dr. Elizabeth Olivet*); John Fiore (*Det. Tony Profaci*); Carey Lowell (*A.D.A. Jamie Ross*); Dianne West (*D.A. Nora Lewin*); Dennis Farina (*Det. Joe Fontana*); J.K. Simmons (*Dr. Emile Skoda*); Annie Parisse (*A.D.A. Alexandra Borgia*); Paul Sorvino (*Det. Sgt. Philip Cerreta*); George Dzundza (*Det. Sgt. Maxwell Greevey*); Christine Farrell (*Arlene Shrier; Forensics Technician*); Larry Clarke (*Det. Morris LaMotte*); Alana De La Garza (*A.D.A. Connie Rubirosa*); Jeremy Sisto (*Det. Cyrus Lupo*); Alicia Witt (*Det. Nola*

Falacci); Linus Roache *(A.D.A. Michael Cutter)*; Anthony Anderson *(Det. Kevin Bernard)*. **Opening Theme Narration:** Steven Zirnkilton.

5200   *Law and Order: Crime and Punishment.* (Series; Reality; NBC; 2003). "In the criminal justice system, Deputy District Attorneys represent the people. The prosecutors you are about to see and they cases they try are real. Nothing has been recreated," said the announcer to the fourth (but short lived) franchise of the *Law and Order* series. Unlike the other versions (which are set in New York City), this version is set in California and deals with real cases in San Diego. All participants, who vary from episode to episode, are real and cases are presented via interviews, witness gathering, trial preparation and the actual trial. Steven Zirnkilton is the announcer.

5201   *Law and Order: Criminal Intent.* (Series; Crime Drama; NBC/USA; 2001–2011). Robert Goren and Alexandra Eames are detectives with the Major Case Squad of the N.Y.P.D. The unit investigates complex crimes (usually murder) that require special investigative work. Stories, which are later a psychological profile of the perpetrators, follow the detectives as they piece together the evidence that ultimately enables an arrest. Later episodes also focus on the investigations of Mike Logan, Carolyn Barek and Zach Nichols.

Program Open: "In New York City's war on crime, the worst criminal offenders are pursued by the detectives of the Major Case Squad. These are their stories."

Cast: Vincent D'Onofrio *(Det. Robert Goren)*; Kathryn Erbe *(Det. Alexandra Eames)*; Courtney B. Vance *(A.D.A. Ron Carver)*; Jamey Sheridan *(Capt. James Deakins)*; Leslie Hendrix *(Dr. Elizabeth Rodgers)*; Chris Noth *(Det. Mike Logan)*; Annabella Sciorra *(Det. Carolyn Barek)*; Jeff Goldblum *(Det. Zach Nichols)*; Julianne Nicholson *(Det. Megan Wheeler)*; Samantha Buck *(Det. G. Lynn Bishop)*; Eric Bogosian *(Capt. Danny Ross)*; Steven Zirnkilton *(Theme Narrator)*.

5202   *Law and Order: Los Angeles.* (Series; Crime Drama; NBC; 2010–2011). *Law and Order* spin off that, set in Los Angeles, follows detectives with the Robbery-Homicide Division of the L.A.P.D. as they investigate "ripped from the headlines crimes." Particular focus is on detectives Rex Winters and Thomas "T.J." Jarusalski. Rex (listed as John on NBC press material) is a clean-cut ex Marine who believes following the letter of the law; T.J., the son of an Oscar-winning Polish cinematographer, is just the opposite and knows too well the dark side of Los Angeles.

Cast: Skeet Ulrich *(Det. Rex Winters)*; Corey Stoll *(Det. Thomas Jaruszalski)*; Alfred Molina *(Deputy D.A. Ricardo Morales)*; Regina Hall *(Deputy D.A. Evelyn Price)*; Megan Boone *(Deputy D.A. Lauren Gardner)*; Rachel Ticotin *(Lt. Arleen Gonzales)*; Terrence Howard *(Assistant D.A. Jonas Dekker)*; Peter Coyote *(D.A. Jerry Hardin)*.

5203   *Law and Order: Special Victims Unit.* (Series; Crime Drama; NBC; 1999–). The Special Victims Unit is a division of the N.Y.P.D. that investigates sexually based offenses. Through the investigations of principal detectives Olivia Benson and Elliot Stabler, graphic but sensitively portrayed stories relate their efforts to not only comfort the victims of such crimes, but apprehend the culprits that are responsible.

Program Open: "In the criminal justice system, sexually based offences are considered especially heinous. In New York City, the detectives who investigate these vicious felonies are members of an elite squad known as the Special Victims Unit. These are their stories."

Cast: Mariska Hargitay *(Det. Olivia Benson)*; Christopher Meloni *(Det. Elliot Stabler)*; Richard Belzer *(Det. John Munch)*; Dann Florek *(Capt. Donald Cragen)*; Ice-T *(Det. Odafin "Fin" Tutuola)*; B.D. Wong *(Dr. George Huang)*; Tamara Tunie *(Dr. Melinda Warner)*; Diane

Neal *(A.D.A. Casey Novak)*; Stephanie March *(A.D.A. Alexandra Cabot)*; Caren Browning *(Off. Judith Siper)*; Joanna Merlin *(Judge Lena Petrovsky)*; Michelle Hurd *(Det. Monique Jefferies)*; Isabel Gillies *(Kathy Stabler)*; Judith Light *(Chief Elizabeth Donnelly)*; Fred Dalton *(D.A. Arthur Branch)*; Leslie Hendrix *(Dr. Elizabeth Rodgers)*; Michaela McManus *(A.D.A. Kim Greylek)*; Steven Zirnkilton *(Theme Narrator)*.

5204   *Law and Order: Trial by Jury.* (Series; Crime Drama; NBC; 2005). *Trial by Jury* is the third spin off from *Law and Order*. But unlike its predecessors (*Law and Order: Criminal Intent* and *Law and Order: Special Victims Unit*), *Trial by Jury* was cancelled shortly after it premiered. Here, the inner workings of the New York judicial system are seen beginning with an arraignment. The process of building a case follows, as does investigating leads, interviewing witnesses and defendants and finally the trial that ends the reign of a criminal.

Cast: Bebe Neuwirth *(A.D.A. Tracey Kibre)*; Amy Carlson *(A.D.A. Kelly Gaffney)*; Fred Dalton *(D.A. Arthur Branch)*; Kirk Acevedo *(D.A. Hector Salazar)*; Scott Cohen *(Det. Chris Ravell)*; Seth Gilliam *(A.D.A. Terence Wright)*; Candice Bergen *(Judge Amanda Anderlee)*.

5205   *Law and Order: U.K.* (Series; Crime Drama; BBC America; 2010). "In the criminal justice system, the people are represented by two separate yet equally important groups: the police who investigate the crime and the Crown Prosecutors who prosecute the offenders. These are their stories" is the opening to the British adaptation of *Law and Order* that divides the program into two segments: the first half establishes the crime and its investigation and ends with the capture of the subject. The concluding half relates the British court system prosecution of the suspect.

Cast: Bradley Walsh *(Det. Sgt. Ronnie Brooks)*; Harriet Walter *(Det. Insp. Natalie Chandler)*; Jamie Bamber *(Det. Sgt. Matt Devlin)*; Ben Daniels *(James Steel; court prosecutor)*; Freema Agyeman *(Alesha Phillips; court prosecutor)*; Gillian Taylforth *(Hannah Masons; court prosecutor)*.

5206   *Law Dogs.* (Pilot; Drama; Unaired; Produced for CBS in 2007). The lives, cases, relationships and personal dramas of a team of public defenders.

Cast: Janeane Garofalo *(Lily Blackwood)*; Josh Cooke *(Matt Harper)*; Mark-Paul Gosselaar *(Jason Marlow)*; Rachael Carpani *(Carly Owen)*; Barry Henley *(Alton MacBride)*.

5207   *The Law Enforcers.* (Series; Crime Drama; NBC; 1969-1970). The relationship between Sam Danforth, a white Deputy Police Chief, and William Washburn, the black District Attorney, as they attempt to maintain law and order in an unnamed California city beset by urban crime. Broadcast as a segment of *The Bold Ones*.

Cast: Leslie Nielsen *(Sam Danforth)*; Hari Rhodes *(William Washburn)*.

5208   *The Law Firm.* (Series; Reality; NBC; 2005). Twelve actual lawyers compete for the top prize of $250,000. The lawyers are split into two teams of six and the competition has them arguing real cases in a real courtroom. The outcome of each case is legally binding, but the teams whose performance, according to legal analyst Roy Black, is the weakest (even if they win a case) is eliminated. The program was dropped by NBC after two episodes (July 28 to August 4) with the remaining episodes airing on NBC's sister station Bravo (to Sept. 21, 2005). Roy Black hosts; Adrienne Allen and Kristen Green are the receptionists.

5209   *Law of the Plainsman.* (Series; Western; NBC; 1959-1960). With his right hand raised and his left hand on the Bible, a

Harvard educated Apache Indian takes the oath to become a U.S. Marshal: "Do you swear to uphold the Constitution of the United States and the territory of New Mexico, to do your duty as a deputy U.S. Marshal without favor or prejudice, so help you God?" The Apache, named Sam Buckhart, responds, "I do." While Sam covers a great deal of New Mexico (1880s), he is based in Santa Fe and must overcome many obstacles to perform his job—especially the prejudices that existed at the time between Indians and whites. But it was a white man who changed the course of Sam's life.

During a battle between the cavalry and the Apache Indians, a 14-year-old brave encounters a wounded army captain. Instead of killing the captain, the brave befriends him and gets help. The captain and the brave, whom the captain names Sam Burkhart, soon become blood brothers. Two years later, after the captain is killed in an Indian ambush, Sam inherits a great deal of money, which enables him to attend Harvard University, as once did the captain. Wishing to help his people, Sam decides to become a law enforcement officer upon graduation.

Tess Logan is Sam's ward, a pretty seven-year-old he rescued from a wagon train massacre; Martha Cominter runs the Santa Fe Boarding House and helps care for Tess; Billy Lordan is Sam's assistant, the marshal of the nearby town of Glorieta; A.L. Morrison is the sheriff of Santa Fe. The town saloon is the Red Bar Saloon and the bank is the Territorial Bank of New Mexico. The pilot episode, "The Indian," aired on *The Rifleman* (Feb. 17, 1959).

Cast: Michael Ansara *(Sam Buckhart)*; Gina Gillespie *(Tess Logan)*; Robert Harland *(Billy Lordan)*; Nora Marlowe *(Martha Cominter)*; Dayton Loomis *(Marshal Andrew Morrison)*.

5210 *Lawbreaker.* (Series; Anthology; Syn.; 1963). Dramatizations based on actual criminal cases. Stories are filmed at the scenes of crimes with the actual people involved. Also known as *Lee Marvin Presents Law Breaker*.

Host-Narrator: Lee Marvin.

5211 *Lawless.* (Series; Crime Drama; Fox; 1997). John Lawless is a former Special Forces operative who resigns from the military to become a private detective. He retreats to Miami's trendy South Beach where his mother (Esther) runs a café and where he establishes a practice. He teams with Reggie, a Jamaican who operates a helicopter charter service and stories follow their case investigations. Canceled after the first episode aired (March 22, 1997) due to dismal ratings.

Cast: Brian Bosworth *(John Lawless)*; Glenn Plummer *(Reggie)*; Janet Hubert-Whitten *(Esther Hayes)*.

5212 *The Lawless Years.* (Series; Crime Drama; NBC; 1959–1961). New York City during the era of Prohibition (1920s) is the setting. It is also an era of mobsters and violence and police efforts to curtail and expose the rackets and racketeers are depicted through the work of Barney Ruditsky, a tough, no-nonsense plainclothes detective with the N.Y.P.D.

Cast: James Gregory *(Barney Ruditsky)*; Robert Karnes *(Max, his assistant)*.

5213 *Lawman.* (Series; Western; ABC; 1958–1962). When a girl, "someone special" to Dan Troop, is killed by a stray bullet in a pointless gunfight, Dan decides to devote his life to upholding the law. As the years pass, Dan becomes a legend—"The Famous Gun from Texas." It is 1879 when Dan, the marshal of Abilene, receives a telegram from the town council in Laramie, Wyoming, asking him to rid the town of three outlaw brothers, one of whom killed the previous marshal. Dan is fast with his guns and tough with his fists. The Laramie town council wants a city where their wives and children can walk down the street without being afraid. Dan realizes that he can't do the job alone and advertises for a deputy (a job that pays $50 a month). A young man named Johnny McKay becomes Dan's deputy. Together they rid the town of the outlaw brothers and stories follow their efforts to uphold the peace.

As a kid Dan worked in a hash house. He believes that a man has to wear a gun because of the way things are now; he also thinks there will be a time when it is not necessary. Lily Merrill owns the town's watering hole, the Birdcage Saloon; Dru Lemp runs the Blue Bonnet Café (where Johnny worked prior to becoming a deputy; it was then called Good Eats); and Julie Tate is the editor of the town newspaper, the *Laramie Weekly* (originally called the *Laramie Free Press*).

Program Open: [bold indicates chorus] "From the entertainment capitol of the world, produced for television by Warner Bros. ... **Lawman**. *Lawman* ... starring John Russell as Marshal Dan Troop. **Lawman** ... and Peter Brown as Deputy Johnny McKay. Produced by Warner Bros."

Cast: John Russell *(Dan Troop)*; Peter Brown *(Johnny McKay)*; Peggie Castle *(Lily Merrill)*; Bek Nelson *(Dru Lemp)*; Barbara Lang *(Julie Tate)*; Dan Sheridan *(Jake the bartender)*.

5214 *The Lawrence Welk Show.* (Series; Variety; ABC; 1955–1971). Champagne (bubbly) music, songs and dances with orchestra leader Lawrence Welk and his family of regulars. Sponsored by Dodge Automobiles and originally titled *The Dodge Dancing Party*.

Host: Lawrence Welk. **Champagne Lady:** Alice Lon, Norma Zimmer. **Regulars:** Dianne Lennon, Kathy Lennon, Peggy Lennon, Janet Lennon, Dick Dale, Gail Farrell, Brian Siebman, Larry Dean, Sandi Jensen, Joe Feeney, Jim Roberts, Bob Lido, Bobby Burgess, Mary Lou Metzger, Buddy Merrill, Barbara Boylan, Jack Imel, Larry Hooper, Art DePew, Bob Havens, Pete Fountain, Bob Ralston, Frank Scott, Jerry Burke, Joe Livoti, Myron Floren, Jo Ann Castle, Neil Levang, Natalie Nevins, Archie Duncan, Cissy King, Clay Hart, Lynn Anderson, Sally Flynn, Steve Smith, Andra Willis, Paula Stewart, Tanya Falan, Barney Liddel, Charlie Parlato, Kenny Trimble, Charlotte Harris, Ralna English, Guy Hovis, Peanuts Hucko, Rocky Rockwell, Aladdin, Clay Hart, Sally Finn, Nancy Sullivan, Tom Neatherland, Ken Delo, Bob Smale, Henry Cuesta, The Blenders, The Hotsy Totsy Boys, The Symanski Sisters. **Announcer:** Bob Warren. **Orchestra:** Lawrence Welk.

5215 *The Lawrence Welk Show.* (Series; Variety; Syn.; 1971–1983). A revised version of the prior title that continues to present wholesome family entertainment (music, songs and dances). Sponsored in part by Geritol.

Host: Lawrence Welk. **Regulars:** Bobby Burgess, Ava Barber, Henry Cuesta, Dick Dale, Ken Delo, Gail Farrell, Arthur Duncan, Myron Floren, Sandi Griffiths, Charlotte Harris, Clay Hart, Larry Hooper, Guy Hovis, Randa Netherton, Bob Ralston, Jim Roberts, Norma Zimmer, Tanya Welk, The Otwell Twins, The Six Symanski Sisters, Joe Feeney. **Announcer:** Bob Warren. **Orchestra:** George Cates.

5216 *Lawrence Welk's Top Tunes and New Talent.* (Series; Variety; ABC; 1955–1959). An extension program based on ABC's *The Lawrence Welk Show* that presents music, songs and performances by aspiring but undiscovered talent. Sponsored by Plymouth Automobiles and also known as *The Plymouth Show Starring Lawrence Welk*.

Host: Lawrence Welk. **Regulars:** Alice Lon, Myron Floren, Buddy Merrill, Dick Dale, Larry Hooper, Larry Dean, Bob Lido, Dianne Lennon, Janet Lennon, Kathy Lennon, Peggy Lennon, Bob Brunner, Brenda Kay, Marjorie Meinert. **Announcer:** Bob Warren. *Orchestra:* Lawrence Welk.

5217   *Laws of Chance.* (Pilot; Drama; Unaired; Produced for ABC in 2005). Chance Morgan, a small town girl who acquired an appreciation of the law from her father, a barber and justice of the peace, is now an Assistant D.A. in Houston, Texas. Chance, a feisty hot head, is seeking the job of D.A. and the proposal was to follow Chance as she prosecutes cases — with outrageous courtroom tactics that always deliver a conviction.

Cast: KaDee Strickland *(Chance Morgan)*; Bruce McGill *(Charles Bauman)*; Viola Davis *(Rebecca)*; Frances Fisher *(Evelyn)*; Michael O'Neill *(Wyatt)*.

5218   *The Lawyers.* (Series; Crime Drama; NBC; 1969–1971). Walter Nichols is an elderly but shrewd Los Angles attorney; bothers Brian and Neil Darrell are his protégés and stories, broadcast as a segment of *The Bold Ones*, relate their case acquisitions (with Brian and Neil doing the necessary legwork and Walter providing the expertise to defend their clients in the courtroom).

Cast: Burl Ives *(Walter Nichols)*; Joseph Campanella *(Brian Darrell)*; James Farentino *(Neil Darrell)*; John Milford *(Lt. Paul Hewitt)*; Todd Martin *(Deputy D.A. Jeff Skinner)*; Marcelle Fortier *(Walter's secretary)*; George Murdock *(D.A. Braddock)*; Charles Brewer *(D.A. Dekker)*; Walter Brooke *(Judge Howe)*.

5219   *LAX.* (Series; Drama; NBC; 2004-2005). A behind-the-scenes look at the inner workings of a large metropolitan airport as seen through the eyes of Harley Random, the Airfield Chief, and Roger DeSouza, the terminal manager of Los Angeles International Airport (called LAX). Harley is single and has no children — "I haven't gotten around to that." Roger has been married twice; he is divorced from Allison and is currently married to Monique. He is also the father of Sophia and Peter (with Allison).

Harley is not one to stand around and do nothing. She actively involves herself with all aspects of the airport's operations. She likes to do things her way to make sure the job gets done. Roger is a bit more laid back and not as much as problem solver as Harley. He prefers to follow the rules and not anger his bosses. Harley can't do that — "The job requires me to have passion and if that makes me a touch cranky too bad."

Shortly after the premiere, Harley and Roger were promoted to co-directors of LAX. Other regulars are Tony, the airline supervisor; Nick, the immigration officer; Henry, the security chief; Betty, the reservations clerk; and Julie, Harley's sister.

Cast: Heather Locklear *(Harley Random)*; Blair Underwood *(Roger DeSouza)*; Paul Leyden *(Tony Magulia)*; Wendy Hoopes *(Betty)*; Frank John Hughes *(Henry Engels)*; Charisma Carpenter *(Julie)*; Sharon Leal *(Monique)*; Brooke Marie Bridges *(Sophia DeSouza)*; Spensir Bridges *(Peter DeSouza)*.

5220   *The Lazarus Man.* (Series; Western; UPN; 1996-1997). It is the 1860s and a man, for reasons unknown, is buried alive in a shallow grave in San Sebastian, Texas, by persons unknown. The man, however, does not die. He awakens, dressed in a Confederate army uniform with Northern gold and a Union Army revolver but no memory of who or what he was. The man takes the name Lazarus (the biblical character who rose from the dead) and stories follow his search to discover who he is.

Cast: Robert Urich *(Lazarus)*.

5221   *The Lazarus Syndrome.* (Series; Drama; ABC; 1979). MacArthur St. Clair is a no-nonsense cardiologist at Webster Memorial Hospital. He is totally dedicated to work and often find this taking a toll on his personal life. It has cost him his marriage (to Virginia), threatening his current marriage (to Gloria) and has also presented him with a delicate situation: the Lazarus Syndrome (wherein a patient believes a doctor is a god-like miracle worker). Stories follow MacArthur as he deals with the situations that develop as a result the syndrome. Joe Hamill is the hospital administrator; and Stacy is Joe's assistant.

Cast: Louis Gossett, Jr. *(MacArthur St. Clair)*; Sheila Frazier *(Gloria St. Clair)*; Ronald Hunter *(Joe Hamill)*; Peggy McCay *(Stacy)*; Peggy Walker *(Virginia Hamill)*; Christina Alvila *(Admissions Nurse)*.

5222   *Lazer Tag Academy.* (Series; Cartoon; NBC; 1986-1987). While escaping from the police, Draxon Drear, an evil criminal from the year 2010, crashes his ship into the ocean. A gas escapes and places him a state of suspended animation. One thousand years later, Draxon is found and revived. When Draxon sees what the future holds and that time travel has become a reality, he devises a plan to control the future — by returning to the past to alter events. When Lazer Tag Academy, the future government, learns that Draxon has stolen a time machine and returned to the past, a team of agents, led by Jamie Jaren, are sent back in time to find Draxon before he can change the past and affect the future.

Voice Cast: Noelle Harling *(Jamie Jaren)*; Booker Bradshaw *(Draxon Drear)*; Christina MacGregor *(Beth Jaren)*; Billy Jayne *(Tom Jaren)*; Sid McCoy *(Professor Olanga)*; R.J. Williams *(Nicky Jaren)*; Tress MacNeille *(Mrs. Jaren)*; Pat Fraley *(Charlie Ferguson)*; Frank Welker *(Mr. Jaren/Skuggs/Ralphie)*.

5223   *Lazy Town.* (Series; Children; Nick; 2004). Stephanie is a very pretty and adorable eight-year-old girl who lives in Lazy Town, a mythical and colorful community with odd-shaped buildings that is run by her uncle, Mayor Milford Meanswell (a puppet). She is friends with puppets Ziggy, Trixie, Stingy and Pixel and the human Sportacus, a very athletic hero. Their nemesis is the human Robbie Rotten, a mean man who can't stand the thought of children (or adults) playing or having fun.

Sportacus watches over Lazy Town from his blimp in the sky. When he senses trouble, he descends to earth to help where needed (he also encourages children to exercise and eat right). Stephanie, who always becomes involved in the antics of her friends, encourages children to sing and dance (she is always featured in at least one song and dance number per show). Their joy always seems to disturb Robbie Rotten and his efforts to destroy the happiness of Lazy Town is the focal point of stories (although his actions are always foiled by Sportacus or by his own misdeeds when one of his wacky ideas backfires). Bessie Busybody is Milford's friend. Produced in Iceland.

Cast: Julianna Rose Mauriello *(Stephanie)*; Magnus Scheving *(Sportacus)*; Stefan Karl Stefansson *(Robbie Rotten)*; David Matthew *(Milford Meanswell)*; Jodi Eichelberger *(Stingy)*; Sarah Burgess, Heather Asch *(Trixie)*; Kobie Powell *(Pixel)*; Gudmundur Thor *(Ziggy)*; Julie Westwood *(Bessie Busybody)*.

5224   *The League.* (Series; Comedy; FX; 2009). Pete, Ruxin, Taco, Andre and Kevin are friends who are connected by their addiction to their fantasy football league in Chicago. The guys live for the sport and stories relate their efforts to balance their sports addiction with other priorities in life — like women and their jobs.

Pete is a charmer and troublemaker who always manages to talk his way out of the troublesome situation he gets into. Although he has a strained relationship with his wife (Meegan), he is a virtual gridiron and has won the league championship three years in a row. Ruxin is a paranoid defense lawyer and feels the whole world is against him. He constantly plots to win the league crown but never succeeds. Ruxin is married to Sofia and they have just become parents. Kevin is the league commissioner who started the league thinking it would be fun — not the nightmare of "babysitting" his team mates that it has become. He is a district attorney and married to Jenny, an outspoken woman whom most people believe is the brains of the league (as she helps develop the teams' draft strategies). Taco is Kevin's younger brother, a spaced-out musician who lacks social skills and is only on the team so Kevin can keep an eye on him. How he managed to one year win the league crown — and be in Thailand at the same time is still a mystery. Andre was picked on in high school and, although the most successful of the group (a plastic surgeon) nothing has changed. He is also known for making idiotic team decisions and tries to do the right thing, but nothing ever goes in his favor.

Cast: Mark Duplass (*Pete*); Nick Kroll (*Ruxin*); Jon Lajoie (*Taco*); Stephen Rannazzisi (*Kevin*); Paul Scheer (*Andre*); Katie Aselton (*Jenny*); Nadine Velazquez (*Sofia*); Leslie Bibb (*Meegan*).

5225   *The League of Gentlemen.* (Series; Comedy; Comedy Central; 2000). Royston Vasey is a fictional village north of England and it is here that dozens of odd characters reside. Performer-writers Mark Gatiss, Steve Pemberton and Reece Shearsmith portray all the characters in three British produced sketch series with horror film like overtones. The first series revolved around a new road that was to be built in Royston Vasey; a deadly epidemic of nose bleeds strikes Royston Vasey in the second series; and, for the third series, individual characters are profiled (such as Tubbs and Edward Tattsyrup, owners of the local shop; Pauline Campbell-Jones, a recruiting officer at the local job center; Barbara Dixon, the transsexual taxi driver; Matthew Chinnery, a vet who suffers from a strange curse: any animal he comes in contact with perishes. Geoff Tipps, a worker in the local plastic factory; Charlie and Stella Hull, whose marriage is on the rocks; the Rev. Bernice Woodall, the priest who does not believe in God; and Hilary Briss, "The Demon Butcher of Royston Vasey" who is known for his "special meals").

Cast: Mark Gatiss, Steve Pemberton, Reece Shearsmith.

5226   *The League of Super Evil.* (Series; Cartoon; Cartoon Network; 2009). The League of Super Evil, called L.O.S.E. for short, sort of sums up the legion as well — a group of misfit super villains with one goal: take over the world. Stories relate their harebrained and always fruitless efforts to become leaders of the world. Voltar, the evil mechanical genius, is the brains of the outfit. He usually devises outlandishly foolish plans that always backfire. Doktor Frogg is a deranged scientist burdened by bad luck. Reginald "Red" Menace is the group's muscle (actually a gentle giant with a streak of goodness who uses his "Fists of Judgment" to squash out those he believes are really evil). Doomageddon is a pan-dimensional hellhound that exemplifies the term "bad dog" (he likes to eat anything that crosses his path but is very lazy and never fully activates his powers of invisibility, telepathy, flying or ability to shrink or grow tall); 17 and 32 are poorly constructed robots (always falling apart) that work as Voltar's henchbots.

Voice Cast: Scott McNeal (*Voltar*); Lee Tucker (*Doktor Frogg*); Colin Murdock (*Reginald "Red" Menace*).

5227   *A League of Their Own.* (Series; Comedy; CBS; 1993). During World War II, candy bar king Walter Harvey, creator of the Harvey Bar, hires washed up ex-ballplayer Jimmy Dugan to manage the Rockford Peaches, an Illinois team in the first All American Girls Professional Baseball League (AAGPBL) to save the game (and make money) when baseball's biggest stars go off to war.

Jimmy was with the 1929 Chicago Cubs and was called "The kid on the team." He had 151 RBI's and went on to a great career. In his youth Jimmy was called "The Carpenter" ("because I nailed all the girls") and took the job because the money was good. Benny the Chimp (whom Jimmy won in a poker game) is the team's mascot.

Evelyn Gardner, Betty Horne, Dottie Hanson, Kit Keeler, Mae Mortibito and Marla Hooch are the Rockford Peaches. Evelyn, jersey

15, plays right field; she is married to Frank. Betty, the catcher, wears jersey 1. She is a widow (late husband, George) and is the quiet one on the team. Betty is a former Miss Georgia and cares for the other girls when they get hurt.

Dottie, jersey 8, plays first base. She is from Oregon and her husband, Bob, is in the army. Dottie is the only girl Jimmy feels he can talk to "man to man" (he considers her to be like one of the players from his old ball club). Kit, the pitcher, wears jersey 23. Mae, jersey 15, plays centerfield; and Marla, a powerful hitter, plays second base (jersey 32).

Jimmy earns $80 a week; Dottie, considered to be the best player, makes $90; Mae, $75; Marla, Kit and Betty, $45. The Suds Bucket is the local watering hole. Based on the 1992 feature film of the same title.

Cast: Sam McMurray (*Jimmy Dugan*); Tracy Nelson (*Evelyn Gardner*); Tracy Reiner (*Betty Horne*); Carey Lowell (*Dottie Henson*); Christine Elise (*Kit Keller*); Wendy Makkena (*Mae Mortibito*); Garry Marshall (*Walter Harvey*); Jon Lovitz (*Ernie Capadino*); Megan Cavanaugh (*Marla Hooch*).

5228   *Leap of Faith.* (Series; Comedy; NBC; 2002). Faith Wardwell is a young woman who works in a Mid-Manhattan advertising agency. She is single and hangs out with her close circle of friends: Dan, her boyfriend; Patty, her aggressive (and sexy) girlfriend and co-worker; Cynthia, her married neighbor; and Andy, her best friend from college who is now a reporter for *Rolling Stone* magazine. Faith had been engaged to be married. In the first episode she broke off the engagement (feeling he was not the right man for her) and took a "leap of faith" to pursue a different path in life. Stories focus on the ups and downs of Faith and her friends. Other regulars are Cricket, Faith's eccentric, socialite mother; and Lucas, Faith's boss.

Cast: Sarah Paulson (*Faith Wardwell*); Lisa Edelstein (*Patty*); Regina King (*Cynthia*); Brad Rowe (*Dan Murphy*); Jill Clayburgh (*Crickett Wardwell*); Ken Marino (*Andy*); Tim Meadows (*Lucas*).

5229   *Leap Years.* (Series; Drama; Showtime; 2001-2002). Athena, Joe, Gregory, Frannie, Josh and Beth are close friends living in New York City. It is the present time (2001) and stories present a look at their current lives as well as their pasts (1993) and what the future holds (2008).

Cast: Michelle Hurd (*Athena*); Bruno Campos (*Joe*); Garret Dillahunt (*Gregory*); Inga Cadranel (*Frannie*); David Julie Hirsh (*Josh*); Nina Garbiras (*Beth*).

5230   *Learning the Ropes.* (Series; Comedy; Syn.; 1988-1989). Robert Randall is a single father (separated from his wife, Anne) who cares for his two teenage children, Ellen and Mark. Robert has a daytime job as a history teacher and vice principal at the Ridgedale Valley Preparatory School, and a second, nighttime job as a wrestler called "The Masked Maniac."

Home to the Randalls is 34 Hampton Street. Even though Ellen and Mark are not wealthy, they attend Ridgedale Prep, "a private school for rich kids," became their father teaches there. Robert's main concern is to see that Ellen and Mark get a college education. (His mind was eased one day when his health club manager asked him to become the Masked Maniac, "the animal of the wrestling ring." Robert originally did it for laughs; but when the character caught on and the money started rolling in, he kept the job to provide for Ellen and Mark's future. Robert must now keep his wrestling job a secret because school regulations prohibit teachers from moonlighting.)

Ellen is the smarter of the two children. She does the cooking (and is very proud of her ability to prepare meals) but does not want to be a housewife and mother — "I want to be a career woman." Mark, the mischievous one, wants "the big bucks job." The Burger Palace is Ellen and Mark's after school hangout; fellow wrestlers call Robert "The Professor."

Anne, who is never seen, is in England studying to become a lawyer. Beth is Ellen's boy-crazy girlfriend; and Carol Dickson is the school's French teacher.

In the original, unaired pilot version, Anne was said to have walked out on her family and Robert was romantically involved with Carol (this episode and two previously taped episodes were re-edited to delete the romantic aspect, which was not a part of the actual series). David Roberts sings the Theme, "Learning the Ropes."

Cast: Lyle Alzado (*Robert Randall*); Nicole Stoffman (*Ellen Randall*); Yannick Bisson (*Mark Randall*); Sheryl Wilson (*Carol Dickson*); Jacqueline Mason (*Beth*).

5231   *Learning to Fly*. (Pilot; Comedy; Unaired; Produced for ABC in 2005). Once charismatic and full of inspiration, Danny Carter had abandoned all that for a job that he finds he now dislikes. Impulsively, he decides to quit and become the man he once was. He begins by pursuing Samantha, the girl who believed he was meant for great things and the proposal was to follow Danny as he maps out a new life designed to fulfill the dreams he once had but abandoned.

Cast: Danny Comden (*Danny Carter*); Bonnie Somerville (*Samantha Boyd*).

5232   *The Leathernecks*. (Pilot; Drama; ABC; Feb. 2, 1963). A proposed spin off from *The Gallant Men* about the experiences of a group of Marines during World War II.

Cast: Van Williams (*Lt. Dave Cameron*); Philip Carey (*Sgt. Matt Barragan*); Armand Alzamora (*Cpl. Vince Mazzini*); George Murdock (*Pvt. Ben Cagel*).

5233   *Leave It to Beaver*. (Series; Comedy; CBS, 1957–1958; ABC, 1958–1963). The house at 211 Pine Street in the town of Mayfield is home to Ward and June Cleaver and their children Wally and Beaver Theodore (called Beaver). Address also given as 211 Maple Street and 211 Pine Avenue; they later move to 211 Lakewood Avenue.

Ward and June are strict but not stern parents. They never spank their sons but when it comes to punishing or disciplining them, Wally and Theodore know what to face: a lecture by their father in the study (Ward often asks his sons what their punishment should be). June rarely disagrees with Ward's decisions.

Wallace, nicknamed Wally, is the older brother. He is in the eighth grade at the Grant Avenue School when the series begins. He later attends Mayfield High School then State College. In high school Wally becomes a three-letter man and Julie Foster (later Mary Ellen Rogers) is his girlfriend.

Theodore acquired the nickname of "Beaver" when Wally couldn't pronounce Theodore and said "Tweder." Ward and June thought "Beaver" sounded better. Beaver, also called the "Beave," attends the Grant Avenue School and then Mayfield High. He wears a green baseball cap, hates "mushy stuff" and likes "to mess around with junk." He would "rather smell a skunk than see a girl" and Miller's Pond is his favorite "fishin' hole." Mary Margaret Matthews (Lori Martin) was the first girl Beaver found attractive (she called him "Teddy").

Edward W. Haskell, better known as Eddie, is Wally's wisecracking friend (he and Wally met in the second grade). Eddie is extremely polite to adults (he fears their authority) but mean to everyone else, especially Beaver (whom he calls "Squirt"; he calls Wally "Sam," "Gertrude" and "Ellwood"). Eddie attends the same schools as Wally and lives at 175 Grant Avenue.

Clarence Rutherford, the overweight friend of Wally and Eddie, is nicknamed "Lumpy." His father, Fred, is Ward's boss at an unidentified company. Fred calls Ward "Lord of the Manor." He is married to Geraldine; his wife in later episodes is named Gwen. Fred originally talked about having three children: a girl, Violet, and two boys who were offered football scholarships. Later, he has only two children, Lumpy and Violet.

Beaver's friends are Larry Mondello, Gilbert Grover and Hubert "Whitey" Whitney. Larry was first credited as Robert Stevens; Gilbert was first introduced as Gilbert Harrison, then Gilbert Gates and finally Gilbert Bates. Judy Hessler is the obnoxious girl who kisses up to teachers and annoys Beaver and his friends with her smug attitude. She was replaced by Penny Woods, a similar character, in last-season episodes.

Cornelia Raeburn is the principal of the Grant Avenue School, Alice Landers is Beaver's caring teacher, and Gus is the old fire chief Beaver visits at Fire Station Number 5. Michael Johnson and Melvyn Lenard composed the theme, "The Toy Parade." See also *It's a Small World* (the series pilot film), *Still the Beaver* and *The New Leave It to Beaver*.

Program Open: "*Leave It to Beaver* ... Starring Hugh Beaumont ... Barbara Billingsley ... Tony Dow ... and Jerry Mathers ... as the Beaver."

Cast: Hugh Beaumont (*Ward Cleaver*); Barbara Billingsley (*June Cleaver*); Tony Dow (*Wally Cleaver*); Jerry Mathers (*Beaver Cleaver*); Ken Osmond (*Eddie Haskell*); Frank Bank (*Lumpy Rutherford*); Richard Deacon (*Fred Rutherford*); Rusty Stevens (*Larry Mondello*); Stanley Fafara (*Whitey*); Jeri Weil (*Judy Hessler*); Karen Sue Trent (*Penny Woods*); Helen Parrish (*Geraldine Rutherford*); Majel Barrett, Margaret Stewart (*Gwen Rutherford*); Wendy Winkelman, Veronica Cartwright (*Violet Rutherford*); Stephen Talbot (*Gilbert Bates*); Cheryl Holdridge (*Julie Foster*); Sue Randall (*Alice Landers*); Doris Packer (*Cornelia Rayburn*); Burt Mustin (*Gus*); Madge Blake (*Larry's mother*); Stanley Fafara (*Harrison "Tuey" Brown; Beaver's friend*); Katherine Warren (*Tuey's mother*); Richard Correll (*Richard Rockover; Beaver's friend*); Buddy Hart (*Chester Anderson; Wally's friend*); Ann Doran, Ann Barton (*Agnes Haskell; Eddie's mother*); Karl Swenson, George O. Petrie (*George Haskell, Eddie's father*); Joey Scott (*Benjy Benjamin; Beaver's friend*); Pamela Beaird (*Mary Ellen Rogers*); Patty Turner (*Linda Dennison; Beaver's classmate*).

5234   *Leave It to Larry*. (Series; Comedy; CBS; 1952). Larry Tucker is a good-natured young man who works as a clerk in shoe store owned by his wife's father, Mr. Koppel. Amy is Larry's wife and Harriet and Steve are their children. Larry is a good husband and father and appears to be just an ordinary guy working at an ordinary job. With no pressure and no worries, Larry is that ordinary guy. Stories relate what happens when circumstances change and Larry must find ways to deal with and solve the new dilemmas that enter his life.

Cast: Eddie Albert (*Larry Tucker*); Betty Kean, Katherine Bard (*Amy Tucker*); Lydia Schaeffer (*Harriet Tucker*); Glenn Walkin (*Steve Tucker*); Ed Begley (*Mr. Koppel*).

5235   *Leave It to the Girls*. (Series; Discussion; NBC; ABC; 1949–1954). Three female panelists and one male guest (the defendant) discuss topical issues. Aired on NBC (April 27, 1949 to Dec. 30, 1951); and ABC (Oct. 3, 1953 to Mar. 27, 1954).

Hostess: Maggi McNellis. **Host:** Eddie Dunn. **Panelists:** Robin Chandler, Faye Emerson, Eloise McElhone, Florence Pritchett, Binnie Barnes, Peggy Ann Garner, Eva Gabor.

5236   *Leave It to the Lamas*. (Series; Reality; E!; 2009). "You've never met a clan like this" is the tagline for a program that follows a blended family "with a genuine show business pedigree" as they work, play and navigate life in California. The featured "clan" members are actor Lorenzo Lamas, his ex-wife, Michele Smith, and their children Shayne (player on ABC's *The Bachelor*), Dakota (aspiring singer) and A.J (soap star). Originally titled *The Lamas Life*.

5237   Leave It to the Women. (Series; Discussion; Syn.; 1981). A panel of women discuss various topical issues with guests.
   Hostess: Stephanie Edwards. **Announcer:** Johnny Jacobs.

5238   Leaving L.A. (Series; Crime Drama; ABC; 1997). Neil Bernstein is the eccentric head of the L.A.P.D. Coroner's Office. It is through his eyes that an off-center look at the work of him and his staff are presented. Libby is his trainee; Reed, the investigator; Tiffany, the lab technician; Dudley, the photographer; Manny, the morgue attendant; Martha, the properties clerk; and Claudia, the assistant medical examiner.
   Cast: Ron Rifkin *(Neil Bernstein)*; Melina Kanakaredes *(Libby Galante)*; Christopher Meloni *(Reed Sims)*; Lorraine Toussaint *(Claudia Chan)*; Billie Worley *(Manny Byrd)*; Anne Haney *(Martha Hayes)*; Hilary Swank *(Tiffany Roebuck)*; Cress Williams *(Dudley Adams)*; Allison Bertolino *(Kate Galante)*.

5239   Leeza. (Series; Talk; NBC; 1993–2000). Entertainment reporter Leeza Gibbons interviews celebrities as well as presenting information concerning movies, TV shows and other related show business news.
   Host: Leeza Gibbons. **Music:** John Tesh.

5240   The Left Over Revue. (Series; Variety; NBC; 1951). A program of music, song and comedy that replaced the cancelled *Broadway Open House* for a short time (Sept. 17 to Nov. 9, 1951).
   Host: Wayne Howell. **Vocalist:** Verna Massey. **Music:** Milton DeLugg.

5241   Leg Work. (Series; Crime Drama; CBS; 1987). Claire McCarron is a former assistant district attorney turned owner of McCarron Investigations, a private detective agency she operates from an office at 17 West 36th Street in New York City. Claire guarantees results and charges $500 a day plus expenses. She has a dog named Clyde and drives a silver Porsche. The car is always in need of repair and Claire must do a lot of walking to accomplish her goals, hence the title. Claire also displays her shapely legs by wearing miniskirts. Claire lives in an apartment at 765 East 65th Street and has a rare collection of pre–World War II Lionel "O" gauge electric trains that she inherited from her father. Claire often eats out and the only two foods she can prepare are oatmeal raisin cookies and coq au vin (chicken in wine sauce). When a case bothers Claire, she resorts to making cookies.
   Claire works with her brother, Fred McCarron, a lieutenant with the Office of Public Relations at One Police Plaza in Manhattan, and Wilhelmina "Willie" Pipal, the Manhattan Assistant District Attorney. The program had two working titles: "Eye Shadow" and "Leg Work." Margaret Colin had the choice of using either title. While she preferred neither, she chose *Leg Work*.
   Cast: Margaret Colin *(Claire McCarron)*; Patrick James Clarke *(Fred McCarron)*; Frances McDormand *(Willie Pipal)*.

5242   Legacy. (Series; Drama; UPN; 1998–1999). Lexington, Kentucky following the Civil War is the setting. It is here that a wealthy Irish American family, the Logans are struggling to build their empire as horse breeders. Despite their wealth, the Logans are not run by money; they are a family who believe in helping others and a family to whom others look in times of need. Ned Logan, the father, is a widower who is raising his four headstrong children alone: Sean, Clay, Alice and Lexy. Also sharing their struggles is Jeremy Bradford, a 17-year-old orphan taken in by Ned.
   Cast: Brett Cullen *(Ned Logan)*; Jeremy Garrett *(Clay Logan)*; Sarah Rayne *(Lexy Logan)*; Lea Moreno Young *(Alice Logan)*; Grayson McCouch *(Sean Logan)*; Ron Melendez *(Jeremy Bradford)*; Lisa Sheridan *(Vivian Winters)*; Sean Bridges *(William Winters)*; Mark Joy *(Col. Henry Griffith)*; Steven Williams *(Isaac)*; Sharon Leal *(Marita)*; Brigid Brannagh *(Molly)*.

5243   Legally Blonde The Musical: The Search for Elle Woods. (Series; Reality; MTV; 2008). A talent search to find an actress to play the role of Elle Woods, the pampered blonde, in the Broadway musical *Legally Blonde*. Ten girls, chosen from a nationwide casting call, are brought together in New York City and placed in a loft where they must live together through the duration of the competition. The girls are mentored by professionals, including cast members from *Legally Blonde*. The girls are then tested in acting, singing and dancing challenges. A panel of judges rates the performances with the weakest performer being eliminated on a weekly basis. The one girl who proves to be the best wins the role of Elle Woods (replacing the current actress, Laura Bell Bundy). Haylie Duff is the mentor. Heather Hatch, Paul Canaan, Bernard Telsey and Jerry Mitchell are the judges.

5244   Legally Mad. (Pilot; Drama; Unaired; Produced for NBC in 2008). Gordon and Brady Hamm are the father-daughter owners of the Chicago firm of Hamm and Hamm, Attorneys-at-Law. The firm handles cases from the most prestigious to the most mundane and the proposal was to follow how the eccentric members of the firm investigate and defend clients.
   Cast: Hugh Bonneville *(Gordon Hamm)*; Charity Wakefield *(Brady Hamm)*; Kristin Chenoweth *(Skippy Pylon)*; Kurt Fuller *(Steven Pearle)*; Loretta Devine *(Janette Harris)*; Jon Seda *(Joe Matty)*.

5245   Legend. (Pilot; Dance; CBS; June 2, 1946). An unsold idea to present a program of dramatic dance music on a weekly basis. Here, Pearl Primus and her troupe of singers and dancers performed "Legend," the tale of an African witch doctor's triumph over an evil sorceress.
   Narrator: Yale Woll. **Performers:** Pearl Primus and Her Dance Company. **Choreographer:** Pearl Primus.

5246   Legend. (Series; Western; UPN; 1995). Ernest Pratt is a 19th century novelist who has created Nicodemus Legend, a western hero. Ernest has written his dime store novels in a first-person narrative and is constantly mistaken for Legend. Unfortunately for Ernest, the real life deeds of Legend that Ernest only wrote about, have resulted in arrest warrants being issued in Colorado.
   Legend is pure fiction — but the warrants are not and Ernest feels he needs to set the record straight. In Colorado, Ernest meets Janos Bartok, an eccentric inventor who convinces him to keep the identity of Legend and use his legend to help people in need. Ernest agrees. Janos is actually the hero behind Legend. His wacky inventions provide Legend with the means to save the day and stories follow Ernest as he tries to be the hero he has written about. Ramos assists Bartok; Chamberlain is the town mayor/undertaker; Grady is the bartender.
   Cast: Richard Dean Anderson *(Ernest Pratt/Nicodemus Legend)*; John de Lancie *(Janos Bartok)*; Mark Adair-Rios *(Huitzilopochtli Ramos)*; Robert Donner *(Chamberlain Brown)*; Robert Shelton *(Grady)*.

5247   The Legend of Butch and Sundance. (Pilot; Western; Unaired; Produced for NBC in 2003). Events in the real life early years of the legendary gentlemen outlaws Butch Cassidy and the Sundance Kid.

Cast: David Rogers (*Butch Cassidy*); Ryan Browning (*The Sundance Kid*); Rachelle Lefevre (*Etta Place*); Blake Gibbons (*Durango*).

5248   *The Legend of Calamity Jane.* (Series; Cartoon; WB; 1997–1998). The Old West is the setting. Martha Jane Canary, called "Calamity Jane" is no calamity. She is tall, slender, dresses in black (with a white scarf and belt) and carries a red whip. She was a runaway who was raised by a Native American tribe. She has honed her skills and uses her abilities to help the downtrodden. Jane is assisted by her partner, Joe Presto, and her romantic interest, Wild Bill Hickok. Stories follow the western heroine as she battles the various villains who plague the good people of the Old West. Quanna Parker is Calamity's Comanche Indian friend; John O'Rourke is the U.S. Army Captain who recruits Calamity for assignments.

Voice Cast: Jennifer Jason Leigh, Barbara Scaff (*Calamity Jane*); Frank Welker (*Joe Presto*); Clancy Brown (*Wild Bill Hickok*); Michael Horse (*Quanna Parker*); Tim Matheson (*Capt. John O'Rourke*).

5249   *The Legend of Custer.* (Series; Western; ABC; 1967). Kansas, 1867 is the setting. Found guilty of dereliction of duty, Major General George Armstrong Custer (U.S. Cavalry) is reduced in rank (to Lieutenant Colonel) and sent to Fort Hays, where he is put in charge of the Seventh Labor Battalion. Custer, who refuses to treat his Company C as a work detail, trains them and, after months of endurance, his squad is recognized as The Fighting Seventh. Stories depict Custer's exploits in Indian affairs, and his personal conflict with Crazy Horse, the Sioux Indian Chief. Also known as *Custer*.

Program Open: "At twenty-four he had been the youngest general in the Civil War. Within five years he had been reduced in rank and sent west to be forgotten. But he was not the type of man to let the world forget. His name. General George Armstrong Custer."

Cast: Wayne Maunder (*Col. George Custer*); Slim Pickens (*Joe Miller, the trail scout*); Peter Palmer (*Sgt. James Bustard*); Grant Woods (*Capt. Myles Keogh*); Robert F. Simon (*Gen. Alfred Terry*); Michael Dante (*Chief Crazy Horse*).

5250   *The Legend of Jesse James.* (Series; Western; ABC; 1965–1966). St. Louis, Missouri, during the 1860s is the setting. Brothers Frank and Jesse James are hard-working farmers whose lives change drastically when their widowed mother is killed by railroad officials when she refuses to sell them her land and they are run off. Bitter and determined to avenge their mother's death, the brothers turn outlaw and not only strike the Great Western Railroad, but attempt to return rightful property to the survivors of innocent victims. The law, however, sees Frank and Jesse as outlaws and a reward has been posted for their capture; Sam Corbett is the Marshal seeking to end their reign of terror. Cole and Bob Younger are the notorious gunfighters that are also featured in stories that depict the violence of the Old West.

Cast: Chris Jones (*Jesse James*); Allen Case (*Frank James*); Robert J. Wilke (*Marshal Sam Corbett*); John Milford (*Cole Younger*); Bob McIntire (*Bob Younger*); Ann Doran (*Mrs. James; first episode*).

5251   *The Legend of Prince Valiant.* (Series; Cartoon; Fox Family Channel; 1991). England during the Middle Ages is the setting for tales of Prince Valiant as he sets out to become a Knight of King Arthur's Round Table. His quest begins with a dream in which he envisions King Arthur requesting that he become a knight. Believing that his dream is an omen, he sets out to fulfill a destiny. As he begins his journey, he meets a peasant (Arn) and a blacksmith's daughter (Rowenne) who join him on his quest. Stories focus on the three as they arrive in Camelot and perform duties to become Knights.

Voice Cast: Robby Benson (*Prince Valiant*); Noelle North (*Rowenne*); Michael Horton (*Arn*); Efrem Zimbalist, Jr. (*King Arthur*); Samantha Eggar (*Queen Guinevere*); Alan Oppenheimer (*Merlin the Magician*); James Avery (*Sir Bryant*); Tim Curry (*Sir Gawain*); Patty Duke (*Lady Morgana*); Jeff Bennett (*Lord Maldon*).

5252   *The Legend of Tarzan.* (Series; Cartoon; ABC Family; 2003). An adaptation of the Disney feature film that continues the story of Tarzan, now the leader of the Apes, and Jane Porter, the girl he rescued and who now lives with him, as they risk their lives to protect their jungle domain from evil doers.

Voice Cast: Michael T. Weiss (*Tarzan*); Olivia d'Abo (*Jane Porter*); Jeff Bennett (*Prof. Archimedes Porter*); Susan Blakeslee (*Kala*); April Winchell (*Terk*); Jim Cummings (*Tantor*).

5253   *Legend of the Dragon.* (Series; Cartoon; Disney; 2006). In ancient China there is a legend of a Dragon Master, a person of special abilities who is chosen to be guardian of the sacred temple. When the current guardian passes, a search is begun to find a new guardian. Ang and Ling are twins who were born in the year of the dragon. Ang and Ling are martial arts experts but each could face a different destiny: Ang is attracted to the powers of goodness (the light) while Ling is prone to evil (the powers of darkness). Both are seeking to become guardians but only one is chosen — the brother (Ling) not the sister (Ang). The balance of power suddenly changes and Ang can go either way — join her brother on the side of good or oppose him with the powers of darkness. Stories relate Ling's efforts to safeguard the temple from evil and Ang's struggles to choose between the light and the dark.

Voice Cast: Alan Marriott (*Ling*); Larissa Murray (*Ang*); Dan Russell (*Master Chin*); Mark Silk (*Xuan Chi*).

5254   *The Legend of the Golden Gun.* (Pilot; Western; NBC; April 10, 1979). During the Civil War, William Quantrill, the Confederate guerilla leader, began a reign of terror in Kansas. His army targeted a farm run by the Coltons and attacked, leaving after they believed they killed the entire family. One man, John Colton, survived and would have died had he not been found and nursed back to health by Joshua Brown, a runaway slave. As John recovers, he vows to avenge his family by killing Quantrill. Joshua believes John is not prepared for such a quest and suggests he seek the help of Jim Hammer, a legendary gunfighter who fights for right. Hammer teaches Colton the art of gunplay — not for revenge, however, but to seek out and destroy evil. Before Hammer and Colton depart company Hammer gives John a gold outfit and a gold-plated seven-barreled gun (the seventh bullet being for evil "because evil doesn't fight fair"). The proposal follows Colton as he assumes the name John Golden and sets out to use his guns for justice.

Cast: Jeff Osterhage (*John Golden*); Carl Franklin (*Joshua "Book" Brown*); Hal Holbrook (*John Hammer; a.k.a. John Swackhamer*).

5255   *Legend of the Seeker.* (Series; Adventure; Syn.; 2008–2010). In a time that has long since been forgotten, a book called *The Book of Counted Shadows* was composed by unknown beings to record the secrets of power. A being called the Seeker used the book to defeat evil. A society of women called Confessors were chosen to protect the book and risk their lives to ensure the safety of the Seeker.

It is many centuries later (in a medieval-like era) when an evil ruler, Darken Rahl, is seeking to rule the world and enslave mankind. He requires *The Book of Counted Shadows* to ensure that power.

In an area called the Midlands, a baby boy, destined to become a Seeker, is born to a woman. To protect the baby from Rahl (who seeks to kill it), the wizard Zeddicus Zul Zorander (called Zedd) takes the baby and gives him to a young couple, George and Mary

Cypher, to raise. The baby grows to become the woodsman Richard Cypher.

It is thirty-three years later when Richard comes to know his true calling. Kahlan, a Confessor, has been assigned to find Richard, present him with the book and have Zedd proclaim him as the next Seeker. Rahl has sensed the presence of a new Seeker and has dispatched soldiers to destroy the Seeker and retrieve the sacred book for him.

Zedd has not revealed his true nature to Richard. They are friends, but Richard believes he is a crazy old man who talks to his chickens. When Kahlan finds Zedd, Zedd reveals his true nature to Richard and presents him with the Sword of Truth — forged metal to ordinary men, but a magical means to destroy evil for the true Seeker. Richard questions what he has been told until Rahl's soldiers attack them. The ensuing battle, in which Richard finds a strength he has never known before, convinces him that what he has been told is the truth. He then learns from Kahlan about Darken Rahl and his mission: to destroy Rahl and save mankind. Stories follow Richard, Kahlan and Zedd as they set out on a dangerous quest to find Rahl and stop him before he can accomplish his goal. Hindering them is Rahl, who has issued wanted posters for Richard's capture (one thousand gold pieces as a reward). Richard destroyed the book in the third episode (his way of acquiring the secrets of power). Rahl's soldiers have informed him of this and now Rahl must capture Richard in order to acquire the power.

Cast: Craig Horner *(Richard Cypher)*; Bridget Regan *(Kahlan Amnell)*; Bruce Spence *(Zedd)*; Craig Parker *(Darken Rahl)*; David de Latour *(Michael Cypher)*; Jay Laga'aia *(Chase)*.

5256 *The Legend of Zelda*. (Series; Cartoon; Syn.; 1989). Zelda, the Princess of Hyrule, and Link, a mighty warrior, jump from the Nintendo game for a TV adaptation in which they battle to protect the Triforce of Wisdom from evil.

Voice Cast: Cynthia Preston *(Zelda)*; Jonathan Potts *(Link)*; Elizabeth Hanna *(Triforce of Wisdom)*; Allan Stewart Coates *(Triforce of Power)*; Colin Fox *(King Harkinian)*; Paulina Gillis *(Spryte)*; Len Carson *(Ganon)*; Jonathan Potts *(Link)*.

5257 *The Legends of the Hawaiian Slammers*. (Pilot; Cartoon; Fox; Nov. 25, 1994). Three thousand years ago a great volcanic explosion caused a warp in time and space and released five evil entities from our world called the Slammers of Darkness (Shadow, Lead, Fire, Storm and Lava). The Slammers wrecked havoc on the world until the five Slammers of Light (Sun, Rain, Cold, Ice and Earth) were sent by the gods to stop them. The immortal Slammers battled for one hundred years before good could defeat evil (each Slammer of Light captured a Slammer of Darkness and transferred their powers into small metal disks — each trapping the other for eternity). The disks were buried deep inside an Hawaiian volcano and left untouched for centuries.

Over the course of time, earthquakes and eruptions jarred the casing that held the Slammers of Sun and Shadow (their energies can only be released by a life force of similar nature: an evil human can control the dark Slammer while a good human can control a light Slammer). It is 1994 when the evil archeologist Von Fragman discovers a Slammer disk. By spinning the disk, as told in the hieroglyphics, Von Fragman releases Shadow and becomes his master. Meanwhile, a young boy (Ronnie) finds a metal disk, which he spins, thinking it is a neat bottle cap, and brings to life Sun. The proposed series was to follow Ronnie and Sun's efforts to stop Van Fragman and Shadow from finding and releasing the dark Slammers in his quest to rule the world.

Voices: Long John Baldry, Jim Byrnes, Babs Chula, Chad Dormer, Ed Glen, Marcy Goldberg, Saffron Henderson, Andrew Kavadas, David Kaye, Shirley Milliner, Jesse Moss, John Noval, Dale Wilson.

5258 *Legends of the Hidden Temple*. (Series; Game; Nick; 1993–1996). Twelve children (six boys and six girls) are divided into specific two-member teams: Silver Snakes, Red Jaguars, Green Monkeys, Blue Barracudas, Orange Iguanas and Purple Parrots. The format places teams in an ancient Mayan-like temple that is built on a stage called Olmec's Temple. Olmec is a talking rock that begins the game by telling the teams what artifact they must find that is hidden in his temple. In round one, each member of each team must cross a moat by any means they can. The first four teams to cross the moat continue with the game while the other two teams are eliminated. In round two, "The Steps of Knowledge," Olmec questions the teams on their knowledge of the artifact that was mentioned at the beginning of the program. Teams answer through buzzer signal recognition and the two highest scoring teams continue onto the next round, "The Temple Games." Here each of the boys and each of the girls must perform a physical task. A pendant is awarded to the best performing players. The team with the most pendants at the end of the round receives the opportunity to win merchandise prizes by entering Olmec's Temple with the object being to find the previously mentioned artifact. It is not as easy as it sounds as it has to be done within three minutes and there are twelve rooms with two doors in each room to navigate. One door holds the artifact but there are also temple guards who could hold a teammate captive if he opens the wrong door (having the pendants won in the prior round on them can set them free; however, if the player does not have a pendant, he is taken out of the game and his teammate must find the artifact alone). If the team fails to find the artifact a lesser value prize is awarded.

Host: Kirk Fogg. **Announcer:** Dee Bradley Baker.

5259 *Legends of the Screen*. (Pilot; Documentary; Syn.; Jan. 1983). Screen legends are recalled via film clips and live interviews with the stars themselves.

Host: Nancy Collins. **Guests:** Rhonda Fleming, Dorothy Lamour, Myrna Loy, Ginger Rogers.

5260 *Legends of the West: Truth and Tall Tales*. (Pilot; Anthology; ABC; Mar. 22, 1981). An attempt to separate western fact from fiction through dramatizations and film clips from various western films.

Hosts: Matthew Laborteaux, Don Meredith. **Guest:** Jack Elam *(as the sheriff)*.

5261 *Legion of the Super Heroes*. (Series; Cartoon; Kids WB; 2006). The Legion of the Super Heroes is a 31st century organization formed by the universe's greatest heroes to protect the United Planets from evil. Its members include Cosmic Boy, Saturn Girl, Triplicate Girl (can change herself into three separate girls), Lightning Boy, Colossal Boy, Ferro Lad, Brainic 5, Bouncing Boy and Superman (who was transported from the 21st century to the future to help battle the super villains of the era.). Stories relate the legion's battle against the diabolical villains who prey on innocent people and vulnerable planets.

Voice Cast: Yuri Lowenthal *(Superman)*; Kari Wahlgren *(Saturn Girl/Triplicate Girl)*; Wil Wheton *(Cosmic Boy)*; Adam Wylie *(Colossal Boy/Brainic 5)*; Dave Wittenberg *(Ferro Lad)*; Michael Cornacchia *(Bouncing Boy)*; Andy Miller *(Lightning Boy)*; Heather Hogan *(Phantom Girl)*; Shawn Harrison *(Timber Wolf)*; Jennifer Hale *(Emerald Empress)*.

5262 *Legmen*. (Series; Crime Drama; NBC; 1984). Jack Gage is a college man studying to be an engineer. David Taylor, his roommate, is studying to become a lawyer. Both are short on cash and find a way to relieve their problems by becoming legmen for Oscar

Amismedi, the owner of the Tri-Star Bail Bonds Agency (later owned by Tom Bannon). Jack and David's efforts to track down bail jumpers is the focal point of stories. Other regulars are Chico, Oscar's assistant; Police Lieutenant Tedisco; and Mrs. Yehudi, Tom's secretary.

Cast: Bruce Greenwood (*Jack Gage*); J.T. Terlesky (*David Taylor*); Don Calfa (*Oscar Amismedi*); Claude Akins (*Tom Bannon*); Anthony Munoz (*Chico*); Robert DoQui (*Lieutenant Tedisco*); Connie Sawyer (*Mrs. Yehudi*).

5263   Legs. (Pilot; Comedy; ABC; May 19, 1978). Stacy Turner and Angie Bates are showgirls at a Las Vegas casino owned by Major Putnam. Stacy cares for her younger sister, Melissa and Angie cares for her younger, mischievous brother, Frankie. The pilot, which became the series *Who's Watching the Kids* with some changes, follows Stacy and Angie as they struggles to divide their time between work and caring for their siblings. Other regulars are Major Putnam, the casino owner; and showgirls Cochise, Bridget, Memphis and Dixie.

Cast: Caren Kaye (*Stacy Turner*); Lynda Goodfriend (*Angie Bates*); Tammy Lauren (*Melissa Turner*); Scott Baio (*Frankie Bates*); Shirley Kirkes (*Cochise*); Elaine Bolton (*Bridget*); Lorrie Mahaffey (*Memphis Blake*); Sayra Hammel (*Dixie*); Dave Ketchum (*Major Putnam*).

5264   The Lennon Sisters Show. (Pilot; Variety; ABC; May 6, 1969). The pilot presentation for *Jimmy Durante Presents the Lennon Sisters Hour* that spotlights the talents of the singing Lennon Sisters (Dianne, Peggy, Janet and Kathy).

Host: Jimmy Durante. **Stars:** Dianne, Janet, Kathy and Peggy Lennon. **Guest:** Bobby Goldsboro. **Orchestra:** Nelson Riddle.

5265   Lenny. (Series; Comedy; CBS; 1990–1991). When Leonard ("Lenny") Joseph Callahan met Shelly Morrison, he had to borrow ten dollars for their first date. When Lenny brought Shelly home to meet the family, his younger brother, Eddie, remarked, "What great torpedoes — and what a tush!" Lenny and Shelly eventually married and set up housekeeping in Boston. Lenny works at two jobs: gasman for Boston Utility, and doorman at an unnamed hotel at night. Shelly is kept busy caring for their three daughters, Kelly, Tracy and baby Elizabeth (played by the Hall twins).

Lenny was born in 1953, and as a kid had a teddy bear named Buzzer. Shelly calls Lenny an easy touch ("A friend in need is a friend of Lenny's"). The Boston Celtics are Lenny's favorite baseball team, and Fielding Insurance handles his life insurance. Lenny enjoys cold pizza in the morning and can belch the song "White Christmas." His favorite robe is a terrycloth one he stole from their honeymoon hotel; he calls Shelly "Shell" and "Love Muffin."

Kelly, their 13-year-old daughter, attends St. Theodore's Catholic Grammar School. She is a complainer, like her father, and has a negative view of everything. She desperately wants "cleavage like my other girlfriends" and feels she is overweight, unattractive and going to be flat-chested.

Tracy, their 10-year-old daughter, is very bright and very knowledgeable for a girl her age (for instance, she watches a lot of television, especially the medical channel, and is thus an expert on all types of diseases). Tracy also attends Saint Theodore's. Lenny remarks that for a ten-year-old girl, Tracy is somewhat unusual. He did ask her, "When you look out into space at night, do you feel homesick?"

Edward ("Eddie") Callahan is Lenny's uncouth brother (he has no respect for anyone and, in the presence of Kelly and Tracy, refers to breasts as "ta ta's," "hooters" and "honkers"). Eddie is on the run from the cops, has 1,500 unpaid parking tickets, writes bad checks, and is wanted for mail fraud and petty theft. Although he should be in jail, he's just smart enough to stay one step ahead of the police. For income, Eddie receives a disability payment (he goes under the name Louie Lonzo and pretends to have a glass eye).

Pat and Mary are Lenny's parents; Megan is Lenny's sister. In the original, unaired pilot film, Alyson Croft played 13-year-old Trisha Callahan (who became Kelly), and America Martin was 10-year-old Kelly Callahan (who became Tracy for the series).

Cast: Lenny Clarke (*Lenny Callahan*); Lee Garlington (*Shelly Callahan*); Jenna Von Oy (*Kelly Callahan*); Alexis Caldwell (*Tracy Callahan*); Peter Dobson (*Eddie Callahan*); Eugene Roach (*Pat Callahan*); Alice Drummond (*Mary Callahan*); Judith Hoag (*Megan Callahan*).

5266   Leo and Liz in Beverly Hills. (Series; Comedy; CBS; 1986). When his bra manufacturing business suddenly begins to show a tremendous profit, Leo Greene, his wife, Liz, and their daughter, Mitzi, leave New Jersey and relocate to the plush and glamour of Beverly Hills. Their misadventures as they attempt to fit in among the rich and famous is the focal point of stories. Other regulars are Lucille, their housekeeper (at 105 North Bevon Drive); Leonard, the handyman; Diane and Jerry Fedderson, their neighbors; and Bunky, Diane's son.

The pilot episode, "The Couch" aired as a segment of *George Burns Comedy Week* on Oct. 16, 1985. Carrie Fisher played the role of Mitzi and the story dealt with Leo and Liz's efforts to get an antique couch to impress the parents of their daughter's fiancé (Bunky Winthrop, played by Mark Steen). Bunky's last name changed for the series, as did his parents (here played by Parker Whitman and Marlena Giovi).

Cast: Valerie Perrine (*Liz Greene*); Harvey Korman (*Leo Greene*); Sue Ball (*Mitzi Greene*); Julie Payne (*Lucille Trumbley*); Michael J. Pollard (*Leonard*); Deborah Harmon (*Diane Fedderson*); Ken Kimmons (*Jerry Fedderson*); Peter Aykroyd (*Bunky Fedderson*).

5267   Leo Little's Big Show. (Series; Children; Disney; 2009). Movie and television show reviews with Leo Little and his younger sister, Amy, giving their perspectives (supported by guests and clips) of the reviewed subjects.

Cast: Leo Howard (*Leo Little*); G. Hannelius (*Amy Little*).

5268   The Les Crane Show. (Series; Discussion; ABC; 1964–1965). The program features discussions on controversial issues. Also known as *ABC's Night Life*.

Host: Les Crane. **Regulars:** Nipsey Russell, Jimmy Cannon. **Announcer:** William B. Williams. **Music:** Don Trenner, Cy Coleman, Elliot Lawrence.

5269   The Les Paul and Mary Ford Show. (Series; Variety; Syn.; 1954). A five-minute filler program consisting of a quick opening, two songs, one commercial and a short closing.

Hosts: Les Paul, Mary Ford.

5270   Lesbian Sex and Sexuality. (Series; Reality; Here!; 2008). A very specialized program (aired on the gay channel Here!) that takes an extremely frank look at what it means to be a lesbian in today's world. The program explores lesbian sexuality through interviews with "sexperts" as well as by visiting erotic dance clubs, lesbian owned adult film companies and sex shops. The program also explores various girl-on-girl fantasies in graphic detail.

5271   The Leslie Uggams Show. (Series; Variety; CBS; 1969). Singer Leslie Uggams hosts a program of music, song and light comedy (including a skit involving the people of a community called Sugar Hill).

Program Open: "From Television City in Hollywood ... it's *The Leslie Uggams Show* with her guests Kaye Ballard, David Frye, Glen Ash, special guest stars The Temptations, the residents of Sugar Hill and Ernie Freeman and his Orchestra."

Host: Leslie Uggams. **Regulars:** Johnny Brown, Lillian Hayman, Alison Mills, Lincoln Kilpatrick, The Donald McKayle Dancers, The Howard Roberts Singers. **Announcer:** Roger Carroll. **Orchestra:** Nelson Riddle, Ernie Freeman.

5272   *Less Than Perfect.* (Series; Comedy; ABC; 2002–2006). GNB is a TV news network in New York City. It is here that Claudia Casey, unflatteringly called Claude, is the assistant to network news anchor Will Butler. Claudia has been working at the station for two years when the series begins. She started as a floater on the fourth floor and worked her way up to the prestigious 22nd floor. Claudia collects troll dolls and is vice president of the American Troll Doll Association.

Kipp Steadman and Lydia Weston are Claudia's condescending co-workers, who conspire to get rid of her to further their own ambitions. Owen Kronsky and Ramona Platt are Claudia's friends, supply room workers on the fourth floor. Carl Monari is the station's cafeteria manager. Stories at this point follow Claudia as she struggles to do her job and overcome the schemes of Kipp and Lydia.

In 2005, Jeb Denton becomes a news personality with the station. A year later, when Claudia returns from her vacation in Italy, she finds that Will has resigned and Jeb has become the new anchor. She also learns that her job as been eliminated and that Lydia (who married Jeb in the prior season finale) has become the show's producer. She also finds one other bit of disturbing news: she has been rehired as Lydia's assistant. Stories now follow Claudia as she begins to evaluate her own ambitions and her struggles to succeed in both her personal and career life.

Claudia has giggle fits and is not use to compliments (although she is very pretty). She lives in Brooklyn and can't lie — "I think it's mean." She is a Pez candy lover (and claims to make her own Pez). Will was called "The Most Trusted Newsman in America." Owen was raised by his two lesbian mothers (Judith and Judy). He uses the ladies restroom "because it's not as scary as the men's room." He is also interested in dirt bikes and aliens but can't find anyone who shares his interests.

Cast: Sara Rue (*Claudia "Claude" Casey*); Sherri Shepherd (*Ramona Platt*); Andrea Parker (*Lydia Weston*); Andy Dick (*Owen Kronsky*); Eric Roberts (*Will Butler*); Patrick Warburton (*Jeb Denton*); Zachary Levi (*Kipp Steadman*); Will Sass (*Carl Monari*).

5273   *Lester and Dr. Fong.* (Pilot; Crime Drama; ABC; Mar. 18, 1976). Dr. Fong is a brilliant criminologist. He also teaches a criminology course at college and has one exceptional student: Lester Hodges, a young man fascinated by crime and who desperately wants to follow in Dr. Fong's footsteps. The proposal, a spin off from *Harry O*, was to follow Lester and Dr. Fong as they team to help the police solve crimes.

Cast: Les Lannom (*Lester Hodges*); Keye Luke (*Dr. Creighton Fong*).

5274   *Let Go.* (Pilot; Comedy; Unaired; Produced for ABC in 2005). Kate Holloway is a pretty, divorced detective with the Pasadena, California, P.D. Her precinct desk represents her life: a mess — but, at least at work, she knows exactly what's what under the clutter. Nick, her long time partner, is just the opposite and her best friend. Kate and Nick are always there for each other and the proposal was to relate events in their lives, mostly at the precinct but also on the street solving crimes.

Cast: Bonnie Hunt (*Kate Holloway*); Michael Landes (*Nick*); Don Lake (*Billy*); Lauren Tom (*Beverly*); Joe Mantegna (*Jack*); Anthony Russell (*Angelo*).

5275   *Let It Go.* (Pilot; Comedy; Unaired; Produced for ABC in 2009). Bridget O'Shea is a gorgeous inspirational talk show host

who rarely follows her own advice until she finds that pursuing the man of her dreams was a fruitless endeavor. She quits the talk show circuit with a plan to write the definitive self-help book. The proposal was to follow Bridget as she sets out to write that book and hopefully score the comeback of the year. Marty is her manager; Chris is her ex-cousin, a professional slacker; Lucy is her assistant.

Cast: Lauren Graham (*Bridget O'Shea*); Lucy Davis (*Lucy St. John*); Jeffrey Tambor (*Marty Roth*); Josh Braaten (*Chris Hopper*); Holly Robinson Peete (*Macy*).

5276   *Let There Be Stars.* (Series; Variety; ABC; 1949). ABC's first series to be broadcast from their new studios in Hollywood. Up and coming actors and actresses performed in revue-like programs with the hope of being discovered.

Cast: Patti Brill, Warde Donovan, Roland Supree, Ward Edwards, Corky Geil, Jane Harvey, Charles Lind, Peter Marshall, Tommy Noonan, Thayer Roberts, Dolores Starr.

5277   *Let's Dance.* (Pilot; Game; ABC; July 2, 1946). Members of the Arthur Murray Dance Studios perform a dance step on stage. A contestant, chosen from the studio audience, is asked to identify the type of dance being presented. A correct answer wins the player a free dance course at the Murray studios. Although Walter Herlihy actually hosted the program, Jim Ameche is seen as the host in the credits (Don, chosen to host the program, refused to do so at the last moment. Walter was brought on in a rush, but there was no time to change the credit cards on the live show).

Host: Walter Herlihy. **Regulars:** Jerry Farr, Velma Smith, The Arthur Murray Dancers, The Flower Dance Company.

5278   *Let's Dance.* (Series; Variety; ABC; 1954). A live musical hour featuring ballroom dancing and broadcast from both New York and Chicago.

Cast: Ralph Mooney (*New York Host*); Martha Wright (*New York Celebrity Table Hostess*); Bud Robinson (*Dancer, New York*); Cece Robinson (*Dancer, New York*); Julius LaRosa (*Vocalist, New York*); Art Mooney (*Chicago Host*); Fran Allison (*Chicago Celebrity Table Hostess*); June Valli (*Vocalist, Chicago*). **Orchestra:** Ralph Flanagan (New York), Art Mooney (Chicago).

5279   *Let's Dance.* (Pilot; Reality; Unaired; Produced for ABC in 2009). Celebrities compete in a dance competition challenges that recreate famous movie, pop and video dance routines.

Host: Kathy Griffin.

5280   *Let's Get Mom.* (Pilot; Comedy; Unaired; Produced for Fox in 1989). A proposal about a vulnerable young housewife named Maureen as she struggles to cope with a husband (Bruce) and four mischievous children (George, Danny, Mickey and Jordan).

Cast: Carol Kane (*Maureen*); Bruce McGill (*Bruce*); P.J. Ochlan (*George*); Robert Oliveri (*Danny*); Robert Gorman (*Mickey*); Joe Schermoly (*Jordan*).

5281   *Let's Go Go.* (Series; Variety; Syn.; 1965). Performances by rock personalities.

Program Open: "From Hollywood, *Let's Go Go* with the swingin' sound. Today's guests Bobby Vee, Eddie Randall, The Cindermen and special guest star Ryan O'Neal. And starring Sam Riddle."

Host: Sam Riddle, John Reynolds.

5282   *Let's Join Joanie.* (Pilot; Comedy; CBS; Jan. 12, 1951). Events in the life of Joan Davis, a misadventure-prone salesgirl for a store called Hats By Anatole. Joan Davis is the only performer who receives credit. Joe Flynn, as Joan's boss, is easily recognizable, but other performers are unknown (there was no review of the program and *TV Guide* lists it only as *Let's Join Joanie* with no cast, storyline or credit information).

Cast: Joan Davis *(Herself)*; Joe Flynn *(Anatole)*.

5283　*Let's Make a Deal.* (Series; Game; NBC; ABC; Syn.; CBS; 1963–). Ten of forty previously selected studio audience members vie for the opportunity to trade their home made articles for cash and/or merchandise prizes. A selected player is usually offered several deals. A first deal most often assures a player a decent prize; a second or third deal tests greed as large amounts of cash and valuable merchandise are at stake — along with everything a player has won up to that point if his deal results in a "zonk" (a nonsense prize). Perhaps the most memorable part of the program is the host offering the day's biggest dealers their choice of "what's behind door number one, two or three" that are displayed on stage.

Program Open: "It's time for *Let's Make a Deal* starring TV's big Dealer, Monty Hall." Six versions appeared:

1. Let's Make a Deal (NBC, 1963–68; aired on NBC in prime time, in 1967). **Host:** Monty Hall. **Model:** Carol Merrill. **Announcer:** Jay Stewart.

2. Let's Make a Deal (ABC, 1969–71). **Host:** Monty Hall.

3. Let's Make a Deal (Syn., 1980). **Host:** Monty Hall. Also known as *The All New Let's Make a Deal.*

4. Let's Make a Deal (Syn., 1984–1986). **Host:** Monty Hall.

5. Let's Make a Deal (NBC, 1990–1991). **Host:** Bob Hilton, Monty Hall.

6. Let's Make a Deal (CBS, 2009–). **Host:** Wayne Brady. **Announcer:** Jonathan Mangum

5284　*Let's Play Post Office.* (Series; Game; NBC; 1965-1966). One line of a fictitious letter, which could have been written by a celebrity or a past figure of history, is revealed. The first of three competing players who associates the content with the author sounds a buzzer. If the player identifies the writer of the letter, he scores one point. If not, the second line is revealed and the game follows in the same manner. The highest scoring player is the winner and receives merchandise prizes.

Host: Don Morrow.

5285　*Let's Play Reporter.* (Pilot; Game; ABC; May 23 and 30; June 6, 1946). A three-episode test program. The host takes on the role of a city newspaper editor while selected members of the studio audience become her cub reporters. Each cub reporter becomes involved in a situation which he must relate back to the editor. Accuracy is the key ingredient as the reporter tells his story. The reporter whose story most closely matches his experience is the winner.

Host: Frances Scott.

5286　*Let's Take a Trip.* (Series; Children; CBS; 1955–1958). The program attempts to help children learn about the world in which they live via visits to places on interest.

Host: Sonny Fox. **Assistants:** Ginger McManus, Brian Flanegan.

5287　*Let's Talk Pep.* (Series; Reality; VH-1; 2010). Sandra "Pepa" Denton, a former member of the singing duo Salt-n-Pepa, has returned to the limelight in an effort to "negotiate the romantic minefield of New York City." After the group broke up, Sandra, frustrated by years of non-fulfilling relationships, went into a state of sexual dormancy. When she realized that this did not improve her situation (didn't evolve, didn't get a rich husband "and the only close relationship she formed was with her exercise bike") Sandra felt it was time to get back into the dating game. But Sandra isn't alone: her three best friends (Kali Troy, Jacque Reid and Joumana Kidd)

are facing the same situation. Episodes follow the four women as they jump start their dating lives to seek their Mr. Right.

5288　*A Letter to Loretta.* (Series; Anthology; NBC; 1953-1954). Responsive dramatizations based on problems expressed in fan letters to actress Loretta Young. After the first season (Sept. 20, 1953 to June 27, 1954), it became *The Loretta Young Show* (which see).

Host-Frequent Star: Loretta Young. **Featured Regular:** Beverly Washburn. **Announcer:** Bob Wilson.

5289　*A Letter to Your Serviceman.* (Experimental Series; Variety; DuMont; April 10 to June 12, 1945). Variety performances geared to servicemen who are in the hospital. The program opens with the host, seated in an office, selecting a letter from a group sent in by actual, hospitalized servicemen. After reading the letter to the audience, the host makes a phone call and arranges for the variety act requested in the letter to perform on the show (servicemen were asked to send in suggestions for future guests).

Host: Bert Bacharach. **Announcer:** Ken Farnsworth.

5290　*The Letters.* (Pilot; Anthology; ABC; Mar. 6, 1973). Interconnected stories about the effects letters, delayed one year in transit due to a plane crash, have on the people to whom they were addressed once they are delivered by the postman (the only regular character). A second pilot, *Letters from Three Lovers*, aired on Oct. 3, 1973.

Cast: Henry Jones *(The Postman)*.

5291　*Letters to Laugh-In.* (Series; Comedy; NBC; 1969-1970). A daily spin-off from *Rowan and Martin's Laugh-In*. Four joke tellers (guest celebrities) relate jokes submitted to *Laugh-In* by home viewers. Jokes are rated by a panel of ten selected studio audience members on a scale ranging from a plus one hundred to a minus one hundred. The winner of the week's highest scoring joke receives merchandise prizes. The lowest scoring joke wins its sender "seven action packed days in beautiful downtown Burbank (California)."

Host: Gary Owens.

5292　*Level 9.* (Series; Crime Drama; UPN; 2000-2001). Level 9 is a state-of-the-art Washington, D.C.–based government agency that has only one function: solve the cases that other law enforcement agencies cannot. It is composed of the government's best cyber operations experts and is tailored to form a rapid response strike force against high tech criminals. The agency is fully mobilized and can go anywhere and anyplace.

Annie Price, a former FBI agent with a remarkable arrest record, heads Level 9. She can think like a computer and figure out a criminal's next move. She has an amazing attention to detail and remarkable recollection abilities. She is rarely distracted by her duties, but is troubled by a computer hacker she dubbed "Crazy Horse." Annie believes Crazy Horse is responsible for half the crimes in America. Her nightmare began in 1998 when, as an FBI agent, she was assigned to a case involving a hacker who broke into a bureau computer and demanded $50 million or he would jam their computers. Annie believed it could be done, but her superiors felt it was a hoax and ignored her — and the hacker. The supposed hoax jammed the computers and now demanded $100 million. With air traffic control computers out and to avoid the worst aviation disaster in history, the ransom was paid. The public never knew what happened — but Annie knew and she hopes with the technology of Level 9 to find Crazy Horse.

While there are a number of agents who work for Level 9, only two are featured: Wilbert "Tibbs" Thibodeaux and Joss Nakano. The featured hackers are Sosh, Roland Travis, Jargon and Jerry Hooten. The hackers, who use screen names, are not permitted to reveal their names and no information is revealed about them. They appear to do nothing else but sit at a computer terminal in bad lighting (the glare of the monitor illuminates the scene).

Cast: Kate Hodge *(Annie Price)*; Michael Kelly *(Wilbert Thibodeaux)*; Susie Park *(Joss Nakano)*; Kim Murphy *(Sosh)*; Fabrizio Filippo *(Roland Travis)*; Esteban Powell *(Jargon)*; Jerry Hooten *(Romany Malco)*.

5293   *Leverage*. (Series; Drama; TNT; 2008–). Nate Ford is an insurance company investigator with an impressive record of recovery (reclaiming millions of dollars in stolen goods for his company). When Nate's son becomes ill and his company refuses to pay the medical bills (that cost his son's life), Nate quits in disgust and soon finds himself descending into alcoholism. He is literally saved by an aeronautics executive who hires him to recover an exclusive airplane design that was stolen by a rival company. To help him accomplish his goal are less than honorable friends he met while working at the insurance company: Alec Hardison, a specialist in Internet and computer fraud; Parker, an expert thief; Eliot Spencer, a retrieval specialist; and Sophie Devereaux, a grifter who is also a talented actress. Once accomplishing his mission Nate forms a unique organization — recover what has been stolen. Stories follow the team's case assignments as they incorporate their unique skills to return stolen objects to their rightful owners.

Cast: Timothy Hutton *(Nate Ford)*; Beth Riesgraf *(Parker)*; Aldis Hodge *(Alec Hardison)*; Christian Kame *(Eliot Spencer)*; Gina Bellman *(Sophie Devereaux)*.

5294   *Lewis and Clark*. (Series; Comedy; NBC; 1981-1982). Tired of working for his wife's father and commuting from his job in Manhattan to his home in Plainview, Long Island, Stewart Lewis purchases, sight unseen, the Nassau County Café, a Texas saloon, from an ad he sees on a train. With the hope of simplifying life for everyone concerned, Stewart uproots his family and moves to Luckenbach, Texas. Stories focus on Stewart's efforts to run his saloon and the misadventures of his family as they struggle to adjust to a life they do not particularly care for. Alicia is Stewart's wife and Kelly and Keith are their children. Roscoe Clark is Stewart's partner (hence the title); Wendy is the waitress; John, the bartender; Silas, the beer distributor; Lester, a bar regular; and Josie is Kelly's friend.

Cast: Gabriel Kaplan *(Stewart Lewis)*; Ilene Graff *(Alicia Lewis)*; Amy Linker *(Kelly Lewis)*; David Hollander *(Keith Lewis)*; Guich Koock *(Roscoe Clark)*; Wendy Holcombe *(Wendy)*; Michael McManus *(John)*; Clifton James *(Silas Jones)*; Aaron Fletcher *(Lester)*; Dana Laurita *(Josie)*.

5295   *Lewis Black's Root of All Evil*. (Series; Comedy; Comedy Central; 2008). A parody of the reality court programs wherein a judge (comedian Lewis Black) presides over cases involving celebrities and pop culture figures he deems as being "the root of all evil."

Host: Lewis Black. **Regulars:** Patton Oswalt, Greg Giraldo, Andrew Daly, Matt Price, Shaun Russell. **Music:** Stephen Phillips.

5296   *Lexx*. (Series; Science Fiction; Syfy; 2000–2002). The *Lexx* is a gigantic, black space ship shaped like a bug. It is from a world called the Light Universe, which is under the rule of the Divine Order (His Divine Shadow is the leader). The *Lexx* is captained by Stanley H. Tweedle, a cowardly security guard; Zev Bellringer, a beautiful love slave, and Kai, a dead assassin, are its crew. Assisting them as best he can is 790, a robot head who constantly professes his love for Kai. Stanley, Zev and Kai were the only survivors of a rebellion against

His Divine Shadow. They became the crew of the *Lexx* when Kai killed His Divine Shadow and Stanley stole the Light Hand Key that controls the ship. Zev, an escaped love slave, joined them.

The *Lexx* needs organic food to thrive (like remnants of stars and planets). It is extremely powerful and is designed to blow up planets — "That is what I do. I blow up planets." Stanley calls it "The Big Bug That Flies Around in the Sky." The Moth (red) is the *Lexx*'s scouting ship.

The *Lexx* is now in the Dark Universe, a cluster of strange planets that is apparently inhabited by evil beings. The experiences of Stanley, Zev and Kai are detailed as they explore strange new worlds.

Cast: Brian Downey *(Stanley H. Tweedle)*; Eva Haberman *(Zev Bellringer; 2000-2001)*; Xenia Seeberg *(Zev Bellringer; 2001-2002)*; Michael McManus *(Kai)*; Jeffrey Hirschfield *(Voice of Robot Head 790)*; Tom Gallant *(Voice of Lexx)*.

5297   *The Liar's Club*. (Series; Game; Syn.; 1969; 1976; 1988). Two players compete. A panel of four liras (guest celebrities) describe in detail the purpose of a real but unusual item. Three explanations are false; one relates the truth. The players must determine which celebrity told the truth. Each correct guess awards the player one point and the player with the highest score at the end of the game is the winner and receives $100.

Program Open: "Welcome to Today's edition of *The Liar's Club*. If you do not know what this object is or what it is used for, we'll settle back, the tall tales are about to begin. First we'd like you to welcome one of America's great story tellers and president of the Liar's Club, Rod Serling." Three versions appeared:

1. The Liar's Club (Syn., 1969). **Host:** Rod Serling. **Resident Liar:** Betty White.

2. The Liar's Club (Syn., 1976). **Host:** Bill Armstrong, Allen Ludden. **Regulars:** Betty White, Dody Goodman, Buddy Hackett, Joey Bishop, Larry Hovis, Dick Gautier.

3. The New Liar's Club (Syn., 1988). **Host:** Eric Boardman.

5298   *The Liberace Show*. (Series; Variety; NBC; Syn.; ABC; CBS; 1952–1969). Music with pianist Wladziu Valentino Liberace (known simply as Liberace).

1969 Program Open: "*The Liberace Show* starring Matt Monroe, Mary Hopkins, Lord Charles; with Richard Wattis and special guest star Eve Arden. All coming to you from London, England." Four versions appeared:

1. The Liberace Show (NBC, 1952). **Host:** Liberace. **Orchestra:** George Liberace.

2. The Liberace Show (Syn., 1953–55). **Host:** Liberace. **Orchestra:** George Liberace.

3. The Liberace Show (ABC, 1958–59). **Host:** Liberace. **Regulars:** Marilyn Lovell, Erin O'Brien, Dick Roman. **Announcer:** Steve Dunne. **Orchestra:** Gordon Robinson.

4. The Liberace Show (CBS, 1969). **Host:** Liberace. **Regulars:** Georgina Moon, Richard Wattis, The Irving Davies Dancers. **Orchestra:** Jack Parnell.

5299   *Liberty's Kids*. (Series; Cartoon; Syn.; 2002). The events leading up to the American Revolutionary War as seen through the eyes of children enlisted by Benjamin Franklin to record the events for his newspaper, *The Pennsylvania Gazette*. James Hiller is a young patriot and the leader of the group; Sarah Phillips is the daughter of an English general; Henri is a French orphan (and the comical aspect as he is forever looking for food). Together the children journey from colony to colony witnessing and reporting the events to Benjamin Franklin. Also known as *Liberty's Kids: Est. 1776*.

Voice Cast: Walter Cronkite *(Benjamin Franklin)*; Chris Lundquist *(James Hiller)*; Kathleen Barr *(Henri LeFevre)*; Reo Jones *(Sarah*

Phillips); Annette Bening (*Abigail Adams*); Warren Buffett (*James Madison*); Aaron Carter (*Joseph Plumb Martin*); Billy Crystal (*John Adams*); Michael Douglas (*Patrick Henry*).

5300   *Libertyville*. (Pilot; Comedy; Unaired; Produced for Lifetime in 2008). Susie is divorced (from Phil), the mother of a 22-year-old lazy daughter (Lorie) and fearful of returning to the dating scene. She lives with her cantankerous father (Henry), younger sister (Tiffany) and stories follow her efforts to cope with the situation that surrounds her.

Cast: Christine Ebersole (*Susie*); Rebecca Creskoff (*Lorie*); Geoff Pierson (*Phil*); Harve Presnell (*Henry*); Misti Traya (*Tiffany*).

5301   *The Lid's Off*. (Series; Interview; Syn.; 1969). Art Linkletter oversees a program of interviews with people from all walks of life.

5302   *Lidsville*. (Series; Adventure; ABC, 1971–1973; NBC, 1973-1974). Intrigued by a magician's performance and the wonders he draws from his hat (at a performance by Merlo the Magician at Six Flags Over Texas) a young boy named Mark (from Jackson City) remains behind as the theater empties. Alone, Mark picks up the magician's hat, which is on stage. The hat suddenly begins to grow larger. Unable to hold it any longer, Mark places it on the floor, where it grows to an enormous size. In an attempt to look inside, Mark climbs on the brim and loses his balance. He falls in and reappears in Lidsville, the Land of Living Hats. Mark is captured and imprisoned by the evil magician Whoo Doo, who believes he is a spy for the good hats. In his cell, Mark meets Weenie, a genie who is also a prisoner and Whoo Doo's slave because he possesses her magic ring. Offering to help her escape from Whoo Doo, and promising to take her back to America with him, Mark convinces Weenie to use her power to set him free. Spotting the magic ring on a table, Mark grabs it and now, in control of Weenie, commands her to take him to safety. Instantly they are transported to the village of the good hats. Gaining the assistance of the good hats, Mark and Weenie struggle to find the secret of the way back to his world. They are opposed by Whoo Doo, who seeks to regain his prisoner, his genie and the magic ring. Characters are the puppet creations of Sid and Marty Krofft.

Cast: Butch Patrick (*Mark*); Charles Nelson Reilly (*Who Doo*); Billie Hayes (*Weenie the Genie*), Sharon Baird, Joy Campbell, Jerry Marling, Angelo Rosetti, Van Snowden, Hommy Stewart, Felix Silla, Buddy Douglas, The Hermine Midgets, Lennie Weinrib, Joan Gerber, Walker Edmiston.

5303   *Lie Detector*. (Series; Reality; Syn; PAX; 1983; 2005). An accuser and an accused appear on stage to relate a real life story. But who is telling the truth and who is lying? A polygraph test is given to both parties after each tells their story. The results are related to the viewing audience (as well as the participants) and, based on the lie detector test results, the record is set straight. Two versions appeared:

1. *Lie Detector* (Syn., 1983). **Host:** F. Lee Bailey.
2. *Lie Detector* (PAX 2005). **Host:** Rolanda Watts.

5304   *Lie to Me*. (Series; Crime Drama; Fox; 2009–2011). Dr. Cal Lightman is a scientist who created the Deception Detection Division of the Department of Homeland Security. Cal is obsessed with truths. He has the ability to tell if a person is lying simply by observing facial features and body movements (a skill he learned by living with primitive African tribes for three years). When he felt his abilities would be better put to use helping corporations and law enforcement authorities, he quit Homeland Security and joined with fellow scientist Dr. Gillian Foster (a psychologist) to start the Lightman Group in Washington, D.C. Also a part of the team is investi-

gator Ria Torres, a former airline security guard whose perceptive skills impressed Cal and he hired her; and Eli Loker, Cal's research analyst.

To Cal and Gillian "the question is not if someone is lying, it's why." Because of Cal's unique abilities and the first impressions he gives people when he questions suspects, most people think he and Gillian are a carnival act. Stories follow Cal and his team as they use their rather unconventional methods to uncover the truth in criminal cases. Emily is Cal's teenage daughter (he is divorced).

Cast: Tim Roth (*Dr. Cal Lightman*); Kelli Williams (*Dr. Gillian Foster*); Monica Raymund (*Ria Torres*); Brendan Hines (*Eli Loker*); Hayley McFarland (*Emily Lightman*).

5305   *The Lieutenant*. (Series; Drama; NBC; 1963-1964). Camp Pendleton is a Marine base in Oceanside California. It is here that young men and women receive their military training and stories focus in particular on the personal and private lives of Lieutenants William Rice and Samwell Panosian. Raymond Rambridge is the base commander and Lily is his secretary. Jeff Alexander composed the theme, "The Lieutenant."

Cast: Gary Lockwood (*William Rice*); Robert Vaughn (*Raymond Rambridge*); Steve Franken (*Samwell Panosian*); Carmen Phillips (*Lily*); Don Penny (*Lieutenant Harris*); Chris Noel (*Various Roles*).

5306   *Life*. (Series; Crime Drama; NBC; 2007). Charlie Crews is a police detective who was framed for a double homicide and sentenced to life in prison (at the Pelican Bay Penitentiary). After 12 years he was freed when the case was reexamined and none of the physical evidence matched. Charlie was exonerated and given his life back (as well as a hefty and unspecified settlement check). Four months after his release, Charlie returns to the force (L.A.P.D.). Now, with a second chance at life, Charlie seeks to prevent what happened to him to happening to someone else.

Charlie was once a by-the-books cop. He is now quite unorthodox and what he learned on the inside gives him the edge on the outside (as he now looks at cases in a whole new light). Stories follow Charlie as he looks beyond the obvious facts to catch the guilty parties on the cases he investigates (stories also focus on Charlie as he attempts to solve his own dilemma—who framed him and why).

Dani Reese is Charlie's partner, who has been instructed by her superior (Lt. Karen Davis) to keep an eye on Charlie (in essence, she is responsible for him). Ted Early is a former CEO (with Alter Cliff Capital) who lives above Charlie's garage and is now Charlie's financial consultant; Constance Griffith is the attorney responsible for Charlie's freedom.

Cast: Damian Lewis (*Charlie Crews*); Sarah Shabi (*Dani Reese*); Robin Weigert (*Lt. Karen Davis*); Brooke Langton (*Constance Griffith*); Adam Arkin (*Ted Early*); Gabrielle Union (*Jane Seever*).

5307   *Life ... and Stuff*. (Series; Comedy; CBS; 1997). Ronnie and Rick have been married for ten years and are the parents of Shawn and Jerry. Ronnie is a housewife who fears Rick will leave her for a 17-year-old cheerleader; she also becomes upset if Rick looks at another woman's chest ("that means he's ignoring me"). Rick met Ronnie in college and began his career in advertising in Portland, Oregon; he is now a creative director but feels his career is unfulfilled, the kids don't appreciate him and he has a troubled marriage. His only pleasure is "my 70-inch projection screen TV with wraparound sound and satellite dish." Rick's dream of married life was like the family on *Leave It to Beaver* and he wonders why his married friends with children didn't talk him out of having children. The kids attend the Putnam (New Jersey) Pre-School.

Adding to Rick's misery is his brother Andy who has no goals, no plans, no money and is always having fun. He lives in the driveway in an old, beat-up Winnebago he calls Casa Del Andy. He calls Ronnie "Mrs. Bro." Jordan and Bernie are Rick's co-workers; Christine is Ronnie's friend

Cast: Pam Dawber (*Ronnie Boswell*); Rick Reynolds (*Rick Boswell*); Brandon Allen (*Shawn Boswell; pilot*); Kevin Keckeisen (*Shawn Boswell; series*); David Bowie (*Andy Boswell*); Anita Barone (*Jordan Emery*); Fred Applegate (*Bernie Skabinsky*); Andrea Martin (*Christine*); Nancy Linstrom (*Ilana Levine*).

5308   *The Life and Legend of Wyatt Earp.* (Series; Western; ABC; 1955–1961). The time is 1873. Wyatt Earp was born in Ohio and into a family of legal professionals; his father is a judge and his relatives are lawyers. Life as a lawyer or judge, however are not in Wyatt's future. He has a dream of operating a cattle ranch and began his career as a shotgun for Wells Fargo. He enjoys buffalo hunting and after one such trek, Wyatt stops off in the town of Ellsworth, Kansas, to meet with an old friend, Sheriff Whitney. Ellsworth is a ruthless town (run by Ben and Bill Thompson) and Whitney needs help. Wyatt, however, is not interested — until Whitney is shot by Bill Thompson. Angered, Wyatt pins on the Marshal's badge in an attempt to bring Bill to justice.

Wyatt is a radical peace officer. He establishes and expects his laws to be obeyed (like no guns in town) and never shoots to kill (he shoots to disable opponents). He has a special gun, the Buntline Special (a longer barrel for long distance shooting) that was given to him in admiration by Ned Buntline, a dime novelist.

When Wyatt feels he has established the peace in one town, he moves onto another (he was next Marshal of Wichita, Kansas, then Dodge City, Kansas, and finally Tombstone, Arizona). While Wyatt not only struggled to dispose of outlaws, he also had to contend with angry citizens who felt his harsh laws were unfair. "When I can wake up in the morning and find citizens not mad at me, that's the day I turn in my badge."

Wyatt Earp is the only regular character. Many recurring characters appeared, especially since there were four town settings. Principal recurring characters are Morgan and Virgil Earp (Wyatt's brothers), Bat Masterson and Doc Holliday (Wyatt's friends), Ben Thompson (the outlaw), Shotgun Gibbs (Wyatt's chief deputy (Tombstone), Marsh Murdock (editor of *The Eagle;* Wichita), Kate Holliday (Doc's daughter), Mayor John Clum (Tombstone); Nellie Cashman, owner of the Birdcage Saloon. The King's Men perform the theme, "The Legend of Wyatt Earp."

Cast: Hugh O'Brian (*Wyatt Earp*); Ross Elliott, John Anderson (*Virgil Earp*); Dirk London (*Morgan Earp*); Mason Alan Dinehart III (*Bat Masterson*); Morgan Woodward (*Shotgun Gibbs*); Douglas V. Fowley, Myron Healey (*Doc Holliday*); Lash La Rue, Steve Brodie (*John Behan*); Denver Pyle (*Ben Thompson*); Don Haggerty (*Marsh Murdock*); Stacy Harris (*John Clum*); Carol Stone (*Kate Holliday*); Randy Stuart (*Nellie Cashman*).

5309   *The Life and Times of Eddie Roberts.* (Series; Drama; Syn.; 1980). Events in the life of Eddie Roberts, an Anthropology Professor at Cranpool College in Anaheim, California. Eddie is married to Dolores and is the father of Chrissy.

Cast: Renny Temple (*Eddie Roberts*); Udana Power (*Dolores Roberts*); Allison Balson (*Chrissy Roberts*); Allen Case (*Harold Knitzer*); Anne O'Donnell (*Dr. Zindell*); Wendy Schaal (*Cynthia Lombocker*); Loyita Chapel (*Vivian Blankett*); Jon Lormer (*Professor Boggs*); Stephen Parr (*Prof. Tony Cranpool*); Daryl Roach (*Turner LaQuatro*); Maria O'Brien (*Chiquita Zamora*); Victoria Carroll (*Gertrude McQuillan*); Lenore Nemetz (*Gertrude McQuillan*); Joan Hotchkis (*Lydia Knitzer*); Billy Barty (*William Billy*).

5310   *The Life and Times of Grizzly Adams.* (Series; Ad-

venture; NBC; 1977–1978). Falsely accused of a crime he did not commit (blamed for a murder that occurred near his home) James Adams flees to the wilderness where, as mountain man Grizzly Adams, he becomes a friend to all living creatures. Stories concern his adventures on the wilderness of the 1850s. Based on the feature film of the same title.

Other regulars are Mad Jack, the series narrator and Grizzly's friend; Nakuma, Grizzly's Indian blood brother; Robbie Cartman, Grizzly's young friend. Grizzly has a pet bear named Ben; Number Seven is Mad Jack's mule.

Program Open: "They call me Mad Jack. And if there is anybody in these mountains that knows the real story of James Adams, that would be me. So I'm puttin' it down in writin' just the way it happened in the hopes of settin' the record straight. My friend Adams was accused of a crime he didn't commit. So he escaped into the mountains, leavin' behind the only life he ever knew. Now that wilderness out there ain't no place for a greenhorn and his chance of survivin' were mighty slim. It were no time at all before he was beaten down, ragged and nearly starved. It was about this time that he found a grizzly bear cub all alone and helpless. Adams knew that little critter couldn't survive without his help so he started right down that cliff, risking his own life to save him. Now that cub took to Adams right off — and that was when he discovered he had a special kind of way with animals; they just come up to him like he was a natural part of the woods. But that bear cub he was extra special. As he growed, he became the best friend Adams ever had and together they became a legend."

Cast: Dan Haggerty (*James "Grizzly" Adams*); Denver Pyle (*Mad Jack*); Don Shanks (*Nakuma*); John Bishop (*Robbie Cartman*).

5311   *The Life and Times of Juniper Lee.* (Series; Cartoon; Cartoon Network; 2005–2007). Orchid Bay City is a city of magical activity and inhabited by both good and evil monsters and demons. The human and magical worlds are separated by a magical barrier that prevents ordinary humans from seeing magic or the creatures related to it. Juniper Lee, an 11-year-old Chinese American girl has been ordained the new Te Xuan Ze, a girl who must maintain the balance between the two worlds. Juniper is magically enhanced, giving her abilities ordinary girls do not have. Stories follow Juniper as she struggles to do her job yet live the life of normal young girl. Jasmine Lee is Juniper's grandmother, and the former Te Xuan Ze; Ray Ray Lee is Juniper's eight-year-old brother; Dennis Lee is Juniper's 16-year-old brother; Monroe is the magical dog; Jody is Juniper's best friend.

Voice Cast: Lara Jill Miller (*Juniper "June" Lee*); Amy Hill (*Jasmine Lee*); Kath Soucie (*Ray Ray Lee*); Carlos Alazraqui (*Monroe*); Alexander Polinsky (*Dennis Lee*); Colleen O'Shaughnessy (*Jody Irwin*).

5312   *The Life and Times of Tim.* (Series; Cartoon; HBO; 2008). Tim is a young man who lives and works in New York City. He has a girlfriend (Amy) and very serious problems: he is self conscious and extremely prone to making the worst decisions each day. Stories, which are adult in nature, follow Tim as he struggles to get through the trying times of each day. Debbie, a prostitute, is Tim's friend; Stu is Tim's friend and co-worker.

Voice Cast: Steve Dildarian (*Tim*); Mary Jane Otto (*Amy*); Nick Kroll (*Stu*); Peter Giles (*Boss*); Edie McClurg (*Amy's grandmother*); Kari Wahlgren (*Amy's mother*).

5313   *The Life and Times of Vivienne Vyle.* (Series; Comedy; Sundance; 2008). A British produced spoof of daytime talk shows that focuses on the hectic on camera and behind-the-scenes life of Vivienne Vyle, the screaming, always harassed host of *The Vivienne Vyle Show*. Helena is her producer; Jared is her husband; Jonathan is her psychotherapist.

Cast: Jennifer Saunders (*Vivienne Vyle*); Miranda Richardson (*Helena de Wend*); Conleith Hill (*Jared*); Jason Watkins (*Dr. Jonathan Fowler*); Helen Griffin (*Carol*); Dave Lamb (*Des*).

5314   Life As We Know It. (Series; Drama; ABC; 2004). A small community in Seattle, Washington, is the setting where the experiences of three sex-on-the-mind high school students are seen: Jonathan Fields, an artistic student with a fascination for photography; Dino Whitman, the all-around athlete who fears revealing his sensitive nature; and Ben Conner, the brainy student who feels that no matter what he does he can never make his parents happy.

Cast: Chris Lowell (*Jonathan Fields*); Sean Farris (*Dino Whitman*); Jon Foster (*Ben Conner*); Lisa Darr (*Annie Whitman*); D.B. Sweeney (*Michael Whitman*); Kelly Osbourne (*Deborah*); Jessica Lucas (*Sue*); Marguerite Moreau (*Monica Young*); Missy Peregrym (*Jackie*); Busy Philipps (*Alex Morrill*).

5315   Life Begins at Eighty. (Series; Discussion; NBC; ABC; DuMont; 1950–1956). A panel of five senior citizens answer questions, either submitted by home viewers or presented by guests relating to the problems of life. Aired on NBC (Jan. 1 to Aug. 25, 1950); ABC (Oct. 3, 1950 to Mar. 10, 1952; July 31, 1955 to Feb. 25, 1956); and DuMont (Mar. 21, 1952 to July 24, 1955).

Host: Jack Barry.

5316   Life Goes On. (Series; Drama; ABC; 1989–1992). Glen Brook, Illinois, is the setting for a dramatic look at the lives of the Thatchers, a Catholic family of five: parents Libby and Drew, and their children, Paige, Becca and Corky. They have a dog named Arnold ("the semi-wonder dog") and live at 305 Woodridge Road. Drew originally worked for the Quentico Construction Company before beginning his own business, the Glen Brook Grill. Libby, a former singer and dancer (under the name Libby Dean) who gave up her career for marriage, now works as an account executive for the Berkson and Berkson Advertising Agency (Jerry Berkson is her boss). They became the parents of a fourth child (Nicholas James Thatcher) in the episode of May 5, 1991 ("Proms and Prams").

Paige is Drew's daughter from a first marriage to Katherine Henning. She loves to paint and first worked as a receptionist at the Matthews Animal Hospital. The original Paige (Monique Lanier) left home at the end of the first season. When Paige (Tracey Needham) returned in November 1990, she moved back home but seemed to lack direction. She worked at several temporary jobs, then enrolled in acting classes at Glen Brook Community College. Paige next worked as a waitress at the family diner, then as a cross worker (doing what is necessary, from picking up metal scraps to stacking pipes) at Stollmark Industries. Shortly after, Paige meets and falls in love with a roustabout sculptor named Michael Romanov. They marry and run off to Europe, but the marriage is short-lived. In the episode "Portrait of a Scandal" (Sept. 27, 1992), Paige leaves Michael ten weeks later and returns home when he chooses his work over her (he left her stranded in Bulgaria). Paige also loses her job at Stollmark but begins the Darlin Construction Company with a former co-worker named Artie.

Rebecca, nicknamed "Becca," is 15 years old and attends Marshall High School. She is a talented ballerina and hopeful writer who fears that her figure will never develop (in the opening theme, Becca looks sideways into a mirror and, referring to her small bust, remarks, "Come on, where are you guys already?"). She wrote for the *Underground Marshal*, the school's forbidden tabloid and had a relationship with Jesse McKenna, a boy who is HIV positive. Prior to Jesse, Becca dated Tyler Benchfield.

Maxene ("Maxie") Maxwell is Becca's best friend. She is physically more developed than Becca, but not as bright (she is somewhat flaky

and boy-crazy). Just the opposite is Rona Lieberman, a blonde bombshell who is the most beautiful girl at school — and the envy of both Becca and Maxie. Rona is an average student who seems to shun the friendship of other girls. She uses her beauty to become the best at everything.

Charles, nicknamed "Corky" and "The Cork," has Down syndrome. He first attended the Fowler Institution, then Marshall High School. Though older than other freshmen, Corky became "one of the guys," proving that despite a handicap, he can become a part of society and do what other kids can do — from playing drums to running for class president. He first worked at the family diner, then as an usher at the Glen Brook Theater. Like Paige, Corky impulsively married, but he is determined to make his marriage work. Amanda Swanson, a girl with Down syndrome, is Corky's wife. She is attending college, and they live on what Corky makes as an usher.

Angela ("Gina") Giordano, Libby's younger sister, was brought on to help Libby care for the family during her pregnancy (Nov. 25, 1990 to May 5, 1991). Gina is the mother of a pretty nine-year-old girl named Zoe and is separated from Zoey's father, Dennis Rydell, who deserted Gina when he learned she was pregnant. Gina is impressed by people who can cook; she ran an unnamed cheesecake business. After the birth of Libby's child, Gina moved out and returned to school.

Cast: Patti LuPone (*Libby Thatcher*); Bill Smitrovich (*Drew Thatcher*); Kellie Martin (*Becca Thatcher*); Monique Lanier, Tracey Needham (*Paige Thatcher*); Chris Burke (*Corky Thatcher*); Mary Page Keller (*Gina Giordano*); Leigh Ann Orsi (*Zoe Giodano*); Tanya Fenmore (*Maxene Maxwell*); Ray Buktenica (*Jerry Berkson*); Lisa Baines (*Katherine Henning*); Michele Matheson (*Rona Liberman*); Lance Guest (*Michael Romanov*); Chad Lowe (*Jesse McKenna*); Tommy Pruett (*Tyler Benchfield*); Andrea Friedman (*Amanda Swanson*); Drew Pillsbury (*Dennis Rydell*); Troy Evans (*Artie*).

5317   Life in Desire. (Pilot; Comedy; Unaired; Produced for Fox in 1990). Shortly after she is released from a psychiatric institution, a wealthy New York woman (Diana) decides to get away from the hustle and bustle of the city and find a simpler life. She moves to Desire, Louisiana, population 5,000, and the proposal was to relate her misadventures as she attempts to begin a new life in a town where the folks are sweet and the living is simple.

Cast: Kate Mulgrew (*Diana Summerfield*); William Daniels (*Beauford Braxton*); Lane Davies (*Buzz Braxton*); Nancy Lenehan (*Miss Penelope Levec*); Kelly Connell (*the Reverend Claude Hooper*); Sarah Abrell (*Taffy Hooper*).

5318   Life Is Wild. (Series; Drama; CW; 2007-2008). Danny is a widower with two children, Katie and Chase. Jo is a divorced mother of two children, Jesse and Mia. Danny is a respected Manhattan veterinarian; Jo is a much sought-after divorce lawyer. The two families have recently merged as a result of marriage but a "Brady Bunch" they are not. The kids have little in common. Katie, although a teenager, is mature beyond her years. She took over the household responsibilities after her mother died and is helping younger brother Chase deal with the loss. Jesse is rebellious and has been cutting school (he disapproves of the marriage); Mia seems to be in her own world and is totally absorbed with the New York Mets.

Realizing that his family is drifting apart, Danny hits on an idea to bring them closer together. He moves the family to the Blue Antelope, a run down lodge in South Africa when he learns there is an urgent need for veterinarians in Africa. Danny's late wife, Claire, grew up at the Blue Antelope, a once prestigious lodge that was run by her father, Art. Since Claire's death, Art has let the lodge fall into a state of disrepair. Now with his grandchildren by his side, Art's life has taken on a new meaning and now seeks to return the lodge to its former glory (with Jo assisting him). In the meantime, Danny finds his time taken up by a need that really exists; Jo has become a full time mother and the kids have to make a new life for themselves. Stories follow the adjustments the family makes as they realize South Africa is their new home. Tumelo is Danny's intern; Emily and Oliver Banks are the children of the owner of the rival Mara Lodge. Katie and Jesse attend the Peacan Wood International School.

Cast: D.W. Moffett *(Danny Clarke)*; Stephanie Niznik *(Jo Clarke)*; Leah Pipes *(Katie Clark)*; K'sun Ray *(Chase Clarke)*; Andrew St. John *(Jesse Weller)*; Mary Matilyn Mouser *(Mia Clarke)*; David Butler *(Art)*; Calvin Goldspink *(Oliver Banks)*; Atandwa Kani *(Tumelo)*; Precious Kofi *(Mbali)*; Tiffany Mulheron *(Emily Banks)*.

5319   *The Life of Riley.* (Pilot; Comedy; NBC; April 13 and 20, 1948). A two episode test (using different performers for the role of Chester A. Riley) for a possible series based on the radio program of the same title about Chester A. Riley, a good-natured, but misadventure-prone aircraft company riveter living in Los Angeles. Peg and Babs are Chester's wife and daughter; Jim and Honeybee Gillis are their neighbors.

Cast: Herb Vigran *(Chester A. Riley; first pilot)*; Buddy Grey *(Chester A. Riley; second pilot)*; Alice Drake *(Peg Riley)*; Arlene Becker *(Babs Riley)*; Lou Krugman *(Jim Gillis)*; Jo Gilbert *(Honeybee Gillis)*.

5320   *The Life of Riley.* (Series; Comedy; DuMont; 1949-1950). In 1932 in Brooklyn, New York, Chester A. Riley, a milkman, and Margaret "Peg" Barker marry. Several years later, after the birth of their daughter Barbara (called "Babs"), the family moves to California where Chester acquires a job as a riveter for Stevenson Aircraft and Associates in Los Angeles. It is here that they also acquire a house at 1311 Blue View Terrace. Although Chester earns only $59 a week, they manage to live comfortably and are soon blessed with a son, Chester Riley, Jr. (called "Junior"). From as early as he can remember, Chester has been plagued by bad luck. That bad luck has followed him to California and stories follow the events that occur as Chester attempts to overcome the situations that occur when his good intentions always backfire.

Jim Gillis (Chester's co-worker) and his wife, Olive (called "Honeybee") are their neighbors; Egbert is Jim's son (he and Junior attend John J. Boskowitz Junior High School; Babs attends North Hollywood High); Carl Stevenson is Chester's boss; Waldo Binny is Chester's friend; Digby "Digger" O'Dell is Chester's pal, "the friendly undertaker"; Millie is Carl's secretary; Simon is Babs' boyfriend.

Cast: Jackie Gleason *(Chester A. Riley)*; Rosemary DeCamp *(Peg Riley)*; Gloria Winters *(Barbara "Babs" Riley)*; Lanny Rees *(Chester Riley, Jr.)*; Sid Tomack *(Jim Gillis)*; Maxine Semon *(Olive "Honeybee" Gillis)*; George McDonald *(Egbert Gillis)*; John Brown *(Digby "Digger" O'Dell)*; Bob Jellison *(Waldo Binny)*; Bill Green *(Carl Stevenson)*; Emory Parnell *(Carl Stevenson; later)*; Mary Treen *(Millie)*; Jimmy Lydon *(Simon Vanderhopper)*. **Announcer:** James Wallington.

5321   *The Life of Riley.* (Series; Comedy; NBC; 1953–1958). A revised version of the prior title that continues to follow events in the life of Chester A. Riley, a good-natured (but trouble-prone) riveter for the Cunningham Aircraft Company in Los Angeles. Chester is married to Peg and they are the parents of Barbara (called Babs) and Chester Jr. (called Junior); they first live at 1313 Blue View Terrace; then 5412 Grove Street and finally 3412 Del Mar Vista. In later episodes, after Babs marries her boyfriend, Don Marshall, they reside at 1451 Blue View Terrace, Apartment 3. Jim and his wife Olive (called "Honeybee") Gillis are the Riley's neighbors; they are the parents of Egbert. Waldo Binny and Otto Schmidlap are Chester's friends. Millicent is Waldo's girlfriend. Calvin and his wife, Belle Dudley are Chester's neighbors in later episodes. Mr. Cunningham is Chester's

boss; Hank Hawkins is the company foreman (Hank is married to Lorna). Cissy Riley is Chester's sister; Annie Riley is Chester's niece; Moose Larkin is Junior's friend. Mitzi Carter is the aircraft company coffee shop waitress; Alvin Winkley is the Riley's landlord (second house); Arnold Willis is the paperboy. Roger Ganaway is Chester's friend; Constance is Roger's wife. Bobbie is Junior's girlfriend; Mrs. Hayes is Babs' baby nurse.

Program Open: "William Bendix in *The Life of Riley* ... with Marjorie Reynolds a Peg, Tom D'Andrea as Gillis ... Lugene Sanders as Babs and Wesley Morgan as Junior."

Cast: William Bendix *(Chester A. Riley)*; Marjorie Reynolds *(Peg Riley)*; Lugene Sanders *(Barbara "Babs" Riley)*; Wesley Morgan *(Chester Riley, Jr.)*; Tom D'Andrea *(Jim Gillis)*; Veda Ann Borg, Marie Brown, Gloria Blondell *(Olive "Honeybee" Gillis)*; Gregory Marshall *(Egbert Gillis)*; Martin Milner *(Don Marshall)*; Melodie Chaney *(Babs and Don's baby)*; Sterling Holloway *(Waldo Binny)*; Stanja Lowe *(Millicent)*; Henry Kulky *(Otto Schmidlap)*; George O'Hanlon *(Calvin Dudley)*; Florence Sundstrom *(Belle Dudley)*; Larraine Bendix *(Annie Riley)*; Mary Jane Croft *(Cissy Riley)*; James Gleason, James Gavin *(Pa Riley)*; Sarah Pudden *(Ma Riley)*; Douglas Dumbrille *(Mr. Cunningham)*; Emory Parnell *(Hank Hawkins)*; Isabel Withers *(Lorna Hawkins)*; Tamara Cooper *(Cunningham's secretary)*; Denny Miller *(Moose Larkin)*; Joe Conley *(Arnold Willis)*; Arthur Shields *(Alvin Winkley)*; Jack Kirkwood *(Peg's Uncle Bixby)*; Reta Shaw *(Mrs. Hayes)*; Victoria King *(Mitzi Carter)*; Carolyn Kearney *(Bobbie)*; Steve Pendleton *(Roger Ganaway)*; Pamela Britton, Sheila Bromley *(Constance Ganaway)*; Bea Benaderet *(Honeybee's mother)*.

5322   *The Life of Vernon Hathaway.* (Pilot; Comedy; NBC; Nov. 9, 1955). A Walter Mitty type of proposal about Vernon Hathaway, a meek watch repairman who daydreams himself into exciting adventures. Aired as a segment of *Screen Director's Playhouse.*

Cast: Alan Young *(Vernon Hathaway)*.

5323   *Life on a Stick.* (Series; Comedy; Fox; 2005). Yippie Hot Dogs is a food court in a Seattle mall. It is here that Laz, his stepsister, Molly, and their friends Fred and Lily work.

Rick is Laz's father and Michelle is Molly's mother. Each was divorced and married eight years ago. Gus is their son together.

Rick and Molly appear as not so typical parents (superficial) and are very lax when it comes to disciplining their children, especially Molly, who has a severe attitude problem. Laz is apparently the only one who can deal with 16-year-old Molly. Molly is extremely jealous of her "totally hot Mom." She feels she isn't pretty and gets angry if someone compliments her on her looks. Laz is a not-easily-motivated 18-year-old who has made a deal with his parents: socialize Molly in return for free room and board. Stories relate events in the lives of Laz, Molly, Fred and Lily as they create havoc at Yippie Hot Dogs and cause numerous problems for their uptight, always-yelling, frantic boss, Mr. Hunt.

Cast: Amy Yasbeck *(Michele Lackerson)*; Matthew Glave *(Rick Lackerson)*; Saige Thompson *(Molly Lackerson)*; Zachary Knighton *(Laz Lackerson)*; Rachelle LaFevre *(Lily)*; Charlie Finn *(Fred)*; Kurt Doss *(Gus Lackerson)*; Maz Jobrani *(Mr. Hunt)*.

5324   *Life on Mars.* (Series; Crime Drama; ABC; 2008). "I had an accident and woke up 35 years in the past. Now that either makes me a time traveler, a lunatic or I'm lying in a hospital bed in 2008 and none of this is real." Sam Tyler, a detective with the N.Y.P.D. 125th Precinct (called 1-2-5) in 2008 who is now a detective with the 1-2-5 in 1973.

In 2008 Sam is romantically involved with fellow detective Maya Daniels. While investigating a case involving a kidnapper-murder, Maya appears to have been kidnapped and Sam is hit by a car. Prior to the accident, Sam was listening to the song "Life on Mars." The viewer sees a brief dream-like sequence as Sam awakens to find himself in 1973 — as a member of the 1-2-5 in Manhattan (he is believed to be a transfer from a precinct in Upstate New York). His identification also reflects 1973 and a case that is identical to the one he is working on in 2008. Sam believes that if he solves this case he can save Maya and return to 2008 (while Sam does solve the case, he is not transported back to his time).

Sam quickly adjusts to the fact that he is where he is. At the precinct Sam meets his team: Gene Hunt, his superior, a rather uncouth lieutenant who believes in rough tactics; Annie Norris, a police woman (at a time when such personnel were part of the Police Woman's Bureau and not permitted to assist on cases as men do). She has a psychology degree from Fordham University in the Bronx and lives with her parents in Queens. She is the only one who is sympathetic to Sam's plight. Chris Skelton is the rookie detective; Ray Carling is the tough, sexist detective with a chip on his shoulder.

At the end of the first episode, Sam hears Maya's voice over his car radio telling him that she is okay and asking him to come home. But how? Stories follow Sam as he seeks that answer and his efforts to incorporate the technologies of 2008 police science in an era where such things as forensic science and finger print analysis and even computers were a far-fetched dream. Based on the British series (see next title).

The final episode explains — in a most unexpected way — Sam's predicament. As Sam finds the words of his father coming true ("Whatever strange place you land on, make that home") and that he is in love with Annie (promoted to detective) the series dissolves to the year 2035. Here astronauts aboard a U.S. mission to Mars (the Aries Project) are just awakening from hibernation and from a neural stimulation program. Sam's program had been that of a detective in the year 2008. But a glitch in the system caused Sam to go back to 1973 — as a cop with the ability of 2008 intact. His fellow astronauts were his fellow cops — and, as the Mars probe lands, the astronauts prepare to explore the planet. Sam is the first one to set foot on Mars.

Cast: Jason O'Mara (*Sam Tyler*); Gretchen Mol (*Anne Norris*); Harvey Keitel (*Gene Hunt*); Michael Imperioli (*Ray Carling*); Jonathan Murray (*Chris Skelton*); Lisa Bonet (*Maya Daniels*).

5325   *Life on Mars.* (Series; Crime Drama; BBC America; 2008). The British series on which the American series of the same title is based (see prior title). Sam Tyler is a Detective Chief Inspector with the Manchester Police Department in England. One day, during a case investigation, Sam is hit by a car and awakens in 1973 as a member of the Manchester and Salford Police Department as a Detective Inspector (his sudden presence is explained as being a transfer from another precinct). Sam quickly adjusts to the fact that he is no longer in 2006 and stories follow his efforts to follow the police procedures of the 1970s world but supplement those techniques with those he learned in the 21st century. Gene Hunt is his superior, an old fashioned cop who will break the rules to get results. Ray Carling, Chris Skelton and Annie Cartwright (also Sam's romantic interest) are fellow officers. The final episode shows Sam awakening from a coma. Believing his experiences in 1973 were real, but now feeling out of place in 2007, he climbs to the top of the police station and jumps off. He appears to return to the past, but the episode is confusing as it can also indicate that Sam may not have returned to the present. Overall, it really doesn't tell the viewer if Sam was insane, in a coma and if he really traveled back in time.

Cast: John Simm (*Sam Tyler*); Philip Glinster (*Gene Hunt*); Liz White (*Annie Cartwright*); Dean Andrews (*Ray Carling*); Marshall Lancaster (*Chris Skelton*).

5326   *Life on the Flipside.* (Pilot; Comedy; NBC; Aug. 29,

1988). When Elroy "Tripper" Day, a rock legend who has been on the road most of his life, learns that his wife has left their three children (Bea, Sonny and Shea) to fend for themselves, he decides to return home and raise the kids himself. The proposal was to relate Tripper's efforts to adjust to a life he has never known and, with the help of his friend, Jonesy, raise three children.

Cast: Trevor Eve (*Elroy "Tripper" Day*); Traci Lin (*Bea Day*); Frank Whaley (*Sonny Day*); Jarrett Lennon (*Shea Day*); Dennis Burkley (*Jonesy*).

5327   *Life on Top.* (Series; Erotica; Cinemax; 2009-2010). A graphic look at the sexual lives of four women living in New York City: Sophie, Bella Marie, Maya and Cassia. Sophie is an ambitious but naïve financial analyst hoping to make her mark in Manhattan; Bella Marie is Sophie's older sister, a gorgeous erotic model who is currently experiencing all the excitement of being on top. She fears as she ages she will fall from those heights. Maya is Sophie's friend (college roommate) who hopes to begin a career as a kick boxer. Cassia is Bella's best friend, a chef at Les Deices Restaurant who one day dreams of owing her own eatery.

Cast: Mary LeGault (*Sophie*); Heather Vandeven (*Bella Marie*); Krista Ayne (*Maya*); Mia Presley (*Cassia*); Clayton Cannon (*D*); Adrian Quinonez (*Andre*); Brandin Rackley (*Regina*); Daniel Messier (*Avi*); Tim Felingham (*Tai*); Danny Crawford (*Vincent*).

5328   *Life Stories.* (Series; Anthology; NBC; 1990-1991). Realistic but fictionalized accounts of the medical problems and daily crisis that people face and how they seek help to overcome their situations — all of which are presented from the patient's viewpoint. "We are a mystery to ourselves and nowhere more so than in our bodies."

Narrator: Robert Prosky.

5329   *Life Unexpected.* (Series; Drama; CW; 2010-2011). It is 1994 and Catherine "Cate" Cassidy and Nathaniel (called Nate) "Baze" Bazile are sophomores at West Mount High School in Portland, Oregon. They have been dating and on the night of the prom become intimate. Sixteen-year-old Cate becomes pregnant and Nate assumes that she will take care of it (have an abortion). Cate, however, does not have an abortion and gives birth to a girl. Unable to care for her, she turns the infant over to a social worker to be put up for adoption. Cate apparently managed to conceal her pregnancy from Nate, her parents and even fellow classmates — as no one knew or even suspected she was pregnant. Unknown to Cate, her baby, named Lux by the social worker, was born with a hole in her heart. Several surgeries were required and Lux was three years old before she was cured. But apparently no one wanted to adopt a three-year-old girl (only babies) and Lux grew up in the foster care system. After almost 16 years and living with seven different foster families, Lux Foster (Lux took the last name of Foster "because I grew up in foster care") decides to take control of her life and declare emancipation. However, to do so, she needs the signatures of her birth parents. For reasons that do not make sense (it was Cate who turned over the baby), only Nate was listed on Lux's case file. Seeing this file, Lux acquires Nate's address and sets out to fulfill her quest. Nate still lives at that address, in an apartment over the bar (The Open Bar) he inherited from his father. A shocked Nate readily accepts Lux as his daughter and signs her document. He tells Lux that her mother is Cate Cassidy, now the co-host of the radio talk show *Morning Madness* on K-100 FM (a show, by coincidence, Lux has always listened to).

Nate's call to Cate is anything but appreciated by Cate — until Nate brings Lux to meet Cate face-to-face. Cate is pleasantly surprised to see Lux and she too signs her document. A judge, however, refuses to grant Lux her request as she has no visible means of support and is ordered to the joint custody of Nate and Cate. Not wanting to see Lux return to foster care, Cate takes her in to become the mother she never was before. Nate feels he should also be a part of Lux's life and both are now forced to deal with one another now that Lux has become a part of their lives. The surprisingly addictive series relates events in the lives of three people as they attempt to become a family that was never meant to be. Ryan Thomas is Cate's co-host (and fiancé); Tracy is Nate's girlfriend; Math is Nate's high school buddy and employee at the bar; Abby is Cate's sister.

Cast: Shiri Appleby (*Cate Cassidy*); Kristoffer Polaha (*Nate Bazile*); Brittany Robertson (*Lux*); Kerr Smith (*Ryan Thomas*); Brittney Irvin (*Tracy*); Justin Basis (*Math*); Alexandra Breckenridge (*Abby Cassidy*); Susan Hogan (*Ellen Bazile, Nate's mother*); Robin Thomas (*Nate's father*).

5330 *Life with Bonnie.* (Series; Comedy; ABC; 2002–2004). Events in the life of Bonnie Molloy, the host of *Morning Chicago*, a daily TV talk show. Bonnie is married to Mark, a doctor, and the mother of Samantha and Charlie.

Bonnie worked as a waitress and Mark was an intern when they first met. After marrying, and when Mark became a doctor, they moved into their comfortable home at 1226 Burton Way. Bonnie has what Mark calls "lateness disease" (as she is late for everything). Bonnie is also a very caring person and often gets involved in the problems of her guests — both on the air and off. Bonnie is never organized and pure dumb luck always seems to get her out of an embarrassing situation. Other regulars are Holly, Bonnie's best friend, her makeup artist; Tony, Bonnie's piano player; Gloria, the Molloy's housekeeper; and David, Bonnie's producer.

Second season episodes dropped the character of Samantha (without any reason given as to why Bonnie and Mark now have only one child) and added the character of Frankie as a friend for Charlie. The change was a mistake as Bonnie and Samantha's relationship was an integral part of the first season episodes. Mark works at Northwestern Memorial Hospital; Bonnie did a TV commercial for Stevenson Soup for the Benson and Stillman Ad Agency.

Cast: Bonnie Hunt (*Bonnie Molloy*); Mark Derwin (*Mark Molloy*); Samantha Browne-Walters (*Samantha Molloy*); Charlie Stewart (*Charlie Molloy*); Holly Wortell (*Holly Brandis*); Anthony Russell (*Tony Russo*); David Alan Grier (*David Bellows*); Frankie Ryan Manriquez (*Frankie Tenucci*); Marianne Muellerleile (*Gloria*).

5331 *Life with Derek.* (Series; Comedy; Disney; 2005). A blended family comedy wherein Nora MacDonald, a single mother with two daughters, Casey and Lizzie, and George Venturi, a single father with three children (Derek, Marti and Edwin) marry and merge their two families. Derek and Casey are each 15 years old and each was the eldest sibling in their prior families. Each is an individualist and now that privilege has since disappeared. They must now live together, fit into each other's life and battle each other for control of the house, their school and literally their own space as they struggle to accept each other — but still try to come out on top when events place them in the same situation at the same time. Stories also focus on the activities of Lizzie, Marti and Edwin — who manage quit well to find mischief on their own away from Casey and Derek's constant feuding.

Cast: Michael Seater (*Derek Venturi*); Ashley Leggat (*Casey MacDonald*); Joy Tanner (*Nora MacDonald*); John Ralston (*George Venturi*); Ariel Waller (*Marti Venturi*); Daniel Magder (*Edwin Venturi*); Jordan Todosey (*Lizzie MacDonald*); Arnold Pinnock (*Paul*); Robbie Amell (*Max*); Shadia Simmons (*Emily*); Kit Weyman (*Sam*).

5332 *Life with Elizabeth.* (Series; Comedy; Syn.; 1953–1957). Elizabeth and Alvin White are newlyweds living in San Francisco. Elizabeth, a bit scatterbrained, enjoys being a housewife while Alvin seems content with his job at Fuddy, Inc., a machine company owned by a Mr. Fuddy. Stormy, a St. Bernard, also lives with them and stories (two-to-three vignettes per episode) are introduced by Jack Narz, an announcer who sets up the plot and invites viewers to watch what happens when Elizabeth and Alvin set out to do something. Chloe is their neighbor.

Cast: Betty White (*Elizabeth White*); Del Moore (*Alvin White*); Lois Bridge (*Chloe*); Ray Erlenborn (*Mr. Fuddy*). **Various Roles:** Frank DeVol, Charlotte Lawrence, Joe Crunston. **Host-Announcer:** Jack Narz.

5333 *Life with Father.* (Series; Comedy; CBS; 1953–1955). New York City at the turn of the 20th century is the setting. In Manhattan at West 48th Street is a quaint little house that is home to the Day family: Clarence Sr., a banker; Vinnie, his wife; and their children Clarence Jr., Whitney, John and Harlan. The early 1900s is a time of great change and many new innovations are changing the way people live. Clarence Day, Sr., is a stubborn man who refuses to accept the progress of a changing world (what was good enough for his father is good enough for him). His family totally disagree, but the times being what they were, live under his rule. Stories follow the daily events in the lives of the Days as Clarence fiercely struggles to hold onto his beliefs despite his family's objections and efforts to change his way of thinking. The Day's maid, Nora, is also known to be Kathleen. Based on the feature film of the same title.

Cast: Leon Ames (*Clarence Day, Sr.*); Lurene Tuttle (*Vinnie Day*); Ralph Reed, Steve Terrell (*Clarence Day, Jr.*); Ronald Keith, B.G. Norman, Fred Ridgeway (*Whitney Day*); Freddie Leiston, Malcolm Cassell (*John Day*); Harvey Grant (*Harlan Day*); Marion Ross (*Nora*). **Announcer:** Bob Lemond.

5334 *Life with Linkletter.* (Series; Variety; ABC; 1950–1952). A casual program of music, interviews and audience participation segments for prizes. A later version appeared on NBC from 1969-1970 with Art Linkletter and his son, Jack Linkletter as the hosts.

Host: Art Linkletter. **Announcer:** Jack Slattery. **Music:** The Muzzy Marcellino Trio.

5335 *Life with Louie.* (Series; Cartoon; Fox; 1994-1995). Incidents in the life of comedian Louie Anderson as a young boy in his hometown of Wisconsin. Louie is one of ten children and no matter what he does or where he goes, he seems to attract trouble. His mother is a sweet, warm-hearted person; his father is loud, obnoxious and a bit eccentric (as he is obsessed with solving problems based on his experiences as a soldier during World War II). Louie Anderson appears as the host in live action segments and his recollections about his childhood are seen in animation. Tommy is Louie's younger brother; Jeannie and Michael are his friends.

Voice Cast: Louie Anderson (*Louie Anderson/Dad Anderson*); Edie McClurg (*Mom Anderson*); Milo Hughes (*Tommy Anderson*); Debi Derryberry (*Jeannie Harper*); Justin Shenkarow (*Michael Grunewald*); Mary Wickes (*Grandma*).

5336 *Life with Lucy.* (Series; Comedy; ABC; 1986). Lucille Barker and Curtis MacGibbon are the elderly co-owners of the M&B Hardware store at 1027 Hill Street in Pasadena, California. Lucy, a widow, lives with her married daughter, Margo MacGibbon, Margo's husband, Ted and their children, Becky and Kevin.

Lucy's late husband was named Sam and her maiden name is Everett. She is a health food nut and financially well off. Curtis was on vacation in Hawaii when Lucy took half interest in the business (Sam and Curtis were partners). When Curtis discovers what Lucy has done — and that she has no business sense (especially with hardware) he suddenly finds his life plagued by Lucy as she attempts to help him run the store. Curtis also feels that his grandchildren are at risk and to safeguard them, he moves into the same house (Ted is his son). Stories follow Curtis as he struggles to cope with Lucy's endless harebrained antics. Eydie Gorme sings the theme, "Life with Lucy."

Cast: Lucille Ball *(Lucille Barker)*; Gale Gordon *(Curtis MacGibbon)*; Ann Dusenberry *(Margo MacGibbon)*; Larry Anderson *(Ted MacGibbon)*; Jenny Lewis *(Becky MacGibbon)*; Philip J. Amelio *(Kevin MacGibbon)*; Donovan Scott *(Leonard Stoner)*.

5337   *Life with Luigi.* (Series; Comedy; CBS; 1952-1953). With a devious plan to get his overweight daughter, Rosa, married, a man named Pasquale arranges for his friend, Luigi Basco, to join him in Chicago's Little Italy. Luigi arrives in the United States (at Ellis Island) from Italy on September 27, 1947 with three dollars to his name. Pasquale sets Luigi up in an antique business, and the struggles of an immigrant to adjust to the American way of life — and escape Pasquale's endless matchmaking attempts — are the focal point of stories. In these early episodes, stories begin and end with Luigi reading a letter he wrote to his "Mama Basco" in Italy.

Pasquale, who calls Luigi "Cabbage Puss" and "Little Banana Nose," runs Pasquale's Spaghetti Palace at 19 North Halsted Street. Luigi runs a shop called Luigi Basco, Antiques at 21 North Halsted Street (he lives in the back of the store). His most cherished possession is a bust of George Washington that was made in 1833). While Luigi is grateful to Pasquale for bringing him to Chicago, he refuses to marry the 250 pound Rosa ("I would rather finda my owna girl"). Despite Luigi's attitude toward Rosa, Pasquale still looks after Luigi ("like Mama tiger help little baby deer") and hopes one day to change Luigi's mind.

Miss Spaulding is Luigi's night school English teacher; Schultz is the owner of Schultz's Delicatessen; Olson and Horowitz are Luigi's classmates. Joe is Pasquale's deadbeat customer.

In 1953 the series returned with a new cast and a slightly revised format. Luigi Basco is now working for Pasquale as a waiter in Pasquale's Spaghetti Palace. Luigi still lives at 21 North Halsted Street and Pasquale's efforts to marry Rosa are still featured. Mary Shipp reprised her role as Miss Spaulding. Based on the radio series of the same title.

Cast: J. Carrol Naish *(Luigi Basco, 1952)*; Vito Scotti *(Luigi Basco, 1953)*; Alan Reed *(Pasquale, 1952)*; Thomas Gomez *(Pasquale, 1953)*; Jody Gilbert *(Rosa, 1952)*; Muriel Landers *(Rosa, 1953)*; Mary Shipp *(Miss Spaulding)*; Sig Rumin *(Schultz)*; Joe Forte *(Horwitz)*; Ken Peters *(Olson)*.

5338   *Life with Roger.* (Series; Comedy; WB; 1996-1997). One day while driving across a bridge, Jason Clark's car stalls. While attempting to fix it, James hears a voice telling him — "Fix the fuel line." Jason looks up and sees a man (Roger Hoyt) standing on the edge of the bridge and contemplating jumping off (something he does two or three times a week to clear his head). Roger is carefree, jobless and homeless. He also finds a friend in Jason and attaches himself to him. Unfortunately, Jason does not want Roger as a friend but finds he can't get rid of him. He also finds himself doing something he would later regret — inviting Roger to become his roommate. Stories, set in Manhattan, follow Jason's efforts to put up with Roger and his carefree ways while attempting to live his own responsible life.

Other regulars are Lanie Clark, Jason's sister; and Myra, Jason's girlfriend. Roger's favorite hangout is Duffy's Bar.

Cast: Mike O'Malley *(Roger Hoyt)*; Maurice Godin *(Jason Clark)*; Hallie Todd *(Lanie Clark)*; Meredith Lynn Scott *(Myra)*.

5339   *Life with Snarky Parker.* (Series; Children; CBS; 1950).

A marionette adventure about Snarky Parker, a deputy sheriff in the town of Hot Rock, as he attempts to maintain law and order. Blackie McGoo is the outlaw; Cuda Barra is the sultry siren; Heathcliff is Snarky's horse; Miss Butterball is the schoolmarm; Slugger is the Hot Rock Café piano player; Noose Nolan is a reformed but evil desperado; Fluffy Webster is Noose's partner.

Voices-Puppeteers: Bil Baird, Cora Baird.

5340   *Life with the Erwins.* (Series; Comedy; ABC; 1950–1955). The alternate title for *Trouble with Father.* See this title for information.

5341   *Life with Virginia.* (Pilot; Comedy; CBS; Sept. 18, 1962). Virginia Carol appears to be the typical American teenage girl. She is pretty and energetic but possesses an uncanny knack for trying to resolve other people's problems. The proposal was to follow Virginia as she tries to mend the problems she created while minding someone else's business. Other regulars are Agnes and Harold, Virginia's parents; Joan, Virginia's sister; and Maggie, the housekeeper.

Cast: Candy Moore *(Virginia Carol)*; Margaret Hayes *(Agnes Carol)*; Karl Swenson *(Harold Carol)*; Roberta Shore *(Joan Carol)*; Margaret Hamilton *(Maggie)*.

5342   *Life's Work.* (Series; Comedy; ABC; 1996-1997). Lisa Ann Hunter is married to Kevin and the mother of two children: Tess and infant Griffin. Lisa Ann is also a working mother and an assistant state's attorney in Baltimore (Kevin works as a basketball coach). Stories follow Lisa Ann as she struggles to juggle her job as an attorney with the responsibilities of running a house and raising two kids.

Cast: Lisa Ann Walter *(Lisa Ann Hunter)*; Michael O'Keefe *(Kevin Hunter)*; Alexa Vega *(Tess Hunter)*; Cameron and Lucas Weibel *(Griffin Hunter)*; Lightfield Lewis *(Matt Youngster)*; Larry Miller *(Jerome Nash)*; Molly Hagan *(Dee Dee Lucas)*.

5343   *Lifestyles of the Rich and Famous.* (Series; Reality Syn.; 1984). The private and personal lives of famous celebrities and people of great wealth.

Host: Robin Leach. **Music:** David Dutcher.

5344   *Lightning Force.* (Series; Adventure; Syn.; 1991). An abandoned shipping yard in the Canadian Northwest is the secret headquarters for an elite intelligence unit called the Lightning Force. It was organized by Mike Rodney (Michael A. Jackson) for the International Organization for Anti-Terrorism. Mike assembled the best of the collective strike forces to help the FBI and CIA battle the growing problem of terrorism. (Mike was killed during the first assignment; the strike force used Mike's nickname of "Lightning" as their official name.)

Matthew ("Matt") Coltrane is a lieutenant in the U.S. Army and now heads the team. He is nicknamed "Trane" and is a very private person (nothing is known about him, other than that he was in the Intelligence Division).

Jo Marie Jacquard was an agent with the French Security Service. She is a combat pilot, computer expert and selective terminator. She is a genius at unscrambling codes and is known to get even with anyone who crosses her (for example, she killed the man who betrayed her father).

Winston Churchill Staples was a lieutenant with the Canadian Forces, Seventh Field Regiment. He is a trained engineer and an expert in demolition. He is the youngest member of the group and the most impetuous.

Sieb Abdul Rahmad is a colonel in the Egyptian Army. He is an expert in operations and intelligence and is also a language specialist.

Cast: Wings Hauser (*Matt Coltrane*); Guylaine St. Onge (*Jo Marie Jacquard*); David Stratton (*Winston Churchill Staples*); Marc Gomes (*Siek Abdul Rahmad*).

5345   *Lights, Camera, Action!* (Series; Variety; NBC; 1950). Performances by promising but undiscovered talent (mostly singers and dancers).
Host: Walter Woolf King.

5346   *Light's Out.* (Pilot; Anthology; NBC; June 30, 1946). Suspense story proposal based on the radio program of the same title. The initial presentation, "First Person Singular," tells of a man (voice of Carl Frank) who resolves the problem of a constantly nagging wife (Mary Wesley) by killing her. The camera enacted the part of the murderer and the viewer saw everything through the murderer's eyes.

5347   *Light's Out.* (Series; Anthology; NBC; 1949–1952). A live program of mystery, suspense and supernatural-based stories adapted from the radio series of the same title.
Typical Opening: (Announcer) "Admiral electric ranges with Flexo Heat and Admiral radio phonographs present *Lights Out.*" The host would then appear: "Hello, tonight's visit into the unknown is called 'A Love Came to Professor Gilder.' Each week on *Lights Out* we ask you to walk with us through the unknown realm of the supernatural. And now, so we won't interrupt tonight's program for commercial, here is our warning: beware the unknown." (Announcer): "Yes, beware the unknown, especially if you're in the market for a new television set...." The host would return after the commercial: "Professor Gilder is waiting to begin tonight's study in terror. Are you? Very well then—*Lights Out!*"
Host: Jack LaRue (*1949-50*); Frank Gallop (*1950–52*).

5348   *Light's Out.* (Pilot; Anthology; NBC; Jan. 15, 1972). Mystery and suspense presentations with a twist ending. In the pilot, "When Widows Weep," Joan Hackett plays a doll maker whose creations trigger a series of bizarre deaths. Herbert Brodkin is the producer.

5349   *Like Family.* (Series; Comedy; WB; 2003-2004). Maddie and Tanya have been friends since childhood. Maddie is white, divorced and the mother of a mischievous son (Keith). She works as the regional director for Windsor and Johnson Consultants in Manhattan. Tanya is black, married to Ed and the mother of Danika and Bobby. Ed and Tanya have been married for 17 years and Ed owns his own car washing business in New Jersey. Tanya was a lawyer who quit to raise a family.

While life went smoothly for Tanya, Maddie had a difficult time. She was living in New York when her husband deserted her and Keith was on the road to disaster. Tanya and Ed are Keith's godparents. With an arrangement with Tanya and Ed, Maddie and Keith move in with Tanya and her family where Maddie hopes Ed can straighten Keith out and lead him on the right path. Stories relate the efforts of the two families to live together. Also helping with Keith is Eugene Ward, Ed's father, a young-at-heart senior citizen who considers Keith "The white grandson I never wanted but got anyway."

Ed is a stern father; Tanya is bossy; together they help turn Keith's life around. Tanya is also opinionated and not only has a vision for her life, but everyone else's. She feels she has to be right about everything. Ed's business has been called Dine and Shine Bar-B-Q (it is a combination car wash and diner) and Ward's Hand Wash.

Danika is Tanya's oldest child. She is beautiful and very smart and a member of the student council at school (St. Mark's High School). She is also the chairman of the Flying Without Wings Dance Committee and is planning on becoming a doctor. Keith also attends St.

Mark's but is not the best student in the world. He had a Big Bird pillowcase and as a kid played with Barbie dolls. Bobby is called "Mama's Little Man" by Tanya and feels his life is ruined if there is no dessert at supper. He looks up to Keith as a role model.
Cast: Holly Robinson Peete (*Tanya Ward*); Diane Farr (*Maddie Hudson*); J. Mack Slaughter (*Keith Hudson*); Kevin Michael Richardson (*Ed Ward*); Megalyn Echikunwoke (*Danika Ward*); B.J. Mitchell (*Bobby Ward*); J. Anthony Brown (*Eugene "Pop" Ward*).

5350   *Like Magic.* (Pilot; Variety; CBS; June 13, 1981). Performances by guest magicians.
Host: Chris Kirby. **Guests:** Melissa Gilbert, Carlton and Company, Goldfinger and Dove, The Great Larcent, Ricky Jay. **Music:** H.B. Barnum.

5351   *Like So Many Things.* (Series; Drama; Internet; 2009). A realistic approach to the problems young adults face in making an emotional connection. The setting is Brooklyn, New York and Lucy and Kari are "two lost souls" who meet after a chance encounter on the street, hit it off and then attempt to begin a relationship.
Cast: Marin Gazzaniga (*Lucy*); Greg Keller (*Kari*).

5352   *Likely Suspects.* (Series; Crime Drama; Fox; 1992-1993). Stanford Marshak is a homicide inspector. He is assisted by Detective Harry Spinosa and the viewer (whom Stanford calls "Rookie"). A case is established at the beginning of an episode. As Stanford and Harry begin their investigation, Rookie joins them (represented by a camera). Stanford talks directly to Rookie and presents him with all the clues and the suspects (the gimmick of the series is to allow the viewer to solve the crimes before or at the same time as Stanford). After the final commercial break Stanford recaps the case and solves the crime (almost always congratulating Rookie for his fine job).
Cast: Sam McMurray (*Insp. Stanford Marshak*); Jason Schombing (*Det. Harry Spinosa*); Melinda Culea (*Capt. Wendy Hewitt*).

5353   *Li'l Abner.* (Pilot; Comedy; ABC; NBC; 1949; 1967; 1971; 1978). Four attempts were made to transform Al Capp's comic strip characters into a weekly series. Each pilot is set in the mythical Ozark community of Dog Patch, USA, and features such characters as the naive Li'l Abner, the beautiful Daisy Mae and Mammy and Pappy Yokum.
1. Li'l Abner (Pilot; Unaired; Produced for ABC in 1949). **Cast:** Craig Shepard (*Li'l Abner*), Judy Bourne (*Daisy Mae*).
2. Li'l Abner (NBC, Sept. 5, 1967). **Cast:** Sammy Jackson (*Li'l Abner*), Jeannine Riley (*Daisy Mae*), Judy Canova (*Mammy Yokum*), Jerry Lester (*Pappy Yokum*), Larry Mann (*Marryin' Sam*), Robert Reed (*Senator Cod*).
3. Li'l Abner (ABC, April 26, 1971). **Cast:** Ray Young (*Li'l Abner*), Nancee Parkinson (*Daisy Mae*), Billie Hayes (*Mammy Yokum*), Billy Bletcher (*Pappy Yokum*), Dale Malone (*Marryin' Sam*), Bobo Lewis (*Nightmare Alice*), Jennifer Narin-Smith (*Snow Bright*), Inga Neilson (*Beautify America*), Jackie Kahane (*Captain Rickeyback*), H.B. Haggerty (*Hairless Joe*), Tom Solari (*Lonesome Polecat*).
4. Li'l Abner in Dog Patch Today (NBC, Nov. 9, 1978). **Cast:** Stephan Burns (*Li'l Abner*), Debra Feuer (*Daisy Mae*), Polly Bergen (*Phyllis Shoefly*), Kaye Ballard (*Bella Asgood*), Louis Nye (*General Bullmoose*), Rhonda Bates (*Appassionata*), Deborah Zon (*Moonbeam McSwine*), Cissy Cameron (*Mitzi Galore*), Diki Lerner (*Lonesome Polecat*), Ben Davidson (*Hairless Joe*), Prudence Holmes (*Sexless*).

5354   *Lil' Bush.* (Series; Cartoon; Comedy Central; 2007). What were President George W. Bush and other members of the White House like when they were children? *Lil' Bush* takes that concept and shows in animated form, events in the lives of Lil' George Bush as a grade school child (with aspirations to become the President). He lives in the White House with his father, George Sr., his mother, Barbara, and his mentally challenged younger brother, Jeb. There are also appearances by Lil' Bush's friends — Lil' Hilary (Hilary Clinton), Lil' Laura (Laura Bush), Lil' Cheney (Dick Cheney), Lil' Rummy (Donald Rumsfeld) and Lil' Kim Jong II. Also known as *Lil' Bush: Resident of the United States.*

Voice Cast: Chris Parson (*Lil' George Bush*); Dave Mitchell (*George Bush, Sr.*); Mara Cary (*Barbara Bush*); Dave Mitchell (*Lil' Jeb*); Iggy Pop (*Lil' Rummy*); Ann Villella (*Lil' Laura*).

5355   *The Lili Palmer Show.* (Series; Interview; CBS; 1951–1953). Celebrity interviews with actress Lili Palmer as the host.

5356   *The Lili Palmer Theater.* (Series; Anthology; Syn.; 1956). Actress Lili Palmer hosts a short-lived syndicated series of dramatic productions featuring virtually unknown actors (at the time) that ran from September through December 1956. Performers include Brenda Hogan, Wendy Hiller, Brian Wilde, Eric Portman, Diana Lynn, Lamont Johnson, Renee Asherson, Sam Wanamaker and Mary Clare.

5357   *Lilo and Stitch.* (Series; Cartoon; Disney; 2003–2006). An adaptation of the animated Disney film of the same title. In the feature film, a scientist (Dr. Jumba Jookiba) on a distant planet creates an illegal genetic creature he calls Number 626. The creature is strong and aggressive and unable to swim in water. When Number 626 is discovered, Dr. Jookiba is arrested and sent to prison in the Grant Council of the Galactic Federation. The creature, while being transported by Captain Gantu to a prison asteroid, manages to escape and takes refuge on Earth — specifically in Hawaii, where he is found by Lilo, a young girl who adopts him as a dog and names him Stitch. She also humanizes Stitch through kindness. As Stitch finds a home with Lilo and her sister Nani, the Galactic Foundation begins a search to find 626 and return him to their planet. The series itself follows the adventures shared by Lilo and Stitch as they seek to find Dr. Jookiba's experimental pods (Stitch's cousins), which have been scattered all over the Hawaiian Islands, and humanize those they find.

Voice Cast: Daveigh Chase (*Lilo*); Chris Sanders (*Stitch*); Tia Carrere, Vanessa Petruo (*Nani*); David Ogden Stiers, Roland Hemmo (*Dr. Jumba Jookiba*); Kevin MacDonald, Oliver Rohrbeek (*Agent Pleakey*); Kevin Michael Richardson (*Captain Gantu*); Liliana Mumy (*Myrtle Edmonds*); April Winchell (*Myrtle Edmonds*); Jillian Henry (*Elena*).

5358   *Lily.* (Pilot; Comedy; NBC; June 12, 1974). Events in the life of a pretty single girl (Lily) with marriage-minded parents (Madge and Ernie) and a marriage-shy boyfriend (Jonathan).

Cast: Brenda Vaccaro (*Lily*); Eileen Heckart (*Madge*); Michael Lombard (*Ernie*); Mike Farrell (*Jonathan*).

5359   *Lily.* (Pilot; Comical Adventure; CBS; June 14, 1986). Lily Miniver is the assistant curator of the Jeffersonian Museum in Washington, D.C. She is eccentric and intrepid and her job takes her around the world. The proposal was to relate her escapades as she fulfills missions for the museum. Other regulars are John Farnsworth, the museum's director; Claudia, Lily's secretary; and Wesley, a staff worker who is seeking Lily's job.

Cast: Shelley Duvall (*Lily Miniver*); Donald Moffat (*John Farnsworth*); Beverly Hope Atkinson (*Claudia*); Peter Jurasik (*Wesley*).

5360   *Lily.* (Pilot; Drama; CW; May 11, 2009). A proposed spin off from *Gossip Girl* that was to focus on Lily Rhodes as a 17-year-old living in Malibu, California in 1983. When Lily's unorthodox activities result in her expulsion from boarding school, she returns to Los Angeles to reconcile with her dysfunctional family: her parents, Rick and CeCe, and her sister, Carol. In the series *Gossip Girl* Lily becomes the matriarch of the van der Woodsen family. Had the series sold, it would have revealed the events leading up to Lily's marriage (to Keith van der Woodsen) as well as relating events in the lives of Rick, a record producer, the superficial CeCe and the free-spirited black sheep of the family, 19-year-old Carol.

Cast: Brittany Snow (*Lily Rhodes*); Cynthia Watros (*Celia "CeCe" Rhodes*); Andrew McCartney (*Rick Rhodes*); Krysten Ritter (*Carol Rhodes*); Matt Barr (*Keith van der Woodsen*); Shiloh Fernandez (*Owen Campos*); Ryan Hansen (*Shep*); Abby Pivaronas (*Veronica*).

5361   *The Lily Tomlin Show.* (Pilot; Variety; CBS; Mar. 16, 1973). Music, songs and comedy sketches with actress-comedienne Lily Tomlin as the host.

Host: Lily Tomlin. **Guests:** Richard Crenna, Nancy Dussault, Richard Pryor. **Orchestra:** Dick DeBenedictis.

5362   *The Lily Tomlin Special.* (Pilot; Variety; ABC; July 25, 1975). Although billed as a special, it was the pilot episode for a proposed weekly series of skits spotlighting the many talents of comedienne Lily Tomlin.

Host: Lily Tomlin. **Guests:** Betty Beaird, Valri Bromfield, Christopher Guest, Doris Roberts, Bill Zuckert. **Orchestra:** Peter Matz.

5363   *Lime Street.* (Series; Crime Drama; ABC; 1985). Lime Street is a British-based insurance company with an American branch in Middleburgh, Virginia (its main branch is located at 55 Lime Street in London). James Greyson Culver heads the Virginia office. Stories relate his case investigations as he seeks the Cheaters — people who defraud insurance companies.

James is a widower and the father of Elizabeth and Margaret Ann. His father, Henry, helps him with the girls as does his nanny, Evelyn. Edward Wingate is James's British colleague; Celia is James's secretary; and Sir Geoffrey Rimbatten is the head of Lime Street.

The series is dedicated to Samantha Smith (played Elizabeth), who was killed in a plane crash after filming four episodes in August of 1985.

Cast: Robert Wagner (*James Greyson Culver*); Lew Ayres (*Henry Wade Culver*); Samantha Smith (*Elizabeth Culver*); Maia Brewton (*Margaret Ann Culver*); Patrick Macnee (*Sir Geoffrey Rimbatten*); John Standing (*Edward Wingate*); Julie Fulton (*Celia*); Anne Haney (*Evelyn*).

5364   *Limelight.* (Pilot; Drama; Unaired; Produced for ABC in 2007). Students at the Public Academy for the Performing Arts are profiled from brutal auditions to classes that test their abilities to become professional performers. Georgia is a Britney Spears wannabe; Zoe is a shy girl with an amazing voice; Kevin, the hip-hop dancer; Romeo, a talented street musician; Jazz, a brilliant dancer; David Laddeman is the artistic director; Vincent is the hopeful actor; Nina is the choreographer.

Cast: Brooklyn Sudano (*Jazz Barkley*); Jessy Schram (*Georgia Beech*); Matthew Davis (*David Laddeman*); Shannon Woodward (*Zoe*); Sharon Leal (*Nina Khari*); Oded Fehr (*Vincent Marlowe*); Noah Gray-Cabey (*Romeo*); Telly Leung (*Kevin Cotton*).

5365   *Limited Partners.* (Pilot; Comedy; CBS; July 19, 1988). Bumberg's Beefeaters in Martindale, Indianapolis, is an English-style fast food chain franchise. It is owned by Sir Freddy Bumberg and managed by a 16-year-old (Kurt). Regis Rogan and Tim Tiffle are two friends who work under Kurt's supervision. Regis is an optimistic dreamer and Tim is his ever-faithful sidekick. The proposal was to relate Regis and Tim's misadventures as they seek to better their lives through hare-brained get-rich-quick schemes. Margie is Tim's girlfriend.

Cast: Joe Flaherty (*Regis Rogan*); Kevin Meaney (*Tim Tiffle*); Holly Fulger (*Margie*); Anthony Newley (*Sir Freddy Bumberg*); Kari Weidergott (*Kurt*).

5366   Lincoln Heights. (Series; Drama; ABC Family; 2007–2009). Eddie Sutton is a police officer who wants to make a difference. He leaves the relative safety of his city beat and moves his family to the inner city neighborhood where he grew up — a neighborhood that is now crime ridden but holds fond memories of his youth. Stories follow Eddie as he patrols the streets and struggles to not only protect his family but make the people of the community feel they have someone on their side. Jen is Eddie's wife; Cassie, Lizzie and Taylor are their children.

Cast: Russell Hornsby (*Eddie Sutton*); Nicki Micheaux (*Jen Sutton*); Rhyon Nicole Brown (*Lizzie Sutton*); Erica Hubbard (*Cassie Sutton*); Misgon Ratliff (*Taylor Sutton*).

5367   Linc's. (Series; Comedy; Showtime; 1998). Linc's Place is a Washington, D.C., bar and grill owned by Russell "Linc" Lincoln. Stories, a somewhat adult version of *Cheers* and *Frank's Place,* focuses on the diverse crowd that frequents the bar.

Cast: Steven Williams (*Russell Lincoln*); Tisha Campbell (*Rosalee Lincoln*); Pam Grier (*Eleanor Winthrop*); Georg Stanford Brown (*Johnnie B. Goode*); Joe Inscoe (*Harlan Hubbard IV*); Daphne Maxwell Reid (*Eartha*); Golden Brooks (*CeCe Jennings*).

5368   The Line. (Pilot; Comedy; NBC; July 29, 1987). Events in the lives of five women (Karen, Jo, Denise, Anna Mae and Lucy) who work side-by-side on an assembly line in a Houston airplane factory. Ken is their supervisor; Alice and Benno are workers.

Cast: Dinah Manoff (*Karen Cooper*); Lori Petty (*Jo Lanier*); Alfre Woodard (*Denise Powell*); C.C.H. Pounder (*Anna Mae Dempsey*); Park Overall (*Lucy Kershaw*); Andrew Rubin (*Ken Morris*); Brian George (*Benno*).

5369   The Line. (Series; Comedy; Internet; Summer 2008). Saga about a young man and his friend who are first in line for a popular science fiction movie — weeks before it opens.

Cast: Bill Hader, Simon Rich, Joe LoTruglio, Paul Scheer, Miriam Tolan.

5370   Line of Fire. (Series; Crime Drama; ABC; 2003-2004). The FBI's battle against crime (specifically Jonah Malloy, the head of the Richmond, Virginia, based Malloy Crime Syndicate). Leading the FBI's battle is Lisa Cohen, a tough as nails agent who is determined to put an end to the syndicate by any legal means she can.

Cast: Leslie Hope (*Agent Lisa Cohen*); David Paymer (*Jonah Malloy*); Jeffrey D. Sams (*Agent Todd Stevens*); Leslie Bibb (*Paige Van Doren*); Anson Mount (*Roy Ravelle*); Julie Ann Emery (*Jennifer Sampson*); Brian Goodman (*Donovan Stubbin*); Kristen Shaw (*Janet Malloy*); Jazsmin Lewis (*Jada*).

5371   The Line-Up. (Series; Crime Drama; CBS; 1954–1960). A line-up is a police department procedure wherein witnesses to crimes are secluded as they attempt to identify suspects from a group of similar looking individuals. Detectives from the San Francisco Police Department are profiled as they begin the grueling task of rounding up suspects in the crimes they investigate. Once the suspects have been collared the eye witnesses are brought to the line-up and stories relate what happens when the procedures are successful or not. Also

known as *San Francisco Beat.* Jerry Goldsmith composed the theme, "San Francisco Blues."

Cast: Warner Anderson (*Lt. Ben Guthrie*); Tom Tully (*Insp. Matt Grebb*); Jan Brooks, Rachel Ames (*Off. Sandy McAllister*); Bob Palmer, Skip Ward (*Off. Pete Larkin*); William Leslie (*Insp. Dan Delaney*); Tod Burton (*Insp. Charlie Summers*); Marshall Reed (*Insp. Fred Asher*); Ruta Lee (*Various Roles*). **Announcer:** Art Gilmore.

5372   The Line-Up. (Pilot; Crime Drama; Unaired; Produced for TNT in 2007). A suspect in a case is seen in a line-up. As he or she is viewed by a witness, the program flashes back to the police investigation into the case.

Cast: Rocky Carroll (*Sean*); Tia Texada (*Jo Jo*); J.R. Cacia (*Ethan*); Michael Raymond-James (*Tommy*).

5373   Lingerie. (Series; Erotica; Cinemax; 2009-2010). A sensual look at the beautiful women who model lingerie in New York City's fashion industry. Stories also focus on the designers and photographers that are also a part of the business. Particular focus is on Lacey Summers, a gorgeous ex-runway model who gave up the hectic modeling life to devote her energies on creating her own line of lingerie. Vanessa is Lacey's roommate, a bisexual model; Jason is the photographer in love with Lacey; Cody is Lacey's younger, protective brother (who lives in the same building as Lacey); Marilyn is the fashion columnist and Lacey's friend; Russ, Cody's roommate, is a bartender at Duncan's Bar; Stephanie is Lacey's perky assistant; Jeffrey is Lacey's gay fashion designer.

Cast: Jennifer Korbin (*Lacey Summers*); Michael Scratch (*Jason*); Lana Tailor (*Vanessa*); Matthew Fitzgerald (*Cody*); Denise Cobar (*Marilyn*); Jonathan Steen (*Russ*); Erin Brown (*Stephanie*); Geoff Stevens (*Jeffrey*).

5374   Lingo. (Series; Game; Syn.; 1987; 2003). Two teams compete, each composed of two members. A partially filled in Lingo card (similar to a Bingo card) is given to each player. A board with twenty-five blank spaces (five lines of five boxes) is displayed. The first letter to a mystery word appears in the first box. Players have to suggest words with the object being to find the mystery word. Words that are too long or too short ends a team's turn at play. The opposing team plays the same type of board (the same one if the opposing team failed to guess the word; a new board is they guessed the word). If the word is guessed the team scores points and receives the opportunity to select two numbered balls from a glass bowl that appears before them. If the balls that are picked have numbers that can complete their Lingo card (a line up and down, diagonally or across) they get Lingo and extra points. Round two plays in the same manner but doubles points. Two versions appeared:

1. Lingo (Syn., 1987). **Host:** Michael Reagan, Ralph Andrews. **Hostess:** Dusty Martell, Marguax MacKenzie.

2. Lingo (GSN, 2003). **Host:** Chuck Woolery, Bill Engvall. **Co-Host:** Stacey Hayes, Shandi Finnessey. **Announcer:** Randy Thomas.

5375   Linus the Lionhearted. (Series; Cartoon; CBS; ABC; 1964–1969). Characters from the Post cereal boxes Crispy Critters, Rice Krinkles, Alpha Bits and Sugar Crisp are brought to life via animation in a series of short segments: *Linus the King of Beasts; Sugar Bear; Lovable Truly; Rory Raccoon; So-Hi, the Asian Boy* and *The Company.* Aired on CBS (Sept. 26, 1964 to Sept. 3, 1966) and ABC (Sept. 25, 1966 to Sept. 7, 1969).

Voice Cast: Sheldon Leonard (*Linus the Lionhearted*); Carl Reiner (*Danny Kangaroo*); Ed Graham (*The Mockingbird*); Jonathan Winters (*The Giant*); Stanley Holloway (*Sugar Bear*).

5376   Lionhearts. (Series; Cartoon; Syn.; 1998–2000). Leo Lionheart, the mascot seen in MGM feature films, is brought to animated life for a look at his life with his family (his wife, Lana, and their children Kate, Spencer and Judy) and his life on the set of Metro Goldwyn Mayer films.

Voice Cast: William H. Macy *(Leo Lionheart)*; Peri Gilpin *(Lana Lionheart)*; Natasha Slayton *(Kate Lionheart)*; Cameron Finley *(Spencer Lionheart)*; Nicolette Little *(Judy Lionheart)*; Harve Presnell *(Grandpa Leo)*.

5377   *Lip Service.* (MTV; 1992-1993). Three two member teams compete in a game wherein they must lip sync both pre-selected songs and randomly chosen songs. The team that proves to be the best lip sync artists wins.

Host: Jay Mohr, John Ales. **Co-Host:** Peter Austin Noto. **DJ:** Monie Love, T-Money.

5378   *Lippy the Lion.* (Series; Cartoon; Syn.; 1962). Mishaps of a trouble-prone lion named Lippy and his friend, Hardy Har Har.

Voice Cast: Daws Butler *(Lippy the Lion)*; Mel Blanc *(Hardy Har Har)*.

5379   *Lipshitz Saves the World.* (Pilot; Comedy; Unaired; Produced for NBC in 2007). There is a secret society of celebrity super heroes headed by Leslie Nielsen. These include actress Jenny McCarthy and sex therapist Dr. Ruth. But also a part of the team is Adam Lipshitz, a 17-year-old high school student who has been chosen to rid the world of danger. The proposal was to follow the celebrity crime fighters, especially Adam, as he not only struggles to save the world, but clean his room, study for exams and be a typical teen when he can.

Cast: Jack Carpenter *(Adam Lipshitz)*; Leslie Nielsen *(Himself)*; Jenny McCarthy *(Herself)*; Ruth Westheimer *(Dr. Ruth)*.

5380   *Lipstick Jungle.* (Series; Drama; NBC; 2008). A look at the lives of three New York women who have weathered the ups and downs to have reached the top of their fields (the top 50 such women in America). Wendy Healey is a gorgeous movie executive; Nico Reilly is editor-in-chief of a fashion magazine; Victory Ford is a fashion designer. Wendy is struggling to balance her career with her family (she is married to Shane and the mother of Maddie and Taylor); Nico is not satisfied with her current position and wants to become a company CEO; Victory still feels she has not achieved her dreams and feels that when she finds Mr. Right she will have accomplished her goals. Stories follow events in the lives of the women.

Cast: Brooke Shields *(Wendy Healey)*; Kim Raver *(Nico Reilly)*; Lindsay Price *(Victory Ford)*; Andrew McCarthy *(Joe Bennett)*; Paul Blackthorne *(Shane Healey)*; Julian Sanda *(Hector Metrick)*; Robert Buckley *(Kirby Atwood)*; David Norona *(Salvador Rosa)*; Dylan Clark Marshall *(Taylor Healey)*; Sarah Hyland *(Maddie Healey)*.

5381   *Liquid Television.* (Series; Anthology; MTV; 1991). A potpourri of short films from producers whose work would not normally be shown on television. The program spotlights mostly animated short subjects (including claymation and computer generated) and features such short subjects as *Beavis and Butthead* [which was spun off into a series of its own; see entry], *Psycho Gram, The Art School Girls of Doom* and *Dog Boy*. Casts and producers vary from show to show.

5382   *The Lisa Hartman Show.* (Pilot; Variety; ABC; June 30, 1979). Actress Lisa Hartman as the host of a program of music, songs and comedy sketches. Lisa Hartman performs the theme, "Hot Stuff."

Host: Lisa Hartman. **Guests:** Andy Kaufman, Bill Kirchenbauer, Rici Martin, Karen Turner. **Orchestra:** Johnny Harris.

5383   *Lisa Raye: The Real McCoy.* (Series; Reality; TV One; 2010–). The beautiful and outspoken actress, Lisa Raye McCoy, first came to the attention of TV viewers via the UPN series *All of Us*. She has appeared in feature films (for example, *The Player, Club* and *Civil Brand*) but all this changed when she married the Premier of the Turks and Caicos in 2006 and she went from living a charmed Hollywood life to the First Lady of a Nation. Lisa Raye was now royalty, had mansions, private jets, maids and servants but she never gave up her love of Hollywood. Suddenly, as fast as a First Lady title was bestowed upon her, it was taken away when rumors of her husband's infidelity caused their marriage to end. Lisa Raye is not one to look back or sit back and feel sorry for herself. Now, determined to reestablish her acting career, Lisa Raye returned to Hollywood and episodes not only to focus on her acting career but her efforts to raise her daughter Kai; keep her troubled sister, rapper DaBrat, in line; and care for her ill mother.

Star: Lisa Raye McCoy.

5384   *The Lisa Whelchel Show.* (Pilot; Comedy; NBC; April 30 and May 7, 1988). When Blair Warner learns that her former grammar school, the Eastland School for Girls in Peekskill, New York, has gone bankrupt and will soon close, she uses the money she had been saving to open a law office to buy the school. When Blair learns that enrollment is down and the administration is not to her liking, she appoints herself as the headmistress and changes the enrollment to allow boys. The proposed series, a spin off from *The Facts of Life* was to relate Blair's experiences as the owner of a school. Other regulars are Noreen, Blair's secretary; Wes, the science teacher; and students Terry, Ashley, Pippa, Rick, Adam, Sara and Beldon.

Cast: Lisa Whelchel *(Blair Warner)*; Kathleen Freeman *(Noreen Grisbee)*; Sam Behrens *(Wes Mitchell)*; Juliette Lewis *(Terry Rankin)*; Mayim Bialik *(Jennifer Cole)*; Meredith Scott Lynn *(Ashley Payne)*; Sherri Krenn *(Pippa McKenna)*; Scott Bryce *(Rick Bonner)*; Seth Green *(Adam Brinkerhoff)*; Marissa Mendenhall *(Sara Bellanger)*; Jason Naylor *(Beldon Glover)*.

5385   *Lisa Williams—Life Among the Dead.* (Series; Reality; Lifetime; 2006). Lisa Williams is an outgoing clairvoyant who claims she is able to communicate with the dead to help bring closure to the deceased's family. The program showcases Lisa's unique psychic abilities as she conducts séances to bring closure to loved ones. Lisa Williams hosts; D.C. Douglas is the narrator.

5386   *Lisa Williams: Voices from the Other Side.* (Series; Reality; Lifetime; 2008). British psychic Lisa Williams seeks to help real people, suffering a loss (friend, lover, family member) find some closure by contacting the spirits of those they lost.

5387   *Listen Up.* (Series; Comedy; CBS; 2004-2005). Tony Kleinman is a columnist (for a paper called *Living*) and also hosts the TV Sports talk show *Listen Up* with Bernie Widmer, a former football player with the NFL.

Tony is married to Dana and is the father of Megan and Mickey. Tony feels his life is a series of trials — shortest kid in his class, wore braces for seven years. Tony hates technology (he especially dislikes cell phones and fears all the waves are dangerous). When he gets upset, Tony does work around the house — but tightening screws is the only skill he has. Dana is an administrator for the Philadelphia Zoo (oversees zoo operations). She doesn't watch Tony's show because she hates sports.

Megan and Mickey attend Clearview High School. Megan, middle name Elizabeth, is a straight A student. She is on the school soccer team and is a member of Project Bully, an organization that provides help to children. Megan is an expert at defying her father — and getting away with it (she also yells at him for all the dumb things he does around the house).

Mickey is not too bright at schoolwork, but he is a golf prodigy and Tony is pushing him to become a pro. Mickey is rather silent compared to Megan and seems to live in his own private world.

Stories follow the events in Tony's life as he struggles to cope with all the problems he encounters at home and at work. His newspaper column, "I Am Champion," is not about sports, "but about life."

Cast: Jason Alexander (*Tony Kleinman*); Wendy Makkena (*Dana Kleinman*); Daniella Monet (*Megan Kleinman*); Will Rothhaar (*Mickey Kleinman*); Malcolm-Jamal Warner (*Bernie Widmer*).

5388 *The Listener.* (Series; Crime Drama; NBC; 2009). "Ever wonder what people are thinking? I don't, I know," says Toby Logan, an EMS paramedic in Toronto, Canada, who has the gift to hear the thoughts of other people (he can also, at times, see briefly into the future as to what will happen). Toby grew up in foster care and never knew his parents. He has had his telepathic abilities since childhood and because of it, it has made him somewhat of a loner. He has kept his abilities a secret and has only just revealed it to his friend, Dr. Ray Mercer, in the hope of exploring its possibilities.

Toby works with Osman "Oz" Bey, an energetic who is unaware of Toby's abilities. Toby keeps his abilities secret "because I'm not a peep show; besides, who would believe me?" Stories follow Toby as he uses his gift (and turns amateur detective) to help people facing a crisis. Dr. Olivia Fawcett is Toby's ex-girlfriend; Charles Marks is the detective Toby helps; George Ryder is Toby's boss; Brian Decker assists Charlie. Produced in Canada.

Cast: Craig Olejnik (*Toby Logan*); Ennis Esmer (*Osman "Oz" Bey*); Lisa Marcos (*Det. Charlie Marks*); Mylene Dinh-Robic (*Dr. Olivia Fawcett*); Colm Feore (*Dr. Ray Mercer*); Arnold Pinnock (*George Ryder*); Anthony Lemke (*Det. Brian Becker*).

5389 *Little Bear.* (Series; Cartoon; Nick; 1995). Little Bear is a young cub who is just discovering the wonders of the world that surrounds her. As Little Bear explores her environment, various learning aspects are related to children through the interactions with other animals (such as Owl and Cat).

Voice Cast: Kristin Fairlie (*Little Bear*); Andrew Sabiston (*Cat*); Tracy Ryan (*Duck*); Amos Crowley (*Owl*); Tara Strong (*Tutu*).

5390 *Little Bill.* (Series; Cartoon; Nick; 1999–2002). An animated program loosely based on comedian Bill Cosby's life as a youngster. Here he is portrayed as five-year-old William Glover, called "Little Bill" by his family (his parents "Big" Bill, a city housing inspector and Brenda, a photographer; his siblings Alice and Bobby; and Brenda's grandmother, called Alice the Great). Stories relate the incidents that Little Bill faces at home, with his friends and at school. Each episode concludes with Little Bill talking directly to children in the audience to tell them what his experiences have taught him that day.

Voice Cast: Xavier Pritchett (*William "Little Bill" Glover*); Gregory Hines (*"Big" Bill Glover*); Phylicia Rashad (*Brenda Glover*); Monique Beasley (*April Glover*); Devon Malik Beckford (*Bobby Glover*); Tyler James Williams (*Bobby Glover*); Ruby Dee (*Alice the Great*); Robin Reid (*Coach Maya*); Melanie Nicholls-King, Ayo Haynes (*Miss Murray*); Vincent Canoles (*Dorado*); Zach Tyler (*Andrew*).

5391 *A Little Bit Strange.* (Pilot; Comedy; NBC; April 23, 1989). The story of a family that is "A Little Bit Strange:" Ben, a widowed father (a sorcerer); Margaret, his mother, a mind reader;

Tasha, his daughter, a witch; T.J. (Tyrone Jeffrey), his son, a warlock; Frank, Margaret's brother, a mad scientist; and Sidney, also known as Mud Man, Frank's "adopted" son (whom Frank created from a pile of mud). Marilyn is Ben's ordinary fiancée, a girl who is having a difficult time adjusting to her soon-to-become family.

Cast: Michael Warren (*Ben Masterson*); Myra J (*Margaret Masterson*); Cherie Johnson (*Tasha Masterson*); Shawn Skie (*T.J. Masterston*); Martin Lawrence (*Sidney*); Finis Henderson (*Frank Masterson*); Vanessa Bell Calloway (*Marilyn McClain*).

5392 *Little Britain.* (Series; Comedy; BBC America; 2008). An exaggerated look at the British Isles (from Scotland to Wales) with a focus on the quirky characters that inhabit the countryside of the United Kingdom (for example, Sebastian Love, the Prime Minister's gay assistant; Vicky Pollard, the teenage troublemaker; Ray McLooney, the eccentric Scottish hotel manager; and Marjorie Dawes, a dietician who makes fun of fat people).

Cast: Matt Lucas, David Walliams, Anthony Head, Paul Putner, Joann London, Steve Furst, Stirling Gallacher, Leelo Ross, Ruth Jones. **Narrator:** Tom Baker.

5393 *Little Britain, U.S.A.* (Series; Comedy; HBO; 2008). Raunchy, fast-paced skit comedy wherein the male leads, portraying an array of character (including females) spoof American culture. Based on the British series *Little Britain* (see prior title).

Stars: Matt Lucas, David Walliams.

5394 *Little Darlings.* (Pilot; Comedy; Unaired; Produced in 1982). Angel Bright is a tough teenage girl who grew up on the mean city streets. Farris Whitney is her complete opposite — from a rich family and pampered all her life. They meet one summer at Camp Little Wolf and become friends when they are assigned to Cabin C. The unsold series, based on the feature film of the same title, was to relate the adventures of two girls who excel in mischief. Other regulars are campers Lisa and Ruthie and the camp counselors (names not given).

Cast: Pamela Segall (*Angel Bright*); Tammy Lauren (*Farris Whitney*); Heather McAdam (*Lisa*); LaShana Dendy (*Ruthie*); Anne Schedeen and Michael McManus (*Camp counselors*).

5395 *Little Dracula.* (Series; Cartoon; Fox Kids; 1991–1999). Mr. and Mrs. Dracula are the parents of a son they call Little Dracula. Little Dracula, however, has been growing up in the shadow of his father, Big Dracula, and feels the time has come to become "a man." Stories relate the mishaps that occur as Little Dracula sets out on a quest to become as great a vampire as his father.

Voice Cast: Edan Gross (*Little Dracula*); Joe Flaherty (*Big Dracula*); Kath Soucie (*Mrs. Dracula*); Jonathan Winters (*Igor/Granny*); Brian Cummings (*Garlic Man*); Joey Camen (*Werebunny*); Neil Ross (*Maggot*); Fran Ryan (*Hannah the Barbarian*).

5396 *Little Einsteins.* (Series; Cartoon; Disney; 2005-2006). Annie, Leo, June and Quincy are four musically gifted children who use their knowledge of song, dance and instruments to familiarize children with music (each episode is a mission with the children combining works of art and musical composers to introduce children to the world of music). Annie is a singer; June, a dancer; Quincy is capable of playing many instruments; and Leo is a conductor.

Voice Cast: Erica Huang (*June*); Jesse Schwartz (*Leo*); Natalie Wojcik (*Annie*); Aiden Pompey (*Quincy*).

5397 *Little House on the Prairie.* (Series; Drama; NBC; 1974–1982). Under the Homestead Act, the Ingalls family receives 160 acres of land in Kansas. Parents Charles and Caroline and their daughters, Mary, Laura and Carrie, leave their home in Wisconsin's Big Woods and journey west to begin new lives. After battling the elements Charles manages to build a home, barn and stable — only to learn that the government has moved their boundaries and they must pack up and start all over again.

Their journey next takes them to Walnut Grove in Plum Creek, Minnesota (1878), where Charles, called "Pa" by Laura, builds his "Little House on the Prairie" for his family. The family's experiences are viewed through the sentimental eyes of Laura, the second-born daughter, who hopes one day to become a writer. Mary is the oldest daughter, and Carrie the youngest, until the birth of Grace later in the series.

Charles ran a lumber mill but found it necessary to take whatever jobs he could find to make money. Mary, who later lost her sight through disease, married Adam Kendall, a blind teacher she met when she attended the Sleepy Eye School for the Blind. (Adam's sight was later restored).

Laura, who later taught at the Plum Creek School, married Almanzo Wilder. Almanzo is the brother of the school's second teacher, Eliza Jane Wilder. (Eliza replaced the original school teacher, Grace Beadle, who left when she married. In 1886 Eliza Jane married Harve Miller and left town; Laura then became the schoolmarm.) Laura's dogs were named Jack and Bandit; Charles called her "Half Pint."

Isaiah Edwards, commonly called Mr. Edwards, is Charles's best friend and, in later episodes, his partner in the lumber mill. Isaiah is married to Grace; they are the parents of three adopted children: Aliscia, John and Carl.

Nels and his bossy wife, Harriet Oleson, run Oleson's Mercantile, Plum Creek's only general store. They have a rather nasty (spoiled) daughter named Nellie and a mischievous son named Willie. When Harriet started a restaurant, she first gave Nellie the responsibility of running it (Nellie's Restaurant); it eventually became Harriet's Restaurant when Nellie, a Protestant, married Percival Dalton, a Jewish accountant. They moved to New York to help Percival's mother after his father's death. Without Nellie, Harriet went into a state of deep depression. Her spirits were lifted when she and Nels adopted an orphan girl named Nancy, a Nellie look-alike who was twice as obnoxious. (Willie also married; a girl named Rachel Brown).

Charles too adopted three children after Mary left to live in Sleepy Eye: Albert, Cassandra and James. Jonathan Garvey purchased a farm in Walnut Grove and became friends with the Ingalls family. He is married to Alice and had a son named Andy. See also *Little House: A New Beginning*.

Cast: Michael Landon (*Charles Ingalls*); Karen Grassle (*Caroline Ingalls*); Melissa Gilbert (*Laura Ingalls*); Melissa Sue Anderson (*Mary Ingalls*); Lindsay and Sidney Green Bush (*Carrie Ingalls*); Wendi and Brenda Turnbeaugh (*Grace Ingalls*); Victor French (*Isaiah Edwards*); Linwood Boomer (*Adam Kendall*); Dean Butler (*Almanzo Wilder*); Lucy Lee Flippen (*Eliza Jane Wilder*); Charlotte Stewart (*Grace Beadle*); James Cromwell (*Harve Miller*); Bonnie Bartlett, Corinne Michaels (*Grace Edwards*); Kyle Richards (*Aliscia Edwards*); Radames Pera (*John Edwards*); Brian Pratt (*Carl Edwards*); Richard Bull (*Nels Oleson*); Katherine MacGregor (*Harriet Oleson*); Alison Arngrim (*Nellie Oleson*); Jonathan Gilbert (*Willie Oleson*); Steve Tracy (*Percival Dalton*); Allison Balson (*Nancy*); Matthew Laborteaux (*Albert Cooper*); Missy Francis (*Cassandra Cooper*); Jason Bateman (*James Cooper*); Merlin Olson (*Jonathan Garvey*); Hersha Parady (*Alice Garvey*); Patrick Laborteaux (*Andy Garvey*); Kevin Hagen (*Dr. Baker*); Ted Gehring (*Ebenezer Sprague*); Ketty Lester (*Hester Sue*); Dabbs Greer (*the Rev. Robert Alden*); Tracie Savage (*Christy Kennedy*); Karl Swenson (*Lars Hanson*).

Note: Three NBC TV movies updating the lives of the Ingalls family also appeared: *Little House: Bless All the Dear Children* (Dec. 17, 1984), *Little House: Look Back to Yesterday* (Dec. 12, 1983) and *Little House: The Last Farewell* (Feb. 6, 1984).

On Jan. 2, 2000, CBS presented the TV movie *Beyond the Prairie: The True Story of Laura Ingalls Wilder* that introduces Laura Ingalls (Alandra Bingham, Meredith Monroe and Tess Harper) as a teenager living on the South Dakota prairie with her father, Charles (Richard Thomas), mother, Caroline (Lindsay Crouse) and sisters Mary (Barbara Jane Reams), Grace (Courtnie Bull and Lyndee Probst) and Carrie (Haley McCormick).

The sequel CBS TV movie, *Beyond the Prairie II: The True Story of Laura Ingalls Wilder* (Mar. 17, 2002) follows Laura (Meredith Monroe), her husband Alonzo Wilder (Walt Goggins) and their daughter, Rose (Skye McCole Bartusiak) as they move to Missouri to begin an apple farm.

5398 *Little House on the Prairie.* (Series; Drama; ABC; 2005). A more realistic adaptation of the *Little House* books by Laura Ingalls Wilder than the 1970s NBC series of the same title.

The ABC version closely follows the book series and presents a very harsh look at the life of the pioneering Ingalls family as they leave their home in Wisconsin to begin a new life (with new land) in the wilds of an unsettled Kansas (Charles, the father, could not find work in Wisconsin and felt that uprooting his family and taking advantage of the Homesteading Act — 160 acres of land — was his only choice). Joining him are his wife, Caroline, their two young daughters, Laura and Mary, and Laura's dog, Jack. With only one wagon and two horses, the Ingalls begin their journey — and their harrowing (and intensely frightening) journey is detailed as they attempt to settle in an untamed territory. The one stranger they meet and befriend, Mr. Edwards, becomes their neighbor (although not right next door). The Indians, the intense heat, the bitter cold, the wildfires, the struggle for survival is so realistically portrayed and captivating that it was a shame only six hours were produced (a two hour pilot and four one hour episodes).

Cast: Cameron Bancroft (*Charles Ingalls*); Erin Cottrell (*Caroline Ingalls*); Kyle Chavarria (*Laura Ingalls*); Danielle Ryan Chuchran (*Mary Ingalls*); Gregory Sporlander (*Mr. Edwards*).

5399 *Little House: A New Beginning.* (Series; Drama; NBC; 1982-1983). A spin off from NBC's *Little House on the Prairie*. When Charles Ingalls is unable to make a living in Plumb Creek, he sells his "little house" to John (a blacksmith) and Sarah Carter, a young couple with two children (Jeb and Jason) and moves (with his wife Caroline and daughters Carrie and Grace) to Iowa (where he becomes a purchasing agent. Laura, Charles's second-born daughter, and her husband, Almanzo, remain behind to continue the lumber mill previously operated by her father). The time is 1887 and stories follow the events in the lives of the people of Plumb Creek.

Other regulars are Royal Wilder, Almanzo's brother; Jenny, Royal's daughter; Etta Plum, the school teacher; Harriet and Nels Oleson, the owners of the general store (Oleson's Mercantile); Willie Oleson, their son; Nancy Oleson, their adopted daughter; Hester Sue, the cook in the Oleson's restaurant; Bill Anderson, the banker; the Rev. Robert Alden; Dr. Baker and Isaiah Edwards, Almanzo's partner.

Cast: Melissa Gilbert (*Laura Ingalls Wilder*); Dean Butler (*Almanzo Wilder*); Stan Ivar (*John Carter*); Pamela Roylance (*Sarah Carter*); Lindsay Kennedy (*Jeb Carter*); David Friedman (*Jason Carter*); Victor French (*Isaiah Edwards*); Nicholas Pryor (*Royal Wilder*); Shannen Doherty (*Jenny Wilder*); Leslie Landon (*Etta Plum*); Richard Bull (*Nels Oleson*); Katherine MacGregor (*Harriet Oleson*); Jonathan Gilbert (*Willie Oleson*); Ketty Lester (*Hester Sue*); Sam Edwards (*Bill Anderson*); Kevin Hagen (*Dr. Baker*); Dabbs Greer (*the Rev. Robert Alden*).

5400 ***Little Leatherneck.*** (Pilot; Comedy; ABC; July 29, 1966). "If I could be the President of the United States, or someone even more important like Santa Claus, it wouldn't mean a thing, 'cause I'd rather be a Marine..." said the opening theme of Cindy Fenton, a pretty pre-teenage girl fascinated by the U.S. Marine Corps, who decides to follow in the footsteps of her father, Marine Drill Sergeant Mike Fenton, and become a "Little Leatherneck." The proposal was to follow Cindy's adventures as she sets out to live the life of a marine. Donna Butterworth performs the theme, "Little Leatherneck."

Cast: Donna Butterworth (*Cindy Fenton*); Scott Brady (*Mike Fenton*); Sue Ane Langdon (*Delores*); Jean Innes (*Miss Raymond*); Ned Glass (*Mess sergeant*).

5401 ***Little Lord Fauntleroy.*** (Pilot; Drama; CBS; Aug. 14, 1982). A proposal that was to continue the Frances Hodgson Burnett novel about Cedric Erroll, an impoverished New York youngster who becomes heir to Dorincourt, a British estate owned by his grandfather, the Earl of Dorincourt. Filmed on location at Belvoir Castle in Leicestershire, England. Other regulars are Mrs. Erroll, Cedric's mother; McGregor, the estate caretaker; Billy, Cedric's friend; Mrs. Lemmy, the cook; Mary, the Earl's wife; and Hustings, McGregor's assistant.

Cast: John Mills (*Earl of Dorincourt*); Jerry Supiran (*Cedric Erroll*); Caroline Smith (*Mrs. Erroll*); Godfrey James (*McGregor*); Dennis Savage (*Billy*); Avis Bunnage (*Mrs. Lemmy*); Carmel McHarry (*Mary*); David Cook (*Hustings*).

5402 ***Little Lulu.*** (Pilot; Comedy; ABC; Nov. 4, 1978). Rocky River is home to a precocious pre-teenage girl named Little Lulu. She is a crusader for girls' rights and believes it is her duty to help people in trouble — whether they want it or not. The proposal was to follow the adventures of a pint-sized whirlwind of energy as she and her friends seem to find misadventure in everything they do. Gloria, Annie and Martha are Lulu's friends; Tubby, Iggie and Willy are the boys they associate with.

Cast: Lauri Hendler (*Little Lulu*); Annrae Walterhouse (*Gloria*); Lulu Baxter (*Annie*); Nita DiGampaolo (*Martha*); Robbie Rist (*Iggie*); Kevin King Cooper (*Tubby*); Eddie Singleton (*Willy*).

5403 ***The Little Lulu Show.*** (Series; Cartoon; HBO; 1995). A television adaptation of the theatrical cartoons that follows events in the life of Little Lulu, a very mischievous girl who can find innocent trouble in anything she does. Annie is her best friend and Tubby is her nemesis, a boy who heads a "For Boys Only Club" that Lulu desperately wants to (and plots to) join but can't ("just because I'm a girl").

Voice Cast: Tracey Ullman, Jane Woods (*Little Lulu*); Michael Caloz, Vanessa Lengies (*Annie Inch*); Bruce Dinsmore (*Tubby Tompkins*); Jonathan Idensgen (*Alvin*); Ricky Mabe (*Willie*); Terrence Scammell (*Officer McNab*); Dawn Ford (*Iggie Inch*); Susan Glover (*Mrs. Tompkins*); Pauline Little (*Mrs. Moppet*); Gary Jewell (*Mr. Moppet*); Angela Boivin (*Gloria*).

5404 ***Little Men.*** (Series; Drama; PAX; 1998-1999). Concord, Massachusetts in the 1880s is the setting. It is here that Josephine Bhaer, called Jo, and her husband, Fritz Bhaer, established Plumfield, a school for children. Jo, one of the March sisters from Louisa May Alcott's book *Little Women,* is a devoted teacher who puts the needs of the children before her own. Jo and Fritz had originally established the school for boys but financial hardships found Jo changing the enrollment to allow girls. Bess Lawrence and Anthena "Nan" Harding are the first two girls to enroll.

Bess is the daughter of Jo's younger sister, Amy. Bess is all girl — "I don't enjoy playing horseshoes, feeding the pigs or breaking nuts on my head." She enjoys the finer things in life like elegant clothes, reading and painting.

Nan is a tomboy and reminds Jo of herself when she was a girl — mischievous and a whirlwind of energy. Nan enjoys doing what the boys do including fishing and pitching horseshoes.

Nathaniel "Nat" Blake, Emil, Isaac, Jack and Dan are the principal boy students. Other regulars are Nick Riley, the handyman; Amy and Laurie, Bess's parents; Asia, the cook; and Margaret "Meg" Brooke, Jo's older sister. The children call Jo "Mrs. Jo; Jo has a horse named Penny (whom she and her sister found stuck in a bog when Jo was 12 years old). Stories follow Jo's struggles to run the school.

Program Open (Jo): "My husband and I founded Plumfield as a school for children from all walks of life. His passing has left a void in my life. But in the children I see the promise of a new day and find the strength to keep our dream alive no matter how hard the struggle."

Cast: Michelle Rene Thomas (*Jo Bhaer*); Rachel Skarsten (*Bess Lawrence*); Brittney Irvin (*Nan Harding*); Trevor Blumas (*Nathaniel Blake*); Spencer Rochfort (*Nick Riley*); Amy Price-Francis (*Amy Lawrence*); Dan Chameroy (*Theodore "Laurie" Lawrence*); Sandra Caldwell (*Asia*); Corey Server (*Dan Maddison*); Jennifer Wigmore (*Margaret "Meg" Brooke*); Michael Oliphant (*Isaac*); Alexander Campbell (*Emil*); Dov Tiefenbach (*Jack Ford*).

5405 ***The Little Mermaid.*** (Series; Cartoon; Disney; 1992–1994). An adaptation of the Disney film of the same title that depicts the adventures of Ariel, the mermaid daughter of Triton (his seventh and youngest) as she shares adventures in the sea with her friends Urchin, Flounder, Gabriella and Sebastian.

Voice Cast: Jodi Benson (*Ariel*); Kenneth Mars (*King Triton*); Samuel E. Wright (*Sebastian*); Edan Gross, Bradley Pierce (*Flounder*); Danny Cooksey (*Urchin*); Pat Carroll (*Ursula, the Sea Witch*).

5406 ***Little Miss Perfect.*** (Series; Reality; WE; 2009). Very attractive young girls (ages five to eleven) compete for the title "Little Miss Perfect" (a real Florida competition) and a $1,000 cash prize. Each episode focuses on two families (a mother and her daughter) as the mothers guide their daughters through the various challenges they must face (from posing to dress to talent). The girl most prolific in all fields receives the crown. The girls are Brandi Jean Pipkin, Ashley Ramkissoon, Shelby Locking, Hadlie Campbell, Alexa Lin Pangonas, Rhonda Meeks, Jayne Dolinskiy, Katelyn Torres, Amber Olive, Sabrina Pendergrass, Emily Tye, Jordan Adcox. Michael Galanes hosts.

5407 ***The Little People.*** (Series; Comedy; NBC). The 1972-1973 title for *The Brian Keith Show.* See this title for information.

5408 ***The Little Prince.*** (Series; Cartoon; Syn.; 1982). A three country (Japan, Germany, France) produced, low budget (fair animation) cartoon about an alien (the Little Prince) and his friend, Swiftee the Space Bird, as they visit their favorite planet, Earth, to explore new things and find adventure.

Voice Cast: Julie McWhirter, Katie Leigh (*The Little Prince*); Hal Smith (*Swiftee the Space Bird*).

5409 ***The Little Rascals.*** (Series; Cartoon; ABC; 1982–1984). A television adaptation of the popular *Our Gang* theatrical comedy shorts of the 1920s, '30s and '40s (*The Little Rascals* is the television title for the series). The adventures of a group of well meaning but mischievous children: Spanky, Alfalfa, Buckwheat, Porky, Darla, Waldo, Butch (the bully), and Woim, Butch's cohort; Petey is the gang's dog.

Voice Cast: Scott Menville (*Spanky*); Julie McWhirter (*Alfalfa/*

Woim/Porky); Patty Maloney (*Darla*); Shavar Ross (*Buckwheat*); B.J. Ward (*Butch/Waldo*); Peter Cullen (*Petie, the dog/Police Officer Ed*).

5410   *The Little Revue.* (Series; Variety; ABC; 1949–1950). A live, half-hour program of music, song and comedy from Chicago (the title is derived from the fact that the series is half as long as other variety series).

Host: Bill Sherry. **Regulars:** Gloria Van, Nancy Evans, Dick Larkin, Billy Johnson, Dick France. **Orchestra:** Rex Maupin.

5411   *Little Rosey.* (Series; Cartoon; ABC; 1990–1991). Sharp-tongued comedienne Roseanne Barr as she might have been as a pre-teenage girl. Rosey hangs out with her friends Buddy, Matthew and Jeffrey and stories relate their adventures with Rosey giving her perspective on life and how to survive childhood. Also featured are Rosey's Nanny and later friends Tess and Tater. After a bout with dismal ratings ABC cancelled the series but revised it as *The Rosey and Buddy Show* (which followed the same basic format).

Voice Cast: Kathleen Laskey, Roseanne Barr (*Little Rosey*); Noam Zylberman (*Buddy*); Tony Daniels (*Rosey's father*); Judy Marshak (*Rosey's mother*); Paulina Gillis (*Tess*); Lisa Yamanaka (*Tater*); Lisa Yamanaka (*Nanny*); Stephen Bednarski (*Jeffrey*); Stephen Bednarski (*Matthew*).

5412   *Little Shop.* (Series; Cartoon; Fox; 1991). An animated adaptation of the feature film *Little Shop of Horrors*. Seymour Krelborn is a high school nerd who, to win a science fair, cross breeds several different species of plants (including a Venus Flytrap). What results is Junior, a crude, rapping plant that has the ability to brainwash people. Stories follow Seymour's misadventures as he struggles to live with a mischievous plant with a mind of its own (and a plant that wants to go everywhere Seymour goes).

Voice Cast: Jana Lexxa (*Seymour Krelborn*); Terry McGee (*Junior*); Jennie Kwan (*Audrey*); Michael Rawl (*Mushnick*).

5413   *Little Shots.* (Pilot; Comedy; NBC; June 25, 1983). Pete, Spitter, Griddy, Linda, Ralph, Wiener and Iris are a group of pre-teenage children known around their neighborhood as the Little Shots, modern-day "Little Rascals" who find misadventure in everything they do.

Cast: Joey Lawrence (*Pete*); Robbie Kiger (*Spitter*); Keri Houlihan (*Griddy*); Mya Akerling (*Linda*); Jeff Cohen (*Ralph*); Kevin Burlat (*Wiener*); Erin Nicole Brown (*Iris*).

5414   *The Little Show.* (Series; Variety; NBC; 1950–1951). The shortened *TV Guide* title for *John Conte's Little Show.* See this title for information.

5415   *Little Vic.* (Series; Drama; Syn.; 1977). Incidents in the life of Gillie Walker, a 14-year-old orphan who becomes a jockey. Little Vic is the horse he trains and later rides in the Santa Anita Derby.

Cast: Joey Green (*Gillie Walker*); Carol Anne Seflinger (*Clara Scott*); Doney Oatman (*Julie Sayer*); David Levy (*Richie Miller*); Del Hinkley (*Mr. Hammer*); Charles Stewart (*Mr. Lawson*); Med Flory (*George Gordon*); J. Jay Saunders (*Dr. Freeman*); Myron Natwick (*Fred Amble*).

5416   *Little Women.* (Experimental; Drama; NBC; Dec. 22, 1939). The first television adaptation of the novel by Louisa May Alcott about the dreams and ambitions of Meg, Jo, Amy and Beth March, four close-knit sisters who live in Concord, Massachusetts, during the late 1860s.

Cast: Molly Pearson (*Margaret "Marmee" March*); Joanna Post (*Margaret "Meg" March*); Flora Campbell (*Josephine "Jo" March*); Frances Reid (*Elizabeth "Beth" March*); Joyce Arling (*Amy March*); Robert Conners (*Jonathan March*); Charles Bryant (*Theodore "Laurie" Lawrence*); Linda Kane (*Hannah*); Wilton Graff (*Friedrich Bhaer*).

5417   *Little Women.* (Series; Drama; Syn.; 1971). A British production based on the novel by Louisa May Alcott. The story, set in Concord, Massachusetts, during the 1880s, follows events in the lives of the close-knit March sisters: Meg, Jo, Beth and Amy, the children of Marmee and Jonathan March. Katharine is their aunt; Hannah is their maid; Theodore "Laurie" Lawrence is Amy's romantic interest; Professor Friedrich Bhaer is Jo's romantic interest; James Lawrence is Laurie's grandfather; Rogers is James's butler.

Cast: Angela Down (*Josephine "Jo" March*); Jo Rowbottom (*Margaret "Meg" March*); Janina Faye (*Amy March*); Sarah Craze (*Beth March*); Stephanie Bidmead (*Margaret "Marmee" March*); Patrick Troughton (*Jonathan March*); Jean Anderson (*Kathryn March*); Stephen Turner (*Theodore "Laurie" Lawrence*); Frederick Jaeger (*Prof. Friedrich Bhaer*); Pat Nye (*Hannah*); John Welsh (*James Lawrence*); Philip Raye (*Rogers*); Martin Jarvis (*John Brooke*).

5418   *Little Women.* (Series; Drama; NBC; 1979). Concord, Massachusetts, during the late 1860s, is the setting. The dreams, ambitions, and frustrations of the March sisters (Jo, Meg, Amy and Beth) as seen through the sentimental eyes of Jo, an aspiring writer. Based on the novel by Louisa May Alcott. In the pilot episode, Beth, the gentle, shy and frail sister, dies after being stricken by scarlet fever. Melissa, her cousin and identical look-alike, replaces her.

Other regulars are Margaret "Marmee" March, their mother; the Rev. Jonathan March, Marmee's husband; John Brooke, Meg's husband; Theodore "Laurie" Lawrence, Amy's husband; Professor Friedrich Bhaer, Jo's fiancé; James Lawrence, Laurie's grandfather; Aunt Kathryn March; Hannah, the March's cook; Amanda, James's housekeeper.

Series Cast: Jessica Harper (*Josephine "Jo" March*); Susan Walden (*Margaret "Meg" March*); Ann Dusenberry (*Amy March*); Eve Plumb (*Beth March*); Eve Plumb (*Melissa Jane Driscoll*); Dorothy McGuire (*Margaret "Marmee" March*); William Schallert (*the Rev. Jonathan March*); Cliff Potts (*John Brooke*); Richard Gilliland (*Theodore "Laurie" Lawrence*); David Ackroyd (*Prof. Friedrich Bhaer*); Robert Young (*James Lawrence*); Mildred Natwick (*Kathryn March*); Virginia Gregg (*Hannah*); Maggie Malooly (*Amanda*).

Pilot Cast: Susan Dey (*Jo March*); Meredith Baxter Birney (*Meg March*); Ann Dusenberry (*Amy March*); Eve Plumb (*Beth March*); Dorothy McGuire (*Margaret "Marmee" March*); William Schallert (*Jonathan March*); Greer Garson (*Aunt Kathryn March*); William Shatner (*Friedrich Bhaer*); Richard Gilliland (*Theodore "Laurie" Lawrence*); Robert Young (*James Lawrence*); Cliff Potts (*John Brooke*); Virginia Gregg (*Hannah*).

5419   *The Littles.* (Series; Cartoon; ABC; 1983–1984). The town of Grand Valley is the setting. It is here that Henry Bigg, a 13-year-old boy befriends the Littles, a family of mouse-high people who live in the walls of homes. William and Lucy are the parents; Dinky, Tom and Little Lucy are their children. Also living with them is Ashley Little, their adopted daughter, and Grandpa Little. Stories also focus on the efforts of the evil Dr. Hunter and his assistant, Peterson, to discover if what he believes is another life form (which he calls the Littles) really do exist, and the efforts of the Littles to remain a secret.

Voice Cast: Jimmy Keegan (*Henry Bigg*); B.J. Ward (*Ashley Little*); Bettina Bush (*Lucy Little*); Donovan Freberg (*Tom Little*); Pat Parris (*Helen Little*); Alvy Moore (*Grandpa Little*); Robert David Hall

(Dinky Little); Gregg Berger *(William Little)*; Hal Smith *(Mr. Finnigan)*; Laurel Page *(Mrs. Bigg)*; Robert David Hall *(George Bigg)*.

5420   The Littlest Groom. (Series; Reality; Fox; 2004). Glen Foster, who stands four feet, five inches tall, is seeking the perfect mate. Through a series of dating challenges, Glen must choose the one woman he feels is best suited for him. The program, considered the worst reality show ever broadcast, was canceled after two episodes (Feb. 16 to 23, 2004).

5421   The Littlest Hobo. (Series; Adventure; Syn.; 1964). Canadian produced program that follows the trail of London, an apparently un-owned German Shepherd as he roams and helps people in trouble. A revised version of the series, also produced in Canada, appeared in syndication in 1980 as *The Littlest Hobo*. Terry Bush performs the latter program theme, "Maybe Tomorrow."

5422   The Littlest Pet Shop. (Series; Cartoon; Syn.; 1995). Elwood Funk owns a pet shop that specializes in miniature versions of full-sized animals (like Chloe the Cat and Stu the Sheep Dog). Stories follow the adventures of the various animals, especially Stu and Chloe, after they are sold but always manage to find their way back to their original home.

   Voice Cast: Babs Chula *(Chloe)*; Michael Donovan *(Stu the Dog)*; Ian James Corlett *(Elwood Funk)*; Ted Cole *(Squeaks)*.

5423   Live and Loud. (Series; Music; VH-1; 2009). A six episode Friday evening program that presents, in an abbreviated form, music concerts by the country's "hottest groups" (for example, Def Leppard, Poison, Nickelback, The Fray and Creed).

   Host: Michele Merkin.

5424   Live Girls. (Pilot; Comedy; Unaired; Produced for Fox in 2000). The lives of three gorgeous young women (Rebecca, Lynne and Kathryn) living in a small New England town and hoping for bigger and better things.

   Cast: Jenny McCarthy *(Rebecca)*; Kiele Sanchez *(Lynne)*; Emily Rutherfurd *(Kathryn)*.

5425   Live-In. (Series; Comedy; CBS; 1989). Sarah Mathews is the manager of the clothing department of Macy's in Manhattan. Her husband, Ed Mathews, owns the Mathews Sporting Goods Store in New Jersey. They are the parents of teenage boys Danny and Peter and infant daughter Melissa. When Sarah decides it is time to return to work after her maternity leave, she applies for a live-in housekeeper at the Broder Domestic Agency.

   The agency finds Lisa Wells, a beautiful Australian girl (it is not explained why the agency had to go to Australia to find the Mathews a nanny/housekeeper). Lisa grew up in the Australia Outback and lived in a small house with seven brothers and sisters. She now has her own room at the Mathews house (30 Hogan Place in New Jersey) and the responsibility of caring for Melissa and watching over Danny and Peter.

   Danny and Peter attend Whitney High School. Peter, a freshman, has yet to become overly concerned about girls and he and Lisa get along fine together. Danny, a sophomore, is just the opposite, a girl-crazy teenager who can't believe a girl like Lisa is living in their house (he has set his goal to catch a peek of Lisa in the nude). Lisa's experiences in America as she cares for the Mathews children are the focal point of stories.

   Cast: Lisa Patrick *(Lisa Wells)*; Kimberly Farr *(Sarah Matthews)*; Hugh Maguire *(Ed Matthews)*; Chris Young *(Danny Matthews)*; David Moscow *(Peter Matthews)*; Allison and Melissa Lindsey *(Melissa Matthews)*; Jenny O'Hara *(Muriel Spiegleman)*; Lightfield Lewis *(Gator)*.

5426   Live Like a Millionaire. (Series; Game; CBS; ABC; 1951–1953). Performances by aspiring but undiscovered talent. The winners, determined by studio audience applause, receive one week's tax on a million dollars as their prize. Aired on CBS (Jan. 5, 1951 to Mar. 14, 1952) and ABC (Oct. 25, 1952 to Feb. 7, 1953).

   Host: John Nelson *(CBS)*, Jack McCoy *(ABC)*. **Music:** Ivan Ditmars.

5427   Live Shot. (Series; Drama; UPN; 1995-1996). A behind-the-scenes look at the world of television news reporting and story gathering as seen through the experiences of Alex Rydell, the news director for KXZX-TV in Los Angeles. Alex is divorced and caring for his son, Sean. Harry Chandler Moore is the station's somewhat vain anchorman (called "The Beacon of Truth") for *Re-Action News*. Sherry Beck is the show's co-anchor, a bright and ambitious girl who has set her goal to become a top news anchor. Nancy Lockridge is the show's news producer; Tommy Greer and "Fast" Eddie Santini are the reckless news crew (they will let nothing stand in their way of getting a story; they have been nicknamed "The News Brothers"); Ricardo Sandoval is a news reporter; Lou Waller is the sportscaster; Liz Vega is the investigative reporter; Marvin Seaborne is the news commentator; Joe Vitale is the show's executive producer; Rick Evers is the assignment editor; and Peggy Traynor is news traffic controller.

   Cast: Jeff Yagher *(Alex Rydell)*; Karen Austin *(Helen Forbes)*; Sam Anderson *(Marvin Seaborne)*; David Birney *(Harry Chandler Moore)*; Wanda DeJesus *(Liz Vega)*; Spencer Klein *(Sean Rydell)*; Bruce McGill *(Joe Vitale)*; Cheryl Pollak *(Nancy Lockridge)*; Rebecca Staab *(Sherry Beck)*; Eddie Velez *(Ricardo Sandoval)*; Antonia Jones *(Peggy Traynor)*; David Coburn *(Rick Evers)*; Michael Watson *("Fast" Eddie Santini)*; Hill Harper *(Tommy Grier)*; Thomas Byrd *(Lou Waller)*; Nia Long *(Ramona Greer)*.

5428   Live Through This. (Series; Drama; MTV; 2000-2001). The Jackson Decker Band was a once famous 1980s band that has since disbanded. Twenty years later the band members unite and decide to perform their last comeback during a summer tour. The band members are Rick Parsons, Annie Baker, Drake Taylor and Keith Rooney. Chase Rooney, Keith's son has just graduated from Stanford and is managing the tour. Keith's daughter, Olivia; Darby, Rick's daughter; Travis Williams, Drake's estranged son, and Tallulah "Lu" Baker, Annie's daughter, are also accompanying the band. Stories follow the band as they tour various cities and the problems that ensue as they struggle to live as a family on the band's tour bus. Pat Benatar performs original songs by Graham Nash.

   Cast: Bruce Dinsmore *(Rick Parsons)*; Tom Lock *(Chase Rooney)*; Jennifer Dale *(Annie Baker)*; Ron Lea *(Drake Taylor)*; David Nerman *(Keith Rooney)*; Matthew Carey *(Travis Williams)*; Jessica Welch *(Olivia Rooney)*; Sarah Manninen *(Tallulah "Lu" Baker)*; Jane McGregor *(Darby Parsons)*.

5429   Live with Regis and Kathie Lee. (Series; Talk; Syn.; 1989–2001). A live daily talk program with Regis Philbin and Kathie Lee Gifford as the co-hosts. Celebrity interviews are mixed with the show's signature attraction, the exchange of conversation between the hosts at the beginning of each episode. In 2001, after co-starring with Regis for 12 years, Kathie Lee opted to leave to pursue other career goals. She was replaced by actress Kelly Ripa who continued the chemistry the show is noted for.

   Hosts: Regis Philbin, Kathie Lee Gifford.

5430   Live with Regis and Kelly. (Series; Talk; Syn.; 2001–). A continuation of *Live with Regis and Kathie Lee* with Kelly Ripa replacing Kathie Lee Gifford as the co-host to Regis Philbin. Programs follow the same format — an exchange of conversation between the two hosts coupled with celebrity interviews.

Hosts: Regis Philbin, Kelly Ripa.

5431   *The Lively Ones.* (Series; Variety; NBC; 1962–1963). An unusual summer program that features music, song and dance set against offbeat electronic background locations. Aired from July 26 to Sept. 13, 1962; and July 25 to Sept. 12, 1963.

Host: Vic Damone. **Regulars:** Joan Staley, Shirley Yelm, Gloria Neil, Quinn O'Hara, The Earl Brown Dancers. **Orchestra:** Jerry Fielding.

5432   *The Lives of Jenny Dolan.* (Pilot; Crime Drama; NBC; Oct. 27, 1975). Jennifer "Jenny" Dolan is a glamorous investigative reporter for the *New World Journal.* Her exploits as she risks her life to uncover the facts behind potentially dangerous stories is the focal point of the unsold series. Joe Rossiter is her editor.

Cast: Shirley Jones (*Jenny Dolan*); Stephen Boyd (*Joe Rossiter*).

5433   *Livin' Large.* (Pilot; Comedy; ABC; April 30, 1989). "Livin' Large" is street talk for "doing fine," "feeling good" or "living well." It is spoken by the young people who live in the poorer sections of Manhattan and who are still full of dreams that have not yet been deflated by the harsh realities of life. The proposal was to focus on 18-year-old Billy Angelo and his wife, Marsha, idealists who hope to one day be "Livin' Large." Other regulars are Billy's friends Kevin (an apartment building super), Sal (the owner of Sal's Barber Shop, the hangout), Luz (works for Sal) and G.Q.

Cast: Eagle Eye Cherry (*Billy Angelo*); Alexia Robinson (*Marsha Angelo*); Jon Polito (*Sal*); Tim Guinee (*Kevin Schaeffer*); Tasia Valenza (*Luz Rodriquez*); Keith Amos (*G.Q.*).

5434   *Livin' Large.* (Series; Reality; MTV; 2002). Carmen Electra and Kadeem Hardison host a program that offers a glimpse into the lives of the rich and famous — from their lavish homes to their exotic getaways.

5435   *Livin' on a Prayer.* (Pilot; Comedy; Unaired; Produced for CBS in 2010). Stephanie is a young, beautiful and single. She lives in Pittsburgh, has had many dates, but finding the perfect mate is not as easy as she thought. The proposal was to follow Stephanie as she returns to the dating scene to find the one man she can spend the rest of her life with.

Cast: Jaime Pressly (*Stephanie*); Lindsay Sloane (*Gina*); Brandon Hardesty (*PK*); Joe Manganiello (*Doug*); Kyle Bornheimer (*Tommy*).

5436   *Living Dolls.* (Series; Comedy; ABC; 1989). Charlene ("Charlie") Briscoe, Caroline Weldon, Emily Franklin and Martha Lambert are beautiful 16-year-old models who live with Trish Carlin, a former high fashion model turned agent (owner of the Carlin Modeling Agency, which she operates from her home at 68th Street and Madison Avenue in New York City).

The girls attend Lexy High School and share two rooms in Trish's home. Charlie is from Brooklyn and first appeared on the "Life's a Ditch" episode of *Who's the Boss?* (as Sam's [Alyssa Milano] friend). She is streetwise and doesn't believe she is as beautiful as people tell her she is. Martha, whose nickname is "Pooch," is from (and constantly talks about) Idaho. Caroline enjoys shopping and her biggest challenge is to decide what to wear each day. She is a "C" student and a bit dense. Emily is a straight "A" student and wants to become a doctor ("Being a doctor is all I ever dream about"); she gets extremely upset if she scores badly on a test. Caroline calls her "M." Despite the fact that the girls strive to do their best, their teachers consider them "Human Hangers" ("Girls who are so pretty that they can't be smart").

Rick (whom Charlie calls "Twerp") is Trish's son; Marion is Trish's sister; Todd Carlin is Trish's ex-husband.

Series Cast: Michael Learned (*Trish Carlin*); Leah Remini (*Charlie Briscoe*); Halle Berry (*Emily Franklin*); Deborah Tucker (*Caroline Weldon*); Alison Elliott (*Martha Lambert*); David Moscow (*Rick Carlin*); Marion Ross (*Marion*); Edward Winter (*Todd Carlin*).

Unaired Pilot Cast: Michael Learned (*Trish Curtis*); Leah Remini (*Charlie*); Melissa Willis (*Caroline*); Vivica A. Fox (*Emily*); Alison Elliott (*Martha*); Jonathan Ward (*Rick Curtis*).

5437   *Living Easy.* (Series; Women; Syn.; 1973). A daily program of guests, interviews, fashion, decorating tips, music, and songs with psychiatrist Dr. Joyce Brothers as the host.

Program Open: "Dr. Joyce Brothers in *Living Easy* ... with Mike Darrow and Bernie Green's Orchestra. Now here's your hostess from the Little Theater off 44th Street, Joyce Brothers."

Host: Dr. Joyce Brothers. **Announcer:** Mike Darrow. **Music:** Bernard Green.

5438   *The Living End.* (Pilot; Comedy; CBS; Mar. 17, 1972). Douglas "Doug" Newman is a veteran defense end for the Chicago Cherokees, a professional football team. The proposal was to relate Doug's misadventures as he tries to divide his time between the two things he loves most — his wife (Nancy) and his team (Bullets, the coach; and players Richie, Mickey, Henry and Stan). See also *Two's Company*, a revised version of this pilot.

Cast: Lou Gossett, Jr. (*Doug Newman*); Diana Sands (*Nancy Newman*); Dick O'Neill (*Bullets*); Paul Cavonis (*Richie Rosen*); John Calvin (*Mickey*); Roger E. Mosley (*Henry*); Don Sherman (*Stan*).

5439   *Living in Captivity.* (Series; Comedy; Fox; 1998). Three couples struggling to co-exist in a gated, planned suburban community is the basis for a program that explores their individual problems as they each face life head on. The couples are Carmen Santucci and his wife, Lisa; Curtis and Tamara Cook; and Will and Becca Merek.

Cast: Lenny Venito (*Carmine Santucci*); Mia Cottet (*Lisa Santucci*); Dondre T. Whitfield (*Curtis Cook*); Kira Arne (*Tamara Cook*); Matt Letscher (*Will Merek*); Melinda McGraw (*Becca Merek*).

5440   *Living in Paradise.* (Pilot; Comedy; NBC; Feb. 1, 1981). Following the death of his wife, Vincent Sherman, a retired businessman, moves to a retirement village called Paradise Park. The proposal was to focus on Vincent as he seeks to live the carefree life of a bachelor, despite Winnie Coogan, his neighbor, who has set her sights on him. Other regulars are Jason, Vincent's son (producer of the TV series *Sorority Sisters*); Hazel, Vincent's landlady; Mel, Hazel's husband; and Donna, Jason's fiancée. Eddie Albert performs the theme, "That's the Way I Am."

Cast: Eddie Albert (*Vincent Slattery*); Georgann Johnson (*Winnie Coogan*); Jerry Houser (*Jason Slattery*); Debralee Scott (*Hazel Adamson*); Alan Oppenheimer (*Mel Adamson*); Patti Townsend (*Donna*).

5441   *Living Lohan.* (Series; Reality; E!; 2008). Dina Lohan is the single mother of Lindsay and Ali Lohan (Dina is divorced from Michael). Lindsay, the troubled (at the time) mega star does not appear on the program. The focus is on Ali, her 14-year-old sister whom stage mother Dina is hoping to launch on a singing career. The program showcases Dina's professional and home life as well as Ali's cutting a record in Las Vegas.

5442   *Living Single.* (Series; Comedy; Fox; 1993–1997). *Flavor* is a contemporary monthly black magazine owned by Khadjah James, a single woman living in Prospect Heights, Brooklyn, New York, with her cousin Synclaire James and friend Regine Hunter.

Khadjah attended Howard University and calls her magazine *Flavor* "because we've got taste." Khadjah's competition is the tacky *Savor* magazine; *Flavor* is located above the Chemical Bank Building in Manhattan.

Snyclaire is from Missouri and works as the magazine's perky receptionist. She has a desk full of good luck troll dolls "to spread joy and happiness in the office" and uses an "emotional filing system. Things that make Khadjah happy are in front; the things that make her weary are in back; and the things that upset her are not within her reach." Before acquiring the job at Flavor, Synclaire worked as a cashier, telephone solicitor, babysitter and order taker at Turkey Burger Hut.

Regine is a buyer for the Boutique. She can't bear to be without a man by her side. She dresses in sexy attire and shows ample cleavage to attract men. She is self-centered, self-absorbed and wants kids — "These genes are too good to waste." Khadjah calls her "loud and busty" (Kim Fields' real-life breast reduction surgery was incorporated into the series, changing the Regine character somewhat. She became less obnoxious and more caring). Regine, real name Regina, is a woman on a mission to marry a man "who knows that fine wine doesn't come with a twist off cap." She believes that she is irresistible to men and that "sometimes life is not fair to me. That's why bras come in different sizes." She believes her breasts ("my double d's") got her into M.I.T. and made her homecoming queen. Regine also lives by her code, "the three c's of men" ("catch, control and conquer"). She also believes that if she is in a room and a man does not look at her "then he must be gay"; the downside: if Regine is without a man, she goes on a chocolate-eating binge.

Maxene "Max" Shaw is a lawyer for the firm of Evans, Bell and Associates in Manhattan. She was born in Philadelphia and later became an attorney for the Public Defenders Office.

Overton "Obie" Wakefield Jones is the building's maintenance man. He is dating Synclaire and lives by the handyman's code "I won't rest until it's fixed." Kyle Barker is Obie's roommate. He is a stockbroker and believes that he is irresistible to women. Kyle was in a band called Water ("the missing element in Earth, Wind and Fire") and had a love-hate relationship with Max.

Cast: Queen Latifah (*Khadjah James*); Kim Fields (*Regine Hunter*); Kim Coles (*Synclaire James*); Erika Alexander (*Max Shaw*); John Henton (*Overton Jones*); T.C. Carson (*Kyle Barker*).

5443   *Living with Fran*. (Series; Comedy; WB; 2005-2006). Reeves Interiors is an interior decorating business run by Fran Reeves, a beautiful and sexy divorcee who is the mother of Josh (21 years old) and Allison (15). Fran, who is in her 40s, but won't admit it, is divorced from Ted, but is not starving for affection — she is dating (and living with) Riley Martin, a handsome contractor who is in his twenties (26).

Fran married Ted, now a doctor, right after high school. Ted's infidelity caused the breakup. Fran got the house and custody of the kids. She decided to redecorate the house and hired Riley to turn Josh's room into a gym. It was a love at first sight and Fran asked Riley to move in with her, Allison accepted the older woman–younger man relationship, but Josh doesn't and has a hard time accepting Riley as his potential step father. (Josh has returned home after being expelled from medical school. During a 72-hour shift, Josh went a bit nuts and chased a male nurse with a bone saw. He was expelled.)

Fran has blossomed into a self-confident, free spirited, emancipated woman with a growing career (she was always sweet and self doubting) — something else Josh has a hard time accepting. As Josh seeks to find his goal in life, he works as the assistant manager of a video tape/DVD store called Video King. Josh was only in medical school for six weeks and it cost Fran $47,000.

Allison is an adorable teenager and takes after her mother and like Fran, considers charisma the family curse — she can't help but flirt with boys. Allison works at I-Hop and delights in needling Josh about Fran and Riley's relationship. The program reunites Fran Drescher (Fran) and Charles Shaugnessy (Ted) who were the co-stars of *The Nanny*.

Cast: Fran Drescher (*Fran Reeves*); Ryan McPartlin (*Riley Martin*); Ben Friedman (*Josh Reeves*); Misti Traya (*Allison Reeves*); Charles Shaughnessy (*Ted Reeves*).

5444   *Lizzie McGuire*. (Series; Comedy; Disney; 2001–2004). The problems faced by a very pretty 13-year-old girl growing up in a small town is the basic premise of *Lizzie McGuire*.

Elizabeth Brooke McGuire, better known as Lizzie, is a seventh (then 8th grader) at Eldridge Elementary School (she later attends Bayridge High School). She lives at 804 Linwood Drive and is the daughter of Sam and Jo McGuire. She has a younger brother, Matt, and is best friends with Miranda and Gordo.

Lizzie always does (or tries) to do what is right. She is considered "a good girl prototype" by her friends mothers. While Lizzie is quite obedient and causes little trouble for her parents, Matt appears to be constantly bored and to relieve his boredom, tries to find something to do — and always winds up in trouble for doing so.

Other regulars are Kate Sanders, the class beauty (and snob); Ethan Craft, the rather simple minded school "hunk"; Larry Tudgeman, the school's number one geek; Lanny Onasis, Matt's friend (who never speaks); and Melina Bianco, Matt's classmate — and cohort in mischief.

Cast: Hilary Duff (*Lizzie McGuire*); Hallie Todd (*Jo McGuire*); Robert Carradine (*Sam McGuire*); Jake Thomas (*Matt McGuire*); Lalaine Vergas (*Miranda Sanchez*); Adam Lamberg (*David "Gordo" Gordon*); Ashlie Brillault (*Kate Sanders*); Clayton Synder (*Ethan Craft*); Kyle Downes (*Larry Tudgeman*); Christian Copelin (*Lanny Onasis*); Carly Schroeder (*Melina Bianco*).

5445   *The Lloyd Bridges Show*. (Series; Anthology; CBS; 1962-1963). Dramatic presentations that recount the stories of free-lance journalist Adam Sheppard.

Cast: Lloyd Bridges (*Adam Sheppard*).

5446   *Lloyd Bridges Water World*. (Series; Reality; Syn.; 1972). Excursions to various tropical islands as well as tips on boating safety and marine band radio use with former *Sea Hunt* star Lloyd Bridges as the host. Harold Haney is the announcer.

5447   *Lloyd in Space*. (Series; Cartoon; Disney; 2001). Lloyd Nebulon is a futuristic alien who lives on the Intredvick Space Station with his mother, Commander Nora Nebulon, and his telepathic sister, Francine. Lloyd has green skin and is a member of the Verdigream race. While his mother commands the space station, Lloyd has befriended Eddie Horton, an American teenager; Kurt Blobberts, a purple blob from a species called Blobullons; and Douglas McNoggin, an alien brain from a species called Cerebellians. Stories relate Lloyd's misadventures with his friends on the space station.

Voice Cast: Courtland Mead (*Lloyd Nebulon*); April Winchell (*Nora Nebulon*); Nicolette Little (*Francine Nebulon*); Justin Shenkarow (*Eddie Horton*); Pamela Hayden (*Douglas McNoggin*); Bill Fagerbakke (*Kurt Blobberts*); Diedrich Bader (*Harvulian "Boomer" Standervault*); Clancy Brown (*Officer Frank Horton*); Warren Sroka (*Rodney Glaxer*); Anndi McAfee (*Brittany*).

5448   *The Lloyd Thaxton Show*. (Series; Variety; Syn.; 1964). Performances by the top names in rock and roll music.

Host: Lloyd Thaxton. **Regulars:** Lynne Marta, Michael Storm.

5449   *Lobo.* (Series; Crime Drama; NBC; 1980-1981). A spin-off from *The Misadventures of Sheriff Lobo.* When the governor of Atlanta discovers that Orly County, Georgia, is virtually crime free due to what he believes is the honest work of the larcenous Sheriff Elroy P. Lobo, he hires Lobo and his deputies to help curb the rising crime rate. The adventures of Sheriff Lobo as he and his deputies, Perkins and Birdie, attempt to do for Atlanta what they did in Orly is the focal point of stories. Perkins is following in Lobo's footsteps; Birdie (real name Birdwell Hawkins) is on the straight and narrow and a thorn in Lobo's back; John E. Carson is the chief of detectives, Metro Atlanta Police; Brandy and Peaches are the gorgeous officers Lobo works with; Hildy is the sergeant who is on to Lobo's dirty deeds; George is the police lab technician. Frankie Laine performs the theme, "Sheriff Lobo."

Cast: Claude Akins (*Sheriff Elroy P. Lobo*); Mills Watson (*Deputy Perkins*); Brian Kerwin (*Deputy Birdwell "Birdie" Hawkins*); Nicholas Coster (*John E. Carson*); Tara Buckman (*Off. Brandy Ames*); Amy Bostwinick (*Off. Peaches McLain*); Nell Carter (*Sgt. Hildy Jones*); William Schallert, Mark Roberts (*The Governor*); Dudley Knight (*George*).

5450   *Local 306.* (Pilot; Comedy; NBC; Aug. 23, 1976). After many years on the job, the middle-aged Harvey Gordon is appointed chief steward of Plumber's Local 306. The proposal was to relate Harvey's efforts to deal with the assortment of problems that arise both at home from a nagging wife and daughter (Rose and Helene) and on the job from fellow union members (Hutchings, Rocco and Fillmore).

Cast: Eugene Roche (*Harvey Gordon*); Miriam-Byrd Nethery (*Rose Gordon*); Susan Sennett (*Helene Gordon*); Milton Parsons (*Hutchings*); Roy Stewart (*Rocco*); Hilly Hicks (*Fillmore*).

5451   *Local Heroes.* (Series; Comedy; Fox; 1996). Jake, Mert, Stosh and Eddie are four men in their twenties who have remained friends since meeting in high school. They live in Pittsburgh, have mundane jobs and hangout together at Blue Lou's Bar and Restaurant. Stories relate their get together meetings at the bar where they talk of their adventures, plan for the future, chase girls and indulge in other male-bonding rituals.

Cast: Jay Mohr (*Jake*); Louis Ferriera (*Mert*); Jason Kristofer (*Stosh*); Ken Hudson Campbell (*Eddie*); Kristin Dattilo (*Bonnie*); Paula Cale (*Gloria*); Brian Doyle Murray (*"Big" Stosh*); Thomas Tevana (*Dan*); Rhoda Gemignani (*Mrs. Trakas*); Tricia Vessey (*Nikki*).

5452   *Locals.* (Pilot; Comedy; Fox; June 23, 1994). Port Ellen is a small town that is also "The Rake Capital of the World." Jerry Hawthorne, the town barber for 25 years, charges $5 for any haircut. His sister, Rita Levine, runs a business adjacent to Jerry's Barber Shop called Pancake Heaven. The town has a motto: "If you think you don't need a rake, then you're really, really wrong" and the unsold series relates life in Port Ellen as seen through the eyes of Jerry (who introduces viewers to the town and its colorful citizens). Other regulars are Mike, Rita's second husband; Fred Wrighter, Rita's son from a first marriage; Old Claude, a barber shop regular; Margie, the town's sexpot (she has eyes for Jerry); and Royce Pruitt, the police chief.

Cast: John Ratzenberger (*Jerry Hawthorne*); Meagen Fay (*Rita Levine*); Kevin Connolly (*Fred Wrighter*); Jeff Corey (*Old Claude*); Jay Acovone (*Mike Levine*); Glenn Shadix (*Royce Pruitt*); Diane Salinger (*Margie Murray*); Ray Baker (*Mayor*).

5453   *The Locator.* (Series; Reality; WE; 2008). Troy Dunn is a real life locator (a person who finds missing people). Emotionally charged episodes follow Tony as he reunites people who have drifted apart and now need to be reunited (from lost loves to childhood friends to adopted children seeking their birth mothers).

5454   *Lock, Stock and Barrel.* (Pilot; Western; NBC; Sept. 24, 1971). The West of the 1880s is the setting for a proposal about Roselle and Clare Bridgeman, newlyweds struggling to begin a new life in the rugged Colorado territory. A second pilot, *Hitched* aired March 31, 1973 that followed the same format but which also failed to produce a series.

First Pilot Cast: Belinda J. Montgomery (*Roselle Bridgeman*); Tim Matheson (*Clare Bridgeman*).

Second Pilot Cast: Sally Field (*Roselle Bridgeman*); Tim Matheson (*Clare Bridgeman*).

5455   *Lock Up.* (Series; Crime Drama; Syn.; 1959). Herbert L. Maris is an attorney based in Philadelphia. He is a man who believes his clients are innocent and will do what it takes to defend them in court. Stories relate Maris's case investigations as he and his legman, Weston, seek the evidence to put the real culprits behind bars.

Cast: Macdonald Carey (*Herbert L. Maris*); John Doucette (*Weston*).

5456   *The Log of the Black Pearl.* (Pilot; Adventure; NBC; Jan. 4, 1975). Following the death of his grandfather (Captain Andrew Sand), stockbroker Christopher Sand, the only living heir, inherits the *Black Pearl*, a deeply in debt three-mast sailing ship. Rather than selling the ship and leaving his grandfather with a bad reputation, Chris assumes ownership to pay off his creditors. The proposed series was to follow Chris's adventures as captain of the *Black Pearl*. Other regulars are Captain "Fitz" Fitzsimmons, the skipper; and Jocko, the first mate.

Cast: Kiel Martin (*Chris Sand*); Ralph Bellamy (*"Fitz" Fitzsimmons*); Jack Kruschen (*Jocko Roper*).

5457   *The Logan's Legacy.* (Series; Drama; UPN; 1989-1990). Lexington, Kentucky, 1861, is home to the Logans, Irish immigrants who have established a tobacco and horse ranch empire. Stories relate their struggles to maintain their empire. Ned Logan, the widowed patriarch, is continuing the legacy established by his ancestors 100 years ago; Sean, the eldest son, grows tobacco and is later appointed the Deputy Director of Lexington; Clay is Ned's hard-working younger son; Lexy is Ned's feisty, younger daughter; Alice, Lexy's older sister, has taken on the responsibility of running the house since her mother, Libby, died giving birth to Lexy. Regine is Libby's sister; Jerry is the orphan taken in by the Logans; Isaac is a ranch hand; Marita is Ned's secretary; Vivian is the banker's daughter; William is Vivian's scheming brother; John is Vivian's family estate manager; Charlotte is the woman Ned later marries; Molly is the town's bad girl.

Cast: Brett Cullen (*Ned Logan*); Grayson McCouch (*Sean Logan*); Jeremy Garrett (*Clay Logan*); Sarah Rayne (*Lexy Logan*); Lea Moreno Young (*Alice Logan*); Ron Melendez (*Jeremy Bradford*); Steven Williams (*Isaac*); Sharon Leal (*Marita*); Chelsea Field (*Aunt Regine*); Brigid Branaugh (*Molly McGuire*); Casey Briggs (*John Hayden Turner*); Lisa Sheridan (*Vivian Winters*); Sean Bridges (*William Winters*).

5458   *Logan's Run.* (Series; Science Fiction; CBS; 1977-1978). In the year A.D. 2319, an atomic holocaust ravages the world. The remaining segment of civilization establishes itself in the City of Domes, a programmed society wherein no one over the age of 30 is permitted to live. At precisely that age, everyone goes willingly into the Carousel for the Ceremony of the Great Sleep, where they are led to believe that their lives will be renewed; in reality, they are exterminated. Those who try to circumvent this tradition are called Runners and become the prey of the Sandmen, whose duty is to pursue and destroy them. Runners are seeking Sanctuary, a supposed haven where all are free to live beyond the age of 30. Logan 5, a Sandman, begins to question the Carousel. Never having seen a reborn citizen, Logan becomes curious. He follows a male Runner to Quadrant 4. There he meets Jessica 6, a girl runner who helps those seeking Sanctuary. Jessica confirms Logan's doubts and tells him that the Carousel means death; she also convinces him that beyond the city there is a Sanctuary. Before Logan is able to do anything, Francis 7, a Sandman, appears and orders Logan to destroy the runners. Logan's hesitation prompts Francis to kill the male; as he is about to kill Jessica, Logan knocks him unconscious. Now, a traitor, Logan becomes a Runner and joins forces with Jessica in an attempt to find Sanctuary.

Concerned about Logan's escape, the Council of Elders, who run the City of Domes (a.k.a. Dome City), assign Francis the task of returning Logan and Jessica so they can be used as an example and testify that there is no Sanctuary. Francis is then told the Carousel is a myth — but necessary because the city can support only a limited number of people. He is promised a seat on the council when he completes his mission. Stories follow Logan and Jessica's adventures with Rem, the android with humanlike qualities who abandoned his robot-run society, as they search for Sanctuary — before Francis finds and captures them. Morgan, Jonathan and Martin are the city leaders with speaking roles. Based on the feature film of the same title.

Cast: Gregory Harrison (*Logan 5*); Heather Menzies (*Jessica 6*); Randy Powell (*Francis 7*); Donald Moffat (*Rem*); Morgan Woodward (*Morgan*); Wright King (*Jonathan*); E.J. Andre (*Martin*); Stan Stratton (*Benjamin*).

5459   *Lois and Clark: The New Adventures of Superman.* (Series; Adventure; ABC; 1993–1997). When the story opens, Clark Kent is seen driving to Metropolis, a city of 12 million people, seeking a job as a reporter for the *Daily Planet*, "The world's greatest newspaper" (according to its editor, Perry White). Clark is, in reality, Kal-El, the only known survivor of the planet Krypton. Before Krypton exploded, the infant Kal-El's parents, Jor-El and Lara (David Warner, Eliza Roberts), placed him in an experimental rocket and programmed the ship to land on Earth, a planet Jor-El knew to be inhabited. On May 17, 1966, the rocket lands in Smallville, Kansas, and the child is found by Jonathan and Martha Kent, a childless farm couple who raise him as Clark Kent. As the child grows, the Kents become aware of the fact their son is no ordinary boy. He demonstrates abilities of amazing strength, keen hearing and amazing eyesight. Clark attended Smallville High School and worked as a reporter on the *Smallville Press*. He yearned to travel to Metropolis but couldn't figure out how to be Clark Kent and secretly use his powers to help mankind. The solution comes when Clark ruins his clothes during a story investigation. He tells his mother "that I need a costume." Martha makes several before coming up with the red and blue one (she uses the blankets that were originally wrapped around Clark. The symbol *S* was a part of those blankets). In Metropolis, Clark meets with editor Perry White and acquires a job as reporter. He then meets his co-workers: Lois Lane, Jimmy Olsen and Cat Grant.

Clark resides at the Apollo Hotel at 344 Clinton in Metropolis. Kryptonite, the green fragments from his planet's explosion, is the only substance that can take away Superman's powers and ultimately destroy Clark.

Lois Lane, who later marries Clark, is "The best damn investigative reporter I've ever seen" says Perry. She attended Metropolis High School (where she was called "Lo Lo") and lives in Apartment 105 at 6304 Chambers Place with her teenage sister, Lucy Lane. Phyllis Coates (TV's original 1952 Lois Lane), then Beverly Garland played Lois's mother, Ellen Lane; Harve Presnell was Lois's father, Dr. Sam Lane. Lois has one bad habit — "I like to pig out at the Fudge Castle."

Perry White, the former mayor of Metropolis, is the paper's no nonsense editor. He is an Elvis Presley fanatic and shouts "Great Shades of Elvis" when something upsets him. Perry is also an ordained minister of the First Church of Blue Suede Deliverance ("I was at Graceland, saw an ad for it on the back of a match cover and the rest is history"). Perry's competition is the *Metropolis Star*.

Jimmy Olsen, the paper's photographer, also likes to dabble in investigating. Perry calls him "Jimbo" and he calls Clark "C.K." Catherine Grant, called Cat, is the paper's society editor/gossip columnist (she is also called "Cat Monger"). The evil Lex Luthor is worth $20 billion and runs a company called LexCorp (a front for his illegal and sinister activities). He appears to have his hands in everything and claims he can't be caught because "Evidence separates the criminal from the successful businessman." Lex also runs LexTel Communications, the city's television station.

See also *The Adventures of Superboy*, *The Adventures of Superman*, *The Adventures of Superpup*, *Smallville* and *Superboy*.

Cast: Dean Cain (*Clark Kent/Superman*); Teri Hatcher (*Lois Lane*); Michael Landis, Justin Whalen (*Jimmy Olsen*); Tracy Scoggins (*Cat Grant*); Lane Smith (*Perry White*); Elizabeth Barondes, Roxana Zal (*Lucy Lane*); John Shea (*Lex Luthor*); Eddie Jones (*Jonathan Kent*); K Callan (*Martha Kent*).

5460   *Lola.* (Pilot; Comedy; CBS; Aug. 1, 1990). When Lola Baltic, a successful attorney, becomes dissatisfied with the fast-paced life of New York City, she and her family (husband, Peter, son Donald, and mother Phoebe) move to Connecticut to begin new lives. The proposal was to follow Lola as she struggles to divide her time between a family, a home and a job — and still find the life of peace and quiet she is seeking. Slim Jim, his wife Annie and their daughter, Francesca, are their neighbors.

Cast: Lesley Ann Warren (*Lola Baltic*); James Read (*Peter Baltic*); Alexis Smith (*Phoebe*); Malachi Pearson (*Donald Baltic*); Don Lake (*Slim Jim Alberino*); Linda Hart (*Annie Alberino*); Jessica Puscas (*Francesca Alberino*).

5461   *Lollipop Louie.* (Pilot; Comedy-Drama; ABC; Jan. 10, 1963). Louie Mastraeani is a happy-go-lucky dreamer who loves lollipops and earns his living as a fisherman in California. The proposal was to relate the various mishaps Louie encounters as he just goes about living life. Aired on *Alcoa Premiere*.

Cast: Aldo Ray (*Louie Mastraeani*).

5462   *London and Davis in New York.* (Pilot; Crime Drama; CBS; Sept. 9, 1984). Photographer Claudia London and journalist John Greyson Davis are lovers who are also a world-famous photojournalist team. Although they are from opposite sides of the track (Claudia is from a wealthy family; John is from a poor one) they find an attraction to each other and cover the globe seeking stories and solving crimes. Other regulars are Paul Fisk, Claudia's chef; Frances Meyers, John's housekeeper; and Brandon Westphal, a rival photographer. Chuck Mangione composed "The Love Theme from London and Davis."

Cast: Season Hubley (*Claudia London*); Richard Crenna (*John Davis*); Roddy McDowall (*Paul Fisk*); Vernee Watson (*Frances Meyers*); James Carroll Jordan (*Brandon Westphal*).

5463   *The London Palladium.* (Series; Variety; NBC; 1966). Entertainment acts from the London Palladium Music Hall in England. Guest celebrities host.

Program Open: "From the world's greatest variety theater, *The*

London Palladium Show starring Roger Moore, Eric Morecombe and Ernie Wise, Millicent Martin and Joe Brown and the Bachelors. *The London Palladium* will return after these messages."

Host: Lorne Greene *(May 26, 1966)*; Kate Smith *(June 3, 1966)*; Jonathan Winters *(June 30, 1966)*; Hugh O'Brian *(July 15, 1966)*; Roger Moore *(Aug. 12, 1966)*. **Regulars:** The Mike Sammes Singers, The Paddy Stone Dancers. **Orchestra:** Jack Parnell.

5464   *The Lone Gunmen.* (Series; Crime Drama; Fox; 2001). John Byers, Melvin Frohike and Richard Langly are the Lone Gunmen, publishers of *The Lone Gunman*, a Tacoma Park, Maryland–based computer oriented newsletter that attempts to expose conspiracies, injustices and criminal activities on all levels of society (the paper is singular in name because it is the only such paper in America). They are backed financially by Jimmy Bond and allies with Yves Adele Harlow, a mysterious woman who seeks to profit from any misfortune she can find (most often cases involving the Lone Gunmen as they set out to right wrongs).

John, Melvin and Richard are, for the most part, geeks or computer nerds who use whatever means they can to bring criminals to justice. Most people believe *The Lone Gunman*, which was started in 1989, is about hunting and fishing. "It's not," says Melvin; "it's called *The Lone Gunman* because we tell the stories others refuse." Melvin was born in Michigan and feels he's the one "who risks his butt doing all the outside work while Langly is behind the scenes" (at his computer in their rundown green, white and rusty van). Prior to becoming one of the Gunmen, Melvin ran the Frohike Electronics Company (his sideline was selling illegal cable boxes).

John, born in Idaho, previously worked for the FCC (Federal Communications Commission) helping the government capture hackers. He quit when he discovered the government was conducting controlled experiments on civilians and concealing the truth about these activities from the public. He is a topnotch hacker and the group's self-proclaimed leader.

Richard, born in Virginia and raised on a farm, has the nickname "Ringo." He loves hard rock music (he is always seen wearing a hard rock T-shirt) and feels he has the computer skills "to become a dot com gazillionaire." Richard also sold illegal cable boxes but quit when he became entangled in a conspiracy to keep the truth from the American public.

Jimmy is a former pro football player whose life savings is providing financial backing for the floundering newsletter. Jimmy helps "because you guys fight for causes I wanna help."

Yves (pronounced Eve) doesn't work for anyone: "I only take their money." She is an expert computer hacker and speaks with a British accent. Her past is unknown, but she is ruthless and will kill if she has to. She wears Ferrari red lipstick and always signs her name in an anagram for Lee Harvey Oswald. While each of the Lone Gunmen likes her, they fear her when she appears at their doorstep (they hope she is not there to kill them). Yves profits off everything she does — whether she works with the Lone Gunmen or against them.

The program is a spin off from *The X-Files* wherein the Gunmen did little more than give information to agents Mulder and Scully. A fourth season episode, "Memento Men," gave them a chance to work with Mulder in the field. Two additional episodes followed — "Unusual Suspects" and "Three of a Kind" before they received their own short-lived series.

Cast: Bruce Harwood *(John Byers)*; Tom Briadwood *(Melvin Frohike)*; Dean Haylund *(Richard Langly)*; Zuleikha Robinson *(Yves Adele Harlow)*; Stephen Snedden *(Jimmy Bond)*.

5465   *The Lone Ranger.* (Series; Western; ABC; 1949–1957). "I wear a mask in the cause of justice," says the Lone Ranger, a mysterious, early west lawman "who cut a trail of law and order across

seven states, forcing the powers of darkness into the blinding light of justice." It was, however, a series of tragic events that transformed Texas Ranger John Reid into the Lone Ranger and teamed him with Tonto, the Potawatomi Indian who saved his life. It began with an assignment to capture Butch Cavendish, the head of the notorious Hole in the Wall Gang. At Bryant's Gap, a canyon about 50 yards wide and bound by cliffs, a team of six Texas Rangers are ambushed by the Cavendish gang and left for dead. Later that day Tonto, who had been hunting for food, finds a lone survivor of the attack — John Reid. Tonto brings Reid to the shelter of a small cave and begins nursing him back to health.

As Reid recovers, he recalls Tonto as the Indian he befriended as a child. Years ago, when Tonto was a child, his village was raided by renegade Indians. His parents were killed and Tonto was left for dead. A young John Reid found Tonto and helped him recover from his wounds. It was at this time that Tonto called Reid "Kemo Sabe" (translated as both "Faithful Friend" and "Trusted Scout").

There is a small patch of grassland that lies amid the rocks broken by countless years of wind and storm. On that land are six graves, each marked by a crudely constructed cross to represent the Texas Rangers who were killed — Captain Dan Reid (John's brother), Jim Bates, Jack Stacey, Joe Brent and Ben Cooper. The sixth cross bears the name of John Reid — put there by Tonto to convince Cavendish that all the Rangers had been killed; to conceal the fact that one Texas Ranger had lived to avenge the others — the Lone Ranger.

To conceal his true identity, Reid fashions a mask from the black cloth of his brother's vest. At first, Reid and Tonto posed as outlaws to enable them to apprehend the Cavendish gang. Once their goal was accomplished, they became a force for good — "Wherever you find a wrong to be righted, that's where you'll find the Lone Ranger" (Reid says also that "keeping my identity a secret makes the pursuit of outlaws easier").

The Lone Ranger's trademark is the silver bullet. The silver comes from a mine Reid inherited. Jim Blaine is the old miner who works the Ranger's silver mine. George Wilson is the Ranger's secret banker in Border City who exchanges the silver for money.

Later episodes feature Dan Reid, John's nephew, as an assistant. The Lone Ranger rides a white horse named Silver (whom he calls "Big Fella"); Scout is Tonto's horse; Victor is Dan's horse. Tris Coffin played Captain Dan Reid; David Leonard is Father Paul, Reid's friend, the padre at the San Brado Mission.

Program Open: "A fiery horse with the speed of light, a cloud of dust and a hearty Hi-yo Silver! The Lone Ranger! With his faithful Indian companion, Tonto, the daring and resourceful masked rider of the plains led the fight for law and order in the early West. Return with us now to those thrilling days of yesteryear; the Lone Ranger rides again!"

Cast: Clayton Moore, John Hart *(John Reid/Lone Ranger)*; Jay Silverheels *(Tonto)*; Chuck Courtney *(Dan Reid)*; David Leonard *(Father Paul)*; Ralph Littlefield *(Jim Blaine)*; Tristin Coffin *(Dan Reid; flashbacks)*; Glenn Strange *(Butch Cavendish)*; Lyle Talbot *(George Wilson)*; Ben Weldon *(Various Outlaw Roles)*. **Announcer:** Fred Foy.

5466   *The Lone Ranger.* (Series; Cartoon; CBS; 1966–1969). An animated version of the live action ABC series (which see for complete background information) that continues to depict the adventures of the Lone Ranger, the mysterious masked rider of the plains, and his Indian companion, Tonto, as they risk their lives to battle injustice.

Voice Cast: Michael Rye *(The Lone Ranger)*; Shepard Menkin *(Tonto)*; Marvin Miller *(Additional Voices)*.

5467   *The Lone Ranger.* (Pilot; Western; WB; Feb. 26, 2003). An unsuccessful attempt to revise the 1949 TV series of the same title. Here, the future Lone Ranger is named Luke Hartman (not John Reid). Luke is from Dallas but attending the Harvard School of Law in Boston while his brother Harmon (not Dan) is a peace officer with the Texas Rangers. After graduating, Luke returns to Texas and joins the Rangers. On an assignment to capture a gang called the Regulators (not the Butch Cavendish Hole in the Wall Gang), the 13 Rangers are attacked by the outlaws and left for dead (it was six Rangers in the series). Later that day, Tonto, an Apache Indian, passing through the area, finds a lone survivor — Luke. Tonto takes the injured Luke to his village, where he is nursed back to health (in the series Tonto helped John recover in a cave). To conceal the identity of Luke, Tonto digs 13 graves to conceal the fact that one Ranger lived to avenge the others — the Lone Ranger. The remainder of the pilot follows Luke's efforts to bring the outlaw gang to justice. Tonto, a Potawatomi Indian in the series, joins Luke to avenge the death of his parents, who were killed by renegade Indians when he was a child. Together they prove to be a powerful symbol for justice in the Old West. Other regulars are Alope, Tonto's sister; and Grace Hartman, Luke's sister, the editor of the Dallas *Enterprise*.

Cast: Chad Michael Murray *(Luke Hartman/Lone Ranger)*; Nathaniel Arcand *(Tonto)*; Fay Masterson *(Grace Hartman)*; Anita Brown *(Alope)*.

5468 *Lone Star*. (Pilot; Crime Drama; NBC; July 31, 1983). Hoping to follow in the footsteps of their uncle, Luther, a retired Texas Ranger who tried to make a difference, two brothers (Ben and George), join the force. They are paired as partners and the proposal was to follow their lighthearted exploits as they battle crime in the Lone Star state. Other regulars are Ranger Captain Sam Mellon and Deputy Cissy Wells.

Cast: Lewis Smith *(Ben McCollum)*; Alan Autry *(George McCollum)*; John McIntire *(Luther McCollum)*; Terri Garber *(Cissy Wells)*; Sandy McPeak *(Sam Mellon)*.

5469 *Lone Star*. (Series; Drama; Fox; 2010). Robert and Bob Allen are actually the same person. He is a brilliant and charismatic schemer who has meticulously created two identities and is living two completely different lives. As Robert Allen, he resides in Houston, Texas, and is married to Kathleen (called Cat), the daughter of Clint Thatcher, patriarch of a wealthy oil family. As Bob Holloway, and more than 400 miles away, he lives in the town of Midland with Lindsay, a sweet and naïve nursing student, who is totally unaware of Cat (as Cat is of Lindsay). Here he is an investment broker who is secretly bilking local depositors of their life savings. In Houston, he is scheming to acquire the family business. Allen has managed to live both lives successfully but always fears exposure, especially from Tremmell, Clint's son, who feels something is not right about him. Serial-like stories relate Allen's efforts to accomplish his pre-set goals while at the same time keep his two worlds secret. Drew is Clint's trusting son; John is Allen's father, the man who raised him in the art of the con. The program was canceled after two episodes.

Cast: Jimmy Wolk *(Robert/Bob Allen)*; Adrianne Palicki *(Kathleen Thatcher-Allen)*; Eloise Mumford *(Lindsay Holloway)*; Jon Voight *(Clint Thatcher)*; David Keith *(John Allen)*; Bryce Johnson *(Drew Thatcher)*; Mark Deklin *(Trammell Thatcher)*.

5470 *The Lone Wolf*. (Series; Adventure; Syn.; 1954). Michael Lanyard, a private detective who works alone, has amazing deductive abilities and has earned the nickname "The Lone Wolf." Michael is also a man who does not want to remain in one place for too long a time; he needs to be where he feels he is needed. Stories follow Michael's adventures as he crusades against the global forces of tyranny and injustice. Based on the stories by Louis Joseph Vance and also known as *Streets of Danger*.

Cast: Louis Hayward *(Michael Lanyard)*.

5471 *The Lonely Wizard*. (Pilot; Drama; CBS; Nov. 15, 1957). A proposed but untitled anthology series that was to dramatize incidents in the lives of great current and past scientists. The pilot story, broadcast on *Schlitz Playhouse of Stars*, told the story of Charles Steinmetz (Rod Steiger), a brilliant electronics engineer who preferred to work in isolation. Rod Steiger also hosts.

5472 *The Loner*. (Series; Western; CBS; 1965-1966). The setting is one month after the surrender at Appomattox ended the Civil War. William Colton was one of many men who fought in the bloody battle. As a union officer he had to do what it took to win, but with the conflict now over, William had time to reflect and has become somewhat disillusioned. He resigns his commission and heads west to search for the meaning of life. Stories follow William's journey as he encounters bitter hatreds in a country still torn apart by war.

Program Open: "In the aftermath of the blood-letting called The Civil War, thousands of ruthless, restless, searching men traveled West. Such a man is William Colton. Like the others he carried a blanket roll, a proficient gun and a dedication to a new chapter in American history, the opening of the West."

Cast: Lloyd Bridges *(William Colton)*.

5473 *The Loner*. (Pilot; Crime Drama; ABC; Aug. 18, 1988). Michael Shane is a man caught between two worlds, neither of which satisfies him. He was raised by his mother, Kate, in an affluent lifestyle, but he rejected it for one he felt would be more meaningful — that of an L.A.P.D. officer. He is partners with a beautiful police woman (Nicole Carver), is seeing a glamorous and wealthy art dealer (Jessica) and displays quiet heroism on the job. But, despite all this, he feels disconnected from the world in which he grew up and not comfortable in the world in which he is currently living. The exploits of a loner, a man who finds true peace only when he is by himself, are detailed as he uses unorthodox methods to apprehend criminals. Abner is his friend, an ex-con who writes poetry.

Cast: John Terry *(Michael Shane)*; Vanessa Bell *(Nicole Carver)*; Constance Towers *(Kate Shane)*; Clare Kirkconnell *(Jessica Grenville)*; Larry Hankin *(Abner Gibson)*.

5474 *Lonesome Dove: The Outlaw Years*. (Series; Western; Syn.; 1995). A spin off that is actually a continuation of *Lonesome Dove: The Series* (see entry). The setting is Curtis Wells, Wyoming. Sadness has befallen the town: Hannah, the wife of Newt Call has died and Newt, unable to face life without her, leaves town to begin a new life as a bounty hunter (but also drinking and womanizing to suppress the memories of his beloved Hannah). After two years Newt returns to Curtis Wells, hoping to settle down. Stories follow Newt as he tries to do just that in a town that is no longer the peaceful place he once knew. Austin, Hannah's brother, is the town's alcoholic sheriff; Josiah, Hannah's father, is now the town's mayor; Clayton Mosby runs the town with an iron fist; the Lonesome Dove Hotel is now run by Amanda Carpenter; and Mattie Shaw, another newcomer to town, is the gunsmith. Ephriam Cleese is the town doctor; Florie and Unbob Finch are other featured townspeople.

Cast: Scott Bairstow *(Newt Call)*; Tracy Scoggins *(Amanda Carpenter)*; Paul Johansson *(Austin Peale)*; Eric McCormack *(Clay Mosby)*; Kelly Rowan *(Mattie Shaw)*; Frank C. Turner *(Unbob Finch)*; Paul Le Mat *(Josiah Peale)*; Bruce McFee *(Deputy Ike)*; Sam Khouth *(Dr. Ephriam Cleese)*.

5475 *Lonesome Dove: The Series*. (Series; Western; Syn.; 1994). A spin off from the 1989 miniseries *Lonesome Dove* (which told the story of Augustus McCrae [Robert Duvall] and Woodrow Call [Tommy Lee Jones], former Texas Rangers and owners of the Hat Creek Cattle Company and Livery Outfit in the town of Lonesome

Dove, Texas). Curtis Wells, Wyoming, is the setting. Events in the life of its citizens, in particular: Newlyweds Newt Call and Hannah Peale (Newt is the son of Woodrow from the miniseries); Clay Mosby, the greedy town owner who is obsessed with Hannah (who resembles his late wife, Mary); Ida Grayson, the owner of the Lonesome Dove Hotel; Austin Peale, Hannah's father, the newspaper editor; and the legendary Buffalo Bill Cody. See also *Lonesome Dove: The Outlaw Years*, the spin off series.

Cast: Scott Bairstow (*Newt Call*); Christanne Hirt (*Hannah Peale Call*); Eric McCormack (*Francis Clay Mosby*); Paul Le Mat (*Josiah Peale*); Paul Johansson (*Austin Peale*); Diahann Carroll (*Ida Grayson*); Sam Khouth (*Dr. Cleese*); Dennis Weaver (*Buffalo Bill Cody*).

5476   The Long Days of Summer. (Pilot; Drama; ABC; May 23, 1980). A nostalgic proposal that recreates the mood of America during the turbulent years just prior to World War II as seen through the eyes of Daniel Cooper, a 13-year-old Jewish boy growing up in Bridgeport, Connecticut. Other regulars are Ed and Millie, his parents; Sarah and Frances, his sisters (the elder Frances is married to Duane Haley); Freddy, Daniel's friend; and Fred Landauer, Freddy's father.

Cast: Dean Jones (*Ed Cooper*); Joan Hackett (*Millie Cooper*); Ronnie Scribner (*Daniel Cooper*); Louanne Ponce (*Sarah Cooper*); Leigh French (*Frances Haley*); John Karlen (*Duane Haley*); David Baron (*Freddy Landauer, Jr.*); Lee deBroux (*Fred Landauer, Sr.*).

5477   Long Distance Relationship. (Series; Comedy; Internet; 2008). Samantha and Sam are high school sweethearts facing the biggest challenge to their relationship as Samantha leaves home to attend Oregon University and Sam, Florida State University. Stories relate the incidents that affect their lives as they each make new friends and try to maintain a long distance relationship via the Internet.

Cast: Rachel Specter (*Samantha*); Dan Levy (*Sam*); Kate Albrecht, Randy Wayne, Jen Zabrowski, Joey Zehr, Lindsay Richards, Audrey Allison.

5478   The Long, Hot Summer. (Series; Drama; ABC; 1965-1966). Ben Quick is a young man who returns to his hometown of Frenchman's Bend, Mississippi, after a long absence, to find that his father has died, his ranch has been abandoned and the town is in control of Will Varner, a powerful banker. Ben is a man of principal and convictions and rather than abandon what was once a prosperous farm, he decides to remain and rebuild it. As Ben contemplates his future, he meets and befriends Clara Varner, Will's beautiful, carefree daughter — a situation that does not sit well with Will, who believes Ben is just a drifter and not worthy of Clara. With only one hope of acquiring the money he needs, Ben approaches Will for a loan. Although Will dislikes Ben, he grants him the loan — provided he leaves Clara alone. Ben agrees. Complications set in when Clara discovers what her father has done and sets her goal to win Ben's love. Serial-like stories depict the conflicts and tensions that exist between Ben and Will as Ben struggles to prove himself worthy of Clara. Based on the feature film of the same title.

Cast: Edmond O'Brien, Dan O'Herlihy (*Will Varner*); Roy Thinnes (*Ben Quick*); Nancy Malone (*Clara Varner*); Lana Wood (*Eula Varner*); Paul Geary (*Jody Varner*); Ruth Roman (*Minnie Littlejohn*); Warren Kennerling (*Lucas Taney*); Paul Bryar (*Harve Anders*); Josie Lloyd (*Agnes*); Michael Zaslow (*Shad Taney*); William Mims (*Sam Ruddabow*); Brian Cutler (*Mitch Taney*); Jimmy Hayes (*Dr. Talicott*); Anne Helm (*Amy*); Tisha Sterling (*Susan*); Jason Wingreen (*Dr. Clark*); Phil Chambers (*Atkinson*); Zalman King (*John Wesley Johnson*); Wayne Rogers (*Curley*); Harold Gould (*Chamberlain*).

5479   Long Island Confidential. (Pilot; Crime Drama; Un-

aired; Produced for Lifetime in 2007). Kate Larkin is a detective with the N.Y.P.D. who transfers from Manhattan to Long Island to be closer to her family (in particular her mother Norah). The proposal was set to relate incidents in Kate's personal and working life.

Cast: Alison Elliott (*Kate Larkin*); Lorraine Bracco (*Norah Larkin*); Jeffrey Pierce (*Mike McCarthy*); Amber Benson (*Liz*); Anthony Carrigan (*Jake*); Ruben Santiago-Hudson (*Calvin Burke*).

5480   Long Island Fever. (Pilot; Crime Drama; ABC; June 27, 1996). Jim McCarty is a New York City homicide detective who yearns for a less hectic life in the suburbs. After his request for a transfer is granted, Jim and his family (his wife Liz and children Matt and Tom) move to Long Island — and what Jim hopes is a better life. Jim's dreams are shattered when he finds it to be even more chaotic than in Manhattan. Jim and his new partner, Scott Parks, are with the Huron County Police Department. Jim is stickler who always wants to do everything by the books; Scott is younger, easy-going and always cracking jokes about the job.

Cast: John C. McGinley (*Jim McCarthy*); Barbara Gulan (*Liz McCarthy*); Adam Baker (*Matt McCarthy*); Spencer Treat Clark (*Tom McCarthy*); Eric Close (*Scott Parks*).

5481   Long John Silver. (Series; Adventure; Syn.; 1956). The shortened title for *The Adventures of Long John Silver*. See this title for information.

5482   Long Time Gone. (Pilot; Crime Drama; ABC; May 23, 1986). When Nick Sandusky's ex-wife, Marilyn, accepts a job that requires frequent traveling abroad, she gives him the responsibility of raising their son, Mitchell. Nick is a screw-up private detective who has a difficult time coping with life, and the unsold series was to relate a father and son's adventures as they work as a team to solve crimes.

Cast: Paul LeMat (*Nick Sandusky*); Wil Wheaton (*Mitchell Sandusky*); Ann Dusenberry (*Marilyn Sandusky*).

5483   Longarm. (Pilot; Western; ABC; Mar. 6, 1988). Action and adventure is combined with light comedy to depict the exploits of Curtis Long, a tough deputy U.S. marshal who undertakes a mission to apprehend the bad guys in New Mexico during the 1870s.

Cast: John Terlesky (*Marshal Curtis Long*).

5484   Longstreet. (Series; Crime Drama; ABC; 1971-1972). Michael Longstreet is an insurance investigator for The Great Pacific Casualty Insurance Company in New Orleans, Louisiana. He is a skilled investigator and known for his expertise in solving crimes. One night, after returning home from an engagement, Michael and his wife, Ingrid, find a gift-wrapped bottle of champagne in the courtyard. Believing it to be from Michael's employer, Duke Paige, Ingrid opens it. The bottle explodes, killing Ingrid and blinding Michael. Michael, now bitter and determined to find Ingrid's killers, enrolls in a clinic for the blind. Here he is taught to use his other senses to their best advantage. Michael acquires a seeing eye dog, Pax (a white German Shepherd), a Braille teacher (Nikki Bell), and a self-defense instructor (Li Tsung) and a job — his former position with Great Pacific. Michael sets out to do what he planned — find Ingrid's killers (whom he uncovers as members of a jewel gang, who having read of Michael's exploits, decided to eliminate him before their next caper). Stories follow Michael attempts to apprehend the people who attempt to defraud his insurance company. Michael lives at 835 Charters Street and is helped by his housekeeper, Mrs. Kingston.

Cast: James Franciscus (*Michael Longstreet*); Peter Mark Richman (*Duke Paige*); Marlyn Mason (*Nikki Bell*); Martine Beswick (*Nikki*

Bell; pilot); Bruce Lee (*Li Tsung*); Ann Doran (*Mrs. Kingston*); Judy Jones (*Ingrid Longstreet; flashbacks*).

5485 Look at Us. (Series; Magazine; Syn.; 1981). Reports on the issues of the 1980s and the lifestyles and achievements of people in the news.

Host: Richard Crenna.

5486 Look Ma, I'm Acting. (Series; Game; DuMont; 1949). The local New York title for *Say It with Acting.* See this title for information.

5487 Look Out World. (Pilot; Comedy; NBC; July 27, 1977). Darcy and Gus are a couple who own a car wash in Santa Monica, California. Benny, Delfi, Beau and Cannonball are their employees, four young men with their heads in the clouds. The proposal, based on the feature film, *Car Wash*, was to relate the hectic goings-on at a busy car wash.

Cast: Maureen Arthur (*Darcy*); Arnold Soboloff (*Gus*); Justin Lord (*Benny*); Bart Braverman (*Delfi*); Steve Doubet (*Beau*); Michael Huddleston (*Cannonball*).

5488 Look Photo Quiz. (Pilot; Game; Unaired; Produced in 1953). A question appears on the screen followed by a series of visual clues. A phone call is placed to a home viewer (pre-selected for the pilot). If the viewer can provide the correct answer, he wins $10. The program is an adaptation of the photoquiz column in *Look* magazine. The pilot was actually a sales-pitch for its sponsor (Shopwell Supermarkets) who provided the prize money for two staged and pre-selected viewers.

Host: Hugh James. **Announcer:** Joe Smith. **Pitchman:** Mike Fitzsimmons.

5489 Look What They've Done to My Song! (Pilot; Comedy; Syn.; July 1980). Spoofs popular melodies via sketches based on the songs.

Host: Norman Fell. **Cast:** Damita Jo Freeman, Gale Garnett, Howard Iskowitz, Marsha Myers, Joe Ristivo, Karen Rushmore, Ty Witney, Sherry Worth. **Orchestra:** Bob Rosario.

5490 Look Who's Here. (Pilot; Interview; DuMont; April 28, 1946). The host talks about a personality prior to his or her entrance. When an off-stage bell sounds, that person walks on stage, the host exclaims "Look Who's Here" and proceeds to interview him. Guests on the pilot: Dr. Frank E. Adair (President of the American Cancer Society), Mary Case (a puppeteer), Bernie Gould (a comedian), Ernest Jones (a one-legged golf pro) and Norman Squires (a USO Camp Show singer).

Host: Geraldine Frazier.

5491 Looking for Love: Bachelorettes in Alaska. (Series; Reality; Fox; 2002). Five gorgeous women are brought to Alaska with the object being to find a husband. Each of the women selects a hopeful mate from a group of perspective bachelors and competes in various, rugged "Alaska-themed dates" to show her worthiness (being able to survive the harsh climate) and win the man she has chosen. Steve Santagati hosts.

5492 Looking Through Gimble's Window. (Experimental; Variety; DuMont; Nov. 24, 1944). A variety format (that featured excerpts from Gilbert and Sullivan by singers from the Savoy Opera Guild) coupled with a long sales pitch by the sponsor (Gimble Brothers Department Store). The sales pitch aspect dealt with merchandise sold by Gimble's (featured was a Botany 500 suit). It was presented like a sketch with one actor (Dick Bradley) meeting a fellow thespian (Tom Grace). Tom admires the suit Dick is wearing and Dick takes him to Gimble's. There they meet a Gimble's buyer (Al Cook), Mike Mutiles (a Gimble's tailor) and Charles Simon (a chemist)—all of whom tell Tom what a great suit the Botany 500 is. Natalie Lauds, Vivian and Lewis Dennison and Charles Kingsley performed the songs.

5493 Lookwell. (Pilot; Comedy; NBC; July 28, 1991). In the 1970s, Ty Lookwell had a TV series called *Bannigan* (wherein he played a tough homicide detective). The show was so realistic that the L.A.P.D. presented him with an honorary badge in 1972. When the series folded, Ty opened Ty Lookwell's Acting Workshop, but the role of a TV cop never left him: he uses the honorary badge as a license to solve crimes. The proposal was to relate Ty's mishaps as he uses his students (Alberti, Suzanne, Chase, Miss Royster, Ben, Jason and Alex) to help him play real life detective. Other regulars are Detective Kennery, the L.A.P.D. cop he helps (or more often helps him out of scrapes) and Ty's housekeeper, June.

Cast: Adam West (*Ty Lookwell*); Ron Frazier (*Detective Kennery*); Ann Weldon (*June*); Bart Braverman (*Alberti*); Molly Cleator (*Suzanne*); Jeff Austin (*Chase*); Deborah Richter (*Miss Royster*); Christopher Daniel Barnes (*Ben*); Todd Field (*Jason*); Brian Bradley (*Alex*).

5494 Loonatics Unleashed. (Series; Cartoon; Kids WB; 2005). It is the year 2772 and likenesses of famous Warner Bros. cartoon characters have become super heroes: Danger Duck (based on Daffy Duck), Ace Bunny (Bugs Bunny), Lexi Bunny (Lola Bunny), Slam Tasmanian Devil (Taz Tasmanian Devil), Rev Runner (Road Runner) and Tech E. Coyote (Wile E. Coyote). The characters are not as looney as their ancestors (nor are they as well drawn or voiced) and stories follow their efforts to preserve peace throughout the universe. Bootsy Collins performs the theme, "Loonatics Unleashed."

Voice Cast: Jason Marsden (*Danger Duck*); Charlie Schlatter (*Ace Bunny*); Jessica DiCicco (*Lexi Bunny*); Kevin Michael Richardson (*Slam*); Kevin Michael Richardson (*Tech E. Coyote*).

5495 The Looney Tunes Show. (Series; Cartoon; Cartoon Network; 2010–). Bugs Bunny and Daffy Duck have been elevated from seven minute theatrical shorts to full-fledged half hours to find misadventure with their friends as they adjust to living in the suburbs. A two-minute music video (a Merrie Melodie) and a two-and-one-half minute Road Runner/Coyote cartoon are interwoven into the proceedings.

Voice Cast: Jeff Bergman (*Bugs Bunny/Daffy Duck*); Billy West (*Elmer Fudd*); Kath Soucie (*Lola Bunny*); Maurice LaMarche (*Yosemite Sam*); Jeff Bennett (*Foghorn Leghorn*); Joe Alaskey (*Sylvester/Tweety Pie/Pepe LePew*); Bob Bergen (*Porky Pig/Speedy Gonzales*).

5496 The Loop. (Series; Comedy; Fox; 2006-2007). Sam Sullivan is 23 years old. He lives in Chicago and shares an apartment with his brother, Sully, and two beautiful girls, Piper and Lizzy. Sam works as an executive for Trans Alliance Airways, a struggling airline on the verge of folding, whose boss (Russ) constantly seeks revolutionary ideas to save it. Russ is assisted by Meryl St. James, the second in command. Working for Sam is Darcy, a girl who is also 23 years old but resents her position as Sam's secretary (she is a graduate of MIT and is a "whiz" at the computer; she has little knowledge of a keyboard but claims she is an expert—"MIT taught me how to e-mail"). Sam is later made head of "a youth oriented, low cost" division of Trans Alliance. Karen is the company executive in second season episodes.

At home Sam's life is not much better. His brother, Sully, is not only a slacker, but idiotic. He chases women, drinks beer, plays practical jokes and enjoys taking naps in the hall closet. He feels he is living the good life through his employment as a counter "boy" at Long John Silver's.

Piper is the girl on whom Sam has a secret crush (but he is too shy to admit it to her). She is a medical student at college and is totally unaware of Sam's feelings toward her. Lizzy works as a bartender and feels everything always goes her way because "I'm so smoking hot."

Stories follow events in Sam's life as he struggles to cope with life at work (as the airline's youngest executive) and at home where he feels he is the only one with a real job.

Cast: Bret Harrison (*Sam Sullivan*); Amanda Loncar (*Piper*); Sarah Mason (*Lizzy*); Eric Christian (*Sully Sullivan*); Mimi Rogers (*Meryl St. James*); Philip Baker Hall (*Russ MacDonald*); Joy Osmanski (*Darcy*); Diora Baird (*Karen*).

5497 *Lopez Tonight.* (Series; Talk; TBS; 2009–). Actor-comedian George Lopez becomes a contender in the late-night talk arena (11:00 P.M. to midnight; later midnight to 1:00 A.M.) with a program that features interviews with people associated with movies, television, sports and politics.

Host: George Lopez. **Announcer:** Big Boy (as identified).

5498 *The Lorenzo and Henrietta Music Show.* (Series; Variety; Syn.; 1976). Music, interviews, songs and comedy sketches with actor/producer/writer Lorenzo Music and his wife Henrietta.

Program Open: "We interrupt these commercials to bring you this important program. And now here are Lorenzo and Henrietta."

Host: Lorenzo Music, Henrietta Music. **Regulars:** Samantha Harper, Dave Willock, Bob Gibson, Erick Darling, Sandy Helberg, Murphy Dunne. **Announcer:** Dave Willock. **Orchestra:** Jack Eskew.

5499 *The Loretta Young Theater.* (Series; Anthology; NBC; 1954–1961). Quality dramatic productions. Attired is a lovely evening gown, host, actress Loretta Young, appears to introduce the evening's story (also often the star). At the conclusion of the story, she reappears and quotes, in accord with the presentation, a proverb from the Bible (these opening and closing segments are often cut from the syndicated prints). A revised version of *A Letter to Loretta*.

Host: Loretta Young. **Regular Performers:** Beverly Washburn, John Newland. **Substitute Host** *(1955)*: Dinah Shore, Merle Oberon, Barbara Stanwyck.

5500 *Losing It with Jillian.* (Series; Reality; NBC; 2010). Physical fitness guru Jillian Michaels takes to the road to battle obesity — one family a time. Once a family has been selected (volunteers) Jillian moves in with them and takes over (setting them up on a special diet and exercise program). Jillian confesses that "I'm sick of hearing excuses" and is determined to show America "that anyone can make a change."

5501 *Lost.* (Series; Reality; NBC; 2001). Two three-member teams are blindfolded and taken to a remote location. They are given little money, have no cell phones and must use their wits to accomplish the series objective: discover where they are and by any means possible, make their way back to New York City. The first team to reach the Statue of Liberty wins $200,000. Al Trautwig narrates.

5502 *Lost.* (Series; Adventure; ABC; 2004–2010). Oceanic Flight 815 is en-route from Australia to Los Angeles when it encounters unexpected turbulence. The plane is literally ripped in half and both halves crash land on an unknown island presumably in the South Pacific. While there are casualties, 48 passengers survive from the front half of the plane (it is later revealed that passengers from the rear half of the plane also survived). When all attempts at rescue fail, the survivors make the island their home (although they find their lives constantly threatened by the mysteries that exist on the strange island).

First season stories are tense, suspenseful and easy to follow. As the series progressed, the simple became complex with confusing flashbacks and flash forwards, difficult to comprehend island happenings and storylines so out of whack that many viewers simply switched to watch something else. Despite a sharp ratings decline, the series was renewed through 2010 (in 2007). A large cast of mostly complex characters also adds to the confusion that is *Lost*. The last season is billed as *Lost: The Final Season* (Feb. 2, 2010 to May 23, 2010). The finale drew a large following (13.5 million viewers) and the producers tried to explain what *Lost* was all about. It is perhaps best to begin with the credit crawl at the end of the episode. Beneath the credits viewers saw the original, horrific plane crash — something from which no one could have possibly survived. And no one did. The island, it appears, was an alternate reality world, a limbo where the passengers gathered to await their journey to the after life together. The incidents encountered on the island, coupled with confusing flashbacks, could be interpreted as what could or would have happened had the crew and passengers survived.

Principal Cast: Matthew Fox (*Dr. Jack Shephard*); Evangeline Lilly (*Kate Austen*); Emilie DeRaven (*Claire Littleton*); Naveen Andrews (*Sayid Jarrah*); Jorge Garcia (*Hugo "Hurley" Reyes*); Josh Holloway (*James "Sawyer" Ford*); Daniel Dae Kim (*Jin Kwon*); Yunjin Kim (*Sun Kwon*); Dominic Monaghan (*Charlie Pace*); Terry O'Quinn (*John Locke*); Harold Perrineau (*Michael Dawson*); Maggie Grace (*Shannon Rutherford*); Adewale Akinnuoye-Agbaje (*Mr. Eko*); Malcolm David Kelley (*Walt Lloyd*); Ian Somerhalder (*Boone Carlyle*); Michele Rodriquez (*Ana-Lucia Cortez*); Elizabeth Mitchell (*Dr. Juliet Burke*); Kiele Sanchez (*Nikki*); Mira Furlan (*Danielle Rousseau*); Henry Ian Cusick (*Desmond*); Jeremy Davies (*Daniel Farraday*); Michael Emerson (*Ben*); Ken Leung (*Miles*).

5503 *Lost and Found.* (Series; Reality; FX; 1995). The program reunites people with lost loves, childhood friends, missing pets and estranged family members. Laura Armstrong is the producer.

5504 *Lost and Found.* (Pilot; Crime Drama; Unaired; Produced for NBC in 2009). Tessa Cooper is a detective with the L.P.P.D. who likes to do things her way. Her superiors, however, want her to follow the rules. When Tessa's continual refusal begins to cause friction within the department, she is demoted and as punishment, regulated to the basement where she is put in charge of solving John and Jane Doe cases. Bitter and determined to regain her prior position, Tessa feels the only way to do so is to solve the cases nobody wants or seems to care about. The proposal was to follow Tessa as she learns a new lesson in law enforcement by solving the cases of people who are somebody not just a name tagged with John or Jane Doe.

Cast: Katee Sackhoff (*Tessa Cooper*); Brian Cox (*Burt Macey*); Andre Holland (*Gayle Dixon*); Damon Herriman (*Anthony Yeckel*); Josh Cooke (*Max Burroughs*); Bahar Soomekh (*Abigail*).

5505 *Lost at Home.* (Series; Comedy; ABC; 2003). Michael Davis works in an ad agency that is 40 miles from his home. He is married to Rachel and is the father of Will, Sarah and Josh. Michael is addicted to work and Rachel would like him to devote less time to work and more time to his family. Michael's devotion to work has cost him a lot. He has missed his kids growing up and feels he doesn't know them anymore. He has succeeded in making a success of himself in the work place, now he feels he needs to succeed as a family man and not become "lost" when he is at home. Stories follow Michael's efforts to get to know his family again — "because I don't know anything."

Rachel was married at 19 and had her first child (now 15-year-old Will) a year later. Other regulars are Jordan King, Michael's boss (who has been married seven times); Sarah revealed that her favorite color is purple, Lisa Kudrow (*Friends*) is her favorite actress and the Dave Matthews Band her favorite group. She likes Cherry Garcia Ice Cream, her monkey pajamas and *The Little Mermaid* (film).

Cast: Mitch Rouse *(Michael Davis)*; Connie Britton *(Rachel Davis)*; Gregory Hines *(Jordan King)*; Stark Sands *(Will Davis)*; Leah Pipes *(Sarah Davis)*; Gavin Fink *(Josh Davis)*.

5506   *Lost in Space.* (Series; Science Fiction; CBS; 1965–1968). The time: October 16, 1997. The place: Alpha Control Center. The mission: Explore the planet Alpha Centauri in the hope that it will provide homes for ten million families a year and reduce the desperate overcrowding on the planet Earth.

A series of deep thrust telescopic probes into neighboring galaxies have established that Alpha Centauri is the only planet within the range of current technology with the ideal conditions for supporting human life. Two million families volunteer for the mission. But only one family, the Robinsons, possess the unique balance of scientific achievement, emotional stability and pioneer resourcefulness that make them the perfect candidates to begin the colonization of deep space. The Robinsons will spend the 98 years of their voyage frozen in a state of suspended animation. They will be traveling at the speed of light in the *Jupiter II*, "the culmination of 40 years of intensive research and the most sophisticated hardware yet devised by the mind of man." The *Jupiter II* has also been shrouded by vigorous security precautions, as other nations, even more desperate for breathing room, may resort to sabotage to beat the United States to the new planet.

Heading the expedition is Dr. John Robinson, a professor of astrophysics, his wife, Maureen, a distinguished biochemist, and their children, "Judith ("Judy"), age 19; Penelope ("Penny"), age 11; and William ("Will"), age nine. Their assistant is Dr. Donald West, a world famous radio astronomer.

As countdown preparations begin, an enemy agent named Colonel Zachary Smith sneaks aboard the *Jupiter II* and reprograms the environmental control robot (called Robot) to sabotage the ship. At minus two minutes and counting, the Robinsons enter the freezing tubes. At zero minus 45 seconds, the freezing units are activated. All hatches are secured and Smith is trapped aboard the craft. The ship is launched and is proceeding normally until Smith's unaccounted-for extra weight alters the ship's flight path. Suddenly the ship encounters a massive meteor shower. Unable to steer the ship, Smith awakens West in the hope of saving the ship. "Who the devil are you?" West asks. "I was trapped just before takeoff." West accepts Smith's explanation and manages to steer the ship clear of the shower; but they are off course. West revives the Robinsons. Smith insists that they reprogram the ship and return to Earth; John thinks it would be best to continue with the mission. Smith attempts but fails to reprogram the robot. The robot's rampage seriously damages the ship before West immobilizes it by disconnecting its power pack.

The Jupiter II is now beyond the range of Alpha Control's tracking. West assumes they are lost two million miles in space. The ship crashlands on an unknown planet that becomes their temporary home. First season episodes relate their adventures on the planet (which Will believes to be Cerberus); second and third season stories find the Robinsons back in space when the *Jupiter II* is repaired and they decide to continue with the mission—despite Smith's persistent efforts to get them to return to Earth.

John was a professor of astrophysics at the University of Stellar Dynamics. Maureen, a biochemist with the New Mexico College of State Medicine, is the first woman in history to pass the International Space Administration's grueling physical and emotional screenings for intergalactic flight. Judy, it was said, "heroically postponed all hopes for a career in the musical comedy field"; Penny, has an I.Q. of 147 and is interested in zoology; Will, who graduated from the Campbell Canyon School of Science at the age of nine, held the highest average in the school's history; his field is electronics.

Donald, a graduate student from the Center for Radio Astronomy, "rocketed the scientific world with his theory of other planets' fitness for human habitation." The relationship between Smith and the Robot provides much of the comic relief. Smith sees the Robot as a slave and calls it such names as "Potbellied Pumpkin," "Bucket of Bolts," "Disreputable Thunderhead," and "Tin Plated Tattletale." His favorite name for it is "Booby." The Robot most often obeys Smith, but does object at times. In the unaired pilot film, the ship was the *Gemini 12*.

Other Roles: Athena, the Green Alien Lady; Nancy Pi Squared, the space beauty; Mr. Zumdish, the space entrepreneur. He was originally the keeper of the Intergalactic Department Store, then owner of a tourist business called Outermost Fundish Ltd. ["Let Fun Be Your Guide"], and finally owner of the Zumdish Insurance Company; and Farnum the Great.

Cast: Guy Williams *(John Robinson)*; June Lockhart *(Maureen Robinson)*; Angela Cartwright *(Penny Robinson)*; Billy Mumy *(Will Robinson)*; Marta Kristen *(Judy Robinson)*; Mark Goddard *(Donald West)*; Jonathan Harris *(Zachary Smith)*; Bob May *(The Robot)*; Dick Tufeld *(Robot's Voice)*; Vittina Marcus *(Athena)*; Dee Hartford *(Athena/Nancy Pi Squared)*; Fritz Field *(Mr. Zumdish)*; Leonard J. Stone *(Farnum the Great)*; Sue England *(Various Computer Voices)*; Dawson Palmer *(Various Alien Roles)*.

Note: On Sept. 8, 1973 ABC aired *Lost in Space*, an animated special in which Craig Robinson (voice of Michael Bell) is the pilot of the *Jupiter II*, now a space shuttle. Other voices: Jonathan Harris (Professor Smith), Sherry Alberoni (Dodi Carmichael), Vincent Van Patten (Linc Robinson). The story finds the crew battling the Tyranos, metallic creatures on a strange planet, when the *Jupiter II* is shot down.

In 2003 the WB commissioned a revival of *Lost in Space* called *The Robinsons: Lost in Space* which, set in 2097, followed the same basic format but without the Dr. Smith character. Adrianne Palicki, Brad Johnson, Jayne Brook, Mike Erwin and Ryan Malgarini were cast.

5507   *Lost on Earth.* (Series; Comedy; USA; 1997). David Rudy is a television reporter who, after on on-the-air blunder, accepts a demotion to host a children's puppet show rather than face unemployment. As he prepares his show he discovers that the puppets who assist him are not props but real aliens that became stranded during their exploration of the universe. Stories follow Rudy as he struggles to do his job and keep the aliens presence a secret. George Greckin is his boss; Sherry is George's daughter, the station manager and David's girlfriend.

Cast: Tim Conlon *(David Rudy)*; Paul Gleason *(George Greckin)*; Stacy Galina *(Sherry Greckin)*; Victor Togunde *(Nick)*.

5508   *The Lost Saucer.* (Series; Comedy; ABC; 1975-1976). While exploring the universe, Fi and Fum, androids from the planet Z-3, penetrate a time warp and land on Earth. Anxious to make friends, they invite two earthlings, Alice and Jerry, aboard their saucer-like spaceship. Suddenly, as curious people begin to gather around the alien craft, Fum becomes alarmed and hurriedly activates the launch mechanism. The ship is sent back into space, where it becomes lost in time. Stories concern their adventures on strange, futuristic planets, and Fi and Fum's efforts to return their passengers to Earth. Also aboard the craft is The Dorse, Fi and Fum's pet (half dog, half horse).

Cast: Ruth Buzzi *(Fi)*; Jim Nabors *(Fum)*; Alice Playten *(Alice)*; Jarrod Johnson *(Jerry)*; Larry Larson *(The Dorse)*.

5509   *Lost Treasure.* (Pilot; Adventure; CBS; June 28, 1971). Andrew Bass, Milovan Drumm and Arleigh Marley are friends who roam the world seeking lost treasures. Their quests often find them encountering people in trouble and the proposal was to relate not only their efforts to uncover the treasures they seek, but help resolve the problems of others.

Cast: James Stacy *(Andrew Bass)*; Bo Svenson *(Milovan Drumm)*; Ben Cooper *(Arleigh Marley)*.

5510   *The Lost World.* (Series; Adventure; Syn.; 1999–2002). It is 1920 when respected British anthropology professor George Edward Challenger expresses his theory that a lost world of unknown civilizations and prehistoric creatures exists within our own world. His evidence is a map drawn by a dying explorer who claims to have seen such a world. Through an arrangement with the Royal Zoological Society, an expedition is arranged for George and fellow explorers John Roxton, Marguerite Krux, Ned Malone and Arthur Summerlee. While traveling down the Amazon River, the group is attacked by a hostile tribe and become stranded on a mysterious plateau of dinosaurs when the hot air balloon they used to escape drifts onto the plateau (but is damaged during the process). Stories follow the adventures of the explorers as they seek to survive and find the secret of the way off the plateau. Along the way they are helped by Veronica Layton, a young woman who is the guardian of the plateau, and allows them to live in the tree house built by her parents; Assai, Veronica's friend, a native girl from a friendly tribe; and Finn, a girl from the future.

George is determined to find a dinosaur egg and bring it back to England with him. John is a famous hunter who is seeking the greatest game of all time: dinosaurs. Marguerite is a beautiful but mysterious woman who helped finance the expedition in a secret attempt to find rare gems. Ned is a newspaper reporter who hopes to write the greatest story of his career; Summerlee is a botanist with a keen interest in unlocking the secrets of the plateau.

Veronica was born on the plateau (like her mother and grandmother who were protectors of the Plateau and cannot leave). Veronica's father, a botanist, is believed to be dead. Veronica believes her mother, who mysteriously disappeared at the same time as her father, may be alive in a land called Avalon. Veronica's search for her mother could lead the Challenger Expedition to the secret of the unknown path to the outside world.

Finn was born in the year 2010. In the year 2033 the plateau has been discovered and has become known as New Amazonia. The world, however, has been devastated by a great holocaust. Finn is propelled back in time (to 1924) through a time warp. Now, in the past, she befriends the Challenger expedition and George feels that her presence in the past has opened a doorway to prevent the future holocaust.

Program Open: "At the dawn of the last century a band of explorers searched for a prehistoric world. Driven by ambition, secret desires and a thirst for adventure and seeking the ultimate story, they are befriended by an untamed beauty. Stranded in a strange and savage land, each day a desperate search for a way out of *The Lost World.*"

Cast: Peter McCauley *(George Challenger)*; Rachel Blakely *(Marguerite Krux)*; Jennifer O'Dell *(Veronica Layton)*; William Snow *(John Roxton)*; David Orth *(Ned Malone)*; Michael Sinelnikoff *(Arthur Summerlee)*; Lara Cox *(Finn)*; Laura Vazquez *(Assai)*; Jerome Ehlers *(Tribune)*.

5511   *Lost Worlds.* (Series; Reality; History Channel; 2006). Archaeologists use modern technology to recreate life in lost civilizations through the artifacts found in ancient cultures. Corey Johnson and Corey Lawson are the narrators.

5512   *Lotsa Luck.* (Series; Comedy; NBC; 1973–1974). Stanley Belmont is a clerk in the lost and found department of the New York City Bus Lines. He is single and lives with his widowed mother, Iris, his married sister, Olive, and Olive's unkempt and unemployed husband, Arthur Swann. Stanley is a man with a big heart who will lend a helping hand to others. Stories relate the simple pleasures and trying times that affect Stanley's life — both at home and at work. Bunny Fitzer is Stanley's neighbor, a bus driver.

Cast: Dom DeLuise *(Stanley Belmont)*; Kathleen Freeman *(Iris Belmont)*; Beverly Sanders *(Olive Swann)*; Wynn Irwin *(Arthur Swann)*; Jack Knight *(Bunny Fitzer)*.

5513   *Lottery.* (Series; Drama; ABC; 1983). Each week a lottery drawing is held by the Intersweep Lottery. When a winning ticket has been drawn, lottery representative Patrick Flaherty visits the winner to present him with a cashier's check. Eric Rush, the IRS agent, accompanies him on every mission to collect the government's share. Stories relate the incidents that occur in the lives of those lottery winners when they suddenly come into unexpected wealth. Three such stories are presented on each program. Alan Graham sings the theme, "Turn of the Cards."

Cast: Ben Murphy *(Patrick Flaherty)*; Marshall Colt *(Eric Rush)*.

5514   *Lou Grant.* (Series; Drama; CBS; 1977–1982). The character of Lou Grant first appeared on *The Mary Tyler Moore Show* (CBS, 1970–1977) as the executive producer of the "The Six O'clock News" on WJM-TV in Minneapolis. When the series ended, Lou relocated to Los Angeles, where he became the city editor of the Los Angeles *Tribune*, the second largest newspaper in the city. Stories take viewers behind the scenes for an accurate look at the working lives of newspapermen and women.

Other regulars are Charlie Hume, the managing editor; Margaret Pynchon, the publisher; reporters Billie Newman, Joe Rossi and Carla Mardigan; Dennis "Animal" Price, the photographer; Art Donovan, Lou's assistant; Adam Wilson, the financial editor; Marion Hume, Charlie's wife; Greg Serantino, Billie's ex-husband; Ted McLovey, the baseball scout who marries Billie; and Heidi, an office worker.

Cast: Edward Asner *(Lou Grant)*; Linda Kelsey *(Billie Newman)*; Robert Walden *(Joe Rossi)*; Mason Adams *(Charlie Hume)*; Nancy Marchand *(Margaret Pynchon)*; Daryl Anderson *(Dennis "Animal" Price)*; Jack Bannon *(Art Donovan)*; Allen Williams *(Adam Wilson)*; Peggy McCay *(Marion Hume)*; Cassandra Foster *(Heidi)*; Vincent Baggetta *(Greg Serantino)*; Cliff Potts *(Ted McLovey)*; Lawrence Haddon, Emilio Delgado *(Foreign Editor)*; Sidney Clute *(National Editor)*; Billy Beck *(Photo Editor)*.

5515   *The Lou Kelly Show.* (Pilot; Interview; Unaired; Produced in 1987). A proposed late night summer interview show with Lou Kelly as host and Dick Clark as producer that failed to generate station interest after the pilot was pitched (via closed circuit) in February 1987.

5516   *Louie.* (Series; Comedy; FX; 2010). Clips of stand-up comedian Louis C.K.'s work are interspersed with short vignettes that detail events in Louie's hectic life (a divorced, early forties father of two daughters).

Cast: Louis C.K. *(Himself)*; Kimberly Barlow *(Tammy)*; Nick DiPaolo *(Nick)*; Max Behren *(Young Louis)*; Nicole Ehringer *(Young Tammy)*.

5517 *The Louie Show.* (Series; Comedy; CBS; 1996). Louie Lundgren is a therapist who lives in Duluth, Minnesota. He was born in Minnesota and is a graduate of Minnesota State University. Louie has always felt a need to help people — ever since he was a child and would help his family solve their problems. Naturally, as he grew, he believed becoming a therapist would be the right career choice for him. Unfortunately the people Louie helps are far more complex ("nuts") than he could ever imagine and stories follow the gruff-voiced Louie as he attempts to help people while also struggling to cope with the numerous problems in his own life.

Gretchen Lafayette is Louie's roommate. Gretchen was born in Los Angeles, went to Pepperdine University and worked as an actress. Her claim to fame was in a Monistat 7 TV commercial. Gretchen didn't want to become known as "the girl with the yeast infection" so she quit, hit the road, wound up in Duluth, answered an ad for a roommate — and become friends with Louie. Helen is Louie's receptionist; Curt is Louie's friend; Sandy is Curt's estranged wife; Dr. Jake Reinhart is Louie's friend; and Kimmy is the waitress at the local diner.

Cast: Louie Anderson *(Louie Lundgren)*; Kate Hodge *(Gretchen Lafayette)*; Bryan Cranston *(Curt Sinic)*; Nancy Beeker-Kennedy *(Helen)*; Paul Feig *(Jake Reinhart)*; Laura Innes *(Sandy Sinic)*; Kimmy Robertson *(Kimmy)*.

5518 *Love, American Style.* (Series; Anthology; ABC; 1969–1974). Comedy vignettes that tackle the world's oldest subject: love. Stories are interspersed with a series of blackouts (that are performed by a regular cast; guests appear in the actual stories). See also *The New Love, American Style.*

Blackout Regulars: Phyllis Elizabeth Davis, Jed Allan, James Hampton, Clifton Davis, Bernie Kopell, Tracy Reed, Stuart Margolin, Buzz Cooper, Marty Grover, Bill Calloway, Barbara Minkus, Lynne Marta, Jacki DeMar, Richard Williams.

5519 *Love and Curses.* (Series; Thriller; Syn.; 1991). A revised version of *She-Wolf of London.* Randi Wallace is a Los Angeles student attending the University in London and preparing her thesis on disproving the supernatural. She is attacked and bitten by a werewolf while doing research on the Moors, and now through a curse, she becomes a beast when the moon is full. Ian Matheson is Kate's love interest, a professor of mythology who teaches at the University.

When the new version begins, it is learned that the University has decided to phase out Ian's classes. He is not upset because his experiences with Randi (encountering supernatural creatures in the *She-Wolf* version) prove that everything he has been teaching is wrong. Ian and Randi relocate to Los Angeles where Ian hopes to find someone who can cure Randi of her curse. Ian acquires a job as the host of the TV show *How Strange, with Dr. Matheson* on Channel 89. Ian sees the show as interviewing "scholars, researchers and academics of the highest order." By the second episode, Randi is working with Ian as his producer. They live in a luxurious apartment and behind the bookcase is a secret room that contains a cell — to keep Randi from killing when she becomes a werewolf. Stories follows Randi and Ian's adventures as they investigate supernatural occurrences in the hope of finding a cure for Randi (they never did). Skip is the show's executive producer.

Cast: Kate Hodge *(Randi Wallace)*; Neil Dickson *(Ian Matheson)*; Dan Gilvezan *(Skip Seville)*.

5520 *Love and Learn.* (Pilot; Comedy; NBC; Aug. 1, 1979). Jason Brewster is a middle-aged college professor who, while on vacation in Las Vegas, meets, falls in love with and marries a beautiful 20-year-old showgirl named Holly. The proposal was to focus on the newlyweds as they struggle to live a normal life despite the problems caused by the differences in their ages and occupations. Other regulars are Mark, Jason's brother; Harvey, Jason's friend; Natalie, Jason's landlady; and Denise, a student of Jason's.

Cast: Lawrence Pressman *(Jason Brewster)*; Candy Clark *(Holly Brewster)*; James Van Patten *(Mark Brewster)*; Earl Boen *(Harvey)*; Natalie Core *(Natalie)*; Kelly Bishop *(Denise Pfeiffer)*.

5521 *Love and Marriage.* (Series; Comedy; NBC; 1959-1960). A behind-the-scenes look at the business of a music publishing company as seen through the eyes of Patricia Baker, the daughter of Bill Harris, a widower who owns the near bankrupt Harris Music Publishing Company in Los Angeles. Bill is behind the times and cannot accept the new wave in music — rock and roll. Patricia knows her father is wrong and must convince him of that fact. Stories follow Patricia as she struggles to save the family business by acquiring Rock and Roll personalities and songs. Steve is Patricia's husband, a lawyer; Susan and Jenny are their daughters; Stubby Wilson is the firm's song plugger; Sophie is the firm's secretary.

Cast: William Demarest *(Bill Harris)*; Jeanne Bal *(Patricia Baker)*; Murray Hamilton *(Steve Baker)*; Susan Reilly *(Susan Baker)*; Jeannie Lynn *(Jenny Baker)*; Stubby Kaye *(Stubby Wilson)*; Kay Armen *(Sophie)*.

5522 *Love and Marriage.* (Series; Comedy; Fox; 1996). Can a happily married but busy couple with two children survive marriage? That is the question posed on *Love and Marriage,* the story of Jack Nardini, the owner of a New York City parking lot garage, who works all day, and his wife, April, a waitress who works at night. Their children are Michael, Gemmy and Christopher. Despite their hectic schedules and little time to actually spend together, Jack and April make their marriage work because they love each other. Stories follow their ups and downs.

Cast: Anthony John Dennison *(Jack Nardini)*; Patricia Healy *(April Nardini)*; Alicia Bergman *(Gemmy Nardini)*; Erik Palladino *(Michael Nardini)*; Adam Zolotin *(Christopher Nardini)*.

5523 *Love and Money.* (Series; Comedy; CBS; 1999-2000). Allison Conklin is the spoiled daughter of billionaire businessman Nicholas Conklin and his wife Effie. She has an air head sister (Puff) and a sarcastic younger brother (Nicky). The Conklins live in a fashionable Manhattan high rise penthouse. Eamon McBride, the building's superintendent, lives in the basement with his father, Finn, the building's doorman. Allison was brought up to respect and marry money. Allison, however, has different feelings and causes a family rift when she falls in love with the blue collar Eamon. With the exception of her champagne-swilling mother, the family disapproves of her new relationship and eagerly seek a way to end the romance. Stories follow Allison as she struggles to make her relationship work despite the obstacles of social status.

Cast: Paget Brewster *(Allison Conklin)*; Brian Van Holt *(Eamon McBride)*; Swoosie Kurtz *(Effie Conklin)*; David Ogden Stiers *(Nicholas Conklin)*; Judy Greer *(Puff Conklin)*; John Livingston *(Nicky Conklin)*; Brian Doyle-Murray *(Finn McBride)*.

5524 *Love and War.* (Series; Comedy; CBS; 1992–1995). Wallis "Wally" Porter, businesswoman and world-famous chef, owns the trendy Chez Wally Restaurant on Manhattan's 72nd Street. After five years, her marriage to Kip Zakar, a conceited actor, breaks up. When Wally loses the restaurant in the divorce settlement, she walks out of the courtroom and wanders into the Blue Shamrock, a quaint 1940s-style bar. After several double vodkas, Wally becomes intoxicated and buys 80 percent of the bar from owner Ike Johnson for $70,000. Ike's brother, Abe, becomes the new bartender when Ike passes away and leaves his 20 percent share to him.

Wally lives at 1016 East 74th Street (Apartment C). She attended the Cordon Bleu School in Paris and can de-bone a chicken in 20 seconds. She can serve 12 dinners in 21 minutes and once received a letter from Julia Child saying that her *coq au vin* was the best she ever tasted. When Wally needed to find herself, she left suddenly for Paris and gave Abe ownership of the bar. Abe hired Dana Palladino, a former chef at the Le Petite Bateau. Dana is the daughter of a famous artist (Dante), worked as a chef for Mick Jagger during his Steel Wheels Tour, and spent a year on the Alaska Pipeline just to learn how to cook salmon. She was raised in Europe and at age ten had her own table at Harry's Bar in Paris.

Wally first met Kip in an off-Broadway production of *Westside Story* (he was Jet number 2). Kip also appeared as the deranged type-setter on an episode of *Lou Grant*; the insane crossing guard in an episode of *Sweating Bullets*; the star of a pilot called *Turf and Surf* (about a meat inspector who drives a Ferrari); and Mr. York, the psychopathic math teacher on *Jake and the Fatman*. When Kip appeared in *Richard III*, the newspapers called him "a nightmare in tights."

Jack Stein, Mary Margaret "Meg" Tynan and Ray Litvak are the bar regulars. Jack writes the opinion column, "The Stein Way" for the New York *Register*. He dated Wally but the relationship just didn't work out. Meg is a sportswriter for the *Register*. She is brash and tends to poke her nose into other people's business. Ray works as a "sanitation engineer" (garbage man) for the New York City Department of Sanitation. Nadine Berkus is the Shamrock's waitress. She lives in Westchester and is afraid to be sexy (the most outrageous thing she ever did was to wear an off-the-shoulder sweater). Her kids are in college and her husband, Charles, is in prison for insider trading.

In the original unaired pilot, *Love Is Hell*, Jay Thomas played columnist Jack Simon and Joel Murray was Joe, the garbage man.

Cast: Susan Dey (*Wally Porter*); Jay Thomas (*Jack Stein*); Michael Nouri (*Kip Zakaris*); Joel Murray (*Ray Litvak*); Annie Potts (*Dana Palladino*); Charlie Robinson (*Abe Johnson*); John Hancock (*Ike Johnson*); Suzie Plakson (*Meg Tynan*); Joanna Cassidy (*Nadine Berkus*).

5525 *Love at First Sight*. (Pilot; Comedy; CBS; Oct. 13, 1980). The problems of a not-so-typical marriage as seen through Karen Alexander, a housewife, and her husband, Jonathan, a blind jingles writer for the Fame Advertising Agency in New York City. Other regulars are Francis Fame, the agency owner; Genevieve, the stylish jingle writer; and Denise, the agency's buxom receptionist. A second pilot aired on Mar. 29, 1982 that kept the same storyline but changed character names. Karen Grant was the housewife and Jonathan, her husband. Other regulars are Heinrich, the building super; and Stan, the Grants' friend.

First Pilot Cast: Susan Bigelow (*Karen Alexander*); Philip Levien (*Jonathan Alexander*); Pat Cooper (*Francis Fame*); Deborah Baltzell (*Genevieve Lamont*); Angela Aames (*Denise*).

Second Pilot Cast: Susan Bigelow (*Karen Grant*); Philip Levien (*Jonathan Grant*); Macon McCalman (*Heinrich Sawyer*); Reni Santoni (*Stan Brotman*).

5526 *Love Bites*. (Pilot; Anthology; Unaired; Produced for NBC in 2010). A proposed program of romantic vignettes. The pilot presents three stories: *The First Time* (focuses on two girls who are the remaining singles in their group of friends. Stars Becki Newton as Annie and Jordana Spiro as Frannie); *First to Go* (a fired accountant [Carter] seeks to hide the fact that he lost his job to his fiancée, Liz. Stars Kyle Howard as Carter and Lindsay Price as Liz); *First in Line* (Jennifer Love Hewitt plays herself in a story about her chance meeting with a man [Judd] who made an agreement with his wife that, if the opportunity arose, she would be the celebrity he would be allowed to sleep with. Greg Grunberg plays Judd).

5527 *The Love Boat*. (Series; Comedy-Drama; ABC; 1977–1986). Merrill Stubing is captain of the *Pacific Princess*, a luxury cruise ship that has been nicknamed "The Love Boat" by her crew: cruise director Julie McCoy, purser Burl ("Gopher") Smith, Dr. Adam Bricker and bartender Isaac Washington. Merrill's daughter, Vicki Stubing became the assistant cruise director (1979), and Julie's sister, Judy McCoy, replaced Julie as the cruise director in 1985. Merrill married Emily Haywood, a wealthy widow, in 1986 (she became the special events director). Ashley ("Ace") Covington-Evans became the ship's photographer in 1984 (later the purser, when Gopher left). To spice up the cruises, the gorgeous "Love Boat Mermaids" were added in 1985. Stories relate brief events in the lives of the passengers.

On May 4, 1985, the *Pacific Princess*, which is owned by the Pacific Cruise Lines in Los Angeles, became the *Royal Princess* in honor of its one-thousandth guest star, Lana Turner. Jack Jones, then Dionne Warwick, perform the theme, "The Love Boat."

Cast: Gavin MacLeod (*Capt. Merrill Stubing*); Lauren Tewes (*Julie McCoy*); Bernie Kopell (*Dr. Adam Bricker*); Fred Grandy (*Burl "Gopher" Smith*); Ted Lange (*Isaac Washington*); Jill Whelan (*Vicki Stubing*); Patricia Klous (*Judy McCoy*); Ted McGinley (*Ashley "Ace" Covington-Evans*); Mary Farrell (*Mary Temple; Adam's nurse*); Sid Gould (*Sidney; ship's waiter*); Marion Ross (*Emily Haywood*). **The Love Boat Mermaids:** Deborah Bartlett (*Susie*); Tori Brenno (*Maria*); Nancy Lynn Hammond (*Jane*); Teri Hatcher (*Amy*); Deborah Johnson (*Patti*); Andrea Moen (*Starlight*); Beth Myatt (*Mary Beth*); Maccarena (*Sheila*).

Note: The actual concept for *The Love Boat* began as the "Luxury Liner" episode of *The Dick Powell Show* (NBC, Feb. 12, 1963), wherein Rory Calhoun played Victor Kihlgren, the captain of a cruise ship. James Stewart was slated to be the host and the series was to chronicle dramatic incidents in the lives of the passengers.

The first pilot, *The Love Boat* (ABC, Sept. 17, 1976) featured crew of the *Sun Princess*: Captain Thomas Allenford (Ted Hamilton), Dr. Adam O'Neill (Dick Van Patten), cruise director Jeri Landers (Terri O'Mara), yeoman purser "Gopher" (Sandy Helberg), and Isaac the bartender (Theodore Wilson).

The Love Boat II pilot (ABC, Jan. 21, 1977) featured Captain Thomas Madison (Quinn Redeker), cruise director Sandy Summers (Diane Stilwell), purser Burl "Gopher" Smith (Fred Grandy), bartender Isaac Washington (Ted Lange) and Dr. Adam Bricker (Bernie Kopell).

The New Love Boat (ABC, May 5, 1977) is the actual pilot that became the series. The series cast appeared in their regular roles.

On February 12, 1990, *The Love Boat: A Valentine Cruise* aired on CBS and reunited most of the original cast for a cruise to the Caribbean via the *Sky Princess*. Kim Ulrich signed on as Kelly Donaldson, the cruise director. Repeating their roles: Gavin MacLeod (Captain Merrill Stubing), Bernie Kopell (Dr. Adam Bricker) and Ted Lange (Isaac Washington, now the chief purser). Vicki Stubing (Jill Whelan) is now a travel agent (she is aboard as part of her vacation); Emily, Merrill's wife, was said to have passed away.

5528 *The Love Boat: The Next Wave*. (Series; Drama; UPN; 1998). An update of the ABC series *The Love Boat* that continues to depict romantic incidents in the lives of the passengers who book passage on *The Sun Princess*, a cruise ship that has been nicknamed *The Love Boat*.

Jim Kennedy III, a 48-year-old ex–Navy man, is the ship's captain (replaced Captain Merrill Stubing). Camille Hunter is the chief of security (a role not in the original series). John Morgan is the ship's doctor (replaces Dr. Adam Brinker). Suzanne Zimmerman is the cruise director (replaces Julie McCoy). Paolo Kaire is the bartender (replaces Isaac Washington). Will Sanders is the purser (replaces Gopher) and Danny is Jim's son (replaced Vicki, Merrill's daughter).

Cast: Robert Urich *(Capt. Jim Kennedy III)*; Joan Severance *(Camille Hunter)*; Corey Parker *(Dr. John Morgan)*; Stacey Travis *(Suzanne Zimmerman)*; Randy Vasquez *(Paolo Kaire)*; Phil Morris *(Will Sanders)*; Kyle Howard *(Danny Kennedy)*.

5529   The Love Connection. (Series; Game; Syn.; 1983). One single person (for example, a male) selects one girl for his date from three videotaped interviews he is permitted to see. Shortly after their date, the male is brought on stage to relate his experiences. Following an interview with the subject, the studio audience is permitted to see excerpts from the videotapes through which the male had made a decision. The audience electronically selects the girl they feel is best for the male. The subject reveals the girl he chose. She is brought on stage and relates her experiences concerning the date. The audience vote is tabulated. If it differs from the subject's choice, he receives the opportunity to date the girl chosen by the audience. If both choices are the same, and if both singles want to date again, the program provides and expenses-paid date. Whatever the subject's final decision, merchandise prizes are awarded for participating.
Host: Chuck Woolery. **Announcer:** Rod Roddy.

5530   Love Cruise. (Pilot; Reality; Unaired; Produced in 2000). Can an ocean voyage bring singles together? Four men and four women are given an all-expenses paid trip with the object being to see which singles make compatible couples. After getting to know each other through compatibility challenges, the singles choose a partner. What results as the voyage continues determines if the right choices were made. With some changes, it became *Love Cruise: The Maiden Voyage* (see next title). A gorgeous oriental girl, identified only as Shane, serves as the host.

5531   Love Cruise: The Maiden Voyage. (Series; Reality; Fox; 2001). Sixteen singles (eight men and eight women) are placed aboard a cruise ship with the intent being to find perfect matches. The singles choose who each would like to be with (they can change partners if they wish as the cruise continues) and compete in various challenges to test compatibility. Singles who do not meet the expectations of the other singles are eliminated (voted off the boat). The two singles who appear to make the perfect couple are the winners. Justin Gunn is the host.

5532   The Love Experts. (Series; Reality; Syn.; 1978). A panel of four celebrities (guests) offers advice to real people on the problems of living and loving in today's world. Eighty-five episodes were produced.
Host: Bill Cullen. **Regular:** Geoff Edwards. **Announcer:** Jack Clark.

5533   The Love Experts. (Series; Magazine; ABC; 1984). The program, broadcast live from Los Angeles, presents up-to-the-minute information on relationships.
Host: Tawny Schneider, Chuck Henry. **Regulars:** Dr. Joyce Brothers, Betty White, Dr. Theresa Crenshaw, Dr. Ruth Westheimer, Dr. Meryle Gellman, Ellie Dylan, Johnny Mountain.

5534   Love Games: Bad Girls Need Love Too. (Series; Reality; Oxygen; 2010). *Bad Girls Club* spin off wherein three former Bad Girls (Amber, Kendra, Sarah) compete against each other to find the man of their dreams from a group of 13 eligible men. The program asks "How bad will these girls be when love is on the line?" Their individual attempts to find the one each believes is right for her is put to the test in a series of challenges and intimate group dates wherein the girls narrow down the field by eliminating those they

feel are unsuitable (the girls can also be eliminated if no one competes for her affections). A match is made when only one Bad Girl and one bachelor remain standing. Whether or not the relationship will last after the competition remains to be seen. Bret Ernst hosts.

5535   Love, Inc. (Series; Comedy; UPN; 2005–2006). Can a girl (Denise Johnson), the owner of a successful dating service (Love, Inc.) find true romance for herself? That is the basic premise of the series. Denise is assisted by Francine, Clea, Viviana and Barry. Denise claims that, "Love is about capability. People with compatible interests being compatible." Denise is intelligent (a graduate of Northwestern University), outgoing and very pretty but she can't seem to find anyone who is compatible. Viviana is an extremely sexy girl from Argentina whose has no trouble finding men (even women are attracted to her) but often finds that the men she becomes attracted to are either gay or married. Clea is the type of girl Denise wishes she could be—compatible with almost everyone and seemingly never without a man. Barry is the typical "everyman," attracted to beautiful girls but not always sure he can score. Shannen Doherty played the role of Denise in the original, unaired pilot version of the series.
Cast: Busy Philipps *(Denise Johnson)*; Reagan Gomez-Preston *(Francine)*; Ion Overman *(Viviana)*; Holly Robinson Peete *(Clea)*; Vince Vieluf *(Barry)*.

5536   Love Incorporated. (Pilot; Reality; Unaired; Produced in 2010). Annabelle and Justin Parfitt are a married couple who operate Fast Life, a matchmaking company. The proposal was to relate events in the couple's daily lives as they seek ways to expand their business.

5537   Love Is a Many Splendored Thing. CBS serial. Sept. 18, 1967 to Mar. 23, 1973. See *Soap Operas*.

5538   Love Life. (Pilot; Comedy; Unaired; Produced for ABC in 2005). Jane and Sam are dating. They believe they are right for each other but their friends think differently as they defy the traditions the friends have set. Jane's girlfriends are attractive women who have sought playboys and rich men; Sam's friends play the field, get what they want then move on. Jane and Sam, once apart of that clique are determined to change and the proposal was to relate their efforts to make their relationship work.
Cast: Julie Bowen *(Jane)*; Tom Everett Scott *(Sam)*; Lucy Davis *(Paige)*; Alan Tudyk *(Oakes)*; Michael Landes *(Todd)*.

5539   Love, Long Distance. (Pilot; Comedy; CBS; July 30, 1985). Leslie Cummings is the assistant anthropologist to Dr. Arthur Ruskin at the Museum of Natural History in New York City. She shares a Manhattan apartment with her friend, Sybil Sylver, but lives in Philadelphia. David Cummings, her husband of five years, runs a construction business with his brother, Stan, and lives in Philadelphia—a situation that forces them to live a commuter marriage with David residing full-time in Philadelphia and Leslie living weekdays in Manhattan and weekends with David. The proposal was to focus on the misadventures that occur as Leslie and David attempt to live a normal married life. John Leffler performs the theme, "Love Long Distance."
Cast: Tricia Pursley *(Leslie Cummings)*; Jack Rose *(David Cummings)*; Cristine Rose *(Sybil Sylver)*; Mike Starr *(Stan Cummings)*; Austin Pendleton *(Dr. Arthur Ruskin)*.

5540   Love Monkey. (Series; Comedy-Drama; CBS; 2006). Tom Farrell is a bachelor who rents a one-room apartment in Manhattan. He is not a good cook, but he feels he has good job and a good life.

He is an A&R (Artist and Repertoire) representative at a major record label (Goliath Records). However, when he objects to his boss's outlook for the company, he is fired.

Tom believes good music always finds its following. He had personally signed 12 successful bands and after he is unable to start his own company (lack of funds) he finds a job with True Vinyl Records, a small company that thinks like he does. Stories follow Tom as he seeks to better his life. Other regulars are Julie, Tom's girlfriend; Brandy, called Bran, Tom's friend ("She's a girl whose a friend, not a girlfriend"); Mike, Tom's oldest buddy (he is married to Tom's sister, Karen); and Jake (an ex-pro athlete) and Shooter (a man-about-town), Tom's friends.

Cast: Thomas Cavanaugh (*Tom Farrell*); Jason Priestley (*Mike Freed*); Judy Greer (*Brandy Lowenstein*); Katherine La Nasa (*Karen Freed*); Christopher Wiehl (*Jake Dunne*); Larenz Tate (*Shooter Cooper*); Ivana Milicevic (*Julia*).

5541   *Love, Natalie.* (Pilot; Comedy; NBC; July 11, 1980). Natalie Miller, wife, mother and overall problem solver, lives at 16 Valley Hart Drive with her husband Peter and children Nora and Franklin. Each program, which satirizes family life, opens with Natalie writing a letter to her mother and closing with "Love, Natalie." Natalie also speaks directly to the audience to relate her feelings about the situations that develop. Other regulars are Mel, Peter's friend; and Ruth, Natalie's friend.

Cast: Judith Kahan (*Natalie Miller*); Christopher Allport (*Peter Miller*); Kimberly Woodward (*Nora Miller*); Corey Feldman (*Franklin Miller*); Jean DeBaer (*Ruth Newman*); Kenneth Tigar (*Mel Orlorfsky*).

5542   *Love Nest.* (Pilot; Comedy; CBS; Mar. 14, 1975). When widowed senior citizens Ned Cooper and Jenny Ludlow find that they can barely live on their social security incomes, they decide to live together in a Florida trailer court. The decision upsets Ned's son, Mort, and Jenny's daughter, Dorothy, who object and want them to move to a senior citizens home. The proposal was to relate the efforts of two young-at-heart senior citizens to enjoy their golden years together without influence from their children. Other regulars are Dick, Ned's friend; and Mary Frances, Jenny's friend.

Cast: Charles Lane (*Ned Cooper*); Florida Friebus (*Jenny Ludlow*); Dana Elcar (*Mort Cooper*); Dee Carroll (*Dorothy Ludlow*); Burt Mustin (*Dick Ewing*); Alice Nunn (*Mary Frances*).

5543   *Love of Life.* CBS serial. 1951–1980. See *Soap Operas*.

5544   *Love on a Rooftop.* (Series; Comedy; ABC; 1966-1967). Dave Willis, an apprentice architect with the firm of Bennington and Associates, earns $85.37 a week. Julie Hammond, the beautiful 22-year-old pampered daughter of a rich car salesman, is studying to become an artist. They meet one day when Dave, preparing to eat lunch at a construction site, drops his liverwurst on rye sandwich. The sandwich falls several stories and lands in Julie's open handbag as she is walking past the site. Dave chases after his sandwich and when he and Julie meet, it's love at first sight. They marry and set up housekeeping in a rooftop apartment at 1400 McDoogal Street in San Francisco.

"You're rich, go ahead and admit it, you're rich" is Dave's reaction when he learns that Julie is wealthy (her reaction: "You make it sound like some sort of disease"). Dave, being the independent type, insists that they live on his income. Julie agrees and relinquishes her world of luxury — a situation that angers her father, Fred Hammond, who was in Europe when she and Dave married. "You may as well know right now," Fred says when he first meets Dave. "If I had been here I would have stopped this marriage." A dumb founded Dave responds simply, "Nice to meet you too, Mr. Hammond."

While Julie's mother, Phyllis Hammond, is hoping only the best for Julie and Dave, Fred firmly believes that Dave will never be able to support her. "We may have some rough times," Dave tells Fred, "but we're going to be all right ... because we love each other and we're gonna do it on our own with no help from you or anyone." Stories follow Dave and Julie as they struggle through the difficult first year of marriage.

Dave and Julie's friends and downstairs neighbors are Stan and Carol Parker. Like the Willises, they too are struggling to make ends meet on a small income. Stan is an idea man who hopes one day to make it big by inventing something that everyone needs (the problem is, "I can't figure out what it is because it is so obvious"). Charles Lane appeared as Dave's boss, Bert Bennington and Hope Summers played his wife, Bertha Bennington.

Cast: Judy Carne (*Julie Willis*); Peter Deuel (*Dave Willis*); Rich Little (*Stan Parker*); Barbara Bostock (*Carol Parker*); Herbert Voland (*Fred Hammond*); Edith Atwater (*Phyllis Hammond*).

5545   *The Love Report.* (Series; Magazine; ABC; 1984). A daily program of celebrity interviews and reports that examine the problems of romantic relationships.

Hosts: Chuck Henry, Tawny Schneider. **Correspondents:** Paul Dandridge, Terry Murphy.

5546   *Love, Sidney.* (Series; Comedy; NBC; 1981–1983). Apartment 405 at 136 East 46th Street in Manhattan is the home of Sidney Shorr, a lonely, middle-aged commercial artist. Sidney, a homosexual, has been depressed since the death of his lover, Martin (seen only in a photograph on the fireplace); he now has no social life and little or no fun. One of the few joys in Sidney's life is seeing Greta Garbo films. It is at a screening of the Greta Garbo movie *Camille* that Sidney meets Laurie Morgan, a spirited young actress who shares Sidney's love for Greta Garbo. However, when Laurie remarks that *Camille* is her least favorite Garbo film, Sidney claims it is one of her best. In an attempt to convince Laurie otherwise, Sidney invites her to his apartment to show her his Garbo photo collection. Sidney's discussion with Laurie seems to make a new man out of him — he is happy. When Laurie is about to leave, a thunderstorm begins. Laurie convinces a reluctant Sidney to let her spend the night. "One thing," she says. "Don't get any ideas." "Me?" responds Sidney. "You don't have to worry about me." "Oh, I get it, that's good," says Laurie. (This exchange of dialogue is virtually the only indication that Sidney is gay. NBC bowed to Moral Majority objections about a gay character and changed Sidney's sexual preference to a point where he could be either straight or gay.)

The following morning, Sidney is changed; he is cheerful and looking forward to the day ahead. He prepares breakfast for Laurie but is saddened again when she leaves. That night, as he is sitting down to dinner, the doorbell rings. It is Laurie. Sidney's eyes light up as she enters and says, "We'll split the rent." Sidney responds by saying he never lived with a woman. "I'll be the best thing that ever happened to you, exclaims Laurie. She immediately begins by redecorating the dreary eight room apartment. Three months later the apartment is cheery and Sidney is a changed man. Sidney also begins to get jealous when Laurie starts daring, and he becomes what he believes is a father figure to her.

On Christmas Eve, 1981, Laurie reveals that she is seeing a married man (not named) and that she is pregnant. She also tells Sidney that the man has given her the money to have an abortion. Sidney, who strongly opposes this, talks Laurie out of having an abortion: "I'll take care of the baby.... Let this be your Christmas gift to me." They agree (Sidney is to become the baby's uncle). Six and a half months later, at Flower Hospital, Laurie gives birth to a girl. Laurie names her Patti (after her favorite song as a kid, "Patty Cake"); Laurie also gives the baby a middle name — Greta — as a reference to how they met. As Laurie finds work on a television soap opera, Sidney becomes more and more of a father to Patti.

Five years later, Laurie falls for a man named Jimmy and decides to marry him. The big blow comes when Laurie tells Sidney she is moving to California. Although it breaks Sidney's heart, he agrees to let Laurie take Patti with her.

One year later, Laurie returns to New York for a visit and eventually decides to stay when she acquires a role on a television soap opera. When Laurie and Jimmy split up, Sidney convinces Laurie to share his apartment once again. Stories follow events in the lives of Sidney Shorr and his adopted family, Laurie and Patti Morgan.

Sidney was originally a freelance commercial artist; he is later employed by Jason Stoller at the Graham and Ludwig Advertising Agency. Laurie first appeared in a television commercial for Amore Soap. She then appeared in four episodes of the TV soap *Another World* and later on the fictional soap *A Time for Loving*. She finally landed the permanent role of Gloria Trenell on the mythical soap *As Thus We Are*.

Mort Harris is Sidney's neighbor; Mrs. Gaffney is Sidney's landlady; Nancy is Jason's secretary. In the NBC pilot film, *Sidney Shorr* (Oct. 5, 1981), Lorna Patterson played Laurie and David Huffman, Jimmy (no last name given).

Cast: Tony Randall (*Sidney Shorr*); Swoosie Kurtz (*Laurie Morgan*); Kaleena Kiff (*Patti Morgan*); Chip Zien (*Jason Stoller*); Graham Beckel (*Jimmy*); Alan North (*Mort Harris*); Barbara Bryne (*Mrs. Gaffney*); Lenka Peterson (*Eve Morgan; Laurie's mother*); Lynne Thigpen (*Nancy; Jason's secretary*).

5547   *Love Songs.* (Series; Music; Syn.; 1985). Music videos coupled with personal ads for singles seeking a mate. The program actually plays matchmaker by running personal ads submitted by viewers. The most appealing ads are shown (over romantic music) and viewers can respond via special box numbers that are provided. The results of matches made by the program are shown as well as the newest music videos.

Host: Dick Summer.

5548   *Love Stories.* (Series; Drama; Syn.; 1991). True stories about people who met and fell in love (and eventually married). The actual people involved in the reenactments that are seen appear to relate their stories.

Host: Kristian Alfonso.

5549   *Love Story.* (Series; Anthology; DuMont; 1954). Live dramatic presentations that emphasize the goodness in nature and the kindness in man. Notable performers include Basil Rathbone, Patricia Breslin, Audra Lindley, Mildred Natwick, Leslie Nielsen, Betty Field and Arthur O'Connell.

5550   *Love Story.* (Series; Game; CBS; 1955-1956). Married or engaged couples are first interviewed then compete in a general knowledge question-and-answer session wherein the highest scoring couple receives and expenses-paid two-week honeymoon in Paris.

Host: Jack Smith. Assistant: Pat Meikle.

5551   *Love Story.* (Series; Anthology; NBC; 1973-1974). Adult and contemporary variations on the theme of love. Notable performers include Janet Leigh, Kay Lenz, Larry Hagman, Lynnette Mettey, Valerie Perrine, Jodie Foster, Don Murray, Susan Oliver, Victoria Principal and Frank Langella. George Schaefer is the producer. Francis Lai composed the "Love Story" theme.

5552   *Love That Bob.* (Series; Comedy; NBC, 1955; 1957–1959;

CBS, 1955–1957). Robert "Bob" Collins, a swinging young bachelor, is owner of Bob Collins Photography in Hollywood. Bob lives with his widowed sister, Margaret MacDonald, and her teenage son, Charles "Chuck" MacDonald, at 804 Grummond Road.

Bob was born in Joplin, Missouri, and is descended from Scottish ancestors. He served in the air force during World War II. Bob is simply a suave and sophisticated ladies' man whose job is to photograph the world's most beautiful women. He considers his models "lumps of clay. I mold them into bright, shimmering butterflies. I give them grace, style and charm." Bob shoots fashion layouts for various magazines and stipulates that his swimsuit models cannot have a waist larger than 23 inches. He can make girls swoon, and he desperately seeks to avoid the path to matrimony. Bob says he is married — to his camera: "Any other type of marriage is a serious commitment and I need my time before settling down. I need to find the right person — no matter how many girls I have to date to find her."

"The Casanova of the Camera," as Margaret calls Bob, simply cannot resist a beautiful woman and insists that he is a confirmed bachelor. "All the Collins men are confirmed bachelors," Margaret says, "until something snaps and they suddenly get married." "Margaret is young and attractive," Bob says. "I keep telling her she should get married again, but does she listen to me? No." Margaret takes care of the house, cooks, cleans, does the shopping and manages to find a little romance — but despite what Bob thinks is best for her, she is not ready to settle down again. (Her longest romance was with Paul Fonda [Lyle Talbot], Bob's World War II air force buddy. Paul is now an airline pilot [a captain] and married one of his stewardesses, Betty Havilland [Dorothy Johnson].)

Margaret considers Bob a father for Chuck: "He's a kind man. He lets us share his house and is putting Chuck through school." But Margaret also says, "Chuck has been raised in an atmosphere of girls, girls, girls." This has been a delight for Chuck, who hopes that whatever his Uncle Bob has, it can be inherited by a nephew.

Chuck first attended Hollywood High School. He joined the National Guard after graduation and in last season episodes enrolled in Gridley College (majoring in pre-med). Francine Williams was Chuck's original girlfriend; Carol Henning replaced her in last season episodes (she enrolled in nearby Beaumont College). Joe DePew and Jimmy Lloyd are Chuck's friends.

"When Bob decides to get married, there is someone waiting for him — me," says Charmaine Schultz, better known as Schultzy, Bob's plain-looking girl Friday. Schultzy is totally dedicated to Bob and in love with him — "I can't compete with the models on the sofa, but give me the kitchen and food and I'll land him."

The hours may be long at times, but Bob rarely complains when it comes to photographing his beautiful models. The voluptuous blonde bombshell, Shirley Swanson, is the model dead set on marrying Bob. Shirley, who measures 38-26-36, is very jealous and called the "Wild Flower" by Bob (Schultzy calls her "Blondie"). Other recurring models included Collette DuBois, a French knockout Bob called his "Sly Little Thief"; Marie DiPaolo is an Italian model Bob calls "My Little Venetian Ambassador of Loveliness"; Mary Beth Hall and Ingrid are two additional models who worked for and drove Bob crazy.

Bob, like his father, is a photographer; but before them there was and still is "Josh Collins — Photography," a business run by Bob's elderly but young at heart grandfather, Joshua ("Josh") Collins, in Joplin, Missouri. Grandpa Collins lives in a drafty old house his father built (and died in from pneumonia). He calls Bob "Young Rooster," Chuck "Chuckie Boy" and Margaret "Mag Pie."

Harvey Helm is Bob's friend, a henpecked wholesale furniture salesman for the Gravener Furniture Company. He calls Bob "Bobby Boy" and was his co-pilot during the war. "Harvey brings home the bacon, but his wife decides how to slice it," says Bob. Harvey is married to Ruthie, a former swimsuit model of Bob's. Carol, Chuck's girlfriend, is Ruthie's niece. Pamela Livingston is Bob's friend, a member of the Bird Watchers' Society. Frank Crenshaw is the sailor with a crush on Schultzy. Kay Michael is the actress Bob dated. Martha Randolph is Schultzy's husband-hunting friend. *Love That Bob* is the now established title for a series that was originally called *The Bob Cummings Show*.

Program Open: [Bob, with camera:] "Hold it, I think you're gonna like this picture." [Announcer:] "And everybody likes new Winston. Winston is the easy drawing, new filter cigarette that tastes good like a cigarette should. King size Winston brings you real flavor in a cigarette and entertainment on *The Bob Cummings Show*."

Cast: Bob Cummings (*Bob Collins*); Rosemary DeCamp (*Margaret MacDonald*); Dwayne Hickman (*Chuck MacDonald*); Ann B. Davis (*Charmaine "Schultzy" Schultz*); King Donovan (*Harvey Helm*); Mary Lawrence (*Ruth Helm*); Charles Herbert (*Tommy Helm*); Joi Lansing (*Shirley Swanson*); Lyle Talbot (*Paul Fonda*); Diane Jergens (*Francine Williams*); Carol Henning (*Olive Sturgess*); Robert Ellis (*Joe DePew*); Jeff Silver (*Jimmy Lloyd*); Nancy Kulp (*Pamela Livingston*); Dick Wesson (*Frank Crenshaw*); Gloria Marshall (*Mary Beth Hall*); Tammy Marihugh (*Tammy Johnson*); Donna Martell (*Marie DiPaolo*); Ingrid Goude (*Ingrid*); Lisa Gaye (*Colette DuBois*); Lola Albright (*Kay Michael*); Bob Cummings (*Josh Collins*); Marjorie Bennett (*Fanny Neemeyer; Margaret's friend*); Kathleen Freeman (*Bertha Krause; Schultzy's friend*). **Announcer:** Bill Baldwin.

5553   *Love That Jill.* (Series; Comedy; ABC; 1958). "They ought to marry so they can argue legally," say friends of Jill Johnson and Jack Gibson, the rival heads of all-female modeling agencies in New York City. Jill, who owns Model Girls, Inc., and Jack, the head of the Gibson Girls Agency, are friendly enemies who snare each other's accounts, publicity and models in an attempt to become the number one modeling agency in Manhattan (both cater to television, film and print ads that require gorgeous girls). Their constant attempts at skullduggery and their continual bickering over accounts has led to an unforeseen love that neither one is willing to admit to under normal circumstances.

To merge agencies or for one even to ask the other out on a date is impossible; hence, each devises elaborate schemes to acquire the other's company — even if it means mixing business with pleasure and snaring the other's account at the same time.

Models Girls, Inc., is located at 670 Madison Avenue; Jill lives in apartment 14A at 1064 Park Avenue; and her favorite ploy to get Jack's attention is to make him jealous by pretending to fall for handsome men.

Jack lives in an apartment at 1360 West 63rd Street, and the Gibson Girls Agency is located at 540 Madison Avenue. In *TV Guide* and other printed sources, Jack's agency is called the House That Jacques Built (Gibson Girls Agency is seen on screen).

Ginger and Peaches are Jill's top models (Ginger is the buxon, dumb blonde type; Peaches is the girl with the hourglass figure). Richard is Jill's secretary (a former crewman at Harvard). Pearl is Jack's secretary; and Brooklyn-born Monty Callahan, a former glass-jawed boxer who was called "One Round Callahan" (he never lasted more than one round) is Jack's masseur.

Cast: Anne Jeffreys (*Jill Johnson*); Robert Sterling (*Jack Gibson*); Betty Lynn (*Pearl*); Jimmy Lydon (*Richard*); Barbara Nichols (*Ginger*); Kaye Elhardt (*Peaches*); Henry Kulky (*Monte*).

5554   *Love Thy Neighbor.* (Series; Comedy; ABC; 1973). At 327 North Robin Hood Road in the Sherwood Forest Estates in San Fernando, California, live Charlie Wilson and his wife, Peggy, a middle class white couple. Charlie, a Democrat, is the shop steward at Turner Electronics. Living next door, at 325 North Robin Hood Road, is Ferguson Bruce and his wife, Jackie, a black couple from Passaic, New Jersey, who are the first to move into an all white neighborhood. Ferguson, a Republican, is the efficiency expert at Turner. Peggy and Jackie quickly become friends; Charlie and Ferguson, on the other hand, are friendly but distrustful of each other. Racial prejudices are satirized as the couples attempt to live side by side and "follow the golden rule, love thy neighbor, you'll find out that it's really cool."

The local bar hangout is Lenny's Tap Room, and the Sherwood Forest Estates were named after the developer: he thought of himself as Robin Hood, only he stole from the poor and made himself rich. Solomon Burke sings the theme, "Love Thy Neighbor."

Cast: Joyce Bulifant (*Peggy Wilson*); Ron Masak (*Charlie Wilson*); Janet MacLachlan (*Jackie Bruce*); Harrison Page (*Ferguson Bruce*); Milt Kamen (*Murray Ferguson*); Louis Guss (*Louie Gordon*).

5555   *Love with a Twist.* (Pilot; Reality; ABC; Jan. 28, 1990). Recreations of tear-jerking, real-life love stories.
Host: Bruce Boxleitner.

5556   *The Lovebirds.* (Pilot; Comedy; CBS; July 18, 1979). Janine and Al Burley are "The Lovebirds" of the title. They are newlyweds and struggling to survive on what Al makes as the manager of the produce department of a local supermarket. The proposal was to follow their romantic ups and downs. Patricia and Fred are their neighbors. Bobby Van performs the theme, "The Lovebirds."
Cast: Lorna Patterson (*Janine Burley*); Louis Welch (*Al Burley*); Ellen Regan (*Patricia Wexelblatt*); Eugene Levy (*Fred Wexelblatt*).

5557   *Loveland.* (Pilot; Drama; Unaired; Produced for Fox in 2000). A large metropolitan hospital is the setting for a proposal about the lives of a group of doctors and nurses.
Cast: Jeremy Sisto (*Mason*); Kristen Wilson (*DeLeon*); Leonard Roberts (*Woods*); Bellamy Young (*Remington*); Mark Harelik (*Quavis*).

5558   *Lover or Loser.* (Series; Game; USA; 2000-2001). Two men stand before a studio audience comprised entirely of women to pitch their dating prowess. The women judge the men on their physical appearance, what they have to say, what they hear from friends, ex-girlfriends and roommates. The women then vote to determine if he is a lover of a loser.
Host: Meredyth Hunt, Scott Sternberg.

5559   *Lovers and Other Strangers.* (Pilot; Comedy; ABC; July 22, 1983). Events in the daily lives of the Delvecchios, a not so-typical American family (parents Frank and Bea; their children, Mike, Mary and Jerry; Mike's wife, Susan; their children, Bruno and Marie; and Bea's sister Pauline).
Cast: Harry Guardino (*Frank Delvecchio*); Carol Teitel (*Bea Delvecchio*); Brian BenBen (*Mike Delvecchio*); Caludia Wells (*Mary Clair Delvecchio*); Alan Hayes (*Jerry Delvecchio*); Keri Houlihan (*Marie Delvecchio*); Helen Verbit (*Pauline*).

5560   *Loves Me, Loves Me Not.* (Series; Comedy; CBS; 1977). Jane Benson is a beautiful grammar school teacher who is constantly hit upon but unable to find the right man for herself. Dick Phillips is a klutzy newspaper reporter who has a hard time impressing girls due to his clumsiness. Jane and Dick are opposites who find an attraction to each other and stories relate their efforts to make it through the travails of a latter 1970s romance. Sue is Jane's friend; Tom is Dick's friend.

Cast: Susan Dey (*Jane Benson*); Kenneth Gilman (*Dick Phillips*); Udana Power, Phyllis Glick (*Sue*); Art Metrano (*Tom*).

5561 *Lovespring International.* (Series; Comedy; Lifetime; 2006). Lovespring International is a Tarzana, California, based matchmaking firm that claims to be in posh Beverly Hills. Victoria Ratchford is its owner and her employees are Lydia, Burke, Tiffany, Steve and Alex.

Lydia Mayhew can't seem to find the right man for herself and has settled on an on-going (now 20 years) relationship with a married man. Burke Kristopher seems to have failed at making a lasting relationship for himself as he is in a marriage of inconvenience. Tiffany Riley Clarke is the sexy but slightly dizzy receptionist; Steve Morris is the staff psychologist; and Alex Odom is the videotographer.

Stories, which are partially scripted, follow an improve cast who ad lib lines as they strive to make perfect matches (bring together romantically challenged individuals). Eric McCormack is the executive producer.

Cast: Jayne Lynch (*Victoria Ratchford*); Wendi McLendon-Covey (*Lydia Mayhew*); Jennifer Elise Cox (*Tiffany Riley Clarke*); Jack Plotnick (*Steve Morris*); Mystro Clark (*Alex Odom*); Sam Pancake (*Burke Kristopher*).

5562 *Low Man on the Totem Pole.* (Pilot; Comedy; CBS; Aug. 1, 1964). Humorous events in the life of H. Allen Smith, a kindhearted author-columnist, who involves himself in the lives of other people. Other regulars are Nelle, Allen's wife; and Mr. Turnbull, Allen's publisher.

Cast: Dan Dailey (*H. Allen Smith*); Diana Lynn (*Nelle Smith*); John McGiver (*Mr. Turnbull*).

5563 *Lowell Thomas Reporting.* (Experimental; Newscast; NBC; July 1, 1941). A one time only simulcast of Lowell Thomas's radio program for Sunoco Oil (broadcast live at 6:45 P.M.). Thomas was seated at a desk while reading the news; the only change from his radio program was that cans of Sunoco Oil were added so the product could be seen while the commercial message was given.

5564 *Lucan.* (Series; Adventure; ABC; 1977–1978). In 1957 an infant is abandoned by his parents and left to die in the forests of northern Minnesota. The infant survives, however, and is raised by a pack of gray wolves. Ten years later, in the summer 1967, a hunting party stumbles upon a strange creature: a humanlike child who eats, sleeps, hunts and howls like a wolf. Authorities are informed and an expedition is organized to find the wolf child.

On October 10, 1967 the wolf boy is captured and brought to the University Research Center in California to begin his journey from the forest to civilization. He is watched over and taught by Dr. Donald ("Don") Hoagland. Progress is slow, but on January 17, 1969, the first breakthrough occurs: the boy learns to eat at the table with utensils.

It is September 5, 1970 when the boy is given a name. When the boy is having difficulty placing geometric shapes in their appropriate places on a board, Don tells him, "You can, you can." When the boy does it, he says "Lu can, lu can."

It is now 1977 and Lucan is 20 years old. His is the first known case in which a human raised in the wild has been successfully treated and restored to human behavior. His senses are remarkably acute, especially his sense of smell. In his ten years of captivity, his sleeping patterns have not changed: his time of greatest activity is still night, and he wanders about restlessly, which reflects the hunting habits of his early childhood — "No amount of training can erase the early struggle for survival. Metabolically, he is more wolf than man."

Shortly after, the school's board of directors tells Don that Lucan is still too wolf like and should be placed in a state sanitarium. Don protests, and all changes when he is injured in a car accident. He speaks to Lucan: "You must leave this place. I've felt for some time you must go ... to find your parents.... Even if you never find them, you promised yourself some day you would search ... I can't protect you anymore."

Lucan leaves the university and begins his search, taking what jobs he can and helping people along the way. In the two month interval between telecasts of the first and second episodes, a dramatic change occurred: instead of Lucan's leaving on his own to search for his parents, the revised storyline finds him escaping from the authorities who tried to keep him captive, fearing he would revert back to being a wolf. The university then hires a bounty hunter named Prentiss to capture him. After another short absence, the series returned with a new storyline: Lucan's adventures as a fugitive from justice. (When two thieves break into the university lab seeking drugs, they encounter Lucan. A fight ensues and one of the thieves is killed. When Lucan is unjustly accused of murder, he escapes to find the only man who can clear him — the other thief. Hindering Lucan's efforts is Prentiss, now a police lieutenant relentlessly pursuing him.) The series ended before Lucan could find his parents or clear his name.

Cast: Kevin Brophy (*Lucan*); John Randolph (*Don Hoagland*); Don Gordon (*Prentiss*).

5565 *Lucas Tanner.* (Series; Drama; NBC; 1974–1975). A realistic portrayal of student-teacher relationships as seen through the eyes of Lucas Tanner, an English instructor at Harry S. Truman Memorial High School in Webster Groves, Missouri. Margaret Blumenthal is the principal (later replaced by John Hamilton); Glendon Farrell is Lucas's young neighbor; Grace Baden is Glendon's grandmother (with whom he lives); Jaytee, Cindy, Terry and Wally are students. Lucas has a dog named O'Casey (later called Bridget).

Cast: David Hartman (*Lucas Tanner*); Rosemary Murphy (*Margaret Blumenthal*); John Randolph (*John Hamilton*); Robbie Rist (*Glendon Farrell*); Alan Abelew (*Jaytee Druman*); Trish Sodik (*Cindy Damin*); Kimberly Beck (*Terry*); Michael Dwight-Smith (*Wally*); June Dayton (*Grace Baden*).

5566 *Los Luchadores (The Wrestlers).* (Series; Adventure; Fox; 2001). Lobo Fuerte is a masked wrestler who entered the ring 15 years ago and quickly became a world champion. Other than being of Spanish descent, his background is a mystery and no one knows where he came from. He has taken up residence in Union City and devotes his life to battling injustice. He fights in the wrestling ring for entertainment "and evil outside of the ring so the people of Union City can sleep at night." Turbine and Maria Valentine are fellow wrestlers who assist Lobo in and out of the ring.

Lobo, Maria and Turbine never remove their masks ("A luchadore's mask is like a reflection of his soul"). Cheating is unthinkable to Lobo, even if it costs him a victory in the ring. He has never lost a fair fight. Lobo is called "the unbeatable champion of the ring" and wrestles for the Lucha Librae Federation at the Union City Sports Arena. Lobo has his headquarters (and appears to live) on the top floor of Lobo Towers, a building that also houses the latest in crime fighting and crime detecting equipment.

A man known only as Laurant commands the equipment. Laurant is a former wrestler who trained Lobo, Maria and Turbine to use their abilities to battle evil. Lobo drives a car called the Lobo Ride, which is capable of amazing maneuvers; it can go from "blast to megablast" in a matter of seconds. The team assists the Metro Police Department. The Tornados is the restaurant-bar frequented by the team.

Turbine is a young, energetic wrestler with a passion for fast cars and motorcycles. He rides a super-powered motorcycle and is called

"Speed Boy" by Maria (villains call him "that speed freak"). He and Lobo met in the ring and became quick friends. Turbine is a mechanical genius and designed many of the gadgets he and Lobo use in their high speed chases.

Maria is an up and coming enmascarada (masked wrestler). She likes speed, action, excitement and defeating the dark forces of evil. In the ring Maria is called "The Battling Beauty" and "The Girl with a Twirl"; Turbine calls her "The Blonde Brainiac."

Cast: Maximo Morrone *(Lobo Fuerte)*; Levi James *(Turbine)*; Sarah Carter *(Maria Valentine)*; Arthur Burghardt *(Laurant)*.

5567   *The Lucie Arnaz Show.* (Series; Comedy; CBS; 1985). WPLE-AM is a radio station nicknamed "Advice Radio 88" (88 KHz is its location on the dial). It is located in Manhattan at 1700 Broadway (at 53rd Street), and 555-WPLE is its advice line phone number. While the station apparently has many programs, we know of only one: *The Love and Lucas Show*, an afternoon comedy and advice program that combines the psychological advice of Dr. Jane Lucas with the comic talents of Larry Love and his invisible dog, Tippy.

Jane lives in Apartment 4A on East 70th Street. She graduated from New York University and also has a daily advice column, "Dear Jane," in the *Daily Mirror*. While Jane seems capable of helping other people resolve their difficulties, she can't seem to work out her own problems — hence the situation for stories.

Thirty-one-year-old Jane plays shortstop on the station's unnamed softball team; the slogan for "The Love and Lucas Show" is "Your spot for music and mental health in the afternoon."

Jim Gordon is the station manager; Jill is Jane's sister (she lives in New Jersey) and Sarah and Billy are Jill's children. Gwyn Gillis appeared as Jim's wife, Peggy Gordon. Based on the British series, "Agony" (with Maureen Lipman as Jane Lucas, an advice columnist who can help people with their problems but is unable to solve her own).

Cast: Lucie Arnaz *(Dr. Jane Lucas)*; Todd Waring *(Larry Love)*; Tony Roberts *(Jim Gordon)*; Lee Bryant *(Jill)*; Melissa Joan Hart *(Sarah)*; Sandy Schwartz *(Billy)*; Gwyn Gillis *(Peggy Gordon)*.

5568   *The Lucille Ball–Desi Arnaz Show.* (Series; Comedy; CBS; 1958–1960). A continuation of *I Love Lucy* in an hour format but broadcast as 13 episodes of *Desilu Playhouse*. Stories follow marrieds Lucy and Ricky Ricardo and their friends, Fred and Ethel Mertz, as they travel to various places and become involved with a different guest star in each episode.

Cast: Lucille Ball *(Lucy Ricardo)*; Desi Arnaz *(Ricky Ricardo)*; William Frawley *(Fred Mertz)*; Vivian Vance *(Ethel Mertz)*; Richard Keith *(Little Ricky Ricardo)*.

5569   *Lucky.* (Series; Comedy; FX; 2003). Michael Linkletter could be considered one lucky man: he won one million dollars in a poker game. However, he could also be considered unlucky: a year later his gambling addiction cost him the million dollars. Michael has tried to overcome his addiction but all efforts have failed — especially since he has mounting bills to pay. One day Michael finds a $100 gambling chip and devises a plan — parlay that chip into another million dollars. Stories follow Michael as he tries to recreate his lucky streak by competing in high stakes, world championship poker games.

Cast: John Corbett *(Michael Linkletter)*; Ever Carradine *(Theresa McWatt)*; Dan Hedaya *(Joey Leggs)*; Kevin Breznahan *(Danny Martin)*; Blaine Pate *(Father Jack)*; Billy Gardell *(Vinny Sticarelli)*.

5570   *Lucky Letters.* (Series; Game; NBC; 1950). The object calls for contestants to unscramble words from clues given through music, visual aids or verse. The players with the most correct answers are the winners and receive merchandise prizes.

Host: Frankie Masters. **Regulars:** Phyllis Myles and the West Twins.

5571   *Lucky Louie.* (Series; Comedy; HBO; 2006). Louie (no last name given) is a man without a dream (or even much ambition). He is married to Kim and is the father of five-year-old Lucy. Louie works part time in a muffler shop and cares for Lucy while Kim works full time as a nurse (to secure benefits). Stories follow the life of a man who constantly complains about life but has no ambition to change it.

Kim and Louie have been married for seven years and it is Kim who wears the pants in the family. She is the breadwinner and she doesn't take "crap" from anyone. She is very foul-mouthed (as is Louie) but has set strict ideals for her family to live by.

Mike and Tina are Louie and Kim's best friends, a married couple who like Louie and Kim, live a simple life in a modest apartment (although here it is Mike who is the breadwinner). Walter and Estelle are also their neighbors, an African-American couple with a daughter named Lisa. Jerry, Kim's eccentric brother, also lives in her building. He is somewhat immature and constantly in need of Kim's direction. Rich is Louie's friend, a schemer who lives with his mother.

Cast: Louis C.K. *(Louie)*; Pamela Adion *(Kim)*; Kelly Gould *(Lucy)*; Mike Hagerty *(Mike)*; Laura Kightlinger *(Tina)*; Jerry Minor *(Walter)*; Jim Norton *(Ellen)*; Rick Shapior *(Jerry)*.

5572   *Lucky Partners.* (Series; Game; NBC; 1958). Two contestants, plus each member of the studio audience are handed a sheet of paper with the word LUCKY printed on one side. Players are then asked to use their own dollar bills and write the last five digits of the serial number under the word LUCKY. The two studio audience players whose numbers match the stage players join them and together they compete for merchandise prizes via a general knowledge question-and-answer session. Winners are the players with the most correct answers.

Host: Carl Cordell.

5573   *Lucky Pup.* (Series; Children; CBS; 1948–1951). Lucky Pup is a dog who lives a life of luxury: he has inherited $5 million from his late master and resides in a mansion. Foodini is an evil magician who, along with his fumbling assistant, Pinhead, are seeking the good life. When Foodini learns that Lucky Pup is rich, he devises a plan to acquire that wealth for himself. Stories, which incorporate marionettes, relate Foodini's endless (and fruitless) efforts to trick Lucky Pup out of his money. When the Foodini character became more popular than Lucky Pup, it was spun off into the series *Foodini the Great*.

Hostess: Doris Brown. **Voices-Puppeteers:** Hope Bunin, Morey Bunin.

5574   *Lucky Us.* (Pilot; Comedy; Unaired; Produced for Fox in 2003). A blind date has unsuspected consequences for Lucy and Alex when Lucy later discovers she is pregnant. Lucy and Alex are now linked by an unplanned for child and the proposal was to relate the mishaps that occur as they plan their future life together.

Cast: Chyler Leigh *(Lucy)*; Ethan Embry *(Alex)*; Jill Ritchie *(Debbie)*; John Ross Bowie *(Charlie)*; Randall Park *(Jimmy)*.

5575   *The Lucy Monroe Program.* (Experimental; Variety; NBC; July 28, 1939). Songs with singer Lucy Monroe and dancing by the team of Josephine and Albert Butler.

5576   *Lucy: Daughter of the Devil.* (Series; Cartoon; Adult

Swim; 2005). Lucy is the 18-year-old daughter of Satan. She has just graduated from art school and has joined her father in a business venture: operating a Tequila Sally restaurant. Unknown to Lucy she is the Anti-Christ. The Vatican is aware of Lucy and has dispatched the Special Sister and Special Fathers to find and destroy her before she can fulfill her destiny (when she reaches 21 years of age).

Lucy's boyfriend is Jesus (pronounced hey-soos) who is actually Jesus Christ in His second coming. Jesus, called D.J. Jesus, is a D.J. known as "The hippest D.J. in San Francisco."

Satan has become aware of D.J. Jesus' real identity but is stopped from killing him by Lucy (but he doesn't hesitate to tempt him into evil). Stories follow Lucy as she dates D.J. Jesus (still unaware of her destiny) and run her father's restaurant; and the efforts of the Special Sister and Fathers to find Lucy before Lucy changes the course of the world. Becky is the Devil's advocate.

Voice Cast: Melissa Bardin Galasky (*Lucy/Becky*); H. Jon Benjamin (*Satan*); Jon Glaser (*D.J. Jesus*); Eugene Mirman (*Special Sister*); Sam Seder (*Special Father*).

5577   *The Lucy Show.* (Series; Comedy; CBS; 1962–1968). Lucy Carmichael is a widow with two children, Chris and Jerry. She lives at 132 Post Road in Danfield, a town in New York State. She shares the house with her divorced friend, Vivian Bagley and her son, Sherman. Lucy and Vivian are former Navy WACS who met during World War II. Vivian is level-headed; Lucy is disorganized and desperate for money (she lives off a trust fund established by her late husband at the Danfield National Bank). The money, however, never seems to be enough and her misguided attempts to acquire additional cash — by whatever legal means she can — is the basic concept of the series from 1962–1965. In the fall of 1965, Lucy moves to San Francisco to begin a new life. She acquires a home at 700 Gower Street and Lucy finds a job as the secretary to Theodore J. Mooney, the vice president of the Westland Bank (in the prior version, he was the president of the Danfield National Bank). Chris and Jerry are not seen (Chris is said to be in college; Jerry has been sent to military school). Vivian had married prior to the format change and is now Vivian Bunson (she appears several times as a guest). Mary Jane Lewis becomes Lucy's new friend (and partner in mischief).

Other regulars are Hughie, Marge's husband; Ted Jr. and Bob Mooney, Theodore's sons; Harrison Cheever, the president of the Westland Bank; Mr. Barnsdahl, the president of the Danfield Bank (before Mr. Mooney); Harry Connors, Lucy's friend; and Marge, Lucy's sister.

Cast: Lucille Ball (*Lucy Carmichael*); Candy Moore (*Chris Carmichael*); Jimmy Garrett (*Jerry Carmichael*); Vivian Vance (*Vivian Bagley*); Ralph Hart (*Sherman Bagley*); Gale Gordon (*Theodore J. Mooney*); Charles Lane (*Mr. Barnsdahl*); Dick Martin (*Harry Connors*); Mary Jane Croft (*Mary Jane Lewis*); Roy Roberts (*Harrison Cheever*); Janet Waldo (*Marge*); Peter Marshall (*Hughie Lewis*); Eddie Applegate (*Bob Mooney*); Michael J. Pollard (*Ted Mooney, Jr.*).

5578   *Luis.* (Series; Comedy; Fox; 2003). Park Avenue Donuts is a pastry shop in New York's Spanish Harlem. It is owned by Luis (no last name given) a 37-year-old constantly harassed man who is longing for a life of peace and quiet.

Luis is divorced from Isabella and is the father of Marlena (Called Marly). Luis owns the building that houses his store. Marly lives in the building with her free-loading boyfriend Greg, a "half Dutch, half Scottish-Irish" artist who hopes to make it big selling his paintings; in short, he's a penniless artist.

Despite the fact that Luis is a landlord and shop owner, he barely has enough money to survive. But also vying for a piece of his near no income is Isabella, who works as a real estate agent (to hopefully make more money Luis tried to get the Jewish community business

by baking salmon donuts). Luis calls Greg (whom he really doesn't like, "Twinkie"); Marly calls Luis "Pop." Luis's one pride and joy is his 1982 Oldsmobile Delta 88 (he calls it Ginger).

Other regulars are Zhing Zhang, a Chinese delivery boy who doesn't speak English; T.K., the schemer who sells "merchandise" he finds in Luis's dumpster; and Mrs. Gallagher, Luis's obnoxious Irish tenant; Rickie, Luis's counter boy.

Cast: Luis Guzman (*Luis*); Diana-Maria Riva (*Isabella*); Jaclyn DeSantis (*Marly*); Wes Ramsey (*Greg*); Charlie Day (*Richie*); Reggie Lee (*Zhing Zhang*); Malcolm Barrett (*T.K.*); Eve Brenner (*Mrs. Gallagher*).

5579   *Luke and the Tenderfoot.* (Pilot; Comedy; CBS; Aug. 6 and 13, 1965). Luke Herkimer is a crooked wagon peddler. Pete Queen is his partner, a young tenderfoot. The proposal was to relate their adventures as they peddle their wares throughout the Old West.

Cast: Edgar Buchanan (*Luke Herkimer*); Carleton Carpenter (*Pete Queen*).

5580   *Luke's Parental Advisory.* (Series; Reality; VH-1; 2008). Luther "Luke" Campbell of the group 2 Live Crew, and his fiancé, Kristin (an attorney) are featured as cameras follow events in their daily lives, focusing mostly on Luke's efforts to deal with his children (Lacresha and Luke Jr.) from a prior marriage.

5581   *Lum and Abner.* (Pilot; Comedy; CBS; Nov. 2, 1949). The Jot 'Em Down General Store in Pine Ridge, Arkansas, is owned by Lum Edwards and Abner Peabody, two friends whose opposing points of view provide the humor for a proposal based on the radio series of the same title. Other regulars are store customers: Moze, Miss Pitts of the Eureka Moth Spraying Company, the Widow Abernathy and Doc Miller. A second pilot aired on Feb. 20, 1951 but only in Los Angeles (on station KTTV). It was used to fill *The Alan Young Show* time slot when a kinescope of Alan's live show from New York was not made available.

Cast: Chester Lauck (*Lum Edwards*); Norris Goff (*Abner Peabody*); Andy Devine (*Moze*); ZaSu Pitts (*Miss Pitts*); Edgar Stehli (*Doc Miller*); Bess McCammon (*Widow Abernathy*). **Announcer:** Wendell Niles.

5582   *The Lush Life.* (Series; Comedy; UPN; 1996). Georgia Sanders (called George) and Margot Hines are best friends who share an apartment together and, despite their lack of riches, attempt to live a lush life (accomplished mostly by scrimping, saving and scheming to increase their earnings).

Cast: Lori Petty (*Georgia "George" Sanders*); Karyn Parsons (*Margot Hines*); Concetta Tomei (*Ann Hines*); Fab Filippo (*Hameton Ford Foster*); Khalil Kain (*Lance Battista*); John Ortiz (*Nelson "Margarita" Marquez*); Sullivan Walker (*Hal Gardner*).

5583   *Luther.* (Series; Crime Drama; BBC America; 2010). John Luther is a brilliant detective "tormented by the darker side of humanity." He is a near genius and hunts only the most diabolical criminals — the fiends who prey on helpless people. The murderer's identity is shown at the opening of each episode. The story itself reveals the psychological duel as the predator seeks the prey. Luther follows his own moral code, but also adheres to the rules of criminal law. Alice Morgan is his friend, a key witness in his first investigation who later assists him; Zoe is Luther's estranged wife (she walked out on him); Mark North is the man seeking Zoe's love (hoping she and Luther will get a divorce); Rose Teller is Luther's superior, the Detective Superintendent; Justin Ripley is Luther's partner; Ian Reed is Luther's friend, the Detective Chief Inspector.

Cast: Idris Elba (*John Luther*); Ruth Wilson (*Alice Morgan*); Steven Mackintosh (*Ian Reed*); Indira Varma (*Zoe Luther*); Paul McGunn (*Mark North*); Saskia Reeves (*Rose Telller*); Warren Brown (*Justin Ripley*).

5584   The Lux Video Theater. (Series; Anthology; CBS; NBC; 1950–1959). Lux soap products sponsored program of quality dramatic presentations. In 1958 it switched from sixty minutes to a half-hour and became *The Lux Playhouse*. Based on *The Lux Radio Theater* and aired on CBS (Oct. 2, 1950 to June 24, 1954) and NBC (Aug. 3, 1954 to Sept. 18, 1959). It also featured adaptations of motion pictures and previews of current films were seen at the end of each episode.

Program Open: "Now, live from Hollywood, *Lux Video Theater*. Lux Presents Hollywood. From the entertainment capital of the world, *Lux Video Theater* presents Scott Brady and Phyllis Thaxter in "Holiday Affair...."

Host: James Mason (*1954-55*); Otto Kruger (*1955-56*); Gordon MacRae (*1956-1957*); Ken Carpenter (*1957*).

5585   Luxury Liner. (Pilot; Drama; NBC; Feb. 12, 1963). Dramatic incidents in the lives of people who book passage aboard a luxury liner as seen through the eyes of Victor Kihlgren, the ship's captain. The program, produced by Aaron Spelling, is his first attempt at what would later set sail as *The Love Boat*. Broadcast as a segment of *The Dick Powell Show*.

Cast: Rory Calhoun (*Captain Victor Kihlgren*).

5586   The Lyon's Den. (Series; Drama; NBC; 2003). Jack Turner is the idealistic offspring of a prestigious line of politicians who works as a lawyer with the firm of Lyon, Lacrosse and Levine. Stories follow Jack as he and his associates tackle difficult cases.

Cast: Rob Lowe (*Jack Turner*); Elizabeth Mitchell (*Ariel Saxon*); Kyle Chandler (*Grant Rashton*); Frances Fisher (*Brit Hanley*); Robert Picardo (*Det. Nick Traub*); Eric Lemier (*Tim Jenkins*); Cliff Robertson (*Hal Malloy*); Matt Craven (*George Riley*); David Krumholtz (*Jeff Fineman*).

5587   The Lyracist Lounge Show. (Series; Comedy; MTV; 2000-2001). Hip Hop music coupled with skits that are interspersed with raps. Based on the Lyracist Lounge, a New York City hip hop showcase that features up-and-coming musical artists.

Rappers: Wordsworth, BabeePower, Master Fuol. **Comics:** Tracee Ellis Ross, Jordan Black, Marty Belafsky, Heather McDonald, Mike Ricca.

5588   The M&M Candy Carnival. (Series; Variety; CBS; 1952-1953). Performances by undiscovered, aspiring talent that is presented against carnival backdrop and sponsored by M&M candies. Winners, determined by a judge, receive a $25 savings bond and a week's pro-booking at the Hamid Steel Pier in Atlantic City, New Jersey.

Host: Gene Crane. **Ringmaster:** Barry Cossell. **Clowns:** Don Lennox, Bill Bailey. **Judge:** George Hammond.

5589   M Squad. (Series; Crime Drama; NBC; 1957–1960). Frank Ballinger is a special plainclothes detective lieutenant with the M Squad Division of the Chicago Police Department. Frank is a no-nonsense cop with a true dedication to his job. Stories follow his investigations into cases that surpass the requirements of systematic law enforcement procedure. Count Basie composed the "M Squad Theme."

Cast: Lee Marvin (*Lt. Frank Ballinger*); Paul Newlan (*Captain Grey*).

5590   M Station: Hawaii. (Pilot; Adventure; CBS; June 10, 1980). M (Makai) Station is a privately funded oceanographic research development company working off the coast of Hawaii. The proposal was to relate the exploits of its five-member team (Dana, Andrew, Karen, Luana and Truck) as they tackle hazardous assignments.

Cast: Jared Martin (*Dana Ryan*); Andrew Duggan (*Andrew McClelland*); Jo Ann Harris (*Karen Holt*); Elissa Dulce (*Luana Sorel*); Moe Keale (*Truck Kealoha*).

5591   Ma and Pa. (Pilot; Comedy; CBS; Mar. 7, 1974). Ma and Pa, as they are known, are a young-at-heart elderly couple who live in a quiet Chicago suburb. They have three grown daughters (Dorothy, Celia and Emily) and many problems as their daughters try to run their lives. Ma and Pa's efforts to overcome their meddling was the focal point of the proposal.

Cast: Mary Wickes (*Ma*); Arthur Space (*Pa*); Dorothy Loudon (*Dorothy*); Marian Hailey (*Celia*); Barbara Sharma (*Emily*).

5592   Mabel and Max. (Pilot; Comedy; CBS; July 31, 1987). Seeking to further her career as an actress, 24-year-old Maxine "Max" Tanner leaves Cedar Rapids and heads for New York City. There, she meets and befriends Mabel Oberdine, a 70-year-old veteran who takes her under her wing. The proposal was to relate their misadventures as they seek work. Other regulars are Harry, Mabel's agent; and Paul, Mabel's son.

Cast: Geraldine Fitzgerald (*Mabel Oberdine*); Mary B. Ward (*Maxine "Max" Tanner*); Shelly Berman (*Harry Kanter*); Tony Goldman (*Paul Oberdine*).

5593   The Mac Davis Show. (Series; Variety; NBC; 1974; 1976). Light comedy, music and songs with singer Mac Davis as the host. Two versions appeared:

1. The Mac Davis Show (NBC, 1974-75). **Host:** Mac Davis. **Regulars:** Kay Dingle, Bo Kaprall, The Tony Mordente Dancers. **Orchestra:** Mike Post.

2. The Mac Davis Show: (NBC, 1976). **Host:** Mac Davis. **Regulars:** Shields and Yarnell, Ron Silver, The Strutts. **Music:** Tom Baher, Mike Post.

5594   The Macahans. (Pilot; Western; ABC; Jan. 19, 1976). The pilot film for *How the West Was Won* (ABC, 1977–79) about the Macahans, a Virginia homesteading family, as they attempt to establish a new life on the Great Plains during the mid–1860s.

Cast: James Arness (*Zeb Macahan*); Eva Marie Saint (*Kate Macahan*); Richard Kiley (*Timothy Macahan*); Bruce Boxleitner (*Seth Macahan*); Kathryn Holcomb (*Laura Macahan*); William Kirby Cullen (*Jeb Macahan*); Vicki Schreck (*Jessie Macahan*).

5595   MacCreedy's Woman. (Pilot; Drama; NBC; Sept. 23, 1958). Brandy MacCreedy is a beautiful singer who inherits a supper club in San Francisco after the sudden death of her husband. Her efforts to run the club and help the people who come there looking for help was the focal point of the proposal.

Cast: Jane Russell (*Brandy MacCreedy*).

5596   MacGruder and Loud. (Series; Crime Drama; ABC; 1985). Malcolm MacGruder and Jennifer Loud are patrol car officers with the L.A.P.D. Malcolm (badge number 459) and Jennifer, called Jenny (badge number 449) are secretly married. Department regulations prohibit married couples from working together. They live at 165 North Veranda — Malcolm in Apartment 2A; Jenny in Apartment 2B. The bookcase in Malcolm's apartment has been secretly converted into a revolving door to allow access to both apartments. Stories relate their efforts to keep their marriage a secret and yet work together as two singles who apparently have little else in common than solving the cases to which they are assigned. Jenny hates a Code 3 ("They're too dangerous"); her badge number was also given as 458 and Malcolm's as 445.

Cast: John Getz (*Malcolm MacGruder*); Kathryn Harrold (*Jennifer Loud*); Frank McCarthy (*Sgt. Bob Myhrum*); Arlen Dean Snyder (*Sgt. Jim Egi*); Ted Ross (*Det. Don Debbin*); Lee deBroux (*Sgt. Hanson*); Rick Rossovich (*Sgt. Geller*); Susan Tyrrell (*Mary Margaret Myhrum*).

5597 *MacGyver*. (Series; Adventure; ABC; 1985–1992). Angus ("Mac") MacGyver is a survival expert and scientific genius who tackles seemingly impossible missions for the government (Mac first worked for Western Tech, then U.S. Intelligence, the Company and finally the Phoenix Foundation).

Peter ("Pete") Thornton is Mac's superior; Nikki Carpenter is Mac's friend and occasional assistant. Jack Dalton is Mac's misadventure-prone friend, a pilot who runs the Dalton Air Service. Maria Romburg appeared as Mac's romantic interest for a short time in 1990. Stories follow MacGyver as he uses his expertise as well as his wits to solve cases for his employers.

The last episode, "The Stringer," was broadcast as a special on April 25, 1992. In it MacGyver meets Shawn A. Molloy (Dalton James), the son he never knew he had. Shawn, who uses the nickname Sam, is the son of Kate Molloy (Lisa Savage), Mac's college sweetheart. Kate, a photo-journalist, was killed by the Chinese while investigating the democratic movement in China. Her son, nine years old at the time (played by Nicholas Matus), survived and later became a photojournalist. While investigating a case involving smuggled goods from China, Mac and Sam meet. The "A" in Sam's name stands for Angus and in a locket he carries a picture of his mother and a man who was unknown to him, until now, MacGyver. After completing the assignment, Mac leaves the Phoenix Foundation to spend time with his son. Harry Jackson is Mac's grandfather; Sue Ling is Mac's foster daughter; Sue Ling; Connie Thornton is Peter's ex-wife; Michael is their son. Although the above episode was promoted as "The Last MacGyver," another first-run episode ("The Mountain of Youth") aired on ABC on May 12, 1992.

Cast: Richard Dean Anderson (*Angus MacGyver*); Dana Elcar (*Peter Thornton*); Bruce McGill (*Jack Dalton*); Brigitta Stenberg (*Maria Romburg*); Dalton James (*Shawn A. Molloy*); John Anderson (*Harry Jackson*); Michele B. Chan (*Sue Ling*); Penelope Windust, Linda Darlow (*Connie Thornton*); Scott Coffey (*Michael Thornton*).

5598 *Mack and Myer for Hire*. (Series; Comedy; Syn.; 1963). Two hapless men, known only as Mack and Myer, are craftsmen with only one ambition in life: to succeed in the two-man business they have established: Mack and Myer for Hire. Stories relate their fumbling attempts to complete the jobs they acquire.

Cast: Mickey Deems (*Mack*); Joey Faye (*Myer*).

5599 *The MacKenzies of Paradise Cove*. (Series; Drama; ABC; 1979). Each Sunday before dinner, Frank and Laura MacKenzie would go sailing. One Sunday afternoon in 1978, a tragic accident claims their lives and leaves their five children, Bridget, Kevin, Celia, Michael and Timothy, orphans.

When authorities threaten to break up the family by sending the children to orphanages, the MacKenzie children convince local fisherman Cuda Weber to pretend to be their uncle, William ("Willie") MacKenzie, so the Child Welfare Department will allow them to live together. Stories, set in Hawaii, follow the adventures of the five MacKenzie children as they struggle to remain together as a family.

Cuda owns the boat, the *Viking*. He held jobs as "dishwasher, grease monkey, bartender, outhouse builder and fish cleaner." He now lives in a cabin by the sea in Oahu; the children live in a house

on Paradise Cove. In the original pilot film, *Stickin' Together* (ABC, April 14, 1978), Sean Thomas Roche played Kevin MacKenzie, the oldest boy.

Cast: Clu Gulager (*Cuda Weber*); Lory Walsh (*Bridget MacKenzie*); Shawn Stevens (*Kevin MacKenzie*); Randi Kiger (*Celia MacKenzie*); Sean Marshall (*Michael MacKenzie*); Keith Mitchell (*Timothy MacKenzie*); Moe Keale ("*Big*" *Ben Kalikini; Cuda's friend*); Sean Tyler Hall ("*Little*" *Ben Kalikini; Ben's son*); Scott Kingston (*Richie Kalikini; Ben's son*); Leinaala Heine (*Ben's wife*); Harry Chang (*Barney; Cuda's friend*).

5600 *MacKenzie's Raiders*. (Series; Adventure; Syn.; 1958). Fort Clark, Texas, 1873, is the base for Ranald S. MacKeznie, a Colonel with the U.S. Fourth Cavalry, as he and his secret team of Raiders (organized by President Grant to bring order back to Texas) battle the savage elements along the Rio Grande between the U.S. and Mexico.

Cast: Richard Carlson (*Ranald S. MacKenzie*); George Gilbreth (*Lt. Tom Paxon*); Riley Hill (*Sgt. Fife*); Dennis Moore (*Sgt. Teal*); Charles Boaz (*Cpl. Dixon*); Jim Brides (*Pvt. Lewis*); Doug McClure (*Cpl. Adam Davis*).

5601 *MacLeish and the Rented Kid*. (Pilot; Comedy; ABC; May 28, 1975). Mac MacLeish is a single newspaper columnist whose life suddenly changes when he agrees to care for Augie, the 12-year-old son of a friend, a widowed foreign correspondent whose travels leave him no time for care for his son. The proposal was set to follow Mac's efforts to care for the mischievous Augie. Other regulars are Suzy, Mac's girlfriend; and Hal, Mac's friend, a wealthy cartoonist.

Cast: Dick Van Dyke (*Mac MacLeish*); Jimmy Baio (*Augie*); Marcia Rodd (*Suzy*); Shelly Berman (*Hal Stark*); John Myhers (*Mac's publisher*).

5602 *MacNamara's Band*. (Pilot; Comedy; ABC; 1977-1978). Seeking a squad of undercover agents for assignments too dangerous for their own operatives, the U.S. government gives five con artists (Johnny MacNamara, Zoltan, Gaffner, Milgrim and Aggie) a choice: spend time in prison or perform hazardous assignments behind enemy lines. They choose to perform the assignments and the proposal was to follow their blundering efforts to complete their missions. Three pilot films were produced.

1. MacNamara's Band (May 14, 1977). **Cast:** John Byner (*Johnny MacNamara*), Sid Haig (*Zoltan*), Bruce Kirby, Sr. (*Gaffney*), Joseph Sicari (*Milgrim*), Lefty Pedroski (*Aggie*).

2. MacNamara's Band II (Dec. 5, 1977). **Cast:** John Byner (*Johnny MacNamara*), Sid Haig (*Zoltan*), Bruce Kirby, Sr. (*Gaffney*), Joe Pantoliano (*Frankie Milano*), Steve Doubet (*Aggie*).

3. MacNamara's Band III (June 10, 1978). **Cast:** John Byner (*Johnny MacNamara*), Sid Haig (*Zoltan*), Bruce Kirby, Sr. (*Gaffney*), Joe Pantoliano (*Frankie Milano*), Steve Doubet (*Aggie*).

5603 *Mad About You*. (Series; Comedy; NBC; 1992–1999). One Sunday evening in December of 1989, Paul Buchman stops at a newsstand to buy the *New York Times*. There is only one copy left, and he is about to pay for it when a girl named Jamie Stemple appears, seeking the *Times* also. She tells Paul that she needs the paper because it contains her parents' obituary ("Beams fell on them during an earthquake"). Jamie is very pretty, has a very sexy voice and Paul half heartedly believes her story; he gives her the paper. As Jamie leaves, she drops a dry cleaning receipt with her name on it. That night, while with a friend, Paul checks the obit page of the *Times* and sees no Stemple — "I knew she was lying." The following day, Paul picks up Jamie's dry cleaning and tracks her down. Jamie is a bit distrustful of Paul (having just broken up with a guy), but Paul knows this is the girl for him. After talking, Jamie feels Paul may be the man she is seeking and invites him to the office Christmas party. They learn they are literally neighbors. Paul resides at 129 West 81st Street (Apartment 5B) and Jamie across the street at 142 West 81st Street (Apartment 11C). The strangers brought together by a newspaper begin dating and marry in 1992 (they are married five months when the series begins). The newlyweds take up residence in Jamie's apartment; Paul sublets his to Kramer (Michael Richards from the series *Seinfeld*).

Jamie is 30 years old and works as regional vice president at a public relations firm called Ferrah-Gantz on Madison Avenue. She was born in New Haven, Connecticut, attended Yale University and likes to be liked by other people; she gets extremely upset if people don't like her and goes out of her way to impress them so they will like her. When she is laid off she and her friend, Fran Devanow, begin their own PR firm (Buchman and Devanow). Paul is a documentary filmmaker and owns his own company (Buchman Films) in Manhattan. He was born in New York City and attended NYU Film School. Paul later works for the Explorer Channel. Riff's Bar is their favorite watering hole.

Dr. Mark Devanow (a gynecologist) and his wife, Fran, are Paul and Jamie's friends (they live downtown on 2nd Avenue). Lila Stemple is Jamie's sister; and Gus and Theresa Stemple are Jamie's parents. In the pilot episode, Paul and Jamie's last name is Cooper.

Cast: Helen Hunt (*Jamie Buchman*); Paul Reiser (*Paul Buchman*); Richard Kind (*Mark Devanow*); Leila Kenzle (*Fran Devanow*); Ann Ramsay (*Lila Stemple*); Paul Dooley (*Gus Stemple*); Nancy Dussault (*Theresa Stemple*).

5604   *Mad Avenue.* (Pilot; Drama; CBS; Aug. 23, 1988). A behind-the-scenes look at the world of advertising as seen through the experiences of Bruce Randall, the senior vice president of the fictional but nationally renowned B.C.D. Ad Agency in Manhattan, and his staff: Ben Lindsey, the senior copyrighter; C.G. and Kirk, his assistants; Meg, the art director; and her assistants, Murph and Dan.

Cast: James B. Sikking (*Ben Lindsey*); James McDonnell (*Bruce Randall*); Jennifer Van Dyck (*Meg Kosar*); M.A. Nickles (*Kirk McNeill*); Elizabeth Ruscio (*C.G.*); Brad Hall (*Dan Montana*); Guy Boyd (*Murph*).

5605   *Mad Jack the Pirate.* (Series; Cartoon; Fox; 1998-1999). Mad Jack is a rather bumbling buccaneer who sails the high seas with his partner, Snuk, for anything that he considers a treasure. Stories follow their madcap adventures as they set sail on their ship, the *Sea Chicken*, battling anyone and anything that stands in their way.

Voice Cast: Bill Kopp (*Mad Jack*); Jess Harnell (*Snuk*), Billy West, Tom Kenny, Cam Clarke, April Winchell, Sandy Fox, Valery Pappas.

5606   *Mad Libs.* (Series; Game; Disney; 1998-1999). Two teams of children, red vs. blue, compete in a four round competition. In round one, "Viewer Mad Lib," teams compete in stunts suggested by home viewers. Twenty points is awarded to the team that best performs the stunt within 45 seconds. "Madder Than You," the second round, has players attempting to supply words that fit categories suggested by the host. Five points is scored per correct word (repeated or unacceptable words disqualify the person who suggested it). Performing a stunt (worth 20 points) comprises round three ("Mega Stunt"); and "Mixed-Up Mad Libs," the final round, has players attempting to correct statements that contain improper words (ten points is scored per word correction). The team with the highest score wins.

Host: David Sidoni.

5607   *Mad Mad House.* (Series; Reality; Syfy; 2004). The reactions of ordinary people who become the roommates to a strange group of individuals: Aguirre (a modern primitive), Iya Ta'shia Asanti (a voodoo priestess), Don Henrie (a vampire) and Avocado (a naturist).

5608   *Mad Men.* (Series; Drama; AMC; 2007–). Sterling Cooper is a prestigious advertising agency on Madison Avenue in New York City. The time is the 1960s and the world of media advertising as it existed at the time is smartly captured (the series has the look and feel of the era of such a business — including the smoke-filled bars). Donald Draper is the creative director of the agency. He is a man who knows his job — and he knows that if he is going to retain that position he must remain one step ahead of the competition. Roger Sterling is the head of the agency; Bertram Cooper is the co-founder. Joan is "the queen bee" of the secretarial pool (Peggy is a featured secretary — "the girl with a heart of gold"); Pete Campbell is the scheming account executive seeking to advance his position by any underhanded method he can. Stories are a behind-the-scenes look at the world of advertising as it once existed, including the intrigues, the deceit and all the other less than ethical ploys that are need to succeed.

Cast: Jon Hamm (*Donald Draper*); John Slattery (*Roger Sterling*); Robert Morse (*Bertram Cooper*); Elisabeth Moss (*Peggy Olson*); Christina Hendricks (*Joan Holloway*); Vincent Kartheiser (*Pete Campbell*); Maggie Siff (*Rachel Menken*); January Jones (*Betty Draper*); Rose Marie DeWitt (*Midge*); Bryan Batt (*Salvatore Romano*); Michael Gladis (*Paul Kinsey*); Aaron Stanton (*Ken Cosgrove*); Rich Sommer (*Harry Crane*); Jared Harris (*Lane Pryce*); Crista Flanagan (*Lois Sadler*); Kiernan Shipka (*Sally Draper*); Julie McViven (*Hildy*).

5609   *Mad TV.* (Series; Comedy; Fox; 1998–2009). A Saturday (11:00 P.M. to Midnight) skit series based on the humor found in *Mad* magazine (which includes spoofs of TV shows, commercials, people and movies and its own creations, like "Spy vs. Spy").

Regulars: Michael McDonald, Debra Wilson, Aries Spears, Alex Borstein, Mo Collins, Nicole Sullivan, Will Sasso, Mary Scheer, Ron Pederson, Jordan Peele, Keegan Michael Key, Pat Kilbane, Nicole Parker, Phil LaMarr, Frank Caliendo, Bobby Lee, Stephanie Weir, Crista Flanagan, Orlando Jones, Bryan Callen, Artie Lange, Josh Meyers, David Herman, Paul Voght, Danielle Gaither, Noel William Berman, Christian Duguay, Andrew Bowen, Criag Antow, Nicole Randall Johnson, Frank Caeti, Nelson Ascencio, Arden Myron, Andrew Daly, Spencer Kayden, Melissa Paul, Simon Helberg, Steven Cragg, Dannah Feinglass, Christina Moore, Jill-Michele Melean, Michael Hitchcock, Tara Killam, Gillian Vigman, Kathryn Fiore, Ramon Hamilton, Lisa Kushell, Chris Hogan, Johnny Sanchez, Erica Ash, Matt Braunger, Eric Price, Lauren Pritchard.

5610   *Madame Sin.* (Pilot; Adventure; ABC; Jan. 15, 1972). Madame Sin, as she is known, is a diabolical, all-powerful woman who has set her goal to rule the world. She operates from a castle in Scotland and is assisted by Malcolm DeVere, a sinister chap who carries out her every command.

Cast: Bette Davis (*Madame Sin*); Denholm Elliott (*Malcolm DeVere*).

5611   *Madame's Place.* (Series; Comedy; Syn.; 1982-1983). Madame is a puppet (controlled by Wayland Flowers) who hosts *Madame's Place*, a late-night talk show, from her mansion in Hollywood (she insists on doing the show from her home because it is titled *Madame's Place*).

Madame was a struggling comedian who worked the dingy night-club circuit before she made it "big" in the movies. She was the star of such films as *A Woman Named Hey You* and *Trampoline Honeymoon.* Madame has been married six times (seven times in the pilot) and had 200 boyfriends; her third husband was a fan who sent her a picture of himself playing polo in the nude. Like many stars, Madame has had her harrowing moments: she was kidnapped by Egbert Tegley, a famous criminal known as "Sweet Tooth" Tegley, who held her hostage at an Atlantic City saltwater taffy stand. Her butler, Walter ("Pinky") Pinkerton, broke down the door and rescued her. Madame was also the target of a crazed fan (played by Archie Hahn) who believed she was the most beautiful woman in the world (he also believed that when the moon is full he turns into a parakeet).

Sara Joy Pitts is Madame's ultra sexy blonde niece. She is the daughter of Madame's sister, Marmalina, and has come to Hollywood (from Georgia, where Madame was born) to become an actress — "just like my Auntie Madame." Sara Joy measures 37-24-36 and is described by Madame as "a sexpot who doesn't realize she is a sexpot." Sara Joy, who wears very low cut and off-the-shoulder blouses, as well as short shorts, watches her favorite soap opera, "The Young and the Stupid," with the sound off ("It's so sad, it makes me cry"). Bernadette Van Gilder, whom Madame calls "Bernie," is her shy, mousy secretary. Buzzy St. James is the 11-year-old kid who lives next door. Lynn LaVecque, a former "two bit band singer," is Madame's competition, the host of *Naked All-Star Bowling.* Barney is Madame's producer.

Lawrence ("Larry") Lunch, the owner of the Lunch Agency, is Madame's exasperating, super-fast talking agent; Rollin Espinoza is the leader of the Madame's Place All-Divorced Orchestra. R. Ray Randall is the never-seen (heard over a speaker phone) head of the unnamed network on which *Madame's Place* airs. Madame calls him "No Face" because "he has no face." Eric Honest (a.k.a. Mr. Honest) is Madame's most frequent and most exasperating guest. Carla and Max are Buzzy's parents. Salaria is the psychic. Denise DeCaro sings the theme, "Here at Madame's Place."

Cast: Wayland Flowers *(Puppet Madame)*; Judy Landers *(Sara Joy Pitts)*; Susan Tolsky *(Bernadette Van Gilder)*; Johnny Haymer *(Walter Pinkerton)*; Ty Henderson *(Barney Wolfe)*; Corey Feldman *(Buzzy St. James)*; Edie McClurg *(Salaria)*; Barbara Cason *(Lynn LaVecque)*; Chandler Garrison *(Voice of R. Ray Randall)*; John Moschitta, Jr. *(Larry Lunch)*; Don Sparks *(Eric Honest)*; Hector Elias *(Rollin Espinoza)*; E.J. Peaker *(Carla St. James)*; John Reilly *(Max St. James)*; George Wyle *(Madame's Place pianist)*.

5612   *Made in America.* (Series; Game; CBS; 1964). A celebrity panel of three must guess how their guests, actual millionaires, acquired their fortunes. Guest millionaires are relatively unknown and panelists are permitted to indirectly question them. Bob Maxwell was originally scheduled to host but was replaced at the last minute by Hans Conried.

Host: Hans Conried. **Panelists:** Jan Sterling, Don Murray, Walter Slezak.

5613   *Made in Hollywood.* (Series; Reality; Syn.; 2005). Interviews with the stars and behind-the-scenes footage of current feature films. The stars of each profiled film serve as the segment host. In 2006 (to 2007) an edition geared to young adults and dealing with non-adult films aired as *Made in Hollywood: Teen Edition.* Kylie Erica Mar is the teen edition host.

5614   *Madeline.* (Series; Cartoon; Family Channel; 1993–1995). Adaptation of the children's books by Ludwig Bemelmans about Madeline, the smallest girl of twelve who live at Miss Clavelle's Boarding School in Paris, France. Her best friend is Pepito and stories relate their misadventures as their curiosity gets them involved in one predicament after another.

Voice Cast: Marsha Moreau, Andrea Libman, Tracey Lee Smythe *(Madeline)*; Judith Orban *(Miss Clavel)*; Anik Matern *(Chloe)*; Kristin Fairlie, Veronika Sztopa, Sonja Ball *(Nicole)*; Sonja Ball *(Marie)*; David Morse, Julian Bailey, A.J. Bond, Kyle Labine, A.J. Bond *(Pepito)*; Louise Vallance *(Genevieve)*; Liz MacRae *(Danielle)*. **Narrator:** Christopher Plummer.

5615   *Madhouse 90.* (Pilot; Comedy; ABC; Dec. 11, 1972). Comedy sketches that spoof movies, TV and everyday life.

Host: Monty Hall. **Regulars:** J.J. Barry, Michael Bell, Vivian Bonnell, Jack Carter, Tom Denver, Kay Dingle, Arnold Dover, Laara Lacey, Pat Proft, Frank Welker, Fred Willard.

5616   *The Madhouse Brigade.* (Series; Comedy; Syn.; 1978). Sketches that satirize politics and culture.

Regulars: Karen Rushmore, Joe Piscopo, Frank Nastagia, J.J. Lewis, Alexander Marshall, Dan Resin, Carlos Carrasco, Rocket Ryan, Nola Fairbanks. **Music:** Tony Monte.

5617   *Madigan.* (Series; Crime Drama; NBC; 1972-1973). Dan Madigan is an embittered plainclothes detective attached to the Manhattan 10th Precinct in New York City. Dan is a loner and tough on suspects; if he believes a suspect is guilty, he will not give up until he has an arrest. While Dan adheres to the rules, he will break them (and often put his job at risk) to get the evidence he needs for a conviction. Based on the feature film of the same title.

Cast: Richard Widmark *(Sgt. Dan Madigan)*.

5618   *Madman of the People.* (Series; Comedy; NBC; 1994-1995). The Brooklyn, New York–based *Your Times Magazine* (owned by Kern Communications) is the setting. Jack Buckner is a columnist who writes "The Madman of the People" column. He has been married to Delia for 30 years. Their daughter, Meg, is the editor of the magazine. Stories relate Jack's often unethical attempts to acquire stories for his column.

Jack, whose favorite bar is the Sandbox, occupies office number 309. He previously worked as night editor on the *New York Post.* He was nominated "Man of the Year" by the Turk Lonigan Society and received the Lonigan Leg (Turk was a two-fisted, one legged reporter — "the best this town has ever seen"). He was also voted "The Knickerbocker Man of the Year" for his hard-hitting columns. Delia, a schoolteacher, calls Jack "A professional eccentric" and "Binky." Meg, the youngest publisher in the history of current communications, previously published a magazine called *Working Mom.* Jack has two other children: Caroline, an interior decorator; and Dillon, who at the age of 23, found his first job — waiter at the Dommo Bean Coffee House. When Jack first saw Dillon in the nursery he said, "I can't wait until he moves out of the house." He is still waiting. As children, Meg had a teddy bear she called Jamboree; Caroline's was Mr. Wooffee. Other regulars are Jonathan Gold, the magazine's technology writer; "Big" Kenny, Caroline's husband; B.J. Cooper, a reporter; and Agnes Davis, Delia's mother

Cast: Dabney Coleman *(Jack Buckner)*; Concetta Tomei *(Delia Buckner)*; Cynthia Gibb *(Meg Buckner)*; Ashley Gardner *(Caroline)*; John Ales *(Dillon Buckner)*; Todd Susman *(Jonathan Gold)*; Craig Bierko *(B.J. Cooper)*; Jane Kean *(Agnes Davis)*; Merrick Deamon *(Kenny)*.

5619   *The Madness of Jane.* (Unaired; Drama; Produced for Lifetime in 2006). Proposal about a brilliant neurologist (Jane) who is diagnosed with a bipolar disorder and the effects it has on those close to her.

Cast: Ever Carradine *(Jane)*; Christine Woods *(Marie)*; Brittany Ishibashi *(Soroya)*; Jeff B. Davis *(John)*.

5620   *Mady Christians: Ode to Liberty.* (Experimental; Stage Play; NBC; April 12, 1940). A television adaptation of the Broadway play by Gilbert Miller about a Communist (Walter Slezak) sought by the police, who finds a hiding place in the home of a flighty female named Mady Christians (Ina Claire).

Cast: Ina Claire, Henry Edwards, Eduard Franz, Colin Hunter, Judson Laire, Boris Marshalor, Walter Slezak, Katherine Stewart.

5621   *The Maggi MacNellis Show.* (Series; Women; NBC; 1949). The alternate title for *Maggi's Private Wire.* See this title for information.

5622   *Maggie.* (Pilot; Comedy; CBS; Aug. 29, 1960). Mark and Annie Bradley are a famous acting couple who, after years of living and working in New York City, decide to take life a bit easier and move to quieter surroundings in Connecticut. Accompanying them is their pretty teenage daughter, Margaret (who prefers to be called Maggie) and the proposal was to relate the mischievous Maggie's misadventures as she (and her parents) struggle to adjust to a life away from show business.

Cast: Margaret O'Brien *(Maggie Bradley)*; Leon Ames *(Mark Bradley)*; Fay Baker *(Annie Bradley)*.

5623   *Maggie.* (Series; Comedy; ABC; 1981–1982). Events in the day-to-day lives of the Westons, a not-so-typical family of five living in Dayton, Ohio. Len Weston, the husband, is the vice principal of Fillmore High School. He is married to Maggie, a woman who sees the family through their difficult times. They are the parents of 12-year-old Mark, eight-year-old Bruce and the mischievous L.J., a 16-year-old who is never seen but shares in family activities and seems to live in the bathroom. Loretta Davenport is Maggie's friend, the owner of the House of Coiffures (a hair salon); Buffy Croft is Maggie's friend; Chris is Loretta's assistant; Tiffany Dietrich is Bruce's friend; and author Erma Bombeck serves as the program host.

Cast: Miriam Flynn *(Maggie Weston)*; James Hampton *(Len Weston)*; Billy Jacoby *(Mark Weston)*; Christian Jacobs *(Bruce Weston)*; Doris Roberts *(Loretta Davenport)*; Judith-Marie Bergan *(Buffy Croft)*; Margie Impert *(Chris)*; Rachel Jacobs *(Tiffany Dietrich)*; Erma Bombeck *(Herself)*.

5624   *Maggie.* (Pilot; Crime Drama; CBS; June 19, 1986). Following the death of her husband, Maggie Webb, a beautiful widow left with numerous debts and back tax problems, finds help from her wealthy sister-in-law, Diane, when she hires her for her London-based PR firm. The proposal was to relate Maggie's misadventures as she attempts to pay her creditors, the tax man and begin a new life. Other regulars are Harry "Pidge" Pidgeon, Maggie's friend; Jeremy Ashton-David, Maggie's boarder.

Cast: Stefanie Powers *(Maggie Webb)*; Ava Gardner *(Diane Webb)*; Herb Edelman *(Harry Pidgeon)*; Jeremy Lloyd *(Jeremy Ashton-Davis)*.

5625   *Maggie.* (Series; Comedy; Lifetime; 1998–1999). Margaret Day, called Maggie, is 40 years old. She is married to Art, a cardiologist, and they are the parents of Amanda, a teenager whose cartoonist boyfriend, Reg, believes he needs to become gay "because all the good cartoonists are gay." Like most people, Maggie begins to develop confused feelings about life. To relieve some of these depressing feelings, Maggie feels she needs to be like she was before she married. She returns to school to become a veterinarian and takes a part time job at a local animal clinic. Stories follow Maggie as she struggles to deal with the incidents that contradict the lifestyle she has established.

Cast: Ann Cusack *(Margaret Day)*; John Slattery *(Art Day)*;

Morgan Nagler *(Amanda Day)*; Todd Giebenhain *(Reg)*; Melissa Samuels *(Amy Sherwood)*; Francesca P. Roberts *(Kimberly Reed)*.

5626   *Maggie and the Ferocious Beast.* (Series; Cartoon; Nick; 2000–2004). Maggie is a five-year-old girl with a very active (and magic) imagination. She has two plush toys (Hamilton Hocks and the Ferocious Beast) and to enjoy adventures with them, she has created an imaginary world called Nowhere Land. Here, Hamilton (a pig) and the Beast become "real" and stories follow Maggie as she uses her vivid imagination to create exciting adventures for herself and her come-to-life friends.

Voice Cast: Kristen Bone *(Maggie)*; Stephen Ouimette *(Beast)*; Michael Caruana *(Hamilton Hocks)*.

5627   *Maggie Brown.* (Pilot; Comedy; CBS; Sept. 23, 1963). Maggie Brown's is a World War II Pacific Island club for American sailors. It is run by Maggie Brown, a former vaudeville song and dance girl, and the proposal was to follow Maggie as she struggles to keep her bistro open despite the objections of John Farragut, the base commander, who feels that the club should be off limits for his men. Other regulars are Jeannie Brown, Maggie's daughter; McChesney, Maggie's competitor; and sailors Joe and Marv.

Cast: Ethel Merman *(Maggie Brown)*; Susan Watson *(Jeannie Brown)*; Roy Roberts *(John Farragut)*; Walter Burke *(McChesney)*; Mark Goddard *(Joe Beckett)*; Marvin Kaplan *(Marv)*.

5628   *Maggie Hill.* (Pilot; Drama; Unaired; Produced for Fox in 2008). Maggie Hill is a brilliant heart surgeon whose life suddenly becomes complicated when she is diagnosed as suffering from schizophrenia. The proposal was to follow Maggie as she struggles to cope with her affliction and serve the patients who need her.

Cast: Christina Cole *(Maggie Hill)*; Alfre Woodard *(Virginia)*; Anna Rose Hopkins *(Christina Cole)*; Denis O'Hare *(Milo Marcus)*.

5629   *Maggie Malone.* (Pilot; Drama; NBC; June 9, 1959). Maggie Malone is a gorgeous singer who also owns a nightclub with Pete, a man with a knack for finding trouble. The proposal, a spin off from *The David Niven Show* was to relate their efforts to run an honest club and help people who find the club a place of refuge.

Cast: Julie London *(Maggie Malone)*; Steve Brodie *(Pete)*.

5630   *Maggie Winters.* (Series; Comedy; CBS; 1998–1999). Margaret Elaine Winters, called Maggie, is a young woman who grew up in the small town of Shelbyville. After graduating from college and attaining her degree in design, she moved to New York to start her career. Maggie became a success and eventually married and thought she found happiness. Then one day she caught her husband cheating on her and her whole world fell apart. She left him, her job and returned to the one place where she knew she could find happiness — Shelbyville.

Although Maggie is much more qualified than the job she soon gets — assistant to the women's apparel buyer at Hendley's Department Store, Maggie accepts it. Maggie is a very sweet girl who simply cannot hurt any one — no matter how mean they are to her. She simply does not have a mean bone in her body. Maggie feels that this is sometimes a drawback because people often take advantage of her. Such a person is Rachel Tomlinson, Maggie's friend (they grew up together) who is now her boss, the store manager. Rachel is pretty but feels she is not as pretty as Maggie and has always been jealous of her because she feels Maggie got everything and she got nothing. The grudge started in Shelbyville Junior High when Rachel first became jealous of Maggie "because you got breasts before me." She now delights in the fact that "I'm the boss of the small town girl who moved away and came crawling back." Despite Rachel's jealousy, they are still friends and frequent Sonny's bar after work. While very pretty Maggie never dresses in revealing clothes or uses her physical attributes to impress anyone. This was not the case when she was three years old — she would embarrass her mother by stripping when guests arrived. Stories relate Maggie's struggles to make a new life for herself in the town where she was born.

Cast: Faith Ford (*Maggie Winters*); Shirley Knight (*Estelle Winters*); Jenny Robertson (*Robin Foster*); Clea Lewis (*Rachel Tomlinson*); Patrick Warburton (*Sonny*); Robert Romanus (*Jeff Foster*); Alex Kapp Horner (*Lisa Harte*); Michael McKean (*Lewis Stickley*); Brittany McConnell (*Katie Foster*); Brian Haley (*Tom Vanderhulst*); Hayden Tank (*Henry Foster*); Vincent Vantresca (*Bobby Campanelli*).

5631   *Maggi's Private Wire.* (Series; Women; NBC; ABC; 1949–1952). A program of celebrity interviews, human-interest accounts, nightclub reviews, fashion previews and gossip. Aired on NBC (as *Maggi's Private Wire*) from July 12 to July 2, 1949; and on ABC (as *The Maggi McNellis Show*) from July 31 to December 11, 1952.

Hostess: Maggi McNellis.

5632   *Magi-Nation.* (Series; Cartoon; Kids WB; 2007). Moonlands is one of eleven parallel worlds to the Earth. It is here that Orwin, the guardian of *The Book of Elders*, awaits the Final Dreamer, an unknown person who can help his people defeat Agram and his evil Shadow Magi, who seek to rule the land.

Eydn is a young girl who believes she is the Final Dreamer. One night, however, while reading *The Book of Elders*, Edyn magically sees the true Final Dreamer, a young Earth boy named Tony Jones. As Edyn reads further, she learns that she is to become Tony's assistant and to meet him at a predestined point. As Edyn finds the secretive meeting place, Tony is magically transported to Moonlands. He meets Edyn and learns that he is the Final Dreamer and must use his abilities to battle Agram. Agram is seeking *The Book of Elders* to encompass its powers of magic for himself. Tony wears a special ring, given to him by his grandfather that signifies he is the Final Dreamer (the ring is magical and through it, Tony can summon Dream Creatures to help him and Edyn battle Agram). Stories follow Tony, Edyn and their assistant, Strag, as they battle the evils of Agram. Korg and Zed are Agram's henchmen.

Voice Cast: Lyon Smith (*Tony*); Martha MacIsaac (*Edyn*); Alan Park (*Furox*); Alex Karzis (*Korg*); Rory O'Shea (*Guardian*); Rick Miller (*Ashio*); Dwayne Hill (*Chud*); Helen King (*Shimmer*).

5633   *The Magic Carpet.* (Pilot; Variety; DuMont; May 16, 1947). Frank Clinton hosts a program of performances by guest magicians under the sponsorship of Alexander Smith Carpets.

5634   *The Magic Clown.* (Series; Children; NBC; 1949–1954). Games, songs and magic geared to children and set against the background of a circus with the Magic Clown as the host and Laffy, his puppet helper in skits (Laffy was derived from the program's sponsor, Bonomo's Turkish Taffy).

Cast: Zovella (*The Magic Clown*); Richard Duois (*The Magic Clown; later*). **Music:** Jack Ward. **Announcer:** Ray Morgan, Jack Gregson.

5635   *The Magic Cottage.* (Series; Children; DuMont; 1949–1951). A magic cottage (where the make believe becomes real) is the setting for stories, fairytales, art instruction, games and other sources of entertainment geared to children.

Hostess: Pat Meikle. **Assistant:** Robert Wilkinson.

5636   *The Magic Garden.* (Series; Children; Syn.; 1974). The Magic Garden is a forest-like area where the make believe becomes real. Sherlock Squirrel and Flap the Bird are the featured animals (puppets) that inhabit the garden. Carole and Paula, two pretty young women, are their friends and through their interactions with Sherlock and Flap's antics, songs, stories and music are presented to acquaint children with various aspects of the world. Carole Demas and Paula Janis perform the opening ("Magic Window") and closing themes ("See Ya").

Cast: Carole Demas (*Carole*); Paula Janis (*Paula*); Cary Antebi (*Voice of Sherlock and Flap*).

5637   *The Magic Hat Shop.* (Experimental; Fashion; DuMont; Oct. 10, 1944). An unusual twist in a fashion show presentation: models displayed the sponsor's product (Knox Hats) by appearing in short dramatic skits and variety performances (songs).

Models: Jede Charles, Erin Kameron, Sharon Shaw, Jeanne Shephard, Leonard Stokes.

5638   *The Magic Hour.* (Series; Talk; Syn.; 1998). Former NBA basketball star Magic Johnson hosts a talk show that not only features celebrity interviews but also monologues and comedy skits.

Host: Magic Johnson. **Co-Host:** Tommy Davidson. **Skit Regulars:** Steve White, Ernest Nyle Brown, Ryan Christian, Jimmy Hodson, Craig Shoemaker, Mike Buttons (*as Mike the Security Guard*). **Announcer:** Jimmy Hodson. **Music:** Sheila E.

5639   *The Magic Lady.* (Series; Children; Syn.; 1951). A program of songs, fairy tales, guests and feats of magic with female magician Geraldine Larsen (The Magic Lady) as the host. Boko, her pixie helper, assists her.

Hostess: Geraldine Larsen. **Assistant:** Jerry Maren (*Boko*).

5640   *The Magic Land of Allakazam.* (Series; Children; ABC; 1960–1964). The magic kingdom of Allakazam is the setting for a program of magic, cartoons, and various adventures geared to children.

Cast: Mark Wilson (*Host*); Nani Darnell, Mike Wilson (*Assistant*); Bev Bergerson (*Rebo the Clown*); Bob Towner (*The King*); Chuck Barnes (*Periwinkle*); Jackie Joseph, Bob Fenton.

5641   *Magic Midway.* (Series; Variety; NBC; 1962-1963). Performances by entertainers from the circus world.

Host: Claude Kirchner. **Regulars:** Bonnie Lee, Bill "Boom Boom" Bailey, Phil "Coo Coo" Kiley, Douglas "Mr. Pocus" Anderson.

5642   *Magic Mongo.* (Series; Comedy; ABC; 1977-1978). While walking on a beach three teenagers (Loraine, Christy and Donald) find a strange looking bottle that has washed ashore. Donald picks it up and opens it. A puff of smoke emerges followed by Magic Mongo, a mischievous genie who becomes their slave. Stories relate the efforts of the teens to conceal the fact that have a genie and a genie's efforts to adjust to life in the 1970s. Other regulars are Ace, the bully; Duncey, Ace's cohort; and Huli, the owner of the beach café hangout. Aired as a segment of *The Krofft Supershow II*.

Cast: Lennie Weinrib (*Magic Mongo*); Helaine Lembeck (*Laraine*); Robin Dearden (*Christy*); Paul Hinckley (*Donald Connelly*); Bart Braverman (*Ace*); Larry Larsen (*Duncey*); Sab Shimono (*Huli*).

5643   *The Magic of Mark Wilson.* (Series; Variety; Syn.; 1977). Magician Mark Wilson, with the assist of his wife, Nani Darnell and son Greg Wilson, perform magic and host a program that also features performances by guest masters of magic.

5644   *Magic on Love Island.* (Pilot; Anthology; NBC; Feb. 15,

1980). Love Island is a beautiful tropical resort that is owned by a mysterious woman named Madge. Madge is assisted by her niece (Cheryl) and nephew (Jimmy) and possesses special powers that can make romance happen. Incidents in the lives of the singles that come to the magical retreat seeking romance is the focal point of the proposal. Bernard Ighner performs the theme, "Love Island, Our Island of Love."

Cast: Janis Paige *(Madge)*; Dominique Dunne *(Cheryl)*; Christopher Knight *(Jimmy)*.

5645   The Magic Ranch. (Series; Children; ABC; 1961). Performances by guest magicians with Don Alan as the host.

5646   The Magic School Bus. (Series; Cartoon; PBS; 1994). Valerie Frizzle is a very special grade school teacher. She has use of the magic school bus, a yellow vehicle that can go anywhere and become anything. As the class begins studying a particular subject, Valerie uses the bus to take them on a field trip. Here, with the help of the bus, the children experience first hand the principals of what they are being taught.

Voice Cast: Lily Tomlin *(Valerie Frizzle)*; Daniel DeSanto *(Carlos Ramon)*; Tara Meyer *(Dorothy Ann)*; Stuart Stone *(Ralphie Tennelli)*; Erica Luttrell *(Keesha Franklin)*; Lisa Yamanaka *(Wanda Li)*; Maia Filar *(Phoebe Terese)*; Danny Tamberelli *(Arnold Perlstein)*; Andre Ottley-Lorant *(Tim)*.

5647   The Magic Slate. (Series; Anthology; NBC; 1950-1951). Dramas, geared to children that feature adaptations of classic and contemporary stories.

Host: Norman Grant. **Regulars:** Valerie McElory, Peter Conlow, Bob Borlek, Homer Yates, Wyley Hancock.

5648   The Magic Trolls and the Troll Warriors. (Pilot; Cartoon; Fox; Nov. 26, 1992). Once upon a time there was a magic village called Troll Land where all lived happily under the leadership of King Laugh. One day, the evil King No Laugh, ruler of Gloom Village, invaded Troll Land and forbade happiness. It was now a crime to smile or be happy and without happiness the magic Trolls (who are slaves in mines to find gold for King No Laugh) cannot survive. Several months later, five trolls (Lokie, Shrimp, Thor, Wartlet and Odine) and the good king's aide Siegfried the Bird, return from a mission to find their beloved kingdom gone. The proposal was to relate the Trolls' efforts to defeat King No Laugh and bring happiness back to Troll Land.

Voices: Cheralyann Bailey, Tony Dakota, Mike Donovan, Alessandro Julian, Cam Lane, Lee Lockar, Scott McNeil, Lelani Marrell, Jesse Moss, Doug Parker.

5649   The Magical Adventures of Quasimodo. (Series; Cartoon; Disney; 1996). Paris in the year 1483, at a time when magic existed, provides the setting for tales of Quasimodo, the hunchback church bell ringer, his lady love, Esmeralda and their friend, Francois, as they join forces to battle villains, especially the notorious Frollo, who is dedicated to the pursuit of evil. Based on the novel *Notre Dame de Paris* by Victor Hugo.

Voice Cast: Daniel Brochu *(Quasimodo)*; Eleanor Noble *(Esmeralda)*; Terrence Schemmel *(Francois)*; Vlasta Vrana *(Frollo)*; Sonja Ball *(Angelica)*; A.J. Henderson *(Dennis)*.

5650   The Magician. (Series; Drama; NBC; 1973-1974). While performing in South America, illusionist Anthony Blake is arrested on a trumped up espionage charge and later imprisoned. Ten years later, he escapes from prison and takes his cellmate, a dying old man, with him. The old man, grateful for the few months of freedom Tony provided for him, leaves Tony a considerable fortune—money he uses, in part, to help people who are unable to turn to the police for help.

Tony now performs regularly at the Magic Castle Club in Los Angeles. Tony's wrists bear the scars of the prison shackles; he can read people (their faces, eyes and hands) and knows when they need help. Tony, however, doesn't interfere; he enlists in a cause and uses the wizardry of his craft to foil evil.

Jerry Anderson is Tony's assistant; Max Pomeroy is an internationally known magazine and newspaper columnist who is also Tony's best friend and a vital source for information. Max keeps a microfilm record of all photos taken of him during his world travels and has a handicapped, wheelchair-bound son named Dennis. While Max is not married, he does live with a charming woman named Lulu. "I'm everything to Max except a wife," she says. When Max relates the story of Tony's prison experiences, he compares it to a book: "Have you ever read the book *The Count of Monte Cristo*? In a sense, Tony lived it...." In the pilot episode (NBC, Mar. 17, 1973), Bill Bixby played Anthony Dorian and Jim Watkins was Jerry Wallace.

Program Open: "All the magic you are about to see is performed without trick photograph of any kind by Bill Bixby—*The Magician*."

Cast: Bill Bixby *(Anthony Blake)*; Keene Curtis *(Max Pomeroy)*; Jim Watkins *(Jerry Anderson)*; Joan Caulfield (Lulu); Todd Crespi *(Dennis)*. **Announcer:** Bill Baldwin.

5651   Magic's Biggest Secrets Finally Revealed. (Series; Reality; My Network TV; 2008). A masked, unknown magician reveals the secrets behind magic tricks and illusions. The illusion is performed then recreated to show how it was accomplished.

Masked Magician: Val Valentino. **Narrator:** Mitch Pileggi.

5652   The Magilla Gorilla Show. (Series; Cartoon; Syn.; 1964). The overall title for three animated segments:

1. Magilla Gorilla. Magilla is a mischievous, fun-loving gorilla and the permanent resident of Mr. Peebles' Pet Shop. Ogee is the young girl ("How much is that gorilla in the window?") who wants Magilla as a pet. Magilla's efforts to remain at the pet shop is the focal point of stories.

2. Ricochet Rabbit. Efforts of Ricochet Rabbit, sheriff of Hootin' Holler, and Droop-a-Long, his slow-moving deputy, to maintain law and order.

3. Punkin Puss and Mush Mouse. Antics of a hillbilly cat (Punkin Puss) and mouse (Mush Mouse).

Voice Cast: Allan Melvin *(Magilla Gorilla/Punkin Puss)*; Howard Morris *(Mr. Peebles/Mush Mouse)*; Jean VanderPyl *(Ogee)*; Don Messick *(Ricochet Rabbit)*; Mel Blanc *(Droop-a-Long)*.

5653   Magnavox Theater. (Series; Anthology; CBS; 1950). Magnavox sponsored program of comedy and drama productions produced by Garth Montgomery. Notable performers include Marjorie Lord, Keith Richards, David Bruce, Kim Stanley, Jean Gillespie, Cecil Kellaway, Don Beddoe, Geraldine Brooks, Hank Patterson, Dane Clark, Steven Hill, Edward Everett Horton, Ilona Massey, Victor Moore and Leora Thatcher.

5654   The Magnificent Marble Machine. (Series; Game; NBC; 1975-1976). Two teams, composed of one celebrity and one non-celebrity contestant, compete. The highest scoring team during a question and answer round receives the opportunity to play the Magnificent Marble Machine—a large, electronic pinball machine. Each team member is given one minute to play, and each bumper that is hit earns the contestant $500.

Program Open: "Today some of these people may win a fortune in cash and prizes when they're picked at random to play *The Mag-*

nificent Marble Machine with one of our all-star teams. Presenting this week — the women: Karen Valentine and Della Reese; battling against the men, Robert Fuller and Jamie Farr. And now here's your host, Mr. Art James."

Host: Art James. **Announcer:** Johnny Gilbert. **Music:** Mort Garson.

5655   *The Magnificent Menasha.* (Pilot; Comedy; NBC; Feb. 20, 1950). A proposal about Menasha, the Jewish manager of a small restaurant, and his efforts to solve the problems of his customers.

Cast: Menasha Skulnik (*Menasha*), Ellen Fenwick, Peggy Hillias, Leonard Scheerer.

5656   *The Magnificent 7.* (Series; Western; CBS; 1998-1999). When Chris Larabee, the leader of a group of hardened recruits, completes a job protecting a Seminole village from a group of renegade Civil War soldiers called The Ghosts of the Confederacy, they find themselves with a new task when Judge Orrin Travis hires them to do something he cannot do alone — uphold the law and establish peace where no laws exist. The group, called The Magnificent 7, are based in the town of Four Corners, and headed by Chris Larabee, a gunfighter who has personal score to settle: find those responsible for killing his wife and son. Vin Tanner is a bounty and buffalo hunter. John "J.D." Dunne is a former stable boy turned gunslinger; Buck Wilmington is a con man and womanizer; Josiah Sanchez is a former gunfighter turned preacher; Ezra Standish is a rogue and gambler; Nathan Jackson is a former slave with medical knowledge. Other regulars are Mary Travis, the newspaper editor; Dana Barron, J.D.'s romantic interest; Maude Standish, Ezra's mother; and Rain, a Seminole Indian girl and Nathan's romantic interest.

Cast: Robert Vaughn (*Orrin Travis*); Michael Biehn (*Chris Larabee*); Eric Close (*Vin Tanner*); Andrew Kavovit (*John Dunne*); Dale Midkiff (*Buck Wilmington*); Ron Perlman (*Josiah Sanchez*); Anthony Starke (*Ezra Standish*); Rick Worthy (*Nathan Jackson*); Laurie Holden (*Mary Travis*); Casey Wells (*Dana Barron*); Michelle Phillips (*Maude Standish*); Siena Goines (*Rain*).

5657   *The Magnificent Six and a Half.* (Series; Comedy; Syn.; 1970). Steve, Whizz, Dumbo, Toby, Stodger and Pee Wee are the Magnificent Six — and a young girl, Liz — the Half, seven British children with only one goal: find fun and adventure wherever and anyway they can.

Cast: Len James (*Steve*); Michael Anderson (*Whizz*); Ian Ellis (*Dumbo*); Brinsley Forde (*Toby*); Lionel Hawkes (*Stodger*); Kim Tallmadge (*Pee Wee*); Suzanne Togni (*Liz*).

5658   *Magnum, P.I.* (Series; Crime Drama; CBS; 1980–1988). Robin's Nest is an estate on Concord Road, later Kalohoa Drive, on the north shore of Hawaii that is owned by the fabulously wealthy but never seen pulp fiction writer, Robin Masters. Jonathan Quayle Higgins is the estate's major domo; private detective Thomas Sullivan Magnum provides security for the estate in return for his living quarters off the main house.

Magnum, born in the town of Tidewater, Virginia, decided on a military career and attended Annapolis. After serving with the VM02 Unit in DaNang during the Vietnam War, he became a naval intelligence officer. He resigned shortly after "when I woke up one morning and realized I was 33 and never 23." He turned his attention to investigating and became a private detective. He charges $200 a day plus expenses; he will lower his fee to $175 if a client can't afford him. He is writing a book called *How to Be a World-Class Private Investigator* and also held a temporary job as house detective at the Hawaiian Gardens Hotel but was angry because he couldn't carry a gun.

Magnum narrates the stories, talks to the camera, acts as a big brother toward women and hangs his head when he becomes frustrated. Magnum claims that the relationship between himself and Higgins is "constant arguing, constant yelling and constant long, boring stories." Jonathan served Her Majesty in five conflicts over 35 years, most notably as a member of England's MI-5 and MI-6 during World War II. In 1957 he ran a hotel called the Arlington Arms which catered to the rich and famous. He is chairman — also called managing director — of the King Kamehameha Club. Higgins has two Great Danes, Apollo and Zeus, who patrol the estate grounds. The dogs, whom Higgins calls The Lads, do not like Magnum but tolerate him. In narration, Magnum tells the audience that "I am 99 percent sure that Higgins is Robin Masters; but it's that one percent that could mean disaster."

Orville Wilbur Wright, called Rick, and Theodore Calvin, called T.C., are Magnum's friends. Rick was born in Chicago and was a Marine Corps weapons expert during the Vietnam War. He came to Hawaii to open his own nightclub, Rick's Place, but gave it up to manage the King Kamehameha Club. He has numerous underworld connections and helps Magnum by obtaining information from the street. T.C., a former chopper pilot in Vietnam, now runs the Island Hopper Helicopter Service. Prior to the war, T.C. was a Golden Gloves Boxer (also said to be a football player). He is divorced from Tina (Fay Hauser) and is the father of Bryant (Shavar Ross).

Carol Baldwin is the assistant D.A. who sometimes works with Magnum. Francis Hofstetler, better known as Ice Pick, is the underworld boss Magnum turns to for help. Robin Masters, who is seen from the back only (Bruce Atkinson) is voiced by Orson Welles. Agatha is Higgins' friend; Mac Reynolds is Tom's naval buddy; Madelyn Jones is the file clerk; Sam is the D.J. at Rick's Place; Luther Gillis is the private eye; Gloria is T.C.'s girlfriend.

Cast: Tom Selleck (*Thomas Magnum*); John Hillerman (*Jonathan Higgins*); Roger E. Mosley (*T.C. Calvin*); Larry Manetti (*Rick Orville*); Elisha Cook, Jr. (*Icepick*); Kathleen Lloyd (*Carol Baldwin*); Kwan Hi Lim (*Police Lt. Tanaka*); Jeff MacKay (*Lt. Mac Reynolds*); Gillian Dobb (*Agatha Chumley*); Margie Impert (*Madelyn Jones*); Deborah Pratt (*Gloria*); Eugene Roche (*Luther Gillis*); Jean Bruce Scott (*Police Lt. Poole*); Mel Carter (*Sam*).

5659   *Mahalia Jackson Sings.* (Series; Variety; Syn.; 1961). Gospel singer Mahalia Jackson performs two songs in a five minute filler program designed to be used by stations as needed (usually between programs or as a filler when movies run short).

5660   *The Mail Story.* (Series; Anthology; ABC; 1954). The alternate title for *Handle with Care*. See this title for information.

5661   *Maisie.* (Pilot; Comedy; CBS; Sept. 12, 1960). Maisie Ravier is a beautiful showgirl who works the small night club circuit hoping to one day make the big time. The proposal was to relate her club performance experiences and the misadventures that occur when she takes outside gigs and tries to help people in trouble. Based on the feature film series starring Ann Sothern.

Cast: Janis Paige (*Maisie Ravier*).

5662   *Maisy.* (Series; Cartoon; Nick; 1999-2000). Maisy is a young female mouse with a quest for knowledge. She and her friends, Tallulah (a chick), Eddy (elephant), Charley (alligator) and Cyril (squirrel) do not speak and stories follow their adventures as they explore the world around them. Brian Greene narrates; David Collins and Shane Douglas provide the songs and babbling noises the characters make.

5663   *Major Adams, Trail Master.* (Western; ABC; 1957).

The ABC daytime title for *Wagon Train* with Ward Bond as the star while the series remained as a prime time attraction.

5664 *Major Annie, M.D.* (Pilot; Drama; CBS; Mar. 1, 1976). A proposed spin off from *Medical Center* about Major Annie Malone, an Army doctor with a decidedly non-regulation outlook.

Cast: Lois Nettleton (*Major Annie Malone*); Della Reese (*Captain Sykes*); John Randolph (*Colonel Mayhill*).

5665 *Major Dad.* (Series; Comedy; CBS; 1989–1993). The story of a tough marine (John D. ["Mac"] MacGillis) who marries a pretty widow (Polly Cooper) with three children (Elizabeth, Robin and Casey) and the misadventures that occur when they set up housekeeping together (first in Oceanside, California, then in Farlough, Virginia).

John was born in Snake River, Mississippi, where his parents owned a farm on Decatur Road. John, a history major at Vanderbilt College, joined the marines in 1967 (in another episode, he mentions being in the marines for 20 years; he joined in 1969). His basic training was done on Parris Island, and he served three tours of duty as a corporal in Vietnam. When the series began, John was stationed at Camp Singleton in Oceanside .On September 17, 1990, John and his family move to Virginia when John is transferred to Camp Hollister (which Polly calls "a military hellhole"). They now live on the base and John becomes "a staff weenie" (the nickname for the job he holds as staff secretary to General Marcus Craig). In the episode of May 13, 1991, John adopts Polly's girls (whose last name changes to MacGillis).

Polly was originally a reporter for the Oceanside *Chronicle*; at Camp Hollister she becomes the managing editor of the camp newspaper, the *Bulldog*, when she is turned down for a reporter's job on the family owned town newspaper, the Farlough *Free Press*. Polly also writes the column "The Suggestion Box" and is in charge of the "At Ease" section of the paper. Polly is a member of the Officers' Wives Club (where once a year she has to participate in Jane Wayne Day, when the wives become marines for a day).

Elizabeth, the oldest daughter, attends Keefer High School (Oceanside episodes). She is the prettiest of the girls; when she looks through the family photo album, she worries about how her hair looked at the time. In Virginia, she attends Hollister Base High School.

Robin, the middle girl, attends Martin Elementary School (Oceanside), where she is a member of the Condors basketball team. In Virginia, where she attends the base school, Robin is a member of the girls' softball league, the Hollister Hornets.

Casey, the youngest of the girls, attends Martin Elementary School (Oceanside) and the base school (Virginia). Ruby and Henrietta are her dolls; Mr. Smithers is her teddy bear.

General Marcus Craig is the commanding officer of Camp Hollister. Alva Lou ("Gunny") Bricker is the administrative chief of the general's office (she replaced Whitney Kershaw as Merilee Gunderson, John's secretary at Camp Singleton). Lieutenant Eugene ("Gene") Holowachuk is John's second in command.

Cast: Gerald McRaney (*John MacGillis*); Shanna Reed (*Polly Cooper*); Marisa Ryan (*Elizabeth Cooper*); Nicole Dubuc (*Robin Cooper*); Chelsea Hertford (*Casey Cooper*); Jon Cypher (*Gen. Marcus Craig*); Beverly Archer (*Alva Lou "Gunny" Bricker*); Whitney Kershaw (*Merilee Gunderson*); Matt Mulhern (*Lt. Eugene Holowachuk*).

5666 *Major Del Conway of the Flying Tigers.* (Series; Adventure; DuMont; 1951-1952). The Flying Tigers is an airline based in Los Angeles. Major Del Conway, a former Word War II Air Force pilot, is its chief pilot. He is assisted by Caribou Jones and stories not only relate their experiences transporting passengers and cargo, but their exploits as investigators for G-2, American military intelligence.

Cast: Eric Fleming, Ed Peck (*Del Conway*); Luis Van Rooten, Bern Hoffman (*Caribou Jones*).

5667 *Major Del Conway of the Flying Tigers.* (Series; Adventure; Syn.; 1953). The Flying Tigers is a U.S. fighter squadron based in China during World War II. Major Del Conway is the head of the Third Pursuit Squadron, one of three such units that are part of General Chennault's Gallant Fighters (in Chinese, "Foo-hoo"; in English, "Flying Tigers").

While the Flying Tigers is a military outfit that fights the forces that oppose liberty, it is made up of volunteers who are only out to make money. Discipline is easy, and their mission is to help the Chinese overcome the invading Japanese. Pilots get $500 for each Japanese Zero they shoot down. Members of Del's squadron are Cashbox Potter, Dick Rossi, Joe Suie and Catfish. The squad's planes (P-40s) are called "Sharks" (the face of a shark is painted on the nose). Their base is called "Firehouse"; Del's air code is "Fire Chief."

Cast: Art Fleming (*Del Conway*); Sandy Kenyon (*Cashbox Potter*); Carl Shanzer (*Dick Rossi*); Warren Nsien (*Joe Suie*); Eddie Luke (*Catfish*).

5668 *Majority Rules.* (Series; Game; ABC; 1949-1950). The object calls for a panel of three players to answer a question based on a majority decision. After a question is read, the players confer on an answer but before it can be stated, at least two players must agree that the answer they have chosen is correct. If they are correct, points are scored and prizes are awarded based on scores: the higher the score, the better the prizes.

Host: Ed Prentiss.

5669 *Make a Face.* (Series; Game; ABC; 1961-1962). Each of the three players who compete sits before three revolving wheels that contain pictures of celebrities that are cut into pieces. The object calls for the players to assemble and identify the celebrities. Each correct identification scores points. The winners, the highest point scorers, receive merchandise prizes.

Host: Bob Clayton. **Assistant:** Rita Mueller.

5670 *Make a Wish.* (Series; Children; ABC; 1971–1977). An attempt to explain, through animation, films, songs and sketches, the differences between fantasy and the real world.

Host: Tom Chapin.

5671 *Make It or Break It.* (Series; Drama; ABC Family; 2009). The Rock, a prestigious gymnastics center in Colorado, is a springboard to the Olympics. It is here that three girls, Payson, Kaylie and Lauren are top students who expect to claim all three spots for the trials (which are the last step before the Olympics). New to The Rock is Emily Kmetko, a talented high school gymnast who won a scholarship to the academy. Emily's abilities impress the coach — but pose a threat to Payson, Kaylie and Lauren who fear she will up seat one of them. Emily has Olympic ambitions but is also burdened by family problems, the most serious of which is her flaky mother, Chloe, who dresses like a hooker and has little grasp of reality. Emily, who is shy and serious, has become the adult of the family, looking for out for her mother since her parents divorced. To help pay the bills, Emily has taken a job at the Pizza Shack. Stories, which present a compelling behind-the-scenes look at the rough and tumble world of gymnastics, relate Emily's efforts to achieve her dream.

Cast: Chelsea Hobbs (*Emily Kmetko*); Ayla Kell (*Payson Keeler*); Josie Loren (*Kaylie Cruz*); Cassie Scerbo (*Lauren Tanner*); Susan Ward (*Chloe Kmetko*); Erik Palladino (*Coach*); Peri Gilpin (*Kim Keeler*);

Candace Cameron (*Summer Van Horne*); Brett Cullen (*Mark Keeler*); Rosa Blasi (*Ronnie Cruz*); Zachary Abel (*Carter Anderson*); Johnny Pacar (*Damon Young*); Mia Rose Frampton (*Becca Keeler*); Wyatt Smith (*Brian Kmetko*); Anthony Starke (*Steve Tanner*).

5672   *Make Me a Super Model*. (Series; Reality; Bravo; 2008). Thirty-five would-be models (both men and women) are chosen from open auditions in five cities. The first program places each of the candidates in several brief modeling chores that eliminate the 21 weakest performers. The remaining 14 models compete for a $100,000 contract with New York Model Management. Like in *America's Next Top Model*, each of the models competes in various photo shoots and modeling challenges that eliminate the weakest performers on a weekly basis. The best at performing all chores wins the contract.

Host: Nicki Taylor. **Co-Host:** Tyson Beckford.

5673   *Make Me Laugh*. (Series; Game; ABC; Syn.; 1958; 1979; 1997). A contestant appears and sits opposite a panel of three guest comedians. At sixty-second intervals, the comedians attempt to make the contestant laugh. For each second that the contestant remains straight-faced, he receives one dollar (up to a limit of $360).

Program Open: "It's the hilarious game, *Make Me Laugh*. And now here's your host, Bobby Van." Three versions appeared:

1. Make Me Laugh (ABC, 1958). **Host:** Robert Q. Lewis. **Assistant:** Penny Peterson.

2. Make Me Laugh (Syn., 1979) **Host:** Bobby Van. **Announcer:** Bill Beery.

3. Make Me Laugh (Comedy Central, 1997-98). **Host:** Ken Ober (1997), Mark Cohen (1998). **Announcer:** Lou DiMaggio.

5674   *Make Mine Music*. (Series; Variety; CBS; 1948-1949). Singer Carole Coleman oversees a program of music and songs.

Host: Carole Coleman. **Regulars:** Larry Douglas, Bill Skipper. **Music:** The Tony Mottola Trio.

5675   *Make My Day*. (Series; Reality; TV Land; 2009). An elaborate prank show that takes the *Candid Camera* concept a bit further to focus on one person for an entire episode. Unknown to a soon-to-be-pranked subject, his family and friends were interviewed to find out what wishes he had. The show then sets up a dream day and hidden cameras capture what results as the subject tries to comprehend what is happening. The episode ends with the subject learning that he was part of an orchestrated prank. Michael Davies is the producer.

5676   *Make Room for Daddy*. (Series; Comedy; ABC, 1953–1957; CBS, 1957–1964). Danny Williams, his wife, Margaret, and their children, Terry and Rusty, live at the Parkside Apartments (Apartment 1204) in Manhattan.

Danny is a night club entertainer who performs at the Copa Club in New York City. He was born in Toledo, Ohio, and, at age 24, met his future wife, Margaret Summers, when she was 17 years old. He was a struggling young stand-up comedian; she worked as a part-time waitress and piano player (in another episode, Margaret mentions she and Danny have known each other since they were children). Margaret was born in Baraboo, Wisconsin, and was cared for by Mom and Pop Finch while her parents were on the road in vaudeville. The family has a pet dog named Laddie.

Actress Jean Hagen (Margaret) wanted to leave the series. The 1955 season ended with Danny's emotional talk with Terry and Rusty that their mother "had gone to Heaven." The following season found Danny as a widower struggling to raise two children with the help of his maid, Louise. Various actresses were brought on to date Danny and win over the affections of his children. At the close of the 1956-57 season, Danny hires Kathleen "Kathy" O'Hara, a widowed nurse, to care for Rusty, who had come down with a case of the measles. Kathy, the mother of a young daughter named Patty (Lelani Sorenson), soon catches the measles and is quarantined in the Williams apartment. A romance develops and Danny proposes to Kathy (ending the ABC series). When the CBS series begins (now called *The Danny Thomas Show*) Danny and Kathy are married and Kathy's daughter is now Linda (Angela Cartwright). Kathy was born in Peoria, Illinois. She and Danny honeymooned in Las Vegas and the CBS episodes find the Williams family now living at 505 East 56th Street (Apartment 542; also given as 781) in Manhattan. Danny calls Kathy "Clancy" and "Irish" and her maiden name is also given as Daly. Prior to becoming a nurse, Kathy was a singer in a band.

Teresa (Terry) is Danny's oldest child. She attended West Side High School then an unnamed college (where she is a member of the Alpha Beta Chi sorority). At this point Terry was written out but returned to marry Pat Hannigan, a night club performer. She had her first job as a sales girl in a women's dress shop.

Russell (Rusty) was born on February 15, 1947. He attended P.S. 54, Claremont Junior High School and then West Side High. Linda attends P.S. 54 and has milk and cookies when she comes home from school.

In Terry's absence, Danny sponsored Italian high school exchange student Gina Minelli. Danny's Uncle Tonoose is the self-proclaimed head of the family. Prior to his role as Uncle Tonoose, Hans Conried played Margaret's Cousin Carl, who "drank and traveled with jugs of wine." Other regulars are Charlie Halper, Danny's boss, the owner of the Copa Club; Bunny, his wife; Jesse Leeds, Danny's first agent; Phil Arnold, Danny's second agent; Ben, Danny's piano player; Elizabeth, Danny's press agent; Frank, Danny's tailor; Harry, Danny's songwriter; Piccola, the young singer discovered by Danny; Jose Jimenez, the building elevator operator; Mr. Heckendorn, the apartment building manager; Debbie, Gina's friend; Sylvia, Linda's friend; Alfie, the Copa Club waiter; and Mr. Daly, Kathy's father. See also *Make Room for Granddaddy*.

***Make Room for Daddy* Program Open:** "It's Dodge [automobiles] for '55. Flashing ahead in style, in value, in performance, Yes, it's the flair-fashioned Dodge for '55, bringing you the brightest family show on television, Danny Thomas ... Jean Hagen as his wife and Sherry Jackson and Rusty Hamer as their children — *Make Room for Daddy*."

***The Danny Thomas Show* Program Open:** "New Aroma Roast Sanka, the best of the coffee bean, aroma flavor but not caffeine, present *The Danny Thomas Show*, starring Danny Thomas. Also starring Marjorie Lord as his wife, Rusty Hamer as their son and Angela Cartwright as their daughter."

Cast: Danny Thomas (*Danny Williams*); Jean Hagen (*Margaret Williams*); Marjorie Lord (*Kathy Williams*); Sherry Jackson, Penny Parker (*Terry Williams*); Rusty Hamer (*Rusty Williams*); Angela Cartwright (*Linda Williams*); Lelani Sorenson (*Patty Williams*); Louise Beavers, Amanda Randolph (*Louise*); Sid Melton (*Charlie Halper*); Pat Carroll (*Bunny Halper*); Jesse White (*Jesse Leeds*); Horace McMahon, Sheldon Leonard (*Phil Arnold*); Mary Wickes (*Elizabeth O'Neal*); Ben Lessy (*Ben*); Frank Jenks (*Frank*); Hans Conried (*Uncle Tonoose*); Pat Harrington, Jr. (*Pat Hannegan*); Harry Ruby (*Harry*); Annette Funicello (*Gina Minelli*); Piccola Pupa (*Piccola*); Bill Dana (*Jose Jimenez*); Bernard Fox (*Alfie*); Gale Gordon (*Mr. Heckendorn*); William Demarest (*Mr. Daly*); Judy Nugent (*Debbie*); Barbara Beaird (*Sylvia Watkins*).

Updates:

1. The Danny Thomas TV Family Reunion (NBC, Feb. 14, 1965). A special that reunites the cast of *The Danny Thomas Show* for a series of skits that continues to depict events in the lives of the Williams family: Danny (Danny Thomas), Kathy (Marjorie Lord), Rusty (Rusty Hamer), Linda (Angela Cartwright), Louise (Amanda Randolph) and Uncle Tonoose (Hans Conried).

2. *Make More Room for Daddy* (NBC, Nov. 6, 1967). A segment of *The Danny Thomas Hour* that reunites Danny Thomas (as Danny Williams) with his former costars: Marjorie Lord (Kathy), Rusty Hamer (Rusty), Angela Cartwright (Linda), and Sid Melton (Charlie Halper). Linda is now in college and Rusty has enlisted in the Army. It is here that Rusty falls in love with Susan MacAdams (Jana Taylor), the daughter of Colonel MacAdams (Edward Andrews).

5677   *Make Room for Granddaddy.* (Series; Comedy; ABC; 1970-1971). An update of *Make Room for Daddy.* Rusty Williams, the son of nightclub entertainer Danny Williams and his wife, Kathy, has enlisted in the army and married Susan McAdams, a colonel's daughter. Terry, Danny's oldest child, is married to Bill Johnson (not Pat Hannegan as in the original series) and is the mother of six-year-old Michael. Linda, the youngest child, is attending a boarding school in Connecticut. When Terry makes plans to join her husband, a serviceman stationed overseas, Danny and Kathy agree to care for Michael until she and Bill return. Rusty, receiving his discharge, and Susan, set up housekeeping away from the family nest and stories relate events in the lives of Danny and Kathy as grandparents. The pilot film aired on CBS on Sept. 14, 1969. Charlie Halper is Danny's boss, the owner of the Copa Club; Uncle Tonoose is the head of the Williams family; Rosey Robbins is Danny's accompanist; Henry is the building elevator operator.

Cast: Danny Thomas (*Danny Williams*); Marjorie Lord (*Kathy Williams*); Sherry Jackson (*Terry Williams*); Rusty Hamer (*Rusty Williams*); Angela Cartwright (*Linda Williams*); Jana Taylor (*Susan Williams*); Michael Hughes (*Michael Johnson*); Sid Melton (*Charlie Halper*); Hans Conried (*Uncle Tonoose*); Rosey Grier (*Rosey Robbins*); Stanley Myron Handleman (*Henry*).

5678   *Make the Connection.* (Series; Game; NBC; 1955). Through a series of question-and-answer rounds with two contestants, a celebrity panel of four has to determine when, where, why and how their paths have crossed with the laymen players. Prizes are awarded to the players if the panel fails to uncover the relationship.

Host: Gene Rayburn, Jim McKay. **Panelists:** Gloria DeHaven, Gene Klavin, Eddie Bracken, Betty White. **Announcer:** Lee Vines.

5679   *Make the Grade.* (Series; Game; Nick; 1989–1991). Three children compete. A game board appears that contains questions based on seventh to twelfth grade studies and six subjects. The object is for players to answer one question from each grade level and one question from each of the subjects. The player with the most correct answer (most squares on the board) wins $500; losers receive a $50 consolation prize.

Host: Lew Schneider, Robb Edward Morris. **Announcer:** Maria Milito.

5680   *Make Your Own Kind of Music.* (Series; Variety; NBC; 1971). The beautiful music of the Carpenters (Richard and his sister, Karen) is interspersed with comedy sketches and performances by guest artists.

Hosts: Karen Carpenter, Richard Carpenter. **Regulars:** Al Hirt, Mark Lindsay, The New Doodletown Pipers, Tom Patchett, Jay Tarses. **Orchestra:** Jack Elliott, Allyn Ferguson. **Announcer:** Dick Tufeld.

5681   *Makeover Ambush.* (Series; Reality; Syn.; 2004). Unsuspecting people, whom a team of stylists feel could benefit from a makeover, are approached, rushed to the studio and given a quickie makeover (clothes, hair and makeup). Surprisingly, even though it is a rush job, the results are quite amazing. The stylists are Nicole Williams, Mary Alice Haney, William Whatley, Nancy Brensson, Anthony Perinelli, Gigi Barry and Rob Talty.

5682   *Makeover Train.* (Series; Reality; Internet; 2007). Three stylists are given a challenge: ride the Boston subway, select an unsuspecting commuter and, within three minutes, work their magic to transform his or her looks. The stylists are Lauren Genatossio, Tasha Forgash, Kevin Lennox.

5683   *Makeup Time.* (Pilot; Women; CBS; Feb. 15, 1945). A program of makeup tips for women by Eddie Senz, an acknowledged camouflage expert. Models were used as Senz demonstrated his magic on hair, lips, eyes and other facial features.

Host: Eddie Senz. **Guests:** Ethel Colby, Julius Colby.

5684   *Makin' It.* (Series; Comedy; ABC; 1979). Billy Manucci is an easygoing young man who lives at home (232 King Street, Passaic, New Jersey) with his parents, Joseph and Dorothy, his sister, Tina, and in the shadow of his swinging older brother, Tony, "a great dancer who just drifts."

Billy is studying to become a teacher at Passaic University. He works for Ivy Papastegios at an ice cream parlor called Tasty Treats and hangs out at a disco called the Inferno. Thirteen-year-old Tina attends Saint Bernadette's Elementary School, and when Billy seeks advice from Tony, he gets the "Manucci Prediction" ("I don't give advice, I predict").

Corky Crandall, an agent for the William Morris Agency in Manhattan, is Billy's girlfriend; and Al ("Kingfish") Sorrentino and Bernard Fusco are Billy's friends. David Naughton performs the theme, "Makin' It."

Cast: David Naughton (*Billy Manucci*); Lou Antonio (*Joseph Manucci*); Ellen Travolta (*Dorothy Manucci*); Denise Miller (*Tina Manucci*); Gary Antonacci (*Tony Manucci*); Rebecca Balding (*Corky Crandall*); Ralph Seymour (*Al "Kingfish" Sorrentino*); Gary Prendergast (*Bernard Fusco*); Jennifer Perito (*Ivy Papastegios*); Wendy Hoffman (*Suzanne*); Diane Robin (*Felice*); Leslie Winston (*Roxanne*).

5685   *Making a Living.* (Series; Comedy; ABC; 1980-1981). A spin off from *It's a Living* that aired from October 24, 1981 to September 10, 1982 and continued to depict events in the lives of a group of waitress at the Above the Top restaurant in Los Angeles. These episodes have been re-titled and syndicated as *It's a Living*. See this title for information.

5686   *Making His Band.* (Series; Reality; MTV; 2009). A spin off from *Making the Band* wherein music icon Sean "P. Diddy" Combs seeks to create a new band for himself (as opposed to creating independent bands). Episodes follow Sean and his partner, choreographer Laurie Ann Gibson, as they test hopeful singers and dancers for the new band.

5687   *Making It.* (Pilot; Comedy; NBC; Aug. 30, 1976). Law students (Steve, Pete, Jay and Greg) from varying backgrounds attempt to live together in a small apartment house run by a much-married woman named Cloris. Other regulars are Janice, Cloris's daughter; and Professor Harry Ebberly.

Cast: Ed Begley, Jr. (*Steve*); Ben Masters (*Pete*); Alvin Kupperman (*Jay*); Evan Kim (*Greg*); Jeanne Arnold (*Cloris*); Sandy Faison (*Janice*); Renny Roker (*Harry Ebberly*).

5688   *Making It Happen.* (Pilot; Magazine; Syn.; May 8, 1988).

A behind-the-scenes look at special events and places of interest to visit.

Host: Rich Little.

5689 *Making Over America with Trinny and Susannah.* (Series; Reality; TLC; 2009). Trinny Woodall and Susannah Constantine are British "fashion gurus" who host the U.K. television series *Trinny and Susannah Undress the Nation* and *What Not to Wear*. Trinny and Susannah have been creating styles for women for 15 years and have decided "to make over America." The women travel from state to state to find style-challenged women and give them a complete makeover to help them feel better about themselves.

5690 *Making the Band.* (Series; Reality; ABC; MTV; 2002–2005). A search to find five male singer-musicians for a new boy band to be called O-Town. The finalists, selected by Lou Perlman (the man noted for creating "pretty boy bands" such as The Back Street Boys and 'N Snyc) are placed together in a large house in Orlando, Florida. As with other reality series, the cameras roll to capture the "drama" that occurs in the house as the boys (who were given a record contract) prepare to become O-Town. The series first aired on ABC but played out on MTV after ABC dropped it for low ratings. A second cycle that ran on MTV in 2002, featured rap artist P. Diddy seeking aspiring rappers for a new hip-hop band. In 2005, a third cycle ran on MTV that sought a mixed (male-female) band with Sean P. Diddy" Combs again overseeing the procedures.

Host: Lou Perlman *(Cycle 1)*; Sean "P. Diddy" Combs *(Cycle 2 and 3)*.

5691 *Making the Grade.* (Series; Comedy; CBS; 1982). The problems that befall the faculty of Franklin High, a school fraught with problems and troublesome students. *Regulars:* Harry Barnes, the dean of boys; Jack Felspar, the assistant principal; Sara, Dave, Anton, and Jeffrey, teachers; students Mindy, Walt and Arnold; and Cynthia, Dave's wife.

Cast: James Naughton *(Harry Barnes)*; Graham Jarvis *(Jack Felspar)*; Alley Mills *(Sara Canover)*; Philip Charles MacKenzie *(Dave Wasserman)*; Zane Lasky *(Anton Zemeckis)*; Steven Peterman *(Jeffrey Kelton)*; Ellen Regan *(Cynthia Wasserman)*; Annabella Price *(Mindy)*; Dan Frischman *(Walt)*; Christopher Blande *(Arnold)*.

5692 *Malcolm and Eddie.* (Series; Comedy; UPN; 1996–2000). Malcolm McGee and Eddie Sherman are friends who live in Kansas City, Missouri. Malcolm, a radio disc jockey at oldies station KZKC (1581 AM) and Eddie, a tow truck driver, share an apartment over their favorite hangout, Kelly's Pub. Malcolm later purchases the pub and renames it Malcolm McGee's Sports Bar; and Eddie begins his own business, Eddie's Tow and Repair with his one faithful truck, Bronkula. A year later Malcolm and Eddie pool their resources and turn the bar into a jazz club called the Fifty/Fifty Club (located at the corner of 4th and Main). Malcolm's competition is McGinley's Bar.

Malcolm and Eddie have a "psycho chef" (Simone), as Eddie calls her, who is in therapy and talks to vegetables. Nicolette, the club's waitress, has a cat named Pokey. She feels chilly at 80 degrees, takes computer classes and uses milk in her bath water "to make my skin baby bottom soft." Nicolette calls Malcolm "Little Bo Cheap" and, at age 30, "has been 24 for the last five years." She has her own unique personality and is hard to live with ("I've been through 12 roommates in two years. Maybe it's me?").

Cast: Malcolm-Jamal Warner *(Malcolm McGee)*; Eddie Griffin *(Eddie Sherman)*; Karen Malina White *(Nicolette Vandross)*; Christopher Daniel Barnes *(Leonard Rickets)*; Ron Pearson *(Doug Rickets)*; Enya Flack *(Bridget Goodwin)*; Kellita Smith *(Danielle)*; Eric Allan Kramer *(Mike McGinley)*; JoNell Kennedy *(Maura McGee)*; Dawn McMillan *(Mia)*; Melissa Chan *(Lisa)*; Charles Robinson *(Marcus McGee)*; Vanessa Marquez *(Janice Ramos)*; Tucker Smallwood *(T.R. Hawkins)*.

5693 *Malcolm in the Middle.* (Series; Comedy; Fox; 2000–2006). Hal and Lois Wilkerson are a happily married couple who often wonder how they produced four troublesome children: Francis, Malcolm, Reese and Dewey (a fifth child, Jamie, is born in 2003). Hal and Lois, however, are not so innocent either. Their antics, coupled with those of their children, have earned them the reputation as "The Most Hated Family in the Neighborhood" (where they live at 123341 Maple Road in an unspecified town). The family is not easily impressed and they care very little about status.

Hal originally worked as a systems supervisor at a company called G.N. Industries ("Making the World Safe with Our Products"). When Hal is laid off, he works at various jobs, including salesman at U Buy It.

Lois was born in Manitoba, Canada. She is totally stressed out by the kids and cares little about modesty (walking around the house topless or in a bra is normal to her). Lois is abrupt, short tempered and rude. She feels she always has to be right even if she is wrong. Lois works as a salesgirl at a department store called Lucky Aide. Because of her temper, Hal lives in total fear of her.

Malcolm is the genius of the family and the only one of the kids who tries to be good (but circumstances just force him to become "bad"). He has an I.Q. of 165 and excels in math. He is the only character who is aware of a viewing audience and talks directly into the camera. He attends North High School and worked with his mother at Lucky Aide.

Francis is the eldest and most troublesome of the children. Because of his uncontrollable ways he was sent to the Marlin Military Academy for rehabilitation. After Marlin, he sought of drifted from job to job. In Alaska, where he worked in a diner, he met and married Piami. He was next a logger then foreman of the Grotto Ranch.

Reese, the third-born son, is following in Francis's footsteps. He is a "D" student at North High School and is quite naïve and easily taken advantage of. He believes he is a ladies' man but he seldom impresses girls.

Dewey is the youngest son before the birth of Jamie and the most conniving. He uses what he calls "Turning on the Cute" to get things from people. He attends Grace Elementary School.

Other regulars are Otto, Francis's boss at the Grotto Ranch; Gretchen, Otto's wife; Stevie, Malcolm's wheelchair bound friend; Craig, Lois's boss at Lucky Aide; Edwin Spangler, the headmaster at Marlin.

Cast: Jane Kaczmarek *(Lois Wilkerson)*; Bryan Cranston *(Hal Wilkerson)*; Frankie Muniz *(Malcolm Wilkerson)*; Christopher Kennedy Masterson *(Francis Wilkerson)*; Justin Berfield *(Reese Wilkerson)*; Erik Per Sullivan *(Dewey Wilkerson)*; Emy Coligado *(Piami Wilkerson)*; Craig Lamar *(Stevie Kenarban)*; David Anthony Higgins *(Craig Feldspar)*; Daniel Von Bargen *(Edwin Spangler)*; Ken Mars *(Otto)*; Meagen Fay *(Gretchen)*; Cloris Leachman *(Lois's mother)*; Laurie Metcalfe *(Susan; Lois's sister)*.

5694 *Malibu.* (Pilot; Drama; ABC; Jan. 23–24, 1983). Serial-like proposal about Linda and Stan Harvey, a young Milwaukee couple who move to California, rent an expensive house in Malibu and become involved in the lives of the rich and beautiful people who reside in the seaside community, including Billie Farnsworth, the real estate agent; Art Bonnell, the womanizing tennis pro; Gail Hessian, the TV journalist; and Clint Redman, a mysterious recluse. Anthony Newely performs the theme, "Malibu."

Cast: Susan Dey (*Linda Harvey*); William Atherton (*Stan Harvey*); Kim Novak (*Billie Farnsworth*); Ann Jillian (*Gail Hessian*); Chad Everett (*Art Bonnell*); Troy Donahue (*Clint Redman*); James Coburn (*Tom Wharton*); Valerie Perrine (*Dee Staufer*); Steve Forrest (*Rich Bradley*); Richard Mulligan (*Charlie Wigham*); George Hamilton (*Jay Pomerantz*); Eva Marie Saint (*Mary Wharton*); Bridget Hanley (*Laura Bonnell*); Jenilee Harrison (*Cherrie*); Anthony Newley (*Wilson Mahoney*).

5695   *Malibu Beach Party.* (Pilot; Variety; Syn.; Aug. 28 to Sept. 1, 1989). A five-episode proposal for a daily program that, set on California's Malibu Beach, features teenagers dancing to recorded and live music, game contests and celebrity guests.

Host: Alan Hunter. **Pilot Co-Host:** Alyssa Milano. **Announcer:** Staci Oki.

5696   *Malibu, Ca.* (Series; Comedy; Syn.; 1998–2000). Peter Collins, a divorced restaurant owner, lives at 11721 Malibu Road in Malibu, California. When his ex-wife, Michelle (Carol Houston), takes a job in Peru, his teenage sons Scott and Jason come to live with him and work as waiters at the Lighthouse, the seafood restaurant owned by Peter. Jennifer Stadler, Samantha Chapman, Murray Updike and Tracee Banks are Jason and Scott's friends.

Scott and Jason attended J.F.K. High School in New York. Scott is now training for the Olympic Swim Team; Jason is a hopeful musician (and singer). Jennifer, nicknamed "Stads," is a lifeguard and a female arm wrestling champion. Samantha, a car nut, knows more about engines than most mechanics, and volunteers her services for charity. Samantha left the series (second season) "to attend college in the east." She was replaced by Lisa, a pre-med student at UCLA who works as a waitress at the Lighthouse. She and Tracee share an apartment Tracee calls "Casa de Fun Fun." Murray runs the Surf Shack, the beach eatery, for its owner (Peter). Murray is a "surfer dude" and hosted an advice radio program called *The Dude of Love* on station KPOV.

Tracee is a gorgeous, busty blonde who believes she is "the most beautiful girl in Malibu and California and the whole U.S. of A. except for alien chicks who may appear on *Star Trek*." She loves to hang out at the beach and wants to be an actress. She did a guest shot on *Baywatch*, hosted a pilot called *Blind Date* and starred in a TV commercial as the Dancing Dorito Chip ("I was the only chip who got dipped in the salsa"). In second-season episodes, Tracee acquires the role of Dr. Sheila Lowenstein, a brain surgeon, on the TV series *Malibu Hospital*. Her favorite color is pink and she says, "I may be an airhead, but I'm one hot babe."

Cast: Ed Blatchford (*Peter Collins*); Trevor Merszei (*Scott Collins*); Jason Hayes (*Jason Collins*); Priscilla Lee Taylor (*Tracee Banks*); Wendi Kenya (*Jennifer Stadler*); Gina Marie May (*Samantha Chapman*); Brandon Brooks (*Murray Updike*); Marguita Terry (*Lisa*).

5697   *Malibu Run.* (Series; Adventure; CBS; 1961). A revised version of *The Aquanauts* that is set in Malibu Beach, California. Larry Lahr and Mike Madison are diving instructors who earn extra money as part time private investigators. While teaching people how to master the water is their primary source of income, Larry and Mike find little excitement in this endeavor. It is when they offer their services to someone in trouble that they find the excitement they are seeking and stories focus on their efforts to solve crimes.

Cast: Jeremy Slate (*Larry Lahr*); Ron Ely (*Mike Madison*); Charles Thompson (*Captain Chaplan*).

5698   *Malibu U.* (Series; Variety; ABC; 1967). The mythical Malibu University on Malibu Beach in California is the setting for a summer program of performances by the top names in rock and roll music.

Program Open: "It's ABC's summer beach-in, *Malibu U.* with the dean, Rick Nelson and this week's *Malibu U.* guests, the popular star, James Darren, the hip glee club, Harpers Bazaar, the Professor of Pop, Frankie Randall; the Bob Banas Dancers; the president of *Malibu U.*'s student body, Robbie Porter — and some *Malibu U.* surprises. Among those contributing to the *Malibu U.* student body are the makers of Clairol, creators of the exciting natural look in beauty and tonight by Midnight Sun, the gentle shampoo lightener that leaves hair shiny. Now, here's the Dean of *Malibu U.*, Rick Nelson...." Harpers Bizarre perform the theme, "Malibu U."

Host: Ricky Nelson (*as the Dean*); **Regulars:** Robbie Porter, Erin Gray, The Bob Banas Dancers, The Malibuties.

5699   *Mall Masters at Mall of America.* (Series; Game; Syn.; 2000-2001). Shoppers at the Mall of America (outside of Minneapolis, Minnesota) are asked questions based on polls and win money if they correctly select the majority opinion.

Host: Scott A. Stone.

5700   *Mallory: Circumstantial Evidence.* (Pilot; Crime Drama; NBC; Feb. 8, 1976). Daniel Mallory was a once-celebrated criminal attorney whose reputation and practice have been tarnished by unfounded perjury charges. He is now struggling to rebuild his reputation and the unsold series was to relate his efforts to help the people who still trust in him.

Cast: Raymond Burr (*Daniel Mallory*); Mark Hamill (*Joe Celli, his aide*).

5701   *Mama.* (Series; Comedy-Drama; CBS; 1949–1957). Incidents in the lives of the Hansons, a Norwegian family living busily in a large American city (San Francisco, 1910), as seen through the eyes of Katrin, the eldest daughter, an aspiring writer who records their daily activities in her diary. Marta ("Mama") and Lars ("Papa") are Katrin's parents. Nels and Dagmar are Katrin's older brother and younger sister. Lars works as a carpenter (for the Jenkins Construction Company) and Marta, called Mama, is a practical woman and the guiding light of the family. The Hansons are not rich and live comfortably at 118 Steiner Street. "Mama can do anything," says Dagmar (Mama says, "It is not the best thing she grew up believing I can do everything"). Mama is content in her way of life and came to America because all her relatives were here — "It's good for family to be together." Katrin, Nels and Dagmar were all born in America; Marta and Lars became American citizens and Mama's greatest desire is to return to Norway to show her children their homeland. Mama wears the silver broach that belonged to her mother; when she becomes upset, Mama scrubs the floors and does other house cleaning. Jenny and Trina are Marta's sisters; Gunnar is Marta's uncle; Ingeborg is Marta's niece; Theodore Roosevelt ("T.R.") Ryan is a friend. Based on the feature film *I Remember Mama*.

Program Open: [Katrin opening an old family album]: "This old album brings back so many memories of San Francisco, of growing up, of all the happy, artless days that seemed so long ago. There is our house on Steiner Street where I was born. And these are the neighbors and friends I recall so well. And my aunts and their children. And I remember my family as we were then. My little sister Dagmar, my big brother Nels and, of course, Papa. But most of all when I think back to those happy days, most of all ... I remember Mama."

Cast: Peggy Wood (*Marta "Mama" Hanson*); Judson Laire (*Lars "Papa" Hanson*); Rosemary Rice, Iris Mann (*Katrin Hanson*); Robin Morgan, Toni Campbell (*Dagmar Hanson*); Dick Van Patten (*Nels Hanson*); Ruth Gates (*Jenny*); Alice Frost (*Trina*); Carl Frank (*Uncle*

Gunnar); Patricia McCormack (*Ingeborg*); Kevin Coughlin (*T.R. Ryan*).

5702   *Mama Malone.* (Series; Comedy; CBS; 1984). The kitchen of the fourth-floor apartment of Ranata Malone in Brooklyn, New York, is where the television program *Cooking with Mama Malone* is taped and broadcast. The comedy stems from Mama's attempts to conduct a show — despite constant interruptions from friends and family members. Ranata is a widow. Her divorced daughter, Connie Taramacopolis works at Paolo's Pizza Patio; Frankie is Connie's son; Dino Forresti is Mama's brother, a pop singer; Austin is the show director; Padre Guardiano is Mama's friend, the parish priest; Father Jose Silva is the Padre's assistant; Stanley is the TV announcer; Jackie is the script girl; Harry is the floor director; Ken is the assistant director; Rosa is Mama's niece; Albert is Rosa's husband; Calvin Klinger is Mama's neighbor; Neta Cavelli is Mama's friend.

Cast: Lila Kaye (*Mama Ranata Malone*); Randee Heller (*Connie Taramacopolis*); Evan Richards (*Frankie Taramacopolis*); Don Amendolia (*Dino Forresti*); Raymond Singer (*Austin*); Ralph Manza (*Padre Guardiano*); Richard Yniquez (*Father Jose Silva*); Sam Anderson (*Stanley*); Joey Jupiter (*Jackie*); Mitchell Group (*Harry*); Pendleton Brown (*Ken*); Candice Azzara (*Rosa*); Robert Costanzo (*Albert*); Paul Benedict (*Calvin Klinger*); Alice Ghostley (*Neta Cavelli*).

5703   *Mama Mirabelle's Home Movies.* (Series; Cartoon; PBS; 2006). Carla (a zebra), Bo (cheetah) and Max (elephant) are three young animals who live in Africa. When they encounter an aspect of nature that they do not understand, they seek the advice of Max's mother, Mama Mirabelle, a wise elephant who solves their problems by showing them wildlife films. The series combines animation (Mama and the young animals) with live action (wildlife footage) to relate aspects of the animal world to children.

Voices: Vanessa Williams, Phillipa Alexander, Julie de Jongh, Teresa Gallagher, Elly Fairman, Alan Marriott.

5704   *Mama Rosa.* (Series; Drama; ABC; 1950). A quaint theatrical boarding house in Hollywood, California, is the setting. The establishment is home to vaudeville performers and young hopefuls and is run by a kindly woman known as Mama Rosa. Mama is a widow and the mother of Nina and Roberto, both of whom have been bitten by the acting bug, although nothing positive has occurred (Nina also works as a stenographer). Stories relate events in the lives of Mama Rosa, Nina and Roberto as well as the celebrities who appear at the boarding house. Nikolai is Roberto's friend, a violin instructor. Aired locally in Los Angeles in 1948 (over KFI-TV) then on ABC (April 23 to June 15, 1950).

Cast: Anna Demetrio (*Mama Rosa*); Beverly Garland (*Nina*); Richard Anderson (*Roberto*); Vito Scotti (*Nikolai*).

5705   *Mama's Boy.* (Series; Comedy; NBC; 1987). When Molly McCaskey loses her money and is forced to leave Florida, she moves to New York to live with her bachelor son, Jake, a writer (of the column "McCaskey") for the *Manhattan Examiner*. Stories deal with Jake's efforts to deal with his mother's attempts to run his life.

The pilot regulars are Victoria, Jake's editor; two characters with no names: Jake's friend and the apartment building manager; and Agnes, Molly's sister.

The series regulars are Jake's friends Officer Mickey Ryan and Lucky; and Molly's sister, Agnes.

Pilot Cast: Bruce Weitz (*Jake McCaskey*); Nancy Walker (*Molly McCaskey*); Susan Blakely (*Victoria*); David Leisure (*Apartment house manager*); Harold Sylvester (*Jake's friend*); Grace Zabriskie (*Agnes*).

Series Cast: Bruce Weitz (*Jake McCaskey*); Nancy Walker (*Molly McCaskey*); James Cromwell (*Lucky*); Dan Hedaya (*Mickey Ryan*); Grace Zabriskie (*Agnes*).

5706   *Mama's Family.* (Series; Comedy; NBC, 1983-1984; Syn., 1986). Residing at 1542 Ray Lane (in some episodes, 1542 Ray Way) in Raytown, USA, are the Harpers, a not so typical American family. Thelma ("Mama") Harper is the cantankerous head of the family. She was married to a man named Carl (deceased) and can extract truth from people with her gift — the look (a stare that forces people to be honest). Mama held a job as a receptionist for the Raytown Travel Agency and her home was originally 10 Decatur Road (at which time it was a brothel called Ma Beaudine's).

Vinton Harper is Mama's second-born child, a locksmith at Kwick Keys, a company that is owned by the Bernice Corporation. His favorite hangout is the Bigger Jigger Bar, and he is a member of the Mystic Order of the Cobra Club.

Naomi Oates, "the sexiest woman in Raytown," and the Harpers' next door neighbor, married Vint in 1983. (Vinton's former wife, Mitzi, ran out on him. Naomi had four previous marriages, to Tom, Bill, Leonard and George.) Naomi is a checker at the local supermarket, Food Circus, and is called "Skeeter" by Vinton (Mama believes Naomi is the kind of girl mothers fear their sons will marry).

Sonia and Vinton Harper, Jr. ("Buzz") are Vint's children from his first marriage. Both attended Raytown High School, and both were dropped from the syndicated version of the series.

Bubba Higgins is Mama's grandson (her daughter, Eunice's son) and attends Raytown Junior College (role began with the syndicated version).

Iola Boylen is Mama's longtime friend and neighbor, a spinster who lives with her never-seen domineering mother. She is a member of the Peppermint Playhouse Theater Company and loves to sew and do arts and crafts.

NBC episodes feature Mama's other children: Ellen Jackson, Thelma's first-born daughter, now a widow and a society woman; and Eunice Higgins, Mama's third-born, neurotic daughter. Fran Crawley, Thelma's sister, writes a column "for the local paper that is thrown on the porch." Ed Higgins is Eunice's husband. In Flashback sequences, Tanya Fenmore and Heather Kerr appeared as Eunice as a girl; Amy O'Neill was Ellen as a girl; David Friedman was Vinton as a boy and Nikki Cox was Iola as a girl. NBC episodes also feature Harvey Korman as Alistair Quince, the program host (sequences that are cut from the program in syndication). Based on a series of skits originally performed on *The Carol Burnett Show*.

Cast: Vicki Lawrence (*Thelma Harper*); Ken Berry (*Vinton Harper*); Dorothy Lyman (*Naomi Harper*); Karin Argoud (*Sonia Harper*); Eric Brown (*Buzz Harper*); Allan Kayser (*Bubba Higgins*); Beverly Archer (*Iola Boylen*); Rue McClanahan (*Fran Crawley*); Betty White (*Ellen Jackson*); Carol Burnett (*Eunice Higgins*); Harvey Korman (*Ed Higgins*); Harvey Korman (*Alistair Quince*); Jerry Reed (*Leonard; Naomi's ex-husband*).

5707   *Man About the House.* (Series; Comedy; Syn.; 1983). The British series on which *Three's Company* is based. Events in the lives of Jo and Chrissy, two girls who share a flat in England, and the problems that ensue when their landlord raises the rent and they sublet a room to Robin Tripp, a male cookery student. See also *Robin's Nest*, the spin off series (which became the *Three's Company* spin off, *Three's a Crowd*). *Man About the House* also led to the British spin off *George and Mildred* (which became the basis for the *Three's Company* spin off *The Ropers*).

Other regulars are George and Mildred Roper, the landlords; Larry Simmons, Robin's friend; Jim, the bartender at the Mucky Duck Saloon, the hangout; Norman Tripp, Robin's brother (who married Chrissy in the last episode).

Cast: Richard O'Sullivan (*Robin Tripp*); Sally Thomsett (*Jo*); Paula Wilcox (*Chrissy Plummer*); Brian Murphy (*George Roper*); Yootha Joyce (*Mildred Roper*); Doug Fisher (*Larry Simmons*); Michael Segal (*Jim*); Norman Eshley (*Norman Tripp*).

5708   *Man About Town.* (Pilot; Comedy; ABC; July 11, 1986). Leon Feddick is a New York bachelor with few friends, few dates and very little excitement in his life. The proposal was to focus on Leon's efforts to turn his life around. Other regulars are Terry, Leon's neighbor (at the Lakeside Vista Apartments in Manhattan at 111489 Becker Avenue), a singer; Vic, Leon's friend, the owner of a bookstore; Sandy, Vic's salesgirl; Mike, the Mailman; and Dean, Leon's cousin.

Cast: Daniel Stern (*Leon Feddick*); Jayne Modean (*Terry Bishop*); Tom Henschel (*Vic LeMeara*); Karlene Crockett (*Sandy*); George Wyner (*Mike the Mailman*); Sam Whipple (*Dean Feddick*).

5709   *Man Against Crime.* (Series; Crime Drama; CBS; Du-Mont; NBC; 1949–1956). Mike Barnett is a tough private detective based in New York City. He upholds the law but when the law prevents him from accomplishing a goal, he will bend it to suit his needs (always to help a client or collar a criminal). Mike's cases are not always the cut and dry as he often takes on the causes of people desperately in need of help. Stories follow one of TVs earliest detectives as he seeks the evidence he needs to clear his clients. Aired on CBS (1949–53), DuMont (1953-54) and NBC (1956).

Cast: Ralph Bellamy (*Mike Barnett*); Frank Lovejoy (*Mike Barnett*); Robert Preston (*Pat Barnett; Mike's brother*); Art Fleming (*Ralph's stand-in*).

5710   *Man Against Crime.* (Pilot; Crime Drama; NBC; Sept. 21, 1958). Dan Garrett is a young, idealistic defense lawyer whose enthusiasm is soon shattered by the realities of the imperfect judicial system. The proposal was to follow Dan as he fights crime, using what tactics he can to see that justice is served.

Cast: Darren McGavin (*Dan Garrett*).

5711   *Man and the Challenge.* (Series; Adventure; NBC; 1959-1960). Glenn Barton is a U.S. government scientist who has volunteered to go beyond the test tube phase and laboratory statistics to become a human guinea pig. His assignment: test the limits of human endurance. Lynn Allen assists Glenn in his research and stories cart his experiences as he sometimes risks his life to make the world a safer place.

Cast: George Nader (*Glenn Barton*); Jayne Meadows (*Lynn Allen*).

5712   *The Man and the City.* (Series; Drama; ABC; 1971-1972). A southwestern metropolis, the fictional equivalent of Albuquerque, New Mexico, is home to Mayor Thomas Alcala, a man who strays from the offices of city hall, mixes with the people, and struggles to solve their problems. Andy Hays is Thomas's assistant; Marian Crane is Thomas's secretary; Josefina is Thomas's housekeeper.

Cast: Anthony Quinn (*Thomas Jefferson Alcala*); Mike Farrell (*Andy Hays*); Mala Powers (*Marian Crane*); Carmen Zapata (*Josefina*).

5713   *The Man Behind the Badge.* (Series; Anthology; CBS; 1953–1955). Dramatizations based on official law enforcement records of the men and women who risk their lives to protect people.

Host-Narrator: Charles Bickford. **Additional Narration:** Norman Rose. **Announcer:** Joel Aldred.

5714   *A Man Called Hawk.* (Series; Crime Drama; ABC; 1989). A spin off from *Spenser: For Hire* where Hawk was a mysterious man who helped Boston private detective Spenser bring criminals to justice. Hawk has now returned to his hometown of Washington, D.C., where he becomes a mysterious figure for justice, a vigilante who seems to come from out of nowhere to help people desperately in need of help. Hawk is assisted by his cousin, Jake and helps Colonel Stoller, a retired army man out to see that justice is done (he gives Hawk a case that he feels needs resolving). An Old Man (as Hawk calls him) is Hawk's mentor.

Cast Avery Brooks (*Hawk*); Moses Gunn (*Old Man*); Jack Ryland (*Colonel Stoller*); Keith David (*Jake*).

5715   *A Man Called Shenandoah.* (Series; Western; ABC; 1965-1966). "O, Shenandoah, you're doomed to wander; so roam in search of home, 'cross this land so lonely." As the theme played, the figure of a man is seen riding through the deep snow. The blistering winds and bitter cold have become part of his life as he wanders from town to town seeking to discover his past, an identity that was lost to him when he was shot in the head for unknown reasons and left to die on the prairie. He was found by two bounty hunters and brought to a nearby town. There he was nursed back to health by a saloon girl named Kate. But upon awakening, he found himself a man without a memory and unaware of who or what he was. Now, as Shenandoah (the Indian name for an amnesiac), he searches for his past throughout the turbulent West of the 1860s ("You can't build a future unless you know the past," he says).

Shenandoah never uncovered his true identity. He learned only that he was a U.S. Army lieutenant assigned to the Western Division of the Second Regiment at Fort Smith and that Fort Todd was the only place he could remember ever having lived. Robert Horton performs the theme, "Shenandoah."

Cast: Robert Horton (*Shenandoah*); Beverly Garland (*Kate; first episode*).

5716   *A Man Called Sloane.* (Series; Adventure; NBC; 1979). Thomas Remington Sloane III is a Priority One Agent for UNIT, a secret U.S. government counterespionage team. Torgue is his assistant, and Mr. Director is the head of UNIT. The front for UNIT is a Los Angeles toy store called the Toy Boutique; the brains behind UNIT is Effie, an E.F.I. series 3000 computer. The enemy of UNIT is KARTEL, an organization that is bent on destroying the world. Sara is Sloane's romantic interest.

In the original 1979 pilot film, *Death Ray 2000* (Mar. 5, 1981), Robert Logan was Thomas R. Sloane, an agent for UNIT and the owner of an antique business called Sloane and Sons in Carmel, California (Penelope Windust played Sloane's business associate, Emma Blessing). Dan O'Herlihy played Mr. Director, but Ji-Tu Cumbuka was a villain named Torgue, who sought to kill Sloane. UNIT was located in Kentucky, where Mr. Director posed as a rural farmer (UNIT's offices were in the back of a barn).

Cast: Robert Conrad (*Thomas R. Sloane*); Ji-Tu Cumbuka (*Torgue*); Dan O'Herlihy (*Mr. Director*); Karen Purcill (*Agent Kelly O'Neal*); Michele Carey (*Voice of Effie*); Diane Stilwell (*Sara*).

5717   *The Man Called X.* (Series; Adventure; Syn.; 1956). Ken Thurston is an American intelligence agent who operates under the code name "X." Stories relate his adventures as he investigates cases on behalf of the government.

Cast: Barry Sullivan (*Ken Thurston*).

5718   *The Man from Atlantis.* (Series; Adventure; NBC; 1977-1978). A storm deep within the Pacific Ocean unearths the sole survivor of the fabled lost kingdom of Atlantis and washes him ashore. A father and son, walking on a beach in California, find the unconscious Atlantian and call an ambulance. The Atlantian, who has webbed hands, is brought to a hospital, where doctors are unable to determine what is wrong with him (other than desiccated lungs and the fact that "he has forgotten how to breathe"). Elizabeth Merrill, a naval doctor, takes an interest in the case and examines the victim. "I know how to save him," she exclaims. With the help of paramedics, she returns Mark to the sea. The water revives and saves the Atlantian's life. The Atlantian, whom Elizabeth names Mark Harris, is brought to the Naval Undersea Center. After a thorough examination, Elizabeth feeds the information to the WRW 1200 computer in Washington, D.C. The computer responds with "Last Citizen of Atlantis?????"

Mark is put through a series of additional tests. He can swim faster than a dolphin and can go to depths of over 36,000 feet. As Elizabeth discovers facts about Mark, Mark becomes fascinated by humans. Although the government allows Mark to return to the sea, he elects to remain and help further humanity's knowledge of the sea and increase his own knowledge of human beings. Stories detail Mark and Elizabeth's work on behalf of the O.R.F. (Oceanic Research Foundation).

C.W. Crawford is the head of the foundation, and Jane, Jimmy and Juno are crew members of the foundation submarine, the *Citation*. Mr. Schubert "is an ocean junkman who wised up, became rich and now gets whatever he wants." Schubert has created what he believes is a perfect world and is seeking to destroy the diseased world above, then make it good once again. Brent is Mr. Schubert's fumbling assistant (Schubert's goal is to capture Mark for his own sinister purposes).

Mark calls himself a citizen of the ocean. He can't talk to fish, but he can understand dolphins and whales. Elizabeth calls Mark "The Project Atlantis Affair."

Cast: Patrick Duffy *(Mark Harris)*; Belinda J. Montgomery *(Dr. Elizabeth Merrill)*; Victor Buono *(Mr. Schubert)*; Kenneth Tigar *(Dr. Miller; Elizabeth's superior)*; Annette Cardona *(Ginny Mendoza)*; Alan Fudge *(C.W. Crawford)*; Robert Lussier *(Brent)*; Jean Marie Hon *(Jane)*; J. Victor Lopez *(Jimmy)*; Anson Downs *(Jumo)*.

5719   *The Man from Blackhawk*. (Series; Western; ABC; 1959–1960). Sam Logan is a special investigator for the Blackhawk Insurance Company during the 1870s. Sam is fast with his guns, rugged and quick with his fists. Stories follow Sam as he travels throughout the lawless west investigating claims filed against his company.

Cast: Robert Rockwell *(Sam Logan)*.

5720   *The Man from Denver*. (Pilot; Western; CBS; April 30, 1959). A proposed spin off from *Zane Grey Theater* about Ward Pendleton, a bank examiner, as he travels throughout the Old West to ferret out corruption.

Cast: Mark Miller *(Ward Pendleton)*.

5721   *The Man from Everywhere*. (Pilot; Comical Western; CBS; April 13, 1961). Old West set spin off from *Zane Grey Theater* about Branch Taylor, a happy-go-lucky drifter who tackles any job to earn money and continue his travels.

Cast: Burt Reynolds *(Branch Taylor)*.

5722   *The Man from Galveston*. (Pilot; Western; Unaired; Produced in 1963). The pilot film for *Temple Houston* (NBC, 1963–64) about Timothy Higgins (later to become Temple Houston), a circuit-riding frontier Texas lawyer whose cases call for more than just defending a client in court. Originally intended for television, but released theatrically instead (it is currently available in syndication).

Cast: Jeffrey Hunter *(Timothy Higgins)*.

5723   *The Man from Interpol*. (Series; Crime Drama; NBC; 1960). Tony Smith is an inspector with New Scotland Yard in England. When the opportunity arises for Tony to study new crime solving techniques, he is assigned to active duty with Interpol (the International Police Force). Stories relate Tony's case investigations.

Cast: Richard Wyler *(Tony Smith)*; John Longden *(Superintendent Mercer)*.

5724   *The Man from the 25th Century*. (Pilot; Science Fiction; Unaired; Produced in 1968). Robert Prentiss was born in Topeka, Kansas, in 1951. Seven years later he was abducted by aliens from a planet 500 years ahead of Earth. For 20 years he was trained for a special mission on Earth: to destroy the Delphi Project, which is designed to protect the Earth from alien invaders (Delphi emits a radium shield that disintegrates alien objects). The aliens' plan begins to take effect when Prentiss, believed to be an important government scientist assigned to perfect Delphi, is taken one mile beneath the earth to its secret location (Prentiss is seen being transported to Earth; but exactly how he comes to be accepted as a scientist is not shown). Prentiss, however, fails to destroy the project when his human qualities override his orders to kill. Prentiss is now considered an enemy by the aliens and the proposal was to follow Prentiss as he aligns himself with the government to battle those who want to destroy him and the planet.

Cast: James Darren *(Robert Prentiss)*; John Napier *(Dr. Carl Baldwin)*; Ford Rainey *(General George Atwood)*; John Crawford *(Alien leader)*.

5725   *The Man from U.N.C.L.E.* (Series; Adventure; NBC; 1964–1968). The United Network Command for Law and Enforcement (U.N.C.L.E. for short) is a U.S. government organization, based in New York City, that battles the evils of THRUSH, an enemy organization bent on world domination. Alexander Waverly heads the New York office and his top agents are Napoleon Solo and Ilya Kuryakin. The Del Flora Tailor Shop on Second Avenue and 40th Street fronts for the agency.

Napoleon is a suave and sophisticated ladies' man. He is an expert at chess, is single and longs for a family. He was born in Kansas City and served a hitch in Korea during the war. Napoleon is not a man of action; he would rather use his considerable charm to talk his way out of a situation rather than use physical force.

Ilya was born in Russia but speaks with what appears to be a British accent. He is knowledgeable in many areas and is well versed in the martial arts (he is also an expert shot and archer). He served a hitch in the Russian Navy and graduated from U.N.C.L.E. Survival School in 1956.

Stories follow Napoleon and Illya's investigations into cases that threaten world security. Other regulars are Lisa Rogers, Alexander's secretary; Del Flora, the owner of the tailor shop; and Heather, a field agent.

Cast: Robert Vaughn *(Napoleon Solo)*; David McCallum *(Ilya Kuryakin)*; Leo G. Carroll *(Alexander Waverly)*; Barbara Moore *(Lisa Rogers)*; Mario Siletti *(Del Flora)*; May Heatherly *(Heather)*; Julie Ann Johnson *(U.N.C.L.E. Girl)*; Sharon Hillyer *(U.N.C.L.E. Girl)*.

5726   *Man in a Suitcase*. (Series; Adventure; ABC; 1968). John McGill is a former American intelligence agent turned private detective. Although now based in London, England, John will travel to wherever the need be to investigate a case for a client (sort of living out of a suitcase). Stories follow John's case investigations.

Cast: Richard Bradford *(John McGill)*.

5727   *The Man in the Family*. (Series; Comedy; ABC; 1991).

When Sal Bavasso learns that his father, Carmine, is dying, he leaves Las Vegas and returns to his home in Brooklyn, New York. Sal, the black sheep of the family (Carmine disapproved of his playboy lifestyle, his friends and his spending habits) promises his father that he will care for the family and run the family business. Carmine's Deli is the business, and the family consists of Sal's mother, Angie, his divorced sister, Annie, his teenage sister, Tina, Annie's son, Robby, and his uncle, Bennie.

Carmine's Deli is located at 38 Benson Drive. Sal and the family live in Apartment 4 on the first floor above the deli.

Sal is a wheeler-dealer and has a shady quality about him (possibly mob connections). He has been knocking around from one job to another since high school. Annie, who is 33 years old, has been divorced for seven years and now works as a salesclerk at Macy's on 34th Street in Manhattan.

Tina, who is 17 years old, attends Saint Vincent's High School. She is very pretty, but sometimes doubts her beauty and ability to attract the opposite sex. Robby attends Saint Vincent's Elementary School; Uncle Bennie shops at Vito's, Sal's competition, "because their prices are lower"; Cha Cha is Sal's not too bright friend. He runs a dry cleaning shop and has a crush on Annie. In the original, unaired pilot, *Honor Bound*, Camille Saviola played Sal's mother, Angie Bavasso. Louis Prima sings the theme, "When You're Smilin'."

Cast: Ray Sharkey (*Sal Bavasso*); Julie Bovasso(*Angie Bavasso*); Leah Remini (*Tina Bavasso*); Billy J. Sullivan (*Bobby Bavasso*); Louis Guss (*Bernie Bavasso*); Billy L. Sullivan (*Robby Bavasso*); Louis Guss (*Bennie Bavasso*); Don Stark (*Cha Cha*).

5728 *Man in the Middle.* (Pilot; Comedy; CBS; April 14, 1972). A conservative family man (Norman) struggles to cope with a life made more complicated by his left-wing daughter (Debbie), a right-wing mother (Belle) and a middle-aged business partner on a youth trip. Harriet is Norman's wife; Kirk is their son.

Cast: Van Johnson (*Norman*); Nancy Malone (*Harriet*); Heather Menzies (*Debbie*); Ruth McDevitt (*Belle*); Michael Brandon (*Kirk*); Allan Melvin (*Harvey*).

5729 *The Man in the Square Suit.* (Pilot; Comedy; ABC; April 22, 1966). Frank Johnson is 37 years old, married (to Marilyn) and the father of a teenage girl (Nancy). He is an accomplished television writer but feels he is a square. He works on a rock and roll TV show but again feels he is square when it comes to such music. The proposal, also known as *The Rambling Wreck from Discotheque* relates Frank's home and working life with his under 25-year-old co-workers: Maxine, his sexy secretary; and Gary Young, the producer.

Cast: Paul Dooley (*Frank Johnson*); Jan Shutan (*Marilyn Johnson*); Diane Sherry (*Nancy Johnson*); Astrid Warner (*Maxine*); Michael Blodgett (*Gary Young*).

5730 *Man of the Comstock.* (Pilot; Western; NBC; Nov. 3, 1953). A proposed spin off from *Fireside Theater* about Bill Stewart, a mining attorney in the Comstock mining area of Colorado during the Civil War, as he attempts to maintain the peace.

Cast: Bruce Bennett (*Bill Stewart*).

5731 *Man of the People.* (Series; Comedy; NBC; 1991). James ("Jim") Doyle is a city councilman who has to pull off scams to survive—"I can't survive on what they pay me in this burg." The "burg" is an unidentified town in the 7th District. Jim is a bookmaker and gambler. When his ex-wife, Margie Patterson, dies, the mayor, Lisbeth Chardin, appoints Jim to replace her for she believes the public wants the appointment to be that of someone close to the de-ceased councilwoman. It is also Lisbeth's plan to manipulate Jim for her own benefit. Unknown to Lisbeth, Jim is aware of her intentions but doesn't let on; he wheels and deals for his benefit, which includes winning the upcoming mayor's race and becoming the man of the people.

Kelly's Pool Hall is Jim's favorite hangout; as a kid, he worked as a shill for an evangelist. Lisbeth has a horse named Jack Hammer, and the Barham Realty Company supplements Lisbeth's income in return for favors.

Constance LeRoy is Jim's former sister-in-law; she now works as his office assistant (she is determined not to let him run scams from the office). Her goal is to keep Jim on the straight and narrow; in her mind she is right and everybody else is wrong. Rita is Jim's ditsy receptionist, an ex-hooker who was arrested twice for prostitution. Kathleen Quinlan played the part of Constance in the unaired pilot version.

Cast: James Garner (*Jim Doyle*); Kate Mulgrew (*Lisbeth Chardin*); Corinne Bohrer (*Constance Le Roy*); Romy Walthall (*Rita*).

5732 *Man of the West.* (Series; Western; Syn.; 1958). The alternate title for *Frontier Doctor*. See this title for information.

5733 *Man of the World.* (Series; Drama; Syn.; 1962). Michael Strait is a world-renowned photojournalist. Stories follow his global assignments as his photo shoots often mean more than just taking pictures. Michael is a man who has a knack for finding trouble—and helping people in distress.

Cast: Craig Stevens (*Michael Strait*).

5734 *Man of Your Dreams.* (Pilot; Comedy; Unaired; Produced for NBC in 2008). Larry Ackerman is considered Chicago's know-it-all bartender. People with problems find relief just by talking to Larry. But it is people with romantic problems that Larry excels. He believes he is an expert on relationships and the proposal was to follow Larry as he dispenses advice to women, revealing the secrets of men to help them find Mr. Right (that is, when his advice doesn't backfire).

Cast: Michael Trucco (*Larry Ackerman*); Constance Zimmer (*Liza*); Christina Chang (*Melinda*); Justina Machado (*Violet*); Rebecca McFarland (*Sally*).

5735 *Man on a String.* (Pilot; Crime Drama; CBS; Feb. 18, 1972). Pete King is a government undercover agent who tackles risky assignments that require precise handling to accomplish. Pete rides a fine line between success and failure and the proposal, an attempt to revise *Tightrope*, was to relate his efforts to single handedly accomplish his missions. William Connaught is Pete's superior.

Cast: Christopher George (*Pete King*); William Schallert (*William Connaught*).

5736 *The Man Who Fell to Earth.* (Pilot; Science Fiction; ABC; Aug. 23, 1987). A small alien space craft, carrying four passengers, crash lands on Earth. The one surviving passenger, John Dorey, is left to carry out his mission: save the remaining population of his dying planet, Athena (which was struck by a meteor and is now doomed as another meteor is approaching). The proposal was to relate Dorey's efforts to somehow find a means by which to return to Athena and transport his people to the safety of the Earth. The pilot finds Dorey teaming with businessman Felix Hawthorne to create World Enterprises as a means of building a ship that can travel the 200 million miles to Athena to save his people. Complicating Dorey's mission is Richard Morse, a U.S. government agent who has become suspicious of his actions.

Cast: Lewis Smith (*John Dorey*); James Laurenson (*Felix Hawthorne*); Robert Picardo (*Richard Morse*).

5737 The Man Who Never Was. (Series; Adventure; ABC; 1966-1967). While being pursued by East German police, who uncovered his identity, American espionage agent Peter Murphy wanders onto an estate where a society party is being held. Straying from the house multimillionaire Mark Wainwright, Peter's exact double, is mistaken for Murphy by the police and killed. Shortly after, when the Wainwright chauffeur mistakes Peter for Mark, and told of an impending meeting, he assumes Wainwright's identity. At first, Peter manages to fool everyone, including Eva, Mark's wife. At the scheduled meeting, in which Eva is to lose control of her family corporation to Roger Berry, Mark's scheming half brother, Peter refuses to sign the necessary papers. Later, when they are alone, Eva questions the stranger posing as her husband. Unable to reveal his true identity, he tells her about Mark and asks her to continue posing as his wife. Mystified, but needing Mark alive to save her family corporation, she agrees. Posing as Mark Wainwright, agent Peter Murphy continues in his capacity as a spy and, assisted by Eva, undertakes hazardous missions for the U.S. government. Jack Forbes is Peter's superior.

Cast: Robert Lansing (*Peter Murphy/Mark Wainwright*); Dana Wynter (*Eva Wainwright*); Alex Devion (*Roger Berry*); Murray Hamilton (*Jack Forbes*).

5738 Man with a Camera. (Series; Crime Drama; ABC; 1958–1960). Mike Kovac is a free-lance photojournalist based in New York City. He was a top combat photographer during the Korean War but suffered hard times after his release from the service (he was barely able to survive and lived in a "broken down old tenement"). It took time, but Mike's photos of celebrities visiting New York got him noticed and back on his feet. Mike's interest waned from celebrities to crime and corruption and he has earned a reputation as a top-notch crime photographer. Stories follow Mike as he attempts to acquire material by assisting the police and solving crimes against insurance companies.

Cast: Charles Bronson (*Mike Kovac*); James Flavin (*Lieutenant Donovan*).

5739 The Man with the Power. (Pilot; Adventure; NBC; May 24, 1977). Eric Smith is a Milwaukee high school teacher with a secret: he is the scion of an alien father and Earth mother. He possesses unique psychokinetic powers and the proposal was to relate his efforts to help the U.S. government when the need arises.

Cast: Bob Neill (*Eric Smith*).

5740 Man Without a Gun. (Series; Western; Syn.; 1958). Yellowstone, Dakota, during the 1870s is the setting. Adam MacLean, editor of *The Yellowstone Sentinel* believes in the power of the press. He also believes gun play is not always the answer and stories follow his efforts to establish peace through the pages of his newspaper. In April of 1957, an unaired pilot episode was filmed with Robert Rockwell as Adam MacLean.

Cast: Rex Reason (*Adam MacLean*); Mort Mills (*Marshal Frank Tallman*).

5741 The Mancini Generation. (Series; Variety; Syn.; 1972). Orchestra leader and composer Henry Mancini hosts a program of popular music with the backing of the forty piece Henry Mancini Orchestra with additional orchestrations by Alan Copeland.

5742 Mancuso, FBI. (Series; Crime Drama; NBC; 1989-1990). Nick Mancuso is a product of the streets of the Lower East Side of New York. He is tough, street smart and turned what could have been a life of crime into something good. He became an FBI agent (assigned to the Metropolitan Field Office in Washington, D.C.). Nick is a widower (his wife, Mary Louise, died in 1964) and he lives in a comfortable apartment at 311 Delaware Street; his favorite hangout is Gertie's Bar (owned by his friend Gertie). Nick's upbringing has given him an edge over other agents as he can better relate to the criminal mind; stories relate his case investigations. Jean is Nick's secretary; Kristen is the FBI agent who assists Nick; Lorraine Kovacs is Nick's married daughter (Andy is her husband and Lee Ann is their daughter).

Cast: Robert Loggia (*Nick Mancuso*); Randi Brooks (*Jean St. John*); Janet Carroll (*Lorraine Kovacs*); Michael Bell (*Andy Kovacs*); Leigh Hughes (*Lee Ann Kovacs*); Lee Garlington (*Gertie*).

5743 Mandrake. (Pilot; Crime Drama; NBC; Jan. 24, 1979). During the twelfth century, wizards carried on the secrets of ancient Egypt and the magic of ancient China. When the hordes of Genghis Khan began to sweep the western world, they destroyed the wizards and their lore. The few who managed to escape established the College of Magic in a secret Tibetan valley wherein the lore was preserved.

It is modern times when a young boy (Mandrake), the lone survivor of a plane crash in the Himalayan Mountains, is found by Tibetan monks and brought to their secret valley. Mandrake is raised and taught the ancient magic by the wizard Theron. When it is time for Mandrake to leave, he is given a special amulet that endows him with special powers. He teams with his servant, Lothar and the proposal was to relate their efforts to use the power of magic to battle crime.

Cast: Anthony Herrera (*Mandrake*); Ji-Tu Cumbuka (*Lothar*); James Hong (*Lothar*); David Hollander (*Young Mandrake; flashbacks*).

5744 Mandrake the Magician. (Series; Adventure; Syn.; 1954). In a secret Tibetan Valley the lore and magic of ancient China is preserved. To ensure its existence, one youth is selected every decade and taught the ancient secrets. It is the 20th century when a young boy is brought to the mysterious valley by his father, a former graduate who has only a short time to live. Theron, the Master of Magic, teaches the young boy, Mandrake, the ancient secrets. Soon, Mandrake becomes greater than his masters. When it comes time for Mandrake to leave, he teams with is servant, Lothar, and together they set out on a crusade against evil. Stories relate their adventures as they use their magical abilities to help people in trouble. Based on the stories by Lee Falk and Phil Davis.

Cast: Coe Norton (*Mandrake*); Woody Strode (*Lothar*).

5745 Manhattan Honeymoon. (Series; Game; ABC; 1954). Three engaged or married couples are first interviewed and then compete in a series of general knowledge question-and-answer rounds. The highest-scoring couple receives an expenses-paid honeymoon in New York City.

Hostess: Neva Patterson.

5746 Manhattan Showcase. (Series; Variety; CBS; 1949). Performances by undiscovered, aspiring talent.

Host: Johnny Downs. **Assistant:** Helen Gallagher. **Music:** The Tony Mottola Trio.

5747 The Manhattan Transfer. (Series; Variety; CBS; 1975). A nostalgic program that recalls the music, songs and dances of the 1930s and '40s.

Host: The Manhattan Transfer (*Tim Hauser, Laurel Masse, Alan Paul and Janis Seigel*). **Regulars:** Archie Hahn, Fayette Hauser, Laraine Newman, Leland Palmer. **Orchestra** Ira Newborn.

5748   *Manhunt.* (Series; Crime Drama; Syn.; 1959). Howard Finucane is a lieutenant with the San Diego Police Department. Ben Andrews is a police reporter for *The San Diego Dispatch*. Stories follow their cases as they team to solve crimes.

Cast: Victor Jory *(Howard Finucane)*; Patrick McVey *(Ben Andrews)*; Charles Bateman *(Det. George Peters)*; Rian Garrick *(Det. Bruce Hanna)*; Chuck Henderson *(Det. Dan Kramer)*; Michael Steffany *(Det. Paul Kirk)*; Robert Crawford *(Det. Phil Burns)*; Todd Armstrong *(Det. Carl Spencer)*.

5749   *Manhunt.* (Series; Game; UPN; 2001). Thirteen players, called the prey, appear opposite three hunters on a remote South Pacific island. To win money, the players must avoid being "shot" by the hunters. Each of the players must appear at specific locations without being detected by a hunter. If a player is "shot" by a hunter (via a paint ball) he is eliminated. The first player to overcome the numerous obstacles of reaching the final destination wins.

Program Open: "On a remote island in the South Pacific, three relentless predators are on the hunt. Their prey: thirteen men and women together in a group. They have six days to cross 50 miles in a treacherous journey and claim a quarter of a million dollars in cash. In the end, only one can emerge victorious in this most dangerous game."

Host: John Cena.

5750   *Manhunt: The Search for America's Most Gorgeous Male Model.* (Series; Reality; Bravo; 2004). A group of handsome men who feel they have what it takes to become a top model compete in a series of modeling challenges based on *America's Next Top Model*. The one contender deemed the most worthy by a panel of judges wins (Jon Johnson won).

Hostess: Carmen Electra.

5751   *Manhunter.* (Series; Crime Drama; CBS; 1974–1975). Cleary County, Idaho, during the public enemy days of the Depression (1934) is the setting. It is here that James and Mary Barrett and their children, Dave and Lizabeth live. Dave is skilled with a gun and has chosen a career path that does not sit well with his family: that of a bounty hunter. Stories detail his work as he assists law enforcement officers by tracking down criminals for their offered rewards. Paul Hogan is the local sheriff; Dave's dog is Beau. In the pilot episode, Shirley O'Hara played Lizabeth Barrett.

Cast: Ken Howard *(Dave Barrett)*; Hilary Thompson *(Lizabeth Barrett)*; Ford Rainey *(James Barrett)*; Claudia Bauer *(Mary Barrett)*; Robert Hogan *(Sheriff Paul Hogan)*.

5752   *Maniac Mansion.* (Series; Comedy; Family Channel; 1990–1992). Maniac Mansion is a large home with a rather unusual "rock" in the basement — an active meteor. Dr. Fred Edison and his family inherited the mansion and stories follow their efforts to cope with all the unusual incidents that occur because of the meteor (which has changed Harry, Fred's brother-in-law, into a fly with a human head; and Turner, his 4-year-old son, into a hulking six-foot giant). Fred is married to Casey; Ike and Tina are their other children; Idella is Harry's wife.

Cast: Joe Flaherty *(Dr. Fred Edison)*; Deborah Theaker *(Casey Edison)*; Kathleen Robinson *(Tina Edison)*; Avi Phillips *(Ike Edison)*; George Buza *(Turner Edison)*; John Hemphill *(Harry)*; Mary Charlotte Wilcox *(Idella)*.

5753   *Manimal.* (Series; Adventure; NBC; 1983). Jonathan Chase is a professor of behavioral science at New York University who helps the police solve crimes as a member of the Special Investigative Division of the N.Y.P.D. (also called the Special Police Task Force). Chase, described as "wealthy, young and handsome," is also "champion of the world's darkest mysteries" — secrets of transmutation that divide animal from man — and man from animal, that he uses to help him defeat evil.

The secret of transmutation is not revealed. In the opening theme it is briefly shown that Jonathan's father (Don Knight) had traveled the world to learn the secret. It was in Africa that his quest came to an end. After being taught the powers by an unknown tribe, he passed the secret on to Jonathan when he was a young boy. No further information is given.

Jonathan now lives in a brownstone on Manhattan's Lower East Side. As himself, Jonathan has a gift of super hearing; as the animals he becomes, he not only possesses their appearance and abilities, he retains his own thinking processes to control his actions. For Jonathan to become an animal he must think about an animal. Jonathan most often becomes a black panther (to spy on criminals) and a hawk (to follow suspects from the air). While the special effects are quite good, the same two sequences are used in each episode (the film is simply reversed to show Jonathan becoming human).

Brooke McKenzie is Jonathan's partner, a police detective with the Special Task Force. She is aware of Jonathan's power (he transformed into the panther to save her life) and has vowed to keep his secret. Tyrone C. "Ty" Earll is Jonathan's friend, a former corporal during the Vietnam War, who now assists him. He too is aware of Jonathan's secret and calls Jonathan "J.C."

Cast: Simon MacCorkindale *(Jonathan Chase)*; Melody Anderson *(Brooke McKenzie)*; Glynn Thurman, Michael D. Roberts *(Tyrone Earll)*; Reni Santoni *(Lt. Nick Rivera)*. **Narrator:** William Conrad.

5754   *Mann and Machine.* (Series; Crime Drama; NBC; 1992). It is "the near future" in Los Angeles and a time when manmade robots assist live police officers in upholding the law. Sergeant Eve Madison, a highly sophisticated and beautiful robot, is such a creation — and the partner of Bobby Mann, an L.A.P.D. detective whose former partner, Warner, was "a bucket of bolts lab-created robot" that was put out of commission by a bullet.

Eve was created through the Artificial Intelligence Program by Dr. Anna Kepler. Eve's body is a combination of plastic compounds and alloy metals. Her brain functions like the human brain and is capable of assimilating artificial material. Eve is the prototype for a project called the Protector, "the future partner of every police officer." Eve is highly advanced in technical terms, but emotionally she is very young (the age of a seven-year-old girl). She has the deductive reasoning of Sherlock Holmes and a genuine sense of humor (she will laugh if she hears something she thinks is funny). Eve eats, sleeps and daydreams. Her eyes are capable of emitting laser beams; her tears are a lubricant and she can speak 40 languages. But the only way Eve can really grow is to experience life — "the good, the bad and the ugly of it." Eve's brain downloads directly to the advanced A.I. Work Station Computer in her apartment (1407 at the Metropolitan Hotel).

Eve believes she was built for only one purpose: to enforce the law. She says, "I'm an information specialist. There isn't a mainframe in the country that I can't access." When first built, Eve was transferred to the San Francisco Bay area (she was created in Danville in the Silicone Valley) and teamed with Bobby (who has to fill out a special report on Eve's actions after each case; they are with the Metropolitan Police Department). Captain Margaret Claghorn is their superior.

Cast: Yancy Butler *(Eve Madison)*; David Andrews *(Bobby Mann)*; S. Epatha Merkerson *(Capt. Margaret Claghorn)*.

5755   *Mannix.* (Series; Crime Drama; CBS; 1967–1975). In the original format (1967-68) Joe Mannix is an investigator for Intertect, a computerized private detective organization headed by Lou Wickersham. The remainder of the series finds the rugged, two-fisted, prone to violence detective, leaving Intertect to strike out on his own as a private detective (working independently from his home at 17 Paseo Verde in Los Angeles). He hires a secretary (Peggy Fair, who occasionally assists him in the field) and helps (and receives help from) L.A.P.D. lieutenants Arthur Malcolm, Adam Tobias and Daniel Ives. Toby Fair is Peggy's young son.

Joe, the son of an American vineyard worker, was a lieutenant in the Air Force during the Korean War. He is a graduate of Western California University (class of 1955) and acquired a private investigator's license a year later. He also possesses a black belt in karate and plays golf to stay fit. Scotch is his favorite drink.

Cast: Mike Connors (*Joe Mannix*); Joseph Campanella (*Lou Wickersham*); Gail Fisher (*Peggy Fair*); Ward Wood (*Lt. Arthur Malcolm*); Robert Reed (*Lt. Adam Tobias*); Jack Ging (*Lt. Daniel Ives*); Mark Stewart (*Toby Fair*).

5756 *MANswers*. (Series; Comedy; Spike TV; 2007–). Comical, if not at times absurd responses to questions that border on the ridiculous (for example, "Who is the richest bitch in America?," "What is the world's smallest legal bikini?" and "What country's armed forces pays for fake boobs?").

Narrator: Matt Short. **Music:** Shawn K. Clement.

5757 *M.A.N.T.I.S.* (Series; Adventure; Fox; 1994-1995). Dr. Miles Hawkins, a biochemist and owner of Hawkins Laboratories, is the third richest man in Ocean City, California (locale later changed to Port Columbia). He grew up in the Lincoln Heights section of the city and graduated from M.I.T. at the age of 18 on a genius scholarship. During the Los Angeles riots of 1991, Miles was shot in the back and crippled by a cop who opposed his beliefs. Miles, however, was unable to prove he was shot by a police officer because the bullet taken from his back is found not to come from a police issued gun. Embittered, the wheelchair bound Miles chose to fight back by waging a war on crime. With the help of his colleague, Dr. John Stonebreak, they created the Hornet (later called the Exo-Skeleton), a black suit that gives him a bug-like appearance, but enables him to walk. In technical terms, the suit is a M.A.N.T.I.S. (Mechanically Augmented Neuro Transmitter Interception System) and with the calling card of the praying mantis, Miles brings criminals to justice as the mysterious Mantis. As the Mantis, Miles will not use a gun (because of what happened to him). His weapon of choice is a paralyzing dart to stop enemies in their tracks ("They thaw out in an hour").

Beneath Hawkins Labs (also called Hawkins Technologies) is the Seapod, an undersea lab Miles built for ocean farming before he was shot, that now serves as his secret base of operations. His modes of transportation are the *Chrysalid* (a ship) and his black car, the Mantis. Unlike the Green Hornet, who was wanted by the police, Mantis works with them (especially Lieutenant Leora Maxwell of the Special Investigation Unit of the Port Columbia Police Department).

Miles was originally assisted by Dr. Amy Ellis, the associate medical director of the Ocean City Police Department. Yuri Barnes is the newscaster for KNCW-TV, Channel 8, who not only reports on Mantis activities, but helps Miles with vital information. Taylor Savidge, a messenger boy for Iron Horse Couriers, is also Miles's legman. When asked who he is, Miles (as Mantis) responds simply "Just one man trying to help."

Cast: Carl Lumbly (*Dr. Miles Hawkins*); Gina Torres (*Dr. Amy Ellis*); Bobby Hosea (*Yuri Barnes*); Christopher Gartin (*Taylor Savidge*); Galyn Gorg (*Leora Maxwell*).

5758 *Mantrap*. (Series; Discussion; Syn.; 1971). One male guest, representing a topic of current interest, appears and sits opposite a panel of three women. Both sides state their opinions then debate the issue.

Host: Al Hamel. **Panelists:** Phyllis Kirk, Meredith MacRae, Jaye P. Morgan, Carol Wayne, Selma Diamond.

5759 *Many Happy Returns*. (Series; Comedy; CBS; 1964-1965). "Every customer is a satisfied customer" is the policy of Krockmeyer's Department Store in Los Angeles. The store's object is "not to accept returns. Talk customers into actually believing the object they are returning is what they actually need."

Walter Burnley is the man hired by Owen Sharp, the store owner, to manage the Adjustments and Refunds Department and follow his rule. Walter is a man who talked a cop out of giving him a ticket for driving the wrong way on a one way street, going through a red light and driving on the sidewalk. He's good, but when it comes to managing his department, he finds it one of the biggest challenges of his life. Lynn Hall, Joseph ("Joe") Foley and Wilma Fritter are his annoying staff.

Lynn is very pretty, but something of a dizzy blonde. She can handle the job, but irritates Walter by using her telephone extension for more personal calls than business calls. Joe is not too bright, has trouble spelling, is forgetful and can't handle a customer with a complaint. Wilma is "the old biddie" who is a combination of both Lynn and Joe and seems to have been working at the store since before it was even built.

Walter, a widower, lives in an apartment at 50 Chestnut Street. His daughter, Joan Randall, her husband, Bob Randall, and their daughter, Laurie Randall, live at 609 North Elm Street — just a short distance from his nephew, Ralph Conway, his wife, Ellen Braddock, and their son, Jimmy, who live at 629 North Elm Street. Walter's involvement with their problems is also depicted. Don Beddoe appeared as Mr. Krockmeyer, the store owner.

Cast: John McGiver (*Walter Burnley*); Elinor Donahue (*Joan Randall*); Mark Goddard (*Bob Randall*); Andrea Sacino (*Laurie Randall*); Elena Verdugo (*Lynn Hall*); Mickey Manners, Richard Collier (*Joe Foley*); Jesslyn Fax (*Wilma Fritter*); Jerome Cowan (*J.L. Fox*); Russell Collins (*Owen Sharp*).

5760 *The Many Loves of Arthur*. (Pilot; Comedy; NBC; May 23, 1978). Dr. Arthur Murdock, a zoo veterinarian who becomes emotionally attached to the animals he treats, often finds it easier to relate to them than to humans. The proposal was to follow Arthur as he finds treating animals a way to help him understand his own problems and those of the people around him. Gail Corbett, Arthur's assistant, would like him to notice her; Dr. Chase is their superior.

Cast: Richard Masur (*Arthur Murdock*); Caroline McWilliams (*Gail Corbett*); David Dukes (*Dr. Chase*).

5761 *The Many Loves of Dobie Gillis*. (Series; Comedy; CBS; 1959-1960). The first season title for what would eventually become *Dobie Gillis*. See this title for information.

5762 *Maple Town*. (Pilot; Cartoon; Syn.; April 13, 1987). The magical land of Maple Town is the setting for a proposed series about the adventures of Patty Rabbit, her family (Mama, Papa and Rachel Rabbit) and her friends, Freddie Fox, Skippy Squirrel, Danny Dog, Bobby Bear and Fanny Fox.

Live Action Host: Janice Adams. **Voices:** Jeff Iwai, Wayne Kerr, Heidi Lenard, Bibi Linet, Lou Pitt, Alice Smith, John Zahler.

5763 *Marblehead Manor*. (Series; Comedy; Syn.; 1987-1988). The luxurious mansion located at 14 Sunflower Lane (city not identified) is called Marblehead Manor. It is owned by the eccentric millionaire Randolph Stonehill and his gorgeous, level-headed wife, Hilary. Randolph is the owner of a company called Stonehill, Inc. (exactly what they do is not said). Hilary is over 40 years old and her fabulous figure still turns men's heads. She has a dog named Albert (whom she named after their ever faithful butler, Albert Dudley). Albert is a third generation butler to a third generation of Stonehills.

Lupe Lopez is the manor's sexy cook and maid and the single mother of a young son (Elvis). Rick is the inept, misadventure-prone estate gardener.

Carol Bruce appeared as Randolph's mother, Margaret Stonehill. In the original pilot episode (shown as the last episode of the series), Charo played Cookie, the ultra sexy maid. Dan Foliart and Howard Pearl composed the theme, "It's a Grand Life."

Cast: Linda Thorson (*Hilary Stonehill*); Bob Fraser (*Randolph Stonehill*); Paxton Whitehead (*Albert Dudley*); Dyana Ortelli (*Lupe Lopez*); Michael Richards (*Rick*); Humberto Ortiz (*Elvis Lopez*).

5764   *March of Time Through the Years.* (Series; Documentary; ABC; 1951–1952). Screenings of old "March of Time" theatrical newsreels.

Host: John Daly. **Narrator:** Westbrook Van Voorhis.

5765   *Marcus Welby, M.D.* (Series; Drama; ABC; 1969–1976). Marcus Welby is an elderly general practitioner who, after suffering a heart attack, decides to lighten his workload by taking on a younger assistant, Dr. Steven Kiley.

Marcus is the wise, kindly physician who still believes in making house calls; Steven is the eager doctor who finds that his years of medical study need the supplementary experience only a man like Marcus can provide. Together, they attempt to treat people as individuals in an age of specialized medicine and uncaring physicians. Marcus and Steven reside in Santa Monica, California, and work part time at Lang Memorial Hospital.

Other regulars are Consuelo Lopez, their nurse; Nurse Kathleen Faverty; Janet Blake, the hospital public relations lady who married Steven (on Oct. 21, 1975); Myra Sherwood, Marcus's romantic interest; Sandy Porter, Marcus's married daughter (Marcus is a widower); Phil Porter, Sandy's husband; Phil Jr., Sandy's son. Penny Santon played Consuelo Lopez in the pilot. See also *The Return of Marcus Welby, M.D.*

Cast: Robert Young (*Marcus Welby*); James Brolin (*Steven Kiley*); Elena Verdugo (*Consuelo Lopez*); Sharon Gless (*Kathleen Faverty*); Pamela Hensley (*Janet Blake*); Anne Baxter (*Myra Sherwood*); Anne Schedeen (*Sandy Porter*); Terry Kiser (*Phil Porter*); Gavin Brandon (*Phil Porter, Jr.*); Alan Hale, Jr. (*Steven's Father*).

5766   *The Marge and Gower Champion Show.* (Series; Comedy; CBS; 1957). Marge and Gower Champion are a real-life husband and wife who are also real-life professional dancers. Stories, based on incidents in their lives, follow their mishaps as they attempt to establish and live a life apart from the hectic demands of show business. Cozy is their friend, a drummer.

Cast: Marge Champion (*Herself*); Gower Champion (*Himself*); Jack Whiting (*Marge's father*); Buddy Rich (*Cozy*); Peg LaCentra (*Amanda*); Barbara Perry (*Miss Weatherly*).

5767   *Marge and Jeff.* (Series; Comedy; DuMont; 1953–1954). New York City is the setting for a peek into the lives of Marge and Jeff Green, a young newlywed couple struggling to survive the difficult first years of marriage. The Green's have a dog-named Paisley.

Cast: Marge Green (*Marge Green*); Jeff Cain (*Jeff Green*).

5768   *Margie.* (Series; Comedy; ABC; 1961–1962). Madison is a small town of the 1920s. It is charming, peaceful and seemingly far removed from the wild and reckless happenings of the larger cities of the era. It is here that the Claytons live: parents Harvey and Nora and their children Margie and Cornell.

Margie is a teenager and a student at Madison High School (where she is the editor of the paper, the *Madison Bugle*). She is pretty, dresses in the latest non-flapper attire and has a tendency to be a do-gooder whose intentions always seem to backfire and cause more problems than she anticipated. Crawford's Ice Cream Parlor is the after school hangout and Margie's closest friends are Maybelle Jackson, Heywood Botts and Johnny Green. Heywood is Margie's on and off again awkward boyfriend; Maybelle is a stunning girl caught up in the world outside of Madison who fancies herself as a Flapper.

Harvey, a loan officer at the Great Eastern Savings Bank, and Nora are understanding parents whose efforts to control Margie's enthusiasm is not always successful. Phoebe is Margie's aunt. Lionel Newman composed the theme adaptation of the 1920s song "Margie."

Cast: Cynthia Pepper (*Margie Clayton*); Dave Willock (*Harvey Clayton*); Wesley Thackitt (*Nora Clayton*); Johnny Bangert (*Cornell Clayton*); Hollis Irving (*Phoebe Clayton*); Tommy Ivo (*Heywood Botts*); Penny Parker (*Maybell Jackson*); Richard Gering (*Johnny Green*); Maxine Stuart (*Mrs. Jackson*); Herb Ellis (*Mr. Jackson*).

5769   *Mariah.* (Series; Drama; ABC; 1987). Mariah is a small country town and the site of a huge maximum security prison. The lives of the people on both sides of the antiquated prison which houses 2,500 men and women are depicted. Regulars are the prison personnel: Deputy Superintendent Ned Sheffield; Dr. Deena Hertz, the psychologist; the Reverend Howard Bouchard; Superintendent James Malone; and corrections officer Lede Cervantes; and the town residents: Brandis LaSalle, Maggie Malone (James's wife), Linda Grancato and Father Timothy Quinlan.

Cast: John Getz (*Ned Sheffield*); Tovah Feldshuh (*Deena Hertz*); William Allen Young (*Howard Bouchard*); Philip Baker Hall (*James Malone*); Wanda DeJesus (*Leda Cervantes*); Kathleen Layman (*Brandis LaSalle*); Susan Brown (*Maggie Malone*); Renne Lippin (*Linda Grancato*); Chris Wiggins (*Timothy Quinlan*).

5770   *Marie.* (Pilot; Comedy; ABC; Dec. 1, 1979). With a dream of furthering her career as a Broadway dancer, Marie Owens leaves her home in Nebraska and moves to New York City. She enrolls in the Carla Coburn Dance Academy and finds an apartment at 368 West 17th Street (which she shares with her new-found friends, K.C. and Sandra). The proposal was to relate Marie's misadventures as she struggles for that big break but encounters setback after setback. Edgar is Marie's landlord; Pancho is Marie's neighbor.

Cast: Marie Osmond (*Marie Owens*); Ellen Travolta (*Carla Coburn*); Telma Hopkins (*K.C. Jones*); Zan Charisse (*Sandra*); Bruce Kirby, Sr. (*Edgar Merton*); Tony Ramirez (*Pancho*).

5771   *Marie.* (Series; Variety; NBC; 1981). Singer-actress Marie Osmond headlines a program that spotlights her talents in musical performances as well her comedic abilities in short sketches.

Host: Marie Osmond. **Regulars:** Jeffrey Barron, Charles Graves, Charles Gray, Doris Hess, Jim Hudson, Debbie Ing, Howard Itkowitz, Shirley Mitchell, Scott Mullaney, Melissa Multray, Greg Norberg, Kathy Primby, Nancy Steen, Steve Stucker, The Lester Wilson Dancers. **Orchestra:** George Wyle.

5772   *Marie.* (Pilot; Talk; Unaired; Produced for Syn. in 2009). A daily talk show featuring celebrity interviews and issues of importance to women.

Hostess: Marie Osmond.

5773   *The Marie Eve, George Lloyd Show.* (Experimental;

Variety; NBC; June 16, 1939). Performances by international night club performers: singer Marie Eve and mimic George Lloyd. The program, broadcast from the Gaumont British projection room in New York City, features Marie performing two French songs and George mimicking a tea leaf reader faking a trance and a man struggling to eat a peanut butter sandwich.

5774   Marilu. (Series; Variety; Syn.; 1994). Actress Marilu Henner hosts a daily program of celebrity interviews and discussions of topical issues with appropriate guests.

Host: Marilu Henner.

5775   The Marilyn McCoo and Billy Davis, Jr., Show. (Series; Variety; CBS; 1977). The husband and wife team of Marilyn McCoo and Billy Davis, Jr., host a program of music, songs and light comedy.

Hosts: Marilyn McCoo, Billy Davis, Jr. **Regulars:** Jay Leno, Tim Reid, Lewis Arquette. **Orchestra:** John Myles.

5776   Marine Boy. (Series; Cartoon; Syn.; 1966). A very special boy, called Marine Boy, possesses the ability to breathe underwater by a special chewing gum called Oxy-gum and is able to swim with his propeller boots. He works on behalf of the Ocean Patrol and is assisted in his battle against evil by Bolton and Piper, pilots of the submarine *P-1*.

Other regulars are Neptina, a topless mermaid (her flowing hair covers her breasts) who can foresee the future (through a magic pearl necklace she wears); Splasher, the unit's dolphin; Professor Fumble, the unit's scientist; and Dr. Mariner, the head of the foundation.

Voice Cast: Corinne Orr (*Marine Boy/Neptina/Cli Cli*); Jack Grimes (*Prof. Fumble/Splasher*); Peter Fernandez (*Piper/Dr. Mariner*); Jack Curtis (*Bolton*).

5777   Mario Lopez: Saved by the Baby. (Series; Reality; VH-1; 2010). Former *Saved by the Bell* co-star Mario Lopez and his wife, Courtney Mazzo, are profiled as they prepare to become parents for the first time.

5778   Mark Saber. (Series; Crime Drama; ABC; 1951–1954). Mark Saber is a plainclothes detective with the Homicide Division of the New York City Police Department. He is tough when he has to be — and fair when he has to be (although he is a bit tough on criminals). Stories relate his case investigations. Originally titled *Mystery Theater* (then *Homicide Squad*, which comprises episodes from 1951–1954; and *The Vise*).

Cast: Tom Conway (*Mark Saber*); James Burke (*Sgt. Tim Maloney*).

5779   Marker. (Series; Drama; UPN; 1995). Richard DeMorra has received a strange inheritance from his late father: markers that he had given to people in his past that helped him achieve success in the rose gardening business in Hawaii (the markers were a promise to repay the favor if it were in his power). To trace his father's legacy and repay those people, Richard uses the markers as a guide and stories relate what happens as he tries to repay the debt. Kimba is Richard's step-mother (his father's much younger wife); Andy is Richard's friend.

Cast: Richard Grieco (*Richard De Morra*); Gates McFadden (*Kimba*); Danny Kahala (*Andy Bumatai*); Shaun Damas (*Young Richard; flashbacks*).

5780   Markham. (Series; Crime Drama; CBS; 1959–1960). Roy Markham is a criminal attorney based in Los Angeles, California. He works for John Riggs, is tough, likes to do his own investigating and will tackle any case as long as he believes his clients are telling him the truth; if they lie, he drops them as a client. Stories relate his case investigations.

Cast: Ray Milland (*Roy Markham*); Simon Scott (*John Riggs*).

5781   Marlo and the Magic Movie Machine. (Series; Children; CBS; 1977–1981). L. Dullo Computer is a company located in the basement of a building in New York City. It is here that a lone computer operator, Marlo Higgins, has secretly perfected the Magic Movie Machine, a computer that can talk, tell jokes and relate a variety of films. Acting as a disc jockey, Marlo and his computer present entertainment geared to children.

Cast: Laurie Faso (*Marlo Higgins*); Mert Hoplin (*Movie Machine Voice*).

5782   Marlowe. (Pilot; Crime Drama; Unaired; Produced for ABC in 2006). An update of author Raymond Chandler's classic detective, Philip Marlowe that literally takes him from the past and propels him into the current day life of Los Angeles. Marlowe is a tough, two-fisted private investigator who believes a case isn't over until justice is served — even if the check bounces. Jessica, a gorgeous girl who is as hard-headed as Marlow, is his Girl Friday.

Cast: Jason O'Mara (*Philip Marlowe*); Amanda Righetti (*Jessica Reede*).

5783   The Marriage. (Series; Comedy; NBC; 1954). Ben Marriott, an attorney with the firm of Burns and Marriott, and his wife, Liz, a former buyer for Hunt's Department Store, live at 31 West 43rd Street in Manhattan. They are the parents of Emily and Peter. Ben's biggest challenge is to balance the checkbook. Emily is not permitted to eat chocolate ice cream (Liz says "It's bad for your skin"). She attends Grant High School and her at home dates consist of "listening to the phonograph and popping corn." Peter likes building antique model cars and reading comic books while taking a bath. The family heirloom is a bible that has been handed down from their grandfather. Stories relate the simple, trying times that test the family's efforts to overcome problems. Based on the radio series (NBC, 1953-54) of the same title.

Cast: Hume Cronyn (*Ben Marriott*); Jessica Tandy (*Liz Marriott*); Susan Strasberg (*Emily Marriott*); Malcolm Broderick (*Peter Marriott*).

5784   A Marriage. (Pilot; Drama; Unaired; Produced for CBS in 2009). Noah and Abby Gabriel are a happily married couple. They are the parents of Maddy and Josh and the proposal was to portray "a marriage that works."

Cast: Bruce Greenwood (*Noah Gabriel*); Miranda Otto (*Abby Gabriel*); Kay Panabaker (*Maddy Gabriel*); Nick Eversman (*Josh Gabriel*).

5785   Marriage A La Mode. (Experimental; Comedy; DuMont; Aug. 28, 1946). A comedy skit about a couple on the verge of divorce who are reunited through an argument with another couple who had come to their home with the intention of buying it after the divorce. An attempt to plug articles sold in the Wanamakers Department Store (where the DuMont studios were located). The idea was to showcase items before, during and after the play.

Cast: John Graham, Madeline Kalleen, Fran Lee, Arthur Page.

5786   The Marriage Broker. (Pilot; Comedy-Drama; CBS; June 12, 1957). When her husband is stolen by another woman, Mae Sweeney begins a matrimonial bureau to pair off lonely hearts for a fee. The proposal, based on the 1952 feature film, *The Model and the Marriage Broker*, was to focus on the changes that occur in the lives of the people Mae matches to each other. Broadcast as a segment of *The 20th Century-Fox Hour*.

Cast: Glenda Farrell *(Mae Sweeney)*.

5787   *Marriage Is Alive and Well.* (Pilot; Anthology; NBC; Jan. 25, 1980). Incidents in the lives of married couples as seen through the eyes of Bryan Fish, a wedding photographer, and his wife, Sarah.

Cast: Joe Namath *(Bryan Fish)*; Susan Sullivan *(Sarah Fish)*.

5788   *The Marriage Ref.* (Series; Comedy; NBC; 2010). A comedy program that is presented like (and mistaken for) a reality series. A real life couple is seen discussing then arguing about a particular incident in their lives. Once the conversation has ended, the tape is shown to a panel of celebrities who then comically discuss the issue and side with either the husband or wife. After hearing the panel's opinions, the Marriage Ref rules for either side. The program is produced by comedian Jerry Seinfeld who, in his first series *(Seinfeld)*, humorously showed the relatable situations facing singles in New York City. Here, he is presenting a revealing series about "the unpredictable and hilarious institution we call marriage."

Host/Marriage Ref: Tom Papa. **Regular Panelist:** Kelly Ripa.

5789   *Married by America.* (Series; Reality; Fox; 2003). Five singles, successful in everything but finding a mate, are matched by relation experts to people of the opposite sex. As the newly formed couple get to know each other, toll free telephone numbers are supplied for viewers to say whether or not the couple are right for each other and whether or not the relationship will lead to marriage.

Host: Sean Valentine.

5790   *Married Not Dead.* (Pilot; Comedy; Unaired; Produced for ABC in 2009). Jessica and Rob are a married couple with children who feel that the romance has gone out of their life. Being parents is rewarding for them, but with each also having a career, they actually spend little time together. The proposal follows Jessica and Rob as they seek a way to bring the romance back into their lives. Christine and Jay are their friends; Susan and Janey are Jessica's children.

Cast: Leah Remini *(Jessica)*; Matthew Lillard *(Rob)*; Kathleen Rose Perkins *(Christine)*; Shaun Majumder *(Jay)*; Janet Varney *(Susan)*; Sam Schuder *(Janey)*.

5791   *Married People.* (Series; Comedy; ABC; 1990-1991). A domestic comedy about incidents in the lives of three married couples who live in a three-family home at 862 Central Park North (at 73rd Street) in New York City. The rent is $500 a month, and the house is a brownstone that is actually located in Harlem — but the tenants prefer to call it "Central Park North" after the street sign on the corner.

Nick and Olivia Williams, a black couple in their fifties, own the building (they live in Apartment 1) and have been married for 32 years. Nick's Fruits and Vegetables is the name of the store Nick operates and has owned for 23 years.

Occupying Apartment 2 are Elizabeth and Russell Meyers, a white couple in their thirties who met in college and married after graduation. Elizabeth is 36 years old, attended Yale University and now works as an attorney for the Wall Street law firm of Michaelson and Michaelson; Elizabeth later adds her name to the firm when she becomes a partner. Russell is a freelance writer who has penned articles for *TV Guide* and the *New Yorker* magazine. He later acquires a monthly column for *Manhattan Life* magazine called "The Worst of New York" (wherein he reviews ten worst things each month). He attended the Columbia School of Journalism and Elizabeth says she

is "36 but looks 32; Russell is 37 but looks 42." When the series began, Elizabeth was already pregnant; in the episode of Nov. 14, 1990, she gave birth to a son she and Russell name Max.

Apartment 3 is rented by Cynthia ("Cindy") Campbell and her husband, Allen, a young white couple (18 years old) from Mineral Wells, Indiana, who moved to New York so Allen could attend Columbia University. Cindy, a cheerleader in high school who has aspirations of becoming a dancer, works as a waitress at the East Side Diner. Allen works after classes in the school's lab; Cindy is extremely jealous of Izzy (Elizabeth Berkley), Allen's gorgeous lab partner at school (her real name is Isabel). Cindy's co-worker at the diner is Madeline (Andrea Elson).

Cast: Bess Armstrong *(Elizabeth Meyers)*; Jay Thomas *(Russell Meyers)*; Barbara Montgomery *(Olivia Williams)*; Ray Aranha *(Nick Williams)*; Megan Gallivan *(Cindy Campbell)*; Chris Young *(Allen Campbell)*.

5792   *Married: The First Year.* (Series; Drama; CBS; 1979). A chronicle of the courtship and marriage of teenagers Billy Baker and Joanna Huffman, and their struggles to survive the difficult first year of marriage. Other regulars are Barbara, Joanna's mother; Mike, Barbara's ex-husband; Cheryl, Mike's second wife; Jennifer, Joanna's sister; Cathy and Bert, Billy's parents; Millie, Billy's sister; Emily, Cathy's sister; Sharon and Cookie, Joanna's friends; and Tom, Billy's friend.

Cast: Leigh McCloskey *(Billy Baker)*; Cindy Grover *(Joanna Baker)*; Claudette Nevins *(Barbara Huffman)*; Joshua Bryant *(Mike Huffman)*; Constance McCashin *(Cheryl Huffman)*; Tracy Justrich *(Jennifer Huffman)*; K Callan *(Cathy Baker)*; Stanley Grover *(Bert Baker)*; Jennifer McAllister *(Millie Baker)*; Christine Belford *(Emily Gorey)*; Stepfanie Kramer *(Sharon Kelly)*; Gee Gee Vorgan *(Cookie Levin)*; Gary Epp *(Tom Liberatore)*.

5793   *Married to the Kellys.* (Series; Comedy; ABC; 2003-2004). Susan Kelly is a young woman who was born in Kansas City, Kansas, but moved to New York City to get away from her possessive family (whom she felt were smothering her). It is here that she meets (and later married) Tom Wagner, a novelist.

After being separated from her family for a time, Susan begins to miss them — "The Kelly family is like an echo system and any small change can cause a ripple." Susan wants to be near her family again and convinces Tom to return to Kansas City with her. He agrees — and is sorry he did when he meets her eccentric family — Bill and Sandy, Susan's parents; Lewis, the babied brother; and Mary, her older sister (who is married to the henpecked Chris). Bill works for the Social Security Administration. He calls Sandy "Mother" and constantly talks about the weather. Sandy is a coupon clipper and constantly worries about her family's eating habits. Mary teaches sociology at college and knits while watching TV. She is very demanding and the total boss of Chris (who lives in fear of her). Chris works for a greeting card company. He likes to smoke cigars but Mary won't let him, so he smokes pretend cigars.

Twenty-one year-old Lewis is still considered a baby by his mother (she still buys his clothes); he has an uncanny interest in insects and is studying entomology at college.

Tom wrote the book *Eight Million Stories* and dreams of writing for *New Yorker* magazine. Susan works as a hostess at Marino's Restaurant. Stories follow Tom as he struggles to adjust to Susan's family — and suggest changes to make them more like a normal family.

Cast: Breckin Meyer *(Tom Wagner)*; Kiele Sanchez *(Susan Wagner)*; Sam Anderson *(Bill Kelly)*; Emily Rutherfurd *(Mary)*; Nancy Lenehan *(Sandy Kelly)*; Josh Braaten *(Chris)*; Derek Waters *(Lewis Kelly)*; Richard Riehle *(Uncle Dave Kelly)*.

5794 *Married to the Mob.* (Pilot; Comedy; CBS; Aug. 7, 1989). Connie Russo is "Married to the Mob" but is not aware of it. Her husband, Tony, is a mobster and his efforts to keep his family from discovering his shady business dealings is the focal point of the unsold series. Other regulars are Nick, Tony's son; Marie, Connie's sister; Frank, Connie's father; and Tony's Mama Russo.

Cast: Richard Romanus (*Tony Russo*); Suzie Plakson (*Connie Russo*); Cynthia Stevenson (*Marie Bondo*); Cory Danziger (*Nick Russo*); Salem Ludwig (*Frank Salerno*); Gina DeAngelis (*Mama Russo*).

5795 *Married ... With Children.* (Series; Comedy; Fox; 1987–1997). At 9674 (also given as 9764) Jeopardy Lane in Chicago, Illinois, live the Bundy family: a husband (Al) who has a pathetic life; a wife (Peggy) who doesn't cook or clean but loves to spend Al's hard-earned money; their beautiful but dense daughter (Kelly); and their girl-crazy son (Bud) who can't get a date. The family dog is named Buck.

Al works as a shoe salesman for Garry's Shoes and Accessories for the Beautiful Woman in the New Market Mall. He attended James K. Polk High School (where he was voted Most Valuable Player of 1966. He made four touchdowns in one game and was offered a college scholarship; he turned it down to marry Peggy). Al believes his life was ruined when he met a fellow student named Margaret ("Peggy") Wanker at a hamburger joint named Johnny B. Goods. She was a sex kitten; Al was a guy. He let his hormones do his thinking for him, and he has been sorry ever since. He drives a run-down Dodge, his most cherished possession.

Peggy was born in Wanker County, a backwoods community that was founded by her ancestors. Peggy knows what will make Al happy, but she will never leave him. Although Peggy is a housewife, she never shops for food, cooks or cleans. Her days are spent watching television and eating Bon-Bons. Finding food has become the family's number one priority. To protect the way women treat men, Al forms NO MA'AM (The National Organization of Men Against Amazonian Masterhood).

Kelly, a blonde bombshell (typically dressed in tight jeans or tight miniskirt and low cut blouses) attends Polk High School. She was born in February ("I'm an aquarium") and says, "Working is a bummer; I'm glad I'm a pretty girl so I don't have to work," but she actually held several jobs. She started as the Weather Bunny Girl on Channel 83's *Action News* program but lost the job when she couldn't read the teleprompter. She was next a roller skating waitress at Bill's Hilltop Drive-In, then Miss Weenie Tots, a model who represented Weiner Tots (hot dogs wrapped in bread and fried in lard) at supermarkets.

After graduating from Polk High, Kelly chose to pursue a career as a model. Although Kelly got tension headaches from smiling, she was told she was a natural leg crosser ("I can do it at will"). She next hosted her own public access television program, *Vital Social Issues 'n' Stuff with Kelly*. With topics like "Slut of the Week," "Hunks" and "Bad Perms," the mythical NBS Network picked up the show (it was canceled when the vital issues became milk and books). When her modeling school closed, Kelly acquired a job at Chicago's TV World Theme Park. She was first the exit gate hostess, then the Verminator Girl (representing the environmentally safe insect killer)

Bud first attended Polk High School then Jermaine College. He has a crush on his next door neighbor, Marcy Rhoades and watches "Dateless Dude Late Night Theater" when he can't get a date. In 1991 Bud pretended to be the street rapper Grand Master B to impress girls and later worked for the Motor Vehicle Bureau before becoming Kelly's modeling agent.

Marcy Rhoades, the Bundys' neighbor, is a loan officer at the Kyoto National Bank. She was first married to Steve Bartholomew Rhoades, a loan officer at the Leading Bank of Chicago. When Steve lost his job he became a cage cleaner at Slither's Pet Emporium, then a ranger at Yosemite National Park (at which time he left Marcy and the series). Shortly after, while at a banking seminar in Las Vegas, Marcy becomes intoxicated and marries Jefferson D'Arcy at Clyde's No Blood Test Needed Chapel. Jefferson is a schemer and apparently married Marcy as a way to avoid working. After putting up with Al's nonsense for years, Marcy chose to battle Al's NO MA'AM organization and formed FANG (Feminists Against Neanderthal Guys). Griff is Al's co-worker; Gary, a woman, is the owner of the shoe store; Miranda Veracruz de la Jolla Cardinal is the local TV reporter. A recording of Frank Sinatra's "Love and Marriage" is used as the theme song.

Cast: Ed O'Neill (*Al Bundy*); Katey Sagal (*Peggy Bundy*); Christina Applegate (*Kelly Bundy*); David Faustino (*Bud Bundy*); Amanda Bearse (*Marcy Rhoades*); David Garrison (*Steve Rhoades*); Ted McGinley (*Jefferson D'Arcy*); Harold Sylvester (*Griff*); Janet Carol (*Gary*); Teresa Parente (*Miranda*).

5796 *Mars: Base One.* (Pilot; Comedy; Unaired; Produced for CBS in 1988). Incidents in the lives of the Ludlows, a family who are part of a pioneer group of earthlings attempting to colonize Mars. Doug Ludlow is the father, an easy-going chap who suffers from bouts of "Earth Sickness"; Ellen, his wife, is a sensible psychologist whose specialty is travelers who can't adjust to life on Mars; Brenda, their teenage daughter, finds it difficult adjusting to life, while their ten-year-old hellion son, Tyrone, has totally conformed to his new surroundings. Dixie, a stripper, her son, Nikki and brother, Mickie, are their annoying neighbors. Also inhabiting Mars: Base One is B.O.B., the environmental robot.

Cast: Tim Thomerson (*Doug Ludlow*); Nancy Youngblut (*Ellen Ludlow*); Christy Johnson (*Brenda Ludlow*); Jonathan Brandis (*Tyrone Ludlow*); Linda Thompson-Jenner (*Dixie*); Stephen Lee (*Nikki*); Dennis Burkley (*Mickie*); Marty Polio (*B.O.B.*).

5797 *Marsha Potter Gets a Life.* (Pilot; Comedy; Unaired; Produced for ABC in 2004). Marsha Potter is a 50-year-old woman facing the world alone. Her kids have grown and moved out of the house; she has just divorced her cheating husband; and she has decided to begin the business of independence. She acquires a small apartment and, even though she has no computer skills, her mothering instincts get her a job at a web design firm. Things are beginning to look up for Marsha and the proposal was to follow her as she learns to live on her own for the first time.

Cast: Brenda Blethyn (*Marsha Potter*); Jenna Von Oy (*Mary Ellen*); Derk Cheetwood (*George*); Michael McMillan (*Eddie*); Erin Hershey Presley (*Jane*).

5798 *The Marshal.* (Series; Crime Drama; ABC; 1995). When you need help you call the police; when the police need help they call the U.S. Marshal. Winston McBride is such a man, a Deputy U.S. Marshal who has vowed to never let a criminal get away.

Winston is married (to Sally) and the father of two girls (Katie and Molly). Winston is not a big fan of violence and would rather talk than fight. Stories follow Winston as he incorporates his unorthodox brand of justice to get the job done.

Cast: Jeff Fahey (*Winston McBride*); Patricia Harras (*Sally McBride*); Kristina Lewis (*Katie McBride*); Carly McKillip (*Molly McBride*); Dey Young (*Sally Caulfield-McBride*).

5799 *Marshal Dillon.* (Series; Western; CBS; 1955–1961). The syndicated title for half-hour episodes of *Gunsmoke* produced between 1955 and 1961. See *Gunsmoke* for information.

5800 *The Marshal of Gunsight Pass.* (Series; Western; ABC;

1950). Gunsight Pass is a growing town of the Old West (1860s) where law and order is upheld by a fearless U.S. Marshal. He is assisted by his deputy sidekick and stories, based on the radio program of the same title (and broadcast live from Los Angeles) follow events that occur in Gunsight Pass.

Cast: Russell Hayden (*Marshal*); Eddie Dean (*Marshal; replaced Russell*); Riley Hill (*Marhsal Riley Roberts; replaced Eddie*); Roscoe Ates (*Deputy*); Jane Adrian (*Ruth, Deputy's niece*); Burt Wenland (*Bud Glover*); Marshall Reed (*Larry Thomas*); Greg Roberts (*Carl Darby*).

5801 *The Marshall Chronicles.* (Series; Comedy; ABC; 1990). High school student Marshall Brightman lives with his parents Michael and Cynthia at 64 Gramercy Place in Manhattan. Michael is a private practice doctor, and Cynthia is a children's storybook editor for Fawn Publishing. Marshall attended P.S. 84 Grammar School and now takes the number 6 IRT subway train to his unidentified high school. Stories relate Marshall's activities at school, where he is intelligent but constantly put down.

Marshall's friends are Melissa Sandler and Sean Bickoff. Melissa is a member of the school's Quiz Bowl team; Sean reads the girlie magazine *Big Babes in Water*. Other students are Leslie Barash, Vincent and Johnny Parmetko. The school is called "our school" or just "the school."

Karen Medak played Johnny's sister, Donna; and Jack Wohl appeared as Leslie's father, Jack Barash. Randy Newman sings the theme, "Falling in Love."

Cast: Joshua Rifkind (*Marshall Brightman*); Steve Anderson (*Michael Brightman*); Jennifer Salt (*Cynthia Brightman*); Nile Lanning (*Melissa Sandler*); Bradley Gregg (*Sean Bickoff*); Meredith Scott Lynn (*Leslie Barash*); Todd Graff (*Vincent*); Gabriel Bologna (*Johnny Parmetko*).

5802 *Marsupilami.* (Series; Cartoon; CBS; 1993). The overall title for three animated shorts:

1. Marsupilami. Marsupilami, a purple jungle creature with spots, feels he needs to help others but often finds misadventure in doing so. He also has to be on the lookout for Eduardo, a suave jaguar who craves Marsupilami morsels for dinner. Norman and Maurice are his friends.

2. Sebastian. The further adventures of Sebastian the Crab (from the Disney movie *The Little Mermaid*) as he tackles life in the sea head on — from lifeguard to crab scout leader to bellhop.

3. Shnookums and Meat. Shnookums the cat and Meat the dog battle each other for leadership in the house in which they live with their human masters.

Voice Cast: Steve Mackall (*Marsupilami*); Samuel E. Wright (*Sebastian*); Frank Welker (*Meat*); Jason Marsden (*Shnookums*); Jim Cummings (*Norman/Maurice*); Steve Landesberg (*Eduardo*).

5803 *The Martha Raye Show.* (Series; Variety; NBC; 1954–1956). Comedienne Martha Raye hosts a program of music and songs coupled with vaudeville-like slapstick sketches.

Host: Martha Raye. **Regulars:** Rocky Graziano, The Martha Raye Dancers. **Orchestra:** Carl Hoff.

5804 *Martha Speaks.* (Series; Cartoon; PBS; 2008). Martha is a friendly dog who, after eating a bowl of Grandma's Alphabet Soup, finds that she suddenly has the ability to speak English. With her new found ability, Martha finds a new meaning to life and through her activities introduces various aspects of life to children.

Voice Cast: Tabitha St. Germain (*Martha*); Vanessa Tomasino (*Carolina*); Alex Ferris (*T.D.*).

5805 *Martha Stewart Living.* (Series; Variety; Syn.; 1991–2004). Home decorating and remodeling ideas, cooking segments, guests, interviews, gardening tips and anything else associated with the home and garden are presented on a daily basis by Martha Stewart. The program was revised in 2005 as *Martha*. It encompassed the same format and ran in syndication until 2010 (at which time it became a Hallmark Channel series).

Host: Martha Stewart.

5806 *The Martha Stewart Show.* (Series; Information; Hallmark; 2010–). Domestic Diva Martha Stewart presents how to projects, cooking segments, gardening tips, scrap booking, decoupage and hand-making gift ideas.

Host: Martha Stewart.

5807 *The Martha Wright Show.* (Series; Variety; ABC; 1954). Singer Martha Wright hosts a program of music and songs under the sponsorship of Packard automobiles and also known as *The Packard Showroom*.

Host: Martha Wright. **Regulars:** The Norman Paris Chorus. **Music:** Bobby Hackett.

5808 *Martial Law.* (Series; Crime Drama; CBS; 1998–2000). Crime solving, comical overtones and karate combine to present a most unusual look at the justice system through Sammo Law, a detective from Hong Kong who is on loan to the Los Angeles Police Department.

Sammo doesn't believe in using guns, but does believe in violence and uses his mastery as a karate master to bring criminals to justice. Stories follow Sammo as he goes about dispensing justice. He is assisted by Kelly Hu, a gorgeous girl who is almost as adapt in karate as Sammo; and detectives Terrell Parker, Dana Dickson, Louis Malone and Amy Dylan.

Cast: Sammo Hung (*Sammo Law*); Arsenio Hall (*Terrell Parker*); Grace Chen (*Kelly Hu*); Tammy Lauren (*Dana Dickson*); Louis Mandylor (*Louis Malone*); Tom Wright (*Lt. Benjamin Winship*); Gretchen Egolf (*Amy Dylan*).

5809 *Martin.* (Series; Comedy; Fox; 1992–1996). Martin Payne and Gina Waters are lovers. Martin, a radio talk show host (*The Insane Martin Payne*) at Detroit station WZUP and Gina, a marketing executive with Whittaker Advertising are later husband and wife. Stories relate incidents in their lives before and after marriage.

Martin, attempted his own business venture, a restaurant called Marty Mart's Meat Loaf and Waffles and later hosted his own TV talk show, *On the Street*.

Gina's friend, Pam James, first worked with her at Whittaker. She then worked as a secretary at Keep It Real Records. Cole Brown, Martin's friend, works as an airport janitor (Gina believes Cole's brain is not connected to the rest of his body for all the dumb things he does). Tommy is Martin's other friend (level-headed). In the last episode, Gina and Martin move to California when Gina is made head of the L.A. office and a network picks up Martin's TV show for a national broadcast.

Other regulars are Sheneneh, Martin's outrageous neighbor who owned Sheneneh's Hair Salon; Stan, Martin's boss at the radio station; Martin's bitter mother, Edna; Jerome, the sleazy con artist; Dr. Cliff Waters, Gina's father; and Nadine Waters, Gina's mother.

Cast: Martin Lawrence (*Martin Payne*); Tisha Campbell (*Gina Waters*); Garrett Morris (*Stan*); Carl Anthony Payne II (*Cole Brown*); Tichina Arnold (*Pam James*); Thomas Mikal Ford (*Tommy*); J.A. Preston (*Dr. Cliff Waters*); Judyann Elder (*Nadine Waters*); Martin Lawrence (*Sheneneh/Edna Lawrence*).

5810 *Martin Kane, Private Eye.* (Series; Crime Drama;

NBC; Syn.; NBC, 1949–1954; Syn, 1957-1958). New York City is the base of operations for Martin Kane, a rugged private detective who takes the cases of people with no where else to turn. He has an office in the Wood Building in Manhattan and charges fees that are appropriate to the case at hand — as much as $500. Martin is not one for following procedure. He uses determination and force of character to achieve results. He refers to women as "Doll Face" and "Sweetheart" and his hangout is McMann's Tobacco Shop. Martin smokes a pipe and uses the sponsor's product, Old Briar pipe tobacco (at 15 cents a pouch). The shop is a vital part of the program as Old Briar is prominently displayed. Hap was replaced in last season by Don Morrow, the new tobacco shop owner. Also known as *Assignment Danger.*

Program Open: "The makers of four distinctive pipe tobaccos — Old Briar, Dill's Best, Model and Tweed present ... *Martin Kane, Private Eye* ... starring William Gargan."

Cast: William Gargan *(Martin Kane; 1949–51)*; Lloyd Nolan *(Martin Kane; 1951-52)*; Lee Tracy *(Martin Kane; 1952-53)*; Frank M. Thomas *(Police Captain Burke)*; Nicholas Saunders *(Sergeant Ross)*; Walter Kinsella *(Happy McMann)*; Don Morrow *(Don)*; Horace McMahon *(Captain Willis)*; King Calder *(Lt. Grey)*; Fred Hillebrand *(Lt. Bender)*. **Announcer:** Fred Uttal

5811   *Martin Lawrence Presents First Amendment Standup.* (Series; Comedy; Starz; 2007). A showcase for established as well as up-and-coming standup comics (who are permitted to use "gutter language," thus explaining the title, that is not bleeped). Produced by Martin Lawrence.

Host: Doug Williams.

5812   *Martin Mystery.* (Series; Comedy; Cartoon Network; 2003). The Center is a secret organization with only one purpose: investigate unexplained phenomena. Its principal agents are Martin Mystery and Diana Lombard, teenagers who must divide their home and school life with their duties as investigators for the Center. Java, a caveman lost in time (and familiar with the unnatural assists them). Stories follow their case investigations as they encounter paranormal phenomena with one thing in common: dripping slime and goo.

Cast: Sam Vincent *(Martin Mystery)*; Dale Wilson *(Billy the Martian)*; Dale Wilson *(Java)*; Kelly Sheridan *(Diana Lombard)*; Teryl Rothery *(MOM)*.

5813   *The Martin Short Show.* (Series; Comedy; NBC; 1994). Marty Short is a comedian who hosts a TV variety series. He is married to Meg and they are the parents of Caroline and Charlie. Stories follow Marty's life at home and his experiences with the guests who appear on the show, including his wife, an actress who often appears as a guest in skits.

Cast: Martin Short *(Marty Short)*; Jan Hooks *(Meg Harper Short)*; Noley Thornton *(Caroline Short)*; Zack Duhame *(Charlie Short)*; Andrea Martin *(Alice)*; Brian Doyle Murray *(Gary)*.

5814   *The Martin Short Show.* (Series; Variety; Syn.; 1999-2000). Celebrity interviews coupled with short comedy skits.

Host: Martin Short. **Regulars:** Mary Scheer, Toby Hill, John Matta, Kelly Carangelo, Kevin McDonald, Jerry Minor, Michael McKean. **Announcer:** Michael McGrath. **Music:** Michael McKean.

5815   *The Marty Feldman Comedy Machine.* (Series; Comedy; ABC; 1972). A blend of contemporary humor with that of the Max Sennett silent film era of slapstick comedy.

Program Open: "From London and Hollywood, *The Marty Feldman Comedy Machine* with tonight's special guest Barbara Feldon, the Honeycombs, Fred Smoot and Spike Milligan."

Host: Marty Feldman. **Regulars:** Barbara Feldon, Orson Welles, Spike Milligan, Fred Smoot, Lennie Schultz, Thelma Houston, Fred Roman.

5816   *The Marty Robbins Spotlight.* (Series; Variety; Syn.; 1977). Tributes to country and western performers by spotlighting a guest and his or her music.

Host: Marty Robbins. **Orchestra:** Tom Tappan.

5817   *The Marvel Super Heroes.* (Series; Cartoon; Syn.; 1965). Adaptation of five Marvel comic book super heroes:

1. Captain America. A secret experiment called Super Soldier Serum endows Steve Rogers with super speed and strength. Adopting the colors of the American flag as his costume, Steve Rogers, alias Captain America, battles evil with the aid of his alloy shield (which can be thrown and used like a weapon).

2. The Incredible Hulk. During an experiment with gamma rays, Dr. Bruce Banner receives an accidental overdose of radiation that changes his DNA and, when he becomes angered, transforms him into a green creature called the Hulk. Unable to control his metamorphous, David uses his other half to battle evil.

3. Iron Man. Tony Stark, owner of Stark Industries, battles evil with a metal suit he built that gives him enhanced strength and the ability to fly.

4. The Mighty Thor. Thor, the son of Oden of Asgard (home of the Norse gods), uses his super strength and mystic hammer to battle the forces of evil.

5. Sub Mariner. Namor, half Atlantian and half human (the son of the Princess Fen of Atlantis and U.S. sea captain Leonard McKenzie), grew up in Atlantis and now uses his power of strength and ability to swim and fly to battle evil.

Voice Cast: Arthur Pierce *(Steve Rogers/Captain America)*; John Vernon *(Tony Stark/Iron Man)*; John Vernon *(Sub Mariner)*; John Vernon *(Major Glenn Talbot)*; Chris Wiggins *(Thor)*; Paul Sols *(Dr. Bruce Banner/Incredible Hulk)*; Peg Dixon *(Betty Ross)*; Peg Dixon *(Pepper Potts)*; Peg Dixon *(Jane Foster)*.

5818   *The Marvelous Misadventures of Flapjack.* (Series; Cartoon; Cartoon Network; 2008). Flapjack is a young boy who was lost at sea and raised by Bubbie, a talking whale. Captain K'Nuckles is a crusty old pirate whose life was saved by Flapjack and Bubbie. Now, as a team, the trio searches for the magical Candied Islands and its treasures of lollipop trees and lemonade springs.

Voice Cast: Thurop Van Orman *(Flapjack)*; Brian Doyle Murray *(Captain K'Nuckles)*; Roz Ryan *(Bubbie)*.

5819   *Mary.* (Series; Variety; CBS; 1978). A comedy-accented program that spotlights the talents of Mary Tyler Moore as a comedienne, singer and dancer. Only three of the eleven produced episodes aired.

Host: Mary Tyler Moore. **Regulars:** Swoosie Kurtz, Judith Kahan, Dick Shawn, James Hampton, Michael Keaton, David Letterman, Leonard Barr, Jack O'Leary. **Orchestra:** Alf Clausen.

5820   *Mary.* (Series; Comedy; CBS; 1985-1986). Mary Brenner is an attractive, middle-aged magazine writer. She lives at 103 South Coast Road in Chicago and writes for a magazine called *Women's Digest.* When her magazine folds, Mary takes a job as the Consumer Helpline columnist for a newspaper called the *Chicago Eagle* (originally called the *Chicago Post*). Mary feels the job is beneath her, but she wants to remain in Chicago, and the Helpline Columnist job is the only one she could find.

Edward ("Ed") LaSalle, the theater critic, writes the column "Stepping Out with Ed LaSalle," and Josephine ("Jo") Tucker pens the column "The Mainline Reporter." Jo is a chain smoker and lives in rather untidy surroundings in an apartment at 704 Holland Street. The fast food service used by the staff is Mr. Yummy.

Dennis Patrick and Doris Belack appeared as Jo's parents, Charles and Norma Tucker. Dan Foliart and Howard Pearl composed "Mary's Theme."

Cast: Mary Tyler Moore (*Mary Brenner*); John Astin (*Ed La Salle*); Katey Sagal (*Jo Tucker*); Carlene Watkins (*Susan Parks*); David Byrd (*Tully*); James Tolkan (*Lester Mintz*); Robert Pastorelli (*Mr. Yummy*).

5821   The Mary Hartline Show. (Series; Children; ABC; 1951). Mary Hartline, a regular on the series *Super Circus* (as "The Queen of the Super Circus") hosts her own series of music, songs and games geared to children.

Hostess: Mary Hartline. **Music:** Chet Robel.

5822   Mary Hartman, Mary Hartman. (Series; Serial; Syn.; 1976-1977). The setting is the mythical town of Fernwood, Ohio, a peaceful little community until the Mass Murderer of Fernwood claimed the lives of the Lombardi family, their two goats and eight chickens, and put the town on the map.

The murders occurred on Mary June Street. A short distance from this street is Bratner Avenue in the Woodland Heights section of town. At 343 Bratner live Mary Hartman, a pretty housewife who constantly worries about the waxy yellow buildup on her kitchen floor, her husband, Tom, an auto plant assembly line worker, and their daughter, Heather, who attends the Woodland Heights Elementary School.

Mary, who is 31 years old (born April 8, 1945), and Tom, who is 35 (born Oct. 4, 1941), met at Fernwood High School (Tom and Mary have been married 14 years when the series begins; Mary married Tom when she was 17).

Mary's parents, George and Martha Schumway, her sister, Cathy, and her grandfather, Raymond Larkin, live at 4309 Bratner Avenue. George works with Tom at the Fernwood Auto Plant and has been married to Martha for 36 years. Grandpa Larkin, now 83, was born in Macon, Georgia, and has been arrested for being the Fernwood Flasher. He is somewhat senile and is always asking, "Where's the peanut butter?" Cathy, who is ten years younger than Mary, is a very pretty, man-crazy free spirit.

Mary's next door neighbors are Charlie and Loretta Haggers, who live at 345 Bratner Avenue. Loretta, age 22, is a sweet and trusting country girl who is hoping to make it big as a recording artist. Charlie, her husband and manager, is 43 years old and works with Tom at the auto plant. Loretta, who calls Charlie "Baby Boy" (also the title of her first hit recording) performs at the local bar, the Capri Lounge. Serial-like stories follow events in their hectic lives. See also *Forever Fernwood*, the spin off series.

Principal Cast: Louise Lasser (*Mary Hartman*); Greg Mullavey (*Tom Hartman*); Claudia Lamb (*Heather Hartman*); Debralee Scott (*Cathy Schumway*); Philip Bruns (*George Schumway*); Dody Goodman (*Martha Schumway*); Mary Kay Place (*Loretta Haggers*); Graham Jarvis (*Charlie Haggers*); Victor Kilian (*Raymond Larkin*); Bruce Solomon (*Sgt. Dennis Foley*).

5823   Mary-Kate and Ashley in Action. (Series; Cartoon; ABC; 2001). The Olsen twins (Mary-Kate and Ashley) as high school girls who are secretly special agents for the government. Mary-Kate, as Agent Misty, and Ashley, as Agent Amber, use their unique abilities to protect the world from evil.

Voice Cast: Mary-Kate Olsen (*Mary-Kate/Agent Misty*); Ashley Olsen (*Ashley/Agent Amber*); Michael Dobson (*Clive Hedgemorton-Smythe*); Sam Vincent (*Capital D*); Brendan Besier (*Quincy*); Terry

Chan (*Rodney Choy*); Lenore Zann (*Renee La Rogue*); Maggie Blue O'Hara (*Romy Bates*).

5824   Mary Kay and Johnny. (Series; Comedy; DuMont; NBC; CBS; 1947–1950). The marital misadventures of Mary Kay and Johnny Stearns, television's first domestic couple. Stories are based on their actual experiences. Aired on DuMont (Nov. 18, 1947 to Aug. 24, 1948); NBC (Oct. 10, 1948 to Feb. 13, 1949); CBS (Feb. 23 to June 1, 1949); and NBC (June 13, 1949 to Mar. 11, 1950).

Cast: Mary Kay Stearns (*Mary Kay Stearns*); Johnny Stearns (*Johnny Stearns*); Christopher Stearns (*Christopher Stearns; their son*); Nydia Westman (*Mary Kay's Mother*); Howard Thomas (*Howie, Johnny's friend*). **Announcer:** Jim Stevenson.

5825   Mary Knows Best. (Series; Reality; Syfy; 2010). Mary Occhino is a psychic, author and host of the daily Satellite radio program, *Angels on Call*. She lives on Long Island (New York) and is the mother of Jacqueline, Carl and Chris. The program charts events in the daily lives of the family. Mary predicts the future, speaks to the dead and offers advice to her listeners on her radio program. Jacqueline, the youngest child, is a business major at Briarcliffe College; Chris is a paranormal expert; Carl is a skeptic who calls himself "the sane one in the family."

5826   The Mary Margaret McBride Show. (Series; Interview; NBC; 1948). Mary Margaret McBride oversees a program of celebrity interviews.

Hostess: Mary Margaret McBride. **Assistant:** Vincent Connolly.

5827   Mary Queen of Shops. (Series; Reality; BBC America; 2009). Cameras follow retail guru Mary Portas as she helps small, struggling shops (in England) regain a foothold in the business world.

5828   Mary Shelley's Frankenhole. (Series; Comedy; Adult Swim; 2010). Dr. Victor Frankenstein, considered a mad scientist, succeeded in mastering immortality by creating a creature from the dead called Frankenstein's Monster (he prefers to be called Creature). With his one success, Victor continued his research and has created a number of such monsters but has also discovered what he calls a "Frankenhole," a wormhole that links his small European village with every time period from the past and future. While stories focus in particular on Victor and his family, it also explores the lives of the historical figures and celebrities who use the Frankenhole to seek Victor's help. Elizabeth is Victor's immortal wife who is sexually frustrated (Victor refuses to have sex with her) and has turned to Count Dracula for love (Dracula, on the other hand, is also seeking to turn her into a vampire). Prof. Sanguinaire Polidori is Victor's assistant; Igor is Victor's hunchback assistant; Heinrich and Gustav are Victor's mortal, elderly children; Stewart Lawrence is the man cursed to be a werewolf; Mother Teresa is Victor's servant. Based on the novel *Frankenstein* by Mary Shelley.

Cast: Jeff B. Davis (*Dr. Victor Frankenstein*); Britta Phillips (*Elizabeth Frankenstein*); Scott Adsit (*Sanguinaire Polidori/Creature/Gustav Frankenstein*); Chris Shearer (*Count Dracula*); Tigger Stamatopoulos (*Igor*); Mark Rivers (*Heinrich Frankenstein*); Jay Johnston (*Stewart Lawrence*); Dino Stamatopoulos (*Mother Teresa*).

5829   The Mary Tyler Moore Comedy Hour. (Series; Variety; CBS; 1979). A show within a show that focuses on the home and working life of Mary McKinnon, a television performer whose program, *The Mary McKinnon Show*, provides a vehicle for guests to perform, and whose off-camera life provides the backdrop for the comedy play and interactions of Mary's staff and friends. Other regulars are Harry, the producer; Iris, Mary's secretary; Ken, the usher;

Artie, the writer-director; Crystal, Mary's housekeeper (first show); Ruby, the housekeeper (series); Mort, the head writer.

Cast: Mary Tyler Moore *(Mary McKinnon)*; Michael Lombard *(Harry Sinclair)*; Joyce Van Patten *(Iris Chapman)*; Michael Keaton *(Ken Christy)*; Ron Rifkin *(Artie Miller)*; Doris Roberts *(Crystal)*; Dody Goodman *(Ruby)*; Bobby Ramsen *(Mort Zimmick)*. **Orchestra:** Alf Clausen. **Theme Vocal:** "Love Is All Around" by Sonny Curtis.

5830   The Mary Tyler Moore Show. (Series; Comedy; CBS; 1970–1977). Following a breakup with her boyfriend, Mary Richards leaves New York and heads for Minneapolis to begin a new life. There she takes Apartment D at 119 North Weatherly in a building owned by her friend, Phyllis Lindstrom. Shortly after, she acquires a job as the assistant producer of the WJM-TV, Channel 12, "Six O'clock News" program and stories follow the life of a single woman as she struggles to make it on her own.

Mary is over 30, single and female — and the first such character to be portrayed on a weekly situation comedy. She is later promoted to producer when her boss, Lou Grant, decided to make himself executive producer.

Lou Grant is a distinguished newsman who knows that his program will never become a ratings winner. He puts up with the antics of his staff, especially anchor Ted Baxter, and finds comfort in alcohol (although he is not addicted) — either from the bottle he keeps in his desk or at the Happy Hour Bar. See also *Lou Grant*.

Ted Baxter, the station's incompetent newscaster, earns $31,000 a year and has trouble pronouncing words (for example, "Arkansas" becomes "Are-Kansas"). He longs for an anchor job in New York with his hero, Walter Cronkite. Ted opened the Ted Baxter's Famous Broadcasting School, hates to part with money, and he calls the station's control room "the Technical Place." Ted married Georgette Franklin, a shy window dresser at Hempell's Department Store. Ted's closing is "Good night and good news."

Murray Slaughter, the only news writer on the show, calls Ted's cue cards "idiot cards," and has been married to his wife, Marie, since 1955. Sue Ann Nivens, the host of WJM's *Happy Homemaker Show*, has advice for everybody and has made it her goal to catch Lou (who wants nothing to do with her).

Mary's upstairs neighbor is Rhoda Morgenstern, a New Yorker who moved to Minneapolis when she couldn't find a job or an apartment in Manhattan. She works as a window dresser at Hempell's Department Store and is struggling to eat right and keep her figure. See also *Rhoda*.

Phyllis Lindstrom is Mary's landlady. She is married to the never-seen Lars and the daughter of Bess. See also *Phyllis*.

The most tragic event to hit WJM was the death of its star performer, Chuckles the Clown (whose real name was given only as George). Chuckles was the Grand Marshal of a parade and dressed as Peter Peanut. He was crushed to death when a rogue elephant tried to shell him. Chuckles was played at various times by Mark Gordon and Richard Schaal. In the last episode, the new station manager (Vincent Gardenia) fires everyone but Ted. Gordie is the weatherman; Bonnie, Laurie and Ellen are Murray's daughters; Edie is Lou's ex-wife; Janie is their daughter; David is Ted's adopted son. Sonny Curtis sings the theme, "Love Is All Around."

Cast: Mary Tyler Moore *(Mary Richards)*; Ed Asner *(Lou Grant)*; Gavin MacLeod *(Murray Slaughter)*; Ted Knight *(Ted Baxter)*; Valerie Harper *(Rhoda Morgenstern)*; Cloris Leachman *(Phyllis Lindstrom)*; Lisa Gerritsen *(Bess Lindstrom)*; Betty White *(Sue Ann Nivens)*; John Amos *(Gordie Howard)*; Georgia Engel *(Georgette Franklin)*; Joyce Bulifant *(Marie Slaughter)*; Sherry Hursey *(Bonnie Slaughter)*; Helen Hunt *(Laurie Slaughter)*; Priscilla Morrill *(Edie Grant)*; Robbie Rist *(David Baxter)*; Nora Heflin *(Janie Grant)*; Lee Vines *(Lee; WJM Announcer)*.

5831   The Mary Van Note Show. (Series; Comedy; Internet; 2008). Comedian Mary Van Note is described as "a cross between Sarah Silverman and Pee Wee Herman." She is intimate yet rude and "strangely innocent." The ten episode web series explores Mary's inner mind as she searches for the man of her dreams. Mary is also seen speaking directly to the camera as well as performing in real and imagined skits.

Cast: Mary Van Note, Moshe Kasher, Alex Koll, Brent Weinbach.

5832   M*A*S*H. (Series; Comedy; CBS; 1972–1983). During wartime the medical corps fights for every life. Helicopters go right to the battlefields to return wounded soldiers to nearby MASH units. One such Mobile Army Surgical Hospital is the 4077, a unit built on barren ground five miles from the Korean War front in one of the most brutal climates on earth — unbearably hot in the summer, sub-zero temperatures in the winter. The 4077 is anything but classy. Its doctors and nurses often operate under battle conditions risking their lives to save others. In order to remain sane amid the insanities of war, the personnel act somewhat abnormally.

Captain Benjamin Franklin Pierce, the doctor most opposed to the war, constantly defies authority. He was born in Crabtree Cove, Maine, and was nicknamed "Hawkeye" by his father (after the main character in *The Last of the Mohicans*). The nurse-chasing Hawkeye was drafted (working in a hospital at the time) and "is the best cutter in the outfit; he is certified in chest and general surgery" and holds the position of chief surgeon. (for which he earns $413.50 a month).

Captain "Trapper John" McIntire is Hawkeye's tent mate. Hawkeye calls him "Champion of the oppressed and molester of registered nurses" and shares in all the shenanigans that Hawkeye pulls to take his mind off the war. Trapper and Hawkeye never had a chance to say goodbye (Hawkeye returns from R&R in Tokyo with "The Mount Rushmore of hangovers" to learn that Trapper was transferred stateside two hours earlier).

Captain B.J. Hunnicutt replaces Trapper John. B.J. (name never revealed) was born in Mill Valley, California. He is a surgeon fresh from civilian residency and is married to Peggy. B.J. attended Stanford Medical School and received the bronze Star (saved a soldier under fire). He is a clean-cut, even-tempered family man who is tempted by nurses but avoids their advances ("I'm hopelessly and passionately in love with my wife").

Major Frank Burns also shares a tent with Hawkeye. Frank, nick-named "Ferret Face," had a lucrative practice before being called up. Frank has set his goal to expose Hawkeye for constantly defying military rules (Hawkeye would like to see Frank transferred to another base — "preferably an enemy base"). Frank is married and fears his wife will discover he is having an affair with Major Margaret Houlihan.

Margaret, nicknamed "Hot Lips," is the head nurse and earns $400 a month. She has a spotless record, has been a chief nurse for ten years and "is a woman of passion but a stickler for rules." Margaret is regular Army; she would like all the doctors and nurses to behave in a military manner but realizes they won't ("They're terribly unruly and undisciplined and I thank God for each and every one of them when those casualties roll in").

Margaret and Frank's affair ended when she left him for Major Donald Penobscott. This caused Frank to have a breakdown and he was transferred to a stateside hospital in Indiana; he also received a promotion to lieutenant colonel.

Charles Emerson Winchester III replaces Frank as Hawkeye and B.J.'s new tent mate. Charles is a pompous Bostonian. He was educated at Harvard and had been working at Tokyo General Hospital before his transfer. He loves classical music and claims that "the meatball surgery that is performed in the OR is causing my skills to deteriorate; they're wasting away."

Colonel Henry Blake first commanded the 4077. He was born in Bloomington, Illinois, and was more like "one of the boys" as opposed to being a leader (he found Hawkeye's antics amusing). Though in charge, he was actually lost without the help of the company clerk (Radar). Henry's joyous transfer turns to sadness when the 4077 learns that his transport plane is shot down over the Sea of Japan and there are no survivors.

Colonel Sherman Potter becomes the new leader of the 4077. Potter, a career army man, was born in Riverbend, Missouri, although he later mentions he is from Hannibal, Missouri. Unlike Henry, Sherman finds Hawkeye's antics a violation of army rules but realizes why he is doing it and never punishes him. Potter finds relief from the insanity by painting and considers his troops at the 4077 "the best group of people I ever worked with."

Corporal Walter Eugene O'Reilly is the company clerk. He was born in Iowa and has the nickname "Radar" (for his ability to perceive what others think). Radar received a hardship discharge when his Uncle Ed died and he became his family's sole support. Maxwell Klinger is the company's "resident loon." He is a corpsman and pretends to be insane to get a Section 8 psychiatric discharge. He is first a corporal then a sergeant and dresses in women's clothes hoping to convince his superiors "that I'm nuts." Klinger became the clerk after Radar and "hates the damned army but I love these people." In the last episode, he married Soon-Lee, a migrant farm worker.

Father Francis Mulcahy is a first lieutenant and the unit's chaplain. He raises money for the Sister Theresa Orphanage and finds his faith in God challenged every day by the horrors he sees. Johnny Mandel composed the theme, "Suicide Is Painless."

Cast: Alan Alda (*Hawkeye Pierce*); Loretta Swit (*Margaret Houlihan*); Wayne Rogers (*Trapper John*); Larry Linville (*Frank Burns*); David Ogden Stiers (*Charles Winchester*); Mike Farrell (*B.J. Hunnicutt*); McLean Stevenson (*Henry Blake*); Harry Morgan (*Sherman Potter*); Gary Burghoff (*Radar O'Reilly*); Jamie Farr (*Maxwell Klinger*); George Morgan (*Father Mulcahy; pilot*); William Christopher (*Father Mulcahy; series*); Karen Philipp (*Lt. Maggie Dish; a nurse*); Timothy Brown (*Dr. "Spearchucker" Jones*); Odessa Cleveland (*Lt. Ginger Ballis; a nurse*); Patrick Adiarte (*Ho-John; Hawkeye's houseboy*); John Orchard (*Ugly John; the anesthetist*); G. Wood (*General Hamilton Hammond*); Linda Meiklejohn (*Lt. Leslie Scorch; a nurse*); Barbara Brownell (*Lt. Jones; a nurse*); Kelly Jean Peters (*Nurse Louise Anderson*); Johnny Haymer (*Supply Sgt. Zale*); G.W. Bailey (*Pvt. Luther Rizzo*); Marcia Strassman (*Nurse Maggie Cutler*); Lynnette Mettey (*Lt. Nancy Griffin; a nurse*); Herbert Voland (*Gen. Brandon Clayton*); Joseph Perry, Jeff Maxwell (*Igor, the cook*); Leland Sung (*Mr. Kwang; Officers Club bartender*); Edward Winter (*Colonel Flagg; the CIA agent*); Allan Arbus (*Major Sidney Freedman; the psychiatrist*); Enid Kent (*Nurse Bigelow*); Judy Farrell (*Nurse Abel*); Beeson Carroll, Mike Henry (*Major Donald Penobscott*); Jean Powell, Lynne Stewart, Linda Kelsey, Jan Jordan (*Nurse Baker*); Mary Jo Catlett (*Nurse Mary Jo Walsh*); Rosalind Chao (*Soon-Lee*).

5833 *MASK.* (Pilot; Cartoon; Syn.; May 20–24, 1985). Mobile Armoured Strike Kommand, MASK for short, is the code name for a top secret U.S. government fleet of sophisticated espionage vehicles that battles crime the world over. The proposal was to relate the exploits of its team (Matt, Gloria, Dusty, Brad, Buddy, Bruce and Thunder) as they battle the evils of Venom, an organization bent on ruling the world. The five part pilot pits MASK against Venom for the first time.

Voice Cast: Doug Stone (*Matt Trakker*); Brendan McKane (*Miles Mayhem*); Graeme McKenna (*T-Bob*); Mark Halloran (*Cliff Dagger*); Sharon Noble (*MASK Computer*); Brennan Thicke (*Scott Trakker*); Brian George (*Lester Sludge/Ali Bombay*).

5834 *The Mask.* (Series; Mystery; ABC; 1954). Walter and Peter Guilfoyle are brothers who are also attorneys. They are based in New York City and not only defend clients, but do their own investigating. Billed as "Television's first hour-long mystery series," stories relate Walter and Peter's investigations into crimes (presented like a mystery and allowing viewers to unravel the clues as the brothers uncover the evidence to not only clear their clients, but bring the actual culprits to justice). Broadcast live on Sunday evenings (with kinescoped re-broadcasts on Tuesday and Wednesday evenings).

Cast: Gary Merrill (*Walter Guilfoyle*); William Prince (*Peter Guilfoyle*).

5835 *The Mask.* (Series; Cartoon; CBS; 1995–1997). An adaptation of the feature film of the same title about Stanley Ipkiss, a nerdy chap who finds an 11th century green mask that when placed on his face transforms him into a zany crime fighting super hero who upholds the peace in Edge City. Stanley is assisted by his girlfriend, Peggy and his dog Milo. Stanley's main nemesis is Pretorius, a mad scientist who seeks to take over the city. The Mask is said to once belong to Noki, the Norse god of Mischief.

Cast: Rob Paulsen, Stefan Fredrich (*Stanley Ipkiss*); Heidi Shannon (*Peggy Brandt*); Tim Curry (*Pretorius*); Kevin Michael Richardson (*Mayor Mitchell Tilton*); Neil Ross (*Lt. Mitch Kellaway*).

5836 *The Masked Rider.* (Series; Science Fiction; Fox; 1995). When the evil Count Dregon and his assistant, Nefaria, begin plans to conquer the Earth, an alien Prince, Dex, is sent to stop them. Dex finds shelter with an Earth family (Hal and Barbara and their children Molly and Albee) and, when the need arises, becomes a powerful but mysterious (to the world) super hero called the Masked Rider, to battle the creatures sent to destroy the planet. Like *The Mighty Morphin Power Rangers* (see entry), *The Masked Rider* is based on a Japanese series (three here—*Kamen Rider, Kamen Rider ZO* and *Kamen Rider J*). The Japanese version battle scenes are incorporated with non-battle sequences shot for the American version and edited together. Unfortunately, the American version tried to take a serious Japanese program and turn it into a comical action *Power Rangers* that just didn't work as the plots are a bit choppy; the editing is quite bad (background buildings do not match; the Japanese Dex's face is visible at times) and the continuity is off. It appears to be that the newly photographed sequences were just shot to be as close as possible to replace the footage that couldn't be salvaged.

Cast: Ted Jan Roberts (*Prince Dex*); Rheannon Silver (*Molly*); Candace Kita (*Barbara*); David Stenstrom (*Hal*); Ashton McArn (*Albee*); Jennifer Tung (*Nefaria*); Ken Merckx (*Count Dregon*); Paul Pistore (*Ferbus*); Steve Kramer (*Cyclopter*); Julie Maddalena (*Fact*); Michael McConnohie (*Gork*); Michael Sorich (*Double Face*); Michi Yamato (*Dex; Japanese version*).

5837 *Masland at Home.* (Series; Variety; CBS; ABC; 1949–1951). Masland Carpets sponsored program of music and songs. Aired on CBS (Sept. 14, 1949 to June 7, 1950) and ABC (Aug. 30, 1950 to Feb. 2, 1951).

Host: Earl Wrightson. **Music:** The Norman Paris Trio.

5838 *Mason.* (Pilot; Comedy; ABC; July 4, 1977). The Bennetts are a seemingly normal American family of four. Howard and Peggy are the parents and Mason and Joyce are their children. Joyce is the typical teenage girl concerned more with makeup and boys than intellectual pursuits. But Mason is different. He is a ten-year-old genius whose misadventures are chronicled as he tries to fit into a world that seems unfit for him.

Cast: Mason Reese (*Mason Bennett*); Barry Nelson (*Howard Bennett*); Barbara Stuart (*Peggy Bennett*); Lee Lawson (*Joyce Bennett*).

5839   *Mason Dixon's Girls.* (Pilot; Crime Drama; CBS; Feb. 29, 1980). Proposed spin off from *The Dukes of Hazzard* about Mason Dixon, a private investigator, with two beautiful assistants, Tinker and Sam, who do the leg work, take the heat and risk their lives to solve crimes while Mason, not one for confrontation, sits back and oversees operations.

Cast: Dennis Rucker *(Mason Dixon)*; Mary Margaret Humes *(Tinker)*; Robin Eisenmann *(Sam)*.

5840   *Masquerade.* (Series; Anthology; PBS; 1971). Improvisational adaptations of classic fairy tales.

Performers: Barbara Sharma, Avery Schreiber, Alice Playten, Bill Hinnant, Barbara Minkus, Seth Allen, Jacque Lynn Colton, Louise Lasser, J.J. Barry, Phil Bruns, Sudie Bond, Barbara Tracy, Abraham Sobaloff.

5841   *Masquerade.* (Series; Adventure; ABC; 1983-1984). Operation Masquerade is a unit of the NIA (National Intelligence Agency) that recruits civilians with no espionage experience but who possess special skills to assist the government in various international cases that require anonymous agents. Mr. Lavender heads the unit and Danny Doyle and Casey Collins are his top assistants. Stories relate Danny and Casey's case assignments and the civilians they recruit for one time only assignments to help them resolve sensitive issues without publicity of any kind.

Cast: Rod Taylor *(Mr. Lavender)*; Greg Evigan *(Danny Doyle)*; Kirstie Alley *(Casey Collins)*. **Announcer:** William Conrad. **Theme Vocal:** "Masquerade" by Crystal Gayle.

5842   *Masquerade Party.* (Series; Game; NBC; CBS; ABC; Syn; 1952–1960; 1974). The object calls for five celebrity panelists to identify elaborately disguised guest personalities. Each panelist is permitted to ask five questions of the guest. Each second of questioning scores one dollar to a maximum of $300. At the end of each five-minute segment, or at any time in between, panelists may attempt to guess their guest's identity. Whether correct or incorrect, the money that is established is donated to charity. In the 1974 version, three celebrity panelists attempt to identify an elaborately disguised guest from a series of indirect question-and-answer rounds. Once the questioning is completed, two players are chosen from the studio audience and asked to identify the guest. The identity of the guest is revealed and players receive prizes if they are correct. Two versions appeared:

1. Masquerade Party (NBC, 1952; 1957; 1960. CBS, 1953-54; 1958; 1959-60. ABC, 1954–56) **Host:** Clayton "Bud" Collyer (1952), Douglas Edwards (1953), Peter Donald (1954–56), Eddie Bracken (1957), Robert Q. Lewis (1958), Bert Parks (1958–60). **Panelists:** Phil Silvers, Ilka Chase, Adele Jergens, Peter Donald, Madge Evans, Buff Cobb, John Young, Johnny Johnston, Betsy Palmer, Jonathan Winters, Jinx Falkenberg, Pat Carroll, Faye Emerson, Gloria De-Haven, Audrey Meadows, Sam Levenson, Lee Bowman, Bobby Sherwood. **Announcer:** Johnny Olson.

2. Masquerade Party (Syn. 1974). **Host:** Richard Dawson. **Panelists:** Lee Meriwether, Bill Bixby, Nipsey Russell. **Announcer:** Jay Stewart.

5843   *Massarati and the Brain.* (Pilot; Adventure; ABC; Aug. 26, 1982). "Mas" Massarati is a wealthy, international soldier of fortune who becomes the guardian of his 12-year-old nephew, Christopher, after the death of his parents. Christopher is an electronics genius who becomes fascinated with his uncle's work — so much so that he joins him on assignments and supplies the necessary contraptions Mas needs to complete his mission. The proposal was to relate Mas and Christopher's battle against the forces of evil. Other regulars are Julie, Mas's government contact; and Anatole, Mas's butler, chef and mansion overseer (in California).

Cast: Daniel Pilon *(Mas Massarati)*; Peter Billingsley *(Christopher Massarati)*; Markie Post *(Julie Ramsdale)*; Christopher Hewett *(Anatole)*.

5844   *Massine's Ballet.* (Experimental; Ballet; NBC; Mar. 11, 1945). A ballet, staged especially for television by Leonide Massine, a dancer-choreographer with the Ballet Theater and produced by Dr. Herbert Graf, stage director of the Metropolitan Opera in New York. The program included Katharine Lee (a solo to Bach's "Chaconne"); Katharine Lee and Ivan Kirov dancing to Rimsky-Korsakov's "Antar"; and Anna Istomina and Serge Ismailoff performing a scene from Leonide Messine's "Blue Danube."

5845   *The Master.* (Series; Adventure; NBC; 1984). John Peter McCallister is a master of the Ninja (the Japanese art of disciplined combat). It was after his service with the Army Air Corps during World War II "that I found myself in Japan. The tranquility and the people kept me there" (in another episode, John mentions he found his way to Japan after the Korean War — where he was a prisoner of war and managed to escape via a motorcycle). Thirty years later, John receives a letter from a girl named Terry McCallister, a daughter he never knew he had. The letter contains a picture of Terry next to an airplane and a postmark from a U.S. city called Ellerston. With these clues, John leaves Japan and begins a quest to find Terry (who is never seen). It is not explained how Terry knew John was her father or how she even knew where or how to contact him. Also not explained is why Terry keeps moving from city to city, always leaving moments before John arrives or is about to find her).

Terry is depicted as a "Jill of All Trades," holding jobs as a pilot, model, waitress, dancer, etc., who always manages to get her picture in some newspaper or magazine. It is from these articles that John finds the clues he needs to track Terry.

John was a member of a secret Ninja society. His decision to leave Japan betrays his destiny and he is sentenced to die by the members of his sect (who fear he may reveal their secrets). Okasa, a former student of John's who is now a Ninja master, has sworn to find John and kill him. John mentions that Terry's mother is Laura Kennedy, a woman he met in Korea. They had a two month relationship "and then one morning she was gone." Max Keller is a young drifter who earns money by competing in motorcycle races and doing odd jobs. Max is in a bar in Ellerston when the local sheriff begins to harass John for carrying a concealed weapon (his Samurai sword). Max steps in, helps John fight off the sheriff and they escape in Max's customized van. While talking, Max learns of John's quest and volunteers to help. Max, intrigued by John's fighting abilities, asks only that John teach him the art of the Ninja. Together they begin a quest to help people threatened by unscrupulous characters while searching for John's long-lost and elusive daughter, Terry (several episodes drop the daughter searching element to focus on John and Max as they help old friends of John's who are in trouble). Cat is Max's friend; Patrick is his father.

Cast: Lee Van Cleef *(John Peter McCallister)*; Timothy Van Patten *(Max Keller)*; Sho Kosugi *(Okasa)*; Tara Buckman *(Cat Hellman)*; Doug McClure *(Patrick Keller)*.

5846   *Master Chef.* (Series; Reality; Fox; 2010). Amateur Chefs compete in various cooking challenges designed to not only test their cooking skills, but bring forth the best of the best — the Master Chef.

Host: Dina Tersago. **Judges:** Gordon Ramsay, Joe Bastianich, Gordon Elliott Bowles.

5847   *Master of Dance.* (Series; Reality; TLC; 2008). Dance competition show with a twist: competing players must be flexible and be able to adapt to a new routine when a song is changed in mid-routine. Dancers unable to adapt quickly enough are eliminated. The most accomplished dancer wins the $50,000 first prize.

Host: Joey Lawrence. **Judges:** Lucinda Dickey, Loni Love, Keith Diorio.

5848   *Masterminds.* (Series; Anthology; Syn.; 2004). In the early 1950s *Racket Squad* dramatized real police files based on the scams used by con men. *Masterminds* tells the real stories of real life crimes executed by brilliant criminals. Reenactments are used to show how the crime was committed (anything from bank robberies to kidnappings) and how law enforcement officials solved the crime.

Narrator: Jamie Watson.

5849   *Masterpiece Playhouse.* (Series; Anthology; NBC; 1950). Live dramatic adaptations of well-known literary works: *Hedda Gabler* (by Henrik Ibsen; July 23, 1950); *Richard III* (by William Shakespeare; July 30, 1950); *The Rivals* (by Richard Sheridan; Aug. 6, 1950); *Six Characters in Search of an Author* (by Luigi Pirandello; Aug. 13, 1950); *The Importance of Being Ernest* (by Oscar Wilde; Aug. 20, 1950); *Othello* (by William Shakespeare; Aug. 27, 1950); and *Uncle Vanya* (by Anon Chekov; Sept. 3, 1950). Fred Coe is the producer.

5850   *Masters of Horror.* (Series; Anthology; Showtime; 2006). Horror yarns directed by Hollywood's top theatrical fright film directors.

Stories include: *Pro Life* (a young woman [Caitlin Wachs] finds her pregnancy anything but normal when she realizes and evil entity is growing inside her; directed by John Carpenter); *The Damned Thing* (Sean Patrick Flanery and Marissa Coughlin in a story about a mysterious force that turns people against each other; directed by Tobe Hooper); *Sounds Like* (Larry Pearce as a man who is suddenly plagued by a heightened sense of sound that threatens to destroy him; directed by Brad Anderson); and *We Scream for Ice Cream* (a man [Lee Tergeson] finds the sins of his past coming back not only to haunt him, but kill him; directed by Tom Holland).

5851   *Masters of Illusion.* (Series; Variety; PAX; 2000). Franz Harary hosts a program that presents performances by magicians, escape artists and illusionists.

5852   *Masters of Illusion.* (Series; Reality; My Network TV; 2009). A weekly showcase for magicians and illusionists who perform truly amazing feats live and in front of a studio audience without camera tricks or computer generated effects. James Romanovich narrates. The Magicians-Illusionists are Ed Alonzo, Danny Cole, Kyle Eichen, Kenrick Ice McDonald, Mark Kalin, Marc King, Jinger Leigh, Jeff McBride, Dan Sperry, Arthur Trace, Adam Wylie, The Amazing Jonathan.

5853   *Masters of Magic.* (Series; Variety; CBS; 1949). Andre Baruch hosts a live program of performances by guest magicians.

5854   *Masters of Science Fiction.* (Series; Anthology; ABC; 2007). "Tales of a present and future Earth." Top name stars and known directors appear on the four week program (Aug. 4 to 25, 2007). *A Clear Escape*, the first story, finds a futuristic psychiatrist (Judy Davis) interrogating and amnesiac whose past holds a secret that can affect the future. Mark Rydell directed. The second story, *The Awakening*, is set in war-torn Baghdad were U.S. soldiers discover a mysterious casualty — one who doesn't appear to be human. Terry O'Quinn, Elisabeth Rohm and William B. Davis star. Michael Petroni directed.

Jerry Was a Man, the third story, is set in the future and stars Anne Heche and Malcolm McDowell as a couple whose lives are changed when they acquire an anthropoid named Jerry. Michael Tolkin directed. The concluding story, *The Discarded*, focuses on three dispensed minorities seeking to find refuge on Earth after they are set adrift in space. Brian Dennehy, John Hurt and James Denton star. Jonathan Frakes directed.

Narrator: Stephen Hawking.

5855   *Masters of the Maze.* (Series; Game; Fox; 1994–1996). Three teams, each composed of three members, compete. An out-of-focus picture, which could be a person, place or thing, is displayed. The first team to buzz in receives a chance to identify the blurred image. A correct guess scores the team ten points. The person who identified the picture is then asked a question regarding the object of the picture. If he answers it correctly the team scores five additional points. The first team to score fifty points wins and receives the first opportunity to win prizes contained in a stage-displayed maze. Here one player remains outside the maze while his partner is placed inside the maze. The maze player must conquer three levels: The Mirror Man, The Honeycomb Man and The Chamber of Knowledge by answering three questions correctly on each level. The time it takes to do so is calculated. The opposing team competes in the same manner. The team that scores the best time competes in the final round, Prize Mountain. Here five monsters are seen flashing "Prize" or "No Prize." One player is given a laser gun; the other teammate must direct his shots (by calling "fire" when he feels the time is right to hit "Prize" on a monster). Three prize hits within the time limit awards the team a shopping spree.

Host: J.D. Roth *(1994-95)*; Mario Lopez *(1995-96)*. **Mirror Man:** Mark Maxwell Smith.

5856   *Matadors.* (Pilot; Comedy; Unaired; Produced for ABC in 2009). Juliana Lodari and Alex Galloway are young lawyers who are also lovers and the offspring of powerful families who have dominated the Chicago justice system for more than thirty years. Juliana's father, Roman, and Alex's father, Victor started a secret society when they were in law school called Matador. They used a matador as it mascot ("a matador must be a showman and strategist, combined with pure killer instinct"). Over time, however, misunderstandings drove the friends apart and created a rivalry that nearly consumed them. Victor become Chicago's most successful defense attorney; Roman became the D.A. Their children followed in their footsteps and became part of the legal system — but their parents oppose their relationship. The proposal was to follow Juliana and Alex as they struggle to maintain their relationship despite the efforts of their families to destroy it.

Cast: Michelle Borth *(Juliana Lordari)*; Zach Gilford *(Alex Galloway)*; Stephen Lang *(Victor Galloway)*; David Strathairn *(Roman Lodari)*; Jonathan Scarfe *(Mitch Galloway)*; Jason Behr *(Gabriel Nicastro)*; Merle Dandridge *(Brooke Comas)*.

5857   *Match Game.* (Series; Game; NBC; Syn.; 1962–2008). A question that contains a blank is read to the two teams that compete (each composed of one celebrity captain and two contestants). Each player writes down the word he feels will best complete the thought. If two players on the same team match, they score $25; if the celebrity matches them, $50 is scored. The first team to score $100 is the winner and the contestants divide the money. A later format had two contestants attempting to match the answers provided by a panel of six celebrities. Money was scored for each match and the player with the highest cash score was the winner. See also *The Match Game-Hollywood Squares Hour.*

Program Open: "From New York City, it's time to play *The Match Game.* This portion of *The Match Game* brought to you by Downey Fabric Softener ... and now here's your host, Gene Rayburn." Eight versions appeared:

1. Match Game (NBC, 1962–69). **Host:** Gene Rayburn. **Announcer:** Johnny Olson.

2. Match Game (CBS, 1973–79). **Host:** Gene Rayburn. **Regulars:** Richard Dawson, Brett Somers, Charles Nelson Reilly. **Announcer:** Johnny Olson (Bern Bennett replaced Johnny for one week in 1975).

3. Match Game P.M. (Syn., 1976). **Host:** Gene Rayburn. **Announcer:** Johnny Olson.

4. Match Game (Syn., 1979–82). **Host:** Gene Rayburn. **Announcer:** Johnny Olson. *Regular Panelists:* Charles Nelson Reilly, Brett Somers.

5. The Match Game-Hollywood Squares Hour (NBC, 1983–84). **Match Game Host:** Gene Rayburn. **Match Game Announcer:** Gene Wood. See entry.

6. Match Game (Syn., 1990-91). **Host:** Ross Shafer. **Announcer:** Gene Wood, Bob Hilton. **Regular Panelist:** Charles Nelson Reilly. Bert Convy hosted the pilot episode.

7. Match Game (Syn., 1998-99). **Host:** Michael Burger. **Announcer:** Paul Boland.

8. Match Game (Unaired TBS Pilot, 2008). **Host:** Andrew Daly. **Regulars:** Bob Einstein, Niecy Nash, Norm MacDonald, Rashida Jones, Sarah Silverman, Scott Thompson.

5858   *The Match Game-Hollywood Squares Hour.* (Series; Game; NBC; 1983-1984). The program combines two former game shows under one title. In *The Match Game* two contestants compete. A question that contains a blank is read to the six celebrities who appear (each of whom writes their answer on card). The contestant at play gives a verbal response. The celebrities reveal their answers one at a time. For each match (same answer) the player scores one point. Three such rounds are played and the contestant with the highest score (up to six points) is the winner. He then competes against the previous champion in *The Hollywood Squares.* Nine celebrity guests appear in a large tic-tac-toe board. One player selects a celebrity. A question is read and the player must determine if the celebrity's answer is either true or false. A correct guess awards that player $25 and either an "X" or an "O" on the board. The first player to score three squares, across, up and down, or diagonally, is the winner of the first round and receives an additional $100 (two additional rounds are played with the money increasing by $100 for each game). The player with the most money is the champion and competes until defeated.

Match Game Host: Gene Rayburn. **Hollywood Squares Host:** Jon Bauman. **Announcer:** Gene Wood.

5859   *Matched in Manhattan.* (Series; Reality; Lifetime; 2008). A dating game type of series combined with the elements of a makeover program. Host Matt Titus is a relationship expert who is said "to specialize in helping straight women and gay men find Mr. Right rather than Mr. Right now." Each program is devoted to the makeover of a relationship challenged woman. The subject is given a complete makeover (from wardrobe and makeup to redecorating her home or apartment). Following the change, the subject is counseled on relationships and dating and given a fresh chance to find her Mr. Right.

5860   *Matches 'N' Mates.* (Series; Game; Syn.; 1967). Two married couples compete. A board that contains a series of answers is revealed for a short period of time. At the end of the time the answers are hidden and a board that contains concealed questions is revealed. One player calls a number to reveal one of the concealed questions. The question is read. If he can recall under which number the correct

answer is, he receives one point. If he is incorrect the answer and question are concealed and the opponent receives a chance to play. The team with the highest score is the winner and receives merchandise prizes.

Host: Art James.

5861   *Matchmaker.* (Series; Game; Syn.; 1987). Three men and three women appear on stage. The host (who cannot see the players) questions each player by asking personal questions. After several such rounds, the host selects the two people he feels are suited for each other. The selected players receive a free trip to a romantic locale in the hopes of sparking a romance (the selected players, however, may elect to take the trip on his or her own or with another person of their choice). The results of each match are related on a future edition of the program after the trip is taken.

Host: David Hull. **Assistant:** Helaine Michaelsen.

5862   *Matinee at the Bijou.* (Series; Anthology; PBS; 1980). Rare or never before telecast theatrical cartoons, serials, shorts and feature films of the 1930s. Set at an old time movie theater where the host invites the audience to join him in that week's presentations. Rudy Vallee performs the theme, "At the Bijou."

Host: W. Scott Devenney. **Usherettes:** Karen Davis, Kathleen Blackerby, Barbara Seuss, Jennifer McPhee. **Theater Patrons:** Linda Van Dusen, Steve Starr, Mark Zewe, Carol Childress, John Zewe.

5863   *Matinee in New York.* (Series; Variety; NBC; 1952). Daytime program, aimed at the housewife, of music, songs, celebrity interviews and game contests.

Hosts: Bill Cullen, Bill Goodwin. **Interviewer:** Ted Collins. **Announcer:** Andre Baruch. **Music:** Jack Miller, John Lesko.

5864   *Matinee Theater.* (Series; Anthology; NBC; 1955–1958). Daily program of dramatic productions produced in California and hosted by actor John Conte. Notable performers include Angie Dickinson, Cara Williams, Shelley Fabares, Maureen O'Sullivan, Victor Jory, George Peppard, Patrick Macnee, Carol Ohmart, Kevin McCarthy, Chuck Connors, Alan Hale, Jr., John Carradine and Gloria Talbott.

5865   *Matlock.* (Series; Crime Drama; NBC, 1986–1992; ABC, 1992–1995). Matlock and Matlock is an Atlanta, Georgia, based law firm owned by Benjamin Layton Matlock and his daughter, Charlene. It became Ben Matlock, Attorney-at-Law, when Charlene left in 1987 to begin her own law practice in Philadelphia. She is replaced by Ben's younger daughter, Lee Ann McIntyre, a prosecuting attorney separated from her husband, Peter; the firm then becomes Matlock and McIntyre, Attorneys-at-Law.

When Lee Ann leaves to start her own practice in California in 1994, Ben replaces her with Attorney Michelle Thomas and changes the firm's name to B.L. Matlock, Attorney-at-Law, with Michelle Thomas, Attorney-at-Law appearing under his name in smaller letters.

Ben charges $100,000 a case and is known for his high rate of success in defending clients. He is a Gemini and was born in the town of Mount Harlan, Georgia. Ben is a graduate of Harvard Law School and worked as a public prosecutor in Atlanta before beginning his own law practice.

Ben is known for two things: eating hot dogs, usually with grape soda, and white suits; he has a closet full of them. This began in 1969 when a case brought Ben to Los Angeles. He became ill after eating several pieces of bad fish and was taken to Community General Hospital. There, he was treated by a young resident intern named Dr. Mark Sloan (Dick Van Dyke, from the series *Diagnosis Murder*).

Ben was just starting his practice and Mark convinced him to invest his life savings, $5,000, in the hottest new item, 8-Track tapes. The 8-Track system proved to be a failure and Ben lost everything. Cheap white suits off the store rack and hot dogs were all he could afford, but he carried on the tradition throughout the years.

Ben has little faith in police labs; "They're not working to help my clients." He prefers to do his own investigating. Ben doesn't make unsubstantiated charges and will occasionally take a case for free.

Julie March is the prosecuting attorney with the Atlanta D.A.'s office. She considers herself one of the best legal minds in the South; Ben calls her the wildest, most ruthless prosecutor the state has. Julie left the series when she moved to Los Angeles to work as a prosecutor in the D.A.'s office.

Les Calhoun is Ben's neighbor, a retired manufacturer who prefers to be called "Ace." Tyler Hudson, Ben's first investigator, is a brilliant stock market investor. He was replaced by Conrad McMasters, a police deputy who doubled as Ben's investigator. Cliff Lewis is a young attorney Ben hires to assist Conrad on investigations.

Carol Huston appeared briefly in 1994 as Jeri Stone, the private detective Ben hired as his investigator when Charlene first left. Cassie Phillips is Ben's law clerk, a student at the Baxter Law School in Atlanta. Betty Lynn is Sarah, Ben's receptionist in first season episodes. In the pilot episode, *Diary of a Perfect Murder* (Mar. 3, 1986), Lori Lethin played Charlene and Alice Hirson was Hazel, Ben's receptionist.

Cast: Andy Griffith (*Ben Matlock*); Linda Purl (*Charlene Matlock*); Lori Lethin (*Charlene Matlock; pilot*); Brynn Thayer (*Lee Ann McIntyre*); Julie Sommars (*Julie March*); Don Knotts (*Les Calhoun*); Kene Holliday (*Tyler Hudson*); Clarence Gilyard, Jr. (*Conrad McMasters*); Daniel Roebuck (*Cliff Lewis*); Kari Lizer (*Cassie Phillips*).

5866 *Matrix*. (Series; Drama; USA; 1993). Steve Matrix is a ruthless hit man. Any job, the right price and someone is eliminated. No matter how careful and brilliant he thought he was, someone was smarter and got the drop on him. Matrix is placed in suspension between Heaven and Hell. It is here that Liz Teel, a representative of the Forces That Be (actually a person from the In-Between) offers him a deal: spend eternity in Hell or redeem his past by helping people in need. Matrix chooses to help people and stories follow his efforts as he is sent back to earth to make up for his deadly past.

Cast: Nick Mancuso (*Steven Matrix*); Carrie-Anne Moss (*Liz Teel*); Phillip Jarrett (*Billy Hicks*).

5867 *The Matt Dennis Show*. (Series; Variety; NBC; 1955). A summer program of music and songs with pianist Matt Dennis as the host.

Host: Matt Dennis. **Off-Camera Introductions:** Frank Sinatra. **Musicians:** Trigger Albert (*Bass*); Mundell Lowell (*Guitar*); Jimmy Campbell (*Drums*).

5868 *Matt Helm*. (Series; Crime Drama; ABC; 1975–1976). Matt Helm is a former U.S. government intelligence agent for the Company turned private investigator. Matt resides at the McGuire Beach House at 2001 Postal Road in Malibu Beach, California, with his girlfriend, Claire Kronski, a private practice attorney.

Matt likes to tackle assignments in ways that he feels will work — not the way he is told to do things. When he becomes frustrated with all the rules he is forced to follow, he resigns and begins his own business, Matt Helm Investigations.

Matt's years of government experience have made him more perceptive and able to see crime in a different light. He knows how to use his wits to outsmart the enemy but still hasn't learned to avoid violent confrontations. Matt also has an eye for the ladies (looking more than anything else)—a situation that doesn't seem to bother Claire (as she knows he will always be faithful to her).

Claire, whom Matt always calls Kronski, most often becomes involved in Matt's cases. Her legal expertise always helps Matt out of a predicament and says of her, "Kronski is the most honest lawyer who ever lived but one of the sneakiest people I have ever known."

Ethel, who calls Matt "Matthew," runs Ethel's Answering Service; Lieutenant Hanrahan, Matt's friend, is with the Homicide Division of the Parker Center of the L.A.P.D.

Cast: Anthony Franciosa (*Matt Helm*); Laraine Stephens (*Claire Kronski*); Jeff Donnell (*Ethel*); Gene Evans (*Lt. Hanrahan*).

5869 *Matt Houston*. (Series; Crime Drama; ABC; 1982–1985). Matlock Houston, called Matt, is a millionaire oil baron, cattle rancher and playboy who helps people in deep trouble. He is the owner of Houston, Inc., a conglomerate at 200 West Temple Street in Los Angeles (address later given as 100 Century Plaza South in Los Angeles) and Houston Investigations, the agency through which he enjoys doing what he likes best — solving crimes. Matt also owns the Houston Cattle Ranch in Texas. Matt is a risk taker (it is what made him wealthy) and often takes unnecessary risks to help his clients.

C.J. Parsons is Matt's business assistant. While C.J. was hired to take care of Matt's corporate matters, she also finds herself his partner when it comes to investigating cases.

Roy Houston is Matt's uncle and assistant in last season episodes. He is a somewhat older private detective whose years of experience as a police officer and detective help Matt use a more logical approach to solving crimes (as opposed to Matt's charging head first into situations without thinking).

Vince Novelli is a lieutenant with the S.C.P.D. (Southern California Police Department); Vince's mother, Rosa, owns Matt's favorite eatery, Mama Novelli's Restaurant; Michael Hoyt is a lieutenant with the L.A.P.D.; and Murray Chase is Matt's harried business manager. Slim (a gorgeous girl) is Matt's accountant; Lamar is Matt's ranch hand; Pam (later called Chris) is Matt's receptionist; Charlie Eagle and Too Mean are Matt's legmen; Ann is Michael's wife; Kathy is his daughter.

Cast: Lee Horsley (*Matt Houston*); Pamela Hensley (*C.J. Parsons*); Buddy Ebsen (*Roy Houston*); John Aprea (*Vince Novelli*); Penny Santon (*Rosa Novelli*); Lincoln Kilpatrick (*Michael Hoyt*); George Wyner (*Murray Chase*); Penny Santon (*Mama Novelli*); D.D. Howard (*Slim*); Paul Brinegar (*Lamar Pettybone*); Cis Rundle (*Pam; later called Chris*); Maureen O'Connor (*Matt's office secretary*); Cal Bellini (*Charlie Eagle*); Rockne Tarkington (*Too Mean*); Judyann Elder (*Ann Hoyt*); Christina Murrill (*Kathy Hoyt*).

5870 *Matt Lincoln*. (Series; Drama; ABC; 1970–1971). Matt Lincoln is a Los Angeles–based psychiatrist who practices preventive psychiatry and struggles to assist people in the early stages of emotional distress to avoid further, more complicated treatment. Stories follow Matt and his young staff (Tag, Ann, Kevin and Jimmy) as they help people facing a variety of crises. In the pilot film, *Dial Hot Line*, Vince Edwards played the lead as Dr. David Leopold. Matt Sr. is Matt's father.

Cast: Vincent Edwards (*Matt Lincoln*); Chelsea Brown (*Tag*); Felton Perry (*Jimmy*); June Harding (*Ann*); Michael Larrain (*Kevin*); Dean Jagger (*Matt Lincoln, Sr.*).

5871 *Matt Waters*. (Series; Crime Drama; CBS; 1996). Matt Waters is a retired naval officer turned science teacher at his alma mater, Bayview High School in New Jersey. Matt was a Navy officer for 20 years and receives a $50,000 a year pension. Matt grew up in New Jersey and chose to become a teacher a year after resigning—

when his brother was killed in a gang shooting. Matt felt he had to make a difference in the lives of young people who may be headed down the wrong path.

Matt's students are rowdy, troubled teenagers. Stories follow Matt as he uses his Navy training to help discipline and set his students on the right path in life.

Cast: Montel Williams *(Matt Waters; a teacher)*; Nicole Moore *(Kristen Wilson; a teacher)*; Sam McMurray *(Charlie Sweet; the coach)*; Cyndi Cartagena *(Angela Perez)*; Amy Hargreaves *(Chloe Drescher)*; Jack Tisdale *(Nathaniel Marston)*; Bob Prysybilski *(Glenn Fitzgerald)*; Richard Chevolleau *(Flea Decker)*.

5872   *Matty's Funday Funnies.* (Series; Cartoon; ABC; 1959–1961). The overall title for a series of Harvey theatrical cartoons, including *Casper, the Friendly Ghost*, *Baby Huey*, *Little Audrey* and *Buzzy the Crow*. Sponsored by Mattel Toys and hosted by the animated Matty and Sisterbelle.

Voices: Jackson Beck, Mel Blanc, Eddie Brandt, Richard Buckley, Daws Butler, Robert Clampett, Sody Clampett, Pinto Colvig, Scatman Crothers, Gwen Davies, Stan Freberg, Paul Frees, Joan Gerber, Norma McMillan.

5873   *Maude.* (Series; Comedy; CBS; 1972–1978). It is October of 1968 at the height of the Presidential campaign (Nixon vs. Humphrey) when Dr. Arthur Harmon introduces his best friend, Walter Findlay to Maude, a three times divorced women with a strikingly beautiful daughter named Carol. Maude is stubborn, opinionated and must have her own way. Walter, divorced once, is stubborn, opinionated and must have his own way. They are also argumentative, especially over politics (Maude is a Democrat; Walter a Republican) and appear to be a mismatched couple. Looks can be deceiving as Walter and Maude fall in love, marry and set up housekeeping at 30 Crenshaw Street in Tuckahoe, New York (address also given as 271 Elm Street). Walter owns Findlay's Friendly Appliance Store and stories relate the incidents that creep in, disrupt and threaten to destroy Maude's lasting relationship with Walter. Her prior husbands were Chester, Albert and Barney and her catch phrase (when someone upsets her) is "God 'ill Get You for That." Walter began his company by selling out of the back of his car and eventually built a successful business. His claim to fame is that he has seen the original 1933 movie, *King Kong*, 153 times. Maude has to interfere in every aspect of Carol's life and they constantly argue, especially over Carol's style of dress.

Carol is voluptuous and likes to dress in revealing tops and short skirts; Maude often claims she can see more than Carol's clothes cover. Carol, a feminist, is 27, divorced (from Vernon), the mother of Philip, and works as an office secretary at Lambert Industries. She is the daughter of Maude's first husband, Barney. Vivian is Arthur's wife (divorced from Jimmy Cavender; Arthur's late wife was named Agnes); Florida, then Nell and finally Victoria worked as Maude's maids. The Florida character was spun off into *Good Times*; Nell was a cockney Brit; Victoria was West Indian. When Walter has too much to drink, he reverts to his childhood—something Maude can't deal with as she has a hard time dealing with him as an adult.

Although Walter prefers that Maude not work, Maude did hold various jobs (in first season episodes she is a real estate agent, then office manager at the Ace Realty Company at $7,000 a year) and later ran for and became a U.S. Congresswoman in the last episode (April 3, 1978).

It was at this time that Walter had retired and became one of Maude's aides when she moved to Washington, D.C. (along with Barbara Rhoades as Maggie Gallagher; Dennis Burkley as Sam Dickey; and Nedra Volz as Pinky Nolan). The episode was also the

pilot for a new version of *Maude* that never materialized as Bea Arthur rejected the role. It was turned into *Onward and Upward*, a series about a black athlete who tries to win a seat in Congress. John Amos, chosen as the star, quit over a format dispute when the title was changed to *Mr. Dooley*. Louis Gossett, Jr., also rejected the role. Cleavon Little was then brought on and several episodes were taped under the title *Mr. Dugan*. But due to the unfavorable portrayal of blacks, this version never actually aired. It was revised one final time as *Hanging In* and ran on CBS for four episodes (Aug. 8 to 29, 1979; see *Hanging In* for information). The last episode also finds Carol and Philip moving to Denver when Carol finds a better job; and Arthur and Vivian relocating to Red River, Idaho, when Arthur decides to begin a new practice.

The "Cousin Maude's Visit" episode of *All in the Family* (Dec. 11, 1971) first introduced Edith's cousin, Maude Findlay to audiences. Here Marcia Rodd played Carol. Ian Harmon is Arthur's grandson; Henry Evans (later to become James Evans) is Florida's husband. Donny Hathaway sings the theme "And Then There's Maude."

Cast: Bea Arthur *(Maude Findlay)*; Bill Macy *(Walter Findlay)*; Adrienne Barbeau *(Carol Traynor)*; Conrad Bain *(Dr. Arthur Harmon)*; Rue McClanahan *(Vivian Harmon)*; Esther Rolle *(Florida Evans)*; Hermione Baddeley *(Nell Naugatuck)*; Marlene Warfield *(Victoria Butterfield)*; Brian Morrison, Kraig Metzinger *(Philip Traynor)*; Charles Siebert *(Vernon Traynor)*; Sparky Marcus *(Ian Harmon)*; John Amos *(Henry Evans)*; Larry Gelman *(Dr. Hubie Binder; Arthur's friend)*; Jan Arvan *(Sam; the bartender)*; Fred Zuckert *(Fred; the bartender)*.

5874   *Maui Fever.* (Series; Reality; MTV; 2007). The lives of a group of twenty something friends who work for the Hawaiian island's resort industry and how their lives and friendships are affected by the different people (tourists) they encounter in each episode. Jesse Beyer, David Corbin, Justin Dutro, Chaunte, Cheyne Magnusson, Sean McClenahan, Anna Stimson, Kevin Sullivan and Anthony Vicar are the workers.

5875   *Maureen.* (Pilot; Comedy; CBS; Aug. 24, 1976). Maureen Langley is a middle-aged department store lingerie salesgirl. She is a widow and lives with her son (Damon) and her mother (Ruth) at 4579 West Caulfield Street. She leads a somewhat boring life and always puts herself out to help others. The proposal was to relate the problems that befall Maureen when she attempts to change her monotonous lifestyle. Mr. Frederick is Maureen's boss; Alice is her friend.

Cast: Joyce Van Patten *(Maureen Langley)*; Sylvia Sidney *(Ruth)*; Jack Bannon *(Damon Langley)*; Alan Oppenheimer *(Mr. Frederick)*; Karen Morrow *(Alice)*.

5876   *Maurice Woodruff Predicts.* (Series; Variety; Syn.; 1969). Celebrity interviews coupled with predictions by mentalist Maurice Woodruff.

Host: Maurice Woodruff. **Co-Host:** Robert Q. Lewis, Vidal Sassoon. **Announcer:** Robert Q. Lewis, Vidal Sassoon.

5877   *The Maury Povich Show.* (Series; Talk; Syn.; 1991). A sensitive talk program wherein host Maury Povich tackles very controversial topics that other shows in the genre overlook. Programs are usually emotional as victims of crimes as well as people with personal or emotional problems appear to tell their stories (and be asked questions by members of the studio audience). Guests, familiar with the problem at hand, appear to offer counseling.

Host: Maury Povich.

5878   *Maverick.* (Series; Western; ABC; 1957–1962). Bret and

Bart Maverick are brothers. They are gentlemen gamblers who roam the Old West in search of rich prey. They are also cowards at heart, but more often than not they find themselves helping people in trouble. They are unconventional, self-centered and untrustworthy, and they possess a genius for conning the con man.

Although they served with the Confederacy during the Civil War, they became Union soldiers when they were captured and figured it would be better to help the enemy than spend time in a Union prison camp. As "Galvanized Yankees" (as Bart puts it), they were assigned to keep the Indians under control out West. At this same time, it is mentioned that another Maverick, Cousin Beauregard (Beau), became a family disgrace when he was honored as a war hero. Beauregard ("Pappy") Maverick, the head of the family, instilled in his sons his cowardice and con-artist genius. When Pappy, as he is called, learned that his nephew, Beau, did something to bring honor to the Maverick name, he branded him "the white sheep of the family" and banished him to England. (Actually, Beau had been captured. While he was playing poker with a Union general, the Confederates attacked the camp. Just as the general lost a game and exclaimed, "Son, I give up," Confederate troops entered the tent. Beau was credited with the capture.) To make up for this family disgrace, Beau spent five years tarnishing his "good" name and was actually brought on (1960-61) to replace James Garner (who left the series in 1960). The following year, and until 1962, another brother, Brent, appeared when Roger Moore left at the end of the 1961 season.

It is against a Maverick's principles to drink alone, and they have one serious vice — curiosity. The Mavericks are from Little Bent, Texas, and a sheriff is not their best friend. A Maverick is not fast on the draw (if there is a way to get out of a gunfight, they will find it). Bart often says, "Sometimes it frightens me what I'll do for money." Bret contends that he is a cautious man — "It's the other faults that bother me."

Besides the Indians, the outlaws and the sheriff, another threat to Bret and Bart was Samantha ("Sam") Crawford, a beautiful con artist who was just as cunning and clever as the Mavericks. A Northern girl at heart, Sam faked a Southern accent and used, besides her genius at the con, her feminine wiles to acquire easy money.

Gentleman Jack Darby and Dandy Jim Buckley are gamblers who also sought easy money and easy prey. See also: *Bret Maverick, The New Maverick* and *Young Maverick.*

Cast: James Garner *(Bret Maverick)*; Jack Kelly *(Bart Maverick)*; Roger Moore *(Beau Maverick)*; Robert Colbert *(Brent Maverick)*; Diane Brewster *(Samantha Crawford)*; Efrem Zimbalist, Jr. *(Dandy Jim Buckley)*; James Garner *(Beauregard "Pappy" Maverick)*; Richard Long *(Gentleman Jack Darby).*

5879   *Maverick Square.* (Pilot; Comedy; ABC; June 29, 1991). Fat Nicky, as he is called, lives in Apartment 3 at 36 Maverick Square in East Boston. His best friend, Sal, lives across town next to the airport in a house that shakes every time a plane takes off. The proposal was to relate incidents in the lives of two best friends who find misadventure in everything they do. Althea is Sal's wife.

Cast: Michael Chiklis *(Fat Nicky)*; David Marciano *(Sal)*; Sharon Cornell *(Rochelle)*; Karla Tamburrelli *(Althea).*

5880   *Max.* (Pilot; Comedy; NBC; April 28, 1983). A proposed spin off from *Gimme a Break* about Max Greene, the owner of Max's Deli, and Danny, an orphan girl he takes under his wing after he catches her shoplifting.

Cast: Don Rickles *(Max Greene)*; LaShana Dendy *(Danny).*

5881   *Max and Me.* (Pilot; Comedy; ABC; July 12, 1985). Max Brennan and his wife Anne (the "Me" of the title) are a middle-aged married couple with a dream: to seek a rejuvenated lifestyle by moving back to New York City to relive the memories of their children who have grown up and moved away from their suburban home on Long Island. The proposal was to relate Max and Anne's misadventures when they do move to a Manhattan brownstone but can't seem to find what they are searching for. Other regulars are Leo and Ginger Winter, their always-battling downstairs neighbors; Mrs. Nelson, an overly protective mother who babies her grown son, Sheldon; Susan, Max's daughter; and Ogden Dust, an undercover police detective who lives in the building.

Cast: Pat Harrington, Jr. *(Max Brennan)*; Dawn Greenhalgh *(Anne Brennan)*; Mary Long *(Susan)*; Brian George *(Ogden Dust)*; Derek McGrath *(Leo Winter)*; Mary Ann McDonald *(Ginger Winter)*; Helen Hughes *(Mrs. Nelson)*; Geoffrey Bowes *(Sheldon Nelson).*

5882   *Max and Ruby.* (Series; Cartoon; Nick; 2002-2003). Max and Ruby are a brother and sister who also happen to be rabbits (and, although they live in a large house, their parents are never seen). Max is three years old and is often at odds with his seven-year-old sister. Max is the mischievous one; Ruby, the obedient child, often has to use her wits to get Max out of the troublesome situations he gets into in his search for adventure. Stories relate the incidents that befall Max, Ruby and their friends (Louise, Valerie and Roger). Also appearing as a parental figure to Max and Ruby is their next-door neighbor, an elderly woman called Grandma.

Voice Cast: Samantha Morton *(Ruby)*; Katie Griffin *(Ruby)*; Bill Rosemberg *(Max)*; Julie Lemieux *(Louise)*; Cameron Ansell *(Morris)*; Kay Hawtrey *(Grandma).*

5883   *Max Headroom.* (Series; Adventure; ABC; 1987). The time is "20 minutes into the future." Television cannot be turned off; ratings are all that matter and Network 23 has become the number one broadcast signal. It has stiff competition from other networks and channel switching during commercials has become a major problem (it causes a dip in Network 23's ratings). To resolve the problem, Bryce Lynch, the head of Network 23's research and development, creates Blipverts, a system that compresses 30 seconds of commercials into only three seconds. The Blipverts work fine at first, until the unexpected happens — viewers begin to explode (spontaneously combust). The human body has millions of nerve endings, each of which contains a small electrical charge. Individually they are harmless and active people burn them off. However, in overweight or inactive people, the electrical charges build up. When a Blipvert is seen, the impulses violently stimulate these nerve endings. They cause a short circuit in inactive people who then explode. Authorities have not yet been able to associate Blipverts with these deaths.

Edison Carter is a world famous journalist who hosts *The What I Want to Know Show* (a news program that goes after stories) on Network 23. His control (newsroom director) is Theora Jones, a beautiful computer genius who worked previously for the defunct World One Network. Edison decides to investigate the mysterious viewer explosions. When he gets too close, hit men are hired to stop him. The hit men's initial attempt to kill Carter fails when he escapes on a motorcycle. Carter is caught, however, when he misjudges a parking lot crossing gate (which reads "Max Headroom 2.3 feet") and crashes into it. He is brought to Bryce's lab. Carter, however, can't be killed; he is too famous and will be missed. Bryce devises a way to resolve this: he creates a computer-generated image of Carter to be seen and programmed to do what Bryce wants. Before the theory is tested, Carter, still unconscious, is given to the hit men for disposal (they sell him for body parts at the Nightingale Body Parts Clinic). When Bryce activates his Edison Carter, he finds that it is not Carter but an image that calls itself Max Headroom (the last image Carter saw before the accident). The image is wisecracking and a joker and only faintly resembles Carter. When Bryce finds that he cannot erase the image, he tells the hit men to dispose of the computer unit that houses it. The hit men sell it to Blank Reg, the operator of Big Time TV. Blank Reg activates Max Headroom and Max soon becomes a top Big Time TV personality. Meanwhile, Edison has regained consciousness and escapes from the body parts clinic. With Theora's help, he exposes Network 23 and its deadly Blipverts. Stories follow Edison's adventures as a reporter for Network 23 and those of his alter ego, Max Headroom.

Cast: Matt Frewer (*Edison Carter/Max Headroom*); Amanda Pays (*Theora Jones*); Morgan Sheppard (*Blank Reg*); Hilary Tindal, Concetta Tomei (*Dominique*); Paul Spurrier (*Bryce Lynch*).

5884   *The Max Headroom Show.* (Series; Talk; Cinemax; 1985). An unusual talk show wherein guests are interviewed by a computerized image (Max Headroom) that appears on a TV screen. (Actually an actor, heavily made up in rubber makeup and enhanced by computer animation, that creates the Max Headroom image).

Cast: Matt Frewer (*Max Headroom*).

5885   *Max Liebman Presents.* (Series; Anthology; NBC; 1954–1956). Monthly program of lavish variety specials produced by Max Liebman: *Satins and Spurs, Sunday in Town, Fanfare, Spotlight, Good Times, Variety, The Big Time, A Connecticut Yankee, Kaleidoscope, The Desert Song, The Chocolate Soldier, Heidi, The Great Waltz, Dearest Enemy, Babes in Toyland, Paris in the Springtime, Panorama, Heaven Will Protect the Working Girl, Marco Polo, The Music of Gershwin, The Maurice Chevalier Show* and *Holiday.* Aired from Sept. 12, 1954 to June 4, 1955 and Oct. 1, 1955 to June 9, 1956.

5886   *Max Monroe: Loose Cannon.* (Series; Crime Drama; CBS; 1990). Maximilian Monroe is a detective with Precinct 57 of the L.A.P.D. Max, as he likes to be called, is rather unorthodox and likes to do things his way. He is also quite reckless when it comes to upholding the law. He feels a cop has to be as unpredictable as the felon he is pursuing in order to achieve positive results (a collar). He constantly defies authorities and has earned a reputation as a loose cannon (surprisingly his actions never get him fired or put on suspension; possibly because he always gets "the bad guy").

While Max is constantly taking the law into his own hands (he operates by what he calls "my own set of books"), his partner, Charlie Evers is his complete opposite. Charlie is a by-the-books detective who often finds working with Max not only contradicting everything he was taught, but also a good bet for losing his job. Charlie is trying to convince Max to stay within the limits of the law, but is not having much success.

Max is single and a ladies' man; Charlie is married to Loretta. Stories follow Max and Charlie as they attempt to uphold the law with totally different perspectives on how it should be done. Yello performs the theme, "Tied Up."

Cast: Shadoe Stevens (*Max Monroe*); Bruce A. Young (*Charlie Ivers*); Arnetia Walker (*Loretta Ivers, Charlie's wife*).

5887   *Max Steel.* (Series; Cartoon; WB Kids; 2000–2002). Josh McGrath is a college student and sportsman with a secret alias: Max Steel, an agent for N-Tek, an organization that incorporates "high tech" secret agents (bodies infused with nanoprobes and periodically charged with trans-phasic energy). Jefferson Smith, Josh's foster father heads N-Tek and stories relate Josh's efforts to secretly perform missions while trying to lead the life of an ordinary college student. Laura is his girlfriend; Pete is his best friend.

Voice Cast: Christopher Campbell (*Josh McGrath/Max Steel*); Chi McBride (*Jefferson Smith*); Lauren Tom (*Laura Chen*); Thomas F. Wilson (*Pete Costas*).

5888   *Max the 2000-Year-Old Mouse.* (Series; PBS; 1970–1979). A museum is the setting. It is here that Max, a pink mouse lives among the many artifacts. As a camera pinpoints a specific artifact, an animated story about it and the key figures and events in Western history that are associated with it are related by a narrator (with Max's help).

Voice Cast: Paul Soles (*Max*); Bernard Cowan (*Narrator*).

5889   *Maxie's World.* (Series; Cartoon; Syn.; 1987). Maxie is a teenage girl who is not only beautiful but also rich and spoiled as well. While she does attend school (Surfside High), thinking about boys, shopping, thinking about boys, dating and thinking about boys are uppermost on her mind. Stories follow Maxie and her equally spoiled girlfriends, Simone, Ashley and Carly as they live the idealistic life that can only be found and enjoyed by cartoon characters.

Voice Cast: Loretta Jafelice (*Maxie*); Susan Roman (*Ashley*); Suzanne Coy (*Simone*); Tara Strong (*Carly*); Nadine Rabinovitch (*Jeri*); Yannick Bisson (*Ferdie*); Geoff Kahnert (*Mushroom*).

5890   *Maximum Exposure.* (Series; Comedy; Syn.; 2000). Do people do idiotic things and do these people ever get the maximum exposure? They do here, as *Maximum Exposure* showcases the home videos of ordinary people caught doing funny and sometimes foolish things (for example, an Evel Knievel wannabe using a bicycle to jump from one rooftop to another). The commentary of the host is also meant to be funny as he says things as idiotic as the people are seen doing in the videos.

Host: Cam Brainard. Music: Mike Greene.

5891   *Maximum Security.* (Series; Drama; HBO; 1985). A gritty, realistic look at prison life as seen through the eyes of Frank Murphy, a long-term inmate (convicted of a crime of passion) at the Riverdale Correctional Facility. Other regulars are Robert McShane, the warden; Dr. Allison Brody, the deputy warden; Leslie, a guard; Bonnie, Frank's wife; and prisoners Benny, Papa Jack, Harry and Puck.

Cast: Geoffrey Lewis (*Frank Murphy*); Stephen Elliott (*Robert McShane*); Jean Smart (*Dr. Allison Brody*); Kerry Sherman (*Leslie Bandercar*); Caroline McWilliams (*Bonnie Murphy*); Robert Desiderio (*Harry*); Trinidad Silva (*Benny*); Stan Shaw (*Papa Jack*); Ponchito Gomez (*Puck*).

5892   *The Maxx.* (Series; Cartoon; MTV; 1995). A spoof of the superhero genre as seen through the adventures of Maxx, a homeless (purple clad) super hero who lives in a cardboard box. While Maxx may think his life has gone by unnoticed, there is Julie Winters, a social worker who cares for him and helps him when she can. While Maxx's situation is not bad enough already, he also suffers from delusions and believes he lives in a surreal world called Pangea. Here, in a fantasy sequence, Maxx is an heroic jungle king and Julie is his queen, whom he must constantly protect from evil. However, just when things are getting good for Maxx in Pangea, he shifts back to the real world and his cardboard box. Stories follow Maxx's adventures as he drifts back and forth between both worlds.

Voice Cast: Michael Haley (*The Maxx*); Glynnis Talken Campbell (*Julie Winters*); Amy Danles (*Sara James*); David Valera (*Isz*); Barry Stigler (*Mr. Gone*); Patty Wynne-Hughes (*Sara's mother*).

5893   *Maya.* (Series; Adventure; NBC; 1967-1968). Terry Bowen, an American boy from Montana, arrives in Bombay, India, to join his father, great hunter Hugh Bowen. At the American Counsel, Terry learns that his father is missing and is believed to have been killed by a man-eating tiger. Believing that no animal can kill his father, Terry decides to begin his own search for his father. Authorities, however, refuse to let him do so. Terry manages to escape and, while seeking refuge in a train's boxcar, meets Raji, an Indian boy who was left alone in the world when a flood destroyed his village, and his pet elephant, Maya. When Raji learned that Maya did not legally belong to him and was to be shipped to the desert for a lifetime of labor, he and Maya fled; and now, a fugitive, he is wanted by the police for stealing the elephant. Stories relate the adventures of two fourteen-year-old boys who join forces to help each other complete their self-imposed missions: Terry to find his missing father; Raji to return Maya to the land of her birth and freedom.

Program Open: "Young Terry Bowen arrives in India from America to join his father, great white hunter Hugh Bowen. But Bowen has been lost on a tiger hunt and is presumed dead, although his body was not found. Convinced that his father is alive, Terry escapes the authorities who wanted to ship him back to America. Teaming with two other fugitives, Raji, an orphan Indian boy, and Maya, his elephant, Terry Bowen searches for his missing father through the strange cities and dangerous jungles of India."

Cast: Jay North (*Terry Bowen*); Sajid Khan (*Raji*). **Narrator:** Marvin Miller.

5894   *Maya and Miguel.* (Series; Cartoon; PBS; 2004). Maya and Miguel Santos are ten-year-old Hispanic twins. They are the children of Rosa and Santiago and the simplistic series relates the twins' adventures at home and at school with stories designed to familiarize children with the Spanish culture. Paco is the family's pet bird; Theo is Miguel's best friend; Chrissie and Maggie are Maya's best friends; Abuela Elena is the twins' grandmother; Senor Felipe is the neighborhood mailman.

Voice Cast: Candi Milo (*Maya Santos*); Nika Futterman (*Miguel Santos*); Elizabeth Pena (*Rosa Santos*); Carlos Ponce (*Santiago Santos*); Carlos Alazraqui (*Paco*); Jerod Mixon (*Theo*); Elizabeth Payne (*Chrissy*); Lucy Liu (*Maggie*); Lupe Ontiveros (*Abuela Elena*); Erik Estrada (*Senor Felipe*).

5895   *Maybe It's Me.* (Series; Comedy; WB; 2001-2002). Molly Stage is a very pretty 15-year-old girl who keeps a daily computer diary of her life — a life that is complicated by her eccentric family — her parents, Jerry and Mary; her twin sisters, Cindy and Mindy; her brothers Rick and Grant; and her grandmother (on her mother's side) Harriet; and her grandfather (on her father's side) Fred.

Molly lives in Wicketstown, Rhode Island and attends Wicketstown High School. She has a best friend (Mia) and likes a fellow classmate (Nick). Because of her wacky family, Molly never invites anybody to her home — except for Mia.

Molly is president of the Chess Club and as a girl was called (and still is by her mother) "Tubby" (not because she was overweight, but because she liked to take baths).

Jerry is an eye doctor (runs Dr. Stage's Optical Services) at the South Street Medical Building. He has an excessive passion for girl's soccer and coaches the Wicketstown Terminators.

Mary is a well meaning mother but insanely frugal "and has no business advising her children," says Molly (she gives ludicrous advice; for example, Mary would say to Molly, "If that boy asks you to try marijuana again you say 'No thanks, my grass is for mowing'"). Mary rings a cowbell to announce breakfast.

Grant is a hopeful Christian rock star and has a band called Behold (he plays guitar and sings). Rick is the black sheep of the family. He is a petty thief and has the street name "Renegade."

Cindy and Mindy take piano lessons "and hate everyone," says Molly (she calls them "the sweet-faced little terrors"). The twins argue about being the same and wanting to be different. But when they become different (like dressing) they become sad and want to be the same again.

Fred, Jerry's father, is a real grouch. As Molly says, "Life stopped making sense to him in 1959 and he has been cranky ever since." Harriet, Mary's mother, is totally absent-minded and has a bad habit of hiding food around the house.

Mia, although Jewish, pretends to be a Christian, as she has a crush on Grant. She is a cheerleader and works at her father's music store, Leiber's C.D. and Vinyl Emporium. Nick, a member of the school's wrestling team, likes Molly but looks upon her as a Marilyn Munster (from the TV series *The Munsters*; Marilyn was the only normal one in an abnormal family).

Cast: Reagan Dale Neis (*Molly Stage*); Fred Willard (*Jerry Stage*); Julia Sweeney (*Mary Stage*); Patrick Lewis (*Grant Stage*); Andrew Walker (*Rick Stage*); Daniella Canterman (*Cindy Stage*); Deanna Canterman (*Mindy Stage*); Vicki Davis (*Mia Leiber*); Ellen Albertini Dow (*Harriet Krump*); Walter Marsh (*Fred Stage; pilot*); Dabbs Greer (*Fred Stage; series*); Shaun Sipos (*Nick Gibson*).

5896   *Maybe This Time.* (Series; Comedy; ABC; 1995-1996). The Coffee Dog Cafe is a small Pennsylvania eatery owned by Shirley Sullivan. Julia Wallace, her recently divorced daughter, has returned home to run the diner and raise her 12-year-old daughter, Gracie. Julia, 35, is a paragon of beauty and virtue. Her honesty often gets her into trouble and she believes men are incapable of having an independent thought. She believes her cheating ex-husband (Frank) will never find a girl "as good as I am." She is delighted when Frank dates "bubble heads" but saddened when he finds a "brainy babe."

Shirley has run the cafe for over 30 years. She has been married five times and worries that Julia keeps herself busy with work and has no social life. She has set her goal to see that Julia finds someone. Stories follow Julia as she seeks to begin a new life and raise her daughter despite her mother's efforts to find her a man. Kay is Shirley's friend; Logan is the diner cook.

Cast: Marie Osmond (*Julia Wallace*); Betty White (*Shirley Sullivan*); Ashley Johnson (*Gracie Wallace*); Amy Hill (*Kay O'Hara*); Craig Ferguson (*Logan McDonough*).

5897   *Mayberry, R.F.D.* (Series; Comedy; CBS; 1968–1971). The simple pleasures and trying times of Sam Jones, a full-time farmer and part-time city councilman in the small town of Mayberry, North Carolina. A spin off from *The Andy Griffith Show*.

Other regulars are Mike Jones, Sam's son (Sam is a widower); Millie Swanson, Sam's romantic interest; Goober Pyle, the gas station attendant; Bea Taylor, Sam's housekeeper (later replaced by Aunt Alice); Howard Sprague, the county clerk; Emmet Clark, the fix-it-shop owner; Martha Clark, Emmet's wife; Ralph and Arnold, Mike's friends.

Cast: Ken Berry (*Sam Jones*); Buddy Foster (*Mike Jones*); Arlene Golonka (*Millie Swanson*); George Lindsey (*Goober Pyle*); Frances Bavier (*Bea Taylor*); Alice Ghostley (*Aunt Alice*); Jack Dodson (*Howard Sprague*); Paul Hartman (*Emmet Clark*); Mary Lansing (*Martha Clark*); Richard Steele (*Ralph*); Sheldon Collins (*Arnold*).

5898   *Mayor of Hollywood.* (Series; Variety; NBC; 1952). Interviews with celebrities and tours of Hollywood with Walter O'Keefe as he attempts to win voters for his fictional quest to become the Mayor of Hollywood. Lou and Bill are his campaign managers; Jeanne and Lina are his campaign office secretaries.

Cast: Walter O'Keefe (*Himself*); Lou Crosby (*Lou*); Bill Baldwin (*Bill*); Jeanne Dyer (*Jeanne*); Lina Romay (*Lina*); . **Announcer:** Lou Crosby, Bill Baldwin. **Music:** Irvine Orton.

5899   *Mayor of the Town.* (Series; Comedy; Syn.; 1954). Springdale is a small American town with a kindly old Mayor

(Thomas Russell) who resides in an old-fashioned house on Elm Street with his nephew Roscoe Gardner and his housekeeper, Marilly. The Mayor enjoys sitting in his easy chair and reading the *Morning Chronicle* by the fireplace. He has an office on Main Street and each night before going to bed, he winds the clock, places the fire screen on the fireplace, puts the damper down and locks the front door. Each year he suffers from "post–Christmas mental hangover" (everything is dull, flat and uninteresting) that takes him the whole month of January to get over. Roscoe, nicknamed Butch, attends Springdale Elementary School. Marilly says the mischievous Butch "can do more damage doing nothing than 20 people doing something." When Butch is naughty, he is sent to bed early. Marilly prepares stewed chicken when guests arrive and talks endlessly about everything. The family has a pet cat (Sweet Alice) and a goldfish (Mr. Weismuller, named after Johnny Weismuller). Capitol City is the nearest metropolis (60 miles away). Minnie is the Mayor's secretary; Joe Ainsley is a member of the city council; June is the Mayor's niece. Based on the radio series (1941–49) with Lionel Barrymore as the mayor.

Cast: Thomas Mitchell *(Mayor Thomas Russell)*; David Saber *(Roscoe Gardner)*; Kathleen Freeman *(Marilly)*; Jean Byron *(Minnie)*; Tudor Owen *(Joe)*; Natalie Wood *(June)*.

5900   McAllister. (Pilot; Crime Drama; ABC; April 30, 1988). Thomas McCallister is a brilliant attorney based in Washington, D.C. He is half Apache and proud of his Indian heritage. Thomas is also determined to see that all people, regardless of their race, receive just treatment form the legal system. The proposed series, a spin off from *Spenser: For Hire* was to relate Thomas's defense of people convicted of a crime but whom he believes are innocent. Maggie is his girlfriend.

Cast: Steve Inwood *(Thomas McAllister)*; Andie MacDowell *(Maggie)*.

5901   McBride. (Series; Crime Drama; Hallmark Channel; 2005). McBride calls himself "A lawyer for the little guy." He has a heart of gold, is independently wealthy and money doesn't matter to him; he often takes cases based on merit. McBride has been a lawyer for eight years when the series begins. He was a member of the L.A.P.D. but became disillusioned as to how easy criminals get back on the street. He quit to attend law school. That was twelve years ago. Now, as a tough but honest defense lawyer, McBride does whatever he can, within the limits of the law, to free clients of criminal charges. Roberta Hansen is a detective with the L.A.P.D. (and McBride's former romantic interest when he was a detective; they still work well together); Phil Newberry is a former public defender that now works as McBride's assistant; Jesse is McBride's dog. John Larroquette, who plays McBride, requested that his character have no first name or even an initial. But through rumors and press material, he is listed as M. McBride or Mike McBride in some sources.

Cast: John Larroquette *(McBride)*; Marta DuBois *(Sgt. Roberta Hansen)*; Matt Lutz *(Phil Newberry)*.

5902   McClain's Law. (Series; Crime Drama; NBC; 1981-1982). When his friend, Sid Lammon is killed and the police investigation into the crime dissatisfies him, Jim McClain, a retired police detective, rejoins the force to solve the crime and do the job as he once did fifteen years ago — "by the gut." Stories relate the exploits of Jim McClain, a 52-year-old veteran cop, and his 30-year-old by-the-books partner, Harry Gates, as members of the San Pedro, California Police Department. Lieutenant Ed DeNisco is their superior; Vangie Cruise is Jim's friend, the owner of the Tides (later called The Flatfish Café), a water-front bar; Susan Cross, Jim's romantic interest; Marie DeNisco, Ed's wife; Detective Jerry Cross and Grace Bannon, Jim's neighbor. Jim wears badge number 127.

Cast: James Arness *(Jim McClain)*; Marshall Colt *(Harry Gates)*; George DiCenzo *(Ed DeNisco)*; Carl Franklin *(Jerry Cross)*; Conchata Ferrell *(Vangie)*; Cheryl Anderson *(Grace Bannon)*; Brooke Bundy *(Marie DeNisco)*; Tanya Boyd *(Susan Cross)*; Gerald S. O'Loughlin *(Sid Lammon; first episode)*.

5903   McCloud. (Series; Crime Drama; NBC; 1970–1977). Sam McCloud is a deputy marshal from Taos, New Mexico, who is assigned to Peter B. Clifford, police chief of the Manhattan 27th Precinct in New York City, to study big city crime detection methods by participating in actual crimes. He is assigned to work with Sergeant Joe Broadhurst and stories follow McCloud as he uses his homespun ways, coupled with what he is learning, to help New York's finest capture criminals. Chris Coughlin is Sam's romantic interest.

Cast: Dennis Weaver *(Sam McCloud)*; J.D. Cannon *(Peter B. Clifford)*; Terry Carter *(Joe Broadhurst)*; Diana Muldaur *(Chris Coughlin)*; Sharon Gless, Nancy Fox *(Sgt. Maggie Clinger)*; Ken Lynch *(Detective Grover)*.

5904   McCoy. (Series; Crime Drama; NBC; 1975-1976). A man known only as McCoy is an engaging private detective who incorporates his unique skills as a con artist to solve crimes. Gideon Gibbs is his assistant; Lucy is the owner of the diner frequented by McCoy.

Cast: Tony Curtis *(McCoy)*; Roscoe Lee Browne *(Gideon Gibbs)*; Lucille Meredith *(Lucy)*.

5905   McDuff, the Talking Dog. (Series; Comedy; NBC; 1976). Calvin Campbell is a somewhat misadventure-prone veterinarian in the small town of Peach Blossom. Calvin cares deeply for the animals he treats and finds his life changing when the ghost of a sheep dog named McDuff appears to him. McDuff feels that Calvin needs help and has materialized to help guide his life. Stories follow Calvin's efforts to cope with the situations that arise as he takes advice from a dog that only he can see and hear. Kimmy is Calvin's sister; Amos is his crusty neighbor; Squeaky is Amos's nephew; Mrs. Osgood is Calvin's housekeeper.

Cast: Walter Wilson *(Dr. Calvin Campbell)*; Michelle Stacy *(Kimmy Campbell)*; Gordon Jump *(Amos Ferguson)*; Johnnie Collins III *(Squeaky)*; Monty Margetts *(Mrs. Osgood)*; Jack Lester *(Voice of McDuff)*.

5906   McGarry and Me. (Pilot; Comedy; CBS; July 5, 1960). Events in the day-to-day lives of Dan McGarry, a kind-hearted but trouble prone police officer, and his wife, Kitty, the woman who looks out for him. Based on the radio series *McGarry and His Mouse*.

Cast: Michael O'Shea *(Dan McGarry)*; Virginia Mayo *(Kitty McGarry)*; Les Tremayne *(Captain)*.

5907   McGee and Me. (Pilot; Comedy; ABC; Jan. 15, 1994). Nicholas Martin is a 12-year-old boy who lives in the town of Eastfield with his parents (Elizabeth and David) and sisters (Sara and Jamie). He is a talented artist and one day creates McGee, a cartoon character who magically comes to life and speaks only to him. McGee's efforts to guide Nicholas's life is the focal point of the unsold series. Louis is Nicholas's best friend; Whatever is the family dog. A second pilot, incorporating the same cast and storyline and title, aired on ABC on Feb. 5, 1994.

Cast: Joseph Dammann *(Nicholas Martin)*; Ken C. Johnson *(McGee's voice)*; Vaughn Taylor *(Elizabeth Martin)*; Terry Bozeman *(David Martin)*; Sarah Dammann *(Sara Martin)*; Chelsea Hertford *(Jamie Martin)*; Brent Kelly *(Louis)*; Poundcake *(Whatever)*.

5908   McGhee. (Pilot; Comedy; CBS; June 28, 1965). Following the death of a distant relative, Walter McGhee, an impoverished artist living in the Bronx, inherits Cleveland, California, a small town populated by 209 people. The proposal was to depict McGhee's efforts to get the town back on its feet after he discovers it is bankrupt. Other regulars are Ann, the town manager; George, the sheriff; and Hilda, McGhee's cousin.

Cast: Jeremy Slate (*Walter McGhee*); Karen Steele (*Ann Dorsey*); George Chandler (*George*); Connie Sawyer (*Hilda*).

5909 *The McGonigle.* (Pilot; Comedy; NBC; July 28, 1961). First Class Boatman's Mate Mac McGonigle and his friend Seaman "Scuttlebutt" Baines are two mischievous but well-meaning sailors stationed aboard the USS *Okinawa*. Their efforts to help people in trouble are the focal point of the unsold series.

Cast: Mickey Shaughnessy (*Mac McGonigle*); Tom D'Andrea (*Scuttlebutt Baines*); Frank Gerstle (*Captain Amboy*); Wally Cassell (*Chief Petty Officer Commissar Jones*); Paul Picerni (*Seaman Bottleneck*); Norman Grabowski (*Seaman Hammerhead*).

5910 *McHale's Navy.* (Series; Comedy; ABC; 1962–1966). Taratupa, an island in the South Pacific during World War II, is the setting. The navy has established a base and has put Wallace B. Binghamton in charge. Binghamton was born in New York and was head of the Long Island Yacht Club before the war; he is somewhat inadequate at being a captain. He is assisted by Lieutenant Elroy Carpenter, who commands PT Boat 16.

Quinton McHale was born in Michigan and was the captain of a tramp steamer in the South Pacific when Admiral Reynolds commissioned him as a lieutenant and assigned him to Taratupa as the commander of Squadron 19 and PT Boat 73. McHale and "his crew of pirates" (as Binghamton calls them) live on the far side of the island in what is called "McHale's Island." The crew, who wheel and deal, have turned Taratupa into "The Las Vegas of the Pacific" and have ruined what Binghamton considers a paradise. His attempts to get the goods on McHale are the focal point of the series. McHale's crew calls Binghamton "Old Lead Bottom," and they have an unreported prisoner of war named Fuji Kobiaji; Fuji is a Japanese soldier who went over the hill and now serves as McHale's cook. McHale's "pirates" are Charles Parker, Lester Gruber, Harrison ("Tinker") Bell, Willy Moss, Joseph "Happy" Haines, Virgil Edwards and Quartermaster ("Christy") Christopher.

Last season episodes are set in Voltafiore, Italy where McHale, his crew and Binghamton have been transferred to the European theater of war.

Cast: Ernest Borgnine (*Lt. Quinton McHale*); Joe Flynn (*Capt. Wallace B. Binghamton*); Tim Conway (*Ensign Charles Parker*); Carl Ballantine (*Lester Gruber*); Billy Sands (*Harrison "Tinker" Bell*); John Wright (*Willy Moss*); Gavin MacLeod (*Joseph "Happy" Haines*); Edson Stroll (*Virgil Edwards*); Gary Vinson (*Quarter Master Christopher*); Bob Hastings (*Lt. Elroy Carpenter*); Jane Dulo (*Nurse Molly Turner*); Yoshio Yoda (*Fuji Kobiaji*); Jacques Aubuchon (*Chief Tali Urulu*); Roy Roberts (*Adm. Bruce Rogers*); Jay Novello (*Mario Lugatto*); Dick Wilson (*Baroni*); Peggy Mondo (*Mama Rosa Giovanni*); Cindy Robbins (*Lt. Gloria Winters*); Henry Beckman (*Col. Harrigan*).

5911 *McKeever and the Colonel.* (Series; Comedy; NBC; 1962–1963). When his father, Major McKeever, is transferred to a U.S. Air Force base in Paris, his son, Gary McKeever, is enrolled in the Westfield Military Academy for Boys in California to allow him to complete his education (it is not made clear if Major McKeever is a widower or married; a mother for Gary is not mentioned).

Harvey Blackwell is the school's commander, a man who relishes in the fact that he runs a well disciplined school. Gary is a mischievous boy and feels that a strict military code prevents him from being a kid or having fun. Gary has set his goal to enjoy his stay at Westfield despite the rules that Colonel Blackwell has set. Harvey's life suddenly becomes anything but peaceful and stories relate Harvey's efforts to discipline Gary and his equally mischievous cadets, Tubby and Monk. Sergeant Claude Barnes is Harvey's assistant; Miss Frances Warner is the dietician.

Cast: Scott Lane (*Gary McKeever*); Allyn Joslyn (*Col. Harvey Blackwell*); Jackie Coogan (*Sgt. Claude Barnes*); Elisabeth Fraser (*Frances Warner*); Keith Taylor (*Cadet Tubby Anderson*); Johnny Eimen (*Cadet Monk*); Peter Hanson (*Major McKeever*); Susan Gordon (*Andrea*); Charlie Ruggles (*Claude's Father*); Ellen Corby (*Harvey's Mother*); Benny Baker (*Tubby's Father*); Doris Singleton (*Tubby's Mother*).

5912 *McKenna.* (Series; Adventure; ABC; 1994–1995). McKenna Wilderness Outfitters is a ranch and guide company based in Bend, Oregon. It is run by Jack McKenna, a widower, who is assisted by his children: Brick, Cassidy, Leigh, Harry and Rose. Stories follow the McKenna's experiences as they struggle to run the ranch and conduct a faltering tour business amid the gorgeous Oregon mountain scenery.

Cast: Chad Everett (*Jack McKenna*); Eric Close (*Brick McKenna*); Jennifer Love Hewitt (*Cassidy McKenna*); Vinessa Shaw (*Cassidy McKenna; pilot episode*); Shawn Huff (*Leigh McKenna*); Ashlee Lauren (*Rose McKenna*); Jacob Loyst (*Harry McKenna*); Jack Kehler (*Walter Maddock*); Rick Peters (*Dale Goodwin*).

5913 *McLaren's Riders.* (Pilot; Adventure; CBS; May 17, 1977). In an attempt to help understaffed police departments, the federal government creates the McLaren Project, a law enforcement program that helps where needed. The proposal was to relate the exploits of its two top agents, highly trained policemen Sam Downing and T. Wood.

Cast: George DiCenzo (*Sam Downing*); Ted Neeley (*T. Wood*).

5914 *The McLean Stevenson Show.* (Pilot; Variety; NBC; Nov. 20, 1975). Comedy sketches that spotlight the talents of McLean Stevenson in his first project after leaving *M*A*S*H*.

Host: McLean Stevenson. **Guests:** Mary Jo Catlett, Brion James, Philip Simms, Ken Stein, Raquel Welch, Edward Winter.

5915 *The McLean Stevenson Show.* (Series; Comedy; NBC; 1976–1977). Evanston, Illinois, is the setting for events in the life of Mac Ferguson, a hardware store owner, as he struggles to cope with life both at home and at work. Peggy is Mac's wife; Janet is their divorced daughter. Chris is their son; Muriel is Peggy's mother. David and Jason are Janet's sons.

Cast: McLean Stevenson (*Mac Ferguson*); Barbara Stuart (*Peggy Ferguson*); Ayn Ruyman (*Janet*); Steve Nevil (*Chris Ferguson*); Madge West (*Muriel*); David Hollander (*David*); Jason Whitney (*Jason*).

5916 *McLeod's Daughters.* (Series; Drama; WE; 2005–2006). Claire McLeod and Tess Silverman McLeod are estranged sisters who are reunited after 20 years when they inherit Drovers Run, a vast cattle ranch. Now, as the owners of the ranch, Claire and Tess form a bond to work together to keep the family legacy alive. Produced in Australia.

Cast: Bridie Carter (*Tess Silverman McLeod*); Lisa Campbell (*Claire McLeod*); Brooke Stacy-Clark, Kaitlyn Stacy-Clark, Tahlia Stacy-Clark (*Charlotte McLeod*); Aaron Jeffrey (*Alex Ryan*); Rachael Carpani (*Jodi Fountain*); Myles Pollard (*Nick Ryan*); Simmone Mackinnon (*Stevie Hall*); Michala Banas (*Kate Manfredi*); Jessica Napier (*Becky Howard*); Sonia Todd (*Meg Fountain*); Brett Tucker (*Dave Brewer*); Inge Hornstra (*Sandra Kinsella*); Michelle Langstone (*Fiona Webb*).

5917 *McMasters of Sweetwater*. (Pilot; Drama; Syn.; Sept. 2, 1974). Marion McMasters is a gentle Boston school teacher who believes he can find fulfillment by teaching out west. Marion, a widower with two children (Claire and Marion Jr.) relocates to the town of Sweetwater, Arizona, and the proposal was to relate the McMasters family as they struggle to adjust to the difficulties of frontier life in the turn-of-the-20th-century settlement town.

Cast: Jack Cassidy (*Marion McMasters*); Tracy Gartside (*Claire McMasters*); Errol Bartine III (*Marion McMasters, Jr.*).

5918 *McMillan*. (Series; Crime Drama; NBC; 1977). A spin off from *McMillan and Wife* without series co-star Susan Saint James (Sally, her character, "died" in an airplane crash). Stories follow Stewart "Mac" McMillan, the Police Commissioner of San Francisco, as he takes an active part in solving crimes. He is assisted by Lieutenant Charles Enright and Sergeant DiMaggio; Aggie Thorton is his housekeeper; Maggie is his secretary.

Cast: Rock Hudson (*Stewart McMillan*); Martha Raye (*Agatha Thorton*); Charles Schuck (*Lt. Charles Enright*); Richard Gilliland (*Sergeant DiMaggio*); Gloria Stroock (*Maggie*); Bill Quinn (*Police Chief Paulson*).

5919 *McMillan and Wife*. (Series; Crime Drama; NBC; 1971–1976). The home at 345 Melrose in San Francisco is the residence of Stewart McMillan, the police commissioner, and his wife, Sally, a woman who loves to play detective and help her husband solve crimes.

Stewart, nicknamed Mac ("Everybody calls me Mac"), is a former lawyer and Korean War veteran (Naval Intelligence). Mac reads a paper called the *Daily Post* and at breakfast he likes his English muffins broken apart ("one breaks an English muffin; one does not cut it"). He has lunch at a health food diner called The Grainery and hates going to Sally's mother's house for Saturday brunch ("She's a terrible cook"). Mac mentioned that his grandfather, John P. McMillan, began a company in 1903 called Kenamack Alfalfa, which was designed but failed to find new uses for alfalfa. Mac played football in college and each year turns lawyer for his annual reserve duty with the Navy's Legal Service Office.

Mac is an unusual police commissioner as he actually involves himself in criminal investigations. This pleases Sally, a bright woman who believes she has the makings of a private investigator. Sally, maiden name Hull, works with deaf children at Century Hospital and when she has a problem, she meditates. Sally has an uncanny knack for finding trouble. She gathers evidence for Mac "by peeking" ("It's not nice to be sneaky"). Sally hopes to surpass her mother in the cooking department and takes gourmet culinary classes at the local high school. She believes she is on the right track because Mac "loved my rattlesnake béarnaise and walnut casserole in goat butter."

Mildred cooks and cleans for Mac and Sally. She considers herself a Jill of all trades for all the work she does — including helping Sally solve crimes. Mildred has a slight drinking problem and is trying to quit. Sergeant Charles Enright is Mac's right hand man. Mildred Natwick played Mac's eccentric mother, Beatrice McMillan; Linda Watkins was Sally's mother, Emily Hull. See also *McMillan*.

Cast: Rock Hudson (*Stewart McMillan*); Susan Saint James (*Sally McMillan*); Nancy Walker (*Mildred*); John Schuck (*Sgt. Charles Enright*); Gloria Stroock (*Maggie; Stewart's secretary*); Bill Quinn (*Police Chief Paulson*).

5920 *McNab's Lab*. (Pilot; Comedy; ABC; July 22, 1966). Andrew McNab hopes to one day invent something that not only works, but what the world actually needs. Andrew, a widowed small town druggist with two children, Ellen and Timmy, is an amateur inventor whose inventions often cause mishap for all concerned. The proposal, broadcast on *Summer Fun*, was to follow Andrew's efforts to invent and care for his children.

Cast: Cliff Arquette (*Andrew McNab*); Sherry Alberoni (*Ellen McNab*); David Bailey (*Timmy McNab*).

5921 *McNaughton's Daughter*. (Series; Crime Drama; NBC; 1976). Laurel McNaughton is a trial lawyer and the Deputy District Attorney of Los Angeles. She is the daughter of the former D.A. (George McNaughton) and is living in his shadow — a shadow she loves to emulate as she stands for justice and will make every effort to see that justice is served. Stories relate not only her case investigations but aspects of her courtroom prosecutions. Lou is her investigator; Charles is the D.A.; Ed is Laurel's associate.

Cast: Susan Clark (*Laurel McNaughton*); James Callahan (*Lou Farragut*); Ricardo Montalban (*Charles Quintero*); John Elerick (*Ed Hughes*).

5922 *McShane*. (Pilot; Crime Drama; NBC; Oct. 28 and Nov. 3, 1986). James L. McShane is a former cop turned district attorney of Atlanta, Georgia. McShane is overweight, has a German shepherd named Max and has vowed to break the back of organized crime. Broadcast on *Matlock* and with some changes, it became the CBS series *Jake and the Fatman*. Other regulars are Lieutenant Frank Daniels; and Palmer, McShane's legman.

Cast: William Conrad (*James L. McShane*); James McEachin (*Frank Daniels*); Alan Campbell (*Palmer*).

5923 *MDs*. (Series; Drama; ABC; 2002). Mission General is a San Francisco hospital whose operators care more about making money than they do about a patient. Shelly Pangborn is the newly appointed administrator who is not really qualified for the job. She is a former theme park manager and struggling to gain the respect of the doctors and nurses who resent her authority. Dr. Bruce Kellerman is the head of the cardio-thoracic unit and manipulates the system to benefit the patient. Dr. Robert Dalgety is the trauma specialist; Dr. Quinn Joyner is the by-the-books physician; Aileen Poole is the head nurse whose main concern is making a profit for the hospital; Dr. Maggie Yang is the young, impressionable intern; Frank Coones is the assistant administrator.

Cast: William Fichtner (*Bruce Kellerman*); John Hannah (*Robert Dalgety*); Leslie Stefanson (*Shelly Pangborn*); Aunjanue Ellis (*Quinn Joyner*); Michaela Conlin (*Maggie Yang*); Jane Lynch (*Ailen Poole*); Robert Joy (*Frank Coones*).

5924 *Me and Benjy*. (Pilot; Comedy; NBC; July 27, 1970). Life in a small American town as seen through the adventures of two mischievous young boys (Homer and Benjy). Other regulars are Ruth and Fred, Homer's parents; Winifred, Homer's sister; Beverly and Joe, Benjy's parents; and Vivian, Benjy's sister.

Cast: Tony Frazer (*Homer Baker*); Audrey Dalton (*Ruth Baker*); John Lupton (*Fred Baker*); Cindy Cassell (*Winifred Baker*); Kevin Herron (*Benjy Smith*); Tracy Reed (*Beverly Smith*); Bernie Hamilton (*Joe Smith*); Kim Hamilton (*Vivian Smith*).

5925 *Me and Ducky*. (Pilot; Comedy; NBC; June 21, 1979). Carol Munday and Cidra Hopnagel, better known as Ducky, are teenage girls who are also best friends. The girls attend San Francisco High School and their misadventures at home and school is the focal point of the proposed series. Other regulars are Dawn, Babs, Toby and Rims, their friends; and Carol's mother and father (no first names given).

Cast: Linda Cook (*Carol Munday*); Jayne Modean (*Cidra "Ducky" Hopnagel*); Dawn Dunlap (*Dawn Duval*); Valerie Landsburg (*Babs*

Hulet); Susan Duvall *(Toby Wells)*; Gary Imhoff *(Rims)*; Kathleen Doyle *(Carol's mother)*; James Karen *(Carol's father)*.

5926 Me and Maxx. (Series; Comedy; NBC; 1980). When a daughter (Maxx) is born to Elaine and Norman Davis, Norman deserts his wife and child, for he feels he cannot handle the responsibility. Eleven years later, Elaine (not seen) decides that it is time to even up the score.

Believing that she is only going to stay with her father for two weeks while her mother is on vacation, Maxx Davis packs a suitcase and crosses the Brooklyn Bridge to Norman's apartment in Manhattan. Norman is surprised by Maxx's visit and shocked when the letter Elaine gave to Maxx for Norman reveals that Elaine is abandoning Maxx and it is now his turn to care for her. Norman has only seen Maxx four times in 11 years. He lives in a small, one bedroom apartment and leads a swinging life-style. When Maxx learns about the letter, she feels unwanted and decides to leave. Norman prevents her from going to New Jersey to live with her elderly grandmother and tells her that she can stay with him. Maxx's attempts to become close to a father she rarely saw and hardly knows are the focal point of stories.

Norman lives in Apartment 738 at 86 East 65th Street in Manhattan and runs Empire Tickets from it (which supplies tickets for sporting, cultural and theatrical events). Barbara is Norman's assistant. Maxx, whose real name is Maxine, attends Public School 135, and says she spells her name with two x's "because my mother says I was double-crossed." Micth is Norman's friend; Gary is the elevator operator. Leonore O'Malley sings the theme, "Is It Because of Love?"

In 1979 a similar series idea was rejected by ABC. *Maxx* is an unaired pilot about a womanizing New York bachelor named Norman (Tim Thomerson) and the complications that set in when he is suddenly made the guardian of his ten-year-old daughter, Maxx (Melissa Michaelsen), whom he deserted at birth.

Cast: Joe Santos *(Norman Davis)*; Melissa Michaelsen *(Maxx Davis)*; Jenny Sullivan *(Barbara)*; Jim Weston *(Mitch Russell)*; Denny Evans *(Gary)*.

5927 Me and Mom. (Series; Crime Drama; ABC; 1985). Morgan, Garfield and Hunnicutt is a Los Angeles–based private detective agency located at 2936 Hampton Boulevard. Lou Garfield, Kate Morgan and Zena Hunnicutt are its operatives. Lou Garfield is a former detective with the Homicide Division of the L.A.P.D. who, after his retirement, started the company to continue his crusade against crime. He has years of experience on the force to guide him and he operates much like he did when he was a cop — everything within the limit of the law.

Kate Morgan, the second partner, is a young criminologist, just out of school, who is eager to solve crimes that the police may not consider important enough or warrant their time to investigate. Kate has a deep desire to help people. She has always been this way and now she feels that when someone needs help but can't get it from the police, they can turn to her company for that help. She is dedicated to each and every cause and will do what it takes (sometimes going against Lou's beliefs) to seek justice.

Zena Hunnicutt, Kate's glamorous mother, is the third partner, a friend of Lou's from the time her late husband and Lou were partners on the police force. Zena, like Kate, is eager to see that justice is served although her participation in cases is more of a background monitor (lookout) rather than as actively involved with criminals as Lou and Kate. Mike Rojas is the L.A.P.D. lieutenant who often becomes involved in their cases. Stories relate the trio's efforts to solve the cases of people with no place else to turn. Amy Holland sings the theme, "Me and Mom."

Cast: Lisa Eilbacher *(Kate Morgan)*; Holland Taylor *(Zena Hun-*

nicutt); James Earl Jones *(Lou Garfield)*; Henry Darrow *(Lt. Mike Rojas)*.

5928 Me and Mrs. C. (Series; Comedy; NBC; 1986-1987). Rather than spend her golden years with her son and his family, Ethel Conklin, an independent 60-year-old widow, decides to remain in her home (at 2709 Webb Street). All is progressing smoothly until she discovers that her Social Security income is not sufficient. To ease the situation, Ethel decides to take in a boarder to help with the expenses. Ethel places a newspaper ad and Gerri Kilgore, an African American girl with a prison record responds. Despite the fact that Gerri is an ex-con (arrested for armed robbery) Ethel feels Gerri deserves a chance and allows her to move in. Gerri works for the Martin, Barton and Fargo computer company and pays Ethel $100 a month plus expenses (she paid $62.50 a month when the series first began). Stories follow Gerri and Ethel's experiences as Ethel finds her life changed for the better due to Gerri's presence and Gerri's experiences as she learns how to get the most out of life from Ethel.

Ethan Conklin is Ethel's son, a private practice certified public accountant. He is married to Kathleen and they are the parents of young Jamie. Ethan is opposed to his mother's living arrangements and is trying to convince her to live with him and his family. Gerri is the daughter of a preacher, the Reverend Kilgore. LaVonne Rucker sings the theme, "Side by Side."

In the original pilot episode (NBC, Mar. 18, 1984), Doris Roberts played 60-year-old Ethel Connelly; Debra Malone was her boarder, Jeri Monroe; Terrence McGovern was Ethel's son, Ethan Connelly and Mary Armstrong was Ethan's wife, Kathleen. Here, Deborah Malone sings the theme, "Me and Mrs. C."

Cast: Peg Murray *(Ethel Conklin)*; Misha McK *(Gerri Kilgore)*; Gary Bayer *(Ethan Conklin)*; Ellen Regan *(Kathleen Conklin)*; Jeremy Brown *(Jamie Conklin)*; Scoey Mitchell *(the Reverend Kilgore)*.

5929 Me and the Boys. (Series; Comedy; ABC; 1994). Following the death of his wife, a hard-working father of three (Steve Tower) suddenly finds his life more complicated than he thought: how to work and care for his three sons (William, Andrew and Artis) without the loving care of his wife? The solution: Mary, his mother-in-law, who has moved in with Steve to help him do what he cannot do alone — raise his sons. Stories follow Steve (and Mary's) efforts to raise three mischievous boys.

Cast: Steve Harvey *(Steve Tower)*; Wayne Collins, Jr. *(William Tower)*; Benjamin LeVert *(Andrew Tower)*; Chaz Lamar Shepherd *(Artis Tower)*; Madge Sinclair *(Mary)*; Wendy Raquel Robinson *(Amelia)*.

5930 Me and the Chimp. (Series; Comedy; CBS; 1972). While playing in the park, Kitty and Scott, the children of Mike Reynolds (a dentist) and his wife, Liz, find an apparently abandoned chimpanzee that they take and unofficially adopt. The chimp, named Buttons by Kitty for his habit of pushing buttons he sees, is actually a lab animal that escaped from an Air Force test lab in San Pascal, California. While Liz is comfortable with the idea of their new "family" member, Mike finds it a bit uneasy living with Buttons as he and Buttons do not always see eye to eye on everything. Stories follow Kitty and Scott's efforts to care for Buttons and the problems that arise when Buttons sets out to do things his way.

Cast: Ted Bessell *(Mike Reynolds)*; Anita Gillette *(Liz Reynolds)*; Kami Cotler *(Kitty Reynolds)*; Scott Kolden *(Scott Reynolds)*; Jackie *(Buttons)*.

5931 Meadowlands. (Series; Drama; Showtime; 2007). Danny and Evelyn Brogan appear to be a happily married couple. They are the parents of two teenage children (Zoe and Mark) and live in what appears to be an ideal neighborhood called Meadowlands. The only thing revealed about the Brogans is that they are in the Witness Protection Program and trying to begin a new life style. Except for the fact that the family is living a lie, nothing is revealed about them — not who they really are, where they previously lived or even why they are in the program (which usually protects witness in murder cases against high profile figures). Stories relate events in the individual lives of the family members. They apparently fear for their safety (always looking over their shoulder) and are struggling to overcome these feelings (and the suspicions of others) as they begin preparations to become part of a community that has many hidden secrets (like everyone seems to be a part of the Witness Protection Program). Also known as *Cape Wrath* in England (where it is produced).

Cast: David Morrissey (*Danny Brogan*); Lucy Cohu (*Evelyn Brogan*); Felicity Jones (*Zoe Brogan*); Harry Treadway (*Mark Brogan*); Sian Brooke (*Lori Marcuse*); Don Gilet (*Freddie Marcuse*); Tom Hardy (*Jack Donnelly*); Emma Davies (*Abigail York*); Tristan Gemmill (*Dr. David York*); Ella Smith (*Jezebel Ogilvie*); Melanie Hill (*Brenda Ogilvie*); Nina Sosanya (*Samantha Campbell*); Ralph Brown (*Bernard Wintersgill*).

5932   The Meant to Be's. (Pilot; Drama; Unaired; Produced for CBS in 2006). Janine Sebring is a young woman who dies, is sent to Purgatory, but in order to achieve heavenly status, is sent back to earth to help people improve their lives. Janine is watched over by "The Man" and the proposal was to follow her spiritual efforts to help those in need.

Cast: Amy Smart (*Janine Sebring*); Ioan Gruffudd (*The Man*).

5933   Meatballs and Spaghetti. (Series; Cartoon; CBS; 1982-1983). Meatballs and Spaghetti is a rock group comprised of Meatball, the plump group leader; Spaghetti, his slim wife; Clyde, their assistant; and Woofer, their dog. Stories relate the mishaps they encounter while playing for their fans.

Voice Cast: Ron Masak (*Meatballs*); Sally Julian (*Spaghetti*); Frank Welker (*Woofer*).

5934   Medallion Theater. (Series; Anthology; CBS; 1953-1954). The shortened *TV Guide* title for *Chrysler Medallion Theater.* See this title for information.

5935   Medic. (Series; Anthology; NBC; 1954–1956). Dramas that present authentic and sophisticated approaches to the medical problems people face and the treatment they receive from doctors. Victor Young and Edward Heyman composed the theme, "Blue Star."

Program Open: "My name is Konrad Styner. I'm a doctor of medicine. Guardian of birth, healer of the sick; comforter of the aged. To the profession of medicine; to the men and women who labor in its cause, this story is dedicated."

Host: Richard Boone (*as Dr. Konrad Styner*). **Announcer:** Lee Vines.

5936   Medical Center. (Series; Drama; CBS; 1969–1976). Dr. Paul Lochner is the administrative surgeon at University Medical Center in Los Angeles. Joe Gannon is a professor of surgery. Stories relate the events in their lives in an adult-oriented and technically accurate drama that depicts the problems faced by doctors in a large city hospital. The pilot film, *UMC* aired on April 17, 1969.

Cast: James Daly (*Dr. Paul Lochner*); Chad Everett (*Dr. Joe Gannon*); Richard Bradford (*Dr. Joe Gannon; pilot*); Tyne Daly (*Jenny Lochner; Paul's daughter*); Jayne Meadows (*Nurse Chambers*); Corinne Comacho (*Dr. Bartlett*); Audrey Totter (*Nurse Wilcox*); Barbara Bal-

davin (*Nurse Holmby*); Chris Huston (*Nurse Courtland*); Catherine Ferrar (*Nurse Higby*); Virginia Hawkins (*Nurse Crawford*); Louise Fitch (*Nurse Bascomb*); Robert Walden (*Dr. Corelli*); Jack Garner (*Dr. Bolton*); Nancy Priddy (*Nurse Loring*); Eugene Peterson (*Dr. Weller*); Fred Holliday (*Dr. Barnes*); Martin E. Brooks (*Lt. Samuels; L.A.P.D.*); Jonathan Lippe (*Sgt. Boyce; L.A.P.D.*).

5937   Medical Investigation. (Series; Drama; NBC; 2004). A somewhat disturbing medical drama that goes beyond the norm to graphically focus on the hypothetical situations that could arise if dangerous outbreaks of diseases should occur. The program focuses on the highly skilled professionals of the National Institutes of Health as they investigate, attempt to resolve situations and prevent a public panic.

Cast: Neal McDonough (*Dr. Stephen Connor*); Kelli Williams (*Dr. Natalie Durant*); Christopher Gorham (*Dr. Miles McCabe*); Anna Belknap (*Eva Rossi*); Troy Winbush (*Frank Powell*).

5938   Medical Story. (Series; Anthology; NBC; 1975-1976). An open, human approach to the problems of medicine as seen through the eyes of the doctor rather than the patient. David Gerber and Abby Mann are the producers. Notable performers include Juliet Mills, Sheila Larken, Kim Richards, Richard Mulligan, Shelley Fabares, Richard Basehart, Broderick Crawford, Deirdre Lenehan, Don Galloway, Diane Baker, Dane Clark, Vince Edwards, Pernell Roberts, Laurie Walters, Meredith Baxter, Howard Duff, Whitney Blake, Julie Cobb, Ann Sothern, Joan Van Ark.

5939   Medicine Ball. (Series; Drama; CBS; 1995). The personal and professional lives of a group of first year residents at the Bayview Medical Center, a teaching hospital in Seattle, Washington.

Cast: Sam McMurray (*Dr. Douglas McGill*); Jensen Daggett (*Dr. Katie Cooper*); Timothy Omunson (*Dr. Patrick Yates*); Harold Pruett (*Dr. Harley Spencer*); Donal Logue (*Dr. Danny Macklin*); Jeffrey D. Sams (*Dr. Clate Baker*); Kai Soremekun (*Dr. Nia James*); Darryl Fong (*Dr. Max Chang*); Vincent Ventresca (*Dr. Tom Powell*); Terri Ivens (*Dr. Elizabeth Vasquez*).

5940   Medicine Man. (Pilot; Comedy; Unaired; Produced in 1962). Old West satire about a fast-talking con man (Doc), his silent Indian partner (Junior) and his eight-year-old ward (Chris) as they roam throughout the West seeking rich prey.

Cast: Ernie Kovacs (*Doc*); Buster Keaton (*Junior*); Kevin Brodie (*Chris*).

5941   Medium. (Series; Drama; NBC; 2005–2011). Allison DuBois appears to be a typical housewife and mother. She is married to Joe, an aero space engineer for Aero Dytech Labs, and is the mother of Ariel, Bridget and Maria (also called Marie). Allison is studying to become a lawyer and works as an intern at the D.A.'s office in Phoenix, Arizona. Allison is also very special: she can see and talk to dead people ("It's like a freaky TV show," she says). Through her visions, Allison can actually see the truth. Spirits appear to her to tell her things. She also has dreams that come true. Allison can't explain why she possesses the ability but she uses it by helping Manny Devalos, the D.A. of Mariposa County, solve crimes. Ariel appears to have the same abilities as her mother but they are not as frequent. Lee Scanlon is a detective with the Phoenix, P.D. who assists Allison (and knows her secret); Cynthia Keener is the missing persons investigator. After Joe is let go from Aero Dytech Labs, he starts (then sells) his own business; he later works for Burroughs-Strauss Engineering. Ariel attends Dartmouth College in last season episodes.

Cast: Patricia Arquette (*Allison DuBois*); Jake Weber (*Joe DuBois*); Sofia Vassilieva (*Ariel DuBois*); Maria Lark (*Bridget DuBois*); Miranda

Carabello (*Maria DuBois*); Miguel Sandoval (*Manuel Devalos*); David Cubitt (*Lee Scanlon*); Anjelica Houston (*Cynthia Keener*); Marki Ann Meyer (*Sarah Donlin, Joe's sister*).

5942 Meego. (Series; Comedy; CBS; 1997). Meego Smith Triangle Not to Scale is an alien from the planet Marmazon Four Point O. Edward Parker is a doctor and widower with three children, Alex, Trip and Maggie. He is also desperately in need of a nanny to care for the kids while he is at work. Fate intervenes in a strange way. While returning from a vacation, Meego, for short, runs into a meteor shower and his ship, the *Bigga 2000* is damaged. The ship enters the earth's atmosphere and Meego is forced to land his ship — in the backyard of the Parker home. There young Alex discovers Meego and asks him to be his nanny. Alex tells Trip, but not Maggie (a blabbermouth) and his father, about Meego, who accepts Alex's offer. Meego then conceals his presence and pretends to be a nanny from the agency. Edward accepts him as an agency nanny and stories follow Meego as he struggles to repair his space ship and care for the Parker children.

Cast: Bronson Pinchot (*Meego*); Ed Begley, Jr. (*Dr. Edward Parker*); Michelle Trachtenberg (*Maggie Parker*); Erik von Detten (*Trip Parker*); Jonathan Lipnicki (*Alex Parker*).

5943 Meet Betty Furness. (Series; Women; CBS; 1953). Guests, interviews, fashion and other topics of interest to housewives.

Hostess: Betty Furness. **Regulars:** Don Cherry, Hank Ford, Bill Stern, David Ross. **Music:** The Buddy Weed Trio.

5944 Meet Corliss Archer. (Series; Comedy; CBS, 1951-1952; Syn., 1954-1955). Sixteen-year-old Corliss Archer, the daughter of Harry and Janet Archer, lives at 32 Oak Street in what appears to be a small American town. Corliss is a pretty high school sophomore with a penchant for getting herself into trouble. She has a weekly allowance of one dollar ("Gee, I wish I could get my father to increase my allowance; a dollar doesn't go far these days") and is jealous of Betty Campbell, a mentioned (but not seen) girl whom she feels will steal her boyfriend, Dexter ("Ooh, I just know that scatterbrain is putting on an act to woo the boys," she says).

Dexter Franklin is the man Corliss plans to marry some day. He also receives an allowance of one dollar a week ("I have an allowance that rattles. I wish I could get one that rustles"). Dexter is the innocent victim of Corliss's endless attempts to improve him (she feels he needs to be more mature). More often than not, Corliss's attempts backfire. "Golly," says Corliss. "How do I manage to mess things up?" "I'll admit it takes talent," says her father, who often resolves the problems at the end of each episode. Despite Harry's help, Dexter still feels, as he says, "lower than a midget with flat feet." Dexter wants to keep on the good side of Harry because if he and Corliss marry, "we may want to live here one day."

Harry Archer is a private practice lawyer (Harold Archer, Attorney at Law) who has been married to Janet for 18 years. Janet, who was a secretary before marrying Harry, is, as Harry says, "a remarkable woman. She is not only attractive and intelligent, but she's also a wonderful housekeeper and an extremely talented cook." Mary and Bill are Dexter's parents.

1951 Program Open: "And now we invite you to *Meet Corliss Archer*, America's teenage sweetheart, starring Lugene Sanders as Corliss with Fred Shields and Frieda Inescort as her parents."

1954 Program Open: "Yes, it's *Meet Corliss Archer* with Ann Baker as Corliss Archer."

Cast: Lugene Sanders (*Corliss Archer, 1951-52*); Ann Baker (*Corliss Archer, 1954-55*); Fred Shields (*Harry Archer, 1951-52*); John Eldredge (*Harry Archer, 1954-55*); Frieda Inescort (*Janet Archer, 1951*); Irene Tedrow (*Janet Archer, 1952*); Mary Brian (*Janet Archer, 1954-55*);

Bobby Ellis (*Dexter Franklin, 1951-55*); Vera Marshe (*Mary Franklin, 1954-55*); Ken Christie (*Bill Franklin, 1954-55*). **Announcer:** John Heistand.

5945 Meet Corliss Archer. (Pilot; Comedy; NBC; Aug. 5, 1956). A rare color pilot for a new version of the prior title about Corliss Archer, a very pretty teenage girl with a penchant for finding trouble. Other regulars are Harry and Janet Archer, Corliss's parents; Dexter, Corliss's boyfriend; Lenny, Corliss's brother; and Mildred, Lenny's girlfriend.

Cast: Robin Morgan (*Corliss Archer*); Jerome Cowan (*Harry Archer*); Polly Rowles (*Janet Archer*); John Connell (*Lenny Archer*); Warren Berlinger (*Dexter Franklin*); Marian Randall (*Mildred Pringle*).

5946 Meet Julie. (Pilot; Cartoon; Syn.; Dec. 1987). While experimenting with a new security device, engineer David McCallister develops a very special doll he names Julie and gives it to his daughter, Carol, as a companion. The doll, which can speak is magically brought to life one night by unknown forces. The doll, now possessed of magical powers, becomes Carol's guardian and protector.

Voice Cast: Nicole Lynn (*Julie*); Karen Burthwright (*Carol*).

5947 Meet Maggie Mulligan. (Pilot; Comedy; Unaired; Produced in 1965). Margaret Mulligan is a gorgeous commercial artist living in New York City. Margaret, who prefers to be called Maggie, finds that looks can be both and advantage and well as a disadvantage. The proposal was to follow her efforts to snare accounts (with her looks) and ward off the unlikely suitors that become attracted to her.

Cast: Janet Leigh (*Maggie Mulligan*).

5948 Meet McGraw. (Series; Crime Drama; NBC; 1957-1958). McGraw, a tough private detective who prefers not to use (or mention) his first name, travels from city to city looking for work (actually, as he says, he minds other people's business). Stories follow the cases McGraw acquires — and the often unorthodox methods he uses to solve them.

Cast: Frank Lovejoy (*McGraw*).

5949 Meet Me in St. Louis. (Pilot; Comedy; ABC; Sept. 2, 1966). Events in the lives of the Smiths, a family of six living in St. Louis, Missouri, at the turn of the 20th century. Anne and Alonzo are the parents; Esther, Glenn, Agnes and Tootie are their children; Katie, their maid; and John Truitt, Esther's boyfriend. Suzanne Cupito, who played Agnes Smith, is now known as Morgan Brittany.

Cast: Celeste Holm (*Anne Smith*); Wesley Addy (*Alonzo Smith*); Shelley Fabares (*Esther Smith*); Larry Merrill (*Glenn Smith*); Tammy Locke (*Tootie Smith*); Suzanne Cupito (*Agnes Smith*); Michael Blodgett (*John Truitt*); Reta Shaw (*Katie*).

5950 Meet Me in the Graveyard. (Series; Drama; Internet; 2008-2009). Viola is a young single woman confined to a mental institution in Georgia after the suicide death of her mother (the situation became too much for Viola to comprehend). Ace, who uses the Internet name Rosehill Cemetery, is a loose cannon living in a halfway house in California. One day, while surfing the Internet, Viola comes across a video posted by Ace (a recovering alcoholic at the time) and responds to it when she spots her mother's headstone in the background. Ace responds to Viola and an unlikely relationship begins. The web episodes relate the love letters each posts to the other.

Cast: Milly Sanders (*Viola*); Adam Saunders (*Ace*).

5951 Meet Millie. (Series; Comedy; CBS; 1952-1956). Millie

Bronson, a beautiful 21-year-old single girl, lives with her mother, Bertha at 137 West 41st Street (Apartment 3B) in New York City. Millie attended Public School 98 and Central High School and now works as a secretary to Johnny Boone, Jr. Johnny's father, John Boone, Sr., is the owner of the company (called both an ad agency and an investment company). Stories focus on the relationship between Millie and Johnny—a romance that Millie originally only dreamed about until one of Bertha's endless attempts to spark a romance between the two finally worked.

Bertha, called "Mama," is a widow who is 48 years old but tells everyone she is 37; in some episodes she says she is "48 minus ten minus five." In last season episodes, Millie and Mama spend time as ranch hands to E.K. Weems, owner of the Weems Cattle Ranch in Texas.

"It all started the day I was born. My father said he wanted a girl and my mother said she wanted a boy. I was born and they were both disappointed," says Alfred E. Printzmetal, Mama and Millie's "life is depressing" seemingly permanently unemployed friend (Bertha says, "Alfred's job is standing in line at the unemployment office"). Alfred can't get along with his parents, especially his father, and hopes one day to build up the courage to leave home and find his own apartment. "I'll never understand women," he says. "They're too complicated. I'll wait until there is something else to marry."

John Boone, Sr., believes that when P.T. Barnum said, "There is a sucker born every minute," he was referring to women. He is henpecked, calls his wife many things behind her back but is a pussycat when he is with her. Based on the radio series of the same title (in which Audrey Totter played Millie).

Program Open: "Live from Television City in Hollywood, Arrid Crème Deodorant, America's largest selling deodorant presents, *Meet Millie*, created by Frank Galen. Starring Florence Halop as Mama, Marvin Kaplan as Alfred and Elena Verdugo as Millie ... a gay comedy about the life and loves of a Manhattan secretary."

Cast: Elena Verdugo (*Millie Bronson*); Florence Halop (*Bertha Bronson*); Ross Ford (*Johnny Boone, Jr.*); Marvin Kaplan (*Alfred E. Printzmetal*); Earl Ross, Roland Winters (*J.R. Boone, Sr.*); Isabel Randolph (*Mrs. Boone; J.R.'s wife*). **Announcer:** Bob Lemond, Bob Shepherd.

5952   *Meet Mr. McNutley.* (Series; Comedy; CBS; 1953-1954). The original title and format for *The Ray Milland Show* (which see for information).

5953   *Meet Mister Mom.* (Series; Reality; NBC; 2005). Do mothers have an easy job running a household? NBC sets out to prove they do not by selecting two families and placing the fathers in charge. While fathers struggle with the kids, the house cleaning, the shopping and the countless other things mothers do, the wives are sent on a vacation and view their husband's activities via closed circuit television. As the mothers watch, the members of each family also compete in various household tasks for cash prizes. Robert Riesenberg and James Bruce are the producers.

5954   *Meet My Folks.* (Series; Reality; My Network TV; 2007). Bachelors are put to the test—meeting the parents of the girls they are dating in a reality show that takes the dating process one step beyond the traditional dating–based series. Here, the bachelors face the girl's parents to prove they are worthy of dating their daughters. But no matter how well they impress the parents they must pass the most crucial challenge—a lie detector test (given at the end of the program). If a bachelor passes he is given permission to date the girl he seeks. Bruce Nash is the producer.

5955   *Meet the Barkers.* (Series; Reality; MTV; 2005). Travis Barker (drummer for the group Blink 812) and Shana Moakler (former Miss USA) have just become newlyweds. Cameras follow the couple as they attempt to balance their show business careers with that of a life away from music and the media.

5956   *Meet the Browns.* (Series; Comedy; TBS; 2009–). Leroy Brown is a mid-sixties church deacon who also runs Brown Meadows, a retirement home he converted from a run-down house he inherited from his father. Leroy is a widower and is assisted running Brown Meadows by his daughter (Cora), his nephew (Will) and Will's wife, Sasha, a nurse. Featured retirees are Miss Daisy, a former B-movie actress; Colonel Cleophus Jackson, a grumpy former Marine; and Ms. Edna, a senior citizen who believes she has the body (and sexuality) of a much younger woman.

Jesus Hernandez is the building's handyman (he is studying to become a lawyer); London Sheraton is a celebrity doing community service at Brown Meadows in compliance with a DUI conviction. Brianna and Joaquin are foster children taken in by Sasha and Will; Carmen Martinez is the children's social worker. Stories relate the events that befall Leroy as he attends church duties and deal with the numerous problems Brown Meadows presents to him.

Cast: David Mann (*Leroy Brown*); Tamela J. Mann (*Cora Brown*); Lamman Rucker (*Will Brown*); Denise Boutte (*Sasha Brown*); K Callan (*Miss Daisy Larue*); Tony Vaughn (*Col. Cleophus Jackson*); Juanita Jennings (*Ms. Edna Barnes*); Jeannette Sousa (*Carmen Martinez*); Arielle Vandenberg (*London Sheraton*); Brianne Gould (*Brianna*); Gunner Washington (*Joaquin*); Antonio Jamarillo (*Jesus Hernandez*).

5957   *Meet the Girls.* (Pilot; Comedy; CBS; Aug. 30, 1960). Maybelle Perkins is a model who is known as "The Shape." Advertising executive Lacey Sinclair is called "The Face" and Josephine Dunning, an assistant buyer for a department store, is nicknamed "The Brain." The girls are roommates and each is searching for fame and fortune via rich husbands. The unsold series, a variation on the feature film and 1958 TV series *How to Marry a Millionaire*, follows the girls as they each attempt to meet the right man—a millionaire.

Cast: Mamie Van Doren (*Maybelle Perkins*); Gale Robbins (*Lacey Sinclair*); Virginia Field (*Josephine Dunning*).

5958   *Meet the Governor.* (Pilot; Comedy; NBC; Oct. 5, 1955). A proposed spin off from *Screen Director's Playhouse* about Clem Waters, a Midwestern lawyer who possesses a dream to become governor of his state. Clem is married to June and Sonny is their son.

Cast: Herb Shriner (*Clem Waters*); Barbara Hale (*June Waters*); Bobby Clark (*Sonny Waters*).

5959   *Meet the Munceys.* (Pilot; Comedy; ABC; May 22, 1988). Following the death of her employer, Esther Lovell-Mingott, a wealthy woman who heads an important Palm Beach philanthropic foundation, maid Billie Muncey inherits her vast fortune and luxurious mansion. Billie invites her mother (Bernice), father (Bud) and brother (Bruce) to move in with her, and the proposal was to relate the slightly off-center Muncey's efforts to adjust to a new lifestyle. Cissie is their snobbish neighbor; Freddie is her son.

Cast: Nana Visitor (*Billie Muncey*); Peggy Pope (*Bernice Muncey*); Carmine Caridi (*Bud Muncey*); Dan Gauthier (*Bruce Muncey*); Joan Hotchkis (*Cissie Vanderplas*); Mark Neely (*Freddie Vanderplas*).

5960   *Meet Your Cover Girl.* (Series; Interview; CBS; 1950-1951). Daytime program in which fashion models discuss various aspects of their careers.

Hostess: Robin Chandler.

5961   *Meet Your Match.* (Series; Game; NBC; 1952). One pre-selected contestant chooses one person from the studio audience as his opponent. A general knowledge question-and-answer session is conducted wherein a correct answer awards a cash prize. If one player fails to answer a question correctly, he is defeated and the opponent (winner) receives whatever cash he has accumulated and the opportunity to select another player with whom to match wits.

Host: Jan Murray.

5962   *The Megan Mullally Show.* (Series; Variety; Syn.; 2006-2007). Megan Mullally, the former co-star of *Will and Grace* (as the rich and spoiled Karen Walker) turns her talents to daytime television as the host of a program of celebrity interviews and chatter.

Host: Megan Mullally. **Music:** Bret Simmons.

5963   *Megan Wants a Millionaire.* (Series; Reality; VH-1; 2009). Megan Hauserman was a contestant on the series *Rock of Love: Charm School* and commented that she would like to become a trophy wife. That comment led to *Megan Wants a Millionaire* wherein Megan is presented with 17 single men, each worth over $1 million, and a choice: to whom to become a trophy wife. With help from her concierge (Niles) and best friends Brooke Cunningham and Cecille Gahr, Megan must decide which of the 17 is the right man for her.

5964   *Megas XLR.* (Series; Cartoon; Cartoon Network; 2003-2005). In a future time, an alien race called the Glorft attack the Earth. Earth defense forces manage to apprehend an alien robot and reprogram it to battle the Glorft. The robot, called a Megas (Mechanized Earth Guard Attack System) is the last hope the Earth has. Earth is on the verge of defeat and their plan is to send Megas back in time to the Battle of the Last Stand to change the outcome of the war from defeat to victory. As Meas is prepared for transportation, an attack by the Glorft cripples Megas (his head is blown off) and the time machine malfunctions, sending Megas to Earth in the year 2000. In a junkyard in New Jersey, two slackers, Coop and Jamie, find Megas and turn him into a hot rod they call XLR (Extra Large Robot). Kiva, a military pilot from the future who was trained to pilot Megas, travels back in time, hoping to retrieve Megas. She is dismayed when she finds him, but is unable to pilot him due to Coop's modifications. Additional complications set in when Kiva learns the Glorft have followed her through time and are now on Earth. With no other choice, Kiva trains Coop and Jamie for fighting and stories relate their battle to save 21st century Earth from its future invaders. Goat is the junkyard owner; Gorath is the head of the Glorft.

Voice Cast: David DeLuise (*Harold "Coop" Cooplowski*); Wendee Lee (*Kiva Andru*); Steven Jay Blum (*Jamie*); Scott Reinecker (*Goat*); Clancy Brown (*Gorrath*).

5965   *Mel and Susan Together.* (Series; Variety; ABC; 1978). Established country singer Mel Tillis and Susan Anton, Miss America runner-up (Miss California) and then TV spokeswoman for Muriel Cigars, host a program of country and western music. Donny and Marie Osmond appeared on the first show to launch the first non–Osmond starring series from the Osmond family's new production facilities in Utah.

Hosts: Susan Anton, Mel Tillis. **Orchestra:** Bob Rozario.

5966   *The Mel Torme Show.* (Series; Variety; CBS; 1951-1952). Daytime program of music and songs with singer Mel Torme as the host.

Host: Mel Torme. **Regulars:** Peggy King, Ellen Martin, Kaye Ballard, Jean Louise Dustine. **Music:** The Red Norvo Trio, The Terry Gibbs Quintet.

5967   *Melba.* (Series; Comedy; CBS; 1986). Melba Patterson is a divorced African-American mother who is the director of the Manhattan Visitors Center in New York City. She lives with her daughter, Tracy, at 623 Bleeker Street. Susan Slater is Melba's "white sister," a carefree single girl who works at the Furth and Preston Ad Agency. She is looking for a husband and hoping to begin a family; she was raised by Melba's mother, Mama Rose, when she was orphaned as a young girl. Stories relate events in the lives of two women who treat each other like a sister. Other regulars are Jack and Gil, Melba's co-workers; and Virginia, Melba's boss. Melba Moore performs the theme, "We're Sisters."

Cast: Melba Moore (*Melba Patterson*); Gracie Harrison (*Susan Slater*); Jamila Perry (*Tracy Patterson*); Barbara Meek (*Mama Rose*); Lou Jacobi (*Jack*); Evan Mirand (*Gil*); Ellen Tobie (*Virginia Atwater*).

5968   *The Melba Moore — Clifton Davis Show.* (Series; Variety; CBS; 1972). A Manhattan brownstone provides the backdrop for a program of music, songs and light comedy.

Hosts: Clifton Davis, Melba Moore. **Regulars:** Ron Carey, Richard Libertini, Timmie Rogers, Liz Torres. **Announcer:** Johnny Olson. **Music:** Charles H. Coleman.

5969   *Melba Moore's Collection of Love Songs.* (Series; Music; Syn.; 1985). A weekly showcase of music videos with the narration hosting of singer Melba Moore.

5970   *Melissa and Joey.* (Series; Comedy; ABC Family; 2010–). Melissa Burke, called Mel, is the beautiful daughter of an Ohio state senator. Although Mel was, as she calls herself, a wild child, she matured and followed in her father's footsteps and became a member of the Toledo city council.

Joey Longo is a commodities trader (for Scanlon Trust) who suddenly loses his job when Mel's sister and brother-in-law create a ponzie scheme that not only costs Joey his job but fosters the arrest of Mel's sister; her brother-in-law flees the country. Their children, Lennox, a rebellious teenage girl, and the adolescent Ryder are placed in Mel's care.

During a speech Mel is giving at City Hall, Mel is interrupted by Joey, who complains about her brother-in-law costing him his job. The complaint falls on deaf ears. Later that day, when Joey stops by Mel's home to apologize and asks for a job at City Hall, he finds there are no jobs there; but when he sees that Mel is having a difficult time caring for Lennox and Ryder, he convinces her that he would be the perfect solution — hire him as a nanny. Mel is reluctant until Joey tells him that after college he ran a center for teens. Joey moves in; Melissa is able to get most of her life back and the *Who's the Boss?*–like series follows Mel and Joey as they not only care for the kids but seek a way to peacefully live with each other. Rhonda is Mel's political aide.

Cast: Melissa Joan Hart (*Melissa "Mel" Burke*); Joey Lawrence (*Joey Longo*); Taylor Spreitler (*Lennox*); Nick Robinson (*Ryder*); Elizabeth Ho (*Rhonda Cheng*).

5971   *Melody, Harmony, Rhythm.* (Series; Variety; NBC; 1949-1950). Singer Lynne Barrett hosts a program of music and songs broadcast on a twice weekly basis.

Host: Lynne Barrett. **Regulars:** Carol Reed, Charles Dobson. **Music:** The Tony DeSimone Trio.

5972   *Melody Street.* (Series; Variety; DuMont; 1953-1954). A cast lip-synchs popular songs (which are played against dramatic scenes).

Host: Elliot Lawrence, Tony Mottola. **Regulars:** Roberta McDonald, Lynn Gibbs, Jo Bowen. **Music:** The Tony Mottola Trio.

5973 *Melody Tour.* (Series; Variety; ABC; 1954). Comedian Stan Freberg oversees a program that features tours of the world via music that is representative of the country visited.

Host: Stan Freberg. **Regulars:** Nellie Fisher, Nancy Kenyon, Norman Scott, Robert Rounseville, Jonathan Lucas, Jane Remes, Peter Gladke. **Orchestra:** Harry Sosnik.

5974 *Melrose Place.* (Series; Drama; Fox; 1992–1999). The dreams and ambitions of a group of young adults living at 4616 Melrose Place, a housing complex in California. The series spawned a spin off (*Models, Inc.*) and set the pace for a number of additional Fox (and WB and UPN) prime time soaps (including *Felicity, The O.C., Savannah, Hyperion Bay, Dawson's Creek* and *South Beach*).

Principal Cast: Heather Locklear (*Amanda Woodward*); Thomas Calabro (*Dr. Michael Mancini*); Josie Bissett (*Jane Andrews Mancini*); Courtney Thorne-Smith (*Allison Parker*); Andrew Shue (*Billy Campbell*); Grant Show (*Jake Hanson*); Doug Savant (*Matt Fielding*); Jack Wagner (*Dr. Peter Burns*); Marcia Cross (*Dr. Kimberly Mancini*); Laura Leighton (*Sydney Andrews*); Daphne Zuniga (*Jo Reynolds*); Rob Estes (*Kyle McBride*); Kelly Rutherford (*Megan Lewis Mancini*); Brooke Langton (*Samantha Reilly*); Jamie Luner (*Lexi Sterling*); Lisa Rinna (*Taylor McBride*); David Charvet (*Craig Field*); Alyssa Milano (*Jennifer Mancini*); Vanessa Williams (*Rhonda Blair*); Kristin Davis (*Brooke Armstrong*); Rena Sofer (*Eve Cleary*); Deborah Adair (*Lucy Cabot*); Amy Locane (*Sandy Louise Harling*); Katie Wright (*Chelsea Fielding*); Dey Young (*Dr. Irene Shulman*); Wayne Tippit (*Palmer Woodward*); Andrew Williams (*Chris Marchette*); Anne-Marie Johnson (*Alycia Barnett*); Perry King (*Hayley Armstrong*).

5975 *Melrose Place.* (Series; Drama; CW; 2009-2010). Remake of the prior title that relates incidents in the lives of a group of young adults who reside at 4616 Melrose Place, a Los Angeles apartment complex. Principal characters are Ella Simms, a gorgeous publicist with a knack for partying; Jonah Miller, a filmmaker; Riley Richmond, his girlfriend, a first grade school teacher; Lauren Yung, a medical student; Auggie, a chef; and Violet, the newcomer to Melrose Place who becomes involved in the intrigue and mysteries surrounding her soon-to-become new friends. Laura Leighton and Thomas Calabro recreate their roles from the original series. Original series regular Heather Locklear reprised her role as the scheming Amanda Woodward, the owner of the WPK Talent Agency beginning with the episode of November 17, 2009.

Cast: Katie Cassidy (*Ella Simms*); Michael Rady (*Jonah Miller*); Jessica Lucas (*Riley Richmond*); Stephanie Jacobsen (*Lauren Yung*); Colin Egglesfield (*Auggie Kirkpatrick*); Shaun Sipos (*David Breck*); Ashlee Simpson-Wentz (*Violet Foster*); Laura Leighton (*Sydney Andrews*); Thomas Calabro (*Dr. Michael Mancini*); Heather Locklear (*Amanda Woodward*).

5976 *The Melting Pot.* (Series; Variety; Syn.; 1978). Comedian Orson Bean oversees a program that combines light comedy as celebrity guests prepare their favorite meals.

Host: Orson Bean. **Music:** Doug Dowdle.

5977 *Melvin Purvis: G-Man.* (Pilot; Crime Drama; ABC; April 9, 1974). The Midwest of the 1930s is the setting for a proposal about the real life exploits of Melvin Purvis, a ruthless FBI agent (then called a G-Man) with an appetite for publicity. Sam Cowley is his assistant. In a TV movie sequel, *The Kansas City Massacre* (ABC, Sept. 19, 1975) Dale Robertson reprised his role as Melvin Purvis with John Karlen as Sam Cowley.

Cast: Dale Robertson (*Melvin Purvis*); Steve Kanaly (*Sam Cowley*).

5978 *Memories with Music.* (Pilot; Variety; NBC; July 28, 1946). A proposal that was set to recall the songs and dances of the 1920s with old time entertainers as its guests. Highlights were songs by Lillian Cornell and Larry Brooks; comedy with silent screen star Mae Murray; and dancing by the team of Blair and Dean.

Performers: Blair and Dean, Larry Brooks, Fairfax Burgher, Sid Cassell, Lillian Cornell, Frederic de Wilder, Dorothy Emery, Jay Gessen, Mae Murray, John Robb.

5979 *The Memory Game.* (Series; Game; NBC; 1971). Five women begin the competition with $50 each. Each is presented with a packet of five questions and given twenty seconds to study them. At the end of the time, the questions are taken back and the host asks one player a question. If she cannot answer it, she is permitted to pass it to any other player by calling her number (1,2,3,4, or 5). The player who correctly answers it scores five dollars; if the player fails to correctly answer it, five dollars is deducted from her total. The player who was the last to give a correct answer becomes the first player top receive the next question. The girl with the highest cash score at the end of two rounds is the winner and keeps what money she has earned.

Host: Joe Garagiola. **Announcer:** Johnny Olson.

5980 *Memphis Beat.* (Series; Crime Drama; TNT; 2010–). Dwight Hendricks is a detective with the Memphis, Tennessee, Police Department. He is the son of a cop who was killed in the line of duty and sees his hometown as "a rich, magical place." In addition to the city, he loves the blues music that is deeply rooted in the city. Dwight considers himself "The Keeper of Memphis" (a man who is protective of his fellow citizens) and stories, which follow Dwight's case investigations, also emphasize the music of the city he so dearly loves (noted blues singer/songwriter Keb "Mo" provides the original songs and performances for the program). Lt. Tanya Rice is Dwight's superior, a by-the-books woman, recently transferred from the suburbs to the city, who finds Dwight's relaxed, laid-back style inappropriate for a member of her team. Davey Sutton is Dwight's partner, a young cop who tries too hard to be perfect (thus complicating their investigations). Paula Ann Hendricks, Dwight's mother, is a door-to-door cosmetics saleswoman. Charlie White, called "Whitehead," is Dwight's hypersensitive, eccentric partner (a seasoned cop from the old school of law enforcement). Reginald Greenback, a detective who loves to eat, is a family man struggling to make ends meet. J.C. Lightfoot, a sergeant who is one-sixteenth Chickasaw Indian, uses his tribal wisdom to help him solve crimes.

Cast: Jason Lee (*Dwight Hendricks*); Alfre Woodard (*Tanya Rice*); Celia Weston (*Paula Ann Hendricks*); D.J. Qualls (*Davey Sutton*); Sam Hemmings (*Charlie White*); Leonard Earl Howze (*Reginald Greenback*); Abraham Benrubi (*J.C. Lightfoot*).

5981 *The Men.* (Series; Crime Drama; ABC; 1972-1973). The overall title for three rotating series: *Assignment: Vienna, The Delphi Bureau* and *Jigsaw*. See individual titles for information.

5982 *Men.* (Series; Drama; ABC; 1989). A talkative program about incidents in the lives of four Baltimore men, friends since high school: Dr. Steven Ratajkowski, a surgeon; Charlie Hazard, a criminal lawyer; Paul Armas, a reporter for the *Sun*; and Danny McDaniel, a police officer. Margaret is Charlie's wife; and Claire is Paul's ex-wife.

Cast: Ted Wass (*Steven Ratajkowski*); Saul Rubinek (*Paul Armas*); Ving Rhames (*Charlie Hazard*); Tom O'Brien (*Danny McDaniel*); Candy Ann Brown (*Margaret Hazard*); Betsy Brantley (*Claire Armas*).

5983 *Men at Law.* (Series; Drama; CBS; 1971). David Hansen, Deborah Sullivan and Gabriel Kay are lawyers attached to the Neighborhood Legal Services Offices in Century City (Los Angeles). Their job is to defend indigent clients and stories, a spin off from *The Storefront Lawyers*, relate their cases and eventual courtroom defenses. Devlin is their superior; Kathy is their secretary.

Cast: Robert Foxworth (*David Hansen*); Sheila Larken (*Deborah Sullivan*); David Arkin (*Gabriel Kay*); Gerald S. O'Loughlin (*Devlin McNeil*); Nancy Jeris (*Kathy*).

5984   *Men at Work.* (Experimental; Music; CBS; May 13, 1942). An informal program of jazz music with the following performers: Henry "Red" Allen (trumpet), Bunny Briggs (singer), Eddie Condon (drummer), Woody Herman (bandleader; clarinet), Max Kaminsky (trumpet), Benny Monten (trombone), Pee-Wee Russell (piano), Zutty Singleton (drummer), and Joe Sullivan (piano).

5985   *Men Behaving Badly.* (Series; Comedy; NBC; 1996-1997). Kevin Murphy and Jamie Coleman are not only best friends, but they are also roommates and sort of an odd couple — Jamie is not only a slacker, but a slob while Kevin, just as immature as Jamie, shows signs of attempting to improve his pathetic life (which consists of watching TV, drinking beer and eating Fudgsciles). Also embroiled in their lives is Sarah Mitchell, Kevin's girlfriend, who finds trying to improve Kevin's life a very difficult task: the immoral Jamie always manages to undo her good intentions. Stories, based on the British series of the same title (1992–1998), follows Kevin and Jamie as they do what they do best — nothing constructive.

Cast: Ron Eldard (*Kevin Murphy*); Rob Schneider (*Jamie Coleman*); Justine Bateman (*Sarah Mitchell*); Dina Spybey (*Brenda Mikowski*); Ken Marino (*Steve*); Jenica Bergere (*Katie*).

5986   *The Men from Shiloh.* (Series; Western; NBC; 1970-1971). Medicine Bow, Wyoming, during the 1890s is the setting. It is here that Colonel Alan MacKenzie has become the owner of the Shiloh Ranch (from its parent series *The Virginian*). The Virginian, the mysterious foreman, and hired hands Trampas and Roy Tate help MacKenzie maintain the ranch. Stories, which feature the regulars on a rotational basis, relate their individual efforts to maintain law and order.

Cast: James Drury (*The Virginian*); Stewart Granger (*Alan MacKenzie*); Doug McClure (*Trampas*); Lee Majors (*Roy Tate*).

5987   *Men in Black: The Series.* (Series; Cartoon; WB; 1997-2000). Jay, Kay and Elle are the Men in Black, members of a top secret government organization established to battle aliens while at the same time keeping their existence a secret from the public (fearing to cause a panic). Stories, adapted from the feature film of the same title, relate the trio's efforts to battle an array of extraterrestrials who manage to find their way to Earth with only one goal: destroy it.

Voice Cast: Jennifer Lien, Jennifer Martin (*Elle*); Keith Diamond (*Jay*); Ed O'Ross, Gregg Berger (*Kay*).

5988   *Men in Trees.* (Series; Drama; ABC; 2006–2008). Marin Frist is a relationship coach. She is the author of two books — *Whose Gonna Love Your Body?* and *If I Can Date, So Can You*. Marin was also commissioned to write a third book — *I'm Getting Married, So Can You*. She is on top of the world as her books are best sellers. She is enjoying a good life, is engaged to be married (to Justin) and has numerous speaking engagements. Marin also believes she knows a lot about men. However, on a speaking engagement in Alaska, Marin finds she knows very little about men and relationships. It all begins when she accidentally grabs her fiancé's computer and sees a slide show of him with other women. In the small town of Elmo, Alaska, where Marin is to give a lecture, she has a rude awakening. In a town where the population is ten men to every one woman, Marin realizes that what she has been writing are all lies (she cannot figure men out and cannot sensibly categorize them). Although frustrated, she becomes fascinated by them. She believes Elmo is the perfect place to learn about men. Stories follow Marin as she struggles to adjust to small town life, learn what men are all about and eventually write the ultimate relationship book (the series title refers to signs posted around town — "Men in Trees" [tree trimmers]).

Other regulars are Annie, Marin's friend; Jack, the fish and wildlife environmentalist; Buzz, the pilot (owner of Buzz Airlines); Ben, the bartender at the bar-hotel (The Chieftain Pub); Patrick, the Jack of all trades; Theresa, Ben's ex-wife; and Sara, a single mother who is also a hooker.

Cast: Anne Heche (*Marin Frist*); Emily Bergl (*Annie*); Abraham Benrubi (*Ben Jackson*); John Amos (*Buzz*); James Tupper (*Jack Slattery*); Sarah Strange (*Theresa*); Derek Richardson (*Patrick*); Suleka Matthew (*Sara*); Justine Bateman (*Lynn*); Lauren Tom (*Mai*); Cynthia Stevenson (*Chief Celia Bachelor*); Orlando Jones (*George*).

5989   *Men Into Space.* (Series; Adventure; CBS; 1959-1960). The U.S. government's attempts to further its space program as seen through the eyes of Colonel Edward McCauley. Mary is Edward's wife; Peter is their son.

Cast: William Lundigan (*Col. Edward McCauley*); Angie Dickinson, Joyce Taylor (*Mary McCauley*); Charles Herbert (*Peter McCauley*); Corey Allen (*Lt. Johnny Baker*); Kem Dibbs (*Capt. Harvey Sparkman*); Tyler McVey (*General Norgath*). **Theme Song:** "Men Into Space" by David Rose.

5990   *Men of a Certain Age.* (Series; Drama; TNT; 2009–). Joe, Terry and Owen are men in their forties who have been friends since college. Now, that they are entering the second stage of their lives, the line that John Lennon once wrote ("life is what happens when you're making other plans") is now beginning to make sense to them and stories, set in Los Angeles, relates events in their lives as they face different challenges.

Joe, separated from his wife Sonia, owns a party store. He is a bit neurotic and dreamed of becoming a professional golfer. His slight addiction to gambling caused his marriage to break up although he is determined to make things right again. Terry is a bachelor who appears intent on staying that way. He has few responsibilities and works (when he feels like it) as an office temp. He also teaches yoga and in his youth he was a popular actor in commercials. Owen is married to Melissa, the father of two children (Michael and Jamie) and works as a car salesman for his overbearing father (Owen Sr.). Owen has diabetes and is worried about what the stress of his job is having on his health. With so many responsibilities, he cannot quit his job, but finds relief when he, Joe and Terry get together.

Cast: Ray Romano (*Joe Theomoni*); Scott Bakula (*Terry Elliott*); Andre Braugher (*Owen Thoreau, Jr.*); Penelope Ann Miller (*Sonia Theomoni*); Lisa Gay Hamilton (*Melissa Thoreau*); Richard Gant (*Owen Thoreau, Sr.*); Lil' JJ (*DaShaun; works for Joe*); Norma Jean (*Diner waitress*); Patricia DeLeon (*Fantasy Woman*); Isaiah Montgomery (*Michael Thoreau*); Kwesi Boakye (*Jamie Thoreau*).

5991   *Men of Annapolis.* (Series; Anthology; Syn.; 1957). Dramatizations based on incidents in the training of men attending Annapolis, the U.S. Naval Academy. The midshipmen of Annapolis perform in all stories, which are produced by William Castle.

Narrator: Art Gilmore.

5992   *Men of the Dragon.* (Pilot; Adventure; ABC; Mar. 20, 1974). Jan and Lisa Kimbro are an American brother and sister and karate experts who, with their Asian friend, Li-Teh, run a self-defense school in Hong Kong. The proposal was to relate their exploits as they use their unique skills to battle crime.

Cast: Jared Martin (*Jan Kimbro*); Katie Saylor (*Lisa Kimbro*); Robert Ito (*Li-Teh*).

5993 *Men, Women and Dogs.* (Series; Comedy; WB; 2001). Jeremiah, Clay, Eric and Royce are four friends who hang out at the dog park (in Los Angeles) to talk about women. The four, however, seem to care more about dogs than anything else — and use their dogs (or lack of them) to attract women.

Jeremiah is a chef at the Strand Restaurant and also tries to impress women with his special recipe chocolate cake. He has a dog named Wolfgang. His dream girl is one who likes food and dogs (but not necessarily in that order). Eric is a surf bum and has a dog named Betsy. He is living with his girlfriend, Michelle (who has issues about playing second fiddle to Betsy). Royce is a penny-pinching miser who likes dogs but doesn't actually have one. He carries a leash with him at the park and pretends to have a dog. Clay is a young idealist who actually loves women more than dogs but is mocked by his friends for thinking so. Stories follow the events in the lives of Jeremiah, Clay, Eric and Royce as they each go about seeking the women of their dreams.

Cast: Bill Bellamy (*Jeremiah*); Mike Damus (*Royce*); Niklaus Lange (*Eric*); Danny Pino (*Clay*); Heather Stephens (*Michele*).

5994 *Menasha the Magnificent.* (Series; Comedy; NBC; 1950). Events in the life of Menasha Skulnik, the manager of a decrepit restaurant that is owned by a domineering woman (Mrs. Davis).

Cast: Menasha Skulnik (*Himself*); Jean Cleveland, Zanah Cunningham (*Mrs. Davis*); Vinton Hayworth, Danny Leane.

5995 *Mental.* (Series; Drama; Fox; 2009). Wharton Memorial Hospital is a psychiatric medical center in Los Angeles. Dr. Jack Gallagher, an unorthodox psychiatrist, is the director of Mental Health Services. Jack has little patience for following the rules and does what he feels is best to help his patients by uncovering the hidden facts that may eventually lead to a cure. Carl Belle is the doctor who opposes Jack's rebellious attitude and is seeking a way to get him dismissed; Veronica Hayden-Jones is Jack's former girlfriend, a psychiatrist who was hoping for Jack's job; Nora Skoff is the hospital administrator; Arturo Suarez is the first year resident; Malcolm Darius Washington is a nurse who overcame poverty to pursue a career; Chloe Artis is a resident psychiatrist.

Cast: Chris Vance (*Jack Gallagher*); Jacqueline McKenzie (*Veronica Hayden-Jones*); Annabella Sciorra (*Nora Skoff*); Derek Webster (*Carl Belle*); Marisa Ramirez (*Chloe Artis*); Nicholas Gonzalez (*Arturo Suarez*); Edwin Hodge (*Malcolm Washington*); Amanda Douge (*Becky Gallagher*).

5996 *The Mentalist.* (Series; Crime Drama; CBS; 2008–). "My name is Patrick Jane, I'm here to help you" is what a victim of crime will hear when Patrick Jane becomes involved in a case. Patrick himself is a victim of crime (his wife and daughter were shot by a serial killer) and thus feels for victims and takes a personal interest in their plight.

Patrick is an independent consultant for the California Bureau of Investigation (CBI). He pays attention to details at a crime scene and notices the little things that can easily be overlooked. He can read people and his past experiences, pretending to be a psychic (to help people) has given him an edge in that some people actually believe he is psychic. Teresa Lisbon is the head of the CBI; Kimball, Wayne and Grace are the other team members. Stories follow the team, in particular Patrick's somewhat unconventional methods, to solve crimes.

First season episodes also focus on Patrick and his CBI team as they attempt to find Red John, an elusive killer who murdered Patrick's wife and daughter. Over time the case becomes such an obsession with Patrick that it causes him to lose focus and he is pulled from the case by Sam Bosco, a no-nonsense department chief who wants him out of the CBI. Patrick wants the Red John case back and the efforts of both men to get their way is a second season recurring storyline (Sam has solved crimes with integrity and honesty and is not impressed with Patrick's methods of charm and trickery).

Cast: Simon Baker (*Patrick Jane*); Robin Tunney (*Teresa Lisbon*); Tim Kang (*Kimball Cho*); Owain Yeoman (*Wayne Yeoman*); Amanda Righetti (*Grace Van Pelt*); Terry Kinney (*Sam Bosco*).

5997 *The Mentor.* (Series; Comedy; Internet; 2010). A four episode Internet spin off from NBC's *The Office* (viewable at NBC.com) that features Dunder and Mifflin office coordinator Erin Hannon contemplating a change in life by taking classes in accounting. Angela is Erin's co-worker and mentor; Kelly is Erin's best friend who now feels their relationship is threatened by Angela.

Cast: Ellie Kemper (*Erin Hannon*); Angela Martin (*Angela Kinsey*); Mindy Kaling (*Kelly Kapoor*); Brian Baumgartner (*Kevin Malone*).

5998 *The Meow Mix Think Like a Cat Game Show.* (Series; Game; GSN; 2008). Cat owners appear with their pets to compete in question and answer rounds (based on their knowledge of cats) as well as in challenges that involve their pet's ability to perform specific tasks. Money is awarded based on the cat's performance as well as how his master scored in the question and answer session. Sponsored by Meow Mix cat food.

Host: Chuck Woolery.

5999 *Mercy.* (Series; Drama; NBC; 2009). The lives of the people who work at Mercy Hospital "as seen through the eyes of those who know it best"— the nurses. Particular focus is on Veronica Callahan, a gruff, hot-tempered nurse who has just returned to Mercy after a tour of duty in Iraq; Chloe Payne, a naïve girl who is just learning how to deal (and cope) with the unsettling challenge of her chosen profession; Sonia Jiminez, a looker (even favored by the camera) who has little trouble getting men but is now seeking a stable relationship. Dr. Chris Sands is the new doctor at the hospital who often butts horns with Veronica; Mike Callahan is Veronica's estranged husband; Dr. Alfred Parks is the hospital administrator; Nurse Klowden is the nurse overseer.

Cast: Taylor Schilling (*Veronica Callahan*); Michelle Trachtenberg (*Chloe Payne*); Jamie Lee Kirchner (*Sonia Jiminez*); James Tupper (*Chris Sands*); Diego Klattenhoff (*Mike Callahan*); Guillermo Diaz (*Angel Lopez*); James Le Gros (*Dr. Harris*); Delroy Lindo (*Dr. Alfred Parks*); Margo Martindale (*Nurse Klowden*); Kate Mulgrew (*Veronica's mother*); Peter Gerety (*Veronica's father*).

6000 *Mercy Point.* (Series; Science Fiction; UPN; 1998-1999). A futuristic medical drama that is set in the 23rd century and follows the lives of the personnel of Mercy Point, a health care center on a colony called Jericho that caters to both humans and aliens.

Cast: Joe Morton (*Dr. Grote Maxwell*); Alexandra Wilson (*Dr. Dru Breslauer*); Maria del Mar (*Dr. Hay Len Breslauer*); Brian McNamara (*Dr. Caleb "C.J." Juardo*); Julia Pennington (*Nurse ANI—Android Nursing Interface*); Gay Thomas (*Dr. Rema Cook*); Jordan Lund (*Dr. Batubg*); Kristen Robek (*Nurse Davies*).

6001 *Merlin.* (Series; Adventure; NBC/Syfy; 2009-2010). In 2009 (July to Sept. 23) NBC broadcast the first season of the British series *Merlin.* (When NBC decided not to air the second season, Syfy purchased the broadcast rights to new episodes and the previously run NBC episodes). A retelling of the Arthurian legend (normally, the legend of King Arthur and his rule over Camelot, is set in the Dark Ages. The series setting is changed considerably and made to look like 15th century England). Arthur is depicted as a teenage prince and his father, King Uther, rules the land. King Uther has outlawed magic and has imprisoned the last talking dragon. It is at this time that a teenage Merlin (who is destined to become the greatest wizard in the world) arrives at the pre-famous Camelot to fulfill his destiny and protect the arrogant Prince Arthur so that he may live to rule the future Camelot. Merlin has been sent by his mother and must keep his magical abilities a secret. He is cared for by Gaius, the court physician and former sorcerer, who is aware of Merlin's secret. The imprisoned dragon, which Merlin befriends and visits when he needs advice, is also aware of Merlin's secret and destiny. Serialized stories follow Merlin as he seeks not only to fulfill his destiny but that of the future King of Camelot. Morgana is King Uther's ward (daughter of his late best friend). Like Merlin, she has powers (ability to see the future) but must keep them a secret. Although privileged, she has missed the love of a family and that void has made her sensitive to the pains and struggles of others. Guinevere (called Gwen) is Morgana's maid servant (but also her best friend). Gwen came from a poor family and the position she now holds is the best thing she could have ever wished for (although unknown to her at this time, she is destined to become to the future Queen of Camelot). Nimueh is a powerful sorceress who is determined to overthrow King Uther and restore magic to Camelot. Uther is a tyrant with a cruel streak who restored peace to the kingdom after he expelled evil magic, defeated the dragons, imprisoned the witches and exposed the mythical beasts. Uther blames evil magic for the death of his wife and thus the reason for his banishment of magic.

Cast: Colin Morgan (*Merlin*); Bradley James (*Prince Arthur*); Anthony Head (*King Uther*); Richard Wilson (*Gaius*); Katie McGrath (*Morgana*); Angela Coulby (*Guinevere*); Michelle Ryan (*Nimueh*); John Hurt (*Dragon's voice*).

6002   *The Merv Griffin Show.* (Series; Variety; NBC; Syn.; CBS; 1962–1972). Music and songs coupled with celebrity interviews. Four versions appeared:

1. The Merv Griffin Show (NBC, 1962-63). **Host:** Merv Griffin. **Orchestra:** Mort Lindsey.

2. The Merv Griffin Show (Syn., 1965). **Host:** Merv Griffin. **Announcer:** Arthur Treacher. **Orchestra:** Mort Lindsey.

3. The Merv Griffin Show (CBS, 1969–72). **Host:** Merv Griffin. **Announcer:** Arthur Treacher. **Orchestra:** Mort Lindsey.

4. The Merv Griffin Show (Syn., 1972). **Host:** Merv Griffin. **Orchestra:** Mort Lindsey.

6003   *Merv Griffin's Crosswords.* (Series; Game; Syn.; 2007). Two players compete (called "The Crossword Solvers") in a game called "Crosswords to the extreme — and winner take all." A crossword puzzle is revealed. The host reads a clue. The first player to buzz in must not only give the correct answer but also spell the missing word correctly. If correct the word appears in the crossword puzzle, the player scores money.

In round two, three additional players (called Spoilers) are introduced. They stand behind the prior two players. If a player makes a mistake (gives the wrong answer) a Spoiler has a chance to steal their spot and their money (by buzzing in and giving the correct answer; if he gives an incorrect response, he is eliminated from further play on that question). The player being replaced then becomes a Spoiler. Money is also doubled in this round from $100 to $200.

The player with the most money (most filled in crossword clues) wins the game and competes in the final round — solving the remain-

ing clues to the puzzle at play within 90 seconds (which adds $2,000 to his score if he is successful; if not he keeps what he earned in the prior rounds). The series is created by Merv Griffin.

Host: Ty Treadway. **Announcer:** Edd Hall.

6004   *The Message.* (Pilot; Reality; TLC; April 9, 2010). A potential series in which private investigator Christopher Bauer grants three people the opportunity to send a message to someone they are desperate to find.

Star: Christopher Bauer.

6005   *Messing Prize Party.* (Series; Game; CBS; 1948-1949). The program features couples performing stunts in return for prizes. Sponsored by Messing Bakeries.

Host: Bill Slater.

6006   *Metalocalypse.* (Series; Cartoon; Adult Swim; 2006). Dethlock is a world-famous heavy metal rock band (they would like to believe the most famous in the world). Nathan Explosion (vocals), William Murderface (bass), Pickles (drums) and guitarists Skwigaar Skwigelf and Toki Wartooth comprise the band. The guys may be able to sing and play instruments but away from the band they are total morons. Stories relate their misadventures as they play gigs but often leave a trail of mayhem and destruction behind.

Voice Cast: Brendon Small (*Nathan Explosion*); Brendon Small (*Pickles*); Brendon Small (*Skwigaar Skwigelf*); Tommy Blacha (*Toki Wartooth*); Tommy Blacha (*William Murderface*).

6007   *Method and Red.* (Series; Comedy; Fox; 2004). After a succession of hot recordings, rappers Method and Red decode to take a break and purchase a home in suburban New Jersey — in a gated community that is predominately white. The neighbors are apprehensive at first then become objectionable when Method and Red disrupt the tranquility of the neighborhood with their rapper friends and wild parties. Hoping to ease the tension is Dorothea, Method's mother, who has moved in with them and has made it her goal to make them respectable neighbors. Stories follow Method and Red as the attempt to fit into a world of suburban living they have never known before. Nancy Blaford is their neighbor, the realtor who sold them the home; Bill is her husband; Skyler their son.

Cast: Clifford Smith (*Method Man*); Reggie Noble (*Red*); Anna Maria Horsford (*Dorothea Smith*); Beth Littleford (*Nancy Blaford*); Peter Jacobson (*Bill Blaford*); David Henrie (*Skyler Blaford*).

6008   *The M-G-M Parade.* (Series; Documentary; ABC; 1955-1956). Metro-Goldwyn-Mayer's first television series; a behind-the-scenes look at the world of filmmaking with guests, interviews, tours of soundstages and clips from various M-G-M films (upcoming and classics).

Host: George Murphy.

6009   *M.I. 5.* (Series; Crime Drama; Syn.; 2009). British produced program (as *Spooks*; *M.I. 5* is the American title) that details the work of the agents attached to Section D of M.I. 5, the United Kingdom's intelligence organization (comparable to America's CIA).

Main characters: Sir Harry Pearce (head of the Department of Counter Terrorism); Ros Myers (Section D Chief); Jo Portman (Case Officer); Lucas North (Senior Case Officer); Malcolm Wynn-Jones (Data Analyst); Nicholas Blake (Head of British Home Security); Sir Richard Dolby (M.I. 5 General Director); Tessa Phillips (Section K Senior Case Officer); Fiona Carter (M.I. 5 agent); Zoe Reynolds (Case Agent); Adam Carter (Section D Chief); Helen Flynn (Case Agent); Danny Hunter (Case Agent); Ruth Evershed (Data Analyst); Connie

James (Senior Analyst); Juliet Shaw (National Security Coordinator).

Cast: Peter Firth *(Harry Pearce)*; Hermione Norris *(Jo Portman)*; Richard Armitage *(Lucas North)*; Hugh Simon *(Malcolm Wynn-Jones)*; Robert Glenister *(Nicholas Blake)*; Robert East *(Richard Dolby)*; Jenny Agutter *(Tessa Phillips)*; Matthew MacFayden *(Tom Quinn)*; Rupert Penry-Jones *(Adam Carter)*; Olga Sosnovska *(Fiona Carter)*; Keeley Hawes *(Zoe Reynolds)*; David Oyelowo *(Danny Hunter)*; Lisa Faulkner *(Helen Flynn)*; Nicola Walker *(Ruth Evershed)*; Gemma Jones *(Connie James)*; Anna Chancellor *(Juliet Shaw)*.

6010   *Miami Ink.* (Series; Reality; TLC; 2005). The world of tattoo artists is explored in a documentary-style presentation that not only profiles the artists but the people who opt for a tattoo and the reasons for their decisions. The program is set at a tattoo shop in Sunset Beach that is owned by Ami James (who also narrates the program).

6011   *Miami Medical.* (Series; Drama; CBS; 2010). "The Golden Hour" is a term used by trauma doctors to indicate that treatment of serious accident victims is critical to saving their lives. Like NBC's *Trauma*, stories relate the work of a team of trauma specialists (The Alpha Team of the Miami Trauma Unit Hospital) as they battle the odds to save lives. Matthew Proctor, a former MASH doctor during the Gulf War, gave up his lucrative private practice to devote his energies as a trauma surgeon; Serena Warren is a recent medical school graduate who is facing a new world of medical challenges with the trauma unit; Christopher Deleo is the playboy surgeon who survives on the adrenaline rush of the unit; Eva Zambrano is the workaholic surgeon who finds her job taking over her personal life; Tuck Brody is the head nurse who holds the team together (balances the needs of the doctors, their patients and their families).

Cast: Jeremy Northam *(Dr. Matthew Proctor)*; Lana Parrilla *(Dr. Eva Zambrano)*; Elisabeth Harnois *(Dr. Serena Warren)*; Mike Vogel *(Dr. Christopher Deleo)*; Omar Gooding *(Tuck Brody)*.

6012   *Miami Undercover.* (Series; Crime Drama; Syn.; 1961). Over a scene of Miami Beach, Florida, we hear: "This is Miami Beach and it's quite a town. The richest ten-mile stretch of sand in the world. We have the simple things of Nature — sun and sea and sand and the tropical breezes. Anybody can go native in half an hour. My name is Jeff Thompson, I'm a personal investigator for the Hotel Association. Most people think I'm a playboy and that's the way it's supposed to be because I work without credentials in *Miami Undercover*." Stories follow Jeff as he goes undercover to investigate problems reported by the Miami Hotel Owners Association. Rocky, a former prizefighter, is Jeff's partner; Mike O'Malley is the Miami Police Department Lieutenant who Jeff helps (and who helps Jeff).

Cast: Lee Bowman *(Jeff Thompson)*; Rocky Graziano *(Rocky)*; Hugh Lawrence *(Lt. Mike O'Malley)*;

6013   *Miami Vice.* (Series; Crime Drama; NBC; 1984–1989). James "Sonny" Crockett and Ricardo Tubbs are detectives with the vice squad division of the Miami Metro Dade County Police Department, also called the Miami, Florida, Police Department. Sonny is divorced from Caroline and the father of Billy.

Sonny lives away from the pressures of society on a boat he calls *The Saint Vidas Dance*. Sonny is "a drug dealer this week, an outlaw biker the next. I'm trying to get by on four hours of sleep a day. I go undercover for weeks at a time. It's disastrous on a marriage, hell on the nervous system." Sonny is a former football player for the University of Miami, the Gators. Although he had a promising career, "I traded the whole thing in for two years in Nam." After the war he became a cop. He started in plainclothes and worked his way up to

vice. He gets a high from the action but suffers from a gambling and drinking problem. Sonny lives on his boat with Elvis, an alligator who was the former mascot of the Gators football team. Elvis was benched for taking a bite out of a player and now works as Sonny's watchdog. To protect his identity around the marina where his boat is docked, Sonny is known as Sonny Brunette.

Ricardo was born in the Bronx, New York, and was a detective with the Armed Robbery Division of the N.Y.P.D., Bronx Division. Another episode claims he was an undercover narcotics detective with the N.Y.P.D. When his brother, Raphael, is killed by a drug kingpin in Brooklyn, Ricardo tracks the killer to Miami and meets Sonny, who is seeking the same man. They solve the case and Ricardo accepts an offer to work with Sonny in vice. When Ricardo visits Sonny on the boat he is known as Ricardo Cooper to protect his identity. Ricardo, called Rico by Sonny, says his name stands for "tough, unique, bad, bold and sassy." Ricardo is single and lives in an apartment on Linden Avenue. He is not as aggressive as Sonny and prefers to take a less gung ho approach when it comes to questioning or chasing suspects.

Sonny and Ricardo work with detectives Gina Calabrese, Larry Zito and Trudy Joplin. Lieutenant Lou Rodriquez is their first superior; he is replaced by Lieutenant Martin Castillo. Last season episodes find Sonny marrying Caitlin Davies. Jan Hammer composed the theme.

Cast: Don Johnson *(Sonny Crockett)*; Philip Michael Thomas *(Ricardo Tubbs)*; Belinda J. Montgomery *(Caroline Crockett)*; Clayton Barclay Jones *(Billy Crockett)*; Saundra Santiago *(Gina Calabrese)*; John Diehl *(Larry Zito)*; Gregory Sierra *(Lt. Lou Rodriquez)*; Edward James Olmos *(Lt. Martin Castillo)*; Sheena Easton *(Caitlin Davies)*; Olivia Brown *(Det. Trudy Joplin)*; Michael Talbott *(Det. Stanley Switek)*; Martin Ferrero *(Noogie Lamont; Sonny's snitch)*; John Hernandez *(Izzy Moreno; Noogie's partner)*; Ellen Greene *(Darlene; Stanley's girlfriend)*.

6014   *Michael and Michael Have Issues.* (Series; Comedy; Comedy Central; 2009). Fast-paced, surreal skits featuring the humor of Michael Ian Black and Michael Showalter, comedians who also write, produce and direct their shows.

Stars: Michael Ian Black, Michael Showalter, Josh Pais.

6015   *Michael Hayes.* (Series; Drama; CBS; 1997-1998). Michael Hayes is a former officer with the N.Y.P.D. turned prosecutor for the U.S. Attorney's Office. When his superior is injured in a bombing, Michael is promoted to the post of Acting U.S. Attorney for the southern district of New York. Michael is an Irish Catholic. He believes in the letter of the law and will not be compromised; if a person is guilty, he will stop at nothing to get the conviction (no matter who he has to expose to pursue justice). Michael lives with Caitlin, the wife of his troubled brother, Danny (who is struggling to find his place in society following his release from prison) and his nephew, Danny Jr., who needs all the guidance he can get to avoid following in his father's footsteps.

Cast: David Caruso *(Michael Hayes)*; Mary B. Ward *(Caitlin Hayes)*; David Cubitt *(Danny Hayes, Sr.)*; Jimmy Galeota *(Daniel Hayes, Jr.)*; Ruben Santiago-Hudson *(Eddie Diaz)*; Peter Outerbridge *(John Manning)*; Hillary Danner *(Jenny Nevins)*; Philip Baker Hall *(William Vaughn)*; Rebecca Rigg *(Lindsay Straus)*.

6016   *Michael Nesmith in Television Parts.* (Series; Comedy; NBC; 1985). Short comedy and musical videos that are strung together "to present the new wave of television comedy."

Host: Michael Nesmith. **Regulars:** Billy Beck, Richard Brunelle, Tina Caspary, Michael Castellano, Randy Doney, Nancy Gregory, John Hobbs, Alan McRae, Dani Minnick, Donna Rupert, Jeff Scott,

Nick Shields, Linda Stayer, Kevin Thompson, The Whispers. **Music:** Joseph Chemay, John Hobbs.

6017   *The Michael Richards Show.* (Series; Comedy; NBC; 2000). Vic Nardozzo is a private investigator for the McKay Detective Agency in Los Angeles. He is a graduate of the USA Detective School and he considers his ability to penetrate any situation, to be chameleon, his greatest asset—"Just ask the judges at the Mr. Universe Contest," he says.

Vic shops at Frugal Simpleton "where simple people shop" and carries Lady Be Brave pepper spray for protection in his inside jacket pocket. Vic uses aliases (his favorite is Roland) and he was the technical consultant for the TV detective series "The Eliminator."

Vic is also a bit of a klutz and stories follow his fumbling attempts to solve crimes for his no nonsense boss, Brady McKay (his bad back often bothers him and he attributes it to an old football injury— "Someone threw a football at me"). When he gets upset, Brady buys a six-pack of beer, goes home and drinks it—"It saved my wife's life several times." Brady also has a TV segment, "On Your Case," for the series *Extra*, where he exposes criminals.

Jack LaMoine is the elderly detective who first met Brady while they were doing security for the Rolling Stones. Jack is also famous for saving 20 people in a Mexican train wreck. Stacy is the office secretary; and Kevin is the eager-to-learn young detective employed by Brady.

Cast: Michael Richards (*Vic Nardozzo*); William Devane (*Brady McKay*); Bill Cobbs (*Jack LaMoine*); Amy Farrington (*Stacy Devers*); Tim Meadows (*Kevin Blakely*).

6018   *Michael Shayne.* (Series; Crime Drama; NBC; 1960-1961). Michael Shayne is a private detective with an office, number 322, at 483 Adams Street in the city of Miami, Florida. Mike, as he is sometimes called, often complains that his mail occasionally gets rerouted to Miami Beach by mistake. Mike enjoys his work despite what some people say—"Mike is practical and realistic and will never get rich at what he is doing." He is relaxed and easygoing and tries not to fly off the handle. He will avoid violence if possible, offers a cigarette to clients and suspects to relax them, and manages to sneak in a kiss when the client is a gorgeous female. Mike gathers the evidence, sorts through the clues and uses every dirty trick in the book to get the truth from both clients and suspects. He uses Brazer's Chemical Lab to do his analysis, and he is a member of the Private Investigators of America.

Angel is the affectionate name Mike uses for Lucy Hamilton, his ever faithful secretary and sometimes "legman." Lucy, who can type 90 words a minute, never lets a client get away.

Tim Rourke is Mike's friend, a reporter-photographer for the Miami *Tribune*; Will Gentry is the homicide police chief based in the Municipal Justice Building who Mike says is "one of the most cooperative police officers I've ever worked with." Leith Stevens composed "The Theme from Michael Shayne."

Cast: Richard Denning (*Michael Shayne*); Patricia Donahue, Margie Regan (*Lucy Hamilton*); Jerry Paris (*Tim Rourke*); Herbert Rudley (*Will Gentry*).

6019   *Michael Shayne, Detective.* (Pilot; Crime Drama; NBC; Sept. 28, 1958). Michael Shayne is a two-fisted private detective who often finds himself going beyond the call of duty to help his clients. Lucy Hamilton is his secretary; Tim O'Rourke is his reporter friend and the proposed series was to relate Shayne's case investigations. Aired on *Decision* and with changes served as the pilot for the NBC series *Michael Shayne, Private Detective*.

Cast: Mark Stevens (*Michael Shayne*); Merry Anders (*Lucy Hamilton*); Robert Brubaker (*Tim Rourke*).

6020   *The Michele Lee Show.* (Pilot; Comedy; CBS; April 5, 1974). Michele Burton is a pretty newsstand clerk at the Beverly Wilshire Hotel in Beverly Hills. She has little excitement in her life but finds great pleasure in helping others. The proposal was to relate her mishaps as her good intentions often backfire. Mr. Zelensky is Michele's neighbor; Gladys is her friend.

Cast: Michele Lee (*Michele Burton*); Herbie Faye (*Mr. Zelensky*); Joyce Bulifant (*Gladys Gooch*).

6021   *Mick and Frankie.* (Pilot; Crime Drama; ABC; July 30, 1989). Mick and Frankie Loomis are brothers who are also modern-day bounty hunters. They are somewhat easygoing and misadventure-prone and flashbacks are used to show them as children when they encounter situations that remind them of childhood incidents.

Cast: Ed Marinaro (*Mick Loomis*); Robert Firth (*Frankie Loomis*); Max Mattino (*Young Mick*); Phillip Glasser (*Young Frankie*).

6022   *Mickey.* (Series; Comedy; ABC; 1964-1965). Mickey O'Grady is retired businessman who purchases the Newport Arms, a hotel in Newport Beach, California, as a means of providing additional income for his family (his wife Nora, and their children, Timmy and Buddy). Unfortunately, for Mickey, the hotel is fraught with problems and stories follow Mickey's efforts to run the hotel. Sammy Ling is the hotel manager; Mr. Swidler is the owner of the nearby gas station.

Cast: Mickey Rooney (*Mickey Grady*); Emmaline Henry (*Nora Grady*); Timmy Rooney (*Timmy Grady*); Brian Nash (*Buddy Grady*); Sammee Tong (*Sammy Ling*); Alan Reed (*Mr. Swidler*).

6023   *Mickey and Nora.* (Pilot; Comedy; CBS; June 26, 1987). Mickey Travis is a former CIA agent turned New York lawyer. He is married to Nora, the manager of a toy store, and the unsold series was to relate the problems that befall the newlyweds when Mickey's past comes back to haunt him (everyone still thinks he is a CIA agent). Other regulars are Vivian, Nora's sister; Adele, Mickey's secretary; and Rip, Mickey's former CIA boss. Cheryl Wheeler performs the theme, "Back in the Main Stream."

Cast: Ted Wass (*Mickey Travis*); Barbara Truetelaar (*Nora Travis*); Nancy Lenehan (*Vivian*); Florence Stanley (*Adele*); George Furth (*Rip*).

6024   *Mickey and the Contessa.* (Pilot; Comedy; CBS; Aug. 12, 1963). When Mickey Brennan, a former all-star football player, retires and acquires a job as the basketball coach at a small college, he hires, sight unseen, a housekeeper for his two children (Sissy and Mike). Several days later, Czigoina, a beautiful but impoverished Hungarian Contessa appears and presents herself as his new housekeeper. The proposal was to depict Contessa Czigoina's efforts to run the Brennan household. Other regulars are Arney, the team manager; and Butch, the team's star player.

Cast: Mickey Shaughnessy (*Mickey Brennan*); Eva Gabor (*Contessa Czigoina*); Ann Marshall (*Sissy Brennan*); Bill St. John (*Mike Brennan*); John Fielder (*Arney Tanner*); Michael Green (*Butch Gorkey*).

6025   *Mickey Daytona.* (Pilot; Crime Drama; Unaired; Produced for CBS in 1992). Mickey Daytona is a private detective, based on the East Coast, who decides that he needs a change of scenery and relocates to Southern California. The proposal was to follow Mickey as he investigates crimes—with a bit of the New York toughness he learned growing up in a tough neighborhood.

Cast: Ray Sharkey (*Mickey Daytona*).

6026   *The Mickey Mouse Club.* (Series; Children; ABC; 1955–1959). For an hour (later half an hour) each weekday afternoon, children of all ages were entertained by a group of talented children (called "Mouseketeers") who were members of the Mickey Mouse Club. There were no rules and there were no fees; the only requirement was to have fun — to sit back, "put on your Mouseke-ears" and join the Mouseketeers in songs, dances and sketches.

While Mickey Mouse appeared in animated form to introduce each episode, it was Jimmie Dodd and co-host Roy Williams who actually conducted the club. The stage was the official Mouse Club House and the Mouseketeers were introduced in many ways via songs. The sight of Mickey, seated at a piano meant it was Monday and "Fun with Music Day." Tuesday found Mickey in a tuxedo and preparing for "Guest Star Day." A flying carpet, carrying Mickey in a sorcerer's suit, meant Wednesday's "Anything Can Happen Day." Thursday's "Circus Day" found Mickey dressed as a ringmaster. And "Talent Round Up Day" was the Friday show, with Mickey outfitted in cowboy duds.

"Meeska, Mooseka, Mouseketeer, Mouse Cartoon Time is now here" (a door to the Mickey Mouse Treasure Mine would then open and a Disney cartoon would be seen). "From the far corners of the Earth; from across the Seven Seas, the stories of today for the leaders of tomorrow" signaled the beginning of "The Mickey Mouse Club Newsreel" (reported by Hal Gibney). "Fun with a Camera" was a segment with photographer Earl Kyser teaching the Mouseketeers aspects of photography. Other segments included the animated Jiminy Cricket in safety segments for children, and "Sooty and His Friend Harry Corbett" (Harry is the straight man for his non-speaking hand puppet, Sooty, who plays songs on his electric organ).

Serialized stories were also a part of the daily program. See the following titles for information on the principal serials: *Annette, Corky and White Shadow, The Hardy Boys and the Mystery of the Applegate Treasure, The Hardy Boys and the Mystery of Ghost Farm, Spin and Marty, The Further Adventures of Spin and Marty* and *The New Adventures of Spin and Marty.*

Host: Jimmie Dodd. **Co-Host:** Roy Williams. **Voice of Mickey Mouse:** Jim MacDonald. **Voice of Jiminy Crickett:** Cliff Edwards. **Mouseketeers:** Annette Funicello, Darlene Gillespie, Carl "Cubby" O'Brien, Karen Pendleton, Bobby Burgess, Tommy Cole, Cheryl Holdridge, Lynn Ready, Doreen Tracy, Linda Hughes, Lonny Burr, Bonni Lynn Fields, Sharon Baird, Ronnie Young, Jay Jay Solari, Margene Storey, Nancy Annate, Billie Jean Beanblossom, Mary Espinosa, Bonnie Lou Kern, Mary Lou Sartori, Bronson Scott, Dennis Day, Dickie Dodd, Michael Smith, Ronald Steiner, Mark Sutherland, Don Underhill, Sherry Allen, Paul Petersen, Judy Harriett, John Lee Johnson, Eileen Diamond, Charley Laney, Mickey Rooney, Jr., Tim Rooney, Johnny Crawford, Larry Larson, Don Grady.

6027   *The Mickey Mouse Club.* (Series; Children; Syn.; 1977). An updated version of *The Mickey Mouse Club* that features twelve new Mouseketeers in songs and dances and an array of never-before televised Disney cartoons and films. The animated Mickey Mouse is the series host; Jiminy Crickett assists him. The daily serial, *The Mystery of Rustler's Cove* was presented. Patty, Stewie, Chris and Bobby are children attending the Circle B Ranch. During a field trip they stumble upon a group of rustlers near a cave at Apache Cliff. Stories follow their efforts to help authorities capture the rustlers. Also known as *The New Mickey Mouse Club.*

Mouseketeers Cast: Lisa Whelchel, Kelly Parsons, Julie Piekarski, Mindy Feldman, Nita DiGiampaolo, Curtis Wong, Shawnte Northcutte, Allison Fonte, Todd Turquand, Angel Florez, William Atmore, Scott Craig. **Voices:** Wayne Allwine (*Mickey Mouse*); Cliff Edwards (*Jiminy Crickett*). **Serial Cast:** Kim Richards (*Patty Bell*); Robbie Rist (*Stuart "Stewie" Withers*); Christian Juttner (*Chris Hollister*); Bobby Rolofson (*Doug Withers*); Tony Becker (*Brett Bell*); Lou Frizzell

(*Buzz*); Bing Russell (*Waco*); Dennis Fimple (*Charlie*); Pete Renoudet (*Bill Logan*); Bill Zuckert (*Will the Cook*).

6028   *The Mickey Mouse Club.* (Series; Children; Disney; 1989). An updated version of the prior titles that presents a group of talented children (the Mouseketeers) who entertain via songs and dances. The program also presents a group of serialized comedies and dramas ("The Daily Serial"):

1. Match Point. Follows a group of young people as they train at a tennis camp run by Holly and Casey Turner. **Cast:** Diana Baines (*Holly Turner*), Danny Sullivan (*Casey Turner*), Kristin D'Atrilo (*Bonnie Stafford*), Renee O'Connor (*Robin*), Brian Krause (*Barton Cummings*), Marisol Cassidy (*Theresa Gonzales*).

2. Teen Angel. A teenager (Dennis) suddenly finds his life more complicated than it already is when authorities from above feels he needs guiding and assign Buzz Gunderson, a fledgling guardian angel to watch over him. **Cast:** Jason Priestley (*Buzz Gunderson*), Adam Biesk (*Dennis Mullen*), Renee O'Connor (*Nancy Nichols*), Sasha Jenson (*Jason*).

3. The Secret of Lost Creek. A sister and brother (Jeannie and Robert), spending the summer at a camp in Lost Creek (in the Sierras) search for a buried treasure when they stumble across a series of mysterious clues. **Cast:** Shannen Doherty (*Jeannie Fogel*), Scott Bremner (*Robert Fogel*), Jody Montana (*Travis Hathaway*), Florence H. French (*Adelaide Murchison*), Ruth Hale (*Augusta Murchison*), Dabbs Greer (*Henry Fogel*).

4. Teen Angel Returns. A sequel to *Teen Angel* that follows fledgling guardian angel Buzz Gunderson as he returns to earth to help Cindy Boone, the teenage daughter of a friend (Rodney) when he was alive. **Cast:** Jason Priestley (*Buzz Gunderson*), Robin Lively (*Cindy Boone*), Randy Oglesby (*Randy Boone*), Jennie Garth (*Karrie Donato*).

5. My Life As a Babysitter. Follows high school seniors Nick and Mitch as they compete for the affections of a girl (Jennifer). **Cast:** Jim Calvert (*Nick Crane*), Sean Patrick Flanery (*Mitch Buckley*), Michele Abrams (*Jennifer Edwards*), Kelli Williams (*Kelly*), Lara Lyon (*Michelle*).

6. Just Perfect. A perfectionist teenager (Trent) finds his life turned upside down when he has to care for Barney, his grandmother's mischievous St. Bernard for three weeks. **Cast:** Christopher Daniel Barnes (*Trent Beckerman*), Jennie Garth (*Crystal*), Sean Patrick Flanery (*Diane*), Judith Jones (*Shelley*), Francesca Jarvis (*Grandmother*).

7. Secret Bodyguard. Comedy about Brittany Belmont, a teenage girl with a seriously overprotective father, who is only allowed to attend high school under the watchful eye of Ernie, a teenage martial arts expert he hired to protect her. **Cast:** Ernie Reyes, Jr. (*Ernie*), Heather Campbell (*Brittany Belmont*), Stephen Burton (*Rick*), Johnny Moran (*Kevin*).

8. Emerald Cove. See title for information (aired as serial here then as a series on its own).

Mouseketeers Cast: Christina Aguilera, Keri Russell, Britney Spears, Justin Timberlake, Josh Ackerman, Rhona Bennett, Nita Booth, Mylin Brooks, Brandy Brown, Marc Worden, Mowava Pryor, Kevin Osgood, Matt Morris, Fred Newman, Braden Danner, Tasha Danner, Nikki DeLoach, T.J. Fantini, Albert Fields, Dale Godboldo, Ryan Gosling, Tiffini Hale, Chase Hampton, Rogue Herring, Tony Lucca, Ricky Lucas, Tate Lynch, Dee Dee Magno, Jennifer McGill, Terra McNair, Ilana Miller, Jason Minor, Terri Misner, J.C. Chasez.

6029   *The Mickey Mouse Clubhouse.* (Series; Cartoon; Disney; 2006–). A daily computer animated program that is set at the Mickey Mouse Clubhouse where the antics of Mickey Mouse, his girlfriend, Minnie Mouse, and their friends Donald Duck and Goofy are depicted as they go about their daily lives.

Voice Cast: Wayne Allwine (*Mickey Mouse*); Russi Taylor (*Minnie*

Mouse); Tony Aneslmo *(Donald Duck)*; Bill Farmer *(Goofy)*; Tress MacNeille *(Daisy Duck)*.

6030 ***The Mickey Rooney Show.*** (Series; Comedy; NBC; 1954–1955). The alternate title for *Hey, Mulligan.* See this title for information.

6031 ***Mickey Rooney's Small World.*** (Series; Children; Syn.; 1975). Eight children, aged four to eight and who vary from program to program, discuss various matters with celebrity guests.
Host: Mickey Rooney.

6032 ***Mickey's Mouse Tracks.*** (Series; Cartoon; Disney; 1993). An updated version of *Good Morning Mickey* that, hosted by an animated Mickey Mouse, showcases various Disney cartoons.

6033 ***Mickie Finn's.*** (Series; Variety; NBC; 1966). The Mickie Finn Nightclub, "America's number one speakeasy," in San Diego, California, is the backdrop for a program that recreates the music, song and dance of yesteryear — from the Gay 1890s to the 1960s. Wife and husband singer-musicians Mickie and Fred Finn host the program.
Host: Mickie Finn, Fred Finn. **Regulars:** The Mickie Finn Waitresses, Spider Marillo, Bobby Jensen, Story Gormely, Owen Leinhard, Don Van Paulta. **Music:** The Mickie Finn Band.

6034 ***Microcops.*** (Pilot; Science Fiction; CBS; June 20, 1989). While pursuing a cosmic criminal named Cloyd, two intergalactic law enforcers from the planet Ich (Nardo and Bidra) land on Earth and discover they are microscopic as compared to humans. In order to function, they befriend a human (Morgan) and enter his body. Through Morgan's eyes, they are able to function here. The proposal was to relate Nardo and Bidra's efforts to apprehend Cloyd and stop him from destroying the universe. Produced in 1988 as *Meganauts.*
Cast: William Bumiller *(Captain Nardo)*; Shanti Owen *(Captain Bidra)*; Page Moseley *(Cloyd)*; Peter Scolari *(Morgan)*.

6035 ***Midas Valley.*** (Pilot; Drama; ABC; June 27, 1985). California's Silicon Valley is the setting for the story of the Hammonds, a wealthy family (head of the Lantern Computer Company), and the romances, intrigues and corporate espionage associated with their high tech business worlds. *Regulars:* Drew Hammond, the head of the family; Molly, his wife; Lillian and Franklin, their children; Sara, Franklin's fiancé; Josh, the computer genius; George, Drew's business rival; and Mitzi, the Japanese industrialist.
Cast: Robert Stack *(Drew Hammond)*; Jean Simmons *(Molly Hammond)*; Shanna Reed *(Lillian Hammond)*; Joseph Hacker *(Franklin Hammond)*; Linda Purl *(Sara Corey)*; James Read *(Josh Landau)*; George Grizzard *(George Carew)*; France Nuyen *(Mitzi Koamoto)*.

6036 ***The Middle.*** (Series; Comedy; ABC; 2009–). Orson, Indiana, is a bustling town in the middle of America's Heartland. It is here that the spunky Frankie Heck works as a car salesgirl at Ehlert Motors. Frankie is also a housewife and mother. She lives at 427 Birchwood Avenue with her husband, Mike (the manager of the Orson Lime Quarry; also works as a delivery man for Little Betty Snack Cakes) and their children Sue, Axl and Brick. Fifteen-year-old Axl and 13-year-old Sue attend Orson High School; Brick, eight years old, constantly whispers to himself and attends Orson Elementary School where his best friend is his backpack (he's mostly ignored by other students).

Axl is a jock who seems to do nothing but raid the refrigerator; Sue is very pretty but cursed with bad luck — from her terrible-looking braces to her failure at everything she attempts. Stories relate events in the lives of the Hecks, especially Frankie, as she attempts to deal with work, her kids and an unemotional husband. Don Ehlert is Frankie's boss; Bob works with Frankie; Carly is Sue's girlfriend.
Cast: Patricia Heaton *(Frankie Heck)*; Neil Flynn *(Mike Heck)*; Eden Shur *(Sue Heck)*; Charlie McDermott *(Axl)*; Atticus Shaffer *(Brick Heck)*; Brian Doyle Murray *(Don Ehlert)*; Chris Kattan *(Bob)*; Blaine Sanders *(Carly)*.
Unaired Pilot Cast: Ricki Lake *(Frankie Heck)*; Lex Medlin *(Mike Heck)*; Bernice O'Brien *(Sue Heck)*; Atticus Shaffer *(Brick Hack)*; Michael Mitchell *(Elvis Heck)*.

6037 ***The Middleman.*** (Series; Science Fiction; ABC Family; 2008). O2STK is a super secret organization that battles comic book–like super villains seeking to wreck havoc on the world. The organization's top agent is the Middleman, a mysterious figure who loves a cool glass of milk and uses high tech weaponry to battle evil. Wendy Watson is a struggling artist who assists Middleman (on her prior job, she encountered a grotesque experiment that escaped from a lab beneath her building. Although Wendy showed courage by attempting to battle the creature, she was unable and grabbed — and saved when Middleman arrived and terminated the creature. Wendy's bravery and ability to act without hesitation impresses Middleman who brings her into the agency). Stories relate their efforts to battle creatures nightmares are made of. Lucy is Wendy's friend, an activist and conceptual artist; Ida is Middleman's cantankerous robotic girl Friday ("a soulless android from outer space who masquerades as a librarian"). Nose is Wendy's eccentric friend, a musician.
Cast: Natalie Morales *(Wendy Watson)*; Matt Keestar *(Middleman)*; Bret Morgan *(Lucy Thornfeild)*; Mary Pat Gleason *(Ida)*; Jake Smollet *(Nose)*.

6038 ***Midnight Caller.*** (Series; Crime Drama; NBC; 1988–1991). Jack Killian is an ex-police inspector who quit the force after accidentally shooting his partner while pursuing a felon. Devon King owns a radio station and is seeking a host for a late night call-in show to help people who are worried about street crime. She hires Jack, and stories relate his efforts to solve crimes that result from listeners' calls.

Jack hosts *Midnight Caller* (12:00 midnight to 3:00 A.M.) on KCJM (93.3 FM) in San Francisco (located at 9009 Howard Street, thirty-eighth floor). Jack, who calls himself "The Nighthawk," lives at 928 Fargo Street, Apt. 3-C and Carmen's Bar is his favorite watering hole.

Foster Castleman of Aradella, Inc., becomes the new owner of the radio station (1990) when Devon becomes pregnant by and later marries stockbroker Richard Clark (Christopher Lawford). Nicky Molloy, Foster's "talent lady" (who programs radio stations) runs KCJM. She previously worked for KSPN (as a tape loader), KLTX (promo copy writer) and KSCO (general manager). When Devon has her baby (at Saint Francis Memorial Hospital), she and Richard name him Jack. Deacon Bridges is a reporter for the San Francisco *Dispatch*; Carl Zymak is a lieutenant with the Homicide Division of the S.F.P.D.; Billy Po is Jack's engineer, Becca Nicholson is the gossip columnist for the *Dispatch*.
Cast: Gary Cole *(Jack Killian)*; Wendy Kilbourne *(Devon King)*; Lisa Eilbacher *(Nicky Molloy)*; Mykelti Williamson *(Deacon Bridges)*; Arthur Taxier *(Carl Zymak)*; Dennis Dunn *(Billy Po)*.

6039 ***Midnight Money Madness.*** (Series; Game; TBS; 2006). Late night (12:00 A.M. to 2:00 A.M.) interactive game that involves home viewers (who become contestants by text, Internet or a 1-900 telephone number). Once a home viewer is selected, he participates in various interactive games that award cash prizes ($100 to $300). Jerilee Bonner, Danny Seckel and Craig T. Jackson host.

6040   *Midnight Mystery.* (Pilot; Mystery; NBC; June 5, 1957). Mystery and suspense stories designed for prime time viewing (the pilot aired on the afternoon series *Matinee Theater*). "Rain in the Morning," the pilot story, tells of a terrified housewife (Peggy McCay) and her attempts to escape from a lunatic (Robert Morse) who traps her in her home.

Host: John Conte. **Announcer:** Paul Davis.

6041   *Midnight Patrol.* (Series; Cartoon; Syn.; 1990). Potsworth is a dog owned by Carter. Keiko, Rosie and Nick are their best friends. Each night, when the five are asleep, they each meet in a magical land called the Dream Zone. Here Potsworth can speak and the five have formed a group called the Midnight Patrol. Not all is peaceful here though. Each evening, the Nightmare Prince awakens to begin a quest to ruin dreams. Stories follow the Midnight Patrol as they attempt to foil the prankish Nightmare Prince.

Voice Cast: Clive Revill (*Potsworth*); George Lemore (*Carter*); Janice Kawaye (*Keiko*); Elisabeth Harnois (*Rosie*); Whit Hertford (*Nick*); Rob Paulsen (*Nightmare Prince*).

6042   *The Midnight Special.* (Series; Music; NBC; 1973–1981). Performances by rock, pop, soul and country and western entertainers. Syndicated in September of 1982 as a sixty minute edited series called *The Best of the Midnight Special.*

Hostess: Helen Reddy. **Regular:** Carol Wayne. **Announcer:** Wolfman Jack, Mike Carruthers.

6043   *Midwestern Hayride.* (Series; Variety; Syn; ABC; 1947–1967). Performances by country and western artists. The long-running program ran in syndication from 1947 to 1967 and on ABC from June 29, 1957 to Sept. 22, 1958.

Host: Paul Dixon, Dean Richards, Willie Thall, Bill Thall. **Regulars:** Bonnie Lou, Phyllis Brown, Helen Scott, Billy Scott, Paul Arnold, Mary Jane Johnson, Clay Eager, Phyllis Holmes, Bill Holmes, Freddy Langdon, Tommy Watson, Zeeke Turner, Wally Praetor, Martha Hendricks, Barney Sefton, Jim Philpot, Ernie Lee, Judy Perkins, Kenny Roberts, Bob Shredi, The Pleasant Valley Boys, The Country Briar Hoppers, The Hometowners, The Kentucky Boys, The Midwesterners, The Lucky Pennies, The Trail Blazers, The Girls of the Golden West, The Brown Ferry Four. **Announcer:** Hal Woodard. **Music:** The Pleasant Valley Rangers.

6044   *The Mighty B!* (Series; Cartoon; Nick; 2008). Bessie Higgenbottom is a ten-year-old girl who dreams of becoming a super hero (the Mighty B!). She lives in San Francisco and is a member of the Honeybees, a Girl Scout–like troop. But, unlike other Honeybees, Bessie is obsessed with acquiring every possible merit bade that exists. As stories follow Bessie's efforts to acquire those badges, they also show her flights of fancy as she imagines she is a buff super hero and can accomplish anything. Ben is Bessie's younger brother; Happy is her dog.

Voice Cast: Amy Poehler (*Bessie Higgenbottom*); Andy Richter (*Ben Higgenbottom*); Dee Bradley Baker (*Happy*); Grey DeLisle (*Portia*); Dannah Feinglass (*Penny*); Jessica DiCicco (*Gwen*).

6045   *The Mighty Boosh.* (Series; Comedy; Adult Swim; 2009). British produced, elaborate skit show that revolves around two friends (Howard and Vince) and the crazy world in which they live. Musical numbers, songs, puppets and animated segments supplement the situations encountered by Howard and Vince and their cast of weird regulars.

Cast: Julian Barratt (*Howard Moon*); Noel Fielding (*Vince Noir*). **Regulars:** Dave Brown, Peter Elliot, Rich Fulcher, Richard Ayoade, Matt Berry.

6046   *Mighty Ducks.* (Series; Cartoon; ABC; 1996-1997). The Mighty Ducks are a half human, half duck team of intergalactic hockey players who, in their spare time, battle the evil Dragaunus. During one of their battles to save the Earth from Dragaunus, the Mighty Ducks become stranded on the planet. Unable (for the present) to return to their own planet (Puckworld), they establish a base in an abandoned hockey rink. The rink is later restored and the Mighty Ducks do what they do best — play hockey. But when the need arises, they use their hockey power to battle crime and eventually defeat Dragaunus and his nasty henchmen.

Voice Cast: Tim Curry (*Lord Dragaunus*); Jim Cummings (*Commander Xenon*); Townsend Coleman (*Canard*); Ian Ziering (*Wildwing*); Steve Mackall (*Nosedive*); Jennifer Hale (*Mallory McMallard*); Brad Garrett (*Grin*); Rob Paulsen (*Dr. Swindle*); April Winchell (*Tanya*); Dennis Franz (*Captain Klegghorn*).

6047   *The Mighty Hercules.* (Series; Cartoon; Syn.; 1960). Hercules, the legendary hero of mythology, struggles to protect the Learirn Valley from the evils of the villainous wizard Deadalus. Helena is the beautiful maiden; Newton is the half human, half horse friend of Hercules; Tweet is another friend of Hercules.

Voice Cast: Jerry Bascombe (*Hercules*); Helene Nickerson (*Helena*); Jimmy Tapp (*Newton/Tweet/Deadalus*). **Theme Vocal:** "The Mighty Hercules" by Johnny Nash.

6048   *Mighty Max.* (Series; Cartoon; Syn.; 1993-1994). On a distant planet intellectual fowls (Lemuroids) have developed the ability to travel from planet to planet through the use of portals. One dissident, Skull Master, sought the secret of the portals but was refused its knowledge. Enraged, he destroyed the Lemuroids — or he thought he did. Virgil, the lone survivor, managed to escape with a magical red cap — a cap that, when its preordained wearer can be found, will endow him with the power to stop Skull Master (who, with his Legion of Warriors, is seeking to take over the Earth). On Earth Virgil finds Max, a boy who, according to ancient prophecy, is the Chosen One. He is bestowed with a mission and responsibilities that he really does not want but must accept. While Max now holds the power to activate the planet portals, he is also a target of Skull Master, who not only wants to conquer Earth, but gain control of the red cap (which will give him ultimate control). In addition to Virgil, Max is assisted by Norman, his Viking guardian, and stories follow the trio as they attempt to vanquish Skull Master and save the planet.

Voice Cast: Rob Paulsen (*Max*); Kath Soucie (*Bea*); Richard Moll (*Norman*); Tony Jay (*Virgil*); Tim Curry (*Skull Master*); Corey Burton (*Felix*); Tress MacNeille (*Max's mother*).

6049   *The Mighty Morphin Power Rangers.* (Series; Science Fiction; Fox; 1993–1998). Zordan (played by David Fielding; voiced by Bob Manahan) is an inter dimensional being caught in a time warp. Rita Repulsa (Soga Machiko, Barbara Goodson, Carla Perez) is an alien, intergalactic sorceress who has set her goal on conquering the Earth. To protect the Earth (as well as the rest of the universe from Rita), Zordan forms an elite team of soldiers to stop her. He chooses Jason (Austin St. James), Trini (Thuy Trang), Zack (Walter Jones), Kimberly (Amy Jo Johnson) and Billy (David Yost), teenagers who attend the Cultural High School in a city called Angel Grove. The teens are magically transported to Zordan's headquarters, the Power Station. There, they meet Alpha 5 (Romy Sharff, Donene Kistler), Zordan's robot aide (voice of Richard Wood, Katerina Luciani) and are told about Rita and why they are needed. Each of the teens is an expert in the martial arts and each is given a special gift to enable them to fight Rita and the monstrous creatures she sends to destroy the Earth.

Jason receives the Power Sword; Kimberly, the Power Bow; Trini, the Power Dagger; Billy, the Power Lance; and Zack, the Power Axe. Each of these weapons can be combined to form a super power weapon. They are next given extraordinary powers drawn from the earth — the Power of Dinosaurs. Jason, bold and powerful, controls the Tyrannosaurus Rex; Zack, clever and brave, controls the mastodon; Kimberly, graceful and smart, controls the pterodactyl; Billy, ancient and wise, controls the Triceratops; and Trini, fearless and agile, controls the saber tooth tiger.

Each of the Power Rangers is given a costume that completely hides their identity. The concealing costumes also serve another purpose: to allow producers to use the original Japanese version fight scenes in the American adaptation.

Unlike most successful series that continue with the same characters and plots, *The Mighty Morphin Power Rangers* changed character and story ideas frequently, making for a complex (if not confusing) history to compile.

The first change occurs in the episode of Nov. 18, 1994 ("The Power Transfer"). Here Jason, Trini, and Zack are chosen to represent Angel Grove in the World Peace Summit in Switzerland. Kimberly also leaves to pursue other interests. Zordan chooses new rangers to replace them: Rocky (Steve Cardenas), Katherine (Catherine Sullivan), Aisha (Karan Ashley) and Adam (John Busch). Also assisting them is Tommy (David Jason Frank). Zordan equips them with new powers called Dragon Zords. Rocky powers the Dragon Thunder Zord; Aisha, the Griffin Thunder Zord; Adam, the Lion Thunder Zord; Billy, the Unicorn Thunder Zord; and Katherine, the Firebird Thunder Zord. These Zords combine to form the Thunder Mega Zord (which they use to battle monsters sent by Rita).

When Rita fails to complete her mission and destroy the Power Rangers, she is replaced by her emperor, Lord Zedd (Robert Axelrod). Although Lord Zedd did exactly what Rita did — create monsters to destroy Angel Grove, he complicated matters by reversing time and giving us another set of Power Rangers — the Young Power Rangers — the second listing of rangers who were turned into preteen children but fought as Power Rangers: young Katherine (Julia Jordan), young Adam (Matthew Sakimoto), young Aisha (Sicilly), young Rocky (Michael J. O'Lasky II), and young Tommy (Michael R. Gotto).

To help the Young Power Rangers, Zordan enlisted the help of the Alien Rangers of Aquitar: Delphine (Rajia Baroudi), Auria (David Bacon), Cesta (Karim Prince), Tidens (Jim Gray) and Corcos (Alan Palmer). The Young Power Rangers became adult again when Zordan found the Zeo Crystal and reversed time.

This also brought about a new version called *Power Rangers Zeo* (1996). Here, Lord Zedd destroys Zordan's base of operations, leaving the Power Rangers without a leader. While sifting through the wreckage of Command Center, the powerless rangers find the Zeo Crystal, which restores not only their powers, but Zordan, Alpha and Command Center. The Zeo is the next step in the Power Rangers' fight against evil. Next, Aisha is replaced by Power Ranger Tanya (Nakia Burrise) and Billy steps down as a ranger to help Alpha because the Zeo Crystal can only power five rangers. The teens are given new powers called Zeo Zords. Katherine and Tanya, Zeo Zords One and Two, control fire power; Rocky and Adam, Zeo Zords Three and Four, control the driving force of the sphinx and Taurus the Bull; and Tommy, Zeo Zord Five, controls flight, the power of the Phoenix. When combined, they control the awesome Zeo Zord.

When it is realized that Lord Zedd has also failed to destroy the Power Rangers, he is replaced by Mondo, the Machine King, his wife, Queen Machina, and their robot son, Prince Sprocket — all attempting to conquer the Earth as it is the last planet they need to control the universe. These characters, from the Japanese version, are not credited.

The series continued under the title *The Power Rangers* (which see for information).

6050   *The Mighty Mouse Playhouse.* (Series; Cartoon; CBS; 1955–1967). Adventures of Mighty Mouse, a courageous and daring defender of the weak and oppressed ("Here I come to save the day" is his cry when he sets out to help someone). He is forever coming to the aid of Pearl Pureheart, the girl always in distress (usually from the evil cat Oilcan Harry). In the episode, "The Johnstown Flood," Mighty Mouse is depicted as an ordinary mouse who invents a potion called Atomic Energy that, when taken, endows him with extraordinary powers. Other show segments are *Dinky Duck, Gandy Goose* and *Heckle and Jeckle.*

Voice Cast: Tom Morrison (*Mighty Mouse/Oilcan Harry*); Carol Lawrence (*Pearl Pureheart*); Anthony Kay (*Gandy Goose*).

6051   *Mighty Mouse: The New Adventures.* (Series; Cartoon; CBS; 1987–1988). Newly animated adventures based on the Terrytoons theatrical cartoon, *Mighty Mouse.* Here the mouse with super strength and ability to fly, uses his abilities to protect a city terrorized by hungry cats. The legend of Mighty Mouse has been changed (see *The Mighty Mouse Playhouse* for the original concept). Here one lone mouse with a self-proclaimed mission to do something enters a supermarket, eats some Super Soup, Super Soap and Super Celery. He then dives into a wedge of Super Cheese. The combination of elements endows him with super powers and changes him into the city's new hero, Mighty Mouse. Mighty Mouse is assisted by his friend, an orphan named Scrappy Mouse. His enemies are The Cow, Petey Pete and The Glove. Also known as *The New Adventures of Mighty Mouse.*

Voice Cast: Patrick Pinney (*Mighty Mouse*); Dana Hill (*Orphan Scrappy*), Charles Adler, Joe Alaskey, Maggie Roswell, Neil Ross, Lisa Raggio, Alan Oppenheimer, Mona Marshall, Tami Holbrook, Candy Candido, Jeannie Elias.

6052   *Mighty O.* (Pilot; Comedy; CBS; Aug. 21, 1962). Joe Slattery and Barney Blaney are chief petty officers assigned to the Coast guard cargo vessel *Ortega,* affectionately nicknamed "Mighty O." Their mishaps as they try to help people in trouble is the focal point of the proposal. Other regulars are Chief Muldoon; and Mary, Barney's girlfriend.

Cast: Craig Stevens (*Joe Slattery*); Alan Hale, Jr. (*Barney Blaney*); Richard Jaeckel (*Chief Muldoon*); Lola Albright (*Mary*).

6053   *The Mighty Orbots.* (Series; Cartoon; ABC; 1984–1985). Rob Simmons, a scientist, and his robots — Tur, Bort, Beau, Crunch and Ono, are members of the Galactic Patrol, the Earth-based futuristic police force. Focal point of the program is their battle against Shadow, a sinister planet of evil whose leader, Umbra, seeks to control the universe.

Voices: Sherry Alberoni (*Bo*); Julie Bennett (*Boo*); Jennifer Darling (*Dia*); Barry Gordon (*Robert Simmons*); Jim MacGeorge (*Bort*); Bill Martin (*Tor*); Don Messick (*Crunch*); Robert Ridgely (*Returns*). **Narrator:** Gary Owens.

6054   *Mike and Buff.* (Series; Interview; CBS; 1951–1953). A program of celebrity interviews with newsman Mike Wallace and his wife Buff Cobb.

6055   *Mike and Maty.* (Series; Talk; Disney; 1994). Mike Burger, a former cruise ship entertainer, and Maty Monfort, a hostess on the Spanish network Univision, are teamed to present a daily talk show that, because of its similarity to *Live with Regis and Kathie Lee* was canceled after one season. (Maty and Mike interviewed celebrities with Mike as the comedy relief and Maty as the voice of reason.)

Hosts: Mike Burger, Maty Monfort.

6056 *Mike and Molly.* (Series; Comedy; CBS; 2010–). Mike Biggs is an officer with the Chicago Police Department. Molly Flynn is a fourth grade teacher at the Walter Payton Elementary School. They meet and find an instant attraction to each other at an Overeaters Anonymous meeting. Stories follow their ups and downs as they struggle to make their relationship work despite all the problems that threaten to break them up. Molly lives with her pot-smoking older sister, Victoria (who flaunts her thin figure) and her doting, widowed mother, Joyce (also thin), who claims Molly is only big boned (a fact she doesn't accept). Mike's life is not easy either. Like Molly, he loves to eat (not sensibly, as Molly does) and has a fast-talking wise acre of a partner, Carl, who constantly teases him about his size; Samuel is the Senegalese waiter; Peggy is Mike's mother; Grandma is Carl's grandmother.

Cast: Bill Gardell (*Mike Biggs*); Melissa McCarthy (*Molly Flynn*); Reno Wilson (*Carl McMillan*); Swoosie Kurtz (*Joyce Flynn*); Katy Mixon (*Victoria Flynn*); Nyambi Nyambi (*Samuel*); Rondi Reed (*Peggy* Biggs); Cleo King (*Grandma*).

6057 *Mike and the Mermaid.* (Pilot; Comedy; ABC; Jan. 5, 1968). While fishing in a river, a young boy (Mike) discovers a legendary creature of the sea — a mermaid. The proposal was to depict Mike's adventures when he befriends and attempts to keep the mermaid's existence a secret. Nellie and Jim are Mike's parents.

Cast: Jeri Lynne Fraser (*Mermaid*); Kevin Brodie (*Mike Malone*); Rachel Ames (*Nellie Malone*); Med Flory (*Jim Malone*).

6058 *The Mike Douglas Show.* (Series; Variety; Syn.; 1966–1981). Daily program of music, songs and celebrity interviews with singer Mike Douglas as the host.

Program Open: "Welcome to *The Mike Douglas Show*. This is Marty Brill and with us on today's show will be Patty Duke, H. Ross Poriot, Joe Harnell and His Band and Mike's co-host for the week, Ethel Merman. And now, here's Mike."

Host: Mike Douglas. **Announcer:** Marty Brill, Jay Stewart. **Music:** Ellie Frankel, Joe Harnell, Frank Hunter, Joe Massimino.

6059 *Mike Hammer.* (Series; Crime Drama; Syn.; 1958). Mike Hammer is a two-fisted private detective working out of New York City. He has an eye for the ladies (friends tell him, "Watch out, Mike, your fangs are showing"). If there is a "doll" or "dish" in trouble, Mike will go out of his way to help her, even waive his fee if necessary. Mike uses force (his fists) to get results and considers roughing up a suspect his social call. Mike takes the law into his own hands and dishes out his own brand of justice — and gets away with it. Mike has an office, Room 812, in Manhattan and lives in a hotel on West 47th Street. For research Mike uses the newspaper morgues of the real *Daily News* at 220 East 42nd Street and the mythical *Chronicle*. Mike's traditional secretary, Velda, is not present in this series, which presents Mike as a loner out to battle injustice and make a buck. The only other regular is his friend, Pat Chambers, a captain with the Homicide Division of the N.Y.P.D.'s 19th Precinct. Brian Keith was originally scheduled to play the role of Mike Hammer but was dropped by the producers when they felt he was not right for the role. Based on the character created by Mickey Spillane and is also known as *Mickey Spillane's Mike Hammer*.

Cast: Darren McGavin (*Mike Hammer*); Bart Burns (*Capt. Pat Chambers*). **Narrator:** Darren McGavin. **Theme Song:** "Riff Blues" by Dave Kahn, Melvyn Lenard.

6060 *Mike Hammer.* (Series; Crime Drama; CBS; 1984–1986). Mike Hammer, a hard-boiled New York City–based private detective, was once a cop — "But I knew all the rules, that's why I'm not a cop now." Mike operates the Mike Hammer Agency at 304 West 16th Street in Manhattan. He has an eye for the ladies and is quite ruthless when it comes to criminals. He resides at 4100 Tenth Avenue, drives a blue 1966 Ford Mustang, carries a gun he calls Betsy and Marty's Bar is his hangout.

Velda is Mike's secretary (as originally written by creator Mickey Spillane, Velda was a brunette with a gift of gab and the ability to handle a gun. For television, her hair color didn't matter; being well endowed did). Pat Chambers is the Homicide Detective with the N.Y.P.D.; Lawrence Barrington is the Manhattan District Attorney; Ozzie the Answer is Mike's information man; Duck Ho Cho, called "Ducky," is the owner of the grocery store where Mike shops; Jenny is the bartender at Marty's; Moochie is the pimp; and the series gimmick is a character called "The Face," a beautiful but mysterious girl who is seen briefly in each episode. In the final episode, Mike uncovered her to be a writer named Laura who wrote *Nick Steele* mystery novels under the pen name Frederick Flynn. She tailed Mike to get story material.

Cast: Stacy Keach (*Mike Hammer*); Lindsay Bloom (*Velda*); Don Stroud (*Pat Chambers*); Kent Williams (*Lawrence Barrington*); Danny Goldman (*Ozzie the Answer*); James Hong (*Duck Ho Cho*); Lee Benton (*Jenny*); Ben Powers (*Moochie*); Donna Denton (*The Face*). **Narrator:** Stacy Keach, Rich Little (last two episodes).

Note: Three TV movies preceded the series:

1. Mickey Spillane's Margin for Murder (CBS, Oct. 15, 1981). **Cast:** Kevin Dobson (*Mike Hammer*), Cindy Pickett (*Velda*), Charles Hallahan (*Pat Chambers*).

2. Mickey Spillane's Mike Hammer: More Than Murder (CBS, Jan. 26, 1983). **Cast:** Stacy Keach (*Mike Hammer*), Lindsay Bloom (*Velda*), Don Stroud (*Pat Chambers*), Kent Williams (*Lawrence Barrington*), Danny Goldman (*Ozzie*).

3. Mickey Spillane's Mike Hammer: Murder Me, Murder You (CBS, April 19, 1983). **Cast:** Stacy Keach (*Mike Hammer*), Tanya Roberts (*Velda*), Don Stroud (*Pat Chambers*), Kent Williams (*Lawrence Barrington*).

Following the series, the TV movie, *The Return of Mike Hammer* aired (CBS, April 18, 1986) and served as the pilot for a revised version called *The New Mike Hammer* (CBS, 1986-1987), which see for information.

6061 *Mike Hammer.* (Pilot; Crime Drama; CBS; Dec. 6, 1994). The name plate on his office door reads "Mike Hammer, Private Eye." The locale, however, is not New York City, Mike's traditional home base, but Miami Beach, Florida. Mike has also gone through some changes — he's 20 years younger and 30 years wiser. Velda, his ultra-sexy secretary, has also relocated to Florida to be with him and Captain Pat Chambers of the N.Y.P.D. is now Detective Sergeant Patricia "Pat" Chambers of the Miami P.D. The proposal was to follow the Mickey Spillane-created character as he dishes out a New York brand of justice in the Sunshine State while attempting to solve crimes.

Cast: Rob Estes (*Mike Hammer*); Pamela Anderson (*Velda*); Darlanne Fluegel (*Pat Chambers*).

6062 *Mike Hammer, Private Eye.* (Series; Crime Drama; Syn.; 1997-1998). Mike Hammer is a tough ex-cop who quit the force because the rules prevented him from taking matters in his own hands to get the job done. He is tough on criminals (a beating is his social call), has an eye for the ladies and a non-holds barred approach to fighting crime — do what it takes. Stories follow Mike's case investigations. Velda is Mike buxom secretary; Lawrence Barrington (formally an Assistant D.A.) is now the Deputy Mayor of New York; and The Face is a mysterious character who trails Mike for story information for her mystery novels.

Cast: Stacy Keach (*Mike Hammer*); Shannon Whirry (*Velda*); Kent Williams (*Lawrence Barrington*); Rebecca Chaney (*The Face*).

6063   Mike, Lu and Og. (Series; Cartoon; Cartoon Network; 2006). Albonquetine is a tropical island with the strange ability to sink then pop up again like a cork. It is here that New York-born Michelene Mazinsky, called Mike, finds herself when she applies for as a foreign exchange student and is sent to Albonquetine. Here she befriends Lu, the self-proclaimed island princess; and Og, Lu's brilliant seven-year-old cousin. Stories relate Mike's adventures as she learns to adjust to her new surroundings and as she and Lu become the innocent victims of Og's experiments and inventions. Wendell is Lu's father and the island governor; Alfred and Margery are Og's parents; Old Queeks is the Island Elder (the Medicine Man), Lancelot is Lu's pet turtle.

Voice Cast: Nika Frost (*Mike*); Nancy Cartwright (*Lu*); Dee Bradley Baker (*Og*); S. Scott Bullock (*Wendell*); Corey Burton (*Old Queeks*); Martin Rayner (*Alfred*); Kath Soucie (*Margery*).

6064   The Mike O'Malley Show. (Series; Comedy; NBC; 1999). Mike O'Malley is a thirty-year-old EMS technician who lives in a small house in New Haven, Connecticut, with his slacker friend, Weasel. Mike is not all that ambitious either. He loves hockey and if there is a way to dodge work he will find a way to do so. Life changes for Mike when one of his friends, the womanizing Jimmy decides to marry (Marcia). Mike suddenly realizes that his life has gone nowhere and decides to make changes. He begins by rekindling his relationship with his ex-girlfriend, Shawna but low ratings ended the series after two episodes and never really changed life for Mike.

Cast: Mike O'Malley (*Himself*); Mark Rosenthal (*Weasel*); Will Arnett (*Jimmy*); Missy Yaeger (*Shawna*); Kate Walsh (*Marcia*); Kerry O'Malley (*Kerry*).

6065   The Mike Wallace Profiles. (Pilot; Reality; CBS; Nov. 17, 1981). In-depth profiles of famous people via film clips, interviews and newsreel footage.

Host-Narrator: Mike Wallace.

6066   The Mikes. (Pilot; Comedy; Unaired; Produced for FX in 2005). The California desert is the setting for a proposal about two down-on-their-luck families (Stanley and Larocca) who live next door to each other and who each blame the other for their economic, social and sexual problems.

Cast: Eve Gordon (*Gwen Stanley*); Josh Laster (*Sam Stanley*); Jenna Gavigan (*Amanda Stanley*); Jeanette Brox (*Faith Larocca*); Jessie Head (*Tyrus Larocca*); Nathan Norton (*Travis Larocca*); Stacy Travis (*Tanya Larocca*); Vincent Angell (*Mike Larocca*).

6067   A Milestone in Television. (Experimental; Variety; NBC; May 15, 1940). Ray Perkins hosts a program that celebrates NBC's first year of regular television programming. Following a speech by then NBC vice president Alfred H. Morton, variety acts were presented: ballet dancing from Alicia Markova and Anton Dolin; a fashion revue hosted by Hildegarde; songs from Avis Andrews, Anna Mary Dickey and Leonard Warren; dances by the Berry Brothers and the Three Peters Sisters; a dramatic skit ("House of Glass") with Gertrude Berg; and a Walt Disney cartoon, "The Ugly Duckling."

6068   Milestones of the Century. (Series; Documentary; Syn.; 1960). An insert series that features newsreel film footage (from Pathe films) that covers one event for each day of the year (thus 365 episodes were produced).

Narrator: Ed Herlihy.

6069   The Milky Way. (Experimental; Stage Play; NBC; Oct. 20, 1939). A television adaptation of the 1934 stage play, "The Cheese Champ," about a scrawny milk delivery man (Burleigh Sullivan) who is turned into a boxer against his will. The story follows Burleigh as he is trained (by Speed) and how he wins the title in a one punch affair (he knocks out the champ by beating him senseless). "The Milky Way" is the first program to use rear projection (filming scenes especially for the live program that were used to heighten the fight scene).

Cast: Fred Stewart (*Burleigh Sullivan*); James Corner (*Speed*); June Blossom (*Mae Sullivan*); Alexander Cross (*Gabby*); Claudia Morgan (*Anne Westley*); Ross Hertz (*Spider*).

6070   Millennium. (Series; Crime Drama; Fox; 1996–1998). Frank Black is a former FBI agent who now works as a profiler for the Millennium Group, a Seattle-based organization that incorporates the abilities of former law enforcement officers to battle the crime that is growing as the new millennium approaches. The group believes the current (1996) and the approaching (2000) crime wave may be the result of an evil that is related to prophecy. Violent stories follow Frank as he investigates unsettling crimes that may be only the start of something he can't even imagine for the future. Catherine is Frank's wife; Jordan is their daughter; Andy McClaren is the unit's assistant director; Peter Watts, Emma Hollis, Bob Bletcher and Lara Means are investigators.

Cast: Lance Henrickson (*Frank Black*); Megan Gallagher (*Catherine Black*); Britany Tiplady (*Jordan Black*); Terry O'Quinn (*Peter Watts*); Klea Scott (*Emma Hollis*); Stephen E. Miller (*Andy McClaren*); Bill Smitrovich (*Bob Bletcher*); Kristen Cloke (*Lara Means*).

6071   Million Dollar Money Drop. (Series; Game; NBC; 2010). "Earlier tonight armed guards picked up one million dollars in cash from a secret vault. It was transported under maximum security to our protective set. The entire million will be handed over to one couple. Their challenge is to hang onto it in the most heart-pounding game ever imagined." Two players compete and work as a team. They receive $1 million in cash but must answer questions to keep it. Two category topics are revealed. The players select one and (in rounds one, two and three) four possible answers are revealed to a question that is then read. Within a sixty second time limit, the players can place money on one answer box, or up to three boxes if they are not sure of the answer; they must leave one answer box empty. Once the money has been bet, they have thirty seconds with which to change their minds. At the end of the time, the trap doors that each box contains open to eliminate any money those boxes may contain. Money that was placed on the correct answer remains and becomes the players' earnings. Rounds four through six eliminate one of the answer boxes but the players are given ninety seconds to place their bets. In the final round, two answer boxes are used and the player must bet all remaining money on the box they feel is the correct response to the question asked. Players either win money or lose everything based on the answer they have chosen.

Host: Kevin Pollak.

6072   Million Dollar Password. (Series; Game; CBS; 2008). A revised version of the 1960s's game show *Password*. Two teams compete, each composed of one celebrity and one non-celebrity contestant. The object is for one player (the giver) to get his partner (the guesser) to identify a key word (for example, Cold) through one word clues (five key words are used for each of the four 30 second rounds that are played). Round one has the celebrity as the guesser; in round two, the celebrity is the giver. Round three has the celebrities switching partners with the celebrity acting as the giver. Round four has the celebrity as the guesser. The player with the highest score is the winner and receives the opportunity to play for $1 million.

A board with six money amounts is shown. Each round is 90 seconds long. The player is teamed with the celebrity with whom he scored the most points. He can choose to be the giver or guesser. In round one ($10,000) he must get five out of ten passwords; round two ($25,000), five out of nine; round three ($50,000), five out of eight; round four ($100,000), five out of seven; round five ($250,000), five out of six; round 6 ($1 million), five out of five. Each money round is limited to three clues per word and the player risks loss of everything if he fails to complete a round (he can quit at any time and leave with what money he has won).

Host: Regis Philbin.

6073   The Millionaire. (Series; Drama; CBS; 1955–1960). A man, seated behind a desk, speaks: "My name is Michael Anthony. For many years, I was executive secretary to the late multibillionaire, John Beresford Tipton. He was one of the very few men who ever earned, by the use of his phenomenal brain, a fortune that ran into the billions of dollars. Among my duties was the unique job of delivering one million dollars which Mr. Tipton frequently gave away tax free, to a total stranger."

Mr. Tipton (never fully seen) lived a life of treasured seclusion and conducted his business activities from Silverstone, his 60,000 acre estate. Here, he indulged in many hobbies, the most unusual of which began when his doctor told him that he must find a means of relaxation. Mr. Tipton, seated in his study, is toying with one of his ivory chess figures, when he sends for his executive secretary, Michael Anthony. "You know, Mike, these chessmen were the first luxury I ever allowed myself ... I decided to make my hobby a chess game with human beings ... I'm going to choose a number of people for my chessmen and give them each a million dollars. The bank will issue the check.... No one is to ever know that I'm the donor. I want a complete report on what happens to each person's life in writing."

After Mr. Tipton's death, the will instructed Michael Anthony to reveal the files of people, selected by a means known only to Mr. Tipton, who were mysteriously presented with a tax free cashier's check for one million dollars. Via flashback sequences, John Beresford Tipton's intrusion on fate is revealed as stories disclose how the money helped or hindered lives.

John Beresford Tipton issued 188 checks for one million dollars (drawn on the Gotham City Trust and Savings Bank). His unique hobby was related to the subject of human nature. "Every subject in his vast store of knowledge was close analysis and was always related to the behavior and destiny of man." Each check recipient must sign a document agreeing never to reveal the exact nature of the gift or its amount. Spouses can be told, but telling anyone else results in a forfeiture of any remaining monies. Also known as *If You Had a Million*.

On Dec. 19, 1978 CBS aired *The Millionaire*, a proposed revival with Robert Quarry as Michael Anthony.

Cast: Marvin Miller (*Michael Anthony*); Paul Frees (*John Beresford Tipton*); Roy Gordon (*Andrew V. McMahon; bank vice president*). **Announcer:** Ed Herlihy.

6074   The Millionaire Matchmaker. (Series; Reality; Bravo; 2008). Patti Stanger is a real life matchmaker. Her clients are millionaires who are unable to find a mate. These millionaires, however, are not your Donald Trump; they are "millionaire losers — men who want Madonna in the bedroom, Martha Stewart in the kitchen and Mary Poppins in the nursery — and they need help." Patti runs what

she calls her "Millionaires Club" ("The hardest club to get into in the world"). She allows beautiful women in for free (her "potential wives") but for men, the fee ranges from $10,000 to $150,000 to meet these women. The viewer is "treated" to the client, the women and the matches Patti tries to establish.

6075   The Milton Berle Show. (Series; Variety; NBC; ABC; 1953–1967). Music, songs and vaudeville-like slapstick comedy combined with performances by celebrity guests (mostly in skits). Four versions appeared:

1. *The Texaco Star Theater* (NBC, 1948–53). See entry for information.
2. *The Buick-Berle Show* (NBC, 1953–55). See entry.
3. *The Milton Berle Show* (NBC, 1955-56). **Host:** Milton Berle. **Orchestra:** Victor Young.
4. *The Milton Berle Show* (ABC, 1966-67). **Host:** Milton Berle. **Regulars:** Bobby Rydell, Donna Loren, Irving Benson, The Berle Girls, The Louis DaPron Dancers. **Announcer:** Dick Tufeld. **Orchestra:** Mitchell Ayres.

6076   The Milton the Monster Show. (Series; Cartoon; ABC; 1965-1966). The overall title for five animated series.

1. *Milton the Monster.* Horrible Hill in Transylvania is the setting for the misadventures of Milton, a lovable Frankenstein-type of monster.
2. *Fearless Fly.* Hyram, a mild-mannered insect, battles evil as Fearless Fly.
3. *Flukey Luke.* The story of a cowboy who doubles as a private detective.
4. *Muggy Doo.* The antics of a fast-talking con artist.
5. *Penny Penguin.* The antics of a very mischievous child.

Voice Cast: Bob McFadden (*Milton the Monster*); Dayton Allen (*Professor Weirdo/Fearless Fly/Flukey Luke*); Larry Best (*Two Feathers/Muggy Doo*); Beverly Arnold (*Penny Penguin*).

6077   Mimi. (Pilot; Comedy; CBS; Aug. 29, 1964). The Garden of Eden is an exclusive California health spa owned by Mr. Peavey. His staff comprises people who have a knack for fouling things up and the proposal was to focus on two of his staff: Mimi, a kind-hearted dietician, and Phil, her friend, the therapist.

Cast: Mimi Hines (*Mimi*); Phil Ford (*Phil*); Dan Tobin (*Mr. Peavey*).

6078   Mimi and Me. (Pilot; Crime Drama; CBS; Sept 7, 1991). The setting is Los Angeles. A free-spirited girl named Mimi Molloy is shopping for clothes when a dying man (shot by crooks) hands her a box and tells her not to let his pursuers get it. Mimi runs but is spotted by the killers. While trying to escape, she bumps into Howard Raney, an uptight orthodontist student, who tries to help but he too is pursued. With the help of Howard's uncle, private detective Al Marr, they solve the mystery of the box (containing German relics needed for a fascist uprising), capture the killers and decide to remain a team. The proposal was to relate Mimi and Howard's adventures as detectives. Other regulars are Amy, Howard's girlfriend; and Rula, Mimi's friend, the owner of a sidewalk boutique.

Cast: Terry Farrell (*Mimi Molloy*); Howard McGillin (*Howard Raney*); Bellina Logan (*Rula*); Kari Lizer (*Amy*); Ken Mars (*Al Marr*).

6079   Mina and the Count. (Series; Cartoon; Cartoon Network; 1996). Mina Harper is a seven-year-old girl with a most unusual best friend — a 700-year-old blue skinned vampire named Vlad the Count (they met when Vlad mistook Mina Harper for Nina Parker, the actual girl he was seeking for his supply of blood). Over time, Nina reformed Vlad, making him less evil. Mina lives with her father and sister Lucy in a small American town and stories follow the mishaps that befall Vlad and Mina. Igor is Vlad's mean, hunchback servant (who loathes Mina for making his master nice); Nick is the school bully. The program, originally intended to become a series, aired as a series of shorts on *What a Cartoon*.

Voice Cast: Ashley Johnson, Tara Strong *(Mina Harper)*; Marc Hamel *(Vlad the Count)*; Jeff Bennett, Robert Galey *(Igor)*; Michael Bell *(Mr. Harper)*.

6080 Mind Control with Derren Brown. (Series; Reality; Syfy; 2007). Derren Brown bills himself as a mentalist (he claims he can make you do something without realizing you are doing it). That concept is put to the test as Derren is set loose on an unsuspecting public to prove what he claims.

6081 Mind of Mencia. (Series; Comedy; Comedy Central; 2005). A look at everyday life as seen through the eyes of comedian Carlos Mencia — from his monologues to man-in-the-street interviews to his interactions with the studio audience.

Host: Carlos Mencia. **Music:** Stephen Phillips.

6082 The Mind of the Married Man. (Series; Drama; HBO; 2001–2002). A male perspective of married life as depicted through the activities of Micky, Doug and Jake, men who work together at a Chicago newspaper. Donna is Micky's wife; Carol is Doug's wife; Kevin is their single friend; Missy is Jake's girlfriend.

Cast: Mike Binder *(Micky Barnes)*; Taylor Nichols *(Doug Nelson)*; Jake Weber *(Jake Berman)*; Sonya Walger *(Donna Barnes)*; Kate Walsh *(Carol Nelson)*; Doug Williams *(Kevin)*; Ivana Milicevic *(Missy)*.

6083 Mindreaders. (Series; Game; NBC; 1979–1980). Two teams of four players, men vs. women, compete. A question calling for a yes or no answer is read to one team. One member of that team (turns rotate) has to predict how each of his teammates answered the question. Each correct prediction score the team $50. The opposing team competes in the same manner. The first team to score $300 is the winner.

Host: Dick Martin. **Announcer:** Johnny Olson.

6084 Mindy Carson Sings. (Series; Variety; NBC; 1949). Singer Mindy Carson hosts a program of music and songs.

Host: Mindy Carson. **Regulars:** Danny Horton, Florian ZaBach. **Announcer:** Don Pardo. **Music:** Earl Sheldon, Norman Cloutier.

6085 Minerva Mink. (Pilot; Cartoon; WB; April 24, 1994). The most beautiful, the most desirable animal in the forest is Minerva Mink (a combination of Marilyn Monroe and Jayne Mansfield). Despite her fabulous looks, she is lonely and looking for "the hunk of my dreams" (a guy with rich parents). Her efforts to find that dream is the focal point of the potential series. Wilfred is the nerd wolf seeking to be that man of her dreams. Aired on *Animaniacs*.

Voice Cast: Julie Brown *(Minerva Mink)*; Peter Scolari *(Wilfred Wolf)*; Frank Welker *(Frog)*.

6086 The Minister of the Divine. (Pilot; Comedy; Unaired; Produced for Fox in 2009). It is a Sunday and church services are being held in the small, conservative farming town of Divine, when its elderly minister is stricken by a heart attack. The following week, Geraldine "Gerry" Granger, a pretty, "chocolate-loving, joke-cracking" lady pastor with a shady past assumes the duties as pastor of the Devine Church. Gerry represents everything the town opposes and the proposal was to relate the mishaps that occur as Gerry sets out to perform her pastoral duties. David Horton is the town council president; Hugo Horton is David's slow-witted son; Alice Tinker is

Gerry's assistant; Owen Nesbitt is the blunt-talking farmer; Frank Boyle is the council secretary.

Cast: Kirstie Alley *(Gerry Granger)*; Kevin McNally *(David Horton)*; Jonathan Tchaikovsky *(Hugo Horton)*; Riki Lindhome *(Alice Tinker)*; W. Earl Brown *(Owen Nesbitt)*; Malcolm Barrett *(Frank Boyle)*.

6087 The Minor Accomplishments of Jackie Woodman. (Series; Comedy; IFC; 2006). Jackie Woodman is an attractive woman with a dream: make it in Hollywood as a TV and movie writer. Ten years have passed since she left New York and her accomplishments are virtually nil (she writes for a second rate magazine called *Image*). Realizing that perhaps the big time is not for her, she embarks on a mission to change her life by accomplishing a series of minor achievements. Stories relate those efforts. Tara is her best friend; Bobby Paterniti (who introduces himself as "Bobby P.") is a semi successful director; Mitchell is Jackie's gay assistant at *Image*; Connor is Tara's boyfriend. Based on the real life experiences of Laura Kightlinger.

Cast: Laura Kightlinger *(Jackie Woodman)*; Nicholle Tom *(Tara)*; Jeffrey Kramer *(Bobby Paterniti)*; Azura Skye *(Skyler)*; Patrick Bristow *(Mitchell)*; Mary Kay Place *(Jackie's mother)*; Colleen Camp *(Angela Birnbaum)*; Butch Klein *(Connor)*.

6088 Minor Adjustments. (Series; Comedy; NBC; 1995–1996). Ron Aimes is a child psychologist who is quite competent at the office and can solve virtually any problem parents face with their children. At home it is a different story. Ron is married to Rachel and is the father of Emma (four years old) and Trevor (ten) — two mischievous kids over which Ron's years of professional training has little effect — until he uses methods a bit unorthodox and is able to deal with them. Stories follow Ron's experiences with his family at home and his attempts to deal with upset parents and rambunctious children at work. Ron shares a medical facility with Dr. Bruce Hampton (a dentist) and Dr. Francine Bailey (a pediatrician); Darby Gladstone, Bruce's niece, is the floor receptionist.

Cast: Rondell Sheridan *(Dr. Ron Aimes)*; Wendy Raquel Robinson *(Rachel Aimes)*; Camille Winbush *(Emma Aimes)*; Bobby E. McAdams II *(Trevor Aimes)*; Linda Kash *(Dr. Francine Bailey)*; Mitchell Whitfield *(Dr. Bruce Hampton)*; Sara Rue *(Darby Gladstone)*.

6089 Minoriteam. (Series; Cartoon; Adult Swim; 2005–2006). El Jefe, a Mexican who fights crime with a leaf blower; Non-Stop, an Arab convenience store owner who is impervious to bullets; Dr. Wang, an Asian human calculator; Fatso, who moves with the speed of lightning; and Jewcano, a man who evokes the powers of the Jewish faith and a volcano, are the Minoritem, ethnic super heroes united for one cause: fight discrimination (such as White Shadow, The Standardized Test, Stuck-Up Girlfriend, Confederate Soldier) wherever it exists.

Voice Cast: Nick Puga *(El Jefe)*; Dana Snyder *(Dr. Wang)*; Keith Lal *(Non Stop)*; Enn Reitel *(Jewcano)*; Rodney Saulsberry *(Fatso)*.

6090 Minute to Win It. (Series; Game; NBC; 2010–2011). A throwback to the early days of television game shows wherein contestants compete in *Beat the Clock* and *Truth or Consequences*–like stunts in an attempt to win money. *Minute to Win It* greatly ups the grand prize money (to $1 million) but players must overcome silly challenges (for example, moving eggs across the floor by fanning them with a pizza box; trying to empty tissues from a box using only one hand). The challenges encompass everyday household items but escalate in difficulty as the players progress. Each player has only one minute to perform a challenge and faces elimination if he fails to complete it. Over the course of the program ten challenges are presented to players. Money is scored for each completed task and players can elect to continue or keep the money they have won up to that point (failure at any level costs a player his winnings). The one player who has not only the ability but the courage to complete all ten challenges wins the money.

Host: Guy Fieri.

6091   *A Minute with Stan Hooper.* (Series; Comedy; Fox; 2003). *A Minute with Stan Hooper* is a weekly segment of *Newsline*, America's highest rated TV news magazine series. In the segment, voted "The Best Moment on Television," Stan relates stories about real people. Stan has always done it from a phony set in a Manhattan studio and feels he can do a better job by meeting "real people," the down-to-earth people of Middle America. To accomplish this, Stan and his wife, Molly, leave the hustle and bustle of New York City for life in Waterford Falls, a sleepy little Wisconsin town.

The town appears to be run by Fred Hawkins, the powerful and rich owner of the Hawkins Cheese Factory. *The Waterford Falls Truth* is the local (and only) newspaper; the Patterson Boys Diner is the local eatery run by gay lovers Pete and Lou. Jimmy's Tavern is the local bar; women in town are not allowed to vote ("It's on the books") and nobody ever loses at pool because nobody ever finishes a game. This is Stan's real life dream town and from the center of the Peterson Boys Diner, *A Minute with Stan Hooper* is broadcast live to the nation (*Newsline* airs at 9:00 P.M. on Wednesday evenings opposite *The Wisconsin Farm Report* in Waterford Falls). Pete and Lou are actually married (when they tied the knot, Lou took Pete's last name).

Stan and Molly reside in a rather lavish house ($500 a month rent) that comes with its own butler (Gary Jameson). Frank's son, Ryan Hawkins, works as Stan's cameraman; Molly is Stan's makeup artist and Chelsea is the diner's sexy waitress. Margie Hawkins is Ryan's dim-witted sister.

Cast: Norm MacDonald *(Stan Hooper)*; Penelope Ann Miller *(Molly Hooper)*; Daniel Roebuck *(Pete Peterson)*; Garrett Diblahunt *(Lou Peterson)*; Reagan Dale Neis *(Chelsea)*; Fred Willard *(Fred Hawkins)*; Brian Howe *(Gary Jameson)*; Eric Lively *(Ryan Hawkins)*; Carolyn Lawrence *(Margie Hawkins)*.

6092   *Miracle at Beekman's Place.* (Pilot; Drama; NBC; Dec. 26, 1988). Following the death of his wife, Dr. Cyrus Beekman, chief of staff of Mid-Mercy Hospital in New York City, quits his job and moves to his old neighborhood on West Wilson Avenue where he opens an inner-city clinic for the needy (The Olivia Beekman Medical Clinic; named after his wife). The proposal was to relate Cyrus's experiences as he attempts to practice what he believes — helping people. Other Regulars are Nurse Sarah Coleman; Dr. Paul Hemingway; Mario, Cyrus's friend; and Isabella, Mario's wife.

Cast: Scoey Mitchell *(Cyrus Beekman)*; Theresa Merritt *(Sarah Coleman)*; Brian Matthews *(Paul Hemingway)*; Robert Costanzo *(Mario D'Agostino)*; Liz Torres *(Isabella D'Agostino)*.

6093   *Miracle at Blaise.* (Experimental; Drama; DuMont; Aug. 22, 1944). A talkative World War II drama about a mysterious American woman (played by Claire Luce) who helps the French underground against the Nazis. As the woman begins her seemingly suicidal mission (to help set a signal for Allied planes), she is visited by a spirit named Tabitha, herself a victim of the war, who provides the guidance she needs to complete the mission.

Cast: Claire Luce, Janet Dowd, Rhodelle Heller, Ruth LeSher, Dorothy South, Nancy Strauss.

6094   *Miracle Pets.* (Series; Reality; PAX; 2001–2003). Inspirational stories about animals and the amazing (and sometimes miraculous) things they do to help humans in trouble or life-threatening situations.

Host: Alan Thicke.

6095   *Miracles.* (Series; Drama; ABC; 2003). Paul Callan is a man with a most unusual job — he investigates the validity of supposed miracles for the Catholic Church (for example, religious images suddenly appearing on the walls of buildings; statues of the Virgin Mary that shed tears; Jesus Christ figures with bleeding palms). What Paul hasn't seen, however, "is the true spirit of God."

Paul is an orphan and never knew his parents. He grew up at Saint Jerome's Orphanage in Boston; he works for Alvin Keel, the head of a secret U.S. government agency that investigates strange happenings. Evelyn Santos assists Paul (she helps Paul investigate but is also there to be a second witness to an event and authenticate what they believe is truly a miracle). Evelyn is a former police officer with knowledge of forensics. Paul says he feels like a doctor — "I never cure anyone. I show up, deliver the bad news and move on."

Cast: Skeet Urich *(Paul Callan)*; Marisa Ramirez *(Evelyn Santos)*; Angus MacFodyen *(Alvin Keel)*.

6096   *The Misadventures of Sheriff Lobo.* (Series; Crime Drama; NBC; 1979-1980). Orly County, Georgia, is home to Elroy P. Lobo, the slightly dishonest sheriff, and his deputies, Perkins (Lobo's flunky) and Hawkins (honest). The characters first appeared on *B.J. and the Bear* and stories follow Sheriff Lobo as he attempts to dispense his own brand of justice — for profit (but never quite achieves his goal and always winds up paying for it in the end).

Sarah Cumberland is the manager of the Orly Hot Springs Hotel; Rose Perkins is Perkins' wife; Margaret Ellen Mercer is the waitress at Danny's Restaurant; Oscar Gorley is the promoter; Mayor Hawkins is Birdie's father. See also the spin off series *Lobo*.

Cast: Claude Akins *(Elroy P. Lobo)*; Mills Watson *(Deputy Perkins)*; Brian Kerwin *(Birdwell "Birdie" Hawkins)*; Leann Hunley *(Sarah Cumberland)*; Cydney Crampton *(Rose Perkins)*; Janet Lyn Curtis *(Margaret Ellen Mercer)*; J.D. Cannon *(Oscar Gorley)*; William Schallert *(Mayor Hawkins)*; Pamela Myers *(Hotel Waitress)*; Dick Winslow *(Hotel Bartender)*; Rosemary DeCamp *(Elroy's Mother)*.

6097   *Misery Loves Company.* (Series; Comedy; Fox; 1995). Nicky St. Hubbins is the Manhattan bar hangout for brothers Joe and Mitchell DeMarco and their friends Perry and Lewis. Joe and Perry are divorced; Mitchell is single and Lewis is married (to Tracy). Stories follow the ups and downs of four close friends who are in various stages of romance and divorce. Other regulars are Nicky, the bar owner; Melanie, Lewis's daughter; and Connor, Perry's son.

Cast: Dennis Boutsikaris *(Joe DeMarco)*; Christopher Meloni *(Mitchell DeMarco)*; Julius Carry *(Perry)*; Stephen Furst *(Lewis)*; Nikki DeLoach *(Tracy)*; Kate E. Mazur *(Nicky)*; Diane Delano *(Melanie)*; Wesley Jonathan *(Connor)*.

6098   *The Misfits of Science.* (Series; Adventure; NBC; 1985-1986). Weird 'R' Us" and the "Misfits of Science" are the nicknames for H.I.T. (the Human Investigative Team) of Humanidyne ("Science to help the human condition"), the largest defense contractor in the United States. Dr. William ("Billy") Hayes and Dr. Elvin ("El") Lincoln are the research scientists who head H.I.T.; Dick Stetmeyer is their easily exasperated supervisor. Billy and El are assisted by Gloria Dinallo, Johnny Bukowski and Jane Miller. They are extraordinary people who happen to be different — but who use their unique powers to help people in trouble.

Billy possesses no special powers; he looks out for the other members of the group. El is very tall (seven feet four inches), has been working on glandular research and developed what Billy calls the "shrinking stuff" (El injected himself with it; when he touches the back of his neck, he can reduce himself to the size of a Ken doll; the condition lasts for 14 minutes). Gloria is a very pretty 17-year-old girl who possesses amazing telekinetic powers. She is also a juvenile delinquent and cared for by her probation officer, Jane Miller (Gloria's father deserted her some months ago). "Glo," as Billy calls her, works as a waitress at the Burger Barn. Johnny, a former rock star known as Johnny B, was "fried" by 20,000 volts of electricity at his last concert and is now a human dynamo. "B Man," as Billy calls him, attracts electricity and discharges lightning bolts. His fingers spark, water can kill him and his eyes glow (he wears sunglasses to cover them). Miss Nance is the agency's pretty receptionist. She is oblivious to what is happening around her and considers it her duty to give recipients their telephone messages — no matter what the circumstances (there is usually a crisis in progress).

Cast: Dean Paul Martin *(Billy Hayes)*; Courteney Cox *(Gloria Dinallo)*; Kevin Peter Hall *(Elvin Lincoln)*; Mark Thomas Miller *(Johnny Bukowski)*; Max Wright *(Dick Stetmeyer)*; Diane Civita *(Miss Nance)*.

6099   Miss America: Countdown to the Crown. (Series; Reality; TLC; 2009). A prequel program to *The Miss America Pageant* that allows viewers to judge and place four girls into the pageant finals. Fifty-two state title holders compete. The women are given living accommodations on the *Queen Mary* luxury ocean liner and face team and individual competitions to help them prepare for the actual Miss America Pageant. Each of the girls are guided by two consultants and viewers rate the girls of their choice via first impression photos, swimsuit photos and You Tube (Internet) videos in TLC's unofficial online polls (which are for entertainment purposes only and have no bearing on the actual pageant). The various competitions are designed to eliminate the majority of the women (weakest performers) to select the 15 gold-sash finalists. It is from this group that viewers can vote for the four girls who show the most promise of becoming the 2009 Miss America. Tyler Harcott hosts.

6100   Miss America Reality Check. (Series; Reality; TLC; 2008). The 52 contestants for the 2008 Miss America pageant are gathered together and placed in a large residence. The girls are profiled via personal interviews and compete in actual beauty pageant challenges to prepare themselves for the actual event. The program is actually a behind-the-scenes look at how the women prepare for the big event. Michael Urie hosts.

6101   The Miss and the Missiles. (Pilot; Comedy; CBS; July 25, 1964). The romantic ups and downs of Connie Marlowe, a magazine writer, and Bill Adams, an Air Force test pilot. Other regulars are Buzz, Connie's brother; Emma, Connie's housekeeper; John P. MacBain, Connie's boss; and Spider, Buzz's friend.

Cast: Gisele MacKenzie *(Connie Marlowe)*; John Forsythe *(Bill Adams)*; Gordon Gebert *(Buzz Marlowe)*; Kathleen Freeman *(Emma)*; John McGiver *(John P. MacBain)*; Michael J. Pollard *(Spider)*.

6102   Miss BG. (Series; Cartoon; Qubo; 2008–2010). BG (Big Girl) is a young girl who experiences the good and bad times with her friends Alex and Gad. She lives with her parents, Jeffrey (a veterinarian) and her mother, Charlotte, a magazine reporter, and younger brother George (who has a pet hamster named Albert). Brittany Ann, is BG's school mate, a rich girl who constantly looks down on her. Alice is BG's aunt; Kayla is Brittany Ann's friend.

Voice Cast: Hannah Endicott-Douglas *(Miss BG)*; Nissae Isen *(George)*; Cameron Ansell *(Gad)*; Billy Rosemberg *(Alex)*; Susan Roman *(Charlotte)*; Neil Crone *(Jeffrey)*; Stephanie Morganstern

(Aunt Alice); Rebecca Brenner *(Brittany Ann)*; Melanie Tonello *(Kayla)*. Laura de Carteret *(Brittany Ann's mother)*; Leah Cudmore *(Terri)*.

6103   Miss Bishop. (Pilot; Comedy; NBC; Sept. 1, 1961). Ella Bishop is a dedicated English teacher in a small Midwestern college town. The proposal, based on the 1941 feature film, *Cheers for Miss Bishop* was to relate Ella's experiences as she sometimes goes out of her way to help her students.

Cast: Jan Clayton *(Ella Bishop)*.

6104   Miss Guided. (Series; Comedy; ABC; 2007). Becky Freeley is a guidance counselor who has returned to her old high school to help students make the right choices in life. In high school, Becky was not the most ambitious of students; she was an underachiever and socially unacceptable; in other words, a geek. But that has all changed. She is now a gorgeous young woman who has shed everything about her former self.

Becky has been given a second chance (to go back and help others who were much like she was) and stories provide an inside look at the lives of the students and faculty who populate the school.

Lisa, a former classmate of Becky's (the beautiful popular girl) now teaches at the school; Tim is the Spanish teacher Becky has an eye for.

Cast: Judy Greer *(Becky Freeley)*; Brooke Burns *(Lisa Germain)*; Kristoffer Polaha *(Tim O'Malley)*; Earl Billings *(Principal Huffy)*.

6105   Miss Jones. (Pilot; Comedy; ABC; July 12, 1991). Shortly after she graduates from law school, Althea "Thea" Jones, a single parent, acquires a job with Ryan, Shapiro and Johnson, a legal firm that specializes in sports figures. The proposal was to relate Althea's efforts to divide her time between defending clients and raising her young son, Spencer. Other regulars are Larry Shapiro, Evanrude Johnson and Buddy Ryan, the senior law partners; Mrs. Mayo, the receptionist, and Bob Nettles, a lawyer. Christine Ebersole performs the theme, "Ain't Life Grand."

Cast: Christine Ebersole *(Althea Jones)*; Charlie Newmark *(Spencer Jones)*; Ernie Hudson *(Evanrude Johnson)*; Ken Welch *(Buddy Ryan)*; Lynn Milgrim *(Mrs. Mayo)*; Larry Haines *(Larry Shapiro)*; Robert Prescott *(Rob Nettles)*.

6106   A Miss Mallard Mystery. (Series; Cartoon; Qubo; 2009). Live action television has its great female detective, Jessica Fletcher *(Murder, She Wrote)*; animation has it animal counterpart: Miss Mallard, a famous duck detective. Accompanied by her nephew Willard Widgeon, Miss Mallard solves the mysteries she and Willard encounter as they embark on a round-the-world journey. Based on the children's books by Robert Quackenbush.

Cast: Kate Hurman *(Miss Mallard)*; Michael Rudder, Terrence Scammell, Arthur Holden.

6107   Miss Match. (Series; Comedy-Drama; NBC; 2003). Kate Fox is a beautiful young attorney who works for her father, Jerry Fox, head of the law firm of Jerrold Fox and Associates. Kate is a brilliant divorce attorney and has an uncanny knack for paring the right man with the right woman. Kate, however, only considers this to be a hobby until a grateful socialite credits Kate in the press on her romantic success and Kate becomes a much sought after matchmaker. Soon Kate finds herself not only handling divorce cases but bringing people together for marriage. Other regulars are Victoria, Kate's friend; Nick, Kate's law partner (who is opposed to her new side line, as is her father); Michael, Kate's boyfriend; and Claire, the office receptionist.

Cast: Alicia Silverstone *(Kate Fox)*; Ryan O'Neal *(Jerry Fox)*; Lake

Bell (*Victoria*); James Roday (*Nick Paine*); David Conrad (*Michael Mendelsohn*); Jodi Long (*Claire*).

6108 ***Miss Pepperdine.*** (Pilot; Comedy; Unaired; Produced for CBS in 1959). Hoping to become a model, Marie Pepperdine, a beautiful mailroom clerk for Pontifore Company Dresses, finds her chances becoming a reality when she is promoted to the position of receptionist. The proposal was to relate Marie's efforts to achieve her dream. Other regulars are Simon Pontifore, the boss; Lily, a model; Herbie, the shipping clerk; Bentley, Simon's nephew; and Hazel and Gus, Marie's neighbors.

Cast: Marie Wilson (*Marie Pepperdine*); Jack Durant (*Simon Pontifore*); Hildy Parks (*Lily Baldwin*); Paul Smith (*Herbie*); Paul Picerni (*Bentley Pontifore*); Mary Beth Hughes (*Hazel*); Harry Clark (*Gus*).

6109 ***Miss Spider's Sunny Patch Friends.*** (Series; Cartoon; Nick; 2004). Miss Spider and Holley are spiders who live in the Hollow Tree in Sunny Patch. They are the parents of Squirt, Wiggle, Spinner and twins Pansy and Snowdrop, and the adoptive parents of Dragon, Shimmer and Bounce. Stories follow Miss Spider and Holley as they attempt to be good parents to a brood of very different children. Squirt is always seeking adventure; Wiggle is shy and introverted; Spinner is very smart; Pansy and Snowdrop may look alike, but they have totally different personalities; Shimmer is a brightly colored jewel beetle; Dragon is a dragonfly who tends to be a bit mean to others; and Bounce loves to eat. Other characters are Grandma Betty Beetle, Beatrice the Queen Bee; and the lazy aunts Ned and Ted.

Voice Cast: Kristin Davis (*Miss Spider*); Robert Smith (*Holley*); Scott Beaudin (*Squirt*); Rebecca Brenner (*Shimmer*); Mitchell Eisner (*Dragon*); Julie Lemieux (*Bounce*); Marc McMulkin (*Wiggle*); Austin Di Iulio (*Spinner*); Alexandra Lai (*Snowdrop*); Tony Jay (*Spiderus*); Kristina Nicoll (*Spindella*); Catherine Gallant (*Queen Beetrice*); Philip Williams (*Ted*).

6110 ***Miss Stewart, Sir.*** (Pilot; Comedy; CBS; Mar. 31, 1972). Kate Stewart is a dedicated teacher who finds her career taking a turn she never expected: becoming the first female faculty member of an exclusive all-male boarding school. In addition to teaching, Kate is also a housemother and coach of the school's dismal football team. The proposal was to relate Kate's experiences as she faces the challenges of her new job. Other regulars are Principal Prentiss; students Buzz, Joe, George and Mike; and Hannah, the cook.

Cast: Joanna Pettet (*Kate Stewart*); Murray Matheson (*Principal Prentiss*); Gary Vinson (*Buzz*); Michael Witney (*Joe*); Don Clarke (*George*); Lee Hollingshead (*Mike*); Nora Marlowe (*Hannah*).

6111 ***Miss Susan.*** (Series; Drama; NBC; 1951). The dramatic story of Susan Peters, a handicapped (wheelchair bound) criminal attorney working out of Ohio. The first program to star a real-life handicapped person (Susan Peters).

Cast: Susan Peters (*Susan Martin*); Katherine Gill (*Mrs. Peck*); Helen Ray (*Laura*); Mark Roberts (*Bill Carter*).

6112 ***Miss Winslow and Son.*** (Series; Comedy; CBS; 1979). Several months after the birth of her son (Edmund), Susan Winslow, a pretty single mother, acquires a job as a commercial artist with the Callahan Agency. Susan's efforts to make a life for herself and her baby are the focal point of stories. Other regulars are Harold, Susan's fussy neighbor; Warren and Evelyn, Susan's parents; Joseph Callahan, Susan's boss; and Rosa and Angelo, Susan's friends. Based on the British series *Miss Jones and Son*.

Cast: Darleen Carr (*Susan Winslow*); Roscoe Lee Browne (*Harold Neistader*); Elliott Reid (*Warren Winslow*); Sarah Marshall (*Evelyn Winslow*); William Bogert (*Joseph Callahan*); Ellen Sherman (*Rosa Vallone*); Joe Rassulo (*Angelo Vallone*); Benjamin Margolis (*Edmund Winslow*).

6113 ***Missing.*** (Series; Reality; Syn.; 2003). Investigations into missing persons cases that present all the known information and asks viewers who may possess additional information to contact authorities. Alex Paen and Pamela Bach host.

6114 ***Missing.*** (Series; Drama; Lifetime; 2003–2005). The desperate search to find missing people is the focal point of stories. There are, however, two versions. In the first version, titled *1-800-Missing*, Brooke Haslett, a by-the books FBI agent, and Jess Mastriani, a special consultant with the FBI with a unique gift, attempt to find people reported as missing. Jess was struck by lightning and is able to receive psychic visions that give her clues to the whereabouts of the people she and Brooke are seeking. Assisting them are Sunny Estrada, a computer and forensics expert, and Alan Coyle, their boss.

Brooke was dropped when the second season began (as *Missing* in 2004) and Jess was teamed with Nicole Scott, a tough, former undercover agent. They work for a special unit out of Washington, D.C., that is run by John Pollock, the assistant director. Antonio Cortez, an evidence expert, assists them. Stories follow their investigations into perplexing (if not bizarre) missing persons cases.

Cast: Gloria Reuben (*Brooke Haslett*); Caterina Scorsone (*Jess Mastriani*); Vivica A. Fox (*Nicole Scott*); Dean McDermott (*Alan Coyle*); Mark Consuelos (*Antonio Cortez*); Justina Machado (*Sunny Estrada*); Justin Louis (*John Pollock*).

6115 ***Missing Links.*** (Series; Game; NBC; ABC; 1963-1964). A story that contains a number of specific blanks is read. A player selects one of the three celebrity guests who appear and bets points on the celebrity's ability to fill in the blanks within a specific time limit. Each word that correctly fits a blank space scores the player one point. The player with the highest score is the winner and receives merchandise prizes. Aired on NBC (Sept. 9, 1963 to Mar. 27, 1964) and ABC (Mar. 30 to Dec. 25, 1964).

Host: Ed McMahon (*NBC*), Dick Clark (*ABC*); **Announcer:** Johnny Olson.

6116 ***Missing Persons.*** (Series; Crime Drama; ABC; 1993). Ray McAuliffe is a detective lieutenant with the Missing Persons Bureau of the Chicago Police Department. Ray is married to Barbara and his team consists of Connie Karadzic, Bobby Davison and Carlos Marrone. While each episode revolves around the team's efforts to find missing people, two-to-three such mini dramas are presented with each involving a singular detective or a team of two investigating a case.

Cast: Daniel J. Travanti (*Lt. Ray McAuliffe*); Patty Lombard (*Barbara McAuliffe*); Jorja Fox (*Officer Connie Karadzic*); Erik King (*Officer Bobby Davison*); Juan Ramirez (*Carlos Marrone*).

6117 ***Missing Persons Unit.*** (Series; Reality; TruTV; 2006). Real life cases of people who have disappeared are chronicled. Stories are investigative in nature and attempt to uncover the reason for the disappearance and the facts that led to both successful and failed conclusions. Originally aired on Court TV. George Deuchar hosts; Sam Fontana narrates.

6118 ***Missing/Reward.*** (Series; Reality; Syn.; 1989). Actual cases involving missing persons are presented through eyewitness accounts, newsreel footage and reenactments in the hope that someone in the viewing audience has knowledge that will help the police solve the case. To entice viewers, large rewards are offered for information that leads to an arrest and conviction.

Host: Stacy Keach.

6119   Mission Genesis. (Series; Science Fiction; Syfy; 1997). In a futuristic time, a deadly virus breaks out on Earth. With no defenses and only one way to save humanity, scientists develop a deep space ark that will enable travel to a new world to reestablish the human race. A crew is selected and will oversee operations: Yuna, the navigator; Bren, the weapons officer; Reb, the engineering officer; Lise, the doctor; Gret, the communications officer; Gen, the onboard computer and Zak the computer and cybernetics expert. Stories follow the crew's efforts to complete their mission amid the numerous dangers posed by the unexplored regions of space. Also known as *Deepwater Black*.

Cast: Nicole deBoer (*Yuna*); Gordon Michael Woolvett (*Reb*); Kelli Taylor (*Gret*); Sara Sahr (*Lise*); Jason Khaner (*Gen*); Craig Kirkwood (*Zak*); Jason Cadieux (*Bren*).

6120   Mission Hill. (Series; Cartoon; WB; 1999). Mission Hill is a fictional neighborhood in an equally fictional city called Cosmopolis. It is here in an apartment at 44 Bow Street, Andy French and his younger brother, Kevin reside. Andy is 24 years old and charming but lazy; he is a hopeful cartoonist who works as a salesman at Ron's Waterbed World. He seems uncomfortable settling on any job or any girlfriend. Kevin, on the other hand, is ambitious, a straight "A" student at school but unable to find a girlfriend. Stories follow events in the brother's lives as they interact with the colorful characters of Mission Hill.

Other regulars are Posey Tyler, Kevin's friend; Jim Kuback, Andy's friend; Natalie and Carlos, the married couple who live across the hall; and Gus and Wally, a senior citizen gay couple.

Fifteen episodes were produced but only seven aired on the WB (cancelled due to dismal ratings). In 2002, the Cartoon Network aired all 15 episodes.

Voice Cast: Wallace Langham (*Andy French*); Scott Melville (*Kevin French*); Brian Poeshn (*Jim Kuback*); Vicki Lewis (*Posey Tyler*); Vicki Lewis (*Natalie Leibowitx-Hernandez*); Herbert Siguenza (*Carlos Hernandez*); Nick Jameson (*Gus Duncz*); Tom Kenny (*Wally Langford*).

6121   Mission: Impossible. (Series; Adventure; CBS; 1966–1973). The cases of the I.M.F. (Impossible Missions Force), a top secret government organization that handles dangerous and highly sensitive international assignments. Stories depict the often suspenseful step-by-step planning and final execution of very tense and complicated missions. Dan Briggs was the original head of the I.M.F.; he was replaced by Jim Phelps. Cinnamon Carter, Rollin Hand, Barney Collier and Willy Armitage were the original members of the team. Paris replaced Rollin; Dana replaced Cinnamon; Casey replaced Dana; and Mimi Davis replaced Casey; Tracy, Lisa, Beth, Monique, Nora and Valerie were the girls used in the interim between Barbara Bain (Cinnamon) and Lesley Ann Warren (Dana).

Dan, then Jim, are the team leaders and present the missions to which they have been charged (heard as a recorded message — that will self destruct after it plays). Jim then selects his agents (usually seen through the photographs he removes from a file and places on a desk). Rollin (and Paris) are masters of disguise; Cinnamon (and the girls who replaced her) is sexy and an expert at distraction; Barney is the electronics expert; and Willie is the strong arm of the team.

Cast: Steven Hill (*Dan Briggs*); Peter Graves (*Jim Phelps*); Barbara Bain (*Cinnamon Carter*); Martin Landau (*Rollin Hand*); Greg Morris (*Barney Collier*); Peter Lupus (*Willy Armitage*); Leonard Nimoy (*Paris*); Lesley Ann Warren (*Dana*); Lynda Day George (*Casey*); Barbara Anderson (*Mimi Davis*); Sam Elliott (*Agent Dr. Doug Lang*);

Bob Johnson (*Recorded Assignment Voice*); Lee Meriwether (*Tracy*); Michele Carey (*Lisa*); Sally Ann Howes (*Beth*); Julie Gregg (*Monique*); Antoinette Bower (*Nora*); Jessica Walter (*Valerie*); Sid Haig (*Various Villainous Roles*). **Theme Song:** "Mission: Impossible" by Lalo Schifrin.

6122   Mission: Impossible. (Series; Adventure; ABC; 1988-1989). A revised of the prior title that deals with the cases of the I.M.F. (Impossible Missions Force), a unit of the government that attempts to solve highly complex assignments. It was headed by Jim Phelps. Following the death of a friend, Jim Phelps, the former head of the I.M.F., comes out of retirement to bring the killer to justice. With the help of a new I.M.F. team Jim accomplishes his goal. Jim feels the need to help prevent crime and the government needs a man with Jim's experience to lead a team. Nicholas Black, Casey Randall, Max Hart, Grant Collier (the son of former I.M.F. member Barney Collier) and Shannon Reed form the new I.M.F team and stories follow Jim as he and his team attempt to solve near impossible cases.

Cast: Peter Graves (*Jim Phelps*); Thaao Penghlis (*Nicholas Black*); Terry Markwell (*Casey Randall*); Tony Hamilton (*Max Hart*); Phil Morris (*Grant Collier*); Jane Badler (*Shannon Reed*). **Theme:** "Mission: Impossible" By Lalo Schifrin.

6123   Mission Magic. (Series; Cartoon; ABC; 1973-1974). Miss Tickle is a schoolteacher who possesses magical powers, which she uses for good over evil. With her students (Carol, Vinnie, Kim, Socks, Harvey and Franklin) and Rick Springfield, a troubleshooter, the group forms the Adventurers Club and travels to fantasy lands to help deserving underdogs. Additional characters include Tomaly, Rick's owl; Mr. Samuels, the school principal; and Tut Tut, Miss Tickle's magic cat.

Voice Cast: Erica Scheimer (*Miss Tickle*); Rick Springfield (*Himself*); Lola Fisher (*Carol*); Lane Scheimer (*Vinnie/Franklin*); Lola Fisher (*Kim*); Howard Morris (*Harvey/Socks*).

6124   The Mississippi. (Series; Drama; CBS; 1983-1984). Ben Walker is a big city criminal lawyer who leaves what he calls "the rat race" for a quieter life in Mississippi as the owner of *The Mississippi*, a river boat. Ben partly finds what he is looking for but also discovers that people need legal help. Stories follow Ben as he forfeits part of his leisure life by establishing a law office to help the defenseless people who live by the river. Stella McMullen is his law assistant; Lafayette "Lafe" Tate is his assistant; Rachel Walker is Ben's daughter (Ben is a widower). Filmed on location in Natchez and also known as *On the Mississippi*.

Cast: Ralph Waite (*Ben Walker*); Laurie Prange (*Rachel Walker*); Linda Miller (*Stella McMullen*); Stan Shaw (*Lafayette Tate*). **Theme Music:** "Theme from the Mississippi" by Lee Holdridge.

6125   The Missus Goes a Shopping. (Series; Game; CBS; 1944; 1947). A mixture of stunts, gimmicks and audience participation aimed at the female members of the viewing audience. The program, based on the CBS radio program of the same title, was first adapted to TV as an experiment and featured such sight gags as a WAC trying to dislodge a coin from the top of her nose without moving her head; and a burly truck driver trying to squeeze his large frame into a girdle. Two versions appeared:

1. The Missus Goes-a-Shopping (CBS, Aug. 3, 1944). **Host:** John Reed King. **Assistant:** Paul Mowry.

2. The Missus Goes-a-Shopping (CBS, 1947–1949). **Host:** John Reed King, Clayton "Bud" Collyer. **Assistant:** Jimmy Brown.

6126   Mr. Adams and Eve. (Series; Comedy; CBS; 1957-1958). Howard Adams and Eve Drake are actors who also happen to be married to each other. Howard first saw Eve on the set of a movie and set his goal to marry her. Two months later they were married. Howard and Eve enjoy their careers and would have it no other way (when Eve was five years old she said she wanted to be an actress and followed through with that statement). Howard and Eve live in Hollywood, California and stories relate incidents in their home and on the set lives (where they star as romantic leads; Eve Drake is Eve's stage name; at home she is Eve Adams). J.B. Hafter is the studio producer; Steve is the Adams's agent; Elsie Carstairs is the Adams's maid; Connie Drake is Eve's mother; and Walter is Elsie's nephew.

Cast: Howard Duff *(Howard Adams)*; Ida Lupino *(Eve Adams)*; Alan Reed *(J.B. Hafter)*; Hayden Rorke *(Steve)*; Olive Casey *(Elsie Carstairs)*; Lee Patrick *(Connie Drake)*; Patrick Wayne *(Walter)*; Lawrence Dobkin *(Director)*; Alan Wood *(Slate Boy)*; Paul Grant *(Assistant Director)*.

6127 *Mr. & Mrs. & Mr.* (Pilot; Comedy; CBS; Sept. 1, 1980). A year after her husband, Jimmy York, an ex-quarterback for the New York Jets, is reported killed in a plane crash in the Caribbean, Jenny Collins (who retained her maiden name) marries Jeff Zelinka, a sportswriter. Shortly after, Jenny's life becomes complicated when Jimmy shows up alive, having been nursed back to health by an Indian fisherman. The proposal was to focus on the problems that exist as Jenny, now with two husbands who each dispute the other's claim on his wife, desperately seeks a way to resolve the situation and live a normal, happily married life—with one husband. Susan is Jenny's friend. Joanie Sommers sings the theme, "Mr. & Mrs. & Mr."

Cast: Rebecca Balding *(Jenny Collins)*; Kale Brown *(Jimmy York)*; Patrick Collins *(Jeff Zelinka)*; Eda Zahl *(Susan Masters)*.

6128 *Mr. & Mrs. Dracula.* (Pilot; Comedy; ABC; Sept. 5, 1980). After 618 years of marriage, vampire Vladimir Dracula, his wife Sonia and their children, Minna and Sonny, relocate from their castle in Transylvania to the Bronx, New York, when angry villagers force them to leave their homeland. The proposal was to relate their misadventures as they attempt to adjust to life in America. Other regulars are Vladimir's Cousin Anton; Mario, their apartment building manager; and Gregor, the bat who forgot how to turn back into a vampire.

Cast: Dick Shawn *(Vladimir Dracula)*; Carol Lawrence *(Sonia Dracula)*; Gail Mayron *(Minna Dracula)*; Anthony Battaglia *(Sonny Dracula)*; Johnny Haymer *(Voice of Gregor)*; Barry Gordon *(Cousin Anton)*; Rick Aviles *(Mario)*.

6129 *Mr. and Mrs. Carroll.* (Series; Variety; DuMont; 1950-1951). The program, also known as *The Most Important People*, features music and songs by musician-singer Jimmy Carroll and his wife, songstress Rita Carroll.

6130 *Mr. and Mrs. Cop.* (Pilot; Crime Drama; CBS; May 3, 1974). Paul and Nancy Roscommon are a married couple who are also police officers. The proposal was to relate their experiences as they try to make their marriage work despite the demands of their jobs.

Cast: Anthony Costello *(Paul Roscommon)*; Marianne McAndrew *(Nancy Roscommon)*; Richard Angarola *(Lieutenant Ocala)*; William Campbell *(Sergeant Baum)*; Redmond Gleeson *(Off. Irv Pyle)*.

6131 *Mr. and Mrs. Mystery.* (Series; Crime Drama; CBS; 1949). John Gay and his wife Barbara live at 46 Perry Street, Apartment 3-C in Manhattan. John works as a criminologist. Barbara, who is not content just being a housewife, feels that living with John has given her the knowledge she needs to become an amateur sleuth

(John doesn't think so and wishes Barbara would go back to being an uncomplicated, loving wife). John's cases always fascinate Barbara; so much so that she attaches herself to John in the hope of helping him solve a crime. Stories follow John's efforts, assisted (and hindered) by Barbara to unravel mysteries.

Cast: John Gay *(Himself)*; Barbara Gay *(Herself)*.

6132 *Mr. and Mrs. North.* (Experimental; Stage Play; NBC; May 19, 1946). A television adaptation of the Broadway show by Frances and Richard Lockridge that relates incidents in the lives of Jerry North, a retired private detective, and his zany but shrewd wife, Pamela, as they try to solve a murder mystery—that of who killed a man and placed the body in the North's Greenwich Village apartment.

Cast: John McQuade *(Jerry North)*; Maxine Stuart *(Pamela North)*; Vinton Hayworth *(Lieutenant Weigand)*; Millard Mitchell *(Detective Mullins)*.

6133 *Mr. and Mrs. North.* (Pilot; Crime Drama; NBC; July 4, 1949). A video adaptation of the radio series of the same title about a private detective turned publisher (Jerry North) and his wife, Pamela, who has a knack for stumbling onto crimes. The pilot episode relates the Norths' efforts to help an attorney find a culprit who is killing heirs to a large estate. Based on characters created by Frances and Richard Lockridge.

Cast: Joseph Allen, Jr. *(Jerry North)*; Mary Lou Taylor *(Pamela North)*.

6134 *Mr. and Mrs. North.* (Series; Crime Drama; CBS, 1952–1954; NBC, 1954). Gerald "Jerry" North, a lieutenant in the navy during World War II, and a former private detective has relinquished the rough life for a peaceful existence as a publisher (for an unidentified house). He is married to Pamela, a beautiful and fashion conscious woman who believes she possesses the mind of a detective (when she sees something that is wrong, she immediately associates it with foul play). Much to Jerry's regret, Pam is most often right and he finds himself playing detective again to solve a crime. It is unfair to give Jerry all the credit. Pam does solve crimes on her own. She is so unassuming that the culprit is unaware of her brilliance and is caught by surprise.

Jerry and Pam live at 24 Sainte Anne's Place, Apartment 6A, in New York's Greenwich Village. (Their address is also given as 23 Sainte Anne's Place, Apartment 408—even though Apartment 6A is seen in the opening theme.) Their closest friend is Bill Weigand, a lieutenant with the Homicide Division of the Police Department of New York City. Based on the novel by Frances and Richard Lockridge.

Cast: Richard Denning *(Jerry North)*; Barbara Britton *(Pamela North)*; Francis DeSales *(Bill Weigand)*.

6135 *Mr. and Mrs. Ryan.* (Pilot; Comedy-Drama; ABC; April 12, 1986). Shortly after she is rescued from kidnappers, Ashley Hamilton, a beautiful Beverly Hills socialite, marries the man who saved her life, Los Angeles police detective Lieutenant Michael Ryan. The proposal was to focus on Ashley's misadventures as she stumbles upon and involves Michael in crimes.

Cast: Sharon Stone *(Ashley Hamilton Ryan)*; Robert Desiderio *(Michael Ryan)*; Joseph Maher *(Stockwell, Ashley's butler)*.

6136 *Mr. and Mrs. Smith.* (Series; Adventure; CBS; 1996). A man, known only as Mr. Smith, and a woman, known only as Mrs. Smith, are sophisticated private detectives who are recruited by a man known only as Mr. Big to work for his organization—The Factory. The man and woman pretend to be a married couple and with the aliases of Mr. And Mrs. Smith to protect their true identities (which are never revealed; also not revealed is any other information for these characters). The Factory is a mysterious organization that appears to be associated with the government as it strives to resolve troublesome situations. Stories relate the cases of Mr. and Mrs. Smith as they solve cases for The Factory.

Cast: Scott Bakula (*Mr. Smith*); Maria Bello (*Mrs. Smith*); Roy Dotrice (*Mr. Big*).

6137   *Mr. and Mrs. Smith.* (Pilot; Adventure; Unaired; Produced for ABC in 2007). Doug Liman and Simon Kirnberg, the original creators of the motion picture *Mr. and Mrs. Smith* have created a TV first: they have personally transformed their movie into a potential TV series. The project picks up where the film left off with John and Jane Smith living undercover as an ordinary professional couple in the suburbs. No one suspects that they actually work as super spies for the nation's top secret intelligence firms. For security reasons, John and Jane are forbidden to totally confide in one another and the proposal was to relate the hazardous assignments they undertake with super high tech gadgets taking front and center stage.

Cast: Martin Henderson (*John Smith*); Jordana Brewster (*Jane Smith*); Julia Ormond (*Mother*); Bridgette Wilson-Sampras (*Ann Burr Clevenger*); Rebecca Mader (*Jordan*).

6138   *Mr. & Ms.* (Pilot; Crime Drama; ABC; 1975). David Robbins, the son of a police lieutenant (Ben Robbins) and his wife, Mandy, the daughter of a private investigator, are a happily married couple who work together as the owners of a private detective agency. Each has been brought up with a slightly differing opinion of how the law works and each encompasses their perspective when it comes to investigating cases. Two pilots were produced that relates their case investigations: *Mr. and Ms. and the Magic Studio Mystery* (Dec. 16, 1975; their efforts to solve the murder of a young woman who tried to blackmail a group of magicians) and *Mr. and Ms. and the Band-stand Murders* (Dec. 23, 1975; their efforts to solve the murder of a British rock star).

Cast: John Rubinstein (*David Robbins*); Lee Kroeger (*Mandy Wagner-Robbins*); Milton Selzer (*Ben Robbins*).

6139   *Mr. Arsenic.* (Series; Anthology; ABC; 1952). Burton Turkus hosts a program of dramatizations based on actual criminal cases.

6140   *Mr. Bean.* (Series; Comedy; PBS; 1992). He is known only as Mr. Bean (no first name given). He lives in a small apartment in North London with Teddy, a teddy bear that appears to be his security blanket. He is fully grown but he is child-like in everything else. He could be considered a buffoon for all the trouble he gets into (but manages to get out of using his wits). But no matter what Mr. Bean does it seems to be something new to him and he must experiment with it to understand it (thus the comical situations). Is Mr. Bean an alien sent to Earth to learn its culture? The opening theme leads one to believe so as he is seen falling from the sky in a beam of light. Or was he just "born yesterday" and totally ignorant about the things that surround him in his everyday life? This, along with what he does for a living is not revealed. Mr. Bean wears a tweed suit with red tie and drives a British Leland Mini. He also rarely speaks and the comedy is completely visual.

Irma Gobb is the only human Mr. Bean appears to be fond of. Although he treats her with little respect (he sees her only as a friend), she sees him in a romantic light. Stories follow Mr. Bean as he goes about exploring the world about him — and getting into endless mischief doing so. Produced in England.

Cast: Rowan Atkinson (*Mr. Bean*); Matilda Ziegler (*Irma Gobb*).

6141   *Mr. Belvedere.* (Pilot; Comedy; CBS; July 12, 1965). Lynn Belvedere is a man-about-town and master of various arts, crafts and professions. The proposal was to relate his experiences as he involves himself in other people's lives.

Cast: Victor Borge (*Lynn Belvedere*).

6142   *Mr. Belvedere.* (Series; Comedy; ABC; 1985–1990). Lynn Aloysius Belvedere appeared on the cover of *World Focus* magazine ("Housekeeper of the Year") and worked for English nobility (valet to Winston Churchill and housekeeper to Queen Elizabeth II). He now resides at 200 Spring Valley Road in Beaver Falls, Pittsburgh, with his new employers, the chaotic Owens family: parents George and Marsha, and their children, Kevin, Heather and Wesley.

Lynn, born in England, lived on Higby Road and attended the Pennington School. He wrote a book on his experiences with the Owens family called *An American Journal: The Suburban Years*. In the last episode, Lynn marries Louise Gilbert (Rosemary Forsyth), an animal behaviorist he met at a Laundromat. Lynn leaves the family to join Louise in Africa when she is asked to return to the University of Boutari to take a gorilla census. In the final minutes of the show, Lynn remarks that he left his weekly journals (the diaries that he was seen writing at the end of each episode) at the Owens home, with a possibility that he may one day return for them.

George originally hosted *Sports Page* (later *Sports Rap*), a radio program on WBK-AM. Later, he is the sports anchor of WBN-TV, Channel 8's *Metro News*, and writer of the "Sports Beat" column for the Pittsburgh *Bulletin*. George calls Lynn "Big Guy" and they are members of the "Happy Guys," a neighborhood crime watch.

Marsha, originally a law student, passed the bar exam in July 1987 and joined the firm of Dawson, Metcalfe and Bach. The following year, she became an attorney for the Legal Hut. Marsha dreamed of helping the underdog; when she couldn't find it at the Legal Hut, she quit and became "Babs," a waitress at the Beaver Falls Diner.

Kevin, their oldest child, attends Van Buren High School. He worked part time at Mr. Cluck's Fried Chicken and as a salesman for Phil's Friendly Motors (a used car lot). He was born in 1967 and was an Eagle Scout. In later episodes, he is a student at the University of Pittsburgh.

Heather, the middle child, is a very pretty girl who attends Van Buren High School (George calls her "Kitten"). Heather's best friend is Angela, a very pretty but kooky girl who has a hanger collection and calls Lynn everything but Mr. Belvedere (for example, "Mr. Bumper Sticker," "Mr. Beaver Dam," "Mr. Beer Belly," "Mr. Bell Ringer"). She and Heather were cheerleaders at school (for the Beavers football team). "Being blonde and pretty are about the only assets Angela has," says Heather. Angela was rarely called by a last name; but when she needed one, she was given three — Shostakovich, Gilbert and Jostakovich.

Wesley, the youngest and most mischievous of the Owens children, attended Conklin Elementary School, Allegheney Junior High and finally Beaver Falls Junior High. He has a dog named Spot, a snake called Captain Nemo and a hamster named Inky. Wesley, called "Wesman" by George, delights in playing practical jokes on his never-seen, but always complaining neighbors, the Hufnagels (in the next to last episode, Teresa Ganzel played the only Hufnagel to be seen, the gorgeous Giselle). To make money, Wesley sold Heather's lingerie, claiming it belonged to Madonna. Leon Redbone sings "The Theme from Mr. Belvedere."

Cast: Christopher Hewett (*Lynn Belvedere*); Bob Uecker (*George Owens*); Ilene Graff (*Marsha Owens*); Tracy Wells (*Heather Owens*); Rob Stone (*Kevin Owens*); Brice Beckham (*Wesely Owens*); Michele Matheson (*Angela*).

6143   *Mr. Bevis.* (Pilot; Fantasy; CBS; June 3, 1960). A proposed but untitled spin off from *The Twilight Zone* about J. Hardy Hempstead, a guardian angel who is assigned to help deserving earthlings. In the pilot titled "Mr. Bevis," Hardy attempts to help James B.W. Bevis (Orson Bean) improve his life.

Cast: Henry Jones (*J. Hardy Hempstead*).

6144   *Mr. Bill's Real Life Adventures.* (Pilot; Comedy; Showtime; Sept. 11, 1986). Mr. Bill, the inches-tall, down-trodden clay figure living in his own world is brought to life to fall prey to countless pit falls. Based on *Saturday Night Live* sketches.

Cast: Peter Scolari (*Mr. Bill*); Mike McManus (*Mr. Sluggo*).

6145   *Mr. Black.* (Series; Anthology; ABC; 1949). Mr. Black, a mysterious individual and crime authority expert, presents mystery and suspense stories in which criminals receive their just deserts.

Host: Anthony Christopher as Mr. Black.

6146   *Mr. Boogedy.* (Pilot; Comedy; ABC; April 20, 1986). In the 1600s, a small group of Pilgrims settled in a section of New England they named Lucifer Falls. William Hanover, an outcast member who delighted in scaring children (hence called Mr. Boogedy), fell in love with the Widow Marion and asked her to marry him. When she refused, Hanover sold his soul to the Devil in exchange for a magic cape that will make Marion fall in love with him. The cape fails to grant Hanover's wish and instead destroys him and his house in an explosion. Hanover, now as the disfigured Mr. Boogedy, remains on his property, seemingly destined to haunt it forever. More than 300 years later (1986), Carlton Davis, a novelty salesman for Gag City, and his family (wife, Eloise, and children, Jennifer, Ahri and Corwin) move into a house that was constructed on the original Hanover land. Immediately they encounter the wrath of Boogedy's ghost who does not relish the idea of sharing his domain with the Davis family. The unsold series was to relate the Davises' efforts to enjoy their new home and find a way to rid their lives of the practical-joke-playing Mr. Boogedy. Neil Witherspoon is head of the town historical society.

On April 12, 1987, ABC presented a two-hour TV movie sequel called *The Bride of Boogedy* wherein Boogedy seeks to find the spirit of his lost love, the Widow Marion. Cast changes were Tammy Lauren as Jennifer Davis, Joshua Rudoy as Ahri Davis, and Leonard Frey as Walter (not Neil) Witherspoon.

Cast: Howard Witt (*Mr. Boogedy*); Richard Masur (*Carlton Davis*); Mimi Kennedy (*Eloise Davis*); Kristy Swanson (*Jennifer Davis*); Benjamin Gregory (*Ahri Davis*); David Faustino (*Corwin Davis*); John Astin (*Neil Witherspoon*).

6147   *Mr. Broadway.* (Series; Drama; CBS; 1964). Michael Bell is a sophisticated Broadway press agent and the owner of the highly successful Michael Bell and Associates, a public relations firm in New York City. Michael's job is to keep people out of the gossip columns as well as in them. He is a man who personally gets involved with his clients and a man who takes a professional interest in his long-time clients. He is, in essence, a P.R. man who acts like a detective when he needs to take action to clear a client of a false charge. A girl named Toki is his girl Friday; Hank McClure is Michael's contact man.

Cast: Craig Stevens (*Michael Bell*); Lani Miyazaki (*Toki*); Horace McMahon (*Hank McClure*).

6148   *Mr. Citizen.* (Series; Anthology; ABC; 1955). Dramas that detail the unselfish acts of ordinary people. The person whose story is selected receives the "Mister Citizen Award."

Host: Allyn Edwards. **Awards Presenter:** Senator Clifford Chase. **Organist:** John Gart.

6149   *Mr. Deeds Goes to Town.* (Series; Comedy; ABC; 1969-1970). Longfellow Deeds is a philosophical country gentleman who becomes misplaced when he inherits the multi-million dollar Deeds Enterprises in New York City after the death of his Uncle, Alonzo Deeds. Now, as the head of the company, Longfellow attempts to run a corporation the way he feels it should be run—to help people—not as a corporation that he feels can easily take advantage of people. Tony Lawrence is Longfellow's assistant (also inherited from his uncle); Henry Masterson is the chairman of the board (who disapproves of Longfellow's simplistic ways of running the company); George is Longfellow's butler. Longfellow has a dog-named Sam.

Cast: Monte Markham (*Longfellow Deeds*); Pat Harrington, Jr. (*Tony Lawrence*); Herbert Voland (*Henry Masterson*); Ivor Barry (*George*).

6150   *Mr. District Attorney.* (Series; Crime Drama; Syn.; 1951). Dramatizations based on the facts of crime from the files of the District Attorney's office (representative of any such office in any city or town). Each story is seen through the eyes of Paul Garrett, alias Mr. District Attorney—"it is my job to prevent crimes as well as solve them. But sometimes you can't prevent them. Sometimes you can only pick up the trail after the violence has begun." Edith Miller is Paul's secretary; Harrington, who has been with the D.A.'s office for 22 years, is Paul's investigator. Based on the long-running radio program of the same title.

Program Open: "*Mr. District Attorney* starring David Brian. Mr. District Attorney, champion of the people, defender of truth, guardian of our fundamental rights to life, liberty and the pursuit of happiness." Mr. District Attorney then speaks: "And it shall be my duty as District Attorney, not only to prosecute to the limits of the law all persons accused of crimes committed within this county, but to defend with equal vigor the rights and privileges of all its citizens."

Cast: Jay Jostyn (*Paul Garrett*); David Brian (*Paul Garrett; later*); Vicki Vola, Jackie Loughery (*Edith Miller*); Len Doyle (*Harrington*). **Announcer:** Fred Uttal.

6151   *Mr. Dugan.* (Series; Comedy; Unaired; Produced for CBS in 1979). Events in the life of Matthew Dugan, a fledgling black Congressman. Three episodes were produced (scheduled to air Mar. 11, 18 and 25, 1979) but outside pressure killed it before it ever got on the air. After a special screening, a caucus of black Congressmen thought *Mr. Dugan* was offensive to black officials and threatened a nationwide switch-off campaign if the series aired. Norman Lear, producer of the show, withdrew it explaining "we have not yet totally fulfilled our intention for the series." See also *Hanging In* for information of the series that evolved from *Mr. Dugan.* Maggie is Matthew's assistant; Sam is his chief of staff; Pinkie is the housekeeper; and Aretha is the press secretary.

Cast: Cleavon Little (*Matthew Dugan*); Barbara Rhoades (*Maggie Gallagher*); Dennis Burkley (*Sam Dickey*); Nedra Volz (*Pinkie Noland*); Sarina Grant (*Aretha Balducci*).

6152   *Mister Ed.* (Series; Comedy; Syn., 1960-1961; CBS, 1961–1966). Shortly after newlyweds Wilbur and Carol Post purchase a home at 17230 Valley Spring Lane in Los Angeles, Wilbur discovers an unusual resident in the barn: a talking horse, named Mister Ed, who was left by the previous owners. Because Wilbur is the only human Ed (as Wilbur calls him) likes well enough to talk to, he will only talk to him (thus begin Wilbur's problems as the owner of a talking horse).

Ed calls himself "the playboy horse of Los Angeles," and considers "filly" the prettiest word in the English language. He weighed 96 pounds at birth (he is Taurus) and inherited the family curse—a fear of heights (begun when his grandfather fell off a cliff while chasing a filly).

Wilbur, an independent architect, operates his office from the barn (which doubles as Ed's home); he was originally slated to be a lawyer (as depicted in sales pitches for the show in early 1960). His address is also given as 17340 Valley Boulevard, 17290 Valley Spring Lane and 1720 Valley Road in Los Angeles. Wilburn was born in Connecticut and his family later moved to California. He studied architecture at UCLA (where he met Carol) and later established his own practice.

Carol, a gorgeous blonde who measures 36-22-36, worked as a dance instructor at Miss Irene's in Hollywood. Her maiden name is Higgins (also given as Carlyle) and is very forgiving of Wilbur when he becomes involved in Mister Ed's antics and often appears as a fool in front of others (his only way to cover up Ed's actions and keep Ed's talking abilities a secret).

Roger and Kay Addison are the Posts' original neighbors (replaced later by Gordon and Winnie Kirkwood). See also *The Wonderful World of Wilbur Pope* for information on the pilot film.

Cast: Alan Young *(Wilbur Post)*; Connie Hines *(Carol Post)*; Allan "Rocky" Lane *(Voice of Mister Ed)*; Larry Keating *(Roger Addison)*; Edna Skinner *(Kay Addison)*; Leon Ames *(Gordon Kirkwood)*; Florence MacMichael *(Winnie Kirkwood)*; Jack Albertson *(Paul Fenton)*; Barry Kelly *(Mr. Carlisle)*; Richard Deacon *(Dr. Baker, the veterinarian)*.

Note: In 2004, Fox produced a pilot for a new version of *Mister Ed* that never materialized as a series. The script was based on the original concept of the series (*The Wonderful World of Wilbur Pope*) and featured David Alan Basche as Wilbur Pope; Sherilynn Fenn as Carlotta Pope; and Sherman Hemsley as the voice of Mister Ed.

6153   *Mr. Garlund.* (Series; Drama; CBS; 1960-1961). Frank Garlund is a financial wizard who, at the age of thirty, has become one of the wealthiest men in America. He is also a key figure in national and international affairs and a man whose ancestry is unknown. All that is known about him is that he was raised by a Chinese gentleman named Po Chang and that he has a foster brother (Kam Chang). Flashback sequences are used to tell the stories of people Frank had come in contact with as he struggled to reach the top of the financial ladder. Also known as *The Garlund Touch*.

Cast: Charles Quinlivan *(Frank Garlund)*; Philip Ahn *(Po Chang)*; Kam Tong *(Kam Chang)*.

6154   *Mr. Glencannon Takes All.* (Pilot; Adventure; ABC; April 19, 1953). Colin Glencannon is the skipper of the *Inchcliff Castle*, a freighter that roams the South Seas. The proposal was to follow his various adventures as he takes on cargo and becomes involved with his customers troubles. See also *Glencannon*.

Cast: Robert Newton *(Colin Glencannon)*.

6155   *Mr. I. Magination.* (Series; Children; CBS; 1949–1952). Imagination Town is a mythical kingdom where children's dreams come true. Fantasy is coupled with education as vignettes dramatize figures and events of past history.

Cast: Paul Tripp *(Mr. I. Magination)*, Ruth Enders, Ted Tiller, David McKay, Donald Devlin, Butch Cavell, Johnny Stewart, Joe Silvan, Don Harris, Clifford Sales, Robin Morgan, Richard Boone, Richard Trask. **Music:** Ray Carter. **Organist:** David Roberts.

6156   *Mr. Inside/Mr. Outside.* (Pilot; Crime Drama; CBS; Mar. 14, 1973). Lou Isaacs and Rick Massi are N.Y.P.D. detectives who buck the system to get the job done. One day during a shootout, Rick is injured and later loses an arm as a result of a criminal's bullet. Rick is forced to retire and becomes the "Mr. Outside" of the title working as a private citizen to help Lou ("Mr. Inside" the system)

solve crimes. Other regulars are Renee, Lou's wife; and Lieutenant Valentine, Lou's superior.

Cast: Hal Linden *(Lou Isaacs)*; Tony LoBianco *(Rick Massi)*; Marcia Jean Kurtz *(Renee Isaacs)*; Paul Benjamin *(Lieutenant Valentine)*.

6157   *Mr. Jericho.* (Pilot; Adventure; ABC; Mar. 3, 1970). Dudley Jericho is a dapper confidence man who devises elaborate schemes to acquire other people's money. The Great Georgina is a beautiful con artist who uses her skills as a thief to relieve people of items she wants. Jericho and Georgina often work separately but sometimes find themselves working together to achieve the same goal. The proposal was to focus on their exploits as they travel the world seeking rich prey. Wally is Dudley's assistant. Lulu performs the theme, "Mr. Jericho."

Cast: Patrick Macnee *(Dudley Jericho)*; Connie Stevens *(Georgia)*; Marty Allen *(Wally)*.

6158   *Mr. Lucky.* (Series; Drama; CBS; 1959-1960). A man, known only as Mr. Lucky (Lucky to his friends) and his partner, Andamo, own the *Fortuna*, a gambling yacht anchored three miles off the Los Angeles shore in international waters (to allow legal gambling). Episodes 1–15 depict Lucky and Andamo's efforts to maintain an honest operation; episodes 16–34 focus on Lucky and Andamo's adventures as the owners of a floating nightclub (Lucky's) when they convert the *Fortuna* into a supper club (Lucky applied for a private club license when he felt it was time for a change and to avoid the hassle of the police trying to arrest him and shut down the club).

Lucky, who gets his name because he is lucky at gambling, is two-fisted and a master of the con (which he will only use to help good defeat evil). He carries a pocket watch that plays the first four notes, when opened, of the song "Mr. Lucky" ("They say I'm lucky"). Andamo, who manages the *Fortuna*, is a Latin and has an eye for the ladies. He is a genius at the con also and calls Mr. Lucky "Lucky" and "Compadre." According to Lucky, "Andamo fights with the police instead of cooperating with them." Lucky and Andamo are not on the best of terms with the police, especially with Lieutenant Rovacs of the L.A.P.D., who, like many other officers of the law, would like to see Lucky and Andamo put away for 20 years. Maggie Shank Rutherford is an old friend of Lucky's; Joe is the *Fortuna's* croupier, then maitre d'; Doris is the *Fortuna* cashier. Henry Mancini composed the theme, "Mr. Lucky."

Cast: John Vivyan *(Mr. Lucky)*; Ross Martin *(Andamo)*; Pippa Scott *(Maggie Shank Rutherford)*; Tom Brown *(Lieutenant Rovacs)*; Joe Scott *(Fortuna Maitre d')*; Paul Genge *(Police Captain)*.

6159   *Mr. Magoo.* (Series; Cartoon; Syn.; 1963). Quincy Magoo is a very kind near-sighted gentleman whose handicap involves him in all sorts of mischief. Charlie is his houseboy; Prezley is Quincy's nephew; Waldo is Quincy's uncle.

Voice Cast: Jim Backus *(Quincy Magoo)*; Jerry Hansen *(Charlie/Prezley/Uncle Waldo)*.

6160   *Mr. Mayor.* (Series; Children; CBS; 1964-1965). Various aspects of the world are related to children through the activities of a kind-hearted mayor of a small, friendly town.

Cast: Bob Keeshan *(Mr. Mayor)*; Jane Connell *(Miss Melissa/Aunt Maude/Mother Homan)*; Bill McCutcheon *(Dudley B. Dudley/Herman Homan)*; Cosmo Allegretti *(Rollo the Hippo/Russell Duck)*.

6161   *Mr. Meaty.* (Series; Children; Nick; 2006). Puppet program about Josh Redgrove and Parker Dinkleman, two lazy teenagers who dream of film careers and pursuing girls, but instead are hampered by a lack of energy and miserable jobs at the local mall food court.

Cast: Jason Hopley (*Parker Dinkleman*); Jamie Shannon (*Josh Redgrove*).

6162 *The Mr. Men Show.* (Series; Cartoon; Cartoon Network; 2008). Sketch program that features Mr. Men and Little Misses characters in various themed situations geared to children. Based on the books by Roger Hargreaves.

Voice Cast: Phil Lollar (*Mr. Lazy/Mr. Small/Mr. Strong*); Susan Ballboni (*Little Miss Scary*); Jeff Stewart (*Mr. Tickle*); Peter Mitchell (*Mr. Messy*); Alicyn Packard (*Little Miss Sunshine/Little Miss Whoops/Little Miss Naughty*).

6163 *Mr. Merlin.* (Series; Comedy; CBS; 1981–1982). Merlin Silvestra, the son of Welsh princess and an incubus father, was born in Wales in A.D. 381. Over time he became a sorcerer, a magician of the highest order who was known as Merlin the Magician. When the series begins, in modern times, Merlin is seen as the owner of a garage in the High Park section of San Francisco. Max Merlin (as he is now known), is 1,600 years old and has fallen behind on the performance of his good deeds. One day, Max receives a visit from Alexandra (whom he calls "Alex"), a gorgeous courier from above, who informs him that he must find an apprentice and teach him the art of sorcery. If he fails, he will lose his immortality and his powers. It has been decided by celestial powers that whoever is able to remove a crowbar from a block of cement at the garage (like King Arthur and his sword, Excalibur), will become the Sorcerer's apprentice.

One day while riding his skateboard, young Zachary ("Zack") Rogers, a girl-crazy, awkward teenager, crashes into Max's supply of oil cans and knocks a car off the hydraulic ramp. Looking for something to help Max lift the car, Zack spots the crowbar and pulls it from the cement. The crowbar glows (and briefly changes to Excalibur), and Max finds his apprentice.

Even though Max hasn't instructed anyone since King Arthur, Zack becomes his new student (Zack works part time at the garage and spends 14 hours a week learning from Mr. Merlin). Stories relate Zack's attempts to learn the art of sorcery, and his and Max's efforts to help people in distress.

Max has an owl named Luther and a secret room called "The Crystal Room" (which contains Max's sorcerer's equipment). In another episode, Max's birth date was given as September 29, A.D. 856.

Zack and his friend, Leo Samuels, attend Mumford High School. Zack lives with his mother, Elizabeth Rogers, at 13761 Havenhurst Road; Diane is Max's mechanic; Laurie is Zach's friend.

Cast: Barnard Hughes (*Max Merlin*); Elaine Joyce (*Alexandra*); Clark Brandon (*Zack Rogers*); Jonathan Prince (*Leo Samuels*); Mickie MacKenzie (*Laurie*); Sandy Rosenberg (*Diane Fishman*); Betty Garrett (*Elizabeth Rogers*).

6164 *Mr. Mom.* (Pilot; Comedy; ABC; Nov. 30, 1984). When Jack Butler, an automotive engineer, loses his job, his wife, Caroline, takes a position with an advertising agency while Jack assumes the household duties. The proposal, based on the feature film of the same title, was to relate Jack's misadventures as a house husband. Other regulars are Kenny, Curtis and Megan, their children; and Joan, their sexy neighbor.

Cast: Barry Van Dyke (*Jack Butler*); Rebecca York (*Caroline Butler*); Brendon Blincoe (*Curtis Butler*); Sean de Veritch (*Kenny Butler*); Heidi Zeigler (*Megan Butler*); Phyllis Davis (*Joan Hampton*).

6165 *Mr. Moon's Magic Circus.* (Series; Variety; Syn.; 1982). Mr. Moon's Magic Circus is the setting for a look at the antics of the show's performers. Mr. Moon is the circus owner; Cosmos is the human-like monkey; Tanzy is the Tiger Girl; Barnaby is the ringmaster; Fatima is the fortune teller; and Stan is the muscle man.

Cast: John Sarantos (*Mr. Moon*); Mark Ganzel (*Cosmos*); Marilyn Magness (*Tanzy*); Hank Adams (*Barnaby*); Marcia Lewis (*Fatima*); Chuck Quinlon (*Stan*). **Music:** Jeffrey Rockwell.

6166 *Mr. Nice Guy.* (Pilot; Comedy; Unaired; Produced for ABC in 2006). Guy is a good natured salesman who tries to be a nice guy—but his good intentions always backfire, get him into trouble and make him feel that he is living under some kind of curse. His only consultation is his loving wife, Annie, who comforts him, and the proposal was to follow Guy as he continues on his mission to do good deeds and figure out a way to reverse the bad results that always occur. Izzy is his best friend.

Cast: Diedrich Bader (*Guy*); Kevin Weisman (*Izzy*); Rena Sofer (*Annie*); Cara DeLizia (*Max*).

6167 *Mr. Novak.* (Series; Drama; NBC; 1963–1965). Incidents in the lives of the students and teachers of Jefferson High School in Los Angeles as seen through the eyes of John Novak, a graduate of Yale University who now teaches English (Room 112 is his homeroom). Albert Vane is the principal (later replaced by Martin Woodbridge); Jean Pagano is the assistant vice principal; Ruth Wilkinson is the girl's vice principal; Rosemary Dorsey is the school secretary (teachers and students are listed in the cast). Filmed at John Marshall and Hamilton High Schools in Los Angeles.

Cast: James Franciscus (*John Novak*); Dean Jagger (*Albert Vane*); Jeanne Bal (*Jean Pagano*); Burgess Meredith (*Martin Woodbridge*); Phyllis Avery (*Ruth Wilkinson*); Marjorie Corley (*Rosemary Dorsey*); Frank Ferguson (*Stan Novak; John's father*).

Teachers: David Sheiner (*Paul Webb*); Stephen Roberts (*Mr. Peeples*); Marian Collier (*Marilyn Scott*); Vince Howard (*Peter Butler*); Peter Hansen (*Mr. Parkson*); Anne Seymour (*Mrs. Vreeland*); Kathleen Ellis (*Ann Floyd*); Andre Phillippe (*Everett Johns*); Donald Barry (*Mr. Galo*); Gloria Talbott (*Miss Harvey*); Steve Franken (*Jerry Allen*); Larry Thor (*Jim Hendrix*).

Students: Kim Darby (*Julie Dean*); Tony Dow (*George*); Jimmy Baird (*Billy Gee*); Marta Kristen (*Gail Andrews*); Noreen Corcoran (*Cathy Williams*); Heather Angel (*Alfreida "Chalky" White*); Brooke Bundy (*Shirley Whittier*); Beau Bridges (*Pat Knowland*); Brenda Scott (*Sue Johnson*); Patricia Morrow (*Gloria*); Shelley Fabares (*Dani Cooper*); Joey Heatherton (*Holly Metcalfe*); Teno Pollock (*Steve Acerno*); Michael Walker (*Bill Russell*); Peter Lazer (*Arnold Frazer*).

6168 *Mr. O'Malley.* (Pilot; Comedy; CBS; Dec. 20, 1959). When Barnaby Baxter, a six-year-old boy, wishes upon a star for a fairy godmother who can make his dreams come true, he is answered by O'Malley, a cigar-smoking, jovial, pink-winged fairy godfather. The proposal was to depict O'Malley's misadventures as the invisible (except to the audience) guardian of a young boy. Alice and George are Barnaby's parents. Aired on *G.E. Theater.*

Cast: Bert Lahr (*Mr. O'Malley*); Ronny Howard (*Barnaby Baxter*); June Dayton (*Alice Baxter*); William Redfield (*George Baxter*).

6169 *Mister Peepers.* (Series; Comedy; NBC; 1952–1955). Jefferson City is a small American town rather than a city. There is the local newspaper, the Jefferson City *Press and Collector*, City High School, City College, Jefferson General Hospital and, most importantly, Jefferson City Junior High School, the focal point of the first series to spoof the public schoolteacher.

Robinson J. Peepers is an army corporal who returns to teaching (general science) after an honorable discharge (poor eyesight). He is gentle and kind, and his students are all his fans. He is also timid and shy and easily taken advantage of. Robinson was born in the neighboring town of Williamsport where his mother, "Ma Peepers," and his sister, Agnes Peepers, still live (Agnes is a teacher at the Jefferson Observatory; Mrs. F.R. Peepers is the name on the mailbox). Robinson talks directly to the audience when he feels the need.

Royala Dean, the school's music teacher, was Robinson's first love interest. When the series, intended only to be a summer replacement for *The James Melton Show*, achieved high ratings, it was quickly brought back to replace the Eddie Mayehoff series, *Doc Corkle*, which was canceled after three episodes. Robinson's new love interest was Nancy Remington, the school nurse. They became engaged in the episode of April 25, 1954 and married on May 23, 1954.

Harvey Weskit is the history teacher. He is married to Marge and is best friends with Robinson (whom he calls "Ace" and "Rob"; Marge calls him "Robbie"). Marge and Harvey became parents of a baby boy (1954) they named Harrison Brookfield Weskit. Marge was born in Chicago, and Robinson calls Harvey, who was best man at his wedding, "Wes."

Mrs. Gurney, the wife of school principal Gabriel Gurney, teaches English. She fusses, mutters to herself, sentimentalizes and forgets what she is about to say. Mr. Bascomb, became the principal in1954; Frank T. Whipp III is the coach.

Cast: Wally Cox (*Robinson J. Peepers*); Tony Randall (*Harvey Weskit*); Norma Crane (*Royala Dean*); Marion Lorne (*Mrs. Gurney*); Joseph Foley (*Gabriel Gurney*); Patricia Benoit (*Nancy Remington*); Georgann Johnson (*Marge Weskitt*); Gage Clark (*Mr. Bascomb*); Ernest Truex (*Nancy's father*); Sylvia Field (*Nancy's mother*); Ruth McDevitt (*Robinson's mother*); Jenny Egan (*Agnes Peepers*).

6170   *Mr. Personality.* (Series; Reality; Fox; 2003). A single, attractive woman (Hayley) is introduced to 20 single men—all of whom are wearing masks. Hayley questions the men to determine compatibility. Those that she feels are a match are brought to "the dark room" where the chosen men can remove their masks and Hayley can feel their faces. Based on what she has learned, Hayley chooses the one man she feels is right for her. In the light, the man removes his mask and Hayley sees her choice for the first time. Produced by Bruce Nash.

6171   *The Mr. Potato Head Show.* (Series; Cartoon; Fox; 1998-1999). A kitchen is the setting for the mishaps that befall Mr. Potato Head, a character based on the toy of the same name, his wife, Mrs. Potato Head and their food friends (such as Mr. Fruitcake, Giblets and Johnny Rotten Apple). Live action puppets are combined with computer animation.

Voices: Brian Jacobs, James Murray, Debra Wilson.

6172   *Mr. President.* (Series; Comedy; Fox; 1987-1988). The Tresch family are America's newest First Family. Sam Tresch is a governor from Wisconsin who ran for and was elected the 43rd President of the United States. Meg Tresch is his wife, the new First Lady and Cynthia, Nick and Jennifer are their children. Stories focus on the efforts of America's "newest First Family" as they struggle to adjust to a life that is more public than private in Washington, D.C.

Charley Ross is Sam's aide; Clifford Tresch is Sam's brother; Fred Hayes is Jennifer's husband; and Lois Guloxton is Meg's sister.

Cast: George C. Scott (*Sam Tresch*); Carlin Glynn (*Meg Tresch*); Maddie Corman (*Cynthia Tresch*); Andrew Gower (*Nick Tresch*); Susan Wheeler Duff (*Jennifer Tresch-Hayes*); Daniel McDonald (*Fred Hayes*); Conrad Bain (*Charley Ross*); Eugene Roche (*Clifford Tresch*); Madeline Khan (*Lois Guloxton*).

6173   *Mr. Rhodes.* (Series; Comedy-Drama; NBC; 1996). Thomas Rhodes is a writer whose book has been critically acclaimed but a commercial failure. With his writing career on hold and with no other choice, Thomas accepts a job to teach English at his former conservative prep school. Stories follow Thomas, a somewhat undisciplined

person, as he attempts to teach but too often presenting his somewhat prejudiced views on his impressionable students.

Cast: Tom Rhodes (*Thomas Rhodes*); Ron Glass (*Ronald Fletcher*); Lindsay Sloane (*Zoey Miller*); Farrah Forke (*Nikki*); Alexandra Holden (*Dani Swanson*); Jensen Ackles (*Malcolm*); Jessica Stone (*Amanda Reeves*); Stephen Tabolowsky (*Ray Heary*).

6174   *Mr. Roberts.* (Series; Comedy-Drama; NBC; 1965-1966). The South Pacific during World War II is the setting. Lieutenant Douglas Roberts is the cargo officer aboard the *Reluctant*, a U.S. Navy cargo ship nicknamed "The Bucket" by its reluctant-to-serve crew. Felling he is displaced, and hoping to serve aboard a fighting vessel, Douglas seeks to acquire a transfer, but, by shouldering the antics of his men, he encounters the hostility of the ship's commander, Captain John Morton who, feeling that the morale of his men preceded Roberts's wants, refuses to forward his letters to the proper authorities. Through Douglas's continual efforts, a rarely seen sentimental picture of the war is seen. Based on the feature film of the same title.

Cast: Roger Smith (*Lt. Douglas Roberts*); Richard X. Slattery (*Capt. John Morton*); Steve Harmon (*Ensign Frank Pulver*); George Ives (*Doc; the surgeon*); Richard Sinatra (*Seaman D'Angelo*); Ronald Starr (*Seaman Mannion*); Roy Reese (*Seaman Reber*); Barry Kelly (*Admiral Weatherby*).

6175   *Mr. Rogers' Neighborhood.* (Series; Children; PBS; 1970–1975). Mr. Rogers is a kind gentleman who lives in a magical neighborhood where, through the antics of the puppet characters who reside there and the live actions guests who visit, various aspects of the world are related to children to help strengthen their emotional development.

Cast: Fred Rogers (*Mr. Rogers*); Lady Aberlin (*Betty Aberlin*); Joe Negri (*Handyman Negri*); Yoshi Ito (*Pilot Ito*); Don Brockett (*Chief Brockett*); Francois Clemmons (*Francois*); Elise Neal (*Elsie*); Audrey Roth (*Audrey Cleans Everything*); Betsy Nadas (*Mrs. McFeely*); William Barker (*Voice of Puppet Dr. Duckbill*); Robert Trow (*Voice of Puppet Henrietta Crow*).

Puppets Voiced by Fred Rogers: King Friday XIII, X the Owl, Queen Sara Saturday, Henrietta Pussycat, Daniel Tiger, Donkey Hodie, Lady Elaine Fairchild.

6176   *Mr. Romance.* (Pilot; Talk; Unaired; Produced in 1987). Langdon Hill, the "Mr. Romance" of the title, first talks with studio audience members, then celebrity guests about romance and concludes with a practical guide on how to keep the romance of passion alive.

Host: Langdon Hill.

6177   *Mr. Smith.* (Series; Comedy; NBC; 1983). While driving from Arizona to California with his act, the Atwood Orangutans (Cha Cha and Bobo) Tommy Atwood is run off the road. Tommy is knocked unconscious and Cha Cha and Bobo, frightened by the approaching police sirens, run away. Cha Cha is found by the Humane Society and is later sent to a government research center in Washington, D.C. Six weeks later, Cha Cha escapes from his cage and, while wandering about the building, enters a lab in which an enzyme designed to increase human intelligence is being developed. Cha Cha mixes some chemicals, drinks the result—and is suddenly endowed with the ability to talk. When tests reveal that he has an I.Q. of 256, he is named Mr. Smith and made a government consultant. Tommy, later traced through Mr. Smith, is summoned to Washington and becomes Cha Cha's assistant. Stories depict the adventures of an articulate genius and government consultant—who happens to be an orangutan—as he attempts to become human.

Other regulars are Raymond Holyoke, Mr. Smith's secretary; Ellie Atwood, Tommy's sister; Judy Tyson, works at the research center; Tracy Randolph, a primate psychologist; Dr. Kline, head of the research center.

Cast Leonard Frey (*Raymond Holyoke*); Tim Dunigan (*Tommy Atwood*); Laura Jacoby (*Ellie Atwood*); Terri Garber (*Judy Tyson*); Lauren Chase (*Tracy Randolph*); Stuart Margolin (*Dr. Kline*); Ed Weinberger (*Voice of Mr. Smith*); C.J. (*Mr. Smith*); Bobo (*Bobo*).

6178   *Mr. Smith Goes to Washington.* (Series; Comedy; ABC; 1962-1963). Eugene Smith is a young patriot. He lives in Jackson County and admires George Washington and Abraham Lincoln (quotes them when the occasion arises). Eugene has no political experience, but after the death of his state senator, he is elected to replace him. Encompassing mature wisdom, boyish charm, warmth and dignity, Eugene relocates to Washington, D.C., and now must adjust to the norms of Capitol life. Patricia Smith is his wife; Cooter Smith is his uncle; Miss Kelly is his secretary; and Arnie is Eugene's butler. Based on the feature film of the same title.

Cast: Fess Parker (*Eugene Smith*); Sandra Warner (*Patricia Smith*); Red Foley (*Cooter Smith*); Rita Lynn (*Miss Kelly*); Stan Irwin (*Arnie*).

6179   *Mister Sterling.* (Series; Drama; NBC; 2003). William Sterling, Jr., is a young, idealistic senator struggling to adjust to the norms of life in Washington, D.C. He is a bit wet-behind-the-ears as he was rushed into the Washington scene to replace the California senator who died unexpectedly. Jackie Brock is his Chief of Staff; Tommy Doyle is the legislative director; Leon Montero is the computer whiz; William Sr. is William's father, the former governor of California; Laura Chandler is the political reporter; Senator Jackson is William's aide; Derek Larner is the Deputy Press Secretary.

Cast: Josh Brolin (*William Sterling, Jr.*); Audra McDonald (*Jackie Brock*); William Russ (*Tommy Doyle*); Chandra West (*Laura Chandler*); James Whitmore (*William Sterling, Sr.*); Graham Greene (*Senator Jackson*); David Norona (*Leon Montero*); Nicole Forester (*William's receptionist*); Dean Cameron (*Derek Larner*).

6180   *Mr. Success.* (Pilot; Comedy; NBC; June 23, 1984). Vernon Silt is the manager of the complaint department of Dorfman's Department Store. He would like to become a success in life, but he is beset by problems, both at home and at work. He feels he is too easy-going and easily taken advantage of. The proposal was to follow Vernon as he tries to assert himself and become a success in life. Other regulars are Helen, Vernon's wife; Libby and Andy, their children; and Lonnie, Vernon's friend. James Coco performs the theme, "Mr. Success."

Cast: James Coco (*Vernon Silt*); Miriam Flynn (*Helen Silt*); Viveka Davis (*Libby Silt*); Pat Cochran (*Andy Silt*); Murphy Dunne (*Lonnie Barst*).

6181   *Mr. Sunshine.* (Series; Comedy; ABC; 1986). Paul Stark is an English professor at Kenyon College whose dry wit and fast thinking have brought him through many crises in his lifetime. Then one day he suffers from an accident that costs him his sight. He is now cynical and has been nicknamed "Mr. Sunshine" by his students. Stories follow events in the life of a man who is anything but "Mr. Sunshine." Other regulars are Chris, Paul's son (Paul is separated from his wife after 16 years of marriage); June, Paul's landlady; Grace, Paul's typist; and Gary, Paul's teaching assistant.

Cast: Jeffrey Tambor (*Paul Stark*); John P. Navin, Jr. (*Chris Stark*); Barbara Babcock (*June Swinford*); Nan Martin (*Grace D'Angelo*); Brian Benben (*Gary Frank*).

6182   *Mr. Sweeney.* (Pilot; Comedy; NBC; Oct. 14, 1953). A spin off from *The Kate Smith Hour* (where it aired as a show segment) and the pilot for *The Wonderful World of Mr. Sweeney.* Cicero P. Sweeney is a kindly old gentleman who owns a small town grocery store. He lives with his daughter, Marge Franklin (a widow) and her young son Kippie. Cicero is also a teller of tall tales and the proposal relates the mishaps that occur due to the exaggerated stories he tells.

Cast: Charlie Ruggles (*Cicero P. Sweeney*); Helen Wagner (*Marge Franklin*); Glenn Walkin (*Kippie Franklin*).

6183   *Mr. T.* (Series; Cartoon; NBC; 1983-1984). Mr. T, co-star of *The A-Team,* as the coach of a U.S. teenage gymnastics team (Kim, Robin, Spike, Jeff, Woody and Toby) as he battles evil at various meets around the world. The program is designed to teach and encourage children to believe in themselves.

Voice Cast: Mr. T (*Himself*); Phil LaMarr (*Woody*); Siu Ming Carson (*Kim*); Shawn Lieber (*Jeff*); Teddy Field III (*Spike*); Takayo Fischer (*Miss Bisby*); Amy Linker (*Robin*).

6184   *Mr. T and Tina.* (Series; Comedy; ABC; 1976). Taro Takahashi is a widowed Japanese businessman who is vice president of a company called Moyati Industries. He is the father of Sachi and Aki and has moved from Tokyo to Chicago to head an American branch of the company. In an attempt to help him care for his children, he hires Tina Kelly, a pretty but dizzy young American woman as a governess. Stories follow the events that spark Taro's life — from his life at home to his life at work. Matsu his Taro's uncle; Michi is his sister-in-law; Miss Llewellyn is the building manager; Harvard is the janitor.

Cast: Pat Morita (*Taro Takahashi*); Susan Blanchard (*Tina Kelly*); June Angela (*Sachi Takahashi*); Gene Profanata (*Aki Takahashi*); Jerry Hatsuo Fujikawa (*Uncle Mitsu*); Pat Suzuki (*Michi*); Miriam Byrd-Nethery (*Miss Llewellyn*); Ted Lange (*Harvard*).

6185   *Mr. Terrific.* (Series; Comedy; CBS; 1967). Stanley Beemish and Hal Waters are partners in Hal and Stanley's Service Station on Northeastern and Wyoming streets in Washington, D.C. Dr. Ned Reynolds is a government scientist who accidentally invents a source of incredible energy he calls the Power Pill. Barton J. Reed is the head of the Bureau of Special Projects, a government organization that seeks to use the pill as a secret weapon in the battle against crime. Henley Trent, Reed's assistant, has been ordered to conduct a search to find a man capable of taking the special pill. His search leads him to the gas station where Stanley is persuaded to test the pill. Seconds after taking the pill, Stanley is transformed into the invincible Mr. Terrific. Stanley is sworn in as an agent and begins a double life: private citizen and "the U.S. government's secret weapon against crime."

Stanley's Mr. Terrific costume is a jacket with wing-like sleeves (which he flaps in order to fly), a pair of goggles and a scarf—all of which he stores in his locker at the gas station. In addition to flying, the pill endows Stanley with incredible strength and speed and an immunity to harm. Stanley is also not your typical superhero. He has difficulty flying and landings become a problem (he can't navigate). He has difficulty finding assigned targets when airborne (his scarf constantly obstructs his vision) and he has a difficult time adjusting to his secret alias. When Mr. Terrific is needed, Reed sounds the Purple Alert. Before each assignment, Reed gives Stanley a box with three pills (one base pill that lasts one hour and gives Stanley the strength of 1,000 men, and two booster pills that last ten minutes each). The pills, which are specially candy coated so Stanley will take them, always wear off at crucial moments and Stanley often has to wrap up cases as his ordinary, bumbling self.

In the original, unaired pilot version, titled *Mr. Terrific*, Stanley Beemish (Alan Young) is a shoe salesman for Mr. Finney (Jesse

White), the owner of Finney's Department Store, and is recruited by the Chief (Edward Andrews) of the Office of Special Assignments, to test a pill that transforms him into Mr. Terrific, a daring but misadventure-prone crime fighter. Stanley did not have a girlfriend in the series, but in the pilot he was in love with Gloria Dickinson (Sheila Wells).

Program Open: "A scientist both wise and bold set out to cure the common cold. Instead he found this power pill which he said most certainly will turn a lamb into a lion, like an eagle he'll be flying; solid steel will be like putty, it will work on anybody. But then 'twas found this potent pill made the strongest men quite ill; so the secret search began to find the one and only man. What they found made them squeamish for only Stanley Beemish, a weak and droopy daffodil could take the special power pill. When he took the pill specific, it made him the most prolific, terrific, Mister Terrific!"

Cast: Stephen Strimpell (*Stanley Beemish*); Dick Gautier (*Hal Waters*); John McGiver (*Barton J. Reed*); Paul Smith (*Henley Trent*); Ned Glass (*Dr. Reynolds*); Ellen Corby (*Hal's mother*).

6186 *Mr. Tutt.* (Pilot; Drama; NBC; Sept. 10, 1958). Ephraim Tutt is a respected, shrewd small town lawyer in New York State. Ephraim believes that the law is meant to be the law, not rest in a set of books and collect dust on a shelf. He is fully aware of the law and the proposal was to relate his efforts to see that justice is served. Olive is his wife; Charlie is his legman. Based on the stories by Arthur Train.

Cast: Walter Brennan (*Ephraim Tutt*); Olive Blakeney (*Olive*); Harry Harvey, Jr. (*Charlie*).

6187 *Mr. Wizard.* (Series; Children; NBC; 1951; 1971). The basics of various scientific experiments are explained to children through demonstrations. Also known as *Watch Mr. Wizard.*

Program Open: "*Watch Mr. Wizard.* That's what all the kids in the neighborhood call him because he shows them the mystery of science in everyday living. *Watch Mr. Wizard* is brought to you by General Mills, makers of Cheerios, the oat cereal that's ready to eat. A Cheerios breakfast gives you power protein to help youngsters grown strong and adults keep feeling fit. And now here he is Don Herbert as Mr. Wizard." Two versions appeared:

1. *Mr. Wizard* (NBC, 1951–1965). **Host:** Don Herbert.
2. *Mr. Wizard* (NBC, 1971-1972). **Host:** Don Herbert.

6188 *Mistresses.* (Series; Drama; BBC America; 2009). A look at the lives of four thirty-something British women, friends since college, whose lives have taken dramatically different turns. Kate is a well respected doctor; Trudi is a 9/11 widow who is unable to achieve closure (her husband's remains were never found); Siobhan, a successful lawyer, is happily married to Hari; and Jessica, a fun-loving girl with an insatiable sexual appetite, whose goal is to avoid marriage (she later finds herself becoming attracted to women despite the fact that she is a mistress to her married boss, Simon). Produced by the BBC.

Cast: Sarah Parish (*Katie Roden*); Sharon Small (*Trudi Malloy*); Orla Brady (*Siobhan Dillon*); Shelley Conn (*Jessica*); Raza Jeffrey (*Hari Malloy*); Adam Astill (*Simon*); Max Brown (*Sam Grey*); Preeya Kalidas (*Carrie*); Lizzie Watkins (*Amy*); Anna Torv (*Alex*); Chris Garner (*Dr. Rob Carrington*); Joanne McQuinn (*Sally Moore*); Alys Thomas (*Lisa*); Adam Rayner (*Dominic*); Patrick Baladi (*Richard*).

6189 *Mistresses.* (Pilot; Drama; Unaired; Produced for Lifetime in 2008). Adaptation of the British series that charts the struggles of several friends from college through their adult years.

Cast: Brooke Burns (*Shannon*); Camille Sullivan (*Kate*); Holly Marie Combs (*Jane*); Rochelle Aytes (*Ava*).

6190 *Mitchell and Woods.* (Pilot; Crime Drama; NBC; Dec. 18, 1981). After a stint as traffic cops, officers Paula Woods and Melanie Mitchell are promoted to plainclothes detectives. Their experiences with the Ocean City, California, Police Department, is the focal point of the proposal.

Cast: Jayne Kennedy (*Paula Woods*); Cindy Morgan (*Melanie Mitchell*); Paul Gale (*Lieutenant Richards*).

6191 *Mixed Doubles.* (Series; Drama; NBC; 1949). New York City provides the backdrop for a look at the Abbotts and the Colemans, newlywed couples who live side by side in one-room apartments. The husbands (Bill Abbott and Eddy Coleman) are underpaid copywriters in the same ad agency, and the wives (Ada Abbott and Elaine Coleman) struggle to make ends meet on scanty paychecks.

Cast: Billy Idelson (*Bill Abbott*); Ada Freeman (*Ada Abbott*); Eddie Firestone (*Eddie Coleman*); Rhoda Williams, Bonnie Baken (*Elaine Coleman*).

6192 *Mixed Nuts.* (Pilot; Comedy; ABC; May 12, 1977). Dr. Sarah Allgood is a psychiatrist who, like her name, tries to help people. She is on staff at the Rosewood State Psychiatric Center and the proposal was to relate her comic adventures as she struggles to deal with her mischievous charges (Bugs, Logan, Moe, Gato and Jamie). Other regulars are Dr. Folder, director of the center; and Nurse Cassidy.

Cast: Zohra Lambert (*Dr. Sarah Allgood*); Emory Bass (*Dr. Folder*); Conchata Ferrell (*Nurse Cassidy*); Dan Barrows (*Bugs*); Richard Karron (*Logan*); Morey Amsterdam (*Moe*); James Victor (*Gato*); Ed Begley, Jr. (*Jamie*).

6193 *Mo and Joe.* (Pilot; Comedy; CBS; Mar. 7, 1974). Maureen, nicknamed "Mo," and her husband, Joe, are a mid-thirties married couple with two children, Julia and Edward. They are also a working couple and have hired a college girl (Iris) to care for their kids. One day, while watching Iris with Julia and Edward, Mo and Joe feel that life may be passing them by. The proposal was to relate the mishaps that befall Mo and Joe when they try to recapture their youth.

Cast: Louise Lasser (*Mo Lambert*); Michael Tolan (*Joe Lambert*); Andrea McArdle (*Julia Lambert*); Matthew Anton (*Edward Lambert*); Judith Kahan (*Iris*).

6194 *Mobile Medics.* (Pilot; Drama; CBS; May 10, 1977). In an effort to help people in extremely critical condition, Dr. Liz Rheiner receives the funding to start Mobile Medics, an experimental project that uses a sophisticated, medically equipped van to help where needed. Pete Vasquez drives the van; Robb Spencer and Craig Bryant are the doctors who ride with him; and Liz heads the unit from Memorial Hospital. The proposal was to relate their experiences as they assist people who do not have the time to make it to a hospital.

Cast: Ellen Weston (*Liz Rheiner*); Jack Stauffer (*Robb Spencer*); Ben Masters (*Craig Bryant*); Jaime Tirelli (*Pete Vasquez*).

6195 *Mobile One.* (Series; Drama; ABC; 1975). Pete Campbell, a top notch reporter for ABC-TV, is fired for excessive drinking. After drying out and getting his life back together, Pete acquires a job as a sportscaster for WQPR radio (103.1 FM) in Crown City, Georgia. When Maggie Spencer, the producer of *The 11 O'clock News* on KONE-TV, Channel 1, in southern California, thinks she needs the hard hitting news stories of the past in order to improve ratings, she hires Pete as a reporter. Doug McKnight is assigned as his cameraman, and stories follow Pete as he uses his ingenuity as a seasoned reporter to go where the news is to get the stories. In the pilot episode

(*Mobile Two*, ABC, Sept. 2, 1975), Pete works for KITE, Channel 10.

Cast: Jackie Cooper (*Pete Campbell*); Julie Gregg (*Maggie Spencer*); Mark Wheeler (*Doug McKnight*); Gary Crosby (*Bruce Daniels; works at KONE*); Warren Stevens (*Police Lt. Baker*).

6196   *Moby Dick and the Mighty Mightor.* (Series; Cartoon; CBS; 1967–1969). The overall title for two animated segments:

1. Moby Dick. Moby Dick, the legendary white whale, struggles to protect his human foundlings, Tom and Tub, from danger.

2. The Mighty Mightor. Tor, a young boy who possesses the power to change his meek self into the Mighty Mightor, battles the evils of a savage era.

Voice Cast: Bobby Resnick (*Tom*); Barry Balkin (*Tub*); Don Messick (*Scooby the Seal*); Paul Stewart (*Mightor*); Bobby Diamond (*Tor*); Patsy Garrett (*Sheera*); John Stephenson (*Pondo/Tog/L'il Rock*); Norma McMillan (*L'il Rock*).

6197   *MoCapp, LLC.* (Series; Comedy; Spike; 2009). Frank, Jeff and Claire are the owners of MoCapp, LLC, a low budget motion capture studio that will go to outrageous lengths to acquire work in the video game industry. Stories, which are comedic in nature, follow the trio as they share their fascinating but rarely exciting or sexy attempts to document the world of video games. Based on the web series of the same title.

Cast: Chris Deluca (*Frank Claxton*); Jonathan Garbus (*Jeff Reynolds*); Kara Klenk (*Claire Owens*); Laura Turek (*Kendall Clement*).

6198   *The Mod Squad.* (Series; Crime Drama; ABC; 1968–1973). The word "mod" is defined as "young people noted for their emphasis on stylish dress; often as a symbol of their alienation from conventional society." Pete Cochran, Julie Barnes and Linc Hayes are three such people — young adults arrested on minor charges and offered a choice by Captain Adam Greer of the L.A.P.D.: spend time in jail or perform specific undercover assignments for him as the Mod Squad. "Times change and cops have to change with it," says Adam. "They can get into a thousand places that we can't. Who is going to suspect kids?"

Pete, Julie and Linc were headed for nowhere and Adam gave them a chance to change the course of their lives. They are not permitted to carry guns and rely on their street smarts to accomplish their goals.

Pete is from a wealthy family and lived in a 14 room, five bathroom Beverly Hills mansion. He simply met the wrong kind of people and was kicked out by his parents for being anti everything. Pete rejected all the efforts his parents made to help him. He was arrested for taking a joy ride in a stolen car.

Julie had no address. Her father had deserted the family and Julie lived with her mother in San Francisco. When Julie discovered her mother was a prostitute, she ran away. She was arrested in Los Angeles for having no visible means of support. Julie couldn't handle her mother's life of one night stands and just "split." She has lost track of her mother and does not know where her mother is or if she is still alive.

Lincoln, nicknamed Linc, was born and raised in the Watts section of Los Angeles. He lived in a three room apartment with 13 people and grew up bitter and disillusioned. He believed in the Black Cause but during the Watts riots, he started a fire and was arrested for arson. He has now come to respect people of all races, and color doesn't matter when arresting criminals although he does say, "I hate to fink on a soul brother."

The whole idea behind the Mod Squad is for Linc, Julie and Pete to melt in, not stand out. Adam believes this is possible although his superior, Chief Barney Metcalf believes the Mod Squad are just kids on probation. Adam becomes upset when the squad is arrested as part of a bust. He feels their attitudes will expose their undercover operations. Julie, Pete and Linc break all the rules — from stealing and breaking and entering — to get the job done. Each feels they are now part of something important for the first time in their lives. Although they like Adam, they feel he is too hard to please. Julie is restless during assignments; Pete is impatient and too anxious to make things happen; Linc is the calm one and usually brings focus to the group. See also *The Return of the Mod Squad*.

Cast: Michael Cole (*Pete Cochrane*); Peggy Lipton (*Julie Barnes*); Clarence Williams III (*Linc Hayes*); Tige Andrews (*Adam Greer*); Simon Scott (*Barney Metcalf*).

6199   *Model by Day.* (Pilot; Crime Drama; Fox; Mar. 21, 1994). When her best friend and roommate, Jae, is injured by carjackers, a beautiful model known only as Lex, decides to do something about it and apprehend the culprits herself. Lex has appeared in *Playboy* magazine, done lingerie ads and was the Prism Lipstick Girl; to hide her true identity, she dons a black outfit and sets out to find Jae's attackers. When she completes her task and figures that the police aren't doing their job, she decides to continue in her dual capacity — a model by day and a mysterious crime fighter by night (called "The Vigilante Vixen" by the press and "Lady X" by medics. A home video caught Lex running from a scene. It showed the shoulder straps of her black leather bra crossed like an "X" in the back. She also wears leather shorts, a hood and dark glasses). Lex, however, does have a problem leading a dual life — getting bruised (wearing makeup solves the problem when modeling). Lex never kills; she disables criminals with her expertise in karate, then handcuffs them for the police to arrest. Other regulars are Master Chang, Lex's martial arts teacher; and Mercedes, Lex's agent.

Cast: Famke Janssen (*Lex*); Traci Lin (*Jae Davis*); Clark Johnson (*Master Chang*); Sean Young (*Mercedes*).

6200   *Model Citizens.* (Series; Reality; PAX; 2004). Female models are commonly thought of as beautiful girls who do nothing but look beautiful, model clothes and make money. PAX-TV chose to show a different side of a model's life (also incorporating some male models). Here ten models (seven women, three men) have agreed to make the world a better place by doing what they can (manual labor) in the poorest regions of the country. Cameras follow their sincere efforts to make a difference. Larissa Meek hosts. Chantille Boudousque, Jacqueline Lord. Nicole Spruill, Daniela Melgoza, Gretchen Eakins, Matthew Schaefer, Kellan Lutz and Rib Hills are the models.

6201   *A Model Life with Petra Nemcova.* (Series; Reality; TLC; 2007). Petra Nemcova, a gorgeous super model, is perhaps best known (or came to world wide attention) when she miraculously survived the 2004 tsunami in Thailand. Petra, as the host of her own series, is seeking a top model (much in the same way Tyra Banks seeks them on *America's Next Top Model*). Here six hopeful models are put through various tasks to test their modeling abilities. The potential models are chosen from around the world and looks take priority over everything else. The one girl Petra feels has the look to be a fashion model is awarded that golden opportunity.

6202   *Models Inc.* (Series; Drama; Fox; 1994-1995). *Melrose Place* spin off that takes an inside look at the cutthroat world of high fashion modeling. Hillary Michaels is the president and CEO of Models Inc., a prestigious Los Angeles modeling agency. Hillary is ruthless and runs her company with an iron fist (although she puts up with her alcoholic employee, Sarah Owens). The prime time soap opera has all the elements of a hit — seductions, blackmail, back stabbing, stalking, murder and betrayal, but it just didn't catch on and was cancelled after one season (29 episodes). *Models Inc.* is not the first show about models to fold. Three other attempts also failed: *Love That Jill* (1958), *Paper Dolls* (1984) and *Living Dolls* (1989).

Cast: Linda Gray *(Hillary Michaels)*; Emma Samms *(Grayson Louder)*; Gracelle Beauvais *(Cynthia Nichols)*; Heather Medway *(Stephanie Smith)*; Cameron Daddo *(Brian Peterson)*; Cassidy Rae *(Sarah Owens)*; Kylie Travis *(Julie Dante)*; Carrie-Anne Moss *(Carrie Spencer)*; Kaela Goldsmith *(Kristy)*; David Goldsmith *(Eric Dearborn)*; Teresa Hill *(Linda Holden)*.

6203 ***Models of the Runway.*** (Series; Reality; Lifetime; 2009). Companion series to the Lifetime version of *Project Runway* that explores the world of the catwalk (runway) from the models perspective. Heidi Klum and Tim Gunn, host.

6204 ***Modern Family.*** (Series; Comedy; ABC; 2009–). Jay is a cranky 63-year-old man who has married a much younger woman (Gloria) and has become the stepfather to her 11-year-old son, Manny. Claire, Jay's daughter from an earlier marriage, and her husband, Phil, have been married 16 years and are the parents of Haley, Alexandra and Luke. Mitchell, Jay's son, is gay and has begun a relationship with Cameron. As Jay and Gloria begin adjusting to an older man–younger woman relationship (they have been married six months), Mitchell and Cameron have just adopted an infant girl (Lily) from Vietnam. While this group is a family, they are from different worlds, "but they somehow fit together." Stories relate incidents in the lives of the individual family members as they struggle to cope with the incidents that somehow manage to invade each other's life.

Cast: Ed O'Neill *(Jay Pritchett)*; Sofia Vergara *(Gloria Delgado Pritchett)*; Julie Bowen *(Claire Dunphy)*; Ty Burrell *(Phil Dunphy)*; Jesse Tyler Ferguson *(Mitchell Pritchett)*; Eric Stonestreet *(Cameron Tucker)*; Sarah Hyland *(Haley Dunphy)*; Ariel Winter *(Alexandra Dunphy)*; Nolan Gould *(Luke Dunphy)*; Rico Rodriguez *(Manny Delgado)*; Ella and Jaden Hiller *(Baby Lily)*.

6205 ***Modern Men.*** (Series; Comedy; WB; 2006). Doug Jessup Reynolds, Tim Clark and Kyle Brewster are three men who love women—but are unable to maintain a steady relationship. The three have been friends since high school and now share an apartment in Chicago. Tim works in his father's bar, The Tug House. He is single and always getting dumped. Doug is divorced from Allie and still holds deep feelings for her. He is hesitant to date other women, fearing Allie will catch him. Kyle, a pharmaceutical salesman, believes he is a ladies' man and although he has numerous one-night stands, they are meaningless because he cannot seem to hold onto a girl.

To solve their problem, Doug, Tim and Kyle, decide to visit a life coach and get the help they need to learn how to romance a woman and maintain a steady relationship. They choose Dr. Victoria Stangel, a gorgeous sex therapist who uses her life experiences coupled with her college degrees to help men (and women) solve their romantic heartaches.

Victoria's philosophy is to figure out what her clients need then help them get it. Stories follow Victoria's efforts to help Tim, Doug and Kyle land the women of their dreams—a situation that proves more difficult than it sounds as Kyle, Tim and Doug know nothing about women—and prove it with each episode. Other regulars are Tug Clark, Tim's father, the bar owner; and Molly Clark, Tim's sister, a law student who also helps tend bar.

Cast: Jane Seymour *(Dr. Victoria Stangel)*; Eric Lovely *(Doug Reynolds)*; Josh Braaten *(Tim Clark)*; Max Greenfield *(Kyle Brewster)*; George Wendt *(Tug Clark)*; Marla Sokoloff *(Molly Clark)*.

6206 ***Modern Romances.*** (Series; Serial; NBC; 1954–1958).

Dramatizations based on modern romance stories. Each story runs five chapters and casts and authors change weekly.

Host-Narrator: Martha Scott, Mel Brandt.

6207 ***Modern Toss.*** (Series; Comedy; IFC; 2009). British produced adaptation of the raunchy cartoon booklet *Modern Toss* that combines live action with animation to literally showcase gross characters, profanity and other inappropriate skits that could never air on broadcast or basic cable without editing.

Cast: Ralph Brown, Camilla Corbett, Mackenzie Crook, Gabrielle Fritz, Simon Greenwall, Paul Kaye, Doon MacKichan.

6208 ***Modesty Blaise.*** (Pilot; Adventure; ABC; Sept. 12, 1982). Modesty Blaise is a beautiful former criminal turned mysterious adventurer who aids people in distress. She is assisted by Willie Garvin, a man whose life she once saved, and most often helps Gerald Tarent, an SIB (Special Intelligence Bureau) agent. Based on the British comic book characters created by Peter O'Donnell. Other regulars are Jack, Tarent's aide; and Wang, Modesty's chauffeur and houseboy.

Cast: Ann Turkel *(Modesty Blaise)*; Lewis Van Bergen *(Willie Garvin)*; Keene Curtis *(Gerald Tarent)*; Sab Shimono *(Wang)*; Douglas Dirkson *(Jack)*.

6209 ***Moe's World.*** (Pilot; Drama; ABC; July 9, 1992). The house on Avenue B in an unnamed inner city is occupied by the Bakers, a family consisting of a widowed mother (Melba), her children (Natalie and Jerome), a grandfather (Gramps), and the spirit of Moe, Melba's 12-year-old son, who was a victim of street violence. The rather unusual series project was to focus on Moe as he looks over his family.

Cast: Deon Richmond *(Moe Baker)*; S. Epatha Merkerson *(Melba Baker)*; Jada Pinkett *(Natalie Baker)*; Kenneth Brown *(Jerome Baker)*; Bill Cobbs *(Abe Baker)*.

6210 ***Moesha.*** (Series; Comedy; UPN; 1996–2001). Moesha Denise Mitchell, called "Mo" for short, lives at 6653 West Post Road in Los Angeles with her father, Frank, stepmother Deidre "Dee" and brother Miles.

Moesha, 15, attends Crenshaw High School, hangs out with her friends at the Den, and works after school as a salesgirl at Class Act, a clothing store. She is a straight "A" student, helps people she believes are in trouble (always making situations worse) and has a knack for defying parental authority and getting into trouble.

In the 1999 season finale (May 25), Moesha graduated from Crenshaw and took a job as a receptionist at *Vibe* magazine (hoping for a break in a career to become a writer). She had planned to attend Northwestern University in Chicago and major in journalism. When the series returned for a new season (Aug. 30, 1999), Moesha is fired from *Vibe* (for interviewing Maya Angelou without permission) and enrolls in college.

Frank, a widower, married Dee three months before the series began. He owns a car dealership, calls Moesha "Pumpkin" and hates for Moesha to wear midriff blouses (he has a "heart attack" when Moesha shows cleavage). He believes "the gray hairs, headaches and wrinkles" he has are "a part of raising a beautiful teenage daughter." Dee, the vice principal at Crenshaw, is desperately trying to win Moesha's love but finding it difficult because Moesha feels no woman can replace her real mother. Miles is a talented dancer and often hears "go to your room" for all the trouble he gets into.

Kim Parker, Nicey Jackson, Quentin Brooks and Lamont Bentley are Moesha's friends. See also *The Parkers*, the spin off series.

Cast: Brandy Norwood *(Moesha Mitchell)*; William Allen Young *(Frank Mitchell)*; Sheryl Lee Ralph *(Dee Mitchell)*; Marcus T. Paulick *(Miles Mitchell)*; Countess Vaughn *(Kim Parker)*; Hakeem Campbell

(Lamont Bentley); Yvette Wilson *(Andell Wilkerson)*; Shar Jackson *(Nicey Jackson)*; Fredro Starr *(Quinton Brooks)*; Bernie Mac *(Uncle Bernie)*.

6211   *The Mohawk Showroom.* (Series; Variety; NBC; 1949). Mohawk Carpets sponsored program of music and songs.

Hosts: Roberta Quinlan, Morton Downey. **Regulars:** Carmen Mastren, The Chieftains. **Announcer:** Bob Stanton. **Music:** Carmen Mastren, Harry Clark.

6212   *The Mole.* (Series; Reality; ABC; 2001–2004). A clever reality series with several versions that allows viewers at home to play along. The basic format had first regular people, then celebrities as contestants. They compete against each other in a series of challenges for a $250,000 prize (later $1 million). One of the players, however, is a mole, a double agent hired by ABC to secretly sabotage the games (which tests the players' abilities to complete certain task challenges). At the end of each episode, the players take "The Quiz," a ten question survey regarding the mole. The person whose test score shows the least knowledge about the mole is "executed" and must leave the competition. The person (other than the mole — who has all the answers to the quiz) that scores highest on the final exam wins the top prize.

The series began as *The Mole* (which featured ten players and a $250,000 prize). The second cycle, *The Mole: The Next Betrayal,* used 13 players and hiked the jackpot to $1 million. The show suffered from a ratings meltdown and was put on hiatus after three episodes; it returned in August of 2002 for a run off of the final episodes. The third cycle, *Celebrity Mole: Hawaii* (January-February 2003) added the celebrity aspect and kept the $1 million jackpot. The final edition, *Celebrity Mole: Yucatan* aired in 2004 and had eight celebrities competing for $250,000. The overall series ran from January 9, 2001 to February 1, 2004.

Host: Anderson Cooper, Ahmad Rashad. **Celebrity Mole Hawaii Players:** Kathy Griffin, Stephen Baldwin, Corbin Bernsen, Michael Boatman, Kim Coles, Erik von Detten, Frederique van Der Wal. **Celebrity Mole Yucatan Players:** Corbin Bernsen, Tracey Gold, Angie Everhart, Dennis Rodman, Mark Curry, Keshia Knight Pulliam, Stephen Baldwin, Ananda Lewis.

6213   *Moll Flanders.* (Series; Drama; PBS; 1980). British produced program that follows the adventures of Moll Flanders, a 17th century woman who was married five times, was twelve years a prostitute, and twelve years a thief. A faithful adaptation of the novel by Daniel DeFoe. Contains nudity and adult situations.

Cast: Julia Foster *(Moll Flanders)*; Karin MacCarthy *(Meg)*; Patrick Newell *(Thomas)*; Paul Lavers *(Robin)*; Ian Ogilvy *(Humphrey Oliver)*; David Bentley *(Henry)*; Lynne Jones *(Catherine)*; Kenneth Haigh *(Jeremy Earl)*; Diana Fairfax *(Lady Verney)*; Jeremy Clyde *(Edward)*; Sheila Reid *(Jenny)*.

6214   *Molloy.* (Pilot; Comedy; Unaired; Produced for Fox in 1989). Following the death of her mother, Maude Molloy, an independent and outspoken 13-year-old girl, is sent to live with her father, Malcolm, in California. Maude's efforts to adjust to a life she finds totally different from what she had come to know living in New York City was the focal point of the original format for the series *Molloy* (see next title). Other regulars are Suzannah, Malcolm's girlfriend; Tripper and Baron, Maude's friends; and Robert, Malcolm's friend.

Cast: Mayim Bialik *(Maude Molloy)*; Robert Desiderio *(Malcolm Molloy)*; Cindy Morgan *(Suzannah Delouca)*; Ashley Maw *(Tripper)*; Bumper Robinson *(Baron)*; Matt Morero *(Robert Hutchins III)*.

6215   *Molloy.* (Series; Comedy; Fox; 1990). Molloy Martin, a pretty 13-year-old girl who attends Beverly Hills Junior High School, works professionally as an actress on the KQET-TV children's show *Wonderland.* She lives at 6113 Fullerton Drive with her father, Paul, stepmother, Lynn, half sister Courtney and half brother Jason.

Molloy has recently moved to Beverly Hills following the death of her mother and is having a difficult time adjusting to her new family, especially Courtney, "a crybaby who puts up a fuss when she gets blamed for something or doesn't get her way." Courtney, 16, attends the Beverly Hills Private School and is called by students (including girls), "the most beautiful girl" at the school. Molloy says, "Courtney is deserving of the title, but beneath all that beauty she is just an airhead." Courtney is totally devoted to herself and looking gorgeous is her number one priority.

For one so young, Molloy is quite knowledgeable and has impressive answers for anything asked of her. "I major in stuff," says Molloy. Despite Courtney's childish behavior, Molloy desperately wants to look like her "and become a woman, but without the dullard interior."

Paul, the program director of radio station KNAP, calls Molloy "Mo." Unlike Molloy, who questions everything and tries to understand what is going on, Paul seems to accept everything that happens and considers it all just a part of life. Lynn runs a business called Martin Interior Decorating. She is a carefree individual and has a lighthearted approach to life.

Simon Lansbury is the host of *Wonderland.* He plays Joey the Squirrel and feels he is worthy of better roles. He is also distressed by the fact that the kid stars get all the attention and fan mail and what fan mail he receives seems to come from "old biddies" who want him to come "and share their trees." Sara is Molly's friend.

Cast: Mayim Bialik *(Molloy Martin)*; Kevin Scannell *(Paul Martin)*; Pamela Brull *(Lynn Martin)*; Jennifer Aniston *(Courtney Martin)*; Luke Edwards *(Jason Martin)*; I.M. Hobson *(Simon Lansbury)*; Ashley Maw *(Sara)*.

6216   *The Molly Picon Show.* (Series; Variety; ABC; 1949). Comedy skits coupled with music and songs with stage and movie star Molly Picon as the host.

6217   *Mom.* (Pilot; Comedy; Unaired; Produced for Fox in 1992). Carol Ann Cooper-Kent-Canelli-Highland-Ulvik is four times widowed, virtually penniless and determined to snare a wealthy man. Carol Ann, otherwise known as Mom, has three daughters (Belinda, Bree and Nash) and is struggling to teach them her gold-digging philosophy so they too may marry rich men. The proposal, a variation of the film *How to Marry a Millionaire,* follows events in the lives of Mom and her daughters as they seek wealthy prospects.

Cast: Loni Anderson *(Carol Ann)*; Amy Yasbeck *(Belinda)*; Erin Reed *(Bree)*; Alanna Ubach *(Nash)*.

6218   *The Mom Show.* (Series; Information; WE; 2009). Real life mothers (see cast) present stories about parenting and marriage as well as offering advice regarding children, fashion, meals, nutrition and medical care.

Host: Laurie Gelman, Catherine Marion.

6219   *Moment of Decision.* (Series; Anthology; ABC; 1957). Rebroadcasts of dramas that originally aired on *Ford Theater.* See this title for information.

6220   *Moment of Fear.* (Series; Anthology; NBC; 1960; 1964; 1965). The plight of people confronted with sudden, unexpected and perilous situations. While most of the series is composed of repeat episodes from other filmed anthology series, the eight programs broadcast in 1960 were first run and featured such stars as Robert

Redford, E.G. Marshall, Laraine Day, Inger Stevens, Macdonald Carey, Fay Spain, Robert Lansing and Peter Mark Richman. Aired from July 1 to Sept. 9, 1960; May 19 to Sept. 15, 1964; and May 25 to Aug. 10, 1965.

6221 *Moment of Fear.* (Pilot; Thriller; Syn.; Feb. 1988). A proposed series of weekly suspense yarns. The pilot, shot under the title *Moment of Fear*, was re-edited as the episode "Attic Suite" and shown on *Tales from the Darkside*. It tells of an unemployed and desperate couple (Paula Trueman, Ray Baker), plagued with caring for a bedridden aunt (Brenda Vaccaro) who each devise a deadly solution for their problem.

6222 *Moment of Truth.* (Series; Drama; NBC; 1965). Events in the life of Dr. Wallace Bennett, a professor and practicing psychologist in a small college town in Canada.

Cast: Douglas Watson (*Dr. Wallace Bennett*); Louise King (*Nancy Bennett*); Lucy Warner (*Helen Gould*); Steven Levy (*Jack*); Bob Christie (*Professor Hamilton*); Lynne Gorman (*Wilma Leeds*); Toby Tarnow (*Carol*); Mira Pawluk (*Barbara Wallace*); Peter Donat (*Vince Conway*); Barbara Pierce (*Sheila*); Ivor Barry (*Dr. Russell Wingate*); Sandra Scott (*Lila*); Tom Fielding (*Steve*); Fernande Giroux (*Monique*); Chris Wiggins (*Dexter*); John Horton (*Eric*); Robert Goodier (*Mr. Leeds*); Michael Dodds (*Johny Wallace*); Anne Campbell (*Diane*); Anna Hagan (*Linda*); John Bethune (*Gil Bennett*).

6223 *The Moment of Truth.* (Series; Game; Fox; 2008). Prior to the broadcast, people who are to appear on stage are hooked up to a lie detector and asked 50 true or false type questions. Each of the responses is recorded but the subjects are not made aware of the results of their answers. On stage a player is placed in the hot seat and appears opposite friends and family members. A pyramid of six money amounts ($10,000 to $500,000) is displayed.

At the first level the player must answer six personal questions correctly (agree with the lie detector results) to win $10,000 (level two is for $25,000 and involves five questions. Level three, for $100,000 has four questions; level four, for $200,000 has three questions; level five, for $300,000 has two questions; the final level, 5, is a one question round worth $500,000.). If, at any time the player gives a false response (opposite of what the lie detector predicted) he loses what money he has. If a player feels unsure about continuing he can quit at the end of a money level and walk away with what he has.

Host: Mark L. Wahlberg. **Music:** William Anderson.

6224 *Momma the Detective.* (Pilot; Crime Drama; NBC; Jan. 19, 1981). She's a housekeeper by profession and an amateur sleuth at heart. She's Momma Sykes, the mother of Sergeant Alvin Sykes of the N.Y.P.D. and the unsold series was to relate Momma's efforts to solve crimes — despite the objections of her son. Jessie and Andy are Alvin's children.

Cast: Esther Rolle (*Momma Sykes*); Kene Holliday (*Alvin Sykes*); Claude Brooks (*Jessie Sykes*); William Walker II (*Andy Sykes*).

6225 *Momma's Boys.* (Series; Reality; NBC; 2008–2009). Thirty-two beautiful women appear and not only have to win the heart of one of three eligible bachelors but that of the boy's mother — who is there to help him choose the right girl. The program relates the conflicts between the mother's wishes and their son's desires as the sons seek the perfect mate (for him and his mother) and the woman of choice's efforts to prove herself to the boy's mother. JoJo Bojanowski, Robert Kluge and Michael Sarysz are the bachelors. Ryan Seacrest is the producer.

6226 *The Mommies.* (Series; Comedy; NBC; 1993–1995). Caryl

Kellogg lives at 13 Oak Way. Her best friend, Marilyn Larson, lives next door at 15 Oak Way. Caryl is married to Paul and is the mother of Blake and Danny. Marilyn is married to Jack; Casey and Adam are her children. The families also share a pet dog named Cosmo.

Jack is an accountant; Paul a computer trouble shooter. Marilyn works from her home as a real estate agent; Caryl, a homemaker, previously worked as a travel agent (she and Marilyn attended Montgomery High School, class of '66).

Adam, 15, attends Valley High School; Blake, Casey and Danny are enrolled in Valley Elementary School. Adam, "not stupid, just highly unmotivated," works at Jolly Meals (a fast food restaurant). Also working there is Tiffany, Adam's girlfriend, the assistant manager. She is a year older than Adam and a year behind him at Valley High. Being pretty is about the only asset Tiffany has ("people say I'm an airhead"). Marilyn calls her "the Giggler" (for her habit of giggling at everything).

Tom Booker is "Mr. Mommy." He is learning the ropes of motherhood when he loses his defense plant job and his wife, Christine, goes to work. Beth and Jason are his kids. Barbara "Babs" Valentine is a spokeswoman for Kitchen Comfort Products. She is the mother of an infant (Zachary) and "has the ability to fold a fitted sheet." She is overly organized and never lies ("I even put my correct weight on my driver's license").

Cast: Caryl Kristensen (*Caryl Kellogg*); Marilyn Kentz (*Marilyn Larson*); Robin Thomas (*Paul Kellogg*); Sam Gifaldi (*Blake Kellogg*); Ryan Merriman (*Danny Kellogg*); David Dukes (*Jack Larson*); Ashley Peldon (*Casey Larson*); Shiloh Strong (*Adam Larson*); Jennifer Blanc (*Tiffany*); Jere Burns (*Tom Booker*); Joanna Kerns (*Christine Booker*); Julia Duffy (*Barbara Valentine*).

6227 *Mommy XXX.* (Series; Reality; Internet; 2009). A profile of Demi Delia, a former Playboy playmate turned adult film star. Demi is also the mother of two teenage children (Chris, a musician, and Brandi, a straight "A" student) and very much involved in making a home for herself and family while at the same time performing in Triple X films. The program does portray Demi's life on the porn set (but no nudity or sexual activity) and is labeled by Crackle.com (where it airs) as a comedy. The program does have its very light humorous moments but is more reality than sitcom (especially, for example, when Demi undergoes breast implants to become a 36DD and suffers painful after effects. Non-upsetting aspects of the surgery are seen and Demi's pain is real, not faked). While the program was filmed with topless scenes, they are digitally altered so nothing offensive is seen. Demi's friends, adult film stars Tory Love, Alanah Rae, Carley Parker and Lexi Belle are also featured.

6228 *Mommywood.* (Series; Reality; Internet; 2009). An extension series (but broadcast only on the Internet) of the Oxygen program *Tori and Dean: Home Sweet Hollywood*. Tori Spelling, the actress daughter of TV producer Aaron Spelling, and her husband Dean McDermott, are the parents of two children, Liam and Stella. Tori is also the author of the book *Mommywood*, wherein she writes about the joys and challenges of parenting in Hollywood. Each episode of the web series is based on a chapter from the book and deals with first time mother anxieties, losing the baby weight, her relationship with her mother (Candy Spelling) and her attempts to deal with the paparazzi.

6229 *Mon Colle Knights.* (Series; Cartoon; Fox Kids; 2001-2002). Professor Hiiragi is a somewhat off-center scientist who has discovered a machine that allows travel from his world (Six Gate World) to Mon World, a world of magical creatures. His daughter, Rockna and her boyfriend, Mondo Ooya, have been assigned a special mission: travel to Mon World to find six monster items that, when combined, could connect their world with the Earth to better both worlds. Rokuna and Mondo become the Mon Colle Knights and stories relate their trek and attempts to overcome Prince Eccentro, a madman who is seeking the monster items to control both worlds. Jane Lovestar is the hamster-like monster Rockna adopts. A Japanese Anime series dubbed in English.

Voice Cast: Brianne Siddall *(Rockna Hiiragi)*; Derek Stephen Prince *(Mondo Ooya)*; Jamieson Price *(Prof. Ichiroubei Hiiragi)*; Wendee Lee *(Jane Lovestar)*; Joe Ochman *(Prince Eccentro)*.

6230   *Mona.* (Pilot; Comedy; ABC; May 12, 1987). Following his retirement from the military, Corneilius Rockwell invites his estranged sister, Mona Robinson, to a reunion in Manhattan. There, he talks Mona into using her savings to purchase a seedy hotel (the Nottingham) that he feels he can turn into a money-making venture. The unsold series, a proposed spin off from *Who's the Boss?*, was to relate Mona's efforts to protect her investment by helping Corneilius run the hotel. Other regulars are Kitty, the reservations clerk; Don, Packard and Eddie, the bellhops; and Tessie, the head bookkeeper.

Cast: Katherine Helmond *(Mona Robinson)*; James B. Sikking *(Corneilius Rockwell)*; Susan Walters *(Kitty McClaren)*; Joe Regalbuto *(Don West)*; Paul Sand *(Packard Vance)*; Robert Petkoff *(Eddie)*; Billie Bird *(Tessie)*.

6231   *Mona McCluskey.* (Series; Comedy; NBC; 1965-1966). Mona McCluskey is a beautiful Hollywood film actress. She works under the name Mona Carroll and earns $5,000 a week. She is married to Mike McCluskey, a U.S. Air Force Sergeant who makes $500 a month. Mona and Mike live in a moderately furnished two-room apartment away from the Affluent Society because Mike insists that he be the breadwinner and live on his income. Mona agrees because she loves him. Incorporating methods that are a bit deceiving, Mona struggles to supplement the strained family budget without arousing Mike's suspicions. Originally scheduled as *Presenting Mona McCluskey* and a pilot episode was filmed under that title.

Other regulars are Mr. Caldwell the studio producer; Sergeant Stan Gruzewsky, Mike's friend; Alice, Stan's girlfriend; General Crone; Jim Stanton, Crone's nephew; Margaret Kincaide, Mona's aunt; and Agatha Kincaide, Mona's aunt.

Cast: Juliet Prowse *(Mona McCluskey)*; Denny Miller *(Mike McCluskey)*; Bartlett Robinson *(Mr. Caldwell)*; Robert Strauss *(Stan Gruzewsky)*; Elena Verdugo *(Alice)*; Herbert Rudley *(General Crone)*; Sal Mineo *(Jim Stanton)*; Madge Blake *(Margaret Kincaise)*; Dorothy Neumann *(Agatha Kincaide)*. **Theme Song Adaptation:** "Yes Sir, That's My Baby" by Sonny Burke.

6232   *Monchhichis.* (Series; Cartoon; CBS; 1983-1984). Monchhia is a city in the clouds above very tall trees. Here its inhabitants, the monkey-like Monchhichis, struggle to preserve their peaceful lives by battling the Grumplins, the evil creatures who want to enslave them.

Voice Cast: Bob Arbogast *(Songs)*; Peter Cullen *(Shreeker/Snitchiff/Gunker)*; Laurie Faso *(Yabbet/Fasset/Scumgor)*; Ellen Gerstell *(Taboo)*; Sidney Miller *(Horrg)*; Robert Morse *(Moncho)*; Frank Nelson *(Wizzar)*; Laurel Page *(Kyla)*; Frank Welker *(Patchitt)*.

6233   *Monday Theater.* (Pilot; NBC; 1970). The overall title for five pilot films that were produced for the 1969-70 season. See: *The Boys, The Kowboys, Me and Benjy, Run, Jack, Run* and *Southern Fried.*

6234   *The Mondo Beyondo Show.* (Pilot; Comedy; HBO; Mar. 19, 1988). Unusual (weird) comedy acts that are presented by Mondo Beyondo, a sexy but off-center woman who hosts a public access channel program called *The Mondo Beyondo Show*. Also known as *Mondo Beyondo* and *Bette Midler's Mondo Beyondo.*

Host: Bette Midler *(as Mondo Beyondo)*. **Music:** Mark Shanin.

6235   *The Money List.* (Series; Game; GSN; 2009). Four players compete, divided into two teams of two. A money list category is revealed (for example, "Brad Pitt Movies," "Saturday Night Live Male Cast Members," "Academy Award Winning Movies"). One team (flip of coin, first show; winning team thereafter) predicts how many subjects they can name that fit the category. The challengers can outbid them or challenge them to do what they predict. The team at play must give the predicted number of subjects without any mistakes. Correctly filling out the money list (succeeding at the prediction) awards the team one win; failure awards the challengers the win. The first team to score two wins receives $25,000 and the chance to compete again for $50,000.

Host: Fred Roggin. **Announcer:** Stefan Ashford Frank. **Music:** Will Slater.

6236   *The Money Maze.* (Series; Game; ABC; 1973-1974). Two married couples compete. One member of each team stands before a large maze; the other members compete in a series of question-and-answer rounds. The first team to score eight points is the winner and plays the Money Maze. Five large boxes, each of which contains one figure of $10,000, are lit. The player must make his way through the maze, touch as many boxes as possible, and return to the starting point — all within sixty seconds. Money is awarded based on the number of boxes touched and what they total — $1, $10, $100, $1,000 or $10,000.

Host: Nick Clooney. **Announcer:** Alan Kalter

6237   *Money Talks.* (Series; Erotica; Playboy; 2009). Will average (but attractive) women strip and pose nude on camera? *Money Talks* seeks to find those women who will not only do that but engage in softcore sexual activities . The program is based in Florida. When a perspective subject is spotted she is approached and offered money to flash or pose nude; even more money to perform in what translates as a drawn out sex act, or "the most outrageous, sexy, out-of-this-world stunts you have ever seen." A girl, identified only as Nadine, hosts.

6238   *Monica: Still Standing.* (Series; Reality; BET; 2009). A profile of Monica, a singer, as she tackles the spotlight while at the same time struggling to be a full time mother to her two young sons.

6239   *The Mo'Nique Show.* (Series; Talk; BET; 2009). "A VIP access to the hottest party on television" is the tagline for a late night cable program hosted by actress-comedienne Mo'Nique and featuring, in addition to celebrity interviews and performances "by the hottest musical artists in the game," humorous segments that pay homage to legendary stars.

Host: Mo'Nique.

6240   *Mo'Nique's Fat Chance.* (Series; Reality; Oxygen; 2008). Ten pretty, plus size women compete in beauty contest–like challenges for the opportunity to win $50,000 in cash and the title "Miss F.A.T." Actress-Comedienne Mo'Nique hosts.

6241   *The Monk.* (Pilot; Crime Drama; ABC; Oct. 21, 1969). Gus Monk is a tough private detective with few friends who wanders from state to state (with his cat Aristotle) minding other people's business. The proposal was to relate his exploits as he tackles dangerous cases.

Cast: George Maharis *(Gus Monk)*.

6242   *Monk*. (Series; Crime Drama; USA; 2002–2009). Adrian Monk is a brilliant detective with the 14th Division of the San Francisco Police Department. In 1998, when his wife Trudy, an investigative reporter for *The Examiner*, is killed in a mysterious car bombing and the case goes unsolved, Adrian develops a rare anxiety disorder that makes him germ phobic and afraid of virtually everything. The condition immediately interferes with Adrian's work and he is given a 315 temporary suspension (a psychological discharge). Adrian regularly sees a psychiatrist (Dr. Charles Kroger; later replaced by Dr. Neven Bell) and is aided by his full time nurse, Sharona Fleming (the divorced mother of young Benjy). Adrian needs to keep busy, but he is deemed too unstable to return to the force. With Sharona's help, Adrian begins a private consulting business and together they set out to help people in trouble (and most often helping police Captain Leland Stottlemeyer, Adrian's former superior, solve crimes).

Adrian has an encyclopedic knowledge of strange and unusual facts. He has a photographic memory and the deductive skills of Sherlock Holmes. Later episodes feature Natalie Teeger, a single mother of 13-year-old Julie, as Monk's assistant when Sharona resigns (in the episode "Mr. Monk and the Red Herring," Sharona remarries her ex-husband and returns to New Jersey. Natalie is a widow [of Mitch, a Navy pilot] who first meets Adrian when she hires him to help her solve a mystery involving a break in her home where nothing was taken. Natalie worked as a waitress in a sleazy bar and accepted Adrian's offer to be his assistant when he found he could tolerate her). Stories follow Monk as he uses his phobias to their best advantage — solving crimes (although most people see him as someone who should be in a mental institution). Julie attends Ashton Jr. High School.

Monk finds closure in the final episode ("Mr. Monk and the End"). To condense a long story: In 1982, fifteen years before she met Adrian, Trudy was a student at Berkeley. She had an affair with her law professor (Ethan Rickover) and became pregnant. To avoid publicity, Ethan hired a midwife (Wendy) to deliver the baby. The baby girl was placed with an adoptive family but Trudy, who never saw the baby, was told she only lived for nine minutes. Twelve years later, when Ethan is appointed as a judge, Wendy attempts to blackmail him. Ethan kills her and buries her in the backyard of his home next to a sun dial. He then arranges to have Trudy killed via the car explosion. Monk learns, through a videotape he found that Trudy made days before she was killed, that she was working on a story about Ethan. Monk, however, hasn't enough evidence to nab Ethan — until he uncovers a newspaper story about Ethan's appointment. The article, accompanied by a picture of Ethan standing by that sun dial, and a statement that he would never sell his house, intrigues Monk. Armed with a gun, Monk approaches Ethan and orders him to dig up the ground surrounding the sun dial. Leland, tipped off by Natalie that Monk has gone after Ethan, arrives just in time to see Monk nail Trudy's killer. Wendy's skeletal remains are found and the telltale clue was the tree that overshadowed the sun dial — "Who would place a sun dial under a tree? Later, Leland has some good news for Monk — he tracked down Trudy's daughter — Molly Evans, a movie reviewer for the *East Bay Chronicle* in nearby Monterey. Adrian and Molly immediately bond. Molly and Adrian will now be a part of each other's lives and Monk and Natalie continue in their capacity as special consultants to the police department. It is also revealed that Lt. Randall Disher, Leland's assistant, has resigned to accept a position as police chief of Summit, New Jersey. Karen is Leland's wife, a documentary film maker. Randy Newman performs the theme, "It's Jungle Out There."

Cast: Tony Shalhoub (*Adrian Monk*); Bitty Schram (*Sharona Fleming*); Kane Ritchote (*Benjy Fleming*); Ted Levine (*Capt. Leland Stottlemeyer*); Traylor Howard (*Natalie Teeger*); Emmy Clarke (*Julie Teeger*); Stanley Kamel (*Dr. Charles Kroger*); Jason Gray-Stanford (*Lt. Randall Disher*); Hector Elizondo (*Dr. Neven Bell*); Glenne Headly

(*Karen Stottlemeyer, Leland's wife*); Stelline Rusich (*Trudy Monk; flashbacks*); Melora Hardin (*Trudy Monk; last episode*); John Turturro (*Ambrose Monk, Adrian's brother*); Aaron Wayne Hill (*Young Monk, flashbacks*); Craig T. Nelson (*Ethan Rickover*); Mary Beth Evans (*Molly Evans*).

6243   *The Monkees*. (Series; Comedy; NBC; 1966–1968). The apartment at 1334 Beachwood Street in a town called Centerville is occupied by Micky Dolenz, Davy Jones, Mike Nesmith and Peter Tork, a rock group known as the Monkees (their address is also given as 1438 Beachwood Street, Los Angeles). A life-size dummy named Mr. Snyder also lives with the band. Davy plays tambourine; Micky, the drums; Peter, keyboard and bass guitar; and Mike, guitar. They have recorded such songs as "I'm a Believer," "Last Train to Clarksville" and "Daydream Believer" but are constantly out of work and seeking gigs.

Davy, born in England, is the most sensible member of the group. Micky was born in Burbank and was called "Goo Goo Eyes" by his mother. In one episode, Micky mentions that "I haven't been to the circus since I was a kid" and proceeds to sing the theme to the TV series *Circus Boy* (in which he starred as a kid under the name Mickey Braddock). Peter was born in Connecticut and is shy around girls. Mike was born in Texas and was an Eagle Scout as a kid. Stories relate their outrageous efforts to find work and become top name recording starts. See also *The New Monkees*.

Cast: Davy Jones (*Himself*); Micky Dolenz (*Himself*); Mike Nesmith (*Himself*); Peter Tork (*Himself*).

6244   *Monopoly*. (Series; Game; ABC; 1988). Three players compete and attempt to acquire a monopoly by answering questions. The Parker Brothers game of Monopoly is displayed in a large format on stage. A question is read. The first player to buzz in and answer it wins one of the properties on the board and its cash value is placed in his bank (an incorrect response deletes that amount of money). Four such rounds are played and the player with the highest cash score acquires a monopoly and wins the game.

Host: Mike Reilly. **Co-Host:** Kathy Davis, Michelle Nicholas, Kathy Karges. **Announcer:** Charlie O'Donnell.

6245   *The Monroes*. (Series; Adventure; ABC; 1966-1967). The year is 1875. With a hope of beginning a new life in Wyoming, Albert and Mary Monroe and their children, Clayt (age 18), Kathleen (16), twins Jefferson and Fennimore (12) and Amy (six), leave their farm in Illinois and head west — to find an unknown valley that Albert laid claim to in 1866.

After a hazardous trek through treacherous country, the Monroes reach the banks of the Snake River, the last crossing before the valley is within reach. Although all precautions are taken, including using float logs for the wagon, a rope becomes loose and pulls Mary into the perilous water. Albert dives in after her, and in a tragic moment both are lost. Suddenly the children are orphaned and Clayt, the oldest, takes charge and proceeds to find the "one valley Pa had marked with a pile of rocks. All I had to guide me was a map Pa had made ten years before." After several days, landscape features begin to appear that fit the map. Soon, they are in "Pa's Valley." "Where are we?" asks Amy. "We're home," a tearful Kathleen responds. "The rocks were just where Pa said." As Clayt lifts them, he finds Albert's U.S. Army belt buckle and his claim to the land: "Now it was ours to root down, to hold if we could."

Shortly after, when Clayt files a claim for the land in Greenwood City, he meets Barney Wales, a roughneck horse rancher who claims the valley is his. (Because of the Monroes' claim, his land now borders on "the dry creek"; he needs the Monroe's land, which is on "the new creek," for its water.) Barney runs horses, not cattle and requires the water; he becomes a constant threat to the Monroes survival as he seeks to get what he wants. Stories follow the efforts of the Monroe children to establish their parent's dream of a new life. "It's just as Pa said, if it were easy, it wouldn't be worth having."

Clayt calls Kathleen "Kath"; Amy calls Kathleen "Sister." Jefferson is nicknamed "Big Twin" and Fennimore, who is slightly shorter, "Little Twin." The family has a white dog named Snow, and the valley they have settled in is called Bear Valley.

Major Mapoy is the Englishman who operates the Mapoy Cattle Company; Jim is the renegade Sioux Indian the Monroes befriended; John Bradford is Mapoy's trail scout; Ruel Jaxon, Sleeve and John Bradford work for Major Mapoy. Sleeve and Ruel are friends of the Monroes, despite some initial scrapes. Dalton Wales and Billy Dan Wales are Barney's rowdy sons; Lorna Wales is Barney's beautiful, mute daughter, who, despite her father's attitude, is sympathetic to the Monroes.

Cast: Michael Anderson, Jr. *(Clayt Monroe)*; Barbara Hershey *(Kathleen Monroe)*; Tammy Locke *(Amy Monroe)*; Keith Schultz *(Jefferson Monroe)*; Kevin Schultz *(Fennimore Monroe)*; Ron Soble *(Jim)*; Liam Sullivan *(Major Mapoy)*; James Westmoreland *(Ruel Jaxon)*; Ben Johnson *(Sleeve)*; Buck Taylor *(John Bradford)*; Russ Conway *(Albert Monroe; first episode)*; Marilyn Moe *(Mary Monroe; first episode)*; Robert Middleton *(Barney Wales)*; James Brolin *(Dalton Wales)*; Tom O'Kelly *(Billy Dan Wales)*; Lisa Jack *(Lorna Wales)*.

6246   *The Monroes.* (Series; Drama; ABC; 1995). The Monroes are a powerful and ambitious family whose patriarch, John Monroe, is seeking the position of governor of the state (Washington, D.C.). John is married to Kathryn and is the father of five children: William (married to Anne), Greer, James, Gabriel and Ruby. The Monroes are a family who do not play by the rules; stories relate the sex scandals, the family betrayals, the bribery and anything else that can cause conflict within the family.

Cast: William Devane *(John Monroe)*; Susan Sullivan *(Kathryn Monroe)*; David Andrews *(William Monroe)*; Lynn Clark *(Anne Monroe)*; Steve Eckholdt *(James Monroe)*; Tracy Griffith *(Ruby Monroe)*; Cecil Hoffman *(Greer Monroe)*; Tristan Tait *(Gabriel Monroe)*.

6247   *Monster Allergy.* (Series; Cartoon; WB Kids; 2006–2007). Zick is a 12-year-old boy burdened by allergies. One allergy, however, is different than all others and enables him to see the invisible monsters that live among us. With the help of his friend, Elena and talking cat Timothy, Zick sets out to help keep people safe from the unseen beasts that seek to do harm.

Voice Cast: Kaley Cuoco *(Elena)*; David Kaufman *(Zick)*; Sam Vincent *(Timothy)*; Candi Milo *(Zick's mother)*.

6248   *Monster Buster Club.* (Series; Cartoon; Jetix; 2008). Single Town is an Earth city that is plagued by trouble-making aliens. In an effort to protect Single Town, Cathy Smith, a girl who appears to be 10 years old, and her grandfather, Mr. Smith, travel from their planet (Rhapsodia) to Earth and establish the Monster Buster Club. Cathy, who is actually 7,000 years old, recruits three Earth children (Samantha, Danny and Chris) and together they set out to stop the alien rampage.

Voice Cast: Andrea Libman *(Cathy)*; Anna Cummer *(Samantha)*; Matt Hill *(Danny)*; Sam Vincent *(Chris)*; Sonja Ball, Ian Corlett, Rick Jones, Matt Hill, Tabitha St. Germain, Michael Yarmush.

6249   *Monster Force.* (Series; Cartoon; Syn.; 1994). Monsters, based on those that appeared in Universal pictures in the 1930s and 40s, are recreated to wreck havoc while seeking to escape from the Monster Force, a group of college students who have banned together to stop the rampage. Dracula leads the monsters, which also include Frankenstein (and his wife, Shelly Frank), Bela the Werewolf, Hotep the Mummy and the Creature from the Black Lagoon.

Voice Cast: Howard Jerome *(Frankenstein)*; Paul Haddad *(Wolfman)*; Caroly Larson *(Shelley Frank)*; David Hewlett *(Lance McGruder)*; Lawrence Bayne *(Dr. Reed Crawley)*; Philip Akin *(Tripp Hansen)*; Robert Bockstael *(Dracula)*.

6250   *Monster in My Pocket.* (Pilot; Cartoon; ABC; Oct. 23, 1993). In a prison on Monster Mountain in Transylvania, the evil Vampire is being guarded by the good monsters (the Invisible Man, the Wolfman, Big Ed — a Frankenstein type, and the Mummy) when he casts a shrinking spell to escape. The spell backfires, shrinking Monster Mountain and blowing it all the way to Los Angeles. Vampire and his evil assistants, Medusa and the Swamp Beast, escape, but they, like their pursuers (the good monsters) are now only one inch tall. Hoping to find help, the good monsters seek out Edgar Raven, a world-famous horror writer who they feel will understand their predicament. Edgar, however, is not at home when they call, but his ten-year-old daughter, Carrie, an avid horror fan, is and agrees to help them recapture Vampire, who now wants to rule the world. (Carrie carries the good monsters around with her in her shirt pocket; both sides are seeking a growth formula to restore them to their normal height.)

Voice Cast: April Winchell *(Carrie Raven)*; Rob Paulsen *(Wolfman)*; Stuart K. Robinson *(Big Ed)*; Dina Sherman *(Medusa)*; Frank Welker *(Swamp Beast)*; Marvin Kaplan *(Mummy)*; Paxton Whitehead *(Vampire/Invisible Man)*.

6251   *Monster Quest.* (Series; Reality; History; 2007). Are ghosts, werewolves, vampires, Big Foot and other such legendary "monsters" real or just folklore? The program explores the lore with an attempt to distinguish fact from fiction. Stan Bernard narrates.

6252   *The Monster Squad.* (Series; Comedy; NBC; 1976-1977). While working as a night watchman at Fred's Wax Museum, Walt, a criminology student, activates a secret crime computer he has invented and, through its oscillating vibrations, brings to life three legendary monsters — Frankenstein, Dracula and the Werewolf. Once wax, but now alive, the monsters hope to make up for their past misgivings by helping people. Stories follow Walt as he and his monster assistants attempt to solve crimes.

Cast: Fred Grandy *(Walt)*; Henry Polic II *(Count Dracula)*; Buck Kartalian *(Bruce W. Wolf)*; Michael Lane *(Frank N. Stein)*; Paul Smith *(Officer McMac Mac)*.

6253   *Monsters.* (Series; Anthology; Syn.; 1988–1991). An aerial view of a neighborhood begins the program. As the camera zooms into a single house, a family is seen inside, discussing what program to watch on TV. The family members are soon revealed to be unearthly creatures dressed as humans. The TV set is on, and as the mother realizes their favorite show is on she exclaims "It's *Monsters*." As her daughter remarks, "Shhh, it's starting," her father turns to the camera and laughs in a sinister tone. Out of the ordinary tales of mayhem that involve seeming ordinary people in perilous situations brought about by greed or deceit. Whether they survive or succumb to a gruesome end is the gimmick of each episode. Richard P. Rubinstein and Jan Saunders are the producers.

6254   *The Monte Carlo Show.* (Series; Variety; Syn.; 1980). American and European variety acts are showcased in a program taped in France.

Host: Patrick Wayne. **Regulars:** Les Girls *(dancers)*; Andre Cahoune. **Music:** Dennis McCarthy.

6255   *The Montefuscos.* (Series; Comedy; NBC; 1975). The trials and tribulations of three generations of Montefuscos, a large Italian-American family living in New Canaan, Connecticut. Tony is the father, a painter. He is married to Rose and they are the parents of Frankie, Joseph, Nunzio and Angelina. Tony is a dentist and married to Theresa; they are the parents of Carmine, Gina and Jerome. Joseph is a priest; Nunzio is an actor; Angelina is married to Jim and they are the parents of Anthony.

Cast: Joseph Sirola (*Tony Montefusco*); Naomi Stevens (*Rose Montefusco*); Ron Carey (*Frankie Montefusco*); Phoebe Dorin (*Theresa Montefusco*); John Aprea (*Joseph Montefusco*); Sal Viscuso (*Nunzio Montefusco*); Linda Dano (*Angelina Cooney*); Bill Cort (*Jim Cooney*); Jeffrey Palladini (*Carmine Montefusco*); Dominique Pinassi (*Gina Montefusco*); Robby Paris (*Jerome Montefusco*); Damon Raskin (*Anthony Cooney*).

6256   *The Montel Williams Show.* (Series; Talk; Syn.; 1991). A distinguished daily talk program that presents controversial topics but not in a wild and racy way (like *The Jerry Springer Show*). The program also has professionals on hand (like psychotherapist Dr. Patricia Johnson) to help people whose situations are overwhelming to them.

Host: Montel Williams. **Psychotherapist:** Maria Setaro, Patricia Johnson.

6257   *Montgomery's Summer Stock.* (Series; Anthology; NBC; 1952–1956). Original dramatic productions with a regular cast of performers that aired as the summer replacement for *Robert Montgomery Presents*. Aired from July 14 to Aug. 25, 1952; July 6 to Aug. 24, 1953; June 28 to Sept. 13, 1954; July 4 to Sept. 5, 1955; and July 2 to Sept. 3, 1956. Produced by Robert Montgomery.

Regular Performers: Elizabeth Montgomery, Vaughn Taylor, Jan Miner, Judy Parrish, John Newland, Margaret Hayes, Anne Seymour, Cliff Robertson, Charles Drake, House Jameson, Augusta Dabney, Dorothy Blackburn, Eric Sinclair, Mary K. Wells, John Gibson, Tom Middleton.

6258   *Monty.* (Series; Comedy; Fox; 1994). Incidents in the life of Monty Richardson, the politically right wing host of *Right Speak with Monty Richardson,* a talk show on Long Island's Channel 35. Other regulars are Fran, his wife; Dave and Greg, their sons; Clifford, Monty's announcer; and Rita, Monty's producer.

Cast: Henry Winkler (*Monty Richardson*); Kate Burton (*Fran Richardson*); David Krumholtz (*Dave Richardson*); David Schwimmer (*Greg Richardson*); Joyce Guy (*Rita Simon*); Tom McGowan (*Clifford Walker*).

6259   *Monty Nash.* (Series; Adventure; Syn.; 1971). Monty Nash is a sophisticated U.S. government special agent who handles top secret White House affairs. He operates by his own set of rules and his only responsibility is to resolve the situations that the President deems are threat to the security of the nation. Stories, based on the spy yarns by Richard Jessup, relate Monty's highly secretive case assignments and efforts to resolve them with as little or no publicity.

Cast: Harry Guardino (*Monty Nash*).

6260   *Monty Python: Almost the Truth — The Lawyers Cut.* (Series; Retrospective; IFC; 2009). Clips from the British series *Monty Python's Flying Circus* are combined with interviews with cast members to recall a series whose unique comedy changed the face of skit shows beginning in 1969.

Original Cast Members: John Cleese, Terry Gilliam, Michael Palin, Terry Jones, Eric Idle, Carol Cleveland. Archival footage is used for the late Graham Chapman. **Guests:** Seth Green, Simon Pegg, Tim Roth, Dan Aykroyd, Russell Brand, Steve Coogan, Eddie Izzard, Hugh Hefner, Jimmy Fallon, Neil Innes, Julian Doyle, Tara Jayn, John Goldstone, Andre Jacquemin, Brett Schlank.

6261   *Monty Python's Flying Circus.* (Series; Comedy; PBS; 1974). An absolutely meaningless title for a program of tasteless, uneven, and insane material that is ingeniously interwoven into an intellectual and entertaining program. Produced in England.

Cast: John Cleese, Graham Chapman, Eric Idle, Terry Gilliam, Terry Jones, Michael Palin. **Regulars:** Carol Cleveland, Donna Reading, Katy Wayech, Dick Vosburgh, Rita Davis, Niki Howorth, Sandra Richards, Ian Davidson, The Fred Tomalson Singers.

6262   *Moolah Beach.* (Series; Reality; Fox Family; 2001). *Survivor* for teenagers (as it was described) that has twelve teenagers competing in Hawaii for a $25,000 cash prize. The teens are divided into six two-member teams (the Red, Purple, Orange, Blue, Yellow and Green). While in no way as grueling as *Survivor*, the show does challenge the teams to use their wits to unravel clues to determine the whereabouts of the money (hidden in an Hawaiian idol). Teams that fail to complete a challenge are banished from the island (eliminated) by the Tiki God. J.D. Roth hosts.

6263   *Moon Over Miami.* (Series; Crime Drama; NBC; 1993). The Walter Tatum Detective Agency, also called Walter Tatum, Inc., is a private investigative firm located at 668 Strand in South Beach in Miami, Florida. Walter Tatum owns the agency; Gwen Cross assists him.

Walter was raised by his grandparents, Nate and Adelaide Tatum since he was two years old, at which time his parents were killed in a plane crash. Walter was fascinated by police and detective shows on television and this influenced his decision to become a lawyer to help people. One summer while working as an apprentice for the Legal Aid Society, Walter's life changed. He saw private detective Gavin Mills (Elliott Gould) help an old lady get her hot water turned back on. The detective did more for the lady than a whole team of lawyers. Walter quit law school and became an apprentice to Mills. He later opened his own agency.

Gwenevere, called Gwen, is the spoiled daughter of Arthur Cross, a wealthy businessman. Arthur has babied Gwen all her life. When he felt the time was right, he arranged a marriage for her — to a man Gwen disliked. Feeling that "My life has no meaning," Gwen refused to get married and deserted her father and fiancé. In an effort to find Gwen, Cross hires Walter Tatum. Walter finds Gwen, but takes her side and tells Cross he is unable to find her. Gwen, without any money and desperately in need of a job, finds employment as Walter's receptionist. She later doubles as Walter's investigator.

Gwen adapts quickly to her new life style but fears her father will one day find her and she will be forced to go back to live a life she hates. The series ended abruptly three months after its premiere with Gwen's relationship with her father still uncertain. She and Walter began a relationship, but this too was left unclear.

Cast: Bill Campbell (*Walter Tatum*); Ally Walker (*Gwen Cross*); Chelcie Ross (*Arthur Cross*).

6264   *Moonlight.* (Pilot; Adventure; CBS; Sept. 14, 1982). When Lenny Barbella, a deliveryman for The House of Wu, a Chinese restaurant in New York City, witnesses a murder, he is secretly recruited by the U.S. government as a spy to help capture the terrorist. When he does, he begins his double life as a spy and deliveryman and the proposal was to relate his fumbling attempts to fulfill his assignments. Other regulars are Thomas Marshall Bibb (a.k.a. Mr. White), Lenny's superior; Clifford Wu, the restaurant owner; and Daphne Wu, Clifford's daughter.

Cast: Robert Desiderio (*Lenny Barbella*); William Prince (*Thomas Marshall Bibb*); Benson Fong (*Clifford Wu*); Rosalind Chao (*Daphne Wu*).

6265   *Moonlight.* (Series; Drama; CBS; 2007–2008). Mick St. John is a private detective based in Los Angeles. He is charming and appears to be about thirty years old — an age he has been for 60 years. In 1947, Mick fell in love with a girl named Coraline who, unknown to him, was a 300-year-old vampire. On their wedding night Coraline turned Mick into a vampire and ever since he has been living a dual life: vampire by day; "normal person" by night (Coraline disappeared shortly after their marriage). An incident 18 years ago changed Mick's life: he saved the life of a child (Beth Turner) and found he no longer wanted to feed on humans for nourishment — nor did he want the embodiment of a vampire. He turned his back on the traditional vampire lifestyle to help humans in trouble. All is progressing well for Mick until he and Beth accidentally cross paths. Beth is now an Internet investigative reporter (for Buzz Wire) and Mick has feelings for her that he can't pursue without revealing who he really is (in later episodes, Beth, who has faint recollections of the man who saved her, discovers Mick's secret when she sees him drinking blood — and vows to keep his secret when she also learns it was he who saved her. Mick acquires his blood in drip-like hospital bags "from a friend"). Stories follow Mick as he uses his vampire abilities to help people (and Beth with her stories). Josef, said to be the oldest living vampire (400), is Mick's friend; Guillermo is the morgue attendant who steals blood from the deceased for himself and other vampires; Lt. Carl Davis is Smith's police department contact; Logan is the vampire computer hacker who helps Mick. Coraline Duvall was a courtesan in 18th century France. She reappears in Mick's life in 2007 as Morgan — who appears to be human, claiming to have found a cure for vampirism (something Mick is seeking to obtain from her).

Cast: Alex O'Loughlin (*Mick St. John*); Sophia Myles (*Beth Turner*); Jason Dohring (*Josef Kostan*); Shannyn Sossamon (*Coraline Duvall*); Jack Vargas (*Guillermo Gasol*); Brian T. White (*Carl Davis*); David Blue (*Logan Griffen*).

6266   *Moonlighting.* (Series; Crime Drama; ABC; 1985–1989). Blue Moon Investigations is a Los Angeles–based private detective organization owned by Maddie Hayes. David Addison is her chief investigator and the agency's manager. Agnes DiPesto is the agency's receptionist; and Herbert Viola is Agnes's romantic interest and the agency's bookkeeper.

Madeline, who prefers to be called Maddie, was a beautiful and sophisticated model who suddenly found herself penniless when her business manager embezzled her funds. With no intent on working for a living, Maddie begins to sell off her business interests, one of which is a detective agency called City of Angels Investigations. Fearful of losing his job, David sweet talks Maddie into saving the company. They become partners and lovers in the reorganized Blue Moon Investigations, also called the Blue Moon Detective Agency.

Maddie is said to be one of the world's most glamorous and most photographed models. She was born in Chicago on October 11 and as a child had a sheep dog named Sport. Her face has graced the covers of such magazines as *Fashion, Glamour, Vanity Fair* and *Vogue* and she appeared in television commercials as the Blue Moon Shampoo Girl.

David was born in Los Angeles on November 27. He is a graduate of UCLA and is optimistic about everything. He constantly jokes, makes lewd sexual remarks and sings whenever the opportunity permits, even when it doesn't. He calls Maddie "Blondie Blonde" and says, "I'm a capitalist — I take my capital wherever I can get it." "Do bears bare? Do bees be?" is his catchphrase.

Maddie is totally honest and forthright; she believes in people despite what has happened to her. David is immature, deceitful and totally distrustful of people. He'll take any case as long as it means money and often goes behind Maddie's back to find clients. Maddie and David constantly bicker about everything, especially the agency, which appears to be a losing proposition for Maddie. "Addison, we need a client, a client we can depend on; a bread and butter client who can help us pay our light bill." David insists that "we have clients" and "we must create our own opportunities. We're sitting on a money machine; we only have to figure out how to turn it on." Maddie feels just the opposite — "We're standing on the decks of the *Titanic*. No one calls, no one comes in and it's bankrupting me. Why am I living this life? I don't deserve this!" Maddie's first sigh of relief came in the episode "Portrait of Maddie" when the agency showed its first profit of $2,035.76.

Despite Maddie's complaints, David does find clients — all of whom Maddie finds unsettling. She especially hates infidelity cases because they are too full of deception and dirt. She also complains about the clients who walk in off the street: "I should have known when a client walks in off the street she'd be nuts" (for example, a girl claiming to be a Leprechaun who hires them to find her pot of gold).

A series like *Moonlighting* comes along once in a blue moon. It was something different at the time but production problems abounded and eventually caused its cancellation. When a new episode could be had, it was heavily promoted by ABC. Despite the fact that Maddie and David have nothing in common, they were brought together in the final few episodes of the 1986-87 season. The following season finds Maddie returning to her parents home in Chicago to sort out her relationship with David. Here, she discovers she is pregnant (to reflect Cybill's real life pregnancy with twins). Maddie had been unfaithful to David and was not sure if the baby was David's or her friend Sam Crawford (Mark Harmon). In a strange turn of events, Maddie marries Walter Bishop (Dennis Dugan), a man she met on a train. The episode, "A Womb with a View," suggested that David is the father.

"Blue Moon Detective Agency. If persons are missing; if objects are lost, we'll find them for you at a reasonable cost" or "Blue Moon Investigations. Get in some trouble, we'll be there on the double. Wife a philanderer, don't worry, we'll handle her" are but two of the many phrases Agnes uses to answer the agency's phones. Agnes talks in rhymes and lives at 633 Hope Street, Apartment 723. Eva Marie Saint and Robert Webber appeared as Maddie's wealthy parents, Virginia and Alexander Hayes. Paul Sorvino was David's father, David Addison, Sr.; and Imogene Coca played Agnes's mother, Clara DiPesto. Al Jarreau performs the theme, "Moonlighting."

Cast: Cybill Shepherd (*Maddie Hayes*); Bruce Willis (*David Addison*); Allyce Beasley (*Agnes DiPesto*); Curtis Armstrong (*Herbert Viola*).

6267   *The Moonman Connection.* (Series; Variety; Syn.; 1979). A disco version of *American Bandstand* wherein young adults dance to disco music.

Host: Moonman-Bacote. **Co-Host:** Alfie Williams.

6268   *Moral Court.* (Series; Drama; Syn.; 2000). People with a moral issue appear before a judge. The accuser speaks first and states why he brought the accused to court (for performing an act that he considers immoral). The accused then speaks and states why he believes he was not immoral. Following the statements and questioning by the judge, a verdict, based on the moral aspects of the issue, is rendered. If the judge finds for the accuser, a monetary award (up to $2,000) is ordered to be paid by the accused; vice versa if the accuser was wrong for bringing the case to Moral Court — "Where it pays to be right."

Judge: Larry Elder. **Bailiff:** Russell Brown. **Court Reporter:** Vivian Guzman.

6269 *More Patience.* (Pilot; Comedy; Unaired; Produced for Fox in 2006). Patience Moore is a New York–based therapist with her own share of personal problems. The proposal was to follow Patience as she struggles to keep her private and professional lives separate. A prior pilot was produced by Fox in 2000 with Mary McCormack as Patience Moore.

Cast: Jennifer Esposito (*Patience Moore*); Bianca Kajlich (*Mia*); Scott McNairy (*Jake*).

6270 *The More Things Change.* (Pilot; Comedy; Unaired; Produced for ABC in 2007). Friends since grade school and now in their thirties, Rick, Wayne, Nesby and Blair have seen each other through thick and thin. Blair is the most successful, with a net worth of over $13 million; Wayne has had relationship success, marrying the girl of his dreams; Rick has had emotional success, just coming to terms with the fact that he is gay; and Nesby, the least successful, appears to enjoy his friends' success. Everything the friends shared made them who they are today and the proposal was to relate the events that test and keep their friendship.

Cast: Chris Johnson (*Rick*); Reno Wilson (*Reno*); Tom Parker (*Blair*); Paulo Costanzo (*Nesby*); Sasha Barrese (*Madeline*); Aimee Garcia (*Diana*).

6271 *More to Love.* (Series; Reality; Fox; 2009). Twenty plus-size women vie for the affection of a 300-pound "husky hunk" in a heavy people take-off on ABC's *The Bachelor* (both of which are created by producer Mike Fleiss). The bachelor, Luke Conley, is a real estate broker who is in the market for a girlfriend with a long term goal of love and marriage. The women (pretty, but in the 200–300 pound range) are really not what Conley wants ("large women with curves and meat on their bones") as most of them admit they hate being big and have tried but failed to lose weight. With nothing new actually here, Conley meets (dates) each of the women and eliminates those he feels are not right for him. The last episode reveals the one he chooses as the girl he feels is right for him (this girl can reject him if she so pleases). Emme, a plus-size fashion model, hosts.

6272 *The Morecambe and Wise Show.* (Series; Comedy; Syn.; 1980). Adult oriented skits that satirize everyday life.

Host: Eric Morecambe, Ernie Wise. **Regulars:** Ann Hamilton, Kenny Ball, Peter Hansen.

6273 *Morel Orel.* (Series; Cartoon; Adult Swim; 2005–2008). Moralton is fictional state that is in the exact center of the United States with its church in the exact center of Moralton. Orel Puppington, a student at Alfred G. Diorama Elementary School, is the son of Clay Puppington, a man who lives by the Protestant Christian Moral Code and a man who seeks to implement this code on his son. Stories follow Orel as he tries to follow a code he really doesn't understand and the mishaps that result by doing so. Clay, the Mayor of Moralton, is a drunk who is also abusive to Orel. Bloberta is Orel's seemingly indifferent mother; Shapey is Orel's younger, spoiled brother; the Reverend Putty is the town pastor; Stephanie is his punk rock lesbian daughter and the owner of a sex store.

Voice Cast: Carolyn Lawrence (*Orel Puppington*); Brita Phillips (*Bloberta Puppington*); Scott Adsit (*Clay Puppington*); Tigger Stamatopoulos (*Shapey Puppington*); William Salvers (*the Rev. Rod Putty*).

6274 *The Morey Amsterdam Show.* (Series; Variety; CBS; DuMont; 1948–1950). The Silver Swan Café provides the setting for a program of music, songs and comedy from a cast of regulars and the guests who happen to stop by for dinner and entertainment. Morey is the restaurant owner; Newton is the waiter; Rosemary the singer; and Jacqueline the cigarette girl. Aired on CBS (Dec. 17, 1948 to Mar. 7, 1949) and DuMont (April 21, 1949 to Dec. 12, 1950).

Cast: Morey Amsterdam (*Morey*); Art Carney (*Newton*); Rosemary Clooney (*Rosemary*); Jacqueline Susann (*Jacqueline*). **Regulars:** Vic Damone, Mary Raye, Francey Lane. **Announcer:** Don Russell. **Music:** Ray McKinley, Johnny Guarnieri.

6275 *Mork and Mindy.* (Series; Comedy; ABC; 1978–1982). Ork, a planet about 200 million miles from Earth, has three moons, and its inhabitants, who resemble humans, evolved from the chicken (their spaceships resemble eggs). Orson, a leader on the planet, assigns Mork, a former dinner diver in a lobster tank turned explorer who charted 16 galaxies, the job of Earth Observer. His assignment is to study life on Earth and to relate his observations to Ork via his Scorpio Reports (which he transmits to Orson via mind transference).

Mork lands on Earth in Boulder, Colorado, and befriends Mindy McConnell, a pretty student who resides at 1619 Pine Street. When she learns about his mission, she agrees to help him. Stories depict their adventures as Mork attempts to learn about life on Earth.

Mork attended Ork Prep School and travels through time via his red sequined Time Traveling Shoes (size eight). He has a pet Orkan Nauger Chump named Beebo and works as a counselor at the Pine Tree Day Care Center.

Mindy attended Boulder High School then the University of Colorado, where she majored in journalism. She first worked in her father's store (McConnell's Music Store), then as a newscaster at KTNS-TV, Channel 31, and finally as the host of *Wake Up, Boulder.*

When Mork and Mindy marry (Oct. 5, 1981), they honeymoon on Ork and shortly after Mork becomes pregnant and lays an egg. The egg hatches and Mork and Mindy become the parents of an elderly, mischievous "baby" they name Mearth (Orkan children are born old and become young with time). Mearth is a combination of Mork, Mindy and Earth. Fred McConnell, Mindy's father, was originally the owner of McConnell's Music Store and later was the conductor of the Boulder City Orchestra. Cathy is Fred's second wife (Mindy's natural mother, Beth, is deceased); she plays flute in the orchestra.

Exidor is Mork's friend, the local loon who has an invisible dog named Brutus (a Doberman) and an invisible aide named Pepe. Frank Bickley, Mindy's downstairs neighbor, is a greeting card writer and has a dog named Bickley. Remo and Jeanie DaVinci are a brother and sister who own DaVinci's Restaurant (later called the New York Delicatessen); Cora Hudson is Mindy's grandmother. Mork's greeting is "Na-nu, Na-nu." Miles is Mindy's boss at Ch. 31; Daniel is the KTNS manager; Jack is the KTNS cameraman; Judy is the KTNS weathergirl; Al is Mindy's landlord; Mrs. Fowler is the head of the day care center.

Cast: Robin Williams (*Mork*); Pam Dawber (*Mindy McConnell*); Conrad Janis (*Fred McConnell*); Jonathan Winters (*Mearth*); Tom Poston (*Frank Bickley*); Robert Donner (*Exidor*); Ralph James (*Orson's Voice*); Elizabeth Kerr (*Cora Hudson*); Jay Thomas (*Remo DaVinci*); Gina Hecht (*Jeanie DaVinci*); Foster Brooks (*Miles Sternhagen*); Charles Bloom (*Daniel Pierson*); Pat Cranshaw (*Jack Loomis*); Jillian Kessler (*Judy*); Vidal Peterson (*The Orkin Elder*); Larry Gelman (*Al Clemens*); Priscilla Morrill (*Mrs. Fowler*).

6276 *Mork and Mindy.* (Series; Cartoon; ABC; 1982-1983). A spin off from *Mork and Mindy* (about Mork, an alien from the planet Ork, who befriends Earthling Mindy McConnell). On orders from Orson, his superior on the planet Ork, Mork and Mindy are ordered to enroll in Mt. Mount High School in an attempt to supply Orson with more information about life on primitive Earth. Stories depict Mork's various misadventures as he attempts to become a typical American high school kid. Fred McConnell is Mindy's father; Mr. Carruthers is the school principal; Eugene and Hamilton are Mork's friends; Doing is Mork's pet.

Voice Cast: Robin Williams *(Mork)*; Pam Dawber *(Mindy)*; Conrad Janis *(Fred McConnell)*; Stanley Jones *(Mr. Carruthers)*; Ralph James *(Orson)*; Shavar Ross *(Eugene)*; Mark L. Taylor *(Hamilton)*; Frank Welker *(Doing)*.

6277   *Morning Court.* (Series; Drama; ABC; 1960-1961). Reenactments of actual metropolitan courtroom cases. Actors portray all of the involved.

Cast: William Gwinn *(Judge)*; Georgiana Hardy *(Judge)*.

6278   *Morning Glory.* (Pilot; Comedy; ABC; July 14, 1989). Blythe Pickney and Connie Briggs are bookers for a local Pittsburgh television program called *The Morning Show*. The program is hosted by Manuel Loco Lopez, is produced by Paul Stengel and airs over station WART. The proposal was to focus on Blythe and Connie as they seek guests for the show. Donna is Paul's secretary. On screen the credit for Manuel reads Christopher Mayer; in *TV Guide* and on press releases the credit reads Chip Mayer.

Cast: Wendel Meldrum *(Blythe Pickney)*; Gail Boggs *(Connie Briggs)*; Joel Brooks *(Paul Stengel)*; Christopher Mayer *(Manuel Loco Lopez)*; Sandra Searles Dickinson *(Donna)*.

6279   *The Morning Show.* (Series; Talk; Syn.; 1969). Music, talk and celebrity interviews designed for an early morning time period.

Host: Ed Nelson. **Regulars:** Rona Barrett, Dr. Julius Sumner Miller, Mr. Blackwell.

6280   *The Morning Show with Mike and Juliet.* (Series; Talk; Fox; 2007–2009). Live morning talk show that features celebrity interviews and discussions on current topics of interest.

Hosts: Mike Jerrick, Juliet Huddy. **Entertainment Reporter:** Jill Dobson. **Theme Music:** Kathryn Korniloff.

6281   *Morning Star.* (Series; Serial; NBC; 1965-1966). New York City provides the setting for the dramatic story of Kathy Elliott, a model caught in the intrigue and excitement of high fashion.

Program Open: "Now matter how the dark the night there is always a new dawn to come. The sun is but a *Morning Star. Morning Star*, a dramatic serial for those who face today and look forward to tomorrow's promise."

Cast: Elizabeth Perry *(Kathy Elliott)*; Adrienne Ellis *(Jan)*; Ed Prentiss *(Edward Elliott)*; Olive Dunbar *(Ann Burton)*; Sheila Bromley *(Aunt Milly)*; Burt Douglas *(George Ross)*; Betty Lou Gerson *(Joan Mitchell)*; Edward Mallory *(Bill Riley)*; Floy Dean *(Eve Blake)*; John Stephenson *(Stan Manning)*; William Arvin *(Dr. Blake)*; Michael Bell *(Jerry)*; Normann Burton *(Joe Bernie)*; Michael Fox *(Marcus Stein)*; Ron Jackson *(Eric Manning)*; Vic Tayback *(The Man)*; Phyllis Hill *(Mrs. Allison)*.

6282   *Morning Star/Evening Star.* (Series; Drama; CBS; 1986). When a fire destroys the Morning Star Children's Orphanage in Birchfield County, California, Debbie Flynn, manager of the Evening Star Retirement Home, arranges for the homeless orphans to remain with her senior citizens. Stories relate incidents in the lives of the Evening Star residents as they open up their home to a group of children. Other regulars are Bob, a social worker; the senior citizens: Binnie, Bill, Kathy, Excell, Martha, Nora and marrieds Gordon and Alice; and the orphans: Lisa, Sarah and Alan (sister and brother), Eugenia and Doug.

Cast: Sherry Hursey *(Debbie Flynn)*; Darrell Larson *(Bob Lane)*; Sylvia Sidney *(Binnie Byrd Baylor)*; Jeff Corey *(Bill MacGregor)*; Elizabeth Wilson *(Kathy Kelly)*; Scatman Crothers *(Excell Davis)*; Mason Adams *(George Blair)*; Teresa Wright *(Alice Blair)*; Ketty Lester *(Nora Blake)*; Kate Reid *(Martha Cameron)*; Tammy Lauren *(Lisa Thurston)*; Missy Francis *(Sarah Bishop)*; Fred Savage *(Alan Bishop)*; Ebonie Smith *(Eugenia Waters)*; Leaf Phoenix *(Doug Roberts)*.

6283   *Mortal Kombat.* (Series; Cartoon; Syn.; 1995-1996). An adaptation of the video game that produced three series: *Mortal Kombat* (1995), *Mortal Kombat: Defenders of the Realm* (1996) and *Mortal Kombat: Conquest* (1998). Mortal Kombat is a tournament where participants duel to the death. In the first series, Rayden, the Lightning God, guides Liu Kang, a warrior; Sonya Blade, a police detective; and Johnny Cage, a martial arts movie star, to a remote island wherein a Shaolin tournament of Mortal Kombat will be held. Here, Liu, Sonya and Johnny must battle alien warriors to save the Earth. Failure to do so, as prescribed in Mortal Kombat, will allow the aliens to enter the Earth's realm and take over.

The second series, *Mortal Kombat: Defenders of the Realm*, finds alien fighters from Mortal Kombat tournaments entering the Earth realm to begin their quest of domination. An elite team of Earth warriors is assembled to stop them. Stories relate the team's efforts to locate and battle the aliens before the tournament is lost and the Earth becomes dominated by aliens. See the following title for information on the final, live action series.

Mortal Kombat Voice Cast: Brian Tochi *(Liu Kang)*; Olivia D'Abo *(Sonya Blade)*; Clancy Brown *(Rayden)*; Luke Perry *(Sub-Zero)*; Cree Summer *(Princess Kitana)*. **Mortal Kombat: Defenders of the Realm Voice Cast:** Clancy Brown *(Rayden)*; Brian Tochi *(Liu Kang)*; Olivia D'Abo *(Sonya Blade)*; Cree Summer *(Princess Kitana)*; Luke Perry *(Sub-Zero)*; Tod Thawley *(Nightwolf)*; Dorian Harewood *(Jax)*; Ron Perlman *(Kurtis Stryker)*.

6284   *Mortal Kombat: Conquest.* (Series; Adventure; Syn.; 1998-1999). A prequel to the *Mortal Kombat* feature films that charts the early adventures of Kung Lao, a martial arts champion who battles to protect the Earth from the evil Shao Khan, an emperor who has opened a portal from Outworld to the Earth Realm and now seeks to absorb the planet into his realm.

Kung Lao is a champion of Mortal Kombat tournaments. He has an advisor (Lord Rayden) and two assistants, Taja and Siro. He has also been assigned the task of training a new generation of warriors for the next tournament. Stories follow Kung Lao as he attempts to accomplish his goal while at the same time battling Shao Khan and the supernatural warriors he has sent to destroy him.

Cast: Paolo Montalban *(Kung Lao)*; Kristanna Loken *(Taja)*; Daniel Bernhardt *(Siro)*; Jeffrey Meek *(Shao Kahn/Lord Rayden)*; Tracy Douglas *(Vorpax)*; Bruce Locke *(Shang Tsung)*; Chris Casamassa *(Scorpion)*.

6285   *Morton and Hayes.* (Series; Comedy; CBS; 1991). Everybody remembers great comedy teams like Laurel and Hardy and Abbott and Costello. But who remembers Morton and Hayes — nobody!" The reason why nobody remembers Morton and Hayes, says host Rob Reiner, is "because their films were thought lost forever in a tragic fire. But recently in Los Angeles, while workers were either in the process of tearing down a Burger King to make way for a Sizzlers, or vice versa, a rusty, battered old vault was discovered." Inside that vault more than 100 black and white "Morton and Hayes" classic comedy shorts of the 1930s and 1940s were found. The prints were restored and presented for the first time on television by Rob Reiner in a weekly series (which aired only six "Morton and Hayes" classics).

Chick Morton and Eddie Hayes began their career in vaudeville with a mind-reading act called the Great Vincenzo (Chick) and Al (Eddie). Chick, who is thin, was the straight man; Eddie, who is overweight, was the foil. They were discovered by Max King, a filmmaker, who produced the comedy shorts. Their earliest known film is "The Vase Shop"; their last film, "Sheeps," made $19 on opening day. They were most famous for their series of detective films, which include "The Case of the Cranky Corpse," "Mr. and Mrs. Murderer," "Morton and Hayes Meet Sherlock Holmes at Charlie Chan's" and "Daffy Dicks" (the first film shown on television).

The success of Morton and Hayes comedies spawned fan clubs. People just couldn't get enough of them. By 1939 virtually every child had in his possession Morton and Hayes hand puppets. In 1948 Max released the boys from their contracts. They last appeared together on *The Glen Campbell Goodtime Hour* on CBS in 1968. Eddie became rich through investments. Chick gambled, drank and was slapped with four paternity suits. He did a guest shot on *Hawaii Five-O* and some television commercials before he retired to the Old Actors' Home in San Fernando. Morton and Hayes were reunited for the first time in 23 years by Rob Reiner in the final two episodes of the series.

In the original CBS pilot, *Partners in Life* (Aug. 31, 1990) Rob Reiner played Max King III, the grandson of Max King, the producer of the classic "Morton and Hayes" comedy films of the 1930s and 1940s. A total of 144 films, thought to be lost forever, were found by workers when they were tearing down the Max King film studios. Each week, one of these lost films was to be seen, hosted by Max King III. Kevin Pollak played Chick Morton and Joe Guzaldo was Eddie Hayes.

Cast: Rob Reiner *(Host)*; Kevin Pollak*(Chick Morton)*; Bob Amaral *(Eddie Hayes)*.

6286   *The Morton Downey, Jr., Show.* (Series; Talk; Syn.; 1988). A talk show that focuses, for the most part, on political issues (as opposed to the personal issues of guests) with opponents from both sides of an issue presenting their views on the topic at hand.

Host: Morton Downey, Jr.

6287   *Morton's by the Bay.* (Pilot; Comedy; NBC; May 29, 1989). When Isidore Morton retires, he turns over operation of his Queens, New York, catering business, Morton's by the Bay, to his incompetent son, Junior. Unknown to Junior, Isidore has made Maggie, his assistant for 13 years, the real boss. The proposal was to relate Maggie's efforts to cover for Junior and keep the business afloat. Other regulars are Patty, Maggie's assistant; Tina, the receptionist; and Harry, the salesman. Nell Carter performs the theme, "To the Top."

Cast: Nell Carter *(Maggie)*; Alan Ruck *(Junior Morton)*; Stephanie Hodge *(Patty)*; Johnnie Karam *(Tina)*; Louis Guss *(Harry)*; Barney Martin *(Isidore Morton)*.

6288   *Moscow Bureau.* (Pilot; Comedy; ABC; June 6, 1986). Christine Nichols, who prefers to be called Chris, is a beautiful magazine reporter for *News Today*. When Chris is assigned to the Moscow Bureau, she has high hopes of becoming the new bureau chief when she hears rumors that the current chief (Herb Medlock) is about to retire. When Chris arrives in the USSR, she finds disappointment when Herb changes his mind and decides to keep his job. The proposal was to relate Chris's misadventures as she seeks stories for the magazine and prove herself worthy of one day replacing Herb. Other regulars are Sasha, the Russian translator; Connie, the American TV reporter; and Tim and Nigel, rival magazine reporters who try to scoop Chris.

Cast: Caroline McWilliams *(Chris Nichols)*; William Windom *(Herb Medlock)*; Elya Baskin *(Sasha Zhukov)*; Nancy Lane *(Connie Uecker)*; Dennis Drake *(Tim Carmichael)*; Barrie Ingram *(Nigel Blake)*.

6289   *Moses the Lawgiver.* (Series; Drama; CBS; 1975). The Biblical story of Moses (drawn from the Book of Exodus) is dramatized as he defies the Egyptian empire to deliver the Jews from their enslavement and lead them to the Promised Land.

Cast: Burt Lancaster *(Moses)*; Will Lancaster *(Young Moses)*; Anthony Quayle *(Aaron)*; Irene Papas *(Zipporah)*; Ingrid Thulin *(Miriam)*; Laurent Terzieff *(Mernephta)*; Simonetta Stefanelli *(Cotbi)*; Ahron Ipale *(Joshua)*; Martina Berti *(Eliseba)*; Didi Lukof *(Gherson)*; Fausto Di Bella *(Zimri)*.

6290   *Most Daring.* (Series; Reality; TruTV; 2007–2009). "Ordinary People in extraordinary danger" is the tag line for a program that showcases real acts of courage that were captured on tape (from rescuing flood victims to extricating victims from a car crash). Harrowing experiences are culled from both law enforcement videos and those captured by amateurs. Originally aired on Court TV. Mitch Lewis narrates.

6291   *The Most Deadly Game.* (Series; Crime Drama; ABC; 1970-1971). Ethan Arcane is a master criminologist with offices in Los Angeles. Although aging, Ethan cannot force himself to retire. In order to continue what he is doing, he hires two young detectives to assist him: Vanessa Smith and Jonathan Croft. Vanessa and Jonathan are recent criminology student graduates. Vanessa is a beautiful young woman who could easily be mistaken for a high fashion model but whose keen interest in helping the police solve crimes led her down a different and more dangerous path. Jonathan, the son of a police officer, also has deep feeling about bringing criminals to justice and has chosen to continue a family tradition. They are both eager to learn from Ethan an stories relate their efforts (working as legmen for Ethan) to solve crimes of the most deadly nature — murder. Originally titled *Zig Zag* and set to star Inger Stevens.

Program Open: "Murder is *The Most Deadly Game*. These three criminologists play it."

Cast: Ralph Bellamy *(Ethan Arcane)*; Yvette Mimieux *(Vanessa Smith)*; George Maharis *(Jonathan Croft)*.

6292   *Most Haunted.* (Series; Reality; TLC; 2002). British produced series wherein a group of ghost hunters explore "the spookiest sites in their home country." The team, like the American series *Ghost Hunters*, incorporates experts in the paranormal field, coupled with the latest technology to find lost souls and explain unexplained paranormal activity. Yvette Fielding is the host-team leader. Karl Beattie, Brian Sheppard, Dr. Ciaran O'Keefe, Matthew Smith, David Wells are Richard Felix are her team.

6293   *The Most in Music.* (Series; Variety; Syn.; 1966). A program of music and songs that are tailored to the talents of its guest hosts, including Barbara McNair, Vikki Carr and Johnny Mathis.

Regulars: The Irving Davies Dancers, The Mike Sammes Singers. **Orchestra:** Jack Parnell.

6294   *Most Likely to Succeed.* (Pilot; Comedy; Unaired; Produced for Fox in 2010). Becca, April, Oliver and Griff are young adults dealing with the harsh aspects of the real world. They were superstars in high school, but since graduation they have come to realize that they can never achieve the "fame" they previously had. The proposal was to follow their efforts to cope with the problems of real life. Kaitlin Doubleday was originally cast as Becca.

Cast: Caitlin Fitzgerald *(Becca)*; Kathryn Hahn *(April)*; Malcolm Barrett *(Oliver)*; Tim Peper *(Griff)*.

6295   The Most Outrageous Moments. (Series; Comedy; NBC; 2006). Outtakes from movies and foreign and domestic television shows; sporting mishaps and home video accidents caught on tape (for which the sender receives $1,000).
Narrator: John Cramer.

6296   Most Popular. (Series; Game; WE; 2009). Seven female contestants appear before an audience of 100 studio members. Based on appearance, the audience eliminates (by electronic voting) one of the players. The remaining six players are then interviewed by the host (who attempts to extract personal information about them). The audience again votes and in succeeding rounds eliminates the four people they find the least desirable. The final two contestants are further interviewed and the audience votes for the one who appears to be the better person. The winner receives $100 per vote received (to a maximum of $10,000).
Host: Graham Norton.

6297   Most Wanted. (Series; Crime Drama; ABC; 1976-1977). The Most Wanted Unit is an elite law enforcement division of the Los Angeles Police Department that is designed to apprehend criminals on the Most Wanted List. The unit is headed by Captain Lincoln Evers and overseen by Dan Stoddard, the city's mayor. Sergeant Charlie Nelson and Officer Kate Manners assist Lincoln and stories relate their case investigations.
Series Cast: Robert Stack *(Capt. Lincoln Evers)*; Shelly Novack *(Sgt. Charlie Nelson)*; Jo Ann Harris *(Off. Kate Manners)*; Hari Rhodes *(Mayor Dan Stoddard)*. **Pilot Cast:** Robert Stack *(Captain Lincoln Evers)*; Shelly Novack *(Sergeant Charlie Benson)*; Leslie Charleson *(Officer Lee Herrick)*; Tom Selleck *(Officer Tom Roybo)*; Percy Rodrigues *(Mayor Dan Stoddard)*.

6298   Mother and Me, M.D. (Pilot; Comedy; NBC; June 14, 1979). Barrie Tucker is a young female doctor who has been assigned to do her internship at Memorial Hospital in New York City. The hospital also employs her mother, Lil Brenner, as one of its head nurses. The proposal was to focus on the problems that arise with mother and daughter working in the same hospital. Other regulars are Evan, Lil's neighbor; and doctors Mace Oatfield and Sam Kanin.
Cast: Leah Ayres *(Barrie Tucker)*; Rue McClanahan *(Lil Brenner)*; Jack Riley *(Evan Murray)*; Kenneth Gilman *(Mace Oatfield)*; Howard Witt *(Sam Kanin)*.

6299   Mother Goose and Grimm. (Series; Cartoon; CBS; 1993). Adaptation of the comic strip, *Mother Goose and Grimm* by Mike Peters that relates the antics of Grimmy, a mutt that lives with fairy tale writer Mother Goose and her cat Attila. Also known as *Grimmy*.
Voice Cast: Mitzi McCall *(Mother Goose)*; Charlie Brill *(Grimmy)*; Eddie Deezen *(Ham)*; Greg Burson *(Attila)*.

6300   Mother, Juggs and Speed. (Pilot; Comedy; ABC; Aug. 17, 1978). The F and B Private Ambulance Company is a near-bankrupt operation owned by the greedy Harry Fishbine. The proposal, based on the feature film of the same title, was to follow the misadventures of three of Harry's employees: Mother, the hard-drinking driver; Juggs, the busty paramedic; and Speed, the embittered ex-cop. Other regulars are Whiplash, Harry's lawyer; Harry's wife (no first name given) and Murdock, an employee.
Cast: Ray Vitte *(Mother)*; Joanne Nail *(Juggs)*; Joe Penny *(Speed)*; Harvey Lembeck *(Harry Fishbine)*; Shay Duffin *(Whiplash Moran)*; Barbara Minkus *(Mrs. Fishbine)*; Rod McCary *(Murdock)*.

6301   Mothers Day. (Series; Game; ABC; 1958-1959). Three mothers compete in various contests based on the operation of a household. The winners, those who successfully complete all tasks, are crowned "Mother for a Day" and receive merchandise prizes.
Host: Dick Van Dyke. **Assistant:** Dotty Mack, Betty Anders. **Announcer:** Bill Brophy.

6302   The Mothers-in-Law. (Series; Comedy; NBC; 1967–1969). Herbert Hubbard is a private practice lawyer who resides at 1805 Ridgeway Drive in Los Angeles with his wife, Eve, and their daughter, Suzie. Living next door, at 1803 Ridgeway are Roger Buell, a television script writer, his wife, Kaye, and their son, Jerry.
Suzie and Jerry grew up together, played together and eventually fell in love with each other. After graduating from high school, they eloped and moved into the Hubbards' garage, which they converted into an apartment (Suzie and Jerry planned on a church wedding, but their meddling mothers-in-law forced them to elope).
Suzie and Jerry are now in college (UCLA); they live next door to their parents and they have a difficult time finding any privacy or peace as Eve and Kaye constantly interfere in their lives. On occasion, Herb and Roger meddle in an attempt to help Suzie and Jerry, but not on a daily, 24 hour basis like their wives (who say, "We only go to the kids' place to advise and suggest").
Roger hardly understands Kaye — "It's probably the one thing that holds our marriage together." Kaye was in show business before she married Roger and sang (as Angelina DiVina, "The Little Girl with the Big Voice") in the Ozzie Snick Orchestra and with Charlie Banks and His Ten Tellers. In the original, unaired pilot film for the series (produced for CBS), Kay Cole played the role of Suzie Hubbard.
Cast: Eve Arden *(Eve Hubbard)*; Herbert Rudley *(Herb Hubbard)*; Kaye Ballard *(Kaye Buell)*; Roger C. Carmel, Richard Deacon *(Roger Buell)*; Deborah Walley *(Suzie Hubbard)*; Jerry Fogel *(Jerry Hubbard)*; Desi Arnaz *(Raphael del Gado)*; Herbert Voland *(Dr. Butler; Suzie's pediatrician)*.

6303   Motor Mouse. (Series; Cartoon; ABC; 1970-1971). A spin off from *The Cattanooga Cats. Motor Mouse* tells the story of a cat (Auto Cat) and his endless but fruitless attempts to beat a mouse (Motor Mouse) in a car race. The second segment, *It's the Wolf,* relates the efforts of Mildew Wolf to acquire a decent meal — in the form of Lambsy, a poor, defenseless lamb.
Voice Cast: Marty Ingels *(Auto Cat)*; Dick Curtis *(Motor Mouse)*; Paul Lynde *(Mildew Wolf)*; Marty Ingels *(Lambsy)*; Allan Melvin *(Bristol Hound)*.

6304   The Motorola Television Hour. (Series; Anthology; CBS; 1953-1954). Motorola Corporation sponsored program of live dramatic presentations from New York City. The program, produced by Herbert Brodkin, includes such performers as Basil Rathbone, Eddie Albert, Vicki Cummings, Jackie Cooper, Hume Cronyn, Walter Matthau, Jack Palance, Roberta Peters, Leora Dana, Charlie Ruggles and Lisa Kirk.

6305   Motown Revue. (Series; Variety; NBC; 1985). A salute to Detroit performers and the hit songs of the 1960s, 70s and 80s.
Host: Smokey Robinson. **Regulars:** Arsenio Hall, Leo O'Brien, The Hitsville Gang Dancers. **Music:** Bruce Miller.

6306   The Mountain. (Series; Drama; WB; 2004). David Carver, Sr., was a man of vision. After winning land (Boundary Mountain) in a poker game, he founded a town and built an escapist playground for sports fanatics and wealthy tourists. After his death, the resort went to his grandson, David Carver, Jr., a free spirit who dreams of becoming a world-class motor cross racer. It was Will, his older brother who was expected to inherit the land (especially since he was already attending business school and had plans for Boundary Mountain) but didn't. Conflict arises within the family as David, saddled with a responsibility he never wanted, finds himself battling his family, as well as outsiders who want the mountain, to maintain and protect his grandfather's legacy.

Cast: Oliver Hudson (*David Carver, Jr.*); Anson Mount (*Will Carver*); Barbara Hershey (*Gennie Carver*); Tara Thompson (*Shelly Carver*); Elizabeth Bogush (*Maxine Dowling*); Tommy Dewey (*Michael Dowling*); Alana De La Garza (*Maria Servano*); Penn Badgley (*Sam Tunney*); Jonathan Urb (*Travis Kurri*); Chad Everett (*David Carver, Sr., pilot*).

6307 *The Mouse and the Monster*. (Series; Cartoon; UPN; 1996-1997). Mo is a bright blue, eight-foot tall, one eyed monster that was created by the demented scientist, Dr. Wackerstein. Chesbro, a mouse, and now Mo's sidekick, saved him from his evil creator. Stories follow the unpredictable Mo and Chesbro as they seek to avoid capture by Wackerstein.

Voices: Buddy Johnson, Marion Kaplan, Herbert Ikatap, Marion Kaplan, Lucille Scrubber, Wes Turner.

6308 *The Mouse Factory*. (Series; Children; Syn.; 1972). Guest celebrities, assisted by clips from various Walt Disney-produced feature films, attempt to explain various aspects of the world to children.

Guests (with Topics Hosted): Annette Funicello (*"Mickey"*); Jo Anne Worley (*"Women's Lib"*); Johnny Brown (*"Folk Tale Favorites"*); Phyllis Diller (*"Spooks and Magic"*); Don Knotts (*"Physical Fitness"*); Dom DeLuise (*"Great Outdoors"*); Joe Flynn (*"Water Sports"*); John Byner (*"Men at Work"*); Jonathan Winters (*"Interplanetary Travel"*); Jim Backus (*"Home Owners"*); Wally Cox (*"Back to Nature"*); John Astin (*"Pluto"*); Shari Lewis (*"Cats"*).

6309 *The Mouse That Roared*. (Pilot; Comedy; Unaired; Produced in 1966). In 1480 an Englishman named Roger Fenwick founded the Grand Duchy of Fenwick, the smallest country in the world (located in the French Alps and only 15¾ square miles) and the only English-speaking European country. Fenwick was not only the founding father, but he also fathered a lot, hence some citizens tend to look alike, such as the current ruler, Duchess Gloriana XII, its prime minister, Count Rupert of Mountjoy, and its forest ranger/Grand Constable of the Armed Forces, Tully Bascomb. Fenwick's major weapon is the long bow and it has been at peace for over 500 years. Its only export is Pino Grand Fenwick, a wine that is sold to the United States. The proposal, based on the feature film, was to focus on life in Fenwick and the efforts of its leaders to make the nation economically strong again after a California wine bottler creates the imitation Pino Grand Enwick, sells it at a lower price and plunges Fenwick into bankruptcy.

Cast: Sid Caesar (*Duchess Gloriana XII*); Sid Caesar (*Count Rupert of Montjoy*); Sid Caesar (*Tully Bascomb*); Joyce Jameson (*Eleanor*); Richard Deacon (*Bender*).

6310 *Mousterpiece Theater*. (Series; Cartoon; Disney; 1983). A series of animated Disney shorts that are broadcast under the umbrella title of *Mousterpiece Theater* (a takeoff on the PBS series *Masterpiece Theater* which broadcast British programs).

Host: George Plimpton.

6311 *The Movie Game*. (Series; Game; Syn.; 1969). Two three-member teams compete in a game based on films and film stars. The team with the highest score at the end of a series of question-and-answer rounds is the winner and receives $250.

Program Open: "It's time to play *The Movie Game* starring today,

Larry Storch, June Lockhart, Dennis Weaver, Carol Channing, Mr. Army Archerd and your Hollywood host, Sonny Fox."

Host: Sonny Fox, Larry Blyden. **Assistant:** Army Archerd. **Announcer:** Johnny Gilbert.

6312 *The Movie Museum*. (Series; Documentary; Syn.; 1954). Screenings of theatrical comedy shorts of the 1920s, 1930s and 1940s. Produced by Paul Killiam who serves as the curator.

6313 *Movie Stars*. (Series; Comedy; WB; 1999-2000). Reese Hardin, "America's Leading Action Star," and Jacey Wyiatt, "America's Favorite Leading Lady," are married. They live in Malibu, California, and are the parents of Apache and Moonglow. Also living with them is Lori Hardin, Reese's daughter from a previous marriage.

Reese is known as "Reese Hardin, Action Star," and has made such films as *Clash of the Titans* (actually starring Harry Hamlin), *Lethal Impact* and *Sudden Vengeance*. It was on the film *Cyber Death 2000* that Reese first met Jacey (she played "the annoying mime who got vaporized"). He is represented by the CAA Agency (Jacey by the William Morris Agency).

Jacey is a three-time Oscar nominee; Reese is a People's Choice Award winner. Jacey "gets the movies that receive praise" while Reese "makes those with the word 'lethal' in the title and gross three billion dollars." Jacey has made such films as *Joan of Arc* and *A Perfect Fool* and is sometimes called "the biggest chick star around." Jacey was raised in Bakersfield by her mother Audrey (Loni Anderson), a stripper (at the Extreme Turbulence Room) who posed nude for *Playboy*'s "Moms of the Stars" pictorial.

Lori came to live with her father "when things got too tense in Ohio. "You burn down one Dairy Queen and they never forget." Lori first attended Buchanan Preschool ("Geek Prep" as she called it), then the "cool" Crosswinds High School. She is 17, gorgeous, and has a love-hate relationship with Jacey (she also borrows much of Jacey's wardrobe—which "looks great on Jacey, but fabulous on me").

Apache and Moonglow attend Buchanan Prep. Apache hates his name and Reese explains "that I was into the American Indian movement and my spiritual guide said for me to name you after a famous Indian." Moonglow seems content with her name.

Todd Hardin is Reese's brother, an actor who gets the least desirable roles. He has been in *Titanic* (frozen corpse number 3), *Starship Troopers* ("the guy who gets crushed by the giant roach"), *Deep Impact* (asteroid victim 702) and *Fargo* (the leg sticking out of the wood chipper). While Reese has a house that overlooks the Pacific Ocean, Todd lives in an apartment that overlooks a homeless guy with a sock puppet called Eddie. Todd attended Juilliard and the Actors Studio, and went to Hollywood with great expectations for a role in *The Sting II*. Reese tagged along "to race motorcycles and chase chicks." Reese got into an altercation with a producer, punched his lights out and got the jobs. Todd frequents the Juice Bar and plays poker with his friends "Stallone, Swayze and Travolta"— Frank Stallone, Don Swayze and Joey Travolta—the brothers of famous stars who feel as Todd does (that their brothers have taken all the glory). Todd, Frank, Don and Joey pooled their resources and opened their own juice bar, "L.A.'s Hottest Spot," Squeeze This.

Cast: Harry Hamlin (*Reese Hardin*); Jennifer Grant (*Jacey Wyatt*); Marnette Patterson (*Lori Hardin*); Zack Hopkins (*Apache Hardin*); Rachel David (*Moonglow Hardin*); Mark Benninghofen (*Todd Hardin*).

6314 *Movieland Quiz*. (Series; Game; ABC; 1948). The object calls for contestants to identify stars and titles of old films from selected scenes. A cash prize is awarded for each correct answer.

Host: Arthur Q. Bryan, Ralph Dumke. **Assistant:** Patricia Bright.

6315   *Movin' On.* (Pilot; Adventure; NBC; July 24, 1972). Clint Daniels, a stock car racer, and cycle racer Johnny Lake are clean-cut young men who share the same dream: to travel around the country to see America. One day they decide to quit the racing circuit, pool their resources and follow their dream. The proposal was to follow their travels across America.

Cast: Patrick Wayne (*Clint Daniels*); Geoffrey Deuel (*Johnny Lake*).

6316   *Movin' On.* (Series; Drama; NBC; 1974–1976). Sonny Pruitt, a tough, uneducated veteran trucker, and Will Chandler, a rebellious, college-educated youth, are gypsy truck drivers who share a truck and haul anything as long as it is legal. Sonny and Will travel the roads from Oregon to Utah to Nevada and stories relate their experiences with the people they encounter as they transport cargo. Betty is Will's girlfriend; Myrna is Sonny's romantic interest; Benjy and Moose are fellow gypsy truckers.

Cast: Claude Akins (*Sonny Pruitt*); Frank Converse (*Will Chandler*); Janis Hansen (*Myrna*); Ann Coleman (*Betty*); Rosey Grier (*Benjy*); Art Metrano (*Moose*). **Theme Vocal:** "Movin' On" by Merle Haggard.

6317   *The Moxy Show.* (Series; Cartoon; Cartoon Network; 1993). The cartoon Network's first original series; a collection of classic Hanna-Barbera produced cartoons that are interspersed with the hosting of Moxy the dog and Flea the flea. Originally titled *The Moxy Pirate Show.*

Voice Cast: Bobcat Goldthwait (*Moxy*); Penn Jillette, Chris Roc (*Flea*).

6318   *Mrs. Columbo.* (Series; Crime Drama; NBC; 1979). The original title for *Kate Loves a Mystery*, the spin off series from *Columbo*. See this title for information.

6319   *Mrs. G. Goes to College.* (Series; Comedy; CBS; 1961-1962). Sarah Green, called Mrs. G. by her friends, has one regret in life: she was never able to attend college. When her husband passes away and Sarah is left with lots of free time, she decides to fulfill her lifelong dream and enroll in college. She enters an unidentified college that resembles the University of Southern California and stories follow the efforts of a middle-age widow to achieve her college education. Professor Crayton is Sarah's advisor; Maxfield is Sarah's landlady; Susan is Sarah's daughter; Jerry is Sarah's son; Joe Caldwell is the featured student. In mid-season, the title changed to *The Gertrude Berg Show.*

Cast: Gertrude Berg (*Sarah Green*); Sir Cedric Hardwicke (*Professor Crayton*); Mary Wickes (*Maxfield*); Skip Ward (*Joe Caldwell*); Marion Ross (*Susan*); Leo Penn (*Jerry*); Paul Smith (*George Howell*); Aneta Corsaut (*Irma Howell*); Karyn Kubcinet (*Carol*); Adrian Ellis (*Student*); Obin Lory (*Student*); Tracy Olsen (*Student*); Bunny Henning (*Student*); Allyson Daniell (*Student*); Martin Dean (*Student*). **Theme Song:** "Alma Mater" by Herschel Burke Gilbert and Alfred Perry.

6320   *Mrs. R.* (Pilot; Crime Drama; NBC; May 20, 1975). Shirley Ridgeway is a homicide detective with the L.A.P.D. She is called Mrs. R., possesses a motherly image but is shrewd and the unsold series was to relate her case investigations.

Cast: Kate Reid (*Shirley Ridgeway*); A Martinez (*Officer Manny Reyes*); John Anderson (*Captain Lewis*).

6321   *MTV: 10 on Top.* (Series; Reality; MTV; 2010). A countdown, with an in-depth look at the top ten most texed and talked about celebrities of the week preceding the broadcast. Also included are behind-the-scenes coverage of TV programs, movies, music videos and the latest bands. Lenay Dunn hosts.

6322   *MTV Top 20 Countdown.* (Series; Variety; Syn.; 1986). Marc Goodman hosts a rundown of the week's (preceding the broadcast) most popular music videos coupled with interviews with music stars and musicians.

6323   *MTV's Top Pop Group.* (Series; Reality; MTV; 2008). A search to find a new music group. Nine groups, chosen from open auditions, are mentored (from stage presence to harmony and style) then compete in various music challenges with the weakest performers being eliminated. The one group that proves to be the best wins $100,000 and the title of "MTV's Top Pop Group."

Host: Mario Lopez. **Judges:** Michelle Williams, Brian Friedman, and, as credited, Eve, Taboo.

6324   *Mucha Lucha.* (Series; Cartoon; Kids WB; 2002–2005). Rikochet, Buena Girl and the Flea are three masked wrestlers who live by the code of Masked Wresting (they never remove their colorful masks). They are also students at the Foremost World Renowned International School of Lucha (wrestling). Stories follow the wrestlers as they train and compete in the ring. Rikochet is skilled at the "Pulverizing Pinball" and "Spinning Top" maneuvers and is seeking to become the school's top wrester. Buena Girl has a move called: "The Buena Bulldozer of Truth." The Flea is a bit nasty and refers to himself in the third person (for example, "The Flea thinks we ought to get of here"). Other characters are Snow Pea, a wimpy guy who hates violence (and often loses matches) and is known for his "Cuddly Hug of Friendship" move; Cindy Slam is a violent young lady who is known for her move, "The Cindy Slammer"; and The Masked Dog is the school's mascot who wrestles under the name "Knocking Paws."

Voice Cast: Carlos Alazraqui, Jason Marsden (*Rikochet*); Kimberly Brooks (*Buena Girl*); Kimberly Brooks (*Snow Pea*); Kimberly Brooks (*Cindy Slam*); Candi Milo (*The Flea*); Janyse Jaud (*Dragon Fly*); James Arnold Taylor (*Kid Wombat*).

6325   *The Mud Show.* (Pilot; Comedy; Unaired; Produced for ABC Family in 2006). The problems that befall the owners and performers of a dilapidated one-ring circus.

Cast: Jackie Kreisler (*Katarin*); David Steinberg (*Arturo*); Gerald Downey (*Robert*); Jay Lay (*Agent Johnson*); Jill-Michele Melean (*Willie*); Melinda Allen (*Sheela*); Steve Little (*Zippy*).

6326   *Muddling Through.* (Series; Comedy; CBS; 1994). Suspecting that her husband, Sonny, is cheating on her, Connie Drego follows him to the Hotel Starlite on Route 5 in Michigan and finds that her suspicions are true. Hoping to scare Sonny, Connie bursts into the room and points a gun at Sonny. The gun accidentally discharges and hits Sonny in the butt. Connie is arrested and sentenced to two-and-a-half years in prison. Two years, four months and six days later Connie is released for good behavior. Connie, now 35, returns to her home and business, a roadside diner/motel called Drego's Oasis. The business is being run by her eldest daughter, Madeline, who is now married to Dwayne Cooper, the trooper who arrested Connie. Connie's younger daughter, 16-year-old Carrie is wild and uncontrollable; and Sonny, who is now broke, returns also, to live off Connie. Stories focus on Connie as she struggles to turn her life around and become the mother Madeline and Carrie never really had. Gidney and Lyle, diner customers.

Cast: Stephanie Hodge (*Connie Drego*); Jennifer Aniston (*Madeline Cooper*); Aimee Brooks (*Carrie Drego*); D. David Morin (*Sonny Drego*); Scott Waara (*Dwayne Cooper*); Hal Landon, Jr. (*Gidney Pace*); Hank Underwood (*Lyle Meriwether*).

6327   *Muggsy.* (Series; Drama; NBC; 1976–1977). Life in an unidentified inner city as seen through the eyes of Margaret "Muggsy" Malloy, a 13-year-old orphan, and her half-brother and guardian, Nick Malloy, a taxicab driver. Other regulars are Gus, their friend; Clytemnestra, Muggsy's friend; T.P., and Clytemnestra's brother.

Cast: Sarah MacDonnell (*Margaret Malloy*); Ben Masters (*Nick Malloy*); Paul Michael (*Gus Gardician*); Star-Shemah (*Clytemnestra*); Danny Cooper (*T.P.*). **Theme Vocal:** "Keepin' It Together" by Blood, Sweat and Tears.

6328   *Mulberry Street.* (Pilot; Comedy; CBS; Aug. 8, 1990). Conchetta "Connie" Savioa is a new-thinking woman with an old world style family. Following a financial setback Connie is forced to move in with her parents, who own Savioa and Sons Grocery on Mulberry Street in New York's Little Italy. The proposal was to focus on Connie as she struggles to rebuild her life but constantly clashes with her family over everything she does. Other regulars are Dominic and Anna, Connie's parents; Vincent, Connie's brother; Joanne, Vincent's wife; Mia and Joseph, Vincent's children; and Connie's Aunt Carmella.

Cast: Connie Sellecca (*Connie Savioa*); Cesar Romero (*Dominic Savioa*); Lila Kaye (*Anna Savioa*); Eddie Mekka (*Vincent Savioa*); Shera Danese (*Joanne Savioa*); Mandy Ingber (*Mia Savioa*); Brad Tatum (*Joseph Savioa*); Penny Santon (*Aunt Carmella*).

6329   *The Mullets.* (Series; Comedy; UPN; 2003–2004). Dwayne and Denny Mullet are spaced-out brothers who work as roofers (owners of Mullet Bros. Roofing) who claim to have "the biggest ladder in the San Francisco area."

Dwayne and Denny are bachelors and live together in an apartment in Reseda, California. They are the sons of Mandi, an absolutely gorgeous divorcee who has married Roger Heidecker, the host of the TV game show *Wizardry*.

Dwayne and Denny hang out at Honk 'n' Go, a convenience store. Drinking beer and getting high is their favorite pastime and stories follow the events that befall two dimwits (most people wonder how such a beautiful and sophisticated woman like Mandi produced two such idiotic sons). Other regulars are Gordo, Dwayne and Denny's equally dim-witted friend; and Melanie, the waitress at the Honk 'n' Go.

Cast: Michael Weaver (*Dwayne Herbert Mullet*); David Hornsby (*Denny Mullet*); Loni Anderson (*Mandi Mullet-Heidecker*); John O'Hurley (*Roger Heidecker*); Anne Stedman (*Melanie*); Ben Tolpin (*Gordo*); Mark Christopher Lawrence (*Bill*).

6330   *Mulligan's Stew.* (Series; Drama; NBC; 1977). Polaris ("Polly") Friedman, Star Shine ("Stevie") Friedman, Adam Friedman and Kimmy Friedman are five orphaned children who have come to live with their uncle, Michael ("Mike") Mulligan, his wife, Jane, and their children, Melinda, Jimmy and Mark, following the death of their parents, Kathy (Mike's sister) and Steve Friedman, who perished in a charter plane crash.

The Mulligans live in a three bedroom, two bathroom home at 1202 Circle Drive. Melinda, Stevie and Kimmy share a room; Mark, Adam and Jimmy also share a room; the den has been converted into a bedroom for Polly; and Mike and Jane have the master bedroom. "We're crowded, but we take it day by day," says Mike, the football coach at Birchfield High School. Jane is the school's consulting nurse, and Polly (age 17), Stevie (14), and Mark (16) also attend the school. Jimmy (age nine) and Adam (age eight) attend Birchfield Elementary School.

Mike and Jane were childhood sweethearts; Mark plays guitar at school dances. Stevie "knows guy things" (like fixing cars) and is the mechanical genius of the family. Melinda "knows girl things" like cooking and cleaning and is struggling to shed her tomboyish ways for her newfound interest in makeup, clothes, boys and dating. Polly, the oldest girl, is approaching her eighteenth birthday and longs for privacy; Kimmy, who is five years old, is a Vietnamese orphan Kathy and Steve, a civil rights lawyer, adopted six months before their death. She calls Jane "Mommy Jane"; Adam, who is nicknamed "Moose" for his stocky build, is well versed in the martial arts. Johnny Whitaker played the role of Mark Mulligan in the pilot film, *Stickin' Together* (NBC, June 20, 1977).

Cast: Lawrence Pressman (*Michael Mulligan*); Elinor Donahue (*Jane Mulligan*); Johnny Doran (*Mark Mulligan*); Julie Anne Haddock (*Melinda Mulligan*); Suzanne Crough (*Stevie Friedman*); Lory Kochheim (*Polly Friedman*); Sunshine Lee (*Kimmy Friedman*); Christopher Ciampa (*Adam "Moose" Mulligan*); K.C. Martel (*Jimmy Mulligan*).

6331   *Mummies Alive!* (Series; Cartoon; Syn.; 1997). When Presley Carnovan, a 12-year-old boy living in San Francisco, is discovered to possess the soul of the Pharaoh Prince Rapses of ancient Egypt, four mummies (Armon, Ja-Kal, Nefertina and Rath) come to life to protect him from Scarab, an evil being who is seeking the spirit of Prince Rapses to gain immortality. The mummies have special powers and their efforts to protect Presley and battle evil at the same time, is the focal point of stories.

Voice Cast: Bill Switzer (*Presley Carnovan*); Cree Summer (*Nefertina*); Dale Wilson (*Ja-Kal*); Scott McNeil (*Rath*); Graeme Kingston (*Armon*); David Kaye (*Talos*); David Sobolov (*Eye of Darkness*); Gerard Plunkett (*Scarab*); Pauline Newstone (*Heka*).

6332   *The Mummy: The Animated Series.* (Series; Cartoon; WB Kids; 2001–2003). In ancient Egypt, Imhotep, an evil and corrupt High Priest, was condemned to death for trying to rule the world. He was wrapped in gauze and buried alive, eventually becoming a mummy. Three thousand years later (1930s), museum curator and archaeologist Evy O'Connell, her husband, Rick, and son, Alex join an expedition to Egypt to uncover the tomb of Imhotep. Accompanying them is Colin Weasler, Evy's co-worker, who, when finding Imhotep's tomb resurrects him (thus becoming his servant). Imhotep is as evil as ever and requires the Manacle of Osirus to gain the power he needs to control the world. The manacle, however, has become attached to Alex's wrist when he found it and it cannot be removed without the Scrolls of Thebes — which both the O'Connell's and Imhotep now seek. Stories, adapted from the feature films *The Mummy* and *The Mummy Returns* follow the O'Connell's as they seek to stop Imhotep.

Second season episodes are titled *The Mummy: Secrets of the Medjai* and finds Alex being trained as a Medjai to combat the Mummy Imhotep as well as other threats he may encounter. Fadil and Yanit are Medjai students; Ninzam is a dark (evil) Medjai; Ardeth Bey is the Medjai leader.

Voice Cast: Chris Marquette (*Alex O'Connell*); John Schneider (*Rick O'Connell*); Grey DeLisle (*Evy O'Connell*); Jim Cummings (*Imhotep*); Michael Reisz (*Colin Weasler*); Jeannie Elias (*Yanit*); Jeff Bennett (*Fadil*); Michael T. Weiss (*Ninzam*); Rene Auberjonois (*Scarab*).

6333   *The Munsters.* (Series; Comedy; CBS; 1964–1966). Herman and Lily Munster, their son Eddie, niece Marilyn and Lily's father, Count Vladimir ("Grandpa") Dracula, live in a spooky, run-down house at 1313 Mockingbird Lane in the town of Mockingbird Heights. The family members resemble movie monsters of the 1930s but believe they are normal and that the rest of the world is strange.

Herman, who resembles Frankenstein, is 150 years old and works as a gravedigger for the Gateman, Goodbury and Graves Funeral Parlor. He was at the Heidelberg School of Medicine — in several jars — for six years. Although he was created in Germany, he left for a new life in England where he was adopted by a family named Munster. He was so grateful for their kindness that he took their last name as his. His body temperature is 62.8 degrees; his pulse is 15; blood pressure, minus three; and his heartbeat, none. Herman is seven feet three inches tall and weights three spins on the bathroom scale. "Darn, darn, darn" is his catchphrase (which he says when something goes wrong).

Lily, Herman's wife, is a vampire whose maiden name is Dracula. She is 304 years old and married Herman in 1865. She is dedicated to her family and makes sure their home is always dusty and full of cobwebs.

Count Vladimir Dracula, called Grandpa, is a 378-year-old vampire and mad scientist. His hometown is in Transylvania, has been married 167 times and has a pet bat named Igor.

Marilyn, their normal-looking (to the viewer) niece, is the black sheep of the family; she attends State University, where she is studying art.

Edward ("Eddie") Wolfgang, Herman and Lily's son, is a werewolf and attends Mockingbird Heights Elementary School. His werewolf doll named Woof Woof.

The family pets are Spot, a fire breathing dragon Grandpa found while digging in the back yard; Kitty Kat, a cat who roars like a lion; and an unnamed raven who says "Never more." Mr. Gateman is Herman's employer; Chet Thornton is Herman's co-worker; Edward Dudley is the Munster family physician.

In the original, unaired color pilot (the series is in black and white) titled "My Fair Munster," Fred Gwynne played Herman; Joan Marshall was his wife, Phoebe; Al Lewis was Grandpa; Beverley Owen was Marilyn; and Happy Derman was Eddie.

Cast: Fred Gwynne *(Herman Munster)*; Yvonne DeCarlo *(Lily Munster)*; Al Lewis *(Grandpa)*; Beverley Owen, Pat Priest *(Marilyn Munster)*; Butch Patrick *(Eddie Munster)*; John Carradine *(Mr. Gateman)*; Chester Stratton *(Chet Thornton)*; Paul Lynde, Dom DeLuise *(Dr. Edward Dudley)*.

Note: The 1966 theatrical film, *Munster Go Home* has Debbie Watson in the role of Marilyn. In the NBC TV movie, *The Munsters' Revenge* (Feb. 27, 1981), Jo McDonnell was Marilyn and K.C. Martel was Eddie. (Fred Gwynne, Yvonne DeCarlo and Al Lewis recreated their roles in both films.) See also *The Munsters Today.*

6334   *The Munsters Today.* (Series; Comedy; Syn.; 1988–1991). An update of *The Munsters.* Parents Herman and Lily Munster, their son Eddie, niece Marilyn, and Lily's father, Count Vladimir Dracula, better known as Grandpa, resemble 1930s movie monsters and consider themselves normal people living in a strange world. In 1966 Grandpa conducts an experiment that backfires and places the family in a state of suspended animation. Twenty-two years later, the family awakens to the new world of the 1980s. Their attempts to adjust to society are depicted. The family still lives at 1313 Mockingbird Lane in the town of Mockingbird Heights.

Herman, who stands six feet eight inches tall, was "born" in Dr. Frankenstein's lab in Transylvania over 300 years ago. He is a gravedigger and works for Mr. Graves of the Gateman, Goodbury and Graves funeral parlor.

Herman worships the ground his wife, the former Lily Ann Dracula, was buried under. Lily is 324 years old and married Herman 299 years ago in Transylvania. Before Lily met Herman, she worked as a singer in Club Dead in Transylvania. She won the beauty pageant title, "Miss Transylvania of 1655" and the Silver Shroud Award for Fashion Design. Herman calls her "Lillikins" and mentioned that he first met Lily when he was walking along the moor in Transylvania

and saw a girl stretched out on the ground. She saw him and it was love at first sight.

Grandpa, the original Count Dracula, is a mad scientist who enjoys conducting experiments in the lab beneath the Munsters home. Grandpa attended the University of Transylvania, majored in philosophy and is a member of the A.V.A. (American Vampire Association). Igor is his pet bat, Stanley his lab rat, and Leonard is the skeleton he befriended in his college days who now lives in the dungeon.

Marilyn is blonde, beautiful and the black sheep of the family. She is 17 years old and attends Mockingbird Heights High School. She first wanted to be an actress, then a magazine writer-editor. Herman mentioned that he was not sure how Marilyn is related to them (in one episode she is Herman's niece; in another she is Lily's niece).

Edward ("Eddie") Wolfgang Munster, Lily and Herman's son, attends Mockingbird Heights High School and wants to become a rock video producer.

Cast: John Schuck *(Herman Munster)*; Lee Meriwether *(Lily Munster)*; Howard Morton *(Grandpa)*; Hilary Van Dyke *(Marilyn Munster)*; Jason Marsden *(Eddie Munster)*.

6335   *Muppet Babies.* (Series; Cartoon; CBS; 1984–1985). While the Muppets have been seen on television and in feature films, their lives a youngsters was kept out of the public eye — until now. Before they became the big stars that they are, they were babies and cared for by a kind woman called Nanny. Stories follow the antics of Jim Henson's beloved characters as they encounter misadventures while seeking things to do.

Voice Cast: Barbara Billingsley *(Nanny)*; Greg Berger *(Fozzie/Scooter)*; Katie Leigh *(Rowlf)*; Laurie O'Brien *(Piggy)*; Dave Coulier *(Beans Bunny/Uncle Waldorf)*; Howie Mandel *(Animal/Skeeter)*; Russi Taylor *(Gonzo)*; Frank Welker *(Beaker)*.

6336   *The Muppet Show.* (Series; Variety; Syn.; 1976–1981). Comedy sketches featuring guest stars in performance with the Muppets, the fanciful puppet creations of Jim Henson. Kermit the Frog and his assistant, Miss Piggy, host and attempt to run a TV station despite numerous obstacles they encounter from their staff. The pilot episode (Mar. 19, 1975) featured the Muppet Nigel as the host and his foils Sam and Floyd. Kermit the Frog, Miss Piggy and other well-known Muppets from *Sesame Street* had only cameos.

Voice Cast: Jim Henson *(Kermit/Rowlf)*; Frank Oz *(Miss Piggy/Fozzie Bear/Sam the Eagle)*; Dave Goelz *(Gonzo/Zoot/Bunsen/Beauregard)*; Richard Hunt *(Sweetums/Scooter/Janis)*; Jerry Nelson *(Pops/Floyd)*.

6337   *Muppets Tonight.* (Series; Variety; ABC, 1996; Disney, 1997–1998). A revised version of the 1980s syndicated series *The Muppet Show* that, despite old and new Muppet characters, failed to impress a new generation of children (and adults). The plot follows the prior series with Kermit the Frog attempting to run a variety show (on KUMP-TV) despite the numerous obstacles that befall him (mainly from his staff of Muppet lamebrains). Name guests stars appear in skits with the various Muppet characters. Unlike the prior series, a new Muppet named Clifford hosts.

Muppet Voices: Brian Henson, Steve Whitmire, Jerry Nelson, Bill Barretta, Frank Oz, Leslie Carrara, Kevin Carlson, Drew Massey, Allan Trautman, Bruce Lanoil.

6338   *Murder.* (Series; Game; Spike TV; 2007). Two teams compete in a rather disturbing game show that uses real life, horrific crime scenes as its basis. A gruesome crime scene is recreated and the players are shown the evidence (in addition to blood-splattered walls and other upsetting details, videotaped interviews with the subjects involved). The host then presents the players, who act as CSI forensic experts, with several clues to help them find the killer (although there are several fake clues added to the crime scene to throw players off). When all the evidence has been examined, the host says, "Present Your Case." After each player does so, what really happened in the presented case is revealed. Players do not receive any prizes; money is donated to a crime victim's charity. Real life 27-year veteran Texas P.D. detective Tommy LeNoir is the host.

6339   *Murder Book.* (Pilot; Crime Drama; Unaired; Produced for Fox in 2004). For each crime that is committed the L.A.P.D. generates a record of it in a "Murder Book." The proposal incorporates that book with each chapter serving as the evidence uncovered by the police before the crime is solved.

Cast: Josh Brolin (*Gilroy*); Nestor Serrano (*Robert*); Gina Motegna (*Claire*); Paula Patton (*Angela*).

6340   *Murder by the Book.* (Series; Crime Drama; Court TV; 2006). The author of a best selling crime novel appears as the guest of a particular episode. As the author discusses the crime he has written about, newspaper clippings, crime scene photos and recreations are used to reconstruct the incidents that led up to and caused the murder — and how it was solved or why it still remains a mystery. Authors appearing on the program include James Ellroy, Michael Connelly, Faye Kellerman, Lisa Scottoline and Jonathan Kellerman.

6341   *Murder in High Places.* (Pilot; Crime Drama; NBC; June 2, 1991). Zenith, Colorado, is a ski village that is billed as "Half Dodge City, Half Beverly Hills." Carson Russell is its mayor and his efforts to keep the peace, with the help of a former cop (Horn) and a former pro football player (Stoney Ptak), is the focal point of the proposal.

Cast: Ted Levine (*Carson Russell*); Adam Baldwin (*Stoney Ptak*); Jamey Sheridan (*Horn*); Joyce Hyser (*Terry Ptak, Stoney's wife*).

6342   *Murder in Small Town X.* (Series; Reality; Fox; 2001). A murder has occurred in Sunrise, Maine. The killer left behind a video tape of the crime and challenges ten amateur investigators (the contestants) to find him and solve the crime. Episodes follow their investigations as each attempts to become the winner by uncovering the culprit. Gary Fredo hosts.

6343   *Murder Ink.* (Pilot; Crime Drama; CBS; Sept. 6, 1983). Murder Ink is a Manhattan bookstore owned by Laura Ireland, an avid mystery fan and amateur sleuth. She is married to Lou Ireland, a sergeant with the N.Y.P.D. and the proposal was to relate Laura's exploits as she attempts to help her husband solve baffling crimes. Other regulars are Sergeant Martin "Willie" Wilkinson, Lou's partner; Claire, Laura's assistant at the bookstore; and Hildy, the post office letter carrier.

Cast: Tovah Feldshuh (*Laura Ireland*); Daniel Hugh Kelly (*Lou Ireland*); Ron McLarty (*Martin Wilkinson*); Marcia Jean Kurtz (*Claire*); Anna Maria Horsford (*Hildy*).

6344   *Murder One.* (Series; Crime Drama; ABC; 1995–1997). A single law case that takes a full season to solve is the idea behind *Murder One*. The season one story (1995-96) follows defense attorney Ted Hoffman as he handles an exceptionally controversial case: the defense of Richard Cross, a wealthy businessman accused of murder. Ted successfully defends Cross and gets him exonerated. However, just as this happens, Neil Avedon, a famous actor with a drinking problem, is framed for the murder Cross was just cleared of. Ted believes Neil is innocent and his season long defense of Neil is the focal point of the stories (bits and pieces from other cases handled by the law firm is interspersed between Ted's defense).

Season two episodes (1996-97) begin with Ted leaving his Los Angles law firm to reestablish a relationship with his family (Annie and Lizzie) whom he had neglected because of work. Also leaving the firm are lawyers Lisa and Lily, who worked alongside Ted.

Attorney Jimmy Wyler becomes the center of attention as he and his associate, Justine Appleton take on the case of Sharon Rooney, a woman (a former mistress of the governor of California) accused of murdering the governor and his current mistress.

Cast: Daniel Benzali (*Ted Hoffman*); Anthony LaPaglia (*Jimmy Wyler*); Grace Phillips (*Lisa Gillespie*); Patricia Clarkson (*Annie Hoffman*); Mary McCormick (*Justine Appleton*); Stanley Tucci (*Richard Cross*); Missy Crider (*Sharon Rooney*); Jack Kehler (*Frank Szymanski*); Gregory Itzin (*Roger Gardfield*); John Fleck (*Louis Hines*); Jason Gedrick (*Neil Avedon*); Barbara Bosson (*Miriam Grasso*); Clayton Rohner (*Vince Biggio*); Kevin Tighe (*Davey Blalock*); Dylan Baker (*Arthur Polson*); J.C. MacKenzie (*Arnold Spivak*); D.B. Woodside (*Aaron Mosley*); Michael Hayden (*Chris Docknovich*); Ralph Waite (*Malcolm Dietrich*); Eileen Heckart (*Frances Wyler*); Jessica Tuck (*Laura Crimmins*); Toni DeRose (*Angela Rosetti*).

6345   *Murder 101.* (Series; Crime Drama; Hallmark; 2006). Dr. Jonathan Maxwell is a senior citizen. He is brilliant when it comes to his job — criminology professor, but away from class he is a bit absent-minded and a bit of a klutz. Jonathan may forget where his next class is being held, but if the police need help to solve a baffling crime, he is there to assist (although he most often helps Mike Bryant, a former cop turned private detective, solve crimes). Stories relate Jonathan's investigations as he and Mike solve complex crimes. Ben Manners is Mike's nephew.

Cast: Dick Van Dyke (*Jonathan Maxwell*); Barry Van Dyke (*Mike Bryant*); Shane Van Dyke (*Ben Manners*).

6346   *Murder, She Wrote.* (Series; Crime Drama; CBS; 1984–1996). The Victorian house at 698 Candlewood Road in Cabot Cove, Maine, is home to Jessica Beatrice Fletcher, a widowed mystery novelist better known as J.B. Fletcher. Jessica is a former high school English teacher who was married to Frank Fletcher, a real estate broker. They had a faithful marriage but were never blessed with children. After Frank's death from natural causes in the early 1980s, Jessica quit her teaching job of 19 years to devote full time to her one indulgence — writing. The publication of her first novel, *The Corpse Danced at Midnight*, became a best seller and began a new career for her as a mystery novelist and amateur sleuth.

Jessica's fascination for writing could be attributed to a college break when she worked as a reporter for a newspaper wire service. Jessica enjoys jogging, gardening, cooking and helping with local charities.

Jessica rarely drinks, but when she does, it's a glass of white wine. She is friendly, talkative and uses her bicycle to get around town. She dislikes driving and refuses to get a license. In later episodes, Jessica acquires a job in New York City as a criminology teacher at Manhattan University. She resides in Apartment 4B at the Penfield Apartments, 941 West 16th Street and teaches creative writing at Inner City High School. Jessica also became a world traveler and wherever she goes she is willing to help a stranger in trouble; she is also eager to help the police figure out "who done it," all of which give her inspiration for her books. Jessica is an expert on poisons due to her research and often says, "I think I know who the murderer is. Now to prove it!"

Jessica's original publisher was Covington House; later it is Sutton Place Publishers then Harper Publishers and finally Consolidated Publishers, all in New York City. Two of Jessica's lead fictional detectives are Inspector Dison and Inspector Gelico. Damain Sinclair is the debonair jewel thief she created.

According to Seth Hazlett, the town's elderly doctor, Cabot Cove leads the nation in the sale of live bait. Doc Hazlett, as he is called, has been practicing medicine for 37 years and lives in a 120-year-old house. Doc is a widower, a bit cantankerous and has a penchant for talking. He has a natural curiosity about life and enjoys fishing off his boat, *Cavalier*.

Amos Tupper was the original town sheriff. He was a bus driver before he joined the police department and is a bit inept at his job — a better talker and eater than he is law enforcer. He was replaced by Sheriff Mort Metzger when Amos retired and went home to Kentucky. Mort was a football player with the LA Rams whose career ended when he injured his knee. He then became a police officer with the N.Y.P.D. but quit for the job of sheriff in Cabot Cove because "I couldn't handle the politics." He also says he came to Maine "because I like it here."

A reformed jewel thief named Dennis Stanton (Keith Michell) is featured in nine episodes that have Jessica Fletcher acting as the host rather than the principal player in the story. In the introductory episode, "A Little Night Work" (Oct. 30, 1988), it is learned that Dennis became a thief to get even with the insurance company, Susquehana Fire and Casualty, that refused to pay for his late wife's medical bills. He would steal jewelry insured by that company. Stanton's second episode, "When the Fat Lady Sings" (Nov. 19, 1989) found him reformed, now working as a claims investigator for the Consolidated Casualty Insurance Company in San Francisco. He is employed by Robert Butler (James Sloyan) and receives assistance from his secretary, Rhonda Markowitz (Hallie Todd). His nemesis is Perry Catalano (Ken Swofford), the police lieutenant who balks at Stanton interfering in police matters.

While the Dennis Stanton character was not spun off into a series of its own, one series did evolve from *Murder, She Wrote—The Law and Harry McGraw* with Jerry Orbach recreating his role as a Boston-based detective (see entry for information).

Cast: Angela Lansbury (*Jessica Fletcher*); Tom Bosley (*Amos Tupper*); Ron Masak (*Mort Metzger*); William Windom (*Doc Hazlett*); Louis Herthum (*Deputy Andy Broom*); Will Nye (*Deputy Floyd McCallum*); Michael Horton (*Grady Fletcher*); Ken Swofford (*Lt. Catalano*); Julie Adams (*Eve Simpson*); Herb Edelman (*Lt. Artie Gelber*); Keith Michell (*Dennis Stanton*); Gregg Henry (*Sheriff Lynn Childs*).

Note: Angela Lansbury returned as Jessica Fletcher in the following TV movies: *Murder, She Wrote: South by Southwest* (1997), *Murder, She Wrote: A Story to Die For* (2000), *Murder She Wrote: The Last Free Man* (2001) and *Murder, She Wrote: The Celtic Riddle* (2003).

6347 *The Murdocks and the McClays.* (Pilot; Comedy; ABC; Sept. 2, 1970). Calvin Murdock and Angus McClay are heads of backwoods families who have been feuding for so long that neither side remembers why; they only know that "hate ain't no good 'less it's likewise." When Julianna McClay, Angus's daughter, and Junior Murdock, Calvin's son, fall in love the families fear that a marriage could lead to an unwanted peace between the two families. The proposal was to relate Angus and Calvin's efforts to break up the relationship and keep the feud going.

Cast: Dub Taylor (*Angus McClay*); Kathy Davis (*Julianna McClay*); Noah Beery, Jr. (*Calvin Murdock*); John Carson (*Junior Murdock*); Nydia Westman (*Grandma Murdock*); James Westerfield (*Sheriff Bates*); George C. Fisher (*Turkey*).

6348 *Murdock's Gang.* (Pilot; Crime Drama; CBS; Mar. 20, 1973). When disbarred criminal attorney B.J. (Bartley James) Murdock, falsely accused of allowing a witness to perjure himself, is released from prison after serving a two-year sentence, he begins a private investigative service to help people by hiring a staff of ex-cons (Bat, Denver, Ed, Mickey and Red). The proposal, set in California, was to follow the adventures of Murdock's gang as they use unorthodox methods to help their clients. Terry is Murdock's secretary; Lawrence is his lawyer.

Cast: Alex Drier (*B.J. Murdock*); Donna Kei Benz (*Terry*); Colby Chester (*Lawrence Devans*); Walter Burke (*Bat Collins*); Ed Bernard (*Ed Lyman*); Dave Morrick (*Mickey Carr*); Norman Alden (*Red Harris*); Charles Dierkop (*Denver Briggs*).

6349 *Murphy Brown.* (Series; Comedy; CBS; 1988–1997). Murphy Brown is a beautiful, hard-hitting investigative reporter for *F.Y.I.* (*For Your Information*), a CBS-TV, Washington, D.C.–based news magazine series.

Murphy has a reputation for getting even with anyone who crosses her. She is easily exasperated, has a tendency to yell a lot. In 1968 Murphy met Jake Lowenstein (Robin Thomas) at the Democratic National Convention. They demonstrated together and were arrested together. It was love at first sight and they were married by the judge who heard their case. Five days later they were divorced. When Jake re-entered Murphy's life in 1990, they had a brief affair, and Murphy became pregnant (beginning Sept. 16, 1991). She chose to raise the baby alone when Jake again deserted her. On May 18, 1992 at 5:32 A.M., Murphy gave birth to a boy she first called "Baby Brown" (she later named him Avery after her late mother).

Corky Lynn Sherwood, an *F.Y.I.* news team reporter, can recite all the books of the Bible by heart and reports fluff-like stories as opposed to hard news stories. She was born on a farm in Louisiana and was crowned Miss America at age 19. At the end of the first season Corky married Will Forrest (Scott Bryce), thus becoming Corky Sherwood-Forrest. Will is a struggling writer and authored a book called *The Dutch Boy.*

Frank Fontana joined the F.Y.I. team as an investigative reporter in 1977 (he previously worked as a reporter for the *New York Times*). Frank and Murphy co-hosted the premiere of the network's early morning newscast, *Overnight News.*

James ("Jim") Dial, the senior anchor, has been with CBS News for 25 years. In 1956 he was the only news correspondent to get an interview with John F. Kennedy when he lost the presidential nomination. If Hubert Humphrey had won the presidency in 1968, he would have made Jim Dial his press secretary. A later episode changed Jim's background somewhat: He was a struggling news reporter for Channel 9 in Chicago who doubled as the host of *Poop Deck Pete and Cartoons Ahoy.* Jim has been called "America's Most Trusted Anchorman."

Myles Silverberg is the executive producer of *F.Y.I.* Murphy's antics have driven Myles to the point of hysteria, and he is a good candidate for ulcers and heart attacks—"I'm 27 years old and living on Mylanta." Myles also hears Murphy's voice in his sleep: "They should pipe it into cornfields to scare the crows away." In 1996 Myles quits *F.Y.I.* to become the head of news operations for CBS in New York; he is replaced by Kay Carter as the new executive producer.

Eldin Stanislaus Bernecky is Murphy's around-the-clock housepainter. He is struggling to paint what appears to be a rather large house but is having difficulty matching colors with Murphy's moods. After several bad experiences with nannies, Murphy appointed Eldin as Avery's nanny.

Phil (no last name given) is the owner of the local watering hole, Phil's Bar and Grill (established in 1919). The bar is located at 1195 15th Street (although number 406 is seen on the front door).

The show's gimmick is to exasperate Murphy even more than she already is by assigning her a different (and rather strange) secretary in virtually every episode (when Murphy felt unappreciated at the network, she contemplated accepting an offer from the rival Wolf network—which offered her an efficient secretary named Barbara

[Patti Yasutake]). Avery and Bill Brown are Murphy's parents; Doris Dial is Jim's wife.

Cast: Candice Bergen (*Murphy Brown*); Faith Ford (*Corky Sherwood*); Joe Regalbuto (*Frank Fontana*); Charles Kimbrough (*Jim Dial*); Grant Shaud (*Myles Silverberg*); Robert Pastorelli (*Eldin Bernecky*); Pat Corley (*Phil*); Lily Tomlin (*Kay Carter*); Colleen Dewhurst (*Avery Brown*); Darren McGavin (*Bill Brown*); Janet Carroll (*Doris Dial*).

6350   *Murphy's Law.* (Series; Crime Drama; ABC; 1988-1989). Daedalus Patrick Murphy is an insurance investigator who not only solves cases of insurance fraud but murders as well. He is a recovering alcoholic and lives in a loft at 3116 Hillside with Kimiko Fannuchi, a beautiful Eurasian model.

Murphy works for Wes Hardin, the claims manager for the First Fidelity Casualty Insurance Company in San Francisco; he originally worked for Triax Insurance. Murphy, divorced from Marissa, is the father of Kathleen. The pressures of work caused Murphy to take up drinking and this, in turn, caused Marissa to divorce him. Ten years later Marissa married Charles Danforth, a wealthy lawyer, and has totally raised Kathleen. Murphy now feels he wants to become a part of Kathleen's life and is in a fierce battle with Marissa to win visitation rights.

Kimiko, who prefers to be called Kim, is much younger than Murphy. She was born of an Italian father and Japanese mother and often helps Murphy solve cases, most often by going undercover. Her claim to fame is being the calendar girl for Morgan Power Tools. While blessed with stunning good looks and a gorgeous figure, Kim can't seem to achieve the status of a model with lesser assets.

Morgan DeSade is Murphy's nemesis, his old boss at Triax Insurance, and Victor Beaudine is Murphy's rival, a sleazy agent for First Fidelity, who uses underhanded methods to solve cases. Al Jarreau sings the theme "Murphy's Law."

Cast: George Segal (*Patrick Murphy*); Maggie Han (*Kimiko Fannuchi*); Josh Mostel (*Wes Hardin*); Kim Lankford (*Marissa*); Bruce Gray (*Charles Danforth*); Sarah Sawatsky (*Kathleen*); Elizabeth Savage (*Morgan DeSade*); Charles Rocket (*Victor Beaudine*).

6351   *Music Bingo.* (Series; Game; NBC; ABC; 1958–1960). A musical selection is played by the orchestra. The first of two players who compete that sounds a buzzer signal receives a chance to identify the song title. If he is correct, a square is marked on a large electronic game board. The first player to complete the board (as in the game of Bingo) is the winner and receives merchandise prizes. Aired on NBC (May 29 to Sept. 11, 1958); and ABC (Dec. 5, 1958 to January 1, 1960).

Host: Johnny Gilbert. Music: Harry Salter.

6352   *Music Central.* (Pilot; Variety; Syn.; Aug. 1981). Live performances by the top names in music coupled with film clips and interviews of the featured performers

Host: Dan Daniel. Guests: Pat Benatar, George Benson, Kim Carnes, Roberta Flack, Deborah Harry, Olivia Newton-John, Paul Simon.

6353   *Music City, U.S.A.* (Series; Variety; Syn.; 1968). Jerry Naylor and Teddy Bart host a program of performances by country and western artists.

6354   *Music '55.* (Series; Variety; CBS; 1955). A summer program, presented as an intimate party, that explores various fields of music (one per week).

Host: Stan Kenton. Guests: Jaye P. Morgan, Peggy Lee, Louis Armstrong, Ella Fitzgerald, Woody Herman, Lena Horne, Frankie Laine. Announcer: Stu Metz. Music: Johnny Richards.

6355   *Music for a Spring Night.* (Series; Variety; ABC; 1960). A springtime program of music and song with orchestra leader Glenn Osser as the host. The Glenn Osser Orchestra and Chorus provide the music and songs.

6356   *Music for a Summer Night.* (Series; Variety; ABC; 1959). Glenn Osser, backed by his orchestra and chorus, present a summer program of music and songs.

6357   *Music from the Meadowbrook.* (Series; Variety; ABC; 1953). Jimmy Blaine, Bill Williams and Frank Dailey host performances by orchestras from Frank Dailey's Meadowbrook in Cedar Grove, New Jersey.

6358   *Music Hall America.* (Series; Variety; Syn.; 1976). Performances by country and western artists. A guest celebrity hosts each show (26 aired) and a cast of regulars also provides light comedy and songs.

Regulars: Sandi Burnett, Dean Rutherford, The Even Dozen. Orchestra: Bill Walker.

6359   *Music in Velvet.* (Series; Variety; ABC; 1949–1951). A program of music, song and dance from Chicago.

Host: Johnny Hill. Regulars: Don Lindley and the Velveteers. Orchestra: Rex Maupin.

6360   *The Music Machine.* (Series; Contest; Syn.; 1987). Three aspiring entertainers compete in a challenge round by performing in original music videos. A panel of three celebrity guest judges score the video (0–100) based on verbal ability and showmanship. The current winner and the week's prior winner compete against each other in the championship round. At the end of the season a grand champion is chosen and receives an array of prizes and the chance to record a professional music video.

Host: Curtis Gadson. Music: Carl Small.

6361   *The Music Maker.* (Pilot; Drama; NBC; Jan. 24, 1963). A proposed spin off from *Alcoa Theater* about Johnny Ballard, a jazz musician who helps people in trouble (basically fellow musicians).

Cast: John Forsythe (*Andy Ballard*).

6362   *The Music Mart.* (Pilot; Comedy; NBC; Feb. 8, 1980). Wally and Carol Coogan are a retired song-and-dance team who run a record store called Coogan's Music Mart. The proposal, which features songs and dance numbers, was to focus on the Coogans as they try to relive their show business past through their music store. Other regulars are Scotty, Wally and Carol's son; Lola, their bookkeeper; and Al, Wally's friend.

Cast: Donald O'Connor (*Wally Coogan*); Gloria DeHaven (*Carol Coogan*); Scotty Plummer (*Scotty Coogan*); Micki McKenzie (*Lola*); Sidney Miller (*Al Coody*).

6363   *Music on Ice.* (Series; Variety; NBC; 1960). Music and songs set against the background of an ice show.

Host: Johnny Desmond, Jill Corey. Regulars: Jacqueline Du Bief, The Skip Jacks, The Dancing Blades. Orchestra: Robert Boucher.

6364   *The Music Scene.* (Series; Variety; ABC; 1969–1970). Performances by the top artists in various fields of music (country and western, ballad, rock, folk and blues). Musical numbers are interwoven with comedy sketches. Broadcast back-to-back with *The New People* to form a 90 minute block of programming (with two 45-minute shows).

Program Open: "It's *The Music Scene*, a super concert of the world's best music, each week featuring the best selling records in the country as selected by the editors of *Billboard*, the weekly record and music industry magazine. This week starring Merle Haggard, Bobby Sherman, Sly and the Family Stone, the Temptations, Pat Williams and the Music Scene Orchestra and the comedy of hosts David Steinberg and Lily Tomlin; and our special guest host, Tommy Smothers."

Host: David Steinberg. **Regulars:** Paul Reid Roman, Lily Tomlin, Larry Hankin, Christopher Ross. **Orchestra:** Patrick Williams.

6365   *Music Scoupe*. (Series; Reality; Syn.; 1993). A music oriented series that showcases relatively unknown garage bands that compete for a chance at a recording contract. Each week several such bands perform and are voted upon by the home audience. The band that receives the most call-in votes is the weekly winner and returns to compete in May (the series began in September) with other weekly winners for the grand prize (based on viewer call-in votes). The program also features clips of established alternative bands as well as musical highlights (video clips) of up-and-coming bands. Dave Kendall hosts.

6366   *The Music Shop*. (Series; Variety; NBC; 1959). The recording industry's top artists perform the music and songs that made them famous.

Host: Buddy Bregman.

6367   *The Music Show*. (Series; Variety; DuMont; 1953-1954). A non-sponsored, solid hour of light classical and popular music and songs from Chicago with orchestra leader Robert Trendler as the host.

Host: Robert Trendler. **Regulars:** Mike Douglas, Eleanor Warner, Jackie Van, Henri Noel, Dolores Peterson. **Orchestra:** Robert Trendler.

6368   *Music World*. (Series; Variety; Syn.; 1978). The White Horse Band provides the musical backing for a program that features performances by country and western entertainers. Guest hosts include Stella Parton, Tommy Cash, Patsy Sleed, Conway Twitty, Karren Wheeler, Ben Dover, Tennessee Tucker, The Fox Brothers.

6369   *Musical Chairs*. (Series; Game; NBC; 1955). Three celebrity panelists compete and play for members of the home audience. A vocal group presents a musically oriented question. The first panelist who is able to give the correct answer by impersonating the original recording artist receives one point. The celebrity with the highest score is the winner and his home viewer receives a cash prize.

Host: Bill Leyden. **Panelists:** Bobby Troup, Johnny Mercer, Mel Blanc. **Vocalists:** The Cheerleaders. **Music:** Bobby Troup.

6370   *Musical Chairs*. (Series; Game; CBS; 1975). A song, either sung by the host or a guest, is stopped one line before its conclusion and three possible last lines of the lyric appear on a board. Four players press a button and lock in their choices. The correct line is revealed and money is awarded to the players choosing the correct line. Three rounds, each containing three songs, are played. The contestant with the highest cash score is the winner. The first game show to be hosted by an African-American.

Program Open: "It's the new musical game show *Musical Chairs* with the Musical Chairs Orchestra directed by Derek Smith and showcasing this week's special guest, featured artist at music festivals, the unique new singing star Jane Oliver; and the young singer whose own record album will be released this summer, Lynn Kellogg; and four young sisters who have thrilled audiences in Africa and Europe, Sister Sledge. And here is the host of *Musical Chairs* the chair-man, Adam Wade."

Host: Adam Wade. **Announcer:** Pat Hernan. **Orchestra:** Derek Smith.

6371   *Musical Comedy Time*. (Series; Anthology; NBC; 1950-1951). Guest performers recreate great moments from hit Broadway musicals. The thirteen adaptations are *Anything Goes, Whoopie, The Chocolate Soldier, Rio Rita, The Merry Widow, Hit the Deck, Babes in Toyland, Miss Liberty, Louisiana Purchase, Mademoiselle Modiste, Revenge with Music, No! No! Nanette* and *Flying High*.

6372   *Musical Merry-Go-Round*. (Series; Variety; NBC; 1947–1949). Live musical performances from relatively unknown performers.

Host: Jack Kilty **Regulars:** Eve Young, Penny Gerard, Frederick DeWilde.

6373   *Mustard Pancakes*. (Series; Children; Ion; 2005). Courtney is a talented woman who lives in a home with three dogs and a cat (puppets). Courtney appears to be a songwriter and each of the dogs (Mo, Tina and Oogenberry) and her brilliant cat (Mr. D) help each other learn about various aspects of life through the activities they encounter in and around the house (which, in turn, relates a learning aspect to children). Each program features a song by Courtney after each commercial break.

Cast: Courtney Campbell *(Courtney)*; Frank Mechkuleit *(Mr. D)*; Frank Mechkuleit *(Oogenberry Ink Dog)*; Trish Leeper *(Mo)*; Lee Armstrong *(Tina Ten Toes)*.

6374   *Mutant League*. (Series; Cartoon; Fox; 1996). Adaptation of the video games *Mutant League Football* and *Mutant League Hockey* that depicts the world of ultimate athletes. The rather violent program (limbs tend to be lost in the extreme sports games that are played) begins with the birth of the Mutant Athletes (humans who were exposed to toxic waste when a stadium was built over a forgotten toxic waste dump). With the mutants established, stories follow one league in particular, Bones Justice of the Midway Monsters (and his teammate Razor Kidd), as they attempt to win at any cost.

Voice Cast: Roman Foster *(Bones Justice)*; Rich Bulloyd, Jerry Lee *(Razor Kidd)*; William Summers *(Joe Magician)*; Robert Panepinto *(Darkstar)*; Barbara Jeanne Harrison *(Sherry Steele/Thrasher Malone)*; Rich Bulloyd *(Liquie Lazer)*; Jim Herbie *(Zelgor)*; Robert Brousseau *(Bob Babble)*; Mark Fleisher *(Kang)*; Roman Foster *(Grim McSlam)*.

6375   *Mutant X*. (Series; Adventure; Syn.; 2001–2004). Genomex is a secret branch of U.S. Intelligence that was established to remake the world by creating perfect men and women through genetic manipulation. Adam, a chief biochemist at Genomex, felt enormous guilt for going against the laws of nature when "genetic mistakes" were created. When he is unable to convince his superior, Mason Eckhart of his beliefs, he breaks loose from Genomex and forms Mutant X, a group of rogue, genetically enhanced agents, who believe Genomex is wrong and now fight to protect the world from Eckhart and his plan to use his creations as super agents for covert missions. Shalimar, Emma, Jesse and Brennan are Adam's main operatives (born mutants).

Shalimar is very territorial and very protective of the people she loves. She has extraordinary martial arts skills and the ability to move at an accelerated rate. Her eyes turn cat-like when she gets angry but she is also reckless and leaves herself wide open to attack.

Emma has the gift of inner vision (as Adam calls it). Her telepathic powers are only the beginning. She has "enormous untapped powers" that have yet to surface (in the second episode, a new power, the ability to sense the feelings of others, emerged). She "is cautious and can be read like a book" says Adam.

Brennan controls electricity. He can discharge such bolts from his fingers and create a ball of energy by placing his hands in a circle. The electricity also gives Brennan incredible strength and a split second burst of invisibility to pass through solid objects. Jesse is the sensitive one of the group. He can control objects by concentrating and can create a force field around his body to absorb the impact of a bullet. He is a computer whiz and skilled in the martial arts.

Proxy Blue is a computer generated female image that reports news events. In last season episodes, the mysterious Lexa Pierce becomes the head of Mutant X. She works for the Dominion (which controls the world's technology) and has the ability to change her molecules to pass through solid objects.

Program Open: "Scientist Adam Kane was a pioneer of genetic research, manipulating DNA to save human lives. But in many their genes unrepentantly mutated and they developed super human abilities. Together four of the most powerful fight to protect the world that doesn't even know they exist. They are *Mutant X.*"

Cast: John Shea (*Adam Kane*); Victoria Pratt (*Shalimar Fox*); Lauren Lee Smith (*Emma DeLauro*); Forbes March (*Jesse*); Victor Webster (*Brennan Mulray*); Tom McCammus (*Mason Eckhart*); Karen Cliche (*Lexa Pierce*); George Buza (*Lexa's Dominion Contact*).

6376   *Mutts.* (Pilot; Comedy; ABC; Oct. 2, 1988). While in a pet store seeking a dog, young Eric Gillman is attracted to a mutt named Jeepers—a canine he discovers can telepathically communicate with him. Eric soon finds his life changed when Jeepers helps him out of his introverted shell. The proposal was to relate the adventures of a boy and his dog. Other regulars are Janice and Stuart, Eric's parents; Christine, the pretty girl next door; and Michelle and Glen, Christine's parents.

Cast: Wendy Schaal (*Janice Gillman*); Geoff Pierson (*Stuart Gillman*); Stephen Dorff (*Eric Gillman*); Amy Hathaway (*Christine Hayden*); Jennifer Darling (*Michelle Hayden*); Ray Buktenica (*Glen Hayden*); David Garrison (*Voice of Jeepers*); Mike the Dog (*Jeepers*).

6377   *M.V.P.* (Series; Drama; Soap Net; 2008). Intimate glimpses into the private lives of the team members (and their "puck bunny women") of the Mustangs, a Canadian hockey team.

Gabe McCall is the captain and team center; Trevor Lemonde is the team's number one draft pick; Malcolm LeBlanc is the CEO of the Mustangs; Damon Trebuchet is the team's enforcer; Connie Lewis is Gabe's romantic interest, the owner of a daycare business. Tabbi is Trevor's girlfriend (dreams of becoming a singer); Evelyn McBride is the widow of Adam McBride, the late captain of the Mustangs; Molly is Evelyn's daughter; Megan Chandler is Connie's friend and the girlfriend of Mustang defense man, Owen Chandler.

Cast: Lucas Bryant (*Gabe McCall*); Dillon Casey (*Trevor Lemonde*); Matthew Bennett (*Malcolm LeBlanc*); Kristin Booth (*Connie Lewis*); Anastasia Phillips (*Tabbi*); Peter Miller (*Damon Trebuchet*); Natalie Krill (*Molly McBride*); Amanda Brugel (*Megan Chandler*); Olivie Wadruff (*Grace Morris*).

6378   *My Adventures in Television.* (Series; Comedy; ABC; 2002). IBS is a mythical broadcast television network. IBS is also a low rated network—even lower than the then real network PAX, which achieves higher ratings with reruns of shows that originally aired on IBS (for example, *Just the Three of Us* and *Reginald Woolworth, M.D.*). In an attempt to improve the network's performance, management hires David Weiss, a stage producer from Minneapolis. Red Lansing, the owner of the network, feels that David "has insight into the average American mind" and can turn the network around. Now, as the program director, a somewhat out of place, but enthusiastic young man struggles to do what is expected of him despite a staff of "quirky" co-workers.

Mike McClarren is David's boss, the senior head of programming; Lindsay Urich is the vice president of comedy development (she believes every man is out to sexually harass her); Paul Weiffler is the president of IBS who has an impressive record but of late has hit a stumbling block (he developed *America's Funniest Home Videos* for ABC and *Yes, Dear* for CBS, both real shows). Joanne Waters is the vice president of programming. The first two episodes aired under the title *Wednesday at 9:30 (8:30 Central)*; six aired as *My Adventures in Television.*

Cast: John Cleese (*Red Lansing*); Ed Begley, Jr. (*Paul Weffler*); Ivan Sergei (*David Weiss*); Melinda McGraw (*Lindsay Urich*); James McCauley (*Mike McClarren*); Sherri Shepherd (*Joanne Waters*).

6379   *My Africa.* (Pilot; Drama; CBS; June 21, 1988). Following the death of their mother, two children (Sara and Davey) are sent to Kenya, East Africa, to live with their estranged father, Dr. Charles Marston. Charles, the son of a British father and an American mother (Millie) was born in Africa and raised in America. He abandoned his family to return to the land of his birth to help its people. The proposal depicts Sara and Davey's attempts to adjust to their new lives; and Charles's efforts, assisted by a British doctor (Maggie) and a native (Peter) to treat the sick.

Cast: Carl Weintraub (*Dr. Charles Marston*); Gennie James (*Sara Marston*); Jaimie McEnnan (*Davey Marston*); Jenifer Landor (*Dr. Maggie Halston-Cray*); Joseph Mydell (*Peter*); Louise Latham (*Millie Marston*).

6380   *My Antonio.* (Series; Reality; VH-1; 2009). Former *General Hospital* heartthrob Antonio Sabata, Jr., has set his sights on finding a mate and has based himself in Hawaii to find that special girl. A group of women vie for Antonio's affections but those that fail to impress him (and his mother, who acts as his judge) are eliminated. The girl who best impresses Antonio (and his mother) receives the opportunity to further date Antonio with the ultimate object being marriage. "This is really important to me and not a game," says Antonio.

6381   *My Bare Lady.* (Series; Reality; Fox Reality Channel; 2006). Four gorgeous U.S. adult film stars travel to London, England, to compete in a series of challenges to establish legitimate careers on the West End Stage. In cycle two of the series, *My Bare Lady: Open for Business* four additional U.S. adult film stars compete in a series of challenges to establish themselves as legitimate businesswomen.

Cycle 1 Girls: Sasha Knox, Kristen Price, Chanel St. James, Nautica Thorn. **Cycle 2 Girls:** Brooke Haven, Casey Parker, Sunny Leone, Veronica Rayne.

6382   *My Big Fat Greek Life.* (Series; Comedy; CBS; 2003). A television adaptation of the feature film *My Big Fat Greek Wedding* that picks up with the newlyweds (Nia and Thomas) returning from their honeymoon and talking about how to set up a modern-day marriage while surrounded by old world Greek customs and loud and obnoxious relatives.

Nia works for her father at the Dancing Zobras (a bar-restaurant in Chicago). Nia and Thomas live in a house across the street from the bar (a wedding gift from her father; they previously lived in a cramped apartment). Nia's family calls Thomas "a non Greek" and the only thing Thomas has in common with his in-laws is that they attend St. Anthony's church together. Stories follow Thomas's efforts to become a Greek and adjust to life not only as a newlywed but to Nia's outlandish family. Other regulars are Maria and Gus, Nia's parents; Nick, Nia's brother; Nikki, Nia's cousin (and best friend) and Nia's Aunt Voula.

In the feature film Nia Vardalos played Toula Portokalos, not Nia, and John Corbett played Nia's boyfriend/husband Ian (Steve Eckholdt plays the role as Thomas on the series)

Cast: Nia Vardalos (*Nia Portokalos-Miller*); Steven Eckholdt (*Thomas Miller*); Lainie Kazan (*Maria Portokalos*); Michael Constantine (*Gus Portokalos*); Gia Caridel (*Nikki*); Andrea Martin (*Aunt Voula*); Louis Mandylor (*Nick Portokalos*); Victoria Adams (*Young Nia*).

6383   *My Big Fat Obnoxious Fiance.* (Series; Reality; Fox; 2004). Randi Coy is a very pretty real life girl who has agreed to be part of a prank in order to win $500,000. She has to pretend to be in love with Steve Williams, a man she met on a reality show and convince friends and family that they are in love and are going to be married. She must also allow a film crew to record all the reactions that occur as Steve meets Randi's family and announces the engagement. The twist — the joke is actually on an unsuspecting Randi. Steve is an actor who has been hired to be the worst fiancé any girl could possibly have — as obnoxious and embarrassing as possible. Randi's reactions and those of her family to Steve's total embarrassment of Randi is the focal point of the program. Claudio DiFolco hosts. Jack Roth is the announcer.

6384   *My Big Redneck Wedding.* (Series; Reality; CMT; 2008). Real weddings, that are all but glamorous, are showcased as mud fights, square dances and monster trucks take center stage.

Host: Tom Arnold.

6385   *My Black Is Beautiful.* (Series; Reality; BET; 2009). An informative program geared toward African American women that features story profiles, interviews, fashion updates and health and beauty tips that "inspire and celebrate the unparalleled beauty" of its target audience. Tasha Smith hosts.

6386   *My Boy Googie.* (Pilot; Comedy; CBS; July 24, 1967). Bill and Kate Wallace are the parents of two children, 12-year-old Frances and eight-year-old Googie. Frances, called "Fannie" is the typical pre-teenage girl who is just discovering boys, while Googie is a problem child who delights is causing mischief. The proposal was to focus on Googie's escapades and the efforts of all concerned to control him.

Cast: Jerry Van Dyke (*Bill Wallace*); Jeanne Ranier (*Kate Wallace*); Teddy Eccles (*Googie Wallace*); Pamela Dapo (*Frances Wallace*).

6387   *My Boys.* (Series; Comedy; TBS; 2006–). P.J. Franklin is a young woman in her twenties who is also a sports writer (baseball); she covers the Chicago Cubs for the *Sun Times*. P.J. has mostly male friends and could be considered a tomboy. She is a low maintenance girl and is the glue that keeps her friends together. P.J. does have a female friend, Stephanie, who attended journalism school with her and who, being more feminine than P.J., offers her tips on how to use her feminine wiles on men. Her male friends are Mike, a ladies' man who is afraid to make a commitment (he also works for the Cubs); Brendan, a D.J. with numerous romantic heartaches; Kenny, a dating challenged sports memorabilia store owner; and Andy, P.J.'s henpecked brother. Adding spice to P.J.'s life is Bobby, a sports writer for the rival newspaper, the *Chicago Tribune*.

Cast: Jordana Spiro (*P.J. Franklin*); Kellee Stewart (*Stephanie Layne*); Michael Bunin (*Kenny Mortitori*); Jamie Kaler (*Mike Callahan*); Reid Scott (*Brendan Dorff*); Jim Gaffigan (*Andy Franklin*); Kyle Howard (*Bobby Newman*).

6388   *My Brother and Me.* (Series; Comedy; Nick; 1994-1995). The Parkers are an African-American family living comfortably in North Carolina. Roger and Jennifer are the parents; Melanie, Alfie and Derek (called Dee Dee) are their children. Alfie and Dee Dee are also best friends and stories relate humorous events in their lives, as well as those of their sister and parents. Milton Berry, called "Goo" is their nosey neighbor; Dionne and Donnel are friends of the children.

Cast: Jim R. Coleman (*Roger Parker*); Karen E. Fraction (*Jennifer Parker*); Aisling Sistrunk (*Melanie Parker*); Arthur Reggie III (*Alfred "Alfie" Parker*); Ralph Woolfolk IV (*Derek "Dee Dee" Parker*); Jimmy Lee Newman (*Milton "Goo" Berry*); Amanda Seales (*Dionne*); Stefan J. Wernli (*Donnel Wilburn*).

6389   *My Buddy.* (Pilot; Comedy; NBC; July 3, 1979). Buddy's Bar is a San Francisco watering hole where people from all walks of life can find a friend in its owner, Woodrow "Buddy" Johnson. One such customer was Albert Worth, a wealthy man who found release from the pressures of work at the bar. One day Buddy is surprised to learn that Mr. Worth has died and he has inherited his multi-million dollar empire, Worth Enterprises. But to keep his inheritance, Buddy must live in the Worth mansion with Albert's snobbish sister, Catherine, and her money-hungry husband, Bernard. Buddy turns over the bar to his friend, Slappy, moves into the mansion and the unsold series was to relate Buddy's misadventures as he attempts to adjust to his new life in high society.

Cast: Redd Foxx (*Buddy Johnson*); Pamela Mason (*Catherine Worth*); Slappy White (*Slappy*); Basil Hoffman (*Bernard Worth*); Irwin C. Watson (*Sumpter, Buddy's friend*).

6390   *My Dad Is Better Than Your Dad.* (Series; Reality; NBC; 2008). Four father and son (or father and daughter) teams compete. A series of various physical contests are held in which the fathers perform the most strenuous part of the stunt with the son or daughter coaching or assisting in aspects that will not cause them any harm. The first competition eliminates the weakest performing team. A second competition eliminates another team. The two final teams compete for a chance to win $50,000. Here one team becomes "The Shooter" while the other "The Blocker." The father of the team at play stands behind a large air gun; his child is "the bullet passer." The gun is designed to shoot paper bullets. The opponent stands before a large wall that contains 44 windows, each worth a different money amount. The child hands her father a bullet, which the father loads into the gun. He aims it at a window, trying to break it to earn its associated points. The blocker must divert the bullet with the paddles he has. After 90 seconds, the teams reverse positions and the game is played in the same manner. The highest scoring team wins and competes for $50,000. Here the father must answer questions based on his child's life. Each correct answer scores $10,000; a wrong answer ends the game and the team wins whatever money they have accumulated.

Host: Dan Cortese.

6391   *My Dad the Rock Star.* (Series; Cartoon; Nick; 2003). William Zilla, called Willy, is the 14-year-old son of Rockford Amadeus Zilla, a world-famous rock star known as Rock Zilla. Willy's life has been anything but normal growing up as his father's tours constantly uprooted the family. Rockford has now settled down and has moved his family to the town of Silent Springs. Willy now has some stability in his life and stories follow his mishaps as he tries to accept a more normal life style. He aspires to be a jazz musician. Created by Gene Simmons (of KISS fame).

Rock has a pet Komodo Dragon (Mosh) and is a bit immature and acts like a teenager. Crystal Zilla is Willy's mother, a spiritualist; Nigel Fanshawe, called Skunk, is Rock's tour bus driver; Sarah, an environmental activist, is Willy's girlfriend; Quincy, who prefers to be called "Q," is Willy's friend; Serenity Zilla is Willy's older sister, a boy crazy teenage girl; Buzz is the local bully; Principal Malfactor is the head of Willy's school; Mr. Kant is Rock's neighbor.

Voice Cast: Joanne Vannicola (*Willy Zilla*); Lawrence Bayne (*Rock Zilla*); Kathleen Laskey (*Crystal Zilla*); Don Francks (*Skunk*); Sarah Gadon (*Alyssa*); Stephanie Anne Mills (*Serenity Zilla*); Martin Cillafana (*Quincy*); Rob Stefaniuk (*Buzz Sawchuck*); Dwight Schultz (*Principal Malfactor/Mr. Kant*).

6392   *My Darling Judge.* (Pilot; Comedy; CBS; April 23, 1961). Cyrus Dunn is a prestigious Beverly Hills judge. He is married to Betsy and is the father of two children, Charlotte and Leila. The proposal was to focus on the problems that befall the good-natured but easily exasperated judge as he tries to put his work aside and spend more time with his family. Willie is the Dunns' gardener.

Cast: Fred Clark (*Cyrus Dunn*); Audrey Totter (*Betsy Dunn*); Melinda Plowman (*Charlotte Dunn*); Anne Whitefield (*Leila Dunn*); Willie Tsang (*Willie*).

6393   *My Enemy, This Town.* (Pilot; Drama; NBC; Feb. 6, 1964). A proposed spin off from *The Kraft Suspense Theater* about Johnny Baroja, a wandering ex-con who helps people in trouble.

Cast: Scott Marlowe (*Johnny Baroja*).

6394   *My Fabulous Wedding.* (Series; Reality; WE; 2007). A look at the preparations that brides-to-be encounter while planning their weddings (although those profiled are rich and do not skimp and purchase what they want—from expensive wedding gowns to exotic reception locales). Brooke Gaston is the producer.

6395   *My Fair Brady.* (Series; Reality; VH-1; 2005–2008). Christopher Knight, the actor who played Peter Brady on *The Brady Bunch* (ABC, 1969–1974) is now 47 years old. Adrianne Curry, the first winner of *America's Next Top Model*, is 22 years old. The two met on *The Surreal Life* and fell in love. A year after their meeting they are still in love and living together. For reasons that are not really explained (other than for publicity) the couple allows cameras in their lives. The program follows Peter and Adrianne as they go about their everyday business—now made more public than private.

Stars: Christopher Knight, Adrianne Curry.

6396   *My Fair Wedding.* (Series; Reality; WE; 2008–2010). Misguided brides are set on the right path to a happy wedding day with a complete makeover from dress to décor. Event planner David Tutera hosts.

6397   *My Family.* (Pilot; Comedy; Unaired; Produced for NBC in 1992.). Monologues, flashbacks and present-day scenes are used to tell the humorous story of Rick Garrison, a survivor of a dysfunctional family, as he goes out of his way to ensure a happy childhood for his two sons Jack (16) and Morgan (6).

Cast: Rick Reynolds (*Rick Garrison*); Maureen Mueller (*Maureen Garrison*); Matt Nolan (*Jack Garrison*); Bradley Pierce (*Morgan Garrison*).

6398   *My Favorite Husband.* (Series; Comedy; CBS; 1953–1955). George Cooper is the subject of the title. He is married to Elizabeth, called Liz, and they live in a lovely home, decorated in Chinese modern, at 1561 Blair Street in Westwood, California. George, an executive with the Sunset State Bank, is level-headed and very understanding (and forgiving) of what results when Liz sets out to do something. Liz is not the typical housewife; she is a bit scatterbrained and her efforts to accomplish something always backfire and involve George in situations that he must always resolve (making him a hero in Liz's eyes).

Liz, as portrayed by Joan Caulfield was tall and blonde; Vanessa Brown, who replaced her in 1955, was petite and brunette. Despite the obvious difference in wives, "the beguiling combination of wit, femininity and attractive sex which has become a hallmark of the role" remained the same. Myrna and Gilmore Cobb are their friends. In 1955 Myrna became Myrna Shepard and she was now married to Oliver Shepard. George's sister, Janice Cooper is a commercial artist; and George's Uncle, Norman, is a former vaudeville performer. Based on the radio series of the same title with Richard Denning as George and Lucille Ball as Liz.

Program Open: "Frigidaire, leader in home appliances, the most famous name in refrigeration, all backed by General Motors, presents *My Favorite Husband* starring Barry Nelson and Vanessa Brown."

Cast: Joan Caulfield (*Liz Cooper; 1953–55*); Vanessa Brown (*Liz Cooper; 1955*); Barry Nelson (*George Cooper*); Bob Sweeney (*Gilmore Cobb*); Alix Talton (*Myrna Cobb; 1953–55*); Alix Talton (*Myrna Shepard; 1955*); Dan Tobin (*Oliver Shepard*); Carolyn Jones (*Janice Cooper*); David Burns (*Uncle Norman*). **Announcer:** Dick Joy.

6399   *My Favorite Martian.* (Series; Comedy; CBS; 1963–1966). One morning, while driving to work, Los Angeles *Sun* newspaper reporter Tim O'Hara witnesses the crash-landing of a UFO (unidentified flying object). He investigates and befriends its pilot, Exagitious 12½, a professor of anthropology from Mars whose specialty is the primitive planet Earth. (During the U.S. Air Force's testing of an X-15 plane, the Martian's spacecraft entered the Earth's atmosphere and locked into a head-on collision course with it. To avoid disaster, Exagitious 12½ strained his ship to get out of the path of the X-15. The strain caused a malfunction and the saucer crashlanded.)

Tim takes the stranded Martian to his apartment at 21 Elm Street, in a home owned by Lorelei Brown, a very pretty but slightly dizzy widow. To protect his true identity, the Martian adopts the alias of Uncle Martin, a relative who has come to live with his nephew, Tim. (Martin's silver spaceship is hidden in Lorelei's garage.) While Martin seeks a way to repair his craft (the materials he needs are still unknown to Earth), he struggles to adjust to a more primitive world and to keep his true identity a secret. His task is complicated by Bill Brennan, a detective with the 12th Precinct of the L.A.P.D., who is suspicious of both Tim and Martin.

Uncle Martin has a superior intellect and claims to be the greatest living authority on the history of Earth. He is puzzled by earthly emotions and thinks humans lack intelligence ("We use all of our brain, not just a portion of it"). He can speak to and understand animals, levitate (with his right index finger) and appear and disappear at will (by raising the antennae at the back of his head).

When Bill, the human bloodhound who is called "Bulldog Brennan," is around, Martin's antennae quiver. Mrs. Brown, who is famous for her fudge brownies, is the mother of two beautiful daughters: Annabel and Angela.

In the unaired pilot version, Martin did not have the power of levitation (he used a control device from his ship to levitate), and Lorelei had only one daughter, Annabel (Ina Victor), who was Tim's romantic interest.

Cast: Ray Walston (*Uncle Martin*); Bill Bixby (*Tim O'Hara*); Pamela Britton (*Lorelei Brown*); Alan Hewitt (*Bill Brennan*); J. Pat O'Malley (*Harry Burns, Tim's boss*); Roy Engle (*Police Captain*); Ina Victor (*Annabel Brown*); Ann Marshall (*Angela Brown*).

6400   *My Favorite Martians.* (Series; Cartoon; CBS; 1973–1975). A spin off from *My Favorite Martian*. When a damaged spacecraft lands on Earth, its occupants, Uncle Martin, his nephew Andy, and their dog Oakie Doakie, are befriended by Tim O'Hara, a newspaper reporter, and his niece Katy—the sole witnesses to their landing. In an effort to help the stranded Martians, Tim shelters them at his home but arouses the suspicions of Bill Brennan, a freelance security officer, who tries to uncover their secret. Stories relate Martin's efforts to maintain his false identity and find the materials he needs to repair his disabled craft and return home. Lorelei Brown is Tim's landlady; Brad Brennan is Bill's son.

Voice Cast: Jonathan Harris (*Uncle Martin*); Lane Scheimer (*Tim O'Hara/Bill Brennan*); Jane Webb (*Katy O'Hara/Lorelei Brown*); Edward Morris (*Andy/Brad Brennan*).

6401 *My Friend Flicka.* (Series; Drama; CBS, 1956–1959; ABC, 1959–1963). Rob McLaughlin and his wife, Nell are the owners of the Goose Bar Ranch in Coulee Springs, Wyoming, during the early 1900s. They are also the parents of Ken and operate a horse ranch. There is one special horse on the ranch, Flicka (Swedish for Little Girl) that was captured by Rob and his foreman, Gus, and given to Ken to care for in an effort to teach him responsibility. Stories, set in an era still governed by lawlessness, relate events in the lives of the family, in particular the adventures shared by Ken and Flicka. Hildy is Gus's niece; Walt is the town sheriff; Tim is Rob's friend. Based on stories by Mary O'Hara.

Cast: Gene Evans (*Rob McLaughlin*); Anita Louise (*Nell McLaughlin*); Johnny Washbrook (*Ken McLaughlin*); Frank Ferguson (*Gus Broeberg*); Pamela Beaird (*Hildy Broeberg*); Hugh Sanders, Sydney Mason (*Walt Sanders*); Tudor Owen (*Tim O'Gara*); Craig Duncan (*U.S. Marshal*); Wahama (*Flicka*).

6402 *My Friend Irma.* (Series; Comedy; CBS; 1952–1954). "If she thinks it could be dangerous," says Jane Stacy, the level-headed roommate of Irma Peterson, a beautiful and shapely "dumb blonde" whose well-meaning intentions always backfire. Irma and Jane share Apartment 3B (later 2C) at Mrs. O'Reilly's Boarding House at 185 West 73rd Street in Manhattan.

Irma was born in Minnesota and loves the excitement of big-city life. She works as a secretary for Milton J. Clyde, owner of the Clyde Real Estate Company at 631 East 41st Street. She is sweet and sensitive and realizes that she is not as smart as other people. She talks to walls "to clear the cobwebs out of my mind" and "when I don't want people to know I know something, I pretend I'm dumb."

Irma is always fashionably dressed; she is a picture of beauty, a good housekeeper and an ample cook, but is head over heels in love with the wrong man—Al, "The best customer at the state unemployment office." The averse-to-work Al is a con artist who calls Irma "Chicken."

Jane was born in Connecticut and lived with her parents at 1362 Post Valley Road before coming to New York to fulfill a dream: marrying a rich man. Jane believes only money can buy happiness and begins her quest by becoming the personal secretary to Richard Rhinelander, the wealthy owner of the Richard Rhinelander Investment Company at 113 Park Avenue. Jane secretly loves Richard and desperately tries to impress him, but feels her chances will be ruined by Irma, who is well below his social scale.

Richard is a graduate of Harvard Business School and, despite his encounters with Irma, finds her delightful. Jane talks directly to the audience to relate her feelings as the story progresses. Jane met Irma quite by accident, when they bumped into each other. When Irma learned that Jane was looking for a place to live, she offered to let her live with her — in "a one-room furnished basement Irma calls home."

When Jane receives a transfer to Panama in 1953, Irma places a newspaper ad for a new roommate. Kay Foster, a reporter for the New York *Globe* answers it and becomes Irma's new roommate.

Kay is bright and beautiful and she too, speaks directly to the audience and comments on the situations that develop as a result of Irma's antics. Kay was born in Ohio and attended Ohio State College (majoring in journalism).

There were plans for Irma to marry and continue the series as *My Wife Irma.* While this never happened, Al was dropped to give Irma a more respectable boyfriend — Joe Vance, a neatly dressed, intelligent, hard-working man (for the Spic and Span Cleaners). Kay's boyfriend is Brad Jackson, a fellow reporter for the *Globe.* Kathleen O'Reilly is the owner of the boarding house; Professor Kropotkin is Irma's neighbor, who plays violin at the Paradise Burlesque Theater (later the Gypsy Tea Room); Bobby is Irma's nephew. Based on the radio program of the same title.

First Season Open: "Lever Brothers Company, makers of Swan, the soap with the exclusive super cleans blend, presents *My Friend Irma* with Marie Wilson as Irma and Cathy Lewis as Jane."

Second Season Open: "Kool cigarettes presents *My Friend Irma* created by Cy Howard and starring Marie Wilson as Irma with Mary Shipp as Kaye." [*Kaye presenting Irma with a cigarette:*] "Have a Kool Irma." [*Irma:*] "Sure thing Kaye. I've switched from hots to Kools, Kool cigarettes I mean. As Willie the Penguin [*animated Kool logo*] says"; "Smoke Kools, smoke Kools." [*Irma:*] "That's right folks, smoke Kools."

Cast: Marie Wilson (*Irma Peterson*); Cathy Lewis (*Jane Stacey*); Mary Shipp (*Kay Foster*); Sid Tomack (*Al*); Hal March (*Joe Vance*); Brooks West (*Richard Rhinelander III*); Gerald Mohr (*Brad Jackson*); Donald MacBride (*Milton J. Clyde*); Sig Arno (*Professor Kropotkin*); Gloria Gordon (*Mrs. O'Reilly*); Richard Eyer (*Bobby Peterson*); John Carradine (*Mr. Corday*); Margaret DuMont (*Richard's mother*). **Announcer:** Frank Bingham, Bob Lemond.

6403 *My Friend Rabbit.* (Series; Cartoon; NBC; 2007). Rabbit is a white hare that lives in a forest. He is close friends with Mouse (a rodent) and together they share exciting adventures with the other animals of the forest (including swans, raccoons and even Thunder the Hippo). Stories follow Rabbit and Mouse as they struggle to solve the problems they encounter.

Voice Cast: Peter Oldring (*Rabbit*); Robert Binsley (*Mouse*); Denise Oliver (*Hazel*); Jeremy Harris (*Thunder*); Milton Barnes (*Jasper*); Hannah Endicott-Douglas (*Amber*); Isabel de Carteret (*Coral*); Nissae Isen (*Jade*); Camden Angelia (*Pearl*); Stacey DePass (*Edweena*).

6404 *My Friend Tony.* (Series; Crime Drama; NBC; 1969). John Woodruff is a private detective and criminologist professor at U.C.L.A. John is a World War II veteran whose partner is Tony Novello, a young boy (now a man) he befriend while serving in Italy (Tony came to the U.S. to look up his old friend, and eventually stayed on to become his partner). Stories relate their case investigations: John is a man who strictly follows the book; Tony is an eager beaver who feels it is necessary to break the rules to get the results they need.

Cast: James Whitmore (*John Woodruff*); Enzo Cerusico (*Tony Novello*).

6405 *My Friends Tigger and Pooh.* (Series; Cartoon; Disney; 2007–). A computer animated adaptation of the *Winnie the Pooh* stories by A.A. Milne that is set in the Hundred Acre Wood where Winnie the Pooh, the honey-loving bear, and his animal friends Tigger (a tiger), Piglet (pig), Rabbit, Eeyore (donkey), Kanga and Roo (kangaroos) live. Christopher Robin is their only human friend. In the new version several new characters are introduced: Darby, a six-year-old tomboyish girl; Buster, her puppy, and Lumpy, a new neighbor in the woods. Stories, aimed at preschoolers, teach learning aspects through the adventures shared by the animals and their human friends.

Voice Cast: Jim Cummings (*Winnie the Pooh/Tigger*); Ken Sansom (*Rabbit*); Chloe Moretz (*Darby*); Struen Erhlinhorn (*Christopher Robin*); Travis Oates (*Piglet*); Dee Bradley Baker (*Piglet*); Max Burkholder (*Roo*); Kath Soucie (*Kanga*); Peter Cullen (*Eeyore*); Oliver Dillon (*Lumpy*).

6406 *My Games Fever.* (Series; Game; My Network TV; 2006-2007). Live, daily game show (1:00 P.M. to 3:00 P.M.) wherein home viewers are the participants (who play via text, Internet or 1-900 telephone numbers). Once a viewer is selected to become a contestant, various interactive games are played, worth from $200 to $500 in cash.

Host: Nikki Stanzione, Natalie Castellanos, Erin Myers, Kourtney Brown, Chris Underwod, Charles Venturi.

6407 *My Generation.* (Series; Game; USA; 1998). Teams, composed of players from various years of high school graduation, are teamed by year and must answer questions based on the year they graduated to the present.

Host: Craig Shoemaker. **Announcer:** Lindsey Stoddart.

6408 *My Generation.* (Series; Drama; ABC; 2010). In 2000, a camera crew began documenting the lives of a group of seniors from Greenbelt High School in Austin, Texas. In 2010, as they return for a reunion, cameras capture what has become of them over the past ten years. Scripted episodes, made to look like a reality series, relate the path each has taken and whether or not they met the goals they originally set for themselves. The students are Kenneth Finley, now a teacher; Dawn Barbuso married Rolly Marks, now serving in Afghanistan (and expecting their first child); Jackie Vachs, the class beauty, failed in an attempt to become an actress and is living with Anders Holt, the rich student. Brenda Serrano, the smartest kid in class, now works for a congressman in Washington, D.C. Steve Foster, the over achiever, has become a surfer; Caroline Chung, the wall flower, is raising Steven's son (who was conceived on prom night, but Steven is unaware of this). And, known only as "The Falcon," is still chasing a dream to become a rock superstar. No one apparently cared as the show was canceled after two episodes.

Cast: Keir O'Donnell (*Kenneth Finley*); Kelli Garner (*Dawn Barbuso*); Jamie King (*Jackie Vachs*); Mehcad Brooks (*Rolly Marks*); Julian Morris (*Anders Holt*); Daniella Alonso (*Brenda Serrano*); Anne Son (*Caroline Chung*); Michael Stahl-David (*Steven Foster*); Sebastian Sozzi (*The Falcon*).

6409 *My Guide to Becoming a Rock Star.* (Series; Drama; WB; 2002). Jace Darnell is a young man with a powerful ambition: become a rock star. He lays out his plan in easy-to-follow steps and stories follow his efforts to make his group, Slip Dog, famous. Doc, Jo, Owen and Danny are the other band members; Eric is Jace's father, a former rock star who is trying to discourage Jace, as musical stardom is very difficult to achieve. Gina is Jace's mother; Sarah Nelson is the DJ mix artist. Based on the British series *The Young Person's Guide to Becoming a Rock Star.*

Cast: Oliver Hudson (*Jace Darnell*); Michael Des Barres (*Eric Darnell*); Kevin Rankin (*Victor "Doc" Pike*); Emmanuelle Vaugier (*Sarah Nelson*); Brian Dietzen (*Owen*); Lauren Hodges (*Josephine "Jo" Delamo*); Rick Overton (*Dole Grevson*); Shannon Tweed (*Gina Darnell*); James DeBello (*Danny Whitaker*).

6410 *My Guys.* (Series; Comedy; CBS; 1996). Sonny DeMarco is the owner of a small limo company in New York City. He is also a widower and the father of Michael and Francis (the "My Guys" of the title). Stories follow Sonny as he attempts to run his business (DeMarco Limousines), care for his sons and find the time for a social

life. Other regulars are Angela, his next-door neighbor; and Dori, the waitress at the coffee shop who hopes to become a professional dancer.

Cast: Michael Rispoli (*Sonny DeMarco*); Francis Capra (*Francis DeMarco*); Mike Damus (*Michael DeMarco*); Marisol Nichols (*Angela*); Sheri Scott (*Dori*).

6411 *My Gym Partner's a Monkey.* (Series; Cartoon; Cartoon Network; 2005). The Charles Darwin Middle School is an institution devoted to educating animals. Adam Lyon is a 12-year-old human boy who also attends the school. A mix-up by the school board (spelling his last name as Lion instead of Lyon) placed him in the animal category and a candidate for the school. Adam adjusts (although he has to be careful as there are signs posted that read "Do Not Eat the Students") and has become friends with Jake Spider Monkey. Stories follow Adam's misadventures (complicated by Jake) in a school where being human is odd. A diminutive frog, Principal Pixiefrog, runs the school; Coach Gillis (a goldfish) is the athletic director; Eugenia Tusk (an elephant) is the lunch lady; Miss Chameleon is the drama teacher; Virgil Sharkowski, called Bull, is the school bully; Slips Python is the school nerd; Ingrid Giraffe is the tallest kid in class; Henry Armadillo anchors the school's news program.

Voice Cast: Nika Futterman (*Adam Lyon*); Tom Kerry (*Jake Spider Monkey*); Maurice La Marche (*Principal Pixiefrog*); Brian Doyle Murray (*Coach Gillis*); Grey De Lisle (*Ingrid Giraffe*); Rick Gomez (*Slips Python*); Phil LaMarr (*Virgil Sharkowski*); Nika Futterman (*Miss Chameleon*); Cree Summer (*Eugenia Tusk*); Tom Kenny (*Henry Armadillo*).

6412 *My Hero.* (Series; Comedy; NBC; 1952-1953). The "hero" of the title is Robert S. Beanblossom, a handsome salesman for the Thackery Realty Company in Los Angeles, who uses his suave and sophisticated style and "power over women" to sell real estate. The girl to whom Robert is a hero is Julie Marshall, a red haired, brown eyed beauty who works as the office secretary. Julie sees Robert as other women do (a playboy bachelor), but she also sees a side of him that other women do not — his somewhat klutzy approach to selling properties when he becomes desperate. Despite Robert's misadventures, he always manages to come out on top (at which time Julie hugs him and says, "My hero").

Willis Thackery, the owner of the company, has been in the real estate game for 27 years. When he likes what Robert is doing, he calls him "Bob," "Bob-O" and "Robin." When he gets angry at Bob, it's "Beanblossom!" Thackery's competition is Yeager's Developments. Leon Klatzkin composed the "My Hero" theme.

Cast: Bob Cummings (*Robert S. Beanblossom*); John Litel (*Willis Thackery*); Julie Bishop (*Julie Marshall*).

6413 *My Kind of Town.* (Series; Reality; ABC; 2005). Two hundred people, chosen from typical American small towns, are brought to New York City to compete in a series of games. At the end of each episode, one player, chosen by the others to be their representative, competes in a game called "Name Your Neighbor." Here the player must identify the names of six players who were featured in the various games that were previously held. If he can, each member of the group wins a prize tailored especially for them; if not, all two hundred lose. Johnny Vaughan hosts.

6414 *My Life and Times.* (Series; Drama; ABC; 1991). "I wouldn't say I've seen it all, but I've seen a lot. I've seen the world change, I've seen myself change. I've watched footsteps on the moon; I've seen myself stumble. I've made a fortune, I've lost a fortune ... I've loved and lost and lived to love again. The one thing I know, life is an adventure. You've got to hold on and let it carry you away. It carried me all the way to the year 2035. And I'm here to tell the tale. I'm Ben Miller and this is my life and times."

From a retirement home in the year 2035, 85-year-old Benjamin ("Ben") Miller spoke those words (over the theme music), and through flashbacks, as Ben recalled his life, we saw his life and times. Unfortunately, ABC canceled the critically acclaimed adult *Wonder Years* after only six episodes, leaving many stories untold. Ben's life was not presented in any specific order; it is the bits of dialogue scattered throughout the various episodes that tie the information presented here together.

On September 17, 1968, Ben began his journalism studies at Northwestern University. It was here that he met and first fell in love with Rebecca Elizabeth Eastman, a student majoring in psychology. After graduation they drifted apart: Ben went to New York to pursue his writing career; she remained in Chicago to attend graduate school; the time is 1972.

We next learn about Ben in 1978. He has written a story about an enchanting girl he met named Jessie (Claudia Christian) for the Illinois Review. At age 35 in 1985, Ben returned to Chicago to look up Rebecca, who is 31. Ben is now a reporter for the New York *Globe*, and he and Rebecca find that they still love each other. She accepted his proposal. They married and returned to New York to live. From this point on, information was not given to link Ben's past.

Ben and Rebecca had two children, Melanie and Daniel. Daniel was born in 1989; Melanie in 1994. At some point between 1989 and 1998, Ben wrote two books: *A Break in the Clouds* and *Come the Redeemer*. Ben also left his job at the *Globe* (possibly in 1986) and began driving a Checker Cab in Manhattan. With only $2,300 in their bank account, Ben bought 900 shares in a company called Lightbridge Systems. He lost virtually everything when the stock market fell 500 points on "Black Monday."

Apparently the times were getting hard for Americans. There was the Crash of 1998, and 50 million people were out of work. It was in 1998 that Ben and his family moved from their home in Seattle to Washington, D.C., where Ben found work as a bookkeeper with Colby-Stern, a government contracting company.

On Memorial Day, 1999, Ben and his family vacationed at Pearl Lake in Illinois. On Labor Day of that year, Rebecca died of cancer. Ben then moved to St. Louis to take a factory job.

We saw Ben celebrate the millennium with his family, and we know from an early episode that in the year 2000 Ben married Lily Matheson. We also know that Rebecca loved working with kids in a Manhattan Welfare center. And, we learn that Ben's favorite candy in the year 2036 (the series progressed one year in the fourth episode) is Milk Duds.

Relatives (Year 2035): Regina Leeds (Ben's daughter, Melanie Miller), Tim Stack (Ben's son, Daniel Miller), Harriet Medin (Daniel's wife, Jessie Miller), Matt McGrath (Daniel's son, Robert Miller), Christopher Pettiet (Daniel's son, Michael Miller).

Flashbacks: Emily Ann Lloyd (Melanie in 1999), Sean Baca (Daniel in 1999), Angela Patton (Ben's mother, Sarah Miller in 1985), Priscilla Pointer (Rebecca's mother in 1985), Paul Dooley (Rebecca's father in 1985).

Cast: Tom Irwin (*Ben Miller*); Helen Hunt (*Rebecca Miller*).

6415   *My Life As a Dog.* (Series; Drama; Showtime; 1997). A television adaptation of the Swedish film *My Life as a Dog* (about a young boy struggling to cope with his mother's illness). The series picks up after the mother's death with the boy (Eric) now living with relatives in a small fishing village called Gimil. It is here that 11-year-old Eric begins a new life and stories follow him as he makes new friends and begins his journey into adulthood. Johnny Johansson is Eric's uncle. Johnny is married to Zoe; Anastasia "A.J." Burke is Eric's

friend (her parents own the Seaside Hotel); Sam, whose father runs an automobile shop, is also Eric's friend.

Cast: Michael Yarmush (*Eric Johansson*); Callum Keith Rennie (*Johnny Johansson*); Jennifer Clement (*Zoe Johansson*); Robin Dunne (*Kris Johansson*); Marley Otto (*Anastasia "A.J." Burke*); Joy Coghill (*Astrid Arnesson*); Bucky Hill (*Sam LaFresne*); David Brown (*Louis LaFresne*); Honoure McIlwain-Collard (*Tiffany Wilson*); Maggie Nagle (*Candice Burke*); Jeff Madden (*Andrew Burke*); R. Morgan Slade (*George Kilodney*).

6416   *My Life As a Teenage Robot.* (Series; Cartoon; Nick; 2003). Jenny Wakeman appears to be an ordinary teenage girl. She is, however, a robot and has been designed to defend the Earth. Her official designation is Global Robotic Response Unit XJ-9. Jenny is brave and powerful, but she has developed human qualities and would like to live the life of a real teenage girl — and even go to school. Jenny (who was created by her mother) is six feet tall and made of metal and is constantly reminded that she has a prime function — saving the world. Brad Carbunkle is Jenny's neighbor and best friend. Tucker Carbunkle is Brad's younger brother. Nora Wakeman is a scientist who has devoted her life to ridding the world of evil. She has created a number of weapons to destroy evil but Jenny is her greatest success. Tiffany and Brittany are the "cool" girls at school. Sheldon is the school geek who finds Jenny to be the true incarnation of the super heroes he reads about in comic books.

Voice Cast: Janice Kawaye (*Jenny Wakeman*); Chad Doreck (*Brad Carbunkle*); Audrey Wasilewski (*Tucker Carbunkle*); Candi Milo (*Nora Wakeman*); Moira Quirk (*Brittany*); Cree Summer (*Tiffany*); Quinton Flynn (*Sheldon Lee*). **Announcer:** Bob Joles.

6417   *My Life As Liz.* (Series; Reality; MTV; 2010). Documentary-like program that follows Liz Lee, a high school senior in Burleson, Texas, as she speaks directly to the camera to relate her life as she navigates different peer groups within the school.

6418   *My Life Is a Sitcom.* (Series; Reality; ABC Family; 2003). Eight families, chosen from video tape submissions chronicling why their family would make the ideal sitcom family, are "invaded" by sitcom writers to determine if they are worthy of starring in a pilot for a potential series. The Zaccagnino family won but a sitcom never materialized.

Judges: Maureen McCormick, David Faustino, Dave Coulier.

6419   *My Life with Men.* (Pilot; Comedy; Unaired; Produced for ABC in 2003). Emily is a middle-aged woman whose life revolves around men: her husband (Patrick), her father (Paul) and her growing sons (Ben, Marty, Sam and Ben). The proposal was to follow Emily as she struggles to cope with a group of Neanderthals and yet retain her sanity amid all the problems they present.

Cast: Wendie Malick (*Emily*); Josh Flitter (*Patrick*); Geoffrey Lewis (*Paul*); Shawn Pyfrom (*Sam*); Sam Ribards (*Jess*); Sam Lerner (*Marty*); Michael Angarano (*Ben*).

6420   *My Little Margie.* (Series; Comedy; CBS, 1952-1953; NBC, 1953-1955). Marjorie Albright, called Margie, is a beautiful 21-one-year-old girl who lives with her widowed father, Vernon Albright, at the Carlton Arms Hotel (Apt. 10-A) in Manhattan. Vern works as an investment counselor at the firm of Honeywell and Todd; Margie, described as "pretty, shapely and attractive," appears to have no job. Men are instantly attracted to her and she uses her beauty to get men to do what she wants them to do. Margie loves to meddle in Vern's business (and private) affairs. When Margie does something, Vern finds out. Vern decides to get even and teach her a lesson. However, as Vern tries to teach her a lesson, she finds out and turns the tables and tries to teach him a lesson for trying to teach her a lesson (the basic plot of virtually every episode).

Freddie Wilson is Margie's impoverished boyfriend. He seems permanently suited for unemployment, and, as Vern says, "Freddie is the only man I know who got fired from five different jobs in the same week." Despite the fact that Vern dislikes Freddie and calls him a "droop," Margie loves him.

Roberta Townsend (Apt. 10-B) is Vern's romantic interest; Mrs. Odetts (Apt. 10-C) is Margie's elderly neighbor and her "cohort in crime." She is an 82-year-old, young at heart widow who had British ancestors at Valley Forge. Her lifelong ambition was to be an actress, and she finds pure delight in helping Margie turn the tables on Vern.

George Honeywell is Vern's boss at the investment agency, and Charlie is the building elevator operator.

Cast: Gale Storm *(Margie Albright)*; Charles Farrell *(Vernon Albright)*; Don Hayden *(Freddie Wilson)*; Hillary Brooke *(Roberta Townsend)*; Gertrude Hoffman *(Clarissa Odetts)*; Willie Best *(Charlie)*; Clarence Kolb *(George Honeywell)*.

6421   *My Little Pony and Friends.* (Series; Cartoon; Syn.; 1986). The overall title for several mini animated series. *My Little Pont* relates the serial-like adventures of Megan, a young girl, and her friends, the multi-colored ponies, as she struggles to protect Dream Valley from evil. *Potato Head Kids* relates the misadventures of the Potato Head family. *Glo and Friends* tells the story of tiny creatures who battle evil Mooligans.

Voice Cast: Ginny McSwain *(Megan)*; Nancy Cartwright *(Gusty)*; Charles Adler *(Spike)*; Katie Leigh *(Baby Shady)*; Russi Taylor *(Morning Glory)*; Susan Blu *(Buttons)*; Sarah Partridge *(Wind Whistler)*; Sherry Lynn *(Galaxy)*; Ellen Gerstell *(Lofty)*; Jill Wayne *(Baby Lofty)*; Keri Houlihan *(Molly)*; Scott Menville *(Danny)*; Jeannie Elias *(Masquerade)*.

6422   *My Living Doll.* (Series; Comedy; CBS; 1964-1965). Rhoda Miller is a beautiful female robot built by Dr. Carl Miller for a U.S. space project designed to send robots into outer space. His creation, AF 709 (AAF 709 in the pilot), is made of low-modulus polyethylene plastics, miniature computers "and assorted components." Rhoda, stands five feet ten inches tall and measures 37-26-36. On her back are four small birthmarks — each of which acts as an emergency control button. Her main "off" switch is located in her right elbow, and her eyes provide a source of power obtained from light (covering her eyes causes a system relaxation). Her microscopic sensors keep her body temperature at a constant 98.6 degrees, making her immune to cold. Rhoda's memory bank contains 50 million items of information, and her computer brain can compute any piece of programmed information in one second.

Carl calls his creation "Living Doll" (the original series title), "It," "709" or "the Robot" — and sees her as just that, not as a beautiful woman. He assigns her to Dr. Robert ("Bob") McDonald, a psychologist at the Cory Psychiatric Clinic, to mold her character. She poses as Rhoda Miller, Carl's niece. At the office, she is Bob's secretary (who types 240 words a minute with no mistakes and no coffee breaks) and at home (an apartment at 5600 Wilshire Boulevard), where Bob lives with his sister, Irene Adams, Rhoda is a patient who requires special attention and is living with them until she can function on her own.

Peter Robinson, Bob's neighbor, is like everyone else and is unaware that Rhoda is a robot (Peter has fallen in love with her and desperately wants to date her; Bob is trying to prevent this from happening, fearing Rhoda will learn all the wrong things, as Peter is a playboy).

After the twenty-first episode, Bob Cummings left the series (he and Julie Newmar simply could not get along together). Bob's hasty departure was explained as his being sent to Pakistan on an assignment. Rhoda became Peter's ward for the remaining five episodes.

Cast: Julie Newmar *(Rhoda Miller)*; Bob Cummings *(Bob McDonald)*; Doris Dowling *(Irene Adams)*; Jack Mullavey *(Peter Robinson)*; Henry Beckman *(Dr. Carl Miller)*.

6423   *My Lucky Penny.* (Pilot; Comedy; CBS; Aug. 8, 1966). Jennifer "Jenny" Penny is the wife of a dental student (Ted) who works as a secretary for an unseen, absent-minded and eccentric boss who communicates with her via tape recordings. The proposal was to relate Jenny's misadventures as she struggles to carry out her boss's sometimes idiotic chores — like, for example, in the pilot episode when she helps her boss get sweet revenge on an unscrupulous gambling friend by paying off $15,000 in pennies. Freddy and Sybil are Penny's friends.

Cast: Brenda Vaccaro *(Jenny Penny)*; Richard Benjamin *(Ted Penny)*; Joel Grey *(Freddy Rockafeller)*; Luana Anders *(Sybil Rockafeller)*.

6424   *My Manny.* (Series; Comedy; TBS; 2009-2010). Jennifer is a recent widow and the mother of a seven-year-old son (Jamel). She runs a catering business and various agency recommended nannies assist her with Jamel when work demands her time. Mike is young, single and working as a male nanny until he completes his master's degree in early childhood education. One hectic day fate intervenes. Jennifer's regular nanny is called away for a family emergency and the agency sends Mike to replace her. Jennifer is a bit taken aback, but Mike loves his job and is not bothered by the people who think it's weird for a man to work with children. The awkward situation soon resolves itself as Jennifer gets use to having another man in her life (she hasn't dated since her husband's passing). An attraction develops and Jennifer finds that Mike may not only be the perfect nanny but the perfect man for her. Stories relate the events that bring Mike and Jennifer closer together. Melanie is Jennifer's best friend, neighbor and co-business partner.

Cast: Elise Neal *(Jennifer)*; Sharif Atkins *(Mike)*; Alanna Ubach *(Melanie)*; Tarren Mason *(Jamel)*; Greg Alan Williams *(Grandpa)*.

6425   *My Mother the Car.* (Series; Comedy; NBC; 1965-1966). On August 23, 1949, Agatha Crabtree, the mother of David Crabtree, passed away. In November 1957, David, now a lawyer, and his high school sweetheart, Barbara Natwick, married. Eight years later, they have two children (Cindy and Randy), a dog (Moon), a comfortable home (at 213 Hampton Street) and the need for a station wagon.

On September 14, 1965, Dave sets out to buy that station wagon. While in a used car lot, he becomes fascinated with a decrepit looking 1928 Porter with the sign "Fixer Upper" on it. Dave gets into the car, touches the radio — and hears a female voice say, "Hello, Davey." Dave responds, "Mother?" and is startled to learn that the voice is emerging from the car's radio. Agatha, who liked automobiles, has been reincarnated as a car to help Dave ("You need help, son") and his family. His mother, however, will speak only to him. Dave pays $200 for the Porter and drives home. He immediately encounters the objections of Barbara (whom he calls "Barb"), who wants a station wagon. In an attempt to make Mother more presentable, Dave takes her to Doc Benson's Auto Clinic for an overhaul and then to A. Schreib's Auto Painting for a new paint job (red). A proud Dave Crabtree returns home — to encounter Barbara's objections once again; she and the kids want a station wagon. Just then Captain Bernard Manzini, an easily exasperated and eccentric antique car collector arrives and offers to buy the Porter for his collection (Dave bought it minutes before Manzini had a chance to acquire it). Dave, of course, refuses to sell, and Manzini's continual efforts to acquire the Porter are a recurring theme. Stories relate Mother's attempts to guide Davey's life and Dave's efforts to conceal the fact that his mother is a car.

Fred and his wife Suzy are Dave's neighbors; Manzini, who considers the Porter "Our Vehicle" (referring to himself and Dave), desperately wants the car and calls Dave everything but Crabtree (for example, Crabmaster, Kravitz, Crabmeat, Kragle); he always responds with "Whatever" when Dave corrects him. Paul Hampton sings the theme, "My Mother the Car."

Cast: Jerry Van Dyke *(Dave Crabtree)*; Maggie Pierce *(Barbara Crabtree)*; Cynthia Eilbacher *(Cindy Crabtree)*; Randy Whipple *(Randy Crabtree)*; Ann Sothern *(Mother's Voice)*; Avery Schreiber *(Bernard Manzini)*; Peggy Miller *(Suzy)*; Chuck Grodin *(Fred)*.

6426 *My Name Is Earl.* (Series; Comedy; NBC; 2005–2009). Earl Hickey is a guy who would steal anything that wasn't nailed down. He was mean to people, took advantage of others and was simply not the nicest guy you'd ever want to meet. He lives at the Pimitt Trailer Park and is married to the very unfaithful Joy. He also has a dim-witted brother named Randy.

One day life appears to be changing for Earl — he wins $100,000 on a scratch-off lottery ticket, but he is hit by a car and loses the ticket. While recuperating in the hospital, Earl sees the TV program *Last Call with Carson Daly.* Carson is discussing a topic regarding success (the direct result of doing good things for other people) and Earl has an epiphany; he vows to improve his life by correcting every bad thing he has ever done. Earl makes a list of his past misdeeds and with Randy's fumbling help, sets out to right what was once wrong. Other regulars are Darnell, the owner of the Crab Shack (Earl's favorite bar) and Joy's new lover (she and Earl are now divorced); and Catalina, a very sexy friend of Earl who also helps him on occasion.

Cast: Jason Lee *(Earl Hickey)*; Jaime Pressly *(Joy)*; Ethan Suplee *(Randy Hickey)*; Eddie Steeples *(Darnell "Crab Man" Turner)*; Nadine Velazquez *(Catalina)*; Noah Crawford *(Young Earl; flashbacks)*; Phoenix Smith *(Young Randy; flashbacks)*; Trey Carlisle *(Earl Jr.)*; Mike O'Malley *(Officer Stuart Daniels)*; Louis T. Moyle *(Dodge)*; Dale Dickey *(Patty)*; Alyssa Milano *(Billie)*; Nancy Lenehan *(Kay Hickey)*; Beau Bridges *(Carl Hickey)*; Mike Cochrane *(Crab Shack regular)*.

6427 *My Own Worst Enemy.* (Series; Drama; NBC; 2008). A secret government organization with subterranean headquarters located beneath a building at 5210 S. Grand Avenue in Los Angeles plays a key role in protecting the U.S. from her enemies. It operates under the guise of the Janus Corporation. Edward Albright is a decorated war hero, a man who can speak 13 languages and hold his breath underwater for five minutes. He believes to prove the existence of free will a person must do something he does not want to do. When he learns of an experiment that will test his beliefs, he volunteers. What results is a split personality ("We manifested a divagate identity dormant in a small portion of the medial temporal lobe, creating a split personality," says Mavis Heller, the head of Janus). Henry Spivey is the result, a part of Edward, but a man who leads a separate life (married to Angie; the father of Ruthy and Jack; and strategic consultant for Janus). Henry, "born" at the facility on March 16, 1969, has no knowledge of Edward although they share the same body (when Henry is asleep Edward functions; when Henry awakens, he is Henry). His disappearances to become Edward when needed are explained as business trips)

All is progressing well until a system malfunction makes Henry aware that something is not right and he soon realizes that he is two different people, but the same person. Although the two can never physically meet, they communicate with each other (through recorded messages each makes and views over a computer). Stories follow Henry and Edward as they thrust into unfamiliar territory where each man is dangerously out of his element. Tom Grady is Henry's friend and co-worker (at Janus) but also an agent named Raymond (for Mavis); Tony is the systems operator responsible for maintaining the balance between Henry and Edward; Norah is Henry's psychiatrist ("who is in tune with the inner workings of both Edward and Henry").

Cast: Christian Slater *(Henry Spivey/Edward Albright)*; Alfre Woodard *(Mavis Heller)*; Madchen Amick *(Angie Spivey)*; Bella Thorne *(Ruthy Spivey)*; Mike O'Malley *(Tom Grady/Raymond)*; Taylor Lautner *(Jack Spivey)*; Saffron Burrows *(Dr. Norah Skinner)*; Omid Abtahi *(Tony)*.

6428 *My Partner the Ghost.* (Series; Comedy; Syn.; 1973). Jeff Randall and Marty Hopkirk co-own Randall and Hopkirk — Private Investigators, at Marshall and Brooks Street in London, England. Marty's wife, Jean Hopkirk works as their secretary-receptionist (Jeff is single).

During a case investigation, Marty is killed by a hit-and-run driver linked to the case. Because of the circumstances surrounding his death, Marty is allowed to return to Earth as a ghost to solve his own murder. Because he is now a spirit, Marty is unable to function as before and must use a person to perform for him. Marty chooses Jeff and appears only to him. With Jeff's help, Marty finds his killer, but he violates an ancient rule and is rejected by his grave: "Before the sun shall rise on you, each ghost unto his grave must go. Cursed be the ghost who dares to stay and face the awful light of day. He shall not to the grave return until a hundred years be gone."

Marty, now forced to remain on Earth, decides to resume his former life as a detective and becomes Jeff's ghostly assistant. The curse also gives Marty the opportunity to watch over his beautiful wife, whom he still worries about. Jean inherited everything from Marty, including trouble from those he convicted who are now seeking revenge: "I've waited eight years to get Hopkirk, now he's dead. But his lovely wife inherited everything, including my revenge. What would have been good enough for him is just as good for her." Also known as "Randall and Hopkirk (Deceased)."

Cast: Kenneth Cope *(Marty Hopkirk)*; Mike Pratt *(Jeff Randall)*; Annette Andre *(Jean Hopkirk)*; Ivor Dean *(Insp. Large)*.

6429 *My Pet Monster.* (Series; Cartoon; ABC; 1987). Max is a young boy who finds friendship in plush toys. One day, while at a toy store, Max spots an unusual animal — a monster with a purple body, pink face and cuffs on its wrists. After purchasing the toy, Max finds a key and unlocks the cuffs. To his amazement, the plush toy grows to a six-foot tall, live monster with an appetite for garbage. Max names the creature Monster and must now keep him a secret (if Monster Land learns that one of its dolls has come to life, it will be whisked back home through a dimensional doorway). The evil Beastur has become aware of Monster and us now trying to retrieve him. Stories follow Max's adventures with Monster — and his efforts to keep him safe from Beastur. Jill is Max's sister; Chuckie is their friend.

Voice Cast: Sunny Besen Thrasher *(Max)*; Jeff McGibbon *(Monster)*; Alyson Court *(Jill)*; Stuart Stone *(Chuckie)*; Dan Hennessey *(Beastur)*; Tara Strong *(Amie)*; Tracey Moore *(Princess)*.

6430 *My Secret Identity.* (Series; Comedy; Syn.; 1988-1989). Dr. Benjamin Jeffcoat is the fifth smartest man in the world. He lives at 45 Meadow Drive in Briarwood, Canada, and enjoys conducting scientific experiments from his garage. Stephanie Clemens, the divorced mother of two children, Andrew and Erin, are his neighbors at 43 Meadow Drive. One day Andrew decides to visit his friend, Dr. Jeffcoat, and wanders into his garage. He is bombarded with blue gamma rays from an experiment Benjamin is conducting and endowed with extraordinary powers (mostly speed and strength) that he uses to foil evil as Ultraman (after his favorite comic book hero). The two keep the secret and stories relate Andrew's efforts to help others as Ultraman. Andrew attends Briarwood High School and hangs out at the Burger Barn. Stephanie is a freelance real estate agent and does volunteer work at the York Community Center. Erin, a very sweet young girl, attends Briarwood Elementary School. Benjamin, called Dr. J by Andrew, attended Broadhurst University. Ruth Shellenbach is Ben's nosey neighbor.

Cast: Jerry O'Connell (*Andrew Clements*); Wanda Cannon (*Stephanie Clements*); Marsha Moreau (*Erin Clements*); Derek McGrath (*Dr. Benjamin Jeffcoat*); Elizabeth Leslie (*Ruth Shellenbach*); Susannah Hoffman (*Rebecca*).

6431   *My Sister Eileen.* (Series; Comedy; CBS; 1960-1961). A basement apartment at the Appopolous Arms at 121 Broadway in New York's Greenwich Village is the residence of Ruth and Eileen Sherwood, sisters from Columbus, Ohio, who moved to the big city to further their career goals.

Ruth is the older sister, a writer who hopes to turn her hometown experiences into a book. She first works as a manuscript reader for the McMann Publishing House, then as a writer for *Manhatter Magazine* (also known as *Manhattan Magazine*). Eileen is the younger, more glamorous sister. She is a hopeful actress and dreams of starring on Broadway. She has an agent named Marty, but few jobs and many struggles as she seeks to achieve her goal. Eileen does have admirers, however — men simply cannot take their eyes off her, and she is constantly wooed by them.

Alan Dahorsameche, better known as "The Wreck" is the Sherwoods' upstairs neighbor. He is a football player for the New York Giants and extremely jealous. He fears that every "wolf" in New York is after his wife, Helen, whom he calls "Princess." Chick Adams is Ruth's friend, a reporter for the *Daily News*; Bertha Bronsky is Ruth's co-worker; and Mr. Appopolous owns the building (in the pilot episode, *You Should Meet My Sister* [NBC, May 16, 1960], Henry Corden played the landlord as Mr. Spevak, the owner of the Spevak Arms). Agnes Moorehead appeared as Ruth and Eileen's aunt, Harriet.

Based on the book by Ruth McKinney, it was first adapted for television on Nov. 30, 1958 in a two hour CBS special with Rosalind Russell (Ruth), Jacqueline McKeever (Eileen), Jordan Bentley (The Wreck), Michelle Burke (Helen) and Joseph Buloff (Mr. Appopolous).

Cast: Elaine Stritch (*Ruth Sherwood*); Shirley Boone (*Eileen Sherwood*); Leon Belasco (*Mr. Appopolous*); Stubby Kaye (*Marty*); Raymond Bailey (*Robert Beaumont*); Jack Weston (*Chick Adams*); Rose Marie (*Bertha Bronsky*); Hal Baylor (*The Wreck*); Treva Frazee (*Helen*).

6432   *My Sister Hank.* (Pilot; Comedy; CBS; Mar. 31, 1972). Henrietta Bennett is a young tomboy who prefers to be called Hank. Her parents, Eunice and Willis, don't quite understand her, but accept her and are trying to change her. Her older sister, Dianne, is mystified (as is Hank about Dianne and her pursuits of such feminine things as makeup). The proposal was to follow Hank's misadventures as she struggles to remain just as she is — a tomboy. Other regulars are Grandpa Bennett; and Arthur, Hank's friend.

Cast: Jodie Foster (*Hank Bennett*); Pippa Scott (*Eunice Bennett*); Jack Ging (*Willis Bennett*); Edgar Bergen (*Grandpa Bennett*); Suzanne Hillard (*Dianne Bennett*); Todd Bass (*Arthur*).

6433   *My Sister Sam.* (Series; Comedy; CBS; 1986–1988). Samantha ("Sam") Russell is a beautiful 29-year-old girl who runs the Russell Scouts Photography Studio from her apartment (5C) at 1345 Benchley Street in San Francisco, California. Sam shares the apartment with her pretty 16-year-old sister, Patti. Patti previously lived in Oregon, where her Aunt Elsie and her Uncle Bob had been caring for her since her parents were killed in a car accident. Patti wanted to be with Sam and moved out. Sam was a straight "A" student at Bennett High School in Oregon (with the exception of a "C-minus" in Spanish); Patti is a sophomore at Millard Fillmore High School; her dream is to quit school and become a rock star.

Jack Kincaid is Sam's neighbor (Apartment 5D) and a photojournalist who got his first cover story in Newsweek magazine when he was 22. Dixie Randazzo, Sam's assistant, is married and the mother of six children (five of whom are not seen). J.D., Sam's agent, attended the University of Bridgeport and has a never-seen wife named Lorraine. Kim Carnes sings the theme "Room Enough for Two."

Cast: Pam Dawber (*Samantha Russell*); Rebecca Schaeffer (*Patti Russell*); Jenny O'Hara (*Dixie Randazzo*); Joel Brooks (*J.D.*); David Naughton (*Jack Kincaid*).

6434   *My So-Called Life.* (Series; Drama; ABC; 1994-1995). Angela Chase is a 15-year-old high school girl struggling to cope with friends, family and first loves. She is somewhat gloomy and has a narrow view of life. She does, however, have a loose cannon of a friend (Rae Ann) who is everything Angela would like to be, but isn't.

Angela likes cookie dough ice cream, attends Liberty High School and has a father (Graham) who thinks everyone in the world is having more fun than him. He works as a salesman for Wood Printing. Betty, Angela's mother, is a go-getter (something Angela would like to be) and is sort of Graham's boss, as her father, Chuck Wood, owns the company, and Betty oversees business operations.

Angela, seen in flashbacks as a girl, was shy and very obedient. She had friends, but never did anything out of the ordinary. As the series begins, Angela decides to change all that and begins by hanging out with Rae Anne. She changes her hair color (to Crimson Glow), which displeases her mother (but not her father) and begins to see life in a new light. Stories follow the events in Angela's so-called life. Other regulars are Danielle, Angela's younger sister; and students Brian, Jordan, Sharon and Rickie.

Cast: Claire Danes (*Angela Chase*); Bess Armstrong (*Patricia "Betty" Chase*); Tom Irwin (*Graham Chase*); Lisa Wilhoit (*Danielle Chase*); A.J. Langer (*Rae Anne Graff*); Paul Dooley (*Chuck Wood*); Devon Odessa (*Sharon Cherski*); Jared Leto (*Jordan Catalano*); Devon Gummersall (*Brian Krakow*); Kaley Cuoco (*Young Angela; flashbacks*); Wilson Cruz (*Rickie Vasquez*).

6435   *My Son, the Doctor.* (Pilot; Comedy; CBS; Aug. 22, 1966). Some doctors are only in the medical profession to make money. This is not the case with Peter Piper, a mother-dominated doctor whose total dedication to work often leaves him little time to spend with his wife, Barbara. The proposal was to focus on Barbara as she tries to change Peter's work habits; and on Peter, as he tries to get out from under his mother's dominance over him. Other regulars are Jenny, Peter's mother; Dr. Jeffrey Berry, Peter's friend, a private practice doctor; and Miss Primrose, Peter's nurse.

Cast: Jefferson Davis (*Dr. Peter Piper*); Julie Gregg (*Barbara Piper*); Kay Medford (*Jenny Piper*); Dick Patterson (*Dr. Jeffrey Berry*); Patsy Kelly (*Miss Primrose*).

6436   *My Super Sweet 16.* (Series; Reality; MTV; 2005). The Sweet 16 parties of real life girls — girls who are the offspring of rich parents and who receive luxurious gifts as they turn "Sweet 16" (while called a reality series, it caters to the upper middle class and does not truly reflect the actual Sweet 16 parties of the average girl). Erin Shockey and Jordana Starr are the producers.

6437   *My Talk Show.* (Series; Comedy; Syn.; 1990). *My Talk Show* was a local talk program on Channel 56 in Derby, Wisconsin. It was hosted by Jennifer Bass and was very amateurish — shaky camerawork, missed cues, out of focus shots. When TV syndication king Perry Flapman sees the show (and dubs Jennifer "a TV Tush") he believes the show is what America is looking for and decides to distribute it nationally. Stories relate the problems Jennifer encounters as she struggles to host a live, national TV talk show.

Other regulars are Angela Davenport, Jennifer's co-host; Mrs. Battle, the show's organist; Anne Marie, Jennifer's neighbor; and Marty, Jennifer's brother-in-law, who lives in a trailer in her driveway (and hosts the "Marty's Corner" segment of the show).

Cast: Cynthia Stevenson (*Jennifer Bass*); Stephanie Hodge (*Angela Davenport*); Debra McGrath (*Anne Marie*); David Packer (*Marty*); Josephine Hinds (*Mrs. Battle*).

6438   *My Three Sons.* (Series; Comedy; ABC, 1960–1965; CBS, 1965–1972). A house at 837 Mill Street in the town of Bryant Park is home to widower Steven ("Steve") Douglas and his three sons: Michael ("Mike") Douglas, Robert ("Robbie") Douglas and Richard ("Chip") Douglas. Also living with them is Steve's father-in-law, William ("Bill") Michael Francis Aloysius O'Casey, who is affectionately called "Bub." (CBS episodes are set in North Hollywood, California.)

The town was named after Seth Bryant, an itinerant pots and pans salesman who founded the town after his wagon broke down and forced him to stay. Steve is an aeronautical engineer (structural design) for Universal Research and Development (he began his career as a test pilot). He is a graduate of Midwest University (class of 1938) and married Louise O'Casey when he was 21 years old (Louise died 12 years later on the night before Chip's first birthday). The family dog is named Tramp. In 1969 Steve married a teacher named Barbara Harper, a widow with a young daughter named Dodie.

Mike is the eldest of Steve's children (18). He attends Bryant Park High School (he is a senior when the series begins) and has a girlfriend named Jean Pearson. He next attends State College (he is a member of the Sigma Gamma Chi fraternity), then joins the air force reserves. Prior to the CBS episodes, Mike marries Sally Ann Morrison, a girl he met in 1963, and moves East to accept a job as a psychology professor.

Robbie (14) first attended Webster Elementary School, then Bryant Park High. In 1967 he marries Katie Miller and becomes the father of triplets two years later: Charley, Steve Jr. and Robbie II.

Chip, the youngest child (seven) attended Webster Elementary School and was a member of the Moose Patrol scouting troop. In 1970, Chip married Polly Williams. They eloped and honeymooned in Mexico.

Ernie Thompson was Chip's friend (beginning with 1963 episodes). When Ernie is orphaned (his parents are killed, but how is not related), he is sent to the King's County Children's Home. Steve then adopts him; at the time Ernie attended the Susie B. Dorsey School. He and Chip were later classmates at Buchanan Elementary School.

Bub, who helps care for the family, was a member of the Brotherhood of the Cavaliers and left the series in 1964. Steve tells the kids that Bub has gone "to visit his mother in Ireland" (actually he went to Ireland to help his aunt, Kate, celebrate her 104th birthday). Bub was in show business (worked as a stage manager at the Royal Theater in Evansberg). To fill the void left by Bub, Steve hires Fedocia Barrett (Reta Shaw) as a temporary housekeeper until Bub returns from Ireland. Shortly after, Bub's brother, Charles ("Charlie") O'Casey, a former merchant marine, arrives at the Douglas home seeking Bub. When Steve learns that Charlie is en route to the Caribbean, he invites him to stay with the family for a few days. Fedocia refuses to cook for another male and gives Steve her notice. Charlie, who comes to be called "Uncle Charlie," agrees to stay and help look after the boys.

Cast: Fred MacMurray (*Steve Douglas*); Tim Considine (*Mike Douglas*); Don Grady (*Robbie Douglas*); Stanley Livingston (*Chip Douglas*); William Frawley (*Bub*); William Demarest (*Uncle Charlie*); Barry Livingston (*Ernie Douglas*); Meredith MacRae (*Sally Ann Morrison*); Tina Cole (*Katie Miller*); Beverly Garland (*Barbara Harper*); Ronne Troup (*Polly Thompson*); Dawn Lyn (*Dodie Harper Douglas*); Cynthia Pepper (*Jean Pearson*); Joseph Todd (*Charley Douglas*); Daniel Todd (*Robbie Douglas II*); Joseph Todd (*Steve Douglas, Jr.*); Russ Conway (*Bob Walters, Steve's boss*); John Gallaudet (*Jim Guthrie, Steve's boss*); Norman Alden (*Tom Williams; Polly's father*); Doris Singleton (*Margaret Williams; Polly's mother*); Jodie Foster (*Priscilla; Dodie's friend*); Victoria Meyerink (*Margaret; Dodie's friend*).

6439   *My Town.* (Pilot; Comedy-Drama; ABC; May 25, 1986). Wheelerville, Ohio, is a small town where people seeking to start new lives can get that chance. The idea came from Lucas Wheeler, the banker and descendant of the town's founder, and the proposal was to relate incidents in the lives of the people who attempt to rebuild their lives as seen through the eyes of Amber Wheeler, Lucas's pretty granddaughter. Other regulars are Tug Wheeler, Amber's brother (they are orphans who live with Lucas); Mrs. McDaniel, Lucas's housekeeper; and Laura Adams, the school teacher.

Cast: Glenn Ford (*Lucas Wheeler*); Meredith Salenger (*Amber Wheeler*); Parker Jacobs (*Tug Wheeler*); Mary Jackson (*Mrs. McDaniel*); Kate Mulgrew (*Laura Adams*).

6440   *My True Story.* (Series; Anthology; ABC; 1950). Dramatic adaptations of stories that appear in *My True Story* magazine. Herbert Duncan is the announcer.

6441   *My Two Dads.* (Series; Comedy; NBC; 1987–1990). Nicole Bradford is a pretty 12-year-old girl who lives in Apartment B at 627 North Brewster Street in Manhattan with her fathers, Joey Harris and Michael Taylor. Joey and Michael, Nicole's co-guardians (she calls them "My Two Dads") are friends who dated Nicole's mother, Marcie Bradford (Emma Samms in a flashback). When Marcie passed away and the actual biological father could not be determined, Joey and Michael were both given the responsibility of caring for her by Judge Margaret Wilbur; Margaret owns the building and resides in Apartment 3B.

Joey is initially an artist (1987-88), then art director for *Financial Update* magazine (1988), artist again (1989) and finally a teacher at New York University (1990). He also wrote the children's book, *Mr. Biggles* (about a leprechaun).

Michael is initially a financial advisor for the Taft-Kelcher Agency (1987–89) then marketing manager for *Financial Update* magazine. He considers his job as a father is to focus on Nicole's needs and wants; Joey's job, he feels, is to help him decide how she is to be punished when she does something wrong. Joey is much more liberal in his parenting and considers Michael a Ward Cleaver (the father on *Leave It to Beaver*) and too strict in raising Nicole.

First-season episodes find Nicole as a typical kid — she likes boys, but is not eager to date; she is experimenting with makeup; and through no fault of her own is growing up and saddening Michael — "She's my little girl. I never want to see her grow up." But grow up she does. She is soon a teenager attending Kennedy Junior High School, and a worry to both her dads as the series focus changed to depict Nicole's growth into young adulthood — and to boys and dating.

Michael and Joey hang out at Klawicki's, a diner located on the ground floor of their building. The diner is owned by Ed Klawicki, a former football player. In final-season episodes, Judge Wilbur takes over the diner and renames it the Judge's Court Cafe.

Cast: Staci Keanan (*Nicole Bradford*); Greg Evigan (*Joey Harris*); Paul Reiser (*Michael Taylor*); Florence Stanley (*Margaret Wilbur*); Dick Butkus (*Ed Klawicki*).

6442   *My Wife and Kids.* (Series; Comedy; ABC; 2001–2005). Michael Kyle, a former UPS truck driver, now owns his own business, Kyle Trucking. He is married to the weight conscious Jay and is the father of Michael Jr., Claire and Cady. Michael longs for a tranquil life but his outrageous family guarantees that his dream will be just that — a dream. Jay also has a dream — to open her own restaurant (which she did in 2004 when she started Jay's Soul Kitchen).

Claire is 12 years old when the series begins. She is beautiful but self-centered and works after school at Ann Tailor, a clothing shop.

Michael, Jr., called Junior, is inspired by pork rinds, naked women and video games (his father calls him "an expert in the dork department" as he is not bright and a very poor student at school). In 2004 Junior married his girlfriend, Vanessa Scott, when he got her pregnant. They had a child they named Michael Jr., but to avoid confusion called him Junior Junior.

Cady is the youngest child (five when the series begins). She attends Crestview Elementary School and is best friends with Franklin Aloysius Mumford, a super-intelligent seven-year-old boy.

Cast: Damon Wayans (*Michael Kyle*); Tisha Campbell (*Jay Kyle*); Jazz Raycole (*Claire Kyle, 2001*); Jennifer Nicole Freeman (*Claire Kyle, 2001–05*); George O. Gore II (*Michael Kyle, Jr.*); Parker McKenna Posey (*Cady Kyle*); Noah Gray-Cabey (*Franklin Mumford*); Brooklyn Sudano (*Vanessa Scott*).

6443   *My Wife Next Door.* (Pilot; Comedy; CBS; Dec. 31, 1975). Suzy and George Barrett gave marriage a chance but found it just wasn't working and filed for divorce. Now, separated, they each go their separate ways. By chance (or did fate step in) they accidentally rent neighboring apartments. The proposal was to relate the problems that arise as the newly separated former lovers become sparring partners again.

Cast: Julie Sommars (*Suzy Barrett*); James Farentino (*George Barrett*); Martha Scott (*Suzy's mother*).

6444   *My Wife Next Door.* (Pilot; Comedy; CBS; Sept. 11, 1980). Lisa Pallick is a television commercials producer; Paul Gilmore is her ex-husband, a big league ball player. Lisa and Paul thought they had seen the last of each other when they got divorced. Then by accident, they rent adjoining apartments in San Francisco. The proposal was to focus on their misadventures as they become sparring partners again. Other regulars are Jan, Lisa's sister; Vinnie, Paul's friend; Lionel, Lisa's co-worker; and Artie, the apartment building super.

Cast: Lee Purcell (*Lisa Pallick*); Granville Van Dusen (*Paul Gilmore*); Desiree Boschetti (*Jan Pallick*); Michael DeLano (*Vinnie Messina*); Frank Dent (*Lionel*); Phil Rubinstein (*Artie*).

6445   *My Wildest Dreams.* (Series; Comedy; Fox; 1985). Lisa McGinnis is a working mother and housewife whose daydreams help keep her family and life together. Lisa is married to Jack and is the mother of seven-year-old Danny. Lisa has been married to Jack for eight years and works at a recording studio called Mound of Sound. Helping Jack and Lisa is Mary, their babysitter. Chandler Trapp is Lisa's boss; Stephanie Benaditto is Lisa's sister; and Gloria Benaditto is Lisa's mother.

Cast: Lisa Ann Walter (*Lisa McGinnis*); John Posey (*Jack McGinnis*); Evan Bonifant (*Danny McGinnis*); Candice Brown (*Mary*); Miguel Nunez, Jr. (*Chandler Trapp*); Kelly Bishop (*Gloria Benaditto*); Mary Jo Keenan (*Stephanie Benaditto*).

6446   *My Wives Jane.* (Pilot; Comedy; CBS; Aug. 1, 1971). Jane Franklin, an actress married to a doctor (Nat), plays a doctor's wife on a television serial. The proposal was to focus on Jane as she struggles to handle both careers — actress and housewife — efficiently. Other regulars are Vic, the serial star; Dirk, the producer; Molly, Dirk's assistant; and Magda, Jane's housekeeper.

Cast: Janet Leigh (*Jane Franklin*); Barry Nelson (*Dr. Nat Franklin*); John Dehner (*Vic Semple*); McLean Stevenson (*Dirk Bennett*); Mia Bendixsen (*Molly*); Nora Marlowe (*Magda*).

6447   *My World ... and Welcome to It.* (Series; Comedy; NBC; 1969–1970). John Monroe is a cartoonist for *Manhattanite* magazine. He is discontented with his job (his boss, Hamilton Greeley constantly complains that "his cartoons talk with their mouths closed"); suspicious of smart children and hostile animals; intimidated by his loving wife and precocious daughter, and scared to death of life. When life becomes intolerable or when he is troubled, John retreats to the secret world of his imagination. His cartoons become real, life becomes tolerable and he is transformed into a person who is irresistible to women and a tower of strength in the eyes of men.

John lives at 130 Post Road in Westport, Connecticut, with his wife, Ellen, and his daughter, Lydia. Ellen is totally dedicated to John and worries that he is much too critical of the world that surrounds him. Lydia is ten years old, very bright, very pretty, and attends Compton Elementary School. She wants to attend Yale University and her attitude ("I better start getting all "A's" now") makes John think he is raising "a girl with the I.Q. of a 55-year-old CPA." Ellen considers Lydia a sensitive child.

The Monroe family dogs are Christabel and Irving; *Manhattanite* magazine is housed in the Manhattanite Building in New York City. Based on "drawings, stories, inspirational pieces and things that go bump in the night, by James Thurber."

Cast: William Windom (*John Monroe*); Joan Hotchkis (*Ellen Monroe*); Lisa Gerritsen (*Lydia Monroe*); Harold J. Stone (*Hamilton Greeley*).

6448   *M.Y.O.B.* (Series; Comedy; NBC; 2000). Riley Veatch is a television character who knows she is a television character. She describes her series as "It's the whole fish out of water, odd couple, unrequited love combo you get most every night on every channel. So you don't want to watch? Hey, that's okay, *Law and Order* is bound to be on somewhere" (refers to the three *Law and Order* series and the repeats on various cable stations).

The odd couple referred to above are Riley and her aunt, Opal Brown. Riley is tough, the product of her all too human experiences. She was abandoned by her working, cult-prone birth mother (Pearl Brown) then left alone when her adoptive mother died (killed when she "went crazy" in a post office and tried to shoot up the place). Riley developed acute personal survival instincts, a fierce independence, a distaste for pretense and an extraordinary ability to sense the needs and desires of others. Riley also needs to do one thing — find her birth mother. With only one known relative, Pearl's sister, Opal, Riley leaves her home in Ohio and heads to California. In the town of Gusset she finds Opal. Opal believes Pearl is with a cult in Finland but is unable to contact her. Until Pearl can be reached, Opal allows Riley to stay with her (thus the odd couple).

Opal is the principal of Gusset High School. She lacks Riley's self-confidence and skepticism about people and their motives. Riley lacks Opal's clear sense of responsibility and fundamental optimism about life. They share sharp intelligence, verbal nimbleness and a not very well hidden loneliness. Stories follow events in their lives and 16-year-old Riley's comments as she speaks directly to the camera.

Cast: Katherine Towne (*Riley Veatch*); Lauren Graham (*Opal Marie*

Brown); Paul Fitzgerald (*Mitch Levitt*); Don McManus (*Stan Peyton*); Colin Martinson (*P.J.*).

6449 Mysteries, Myths and Legends. (Series; Reality; Syn.; 1981). The program explores various legends and myths that surround us in everyday life.
Narrator: Steve Marshall.

6450 The Mysteries of Alfred Hedgehog. (Series; Cartoon; Qubo; 2010). Gnarly Woods is an area where mysteries abound. It is here that Alfred Hedgehog, a ten-year-old hedgehog with the mind of Sherlock Holmes, lives. He and his two best friends, Camille and Milo, constantly stumble upon mysteries (like trees turning blue, giant footprints, fish raining from the sky) and stories follow their efforts to uncover the reason behind the strange occurrences.
Voice Cast: Carolina Bartczak (*Alfred Hedgehog*); Angela Galuppo (*Milo Skunk*); Emma Taylor-Isherwood (*Camille Wallaby*); Lisa Norton (*Cynthia Payne*); Stephanie Beard (*Lily Hedgehog*).

6451 Mysteries of Chinatown. (Series; Crime Drama; ABC; 1949-1950). Yat Fu's is a curio shop at 1302 Golden Avenue in San Francisco's Chinatown. Dr. Yat Fu is its owner, an amateur crime sleuth who helps the police solve crimes. Ah Toy is his beautiful niece and shop assistant and sometimes partner in crime solving; she lives with her uncle at 0734 Magnolia Street.

Dr. Yat Fu works closely with Lieutenant Hargrove of the S.F.P.D.'s Homicide Bureau. When East Coast commitments forced Bill Eythe to leave the live West Coast-produced series, his character, Hargrove, was killed during "a volley of slugs pouring out of a Chinatown alley." He was replaced by Richard Crane as Lieutenant Cummings (when commitments called Crane away from the show, Cummings was not killed off; he was simply contacted by phone and not seen).

"Mysteries of Chinatown" is a unique show for its time, as no expense was spared to make authentic sets. While shows like "Captain Video" had a weekly props budget of $25 in 1949, "Mysteries" spent more than $10,000 just to furnish the set. Some of the most notable props were a genuine teakwood tabaret valued at $3,000, a real Chinese sacred urn (so ornate it couldn't be replaced; valued at $1,500) and two genuine opium pipes, each over 155 years old. The program also employed four exterior sets and four interior sets (which cost many thousands of dollars and took one thousand man hours to build). Topping it off was $5,000 worth of theatrical lights to illuminate the eight sets.
Cast: Marvin Miller (*Dr. Yat Fu*); Gloria Saunders (*Ah Toy*); Bill Eythe (*Lt. Hargrove*); Richard Crane (*Lt. Cummings*).

6452 Mysterious Forces Beyond. (Series; Reality; TLC; 1994). Are ghosts real? Are there actually powers that can heal the sick? Are visions of the future people say they experience real? These are the types of questions the program attempts to answer thorough examinations of paranormal phenomena. It basically asks, after all the evidence is presented, for the viewer to decide for himself.
Host: Nick Mancuso.

6453 The Mysterious Mummy Case. (Experimental; Mystery; NBC; May 17, 1938). Newsreels, travelogues, speeches and live talent were combined with story telling to relate the tale of an evil influence that has been responsible for several deaths and eventually caused the sinking of the SS *Titanic*. Variety exclaimed the program "as cathode ray television's first important milestone from a purely story-telling entertainment technique standpoint." Five sets were used and fades to black, slides and film inserts were also used for transitions (allowing actors costume changes). The action, Variety said, "was cramped and

rigid due to the present limited range of the iconoscope." It also said that "the close-up ... is still an unsolved television problem" (close-ups back then tended to blur the other characters when focusing on a speaker).
Cast: Tom Terriss (*Himself*); Dorothy McGuire (*Miss Clark*); William David (*Edward Lawson*); J. Malcolm Dunn (*Colonel*); Aristes DeLeone (*Egyptian*); Arthur Maitland (*Dr. Harvey*); Anthony Cooper (*Wilson Ellis*); Ned Weaver (*Curt*).

6454 The Mysterious Two. (Pilot; Science Fiction; NBC; May 31, 1982). Tim Armstrong is an Earthling with a self-imposed mission: destroy He and She, aliens who pose as evangelists to recruit people (by brainwashing) to abandon their worldly goods and join them in their world of serenity called New Tomorrow (located in an abandoned missile site outside of Santa Fe, New Mexico). Originally titled *Follow Me if You Dare* and filmed in 1979.
Cast: James Stephens (*Tim Armstrong*); John Forsythe (*He*); Priscilla Pointer (*She*).

6455 Mysterious Ways. (Series; Drama; PAX; 2001-2002). Declan Dunn is an anthropologist and teacher at Northern Oregon University. He says, "I've seen some strange things. Some explainable, some that defy all logic. Maybe it's just plain luck, coincidence or maybe they're miracles, a higher power at work. This is the stuff I investigate because Albert Einstein once said, 'The most beautiful things we can experience is the mysterious.'"

Declan is assisted in his attempts to prove strange happenings are miracles by Peggy Fowler, a psychiatrist in private practice and on staff at Oregon Hospital. Stories follow Declan and Peggy as they probe mysterious happenings. Other regulars are Miranda, a college coed majoring in physics who helps Declan.
Cast: Adrian Pasdar (*Declan Dunn*); Rae Dawn Chong (*Dr. Peggy Fowler*); Alisen Down (*Miranda Feigelsteen*).

6456 Mystery. (Series; Anthology; PBS; 1980–2010). British produced mysteries based on the works of noted authors and hosted by Vincent Price, Gene Shalit and Diana Rigg.

6457 Mystery and Mrs. (Pilot; Crime Drama; ABC; Sept. 27, 1950). George Fame and his wife Sally are newlyweds and partners in the Fame Detective Agency. Sally is young, beautiful and somewhat trouble prone. She enjoys the thrill of a case but often plunges into sometimes dangerous situations without thinking first. She does have a keen sense for crime solving and often relies on her feminine intuition to help George, a master of deductive reasoning, uncover the clues they need to solve a crime. The proposal was to relate their joint investigations and the comical incidents that arise due to Sally's over eagerness.
Cast: Gale Storm (*Sally Fame*); Don DeFore (*George Fame*), George Pelham, Robert Shayne, Eve Whitney.

6458 Mystery Chef. (Series; Cooking; NBC; 1949). The program, one of NBC's first daytime shows, features step-by-step cooking instruction. The title refers to the host, who was not identified when the program first began.
Host: John McPherson.

6459 Mystery Dance. (Pilot; Crime Drama; ABC; June 29, 1995). Susan Baker is a community affairs reporter (for example, covering the PTA, the art center) for a Los Angeles paper called the *L.A. Paid Reader*. She is married to Alan Baker, a college biology professor who leads a boring life. Susan has a daughter (Emily), who is busy with high school and work and a son (not seen) who is away at college. Susan seems to be content until a professor is found dead at her husband's unnamed college. The police have ruled it as a suicide, but Susan, being a friend of that professor, believes differently and decides to investigate. She brings in Alan and together they prove it was murder. "That murder was fun, wasn't it," Susan remarks; then she tells Alan the rest—that she is taking out a personal ad to hire her services out as a private detective. The proposal was to follow Susan's efforts to solve crimes—with a little help from Alan. Other regulars are Colleen, their neighbor; Bob, Colleen's husband; Nancy, the paper's receptionist; and Beth, the dean of the college.

Cast: Jane Curtin *(Susan Baker)*; Peter Riegert *(Alan Baker)*; Kate Bayley *(Emily Baker)*; Nancy Lenehan *(Colleen Wilson)*; William H. Macy *(Bob Wilson)*; Gates McFadden *(Nancy Maxwell)*; Karen Trumbo *(Beth Hillyard)*.

6460 *Mystery File.* (Series; Game; ABC; 1951). The alternate title for *Q.E.D.* See this title for information.

6461 *Mystery Files.* (Series; Reality; Investigation Discovery; 2010). Dramatic recreations that explore (and try to solve the mysteries) that surround some of histories most captivating figures (from Cleopatra to King Arthur). Carl Hall and Danny Tipping are the producers.

6462 *The Mystery Files of Shelby Woo.* (Series; Comedy; Nick; 1996–1998). Shelby Woo is a young girl who excels in school (she is a straight *A* student and is fascinated by crime and crime solving). Shelby has, for one so young, developed a keen sense of deduction and uses that ability to help the local police (especially Detectives Sharon Delancey and Whit Hineline) solve baffling crimes. Shelby lives with her grandfather, Mike "Grandpa" Woo, and Noah, Cindy and Vince are her friends (who help her solve crimes and provide some comic relief).

Cast: Irene Ng *(Shelby Woo)*; Pat Morita *(Mike "Grandpa" Woo)*; Ellen David *(Det. Sharon Delancey)*; Steve Purnick *(Det. Whit Hineline)*; Adam Busch *(Noah Allen)*; Preslaysa Edwards *(Cindy Ornette)*; Noah Klar *(Vince Rosania)*.

6463 *Mystery Is My Business.* (Series; Crime Drama; DuMont; 1950-1951). The syndicated title for *The Adventures of Ellery Queen*. See this title for information.

6464 *Mystery, Magic and Miracles.* (Series; Reality; Syfy; 1994-1995). An attempt to uncover the answers to the legends and myths that surround us in everyday life.

Host: Patrick Macnee.

6465 *Mystery Science Theater 3000.* (Series; Science Fiction; Comedy Central/Syfy; 1989-1999). Dr. Clayton Forrester is a mad scientist with an insane idea: take over the world by inflicting the worst movies ever made on the population. But what movie? With the help of his equally insane assistant, Frank at the Deep Thirteen Research Center, Clayton kidnaps the unit's janitor, Joel, and "shoots" him into orbit in a satellite called the Satellite of Love. Here Joel, who later builds two robots for company, Tom Servo and Crow T. Robot, is forced to watch an endless supply of the worst science fiction movies ever made. As Joel (later replaced by Mike) watches the films, he is seen in silhouette with his robots at the bottom of the screen commenting on the film. The series ran on Comedy Central from 1989 to 1996 and concluded its run on Syfy from 1997–1999.

Cast: Joel Hodgson *(Joel)*; Michael J. Nelson *(Mike)*; Kevin Murphy, J. Elvis Weinstein *(Tom Servo)*; Trace Beaulieu, Bill Corbett *(Crow T. Robot)*; Trace Beaulieu *(Dr. Clayton Forrester)*; Frank Conniff *(Frank)*; Jim Mallon *(Gypsy)*; Mary Jo Pehl *(Magic Voice)*.

6466 *Mystery Woman.* (Series; Crime Drama; Hallmark; 2006). Samantha Kinsey is a young woman who operates a bookstore called Mystery Woman. As a young girl, Samantha read every mystery novel she could find. Her Uncle, Bob, a crime novel aficionado, would read her a detective story each night at bedtime. As the years passed Samantha became more and more of an expert at solving baffling crimes (even before she finished reading a whodunit). When her Uncle Bob passed away, Samantha inherited not only his bookstore (Mystery Man) but also Ian Philby, the store's crime connoisseur (a former CIA agent) and a mysterious friend of the family. Samantha takes over the bookstore (changing its name to Mystery Woman) and soon finds herself using her expertise to solve real life baffling crimes. It seems that wherever Samantha is (or goes) murder seems to follow. Stories relate Samantha's (and Ian's) efforts to take what they only read about in books into the real world and solve real crimes. Cassie is Samantha's friend, the Assistant D.A.; Connors is the police chief. In the pilot episode, Cassie was credited as Cassie Thomas (she is Cassandra "Cassie" Hillman in the series).

Cast: Kellie Martin *(Samantha Kinsey)*; J.E. Freeman *(Ian Philby; pilot)*; Clarence Williams III *(Ian Philby; series)*; Constance Zimmer *(Cassie Thomas; pilot)*; Nina Siemaszko *(Cassie Hillman; series)*; Casey Sanders *(Chief Connors)*.

6467 *Mystic Knights of Tir Na Nog.* (Series; Adventure; Fox; 1998-1999). Terma is a mystic island that has been ruled by two families: those of Queen Maeve and those of King Conchobar. Maeve's thirst for power, however, causes her to form an alliance with Mider, a dark fairy, to gain the abilities of a sorceress. Maeve believes the rule of the land is her birthright and no one will be able to stop her. Conchobar, powerless to stop her, is about to give up the battle when fate intervenes. Rohan, a young warrior, finds an ancient Terma scroll that speaks of Draganta, a warrior that is destined to bring peace to Terma. When Rohan notices that the birthmark on his arm matches that of the mark on the scroll, he realizes he is the chosen one. However, to fulfill his destiny, he must find Draganta, whose whereabouts lies in the mystery of the four scrolls. Rohan is not alone in his journey. He is joined by his friend, Angus; the king's daughter, Deirdre; Ivar, a prince and Cathbad, a druid who becomes their guide. Cathbad's first instincts lead them to a land of little people called Tir Na Nog. Here, the king endows each member of the team with a power to become the Mystic Knights of Tri Na Nog (Rohan is the Mystic Knight of Fire; Deirdre is the Mystic Knight of Air; Angus is the Mystic Knight of the Earth; Ivar is the Mystic Knight of Water. In later episodes a young warrior named Garrett joins them and becomes the Mystic Knight of the Forests). Stories follow the Mystic Knights as they search for Draganta while at the same time battling Queen Maeve, who is determined to stop them by conjuring up mythical beasts to destroy them.

Cast: Lochlainn O'Meararn *(Rohan)*; Lisa Dwan *(Deirdre)*; Vincent Walsh *(Angus)*; Justin Pierre *(Ivar)*; Ben Palmer *(Garrett)*; Charlotte Bradley *(Queen Maeve)*; Stephen Brennan *(King Conchobar)*.

6468 *Myth Busters.* (Series; Reality; Discovery Channel; 2003–). A group of "myth busters" attempt to disprove myths, urban legends and folklore sayings by putting the chosen subject to the test. With the help of Buster, the crash dummy, the group does what it takes to debunk supposed facts. Adam Savage and Jamie Hyneman host. Robert Lee is the narrator.

6469 *Mythic Warriors: Guardians of the Legend.* (Series; Cartoon; CBS; 1998-2000). A modernized Mt. Olympus is the setting where tales of the ancient Greek gods are retold, including Zeus, King of the gods and the ruler of Mt. Olympus; Hera, Queen of the gods; Hades, Lord of the Underworld; Demeter, Goddess of Fertility, Poseidon, God of the Sea; Hermes, Messenger of the Gods' and Athena, Goddess of Wisdom.

Voice Cast: James Blendick (*Narrator*); Gary Krawford (*Zeus*); Janet-Lanie Green (*Hera*); Lally Cadeau (*Athena*); Richard Clarkin (*Hermes*); Francis Diakowsky (*Poseidon*).

6470   *The Naked Brothers Band.* (Series; Reality; Nick; 2007). The Naked Brothers Band is a rock band started by Nat and Alex Wolff, the teenage sons of composer Michael Wolff. Cameras follow the brothers as they experience all the problems of starting a band and journeying up that rocky road to musical stardom. Polly Draper is the off screen voice of Alex and Nat's mother.

6471   *Naked City.* (Series; Crime Drama; ABC; 1958-1959; 1960–1963). Naked city Producer Herbert B. Leonard opens the program: "Ladies and gentlemen, you are about to see the Naked City. This story was not photographed in a studio; quite the contrary. The actors played out their roles in the streets and buildings of New York itself." *Naked City* appeared as two separate series: a half-hour version (1958-1959) and a longer running hour version (1960–1963). Each version was filmed in black and white and focused on the grueling investigations of police officers as they solved crimes.

1958 Version: Jim Halloran and Dan Muldoon are detectives with the 65th Precinct in Manhattan. Jim is married to Janet and is the father of Evie. Dan, an older detective, was killed off in the episode "Ten Cent Dreams" (Mar. 10, 1959) when his car blew up after hitting a gasoline truck during a high speed car chase. He was replaced by Mike Parker, a somewhat gruff lieutenant who now worked alongside Jim. Also assisting Jim and Mike was Sergeant Frank Arcaro. George Duning and Ned Washington composed the theme "This Is the Naked City."

1960 Version: Lieutenant Mike Parker and Sergeant Frank Arcaro reprised their roles with Detective Adam Flint becoming their new partner. Adam is romantically involved with Libby Kingston, an actress who works at an unidentified television studio in Manhattan.

Each episode ended with one of the most famous lines in television history: "There are eight million stories in the Naked City. This has been one of them." Billy May composed "The Naked City Theme" (1960–62); Nelson Riddle composed "The New Naked City Theme" (1962-1963).

Cast: James Franciscus (*Det. Jimmy Halloran*); John McIntire (*Lt. Dan Muldoon*); Horace McMahon (*Lt. Mike Parker*); Harry Bellaver (*Sgt. Frank Arcaro*); Suzanne Storrs (*Suzanne Halloran*); Paul Burke (*Det. Adam Flint*); Nancy Malone (*Libby Kingston*); Edward Asner (*Lt. Vincent Busti*); Marco Lungreen (*Evie Busti; Vincent's wife*).

6472   *Naked Hotel.* (Pilot; Drama; Unaired; Produced for ABC in 2003). The Hotel de Bleu is a Bahamas hideaway for the rich and famous and the proposal was to relate events in the lives of the staff and the jet-setters who find the serenity they are seeking away from their corporate worlds.

Cast: John Corbett (*Manager*); Jenny Wade (*Assistant Manager*); Sara Ramirez (*Maid*); Michael Rispoli (*Security Chief*); Laura Jordon (*Desk clerk*).

6473   *The Naked Trucker and T-Bones Show.* (Series; Comedy; Comedy Central; 2007). Dave Allen and David Koechner are the stars of a live comedy act that plays at comedy clubs in Los Angeles. Dave is "The Naked Trucker," a big rig trucker who drives in the nude; David is his sidekick, Gerald "T-Bones" Tibbons. The program is an adaptation of the stage show with the two characters relating some of their outrageous trucking experiences to the TV audience. A guitar covers the Naked Trucker (who sings and preaches the gospel, so he is not fully naked); T-Bones is a drifter who rides with the Naked Trucker. Songs and stories of life on the road are featured.

Cast: Dave Allen (*The Naked Trucker*); David Koechner (*Gerald "T-Bones" Tibbons*).

6474   *The Naked Truth.* (Series; Comedy; ABC, 1995-1996; NBC, 1996-1997). Nora Wilde can be described simply as gorgeous. But for Nora, being gorgeous does not always get her what she wants; it sometimes has the opposite effect. Nora attended Sarah Lawrence University where her experiences as editor of the school newspaper gave her the incentive to become a writer (especially when her story on campus lesbians caused a sensation). After college, Nora married (but later divorced Paul, whom she felt was inhibiting her career). She became a Pulitzer Prize nominee and worked for a short time for the *Washington Post*. Paul, however, is bitter over the divorce and has begun his campaign of revenge against her by using his extreme wealth to make sure Nora never achieves real success. She loses her job at the paper and with no other choice, she becomes a writer-photographer for *The Comet*, a tabloid that thrives on celebrity dirt (and stories following Nora she goes undercover to find them — from attempting to get a picture of a supposed pregnant Anna Nicole Smith to going undercover as a stripper for an expose on big breasted girls).

Although the doors have been closing on Nora, she does find a better job as a reporter when Camilla Dane becomes the new owner of *The Comet*, changes its name to *The Inquisitor* and promotes Nora. Other staffers for *The Comet* are Les, Chloe, Nick, Dave and Jake. Originally titled *Wilde Again*.

Cast: Tea Leoni (*Nora Wilde*); Holland Taylor (*Camilla Dane*); George Wendt (*Les Polonsky*); Amy Ryan (*Chloe Banks*); Jack Blessing (*Mr. Donner*); Darryl Sivad (*T.J.*); Jonathan Penner (*Nick Columbus*); Mark Roberts (*Dave Fontaine*); Mary Tyler Moore (*Catherine Wilde; Nora's mother*); George Segal (*Fred Wilde; Nora's father*); Tom Verica (*Jake Sullivan*).

6475   *Nakia.* (Series; Crime Drama; ABC; 1974). Nakia Parker is a Navaho Indian and the deputy sheriff of Davis County, New Mexico. He works under Sheriff Sam Jericho and often finds his heritage and beliefs clashing with the law he has sworn to uphold. Stories follow Nakia as he attempts to uphold the law — despite the situations he encounters. Irene James and Hubbel Martin are fellow deputies; Ben Redearth and Half Cub are fellow Indians. In the pilot episode, Joe Kapp played Hubel Martin.

Cast: Robert Forster (*Nakia Parker*); Arthur Kennedy (*Sam Jericho*); Gloria DeHaven (*Irene James*); Taylor Lacher (*Hubel Martin*); Victor Jory (*Ben Redearth*); John Tenorio, Jr. (*Half Cub*).

6476   *The Name Game.* (Pilot; Game; Unaired; Produced for ABC in 1990). Four players compete, divided into two teams of two. The object calls for one player to guess the identity of a famous person from indirect clues given to him by his partner.

Host: Bob Eubanks.

6477   *The Name of the Game.* (Series; Crime Drama; NBC; 1968–1972). Glenn Howard, the publisher of *Crime* magazine, built the then-fictional and defunct *People* magazine into a multimillion-dollar empire (Howard Publications); Dan Farrell is the senior editor, a former FBI agent who is conducting a personal battle against the underworld (who killed his wife and child); Jeff Dillon is the editor of the "People" section of *Crime* magazine. Their individual attempts to uncover story material are depicted on a rotating basis. Peggy Maxwell is their Girl Friday; Joe Sample, Andy Hill and Ross Craig are fellow reporters. In the pilot film, *Fame Is the Name of the Game* (Nov. 26, 1966) George Macready played Glenn Howard.

Cast: Gene Barry (*Glenn Howard*); Robert Stack (*Dan Farrell*); Tony Franciosa (*Jeff Dillon*); Susan Saint James (*Peggy Maxwell*); Ben Murphy (*Joe Sample*); Cliff Potter (*Andy Hill*); Mark Miller (*Ross Craig*).

6478   *Name That Tune*. (Series; Game; NBC; CBS; 1953–2007). The object calls for players to identify song titles after hearing only a few bars. Each correct identification scores a player a point and the player with the highest point total is the winner. Six versions appeared:

1. Name That Tune (NBC, 1953-54; CBS, 1954–59). **Host:** Red Benson, Bill Cullen, George DeWitt. **Vocalist:** Vicki Mills. **Announcer:** Johnny Olson, Wayne Howell. **Orchestra:** Harry Salter, Ted Rapf.

2. Name That Tune (NBC, 1974-75; 1977; Syn., 1974–77). **Network Host:** Dennis James. **Syndication Host:** Tom Kennedy. **Orchestra:** Tommy Oliver. **Announcer:** John Harlan.

3. The $100,000 Name That Tune (Syn., 1976–1981). See entry for information.

4. The New $100,000 Name That Tune (Syn., 1984). See entry for information.

5. Name That Tune (Unaired Pilot; Produced in 1989). **Host:** Peter Allen. **Announcer:** Charlie O'Donnell.

6. Name That Tune (Unaired Pilot; Produced for CBS in 2007). **Host:** Donny Osmond.

6479   *Name That Video*. (Series; Game; VH-1; 2001). Three contestants compete in a game wherein they must answer questions based on music videos. Rounds vary in presentation, but the two most frequently used formats are "Say It Again" (players have to figure out the correct lyrics from hard to understand songs from a choice of three possible answers) and "Finish the Phrase" (players hear part of a song then must sing the next line). The player with the highest score competes in a final round wherein he must name ten videos to win a new car; failure to do so award him $500 per correct identification.

Host: Karyn Bryant.

6480   *Name Your Adventure*. (Series; Reality; NBC; 1992). A Saturday morning program that allows teenagers the opportunity to fulfill their most exciting dreams. Subjects are selected from letters sent into the program and chosen entries are granted that dream (from rafting down the Colorado River to riding in an air balloon).

Host: Mario Lopez. **Co-Host:** Jordan Brady, Tatyana M. Ali.

6481   *The Namedroppers*. (Series; Game; NBC; 1969-1970). The game involves three guest celebrities who comprise the panel; twenty contestants selected from the studio audience; and two Namedroppers (people who are in some way related to the celebrities). One Namedropper appears and briefly tells how he is related to one of the celebrities but does not say to whom. Each celebrity relates a story concerning their relationship, but only one story is true. Of the twenty studio audience members, two compete at a time. The eighteen remaining players each press a button and select the celebrity they believe is related to the Namedropper. The stage players verbally divulge their choice. The celebrity identifies the Namedropper. The studio audience votes are revealed and each incorrect vote awards the correct player ten dollars; if neither of the two players is correct, the Namedropper receives the money. Two such rounds are played per game, enabling all twenty contestants to compete during a five-day period.

Host: Al Lohman, Roger Barkley. **Announcer:** Kenny Williams.

6482   *The Name's the Same*. (Series; Game; ABC; 1951–1955).

The object calls for a celebrity panel to identify the birth names of guests who have the same names as famous celebrities. Players receive cash prizes based on the number of probing questions asked of them by the panel. Ten questions is the limit and $25 is the amount that is awarded if the panel fails to identify the name.

Host: Robert Q. Lewis (*1951–54*); Dennis James (*Oct. 1954*); Bob Elliott, Ray Goulding (*April 1955*); Clifton Fadiman (*June 1955*). **Panelists:** Joan Alexander, Bess Myerson, Gene Rayburn, Arnold Stang, Abe Burrows, Meredith Wilson, Audrey Meadows, Laraine Day, Walter Slezak, Roger Price. **Announcer:** John Reed King, Lee Vines.

6483   *Nancy*. (Series; Comedy; NBC; 1970-1971). Nancy Smith is the daughter of the President of the United States. She is young and beautiful and longs for a life she once lived in Iowa (where her family owns a horse ranch). However, being in the position she is in, she stays by her father's side and is sort of a First Daughter as her father is a widower. She appears to be content with life in Washington, D.C., although she does take periodic trips back home to tend to the ranch in Center City. On one such visit, Nancy's favorite horse, Lady, suddenly becomes ill. Nancy calls the local veterinarian, Adam Hudson, and it is a love at first sight when Nancy and Adam meet. They date, marry and set up housekeeping in Center City on the former Swenson farm. Adam is an easy-going young man who often offers his services at no charge when people can't afford to pay him. He also realized one thing now that he really hadn't considered before his marriage — he is married to the president's daughter and must now lead a life that is more public than private. Stories follow the somewhat shy Adam as he and Nancy attempt to make their marriage work despite the constant press attention and the bodyguards who must protect Nancy at all times.

Abby Townsend is Nancy's guardian; Willie Maxwell is Adam's friend, a reporter for the *Daily Clarion*; Everett McPherson is Adam's uncle; Turner and Rodriquez are the Secret Service Agents assigned to protect Nancy.

Cast: Renne Jarrett (*Nancy Smith*); John Fink (*Adam Hudson*); Celeste Holm (*Abby Townsend*); Eddie Applegate (*Willie Maxwell*); Robert F. Simon (*Everett McPherson*); William H. Bassett (*Secret Serviceman Turner*); Ernesto Macias (*Secret Serviceman Rodriquez*).

6484   *Nancy Drew*. (Pilot; Mystery; ABC; Dec. 15, 2002). Pamela Sue Martin (then Janet Louise Johnson) played Nancy Drew, the teenage sleuth and daughter of criminal attorney Carson Drew in 1977 on ABC's *The Nancy Drew Mysteries*. In 1995 Tracy Ryan played the pretty sleuth as a 21-year-old in the syndicated *Nancy Drew*. In 2002, ABC presented the pilot episode for another version of Nancy Drew with Maggie Lawson as Nancy (back to being a teenager). Here Nancy has just graduated from River Heights High School and has enrolled in River Heights University. She is accompanied by her close friends, George Fayne and Bess Marvin. New to the format is Christina Louisa Maria Timkins, Teeny for short, Nancy's friend, a rich debutante from Rockport, Texas. The proposal was to follow Nancy as she stumbles upon and attempts to solve crimes. Other regulars are Carson Drew, Nancy's father; and Ned Nickerson, Carson's investigator.

Cast: Maggie Lawson (*Nancy Drew*); Lauren Birkell (*George Fayne*); Jill Ritchie (*Bess Marvin*); Marieh Delfino (*Teeny*); Brett Cullen (*Carson Drew*); Nick Stabile (*Ned Nickerson*).

6485   *Nancy Drew*. (Series; Mystery; Syn.; 1995-1996). An update of the *Nancy Drew* mystery stories by Carolyn Keene. The series takes Nancy Drew, the pretty daughter of attorney Carson Drew, away from her traditional setting of River Heights in Illinois. Nancy is now 21 years old and lives on her own in Apartment 603 of the

Callisto Hotel at 306 Marsh Avenue in an unidentified city. While still hoping to become a detective, Nancy works at various jobs as an employee of the Temp Agency. She is also attending an unnamed college and studying criminology. Nancy has a knack for stumbling upon crimes (and enjoying solving them) and is assisted in her capers by her best friend, Georgia "George" Fayne and George's cousin, Bess Marvin. George and Bess share Apartment 3 over a store called Phillips Shoes. George is studying film (and hopes to become an editor) and works part time as a messenger for Quick Draw Couriers. Bess is studying journalism and works part time on a newspaper called *The Rag*, the city's alternative paper. Ned Nickerson, Nancy's boyfriend, appears occasionally.

Cast: Tracy Ryan (*Nancy Drew*); Jhene Erwin (*Bess Marvin*); Joy Tanner (*Georgia Fayne*); Scott Speedman (*Ned Nickerson*).

6486   ***The Nancy Drew Mysteries.*** (Series; Crime Drama; ABC; 1977–1978). Nancy Drew is a pretty, smart and adventurous girl who yearns to become a detective. She is being raised by her widowed father, Carson Drew, an attorney whose wife died when Nancy was three years old. Nancy and her father live at 8606 Bainbridge Street in the town of River Heights and Nancy is a recent graduate of River Heights High School. She now works as a part-time investigator for her father, but mostly researches legal files and checks driving records. However, when a case turns into a mystery for Carson, Nancy becomes a detective and tries to help Carson solve it. Nancy constantly takes chances and often places her life in jeopardy. "Nancy is a girl with a very inquisitive mind who loves to solve a mystery," says Carson. "But the day she began part time investigative work for me was the start of my gray hairs."

Nancy dislikes being told she is wrong; it angers her and sets her into motion to prove what she saw or feels is right. While Nancy does do investigating, she doesn't consider what she does prying — "I just observe." Nancy is assisted on all her cases by her best friend, Georgia "George" Fayne. George, who attended River Heights High School with Nancy, lives at 16 River Street. A job is not mentioned for George but she does want to become a detective. Nancy feels George is not ready and lets her practice by doing undercover work for her. While Carson is shrewd and can read people, George is often in a daze as to what is going on when she and Nancy are on a case. George often comes up with "clues that don't seem to mean anything except to Nancy," she says. She often paints a graphic picture of what could happen if she and Nancy go any further.

Ned Nickerson was first Carson's assistant and Nancy's shy boyfriend although Nancy was never quite sure what Ned's intentions were. Ned is afraid to ask Nancy for a date and George believes "Nancy has turned your brains into mush. Your mistake was to become her friend. She thinks of you as a big brother." Ned also believes "Nancy is not interested in romantic things like moonlit rides. She's a very serious girl." This indecisive Ned was dropped in favor of a more forceful Ned. Here Ned, who had an eye for Nancy, was an investigator for the Boston D.A.'s office who worked with Carson.

Cast: Pamela Sue Martin, Janet Louise Johnson (*Nancy Drew*); William Schallert (*Carson Drew*); Jean Rasey, Susan Buckner (*George Fayne*); George O'Hanlon, Jr., Rick Springfield (*Ned Nickerson*); Robert Karnes (*Sheriff Kane*).

6487   ***The Nancy Dussault Show.*** (Pilot; Comedy; CBS; May 8, 1973). After several years as a Broadway understudy actress Nancy Clancy finally gets a break when her leading lady becomes ill. Nancy steps into the spotlight and becomes an overnight sensation. The proposal, set in New York City, was to relate Nancy's misadventures as a newly discovered star and as a new wife, having just married Bill Clancy. Clare is Nancy's friend.

Cast: Nancy Dussault (*Nancy Clancy*); Lawrence Pressman (*Bill Clancy*); Karen Morrow (*Claire*).

6488   ***The Nancy Walker Show.*** (Series; Comedy; ABC; 1976–1977). Nancy Kitteridge is a Hollywood theatrical agent. She is married to Kenneth and is the mother of Lorraine. Nancy's clients are not always the typical actor or actress seeking a job, but unusual people seeking to break into show business. Stories follow Nancy as she struggles to cope with clients and deal with her neurotic family. Glen is Lorraine's husband; Terry Folson assists Nancy.

Cast: Nancy Walker (*Nancy Kitteridge*); William Daniels (*Kenneth Kitteridge*); Beverly Archer (*Lorraine*); James Cromwell (*Glen*); Ken Olfson (*Terry Folson*). **Theme Vocal:** "Nancy's Blues" by Nancy Walker.

6489   ***The Nanette Fabray Show.*** (Series; Comedy; NBC; 1961). The alternate title for *Yes, Yes Nanette*. See this title for information.

6490   ***The Nanny.*** (Series; Comedy; CBS; 1993–1999). The fashionable 19-room dwelling on New York's Park Avenue is home to Maxwell Sheffield, a widow with three children (Maggie, Gracie, Bryton), a butler, Niles and a live-in nanny, Fran Fine.

Maxwell, a successful Broadway producer is responsible for such plays as *Annie 2*, *Moby*, *Regardless* and *Loves Me Not*. He is a partner with C.C. Babcock in Sheffield-Babcock Productions (originally Maxwell Sheffield Productions). Before moving to California to produce a TV series (final episode), Max produced one last play — *Yetta's Letters* (based on the love letters of Fran's grandmother). Ann Guilbert, who plays the somewhat senile Yetta Rosenberg, believes Max and Fran are Rob and Laura Petrie from *The Dick Van Dyke Show*. (Ann played neighbor Millie Halper on that show.)

Francine, nicknamed Fran, is 29 years old and believes some women think she is a stripper or a hooker "by the clothes I wear." After losing her job at the Bridal Shoppe in Flushing, Queens, she began selling Shades of the Orient Cosmetics door to door. At the Sheffield home she was mistaken for an agency nanny, impressed Max's kids and was hired as their nanny. Fran is a graduate of the Ultissima Beauty Institute. She later attended the Barbizon School of Modeling and was a foot model for two years. Fran's favorite performer is Barbra Streisand (she believes *Yentl* is the best movie ever made). She and Maxwell married in last season episodes (she later gave birth to twins she and Maxwell named James Samuel and Eve Kathryn).

Margaret, nicknamed Maggie, is 14 years old and very pretty but feels she is "a worthless, pathetic, unlovable nothing." Maggie also believes she has no personality. Fran, who cured Maggie of her false beliefs, feels more like her girlfriend than her nanny. Maggie attended the Holy Cross Grammar School, then the Lexington Academy.

Gracie, the middle child (called "Angel" by Fran), is "a complicated girl" with multiple personalities. She is six years old when the series begins and is in therapy sessions to treat her introversion and insecurities. Gracie has an imaginary friend (Imogene) and two hamsters (Miss Fine and Mr. Sheffield). Gracie attends the Holy Cross School (later Lexington Academy) and can't have fun at school because she worries about the polar ice caps melting. She believes the showgirls that audition for her father are "giant Barbie dolls."

Bryton is ten years old and mischievous. He attends the Lexington Academy and overindulges on junk food. Bryton is interested in sports "if I can own the team."

By 1999, Niles has been in service to Maxwell for 25 years. He is a member of the Professional Butler's Association and says about his name "It's Niles, just Niles, like Cher." His favorite part of the job is watching gorgeous showgirls audition at the house. He has written a play he hopes Maxwell will produce called *Love, Valet, Compassion.*

Chastity Claire "C.C." Babcock is Maxwell's business partner and calls herself C.C. (her mother is B.B.; her sister, D.D.). She is constantly trying to impress Maxwell (in hopes of marrying him) and calls Fran "Nanny Fine." She has a dog (given to her by Maxwell) named Chester, and calls the kids "Macy, Bob and Nancy." C.C. believes people think she is "a self-centered, cold-hearted witch." She and Niles are constantly at odds, but fell in love and later married. C.C. tries to be nice and sensitive "but my nasty attitude can't make it happen." Val is Fran's friend; Sylvia is Fran's mother.

Cast: Fran Drescher *(Fran Fine)*; Charles Shaughnessy *(Maxwell Sheffield)*; Daniel Davis *(Niles)*; Lauren Lee *(C.C. Babcock)*; Nicholle Tom *(Maggie Sheffield)*; Madeline Zima *(Gracie Sheffield)*; Benjamin Salisbury *(Bryton Sheffield)*; Renee Taylor *(Sylvia Fine)*; Rachel Chagall *(Val Toriello)*; Ann Morgan Guilbert *(Yetta)*.

6491   *Nanny and the Professor.* (Series; Comedy; ABC; 1970-1971). Phoebe Figalilly is not a witch or a magician, but she possesses the ability to spread love and joy. She drives an antique car she calls Arabella and magically appears when someone needs help. She can understand animals and seems to make the impossible happen. Professor Harold Everett is a widowed college professor and the father of three mischievous children: Harold ("Hal") Jr., Prudence and Bentley. Professor Everett is having a difficult time caring for his kids (housekeepers are frightened off by the children), until Phoebe, who prefers to be called Nanny, arrives to help him and take charge of his household. The Everetts live at 10327 Oak Street in Los Angeles. Professor Everett teaches math at Clinton College, and the family pets are Waldo (a dog), Sebastian (a rooster), Mike and Myrtle (guinea pigs) and Geraldine and Jerome (baby goats). Hal is interested in science and has a lab set up in the basement (his father believes Hal is too dedicated to his experiments, which rarely work). Bentley's nickname is Butch. Henrietta is Phoebe's aunt; Francine Fowler is the girl with a crush on Hal; Florence is Francine's mother. Harry Nilsson sings the theme, "Nanny."

Cast: Juliet Mills *(Phoebe Figalilly)*; Richard Long *(Harold Everett)*; David Doremus *(Hal Everett)*; Kim Richards *(Prudence Everett)*; Trent Lehman *(Butch Everett)*; Eileen Baral *(Francine Fowler)*; Patsy Garrett *(Florence Fowler)*; Elsa Lanchester *(Aunt Henrietta)*; Harry Hickox *(College Dean)*.

Note: On Sept. 15, 1973, ABC presented *Nanny and the Professor,* an animated pilot that used the voice of the live action cast but failed to produce a new version of the series (that would have continued to follow events in the magical life of Nanny).

6492   *Nanny 911.* (Series; Reality; Fox; 2004). Real life nannies, each with a specific skill for dealing with unruly children, appear at the home of a family with a problem child (or children) and take over — giving the parents a rest while they attempt to turn wild children into obedient children. The nannies rules are not easily accepted by the child (who usually goes into a faked crying tantrum) when put to the test. The nannies also advise the parents and when they feel their job is done, leave, and the parents are left to deal with the aftermath. The nannies are identified as Head Nanny Lillian, Nanny Stella, Nanny Debbie and Nanny Yvonne.

6493   *Naomi's New Morning.* (Series; Talk; Hallmark; 2006). Singer Naomi Judd is the host of a no topics is off limit talk show. In addition to celebrity interviews, the program presents discussions with experts in psychology, neuroscience and the paranormal.

6494   *Naruto.* (Series; Cartoon; Cartoon Network; 2002). Uzumaki Naruto is a young ninja who is seeking to become a master

ninja and a Hokage (leader) of his village (Konoha in the Land of Fire). Naruto, however, is not an ordinary boy. Twelve years earlier, a Kyubi (a nine tailed demon fox) attacked Konoha. The village chief, the Fourth Hokage, captured the spirit of the fox and sealed it within a baby boy named Naruto. Although adults fear Naruto for the demon that lives within him, he has shown not to have turned evil. Stories follow Naruto as he and three friends (Sasuke, Sakura and ninja instructor Kakashi) join forces to battle evil wherever they find it.

Voice Cast: Maile Flanagan *(Naruto Uzumaki)*; Danielle Judovitt *(Tenten)*; Kate Higgins *(Sakura Haruno)*; Kyle Hebert *(Kiba Inuzuka)*; Tom Gibis *(Nara)*; Grant George *(Yoroi)*; Crispin Freeman *(Ebisu)*; Quinton Flynn *(Iruka Umino)*; Susan Dalian *(Haku)*; Julianne Buescher *(Anko)*; Colleen O'Shaughnessy *(Ino)*; Tara Platt *(Temari)*.

6495   *NASCAR Angels.* (Series; Reality; Syn.; 2006). Members of the NASCAR racing circuit perform good deeds across the country. The emotional reactions of the people helped close out each episode. Rusty Wallace, Shanna Wiseman host. Steve Wood is the announcer.

6496   *NASCAR Racers.* (Series; Cartoon; Fox; 2000). A team of good NASCAR racers (Team Fastex) vs. the evil Team Rexcor. Car designer Jack Fassler developed the concept for the cars; his daughter, Megan, created the cars. Members of the Fastex team include Steve, Sharp, Carlos Rey and McCutchen. Jack's rival, Garner Rex Rexton stole Jack's concept and created his own brand of cars and now each strives to beat the other to become number one on the NASCAR circuit.

Voice Cast: Paul Dobson *(Jack Fassler)*; Kathleen Barr *(Megan Fassler)*; Ron Halder *(Garner Rexton)*; Roger R. Cross *(Steve Sharp)*; Ian James Corbett *(Mark McCutchen)*; Scott McNeil *(Lyle Owens)*; Kirby Morrow *(Redline)*; Rino Romano *(Carlos Rey)*.

6497   *The Nash Airflyte Theater.* (Series; Anthology; CBS; 1950-1951). Nash Products sponsored program of dramatic productions that feature such stars as Jane Wyatt, Joan Bennett, Van Heflin, Laraine Day, Dane Clark, Ronald Reagan, Basil Rathbone, David Niven Joan Blondell, Kitty Carlisle, Ann Rutherford and Richard Arlen.

6498   *Nash Bridges.* (Series; Crime Drama; CBS; 1996–2001). Nash Bridges is an inspector with the San Francisco Police Department. He is partners with Joe Dominquez and the father of Cassidy. He is twice divorced and lives with his father and Cassidy at 855 Sacramento Street.

Nash was born on December 7, 1955. He attended the San Francisco Police Academy and was the youngest cop to ever receive a Gold Star. Nash has a tendency to call people "Bubba." Nash drives a 1971 yellow Plymouth Barracuda convertible. Only 14 such cars were made and he calls his The Cuda. In some episodes, Nash claims the car was made in 1970. Nash has a photographic memory and loses his temper when he becomes angry.

Lisa is Nash's first ex-wife; Kelly was the second Mrs. Bridges. Lisa, the owner of a catering company, is Cassidy's mother. Though divorced, Nash and Lisa are still close; he and Kelly are further apart.

Nash is first an inspector, then Captain, and heads the S.I.U. (Special Investigative Unit of the S.F.P.D.). Headquarters was first located in a building in downtown San Francisco. When an earthquake partially destroyed the building, operations were transferred to a docked ferry boat called the *Eurika* on Hyde Street. Two years later, the ferry is replaced by a 177 foot barge that once housed the Allied Cannery Company, then a rave club.

Nash often breaks the rules to get the job done and takes the heat for doing so. He prefers to work with his team and balks at sharing cases and information with the FBI. "They're too damned sure about everything," says Nash.

Joe was originally introduced as Nash's ex-partner who quit the force to become a private detective. He is semi-retired when the series begins and helps "The Nashman," as he calls Nash, solve crimes. He is later back on the force, first as an inspector then lieutenant. He is married to Inger and lives in an apartment at 4665 Laguna. In last season episodes, he and Inger become the parents of a girl they name Lucia. Joe is the owner of a gay bar called the Tender Loin through a get-rich scheme that backfired and partners with Nash in a moonlighting business called Bridges and Dominquez — Private Investigators. They have offices at 427 Grey Street in a building full of psychiatrists. They often become involved in private capers while working on departmental matters.

Cassidy, Nash's only child, first attended Bay High School then Berkeley College. She originally had aspirations to become an actress but later found an interest in law enforcement and attended the police academy. As an actress, Cassidy appeared topless in an avant garde play called *Tears of the Monkey*. Cassidy then became a police officer and was first assigned to the Seacliff section of San Francisco. She was later reassigned to Nash's unit as a uniformed officer. Cassidy is rarely defiant and loyal to her father.

Nash was uneasy with Cassidy becoming a cop as he was with her doing nude scenes in plays. Cassidy was involved in a fatal shooting and exonerated but quit the force when she felt her father was against her becoming a police officer. The series ended with an unresolved cliff hanger on May 4, 2001 when Cassidy is seen weighing the possibilities of returning to the force or leaving to begin a new life in Paris.

Nick Bridges is Nash's father, a former longshoreman who lived at the Three Oaks Retirement Home before he came to reside with Nash. Nick could not get along with "management" as he calls it. Nick served aboard the USS Phoenix during World War II and now cares for the house and does the cooking. He is suffering from the early stages of Alzheimer's disease. Nash's sister, Stacey Bridges, is an assistant district attorney.

Inspector Caitlin Cross is a beautiful internal affairs officer Nash calls "The Grand Inquisitor." Caitlin has been assigned to perform an audit investigation of the S.I.U.'s prior cases. She first worked for the FBI but quit "when I couldn't tell lies from truths." She next worked as an analyst for the CIA, Russian Intelligence Division; "I analyzed Russian documents all day long." As a result, she can read and speak Russian. She resigned after five years. The mayor of San Francisco then hired her to oversee S.I.U. procedures.

Harvey Leek, Evan Cortez and Antwon Babcock are other members of Nash's team. Antwon is a tough black inspector whose attitude has fostered his transfer to five different investigative units in three years. He is street smart and appears to have found a permanent station with the S.I.U.

Nash is the only cop at the S.I.U. with his personal guardian angel — Angel, an apparent homeless person who dresses in white with a pair of wings. He came from out of nowhere to save Nash's life during a case and has now taken it upon himself to watch over Nash. Angel, as Nash calls him, has no apparent means of income and no background after 1958. As best as Nash can determine, Angel is really Peter Spellman. He was born at Saint Mary's Hospital on January 27, 1949. He was adopted by Dr. Alvin Spellman and his wife Helen. After Helen's death, Peter was sent to a foster home where he lived until the age of nine. In the summer of 1958 his records stopped. He became non-existent. He never paid taxes, never had a job, has no social security number, was never in the service. No school records exist either.

Elia Cmiral composed the original theme "Nash Bridges." Eddie Jobson composed the revised theme "I've Got a Friend in You" and Ray Bunch composed the final season "New Nash Bridges Theme."

Cast: Don Johnson (*Nash Bridges*); Cheech Marin (*Joe Dominquez*); Jodi Lyn O'Keefe (*Cassidy Bridges*); Annette O'Toole (*Lisa Bridges*); Serena Scott Thomas (*Kelly Bridges*); James Gammon (*Nick Bridges*); Yasmine Bleeth (*Caitlin Cross*); Angela Dohrman (*Stacey Bridges*); Jeff Perry (*Harvey Leek*); Jaimie P. Gomez (*Evan Cortez*); Cress Williams (*Antwon Babcock*); Tracey Walter (*Angel*).

6499 *Nash's Vision.* (Pilot; Fantasy; Unaired; Produced for NBC in 1991). A rather unusual approach to fighting crime: After his son is killed in a hit-and-run accident, David Nash, an undercover detective who possesses telepathic powers, finds assistance in his battle against crime from his deceased son's little toy dinosaur — which is capable of transforming itself into a real 50 foot dinosaur. The proposal was to relate David's unusual methods to deal with the city's criminal population.

Cast: Robert Taylor (*David Nash*).

6500 *Nashville.* (Series; Reality; Fox; 2007). A short lived (cancelled after its second episode) program that follows a group of hopeful country-western singers as they try to make their mark in Nashville. The series, which only managed to introduce the hopefuls and give a glimpse into what they were to face, showed them meeting managers and preparing for performances. The hopefuls are Jeff Aleen, Rachel Bradshaw, Mika Combs, Sarah Gunsolus, Lindsey Hager, Matt Jenkins, Jamey Johnson, Clint Moseley, Monty Powell and Chuck Wickes.

6501 *Nashville 99.* (Series; Crime Drama; CBS; 1977). Nashville 99 is the badge number of Stonewall "Stoney" Huff, a dedicated detective lieutenant with the Nashville Metropolitan Police Department in Tennessee. Detective Trace Mayne is his partner and stories relate their efforts to solve crimes. Birdie Huff is Stoney's mother; R.B. is a deputy.

Cast: Claude Akins (*Stoney Huff*); Jerry Reed (*Trace Mayne*); Lucille Benson (*Birdie Huff*); Charley Pride (*Deputy R.B.*). **Theme Vocal:** ("Nashville 99") by Jerry Reed.

6502 *The Nashville Palace.* (Series; Variety; NBC; 1981–1982). Performances by country and western entertainers coupled with a weekly skit called "The Coots" (about a wacky family living in Looney Corners, Tennessee). Taped at the Nashville Palace Theater. The pilot episode aired on Oct. 25, 1980 and featured Roy Clark as the host.

Host/Announcer: Slim Pickens. **Cast:** Hamilton Camp (*Pa Coot*); Donna Siegel (*Ma Coot*); Terri Gardener (*Daughter Amelia Coot*); Harry Murphy (*Son Thomas Alva Coot*); Wendy Suits (*Granny Coot*). **Music:** Charlie McCoy and His Palace Pickers.

6503 *Nashville Star.* (Series; Reality; NBC; 2008). A talent search to find "the next great country music artist." Ten promising finalists are selected from open auditions across the country. These contenders compete in Nashville in a talent contest for a recording contract with RCA records. Contestants are judged by a panel and each week one hopeful faces elimination. The one remaining singer, chosen from three finalists in the last episode, wins the contract. Buddy Jewell was the winner.

Host: Nancy O'Dell, Le Ann Rimes, Billy Ray Cyrus.

6504 *Nashville Tonight.* (Series; Talk; Nashville Network; 1993–1996). Lorianne Crook and Charlie Chase host a program of interviews with country and western performers.

6505 *Nasty Boys.* (Series; Crime Drama; NBC; 1990). Fact-based program about the Northern Narcotics Bureau of the Las Vegas Police Department, an elite (and rather unorthodox) team of five undercover cops known as the Nasty Boys (Eduardo, Paul, Wheeler, Danny and Tommy). Other regulars are Serena, Eduardo's wife; Lieutenant Max Krieger; and Chief Bradley.

Cast: Benjamin Bratt (*Eduardo Cruz*); Jeff Kaake (*Paul Morrisey*); Don Franklin (*Al Wheeler*); Craig Hurley (*Danny Larsen*); James Pax (*Tommy Kee*); Dennis Franz (*Max Krieger*); Nia Peeples (*Serena Cruz*); Sandy McPeak (*Chief Bradley*). **Theme Vocal:** ("*Nasty*") by Lisa Keith.

6506   The Nat King Cole Show. (Series; Variety; NBC; 1956-1957). A charming half-hour of music and songs with singer Nat King Cole (the first African-American singer to host a major network variety series).

Program Open: "From the Copa Room of the Sands Hotel in Las Vegas, *The Nat King Cole Show* with Ella Fitzgerald, the Four Lads, music conducted by Nelson Riddle, the Randy Van Horne Singers and now our show."

Host: Nat King Cole. **Regulars:** The Randy Van Horne Singers, The Boataneers. **Orchestra:** Gordon Jenkins, Nelson Riddle.

6507   National Bingo Night. (Series; Game; ABC; 2007). A large plastic sphere that stands 2 and-one-half stories high contains 75 numbered balls (1–75). Three games of Bingo are played—the Red Card, Blue Card and White Card. Descriptions for each of the games is based on the first episode (they vary slightly from there on). Each member of the studio audience receives a normal Bingo card. Three players compete, one at a time (one per color card). The Red Card game is called "500 Mile Run." The Bingo balls are activated (sent spinning by an air machine) and the player has to predict whether the ball that comes out will be higher or lower than the first number given by the host. If he is correct, that ball's total is added to the mileage (he must drive 500 miles); studio audience members mark that number on their Bingo cards. The player must then predict whether the next ball will be higher or lower than the prior ball. An incorrect prediction stalls the player but allows the studio audience to use that number on their Bingo cards. If a studio audience member makes Bingo (five numbers in a line) before the stage player reaches the 500 miles (points) he loses his chance at $50,000 and the studio audience player receives $5,000.

Round two is the White Card game. Here, a stage player chooses one car from three that are displayed on stage. The vin number of that car is displayed on a board. The object is for the player to win that car by eliminating the vin number. He must predict whether the Bingo balls that will exit the machine will be odd or even. If a correct guess is made and a number that appears on the ball matches a number on the board, that number is eliminated. He must, however, eliminate all the numbers before a studio audience member calls Bingo. The third round, the Blue Card, has the Bingo balls marked with a black or red decal. A bride and groom mannequin are displayed in a diorama. The bride needs to make seven steps to reach the groom. The player has to predict whether a ball will be black or red. Correct predictions move the bride one step closer to the groom. The player must get the bride to the groom before a studio audience player calls Bingo.

Host: Ed Sanders. **Bingo Girl:** Yesenia Adame. **Bingo Verifier:** Sunil Narkar.

6508   National Lampoon's Funny Money. (Series; Game; GSN; 2003). Two contestants compete. In round one, a question based on the world of comedy is asked. The first player to buzz in and correctly answer it scores two points (called Funny Money Dollars) and chooses one of three guest comedians who must then perform a routine on stage. Audience laughs are registered on a meter

and each time the needle hits the green zone one additional point is scored. Additional rounds include players having to determine which celebrity supplied the caption for an unusual picture and players answering questions based on a comedian's stage performance. The player with the highest point score wins a vacation as a prize.

Host: Jimmy Pardo. **Announcer:** Budd Friedman.

6509   National Lampoon's Greek Games. (Series; Game; GSN; 2006). Four fictional college fraternities and four fictional sororities compete against each other in various frat party games for a trip to the Greek island of Mykonos. Twenty-six events are held and the players compete in such outlandish games as "The Gooey Ten-Yard Dash," "The Reclining Chariot Race" and "Slip and Slide Long Slide."

Host: George Gray. **Sideline Reporters:** Daphne Brogdon, Petros Papadakis.

6510   National Lampoon's Hot Flashes. (Series; Comedy; Syn.; 1984). A limited run (five episode) program that takes an off-the-wall look at the antics of the staff of *National Lampoon's Hot Flashes,* an evening TV news show as they prepare for broadcast. Kimberly Clark and John B. Goode are the anchors; Barry Gold is the entertainment reporter; Walter Conkrite (take-off on Walter Cronkite) is the consumer reporter; Samantha is the production assistant Ali is the floor manager; Juan Jones is the investigative reporter; Chuck Fodder is the roving reporter.

Cast: Lois Robbins (*Kimberly Clark*); Mark King (*John B. Goode*); Kevin Pollak (*Barry Gold*); Franklyn Ajaye (*Walter Conkrite*); Wendy Goldman (*Samantha*); Blake Clarke (*Ali*); Jeff Marder (*Juan Jones*); Rodger Bumpass (*Chuck Fodder*).

6511   National Lampoon's Two Reelers. (Pilot; Comedy; NBC; Aug. 28, 1981). Stephen and Rodger (last names not given) are college students who decide to leave school and travel around the world. They pool their resources and the proposal was to relate their experiences as they seem to encounter nothing but misadventure.

Cast: Stephen Furst (*Stephen*); Rodger Bumpass (*Rodger*).

6512   The National Snoop. (Pilot; Comedy; NBC; Aug. 18, 1983). A satirical television newsmagazine that, set at the newsroom of the "National Snoop," presents unusual news and human interest stories.

Co-Anchors: Catherine Bergstrom, Phil Hartman, Lennie Weinrib. **Regulars:** Dr. Joyce Brothers, Don Calfa, Sheila Frazier, Allan Katz, Rose Lau, Greg Lewis, K.C. Winkler, Bob Yerkes. **Music:** Perry Botkin, Jr.

6513   National Velvet. (Series; Drama; NBC; 1960–1962). Velvet Brown is the pretty 12-year-old daughter of Herbert and Martha Brown, the owners of the Brown Dairy Ranch in a Midwestern community called the Valley (on the outskirts of Birch City). Velvet has a beautiful 16-year-old sister (Edwina) and a curious and mischievous six-year-old brother (Donald). Velvet also has a dream: to train her horse King to win the Grand National Sweepstakes.

Velvet receives help in training King from Mi Taylor, the ranch hand, a former steeplechase rider whose career ended when he was thrown from a horse during a race and injured his leg; he now walks with a limp.

Edwina, called "Winna," shares a bedroom with Velvet. She is very feminine (Velvet is more like a tomboy) and is a sophomore at Valley High School. She breeds canaries and had two boyfriends: the more steady Theodore P. Nelson, an anthropology professor at State College, and the occasional Carl Evans, a local boy. Donald is a realistically typical little boy. He gets hurt (for example, falling down the stairs), adopts stray animals, fibs, blames his sisters for something he did and is often confused by "big words" (like elopement). While stories relate incidents in the lives of the Brown family, particular focus is on Velvet as she trains King for the Grand National Steeplechase. Based on the Elizabeth Taylor film of the same title.

Cast: Lori Martin (*Velvet Brown*); Arthur Space (*Herbert Brown*); Ann Doran (*Martha Brown*); Carole Wells (*Edwina Brown*); Joey Scott (*Donald Brown*); James McCallion (*Mi Taylor*); Carl Crow (*Theodore P. Nelson*); Michael Vandever (*Carl Evans*).

6514   The Natural Look. (Pilot; Comedy; NBC; July 6, 1977). Reedy Harrison is a cosmetics executive for Contessa Toiletries. She is married to a pediatrician (Bud) and the proposal was to relate Reedy's efforts to divide her time between a monopolizing job and her husband, who yearns for a wife who is more at home than at work. Other regulars are The Countess, the owner of the company; Edna, Reedy's friend; and Arthur, the Countess's son, the director of the company.

Cast: Barbara Feldon (*Reedy Harrison*); Bill Bixby (*Dr. Bud Harrison*); Brenda Forbes (*Countess*); Sandy Sprung (*Edna*); Michael MacRae (*Arthur*).

6515   Naturally, Sadie. (Series; Comedy; Disney; 2005). Is being smart the new in thing for a pretty teenage girl? Sadie Hawthorne is a high school girl who is determined to answer that question. Sadie is a girl who not only loves Nature, but also loves to study and observe animals ("I'm amazed by everything that is wild—animals, bugs and even the wild people in my own life. Guess it just comes ... naturally"). While Sadie's dream is rather weird ("to go to the Rain Forest to study bugs and fungus and weird microbes") she uses her research in studying animals and their behavior to analyze people (mostly her school mates) and help them overcome any problem they may have—a situation that seems sound—until Sadie intervenes and mishap occurs.

Cast: Charlotte Arnold (*Sadie Hawthorne*); Collette Micks (*Jean Hawthorne*); Justin Bradley (*Hal Hawthorne*); Jasmine Richards (*Margaret Browning-Levesque*); Richard Clarkin (*Walter Hawthorne*); Michael D'Ascenzo (*Rain Papadaki*); Alex Hood (*Ron Yuma*); Mallory Margel (*Mallory Randell*); Shenae Grimes (*Arlene Alcott*); Kyle Kass (*Owen Anthony*); Alison Sealy-Smith (*Ms. Mann*); Mandy Butcher (*Chelsea Breuer*).

6516   Naughty Amateur Home Videos. (Series; Erotica; Playboy; 1999–). Real people performing soft core sexual acts are profiled (not as explicit as amateur videos found in the adult sections of video stores). The program's gorgeous host travels to various cities and towns to record the sexual activities of people—alone, together or in groups. Episode titles are as suggestive as the programs themselves (for example, "West Virginia Vixens," "Tennessee Teasers," "Kansas Cougars," and "Arkansas Amateurs").

Hostess: Jesse Jane.

6517   Navy Log. (Series; Anthology; CBS; ABC; 1955–1958). Incidents in the lives of the men of the U.S. Navy are dramatized in stories based on official files. Notable performers include Leonard Nimoy, Beverly Garland, Clint Eastwood, Ernest Borgnine, James Cagney, Robert Montgomery, Sally Fraser, Martin Milner and Jimmy Lydon.

6518   NBC Action Playhouse. (Series; Anthology; NBC; 1971-1972). Peter Marshall hosts dramas that originally aired on *The Bob Hope Chrysler Theater*. Aired from June 24 to Sept. 7, 1971; and May 23 to Sept. 5, 1972.

6519   NBC Adventure Theater. (Series; Anthology; NBC; 1971-1972). Rebroadcasts of dramas, hosted by Art Fleming (1971) and Ed McMahon (1972) that originally aired on *The Bob Hope Chrysler Theater*. Aired from June 24 to Sept. 4, 1971; and June 15 to Aug. 31, 1972.

6520   The NBC Comedy Hour. (Series; Variety; NBC; 1956). Music, songs and comedy sketches coupled with performances by new talent discoveries.

Host: Gale Storm. **Regulars:** Jonathan Winters, Hy Averback. **Announcer:** Hy Averback.

6521   NBC Comedy Theater. (Series; Anthology; NBC; 1971-1972). Jack Kelly hosts a summer program that comprises comedy episodes that originally aired on *The Bob Hope Chrysler Theater*. Aired from July 7 to Aug. 30, 1971; and July 8 to Sept. 4, 1972.

6522   The NBC Comics. (Series; Cartoon; NBC; 1950). The network title for *The Telecomics* when the series moved from syndication to NBC.

6523   The NBC Follies. (Series; Variety; NBC; 1973). A revue based on the music, song, dance and comedy of vaudeville. The pilot episode aired on Feb. 8, 1973.

Host: Sammy Davis, Jr. **Regulars:** Mickey Rooney, The Carl Jablonski Dancers. **Orchestra:** Harper MacKay.

6524   NBC Playhouse. (Series; Anthology; NBC; 1960). Actress Jeanne Bal hosts a summer program of filmed dramas that originally aired on other anthology programs. Ran from June 28 to September 6, 1960.

6525   NBC Repertory Theater. (Series; Anthology; NBC; 1949). Live dramatic program that ran from April 17 to July 10, 1949 and featured a different cast and story each week.

6526   The NBC Revue. (Experimental; Variety; NBC; May 17, 1939). A potpourri of variety acts with magician Robert Reinhart as the host: comical dancing by Hal Sherman; a fashion show from the Ritz Carlton Hotel with Nancy Turner as the commentator; vocals from the Smoothies (a night club trio); circus-like stunts with the Flying Ginsbergs; and a comic playlet called "The Smart Thing" with Martha Sleeper, Ned Wever and Buford Hampden in a story about a man who is about to elope with his friend's wife until he finds the husband too eager to let his wife go.

6527   The NBC Saturday Prom. (Series; Variety; NBC; 1960-1961). Singer Merv Griffin oversees a program that features performances by the top names in music.

6528   The NBC Sunday Mystery Movie. (Series; Crime Drama; NBC; 1971–1977). The overall title for nine rotating series: *Amy Prentiss, Columbo, Hec Ramsey, Lanigan's Rabbi, McCloud, McCoy, McMillan, McMillan and Wife* and *Quincy, M.E.* See individual titles for information.

6529   N.C.I.S. (Series; Crime Drama; CBS; 2003–). The Navy Criminal Investigative Service (N.C.I.S.) is an organization that operates outside of the U.S. military to investigate crimes associated with service men and women. Stories follow Special Agent Jethro Gibbs and his specialized team as they probe incidents that could eventually embarrass the military if not discreetly handled. Ziva David, Anthony DiNozzo, Jimmy Palmer, Caitlin Todd and Timothy McGee assist Jethro, Abby Sciuto is their lab assistant; Dr. Donald

"Ducky" Mallard is the unit's medical examiner. The program is a spin off from *JAG*.

Cast: Mark Harmon (*Leroy Jethro Gibbs*); Sasha Alexander (*Caitlin Todd*); Michael Weatherly (*Tony DiNozzo*); Pauley Perrette (*Abby Sciuto*); David McCallum (*Dr. Donald Mallard*); Lauren Holly (*NCIS Director Jenny Shepard*); Joe Spano (*FBI Agent T.C. Fornell*); Brian Dietzen (*Jimmy Palmer*); Sean Murray (*Timothy McGee*); Cote de Pablo (*Ziva David*); Rocky Carroll (*Leon Vance, NCIS Director, 2008*).

6530 N.C.I.S.: Los Angeles. (Series; Crime Drama; CBS; 2009–). A spin off from *N.C.I.S.* that focuses on the Los Angeles–based Naval Criminal Investigative Service of Special Projects, a unit that specializes in undercover surveillance and counter surveillance (unlike its parent show, there are no dead bodies at the beginning of each episode or lab scenes scattered throughout the story).

Special Agent Lara Macy heads the unit, a former military police major. Her agents include G. Callen, Sam Hanna, Nate Getz and Kenji Blye. Callen had previously worked for the CIA, FBI and DEA. He is brilliant but a loose cannon and constantly breaks the rules. Sam is a former Navy SEAL who has "seen service in every incident, skirmish or battle the U.S. has been involved in the past 20 years." Nate is the unit's operational psychologist (profiles the target and briefs the agents before they go undercover). Kenji is an army brat (she grew up in a military family) with a background in forensics and criminology. The two-part pilot episode, titled "Legend," aired on *N.C.I.S.* on April 28 and May 5, 2009.

Cast: Louise Lombard (*Lara Macy*); Chris O'Donnell (*G. Callen*); LL Cool J (*Sam Hanna*); Daniela Ruah (*Kenji Blye*); Peter Cambor (*Nate Getz*); Eric Christian Olsen (*Det. Liaison Marty Deeks*).

6531 Nearly Departed. (Series; Comedy; NBC; 1989). While on vacation, Professor Grant Pritchard and his wife Claire perish in a rock slide. The spirits of Grant and Claire return to their earthly home and find it inhabited by the Dooley family, a prospect that annoys Grant who desperately wants his house back. Grant's continual complaints (to the audience) and attempts to live with the Dooleys (who cannot see him) are the focal point of stories. The Dooleys are Michael, the father, a plumber; Liz, his wife; Derek, their son; and Jack Garrett, Liz's father.

Cast: Eric Idle (*Grant Pritchard*); Caroline McWilliams (*Claire Pritchard*); Stuart Pankin (*Michael Dooley*); Wendy Schaal (*Liz Dooley*); Jay Lambert (*Derek Dooley*); Henderson Forsythe (*Jack Garrett*).

Theme Vocal: ("Nearly Departed") by Eric Idle.

6532 Neat and Tidy — Adventures Beyond Belief. (Pilot; Satire; Syn.; Dec. 1986). Valentena Tidelio, the daughter of a mobster, runs away from her father's jailer, music school conservatory Headmistress Bruno Van Kleef, seeking to find her mother, presumed killed in a car accident 15 years ago. Nick Pratt, a mechanic who fears he killed his partner during a heated argument, flees, thinking the police are seeking him. By chance Valentena, who pretends to be Tena Tidy, and Nick, who uses the alias Nick Neat, meet and team to help each other out. The proposed series was to relate Tena and Nick's outrageous world-wide adventures as they seek Tena's mother and attempt to escape from their relentless pursuer — Headmistress Van Kleef.

Cast: Jill Whitlow (*Tena Tidy*); Skyler Cole (*Nick Neat*); Elke Sommer (*Bruno Van Kleef*).

6533 Ned and Stacey. (Series; Comedy; Fox; 1995–1997). Ned Dorsey is an executive at the Spencer Advertising Agency on Madison Avenue. Stacey Colbert is a newspaper columnist (for *The Village Voice*) and later a freelance writer. Ned lives in a two-bedroom Manhattan apartment and has a boss who believes in married executives — no marriage, no promotion.

Stacey works in Manhattan but lives on Long Island. Ned and Stacey meet by chance at a bar and become friends although they are not fully compatible — she's politically right wing and "he's no wings at all." They find they each have something the other wants. Stacey agrees to pose as Ned's wife; Ned agrees to let Stacey live in his second bedroom apartment so she can be closer to her job.

Although Ned is "married," he hits on other women — and Stacey would like to know whom he is dating — "I'm your wife, I have the right to know." Ned, 35, is neat, loves to cook, and enjoys growing vegetables and flowers on his balcony. He maneuvers and manipulates his way through life. "I exploit people, that's what I do."

Stacey, born in Trenton, New Jersey, attended Brandice College. As a kid she was gawky, wore braces and was a head taller than other girls. For Stacey, a good day can only happen "if I have a great hair day." When Ned takes Stacey out for a meal, they dine at Dugan's Café; they each enjoy snacks at Amanda's-A-Muffins, a coffee shop owned by Stacey's sister, Amanda Moyer (she is married to Eric "Rico" Moyer).

The program is a reworking of the 1966 series *Occasional Wife* and follows Ned's efforts to get ahead in business with a pretend wife.

Cast: Thomas Hayden Church (*Ned Dorsey*); Debra Messing (*Stacey Colbert*); Nadia Dajani (*Amanda Moyer*); Greg Germann (*Eric Moyer*); Harry Goz (*Saul Colbert*).

6534 Ned Blessing: The Story of My Life and Times. (Series; Western; CBS; 1993). Ned Blessing is an Old West outlaw with many people gunning for him. After six years Ned, called "The bad boy of Texas," decides to return to his home town of Plum Creek to see his father. When Ned and his amigo, "Old" Crecencio Salos, arrive in town, they discover it is a hell-hole and filled with riff-raff (taken over by an outlaw gang. Ned's father has left to find his son). Seeing that the citizens are in need of help — and with the aid of a brave townsperson (Tim "Sticks" Packwood) Ned faces the outlaws and in the ensuing gunfight, ends their reign. Grateful for what Ned has done, Judge Longley approaches Ned and asks him to become their sheriff. Ned, however, wants to search for his father; his mind is changed when the judge tells him that before he left Ned's father said he would return. Figuring that the best way to see his father would be to wait for him, Ned accepts the job, although it means he and Old "will have to give up stealing for a while."

Ned wears a bracelet made from a girl's hair on his right wrist (it was made by Jilly Blue, a girl who lived in the town when he "was just a spud") and fears one man — General Pelo Blanco, who is after him for stealing his cattle in Mexico. Stories follow Ned as he becomes a good guy — for the time being and help rebuild the town of Plum Creek. Other regulars are Wren, the saloon girl; One Horse, the "crazy" Indian who carries a bag that he won't let anyone touch; and Big Emma, the saloon owner.

Cast: Brad Johnson (*Ned Blessing*); Luis Avalos (*Crecencio Salos*); Brenda Bakke (*Wren*); Wes Studi (*One Horse*); Tim Scott (*Tim Packwood*); Rusty Schwimmer (*Big Emma*); Tony Genaro (*General Pelo Blanco*); Richard Riehle (*Judge Longley*).

6535 Ned's Declassified School Survival Guide. (Series; Comedy; Nick; 2004–2007). How does a kid get through school? For 13-year-old Ned Bigby, a seventh grader at the James K. Polk Middle School, it is using his wits to overcome the hurdles of junior high. Ned is a witty kid who shares tips on surviving the obstacles that plague most school kids with the viewing audience. Ned is not a special kid; he is just a normal kid who has to overcome the tests, crushes, teachers and whatever else life throws at him as he struggles to achieve his education. There are mishaps and misadventures for him too, and he shares those good and bad times with his two best friends, Jennifer "Moze" Mosley and Simon "Cookie" Cook. Billy Loomer, called Bully, has a crush on Jennifer; Coconut Head is a student whose hair is oddly enough, shaped to look like half a coconut; Gordy is the school janitor; Ms. Derga is the P.E. teacher; Mr. Monroe, the science teacher; and Mr. Copsaw, the shop teacher.

Cast: Devon Werkheiser *(Ned Bigby)*; Lindsey Shaw *(Jennifer "Moze" Mosley)*; Daniel Curtis Lee *(Simon "Cookie" Cook)*; Rob Pinkston *(Coconut Head)*; Kyle Swann *(Billy "Bully" Loomer)*; Dave Florek *(Mr. Copsaw)*; Kim Sava *(Ms. Derga)*; Jim J. Bullock *(Mr. Munroe)*; Teo Olivares *(Crony)*; Don Creech *(Mr. Sweeney)*; Christian Serratos *(Susie Crabgrass)*; Steve Bannos *(Mr. Cambover)*; Carlie Casey *(Missy Meany)*; Rachel Sibner *(Lisa Zemo)*; Cathy Immordino *(Sandy Crew)*.

6536   Ned's Newt. (Series; Cartoon; Fox; 1997–1999). Ned Flemkin is a hyperactive boy with a normal pet, a salamander (a newt) until he feeds it Zippo Newt Food. The food transforms the four-inch creature into a mischievous, fun-loving (but gluttonous) 500-pound monster called Newton. Newton is also very curious and lives to cause trouble for Ned; however, when the trouble becomes too much for Newton to handle, he shrinks down to four inches and leaves it to Ned to deal with the situation. Eric and Sharon are Ned's parents (who are unaware of Newton's actual size); Linda, Renfrew and Doggle are Ned's friends.

Voice Cast: Tracey Moore *(Ned Flemkin)*; Harland Williams, Ron Pardo *(Newton)*; Carolyn Scott *(Sharon Flemkin)*; Peter Keleghan *(Eric Flemkin)*; Tracy Ryan *(Linda Bliss)*; Colin O'Meara *(Renfrew)*; Colin O'Meara *(Doogle)*.

6537   Needles and Pins. (Series; Comedy; NBC; 1973). Life in the aggravating world of the garment industry as seen through the experiences of Wendy Nelson, a struggling young fashion designer with Lorelei Fashions in New York City (located at 463 7th Avenue). Nathan Davidson is in charge of manufacturing; Harry Karp is Nathan's partner; Charlie Miller is the salesman; Sonia Baker is the bookkeeper; Max is the material cutter; Myron Russo is the pattern maker; Julius Singer is the owner of the competing Singer Sophisticates; Elliott is the restaurant waiter.

Cast: Deirdre Lenihan *(Wendy Nelson)*; Norman Fell *(Nathan Davidson)*; Louis Nye *(Harry Karp)*; Bernie Kopell *(Charlie Miller)*; Sandra Dee *(Sonia Baker)*; Larry Gelman *(Max)*; Alex Henteloff *(Myron Russo)*; Milton Selzer *(Julius Singer)*; Joshua Shelley *(Elliott)*.

6538   The Neighbors. (Series; Game; ABC; 1975-1976). Of the five actual female neighbors who appear on each program, two are selected as the players; the remaining three become the panel. The object calls for a player to determine if a statement made by the panel refers to her or her neighbor. Each correct guess scores the player money and the highest scoring player is the winner.

Program Open: "It's time for *The Neighbors* and here's the neighbors' best friend and your host, Regis Philbin."

Host: Regis Philbin. **Models:** Jane Nelson, Sylvia Neils. **Announcer:** Joe Sinan.

6539   Neighbors. (Pilot; Comedy; Unaired; Produced for ABC in 2005). Clem and his wife, Judy, and Hal and his wife Leslie are suburban neighbors. Clem is the epitome of the elite, suburban neighbor — quite and refined; Hal is the city bred–like neighbor, careless and loud. Clem and Hal simply do not get along, but Judy and Leslie have become friends and the proposal was to follow the mishaps that occur as Clem and Hal attempt to adjust to each other and eventually become friends.

Cast: Brian Benben *(Clem)*; Lenny Clarke *(Hal)*; Ann Cusack *(Judy)*; Melinda McGraw *(Leslie)*.

6540   Neighbors from Hell. (Series; Cartoon; TBS; 2010). Balthazor Hellman, a demon from the netherworld, has been caught watching television. In Hell, television is outlawed because "it rots the mind." Balthazor was an avid TV viewer and through sitcoms, he has acquired an amazing knowledge about humans. In recent days, the Devil has become worried as an earth company, Petromundo, has developed a super drill that is capable of reaching the center of the earth and exposing Hell. Balthazor's wrong doing has put him at the bottom of the Devil's list and, in punishment, he and his family have been banished to earth to blend in with humans and figure a way to destroy the super drill and protect Hell. The first original animated series for TBS follows Balthazor as he begins his quest (by acquiring a job at Petromundo) and how he and his family attempt to adjust to life as humans.

Balthazor is a low level Hell torturer who, in addition to his TV addiction, loves cars and seeing the good in people. Tina Hellman is Balthazor's no nonsense wife. She detests being on earth and can't wait to get back to her old life. She spends her days surfing the Internet for celebrity gossip. Mandy and Josh are their children. Mandy is a teenage girl who uses her devilish feminine wiles to get what she wants from the humans she must associate with. Josh is a mischief maker who loves video games, setting fires and conversing with animals. Don Killbride is Balthazor's boss, the CEO of "the most evil corporation on earth, Petromundo." Don, a ruthless billionaire, has no respect for the environment and will destroy what he has to find oil and make money. Chevdet is a Turkish immigrant who becomes Balthazor's best friend. He is the chief engineer behind the super drill and Balthazor's best chance of achieving his goal. Marjoe is the Hellman's annoying neighbor. She enjoys racial profiling and inappropriate relations with her suicidal French poodle Champers. Puzuzu is a goblin who was forced by the Devil to pose as the Hellman's dog. In addition to his enjoyment of spinning in the microwave oven, he likes Lady Gaga and French salad dressing. Uncle Vlaartark is Balthazor's somewhat senile uncle.

Voice Cast: Will Sasso *(Balthazor Hellman)*; Molly Shannon *(Tina Hellman)*; Tracey Fairway *(Mandy Hellman)*; David Soren *(Josh Hellman)*; Kurtwood Smith *(Don Killbride)*; Dina Waters *(Marjoe Saint Sparks)*; Patton Oswalt *(Pazuzu)*; Kyle McCulloch *(Chevdet Tevetog/Uncle Vlaartark)*.

6541   The Neistat Brothers. (Series; Comedy; HBO; 2010). Casey and Van Neistat are brothers who, in 1999, purchased an iMac computer that made video editing possible for amateurs. Over time the brothers produced over 200 short films. Now, considered professionals (but still working on a shoestring budget), the brothers have come to cable TV to present a behind-the-scenes look at how they shoot their reality-based films (which are also seen as completed projects with the brothers narrating).

Stars: Casey Neistat, Van Neistat.

6542   Neon Rider. (Series; Drama; Syn.; 1990-1991). Michael Terry has a Ph.D. in child psychology and taught science and human behavior at the university level for five years. He had an article published in the most highly regarded sociology magazine in the world and is the author of a book called *The Development of Teenage Behavior*. Despite his achievements, Michael feels it's all talk and no action. He decides to put his schooling to work and get firsthand experience working with troubled teens and developing their character.

Michael quits his job and purchases a ranch in Canada's Fraser Valley. There, with the cooperation of the juvenile court, he begins his program of helping troubled teens deal with poverty, parental neglect, gang wars and drug abuse. The court considers the juveniles on the Ranch (as it is called) to be in confinement; if they attempt to leave, it will be considered an escape; if they are caught it means being tried as adults and prison. Michael's former colleagues call the Ranch "Michael's Folly."

Fox Devlin, who has a white horse named Saddles, is the Ranch foreman. Vic is a Native American who works as a ranch hand; he has a horse named Dundee. C.C. Dechardon is the cook; Rachel Woods is the social worker assigned to assist Michael. Bill Henderson sings the theme, "Neon Rider."

Cast: Winston Rekert (*Michael Terry*); Antoinette Bower (*Fox Devlin*); Samuel Sarker (*Vic*); Alex Bruhanski (*C.C. Dechardon*); Suzanne Errett-Balcom (*Rachel Woods*).

6543   *The Nerd.* (Pilot; Comedy; NBC; Mar. 2, 1996). Rick Steadman is the kind of guy who gets under your skin. He is annoying and considered a nerd. Although awkward he is also a hero. He risked his life to save an unconscious man (William Boyd) from a burning building. Years later, when William learns that his rescuer has fallen on hard times and has no place to live, he repays the kindness by letting Rick move in with him and his wife, Tanzy. The proposal relates William and Tanzy's efforts to cope with the unwanted help they receive from Rick.

Cast: John Dye (*Rick Steadman*); Robert Joy (*William Boyd*); Harley Jane Kozak (*Tanzy Boyd*).

6544   *Nero Wolfe.* (Pilot; Crime Drama; ABC; Dec. 18, 1979). Nero Wolfe, the fictional character created by Rex Stout, is a gourmet, horticulturist and master criminologist who helps the police and FBI solve baffling crimes. Nero rarely leaves his home; Archie Goodwin, his legman, does the actual detective work, which he brings to Nero for his final analysis. Nero then gathers all the suspects at his home and reveals the culprit. Other regulars are Inspector Cramer of the N.Y.P.D.; and Fritz Brenner, Nero's butler.

Cast: Thayer David (*Nero Wolfe*); Tom Mason (*Archie Goodwin*); Biff McGuire (*Inspector Cramer*); David Hurst (*Fritz Brenner*).

6545   *Nero Wolfe.* (Series; Crime Drama; NBC; 1981; A&E, 2001-2002). Nero Wolfe is an overweight master criminologist, gourmet cook, horticulturist and connoisseur of fine wine. He is also wealthy, reclusive, abrupt, insulting and arrogant. He lives in a New York brownstone but seldom leaves the house to solve crimes. His legman, private detective Archie Goodwin, collects the evidence for him. Nero considers the evidence Archie gathers to be pieces of a puzzle. When a case is solved in Nero's mind, he gathers all the suspects at his home. He recaps the crime, questions the suspects and reveals the culprit. While operating as a private investigative agency, Nero also helps the police, namely Inspector Cramer, solve crimes. On NBC, Nero's address was given as 918 West 35th Street; on A&E, he resides at 454 West 35th Street in Manhattan.

Nero raises orchids and enjoys sitting "in my nice big easy chair and enjoying a delectable glass of beer." Nero claims he doesn't leave the house "because I hate traffic." When a circumstance forces Nero to leave his home, he immediately misses the comforts of his home and avails himself to the comforts of other people's homes. It is at these times that Nero hopes for one thing — a meal prepared by a gourmet cook. These occasions also give Nero the opportunity to pick up minute details the police often overlook.

Nero solves cases by hard facts not by imagining who did it. Nero usually sets a trap to catch a killer — "We can't go to him, so we have to make him come to us." Nero depends on Archie and Archie depends on Nero. "I do nothing without Archie," says Nero. "He's inquisitive, charming, impetuous, alert and forceful. He gets me what

I need to solve crimes." Archie lives at 237 East 46th Street and doesn't take notes when he questions a suspect — "I have a photographic memory." Nero sometimes believes Archie's last name should be Wolf because he has an eye for the ladies. Deep down Nero fears that Archie is going to leave him when he meets the right girl and marries. Archie believes Nero has only two passions — orchids and beer. Both versions are based on the character created by Rex Stout.

NBC Cast: William Conrad (*Nero Wolfe*); Lee Horsley (*Archie Goodwin*); Allan Miller (*Inspector Cramer*); George Voskovec (*Fritz Brenner*); Robert Coote (*Theodore Hortsman*). **A&E Cast:** Maury Chaykin (*Nero Wolfe*); Timothy Hutton (*Archie Goodwin*); Colin Fox (*Fritz Brenner*); Bill Smitrovich (*Inspector Cramer*).

6546   *The Net.* (Series; Drama; USA; 1998-1999). Angela Bennett is a computer expert who accidentally receives a top secret e-mail meant for members of an evil organization called Praetorians, who are planning to control people through computers. When the organization learns that Angela has received their message, they erase her identity and rework it to make her a criminal, one of the FBI's ten most wanted. Angela, unable to reverse what has been done to her sets her goal to bring down the Praetorians and clear her name. She is assisted by a mysterious voice called The Sorcerer, whom she hears over her laptop and guides her, and her friend, Jacob Resh as they set out on dangerous quest: bring down the Praetorians while at the same time staying one step ahead of the FBI and the Praetorians hit men, Sean Trelawney and Greg Hearney. Based on the Sandra Bullock motion picture of the same title.

Cast: Brooke Langton (*Angela Bennett*); Tim Curry (*Sorcerer's voice*); Eric Szmanda (*Jacob Resh*); Joseph Bottoms (*Sean Trelawney*); Mackenzie Gray (*Greg Hearney*); Kelli Taylor (*Anna Kelly*).

6547   *Nettie.* (Experimental; Stage Play; NBC; April 22, 1945). A television adaptation of the play by George Ade. The story is set in a swanky night club called the Palm Room (where a beautiful girl named Nettie entertains). Here, three men-about-town (played by Steve Chase, Richard Maloy and Mort L. Stevens) have an appointment to meet with Nettie (Leila Ernst) at her favorite corner table. Each is unaware that the other knows Nettie (each met her on Fifth Avenue; and each has given her a piano to help her fledgling music career) and their reactions to this discovery is the focal point of the play.

Cast: Steven Chase, Gilbert Douglas, Leila Ernst, Richard Maloy, Mort L. Stevens, Ann Travers. **Floor Show Performers:** Shirley Conklin (*singer*); Richard Gibson (*tap dancer*); Janice Thompson (*dancer*).

6548   *Nevada Smith.* (Pilot; Western; NBC; May 3, 1975). Nevada Smith, a half-breed gunslinger, and Jonas Cord, a famous exgunfighter and Nevada's mentor, team to enforce justice on the ruthless frontier. The proposal, based on the 1966 feature film of the same name was to relate their adventures as they dispense justice.

Cast: Cliff Potts (*Nevada Smith*); Lorne Greene (*Jonas Cord*).

6549   *Never Again.* (Pilot; Comedy; ABC; Nov. 30, 1984). Abigail "Abby" Cartwright is a lawyer; Lawrence "Larry" Newman is a radio sportscaster; and Mitchell "Mitch" Franklin is a bookkeeper. The three are friends, single and share adjoining apartments; the proposal was to relate incidents in their lives as they help each other out. Denise is their friend, a waitress.

Cast: Jamie Rose (*Abby Cartwright*); Judge Reinhold (*Larry Newman*); Allen Garfield (*Mitch Franklin*); Margot Rose (*Denise*).

6550   *Never Better.* (Pilot; Comedy; Unaired; Produced for ABC in 2008). Keith, a recovering alcoholic, is trying to be the family man he once was. He is married to his college sweetheart (Allison)

and they are the parents of Claire and Doug. Keith attends AA meetings; Linda is his no-nonsense sponsor and the proposal was to follow Keith as he tries to reform.

Cast: Damon Wayans *(Keith)*; Nicole Ari Parker *(Allison)*; Jane Lynch *(Linda)*; Kathleen Rose Perkins *(Claire)*; Matt Winston *(Doug)*.

6551   *Never Say Never.* (Pilot; Comedy; CBS; July 11, 1979). Harry Walter is a hard-working 54-year-old plumbing supply company businessman; Sarah Keaton is a poised and beautiful pediatrician. They meet, fall in love and plan to marry — and the proposal was to relate their courtship, eventual marriage and efforts to make their marriage work. Other regulars are Florence, Harry's mother-in-law; Paul, Harry's son; and Ronnie, Sarah's friend.

Cast: George Kennedy *(Harry Walter)*; Anne Schedeen *(Dr. Sarah Keaton)*; Irene Tedrow *(Florence)*; Bruce Kimmel *(Paul Walter)*; Rick Podell *(Ronnie)*.

6552   *Never Too Young.* (Series; Serial; ABC; 1965-1966). "... We're young but never too young to set this whole world spinning, say you'll be my girl and we'll show the world we're never too young...." Malibu Beach, California, provides the backdrop for a look at the lives of a group of young people as seen through the eyes of Alfie, the owner of the local beach hangout (Alfie's Café).

Cast: David Watson *(Alfie)*; Michael Blodgett *(Tad)*; Robyn Grace *(Joy)*; Tommy Rettig *(Jo Jo)*; Tony Dow *(Chet)*; Cindy Carol *(Susan)*; Pat Connolly *(Barbara)*; Dack Rambo *(Tim)*; Patrice Wymore *(Rhoda)*; Merry Anders *(Joyce)*; John Lupton *(Frank)*. **Announcer:** Roger Christian. **Music:** Ray Martin.

6553   *The New Adam-12.* (Series; Crime Drama; Syn.; 1989-1990). An updated version of the NBC series *Adam-12* (1968–1974) that follows the daily assignments of Matt Doyle and Gus Grant, Los Angeles police officers who are assigned patrol duty in a car whose code is Adam-12. Matt and Gus hangout in a bar-café called Scruffy's and the number 012 can be seen as the identification number on the car's roof.

Cast: Ethan Wayne *(Off. Matt Doyle)*; Peter Parros *(Off. Gus Grant)*; Miguel Fernandez *(Sgt. Harry Santos)*.

6554   *The New Addams Family.* (Series; Comedy; Fox Family; 1998–2002). A revised version of the 1964–66 ABC series *The Addams Family*. The Addams are an eccentric family who live in a spooky mansion on Cemetery Ridge. Gomez, a wealthy eccentric, is married to the beautiful, always dressed in black, Morticia. They are the parents of Wednesday and Pugsley. Also living with them is Gomez's brother, Fester (called Uncle Fester), Gomez's Grandmama, Eudora; Lurch, the zombie-like butler; and Thing, a human right hand, the family servant.

Gomez dabbles in the stock market (apparently how he made his money). He is of Spanish ancestry and an excellent swordsman. He and Morticia celebrate Halloween and Bastille Day as major holidays. Morticia makes curses on shooting stars, carves statues out of stone and uses swamp water for cooking.

Eleven-year-old Wednesday and eight-year-old Pugsley attend the Sherman School. Wednesday dresses in black like her mother and appears to have one primary goal in life: kill Pugsley. She considers Pugsley to be "an expendable guinea pig." Pugsley enjoys playing with dynamite caps. Fester is an explosives expert (or so he thinks) and generates his own electricity. He sleeps on a bed of nails and is a member of the Global Mercenaries. Lurch loves to play the piano and responds with "You Rang" when he is summoned.

Stories follow the family as they go about their "normal" daily lives, always trying to figure out why the outside world is so strange and won't accept them as members of society. Based on characters created by Charles Addams.

Cast: Glenn Taranto *(Gomez Addams)*; Ellie Harvie *(Morticia Addams)*; Nicole Fugere *(Wednesday Addams)*; Brody Smith *(Pugsley Addams)*; Michael Roberds *(Fester Addams)*; Betty Phillips *(Eudora Addams)*; John DeSantis *(Lurch)*; Steven Fox *(Thing)*.

6555   *The New Adventures of Batman.* (Series; Cartoon; CBS; 1977-1978). A continuation of the live action 1966 series *Batman* with Bruce Wayne, Dick Grayson and Barbara Gordon (alias Batman, Robin the Boy Wonder and Batgirl) upholding the law in Gotham City. Batmite, the mouse, assists them.

Voice Cast: Adam West *(Batman)*; Burt Ward *(Robin)*; Melendy Britt *(Batgirl)*; Lennie Weinrib *(Batmite)*.

6556   *The New Adventures of Beans Baxter.* (Series; Comedy; Fox; 1987-1988). Benjamin ("Beans") Baxter is a typically normal 17-year-old boy. He lives in the small town of Witches Creek, Kansas, with his mother, Susan, father, Benjamin Sr., and younger brother, Scooter. Unknown to the family, Ben Sr. is a courier for the Network, a postal service for the secret agencies of the U.S. government, which is headed by Number One. When the series begins, Ben Sr. is transferred to Washington, D.C. He and his family take up residence at 1341 Maple Street, and Beans enrolls in Georgetown High School. Shortly after, Beans stumbles into his father's secret life (he believes he is a mailman) when he sees him being kidnapped by U.G.L.I. (Underground Government Liberation Intergroup), an evil organization headed by Mr. Sue. In an attempt to rescue his father, Beans comes in contact with Number One and is recruited by the Network as a spy-courier to help him in his quest to find his missing father (his "new adventures").

Darla (Kristin Cumming) was Beans' original girlfriend (in Witches Creek); in Washington, he is pursued by Cake Lase, "the most gorgeous girl on his high school campus." Beans, however, sees no other girl but Svetlana, a beautiful Soviet defector, when he learns he is going to be working with her. Scooter, "a pint-sized Albert Einstein," has a pet guinea pig named Alvin.

Cupcake Lase is Cake's sister; Mrs. Number One is Number One's wife; Little One is their son.

Theme: "The New Adventures of Beans Baxter," by Joseph Birtelli.

Cast: Jonathan Ward *(Beans Baxter)*; Elinor Donahue *(Susan Baxter)*; Scott Bremner *(Scooter Baxter)*; Karen Mistal *(Cake Lase)*; John Vernon *(Number One)*; Kurtwood Smith *(Mr. Sue)*; Shawn Weatherly *(Svetlana)*; Rick Lenz *(Ben Baxter, Sr.)*; Sarah Sawatsky *(Cupcake Lase)*; Lorraine Foreman *(Mrs. Number One)*; Shawn Clements *(Little One)*.

6557   *The New Adventures of Charlie Chan.* (Series; Crime Drama; Syn.; 1957-1958). Charlie Chan, a courteous, shrewd and philosophical Chinese detective created by Earl Derr Biggers, is taken from his traditional American setting and placed in Europe. His number One Son, Barry assists him and stories relate their efforts to solve baffling crimes. Inspector Duff and Inspector Carl Marlowe of New Scotland Yard are the featured police official Charlie assists.

Cast: J. Carrol Naish *(Charlie Chan)*; James Hong *(Barry Chan)*; Rupert Davies *(Inspector Duff)*; Hugh Williams *(Inspector Carl Marlowe)*.

6558   *The New Adventures of Gilligan.* (Series; Cartoon; ABC; 1974–1977). A spin off from *Gilligan's Island* that continues to relate the misadventures that befall the shipwrecked survivors of the sightseeing ship *S.S. Minnow* as they struggle for survival and seek a way off the island. Jonas Grumby is the skipper; Gilligan is his first mate; Ginger Grant is the actress; Mary Ann Summers is the clerk from Kansas; Thurston and Lovey Howell are the millionaires; Roy Hinkley is the Professor.

Voice Cast: Alan Hale, Jr. *(The Skipper)*; Bob Denver *(Gilligan)*; Jane Webb *(Ginger Grant)*; Jim Backus *(Thurston Howell)*; Natalie Schafer *(Lovey Howell)*; Russell Johnson *(The Professor)*; Jane Edwards *(Mary Ann Summers)*.

6559　The New Adventures of He-Man. (Series; Cartoon; Syn.; 1990). An updated version of *He-Man and the Masters of the Universe* (see entry) that takes the super warrior away from his home planet of Eternia to battle the evil Skeletor on the planet Primus (where Skeletor has waged a war using the mutants of the planet Denebria, as his army). Skeletor plans to conquer the universe but he faces the opposition of He-Man who, with the Galactic Guardians, attempt to stop him and his mutant army. The Galactic Guardians are Captain Hydron, Lieutenant Flipshot, Drissi (a teenage girl), her brother Caz and Darius, the head of the Galactic Council.

Voice Cast: Gary Chalk *(He-Man)*; Tracy Eisner *(Drissi)*; Mark Hildreth *(Caz)*; Campbell Lane *(Skeletor)*; Scott McNeil *(Lt. Flipshot)*; Don Brown *(Capt. Hydron)*.

6560　The New Adventures of Huckleberry Finn. (Series; Adventure; NBC; 1968–1969). A live action-animated series adapted from the novel *The Adventures of Huckleberry Finn* by Mark Twain. Pursued by the vengeful Injun Joe, Huckleberry Finn, Becky Thatcher and Tom Sawyer run into a cave where they are engulfed by a raging river and transported to a strange fantasyland that is inhabited by cartoon characters. Stories relate their adventures as they, pursued by Joe, wander through various lands, help people in need, and try to find the way home to 1845 Hannibal, Missouri. Live action is played against superimposed animated backgrounds.

Cast: Michael Shea *(Huckleberry Finn)*; Lu Ann Haslam *(Becky Thatcher)*; Kevin Schultz *(Tom Sawyer)*; Ted Cassidy *(Injun Joe)*; Anne Bellamy *(Tom's Aunt Polly)*; Dorothy Tennant *(Becky's mother)*.

6561　The New Adventures of Madeline. (Series; Cartoon; ABC; 1995). An updated version of *Madeline* (see entry) that is set in France (where Madeline is a student at a school run by Miss Clavel). Here Madeline has befriended Pepito, a boy from a nearby school, and stories relate the misadventures they encounter together.

Voice Cast: Andrea Libman *(Madeline)*; Louise Vallance *(Miss Clavel)*; Louise Vallance *(Genevieve)*; David Morse *(Pepito)*.

6562　The New Adventures of Martin Kane. (Series; Crime Drama; NBC; 1953-1954). A revised version of *Martin Kane, Private Eye* that transplants private detective Martin Kane from America to Europe. Kane is still as tough as he was in the prior version and, although he prefers to work alone, he now finds business booming as a consultant (who actively investigates crimes) to various international police departments. Also known as *Assignment Danger* (its title when first syndicated).

Cast: Mark Stevens *(Martin Kane)*; William Gargan *(Martin Kane; later)*; Brian Reece *(Scotland Yard Inspector)*.

6563　The New Adventures of Mighty Mouse and Heckle and Jeckle. (Series; Cartoon; CBS; 1979–1982). The overall title for two series. The first, *Mighty Mouse*, updates the 1940s theatrical cartoon with newly animated segments about Mighty Mouse as he battles the forces of evil. Pearl Pureheart is his girlfriend; Oilcan Harry is the villain. *Heckle and Jeckle*, the second segment, features newly animated sequences that relate the adventures of the mischievous talking magpies. Mighty Mouse first appeared on TV (CBS,

1955–1967) via *The Mighty Mouse Playhouse* with Tom Morrison as the voice of Mighty Mouse. The *Heckle and Jeckle* theatrical cartoons, featuring the voice of Paul Frees, were first syndicated in 1955.

Voice Cast: Alan Oppenheimer *(Mighty Mouse)*; Diane Pershing *(Pearl Pureheart)*; Alan Oppenheimer *(Oilcan Harry)*; Frank Welker *(Heckle/Jeckle)*.

6564　The New Adventures of Ocean Girl. (Series; Cartoon; Syn.; 2000). An animated version of the live action series *Ocean Girl* (see entry) that changes the original concept. Here Neri is a princess (daughter of King Nemon) and lives on a planet of water called Oceana. A series of crystal keys is the planet's balance and they are guarded by the sacred whales. Galiel, an evil space wizard, is seeking the crystals to gain absolute power. When Galiel tricks the whales and manages to steal one of the crystals, it upsets the planet's balance and causes it to become totally immersed in water. Stories follow Neri as she embarks on a mission to stop Galiel from acquiring the other crystals and return the crystal he has stolen to save her planet.

Voice Cast: Marnie Reece-Wilmore *(Princess Neri)*; Michael Carman *(Galiel)*; Dennis Pryor *(King Nemon)*; Stephen Whittaker *(Moza)*; Samuel L. Jackson *(Prince Jobah)*; Gary Files *(Zardor)*; Marg Downey *(Elgar)*; Doug Trimlett *(Neanda)*; Sigrid Thornton *(Narrator)*.

6565　The New Adventures of Old Christine. (Series; Comedy; CBS; 2006–2010). Christine Campbell is the owner (with friend Barb) of 30 Minutes to Bloom, a female only health spa in Los Angeles. She is divorced from Richard (a contractor) and the mother of Richie Jr. Christine has not dated since her divorce and becomes the "old Christine" when Richard begins a relationship with a younger woman named Christine Hunter (who becomes "the new Christine"). The situation angers "old" Christine (who still has feelings for Richard) and her adventures as she goes about seeking love are the program's focal point. Lindsay and Marly are the snooty mothers Christine befriends at Richie's school (Westbridge Elementary); Matthew is "Old" Christine's brother; Lucy is Matthew's girlfriend; Allie is the spa receptionist. "New" Christine works as a receptionist at a law firm called Schwartz, Chervin, Jacobs, Young, Loder and White; Matthew is later a therapist.

Cast: Julia Louis-Dreyfus *(Christine Campbell)*; Clark Gregg *(Richard Campbell)*; Trevor Gagnon *(Richard Campbell, Jr.)*; Emily Rutherfurd *(Christine Hunter)*; Tricia O'Kelley *(Marly)*; Alex Kapp Horner *(Lindsay)*; Hamish Linklater *(Matthew Kimball)*; Wanda Lewis *(Barb)*; Michaela Watkins *(Lucy)*; Amy Farrington *(Allie)*; Scott Bakula *(Jeff, New Christine's father)*.

6566　The New Adventures of Pinocchio. (Series; Children; Syn.; 1961). Pinocchio is the wooden boy who was brought to life to please Gepetto, the lonely old man who created him. Stories, based on the Italian fairy tale (not so much the Disney movie) follows Pinocchio as he and his friend, Jiminy Crickett seek adventure. Other friends are Pedro Pistol, the private detective; Simoro, Pedro's dog; Cool S. Cat, a female beatnik; and the con artist Foxy Q. Fibble. Characters are puppets brought to life by a process called Animagic. Arthur Rankin and Jules Bass are the producers.

Voice Cast: Joan Fowler *(Pinocchio)*; Stan Francis *(Gepetto)*; Larry D. Mann *(Foxy)*.

6567　The New Adventures of Robin Hood. (Series; Adventure; TNT; 1997-1998). An update of the Robin Hood legend that finds the English outlaw hero of Sherwood Forest a bit more daring and a master swordsman (forsaking the customary bow and arrow) to battle for the rights of the common man. His band of outlaws include Little John, Friar Tuck, his mentor Olwyn and his love interest,

Lady Marian Fitzwalter; his enemies are Prince John and the Sheriff of Nottingham.

Cast: Matthew Poretta, John Bradley (*Robin Hood*); Anna Galvin, Barbara Griffin (*Marian Fitzwalter*); Richard Ashton (*Little John*); Martyn Ellis (*Friar Tuck*); Christopher Lee (*Olwyn*); Andrew Bicknell (*Prince John*); Christine Woods (*Rowena*).

6568   *The New Adventures of Spin and Marty.* (Series; Comedy; ABC; 1958). A second spin off from *Spin and Marty* (which see, along with *The Further Adventures of Spin and Marty*). Further events in the lives of Triple R Ranch campers Spin Evans and Marty Markham. The story concerns the efforts of Spin and Marty to stage a variety show to pay for the damages caused by Marty's Jalopy when it ran into the ranch house. Broadcast as 12 segments of *The Mickey Mouse Club.* Jim Logan is the ranch owner; Bill Burnett is the counselor; Ollie is the wrangler; Speckle, Ambitious, Joe, Moochie and George are campers; Annette and Darlene are campers at the all-girl Circle H Ranch.

Cast: Tim Considine (*Spin Evans*); David Stollery (*Marty Markham*); Roy Barcroft (*Jim Logan*); Harry Carey, Jr. (*Bill Burnett*); Dennis Moore (*Ollie*); Annette Funicello (*Annette*); Darlene Gillespie (*Darlene*); Kevin Corcoran (*Moochie O'Hara*); Tim Hartnagel (*Speckle*); Joe Wong (*George*); Sammy Ogg (*Joe*); B.G. Norman (*Ambitious*).

6569   *The New Adventures of Superman.* (Series; Cartoon; CBS; 1966-1967). An animated series that is composed of two segments. The first deals with the crime-fighting adventures of Clark Kent, alias Superman, and reporter Lois Lane (see *The Adventures of Superman* for background information). The second depicts the adventures of Clark Kent as Superboy (see *The Adventures of Superboy* for background information).

Voice Cast: Clayton "Bud" Collyer (*Superman/Clark Kent*); Joan Alexander (*Lois Lane*); Ted Knight (*Editor Perry White*); Bob Hastings (*Superboy/Clark Kent*).

6570   *The New Adventures of Winnie the Pooh.* (Series; Cartoon; ABC; 1988–1991). The Hundred Acre Woods is the setting for the adventures of a group of close animal friends. Winnie the Pooh is a fun-loving, caring, honey-seeking bear that is always helping others; Tigger is a dim-witted but energetic tiger that loves to bounce on his tail; Piglet is a small pig with big dreams and, despite his small size, hopes to achieve those dreams. Rabbit is the eldest of the animals and also the wisest. His passion is planting vegetable gardens. Eeyore is the slow-talking and slow walking donkey that puts up with his friends antics but would like to find some peace and quiet away from them. Kanga and Roo are mother and son kangaroos; Christopher Robin is the only human character that is fully seen (his mother is seen but not in full figure). Christopher often shares adventures with Pooh and is the only one who knows his animal friends can talk. Based on the characters created by A.A. Milne.

Voice Cast: Jim Cummings (*Winnie the Pooh*); Paul Winchell (*Tigger*); John Fiedler (*Piglet*); Ken Sansom (*Rabbit*); Peter Cullen (*Eeyore*); Michael Gough (*Gopher*); Hal Smith (*Owl*); Tim Hoskins (*Christopher Robin*); Patricia Parris (*Christopher's mother*).

6571   *The New Adventures of Wonder Woman.* (Series; Adventure; CBS; 1977). A revised, modern-day version of the ABC series *Wonder Woman.* See the 1977 version of *Wonder Woman* for information.

6572   *The New American Bandstand.* (Series; Variety; Syn.; 1987–1989). A revised version of ABC's Saturday Afternoon 1950s hit *American Bandstand* that features performances by popular music artists as well as a new segment that spotlights promising comedians.

Host: David Hirsch. **The New American Bandstand Theme:** David Russo.

6573   *New Amsterdam.* (Series; Crime Drama; Fox; 2008). In the 1640s when New York was known as New Amsterdam, John Amsterdam was a soldier in the Dutch army. During a battle with a Native American tribe, John stepped in front of a sword to save the life of a young Indian girl. The girl brought Jack to a place of refuge and saved his life by casting an ancient spell that made him immortal. John will never age and the spell can only be broken (to make him mortal again) when he finds his one true love. The centuries pass and John has devoted his life to upholding the law. It is 2008 when viewers are introduced to John Amsterdam. He lives in Manhattan and is a detective with the N.Y.P.D. John has seen New York grow from its colonial beginnings to its present day metropolis. He and Manhattan are a part of each other and his 400 years of experiences have made him an invaluable addition to the police department. Only one man, Omar, the owner of a jazz club and his life-long friend, knows John's secret. Over the course of time, John has met and known and lost many women — but none have been the one that can change his life.

One day while chasing a suspect, John suffers a heart attack and nearly dies. He realizes that during that pursuit he must have crossed paths with his one true love. He now realizes that his life has changed forever. Stories follow John as he not only upholds the law, but seeks the mysterious woman the Indian girl spoke of in her prophecy. Eva Marquez is John's partner; Sarah is a doctor at St. Francis Hospital.

Cast: Nikolaj Coster Waldau (*John Amsterdam*); Zuleikhla Robinson (*Eva Marquez*); Stephen Henderson (*Omar*); Alexie Gilmore (*Dr. Sarah Dillane*).

6574   *The New Andy Griffith Show.* (Series; Comedy; CBS; 1972). Andy Sawyer is a former sheriff and justice of the peace turned the mayor of Greenwood, North Carolina. Andy is married to Lee and they are the parents of Lori and T.J. Andy is a peace-loving, easygoing politician who wants only the best for his town. He listens to the people's wants and tries to fulfill their requests. Stories relate his simple pleasures and trying times as he deals with problems at work and at home. Nora is Lee's sister; Buff MacKnight is the senior town councilman.

Cast: Andy Griffith (*Andy Sawyer*); Lee Meriwether (*Lee Sawyer*); Lori Ann Rutherford (*Lori Sawyer*); Marty McCall (*T.J. Sawyer*); Ann Morgan Guilbert (*Nora*); Glen Ash (*Buff MacKnight*); Ruth McDevitt (*Mrs. Gossage*).

6575   *The New Archies.* (Series; Cartoon; NBC; 1987). An updated version of *The Archie Show* (see entry) that presents junior high school versions of Archie Andrews and his friends Veronica Lodge, Betty Cooper, Jughead Jones, Big Ethel and Big Moose, all of whom live in the town of Riverdale. Miss Grundy is still the teacher (only a bit younger from when she would later be teaching them in Riverdale High School) and sight gags are still used to complicate their lives as adolescents.

Voice Cast: J. Michael Roncetti (*Archie Andrews*); Alyson Court, Sunny Besen Thrasher (*Veronica Lodge*); Lisa Coristine (*Betty Cooper*); Michael Fantini (*Jughead Jones*); Victor Erdos (*Big Moose*); Jazzmin Lausanne (*Big Ethel*); Linda Sorenson (*Miss Grundy*).

6576   *New Attitude.* (Series; Comedy; ABC; 1990). Beauticians Vicki St. James and her younger sister, Yvonne St. James, own New Attitude, a beauty salon located at 41 South La Brea in Los Angeles.

Vicki, the prettier sister, is also the smarter one; she is seeking Mr. Right and wants to settle down. Yvonne, who attended Carver High School (as did Vicki), looks to Vicki for guidance. While not exactly a flake, she seems to have a knack for complicating everything she does.

Selena's Hair Affair, located at 44 South La Brea (and run by Jedda Jones as Selena) is New Attitude's main competition. The store located directly across the street from New Attitude is Checks Bakery.

Lamaar is Vicki's hairstylist and runs the "Hair by Lamaar" corner of New Attitude. Audrey Laker is the manicurist; Taylor is the assistant who is hoping to pass her beautician's test (which she had failed 12 times); Leon is Vicki's landlord. Sheryl Lee Ralph sings the theme, "New Attitude."

Cast: Sheryl Lee Ralph (*Vicki St. James*); Phyllis Yvonne Stickney (*Yvonne St. James*); Jedda Jones (*Selma*); Morris Day (*Lamaar*); Karen Bankhead (*Audrey Laker*); Larenz Tate (*Taylor*); Earl Billings (*Leon*).

6577   *The New Avengers.* (Series; Adventure; CBS; 1978-1979). An update of *The Avengers* that continues the British government's battle against diabolical villains as seen through the assignments of John Steed, the Ministry's top agent, and his partners, Purdy and Mike Gambit.

The dashing and debonair John Steed is basically the same character as in the prior series. He believes that Britain rules and has sworn to defend her against all her enemies. While he still lives at 3 Stable Mews in London, he also owns a country estate called Steed's Stud (where he entertains the ladies and breeds horses. It also serves as his headquarters for issuing orders to agents). Steed is still a master of Old World charm and courtesy, still carries his sword-in-the-handle umbrella, and still wears bowler hats (which have been lined with metal). Steed, Purdy and Gambit work well as a team because they have mutual respect for each other.

Purdy, named after the most respected and expensive shotgun in the world, was born in India. Because her father, a Brigadier in the British army, was constantly on the move, Purdy had an international education and attended exclusive private schools. She studied dance and eventually became a professional ballerina. After her father's death (shot as a spy after joining the Secret Service), Purdy became a Ministry agent. She is well versed in the martial arts and an expert on firearms.

Mike Gambit has a long and distinguished military background. He spent time in the British army (Parachute Regiment) and was later with the Special Air Services. He acquired knowledge of guerrilla warfare when he worked as a mercenary in Africa and the Middle East. He also wrestled crocodiles in the Congo and became a professional race car driver before becoming a Ministry agent. Gambit is an expert in unarmed combat, and a skilled pilot, shot and archer.

Cast: Patrick Macnee (*John Steed*); Joanna Lumley (*Purdy*); Gareth Hunt (*Mike Gambit*).

6578   *The New Bill Cosby Show.* (Series; Variety; CBS; 1972-1973). Various songs, dances and comedy sketches that depict the world as seen through the eyes of comedian Bill Cosby.

Host: Bill Cosby. **Regulars:** Susan Tolsky, Lola Falana, Foster Brooks, Oscar DeGrury, Erin Fleming, The Donald McKayle Dancers. **Announcer:** Lola Falana. **Orchestra:** Quincy Jones, Bobby Bryant.

6579   *The New Bob Cummings Show.* (Series; Comedy; CBS; 1961-1962). Bob Carson is a freelance pilot based in Palm Springs, California who is not only a ladies' man but also a man who will go out of his way to help people (he thinks) are in trouble (especially beautiful women). Bob also has numerous monetary problems and

stories follow Bob as he struggles to cope with the various, aggravating situations that confront him every day. Lionel is Bob's sidekick and Henrietta Gregory, a very pretty teenage girl who is part tomboy and called "Hank" is Bob's neighbor. Bob owns the never marketed Aero Car (a car that could be converted into a plane in ten minutes. Its inventor could never get it mass-produced and Bob flew the prototype model; it was slated to sell for $13,000, a considerably large sum for 1961).

Cast: Bob Cummings (*Bob Carson*); Murvyn Vye (*Lionel*); Roberta Shore (*Henrietta "Hank" Gregory*).

6580   *The New Breed.* (Series; Crime Drama; ABC; 1961-1962). Price Adams, a lieutenant with the Los Angeles Police Department, is a man who believes that to battle the new breed of criminals the police need to be just as clever and deceiving as the thugs they purse. To do so, Price establishes the Metropolitan Squad, an experimental unit of the city's best officers. Price, a veteran of the force, believes in caution and working within the limits of the law when possible. Stories relate the unit's efforts to disrupt the workings of organized crime. Keith Gregory is the captain; Vince, Joe and Peter are other members of the unit.

Cast: Leslie Nielsen (*Lt. Price Adams*); John Beradino (*Sgt. Vince Cavelli*); Byron Morrow (*Capt. Keith Gregory*); John Clark (*Off. Joe Huddleston*); Greg Roman (*Off. Pete Garcia*).

6581   *New Car Smell.* (Pilot; Comedy; Unaired; Produced for Fox in 2004). A prestigious Las Vegas car dealership is the backdrop for a proposal that focuses on a group of sales people who devise ingenious ways to outdo each other to win the spot of top salesman.

Cast: Brooke Shields (*April*); Christopher McDonald (*Mac*); Dana Daurey (*Holly*); Dave Attell (*Harry*); Victor Togunde (*Jamal*).

6582   *The New Card Sharks.* (Series; Game; CBS; 1986). A revised version of *Card Sharks*. A question, based on a survey of 100 people, is stated. The player (two compete) who comes closest to predicting the number of people who said yes, plays high-low card. The first card of five playing cards is shown. The player has to predict whether the next card will be higher or lower. The first player to correctly predict his line of cards is the winner.

Host: Bob Eubanks. **Card Dealers:** Susanna Williams, Lacey Pemberton. **Announcer:** Gene Wood.

6583   *The New Christy Minstrels Show.* (Series; Variety; NBC; 1964). Summer program of music and songs starring the singing group the New Christy Minstrels.

The New Christy Minstrels: Ann White, Paul Potash, Barry Kane, Karen Gunderson, Barry McGuire, Clarence Treat, Larry Romos. **Regulars:** The Chuck Cassey Singers, The Doerr-Hutchinson Dancers. **Orchestra:** Peter Matz.

6584   *New Comedy Showcase.* (Pilot; Comedy; CBS; 1960). The overall title for seven unsold pilot films. See: *Johnny Come Lately, Maggie, Maisie, Slezak and Son, They Went Thataway, You're Only Young Once* and *You're Only Young Twice*.

6585   *A New Day.* (Pilot; Comedy; Unaired; Produced for ABC in 1992). The Watsons are a suburban, white middle-class family of five. Cathy, the mother, is a social worker with a heart of gold who dramatically changes her family when she brings home Demond Carter, a black teen who has a tough inner-city background. Cathy sees untapped potential in Demond, who has exhausted all his foster care possibilities. She feels his presence will broaden the perspective of her three pretty, self-involved daughters (Lori, Julie and Tammy) and provide for her husband (Kevin) the son he never had. The proposal was to follow events in the lives of the Watsons as they unofficially adopt a new member.

Cast: Cindy Williams *(Cathy Watson)*; Richard Gilliland *(Kevin Watson)*; Lackey Bevis *(Lori Watson)*; Megan Parlen *(Julie Watson)*; Ashleigh Blair Sterling *(Tammy Watson)*; Merlin Santana *(Demond Carter)*.

6586   A New Day in Eden. (Series; Drama; Showtime; 1982-1983). Television's first "adult serial" (as it was billed, although it lasted only for 13 episodes), that focuses on the sexual desires of a group of people who live in a community called Eden. Contains nudity and adult situations.

Cast: Lara Parker *(Betty Franklin)*; Jane Elliot *(Maggie Sinclair)*; Wendy Barry *(Shelly Novak)*; Steve Carlson *(Josh Collier)*; Grant Wilson *(Biff Lewis)*; Ann Wilkinson *(Laurel Franklin)*; Jack Wagner *(Clint Masterson)*; Maggie Sullivan *(Miranda Stevens)*; Don Matheson *(Lockhart)*; Jim McMullan *(Bryan Lewis)*; Larry Poindexter *(Greg Lewis)*.

6587   The New Dick Van Dyke Show. (Series; Comedy; CBS; 1971-1974). Richard ("Dick") Preston, his wife, Jennifer ("Jenny"), and their children, Annie and Lucas, reside in a ranch-style house on Hayes Creek Road in Carefree, Arizona. Dick is the host of *The Dick Preston Show*, a 90 minute talk-variety program that is produced by KXIU-TV, Channel 2, in Phoenix (the station is owned by the Compton Broadcasting Company).

Michelle ("Mike") Preston is Dick's sister, booking agent and secretary at Channel 2; Bernard ("Bernie") Davis is Dick's agent and business manager; and Carol Davis is Bernie's wife.

Annie is nine years old and attends Camelback Grammar School. Dick calls Annie "Pumpkin," and Bernie's affectionate name for her is "Sweetness."

Lucas is 16 years old. He is a young Romeo and seems to have a never-ending supply of girlfriends. The episode of October 2, 1971 ("Interracial Dating") was very controversial for its time and showed Lucas dating a black girl named Judy Williams (Ta-Tanisha). The family's acceptance of Judy was made easier when Annie wrote a poem ("Roses are red, violets are blue, so why can't people be colors too?").

Dick and Jenny also have an infant son named Chris (Tiffany Graff). Dick closes his show with "Bye, have a nice rest of the day." The family cat is Mr. Rosenbloom (named after Annie's music teacher). Carl Reiner's voice is heard as that of the studio director; and Dick's real life children, Barry and Stacy Van Dyke, played various roles.

In 1973 the series switched locales (to California) when Dick quit his local talk show to play Dr. Brad Fairmont on the television soap opera *Those Who Care*. The Prestons now live in Tarzana at 747 Bonnie Vista Road. New to the cast are Max Mathias, the show's producer; Alex Montez, the director; and Dennis Whitehead, the show's writer.

Richard Richardson is Dick's neighbor, an actor who stars in the TV series *Harrigan's Hooligans*; Connie is Richard's wife; and Margot Brighton is the star of *Those Who Care* (she plays Dr. Susan Allison, Brad's supervisor at Pleasant Valley Hospital). Stories for both versions relate Dick's efforts to cope with family and job related problems.

Cast: Dick Van Dyke *(Dick Preston)*; Hope Lange *(Jenny Preston)*; Angela Powell *(Annie Preston)*; Michael Shea *(Lucas Preston)*; Marty Brill *(Bernie Davis)*; Nancy Dussault *(Carol Davis)*; Fannie Flagg *(Michele "Mike" Preston)*; David Doyle *(Ted Atwater)*; Dick Van Patten *(Max Mathias)*; Henry Darrow *(Alex Montez)*; Barry Gordon *(Dennis Whitehead)*; Richard Dawson *(Richard Richardson)*; Chita Rivera *(Connie Richardson)*; Barbara Rush *(Margot Brighton)*.

6588   The New Dragnet. (Series; Crime Drama; Syn.; 1989).

An updated version of the 1951 series *Dragnet*. The day-to-day grueling assignments of Vic Daniels and Carl Melina, detectives with the West Los Angeles Police Department. Vic and Carl are partners whose case investigations are profiled on a weekly basis. Stories, while not as dramatic as those presented on the original series, are based on true events (with only the names and places changed "to protect the innocent"). Vic and Carl are good at their job, but not as persistent and determined as Jack Webb's Joe Friday character (nor as droll and somber). Here Vic and Carl had equal rankings; on the original series, Joe was a sergeant and outranked his partners. Bill Fulton composed "The New Dragnet Theme."

Cast: Jeff Osterhage *(Vic Daniels)*; Bernard White *(Carl Melina)*; Don Stroud *(Captain Lussen)*; Thalmus Rasulala *(Captain Bolz)*.

6589   The New Ernie Kovacs Show. (Series; Variety; ABC; 1961-1962). Sketches and blackouts that satirize life. See also: *The Ernie Kovacs Show, It's Time for Ernie, Kovacs on the Corner* and *Kovacs Unlimited*.

Host: Ernie Kovacs. **Regulars:** Jolene Brand, Maggi Brown, Bobby Laugher, Joe Mikalos, Leonard Allstar, Alice Novice, Francis McHale, Bob Warren. **Orchestra:** Harry Geller.

6590   The New Ghost Writer Mysteries. (Series; Adventure; CBS; 1997-1998). Camela Gorrick, Emily Robson and Henry Strickland are eighth graders at Jesse Owens Junior High School in the Fort Greene section of Brooklyn, New York. While they appear to be ordinary 13-year-olds, they are actually amateur detectives who solve crimes in and around their school. What makes them so unusual is that they receive help from Ghost Writer, a silver (sometimes gold) entity that fights for right.

Ghost Writer appears as a round, glowing object that can only be seen by Camela, Emily and Henry. Although the series is an update of *Ghost Writer* (see entry), it is not explained what Ghost Writer is or how it attached itself to the teenagers. Ghost Writer cannot speak. It communicates through words and has the ability to rearrange any printed matter to get its message to Camela, Emily and Henry. They, in turn, can communicate with Ghost Writer by writing their instructions on a piece of paper or typing it into a computer. Ghost Writer reads the message (seen in a glowing light) then does what it is asked (usually to investigate as Ghost Writer can get into places no one else can — like computer circuits, inside sealed envelopes).

Once the Ghost Writer Team (as they call themselves) have the facts they proceed to investigate and eventually solve crimes.

Camela, called Cam, lives at 207 Fulton Street. She is an amateur photographer and loves sports (her mother, a lawyer, was a star sprinter on her high school track team). Emily, called Em, lives in a brownstone at 61 Bridge Street. She is the daughter of a district attorney and a reporter for the school's newspaper, *The Ratler*. Henry, called Strick, lives in a cluttered, basement-like area he calls "The Batcave" (no mention is made of Strick's parents or exactly what or where "The Batcave" is). Strick helps Cam and Em as an unofficial member of the school paper (Cam appears to be the paper's photographer in some episodes while in others she just seems to be helping Em get the facts for stories).

Cast: Charlotte Sullivan *(Camela Gorrick)*; Erica Luttrell *(Emily Robson)*; Kristian Ayre *(Henry Strickland)*.

6591   The New Gidget. (Series; Comedy; Syn.; 1986-1988). The home at 656 Glendale Avenue in Los Angeles is owned by Frances and Jeff Griffin, a young married couple who met as teenagers on Malibu Beach — when Jeff was a surfer called "Moondoggie" and Frances was nicknamed "Gidget" ("a girl who is not a giant or a midget — a Gidget"). Gidget now owns her own business (Gidget Travel) and Jeff is a city planner.

Gidget and Jeff attended Westside High School. Jeff was taught to surf by the Great Kahuna (Don Stroud), a legendary surfer. Gidget turned her love for surfing into a home video called *Gidget's Guide to Surfing*. Jeff was originally a construction worker for the Bedford Construction Company.

Danielle ("Danni") Collins is Gidget's pretty niece (the daughter of her unseen sister, Anne and her husband John). Danni is temporarily living with Gidget and Jeff while her parents are away on business. Gidget and Jeff are new to being parents "and we make it up as we go along in raising Danni." Danni is tall, slender and very attractive, and she inherited Gidget's love for surfing. She and her friend, Gail Baker, attend Westside High School and their favorite hangout is Malibu Beach.

Gidget's father, Russell ("Russ") Lawrence, is now retired (he was an English professor at UCLA) and assists Gidget at the travel agency (as does her longtime friend, Larue).

In the pilot episode, *Gidget's Summer Reunion* (Syn., June 1985), Gidget's niece is Kim (Allison Barron), not Dani; Russell Hoover (not Lawrence) is Gidget's father; Larue Powell became Larue Wilson.

Cast: Caryn Richman (*Gidget Griffin*); Dean Butler (*Jeff Griffin*); Sydney Penny (*Danni Collins*); William Schallert (*Russ Lawrence*); Lili Haydn (*Gail Baker*); Jill Jacobson (*Larue Powell*).

6592 *The New Healers.* (Pilot; Drama; ABC; Mar. 27, 1972). The work of Dr. Robert Kier, the director of the Institute for Medical Research in California. Other regulars are Joe Tate, the financial director; Laura, Robert's ex-wife; Nikki and Vince, Robert's children; Barbara, Robert's secretary; and Claire, a doctor.

Cast: John Forsythe (*Robert Kier*); Pat Harrington, Jr. (*Joe Tate*); Kate Woodville (*Claire*); Beverly Garland (*Laura Kier*); Shelly Juttner (*Nikki Kier*); Christian Juttner (*Vince Kier*); Ellen Weston (*Barbara*).

6593 *The New Howdy Doody Show.* (Series; Children; Syn.; 1976). An updated version of *Howdy Doody*, the NBC 1947–1960 series about the puppet Howdy Doody and his friend, Buffalo Bob Smith, and their efforts to run a circus in Doodyville. The new version follows the same basic format with songs, stories and sketches geared to children. Clarabell Hornblow is the circus clown (honks a yes or no horn instead of speaking); Happy Harmony is the schoolteacher; Cornelius Cobb is the prop man; Nicholson Muir is the producer (a takeoff on the real producers, Roger Muir and Nick Nicholson); Jackie is the singer; Phineas T. Bluster (puppet) is the mean old man who is opposed to Howdy and his circus; Fletcher is the sketcher.

Cast: Bob Smith (*Buffalo Bob Smith*); Lew Anderson (*Clarabell Hornblow*); Marilyn Patch (*Happy Harmony*); Milt Neil (*Fletcher the Sketcher*); Nick Nicholson (*Cornelius Cobb*); Bill LeCornec (*Nicholson Muir*); Jackie Davis (*Jackie*); Bob Smith (*Voice of Howdy Doody*); Dayton Allen (*Voice of Phineas T. Bluster*). **Music:** Jackie Davis.

6594 *The New Jetsons.* (Series; Cartoon; Syn.; 1985). An update of the 1960s series *The Jetsons* that continues to depict events in the lives of the futuristic (21st century) Jetson family: George, his wife, Jane and their children Judy and Elroy.

Voice Cast: George O'Hanlon (*George Jetson*); Penny Singleton (*Jane Jetson*); Janet Waldo (*Judy Jetson*); Daws Butler (*Elroy Jetson*); Jean VanderPyl (*Rosie*); Brenda Vaccaro (*DiDi*).

6595 *The New Kids on the Block.* (Series; Cartoon; ABC; 1990). The rock group, The New Kids on the Block, are animated and the adventures they find as they perform throughout the world are the focal point of stories. The New Kids on the Block (Jordan Knight, Jonathan Knight, Joseph McIntyre, Donnie Wahlberg and Danny Wood) appear as themselves in live action introductions and closing segments while actors for their animated antics voice them.

Voice Cast: Matt E. Mixer (*Jonathan Knight*); Scott Menville (*Joe McIntyre*); David Coburn (*Donnie Wahlberg*); Brian Stokes Mitchell (*Danny Wood*); Dave Fennoy (*Dick Scott*); J.D. Hall (*Bizcut*).

6596 *A New Kind of Family.* (Series; Comedy; ABC; 1979–1980). The house at 1836 Loma Linda Drive in Los Angeles is shared by two families: The Flanagans and the Stones (later dropped in favor of the Ashtons). The families agreed to share expenses and stories relate the problems they encounter living in the same residence. Kit Flanagan is a widow and the mother of Hilary, Tony and Andy. Abby Stone is a divorcee and the mother of Jill. Jessica Ashton, is a divorcee who runs the Elegant Eats Catering company; she has a daughter named Jo Jo. Harold Zimmerman is their landlord; Michael Jansen is Kit's romantic interest; Carl Ashton is Jessica's ex-husband. Harold is the host of a TV show called *The Homemaker's Midday Matinee*; Kit has a dog named Heinz.

Cast: Eileen Brennan (*Kit Flanagan*); Lauri Hendler (*Hilary Flanagan*); Rob Lowe (*Tony Flanagan*); David Hollander (*Andy Flanagan*); Gwynne Gilford (*Abby Stone*); Connie Hearn (*Jill Stone*); Telma Hopkins (*Jessica Ashton*); Janet Jackson (*Jo Jo Anderson*); Chuck McCann (*Harold Zimmerman*); Robert Hogan (*Michael Jansen*); Scoey Mitchell (*Carl Ashton*).

6597 *The New Land.* (Series; Drama; ABC; 1974). The life and struggles of the Larsen family, Scandinavian immigrants, as they seek to build a new life for themselves in Minnesota in 1858. Christian Larsen is the father; he is married to Ann and they are the parents of Tuliff and Annaliase. Bo Larsen is Christian's brother; Lars and Molly Lundstrom are their neighbors; Rhodie is Lars and Molly's daughter; Mr. Murdock is their friend.

Cast: Scott Thomas (*Christian Larsen*); Bonnie Bedelia (*Ann Larsen*); Todd Lookinland (*Tuliff Larsen*); Debbie Lytton (*Annaliase Larsen*); Kurt Russell (*Bo Larsen*); Donald Moffat (*Lars Lundstrom*); Gwen Arner (*Molly Lundstrom*); Stephanie Steele (*Rhodie Lundstrom*); Lou Frizzell (*Mr. Murdock*).

6598 *The New Lassie.* (Series; Drama; Syn.; 1989–1991). Glen Ridge is a small town in California. At 415 Latimor Road live the McCullochs: parents Dee and Chris, their children, Megan and Will, and their dog, Lassie, a descendant of television's original 1954 Lassie, who became a part of the family (1986) when Chris rescued her from a car wreck and named her (a puppy at the time) Lassie.

Chris runs the McCulloch Construction Company. Dee works at the Willingham Pet Adoption Center. When the pet agency closed, Dee acquired a job as a placement officer at the Glen Ridge Employment Agency. Megan attended Glen Ridge Elementary (first season), then Glen Ridge High. She is a cheerleader (for the Gophers football team) and worked after school with her mother at the pet adoption center. Megan is a budding photographer and in one episode, she mentioned attending Madison High School. Will, the youngest McCulloch, attends Glen Ridge Elementary School (first season) and the Evergreen School (second season).

Steve, a freelance writer is Chris's adopted brother. Steve is actually Timmy Martin, the second owner of Lassie (*Timmy and Lassie*, 1957–64. In this series, Timmy was the adopted son of Paul and Ruth Martin and lived on a farm in Calverton). In the episode "Roots" (Nov. 1989) it is learned that 25 years ago young Timmy was taken away from his foster parents. Later, Timmy began using his middle name of Steve and was adopted by the McCulloch family. In 1989 Ruth Martin-Chadwick (June Lockhart), Timmy's first adoptive mother (now remarried) tracks Chris down to reclaim her dog — the puppy Chris rescued from the car wreck. Ruth is unaware that Timmy is now Steve or part of a new family. It is a bittersweet reunion — Timmy blames Ruth for abandoning him — until Ruth explains that she fought tooth and nail to get him back but couldn't. When Ruth sees how much Will and Lassie love each other, she allows the Mc-Cullochs to keep Lassie.

In the episode of November 25, 1990, Tommy Rettig, Lassie's original owner (*Jeff's Collie*, 1954–57), appeared as Professor Jeff Miller and was reunited with Jon Provost when Steve and Will bring Lassie to the university for an experimental project involving dogs and computers.

Roddy McDowall appeared in several episodes as Andrew Leeds, a famous writer and friend of the McCullochs; in first season episodes, a stray cat named Sam frequented the McCullochs' house for food.

Cast: Dee Wallace Stone (*Dee McCulloch*); Christopher Stone (*Chris McCulloch*); Wendy Cox (*Megan McCulloch*); Will Niper (*Will McCulloch*); Jon Provost (*Steve McCulloch*).

6599 *The New Leave It to Beaver.* (Series; Comedy; TBS; 1986–1989). An updated version of *Leave It to Beaver* that continues to depict events in the lives of the Cleaver family. June is now a widow and a member of the Mayfield City Council. She lives in the original series house at 211 Pine Street with her younger son, Theodore ("Beaver") Cleaver, and his two sons, Kip and Ollie; Beaver is divorced from Kimberly. Kip attends Mayfield High School, and Oliver, the Grant Avenue School. Beaver is now partners with Clarence ("Lumpy") Rutherford in the Cleaver and Rutherford Company (exactly what they do is not revealed). Lumpy is now married and the father of a daughter (J.J.).

Wally, June's older son, is an attorney and lives at 213 Pine Street. He is married to Mary Ellen, and they have a daughter named Kelly. Mary Ellen was Wally's high school sweetheart (played in the original series by Pamela Beaird); Kelly attends the Grant Avenue Grammar School and is a member of the Junior Chipmunks. Oliver, called "Ollie" by Beaver, hangs out with Kelly.

Eddie Haskell is now married to Gert and is the father of two boys, Freddie and Bomber. He is still the same wisecracking character he was in the 1960s. Eddie owns the rather slipshod run Eddie Haskell Construction Company. Freddie (who takes after Eddie), attends Mayfield High School. Bomber (also mischievous) is enrolled at the Vicksburg Military School.

Cast: Barbara Billingsley (*June Cleaver*); Tony Dow (*Wally Cleaver*); Jerry Mathers (*Beaver Cleaver*); Ken Osmond (*Eddie Haskell*); Janice Kent (*Mary Ellen Cleaver*); Kaleena Kiff (*Kelly Cleaver*); John Snee (*Oliver Cleaver*); Kipp Marcus (*Kip Cleaver*); Ellen Maxted (*Gert Haskell*); Eric Osmond (*Freddie Haskell*); Christian Osmond (*Bomber Haskell*); Frank Bank (*Lumpy Rutherford*); Keri Houlihan (*J.J. Rutherford*).

6600 *The New Lorenzo Music Show.* (Pilot; Comedy; ABC; Aug. 10, 1976). A satirical behind-the-scenes look at a television talk-variety show as seen through the experiences of Lorenzo Music, the nervous, anxiety-ridden host, and his wife, Henrietta, the relaxed and poised co-host. The pilot led to the syndicated (Sept. 1976) *The Lorenzo and Henrietta Music Show* which featured the real-life husband and wife team co-hosting a talk-variety series.

Host: Lorenzo Music, Henrietta Music. **Guests:** Steve Anderson, Lewis Arquette, Jack Eagle, Roz Kelly, David Ogden Stiers.

6601 *The New Loretta Young Show.* (Series; Comedy; CBS; 1962-1963). Christine Massey is a beautiful, charming and sophisticated woman who lives in a conservative neighborhood at 7816 Willow Road in the small town of Ellendale, Connecticut. Christine is a widow and the mother of seven children (Vickie, Maria, Marnie, Judy, Binkie and twins Peter and Paul). She moved to Ellendale 14 years ago to raise her children away from the congestion of a big city. She earns a living as a children's storybook writer. Hoping to secure a position as a writer for *Manhattan* magazine, Christine submits a story idea. She is granted an interview and meets with its editor, Paul Belzer, in Manhattan. Paul likes her style and is willing to hire her if she will upgrade her writing to accommodate the sophisticated publication. Her decision to comply prompts him to request her presence at dinner to discuss matters. She accepts and stories, which are presented in a serial-like format, depict their courtship, their marriage and their establishing a home in Connecticut. Following their marriage, stories focus on the trails and tribulation of the nine-member Massey-Belzer family. It is called "New" because it is a departure from Loretta's prior anthology series, *A Letter to Loretta* and *The Loretta Young Show*.

Cast: Loretta Young (*Christine Massey*); James Philbrook (*Paul Belzer*); Beverly Washburn (*Vickie Massey*); Tracy Statford (*Maria Massey*); Celia Kaye (*Marnie Massey*); Sandy Descher (*Judy Massey*); Dack Rambo (*Peter Massey*); Dirk Rambo (*Paul Massey*); Carol Sydes (*Binkie Massey*); Leif Erickson (*Bascombe Beebee*); Regina Gleason (*Rain Beebee*); Hope Summers (*Mrs. Teasdale*).

6602 *The New, Love American Style.* (Series; Anthology; ABC; 1985-1986). Comedy vignettes that tackle the ups and downs of love, marriage and divorce. An updated version of *Love, American Style* whose stories are interspersed with blackouts (performed by a regular cast; guests appear in the actual stories). Lou Rawls performs the theme, "Love, American Style."

Blackout Regulars: Marcia Wallace, Damita Jo Freeman, Norm Crosby, Amy Yasbeck, Barry Pearl, Arsenio Hall.

6603 *The New Maverick.* (Pilot; Western; CBS; Sept. 3, 1978). A revised version of *Maverick* (ABC, 1957–62) and the pilot for *Young Maverick* (CBS, 1979-80). *Maverick* dealt with the exploits of three less-than-honorable gamblers: brothers Bret and Bart Maverick (James Garner, Jack Kelly) and their English cousin, Beau (Roger Moore). *The New Maverick* follows the adventures of Ben Maverick, the young, eager and inexperienced son of Beau, as he, like those before, becomes involved in the troubles of others. Nell is Ben's friend.

Cast: Charles Frank (*Ben Maverick*); Susan Blanchard (*Nell McGarahan*).

6604 *The New Mike Hammer.* (Series; Crime Drama; CBS; 1986-1987). A revised version of the 1984 CBS series *Mike Hammer* that is actually a continuation of it with Mike, the tough private detective working out of New York City, dishing out his own brand of justice to law breakers. Based on the character created by Mickey Spillane. Velda is Mike's secretary; Pat Chambers is the Homicide Captain; Lawrence Barrington is the D.A; Ozzie the Answer is Mike's information man; and The Face is the girl who tails Mike for research for her "Nick Steele" mystery novels.

Cast: Stacy Keach (*Mike Hammer*); Lindsay Bloom (*Velda*); Don Stroud (*Pat Chambers*); Kent Williams (*Lawrence Barrington*); Danny Goldman (*Ozzie the Answer*); Donna Denton (*The Face*). **Theme Song:** "Harlem Nocturne" by Earle Hagen.

6605 *The New Monkees.* (Series; Comedy; Syn.; 1987). The New Monkees (Marty, Dino, Larry and Jared) are a struggling rock group seeking that road to stardom. They live is a very large and bizarre mansion and stories, an update of the 1966 series *The Monkees*, relate the mishaps they encounter at home and in performance. Manfred is their butler; Rita is the café waitress; Helen is the voice of the group's computer.

Cast: Marty Ross (*Marty*); Dino Kovacs (*Dino*); Larry Saltis

(Larry); Jared Chandler *(Jared)*; Gordon Oas-Heim *(Manfred)*; Liz Godfrey *(Helen)*; Bess Motta *(Rita)*.

6606   *The New Odd Couple.* (Series; Comedy; ABC; 1982). An updated version of *The Odd Couple*. Felix Unger is a perfectionist photographer; *New York Herald* sports writer Oscar Madison is his rather untidy Manhattan apartment roommate and stories relate their efforts to live together despite their differing life styles. Most episodes are recast versions of original *Odd Couple* scripts. Other regulars are Mira, Oscar's secretary; Cecily and Gwendolyn Pigeon, Oscar and Felix's neighbors; Murray Greschner, the cop; Frances Unger, Felix's ex-wife; Roy, Vinnie and Speed, Oscar's poker-playing pals; Henry and Vivian, members of Felix's theater group; Barney, the pool hall owner.

Cast: Ron Glass *(Felix Unger)*; Demond Wilson *(Oscar Madison)*; Liz Torres *(Mira)*; Sheila Anderson *(Cecily Pigeon)*; Ronalda Douglas *(Gwendolyn Pigeon)*; John Schuck *(Murray Greschner)*; Telma Hopkins *(Frances Unger)*; Bart Braverman *(Roy)*; Marvin Braverman *(Vinnie)*; Christopher Joy *(Speed)*; Wally Taylor *(Barney)*; Michael Rapppaport *(Henry)*; Jill Jaress *(Vivian)*.

6607   *The New $100,000 Name That Tune.* (Series; Game; Syn.; 1984). A revised version of *The $100,000 Name That Tune*. Two contestants compete in various contests wherein they must identify song titles after hearing only a few bars. The winner, the highest scorer, receives the opportunity to win $100,000 by identifying a very difficult mystery tune after hearing only one note.

Host: Jim Lange. **Announcer:** John Harlan. **Music:** The Tommy Oliver Orchestra.

6608   *The New Operation Petticoat.* (Series; Comedy; ABC; 1978-1979). An update of *Operation Petticoat* (which dealt with the crew of the World War II pink submarine, *Sea Tiger*). When most of the crew transfers, the *Sea Tiger* is re-staffed and assigned to duty as a sea going ambulance. Stories relate their experiences as they roam the South Pacific during World War II. Sam Haller is the captain; Michael Bender is his lieutenant. The nurses are Dolores Crandall, Katherine O'Hara and Betty Wheeler. Other crew members are listed in the cast.

Cast: Robert Hogan *(Capt. Sam Haller)*; Randolph Mantooth *(Lt. Michael Bender)*; Melinda Naud *(Lt. Dolores Crandall)*; Jo Ann Pflug *(Lt. Katherine O'Hara)*; Hilary Thompson *(Lt. Betty Wheeler)*; Warren Berlinger *(Chief Stanley Dobritch)*; Richard Brestoff *(Yeoman Alvin Hunkle)*; Sam Chew, Jr. *(Lt. Travis Kern)*; Jim Varney *(Seaman Broom)*; Don Sparks *(Seaman Horner)*; Fred Kareman *(Seaman Doplos)*; Martin Azarow *(Chief Manhiannini)*; Peter Mamakos *(Seaman Kostos)*.

6609   *New Orleans Force.* (Pilot; Crime Drama; ABC; April 2, 1975). Jim Gideon is the head of an elite team of U.S. Department of Justice investigators based in New Orleans. He is assisted by Meg and the proposal was to relate their case assignments.

Cast: Peter Graves *(Jim Gideon)*; Diana Douglas *(Meg)*.

6610   *The New People.* (Series; Drama; ABC; 1969-1970). A small inter-island charter en-route from Southeast Asia to the Manila, is caught in a fierce storm and damaged. The plane crash-lands on Bonamo, a remote Pacific island once operated by the Atomic Energy Commission as a hydrogen bomb test site but abandoned due fear of contamination by the trade winds. Of the fifty passengers on board, forty American college students in a cultural exchange program survive. Stories relate their struggles to find a way back to civilization while, at the same time, establishing a society untouched by the destruction of modern man. In the first episode Hanachek (Richard

Kiley) of the American Counsel, helps "The New People" establish themselves on the island (he later dies from injuries suffered in the crash). Broadcast back-to-back with the 45-minute *Music Scene* (thus creating a 90-minute block).

Program Open *[Male:]* "Our tour of the Pacific was over. *[Girl:]* We were going home. Forty of us. *[Male:]* Forty kids. The storm was getting worse. We prayed. Then we crashed. *[Girl:]* The pilots were dead, We were all alone on this island. Two thousand miles from nowhere. A few hours later we found the town. *[Male:]* A town built for an atomic bomb test. The Atomic Energy Commission had cancelled the test and deserted this island. *[Girl:]* We had food and shelter and one thing more — a frightening realization we'd never leave here again. *[Male:]* This was our home forever. No more friends, family. *[Girl:]* No more anything. Just us. And God, are we scared."

Cast: Tiffany Bolling *(Susan Bradley)*; Zooey Hall *(Robert Lee)*; David Moses *(Eugene "Bones" Washington)*; Peter Ratray *(George Potter)*; Lee Jay Lambert *(Errol "Bull" Wilson)*; Kevin Michaels *(Dexter)*; Brenda Sykes *(Brenda)*; Nancy DeCarol *(Gloria)*; Dennis Olivieri, Kevin O'Neal *(Stanley)*; Jill Jaress *(Ginny)*; Elizabeth Berger *(Laura)*; Clive Clerk *(Jack)*; Donna Baccala *(Wendy)*; Carl Reindel *(Dan Stoner)*.

6611   *The New Perry Mason.* (Series; Crime Drama; CBS; 1973-1974). Perry Mason is a brilliant criminal defense attorney working out of Los Angeles. He is not a man to stand by and let others do all the work; he often takes an active part in his case investigations. He is also a man who is known for his brilliant courtroom defenses — often waiting for the last possible moment to present a surprise witness that inevitably wins him the case. Della Street is Perry's ever-faithful secretary; Paul Drake is his investigator; Hamilton Burger is the District Attorney and Perry's chief adversary; Arthur Tragg is a lieutenant with the Los Angeles Police Department; Gertie Lade is Perry's office receptionist. An update of *Perry Mason* and based on the character created by Erle Stanley Gardner.

Cast: Monte Markham *(Perry Mason)*; Sharon Acker *(Della Street)*; Harry Guardino *(Hamilton Burger)*; Albert Stratton *(Paul Drake)*; Dane Clark *(Arthur Tragg)*; Brett Somers *(Gertie Lade)*.

6612   *The New Phil Silvers Show.* (Series; Comedy; CBS; 1963). Plant 4 of Osborne Industries in Los Angeles is the location. Office B-116 of Factory D is the base of operations. Harry Grafton, the maintenance department foreman, is the man assigned to that office.

While Osborne Industries makes everything from plumbing supplies to machinery parts, Harry has his own business called Grafton Enterprises, which he runs from his office and struggles to keep secret from his superiors. Harry is the only man who can get the assembly line started again when it breaks down; he is also a master manipulator who is totally dedicated to acquiring money. Stories relate Harry's efforts to not only keep the assembly line moving, but ways he can profit from it. Fred H. Brink is the plant supervisor. Waluska, Roxy and Lester are Harry's assistants; Audrey is Harry's widowed sister (Susan and Andy are her children); Mr. Osborne is the company owner; Della is his niece. In the opening theme, Harry is seen in animated form, and he says, "Glad to see ya." When the factory whistle blows smoke for the show's title and star, Phil Silvers' name appears in various combinations (for instance, Slip Hilvers, Shil Pilvers). A reworking of the Sergeant Bilko character from *The Phil Silvers Show* (see entry).

Cast: Phil Silvers *(Harry Grafton)*; Stafford Repp *(Fred Brink)*; Herbie Faye *(Waluska)*; Jim Shane *(Lester)*; Pat Renella *(Roxy Klinger)*; Elena Verdugo *(Audrey)*; Sandy Descher *(Susan)*; Ronnie Dapo *(Andy)*; Douglas Dumbrille *(Mr. Osborne)*; Evelyn Patrick *(Della Osborne)*.

6613   The New Shmoo. (Series; Comedy; NBC; 1979). The Shmoo is an Al Capp comic strip character that is mischievous and enjoys the company of humans. Nita, Mickey and Billy Joe are its human friends, teenagers who have a keen interest in anything supernatural (like the Shmoo). With the help of the Shmoo, the teens investigate psychic phenomena.

Voice Cast: Frank Welker (*The Shmoo*); Dolores Cantu-Primo (*Nita*); Chuck McCann (*Billy Joe*); Bill Idelson (*Mickey*).

6614   The New Show. (Series; Comedy; NBC; 1984). Topical comedy sketches coupled with music and songs by top name guest stars.

Cast: Dave Thomas, John Candy, Buck Henry, Valri Bromfield, Maggie Jacobson, Tom Davis, Laura Monahan, J.D. Smith. **Announcer:** Jeff Bergman. **Music:** Howard Shore.

6615   The New Soupy Sales Show. (Series; Comedy; Syn.; 1979). An update of comedian Soupy Sales' programs of the 1950s and 60s that continues to spotlight him in various mishaps that occur in and around his home (where he lives with his dogs White Fang and Black Tooth).

Host: Soupy Sales. **Regulars:** Clyde Adler, Marty Brill.

6616   The New Stu Erwin Show. (Series; Comedy; ABC; 1954-1955). The later title for *Trouble with Father*. See this title for information.

6617   The New Super Friends Hour. (Series; Cartoon; ABC; 1977-1978). A spin off from *The Super Friends* that continues to relate the exploits of the world's mightiest heroes (listed in the cast) as they battle injustice throughout the world.

Voice Cast: Danny Dark (*Superman*); Shannon Farnon (*Wonder Woman*); Olan Soule (*Batman*); Casey Kasem (*Robin*); Norman Alden (*Aquaman*); Michael Bell (*Zap*); Liberty Williams (*Jana*); Casey Kasem (*Computer Voice*); Michael Bell (*Gleek*). **Narrator:** William Woodson, Bob Lloyd.

6618   The New Temperatures Rising Show. (Series; Comedy; ABC; 1973-1974). A satire of medical dramas as seen through the antics of the staff of Capitol General Hospital in Washington, D.C. A spin off from *Temperature's Rising*. Paul Mercy is the harassed head of the hospital; Jerry Noland is the scheming doctor; Charles Claver is the by-the-books doctor seeking to expose Jerry; Wendy, Kelly and Tillis are the principal nurses; Agatha is Paul's mother; Edwina is Paul's sister.

Cast: Paul Lynde (*Dr. Paul Mercy*); Jennifer Darling (*Nurse Wendy Winchester*); Barbara Cason (*Admissions Nurse Tillis*); Cleavon Little (*Dr. Jerry Noland*); John Dehner (*Dr. Charles Claver*); Jeff Morrow (*Dr. Lloyd Axton*); Alice Ghostley (*Edwina Mercy*); Sudie Bond (*Agatha Mercy*); Barbara Rucker, Sharleen Cotright (*Nurse Kelly*); Jerry Houser (*Orderly Haskell*); Ken Smedberg (*Orderly Jackson*); Mary Batten (*Nurse Reed*); Sandy Freeman (*Nurse Hamlin*).

6619   The New Three Stooges. (Series; Cartoon; Syn.; 1966). Moe, Larry and Curly, three trouble prone men known as the Three Stooges (from a series of 1930s and 40s theatrical shorts) face life head on only to find slapstick mishaps in everything they do.

Voice Cast: Moe Howard (*Moe*); Larry Fine (*Larry*); Curly Joe Howard, Joe DeRita (*Curly*).

6620   The New Tom Greene Show. (Series; Talk; MTV; 2003). A talk program that is more comedy than talk. Although celebrity interviews make up the bulk of the program, Tom's exchange of talk with his sidekick, Glenn Humplick and his comedy bits make the show a tad different than others of its type.

Host: Tom Greene. **Regulars:** Glenn Humplick, Ed Scott, Rita de Leon (*as Tom's blind date in skits*).

6621   The New Treasure Hunt. (Series; Game; Syn.; 1973–1977). Three players each stand before a jack-in-the-box. The contestant whose box contains a Treasure Hunt card receives the opportunity to win $25,000. The player chooses one of thirty boxes that are displayed on stage. The contents, or a cash bribe not to take the box, becomes the player's prize. An updated version of *Treasure Hunt*, which ran from 1956–1959 with Jan Murray as the host.

Program Open: "From Hollywood, it's *The New Treasure Hunt*. And here's the star of our show, Geoff Edwards."

Host: Geoff Edwards. **Assistant:** Jane Nelson, Siv Aberg (a.k.a. Sivi Aberg). **Check Guard:** Emil Autre. **Announcer:** Johnny Jacobs.

6622   The New $25,000 Pyramid. (Series; Game; CBS; 1982). Two teams, each composed of one celebrity and one non-celebrity contestant, compete. One team chooses one of six subject categories that are displayed on a large pyramid. Each subject contains seven related objects; one player has to relate each subject to his partner in one-word clues (within a 30-second time limit). The player who scores highest (each plays three categories) wins the game and receives the opportunity to win money (originally $50,000; then $25,000) by attempting to guess seven subjects on a large pyramid board within 60 seconds. The program was originally syndicated in January 1980 as *The $50,000 Pyramid* before becoming a daily CBS series in September of 1982.

Host: Dick Clark. **Announcer:** Jack Clark, Charlie O'Donnell, Johnny Gilbert, Rod Roddy, Charlie Tuna.

6623   The New Voice. (Series; Comedy-Drama; PBS; 1981-1982). The experiences of a group of students who write for *The New Voice*, the newspaper of Lincoln High School in Boston. Lorraine, Millie, Ken, Claudio, Larry and Kiko are students; Mr. Morfi is the paper's advisor; Mrs. Carrington is the school's principal.

Cast: Lorraine Gauli (*Lorraine George*); Millie Santiago (*Millie*); Ken Mochizuki (*Ken*); Claudio Martinez (*Claudio*); Kiko Mckee Redwing (*Kiko*); Shawn Elliott (*Mr. Morfi*); Carmen DeLavallad (*Mrs. Carrington*). **Music:** Chico O'Farrell.

6624   The New WKRP in Cincinnati. (Series; Comedy; Syn.; 1991–1993). A revised version of *WKRP in Cincinnati*. WKRP, 1530 on the AM dial, is a 5,000 watt rock station in Ohio. The station made its premiere broadcast on December 7, 1941, with the news story "The Japanese have just attacked Pearl Harbor." The station is still located on the fourteenth floor of the Flimm Building and is still very low rated. Its slogan is "The Mighty 1530 AM."

Arthur Carlson manages the station for his mother, Lillian ("Mama") Carlson; his late father founded WKRP. Arthur has high hopes that one day the station will crack the top ten. Arthur's wife, Carmen, runs a business called Carmen's Crystal Critter Corner in the Pinedale Mall.

Les Nessman is WKRP's news director. He has been with the station for more than 20 years and won the Buckeye Hawk News Award nine times. He still wears a bandage (to remind him of an injury he received in 1978 on the original series) and still has "invisible walls" that surround his desk in the bull pen office. Les calls himself "The News Beacon of the Ohio Valley."

Herb Tarlek is the station's salesman. He is married to Lucille, and hits on every beautiful girl he sees. He continues to call Arthur "Big Guy."

Mona Loveland is the late night D.J. (hosts *Mona Till Midnight*; her character replaced Venus Flytrap from the original series). Mona's sexy voice has made her a hot item at the station.

Dana Burns and Jack Allen are divorced D.J.'s who host a music and talk program called *The Burns and Allen Show* (the replacement for Dr. Johnny Fever). Radical D.J. Razor Dee replaced "Burns and Allen" in second season episodes. Dee works as "The Razor Man" and was a monks' barber for two years in the Order of Our Lady of the Forgetful.

Ronnie Lee was the first receptionist (Jennifer Marlowe's replacement). Ronnie was not as glamorous or buxom as Jennifer and was dropped (she was said to be attending night school to get her master's degree). She was replaced by Nancy Brinkwink, a busty blonde who has the hots for "the only man for me—Herb." Nancy has a B.A. in communications from Dennison College and was a former buyer for Studor and James in Cincinnati (she left the job because all the men she worked with were either married or gay).

Claire Hartline is the traffic manager (arranges commercial time); her character replaced Bailey Quarters. Donovan Aderhold is the new program director (his character replaced Andy Travis). New to the concept is Arthur's son, Arthur Carlson, Jr., the obnoxious junior salesman (Herb calls him "Little Big Guy").

Several regulars from the original show appeared: Jennifer Marlowe (Loni Anderson) was first a wealthy widow ("My husband, Cesare, died on our honeymoon; he was smiling at the time"); she later announced her engagement to Reynaldo Roberio Ricky Ricardo Goulegant III (Robert Goulet), the prince of a small European country called Rosario Roberto. Venus Flytrap (Tim Reid) now lives in Washington, D.C. After leaving WKRP he acquired a job with BET (Black Entertainment TV), first in marketing, then as chief executive officer.

Dr. Johnny Fever (Howard Hesseman) was first living in New York's Greenwich Village and writing a book about rock and roll music. Hesseman received special guest star billing in second season episodes when Johnny returned to WKRP as the new overnight D.J.—the midnight to 6:00 A.M. shift. (He replaced the unseen Moss Steiger).

Cast: Gordon Jump (*Arthur Carlson*); Richard Sanders (*Les Nessman*); Frank Bonner (*Herb Tarlek*); Tawny Kitaen (*Mona Loveland*); Kathleen Garrett (*Dana Burns*); Michael Des Barres (*Jack Allen*); French Stewart (*Razor Dee*); Wendy Davis (*Ronnie Lee*); Marla Jeanette Rubinoff (*Nancy Brinkwink*); Hope Alexander-Willis (*Claire Hartline*); Mykelti Williamson (*Donovan Aderhold*); Lightfield Lewis (*Arthur Carlson, Jr.*).

6625 New Year. (Pilot; Drama; ABC; July 17, 1993). Daniel J. "Danny" Hartman is the wealthy co-owner of Hartman, Fishkin and Mavis Pharmaceuticals. He represents the established, empowered older generation. Elsie Robertson is his competition, the owner of Robertson, Inc., a struggling company run by the younger generation who feel that they've been robbed of the American Dream that no longer exists. The story opens on New Year's Eve in 1999. Danny is hosting a lavish party to welcome the new millennium when a mysterious young man approaches him and says, "I'm going to destroy you." Thus the plot is as the older battles the younger for control of the pharmaceutical world. Other regulars are Suzanne, Jimi and Katie, Danny's children; Larry, Danny's partner; Alan, Elsie's aide; and Eudora, Danny's associate.

Cast: Stacy Keach (*Danny Hartman*); Jane Alexander (*Elsie Robertson*); Roma Downey (*Suzanne Hartman*); Linden Ashby (*Jimi Hartman*); Joanna Going (*Katie Hartman*); Mark Matheisen (*Alan Dale Masters*); Zelijko Ivanek (*Larry Fishkin*); C.C.H. Pounder (*Eudora Kellogg*); Giancarlo Esposito (*Marcus Foster*); Amelia Campbell (*Dr. Barbara Beck*); Socorro Santiago (*Izabella Gallardo*).

6626 New York Confidential. (Series; Crime Drama; Syn.; 1958). Lee Cochran is a New York City–based newspaper reporter-columnist. He is tough, determined and obsessed with solving crimes.

He doesn't write from what the wire services report. He goes into the field and takes the punches to get the goods on criminals and write the headline making stories.

Cast: Lee Tracy (*Lee Cochran*).

6627 New York Goes Hollywood. (Series; Reality; VH-1; 2008). Tiffany Pollard, known as New York on *The Flavor of Love* and *I Love New York*, leaves Manhattan to pursue her dream of becoming an actress. Cameras chart those efforts.

6628 New York Goes to Work. (Series; Reality; VH-1; 2009). Reality television star Tiffany Pollard (better known as New York) is featured as she seeks to acquire a job. While Tiffany would like to accept a job in show business, she finds that "the acting biz is hard and unpredictable." To pay the bills, Tiffany, a girl with a nasty attitude, will attempt to perform a job based on what viewers think will best suite her (or best aggravate her). Each week a list of three jobs are presented to viewers along with toll free telephone numbers. The job that receives the most votes becomes the job Tiffany must tackle. Cameras follow Tiffany as she tackles the job (anything from Burger King employee to sewer worker) with her object being to impress her employer for a $10,000 bonus (if she should quit or get fired, she loses the money).

6629 New York News. (Series; Drama; CBS; 1995-1996). A behind-the-scenes look at the workings of a daily newspaper (the *New York Reporter*) as seen through the activities of its editorial staff and reporters. Louise Felcott is the tough publisher ("Get me the story at any cost"); Nan Chase is the gossip columnist, with Angela, Ellie, Mitch, Jack, Tommy and Victor as reporters.

Cast: Mary Tyler Moore (*Louise Felcott*); Madeline Kahn (*Nan Chase*); Melina Kanakaredes (*Angela Villlanova*); Kelli Williams (*Ellie*); Anthony DeSando (*Tony Amato*); Kevin Chamberlain (*Victor*); Gregory Harrison (*Jack Reilly*); Joe Morton (*Mitch Cotter*).

6630 New York Undercover. (Series; Crime Drama; Fox; 1994–1998). The personal and professional lives of a group of N.Y.P.D. undercover detectives. The main characters are Detectives J.C. Williams and Eddie Torres. J.C. has just divorced his wife, Chantal, and is trying to be a good father to their son, Gregory (called "G"). Eddie is an over-eager cop who strives to do the best he can while struggling to deal with family problems and his Puerto Rican heritage. The only relaxation that J.C. and Eddie seem to have is at a bar called Natalie's. Their strict (no nonsense) lieutenant is Virginia Cooper; Detective Nina Moreno is a young Puerto Rican cop who is also struggling to become the best cop she can. Tommy MacNamara is an Irish detective with a know-it-all attitude; Alec Stone is a detective who will do what it takes to get the job done. Nell Delaney is a tough detective who uses her intelligence not violence to deal with criminals. Malcolm Baker is a lieutenant who joins the team in last season episodes as the unit's supervisor (replacing Virginia).

Cast: Malik Yoba (*J.C. Williams*); Michael DeLorenzo (*Eddie Torres*); Patti D'Arbanville (*Virginia Cooper*); Lauren Velez (*Nina Moreno*); Jonathan LaPaglia (*Tommy MacNamara*); Thomas Mikal Ford (*Malcolm Baker*); Josh Hopkins (*Alec Stone*); Marisa Ryan (*Nell Delaney*); Fatima Faloye (*Chantal Williams*); George O. Gore II (*Gregory "G" Williams*); Gladys Knight (*Natalie, the bar owner*).

6631 The New Zoo Revue. (Series; Children; Syn.; 1972). Various aspects of the world are related to children via songs, sketches, dances and stories via the animals at a zoo (actors dressed in costumes).

Cast: Doug Momary, Emily Peden (*Host*); Sharon Baird (*Charlie the Owl*); Bill Galloway, Bob Holt (*Voice of Charlie*); Yanco Innone

(Freddie Frog); Joni Robbins *(Voice of Freddie)*; Thomas Carri, Larri Thomas *(Henrietta Hippo)*; Hazel Shermit *(Voice of Henrietta)*; Chuck Woolery *(Mr. Dingle, the store owner)*; Fran Ryan *(Miss Goodbody)*.
Music: Denny Vaughn, Milton Greene.

6632   Newhart. (Series; Comedy; CBS; 1982–1990). Richard ("Dick") Loudon, a history buff and "how-to" book author, and his wife, Joanna, own the 200-year-old Stratford Inn at 28 Westbrook Road in River City, Vermont. In addition to running the inn, Dick hosts the TV show *Vermont Today* on WPIV, Channel 8. Dick and Joanna met when they both worked for an ad agency in New York City. Joanna is a real estate broker and hosts a television show called *Your House Is My House* on Channel 8 (later called *Hot Houses*).

George Utley, Dick's handyman, is a member of the Beaver Lodge and invented the board game "Handyman: The Feel Good Game." Stephanie Vanderkellen is Dick and Joanna's maid. She is the spoiled daughter of a wealthy family (who live in Newport) and took the job to experience real life. Stephanie replaced her sister, Leslie Vanderkellen, the original maid, when she left to complete her education at Oxford.

Stephanie is very moody and looks down on people of lower social status. She had a show on WPIV called *Seein' Double* (in which she played twins Jody and Judy Bumpter; Dick Loudon played her father, Henry Bumpter, and the show was produced, written and directed by Stephanie's boyfriend, Michael Harris).

Michael was an executive at WPIV (he produced Dick's show), then a salesman at Circus of Shoes after he was fired for insulting the boss's daughter. He was then a produce clerk at Menke's Market, a mime, and finally a resident of the Pine Valley Psychiatric Hospital. Michael is totally devoted to Stephanie, calls her "Cupcake," "Gumdrop" and Muffin" and constantly showers her with gifts. To give Stephanie even more gifts, Michael created "Cupcake Day," which comes between Valentine's Day and Easter. In 1989 Stephanie became pregnant and gave birth to a girl she and Michael named Baby Stephanie (played at age five by Candy Hutson).

Larry and his two non-speaking brothers, Darryl and Darryl, are rural types who own the local diner, the Minuteman Café. Larry attended the Mount Pilard Technical School; Darryl One was enrolled at Oxford University; and Darryl Two, who majored in royalty, attended Cambridge University under a rowing scholarship. Larry does all the talking for his brothers. When he enters a scene, he starts by saying, "Hello. My name is Larry. This is my brother, Darryl, and this is my other brother, Darryl."

On May 21, 1990, the final first-run episode aired: "The Last Newhart." Mr. Takadachi (Gedde Watanabe) offers each resident of the town one million dollars for their property with a plan of building the 5,000-room Takadachi Hotel and golf course. All but Dick and Joanna sell. Michael and Stephanie, with plans to build "Stefi Land," move to Switzerland; George, who once bought some land when he was drunk to build "Utley Land" (an amusement park for handymen), sells it; and Larry and the Darryls move to Chicago to live with an uncle.

Five years later, the Stratford Inn is on the fourteenth fairway, and it has a Japanese motif. It is also the site for a reunion of the old gang. With the exception of Larry and the Darryls, all have remained the same. Larry is now married to Rhonda (Christie Mellor), Darryl One has wed Sada (Lisa Kudrow) and Darryl Two is married to Zora (Nada Despotovich). The occasion marks the first time the Darryls speak — to yell "Quiet!" at their arguing wives ("They never spoke before," Larry says, "because nothing ever pissed them off before"). As the reunion becomes unruly, Dick decides to leave. He is standing in the doorway when he is hit by a golf ball. He passes out and the screen goes black. A figure is seen in bed. He switches on the light, and we see that it is not Dick Loudon but Dr. Bob Hartley (from

The Bob Newhart Show). His wife, Emily (Suzanne Pleshette), asks what is wrong, and Bob proceeds to tell her about a horrible nightmare in which he was an innkeeper and married to a beautiful blonde; about an heiress for a maid; about three strange brothers....

Apparently, the eight years of *Newhart* were but the one night's dream of Dr. Bob Hartley. Kirk was the original owner of the Minuteman Café; Arthur and Mary are Stephanie's parents; Florence is Joanna's mother; Jim and Chester are Bob's friends. Henry Mancini composed "The Newhart Theme."

Cast: Bob Newhart *(Dick Loudon)*; Mary Frann *(Joanna Loudon)*; Julia Duffy *(Stephanie Vanderkellen)*; Tom Poston *(George Utley)*; Peter Scolari *(Michael Harris)*; William Sanderson *(Larry)*; Tony Papenfuss *(Darryl One)*; John Volstad *(Darryl Two)*; Jennifer Holmes *(Leslie Vanderkellen)*; Steven Kampmann *(Kirk Devane)*; Richard Roat, Jose Ferrer *(Arthur Vanderkellen)*; Priscilla Morrill *(Mary Vanderkellen)*; Zoaunne LeRoy *(Rose; Vanderkellen's maid)*; Peggy McCay *(Florence McKenna)*; Thomas Hills *(Jim Dixon)*; William Lanteau *(Chester Wanamaker)*.

6633   The Newlywed Game. (Series; Game; ABC; Syn.; GSN 1966–). Four husband-and-wife couples compete. The object calls for the wives to predict how their husbands answered certain questions, and vice versa. The team with the most correct answers is the winner and receives merchandise prizes. Seven versions appeared:

1. The Newlywed Game (ABC, 1966–74). **Host:** Bob Eubanks. **Announcer:** Johnny Jacobs.

2. The Newlywed Game (Syn, 1977–80). **Host:** Bob Eubanks. **Announcer:** Johnny Jacobs.

3. The All-New Newlywed Game (Syn., 1985–89). **Host:** Bob Eubanks, Paul Rodriquez. **Announcer:** Bob Hilton, Charlie O'Donnell. **Model:** Shelley Taylor-Morgan.

4. The Newlywed Game (Syn, 1996–97). **Host:** Gary Kroeger. **Announcer:** Ellen K.

5. The Newlywed Game (Syn., 1997–99). **Host:** Bob Eubanks. **Announcer:** John Cramer.

6. The Newlywed Game (GSN, 2009-10). **Host:** Carnie Wilson. **Announcer:** Brad Aldous, Randy West.

7. The Newlywed Game (GSN, 2010–). **Host:** Sherri Shepherd. **Announcer:** Gary Evans.

6634   Newlywed — Nearly Dead. (Series; Reality; Fine Living Network; 2008). Therapist Gary Direnfeld attempts to help newlyweds on the verge of a breakup overcome their differences and rekindle the spark that brought them together in the first place. Gary Direnfeld hosts; Paul Ackerley is the narrator.

6635   Newlyweds: Nick and Jessica. (Series; Reality; MTV; 2003). Jessica Simpson and Nick Lachey have married, They are now newlyweds and cameras follow them virtually everywhere as the pop stars begin their new life together.
Cast: Jessica Simpson, Nick Lachey, Tina Simpson, Joe Simpson, Ashlee Simpson, Drew Lachey, Lea Lachey, Cacee Cobb.

6636   Newman's Drugstore. (Pilot; Comedy; NBC; Aug. 30, 1976). Brooklyn, New York, during the Great Depression is the setting. Charles Newman, a widower and the father of a 12-year-old son (Woody) owns a corner pharmacy called Newman's Drugstore. Charles is overly generous with his hard-luck customers and his efforts to keep his business afloat is the focal point of the proposal.
Cast: Herschel Bernardi *(Charles Newman)*; Michael LeClair *(Woody Newman)*.

6637   Newport Harbor. (Series; Reality; MTV; 2007). *Laguna Beach* spin off that documents (in dramatic soap opera–like style)

the lives of a group of teenagers living in Newport Beach, California (the beachside community in Orange County). Also known as *Newport Harbor: The Real Orange County*. The teens are Clay Adler, Chase Cornwell, Sasha Dunlap, Taylor Geiney, Grant Newman, Chrissy Schwartz, Allie Stockton.

6638   The News. (Pilot; Comedy; Unaired; Produced for ABC in 2007). April Tarnoff is young, pretty, sharp and hard-working. She is a news producer at a local television station who suddenly finds her life changing when she is promoted to executive producer and presented with a whole new world of problems. The proposal was to follow April as she struggles to get the station's live newscasts on the air and deal with a staff of on-air reporters who are anything but conventional (from Judd, a reporter who mocks stories; Gretchen, the gorgeous reporter who is seeking the anchor seat; Terry, the aging reporter who fears losing her looks; and Harvey, the anchor who stages stories by becoming a part of them).
    Cast: Rachel Boston *(April Tarnoff)*; Barry Bostwick *(Harvey Deegan)*; Amy Yasbeck *(Terry Lynn Collins)*; Jay Harrington *(Judd Brinkmeyer)*; Julie Gonzalo *(Gretchen Holt)*; Kristy Wu *(Darla)*; Andre Holland *(Deshawn Burkett)*.

6639   The News Is the News. (Series; Comedy; NBC; 1983). A live program of skits that poke fun at TV newscasters and news programs.
    Newscasters: Michael Davis, Simon Jones, Charlotte Moore, Lynne Thigpen, Trey Wilson.
    London Correspondent: Michael Palin. **Announcer:** Karen Dale. **Music:** Bob Mounsey.

6640   News Radio. (Series; Comedy; NBC; 1995–1999). WNYX, 585 on the Am dial, is an all news radio station located in the Criterion Building on 58th Street in Manhattan. Dave Nelson is its young director and his efforts to curtail the antics of his staff and run the station is the focal point of stories. Although played for laughs, the program does present a look at the office politics and relationships in a radio station. Other regulars are newscasters Matthew Brockwell, Bill McNeal, Lisa Miller, Max Lewis and Catherine Duke; Beth, Dave's secretary; Joe, the electrician. Bill McNeal is also called Bill McIntire.
    Cast: Dave Foley *(Dave Nelson)*; Phil Hartman *(Bill McNeal)*; Maura Tierney *(Lisa Miller)*; Ella Joyce *(Catherine Duke; pilot)*; Khandi Alexander *(Catherine Duke; series)*; Andy Dick *(Matthew Brockwell)*; Vicki Lewis *(Beth)*; Jon Lovitz *(Max Lewis)*; Stephen Root *(Jimmy James)*; Joe Rogan *(Joe Garrelli)*.

6641   News to Me. (Pilot; Comedy; Unaired; Produced for ABC in 2004). *American Weekly* is the largest selling magazine in the U.S. despite its dull writing and non-sensational stories. Joel Stein, a British journalist is hired to breathe some new life into the magazine and the proposal was to follow Joel as he faces resentment from staffers while trying to implement a new, modern approach for the magazine.
    Cast: Colin Hanks *(Joel Stein)*; Andrea Anders *(Emma Leeds)*; David Hasselhoff *(Stryker Langley)*; Sharon Lawrence *(J.D. Cooper)*; Sheryl Lee Ralph *(Cicely Dupree)*; Roger Rees *(Marshall Cahill)*.

6642   Newsstand Theater. (Series; Anthology; ABC; 1952). Adaptations of short stories produced by Wilbur Stark.

6643   The Newz. (Series; Comedy; MTV; 1999–2002). Comedy skits that spoof everything from news events and political figures to movies and television shows.
    Cast: Mystro Clark, Tommy Blaze, Nancy Sullivan, Lou Thornton, Stan Quash, Dan O'Connor, Deborah Magdalena, Brad Sherwood.

6644   The Next Action Star. (Series; Reality; NBC; 2004). A search to find the next male and female action star from a group of gutsy contenders (not afraid of explosions, jumping off buildings, dodging cars, etc.). Each is competing for the opportunity of starring in the made-for-TV action film *Bet Your Life* (to be directed by action movie director Joe Silver). Each of the participants must perform stunts and are judged by a panel for their authenticity. Each of the fourteen participants (seven men, seven women) receives six weeks of training (including acting and weapons precaution) before actually performing stunts. At the end of the session, they are put through their paces and judged on an acting sequence and a stunt scene. The least satisfactory performers are eliminated on a weekly basis by the judges. The two remaining players (one male, one female) receive the co-starring movie roles. Tina Malave hosts. Sean Carrigan and Corinne Van Ryck de Groot won.

6645   The Next Best Thing: Who Is the Greatest Celebrity Impersonator? (Series; Reality; ABC; 2007). A search for "The world's greatest celebrity impersonator." Celebrity look-alikes, chosen from open auditions, appear before a panel of three judges. The impersonator must provide three aspects in order to become a finalist: the look, the voice and the performance. Impersonators who fail in any aspect (no matter how much they resemble the celebrity) are sent home. When the finalists are chosen (the best from auditions across the country) they perform again in California — this time to be judged by viewers, whose call-in votes determine who goes and who stays. The last remaining impersonator is crowned "The World's Greatest Celebrity Impersonator." Michele Merkin hosts; Elon Gold, Lisa Ann Walter and Jeffrey Ross are the judges.

6646   The Next Food Network Star. (Series; Reality; Food Network; 2005–). Ten chefs compete in various cooking challenges for the opportunity to become the network's next star and host of his or her own cooking series. The contestants are judged by Bob Tuschman, the senior vice president of programming and production and Susie Fogelson, vice president of marketing and brand strategy, and Food Network host Bobby Flan. The executive's decision are final as they have a stake in the winner's show. Marc Summers and Bobby Flay host.

6647   The Next Great American Band. (Series; Reality; Fox; 2007). An attempt to find "the next great American band." Following programs dedicated to highlighting the good and bad to downright awful bands that auditioned, the series becomes serious and focuses on the best musicians from the auditions, Each week the bands perform and each week the home audience votes via toll free numbers, for the bands they feel should advance. Each week the band with the lowest call-in-votes is eliminated. The one band that proves to be a favorite with viewers receives a recording contract. Dominic Bowden hosts; Sheila E., Ian Dickson and John Rzeznik are the judges.

6648   The Next Iron Chef. (Series; Reality; Food Network; 2007–). Ten professional chefs compete in various food preparation challenges in the Kitchen Stadium for the culinary title "Iron Chef." Alton Brown hosts.

6649   The Next Step Beyond. (Series; Anthology; Syn.; 1978). John Newland returns to host an updated version of his original series, *One Step Beyond* that continues to present true stories of psychic happenings.

6650   *Ni Hao, Kai-Lan.* (Series; Cartoon; Nick; 2008). An attempt to introduce children to the Chinese culture and the Mandarin language through Kai-Lan Chow, a pre-schooler who shares colorful adventures and story telling with other children her age. The title translates as "Hello, Kai-Lan.

Voice Cast: Jade-Lianna Gao Jian Peters *(Kai-Lan Chow)*; Beverly Duan *(Lulu)*; Angie Wu *(Ho Ho)*; Laura Marano *(Mei Mei)*; Zachary Gordon *(San San)*; Clem Cheung *(Ye Ye)*; Tommy Nightingale *(Fluffy)*; Jack Samson *(Rintoo)*.

6651   *Nice Girls Don't Get the Corner Office.* (Pilot; Comedy; Unaired; Produced for ABC in 2007). Masterlord Realty is a high-end corporate real estate firm that employs Angela, a bright and competent girl who is totally dedicated to her job. Angela has dreams of becoming a vice president but she is too nice — not the kind of cutthroat needed to advance within the company. Angela's dreams are shattered when charismatic co-worker Deef tells her being nice will get her nowhere. But Angela is not defeated. She befriends a new secretary, Joy, an older woman who knows how to rise within the ranks of a company. The proposal was to follow Angela and Joy as they work together with Angela having a very difficult time trying to be someone she is not (and Joy trying to resist Angela's efforts to make her nice).

Cast: Jayma Mays *(Angela)*; Jane Curtin *(Joy)*; Flex Alexander *(Deef)*; Caroline Chikezie *(Rachel)*; Kathryn Hahn *(Price)*; Gregory Itzin *(Gary Stone)*.

6652   *Nichols.* (Series; Comedy; NBC; 1971-1972). Nichols, Arizona, in 1914 is the setting. A former cavalry officer called only Nichols returns to his hometown after an 18 year absence. He discovers that the town, which was founded by his parents, no longer belongs to him; it has been taken from his late mother by two mean brothers named Scully One and Scully Two. With no plans to stay in town, Nichols decides to drown his sorrows. At the Salter House Bar, Nichols begins to talk with Ruth, the barmaid. When a man named Ketcham thinks Nichols is flirting with Ruth (whom he considers his girlfriend), a fight breaks out. Nichols is arrested and held responsible for $300 in damages. When Sara ("Ma") Ketcham, Ketcham's mother and the town's self-appointed law, finds that Nichols cannot pay what he owes, she sentences him to six months' duty as sheriff. Though reluctant, Nichols becomes the sheriff—"But don't let that worry you, it's only a sideline." His real genius, though, is at the con — which he uses to outwit the bad guys and help maintain the peace.

Nichols is assisted by "Mitch" Mitchell, a deputy who reports directly to Sara and obeys her every command. Mitch has a dog named Slump.

The series, which was expected to be renewed, was not, and the last episode introduced a more courageous and forceful hero named Jim Nichols, Nichols's twin brother. When Nichols attempts to break up a barroom brawl, he is killed. Several days later, Jim arrives in town. After learning what has happened, he apprehends his brother's killer. Sara offers him the job of sheriff, but Jim refuses. In a substituted ending, Jim leaves town, never to return.

Cast: James Garner *(Nichols/Jim Nichols)*; Margot Kidder *(Ruth)*; John Beck *(Ketcham)*; Neva Patterson *(Sara "Ma" Ketcham)*; Stuart Margolin *(Mitchell)*; John Harding *(Salter)*; Paul Hampton *(Johnson)*; Alice Ghostley *(Bertha)*; Richard Bull *(Judge Thatcher)*; M. Emmet Walsh *(Gabe)*; John Quade *(Scully One)*; Jesse Wayne *(Scully Two)*.

6653   *Nichols and Dymes.* (Pilot; Crime Drama; NBC; Oct. 7, 1981). When local law enforcement agencies need help they turn to the federal government. When such is the case, Bureau Section Chief Whitney assigns his two best agents — Buck Nichols and Willy Dymes — to resolve the situation. The proposal was to relate their lighthearted exploits as the fun-loving Nichols and Dymes go undercover and use unconventional methods to get the job done ("What the boss don't know won't hurt him").

Cast: Rocky Bauer *(Buck Nichols)*; Robin Strand *(Willy Dymes)*; George McDaniel *(Chief Whitney)*.

6654   *Nick and Hillary.* (Series; Comedy; NBC; 1989). A revised version of *Tattinger's* (about Nick Tattinger and his efforts to run a swanky restaurant called Tattinger's). When Nick learns that his accountant made off with all his money, he leaves the restaurant in his ex-wife, Hillary's hands so he can try to find the accountant. After an unsuccessful search, Nick returns to New York to find that Hillary has turned Tattinger's into a jazzed-up, now successful eatery. Nick's mishaps as he and Hillary operate the restaurant are the focal point of stories. Other regulars are Nina and Winifred, Nick's daughters; Sid, the bartender; Sheila, the chef; Spin, the maitre d'; and Louis, a waiter.

Cast: Stephen Collins *(Nick Tattinger)*; Blythe Danner *(Hillary Tattinger)*; Patricia Colinhan *(Nina Tattinger)*; Jessica Prunell *(Winifred Tattinger)*; Jerry Stiller *(Sid Wilbur)*; Mary Beth Hurt *(Sheila Brady)*; Chris Elliott *(Spin)*; Roderick Cook *(Louis)*.

6655   *Nick and Nora.* (Pilot; Mystery; ABC; Mar. 4, 1975). Nick and Nora Charles are a sophisticated married couple who have a knack (especially Nora) for stumbling upon crimes. Nick was a former editor of crime books and Nora, a socialite. Nora, however, also believes she has the instincts of a detective and relishes in the fact that she and Nick will be working on a case. The proposal, based on the characters created by Dashiell Hammett, was to relate their efforts to solve crimes (usually murder). William Powell and Myrna Loy first portrayed Nick and Nora Charles in a series of theatrical films beginning in 1934. On television (NBC, 1957–59) Peter Lawford and Phyllis Kirk portrayed Nick and Nora Charles.

Cast: Craig Stevens *(Nick Charles)*; Jo Ann Pflug *(Nora Charles)*.

6656   *Nick and Shelly.* (Pilot; Crime Drama; Unaired; Produced for Lifetime in 2003). Nick and Shelly are divorced, but still partners in their private detective firm. Shelly is brilliant and has the instincts of Sherlock Holmes; Nick is more the Mike Hammer type of detective, an eye for the ladies and quick with his fists. The proposal was to follow Nick and Shelly as they combine their unique skills to solve cases.

Cast: Adrian Pasdar *(Nick)*; Julie Warner *(Shelly)*.

6657   *Nick and the Dobermans.* (Pilot; Crime Drama; NBC; April 25, 1980). Duke, Erskine and Pee Wee are three smart Doberman Pinschers owned by Nick Luchese, a New York–based private detective who inherited them from a late carnival performer. The proposal, a revised version of *Alex and the Doberman Gang* was to relate Nick's efforts to solve crimes with the assist of the dogs.

Cast: Michael Nouri *(Nick Luchese)*; Robert Davi *(Lt. Anthony Elbone)*.

6658   *Nick Cannon's Star Camp.* (Series; Reality; Internet; 2007). A Nickelodeon-produced Internet series that attempts to create a group of talented children and turn them into "multimedia mega stars." Ten children who possess various musical abilities (from singing, rapping and dancing) are trained (with the help of music industry singers, musicians and producers) to become "the next big stars." Nick Cannon hosts.

6659   *Nick Derringer, P.I.* (Pilot; Comical Crime Drama; ABC; May 4 and 11, 1988). Nicholas Derringer, who prefers the more rugged Nick, is four feet tall. He runs a successful private detective company in San Francisco and his motto is "No Case Too Small." The proposal, a spin off from *Hooperman* was to relate Nick's efforts to serve clientele that respect his professional skill.

Cast: David Rappaport (*Nick Derringer*); Laura Bassett (*Yolanda, his secretary*).

6660   *Nick Freno: Licensed Teacher.* (Series; Comedy; WB; 1996–1998). Nick Freno is an out-of-work actor who takes a job as a substitute English teacher to pay the bills. He first works at the Gerald R. Ford Middle School (1996-97) then at the Gerald R. Ford High School (1997-98). Kurt Fust is the vice principal at the middle school; Dr. Katherine Emerson, author of the book *School of Thought* is the principal at the high school.

Stories follow Nick as he tries to make a difference in the lives of his students. Nick is a natural comedian and has an outrageous sense of humor — assets he uses to deal with students who think they know more than he does.

Other regulars are Mitch "Mezz" Crosby, a science teacher who also hosts a live TV show on WWEN-TV called *Science with Mitch Crosby;* teachers Al Yaroker, Mrs. Fox and Elana Lewis; and the students: Sarah, Davey, Orlando, Jordan, Anna Marie, Tyler, Sophia, Tasha and Jared.

Cast: Mitch Mullany (*Nick Freno*); Stuart Pankin (*Kurt Fust*); Jane Sibbett (*Katherine Emerson*); Portia de Rossi (*Elana Lewis*); Charles Cyphers (*Al Yaroker*); Estelle Harris (*Mrs. Fox*); Mila Kunis (*Anna Marie Del Bruno*); Christina Vidal (*Sophia Del Bruno*); Malinda Williams (*Tasha*); Cara DeLizia (*Sarah*); Kyle Gibson (*Davey*); Jonathan Hernandez (*Orlando Diaz*); Blake Heron (*Jordan*); Andrew Levitas (*Marco*); Arjay Smith (*Jared*).

6661   *Nick Knight.* (Pilot; Crime Drama; CBS; Aug. 20, 1989). Many years ago a man named Nicholas wished for immortality. A master vampire named LaCroix arranged for Nicholas to have his wish by making him a creature of the night who must live on human blood. But Nicholas was unable to kill anyone and turned his back on vampirism — making an enemy of LaCroix but using his powers to help good defeat evil. It is now 1989. Nick Knight (the name Nicholas has assumed) is a homicide detective who works the night shift with his obnoxious partner, Don Schanke (who is unaware that Nick is a vampire). The proposal was to relate Nick's efforts to apprehend criminals via his special powers: super strength, the ability to fly (as a bat), super sensitive vision and hearing and his ability to work well at night. Other regulars are Janette, the beautiful vampire from Nick's past; and Dr. Jack Brittington, the police coroner who knows Nick's secret and is trying to develop an artificial blood that can help cure him. With changes, the idea sold as *Forever Night* (see entry).

Cast: Rick Springfield (*Nick Knight*); John Kapelos (*Don Schanke*); Cec Verrell (*Janette*); Michael Nader (*LaCroix*); Robert Harper (*Dr. Jack Brittington*).

6662   *Nick Swardson's Present Time.* (Series; Comedy; Comedy Central; 2010). Skits that satirize everyday life with Nick Swardson as the host and Valorie Hubbard and Gregory Allen Gabroy as regulars.

6663   *Night Calls.* (Series; Erotica; Playboy; 1995–). Live call-in program wherein female hosts answer viewers sexually based questions. During the program's run, two spin offs aired: *Night Call 411* (2000–05) which featured sex advice and a "net nympho" who read e-mails submitted by viewers; and *Night Calls Hot Line* (2004-05) which also presented sexual advice. Adult film stars Christy Canyon and Ginger Lynn host Night Calls on Playboy Radio.

Night Calls Host: Juli Ashton, Doria Rone, Tiffany Graneth, Jesse Jane, Kristen Price. **Night Calls 411 Host:** Crystal Knight, Flower Edwards. **Net Nympho:** Tera Patrick, Kitana Baker, Nicole Oring. **Night Calls Hot Line Host:** Ashley Blue, Nautica Thorn, Ann-Marie.

6664   *Night Club Review.* (Experimental; Variety; NBC; June 9, 1939). Performances by night club and vaudeville artists: Frank and Jean Huber (comedy drunks), Bob Nellor (a ventriloquist), Charles Carrer (a juggler), Ella Logan (singer), Buck and Bubbles (black comedians), Joe Jackson, Jr. (comical bike rider) and the California Jitterbugs.

6665   *Night Court.* (Series; Drama; Syn.; 1965). Dramatizations based on the files of New York and Los Angeles Night Court hearings.

Cast: Jay Jostyn (*Judge*); Sandy Spillman (*Public Defender*); Barney Biro (*Public Defender*).

6666   *Night Court.* (Series; Comedy; NBC; 1984–1992). The Manhattan Criminal Courts Building in New York City is the setting for a comical look at life inside the night court of arraignment judge Harold T. ("Harry") Stone. The building is also called the Municipal Court House, and Harry's sessions are held on the eighteenth floor in Room 808 (1808 in some episodes).

Harry attended East Chesapeake State College and attempted to break into show business as a magician. His idol is singer Mel Tormé (he owns every record Mel ever made and has decided to marry the first girl who is impressed by that). Harry's inability to meet Mel under normal circumstances is a recurring gimmick of the program.

Harry, voted "Most Fascinating Judge in New York" by the Empire Magicians' Society, processes 12 percent fewer cases than any other judge in his position (the reason: he talks to defendants and lectures them). Harry's true love is magic: his hero is Harry Houdini and he teaches law classes at the Ed Koch Community College (Ed Koch is the former mayor of New York). Harry is also famous for his "$55 and time served" sentences.

Christine Sullivan is the legal aid attorney. She was born in the small town of North Tonawanda near Buffalo, New York. At age 19 she was a junior in Buffalo State College and majored in psychology (she is now an expert on depression). Christine is very beautiful and always fashionably dressed. She is a member of "Ha Ha" (Happy Alone, Happy Adults; their slogan is "Happy to Be Happy") and says, "The most artistic people I get as clients are hookers with makeup skills." In 1990 Christine had a one night stand with an undercover cop named Tony Juliano (Ray Abruzzo). She became pregnant and married Tony in an Italian restaurant. Tony left the following day to track down a criminal in Colombia. In the episode of May 2, 1990, Christine becomes trapped in an elevator and gives birth to a boy (whom she names Charles Otis). She and Tony divorced in the episode of Feb. 6, 1991. In the episode of Feb. 12, 1992 Christine ran for congresswoman of the 13th District; she was elected to Congress in the final first-run episode (May 13, 1992) and moved to Washington, D.C., to begin her new career.

Reinhold Fielding Elmore (he assumed the name Dan Fielding when he started school) was born in Paris, Louisiana. His parents were rural, and he lived with pigs in his room. He was six before he realized he wasn't related to them. Dan, the prosecuting attorney, is a ladies' man, has stock in a company called the Fletko Corporation (which is famous for tearing down landmarks) and he is the overseer of the Phil Foundation, a charity that supports needy causes. Dan hosted a television show called *In Your Face* (a putdown show) and left his job in the last episode to pursue the woman of his dreams — Christine — in Washington.

On a judicial system I.Q. test, bailiff Bull Shannon scored 181; despite this, his friends still think he is "dumber than dirt." His real first name is Nostradamus; he got the name Bull from his mother (she said "Bull" when she found out she was pregnant). Because Christine is so sweet and kind to Bull, he calls her "a lily pad in a pond full of sludge." Bull is very devoted to Harry — "I'd swallow molten lava for that man. Fortunately, he never asked me." He also says people mistake his humor for a rare pituitary disease. In the episode of Nov. 20, 1991 Bull married Wanda (Cathy Appleby) on the roof of the courthouse. In the last episode, Bull is taken to the planet Jupiter by two aliens to become somebody — "The man who can reach the items on our top shelves."

Mac Robinson is the court clerk. He is married to a pretty Vietnamese women named Quon Le Dac, who works as a checker at the Vegetable Mart. Mac met Quon Le in Vietnam during the war. She was only 12 years old and fell in love with him when he helped her family overcome the ravages of recent bombings. In 1985 Quon Le left Vietnam when the new regime took over and came to New York to find Mac. Mac married her in an attempt to keep her in the United States.

Rosalind ("Roz") Russell is a bailiff and earns $410 a week. Before her current job Roz was a stewardess for Paramus Airlines (it was here that she found her goal in life "was to kick butt"; a group of annoying passengers made her "see the light").

Lana Wagner was the original court clerk; she was replaced by Charli Tracy; Mac Robinson then replaced Charli.

In the original pilot, Gail Strickland played Sheila Gardner, the public defender. Sheila was replaced by Liz Williams. Wilhelmina ("Billie") Young replaced Liz. Mary replaced Billie and Christine replaced Mary as the legal aid lawyer.

Selma Hacker and Florence Kleiner were the female bailiffs before Roz. Lisette is the pretty, curly haired blonde court stenographer. She is a sweet girl who knits sweaters for birds and gets a kick out of folding socks. Craven is the sleazy court reporter for the New York *Herald.*

Cast: Harry Anderson (*Harry T. Stone*); Markie Post (*Christine Sullivan*); Richard Moll (*Bull*); John Larroquette (*Dan Fielding*); Charles Robinson (*Mac Robinson*); Marsha Warfield (*Roz Russell*); Joleen Lutz (*Lisette Hocheiser*); Gail Strickland (*Sheila Gardner*); Selma Diamond (*Selma Hacker*); Paula Kelly (*Liz Williams*); D.D. Howard (*Charli Tracy*); Ellen Foley (*Billie Young*); Terry Kiser (*Al Craven*); Denice Kumagai (*Quon Le*).

6667   *Night Editor.* (Series; Anthology; DuMont; 1954). The work of newspapermen as seen through the eyes of Hal Burdick, the night editor of a newspaper. Irving Mansfield and Ward Byron are the producers.

Host-Narrator: Hal Burdick.

6668   *Night Gallery.* (Series; Anthology; NBC; 1971–1973). Each episode opens with the host, situated in an art gallery, approaching a painting and explaining its significance to the audience. A story, usually with supernatural overtones, is then presented as people face the horrifying confrontation between nightmare and reality. Originally broadcast as a segment of *Four-in-One* and also known as *Rod Serling's Night Gallery.*

Host: Rod Serling.

6669   *Night Games.* (Series; Game; CBS; 1991). Three women and three men appear on stage in their pajamas. In round one each of the girls has to answer a personal question. Her answer is rated from one to ten by the remaining five players. Round two has the men each answering a personal question. Rounds Three and Four are worth from one to twenty points and the questions explore creativity and sensuality (Rounds One and Two deal with openness and honesty). The player with the highest score is the winner. He or she then selects the player he or she would most like for a date.

Host: Jeff Masters. **Music:** Scott Harper.

6670   *Night Heat.* (Series; Crime Drama; CBS; 1985). Tom Kirkwood is a reporter for a newspaper called *The Eagle* who works closely with the detectives of the Midtown South Police Station of the Toronto, Canada, Police Department. Tom writes the column "Night Heat" and through his eyes, as he follows the detectives on and off the job, the rewards, frustrations and comradeship of the detectives who work the night beat are seen. In addition to the detectives listed in the cast, other regulars are Nicole, the owner of the local hangout, Nicole's Bar; Helen Hogan, the wife of Lieutenant Bob Hogan; Bob Hogan, Jr., Bob's son; and Dorothy Fredericks, the prosecuting attorney. B.J. Cook performs the theme, "Night Heat."

Cast: Allan Royal (*Tom Kirkwood*); Jeff Wincott (*Det. Frank Giambone*); Scott Hylands (*Det. Kevin O'Brien*); Lynda Mason Green (*Det. Florence "Fleece" Toland*); Wendy Crewson (*Dorothy Fredericks*); Sean McCann (*Lt. Bob Hogan*); Stephen Mendel (*Det. Freddie Carson*); Eugene Clark (*Det. Colby Burns*); Susan Hogan (*Nicole*); Debra Grover (*Off. Elaine Jeffers*); Maxine Miller (*Helen Hogan*); Louise Vallance (*Off. Stephanie Brody*); Robert McClure (*Robert Hogan, Jr.*).

6671   *Night Partners.* (Pilot; Crime Drama; CBS; Oct. 11, 1983). Feeling the need to help the police, two women (Elizabeth and Lauren) form a police auxiliary to aid the victims of violent crimes. Elizabeth is the wife of a police officer (Glen) and the mother of two children (Francine and Sam); Lauren is a divorced secretary and the mother of a son (Josh). The proposal was to relate Elizabeth and Lauren's experiences as they patrol the night beat (5:30 P.M. to 1:00 A.M.) under the code name Crisis One. Other regulars are Police Chief John Wilson and Detective Roy Henderson.

Cast: Yvette Mimieux (*Elizabeth McGuire*); Diana Canova (*Lauren Hensley*); Arlen Dean Snyder (*Glen McGuire*); Tricia Cast (*Francine McGuire*); Patrick Brennan (*Sam McGuire*); Michael Evans (*John Hensley*); Larry Linville (*John Wilson*); Michael Cavanaugh (*Roy Henderson*).

6672   *Night Prowl.* (Pilot; Drama; Syn.; Mar. 1958). Dick Richards is a former attorney who gave up his successful practice to become the editor of a music magazine called *Take 5.* Dick prowls from cafe to cafe in New York City meeting the stars of today and trying to pick the stars of tomorrow. The proposal was to follow Dick's experiences when his work involves him with shady characters — and the police, especially his friend, Lieutenant Pete Lonigan, whom he helps solve crimes. Aired on *Studio '57* under the title *Take 5.*

Cast: Dennis O'Keefe (*Dick Richards*); Jack Straw (*Pete Lonigan*).

6673   *The Night Rider.* (Pilot; Western; Unaired; Produced in 1962). It is the 1860s and Johnny Laredo is a gunfighter who travels at night to avoid those seeking him (people out for revenge; lawmen). Johnny was born in Wyoming and is wanted for a series of gunfight related killings. With a bounty on him, he travels across the western frontier, helping people where he can but seeking an opportunity for redemption.

Cast: Johnny Cash (*Johnny Laredo*).

6674   *The Night Rider.* (Pilot; Adventure; ABC; May 11, 1979). Shortly after the murder of his parents (Marie and Jim Hollister) in New Orleans, a wealthy British woman (Lady Earl) adopts the surviving son (Charles) and takes him home to England with her. Charles is raised and educated in the finest schools and eventually becomes Sir Thomas Earl. But the memories of the past still haunt him. With a plan to avenge his parents' deaths, Sir Thomas returns to the home of his birth (New Orleans, now the 1870s). He poses as a dandy by day but becomes the mysterious Night Rider by night — a daring and powerful figure who avenges the wrongs done to innocent people. The proposal was to relate his exploits.

Cast: David Selby *(Sir Thomas Earl)*; Percy Rodrigues *(Robert, his friend)*.

6675   *Night Rose.* (Pilot; Anthology; Syn.; Nov. 2, 1987). An proposed series of weekly thrillers. The pilot presentation, titled "Akhbar's Daughter," tells of a young man (Bill) and his involvement with the mysterious daughter (Kara) of a wealthy Arabian (Akhbar) — a girl who is icy by day and passionate by night.

Cast: Christopher Atkins *(Bill Bitterman)*; Roya Megnot *(Kara)*; Ed Setrakian *(Akhbar)*.

6676   *Night Stalker.* (Series; Crime Drama; ABC 1974–1975). The shortened title for the Darren McGavin series *Kolchak: The Night Stalker.* See this title for information.

6677   *Night Stalker.* (Series; Crime Drama; ABC; 2005). A remake of the 1970s cult classic *Kolchak: The Night Stalker.* Carl Kolchak is a seasoned crime reporter for the Los Angeles *Beacon.* He previously worked in Las Vegas and has been with the *Beacon* for 18 months when the series begins. Carl also has a personal vendetta to settle: find and kill the supernatural creature that killed his wife and caused him to have a mental breakdown and spend six months in a psychiatric ward. Carl believes creatures of the supernatural exist. Since the death of his wife, he now associates the unnatural with the various crimes he investigates (but the execution of such stories pales in comparison to the suspenseful presentation of the original series). Complicating Carl's efforts to find his wife's killer are the FBI — who consider Carl the prime suspect but can't prove it (Carl and his wife were in a car when an unknown being with considerable fur and sharp fangs, crashed through their windshield. It killed Carl's wife and left him with a huge chip on his shoulder; in turn, Carl is rarely nice to anyone).

Other regulars are Perri Reed, the senior reporter who works with Carl; Tony Vincenzo, the editor; and Jain McManus, the photographer who accompanies Carl and Perri.

Cast: Stuart Townsend *(Carl Kolchak)*; Gabrielle Union *(Perri Reed)*; Cotter Smith *(Tony Vincenzo)*; Eric Jungmann *(Jain McManus)*.

6678   *Night Stand with Dick Dietrick.* (Series; Satire; Syn.; 1995). A spoof of talk programs with a dim-witted, self-absorbed, obnoxious host (Dick Dietrick) and comical discussions on topical issues (such as sex addicts with Dick setting two such people up on a date; a salute to the post office); actors play the guests brought on to discuss topics.

Host: Timothy Stack as Dick Dietrick. **Regulars:** Lynne Marie Stewart, Robert Alan Beuth, Tim Silva, Christopher Darga, Jordana Capra. **Music:** Fred Lapides.

6679   *Night Talk with Jane Whitney.* (Pilot; Talk; Unaired; Produced for Syndication in 1992). A proposed late night talk show that was to focus on a specific topic each day (for example, the human stories behind the headlines; the issues and concerns of the working man; believable stories about personal relationships).

Host: Jane Whitney.

6680   *Night Visions.* (Series; Anthology; Fox; 2001). Dramas, some with supernatural overtones, that focus on people who are sud-

denly confronted with unexpected (and sometimes) perilous situations.

Host: Henry Rollins.

6681   *The Nightingales.* (Pilot; Crime Drama; NBC; May 19, 1979). As part of an experiment to team female officers as patrol car partners, the L.A.P.D. launches a program called the Nightingales and selects two beautiful undercover cops (Jenny and Cotton) to become the first team. The proposal was to relate Jenny and Cotton's exploits as they patrol the Hollywood beat at night. Other regulars are Big Duane, Jerry and Cotton's contact at Radio Station KIRA; and Sergeant Donovan, their superior.

Cast: Marcia Strassman *(Jenny Palmermo)*; Colette Blonigan *(Cotton Gardner)*; James Spinks *(Big Duane)*; Richard Hatch *(Sergeant Donovan)*.

6682   *Nightingales.* (Series; Drama; NBC; 1989). Nightingale House is a dorm for student nurses in Los Angeles. It has 20 rooms and two clothes dryers. Christine Broderick, the director of student nursing at Wilshire Memorial Hospital, is the den mother to the featured nurses: Samantha ("Sam") Sullivan, Allyson Yates, Bridget Loring, Becky Grainger and Yolonda ("Yoyo") Puente.

Christine attended the Wellington School of Nursing in 1968; she took the job as den mother when the previous woman "took a job up north and suddenly left." At Wilshire Memorial, a teaching hospital, Christine has office 728. Samantha, who teaches "Cardio Funk" (aerobics) at the Health Club, was an alcoholic who lost custody of her daughter, Megan, to her mother, Effie Gardner; Sam is now waging a court battle to regain custody of Megan. Bridget is in the witness protection program (she witnessed a murder and has been given a new identity). Room 124 is the nurses' lounge at the hospital. The program has many "lingerie scenes." (Each episode features some or all the student nurses in their bras and panties. The scenes, which included some in the opening theme, were blasted by critics and eventually caused the show's cancellation when it became "to hot to handle.")

Dr. Paul Petrillo is Christine's ex-husband; Dr. Garrett Braden is head of the hospital; and Charlene Chasen is the "evil" doctor who opposed Christine. In the original pilot film (June 27, 1988), Mimi Kuzak played Liz McCarren, the den mother.

Cast: Suzanne Pleshette *(Christine Broderick)*; Chelsea Field *(Samantha Sullivan)*; Kim Ulrich *(Allyson Yates)*; Susan Walters *(Bridget Loring)*; Kristy Swanson *(Becky Grainger)*; Roxann Briggs *(Yolonda Puente)*; Taylor Fry *(Megan)*; Jennifer Rhodes *(Effie Gardner)*; Gil Gerard *(Paul Petrillo)*; Barry Newman *(Garrett Braden)*; Doran Clark *(Charlene Chasen)*.

6683   *NightMan.* (Series; Adventure; Syn.; 1997–1999). Jonathan Dominus, better known as Johnny Domino, is a musician who plays sax at the House of Soul, a jazz club in Bay City.

Johnny is the son of ex cop Frank Dominus and secretly NightMan, a daring crusader who helps the police, especially Lieutenant Brianni Branca, capture felons.

Johnny's life changed one day when a sudden, freak storm erupted and engulfed him in a strange light that endowed him with the ability to hear evil (the crimes others are planning to commit). Johnny's first such "hearing " is that of a terrorist planning to bomb a communications peace conference.

Johnny, scheduled to play at the conference, alerts authorities about a potential problem, but is too late: a bomb explodes and Johnny takes the full impact of the explosion. Doctors are amazed that he is not only alive, but apparently unhurt. At Bay City Hospital, Johnny meets Raleigh Jordan, a U.S. government scientist who developed a military defense system being sought by the enemy. Because Johnny saved Raleigh's life at the conference (by clearing people out before the bomb exploded), the terrorists are now seeking to kill both Raleigh and Johnny. At a warehouse, Raleigh shows Johnny the reason why he is being sought: for a defense system of the future that will be sold to the highest bidder. These include a bulletproof suit with advanced stealth capabilities, a lens with targeting scanners, a laser beam, and an antigravity belt. As they speak, terrorists approach the warehouse. Johnny and Raleigh escape, undetected, by using what will be called the NightMan gear, to fly over their heads.

Johnny lives at 1943 Ward Court in an apartment over the House of Soul. This becomes his and Raleigh's base of operations (later episodes find Raleigh as the club's manager). NightMan, called "Evil's worst nightmare," is said to be "tuned to the frequency of evil" and "hunts the evil that walks in the dark." To make it appear that Johnny and NightMan are two distinct people, Raleigh has devised a special holographic image that projects a 3-D image of Johnny performing on stage at the House of Soul. This gives Johnny the perfect cover to convince everyone he is not NightMan.

Brianni, the daughter of an army master sergeant, has a photographic memory (when it comes to criminal case details) and suspects Johnny is NightMan but can't prove it. Johnny's greatest enemy is Kieran Keyes, an evil billionaire who runs the Keyzar Corporation, a computer software company he uses as a front for his plans to control the world.

Helping NightMan on occasion is Laurie Jarvis, an ex-cop Johnny calls "NightWoman." Laurie suffered a spinal injury that crippled her. After experimental spinal surgery at the Leander Institute in Switzerland and with the aid of an energizer suit she developed, Laurie can walk. The suit also gives her special powers to battle evil. Laurie uses her costume to help her as a detective for her company, Woman Trouble ("I help women in trouble"). Based on the comic book of the same name.

Cast: Matt McColm (*Jonathan Dominus*); Earl Holliman (*Frank Dominus*); Jayne Heitmeyer (*Brianna Branca*); Derek Webster, Derwin Jordan (*Raleigh Jordan*); Kim Coates (*Kieran Keyes*); Deanna Milligan (*Laurie Jarvis*).

6684 *Nightmare.* (Series; Anthology; Syn.; 1958). Dramatizations that depict the plight of people who are suddenly involved in unexpected and perilous situations.

6685 *Nightmare Cafe.* (Series; Drama; NBC; 1992). The All Night Café is located near the docks in Los Angeles. The café has strange powers: it gives people a second chance at life, the opportunity to go back and relive a crucial moment that can alter their future existence. A mysterious man named Blackie operates the café "for a higher authority." Fay Peronovick is the waitress, and Frank Novak is the cook. (The café needed a new waitress and cook; Fay and Frank's lives ended in the waters overlooking the café; Fay, when she was jilted and committed suicide; Frank, when he stumbled upon toxic waste polluters. Both were given a second chance to right their wrongs—by working at the café and helping other people through personal crises.)

Blackie seems sinister (possibly a messenger of the devil) and appears to delight in the circumstances that cause a person's downfall (he views second chance lives via a special television set in the café; he can also send Fay or Frank into that person's life to help). Blackie calls Fay "Faysie." Fay was born in Tulsa, and her middle name is Petula; she lived at 341 Gateway. Penny Fuller appeared as her mother, Victoria, and Molly Parker was Fay's sister, Ivy. J. Peter Robinson composed the "Nightmare Café Theme."

Cast: Robert Englund (*Blackie*); Lindsay Frost (*Fay Pernovick*); Jack Coleman (*Frank Novak*).

6686 *Nightmare Classics.* (Series; Anthology; Showtime; 1989). Condensed adaptations of famous horror stories that feature such stars as Laura Dern, Roddy McDowall, Amy Irving, Debholm Elliott, Linda Hunt, Rue McClanahan, David Hemmings and Lisa Marie Russell. Shelley Duvall is the producer.

6687 *Nightmare Room.* (Series; Anthology; WB; 2001-2002). "When the light fades and the moon rises anything can happen. The world becomes a carnival of shocks and chills. A whirling merry-go-round that never stops. Spinning faster and faster, taking you on a frightening ride. I'm R.L. Stein. Don't fall asleep or you may find yourself in *The Nightmare Room*." Chilling stories, aimed at teenagers, that are based on the *Nightmare Room* books by R.L. Stine. Adults appear in minor roles and while children are placed in vicarious situations, they are never harmed.

Narrator: R. L. Stine.

6688 *Nightmares and Dreamscapes.* (Series; Anthology; TNT; 2006). Eight horror tales (each featuring a different cast) based on short stories by Stephen King. Each story begins as a normal presentation. A twist happens and it suddenly becomes abnormal (for example, in the first story, "Battleground," a hit man [William Hurt] assassinates the CEO of a toy company. Suddenly toy soldiers created by the toy king come to life and attack the hit man). Stars include William Hurt, William H. Macy, Jeremy Sisto, Steven Weber, Kim Delaney, Samantha Mathis, Tom Berenger, Richard Thomas, Sigrid Thorton and Andy Anderson.

6689 *Nightside.* (Pilot; Drama; ABC; April 15, 1973). Carmine Kelly is a press agent who covers the Midnight action in New York City. His experiences "with the people who brighten up when the sun goes down" was to be the focal point of the unsold series. Smitty is his friend, the restaurant owner; Aram is the private detective who helps Carmine.

Cast: John Cassavetes (*Carmine Kelly*); Alexis Smith (*Smitty*); Mike Kellin (*Aram Bessoyggian*).

6690 *Nightside.* (Pilot; Crime Drama; ABC; June 8, 1980). Danny and Ed are L.A.P.D. police officers who patrol the city at night. They relax, when they can, by listening to the sexy-voiced D.J., Janie Moody over KDEV radio; they find aggravation from their hot-headed watch commander (Sergeant Duckman); they get interference from Eddie Kopeck, the free-lance reporter who seeks to get the stories Danny and Ed are covering; and they find mishap from Redlight and Greenlight, two reckless ambulance drivers. The proposal was to relate Danny and Ed's experiences with the various characters they meet.

Cast: Doug McClure (*Danny Dandoy*); Michael Corneilson (*Ed Macey*); Roy Jenson (*Sergeant Duckman*); Melinda Naud (*Janie Moody*); Danny Wells (*Eddie Kopeck*); Michael D. Roberts (*Greenlight*); Michael Winslow (*Redlight*); Janice Lynde (*Lily, the radio dispatcher*).

6691 *Nightwatch.* (Pilot; Drama; CBS; July 15, 1968). James Van Ducci and Owen Kerr are investigators for The Great Lakes Interstate Bureau in Chicago. James and Owen are seasoned investigators who take great pride in their work and the proposal was to focus on the methods they use to resolve cases. Ellie is James's wife.

Cast: Carroll O'Connor (*James Van Ducci*); Andrew Duggan (*Owen Kerr*); Michael Murphy (*William Smith*); Jacqueline Betton (*Ellie Van Ducci*).

6692 *Nikita.* (Series; Drama; CW; 2010–). A continuation of

La Femme Nikita. Division is a top secret U.S. agency that recruits assassins. Nikita was one of its reluctant recruits but has since escaped. Nikita was adopted as a child by parents who neglected her. She ran away from home and at the age of 16 lived on the streets. Two years later, she was arrested for killing a police officer. Although innocent, she was convicted and sentenced to death. Shortly after, she was taken from her cell by Division to become one of their agents. To cover up her disappearance, it was reported that Nikita had died (on Sept. 3, 2004 by lethal injection). Nikita is trained and soon becomes one of its top assassins. But Nikita makes one fatal mistake—she breaks a rule when she falls in love with Daniel Monroe. The affair lasted for three months before Division, fearing to lose Nikita, had Daniel killed. The act had an opposite effect and enraged Nikita, who broke away from Division to become a fugitive with one determined goal: destroy Division. Action stories follow Nikita as she attempts to evade the Division agents pursuing her and achieve her goal.

Stories also focus on a young girl (Alex), framed for the murder of her family by Division who becomes a reluctant recruit (do what they say or die. Shortly after the murders and before Division acquired her, Nikita rescued Alex and trained her in secret to resist Division and help her bring it down. Alex works from the inside to help Nikita and later becomes an agent. Alex is unable to kill and receives the secret help of Nikita to fulfill her assignments). Through Alex, Division's training sessions are detailed. Michael is Division's top assassin and Nikita's former trainer (who is now out to kill her); Percy is the agency's chief; Amanda is his cold hearted assistant; Birkoff is the agency's computer genius. Series star Maggie Q is also known as Margaret Quigley.

Program Open: "Six years ago I was taken from prison and forced to become an assassin for a secret unit of the government, a black ops program called Division that has now gone rogue. They destroyed my identity and they destroyed the man I loved. I escaped and now the man that trained me, someone I trusted, is hunting me. Division's power and influence continues to grow and no one is beyond their reach. They'll annihilate any person, any government that stands in their way. But along with my partner, Alex, who's undercover inside Division, I will stop them. I will protect the innocent they target and I will make them pay."

Cast: Maggie Q *(Nikita)*; Lyndsy Fonseca *(Alex)*; Shane West *(Michael)*; Melinda Clarke *(Amanda)*; Xander Berkeley *(Percy)*; Aaron Stanford *(Birkoff)*.

6693   *Nikki*. (Series; Comedy; WB; 2000–2002). Nikki and Dwight White are a happily married young couple with vastly different jobs. Nikki is a gorgeous chorus girl (a calf dancer) at the Golden Calf Hotel and Casino in Las Vegas; Dwight is a wrestler who performs under the name "The Cry Baby" at the Las Vegas Pavilion (as a member of the CWF Wrestling Federation). Nikki and Dwight live at 262 Lincoln Drive, Apartment C (also seen as Apartment 25) and stories follow their efforts to survive the difficult first years of marriage. As the series progressed, Nikki loses her job when the Golden Calf closes. She first worked as the Meat Girl (hands out meat samples), then as Orchida (a super hero who is part girl and part flower) at the Comics Fair; a CWF cheerleader (she also wrestled as the Cheerleader of Doom) and finally as a salesgirl at American Auto Parts.

TV Fate was not kind to Dwight either. When the CWF folded, Dwight became a wrestler with the WXL league. When this was not to his liking he joined the VWF (Very Violent Wrestling). The series ended before establishing any further information. Other regulars are Jupiter, Dwight's boss; Mary and Luna, dancers; Martine, the choreographer; Marion, Dwight's domineering mother; and Thor, a wrestler.

Cast: Nikki Cox *(Nikki White)*; Nick von Esmarch *(Dwight*

White); Toby Huss *(Jupiter)*; Christine Estabrook *(Marion White)*; Susan Egan *(Mary)*; Steve Valentine *(Martine)*; Brad William Henke *(Thor)*; Marina Benedict *(Luna)*.

6694   *Nikki and Alexander*. (Pilot; Comedy; NBC; Aug. 16, 1989). While writing an article, free-lance journalist Alexander Bowman is interrupted by a knock at the door. A beautiful Russian girl named Nikki Simka, a delegate to the United Nations in New York City, enters and begins crying (having found out that the man she loves is married). When Alexander learns that Nikki has also lost her apartment, he offers to rent her the spare bedroom in his Greenwich Village apartment. Although the pilot ended with Nikki and Alexander as just friends, the series would have followed their romantic misadventures.

Cast: Irena Ferris *(Nikki Simka)*; Tim Matheson *(Alexander Bowman)*.

6695   *Nilus the Sandman*. (Series; Cartoon; Family Channel; 1991). Live action combines with animation and music to follow Nilus, a magical Sandman, who enters the minds of sleeping people to allow them to visit the fantasy worlds they create in their dreams.

Voice Cast: Long John Baldry *(Nilus)*; Donny Osmond *(Trendoid)*; Holly Cole *(Trendet)*.

6696   *The Nine*. (Series; Drama; ABC; 2006). It was a regular day. A group of people went to work but destiny brought them each to the Federal Republic Bank (also called Fidelity National Bank). Outside, two men are seen observing the bank. When it seems like the perfect opportunity, they enter the bank (with an intent to rob it) but something goes terribly wrong and nine patrons are taken hostage. The action quickly switches to a SWAT team recovering the hostages after a 52-hour standoff. But what happened during those 52 hours? That is the premise of this serialized drama as flashbacks are used to convey the lives of these nine people before, during the hostage standoff and the after effects.

The principal players are Dr. Jeremy Kates, a noted surgeon; Nick Cavanaugh, a gambling addicted homicide cop; Kathryn Hale, an Assistant D.A.; Malcolm Jones, the bank manager; Egan Foote, a depressed and henpecked man who came to the bank to commit suicide in the men's room; Franny and Eva Rios, sisters who are bank tellers; Felicia, Malcolm's daughter (who was visiting her father at the time); and Lizzie Miller, a hospital social worker. Of the nine hostages, one is killed (Eve—although she is seen in flashbacks); as for the two bank robbers—Randall Reese is shot; the other, Lucas Dalton is captured.

Cast: Tim Daly *(Nick Cavanaugh)*; Kim Raver *(Kathryn Hale)*; Chi McBride *(Malcolm Jones)*; Camille Guaty *(Franny Rios)*; John Billingsley *(Egan Foote)*; Jessica Collins *(Lizzie Miller)*; Scott Wolf *(Jeremy Kates)*; Dana Davis *(Felicia Jones)*; Jeffrey Price *(Randall Reese)*; Tom Verica *(Ed Nielsen)*; Lourdes Benedict *(Eva Rios)*; Owain Yeoman *(Lucas Dalton)*; Michael Emmanuel *(Tom Mitchell)*; Kim Stanton *(Naomi Jones)*.

6697   *905-Wild*. (Pilot; Drama; NBC; Mar. 1, 1975). Doc Coolidge is the head of the Los Angeles County Bureau of Animal Control. He is assisted by officer Walt Marsh, Dave Gordon and Les Taylor and the proposal, a spin off from *Emergency* was to relate the team's various experiences rescuing animals. Rose is their secretary-dispatcher (905-Wild is the unit's telephone number).

Cast: Leslie Nielsen *(Doc Coolidge)*; Mark Harmon *(Dave Gordon)*; Albert Popwell *(Les Taylor)*; Gary Sandy *(Walt Marsh)*; Roseanne Zecker *(Rose)*.

6698   *90210*. (Series; Drama; CW; 2008–). An revised version of the Fox series *Beverly Hills, 90210.* Life in fashionable Beverly Hills, especially West Beverly Hills High School, as seen through the eyes of Annie Wilson and her adopted brother, Dixon, the new kids at school (having just relocated from Kansas with their parents, Harry and Debbie, to be closer to their grandmother [Harry's mother], Tabitha, a former television star and a charter member of the Betty Ford Clinic.

Annie is sweet and friendly and has a passion for the theater; Dixon is the star athlete. Their father is the school's new principal. Naomi is the spoiled, rich girl; Ethan is the popular jock; Navid is the aspiring journalist; Silver is the rebel student who produces a You Tube Internet blog. Kelly Taylor (a student on the original series) is now the school's guidance counselor; Ryan is a teacher; Nat owns the local hangout, the Peach Pit. Shannen Doherty, Joe E. Tata and Ann Gillespie also revise their roles from the original version.

Cast: Lori Loughlin (*Debbie Wilson*); Rob Estes (*Harry Wilson*); Shenae Grimes (*Annie Wilson*); Tristan Wilds (*Dixon Wilson*); Anna Lynne McCord (*Naomi Clark*); Ryan Eggold (*Ryan Matthews*); Jessica Stroup (*Erin Silver*); Michael Steger (*Navid Shirazi*); Jessica Lowndes (*Adrianna Tate-Duncan*); Dustin Milligan (*Ethan Ward*); Matt Lanter (*Liam Court*); Jennie Garth (*Kelly Taylor*); Jessica Walter (*Tabitha Wilson*); Trevor Donovan (*Teddy Montgomery*); Sara Foster (*Jen Clark*); Christina Moore (*Tracy Clark*); James Patrick Stuart (*Charles Clark*); Zachary Ray Sherman (*Jasper Herman*); Adam Gregory (*Ty Collins*); Shannen Doherty (*Brenda Walsh*); Maeve Quinlan (*Constance Tate-Duncan*); Gillian Zinser (*Ivy Sullivan*); Meika Cox (*Sasha*); Ann Gillespie (*Jackie Taylor*); Joe E. Tata (*Nat Bussichio*).

6699   9 to 5. (Series; Comedy; ABC, 1982-1983; Syn., 1986–1988). Events in the lives of a group of secretaries at Consolidated Industries in Cleveland, Ohio (the original setting). American Household Products (AHP) in New York City became the locale in second season episodes. In 1986–87 it was Berkley Foods International, and finally (1987-88) Barkley Foods International — both of which were located at 36 East 46th Street in Manhattan.

Franklin Hart, Jr., Dag Larson, William ("Bud") Coleman and E. Nelson Felb are the sexist bosses. Roz Keith assists Hart, the Budget Department head; Charmin Cunningham is Bud's girl Friday. Harry Pearlman, Mike Henderson and Russ Merman are company salesmen.

Violet Newstead is the secretarial supervisor; Doralee Rhoades is Hart's secretary in ABC episodes; in syndicated episodes, she is Doralee Brooks, secretary to Bud and married to the never-seen Curtis Brooks.

Judy Burnley is originally an office secretary; later she is Russ's secretary. Marsha McMurray is first Charmin's secretary, then Felb's. Linda Bowman is the office secretary.

Violet is the mother of a young son (Tommy) and sold Loverware (sexy lingerie). Franklin is a Republican and, while he may be a sexist, does go out on a limb for his secretaries — "Didn't I break all the rules to get you Sweet and Low for the coffee room?" The *E* in Nelson's name stands for Excellent, and his nickname is "Spanky." Bud was the vice president of acquisitions. While the president of Berkley Foods is not seen, his daughter, Evelyn Berkley was. In a rare sitcom appearance, Jane Fonda played O'Neal, the security guard, in the episode of Oct. 12, 1982; her guard dog was named Nunzio. Based on the Dolly Parton feature film. Phoebe Snow, then Dolly Parton sing the theme, "9 to 5."

Cast: Rita Moreno (*Violet Newstead*); Rachel Dennison (*Doralee Rhoades*); Valerie Curtin (*Judy Burnley*); Leah Ayres (*Linda Bowman*); Jeffrey Tambor, Peter Bonerz (*Franklin Hart, Jr.*); James Komack (*Dag Larson*); Jean Marsh (*Roz Keith*); Herb Edelman (*Harry Pearlman*); George Deloy (*Mike Anderson*); Robin Dearden (*Evelyn Berkley*); Gail Strickland (*Lois Hart, Franklin's wife*); Tony LaTorre (*Tommy Newstead*).

6700   *The 1900 House.* (Series; Reality; PBS; 1999). A British produced reality series that goes back in time — to the year 1900 for a family to experience life as it was then. A volunteer family (the Bowlers) are placed in a house just as it would have appeared in 1900. The family must wear clothes of the era and live just as a real family would have at the time (they are not permitted to use any items invented after 1900). Individual family members are allowed only one modern convenience — a TV camera placed in a special room to allow them to speak directly to it and convey their feelings as they live in the past. Henry Strozier is the narrator; the Bowlers are parents Paul and Kathryn and their children Ruth, Hilary, Joseph and Joyce.

6701   *90 Bristol Court.* (Series; Comedy; NBC; 1964-1965). The overall title for three family comedies that are set against the background of 90 Bristol Court, a fashionable but fictitious apartment-motel in Southern California. For information see *Harris Against the World, Karen* (1964 version with Debbie Watson) and *Tom, Dick and Mary.*

6702   *Ninja Turtles: The Next Mutation.* (Series; Adventure; Fox; 1997-1998). A live action series based on the animated *Teenage Mutant Ninja Turtles* (see entry). Five turtles (not four as in the original version) are abandoned and fall into a New York City sewer. They come in contact with a mysterious green substance that transforms them into human-like creatures. Four (Michelangelo, Donatello, Leonardo and Raphael) are found by Master Splinter, a ninja master (turned into a rat by the green substance); the fifth turtle, a girl (Venus de Milo), is found by Chung I, a Shinobi Master (who whisked her off to China to teach her the way of the Shinobi [Ninja]). Her brothers were taught the martial arts by Master Splinter to battle the Dragon Lord, an evil dictator and leader of an army of dragons called the Rank. The new series reunites Venus (who returns to New York) with her brothers to help them battle evil and keep the city safe from the Dragon Lord.

Cast: Stephen Mendel (*Master Splinter*); Fiona Scott (*Master Splinter; voice*); Kirby Morrow (*Michelangelo*); Jarred Blancard (*Michelangelo; voice*); Michael Dobson (*Leonardo*); Gabe Khouth (*Leonardo; voice*); Matt Hill (*Raphael*); Jason Gray-Stanford (*Donatello*); Richard Lee (*Donatello; voice*); Lalainia Lindbjerg (*Venus de Milo*); Christopher Gaze (*Dragon Lord*); Andrew Kavadas (*Rank Lieutenant*); Chang Tseng (*Chung I*).

6703   *Nip/Tuck.* (Series; Drama; FX; 2003–2010). Christian Troy and Sean McNamara are Miami Beach–based plastic surgeons. Christian is an arrogant ladies' man who worships money; Sean is a timid family man who is devoted to his dysfunctional family (his vengeful and oversexed wife, Julia; Matt, his rebellious teenage son; and Annie, his pre-teenage daughter). In addition to relating events in the private and work lives of Sean and Christian, stories also follow the lives of the patients who come to them for life-changing surgery.

Beginning with the episode of October 30, 2007, Sean and Christian leave Florida for greener pastures in Hollywood, California. Stories, which still focus on people seeking plastic surgery to improve their looks, also detail Sean and Christian's efforts to establish a new practice. Fiona becomes their agent when the doctors become consultants for the TV series *Hearts 'n Scalpels.* Freddy Prune is the show's producer; Kimber is the former porn star turned director; Dr. Theodora "Teddy" Lowe is Sean's girlfriend; Mike Hamond is the younger doctor who joins Sean and Christian's practice (2009).

Cast: Dylan Walsh (*Sean McNamara*); Julian McMahon (*Christian Troy*); Joely Richardson (*Julia McNamara*); John Hensley (*Matt McNamara*); Kelsey-Lynn Batelaan (*Annie McNamara*); Roma Maffia (*Dr. Liz Cruz*); Bruno Campos (*Dr. Quentin Costa*); Valerie Cruz

(*Grace Santiago*); Linda Klein (*Nurse Linda*); Katee Sackhoff, Rose McGowan (*Dr. Theodora Lowe*); Oliver Platt (*Freddy Prune*); Portia de Rossi (*Olivia Lord*); Kelly Carlson (*Kimber Henry*); Mario Lopez (*Dr. Mike Hamond*); Lauren Hutton (*Fiona*); Brooke Shields (*Faith Wolper*); Famke Janssen (*Ava More*); Tia Carrere (*Mistress Dark Pain*); Oliver Platt (*Freddy Prune*); Daphne Zuniga (*Carly Summers*).

6704   Nitro Circus. (Series; Reality; MTV; 2009). Travis Pastrana is considered the world's greatest motocross rider. The program charts Travis and his crew's (Nitro Circus) exploits as they travel around the world performing outrageous stunts that test the limits of human endurance. Travis is assisted by Jolene Van Vugt, Andy Bell, Jim DeChamp, Erik Runer, Tommy Passamonte.

6705   No — Honestly. (Series; Comedy; PBS; 1975). The courtship and early-married life of the Danbys: Charles, an actor, and his scatterbrained wife, Clara, author of "Ollie the Otter" stories for children. Other regulars are Lord and Lady Burrell, Clara's parents; and Royal, the Burrell's butler.

Cast: John Addison (*Charles Danby*); Pauline Collins (*Clara Danby*); James Berwick (*Lord Burrell*); Fanny Rowe (*Lady Burrell*); Kenneth Benda (*Royal*).

6706   No Complaints. (Pilot; Comedy; NBC; July 24, 1985). After a 12-year absence, former college roommates and best friends Valerie Anastas (a housewife with two children, Melanie and Raymond) and Joanna Newman (a vice president with the advertising firm of Burkin, Wain and Burkin) resume their friendship when they meet again. The proposal was to relate the misadventures of two best friends. Other regulars are Nick, Valerie's husband; Jack, Joanna's boss; and Michael, Jack's junior partner.

Cast: Diana Canova (*Valerie Anastas*); Anne Twomey (*Joanna Newman*); James Sutorius (*Nick Anastas*); Emily Moultrie (*Melanie Anastas*); Matt Dill (*Raymond Anastas*); Harold Gould (*Jack Wain*); Brad O'Hare (*Michael Burken*).

6707   No Heroics. (Pilot; Comedy; Unaired; Produced for ABC in 2009). The Watch Tower is a bar where a group of less-than-heroic super heroes hangout. These include Pete, alias Chillout, whose ability is to freeze water (he is a hit at parties for making ice cubes for scotch); Nigel, alias Brainstorm, can read minds (if he is close enough to you and feels in the mood); Callie, alias Crossfade, is cool, but bitter and jaded; Sandy, alias Slamazon, is strong, but her abilities scare men off and she can never find a date; and Bradley, alias Infinitum, a square-jawed, square-brained stud. The proposal was to follow the heroically-challenged heroes as they wait for the call for help.

Cast: Freddie Prinze, Jr. (*Bradley*); Arielle Kebbel (*Sandy*); Eliza Coupe (*Callie*); Paul Campbell (*Pete*); Tom Riley (*Nigel*).

6708   No Holds Barred. (Series; Comedy; CBS; 1980). A look at the crackpot side of contemporary American life via film and video-taped segments.

Host: Kelly Monteith.

6709   No Ordinary Family. (Series; Adventure; ABC; 2010-2011). Jim Powell, a Pacific Bay police sketch artist, his wife, Stephanie, a research scientist for Global Tech, and their teenage children, Daphne and J.T., are, for the most part, an ordinary family. They have their differences and each appears to be living in his or her own world. Hoping to change this and bring the family together, Jim arranges for a trip to the Brazilian Rain Forest. During the flight, a sudden electrical storm damages the plane and it plunges into a river. The pilot is killed but the Powell family survives. The family

is rescued and they appear to be fine. Several days later they change. Jim has acquired incredible strength and can leap to fantastic heights; Stephanie has acquired supersonic speed; Daphne becomes telepathic (can hear other people's thoughts); and J.T., who has a learning disability, acquires academic brilliance. Stephanie believes the phosphorescence in the river water has affected them and given them their extraordinary abilities. Stories relate events in the lives of a family who are no longer just ordinary as they attempt to adjust to their new powers and use them for good (especially Jim, who sets his goal to capture criminals). George is Jim's confidante, a D.A., who helps him in his quest; Katie is Stephanie's confidante, a lab technician. Yvonne is a detective on the force; Drayton is Stephanie's superior, a man with sinister motives (he appears to know about the river water and what it can do).

Cast: Michael Chiklis (*Jim Powell*); Julie Benz (*Stephanie Powell*); Kay Panabaker (*Daphne Powell*); Jimmy Bennett (*J.T. Powell*); Romany Malco (*George St. Cloud*); Autumn Reeser (*Katie Andrews*); Christina Chang (*Yvonne Cho*); Stephen Collins (*Drayton King*).

6710   No Place Like Home. (Pilot; Comedy; CBS; Sept. 6, 1985). When Diana Bellamy and Marsha Brayfield, friends since childhood, come to the conclusion that the only way they can afford their lifelong dream of owning a home is to buy one together, they convince their mates of the decision. The proposal was to relate the misadventures of Diana (and her live-in boyfriend, Murray) and Marsha (and her husband, Paul) as they attempt to share a house.

Cast: Susan Hess (*Diana Bellamy*); Molly Cheek (*Marsha Brayfield*); Rick Lohman (*Paul Brayfield*); Jack Blessing (*Murray McCoy*).

6711   No Soap, Radio. (Series; Comedy; ABC; 1982). The floundering Hotel Pelican in Atlantic City, New Jersey, is the setting for a look at the staff and residents of the establishment. Stories are frequently interrupted by nonsensical skits and anything that can generate a laugh — from sight gags to sound effects — creating "comedy that's impossible to describe." The regulars are Roger, the proprietor; Sharon, the desk clerk; Al, the house detective; Morris, the bellboy; and hotel residents Mr. Plitzky, Mrs. Belmont, Marian, Gunther (Marian's husband) and Victoria.

Cast: Steve Guttenberg (*Roger*); Brianne Leary, Hillary Bailey (*Sharon*); Bill Dana (*Mr. Plitzky*); Jerry Marin (*Morris*); Stuart Pankin (*Al Tuttle*); Fran Ryan (*Mrs. Belmont*); Edie McClurg (*Marian*); Johnny Haymer (*Gunther*); Victoria Carroll (*Victoria*); **Skit Regulars:** Ed Arnold, Joe Baker, Gregg Berger, Bill Callaway, Brett Clark, Mike Darnell, Bob Hastings, Michael Jacobs, Jack Kruschen, William Lanteau, Sidney Miller, Warren Munson, Gary Owens, Renny Peterson, Ron Richards, Roselyn Royce, Phil Rubinstein.

6712   No Time for Sergeants. (Series; Comedy; ABC; 1964-1965). Will Stockdale is a naïve Georgia farm boy who suddenly finds his life turned upside down when he is drafted into the United States Air Force. Will has a philosophy of kindness (which displeases his superior officers) and is lost in a world he has never known before. Will is awkward and amazed by what he sees and is determined to make the Air Force proud of him. Stories follow Will as he tries to do what is best for the Air Force — no matter how many times he receives KP (Kitchen Patrol) for all the foul ups he causes. Millie is Will's girlfriend; Tilda Jay is Will's sister. Will has a dog named Blue. Based on the feature film.

Cast: Sammy Jackson (*Will Stockdale*); Harry Hickox (*Sgt. Orville King*); Paul Smith (*Capt. Paul Martin*); Kevin O'Neil (*Pvt. Ben Whitledge*); Laurie Sibbald (*Millie Anderson*); Andy Clyde (*Grandpa Anderson*); Greg Benedict (*Pvt. Irving Blanchard*); Michael McDonald (*Pvt. Jack Langdon*); Joe E. Tata (*Private Neddick*); Hayden Rorke

(Colonel Farnsworth); Stacey Maxwell *(Tilda Jay Stockdale)*; Frank Ferguson *(Pa Stockdale)*.

6713   No Warning. (Series; Anthology; NBC; 1958). A revised version of *Panic* that continues to present dramas that depict the plight of people whose lives are suddenly thrown into turmoil by an unexpected crisis. Al Simon is the producer.

Narrator: Westbrook Van Voorhis.

6714   Noah Knows Best. (Series; Comedy; Nick; 2000-2001). Noah Beznik is a teenager who lives with his parents, Jeff and Martine, and sister, Megan, in an apartment house in Manhattan. He is the manipulative 14-year-old son of a playwright who takes advantage of other people to accomplish a goal. As Noah, who attends Hudson Prep School, speaks directly to the camera to relate proceedings, stories follow his efforts to do what he feels is best — to help himself. Alton and his brother, D.J., are Noah's friends; Camille Ruiz is Megan's girlfriend.

Cast: Philip Glenn Van Dyke *(Noah Beznik)*; Richard Kline *(Jeff Beznik)*; Marcia Strassman *(Martine Beznik)*; Rachel Roth *(Megan Beznik)*; Cori Ann Yarckin *(Camille Ruiz)*; Willie Green *(Alton Martin)*; Stacy Matthews *(D.J. Martin)*.

6715   Noah's Arc. (Series; Drama; Logo; 2006). While Showtime's *The L-Word* focuses on lesbians, Logo's *Noah's Arc* tells the story of a group of gay men living in Los Angeles. The principals are Noah Nicholson and his romantic interest Wade, both screenwriters (although Wade is an established pro and Noah is struggling to make his mark in the film industry); Alex Kirby, an HIV/AIDS counselor; Trey, an anesthesiologist; and Ricky, the owner of an exclusive clothing store. Stories follow the men as they face the pressures of everyday life — made much more difficult by the fact that they are gay.

Cast: Darryl Stephens *(Noah Nicholson)*; Rodney Chester *(Alex Kirby)*; Christian Vincent *(Ricky Davis)*; Douglas Spearman *(Chance Counter)*; Jensen Atwood *(Wade)*; Gregory Keith *(Trey)*; Jennia Fredeique *(Brandy)*; Merwin Mondesir *(Dre)*; Wilson Cruz *(Junito)*; Benjamin Patterson *(Guy)*; Jonathan Julian *(Eddie)*; Sahara Davis *(Kenya)*.

6716   Noah's Ark. (Series; Drama; NBC; 1956-1957). Dr. Sam Rinehart is an aging and ill veterinarian who is also wheelchair bound. Dr. Noah McCann is the young assistant he hires to help him at his animal clinic. Stories follow the dedicated doctors as they use time tested methods (those of Sam) coupled with the new theories of animal treatment (as introduced by Noah) to serve the people of their community. Liz is their nurse-secretary; Agnes is Sam's daughter (a widow); Davy is her son.

Cast: Paul Burke *(Noah McCann)*; Vic Rodman *(Sam Rinehart)*; May Wynn *(Liz Clark)*; Natalie Masters *(Agnes Marshall)*; Paul Engle *(Davy Marshall)*; Russell Whitney *(Glenn White)*. **Theme Vocal:** "Noah" by the Hi-Lo's.

6717   Noble Quest. (Pilot; Drama; Unaired; Produced for ABC in 1991). Ty Nuygen was born in Vietnam during the war. Twenty years later, Ty makes a pledge to his dying mother to find his American father. The proposal was to relate Ty's travels across the U.S. as he searches for the father he has never known.

Cast: Keith Cooke *(Ty Nuygen)*.

6718   Nobody. (Pilot; Drama; Unaired; Produced for ABC Family in 2006). Jessica Drake is a Nobody, a girl with the unique ability to physically change her features (Nobodies are blessed — or cursed — individuals who give up their own lives to safeguard society

as someone else). The eerie proposal was to follow Jessica as a paranormal investigator who, with her trusted confidante, Marcus, battle the elements of the unknown.

Cast: Dawn Stern *(Jessica Drake)*; Ryan Belleville *(Marcus)*.

6719   Nobody's Perfect. (Series; Comedy; ABC; 1980). As part of an exchange program, Roger Hart, a brilliant Scotland Yard inspector is assigned to duty with the San Francisco Police Department's 22nd Precinct. Hart is teamed with a beautiful officer (Jennifer Dempsey) and the program relates Hart's exploits as he investigates crimes and struggles to overcome his one imperfection: he is calamity-prone. Other regulars are Lieutenant Vince DeGennaro, their superior; Dreyfus, the lab technician; and Careful Eddie, Hart's informant. Originally titled *Hart of San Francisco* but changed due to a possible title confusion with *Hart to Hart*.

Cast: Ron Moody *(Roger Hart)*; Cassie Yates *(Jennifer Dempsey)*; Michael Durrell *(Vince DeGennaro)*; Greg Monaghan *(Dreyfus)*; Danny Wells *(Careful Eddie)*.

6720   The Noel Edmonds Show. (Pilot; Comedy; ABC; June 21 to 27, 1986). A late night potpourri of music, comedy, unusual variety acts and celebrity interviews with British comedian Noel Edmonds as the host. Kevin Kiner provides the music.

6721   Nolan Knows Best. (Pilot; Comedy; Unaired; Produced for ABC in 2010). Dana Nolan is a young man who grew up in the shadow of his father, Phil, a legend (school coach) in their hometown. Dana is now married (to Julie) but has always regretted that he was never be able to please his father (whom Dana believes loves his older brother, Stan, more). Life changes for Dana when Phil, a widower, moves into the apartment above Dana's garage and Dana feels he now has an opportunity to get to better know his father. The proposal was to follow Dana, a school guidance counselor, as he tries to become the man his father believes he should be. Elaine and Abby are Dana and Julie's daughters (who consider the obnoxious Phil to be a lovable grandfather); Julie is an anesthesiologist.

Cast: Dana Gould *(Dana Nolan)*; Brian Dennehy *(Phil Nolan)*; Traylor Howard *(Julie Nolan)*; Lexi Jourdan *(Abby Nolan)*; Payton Lucas *(Elaine Nolan)*; Todd Stashwick *(Stan Nolan)*.

6722   Noonbory and the Super 7. (Series; Cartoon; CBS; 2009). In a colorful place called Boryland, there exists the island of Toobalooba, which is inhabited by playful characters called Borys. Here, seven Borys unite and use their senses of sight, sound, smell, taste, hearing and touch to protect Toobalooba from an array of comical villains that seek to conquer it. Noonbory leads the team. He is assisted by Jettybory, Cozybory, Totabory, Pongdybory, Lukybory and Mambybory.

Voices: Kevin Aichles, Nolan Balzer, Rod Benfield, Stead Crandall, Melanie Dahling, Jolie L'Esperanza, Jacqui Fox, Brent Hirose, Laura Kolisnyde, Reagan McCheyne, Margoux Miller, Duade Montsbruno, Jade Repita, Trevor Toffan, Todd Schlick.

6723   The Noonday Show. (Pilot; Variety; NBC; Dec. 15 to19, 1985). Proposal for a daily program of news, music and comedy.

Host: David Steinberg. **Regulars:** Carol Androsky, Stan Cann, Jane Dulo, Gailard Sartain, Bill Saluga. **Music:** David Foster.

6724   N.O.P.D. (Series; Crime Drama; Syn.; 1956). Victor Beaujac and John Conroy are detectives with the homicide division of the New Orleans Police Department (N.O.P.D.). Stories, based on official N.O.P.D. files, relate their investigations. The program is filmed on location, and it appears that actual citizens were used in the dramas (acting is not their forte; only the two stars receive credit).

Stacy Harris plays his character like Jack Webb's Sergeant Joe Friday on *Dragnet*. He narrates and questions the suspects while Conroy, whom Victor calls "John-O," takes notes. Victor resides in an apartment on Bourbon Street, while John was said to have a home on Shady Pine Avenue.

Program Open: "This is the official emblem [police badge] of the New Orleans Police Department. You are about to witness a true story of a crime from the official files of the N.O.P.D. The names of all persons actually involved have been changed."

Cast: Stacy Harris (*Det. Victor Beaujac*); Louis J. Sirgo (*Det. John Conroy*).

6725   *Norby.* (Series; Comedy; NBC; 1955). Events in the lives of the Norby family, in particular Pearson, the father, the vice president of small loans at the First National Bank in Pearl River, New York. Pearson is married to Helen and they are the parents of Diane and Hank. Bobo and his wife Maureen are their neighbors; Wahleen Johnson is the bank telephone operator; Maude Endles is the bank president; Mr. Rudge is the bank efficiency expert.

Cast: David Wayne (*Pearson Norby*); Joan Lorring (*Helen Norby*); Susan Holloran (*Diane Norby*); Evan Elliott (*Hank Norby*); Jack Warden (*Bobo*); Maxine Stuart (*Maureen*); Janice Mars (*Wahleen Johnson*); Paul Ford (*Bank President*); Carol Veazie (*Maude Endles*); Ralph Dunn (*Mr. Rudge*).

6726   *Norfin Adventures.* (Pilot; Cartoon; Syn.; Oct. 31, 1993). Norfins are "the original trolls" as they call themselves. Sherlock, Aggie, Bogie and Herc are the good Norfins. Dr. Doom is an evil Norfin who is seeking the key to unlimited power. The proposal was to follow the good Norfins as they attempt to find Olaf's Opal — the key to unlocking the mystery of ultimate power — before Dr. Doom.

Voices: Don Brown, Mike Donovan, Michael Benyaer, Saffron Henderson, Andrew Kavadas, Sam Kouth, Doug Parker, Cathy Weseluck.

6727   *The Norliss Tapes.* (Pilot; Thriller; NBC; Feb. 21, 1973). David Norliss is a San Francisco–based writer who investigates supernatural occurrences. As he covers stories he records his notes on audio tape (hence the title) and later transcribes them for a book. The proposal was to relate David's adventures as he becomes involved in unearthly situations. Sanford Evans is David's publisher.

Cast: Roy Thinnes (*David Norliss*); Don Porter (*Sanford Evans*).

6728   *The Norm Show.* (Series; Comedy; ABC; 1999–2001). Norm Henderson is a man who likes to gamble. He was also a professional hockey player but not considered very good. Combine sports with gambling and tax evasion and you have the predicament Norm finds himself — caught, busted and banned from playing hockey. As part of his sentence, Norm is assigned to community service with the New York City Department of Social Services. Stories follow Norm's antics as he tries to pay off his tax bill, avoid gambling and try to help people who really need help (despite the fact that Norm is not overly qualified to help people).

Other regulars are Laurie Freeman, Norm's co-worker; Max Denby, the harassed head of the agency; and Shelley Kilmartin, Danny Sanchez, Taylor Clayton and Amy Wilson, other social service workers.

Cast: Norm MacDonald (*Norm Henderson*); Laurie Metcalf (*Laurie Freeman*); Max Wright (*Max Denby*); Faith Ford (*Shelley Kilmartin*); Ian Gomez (*Danny Sanchez*); Nikki Cox (*Taylor Clayton*); Amy Wilson (*Molly Carver*); Artie Lange (*Artie Henderson*).

6729   *Norma Rae.* (Pilot; Drama; NBC; Nov. 21, 1981). Norma Rae Webster is a mill hen (a textile mill worker) in the small town of Oakalona. She is a widow and the mother of two children (Willie and Craig). Norma is also a fighter and is struggling to unionize the workers at the mill. The proposal, based on the 1979 feature film of the same title, was to relate Norma Rae's experiences at work and at home. Other regulars are Frank Osborne, the father of Norma's illegitimate son, Craig; Vernon, Norma's father; Alma, the woman who boards at Vernon's home; Reuben, Norma's friend; and William and Emery, mill workers.

Cast: Cassie Yates (*Norma Rae Webster*); Nancy Jarnagin (*Willie Webster*); Keith Mitchell (*Craig Webster*); Barry Corbin (*Vernon Witchard*); Jane Atkins (*Alma Woodruff*); Jordan Clarke (*Frank Osborne*); Gary Frank (*Reuben*); Ernest Hardin, Jr. (*William Poole*); Mickey Jones (*Emery*).

6730   *Normal Life.* (Series; Comedy; CBS; 1990). Incidents in the lives of the Harlows, a "normal" family of five living in Los Angeles. Max Harlow, the father, is a novelist. Anne, his wife, is seldom content, harassed either by her job or by the antics of her children. Since the series was not broadcast in the order the episodes were made, information on Anne is not consistent. When first seen, Anne apparently worked for a lawyer (based on a conversation with Max). She next worked as a member of the school board. She quit this job when she got fed up with the school board's ignoring her suggestions. Two episodes later, she is now head of the public school board, 5th District. In an episode after this, she is unemployed. When something upsets Anne, she takes a long bath.

Information on Tess, their oldest child, is also conflicting. When first introduced, she is 22 years old and working for New Market Films in Hollywood. Later, she is 21 years old and looking for a job (having just quit her job as a tour guide at the Hollywood Wax Museum). One week she is living at home, the next she has her own apartment "seven blocks away." In one episode, when she is not living at home, Tess has a job in an unnamed art gallery. She is best friends with Prima, a seemingly spaced-out girl.

Jake, the middle child (19 years old), plays guitar in a professional (but unnamed) band. While it is difficult to tell, it seems that he is attending college.

Simon, the youngest child, attends Valley Junior High School and is a member of the Wildcats basketball team. Sharing the Harlows ups and downs is their neighbor, Dr. Bob Gordon.

In the unaired pilot version (produced in 1989), Janet Margolin played Anne Harlow and Max Gail was Jack Harlow.

Cast: Cindy Williams (*Anne Harlow*); Max Gail (*Max Harlow*); Moon Unit Zappa (*Tess Harlow*); Dweezil Zappa (*Jake Harlow*); Josh Williams (*Simon Harlow*); Bess Myer (*Prima*); Jim Staahl (*Bob Gordon*).

6731   *Normal, Ohio.* (Series; Comedy; Fox; 2000). Butch Gamble is a construction worker who lives in Normal, Ohio. He is the son of Bill and Joan Gamble, divorced from Elizabeth, and the father of Charlie. Butch also has a sister (divorced), Pamela. Elizabeth has now re-married (to Danny). Butch's life, however, is not normal, He has a deep dark secret and after years of living with it, he chose to come out of the closet and profess to being gay. Butch is now happy although living his new life style is not as easy as he thought it would be as he is the guiding light of his eccentric family. Stories follow Butch's efforts to help his family overcome their numerous problems — while attempting (but never really succeeding) to start his new life style.

Other regulars are Kimberly and Robbie, Pamela's children. Pamela is a beautician who yearns to start her own business in a nail salon. To earn extra money for her salon, Pamela attempted to strip — as the Blushing Bride — at the Nude Ranch (but when it came to actually doing it, she couldn't). But Pamela's dream did come true;

her father loaned her the money to take her Nails by Pamela basement business to a store called Pamela's Institute of Cuticle Care.

Bill is a member of the Southside Poker Club; Joan teaches Sunday school at the local church. Kimberly works as the maitre'd at Joshua's Grill, a restaurant. Butch likes left over cake for breakfast and as a kid had a doll named Sally (that he stole from Pamela). Danny is addicted to the Weather Channel (especially the girls) and calls such people "Weatherheads."

Cast: John Goodman (*Butch Gamble*); Orson Bean (*Bill Gamble*); Anita Gillette (*Joan Gamble*); Joely Fisher (*Pamela Miller*); Julia McIlvaine (*Kimberly Miller*); Cody Kasch (*Robbie Miller*); Mo Gaffney (*Elizabeth Gamble*); Charles Rocket (*Danny Miller*); Greg Pitts (*Charlie Gamble*).

6732   *Normal People.* (Pilot; Comedy; Unaired; Produced for Fox in 2001). Work place proposal about four friends in their twenties who have dull, dead-end jobs but find bliss in their off-work lives.

Cast: Tori Spelling (*Carol Ann*); Heidi Mokrycki (*Evie*); Christopher Gartin (*A.J.*); Marc Worden (*Bradley*).

6733   *Norman Corwin Presents.* (Series; Anthology; Syn.; 1971). Author Norman Corwin hosts a program of original dramatic productions.

6734   *The North Shore.* (Series; Drama; Fox; 2004). The Grand Waimea is a luxurious hotel located on the North Shore of Hawaii. Jason Matthews is the hotel's general manager while his ex-girlfriend, the gorgeous Nicole Booth heads up guest relations, a position she took to make it on her own in the business world (she felt stifled by her father, the owner a hotel empire). Stories focus on the events in the lives of both the staff and guests of the hotel. Other regulars are Chris Remsen, the owner of the adventures company that works the hotel; M.J. Bevans, the hotel waitress; Gabriel Miller, the lifeguard; Frankie Seau; and Tessa Lewis, a con artist who works as the hotel's receptionist.

Cast: Brooke Burns (*Nicole Booth*); Kristoffer Polaha (*Jason Matthews*); Jay Kennedy Johnson (*Chris Remsen*); Nikki DeLoach (*M.J. Beavans*); Jason Momoa (*Frankie Seau*); Corey Sevier (*Gabriel Miller*); Amanda Righetti (*Tessa Lewis*); James Remar (*Vincent Colville*).

6735   *Northern Exposure.* (Series; Drama; CBS; 1990–1995). After 74 rejections for a medical school scholarship, Joel Fleischman finds that the state of Alaska will pick up the $125,000 tab if he will begin his practice (and spend four years) in Alaska. Joel attended Richfield High School, Columbia University Medical School and did his internship at Beth Sinai Hospital in New York City.

In Anchorage, Joel finds that he has been assigned to the remote town of Cicely, a growing community in the borough of Arrowhead that was founded by Maurice Minifield, a former NASA astronaut, who arranged for Joel's scholarship. Cicely is a small town desperately in need of a doctor. Joel's office is established in the abandoned Northwestern Mining building, and a native woman named Marilyn Whirlwind serves as his nurse.

Margaret ("Maggie") Mary O'Connell, a pretty brunette who was born in Michigan, is Joel's landlady and the owner of the one plane O'Connell Air Taxi Service. Shelley Tambo, the beautiful young wife (age 23) of Holling Vincoeur (age 68), is the waitress at the Brick Bar (owned by Holling). Chris Stevens is the only D.J. on the town's only radio station, KBHR (57 on the AM dial; "Great Bear Radio," as it is called, is owned by the Minifield Communications Network). Ed Chigliak is a native Alaskan who assists Joel.

Cast: Rob Morrow (*Joel Fleischman*); Janine Turner (*Maggie O'Connell*); Barry Corbin (*Maurice Minifield*); John Cullum (*Holling Vincoeur*); Cynthia Geary (*Shelley Tambo*); John Corbett (*Chris Stevens*); Darren E. Burrows (*Ed*).

6736   *Northstar.* (Pilot; Science Fiction; ABC; Aug. 10, 1986). During a NASA mission to photograph an eclipse in space, a solar disturbance releases a beam of light that enters the camera lens of astronaut Jack North. Jack is temporarily blinded but on his first exposure to sunlight (after a two-week hospital stay) it is discovered that ultra violet sun light can accelerate his IQ to 1000. It is also learned that Jack has the ability to command his brain and accelerate his senses — but also that prolonged exposure to the sun can kill him. By wearing a special pair of sunglasses developed by Dr. Allison Taylor, Jack can now live like a normal person. The proposal was to relate Jack's exploits, as an agent for Operation Northstar, as he uses his unique abilities to solve impossible problems. Col. Evan Marshall is their superior.

Cast: Greg Evigan (*Major Jack North*); Deborah Wakeham (*Dr. Allison Taylor*); Mitchell Ryan (*Evan Marshall*).

6737   *Northwest Passage.* (Series; Adventure; NBC; 1958–1959). The era of the French and Indian Wars (1754–1759) is the setting. It is at this time that Major Robert Rogers, an explorer and Indian fighter, organizes a group of men (his Rogers Rangers) to search for the fabled Northwest Passage, a waterway that links the East and West. Stories, based on fact, relate the experiences of Rogers and his men as they brave the American wilderness (in upper New York State and Eastern Canada) and help settlers in a savage era.

Cast: Keith Larsen (*Major Robert Rogers*); Buddy Ebsen (*Sgt. Hunk Marriner*); Don Burnett (*Ensign Langdon Towne*); Philip Tonge (*General Amherst*); Lisa Davis (*Natula*); Larry Chance (*Black Wolf*); Jim Hayward (*Jonas*); Pat Hogan (*Rivas*).

6738   *Northwest Passage.* (Pilot; Crime Drama; Unaired; Produced for ABC in 1989). Crime prevention in a small Pacific Northwest town as seen through the eyes of its sheriff, Harry Truman. In the pilot episode, FBI agent Dale Cooper assists Truman in the search for a serial killer. With changes, it became the basis for the series *Twin Peaks* (ABC, 1990-91).

Cast: Michael Ontkean (*Harry Truman*); Kyle MacLachlan (*Dale Cooper*); Piper Laurie (*Katherine Packard*); Joan Chen (*Jocelyn Packard*); Brad Dourif (*Jerry Horne*); Richard Beymer (*Benjamin Horne*); Jim Marshall (*James Hurley*); Lara Flynn Boyle (*Donna Hayward*); Everett McGill (*Ed Harley*); Dana Ashbrook (*Bobby Briggs*).

6739   *Not Another High School Show.* (Pilot; Comedy; Unaired; Produced for Comedy Central in 2005). A spoof of the endless parade of teen oriented dramas — from *One Tree Hill* to *Dawson's Creek* as seen through the activities of a group of not-so-typical teenagers.

Cast: Anna Osceola (*Charlie*); Rachel Specter (*Autumn*); Jeffrey Christopher Todd (*Lawson*); Jocelin Donahue (*Melissa*); John Keefe (*Brian*); Brendan Miller (*Sean*).

6740   *Not for Hire.* (Series; Crime Drama; Syn.; 1959). The Criminal Investigation Unit is a division of the U.S. Army that has been established to investigate crimes within the military. Steve Dekker, a sergeant, heads the unit; Sonica Zametoo, a WAC officer and Army Corporal Zimmerman assist him. Stories relate their efforts to solve cases (from desertion to sabotage) without help from outside sources (such as the FBI). Also known as *Sergeant Steve Dekker*.

Cast: Ralph Meeker (*Sgt. Steve Dekker*); Elizabeth Rush (*Sonica Zametoo*); Ken Drake (*Corporal Zimmerman*).

6741   *Not for Publication.* (Series; Drama; DuMont; 1951).

Stories of human interest (later, the facts behind the headline making stories) as seen through the eyes of a man known only as Collins, a reporter for the New York *Ledger*. Also known as *Reporter Collins*.

Cast: William Adler, Jerome Cowan *(Reporter Collins)*.

6742   *Not for Women Only.* (Series; Discussion; Syn.; 1972). Topical issue discussions designed to attract male members of the viewing audience.

Hostess: Aline Saarinen, Barbara Walters, Polly Bergen, Lynn Redgrave. **Host:** Hugh Downs, Frank Field.

6743   *Not in Front of the Kids.* (Pilot; Comedy; ABC; June 16, 1984). Ben and Millie Rosen are a middle-aged couple caring for Amy and Jimmy, their grandchildren, while their parents are away on business. The proposal was to relate the mishaps that occur as the older and younger generations attempt to adapt to each other. Iris is their neighbor.

Cast: Don Ameche *(Ben Rosen)*; Katherine Helmond *(Millie Rosen)*; Amanda Herman *(Amy)*; Jason Naylor *(Jimmy)*; Bette Ford *(Irish Bunch)*.

6744   *Not Necessarily the News.* (Series; Comedy; HBO; 1983). Actual news footage (slightly edited for laughs) with sketches and blackouts that satirize television news programs. Based on the British series *Not the Nine O'clock News*.

Cast: Anne Bloom, Danny Breen, Rich Hall, Mitchell Lawrence, Audrie Neenan, Stuart Pankin, Lucy Webb.

6745   *Not the Nine O'clock News.* (Series; Comedy; Syn.; 1981). Topical skits that spoof current events and television news programs. The British series that served as the basis for *Not Necessarily the News*.

Reporter: Rowan Atkinson, Pamela Stephenson, Mel Smith, Griff Rhys Jones. **Regulars:** Chris Langham, Oscar James, Vicki Silva, Nick Rowley, Phil Goddard, David Renwick, Hugh Thomas, Bill Connelly, Andy Hamilton, Sue Chisholm, Stewart Fell.

6746   *Not Until Today.* (Pilot; Comedy; NBC; June 27, 1979). Jason Swan is a small town police chief whose life suddenly changes when a young man (Jake Warren) shows up claiming to be his illegitimate son. The proposal was to focus on the relationship between a father and son as they struggle to become a family and share each other's interests. Other regulars are Mae, Jason's sister; Father Francis Dacey, Jason's friend; and Sally, the waitress.

Cast: Darren McGavin *(Jason Swan)*; Michael Horton *(Jake Warren)*; Lynn Carlin *(Mae)*; Dick Sargent *(Father Francis Dacey)*; Alexandra Stoddart *(Sally)*.

6747   *Notes from the Underbelly.* (Series; Comedy; ABC; 2007). Lauren and Andrew Stone are a married couple who live at 446 Citrus Avenue in Los Angeles, California. Lauren is a guidance counselor at Oakmont High School; Andrew works as a landscape architect. Andrew loves Lauren — "But she's a huge pain in the ass." Lauren and Andrew are also in their early thirties and looking forward to (but facing all the obstacles of) their first pregnancy. Andrew had wanted children and had tried everything to convince Lauren — who felt she was not ready (she still had a lot to accomplish). Then one day, three years later, Lauren felt her life was suddenly missing something. She stopped taking the pill and on the first night without it, she became pregnant. Lauren and Andrew now look at life in a whole new light as they are about to become parents. Lauren is especially affected as she experiences the joys, frustration and strange food cravings her first pregnancy causes her. Andrew does her every bidding. Still she's a pain, he says, "but sometimes I can be a pain in the ass

too." Cooper, a gorgeous divorce lawyer, is Lauren's friend; Julie and Eric are Andrew and Lauren's married friends (Julie is also pregnant); Danny is Andrew's friend, a slacker who plays piano near the escalator of the women's shoe department at Nortsrom's.

Cast: Jennifer Westfeldt *(Lauren Stone)*; Peter Cambor *(Andrew Stone)*; Rachael Harris *(Cooper)*; Melanie Paxon *(Julie)*; Sunrish Bala *(Eric)*; Michael Weaver *(Danny)*.

6748   *Nothing But the Best.* (Series; Variety; NBC; 1953). A summer program of celebrity interviews and performances by guests with actor Eddie Albert as the host and the music of Skitch Henderson and His Trio.

6749   *Nothing in Common.* (Series; Comedy; NBC; 1987). David Basner is head of David Basner & Associates, a struggling advertising agency in Chicago. Max Basner, his recently divorced father, is a salesman for the Applebaum Toy Company. David is also struggling to live his own life, but finds constant interference from Max, who feels it is his duty to guide him. Stories relate the efforts of a father and son who have nothing in common to get along with one another. Based on the 1986 feature film of the same title. Other regulars are David's employees: Jacqueline, Victoria, Norma, Roland, Mark, Myron and Joey D.

Cast: Todd Waring *(David Basner)*; Bill Macy *(Max Basner)*; Wendy Kilbourne *(Jacqueline North)*; Elizabeth Bennett *(Victoria Upton-Smythe)*; Mona Lyden *(Norma Starr)*; Paul Tinder *(Roland Reed)*; Bill Applebaum *(Mark Glick)*; Patrick Richwood *(Myron Nipper)*; Billy Worth *(Joey D.)*.

6750   *Nothing Is Easy.* (Series; Comedy; CBS; 1987). A revised version of *Together We Stand*. Following the death of her husband in a car accident, Lori Randall secures a job and enrolls in school to become a court stenographer. She is now a single mother to her natural children, Amy and Jack and her adopted children, Sally and Sam. Stories relate events in the lives of the Randall's as Lori struggles to cope with work, school and raising four mischievous children. Marion is Lori's neighbor and best friend.

Cast: Dee Wallace *(Lori Randall)*; Katie O'Neill *(Amy Randall)*; Scott Grimes *(Jack Randall)*; Ke Huy Quan *(Sam)*; Natasha Bobo *(Sally)*; Julia Migenes *(Marion)*.

6751   *Nothing Sacred.* (Series; Drama; ABC; 1997–1998). St. Thomas is a Catholic parish in Chicago. It is here that Father Francis Xavier Reyneaux, called Father Ray, has been assigned (with Fathers Leo and Eric). Father Ray is not only a priest, but a teacher at St. Francis Grammar School. He is also a man who is beginning to question his faith, his calling and even his existence. Stories relate the personal demons Father Ray battles as he deals with the poor and troubled of his parish.

Cast: Brad Sullivan *(Father Leo)*; Kevin Anderson *(Father Francis Reyneaux)*; Scott Michael Campbell *(Father Eric)*; Ann Dowd *(Sister Maureen "Mo" Brody)*; Tamara Mello *(Rachel)*; Bruce Altman *(Sidney Walters)*; Stephen Bridgewater *(Organist)*.

6752   *Nothing Upstairs.* (Pilot; Comedy; CBS; Aug. 10, 1990). A proposed late night (1:30–2:30 A.M.) program that blends elements of situation comedy, variety show, stand-up comedy and fantasy sequences to present life backstage at a fictional New York Club.

Cast: Larry Keith *(Club owner)*; Coati Mundi *(Bartender)*; Amy Stiller *(Waitress)*; Gene Baylos *(Has-been comic)*; Neill Gladwin, Stephen Kearney *(Oddball customers)*.

6753   *Novel Adventures.* (Series; Drama; Internet; 2008). Lizzie, Amy, Laura and Joanna are four Los Angeles women who belong to a book club. As the sessions become boring to them, they decide to ditch the club and live the adventures they would normally only read about. Stories relate their experiences as they transform their ordinary lives into once in a lifetime experiences.

Cast: Daphne Zuniga *(Laura French)*; Ashley Williams *(Lizzie McKenzie)*; Jolie Jenkins *(Amy Pierson)*; Paola Turbay *(Joanna Ruiz)*.

6754   *Now and Again.* (Series; Drama; CBS; 1999-2000). Michael Newman is a unique individual. He is a product of bio engineering. He has incredible strength, increased mental abilities and the brain of Michael Wiseman, an insurance executive who was killed by a train in a subway accident. Dr. Theodore Morris created Michael Newman and performed the brain transplant as a government experiment to create super agents with the needed abilities to perform hazardous assignments. Michael Wiseman was married to Lisa and the father of Heather. Michael Newman retains memories of his benefactor's life and while not permitted by the government to make contact, he feels that he must do just that. Stories follow Michael as he performs the tasks he was created for.

Cast: Eric Close *(Michael Newman)*; Dennis Haysbert *(Dr. Theodore Morris)*; Margaret Colin *(Lisa Wiseman)*; Heather Matarazzo *(Heather Wiseman)*; Gerrit Graham *(Roger Bender)*; John Goodman *(Michael Wiseman; pilot)*.

6755   *Now and Then, Here and There.* (Series; Cartoon; Syfy; 2008). While attempting to rescue a mysterious girl with strange eyes (Lala-Ru) a young Japanese boy (Shu) is magically transported to her desert world and into the midst of a battle between her people and the evil ruler General Hamdo. Stories follow Shu and Lal-Ru, who possesses the power to create water, as they battle the cruelties of Hamdo.

Voice Cast: Eddie Paulson *(Shu)*; Lisa Ortiz *(Lala-Ru)*; Jack Taylor *(Hamdo)*; Dana Halsted *(Abelia)*; Henry Tenney *(Captain)*; Dan Green *(Nabuca)*; Crispio Freeman *(Tabool)*.

6756   *The Now Generation.* (Pilot; Interview; ABC; Mar. 6, 1968). Interviews with people of the 1960s "Now Generation." The pilot presents an in-depth interview with Mia Farrell wherein she reflects on her youth, the Vietnam War, her family, career and relationships.

Host: Ryan O'Neal. **Guest:** Mia Farrow.

6757   *Now Is Tomorrow.* (Pilot; Anthology; Unaired; Produced in 1961). A proposed series of dramas about people of today pursuing their destinies in the world of tomorrow ("We all have a role to play in tomorrow's world and some of us may affect that world considerably"). The pilot episode follows Captain David Blair (Robert Culp) as he trains for one of the most important jobs in the military: War Room monitor who has the power to destroy the world (by pushing the war button) should the U.S. be attacked.

Host: Charles Bickford.

6758   *Now We're Cookin'.* (Pilot; Comedy; CBS; April 19, 1983). Hoping to turn their lives around when they are released from prison, three ex-cons (Cookie, Rolly and Tony) find work at a diner owned by a woman named Marge. The proposal was to focus on the ex-cons as they struggle to go straight and keep out of trouble. Other regulars are Janine, the parole officer; Vern, the man who yearns for Marge; and Ernie, the detective.

Cast: Lyman Ward *(Cookie Porter)*; Cleavon Little *(Rollin "Rolly" Hutton)*; Paul Carafotes *(Anthony "Tony" Tarzola)*; Carole Cook *(Marge)*; Lynne Moody *(Janine Rogers)*; Gary Allen *(Vern)*; Joe Mantegna *(Ernie)*.

6759   *Now You See It.* (Series; Game; CBS; 1974–1975). Two teams compete, each composed of two members. A board is displayed that contains four vertical lines of run-on letters. The four vertical lines, numbered one through four, become the "line"; and the 14 letters each line contains (numbered 1 through 14) become the "position." One player sits with his back to the board. A question is read and his teammate must locate the answer on the board by calling a "line" (1, 2, 3 or 4). If the player is correct, his partner then faces the board and has to call the "position" of the answer (1 through 14). Points are awarded to the line and position total (for example, Line 2, Position 5 equals 7 points). The other team competes in the same manner. The team with the highest score is the winner.

Host: Jack Narz. **Announcer:** Johnny Olson, Gene Wood. **Music:** Michael Malone.

6760   *Nowhere Man.* (Series; Drama; UPN; 1995-1996). Thomas Veil is a photojournalist. In 1994, while in South America, Veil snaps a picture of four men being hanged by what appears to be American soldiers. John labels the picture "Hidden Agenda" and files it away. One year later, while in a restaurant with his wife (Alyson) his life changes. After returning from the restroom, he finds that he is a man without a past. Alyson doesn't recognize him (she is with another man — her husband), his friends and family are strangers. His studio has been ravaged (his "Hidden Agenda" photograph has been taken — but not the negative). No trace of Veil's past appears to exist. While it is not really explained why this all happened a year after the photo was taken (as opposed to when the photo was taken) Veil realizes the negative he has is the key to unraveling the mystery. It is made clear that "some mysterious organization" is pursuing him but why has his wife, friends and family gone along with the conspiracy? Although captured and placed in a sanitarium (a failed attempt to break him) Veil does manage to escape and begins a treacherous search to find who is pursuing him and why the negative to "Hidden Agenda" is so important.

Program Open: "My name is Thomas Veil, or at least it was. I'm a photographer. I had it all: a wife, Alyson, friends and a career. And in one moment it was all taken away. All because of a single photograph. I have it; they want it and they will do anything to get the negative. I'm keeping this diary as proof that these events are real. I know they are. They have to be."

Cast: Bruce Greenwood *(Thomas Veil)*; Megan Gallagher *(Alyson Veil)*.

6761   *Nowhere to Hide.* (Pilot; Crime Drama; NBC; June 5, 1977). Ike Scanlon, an agent for the U.S. Marshals Service, is a dedicated law enforcer who stops at nothing to get the job done. He is assisted by Deputy Ted Willoughby and the proposal was to relate their case assignments.

Cast: Lee Van Cleef *(Ike Scanlon)*; Charles Knox Robinson *(Ted Willoughby)*; John Randolph *(Narrator)*.

6762   *Number 96.* (Series; Comedy; NBC; 1980-1981). The outrageous sexual activities of a group of people who reside at Number 96 Pacific Way, a Los Angeles apartment building. Based on the Australian series of the same title. The regulars are Lou, the owner of a bar; Rita, his sister; Max, an architect; Marion, Max's wife; Mark, a baseball player for the Bullets; Jill, Mark's wife; Sharon, an actress; Ginny, Sharon's roommate, Anthea, a boutique shop owner; Horace, a retired army officer; Sandy, a nurse; Maureen, Sandy's mother; Nathan, Lou's brother, a cop; Chick, the movie director; Lyle, the janitor; Roger, a resident; Dorothy, Roger's ex-wife; Lisa, a resident; and Hildy, Roger's girlfriend.

Cast: Eddie Barth *(Lou Sugarman)*; Ellen Travolta *(Rita Sugarman)*; Greg Mullavey *(Max Quintzel)*; Randee Heller *(Marion Quintzel)*;

Howard McGillin (*Mark Keaton*); Sherry Hursey (*Jill Keaton*); Hilary Thompson (*Sharon St. Clair*); Maria O'Brien (*Ginny Ramirez*); Rosine Widdowson-Reynolds (*Anthea Bryan*); Barney Martin (*Horace Batterson*); Jill Choder (*Sandy Galloway*); Betsy Palmer (*Maureen Galloway*); Todd Susman (*Nathan Sugarman*); John Reilly (*Chick Walden*); Charles Bloom (*Lyle Bixler*); James Murtaugh (*Roger Busky*); Sharon Spelman (*Dorothy*); Elaine Giftos (*Hildy*).

6763   *The No. 1 Ladies' Detective Agency.* (Series; Crime Drama; HBO; 2009). Precious Ramotswe was born in Botswana, a nation of Africa. She was raised by a father who taught her the powers of observation. Later, after her father's passing and leaving her abusive husband, Precious decides to follow her dream to help other people by opening her own (and the only female) detective agency — The No. 1 Ladies' Detective Agency, in the Kagle Hill Shopping Center on the outskirts of Gaborone. Assisting Precious is Grace Makutsi, her efficient but highly strung secretary (a graduate of the Botswana Secretarial College); J.L.B. Matakoni is the owner of the Tiokweng Road Speedy Motors Garage (and Precious's suitor); B.K. is the owner of the Last Chance Hair Salon, the business next door to Precious's agency. The series, filmed on location in Botswana, follows Precious as she attempts to help others based on the belief that a woman knows what's going on more than a man.

Cast: Jill Scott (*Precious Ramotswe*); Anika Noni Rose (*Grace Makutsi*); Lucian Msamati (*J.L.B.*); Desmond Dube (*B.K.*).

6764   *Number Please.* (Series; Game; ABC; 1961). A line of twenty spaces is placed before each player. After a clue is given, the host calls a number. Players remove that number. A letter is revealed and players attempt to identify the concealed phrase that the line contains. The game continues until one player correctly identifies the message. Incorrect answers disqualify players from that particular round. The player with the most correct identifications is the winner and receives merchandise prizes.

Host: Clayton "Bud" Collyer.

6765   *Number 13 Demon Street.* (Pilot; Thriller; Syn.; 1962). When Satanya, a 17-year-old girl kills herself over a lover's quarrel, she is sent to Hell. Because suicide is a special case, Satanya is offered the opportunity to escape Hell if she becomes a messenger of the Devil. Her assignment: To deliver a special invitation called a "Passport" which contains the evil necessary to make people candidates for Hell.

Also known as *The Devil's Messenger.* In May of 1959, Official Films had negotiated with Herts-Lion Productions to film a half-hour series called *Number 13 Demon Street* for syndication beginning in September. In July, Burl Ives was chosen to play the Devil, but was replaced by Lon Chaney, Jr., when production moved to Sweden. A series was apparently filmed (14 episodes are known to exist) but was never telecast in the U.S. as individual segments. Instead, three segments were edited to form a feature length pilot that aired via syndication in 1962.

Cast: Lon Chaney, Jr. (*The Devil*); Karen Kadler (*Satanya*).

6766   *NUMB3RS.* (Series; Crime Drama; CBS; 2005–2009). *The Attraction Equation: The Power of Pi* is a book written by Charlie Eppes, a professor of applied mathematics at Cal Tech University in California. Charlie believes that mathematics can be used to solve crimes by revealing patterns and predict behavior. This has only been a theory for Charlie until his brother, Don, an FBI agent with the Metro Bureau in Los Angeles, decides to put his theory to the test to help him and his team solve baffling crimes. Armed with his knowledge of mathematics, Charlie sets out to prove that numbers can actually capture criminals. Other regulars are Alan, Charlie's widowed

father (a former urban planner); Larry, Amita and Terry, Charlie's associates; and FBI agents David Sinclair and Megan Reeves; Dr. Mildred French is head of the math department; Oswald is Charlie's friend.

Cast: Rob Morrow (*Don Eppes*); David Krumholtz (*Charlie Eppes*); Judd Hirsch (*Alan Eppes*); Peter MacNichol (*Larry Fleinhardt*); Alimi Ballard (*David Sinclair*); Sabrina Lloyd (*Terry Lake*); Diane Farr (*Megan Reeves*); Navi Rawat (*Amita Ramanujan*); Kathy Najimy (*Dr. Mildred Finch*); Dylan Bruno (*Colby Granger*); Aya Sumika (*Special Agent Liz Warner*); Sabrina Lloyd (*Terry Lake*); Jay Baruchel (*Oswald Kittner*).

6767   *Nurse.* (Series; Drama; CBS; 1981–1982). Mary Benjamin is a widow who resumes her career as a nurse after her son (Chip) departs for college. She finds work as the head nurse at Grant Memorial Hospital in New York City (working in the general medical surgical ward and tenuously supervising patients and staff — where her self-confidence is put to the test by Dr. Kenneth Rose, the hardnosed staff surgeon). Stories follow Mary as she struggles to balance her personal and professional life, adjusting to her role as a single parent and enjoying her independence. Stories also show what it means to be a nurse — no longer a doctor's handmaiden but rather an accomplished medical professional who is responsible for the lives of the patients in her charge. Dr. Kenneth Rose was later called Dr. Adam Rose. Joseph Calvo is Mary's neighbor, a lawyer.

Cast: Michael Learned (*Mary Benjamin*); Robert Reed (*Kenneth Rose/Adam Rose*); Christopher Marcantel (*Chip Benjamin*); Dennis Boutsikaris (*Joseph Calvo*); Hattie Winston (*Nurse Toni Gillette*); Bonnie Hellman (*Nurse Penny Brooks*); Hortensia Colorado (*Nurse Betty LaSada*).

6768   *Nurse Bob.* (Pilot; Comedy; Unaired; Produced for NBC in 1988). Bob Wykowski is a male nurse who has broken the rules of society so often that he has spent much time in jail. After his current release, Bob seeks an honest job to fulfill his parole obligations and agrees to take a job caring for an elderly man (Ted Palmer) in his house. The proposal was to relate Bob's efforts to care for Ted despite the antics of Mr. Palmer's wacky family: Natalie, his off-the-wall daughter-in-law; Frank, Natalie's nasty boyfriend, a lawyer; Carl, Natalie's rebellious young son; and Chloe, Natalie's teenage daughter, the apparently only normal person in the family.

Cast: Tim Thomerson (*Bob Wykowski*); Norman Fell (*Ted Palmer*); Valerie Curtin (*Natalie Palmer*); Todd Susman (*Frank*); Moya Kordick (*Chloe Palmer*); Andrew Bednarski (*Carl Palmer*).

6769   *Nurse Jackie.* (Series; Comedy-Drama; Showtime; 2009–). Jackie Peyton is an ER nurse in a New York City's All Saints Hospital struggling to navigate the rough waters of the crumbling healthcare system. She is a dedicated nurse who strives to provide her patients with the best care possible; but she is also a woman battling her own demons: a lapse of her Catholic faith and her addiction to the prescription drug Percocet (due to a job-related bad back). While Jackie sports an unattractive short haircut and a cynical approach to the doctors with whom she works, she is also quite unethical for reasons that she feels will benefit others (for example, stealing money from a wealthy man who stabbed a prostitute and giving it to a needy pregnant woman; forging an organ donor card of a patient who just died). Eleanor O'Hara is Jackie's best friend, a British doctor who respects Jackie for what she does; Fitch Cooper is the smug Ivy League doctor who prefers golf to patients and leaves his nurses to deal with his drive-by diagnosis; Eddie Walzer is the hospital's pharmacist (supplies Jackie with her drugs); Zoey Barkow is the impressionable first year nursing resident; Mohammed de La Cruz, called "Mo Mo" is Jackie's street-smart confidante; Kevin is Jackie's husband; Grace and Fiona are their daughters.

Cast: Edie Falco (*Jackie Peyton*); Eve Best (*Eleanor O'Hara*); Pete Fancinelli (*Fitch Cooper*); Paul Schulze (*Eddie Walzer*); Merritt Wever (*Zoey Barkow*); Haaz Sleiman (*Mo-Mo*); Dominic Fumusa (*Kevin Peyton*); Ruby Jerins (*Grace Peyton*); Mackenzie Aladjem (*Fiona Peyton*).

6770   *The Nurses*. (Series; Drama; CBS; 1962–1965). The personal and professional lives of Liz Thorpe and Gail Lucas, dedicated nurses at Alden General Hospital in New York City. During its last season the title changed to *The Doctors and the Nurses* and also focused on the lives and experiences of doctors Alex Tazinski and Ted Steffen. Revised for daytime television in a serialized version called *The Nurses* (see next title). Aired as *The Nurses* from Sept. 27, 1962 to Sept. 17, 1964 (67 episodes); and as *The Doctors and the Nurses* from Sept. 22, 1964 to Sept. 7, 1965 (30 episodes).

Cast: Shirl Conway (*Nurse Liz Thorpe*); Zina Bethune (*Nurse Gail Lucas*); Joseph Campanella (*Dr. Ted Steffen*); Michael Tolan (*Dr. Alex Tazinski*); Hilda Simms (*Nurse Ayres*); Stephen Brooks (*Dr. Lowry*); Edward Binns (*Dr. Kiley*); John Beal (*Dr. Henden*); Fred Stewart (*Dr. Felix Reisner*).

6771   *The Nurses*. (Series; Serial; ABC; 1965–1967). A daily afternoon version of the prior prime time title that set at Alden General Hospital, continues to depict events in the working lives of nurses Liz Thorpe and Gail Lucas.

Cast: Mary Fickett (*Liz Thorpe*); Melinda Plank (*Gail Lucas*); Patricia Hyland (*Brenda*); Leonie Norton (*Dorothy Warner*); Nat Polen (*John Crager*); Carol Gainer (*Donna*); Polly Rowles (*Mrs. Grassberg*); Darryl Wells (*Mike*); Arthur Franz (*Hugh*); Muriel Kirkland (*Cora*); Paul Stevens (*Paul*); Joan Wetmore (*Martha*); Dick Van Patten, Alan Yorke, Nicholas Pryor, John Beal.

6772   *Nurses*. (Series; Comedy; NBC; 1991–1994). The Community Medical Center, 3 West (Third Floor) in Miami Beach, Florida, provides the setting. Sandy Miller, the head nurse, is bitter over her recent divorce from plastic surgeon Howard Miller. She lives in an apartment with an ocean view "But they built a high rise that obstructs the view—and I'm still paying for the view." Nurse Julie Milbury previously worked as a psychiatric social worker but had to quit—"I got too nervous around the patients; they had mental problems." She is a hypochondriac and has a number of phobias (for example, afraid to ride a crowded elevator; fearful of flying over water). Her favorite eatery is Trader Vick's and her middle name is Ronald (her parents were expecting a boy).

K.C. McAfee oversees hospital operations (she wants a corporate job and sees this as "a pit stop on my way to the top"). Her father was a puppeteer and she had an unsettled childhood ("We had to go where the work was"). K.C. puts twelve minutes aside each day for what she calls "Me time." She previously worked at a snack food company called Little Stephanie International but quit because "all the girls looked like me." Her hobby is collecting snowball domes ("The ones you shake"). Jack Trent is a businessman, convicted of insider trading, who was sentenced to 3,000 hours of community service at the hospital. He lived at 545 Park Avenue in New York City and now pulls cons to survive.

Cast: Stephanie Hodge (*Nurse Sandy Miller*); Loni Anderson (*K.C. McAfee*); Jeff Altman (*Nurse Greg Vincent*); Arnetia Walker (*Nurse Annie Roland*); Mary Jo Keenan (*Nurse Julie Milbury*); Gina Cuevas (*Nurse Ada Maris*); Kip Gilman (*Dr. Hank Kaplan*); Matt McCoy (*Dr. Howard Miller*); David Rasche (*Jack Trenton*); Florence Stanley (*Dr. Riskin*). **Theme:** "Here I Am" by George Aliceson Tipton and John Bettis.

6773   *Nurses*. (Pilot; Drama; Unaired; Produced for Fox in 2006).

Philadelphia General Hospital is the backdrop for a look at the work of the dedicated nurses who are at the beck and call of the doctors they serve. Eve Morrow is the newest nurse at the hospital, the daughter of Dr. Richard Morrow, the head of surgery; Kurt Taylor is a rising doctor; Becca Dimato is the flirtatious nurse who steals medication to help patients she feels are not getting the right care; Joanne "Jo" Mazur is a nurse who is also a single mother; Patrick DeLeon is a male nurse who is romancing Joanne; Chris Korenek is a nurse, bored with her marriage, who wonders if she has what it takes to become a surgeon; Margo MacDonald is the head nurse.

Cast: Eliza Dushku (*Eve Morrow*); Gregory Harrison (*Richard Morrow*); Brett Dalton (*Kurt Taylor*); Drew Sidora (*Becca Dimato*); Jaclyn DeSantis (*Joanne Mazur*); Melinda Page Hamilton (*Margo MacDonald*); Sara Rue (*Chris Korenek*); Ramon Rodriquez (*Patrick DeLeon*).

6774   *The Nut House*. (Pilot; Comedy; CBS; Sept. 1, 1964). Rapid-fire, burlesque-like dramatizations that spoof the American scene.

Regulars: Ceil Cabot, Jane Connell, Fay DeWitt, Andy Duncan, Don Francks, Tom Holland, Adam Keefe, Muriel Landers, Marilyn Lovell, Mara Lynn, Jack Sheldon, Alan Sues. **Music:** Jerry Fielding.

6775   *Nuts and Bolts*. (Pilot; Comedy; ABC; Aug. 24, 1981). Primo is a caring, out-of-date robot. Victor is a caustic, sophisticated robot; and Beeper is a vacuum cleaning robot. All are the creations of Miles Fenton, a widowed computer engineer who created the robots to help him raise his children, Lucy and Alex. The proposal was to relate the mishaps that arise when human and machine clash. Other regulars are Karen Prescott, Miles's girlfriend; and Martha, Miles's mother.

Cast: Rich Little (*Miles Fenton*); Tammy Lauren (*Lucy Fenton*); Justin Dana (*Alex Fenton*); Eve Arden (*Martha Fenton*); Jo Ann Pflug (*Karen Prescott*); Mitchell Young Evans (*Primo*); Douglas V. Fowley (*Primo's Voice*); Tommy McLoughlin (*Victor*); Garnett Smith (*Victor's Voice*).

6776   *The Nutt House*. (Series; Comedy; NBC; 1989). Reginald J. Tarkington is the manager of the Nutt House, a once prestigious New York hotel that has fallen on hard times. The elderly and eccentric Edwina Nutt owns the hotel, a miser who refuses to renovate or invest new monies in the hotel. Reginald also has to contend with a staff he feels are desperately in need of psychiatric help. Reginald is assisted by the lame-brained Dennis; Mrs. Frick, the nasty housekeeper; Sally, Edwina's sexy but naïve secretary; Freddy, the almost blind elevator operator; Stanley, the doorman; and the annoying Charles Nutt III, Edwina's grandson, who oversees the hotel's operations. Stories follow Reginald as he attempts to run a hotel that he feels will soon drive him to the psychiatric ward.

Cast: Harvey Korman (*Reginald J. Tarkington*); Cloris Leachman (*Edwina Nutt/Mrs. Frick*); Molly Hagan (*Sally Lonnaneck*); Mark Blankfield (*Freddy*); Brian McNamara (*Charles Nutt III*); Gregory Itzin (*Dennis*); Ronny Graham (*Stanley*).

6777   *N.Y.C. Prep*. (Series; Reality; Bravo; 2009). A profile of six not-so-typical New York teenagers: Camille Hughes, Jessie Leavitt, Kelli Tomashoff, Taylor DiGiovanni, Sebastian Oppenheim and Peter "P.C." Peterson. The selected teens are rich, over privileged and bratty (sort of an underage version of Bravo's successful *Real Housewives* franchise). Little attention is paid to the schools the teens attend (mainly because their exclusive private schools [Nightingale-Bamford, Birch Walthen Lenox and Dwight] would not allow filming or even their name being mentioned). The one exception was for Taylor, a 15-year-old student at a public high school (Stuyvesant).

Although portrayed as "the token public school student," Taylor is determined to join the Upper East Side scene like her friends. Episodes focus in particular on their high-end side of life: the fashion, parties and swank restaurants.

6778   N.Y.P.D. (Series; Crime Drama; ABC; 1967–1969). Mike Haines, Johnny Corso and Jeff Ward are detectives with the 27th Precinct of the N.Y.P.D. Stories, which are quite gritty, follow the squad car detectives as they investigate crimes from robbery to homicide with a focus on the details each case presents and how suspects are determined, questioned and brought to justice.

Cast: Jack Warden *(Mike Haines)*; Frank Converse *(Johnny Corso)*; Robert Hooks *(Jeff Ward)*.

6779   N.Y.P.D. Blue. (Series; Crime Drama; ABC; 1993–2005). A gritty, groundbreaking series that focuses on the day-to-day lives of the officers of the 15th Detective Squad of the New York City Police Department. The program introduced foul (gutter) language and partial nudity to prime time broadcast network TV; it was so controversial that 57 ABC affiliates refused to air the first episode.

Detective Andy Sipowitz is the principal focus of attention. He is a hard working cop who worked previously with the 25th Precinct. He does drink (Patrick's Bar is his favorite watering hole) and it does affect his job. Over the course of the series, Andy has been a partner with John Kelly (1993-94), Bobby Simone (1994–98), Danny Sorenson (1998–2001) and John Clark, Jr. (2001–05). In addition to the detectives listed in the cast, other regulars are Sylvia Costas, the Assistant District Attorney; Laura Kelly, a lawyer and John's ex-wife; and Donna Abandando, the squad room secretary. Steven Bochco created the series.

Cast: Dennis Franz *(Det. Andy Sipowitz)*; David Caruso *(Det. John Kelly)*; Jimmy Smits *(Det. Bobby Simone)*; Rick Schroder *(Det. Danny Sorenson)*; Sharon Lawrence *(Sylvia Costas)*; James McDaniel *(Lt. Arthur Fancy)*; Sherry Stringfield *(Laura Michaels Kelly)*; Nicholas Turturro *(Det. James Martinez)*; Gordon Clapp *(Det. Greg Medavoy)*; Gail O'Grady *(Donna Abandando)*; Justine Miceli *(Det. Adrienne Lesniak)*; Andrea Thompson *(Det. Jill Kirkendall)*; Bill Brochtrup *(Det. John Irvin)*; Jacqueline Obradors *(Det. Rita Ortiz)*; Henry Simmons *(Det. Baldwin Jones)*; Amy Brenneman *(Det. Janice Licalsi)*; Kim Delaney *(Det. Diane Russell)*; Mark-Paul Gosselaar *(Det. John Clark, Jr.)*.

6780   N.Y.P.D. 2069. (Pilot; Crime Drama; Unaired; Produced for Fox in 2003). Alex Franco, an officer with the New York City Police Department in 2003 is mysteriously transported to the year 2069 where his experiences battling crime with antiquated methods, but learning to accept new ones, was to be the focal point of the series.

Cast: Josh Hopkins *(Alex Franco)*; Annie Parisse *(Gina Zahl)*; Anna Gunn *(Natalie)*; Giancarlo Esposito *(Lt. Gardner)*; Danny Pino *(Eric Cavanaugh)*.

6781   The O. Henry Playhouse. (Series; Anthology; Syn.; 1957). Dramatizations based on the stories of William Sidney Porter, who, while in prison, wrote under the pen name O. Henry.

Host-Narrator: Thomas Mitchell *(as O. Henry)*.

6782   Oakmont. (Pilot; Drama; NBC; June 19, 1988). In the small New England town of Barrington stands a boarding school called Oakmont that was once attended by Michael Fields, now a high-powered successful publisher in New York City. When the opportunity arises for Michael to become the school's headmaster, he quits his job and moves back home with his daughter, Rebecca (his son, David, is already attending the school). Girls are now admitted at the formerly all-male prep school and Rebecca becomes one of its students, causing mixed feelings in David — his sister is a student and his father is the headmaster. The proposal was to focus on Michael's experiences as headmaster and on the students, faculty and community surrounding Oakmont. Corry and Eric are David's friends.

Cast: Michael McKean *(Michael Fields)*; Jonathan Ward *(David Fields)*; Marcianne Warman *(Rebecca Fields)*; Brandon Douglas *(Corry)*; Byron Thomas *(Eric)*.

6783   The Oaks. (Pilot; Drama; Unaired; Produced for Fox in 2007). A home in 1967, 1987 and 2007 is the setting for a look at three different couples who inhabited the residence at three different times and appear to be connected by the mysterious spirits that haunt it.

Cast: Sienna Guillory *(Jessica)*; Shannon Lucio *(Sarah)*; Bahar Soomekh *(Hollis)*; Jeremy Renner *(Dan)*; Matt Lanter *(Mike)*; Michael Rispoli *(Frank)*; Romy Rosemont *(Molly)*.

6784   The Oath. (Pilot; Drama; ABC; Aug. 24, 1976). Dramas depicting the work of doctors dedicated to the profession of healing. Two pilots were produced. The first story, "33 Hours in the Life of God," tells of a cold, impersonal cardiologist (Hal Holbrook) whose total dedication to his work begins to affect his health. The second pilot story, "The Sad and Lonely Sundays" (Aug. 26, 1976) tells of an aging doctor (Jack Albertson) who reenters medical school to catch up on 40 years of medical progress.

6785   The Object Is. (Series; Game; ABC; 1963-1964). Six players compete in a game wherein they must identify personalities from object clues. The player with the most correct identifications is the winner and receives merchandise prizes.

Host: Dick Clark. **Announcer:** Mike Lawrence.

6786   The Oblongs. (Series; Cartoon; WB; 2001). The Oblongs are a family who live in Hill Valley, a toxic town next to an industrial waste site. The Oblongs are also a family who have been seriously affected by pollution emanating from the site: each has bizarre physical and emotional abnormalities. Bob, the father, manages quite well without arms and legs. Pickles, his wife, is bald (she wears a wig) and is addicted to cigarettes and alcohol. Biff and Chip are their conjoined sons; Beth, their youngest child (4 years old) has a cucumber-like growth coming out of her head; and Milo, their youngest son, is an optimist who has only one strand of hair on his head. Bob's mother, called Grammy, is a vegetable. The family cat, Lucky, is a chain smoker; and their dog, Scottie, is a narcoleptic.

Bob works on the assembly line (screwing lids on jars with his teeth) at Globocide, a company that makes pesticides, defoliants and baby formula. Stories, based on the book *Creepy Susie and 13 Other Tragic Tales for Troubled Children* by Angus Oblong, follows the Oblongs as they attempt to live a normal life.

Other regulars are George Kilmer, Bob's boss; Pristine, George's wife; Debbie, George's daughter; Jared, George's son; School Principal Davis; School Nurse Rench; Leland the homeroom teacher; and Milo's friends, Helga, Creepy Susie, Mikey Butts and Peggy Weggy.

Voice Cast: Will Ferrell *(Bob Oblong)*; Jean Smart *(Pickles Oblong)*; Pamela Segall *(Milo Oblong)*; Randy Sklar *(Biff Oblong)*; Jason Sklar *(Chip Oblong)*; Billy West *(George Kilmer)*; Pamela Segall *(Jared Kilmer/Debbie Kilmer)*; Lea DeLaria *(Helga Phugly)*; Jeannie Elias *(Creepy Susie/Mikey Butts)*; Becky Thyre *(Peggy Weggy/Pristine Kilmer)*.

6787   Oboler's Comedy Theater. (Series; Anthology; ABC; 1949). Arch Oboler, a prolific writer for programs on radio during its golden age, oversees a series of comedic stories that he has written especially for television. Also known as *Arch Oboler's Comedy Theater*.

Performers: Sara Berner, Ken Christy, Hans Conried, Marna Kenneally, Frances Rafferty, Olan Soule, Louis Merrill, Olive Deering, Danny Richards, Jr. **Music:** Rex Koury.

6788 *The O.C.* (Series; Drama; Fox; 2003–2007). The upscale community of Newport Beach in Orange County (the O.C.), California provides the backdrop for a look at the lives of the wealthy and not so prosperous members of the community.

Cast: Peter Gallagher (*Sandford "Sandy" Cohen*); Kelly Rowan (*Kirsten Cohen*); Benjamin McKenzie (*Ryan Atwood*); Adam Brody (*Seth Cohen*); Mischa Barton (*Marissa Cooper*); Melinda Clarke (*Julie Cooper-Nichol*); Tate Donovan (*Jimmy Cooper*); Chris Carmack (*Luke Ward*); Rachel Bilson (*Summer Roberts*); Gary Grubbs (*Gordon Mullit*); Kevin Sorbo (*Frank Atwood*); Autumn Reese (*Taylor Townsend*); Cam Gigandet (*Kevin Volchok*); Samaire Armstrong (*Anna Stern*); Michael Nouri (*Dr. Neil Roberts*); Autumn Reeser (*Taylor Townsend*); Michael Cassidy (*Zach Stevens*); Jeff Hephner (*Matt Ramsey*); Olivia Wilde (*Alex Kelly*); Navi Rawat (*Theresa Diaz*); Amanda Righetti (*Hailey Nichol*); Shannon Lucio (*Lindsay Gardner*); Ryan Donowho (*Johnny Harper*); Wayne Dalglish (*Brad Ward*); Corey Price (*Eric Ward*); Chris Pratt (*Che*); Logan Marshall-Green (*Trey Atwood*); Johnny Lewis (*Dennis "Chili" Childress*); Ashley Hartman (*Holly Fischer*); Kimberly Oja (*Taryn Baker*); Paula Trickey (*Veronica Townsend*); Jeri Ryan (*Charlotte Morgan*); Nikki Griffin (*Jess Sathers*).

6789 *Occasional Wife.* (Series; Comedy; NBC; 1966-1967). Peter Christopher, called "The Company Bachelor" at work, is a ladies' man who is best at romancing women. He has a nice apartment on East 57th Street in Manhattan and a good job with the Brahms Baby Food Company. On one night his world suddenly changed. It began with his mother — "Peter, a man of your age should be married" — and concluded with his family-and corporate image-minded boss, Max Brahms — "A man should be judged by his ability. The only thing that counts around here is whether you are married or not."

When an executive position becomes available, Peter applies but is refused — "I'm sorry, Peter. I believe in married executives. No marriage, no promotion." Later that day, while drowning his sorrows in a bar, he begins talking with his friend, Greta Patterson, the hatcheck girl. Greta has problems too, with men hitting on her, and she remarks, "Too bad you can't do what I do to protect myself in this place — pretend you're married."

An idea forms in Peter's mind. "Greta, you've given me the solution to my problem, a fake wife, that's the answer for Brahms." "You must be out of your mind," Greta says. "No, Greta, I mean it. I want you to be my wife ... occasionally." Greta refuses until Peter offers to find her an apartment and pay for her rent and art classes (she is studying to be a dress designer). Peter buys her a damaged wedding ring for $15, and she goes on salary as his occasional wife.

Peter, who lives in Apartment 7C, sets Greta up in Apartment 9C in his building. For access to each other's apartments, Peter and Greta use the back fire escapes (they fear getting caught if they use the elevators or their front doors). Apartment 8C is between them — the residence of "The Man in the Middle" (who witnesses their antics and has come to enjoy watching them).

Peter and Greta then devise a story for Mr. Brahms: they met at the Huntington Yacht Club. It was love at first sight, and they married immediately after (Greta pretends to be a dancer turned librarian who lived in Boston).

"How long will the marriage last?" asked Greta. "The marriage is going to last until I get a vice presidency," Peter says. "Then Greta

will have a boating accident, then you'll be lost, I'll be a widower and Brahms will love me." Peter's plan begins to work — he is made an advertising executive when Brahms learns of his marriage.

Greta pretends to be Peter's wife whenever the need arises. Peter has a girlfriend named Marilyn Granville. Mr. Brahms believes that she is Peter's sister. Greta has a boyfriend named Bernard ("Bernie") J. Cramer. Brahms believes Peter is Greta's brother. Peter's mother believes Peter and Greta are really married and that it was love at first sight.

To pay for a third day of art school, Greta took a job as a receptionist for the Bellfield General Employment Agency at $65 a week. The slogan of the Brahms Baby Food Company is "Every Meal a Lullaby."

Wally Frick is Peter's office rival and will stop at nothing to advance his position within the company. He is married to a pretty, power seeking woman named Vera. Vera is unable to make Wally as aggressive as she is; to compensate for this, she stays by Wally's side and coaches him on how to "kiss up" to the boss.

Program Open: "There are eight million stories in the Naked City. Some are violent; some happy, some sad. But one of them is just plain cuckoo. This is a modern fable about two young people who make a bargain only to find that they were going to get a lot more than they bargained for. We call our fable *Occasional Wife* and it stars Michael Callan and Patricia Harty and it features among other things, a fire escape" (refers to the way the principals sneak in and out of each other's apartments so nobody will realize they are not really married).

Cast: Michael Callan (*Peter Christopher*); Patricia Harty (*Greta Patterson*); Jack Collins (*Max Brahms*); Susan Silo (*Vera Frick*); Jack Riley (*Wally Frick*); Chris Noel (*Marilyn Granville*); Stuart Margolin (*Bernie Cramer*); Bryan O'Byrne (*Man in the Middle*). **Narrator:** Vince Scully.

6790 *Ocean Force.* (Series; Reality; TruTV; 2008). The work of life guards (here representing Huntington Beach in California) are depicted in a more serious light than on the series *Baywatch*. While *Baywatch* did show that beach rescues can be dangerous, *Ocean Force* relates the real life rescues with all the hazards such rescues involve. Michael Bartlett, Eric Dieterman, Jon Elser and Matthew Norton are the lifeguards.

6791 *Ocean Girl.* (Series; Adventure; Disney; 1994–1997). Neri is a mysterious girl who lives on an island off the coast of Australia. Many years ago she and her father (who has since died) came to Earth by space ship (from their home world, the Planet of the Oceans [also called Ocean Planet]) to save the Earth's oceans, a responsibility that has since fallen on her shoulders. Neri can breathe under water and communicate with whales (she has befriended one she calls Charley). Dr. Diane Bates is a marine biologist and the single mother of teenagers Brett and Jason. Diane has been assigned to ORCA (Oceanic Research Center of Australia), an underwater research and environmental protective facility. When Diane begins a study of whales (with her sons as assistants) she begins using whale songs — and attracts Neri, who appears in the middle of the ocean (later, when Brett's inoperable boat strands him on Neri's island, the two become friends and Neri becomes a part of Diane's team). Neri seeks Diane's help in protecting the oceans and Diane requires Neri's help in furthering her knowledge of the sea and whales. Stories follow Neri's adventures as she interacts with humans for the first time and battles the enemies of the oceans. Dr. Winston Seth is Diane's research partner; Vanessa, Zoe and Froggy are interns at the center. See also *The New Adventures of Ocean Girl* (which incorporates the character of Neri but changes everything else).

Cast: Marzena Godecki (*Neri*); Kerry Armstrong, Liz Burch (*Dr.*

Diane Bates); Jeffrey Walker *(Brett Bates)*; David Hoflin *(Jason Bates)*; Alex Pinder *(Dr. Winston Seth)*; Jacalyn Prince *(Vanessa Lane)*; Cassandra Magrath *(Zoe Kondelos)*; Joel de Carteret *(Jake "Froggy" Reilly)*; Nicholas Bell *(Dr. Hellegren)*; Lauren Hewett *(Mera)*.

6792 *Ocean Quest.* (Series; Reality; NBC; 1985). A beautiful girl's experiences as she explores the oceans of the world. The girl, former Miss Universe Shawn Weatherly is chosen for the quest (a woman of courage with no knowledge of diving) to devote one year of her life to the greatest adventure of her life: documenting the myths, mysteries and monsters of the ocean. Shawn's amazing experiences as she trains with undersea photographer Al Giddings and his crew to her one-year true experiences are presented in documentary style.

Cast: Shawn Weatherly *(Herself)*; Al Giddings *(Himself)*. **Narrator:** Ray Willes.

6793 *Ochoc Cinco: The Ultimate Catch.* (Series; Reality; VH-1; 2010). Twenty women chosen from a group of 85 contestants vie for a chance to become the woman for former pro football star (Cincinnati Bengals), Chad Ochocino. After completing "Dating Camp" training, each of the women is ranked as the best possible matches for Chad. The women then compete in various "getting to know you" challenges and the one woman who most impresses Chad could become the next Mrs. Ochocino.

6794 *O'Connor's Ocean.* (Pilot; Adventure; NBC; Dec. 13, 1960). Torin O'Connor is a marine ocean firm lawyer who, in his spare time enjoys yachting. The proposal was to follow Torin as he tackles cases involving the high seas.

Cast: John Payne *(Torin O'Connor)*.

6795 *Octavius and Me.* (Pilot; Comedy; CBS; July 17, 1962). Octavius, nicknamed "Ockie," and his wife, Hattie, are a retired couple who decide to travel around the country in a most unusual way: from trailer camp to trailer camp. The proposal was to focus on their efforts to help the people they meet during their stopovers.

Cast: Dub Taylor *(Octavius Todd)*; Lois Bridge *(Hattie Todd)*.

6796 *October Road.* (Series; Drama; ABC; 2007). Knights Ridge, Massachusetts, is a small, picturesque New England town. It is also the home of a group of close knit friends: Nick Garrett, Hannah Daniels, Ray "Big Cat" Cataldo, Eddie Latekka, Ikey and Physical Phil. But that was in 1997. Since then, Nick has become the successful author of a book (*Turtle on a Snare Drum*, which is a not-so-flattering look at his home town and his friends) and has been living in New York City. One day in the spring of 2007, Nick accepts an offer to give a speech on novel writing in his hometown at Duframe College. Nick never returned, "because I got sidetracked." Once he stayed away, staying away became the way for him. But now he has come home to face everything he left behind; he never kept in touch (Hannah says, "Nick just vanished into the ether"). His return is not so welcomed and he faces mixed emotions from his friends (who are bitter for his portrayal of them in his book). He finds that his former love, Hannah, has a ten-year-old son (Sam); Ray is now the owner of Cataldo Builders (a construction company); Physical Phil hasn't stepped outside of the town since 9-11; Iky still feels he is friends with Nick (although he is a bit angered that he wasn't represented in the book); and Eddie, his best friend, now feels they can no longer be friends. Nick also believes that Sam is his son (although Hannah denies it) because both he and Sam are allergic to any kind of nut. Nick realizes he made a mistake by never coming home. He also knows there are a lot of unexpected adventures in town — and he is not about to leave again. Stories follow Nick as he reacquaints himself with old friends — and new experiences for a follow-up book that is true to life and honest.

Cast: Bryan Greenberg *(Nick Garrett)*; Laura Prepon *(Hannah Daniels)*; Warren Christie *(Ray Cataldo)*; Evan Jones *(Ikey)*; Jay Paulson *(Physical Phil)*; Geoff Stults *(Eddie Latekka)*; Slade Pearce *(Sam Daniels)*; Tom Berenger *(The Commander)*; Brad William Henke *(Owen Rowan)*; Odette Yustman *(Aubrey)*.

6797 *The Odd Couple.* (Series; Comedy; ABC; 1970–1975). Felix Unger is an excessively neat perfectionist; Oscar Madison is an irresponsible slob. Both men are divorced and live together at 1049 Park Avenue (at 74th Street and Central Park West in New York) in Apartment 1102. Felix and Oscar first met when they were chosen as jurors for the trial of Leo Garvey, a man accused of driving his roommate crazy (Oscar was a sportswriter for the *New York Times* at the time).

Felix, who suffers from sinus attacks, was born in Chicago, moved to Oklahoma and grew up on a farm in Glenview, New York (another episode mentions Toledo, Ohio, as his hometown). He is a member of the Radio Actors' Guild (as a kid he appeared on *Let's Pretend*), and in college he had his own radio show called *Felix*. Felix is now an established photographer and operates Portraits a Specialty. Before moving in with Oscar, Felix, his wife, Gloria, and their children, Edna and Leonard lived in New Rochelle, New York.

Oscar, a sportswriter for the *New York Herald*, was born at Our Lady of Angels Hospital in Philadelphia (another episode states that Oscar was born in Chicago — where he and Felix met briefly as kids). Oscar's first job in New York was as a copywriter for *Playboy* magazine; he had a radio show called *The Oscar Madison Sports Talk Show* (later changed to *Oscar Madison's Greatest Moments in Sports*). Oscar and his wife, Blanche, divorced after eight years of marriage due excessive arguing (Felix and Gloria divorced because of his excessive neatness). Based on the play by Neil Simon.

Murray Greschner is a police officer with the N.Y.P.D. Myrna Turner is Oscar's secretary. She was born in the Bronx, is disorganized, sloppy and lazy. Myrna is forever having boyfriend trouble, especially with "Sheldn" ("They forgot the 'O' on his birth certificate"). She calls Oscar "Mr. M." Miriam Welby is Felix's romantic interest; and Dr. Nancy Cunningham is Oscar's lady love; Mimi is Murray's wife. Sisters Cicely and Gwen Pigeon are Oscar and Felix's neighbors; Speed, Vinnie and Roy are Oscar's poker-playing pals.

Program Open: "On November thirteenth Felix Unger was asked to remove himself from his place of residence. That request came from his wife. Deep down he knew she was right. But he also knew that someday he would return to her. With nowhere else to go, he appeared at the home of his childhood friend, Oscar Madison. Sometime earlier, Madison's wife had thrown him out, requesting that he never return. Can two divorced men share an apartment without driving each other crazy?"

Cast: Tony Randall *(Felix Unger)*; Jack Klugman *(Oscar Madison)*; Al Molinaro *(Murray Greschner)*; Penny Marshall *(Myrna Turner)*; Elinor Donahue *(Miriam Welby)*; Joan Hotchkis *(Nancy Cunningham)*; Janis Hansen *(Gloria Unger)*; Brett Somers *(Blanche Madison)*; Pamelyn Ferdin, Doney Oatman *(Edna Unger)*; Leif Garrett, Willie Aames *(Leonard Unger)*; Jane Dulo, Alice Ghostley *(Mimi Grescher)*; Monica Evans *(Cicely Pigeon)*; Carole Shelley *(Gwen Pigeon)*; Garry Walberg *(Speed)*; Larry Gelman *(Vinnie)*; Ryan MacDonald *(Roy)*.

6798 *Odd Man Out.* (Series; Comedy; ABC; 1999-2000). Julia Whitney is a single mother (a widow) with four children: Paige, Elizabeth, Valerie and Andrew, the only male is a house full of women — the odd man out.

The Whitney's live in South Beach, Florida, where Julia works as a caterer; her late husband was named Bill. She was born in Cincinnati and attended the University of Miami.

Paige, the eldest child, is absolutely gorgeous. She is a sophomore at South Beach High School and yearns to be a model (Julia wants her to wait, attend college, then follow her dream). She believes being beautiful is her goal in life and she is determined to let the world know that. Valerie, the second born daughter, idolizes Paige and can't wait until she is older (she is 13; Paige is 16) so she can become as glamorous as Paige. Right now, she feels her slowly developing figure is hindering those chances. Elizabeth is 10 years old and is slowly becoming influenced by Paige and Valerie. She is more into academics than her sisters and enjoys playing the oboe.

Andrew has learned a lot from living with four females; he can even tell what shampoo a girl uses and what perfume she wears. He finds the bathroom unsafe—the girls have lip gloss emergencies and throw him out—"Changing the locks won't work," says Julia, "because your sisters are like jewel thieves." Andrew considers himself the man of the house—although his sisters think it is a big joke.

Andrew pals around with his best friend, Keith Carlson, a girl crazy teenager who has the hots for Paige (the feeling is not mutual, however). He plays the drums and started a garage band called Exhaust Pipe (Andrew plays the guitar).

Also hanging out at the Whitney home is Julia's sister, Jordan, a modeling agency representative who is self-absorbed and constantly thinks about herself. She is very close to Paige and even got her a job as a lingerie model—although they only used her as a foot model. When Bill passed away, Jordan said she would help steer the ship—"But she torpedoed it," says Julia. Lynsey Bartilson was originally chosen to play the role of Valerie Whitney.

Cast: Markie Post (*Julia Whitney*); Natalia Cigliuti (*Paige Whitney*); Vicki Davis (*Valerie Whitney*); Marina Malota (*Elizabeth Whitney*); Erik von Detten (*Andrew Whitney*); Jessica Capshaw (*Jordan*); Trevor Fehrman (*Keith Charles*).

6799   The Oddball Couple. (Series; Cartoon; ABC; 1975–1977). *Odd Couple* spoof that relates the antics of two trouble-prone magazine writers: Fleabag, a natural-born canine slob; and Spiffy, a perfectionist cat. Goldie Hound is their secretary.

Voice Cast: Paul Winchell (*Fleabag*); Frank Nelson (*Spiffy*); Joan Gerber (*Goldie Hound*).

6800   Oddville, MTV. (Series; Comedy; MTV; 1997). A program that presents odd things—from boring (and pointless interviews) bad talent acts, awful celebrity impersonations and people who just sit there and say or do nothing.

Host: Frank Hope. **Co-Host:** David Greene. **Featured:** John Walsh as Joey the Monkey. **Announcer:** Melissa Gabriel.

6801   Odyssey. (Series; Anthology; CBS; 1957). Charles Collingwood hosts and narrates stories based on events that shaped the world.

6802   Odyssey 5. (Series; Science Fiction; Showtime; 2002). On August 7, 2007, the Earth is destroyed in a fiery explosion. With the exception of a group of people aboard the space shuttle *Odyssey*, all life on Earth has been destroyed by an entity called Leviathan, an artificial intelligence developed by scientists. Shortly after the explosion, a non-organic being called the Seeker appears to the members of the *Odyssey:* Commander Chuck Taggert, reporter Sarah Forbes, astronaut Angela Perry and scientist Kurt Mendel. The Seeker informs them that 50 other such worlds have been destroyed but it has always arrived too late to find survivors. Now, for the first time, the Seeker can change what happened. It sends the crew back in time five years so they can hopefully change the past to prevent a disastrous future.

Stories follow the crew as they confront their pasts and seek the people responsible for creating Leviathan.

The twenty-episode series was produced in Canada. Fourteen episodes aired on Showtime in 2002; the remaining six episodes aired on Showtime in 2004.

Cast: Peter Weller (*Chuck Taggert*); Leslie Silva (*Sarah Forbes*); Tamara Craig Thomas (*Angela Perry*); Sebastian Roche (*Kurt Mendel*); Christopher Graham (*Neil Taggert*); Gina Clayton (*Paige Taggert*); Kenneth Mitchell (*Marc Taggert*); Jim Codrington (*Troy Johnson*); Sonja Smits (*Cynthia Hodge*); Lindy Booth (*Holly Culverson*); Phillip Jarrett (*Paul Forbes*).

6803   Of All Things. (Series; Variety; CBS; 1956). A summer program of music and songs with actress Faye Emerson as the host.

Host: Faye Emerson. **Regulars:** Jack Haskell, Ilene Woods. **Announcer:** Del Sharbutt. **Music:** Billy Clifton.

6804   Of Men, of Women. (Pilot; Anthology; ABC; Dec. 17, 1972). Dramatic as well as comedic stories about the many faces of love. A second pilot aired on May 6, 1973 and stories included "All Her Own" (Lee Remick as woman who fears she may have caused her husband's suicide), "Hot Machine, Cold Machine" (widower Jackie Cooper and widow Cloris Leachman meet by chance at a coin operated laundry), "Margie Pssses" (Deborah Raffin as an effervescent teenage girl with an everlasting effect on people), and "The Brave and the Free" (Marlyn Mason and George Maharis struggling to iron out the problems in their marriage).

Host: Lee Remick (Pilot One), Stephen Boyd (Pilot 2).

6805   Off Broadway. (Pilot; Crime Drama; ABC; May 12 and 20, 1995). Consuela "Connie" Muldoon is a tough, dedicated N.Y.P.D. homicide detective who prefers to work alone. Connie is also a single mother struggling to raise a 13-year-old daughter (Julianna). The proposal, a spin off from *The Commish* was to focus on her relentless investigations into the cases she tackles.

Cast: Lisa Vidal (*Connie Muldoon*); Christina Vidal (*Julianna Muldoon*); Robert Hooks (*Captain*).

6806   Off Campus. (Pilot; Comedy; CBS; June 8, 1977). Life in a co-ed rooming house as seen through the eyes of a group of college students (Janet, Steve, Bonnie, Josh, Stanley, Weineke and Alexis) preparing for graduation and adulthood.

Cast: Marilu Henner (*Janet*); Josh Mostel (*Steve*); Ann Risley (*Bonnie*); Chip Zien (*Josh*); Paul Reigert (*Stanley*); Joe Bova (*Weineke*); Alexa Kenin (*Alexis*).

6807   Off Center. (Series; Comedy; WB; 2001). Euan Pearce and Mike Platt are friends who met at Oxford University. They now share Apartment 6-D at the posh Hadley Building off Center Street in Manhattan. Euan is a free spirited, girl-chasing investment counselor. Mike is his direct opposite, a laid-back and simplistic young man who seeks a meaningful relationship with a girl, hopefully with his current girlfriend, Liz. Mike does have one obsession though—for adult films starring nurses; Liz calls it "Nurse Porn." Stories follow the lives of two mismatched roommates who happen to be best friends. Other regulars are Status Quo, the music store owner who is also the building landlord; Vee, Liz's friend, a model (although she calls herself a supermodel); and Chan, the owner of the Vietnamese restaurant frequented by Mike and Euan.

Cast: Sean Maguire (*Euan Pearce*); Eddie Kay Thomas (*Mike Platt*); Lauren Stamile (*Liz*); Berglind Icey (*Vee*); Jason George (*Ethan "Status" Quo*); John Cho (*Chan Presley*).

6808   Off Duty. (Pilot; Drama; CBS; Aug. 16, 1988). Off Duty is a fabled policeman's bar in Chicago. It is owned by a woman named Siobhan, a cop's widow, and the proposal was to focus on the after-hours lives of the cops who assemble there: Zack, the bartender, who is working at Off Duty while recovering from a car accident while on active duty as a cop (he has broken hips and gets around on a special wheeled stool); Pat, his female ex-partner; Charles, the rookie cop; his brother, Vincent, who watches over Charles and has been nicknamed "Mother"; and Tom, the permanent fixture at the bar, a legendary retired cop.

Cast: Eileen Brennan (*Siobhan*); Charles Frank (*Zack Scott*); Lisa Blount (*Pat Yaraslovsky*); Charles Stratton (*Charlie DiAntha*); Ray Abruzzo (*Vincent DiAntha*); Tony LoBianco (*Tom Cooper*).

6809   *Off Duty*. (Pilot; Comedy; Unaired; Produced for NBC in 2009). Glenn Falcon is a legendary police detective who is nearing retirement and whose ability to solve crimes as he once used is starting to fade. Matthew Roberts is a young, ambitious detective who has been partnered with Glenn. The proposal was to follow Matthew as he struggles to work his way up the departmental ladder despite the problems Glenn creates for them.

Cast: Bradley Whitford (*Glenn Falcon*); Antonio Ortiz (*Matthew Roberts*); Bonnie Somerville (*Kim Roberts*); Capethia Jenkins (*Chief Cannery*); Ken Jeong (*Jackie Chan*); Romany Malco (*Mike Roberts*).

6810   *Off the Leash*. (Series; Reality; Lifetime; 2006). A search to find the next great canine star. Seven finalists are chosen from open auditions by the Le Paws animal agency in Los Angeles. The dogs (who appear with their masters) compete in a number of "acting scenes" to weed out the worst "performers." The last remaining dog in episode six wins a role in a feature film — and will hopefully become the next Lassie. Addison Witt hosts.

6811   *Off the Rack*. (Series; Comedy; ABC; 1985). Following the death of his partner in the H&W Garment Company, Sam Waltman suddenly finds himself with a new partner — Kate Halloran, his late partner's wife. Sam is gruff, miserable and likes to conduct business alone. Kate is cheerful, outgoing and loves working with people. Stories relate the mishaps that occur as the incompatible Sam and Kate attempt to run a business together. Kate is the mother of Shannon and Timothy; Brenda is Sam's secretary; Skip Wagner is the designer; Cletus is the office assistant. In the pilot episode, R.J. Williams played Timothy; and William Brian Curran was J.P., the designer.

Cast: Ed Asner (*Sam Waltman*); Eileen Brennan (*Kate Halloran*); Claudia Wells (*Shannon Halloran*); Cory Yothers (*Timothy Halloran*); Pamela Brull (*Brenda Patagorski*); Sandy Simpson (*Skip Wagner*).

6812   *Off the Record*. (Series; Comedy; DuMont; 1948). New York City is the setting for a story about a millionaire Park Avenue radio disc jockey and his Man Friday. One of the earliest situation comedies and one of the first to be cancelled shortly after its premiere (due to a dispute between the star and producer). The live series was originally scheduled to premiere on Oct. 12, 1948 but was delayed one week due to the illness of its announcer. It produced two episodes and ran from Oct. 19 to Oct. 26, 1948.

Cast: Zero Mostel (*Disc Jockey*); Joey Faye (*His Man Friday*). **Announcer:** Ken Roberts.

6813   *Off the Wall*. (Pilot; Comedy; NBC; May 7, 1977). Hopkins Hall is a co-ed dorm on the campus of Ohio Western College. Matt, Jeannie, Flash, Lennie, Gordon, Tammy, Melvin, Arthur and George are the featured students and a former male army chef called "Mother" is overseer of the dorm. The proposal was to follow incidents in the lives of the students. Harry Gold performs the theme, "Off the Wall."

Cast: Todd Susman (*Matt Bozeman*); Dana House (*Jeannie*); Harry Gold (*Flash*); Cindy Helberg (*Lennie*); Sean Roche (*Gordon*); Sally Hightower (*Tammy*); Sandy Helberg (*Melvin*); Frank Helberg (*Arthur*); Frank O'Brien (*George*); Hal Williams (*Mother*).

6814   *Off the Wall*. (Series; Comedy; Syn.; 1986). Sketches performed by a repertory company that poke fun at TV, commercials, politics, life and even fairy tales.

Regulars: Joe Baker, Louise Duart, Susan Elliot, Pat Fraley, Shelley Herman, Terry Kiser, John Roarke, Cynthia Stevenson.

6815   *Off to See the Wizard*. (Series; Anthology; ABC; 1967-1968). Adventure films geared to children (including reedited theatrical films and unsold TV pilot films). For information on the pilot films that aired, see: *Alexander the Great, The Hellcats, Mike and the Mermaid* and *Tarzan, the Ape Man.* The episodes are introduced by animated *Wizard of Oz* characters Dorothy and Scarecrow.

Voice Cast: June Foray (*Dorothy*); Daws Butler (*Scarecrow*).

6816   *Off We Go*. (Pilot; Comedy; CBS; Sept. 5, 1966). Anxious to participate in the war effort (during World War II), Rod Ryan, a brilliant 16-year-old who looks older than he is, enlists with the U.S. Army Air Corps. Quickly he rises to the rank of colonel and is placed in charge of a small base in England. The proposal was to depict the experiences of Colonel Rod Ryan and his men as they attempt to carry out dangerous assignments. Other regulars (non-military) are Debbie, Rod's girlfriend; and Josie and Carl, Rod's parents.

Cast: Michael Burns (*Col. Rod Ryan*); Ann Jillian (*Debbie Trowbridge*); Dick Foran (*Lt. Casey Slade*); Nancy Kovack (*Lt. Sue Chamberlain*); Alan Sues (*Lt. Col. Jefferson Dale*); Elisabeth Fraser (*Josie Ryan*); Dave Willock (*Carl Ryan*).

6817   *The Office*. (Series; Comedy; CBS; 1995). A look at corporate life as seen through the eyes of Rita Stone, a career secretary in the packaging department of an ad agency called Package, Inc. Other regulars are Mae, a former Club Med worker who has been married three times. She is blonde, sexy, outspoken and works as the office secretary; Deborah, an MBA student and secretary to boss Steve Gilman; Beth, a working mother whose problems seem to follow her to work; she is secretary to boss Natalie Danton; Frank, Rita's boss; and Bobby, an artist/designer.

Cast: Valerie Harper (*Rita Stone*); Andrea Abbate (*Mae D'Arcy*); Kristin Dattilo (*Deborah Beaumont*); Debra Jo Rupp (*Beth Avery*); Lisa Darr (*Natalie Stanton*); Dakin Matthews (*Frank Gerard*); Gary Dourdan (*Steve Gilman*); Kevin Conroy (*Bobby Harold*).

6818   *The Office*. (Series; Comedy; NBC; 2005–). The Dunder Mifflin Paper Supply Company is a business located in Scranton, Pennsylvania. Michael Scott is the regional manager, an insensitive boss who seems to care for the welfare of his employees but tries to put his own spin on company policy (something that always causes him to get into trouble). Jim Halpert is the talented but easily bored salesman; Dwight K. Schrute, the kiss-up; Pamela Beesley, the receptionist who yearns to become an illustrator; and Ryan Howard is the temp. Stories are a tongue-in-cheek look at the nine-to-five white-collar world; based on the British TV series of the same title.

Cast: Steve Carell (*Michael Scott*); Rainn Wilson (*Dwight K. Schrute*); John Krasinski (*Jim Halpert*); Jenna Fischer (*Pamela Beesly*); B.J. Novak (*Ryan Howard*); Leslie David Baker (*Stanley Hudson*); Brian Baumgartner (*Kevin Malone*); Angela Kinsey (*Angela Martin*); Phyllis Smith (*Phyllis Lapin*); Kate Flannery (*Meredith Palmer*); Mindy Kaling (*Kelly Kapoor*); Creed Bratton (*Himself*); Oscar Nuñez (*Oscar Martinez*); Paul Lieberstein (*Toby Flenderson*); Ed Helms (*Andy Bernard*); Craig Robinson (*Darryl Philbin*); Melora Hardin (*Jan*

Levinson); David Denman (*Roy Anderson*); Rashida Jones (*Karen Filippelli*); Andy Buckley (*David Wallace*); Ellie Kemper (*Kelly Erin Hannon*); Robert R. Shafer (*Bob Vance*); Amy Ryan (*Holly Flax*).

6819 *The Office.* (Series; Comedy; BBC America; 2008). The British program on which the American series is based. Documentary style presentation that follows the staff of the Wernham Hogg Paper Company. David Brent is the office manager; Gareth Keenan, the workers team leader; Tim, the sales rep; Dawn, the receptionist; Neil and Jennifer are the bosses.
Cast: Ricky Gervais (*David Brent*); Mackenzie Crook (*Gareth Keenan*); Martin Freeman (*Tim Canterbury*); Lucy Davis (*Dawn Tinsley*); Patrick Baladi (*Neil Godwin*); Stirling Gallacher (*Jennifer Taylor-Clarke*).

6820 *Official Detective.* (Series; Anthology; Syn.; 1957). Dramatizations based on stories that appear in *Official Detective* magazine.
Host-Narrator: Everett Sloane

6821 *O'Grady.* (Series; Cartoon; The N; 2004). Beth, an activist; Abby, a girl who wants to be (but isn't) cool; Kevin, called "the Man with the Plan" (which often backfire) and Harold, a teenage ladies' man (or so he thinks) are students at O'Grady High, a school were strange things occur. The friends are continually caught in mysterious happenings and stories relate their efforts to overcome the weirdness they encounter.
Voice Cast: Holly Schlesinger (*Beth Briggs*); Melissa Bardin Galsky (*Abby Wilde*); Patrice O'Neal (*Harold Jenkins*); H. Jon Benjamin (*Kevin*).

6822 *Oh, Baby!* (Series; Talk; Syn.; 1952). Host Jack Barry converses with infants (who respond via voice-over dubbing).

6823 *Oh Baby.* (Series; Comedy; Lifetime; 1998–2000). Tracy Calloway is a middle-aged businesswoman. She is happy, giving and enjoys what she is doing. Suddenly, she realizes that her biological clock is ticking and becomes overwhelmed with the prospect of settling down and having children. Tracy, however, would like to have children without the hassle of a marriage and figures that artificial insemination is the right path for her — or is it? Her best friend, twice divorced Charlotte, a psychiatrist, feels that Tracy is rushing into a situation she is not prepared to handle. With that thought established, stories follow Tracy as she struggles to make the right decision while coping with the situations that make her see what life would be like as a single mother and those that suggest she should wait for the right man to come along. Celia is Tracy's mother; Ernie, her brother, is a frustrated painter.
Cast: Cynthia Stevenson (*Tracy Calloway*); Jessica Walter (*Celia Calloway*); Joanna Gleason (*Charlotte*); Matt Champagne (*Ernie Calloway*); Julie Neumark (*Tracy as a teenager*); Doug Ballard (*Dr. Doug Bryan*); Don McManus (*Don Lewis*); Jack Coleman (*Rick*).

6824 *Oh, Boy!* (Series; Variety; ABC; 1959). A summer program of performances by country and western artists.
Host: Tony Hall. **Regulars:** Brenda Lee, Cherry Warner, Lorie Mann, Don Lang, Dickie Pride, Mike Preston, Red Price, Chris Andrews, Neville Taylor, Tony Sheridan, Dudley Helsop, The Cutters, Lord Rockingham XI, The Vernons, The Wreckers.

6825 *Oh Grow Up.* (Series; Comedy; ABC; 1999). Ford, Norris and Hunter are three men who never really grew up. Ford is a lawyer with the firm of Tattleman and Keeler. He is gay, although he was married to Suzanne. Norris is an artist who only paints when he is mad. He sold medical equipment before deciding to become an artist.

Hunter cleans when he gets upset and runs the Peretti Brothers Construction Company. Ford, Hunter and Norris share an apartment together and dine at the Chelsea Diner. Norris worked as a Psychic Buddy to pay off a $600 phone bill for calling a hotline and falling asleep before hanging up. When Hunter gets upset he listens to a singer named Suzanne Vega. He is also the father of Chloe. Hunter had an affair with a girl named Julie when he was in college. When he returned from spring break Julie was gone (transferred to another college). Julie became pregnant but never told Hunter. Chloe tracked Hunter down via the Internet and came to New York (from San Francisco) to begin college at NYU.
Cast: John Ducey (*Ford Vandemear*); David Alan Basche (*Norris Machelsky*); Stephen Dunham (*Hunter Sheffield*); Niesha Trout (*Chloe Sheffield*); Rena Sofer (*Suzanne Vandemear*).

6826 *Oh Henry!* (Pilot; Comedy; NBC; Aug. 12, 1989). The Bayou Burger fast food franchise in Kansas City is owned by Henry Gibbs, a widower with two children (Megan and Donny) and a nagging sister-in-law ("Aunt" Mildred). The proposal was to focus on Henry as he struggles to run the restaurant, raise two kids, contend with his staff (Paul, Sally and Carl) and somehow find some tranquility in life. Paul and Sally are waiters; Carl is the cook.
Cast: Blake Clark (*Henry Gibbs*); Marian Mercer (*Aunt Mildred*); Stefanie Ridel (*Megan Gibbs*); Raffi DiBlasio (*Donny Gibbs*); Kirk Geiger (*Paul*); Christine Cavanaugh (*Sally*); Al Fann (*Carl*).

6827 *Oh, Kay!* (Series; Variety; ABC; 1951). A live, Chicago-based program of music, songs and interviews.
Host: Kay Westfall. **Regulars:** Mary Ellen White, Jim Dimitri. **Music:** David LeWinter.

6828 *Oh, Madeline.* (Series; Comedy; ABC; 1983-1984). Madeline and Charlie Wayne are married and live at 217 Faircourt Avenue in the Eastfield section of Chicago. Charlie is a romance novelist who writes under the pen name Crystal Love (he has written such novels as *Love's Burning Blazing Tender Purple Passion* and *Love in the End Zone*). He also writes romantic stories for the Sunday magazine section of a newspaper called *The Outlook*. Madeline has been married to Charlie for ten years and enjoys her life as a housewife. She is a graduate of the Julia Faraday High School and feels that "all the horrible things that happen to me could happen to someone else — but they happen to me in front of someone else." Stories relate incidents that spark the lives of Madeline and Charlie. Robert is Charlie's friend, a womanizing travel agent Madeline calls "Mr. Gunk Face." Doris is Robert's ex-wife; Annie is Charlie's agent. Reese and Charlotte are Madeline's parents; Joyce is Madeline's younger sister.
Cast: Madeline Kahn (*Madeline Wayne*); James Sloyan (*Charlie Wayne*); Francine Tacker (*Annie McIntyre*); Louis Giambalvo (*Robert Leone*); Jesse Welles (*Doris Leone*); Melanie Chartoff (*Joyce*); Geraldine Fitzgerald (*Charlotte Vernon*); Ray Walston (*Reese Vernon*).

6829 *Oh, Nurse!* (Pilot; Comedy; CBS; Mar. 17, 1972). Kathi, LuAnn, Maria and Gail are student nurses residing in a dorm run by Patricia Conklin, a no-nonsense chief nurse. Jimmy and Steve are male interns also residing at the dorm and the proposal was to relate the mishaps that occur as the students adjust to Nurse Conklin's military-like rule.
Cast: Pat Carroll (*Nurse Conklin*); Susan Foster (*Kathi*); Heather Young (*LuAnn*); Lori Saunders (*Maria*); Judy Pace (*Gail*); Stephen Young (*Jimmy*); Norman Grabowski (*Steve*).

6830 *Oh! Susanna.* (Series; Comedy; CBS; 1956–1959). The shortened title for *The Gale Storm Show — Oh! Susanna.* See this title for information.

6831   *Oh, Those Bells.* (Series; Comedy; CBS; 1962). Hoping to begin new lives in America, the three Bell brothers leave Germany and head for California. Shortly after, Herbert Bell, Harry Bell and Sylvester Bell are flat broke and hungry. It is not stated exactly how the Bell brothers met their future employer, Henry Slocum, other than "We were broke and hungry and taken in by Mr. Slocum."

The boys, as they are sometimes called, are put to work by Slocum as custodians in Cinema Rents, a motion picture and television show prop rental business located at 4 Ridgeway Drive in Hollywood. They live together in a bungalow at a complex referred to as Mrs. Stanfield's, and the comedy stems from the antics of the insecure brothers as they attempt to adjust to life in America and do the best job that they can for Mr. Slocum. Kitty is Slocum's secretary. Cinema Rents (as seen on the screen) is called the Hollywood Prop Shop in printed sources. Tutti Camarata composed the theme.

Cast: Herbert Wiere (*Herbert Bell*); Harry Wiere (*Harry Bell*); Sylvester Wiere (*Sylvester Bell*); Henry Norell (*Henry Slocum*); Carol Byron (*Kitty Matthews*); Reta Shaw (*Mrs. Stanfield*). **Theme:** "Oh Those Bells" by Tutti Camarata.

6832   *Oh Yeah! Cartoons.* (Series; Cartoon; Nick; 1995–1997). Kenan Thompson then Josh Server host a series of seven minute cartoons produced especially for television by independent film makers. Nearly 100 animated projects were produced with four of them, *Chalk Zone*, *The Fairly Odd Parents*, *Mina and the Count* and *My Life As a Teenage Robot* eventually becoming series (see titles for information).

6833   *Ohanian.* (Pilot; Crime Drama; ABC; April 4, 1976). Following the death of his wife in a bombing incident that the police are unable to solve, homicide detective Kirk Ohanian quits the force and moves to Hawaii to become the owner of the *Quest*, a charter boat for hire. The proposal was to relate Kirk's adventures as he uses his former training as a cop to solve the crimes he encounters. Other regulars are Uncle Ara, his mate on the *Quest*; Heather McDougall, Kirk's friend, a widow; and Steve and Doug, Heather's children.

Cast: Mike Connors (*Kirk Ohanian*); Gregoire Aslan (*Uncle Ara*); Mariette Hartley (*Heather McDougall*); Tony Becker (*Steve McDougall*); Christopher Gardner (*Doug McDougall*).

6834   *Ohara.* (Series; Crime Drama; ABC; 1987-1988). Lieutenant (no first name) Ohara (pronounced O-Ha-Ra) is a compassionate but offbeat Asian police officer with the L.A.P.D. He can boast of 20 years hard experience and is considered one of L.A.'s finest. Ohara has a tremendous insight into what makes people tick. He is streetwise and will open up his home and heart to anyone in need of a little advice — and a home-cooked meal.

Ohara is also a karate master but prefers to use his mental acuity to solve crimes. He works with Detectives Cricket Sideris, Jesse Guerrera, Shaver and Sergeant Phil O'Brien. Captain Ross, then Captain Lloyd Hamilton, are their superiors. Other regulars are Gussie, the diner owner, and Roxy, the police department computer operator.

In the fall of 1987 (the series premiered in Jan. of 1987) the format switched to find Ohara as a member of the Federal State Anti Crime Unit. Six months later (with the episode of Mar. 26, 1988), the format changed again when Ohara and his partner, Shaver, resign from the police force to open their own detective agency — Ohara and Shaver Investigations. New to the cast is Teresa Storm, their superior at the Anti Crime Unit.

Cast: Pat Morita (*Lt. Ohara*); Catherine Keener (*Det. Cricket Sideris*); Richard Yniquez (*Det. Jesse Guerrera*); Jack Wallace (*Sgt. Phil O'Brien*); Robert Clohessy (*Det. Shaver*); Rachel Ticotin (*Teresa Storm*); Meagen Fay (*Roxy*); Jon Polito (*Captain Ross*); Kevin Conroy (*Capt. Lloyd Hamilton*).

6835   *O'Hara: United States Treasury.* (Series; Crime Drama; CBS; 1971-1972). James O'Hara is a top agent with the United States Treasury Department. He is a man who carefully plans his every move. He feels caution and careful planning, not force tactics, will net him the criminals he is seeking. Stories relate his investigations into crimes perpetrated against Customs, Secret Service and Internal Revenue. James works with Inspector Ed Miller; Ben Hazzard is their superior.

Cast: David Janssen (*James O'Hara*); Paul Picerni (*Ed Miller*); Stacy Harris (*Ben Hazzard*).

6836   *Ohh, Nooo!!! Mr. Bill Presents.* (Series; Comedy; Fox Family; 1998). Mr. Bill, the abused clay figure from *Saturday Night Live* has moved to Los Angeles to become an actor. Success, however, is not on Mr. Bill's side and to make ends meet, he becomes the host of a TV show called *Ohh, Nooo!!! Mr. Bill Presents*, wherein he hosts comedy clips from around the world (in particular the British series *Mr. Bean* starring Rowan Atkinson). Unfortunately for Mr. Bill, his arch enemy, Sluggo, has also relocated to Los Angeles and has resumed his enjoyable habit of squashing him.

Cast: Walter Williams (*Mr. Bill*); John Borkowski (*Mr. Hands*).

6837   *O.K. Crackerby.* (Series; Comedy; ABC; 1965-1966). O.K. Crackerby is the world's richest man. Shortly after the death of his wife, he decides to relocate to Palm Springs, California. There, with his three children, Cynthia, Hobart and O.K. Jr., they find themselves misplaced, hampered by their simple ways and unable to fit into the genteel society circle. Stories focus on O.K's battle of wits against snobbery. St. John Quincy is the society tutor hired by O.K. to tutor his children; Susan Wentworth is Quincy's girlfriend; Slim is O.K.'s friend; Davey is O.K.'s nephew.

Cast: Burl Ives (*O.K. Crackerby*); Brooke Adams (*Cynthia Crackerby*); Joel Davidson (*Hobart Crackerby*); Brian Corcoran (*O.K. Crackerby, Jr., series*); Billy King (*O.K. Crackerby, Jr., unaired pilot*); Hal Buckley (*St. John Quincy*); Laraine Stephens (*Susan Wentworth*); Dick Foran (*Slim*); John Indrisano (*O.K.'s Chauffeur*); Jonathan Daly (*Davey*).

6838   *Okay Mother.* (Series; Testimonial; DuMont; 1948–1951). The program salutes mothers of celebrities or mothers who have become famous on their own.

Host: Dennis James.

6839   *The O'Keefe's.* (Series; Comedy; WB; 2003). Harry and Ellie O'Keefe are the parents of Lauren, Danny and Mark and believe in a strict education; so much so that Ellie home schools them. The children are brilliant but have not experienced a school life outside of their home.

The O'Keefe children speak six languages, read Shakespeare for fun and use swear words like "Ogsblood." Harry and Ellie have given their children so much knowledge but it is all book smarts — they have no street smarts. The situation changes when Danny turns 15 and Lauren becomes 14 and they are enrolled in Hearst High School. This occurs because of Article Two, Section A of an agreement (written on a napkin) that Harry and Ellie made while they were attending Columbia University (where they met and fell in love). It was on that napkin that Harry and Ellie agreed to let their future children attend a public school to be heard when they became of age (teenagers). Stories follow the experiences of Lauren and Danny as they begin their public school careers (Mark has not yet become a teen and is thus still home schooled by Ellie). Harry believes in family and is scared for his kids. He is a veterinarian and runs the O'Keefe Veterinary Clinic. Ellie was a stocks and bonds trader on Wall Street before she became pregnant.

Cast: Judge Reinhold (*Harry O'Keefe*); Kristen Nelson (*Ellie O'Keefe*); Tania Raymonde (*Lauren O'Keefe*); Joseph Cross (*Danny O'Keefe*); Matt Weinberg (*Mark O'Keefe*).

6840 *Old American Barn Dance*. (Series; Variety; DuMont; 1953). Summer program of performances by country and western entertainers.

Host: Bill Bailey. **Regulars:** Tennessee Ernie Ford, Pee Wee King.

6841 *Old Dogs*. (Pilot; Crime Drama; ABC; Aug. 10, 1987). James "Jimmy" Bryce works as a security guard at a bingo parlor. He was once a tough cop who broke too many rules and was suspended. Mayo Dunlap is a retired by-the-books captain who lives for his job. He is now a volunteer (basically a file clerk) at his old precinct. When a cop's murder sparks a police department scandal, the two "old dogs" meet when they each begin their own investigation into the crime. They solve the case, impress the brass and are appointed special consultants to the police department. The proposal was to relate the investigations of two opposite-in-procedure cops as they solve difficult crimes.

Cast: Robert Loggia (*Jimmy Bryce*); Robert Prosky (*Mayo Dunlap*); Franc Luz (*Lt. Randy Granville*); Alex Rocco (*Capt. Rudy Luchese*); Les Lannom (*Off. Ned Haas*).

6842 *Old Friends*. (Pilot; Comedy; ABC; July 12, 1984). After his wife deserts him, Jerry Forbes, a successful New York lawyer, relinquishes his job and with his son, Mark, returns to his hometown of Columbus, Ohio, to begin a new life. The proposal was to relate Jerry's attempts to establish his new lifestyle. Other regulars are Laura King, Jerry's love interest, a radio disc jockey.; Phil, Jerry's father, the owner of the Forbes Pharmacy; Susan, Laura's sister; and Charlie and George, Jerry's friends.

Cast: Christopher Lloyd (*Jerry Forbes*); Jennifer Salt (*Laura King*); Grant Forsberg (*Mark Forbes*); John Randolph (*Phil Forbes*); Deborah Goodrich (*Susan King*); Stanley Kamel (*Charlie*); Steve Ryan (*George Neal*).

6843 *Old Money*. (Pilot; Comedy; CBS; June 28, 1988). The lives of the Palmers, a fabulously wealthy but eccentric family living in the city of Palm Grove. Charles Palmer, the industrious head of the family, made his money the old-fashioned way — he married it. His wife, Arabia, is a blue-blood who enjoys writing romance novels. They have three daughters: Countess Celia, a fashionable jet setter with countless husbands; Felicity, an overly generous philanthropist; and the mysterious Meg, who has returned to the family after a 20-year absence. Other regulars are Celia's illegitimate sons, Steven (kind) and Chip (sneaky); Hank, Felicity's slightly dense husband; Roberto, the groundskeeper who indulges in insider trading on the side; Brian, Charles's personal assistant; Kate, the strict housekeeper; and Tammy, the seemingly naive country girl who invites trouble.

Cast: Don Porter (*Charles Palmer*); Nan Martin (*Arabia Palmer*); Carolyn Seymour (*Celia*); Sandy Faison (*Felicity*); Terri Treas (*Meg Palmer*); Tom Isbell (*Steven*); John Dye (*Chip*); Abraham Alvarez (*Roberto*); William Thomas, Jr. (*Brian*); Jim Piddik (*Hank*); Conchata Ferrell (*Kate*); Lori Loughlin (*Tammy Cooper*).

6844 *The Old Nickerbocker Music Hall*. (Pilot; Mystery-Game; CBS; Oct. 9, 1948). A combination mystery drama and game show broadcast live from the Old Nickerbocker Music Hall, a Gay Nineties Revue, in New York City. The program begins with a dramatization (in the test, "The Times Square Story") during which a crime is committed. Customers of the hall then receive the opportunity to win prizes by attempting to identify the culprit. One of the first programs to experiment with live, remote pickups.

Performers: Sally Gracie, Henry Lascoe, Madeleine Lee, Jack Lemmon, Darren McGavin, Farrell Pelley and Maureen Stapleton.

6845 *The Oldest Rookie*. (Series; Crime Drama; CBS; 1987-1988). When his friend, Officer Harry Clark, is killed in the line of duty, Ike Porter, a 25-year veteran, resigns from his job (Deputy Chief of Public Affairs for the L.A.P.D.) to become a street cop. Following his retraining at the academy and a brief stint as a patrol cop, Porter calls in an old favor (from the mayor) and is promoted to detective. Ike's experiences as "The Oldest Rookie" (age 50) as he and his partner, Tony Jonas, attempt to solve crimes is the focal point of stories. Ike spent 25 years on the force and attended 416 press conferences and ate 512 "rubber chicken banquets." Ike does not always go by the books and uses his years of experience to know what is right (his hunches often compel him to go by his gut instinct, not by what the book says). Tony is a somewhat wet-behind-the-ears detective who finds it a whole new ball game working with Ike. Other regulars are Lieutenant Marc Zaga, Detective Gary Lane; Chief Black; Sandy Porter, Ike's niece; and Nina Zaga, Marc's daughter.

Cast: Paul Sorvino (*Ike Porter*); D.W. Moffett (*Tony Jonas*); Raymond J. Barry (*Marc Zaga*); Marshall Bell (*Garry Lane*); Patrick Cronin (*Chief Black*); Mira Sorvino (*Sandy Porter*); Leah Ayres (*Nina Zaga*).

6846 *The Oldsmobile Music Theater*. (Series; Anthology; NBC; 1959). Oldsmobile cars sponsored program that interweaves songs from the past and present with contemporary dramas. Also known as *Hayes and Henderson*. Produced by David Susskind and Jacqueline Babbin.

Host-Singers: Bill Hayes, Florence Henderson. **Music:** The Herbie Mann Quartet.

6847 *Oliver Beene*. (Series; Comedy; Fox; 2003–2005). Oliver Beene is an 11-year-old boy who lives in Apartment 10M of the Central Apartment Building in Rego Park, Queens, New York during the early 1960s. He is the son of Jerry and Charlotte Beene and has a 14-year-old brother named Ted. Borrowing aspects of *The Wonder Years*, stories of Oliver's youth are narrated by Oliver as an adult.

Jerry is a dentist who feels the whole world is against him. His one goal in life is to get a parking space in front of the building. He is also an amateur inventor whose inventions seldom work. Charlotte's social life consists of "the laundry room and the elevator," she says. She is president of the building's Tenant Association. Her claim to fame: "I was on TV in 1939 at the New York's World's Fair. The cameraman was told to find a pretty girl and show her. I was that girl."

Oliver likes to help people he believes are in trouble (although his interference always causes more problems than solutions). He and Ted attend P.S. 206 (also said to be Public School 304). Oliver believes everybody listens to his conversations. He has a dog named Scruffles and had a first job delivering papers for the *Tribune* at $6 a week. Oliver had a band called Oliver and the Otters and helps his mother make cookies. His favorite TV show is "Romparama" hosted by Ringmaster Bob.

Ted is a ladies' man (or so he believes) and his greatest weakness is chocolate éclairs. He is on the track team at school (the fastest runner they have) and Oliver says, "He always fails to impress girls by the dumb things he says." Other regulars are Joyce and Michael, Oliver's friends. Press release information gives the following full names for characters (although they are not used on the program): Oliver David Beene; Dr. Jeremiah "Jerry" Beene; Charlotte Caroline Beene; Tayler "Ted" Mark Beene.

Cast: Grant Rosenberg (*Oliver Beene*); Grant Shaud (*Jerry Beene*); Wendy Makkena (*Charlotte Beene*); Andrew Lawrence (*Ted Beene*);

David Cross (*Voice of Adult Oliver*); Taylor Emerson (*Michael*); Daveigh Chase (*Joyce*).

6848   *Olivia*. (Series; Cartoon; Nick; 2009). British produced, computer animated program about Olivia, a six-year-old girl (seen as a cute pig) whose main goal is to survive the daily pressures of life. She lives with her mother and four-year-old brother Ian. Olivia has big dreams. As Olivia tries to live those dreams, learning experiences are presented to children. Francine is her neighbor; Julian is her best friend. Based on the books by Ian Falconer.

Voice Cast: Emily Gray (*Olivia*); Michael Van Citters (*Ian*); Brianna McCracken (*Francine*); Jeremy Herzig (*Julian*).

6849   *O'Malley*. (Pilot; Crime Drama; NBC; Jan. 8, 1983). Michael "Mike" O'Malley is a throwback to the past: a 1940s style private detective working out of a 1980s New York City. The proposal was to relate his dated but still effective methods to solve crimes. Other regulars are Amanda, Mike's ex-wife; Guy, Mike's friend, the owner of the Fleming Art Gallery; and Denny, Guy's secretary.

Cast: Mickey Rooney (*Mike O'Malley*); Anne Francis (*Amanda O'Malley*); Peter Coffield (*Guy Fleming*); Sarah Abrell (*Denny*).

6850   *Omba Mokomba*. (Series; Children; Disney; 1997). Omba Mokomba is Swahili for "Ask Mokomba." And "Ask Mokomba" is a fictional television series in Africa where Mokomba, the show's host, answers viewers' questions about animals (which are seen via wildlife footage).

Cast: Benjamin Brown (*Mokomba*); Natasha Pearce (*Candace; his assistant*).

6851   *The Omega Factor*. (Series; Mystery; Syn.; 1981). Tom Crane is a newspaper journalist who is secretly a member of Department 7, a British government organization that uses people possessed of special occult powers to investigate and solve crimes (the title refers to the ultimate potential that is possible from the human mind). Dr. Anne Reynolds assists Tom; Andrew Scott-Erskine is the head of Department 7; Julia Crane is Tom's wife; Michael Crane is Tom's brother; Edward Drexel is an enemy of Department 7 (a dabbler in the occult); Morag and Paul are members of Department 7. Paul is also assisted by The Mysterious Spirit (who only appears to him). Mrs. Coleman is the medium; Dr. Roy Martindale is Erskine's assistant.

Cast: James Hazeldine (*Tom Crane*); Louise Jameson (*Dr. Anne Reynolds*); Brian Derby (*Andrew Scott-Erskine*); John Carlisle (*Dr. Roy Martindale*); Joanna Tope (*Julia Crane*); Nicholas Coppin (*Michael Crane*); Cyril Luckham (*Edward Drexel*); Natasha Gerson (*Morag*); Jack D'Arcy (*Paul*); Monica Brady (*The Mysterious Spirit*); Sheila Latimer (*Mrs. Coleman*); Sheila Duffy (*Spirit Voices*).

6852   *The Omen*. (Pilot; Thriller; NBC; Aug. 9, 1991). Jack Mann is a writer-reporter for the *Associated Press*. Annalisse Summer is an ER nurse dedicated to helping people; Dr. Linus is a doctor who has seen what Jack and Annalisse have: an evil entity that seeks to destroy and has joined them to help stop it (the entity possesses people and controls them to do its bidding).

Cast: Brett Cullen (*Jack Mann*); Chelsea Field (*Annalisse Summer*); William Sadler (*Dr. Linus*).

6853   *Omni: The New Frontier*. (Series; Magazine; Syn.; 1981). Peter Ustinov hosts and narrates stories that, based on *Omni* magazine, explore the scientific wonders that will shape the future.

6854   *Omnibus*. (Series; Anthology; CBS; ABC; NBC; 1952–1961; 1988). Programs devoted to people and "living ideas"; dramatic presentations, explanations, discussions and demonstrations concerning music, dance, history, theater, opera, ballet and literature. Two versions appeared:

1. Omnibus (CBS, 1952–56; ABC, 1956-57; NBC, 1957–1961). **Host:** Alistair Cooke.

2. Omnibus (ABC Pilot; May 26, 1988). **Host:** Beverly Sills. **Guests:** Rosemary Clooney, Michael Feinstein.

6855   *On Broadway Tonight*. (Series; Variety; CBS; 1964-1965). Aspiring singers and dancers receive the opportunity to showcase their talents with the object being to impress producers and achieve their first step on the walkway to fame.

Program Open [after announcer introduces four guests]: "These are four of America's finest young entertainers in Irving Mansfield's production of *On Broadway Tonight* with your host Rudy Vallee. Presented by Ralston Purina of Checkerboard Square, makers of Purina Dog Chow and many more products in the famous checkerboard packages."

Host: Rudy Vallee. **Orchestra:** Harry Sosnik.

6856   *On Our Own*. (Series; Comedy; CBS; 1977-1978). Toni McBain, the creative director, and copywriters April Baxter and Maria Teresa Bonino work for the Bedford Advertising Agency at 605 Madison Avenue in New York City. The agency is owned by J.M. Bradford and stories relate events in the home and working lives of April, Toni and Maria. Craig is the agency salesman; Edie is the commercials' producer; Vanessa is Julia's land lady. Julia lives at 345 East 45th Street; Maria at 62 West 72nd Street. Julia is neat; April is a perfectionist; and Maria is a rather untidy housekeeper.

Cast: Gretchen Wyler (*Toni McBain*); Bess Armstrong (*Julia Peters*); Dixie Carter (*April Baxter*); Lynnie Greene (*Maria Teresa Bonino*); Bob Randall (*J.M. Bedford*); Dan Resin (*Craig Boatwright*); John Christopher Jones (*Eddie Baines*); Sasha von Scherler (*Mrs. Oblensky*); Larry Haines (*Maria's father*); Kay Medford (*Maria's mother*).

6857   *On Our Own*. (Series; Comedy; ABC; 1994-1995). Josh Jerrico is the oldest child of a family of nine. When his parents are killed in a car accident, Josh feels the only way he can keep the family together is to pretend to be their Aunt Jelcinda, who has come to Los Angeles from Memphis to care for her nieces and nephews (Jami, Jai, Jesse, Jordie, Joe and Jarreau). Alana Michaels is the social worker who is aware of the charade (but promises to keep Josh's secret); complications arise when Gordon Ormsby, Alana's supervisor, meets Jelcinda and develops a crush of her (err him) without knowing that she is really a he. Stories from Sept. to Dec. 1994 follow Josh as he struggles to keep the family together by pretending to be the Jerrico's aunt. After a hiatus, the series returned (from March-April 1995) with a revised format wherein Josh still had to care for his siblings — but this time as their legal guardian as he was granted custody of his siblings (thus ending the charade aspect).

Cast: Ralph Louis Harris (*Josh Jerrico/Aunt Jelcinda*); Jazz Smollett (*Jai Jerrico*); Jojo Smollett (*Jimi Jerrico*); Jurnee Smollett (*Jordee Jerico*); Jussie Smollett (*Jesse Jerrico*); Jake Smollett (*Joe Jerrico*); Jocqui Smollett (*Jarreau Jerrico*); Laura Ponce (*Nails*); Karen Kim (*Suki*); Kimberly Kates (*Alana Michaels*); Roger Alan Brown (*Gordon Ormsby*); T'Keyah Crystal Keymah (*Scotti Decker*).

6858   *On Our Way*. (Pilot; Drama; CBS; June 29, 1985). Kate and Sam Walsh are a retired couple who purchase a motor home and decide to explore America. The proposal was to relate their experiences as they run into adventure, spurred by his nose for news as a one-time crime reporter and her lively interest in people.

Cast: Janet Leigh (*Kate Walsh*); Harry Guardino (*Sam Walsh*).

6859 *On Parade.* (Series; Variety; NBC; 1964). Performances by internationally known entertainers (each of whom appears as the host of their particular program).

Host: Rosemary Clooney *(July 17)*; Tony Bennett *(July 24)*; Henry Mancini *(July 31)*; Mimi Hines *(Aug. 7)*; Juliet Prowse *(Aug. 14)*; Diahann Carroll *(Aug. 21)*; Julius LaRosa *(Aug. 28)*; Jane Morgan *(Sept. 4)*; The Limelighters *(Sept 11)*. **Orchestra:** Nelson Riddle.

6860 *On Stage America.* (Series; Variety; Syn.; 1984). Magazine-like program that presents in-depth celebrity profiles and performances.

Hosts: Randi Oakes, Susie Bono, Steve Edwards, Todd Christianson. **Regulars:** Minnie Pearl, John Brakaw. **Orchestra:** Dennis McCarthy.

6861 *On Stage Everybody.* (Experimental; Variety; DuMont; Mar. 6, 1945). Performances by various entertainment acts: comedy from Cyril Smith and Danton Walker; impressions from Jimmy McColl; songs by Hildegarde Halliday; and dancing by Pearl Primus.

Host: Billy Rose. **Announcer:** Walter Herlihy.

6862 *On the Air.* (Series; Comedy; ABC; 1992). The time is 1957, and television is still relatively new. One New York–based network, the Zoblotnick Broadcasting Corporation (ZBC), decides that the only way to attract viewers (and save their network) is to give movie idols their own shows. They begin by hiring Lester Guy, a fading matinee idol who is hoping to make a comeback via *The Lester Guy Show*, an 8:00 P.M. music, comedy and variety show that is plagued by the (over exaggerated) mishaps that actually occurred on live television during its "Golden Years."

Lester was a contract player at Amalgamated Studios and got his start with a bit part in the film *The White Cliffs of Dover*. Betty Hudson is Lester's co-star. She is from Westport, Connecticut, and the sister of movie star Sylvia Hudson. Betty, however, has no acting experience and is a bit dim witted. To make Guy look good, Betty was chosen to be his co-star.

Buddy Budwaller is the tyrannical head of the network and the "yes man" for the never-seen Mr. Zoblotnick. Vladja Gochtch is the inexperienced, impossible to understand foreign director who directs Guy's show. Ruth Trueworthy is Vladja's assistant (she translates his thick German accent into English for the crew). Dwight McGonigle is the often distressed producer of *The Lester Guy Show*. Blinky Watts appears to be blind—"He's not. He suffers from Bozman Symplex; he sees 25.6 times as much as we do." He is the sound effects man (he has pre-set levers on his control board and operates from memory rather than sight).

Wembley Snaps dog food sponsors *The Lester Guy Show*; Everett Greenbaum is the show's announcer; and Susan Russell is the announcer's assistant.

Cast: Ian Buchanan *(Lester Guy)*; Marla Rubinoff *(Betty Hudson)*; Anne Bloom *(Sylvia Hudson)*; Miguel Ferrer *(Buddy Budwaller)*; David L. Lander *(Vladja Gochtch)*; Nancye Ferguson *(Ruth Trueworthy)*; Marvin Kaplan *(Dwight McGonigle)*; Tracey Walter *(Blinky Watts)*.

6863 *On the Case with Paula Zahn.* (Series; Crime Drama; Investigation Discovery; 2009–). An inside look at crime stories. Each selected case is real and is detailed with crime scene photos, police videos and interviews with the people involved in the case by the program's host, news woman Paula Zahn, who has an uncanny knack to get her subjects to speak candidly about their involvement. While not really needed (due to the actual information that is available), reenactments are also incorporated.

Host: Paula Zahn.

6864 *On the Corner.* (Series; Variety; ABC; 1948). Talent performances culled from the *Vaudeville* section of the entertainment industry newspaper, *Variety*.

Host: Henry Morgan. **Regulars:** Virginia Austin, George Guest, Roy Davis, The Clark Sisters.

6865 *On the Cover.* (Series; Game; PAX; 2004). A game show based on headlines or blurbs that could appear on magazine, CD or DVD covers. Three contestants compete. Players are shown a series of covers with a blurb (made up by the show's writers). A question relating to one of the pictured covers is asked (for example, "What movie co-starred…"). The first player to sound a buzzer and answer it correctly scores points. The lowest scorer at the end of the round is eliminated. The remaining two players compete in a similar round two. Here the highest scorer wins the game and a chance to compete in the bonus round. A board with a concealed (by the numbers 1–9) picture of a celebrity is displayed. The host reads nine questions, one at a time. Each question the player answers correctly (within 90 seconds) removes the corresponding number from the picture (which reveals one segment of the picture; rarely would all nine segments be revealed). If the player can identify the celebrity he wins a valuable prize; if not, a less expensive prize is awarded.

Host: Mark L. Wahlberg. **Announcer:** Vanessa Marshall, Mitch Lewis.

6866 *On the Edge.* (Pilot; Crime Drama; NBC; June 4, 1987). Jack Shake is a hard-nosed L.A.P.D. detective; M.R. Baker is his partner, a hotshot rookie. The proposal was to relate their efforts to solve complex crimes.

Cast: Tom Skerritt *(Jack Shake)*; Tom O'Brien *(M.R. Baker)*; J.T. Walsh *(Capt. Alan Quail)*; Peter Iacangelo *(Detective D'Agostino)*.

6867 *On the Go.* (Series; Variety; CBS; 1960). Guests, interviews and visits to various areas around Los Angeles.

Host: Jack Linkletter. **Announcer:** Johnny Jacobs.

6868 *On the Lot.* (Series; Reality; Fox; 2007). A search to find "the next great American director." Fifty finalists, chosen from 12,000 short film submissions from around the world, are gathered together in Hollywood. Here, various film related competitions are held to determine the best of among the group of talented but still undiscovered film directors. The first challenge is to present a pitch. A log line (one sentence plot) is given to each of the competitors. Within 24 hours each must devise a complete story (beginning, middle and end) and sell that story to a panel of three judges (two regulars and one guest). The 18 worst presenters are eliminated. The remaining 32 directors are given equipment, actors and a shooting site and must, within 24 hours, produce a two-and-one-half minute film. Cameras follow the frustrations of each director (who are working in teams of three) as the pressure mounts to get the film made. Each of the films is then screened. Twelve directors, whose films do not meet the judge's demands, are eliminated. The twenty remaining directors now work independently and must produce films based on the instructions given to them. The results are judged by the panel—but it is the votes from viewers that determine who stays and who goes. Potential directors are eliminated each week and the one remaining director receives a $1 million deal with Dream Works Studios (and the opportunity to work with director Steven Spielberg).

Hostess: Adrianna Costa. **Judges:** Carrie Fisher, Garry Marshall.

6869 *On the Rocks.* (Series; Comedy; ABC; 1975-1976). Life in the Alamesa State Minimum Security Prison as seen through the eyes of convict Hector Fuentes, a streetwise petty thief. Based on the British series *Porridge*. Lester, Cleaver, Nick and Gabby are fellow convicts; Mr. Gibson and Mr. Sullivan are the correctional officers; Wilbur Poindexter is the warden; Dorothy Burgess is Wilbur's secretary.

Cast: Jose Perez (*Hector Fuentes*); Hal Williams (*Lester DeMott*); Rick Hurst (*Cleaver*); Bobby Sandler (*Nick Palik*); Mel Stewart (*Mr. Gibson*); Tom Poston (*Mr. Sullivan*); Pat Cranshaw (*Gabby*); Logan Ramsey (*Wilbur Poindexter*); Cynthia Harris (*Dorothy Burgess*).

6870   On Top All Over the World. (Pilot; Reality; Syn.; April 11, 1985). A survey of the entertainment industry world wide (the best in television, movies and music).

Hosts: Morgan Brittany, Stephen J. Cannell. **Guests:** Edward Asner, Linda Blair, Joan Collins, Morgan Fairchild, Bonnie Franklin, Ben Gazzara, David Hasselhoff, Roger Moore, Olivia Newton-John, Victoria Principal, Jane Seymour, Elizabeth Taylor, Raquel Welch. **Announcer-Narrator:** Steve O'Brien.

6871   On Trial. (Pilot; Drama; ABC; Nov. 8, 1948). Reenactments of actual court cases that feature real judges. In the pilot episode, New York Supreme Court judge Ferdinand Pecora hears a case on the legality of wire-tapping in crime detection. The television program was also an audition for a possible radio series. The audio portion was broadcast on ABC-AM, but neither went beyond the initial test.

Cast: William G.H. Finch, Charles P. Grimes, William P. Herlands, Judge Ferdinand Pecora, Lloyd Paul Stryker. **Announcer:** Bob Sabin.

6872   On Trial. (Series; Anthology; CBS; 1956-1957). Dramatizations based on actual court cases. Two pilots were produced: *On Trial* (Sept. 23, 1955; aired as a segment of *Star Stage*) and *On Trial* (May 18, 1956). The first pilot story, "The U.S. Versus Alexander Holmes" starred Joseph Cotten as a lawyer prosecuting a sailor charged with homicide; the second pilot story, "The Man in the Black Robe," stars John McIntire as a judge seeking to prosecute a powerful racketeer.

Host-Narrator: Joseph Cotten.

6873   On Trial. (Pilot; Drama; NBC; April 29, 1994). A proposed series of dramas based on real life trials. The pilot, "The Dark Place," tells of a woman (Elaine Bilstad) with multiple personalities who, after an affair with a man (Don Bloomfield) accuses him of raping a six-year-old girl.

Host-Narrator: F. Lee Bailey.

6874   On Your Account. (Series; Game; NBC, 1953-1954; CBS, 1954–1956). Contestants appear on stage and relate their sorrows. A panel then questions them to determine the seriousness of their individual situations. Each question that is asked deposits five dollars in a bank. After a specified time, the panel chooses the person they feel is the most desperate. That contestant receives the money that has been deposited in the bank.

Host: Win Elliot, Dennis James. **Announcer:** Bill Rogers. **Music:** Paul Taubman.

6875   On Your Mark. (Series; Game; ABC; 1961). Children, aged from nine to thirteen, and who are pursuing the same career goal, compete. A series of question and answer rounds, based on the contestant's career potential, follow, with the player scoring the highest being declared the winner.

Host: Sonny Fox.

6876   On Your Way. (Series; Game; DuMont; ABC; 1953-1954). Selected members of the studio audience compete. The host reads a general knowledge type of question. The first player to identify himself through a buzzer signal receives a chance to answer. Points are scored if he is correct. The winner, the highest scoring player, receives an all-expenses paid trip to his place of desire. Aired on DuMont (Sept. 9, 1953 to Jan. 20, 1954) and ABC (Jan. 23 to April 17, 1954).

Host: Clayton "Bud" Collyer, John Reed King, Kathy Godfrey.

6877   Once a Hero. (Series; Adventure; ABC; 1987). There is a world beyond the third dimension called Comic Book World. Here, the characters live their lives based on the adventures drawn by their creators. Abner Bevis is one such cartoonist whose character, Captain Justice, is the heroic savior of Pleasantville. Captain Justice is, in reality, beloved schoolteacher Brad Steele. There are good citizens in Pleasantville, like the lovely Rachel Kirk and her sister, Tippy Kirk. But there is also the Captain's arch enemy, the evil Max Mayhem.

Abner has been drawing the comic strip for 30 years and is running out of fresh ideas. When he begins using plots from earlier adventures, people begin to lose interest and sales plummet. In Pleasantville, Captain Justice begins to fade. "This is no good," the Captain says. "We are dependent upon the affections of people in the real world. As long as we remain in their hearts, we are safe. Should they start to forget us, we simply fade away ... I won't let this happen. I'll go to the third dimension and force them to remember." To do this, Captain Justice flies through the Forbidden Zone into the real world.

As Captain Justice seeks Abner in Los Angeles, the ruler of Comic Book World, the Great and Magnificent One, summons Gumshoe, a 1940s-style private detective, and hires him to find Captain Justice and bring him back — "If he stays he will experience a fate more horrific than a superhero can endure. He should spend his remaining days here, with dignity and honor."

Gumshoe finds Captain Justice and learns he met with Abner and discovered that Pizazz Comics is planning to discontinue Captain Justice because "the kids don't go for it like they used to." Justice tells Gumshoe he is determined to change that and save Pleasantville by getting people to remember him. With Gumshoes help, the Captain begins a crusade against injustice and soon becomes a hero. The comic is reinstated and Pleasantville is saved. Stories follow Captain Justice and Gumshoe as they continue to fight for right. Emma Greely is the reporter for the Los Angeles *Gazette*; Lobsterman assists the Captain (in Pleasantville); Victor Lazarus is the real world villain seeking to do away with the Captain. In the real world, T.J. North (Adam West) plays Brad Steele/Captain Justice on the TV series *Captain Justice*. Jim Turner played Captain Justice in the unaired pilot version.

Cast: Jeff Lester (*Brad Steele*); Robert Forster (*Gumshoe*); Dianne Kay (*Rachel Kirk*); Dana Short (*Tippy Kirk*); Harris Laskaway (*Max Mayhem*); Milo O'Shea (*Abner Bevis*); Caitlin Clarke (*Emma Greely*); Trevor Henley (*Lobsterman*); Richard Lynch (*Victor Lazarus*).

6878   Once a Thief. (Series; Crime Drama; Syn.; 2002). Victor Mansfield is an intelligence agent and ex cop who was framed on a false drug charge. He was imprisoned but freed by a mysterious woman (known only as the Director) to work for her in law enforcement.

Lee Anne Sai and Mac Ramsey are master thieves who are on the run from "the Hong Kong Family" (mob) for stealing. They are given refuge by the Director on condition that they work with her and Victor. Stories follow the Director's team as she assigns them cases that require expert thievery skills to solve.

The team enjoys meals at the Jade Swan Restaurant. Mac and Lee Anne are skilled in the martial arts. Mac has a $3 million bounty on his head; Lee Anne's downfall is that she has a sense of morals; Mac is considered the underachiever member of the team according to the Director.

Cast Nicholas Leo (*Victor Mansfield*); Sandrine Holt (*Lee Anne Sai*); Ivan Sergei (*Mac Ramsey*); Jennifer Dole (*The Director*).

6879   *Once and Again.* (Series; Drama; ABC; 1999–2002). Rick Sammler is the divorced father of two children, Eli and Jesse. Lily Manning is the newly divorced mother of two children, Grace and Zoe. They are also romantically involved and stories, set in Chicago, follow the lives of two single parents and their efforts to balance their careers to spend time together.

Rick is an architect and divorced from Karen (whom he considers spiteful). Lily is an on-line salesperson (later radio talk show host) who is newly separated from her selfish husband Jake, a restaurateur. Lily's children are insecure (Grace) and troubled (Zoe). Eli, Rick's oldest child, appears tough but is actually soft hearted; Jesse is a bit troubled over the divorce of her parents. The program allows viewers to get into the minds of the characters through mini interviews mixed throughout each episode.

Cast: Bill Campbell (*Rick Sammler*); Sela Ward (*Lily Manning*); Shane West (*Eli Sammler*); Evan Rachel Ward (*Grace Manning*); Meredith Deane (*Zoe Manning*); Susanna Thompson (*Karen Sammler*); Jeffrey Nordling (*Jake Manning*); Ever Carradine (*Tiffany*); Marin Hinkle (*Judy Brooks*).

6880   *Once Upon a Fence.* (Series; Children; NBC; 1952). Stories, songs and music for children with Katherine Heger as the host and music by Dave Kargler.

6881   *Once Upon a Spy.* (Pilot; Adventure; ABC; Sept. 19, 1980). The Organization is a special investigative agency of the U.S. government that is run by a mysterious woman known only as "The Lady." Jack Chenault and Paige Tannehill are her top operatives and the proposal was to relate their case assignments. Burkle is The Lady's aide.

Cast: Eleanor Parker (*The Lady*); Ted Danson (*Jack Chenault*); Mary Louise Weller (*Paige Tannehill*); Burke Byrnes (*Burkle*).

6882   *Once Upon a Tune.* (Series; Anthology; DuMont; 1951). A complete musical is presented each week, usually an adaptation of a Broadway play.

Regulars: Phil Hanna, Sondra Lee, Holly Harris, Bernice Parks, Ed Holmes. **Music:** Reginald Beane.

6883   *One Big Family.* (Pilot; Comedy; Unaired; Produced for CBS in 1987). Schenectady, New York, in the late 1940s is the setting. WINT is a small radio station owned and run by the McAllister family from their home. Maggie, the mother, hosts a morning chit chat show called *Morning Maggie;* her husband, Mack, is the station's dapper newscaster and business affairs manager; Dorothy, their strong-willed 19-year-old daughter, writes the station's daily soap opera; and Bradley, their 15-year-old son, is a budding 1940s-style hipster. The station's music director is Maggie's 70-year-old Aunt Esther. Other regulars are Mack's younger brother, Philly, a would-be entrepreneur who is married to a wide-eyed Japanese war bride (Sayoko); and George, the only non-family member, a black announcer who affects a "refined" accent on the air. The proposal was to relate the mishaps that befall "One Big Family" as they perform multiple roles to keep the station going. Originally titled *Morning Maggie.*

Cast: Ellen Greene (*Maggie McAllister*); John Vickery (*Mack McAllister*); Marita Geraghty (*Dorothy McAllister*); Matthew Perry (*Bradley McAllister*); Eileen Heckart (*Aunt Esther*); Hank Azaria (*Philly McAllister*); Marilyn Tokuda (*Sayoko McAllister*); Larry Riley (*George*).

6884   *One Big Family.* (Series; Comedy; Syn.; 1986). Don Hatton is an officer with the Seattle, Washington, Police Department. He lives at First and Hastings with his wife, Jan, and his siblings, Mary Ann, Kate, Brian and Roger. Also living with them is Jake Hatton, Don's uncle, who has moved in to help Don care for his younger brothers and sisters. Jake became an active part of the family when Don's parents were killed in an automobile accident shortly after Don and Jan were married (they are still newlyweds). Jake is an old-time vaudeville performer and, with age, he becomes a bit grumpy, but his old-age wisdom provides the guidance Don and Jan can't. Stories follow the events that befall the various members of the younger Hatton family as Jake struggles to keep the family together. Brian (the mischievous one) and Kate, the eldest children, attend Fillmore High School. Other regulars are Phil, Jake's friend — and occasional helper in guiding the lives of the children.

Cast: Danny Thomas (*Jake Hatton*); Anthony Starke (*Don Hatton*); Kim Gillingham (*Jan Hatton*); Anastasia Fielding (*Mary Ann Hatton*); Allison McMillan (*Kate Hatton*); Michael DeLuise (*Brian Hatton*); Gabriel Damon (*Roger Hatton*); Barney Martin (*Phil*).

6885   *One Day at a Time.* (Series; Comedy; CBS; 1975–1984). Ann Romano is a liberated, 34-year-old divorcée (who has resumed her maiden name) who lives with her two daughters, Barbara and Julie Cooper (who carry their father's last name), at 1344 Hartford Drive, Apartment 402, in Indianapolis, Indiana.

Ann was born in Logansport, Indiana, and attended Logansport Hgih School. She was first an account executive at the Connors and Davenport Advertising Agency, then co-owner of the Romano and Handris Ad Agency with Nick Handris; the agency was later called Handris and Associates. When the business folded, Ann and her former co-worker (and rival) at Connors and Davenport, Francine Webster, pooled their resources and opened the Romano and Webster. Claude Connors was Ann's first boss.

Ann's first season boyfriend was David Kane, her divorce lawyer (with the firm of McInerney, Wollman, Kollman and Schwartz). She later married architect Sam Royer on May 16, 1983, and moved to 322 Bedford Street, Apartment 422.

Julie, Ann's oldest and more troublesome daughter, attended Jefferson High School. Julie, who did not attend college, was a receptionist for a veterinarian at the Curran Animal Center, a freelance fashion designer and a counselor at the Free Clinic. Julie later married Max Horvath, a flight attendant for PMA Airlines, on Oct. 10, 1979. When Max is laid off, he turns to writing. When he is unable to make a go of it, he takes a job as a waiter at Barney's Tavern. He and Julie became the parents of a daughter they named Annie (J.C. and R.C. Dilley and Paige and Lauren Maloney).

Barbara, Ann's younger daughter, began the series as a tomboy and evolved into a beautiful young woman. She attended Jefferson High School and later City College (but dropped out), and held the following jobs: cook at Quickie Burger, salesclerk at Olympia Sporting Goods and travel agent at the Gonagin Travel Agency. Barbara's greatest disappointment occurred shortly after her marriage (on Oct. 3, 1982) to Mark Royer, a dentist. Having always dreamed of raising a family, Barbara learned that she cannot bear children (an inability to conceive that even surgery cannot cure).

Dwayne F. Schneider, the building superintendent, lives in the basement (Apartment 1) and is a member of I.B.M. (Indianapolis Building Maintenance). He married in 1957, but the marriage lasted only one week. (His wife got up one morning, hot-wired his truck and just took off. However, in the pilot episode, Dwayne is married; in a later episode, Dwayne was married for five days and got a divorce.)

Ginny Wrobliki, Ann's sexy neighbor, is a waitress at the Alibi Room bar; Bob Morton is Barbara's friend; Kathryn Romano is

Anne's mother. Ed is Ann's ex-husband; Alex is Nick's son; Marge is Sam's ex-wife; Felicia is Nick's ex-wife; Beerbelly is Dwayne's friend.

Cast: Bonnie Franklin (*Ann Romano*); Valerie Bertinelli (*Barbara Cooper*); Mackenzie Phillips (*Julie Cooper*); Michael Lembeck (*Max Horvath*); Shelley Fabares (*Francine Webster*); Boyd Gaines (*Mark Royer*); Nanette Fabray (*Kathryn Romano*); Richard Masur (*David Kane*); Mary Louise Weller (*Ginny Wroblinki*); Joseph Campanella (*Ed Cooper*); John Hillerman (*Claude Connors*); Charles Siebert (*Jerry Davenport*); John Putch (*Bob Morton*); Ron Rifkin (*Nick Handris*); Glenn Scarpelli (*Alex Handris*); Elinor Donahue (*Felicia Handris*); Chuck McCann (*Beerbelly*); Howard Hesseman (*Sam Royer*); Claudette Nevins (*Marge Royer*); Jack Riley (*Mr. Gonagin; Barbara's boss, 1984*).

6886   *1-800-Missing.* (Series; Drama; Lifetime; 2003). The original title for *Missing* (which see for information).

6887   *One-Eyed Jacks Are Wild.* (Pilot; Drama; Unaired; Produced for ABC in 1966). Proposal about an American (George Grizzard) who takes a most unusual job: replacing the Prince of a European Kingdom until such time as those seeking to assassinate him can be uncovered and brought to justice. Diana Dors co-stars.

6888   *One Happy Family.* (Series; Comedy; NBC; 1961). Penny and Dick Cooper are a young married couple who, due to a financial setback, are forced to move into the home of her parents, Barney and Mildred Hogan. Also living in the house are Penny's grandparents, Charley and Lovey Hackett. Stories follow the misadventures that occur as three generations of one family attempt to live under the same roof. Dick works as a meteorologist; Charley is a plumber.

Cast: Judy Warner (*Penny Cooper*); Dick Sargent (*Dick Cooper*); Chick Chandler (*Barney Hogan*); Elisabeth Fraser (*Mildred Hogan*); Jack Kirkwood (*Charley Hackett*); Cheerio Meredith (*Lovey Hackett*).

6889   *101 Dalmatians: The Series.* (Series; Cartoon; Disney; 1997). A television adaptation of the 1961 animated feature film and the 1996 live action movie, *101 Dalmatians*, that dealt with the evil Cruella DeVil and her efforts to make a fur coat from the skins of the 101 dogs of Roger and Anita Dearly. Their main dogs are Perita and Pongo (who have 15 birth puppies; the Dearly's adopted 84 additional puppy Dalmatians). Roger and Anita live on a farm and three Dalmatians, Lucky, Rolly and Cadpig, have joined with Spot the chicken to defend their home and keep Cruella's from achieving her dream of a dog fur coat.

Voice Cast: Pamela Adlon, Debi Mae West (*Lucky*); April Winchell (*Cruella de Vil*); Rob Paulsen (*Cecil B. de Vil*); Kevin Schon (*Pongo*); Pam Dawber (*Perdy*); Kath Soucie (*Rolly/Cadpig*); Tara Strong (*Spot*); Toran Caudell (*Tripod*); Michael McKean (*Jasper*); David L. Lander (*Horace*); Charlotte Rae (*Nanny*); Jim Cummings (*Colonel*); Danny Cooksey (*Mooch*); Thom Adcox-Hernandez (*Dipstick*); Christine Cavanaugh (*Dumpling*); Marla Gibbs (*Duchess*); Justin Shenkarow (*Patch*).

6890   *100 Centre Street.* (Pilot; Comedy; ABC; Aug. 31, 1984). Charles Felt, Nell Hartigan, Earl Doucette and Ramon Robledo are judges who try cases at the Hall of Justice at 100 Centre Street in New York City. Incidents that affect their lives and the people that stand trial before them is the focal point of the proposal. Other regulars are Pam, the public defender; Louis, the prosecuting attorney; Leo, the bailiff; Harry, the newsstand owner; Fran, Charles's wife; and Andre, the court stenographer.

Cast: Len Cariou (*Judge Charles Felt*); Dee Wallace (*Judge Nell Hartigan*); J.A. Preston (*Judge Earl Doucette*); Henry Darrow (*Judge Ramon Robledo*); Lela Levy (*Pam Verderamo*); James Canning (*Louis Keck*); Ernie Hudson (*Leo Kelly*); Ernie Sabella (*Harry Pike*); Christine Belford (*Fran Felt*); Wright Dorsey (*Andre Bussey*).

6891   *100 Center Street.* (Series; Drama; A&E; 2001-2002). A behind-the-scenes look at the proceedings of New York City's arraignment court as seen through the cases of Joe Rifkind, a liberal judge known as "Let 'em go Joe." His conflicts with the court system, especially with the strict Judge Attalla Sims (called "Attalla the Hun") and the Manhattan District Attorney's office are also a focal point of the program.

Cast: Alan Arkin (*Joe Rifkind*); LaTanya Richardson (*Attalla Sims*); Phyllis Newman (*Sarah Rifkind, Joe's wife*); Paula Devicq (*ADA Cynthia Bennington*); Joseph Lyle Taylor (*ADA Bobby Esposito*); Manny Perez (*Ramon Rodriquez*).

6892   *The 100 Deeds for Eddie McDowd.* (Series; Comedy; Nick; 1999–2002). Eddie McDowd is 17 years old and a school bully. When a mysterious man (called the Drifter) sees the harm Eddie is causing, he intervenes and transforms Eddie into a dog. In order for Eddie to become human again, he must perform 100 good deeds. Justin Taylor is the last kid Eddie bullied as a human. While at the pound with his parents looking for a dog, he spots Eddie and adopts him. He later learns what has happened when he becomes the only person who can hear Eddie talk. Eddie now lives with Justin, his parents (Doug and Lisa) and his sister (Gwen) and stories follow Justin as he helps Eddie complete his task to become human again. Sharifa is Justin's best friend.

Cast: Brandon Gilberstadt (*Justin Taylor*); William Francis McGuire (*Doug Taylor*); Catherine MacNeal (*Lisa Taylor*); Morgan Kibby (*Gwen Taylor*); Brenda Song (*Sharifa Chung*); Jason Hervey (*Voice of Eddie*); Richard Moll (*Drifter*).

6893   *100 Grand.* (Series; Game; ABC; 1963). One contestant, possessing knowledge in at least one specific field, is placed opposite a panel of five professional authorities. The panelists then ask him a series of questions. Each correct response awards him a large amount of cash. The contestant is permitted to continue or quit playing and leave with his earnings at any time. One incorrect response and the player is defeated. If the player survives several of these knowledge battles, he then faces the final competition: to answer five questions sent in by home viewers. If he is successful, he receives $100,000; if he fails, he is defeated and loses everything.

Host: Jack Clark. **Announcer:** Arthur Van Horn.

6894   *The 100 Lives of Black Jack Savage.* (Series; Adventure; NBC; 1991). On the Caribbean island of San Pietro in the 1790s, a pirate named Black Jack Savage is hanged. His ghost remains on the island and haunts his former residence, Blackbird Castle. Three hundred years later in New York City, billionaire Barry Tarberry, the owner of Tarberry Enterprises, is arrested for insider trading. While out on bail, Barry gathers his available assets and goes into exile — on the island of San Pietro. Shortly after purchasing the haunted Blackberry Castle, Barry encounters and must learn to live with Black Jack (Barry is now wanted by the FBI and broke — the government seized all his other assets).

The current owner of Blackbird Castle is the only person who can see and hear Black Jack. Barry also learns that Black Jack killed 100 people as a pirate and is now cursed to remain on Earth until he can save an equal number of lives to make up for those he took. Black Jack has a spiritual advisor named Larry. Through Larry, Black Jack learns that Barry is headed all the way down for his past deeds — "Right now they've got you scheduled in the Ivan the Terrible chamber in the southeast corner of hell." Now that both are virtually in the same predicament, they agree to help each other by saving lives. Each life they save they split (51 percent goes to Jack, 49 percent to Barry). It's the only chance Barry has to save his soul, and it's Jack's only chance to find eternal peace. Stories relate their somewhat bumbling efforts to save lives.

Assisting Barry and Jack (but he doesn't know about Jack) is Logan Murphy, a brilliant scientist who once worked for the Pentagon as a defense specialist. Logan believes that Barry is crazy (he sees Barry talking to air), and he invented the *Blackbird*, a high tech speedboat made from the body of a SR71 spy plane, which Barry uses to battle crime (Barry hides the boat at a secret dock near the castle).

Black Jack fears Snarks—"Little Dirt Bags" that will send him to hell if he leaves the castle. (Snarks are actually ghostly creatures in a different dimension, and they can cause Black Jack harm. If the Snarks catch Jack, they can transport him to hell by bringing him to the roots of the tree where he was hanged; the roots lead to hell.) To combat the Snarks, Barry had Logan create an anti-Snark weapon he calls "The Snark Buster." (It resembles a vacuum cleaner, and Logan's official name for it is the "Proton Ion Positive Negative Field Adjuster.") Each episode concluded with the number of lives left to save. At the end of the last episode, "89 Lives Left to Save" appeared. Abel Vasquez is the island's corrupt governor; Reya is his niece.

Cast: Daniel Hugh-Kelly *(Barry Tarberry)*; Stoney Jackson *(Black Jack Savage, Pilot)*; Steven Williams *(Black Jack Savage, Series)*; Steve Hytner *(Logan Murphy)*; Bert Rosario *(Abel Vasquez)*; Roya Megnot *(Reya Montegro)*.

6895   *100 Questions.* (Series; Comedy; NBC; 2010). Charlotte Payne is a young British woman who now lives and works in New York City. She is pretty, ambitious but feels she will never really meet the perfect soul mate. After a succession of failed relationships, Charlotte decides to seek professional help and joins Soul Mate Specialists, a computer dating service. Before accepting any client, the client must answer 100 scientifically formulated questions that are designed to determine his or her perfect soul mate. As Charlotte answers each of the questions (for example, "What brought you here?," "Are you open minded?," "Are you romantic?") a flashback sequence is shown that relates Charlotte's associated comic mishaps. Sharing Charlotte's experiences are her close friends: Jill, Leslie, Wayne and Mike, all of whom are single and seeking the perfect mates also. Jill is a gorgeous kindergarten teacher who sees every man as a potential mate (unfortunately for Jill, the feelings are most often not mutual as Jill is too pushy and intimidates men). Leslie is a laid back young woman who is very choosey about the men she dates but never seems to find one who can meet her standards. Mike is a public defender; Wayne is the son of a billionaire who was cut off from the family for being a slacker. Wayne knows that his family wants him to gain a sense of responsibility, but always getting what he wanted has made that a difficult goal to achieve. He has never had a job and lives with Mike. Originally titled *100 Questions for Charlotte Payne*. Andrew is Charlotte's dating service counselor (seen at the beginning of each episode before the flashback).

Cast: Sophie Winkleman *(Charlotte Payne)*; Colette Wolfe *(Jill; series)*; Joy Suprano *(Jill; pilot)*; Smith Cho *(Leslie; series)*; Elizabeth Ho *(Leslie; pilot)*; Christopher Moynihan *(Mike Poole)*; David Walton *(Wayne Rutherford)*; Amir Tolai *(Andrew; pilot)*; Michael Benjamin Washington *(Andrew; series)*.

6896   *106 and Park.* (Series; Music; BET; 2000–). A modern version of the 1950s series *Your Hit Parade* that presents a countdown of the top music videos. The program is broadcast live from New York City and features, in addition to a live audience, the biggest superstars as guests.

Host: Joseph Forrester, Terrence Jenkins, Raquel Roxanne Diaz (a.k.a. Rocsi).

6897   *The $100,000 Big Surprise.* (Series; Game; CBS; 1956–1957). Each of the contestants who appear selects one of two sets of questions, the "easy" or the "difficult." Players are quizzed in their choices and receive cash prizes for each correct response. Players, who are defeated and lose everything if they give an incorrect response, can continue or stop at any point, Players vie for the opportunity to win $100,000 by answering increasingly difficult questions in their chosen categories.

Host: Jack Barry, Mike Wallace. **Assistant:** Sue Oakland, Mary Gardiner.

6898   *The $100,000 Name That Tune.* (Series; Game; Syn.; 1976–1981). An update of *Name That Tune*. Two contestants compete in a game wherein they must identify song titles after hearing only a few bars played by an orchestra. Several rounds are played (worth different amounts of money) and the highest scoring cash player is the winner. The champion receives the opportunity to win $100,000 by identifying a very difficult mystery tune from three notes of music. Revised as *The New $100,000 Name That Tune*.

Host: Tom Kennedy. **Model:** Jeri Fiala. **Orchestra:** Tommy Oliver, Stan Worth. **Music Performer:** Dan Younger and the Sound System. **Vocalists:** Steve March, Monica Buris.

6899   *The $100,000 Pyramid.* (Series; Game; Syn.; 1985–1988; 1991–1993). A revised version of *The $25,000 Pyramid*. Two teams, each composed of one celebrity and one non-celebrity contestant, compete. One team chooses one subject (from six that are displayed on a pyramid board). Each subject contains seven related objects. One player must use one-word clues and relate the meaning of each object to his partner within thirty seconds. Each correct association scores one point. Three rounds are played and the player with the highest score is the winner and receives the opportunity to win up to $25,000 by guessing seven subjects in 60 seconds. At a later date (seven weeks) the three players who used the least amount of time at the pyramid compete for $100,000.

Host: Dick Clark *(1985–88)*; John Davidson *(1991–92)*. **Announcer:** Johnny Gilbert.

6900   *The $100,000 Video Challenge.* (Pilot; Comedy; Unaired; Produced in 1990). Amateur home videos are screened with prizes awarded for each of the three funniest productions (as voted by the studio audience). While the big money prize was never awarded, winners of the weekly contests were screened again with the best video winning its maker $10,000.

Host: Chuck Henry.

6901   *The $128,000 Question.* (Series; Game; Syn.; 1976–1977). Players who possess knowledge in at least one specific field, compete. Each is asked a series of questions ranging in value from $64 to $64,000. The player, who risks loss of everything if he should give an incorrect response, can either continue playing or quit after answering each question. Once a player earns $64,000, he receives the opportunity to return at a later date and compete for another $64,0000.

Host: Mike Darrow *(Season One)*; Alex Trebek *(Season Two)*. **Announcer:** Alan Kalter *(First Season)*; Sandy Hoyt *(Second Season)*.

6902   *One in a Million.* (Series; Game; ABC; 1967). The object calls for contestants to discover (through question and answer probe rounds) the secrets that are shared by a panel of four guest celebrities.

Host: Danny O'Neill.

6903   *One in a Million.* (Series; Comedy; ABC; 1980). Shirley Simmons is a cab driver who inherits controlling interest in the $200 million Grayson Enterprises after the death of its founder, Jonathan Grayson, a friend of Shirley's. Shirley's efforts to fulfill Grayson's wishes and run his company as the Chairman of the Board, is the focal point of stories. Other regulars are Roland Cushing, the company vice president; Nancy Boyer, Shirley's secretary; Barton Stone, Cushing's attorney; Raymond and Edna, Shirley's parents; Max, the diner owner; Grace, Roland's wife; Michael Boyer, Nancy's son; Duke, Shirley's friend.

Cast: Shirley Hemphill *(Shirley Simmons)*; Keene Curtis *(Roland Cushing)*; Dorothy Fielding *(Nancy Boyer)*; Richard Paul *(Barton Stone)*; Mel Stewart *(Raymond Simmons)*; Ann Weldon *(Edna Simmons)*; Carl Ballantine *(Max Kalamo)*; Louise Sorel *(Grace Cushing)*; Jimmy Heth *(Michael Boyer)*; Ralph Wilcox *(Duke)*.

6904   *One Life to Live.* ABC serial. Premiered: July 15, 1968. See *Soap Operas.*

6905   *The One: Making of a Music Star.* (Series; Reality; ABC; 2006). Not only is *The One* a copy of *American Idol* but it also achieved the worst ratings in the history of ABC for a premiere (1.1 million viewers or a three share of the available audience). The program follows a group of amateur singers as they compete for a contract from a major music company. The contestants are seen at Music Academy (where they are trained and mentored). From this point on, each performs on stage and is judged by a panel. But it is viewer votes that determine who stays and who is eliminated. Cancelled after three episodes and before a winner was chosen. George Stroumboulopoulos hosts; Kara Dio Guardi, Mark Hudson and Andie Harrell are the judges.

6906   *One Man Show.* (Series; Comedy; Syn.; 1969). Performances by guest comedians (who also serve as hosts for that particular program).

Guests Include: Morey Amsterdam, Bob and Ray *(Bob Elliott, Ray Goulding)*; Groucho Marx, Rip Torn, Steve Allen. **Announcer:** Ed Jordan.

6907   *One Man's Experience.* (Series; Anthology; DuMont; 1952-1953). Human interest accounts that depict the joys and sorrows of men. Guests appear in stories that run four days each. See also *One Woman's Experience.* Also known as *One Man's Story.*

6908   *One Man's Family.* (Series; Drama; NBC; 1949–1955). The life, sex values and worthiness of the American family as seen through the experiences of the Barbour's, a seven-member family living in the swank Sea Cliff section of Bay City in California. Henry Barbour, a stockbroker, is the head of the family. He is married to Frances (called "Fanny") and they are the parents of Hazel, Claudia, Jack, Clifford and Paul. Adapted from the radio program of the same title.

Principal Cast: Bert Lytell, Theodore Van Eltz *(Henry Barbour)*; Marjorie Gateson, Mary Adams *(Frances Barbour)*; Lillian Schaff, Linda Reighton *(Hazel Barbour)*; Nancy Franklin, Eva Marie Saint, Ann Whitfield *(Claudia Barbour)*; Robert Wigginton, Martin Dean, Arthur Cassell *(Jack Barbour)*; Frankie Thomas, Jr., Billy Idelson, James Lee *(Clifford Barbour)*; Paul Thompson *(Paul Barbour)*; Madeline Bugard *(Teddy Barbour)*; Mercedes McCambridge, Susan Shaw *(Beth Holly)*; Michael Higgins, Jack Edwards *(John Roberts)*; Nancy Franklin *(Ann White)*; Les Tremayne, Walter Brooke *(Billy Herbert)*.

6909   *The $1,000,000 Chance of a Lifetime.* (Series; Game; Syn.; 1986). Two teams, each composed of two members, compete.

One member of each team stands before a line of blank spaces. Letters to the formation of a clue word appear, one at a time. The first player to identify the word receives money and the chance to identify the mystery puzzle by selecting two letters that appear in the unknown name, place or object. The first player to identify the puzzle wins money. Players rotate turns and the highest scoring team plays the bonus round. To win one million dollars the team first selects one category from three that are shown, then has to guess six related subjects (from letters that appear) within sixty seconds. Successful players win $5,000 and the chance to compete again. Ten thousand dollars is awarded if the team wins the next day's game and is successful in the bonus round. The one million dollars is awarded if the team can win both a third game and successfully complete a third bonus round.

Host: Jim Lange. **Assistant:** Karen Thomas. **Announcer:** Johnny Gilbert, Marc Summers.

6910   *The $1,000,000 Video Challenge.* (Series; Contest; Syn.; 1990). Guest Hollywood directors, producers and actors judge amateur home videos each week. Each video is judged in four categories: comedy appeal, kids stuff, music and that's life. The winning video chosen by the panel awards its producer cash or merchandise prizes. The deceiving title refers to the total amount of money and merchandise that will be awarded over a 39 week run.

Host: Steven Kelley.

6911   *One Minute from Broadway.* (Pilot; Comedy; NBC; July 23, 1956). Wayward Inn is an off-Broadway hotel in New York City that houses literary and theatrical people; it is literally "One Minute from Broadway" (the pilot episode title). Gloria is a small town Philadelphia girl with big dreams: becoming a star on the Great White Way. The proposal was to focus on Gloria's mishaps as she resides at the hotel and seeks acting jobs. Aired on *Sneak Preview.* Had the project sold it would have been titled *Wayward Inn.*

Cast: Gloria Talbott *(Gloria)*; Brian Aherne *(Hotel operator)*.

6912   *One Minute Please.* (Series; Game; DuMont; 1954-1955). Two teams, each composed of three members, compete. A topic is stated (for example, "The Perfect Woman," "How to Drive a Car") and each panelist must incorporate it into a conversation for one minute without undue repetition, hesitation, or straying from the point. Winners are the wordiest talkers. Prizes are awarded to the studio audience members who are represented by the individual panelists. Based on the BBC radio and TV program of the same title.

Host: John K.M. McCaffery, Allyn Edwards. **Panelists:** Ernie Kovacs, Beatrice Straight, Hermione Gingold, Alice Pearce, Jimmy Cannon, Marc Connolly.

6913   *One More Try.* (Pilot; Comedy; CBS; Aug. 31, 1982). Dede March is the owner of the Creative Catering Service in New York City. Adam Margolin is the curator of the Museum of Natural History and the father of two children (Paul and Daniel). The proposal was to follow the ups and downs of marriage as Dede and Adam, both victims of previous marriages that ended in divorce, decide to marry and give it one more try (they set up housekeeping in Adam's apartment at 421 West 71st Street). Other regulars are Jenny, Dede's business partner; and Mr. Liebowitz, the building's elevator operator. Lucie Arnaz performs the theme, "One More Try."

Cast: Lucie Arnaz *(Dede March)*; Laurence Luckinbill *(Adam Margolin)*; Randall Batinkoff *(Paul Margolin)*; Benjamin Bernouy *(Daniel Margolin)*; Judy Gibson *(Jenny Marlowe)*; Maurice Shrong *(Mr. Liebowitz)*.

6914   *One Night Band.* (Pilot; Drama; CBS; May 28, 1983).

Michael is the lead guitar; Vikki, the singer; Tony, the drummer; and Zack, second guitar. Together they are One Night Band, a struggling country and western group. The proposal was to chart their rocky road to stardom.

Cast: Brad Maule *(Michael Harrison)*; Stepfanie Kramer *(Vikki Royelle)*; George Deloy *(Tony Glazer)*; George Cassel *(Zack Radford)*.

6915   *One Ocean View.* (Series; Reality; ABC; 2006). A look at the activities of a group of New Yorkers who flock to the waterfront resort of Fire Island for a weekend of fun in the sun. The participants are Heather Lutz, Usmon Shaikh, K.J. Nies, John Healy, Radha Agrawal.

6916   *One of the Boys.* (Series; Comedy; NBC; 1989). The Lukowski Construction Company in Queens, New York, is owned by Mike Lukowski and managed by Maria Navarro. Mike is a widower with three sons (Luke, Nick and Steve) and Maria is a beautiful Venezuelan girl. The first four episodes focus on Mike and Maria's courtship; they married in the fifth episode and had the series been renewed it would have focused on what the sixth episode showed: Maria's new position as a wife and business partner in the company. Other regulars are Bernice, Maria's friend; Vanessa, the steady client; and Ernie, a worker.

Cast: Maria Conchita Alonso *(Maria Navarro)*; Robert Clohessy *(Mike Lukowski)*; Michael DeLuise *(Luke Lukowski)*; Justin Whalen *(Nick Lukowski)*; Billy Morrissette *(Steve Lukowski)*; Amy Aquino *(Bernice)*; Melody Rogers *(Vanessa Orloff)*; Dan Hedaya *(Ernie)*.

6917   *One on One.* (Series; Comedy; UPN; 2001–2006). Flex Washington is a sportscaster at Baltimore TV station WYNX (host of *The Flex Files*). He is divorced (from Nicole) and the father of 14-year-old Breanna Barnes. Breanna had been living with her mother until Nicole acquired a grant to study aquatic wild life in Nova Scotia and Flex became her guardian. Stories follow the relationship between a single father and his gorgeous, boy-crazy teenage daughter.

Flex excelled in basketball in high school and won a scholarship to college (where he majored in communication arts as a backup to his professional sports career). After graduating from Maryland State University he joined the NBA. During his second season he threw his knee out and was unable to continue playing.

Breanna attends McKinley High School and has ambitions to become an actress. In 2005 she moves to Los Angeles to attend Chaplin University of the Arts. She acquires several roommates (Sara, D-Mack, Lisa and Cash) and the revised series storyline follows Breanna's mishaps as she sets out to attend college and live on her own.

Spirit and Arnaz are Breanna's friends (Arnaz is later Breanna's boyfriend, a hopeful musician). He works with her in a diner called The Blog; Duane Odell Knox, Flex's friend is a used car salesman at Big Sal's Used Cars.

Cast: Flex Alexander *(Flex Washington)*; Kyla Pratt *(Breanna Barnes)*; Kelly Perine *(Duane Odell Knox)*; Robert Ri'chard *(Arnaz Ballard)*; Sicily *(Spirit Jones)*; Nicole Paggi *(Sara)*; Camille Mana *(Lisa)*; Jonathan Chase *(Cash)*; Ray J *(D-Mack)*; Tichina Arnold *(Nicole Barnes)*; Shondrella Avery *(Candy)*; Saskia Garel *(Danielle)*; Rashaan Nall *(Walt)*; Melissa DeSousa *(Natalie)*.

6918   *One Piece.* (Series; Cartoon; Cartoon Network; 1999). In a time long ago, a vicious pirate named Gold Roger ravaged ships to obtain a fabulous wealth, His exploits earned him the name Pirate King. His reign, however, came to an abrupt end when he was captured and sentenced to death. Rather than turn over his booty to authorities and come clean, Gold Roger reveals only that his treasure (called One Piece) is hidden somewhere in a treacherous place called the Grand Line. As the years pass the treasure becomes a legend that

no one has ever been able to find. One day, many years later, a young boy named Monkey D. Luffy embarks on a mission to find the treasure and become the next great pirate king. He is assisted by Roronoa Zolo (a swordsman), Usopp (a mechanic), Chopper (a doctor), Sanji (a cook) and Nami (a navigator) and stories relate their dangerous quest.

Voice Cast: Bella Hudson *(Monkey D. Luffy)*; Erica Schroeder *(Monkey D. Luffy)*; Marc Diraison *(Roronoa Zolo)*; Andy Rannells *(Roronoa Zolo)*; Kerry Williams *(Nami)*; David Moo *(Sanji)*; Lisa Ortiz *(Chopper)*; Eric Stuart *(Narrator)*; Jason Griffith *(Yasopp)*; Jason Griffith *(Usopp)*.

6919   *One Step Beyond.* (Series; Anthology; ABC; 1959–1961). Dramas based on true events that are strange, frightening and unexplainable in terms of normal human experience. Originally sponsored by the Alcoa Corporation and titled *Alcoa Presents One Step Beyond*.

Program Open: "Come, you'll witness things strange, unexplained, mysterious, but no to be denied. Join me now and take *One Step Beyond*."

Host: John Newland.

6920   *110 Lombard Street.* (Pilot; Comedy; CBS; Sept. 14, 1988). The mishaps that befall three single men (Bob, Mike and Ryan) who share an urban apartment at 110 Lombard Street. Other regulars are Linda, Mike's sister. The proposal was also set to present musical guests and a regular cast performing various roles each week.

Cast: Bob Bainborough *(Bob)*; Mike Myers *(Mike)*; Ryan Stiles *(Ryan)*; Linda Kash *(Linda)*. **Regulars:** Dana Anderson, Bonnie Hunt, Debra Jarvis, Richard Kind, Jane Morris, Don Lake, Audrey Webb, Mark Wilson.

6921   *One Tree Hill.* (Series; Drama; WB, 2003–2006; CW, 2006–). Teenagers living in the small North Carolina town of Tree Hill and struggling to find their place in the world is the focal point of stories. Particular focus is on brothers Lucas and Nathan Scott and the romantic entanglements both face, especially when they fall for the same girl, the beautiful Peyton. The fifth season (2008) advances the storyline four years (to deal with the characters as young adults instead of high school students). Focus is now on Lucas (a published novelist) and Brooke Davis (a fashion designer).

Cast: Chad Michael Murray *(Lucas Scott)*; James Lafferty *(Nathan Scott)*; Paul Johansson *(Dan Scott)*; Moira Kelly *(Karen Roe)*; Bethany Joy Lenz *(Peyton Elizabeth Sawyer)*; Sophia Bush *(Brooke Penelope Davis)*; Barbara Alyn Woods *(Deborah Helen Scott)*; Lee Norris *(Marvin "Mouth" McFadden)*; Craig Sheffer *(Keith Scott)*; Barry Corbin *(Coach Whitey Durham)*; Cullen Moss *(Junk)*; Vaughn Wilson *(Fergie)*; Bryan Greenberg *(Jake Jagielski)*; Brett Claywell *(Tim Smith)*; Bevin Prince *(Bevin Mirskey)*; Antwon Tanner *(Skills)*; Danneel Harris *(Rachel Gatina)*; Craig Sheffer *(Keith Scott)*; Bethany Joy Galeotti *(Haley James Scott)*; Shawn Shepard *(Principal Turner)*; Kieren Hutchinson *(Andy Hargrove)*; Tyler Hilton *(Chris Keller)*; Kelsey Chow *(Gigi Silveri)*; Michael Copon *(Felix Taggaro)*; Emmanuelle Vaugier *(Nicki)*; Sheryl Lee *(Ellie Harp)*.

6922   *One, Two, Three— Go!* (Series; Children; NBC; 1961-1962). Filmed and taped explorations to places of interest to children.

Host: Jack Lescoulie. **Assistant:** Richard Thomas.

6923   *1 vs. 100.* (Series; Game; NBC, 2006; GSN, 2010). One player stands before a large set that seats 100 opponents. A question, worth $1,000 is asked of the player. Three possible answers appear (A, B and C). Each member of the Mob (as the opponents are called) selects one answer. The player is asked to verbally select an answer.

When the correct answer is revealed, the player, if correct, receives $1,000 for each Mob member who answered incorrectly. If the player is wrong, he is defeated and wins nothing (the remaining Mob members split his money). Further questions increase the money amount at stake and the player can win $1 million if he defeats all of the Mob; he also has the option of leaving with the money he has won after each plateau (answering three same money amounts correctly).

In 2008, a ten line prize board is used. Money amounts range from $1,000 to $1,000,000. Each money amount contains 10 spaces. A player wins money by those mob members who give a wrong answer to a question. Each 10 incorrect answers wins the player a row and like in the prior format, he can quit with what money he has won or face the mob hoping for a higher cash prize. If the player gives the wrong answer, the mob splits what money he has won. The GSN version lowers the prize money and has The Mob appearing on monitors as opposed to live on stage.

Host: Bob Saget (NBC), Carrie Ann Inaba (GSN).

6924   *One West Waikiki*. (Series; Crime Drama; CBS; 1994). While in Hawaii to address the annual Homicide Symposium, Dr. Dawn "Holli" Holliday, the deputy chief medical examiner with the L.A.P.D., finds the body of a young woman while swimming in Macaha Bay on Waikiki. Because of her status, Holli is permitted to assist the local coroner in the autopsy. Holli concludes by the marks on the victim's chest, that she was pushed and drowned. Later, during the post op, Holli finds that the girl is missing a kidney that was surgically removed and calls her death a homicide. A maverick cop named Lieutenant Mack Wolfe is assigned to investigate Holli's Jane Doe case. Their investigation uncovers an organization that brings girls in for prostitution and the sale of organs (the girls receive extensive plastic surgery to make them beautiful; in return they "donate" a kidney). When the case is solved, Holli is asked to remain in Hawaii and become the new medical examiner (to replace the retiring Dr. Reeves). She accepts and finds a new business address at One West Waikiki — the medical examiner's building.

When Holli was a kid her mother died. She was never able to obtain the cause of death (listed as unascertainable). That is why Holli went into forensics — and why she never gives up on a homicide. With that determination and with new solutions to unmask old secrets, stories follow Holli and Mac's case investigations. Other regulars are Nui, the coroner's office field investigator; Kimo, Mac's assistant; and police captain Dave Herzog.

Cast: Cheryl Ladd (*Dawn Holliday*); Richard Burgi (*Mack Wolfe*); Elsie Sniffen (*Nui*); Ogie Zulueta (*Kimo*); Paul Gleason (*Dave Herzog*).

6925   *One Woman's Experience*. (Series; Drama; DuMont; 1952–1953). Human interest accounts that depict the joys and sorrows of women. Guests appear in stories that run four days each. Also known as *One Woman's Story*. See also *One Man's Experience*.

6926   *One World*. (Series; Comedy; NBC; 1998–2000). Karen and Dave Blake are a childless couple who adopt the worst kids they can find in hopes of straightening them out. They live in Florida and their kids are Jane, Ben, Marcie, Sue, Neil, and Cray. Stories relate events in their lives.

Jane is the wild one. She has been abandoned, abused and ignored and feels she is everybody's problem (and always in trouble). She dates guys who know how to use a phone — "but it's usually one call and it's to their lawyer." Jane, who believes she is living with "the Brady Bunch," is pushy, rude "and worst of all," says Marcie, "she doesn't like to shop." Marcie, the assistant manager of the Warehouse, "the hippest under-21 club in town," loves to shop and claims she can get anything for half price. Sue, 16, plays midfield on the girls'

soccer team at South Beach High School (where Dave is athletic coach). She is a hopeful for the Olympic Soccer Team.

"If we don't have each other, we don't have anything" says Neil, the brainy one of the kids, who feels their constant squabbling may break up the only family he has ever known. He hopes to become a stockbroker. Cray, 12, the youngest, plays the harp in the school orchestra and is a member of the Skateboard Club. He enjoys sitting on the front porch waiting for hurricanes (he chains himself to the porch chair so it won't get blown away).

Cast: Elizabeth Moreland (*Karen Blake*); Michael Tolan (*Dave Blake*); Arroyn Lloyd (*Jane Blake*); Bryan Kirkwood (*Ben Blake*); Alisa Reyes (*Marcie Blake*); Michelle Krusiec (*Sue Blake*); Harvey Silver (*Neil Blake*); Brandon Baker (*Cray Blake*).

6927   *The Onedin Line*. (Series; Drama; Syn.; 1976). Liverpool, England, during the 1860s provides the backdrop for tales of tradesman James Onedin, captain of the *Charlotte Rhodes*, a three-mast top sail schooner as he attempts to maintain a cargo transporting business.

Cast: Peter Gilmore (*James Onedin*); Anne Stallybrass (*Anne Onedin*); Brian Rawlinson, James Garbutt (*Robert Onedin*); Jessica Benton (*Elizabeth Frazer*); James Hayter (*Joshua Webster*); Mary Webster (*Sarah Onedin*); Philip Bond (*Albert Frazer*); Jane Seymour (*Emma Fogarty*); John Phillips (*Jack Frazer*); Edward Judd (*Manuel Ortega*).

6928   *The O'Neills*. (Series; Drama; DuMont; 1949-1950). Peggy O'Neill is a young widow and the mother of two children, Janice and Eddie. Peggy works as a fashion designer and stories, based on the radio program of the same title, relate her efforts to provide a decent life for herself and children.

Cast: Vera Allen (*Peggy O'Neill*); Janice Gilbert (*Janice O'Neill*); Michael Lawson (*Eddie O'Neill*); Ian Martin (*Bill O'Neill*); Celia Bubkin (*Mrs. Levy*); Ben Fishbein (*Mr. Levy*); Jane West (*Mrs. Bailey*).

6929   *Only in America with Greg Jackson*. (Series; Interview; Syn.; 1986). A daily program of in-depth celebrity interviews with Greg Jackson as the host.

6930   *Only Temporary*. (Pilot; Comedy; NBC; Sept. 1, 1989). Just Temporary is a Hollywood temporary employment agency owned by Arnie Kaznoff. Barbara Myer is the supervisor and Amy, Ken and Sookie are the featured employees. Barbara has a ditsy sister named Nicole and Nicole has an equally empty-headed girlfriend named Torie. The proposal was to focus on Barbara as she struggles to run the agency and solve the problems created by Nicole and Torie who don't look for trouble, but seem to attract it like a magnet. Judy is Barbara's friend. Tisha Campbell performs the theme, "Just Temporary."

Cast: Chelsea Field (*Barbara Myer*); Christine Mellor (*Nicole Myer*); Lisa Kudrow (*Torie*); Herb Edelman (*Arnie Kaznoff*); Marcia Cross (*Amy Jones*); Jonathan Stark (*Ken Lugee*); Kate Benton (*Sookie*); Lisa Jane Persky (*Judy*).

6931   *Open All Hours*. (Series; Comedy; The Entertainment Channel; 1982). The British program on which *Open All Night* is based. Arkwright (as he is called) is a stubborn survivor of the supermarket age who owns a corner grocery shop and competes by staying open all hours. His interactions with the unusual characters that frequent the store — and his endless attempts to seduce the luscious nurse, Gladys Emmanuel — are the focal point of stories.

Cast: Ronnie Baker (*Arkwright*); Lynda Brown (*Gladys Emmanuel*); David Jason (*Granville; his nephew*).

6932   Open All Night. (Series; Comedy; ABC; 1981–1982). Gordon Feester is the owner-operator of an Englewood, California "364 Store," a 24-hour-a day grocery store fraught with problems. Gordon's attempts to cope with the unusual customers who frequent his store, as well as his somewhat wacky family, is the focal point of stories. Based on the British series *Open All Hours* (which see for information). Other regulars are Gretchen, Gordon's wife; Terry, Gordon's stepson; Robin, the night manager; Larry Bud, Gretchen's ex-husband; Wayne and Connie, Gordon's parents. Police Officers Steve and Edie are regular visitors to the store.

Cast: George Dzundza (*Gordon Feester*); Susan Tyrrell (*Gretchen Hofmeyster-Feester*); Sam Whipple (*Terry Hofmeyster*); Bubba Smith (*Robin*); Jay Tarses (*Officer Steve*); Bever-Leigh Banfield (*Officer Edie*); James Gallery (*Larry Bud Hofmeyster*); Art Kassul (*Wayne Feester*); Mary Jackson (*Connie Feester*).

6933   Open House. (Series; Comedy; Fox; 1989–1990). A spin off from *Duet* wherein Laura Kelly and Linda Phillips become brokers with the Juan Verde Real Estate Company in Los Angeles.

Laura, who had a catering business, gave it up when she and her husband, Ben, divorced. She lives at 13205 Ocean Avenue, is sweet, innocent, a bit naive and troubled by a drinking problem. She has one regret: having had her address tattooed on her left breast (which she had done so she could remember where she lives when on a drinking binge).

Linda is still married to Richard; they later separate and divorce. Their daughter, Amanda, appears in the first episode and is then said to be cared for by Geneva, Linda's housekeeper.

Linda is a high powered sales agent and is constantly engaged in a battle of wits with fellow agent Ted Nichols to make the most sales. Richard plays piano at Jasper's Bar and Restaurant. (Richard lives in an apartment at 549 Palisades Avenue; Linda resides in their former home at 10 West Florist Street.) Margo Van Meter, the receptionist, has a cat named Boris; Roger McSwain is the agency's owner, and Scott Babylon is an agent who uses celebrities' voices to make sales.

Phoebe is Roger's man-crazy daughter; Dorothy is Ted's mother. In the first few episodes, John Greene owned Juan Verde (he was bought out by McSwain).

John Beasley and John Veiter composed the "Open House" theme.

Cast: Mary Page Keller (*Laura Kelly*); Alison LaPlaca (*Linda Phillips*); Chris Lemmon (*Richard Phillips*); Ginger Orsi (*Amanda Phillips*); Arleen Sorkin (*Geneva*); Philip Charles MacKenzie (*Ted Nichols*); Ellen DeGeneres (*Margo Van Meter*); Nick Tate (*Roger McSwain*); Sherri Krenn (*Phoebe McSwain*); Marian Mercer (*Dorothy Nichols*); Jon Cypher (*John Greene*).

6934   Opening Night. (Series; Anthology; NBC; 1958). Actress Arlene Dahl hosts a summer program of selected repeat episodes from *Ford Theater.*

6935   Opera Cameos. (Series; Variety; DuMont; 1953–1955). Opera singer Giovanni Martinelli oversees a program that presents condensed versions of popular operas.

6936   Opera vs. Jazz. (Series; Variety; ABC; 1953). A musical symposium in which two guests (per week) discuss and perform operatic arias and standard tunes.

Host: Nancy Kenyon. **Regulars:** Don Cornell, Jan Preece, Robert Merrill, Alan Dale, The Strawhatters. **Music:** Johnny Reo.

6937   Operating Instructions. (Pilot; Drama; Unaired; Produced for USA in 2009). Rachel Scott, newly returned from the Iraq battlefields where she served as a top trauma surgeon, finds a position in an inner-city hospital where she soon discovers the bureaucratic minefields of the public health care system. The proposal was to follow Rachel as she challenges the system to do what she was trained to do — save lives.

Cast: Emily Rose (*Rachel Scott*); Christine Lahti (*Helen Keller*); Johnny Sneed (*Will McKay*); Assaf Cohen (*Eli Funston*); Diana Maria Riva (*Amani*); Nick Zano (*Luke*).

6938   Operating Room. (Pilot; Comedy; NBC; Oct. 4, 1979). Jim Lawrence, Charles Webner and Robert Robinson are doctors attached to Los Angeles Memorial Hospital. Charles and Robert are single; Jim is married to Jean and the proposal was to relate their efforts to cope with problems at home and at work.

Cast: David Spielberg (*Jim Lawrence*); Oliver Clark (*Charles Webner*); James Sutorius (*Robert Robinson*); Barbara Babcock (*Jean Lawrence*).

6939   Operation: Entertainment. (Series; Variety; ABC; 1968–1969). Entertainment, from songs and dances to musical numbers and comedy skits that are presented in the style of World War II U.S.O. (United Servicemen's Organization) clubs.

Program Open: "From the U.S. Naval Amphibious Base in Coronado, California, ABC's *Operation Entertainment* presents in alphabetical order Roosevelt Greer and the L.A. Rams Fearsome Foursome, Charlie Manna, the McGuire Sisters, Kaye Stevens, Donna Jean Young, the Operation Entertainment Girls and Terry Gibbs and the All-Star Band."

Host: Jim Lange. **Announcer:** Johnny Jacobs. **Music:** Terry Gibbs.

6940   Operation Greasepaint. (Pilot; Comedy; CBS; Aug. 12, 1968). Spivak, Minihane, Bower, Brown and Keller are a ragtag entertainment unit assigned to the Normandy Combat Zone during World War II. The proposal was to relate their mishaps as they attempt to entertain the troops.

Cast: Avery Schreiber (*Spivak*); Jack Burns (*Minihane*); Fred Willard (*Bower*); Johnny Haymer (*Brown*); Robert Fitch (*Keller*).

6941   Operation: Neptune. (Series; Adventure; NBC; 1953). Bill Hollister is the commander of a U.S. Navy submarine whose extensive undersea work has earned him the nickname of "Captain Neptune." Serialized stories, set in the undersea kingdom of Nadiria, relate Bill's attempts to stop the evil Kabeda from a power-mad plan to control the world by killing the surface population. Broadcast live and also known as *Captain Neptune.* Other regulars are Dink Melvin, Bill's assistant; Admiral Bigelow, Bill's superior; Dick Saunders, Bill's assistant; Thirza, the Empress of Nadiria; and Mersennus, Kabeda's henchman.

Cast: Tod Griffin (*Bill Hollister*); Humphrey Davis (*Dink Melvin*); Rusty Lane (*Admiral Bigelow*); Richard Holland (*Dick Saunders*); Margaret Stewart (*Thirza*); Harold Conklin (*Kabeda*); Dehl Berti (*Mersennus*).

6942   Operation Petticoat. (Series; Comedy; ABC; 1977–1978). Lt. Cmdr. Matthew Sherman commands the USS *Sea Tiger,* a Navy submarine that was christened in 1941. In August 1942, just 45 minutes before Sherman arrives to take command, the *Sea Tiger* is attacked by Japanese planes and sunk. With the help of his crew, the 2,000 ton *Sea Tiger* is made seaworthy — put back together again with junk, from bathroom fixtures to car parts.

On the island of Marquis, the *Sea Tiger* (called "The Boat" by Sherman), is brought in for minor repairs and a paint job. Shortly after an undercoat of shocking pink paint is put on the sub, an enemy plane attacks the base and destroys the supply of gray paint. For reasons that are never really explained (other than that the *Sea Tiger* is always on patrol and can't get into a port for repainting), the sub remains pink. Stories relate the crew's adventures as they roam the South Pacific.

Lt. Nick Holden is the supply officer who uses cons to get what he needs. Chief Herbert Molumphrey is the sub's mechanic; he can work miracles when it comes to jerry-rigging. Alvin Hunkle is the overeager yeoman; Seaman Broom is called "Doom and Gloom Broom" for his negative outlook on everything; Ensign Stovall is the navigator; and Seaman Williams is the radio technician.

When a group of Army nurses (Edna, Dolores, Barbara, Ruth and Claire) become stranded on an island, they become a part of the crew when they are rescued by Sherman. They now seem to be trapped aboard the sub (every time they are supposed to leave, something comes up to prolong their stay). Despite the fact that their lingerie hangs here and there to dry, and Molumphrey believes substituting bras for springs is indecent "and not navy," Sherman is most often content — "Rather this than a desk in Washington."

Major Edna Howard can work wonders by substituting clothes for scarce items (for instance, a girdle became a much needed valve spring). Lt. Dolores Crandall is the sexiest of the girls. She is a health nut, sweet and a bit clumsy. Dolores means well, tries so hard to do her best, but things just don't work out her way. Lt. Barbara Duran is the most sophisticated of the nurses and is fascinated with Holden (his schemes impress her). Lt. Ruth Colfax and Claire Reid are the remaining bombshells who Sherman believes are distractions to his crew (although when duty calls, the guys seem to forget the girls and become the crew Sherman needs). *See also The New Operation Petticoat.*

Cast: John Astin (*Matthew Sherman*); Richard Gilliland (*Nick Holden*); Yvonne Wilder (*Edna Howard*); Melinda Naud (*Dolores Crandall*); Jamie Lee Curtis (*Barbara Duran*); Dorrie Thompson (*Ruth Colfax*); Bond Gideon (*Claire Reid*); Richard Brestoff (*Yeoman Alvin Hunkle*); Christopher J. Brown (*Ensign Stoval*); Wayne Long (*Herbert Molumphrey*); Jim Varney (*Seaman Broom*); Richard Marion (*Seaman Williams*).

6943   Operation: Runaway. (Series; Drama; NBC; 1978). David McKay is a former vice squad detective who is now a private practice psychiatrist. He teaches psychology at Westwood University in Los Angeles and is devoted to helping children and teenagers in trouble — a habit he picked up from his days on the force. David's efforts to track down runaways are the focal point of stories. Other regulars are Kate Wingate, the dean of women at Westwood; Mark, David's assistant; and Susan, David's ward.

Cast: Robert Reed (*Dr. David McKay*); Karen Machon (*Kate Wingate*); Michael Biehn (*Mark Johnson*); Ruth Cox (*Susan Donovan*).

6944   Operation Secret. (Pilot; Adventure; ABC; Feb. 16, 1963). Hugo Pietra and David Storm are agents for the O.S.S. (Office of Strategic Services) during World War II. The proposal, a spin off from *The Gallant Men* was to relate their assignments behind enemy lines.

Cast: Ray Danton (*Hugo Pietra*); Earl Hammond (*David Storm*).

6945   Opportunity Knocks. (Series; Game; ABC; 2008). A game show where the stage is set up on the street opposite the home of the family chosen to be the contestants. Friends and neighbors are the "studio audience" and each member of the chosen family are asked questions that refer to how well they know each other (compiled from interviews with family and friends). Correct answers earn the family cash (up to $250,000 if each member can answer each of the questions correctly).

Host: J.D. Roth.

6946   Opposite Sex. (Series; Comedy; Fox; 2000). Evergreen Academy was an all girls' school that, due to financial difficulties, has changed enrollment to allow boys. Cary, Jed and Phil are currently the only male students and stories relate the awkward moments and trying times the students face. Miranda, Kate and Stella are the featured female students. Rob is Jed's widowed father; Maya Bradley and Mr. Oslo are teachers.

Cast: Allison Mack (*Kate Jacobs*); Lindsey McKeon (*Stella*); Margot Finley (*Miranda Mills*); Kyle Howard (*Phil Steffan*); Milo Ventimiglia (*Jed Perry*); Chris Evans (*Cary Baston*); Gracelle Beauvais (*Maya Bradley*); Chris McKenna (*Rob Perry*); Chris Hogan (*Mr. Oslo*).

6947   The Oprah Winfrey Show. (Series; Talk; Syn.; 1986–2011). A daily program with actress/producer Oprah Winfrey as the host. Topics of discussion are often controversial and often bring considerable press and media coverage. She is, perhaps best known, for conducting her book club segment (where she comments on books with guests and recommends them to her audience).

Host: Oprah Winfrey.

6948   Oprah's Big Give. (Series; Reality; ABC; 2008). Ten ordinary people, divided into five teams of two, are involved in a charitable-like game show. Each team is assigned specific tasks. Each do-gooder's efforts are evaluated by a panel and the poorest performers are eliminated. The object is to find the most charitable person who will, on the last program, be awarded $1 million. Nate Berkus hosts; Oprah Winfrey is the producer.

6949   Opryland: Night of Stars and Future Stars. (Pilot; Variety; NBC; June 16, 1981). Eight promising country and western hopefuls perform in bids to be named "Future Stars." Of the eight contestants who perform, one male and one female is chosen; each receives $5,000 and an appearance on an NBC-TV special. The contestants are Mark Barnett, Jerry Dixon, Diane Goodson, Tammy Gregg, Jeff Myers, Ginger Nickerson, Cindy Smith and Perry Stevens.

Host: Gene Kelly. **Judges:** Glen Campbell, Martin Charnin, Sheila Robinson, Doro Wilson, Texie Waterman. **Orchestra: Bill Walker.**

6950   The Orchid Award. (Series; Variety; ABC; 1953-1954). A program of show business achievement awards in which selected individuals are presented with a real orchid and then perform their material.

Host: Bert Lytell, Ronald Reagan, Donald Woods. **Announcer:** John Heistand. **Orchestra:** Paul Weston.

6951   The Oregon Trail. (Series; Western; NBC; 1977). It is the 1840s and Evan Thorpe has organized a wagon train to transport settlers from Illinois to the hope of a new and better life in Oregon. Evan is a widower and he is accompanied by his children, Andrew, Rachel and William. Stories relate events that occur in the lives of the pioneers as they journey to a new land. Margaret Devlin is the featured pioneer; Luther Sprague is the trail scout; Mr. Cutler is the captain.

Cast: Rod Taylor (*Evan Thorpe*); Andrew Stevens (*Andrew Thorpe*); Gina Maria Smika (*Rachel Thorpe*); Tony Becker (*William Thorpe*); Darleen Carr (*Margaret Devlin*); Charles Napier (*Luther Sprague*); Ken Swofford (*Mr. Cutler*). **Theme Vocal:** "The Oregon Trail" by Danny Darst.

6952   The Orient Express. (Series; Anthology; Syn.; 1953). Intriguing stories, featuring a different cast each week, that are set on the Orient Express, a famous European passenger train. Robert Spafford is the producer.

6953 *Original Sins.* (Pilot; Crime Drama; CBS; April 12, 1991). By calling 555-WPOV you'll reach radio station WPOV, 88.7 FM and the talk show *True Confessions*, which is hosted by Father Jonathan Frain, a Catholic priest who is there to help people, not judge them. Facing his own personal problems, Jonathan has taken a leave of absence to work things out and by helping others he feels he may be able to help himself. The proposal was to follow Jonathan as he tries to help people in need. Other regulars are Becka, the program director; Chas, the station manager; Jimbo, Jonathan's engineer.

Cast: Mark Harmon (*Jonathan Frain*); Julianne Phillips (*Becka Sharp*); Ron Perlman (*Chas Brawley*); David Clennon (*Jimbo*).

6954 *Orleans.* (Pilot; Drama; Unaired; Produced for NBC in 1989). In an attempt to keep her 15-year-old troubled son, Nick, out of juvenile detention, Jessica Filley, a Los Angeles lawyer, convinces a judge that she will move to New Orleans so that Nick can have the supervision of his father, Jay, a police officer. The proposal was to relate Jessica's cases as an assistant D.A. in New Orleans and Nick's efforts to stray from trouble.

Cast: Alfre Woodard (*Jessica Filley*); Mario Van Peebles (*Jay Filley*); Keith Williams (*Nick Filley*); Roy Thinnes (*Barney Fontenot*); Elizabeth Ashley (*Lolly Fontenot*).

6955 *Orleans.* (Series; Drama; CBS; 1997). New Orleans provides the setting for a look at the Charbonnets, a powerful family. Luther, a respected (and ruthless) judge heads the family. He is a widower and the father of Chade (a police officer), Jesse (an Assistant District Attorney) and Paulette (the manager of a riverboat casino). Incidents in the lives of each of the family members (more often than not each coming to the other's defense in times of need) are the focal point of stories. Rosalee Clark is the District Attorney; Curtis Manzant is a lawyer.

Cast: Larry Hagman (*Luther Charbonnet*); Colleen Flynn (*Paulette Charbonnet*); Michael Reilly Burke (*Jesse Charbonnet*); Brett Cullen (*Clade Charbonnet*); Vanessa Bell Calloway (*Rosalee Clark*); O'Neal Compton (*Curtis Manzant*).

6956 *The Orphan and the Dude.* (Pilot; Comedy; ABC; July 18, 1975). Oliver Smith is a white garage mechanic who was raised in an orphanage. Curtis Brown is his friend, a black street hustler known as "The Dude." Curtis has an adopted son (Leonard) and the three share a small apartment in California. The proposal was to relate the misadventures that befall a most unusual "family."

Cast: Oliver Clark (*Oliver Smith*); Art Evans (*Curtis Brown*); Todd Bridges (*Leonard Brown*).

6957 *Orson Bean and Other People.* (Pilot; Reality; Syn.; Sept. 7, 1974.). Ordinary people are first interviewed then asked to give their opinions on contemporary subjects.

Host: Orson Bean.

6958 *Orson Welles' Great Mysteries.* (Series; Anthology; Syn.; 1973-1974). Actor-writer-director Orson Welles hosts a program of mystery presentations produced by Alan P. Sloane.

6959 *The Osbournes.* (Series; Reality; MTV; 2002–2005). A behind-the-scenes look at the real life of Ozzy Osbourne, the millionaire heavy metal rock star, and his family (his wife, Sharon, and their teenage children Kelly and Jack). Cameras follow each family member as they go about their daily lives.

Cast: Ozzy Osbourne, Sharon Osbourne, Kelly Osbourne, Jack Osbourne.

6960 *Osbournes Reloaded.* (Series; Variety; Fox; 2009). On MTV, from 2002 through 2005, the Osbournes (parents Ozzy and Sharon and their children Jack and Kelly) were featured in a reality series (*The Osbournes*) that depicted events in their daily lives. Four years later, the Osbournes return to TV for a strange "variety" show. Here the family present (and perform in) a series of bizarre skits coupled with musical performances, guests, hidden camera pranks and, not common to any other normal variety series, numerous bleeped expletives. Cancelled the same night it premiered (April 1, 2009).

Cast: Ozzy Osbourne, Sharon Osbourne, Jack Osbourne, Kelly Osbourne.

6961 *Oscar's Orchestra.* (Series; Cartoon; Syn.; 2002). Oscar is a blue piano that loves to play classical music. He is also capable of talking. Oscar lives in a futuristic Vienna that is ruled by Thaddeus Vent, a dictator who has banned music. Because Oscar is a musical instrument he is no longer allowed to play music. This upsets Oscar who decides to revolt. He joins with his friends (Trevor the Tuba, Eric the Triangle, Monty the Violin and Kevin the keyboard) to find a way to restore classical music to Vienna. They find help from two humans (Rebecca and her grandfather, Mr. Crotchet) who allow them to use their home as a place of refuge. Stories follow Oscar as he schemes to outwit Vent and bring the joy of music to the people.

Voice Cast: Dudley Moore (*Oscar*); Elly Fairman (*Rebecca*); Colin McFarlane (*Thaddeus Vent/Tank*); Michael Kilgarriff (*Mr. Crotchet*). **Narrator:** David DeKeyser.

6962 *The Osmond Family Show.* (Series; Variety; ABC; 1979). Marie and Donny Osmond, backed by their brothers, Alan, Jay, Jimmy, Merrill and Wayne, perform songs, dances and comedy skits with guests.

Hosts: Marie Osmond, Donny Osmond. **Family Members:** Alan Osmond, Jay Osmond, Jimmy Osmond, Merrill Osmond, Wayne Osmond. **Regulars:** Johnny Dark, The Ice Angels. **Announcer:** Wayne Osmond. **Orchestra:** Bob Rozario.

6963 *The Osmonds.* (Series; Cartoon; ABC; 1972–1974). The United States Global Committee has elected the Osmond Brothers as their goodwill ambassadors. Stories follow the pop group as they attempt to promote understanding between nations.

Voice Cast: Alan Osmond, Jay Osmond, Donny Osmond, Merrill Osmond, Wayne Osmond, Jimmy Osmond (*Themselves*); Paul Frees (*Fugi the dog*).

6964 *O.S.S.* (Series; Adventure; ABC; 1957-1958). Europe during World War II is the setting. Frank Hawthorn is an agent for the United States Intelligence Service, otherwise known as the O.S.S. (Office of Strategic Services). Stories, based on actual case histories, relate Frank's undercover assignments behind enemy lines.

Cast: Ron Rondell (*Frank Hawthorne*); Robert Gallico (*Sergeant O'Brien*); Lionel Murton (*O.S.S. Chief*).

6965 *Oswald.* (Series; Cartoon; Nick; 2001). Oswald is a blue octopus. He has a frankfurter-shaped dog named Weenie and stories relate their daily adventures in a place called Big City with their friends Daisy (a talking flower), Pongo (a dragon), Madame Butterfly and her daughter, Katrina, Bingo (a rabbit), Andy (a pumpkin), Johnny Snowman (a snowman who runs an ice cream store), and Steve (a walking and talking tree).

Voice Cast: Fred Savage, Richard Pierce (*Oswald*); Crystal Scales, Moir Leslie (*Daisy*); Laraine Newman (*Madame Butterfly*); Debi Derryberry (*Katrina*); Michael McKean (*Bingo Bunny*); Eddie Deezen (*Andy Pumpkin*); Mel Winkler (*Johnny Snowman*); Fred Stoller (*Steve Tree*).

6966   *Other People, Other Places.* (Series; Documentary; Syn.; 1973). The alternate title for *Strange Places.* See this title for information.

6967   *The Others.* (Series; Drama; NBC; 2000). The Others is a group of gifted individuals who help people threatened by ghosts or the supernatural. It was founded by Elmer Greentree, a famous medium who uses his home (at 36 Pleasant Way) as the group's headquarters. Elmer, now 83, was ten years old when he had his first vision in 1927; "I called them nightmares." Marian, Ellen, Miles, Professor Warren, Albert and Mark are the six strangers who provide a gateway to the other side.

Marian Kitt was born in Iowa and is the youngest member of the group. She is a college student (at Massachusetts University) and is gifted but doesn't want her gifts: ability to channel spirits through her body; visions (which she considers bad dreams) and sleep walking (often bringing her to the scene of a crime or leading the Others to a suspect in a case).

Ellen Satori is a psychic and considers herself a spirit medium. She is the quiet one of the group and only intervenes when she receives a message from the other side.

Miles Ballard is a professor of folklore and mythology at the University (Marian is one of his students). He brought her into the group after she witnessed the spirit of a girl who was killed in her dorm room). Miles "sees things that aren't there" but can't quite interpret what he sees.

Albert is blind and uses his sixth sense "to see the other world" (which the viewer sees in the form of negative images).

Dr. Mark Gabriel is a first year resident at Saint Joseph's Hospital. He is an impasse and can see what is ahead. Professor Warren keeps a video record of the group's investigations and sets them up with people they need to help. He teaches at the University and is working to improve his self image.

Cast: Julianne Nicholson (*Marian Kitt*); Bill Hobbs (*Elmer Greentree*); Melissa Crider (*Ellen Satori*); John Billingsley (*Miles Ballard*); John Alyward (*Albert*); Gabriel Macht (*Mark Gabriel*).

6968   *The Othersiders.* (Series; Reality; Cartoon Network; 2009). A teenage version of *Ghost Hunters.* Five friends, interested in the paranormal, use state of the art technology to investigate reports of ghostly happenings ("They're not just hunting ghosts. They're hunting for the truth"). The team (identified by first names only) are: Riley (lead investigator), K.C. (case manager), Jackie (researcher), Sam (web manager), Zack (equipment manager).

6969   *Otherworld.* (Series; Fantasy; CBS; 1985). While sightseeing in Egypt (touring the Great Pyramid of Cheops), Hal Sterling, an American engineer, his wife, June, and their children (Gina, Trace and Smith) are engulfed by a space time warp when an alignment of six planets occurs and opens a mysterious time portal that transfers them into the Otherworld (a world that resembles ours in appearance but has its own history and evolution). Immediately, they encounter Kommander Kroll, a paramilitary policeman on patrol, who becomes suspicious of them (believing they are terrorists). As the Sterlings attempt to blend in (in the Sarlex Zone) they discover that the inhabitants, who seem like normal humans, are highly sophisticated androids; they learn also that the Masters of Inmar, the Supreme Governors in the Capitol, have the power to return them to their world. As Kroll and his Storm Troopers enter Sarlex, the Sterlings flee to the Forbidden Zone to seek Inmar and the secret of the way back. Stories relate the Sterlings journey into the various provinces and attempts to escape Kroll who is now seeking to kill them. Nova is the android who helps Hal and his family.

Program Open: "Other worlds lie outside our seeing beyond the beyond, at the edge of within. The Great Pyramids, erected by the Ancient Ones as a barricade, at a portal between two dimensions — two separate realities. This is the story of one family, drawn through a mysterious vortex into the Otherworld and of their perilous trek homeward."

Cast: Sam Groom (*Hal Sterling*); Gretchen Corbett (*June Sterling*); Jonna Lee (*Gina Sterling*); Tony O'Dell (*Trace Sterling*); Brandon Crane (*Smith Sterling*); Jonathan Banks (*Kommander Kroll*); Amanda Wyss (*Nova*).

6970   *Our Family Business.* (Pilot; Drama; ABC; Sept. 20, 1981). An unusual proposal for what would have been an equally unusual series: a look at organized crime from the syndicate's point of view, namely that of underworld boss Ralph Lazara and his family: his wife, Patricia; Gep, his mobster son; Gep's wife, Annie; Phil, Ralph's honest son, a banker (he despises what his family stands for); Susan, Phil's wife; Jamie, Ralph's youngest son; and the Leeper, Ralph's right-hand man.

Cast: Sam Wanamaker (*Ralph Lazara*); Vera Miles (*Patricia Lazara*); Ted Danson (*Gep Lazara*); Ayn Ruyman (*Annie Lazara*); David Morse (*Phil Lazara*); Deborah Carney (*Susan Lazara*); Chip Mayer (*Jamie Lazara*); Steve Apostl'e (*The Leeper*).

6971   *Our Family Honor.* (Series; Crime Drama; ABC; 1985-1986). Vincent Danzig and Patrick ("Pat") McKay were childhood friends who grew up in "the old neighborhood" in New York City. Vincent took the criminal path and is now a syndicate boss. Pat followed in a proud family tradition and became a policeman; he is now dedicated to destroying the Danzig criminal empire (he also blames the family for killing his eldest son, Officer Patrick McKay, Jr.). Serial-like episodes relate events within the two rival families.

The Danzigs live in a mansion at 63-1432 Southcrest Lane on Long Island. Vincent is married to Marianne, his second wife (his first wife died two years after the birth of his son, August). His children are August ("Augie") Danzig and Jerry Danzig. Augie is married to Rita and is the father of a young son named Mark. Jerry is a lawyer for the First Federated Bank in Manhattan; he uses the name Jerry Cole in order to have his own life away from the Danzig family.

The McKays are a hard working family living in Manhattan. Patrick and his wife, Katherine, reside at 6340 Bridge Street. Patrick began his career as a patrolman and was the chief of operations when first introduced; by the end of the first episode, he was the police commissioner — and a threat to Vincent.

Frank McKay is Pat's son and a detective with the 8th Precinct in Manhattan. Elizabeth ("Liz") McKay is Pat's granddaughter. She is a police officer with Unit 41 of the 8th Precinct. Liz rides in patrol car 2708 with her partner, Officer Ed Santini. Her father was Patrick Jr.; her mother is Rose. Liz is romantically involved with Jerry Cole. Matthew ("Matt") McKay is Pat's second-born son, a criminal attorney who is seeking to destroy the Danzig family. His wife is Roxanne.

Cast: Eli Wallach (*Vincent Danzig*); Kenneth McMillan (*Pat McKay*); Tom Mason (*Frank McKay*); Daphne Ashbrook (*Liz McKay*); Georgann Johnson (*Katherine McKay*); Michael Madsen (*Augie Danzig*); Michael Woods (*Jerry Danzig/Jerry Cole*); Sheree J. Wilson (*Rita Danzig*); Scott Shrek (*Mark Danzig*); Ray Liotta (*Ed Santani*); James O'Sullivan (*Matthew McKay*); Juanin Clay (*Roxanne McKay*); Patricia Duff (*Rose*).

6972   *Our Five Daughters.* (Series; Drama; NBC; 1962). Jim and Helen Lee are a married couple and the parents of five daughters (Ann, Marjorie, Barbara, Jane and Mary). Stories relate the incidents that befall the individual family members. Mary is married to Don; Charlie is Helen's brother.

Principal Cast: Michael Keene (*Jim Lee*); Esther Ralston (*Helen Lee*); Wynne Miller (*Mary Lee Weldon*); Patricia Allison (*Barbara Lee*); Nuella Dierking (*Jane Lee*); Iris Joyce (*Marjorie Lee*); Jacqueline Courtney (*Ann Lee*); Ben Hayes (*Don Weldon*); Robert W. Stewart (*Uncle Charlie*).

6973 Our House. (Series; Drama; NBC; 1986–1988). Jessica ("Jessie") Witherspoon is a widow and the mother of three children: Kris, Molly and David. They live at 14 Ashton Street in Los Angeles with Jessie's father-in-law, Gus Witherspoon, a widower who extended an invitation to Jessie and her family to live with him after the death of her husband, John. Gus is a retired railroad engineer. He and his friend Joe Kaplan are members of the Monona Service Club.

Jessie was originally a models photographer for Cathcart Architects, then a photographer for the Los Angeles *Post-Gazette*. Kris, her oldest daughter, attends James K. Polk High School (also given as Highland Park Hugh) and is determined to become an astronaut. David, her middle child, is enrolled in Naismith Junior High, and Molly, her youngest, attends Naismith Elementary School. Jessie and her family, who have a dog named Arthur, originally lived in Fort Wayne, Indiana.

Ben Witherspoon is Gus's estranged son; Gail is Ben's wife; and Sheila is Jessie's sister. Gus's late wife was named Mary; Patrick Duffy played Jessie's husband, John, in a flashback sequence.

Cast: Wilford Brimley (*Gus Witherspoon*); Deidre Hall (*Jessie Witherspoon*); Shannen Doherty (*Kris Witherspoon*); Chad Allen (*David Witherspoon*); Keri Houlihan (*Molly Witherspoon*); Gerald S. O'Loughlin (*Joe Kaplan*); William Katt (*Ben Witherspoon*); Rebecca Balding (*Gail Witherspoon*); Laurie Burton (*Sheila*).

6974 Our Little Genius. (Series; Game; Unaired; Produced for Fox in 2010). Child geniuses from six to twelve years of age are involved. Each child is quizzed in their field of expertise then face a panel of experts for further questioning, including Ivy League professors. Children can win up to $500,000 but can be stopped at any time by their parents (who fear the money already won will be lost if their child answers a question incorrectly). The series was scheduled to air beginning January 12, 2010 but was pulled on January 8 by the request of producer Mark Burnett who was not comfortable with the episodes already taped (it was revealed that some information was relayed to the children during the pre-production stage).

Host: Kevin Pollak.

6975 Our Man Flint. (Pilot; Adventure; ABC; Mar. 17, 1976). Derek Flint is an agent for the U.S. government who tackles dangerous international assignments. The proposal, adapted from the theatrical films *Our Man Flint* and *In Like Flint* was to follow the ladies' man and smooth operator as he institutes his own set of rules to defeat enemies of the country.

Cast: Ray Danton (*Derek Flint*).

6976 Our Man Higgins. (Series; Comedy; ABC; 1962-1963). When the MacRoberts, a middle-class American family inherit a rare and expensive silver service from a titled British relative, they also receive Higgins, a high-tone English butler whom they must retain in order to keep the silver service. Stories depict the problems that befall both Higgins and the MacRoberts family as they struggle to rearrange their lives and adjust to each other. Based on the radio program *It's Higgins, Sir*. Duncan and Alice MacRoberts are the parents of Joanne, Tommy and Dinghy.

Cast: Stanley Holloway (*Higgins*); Frank Maxwell (*Duncan Mac-*

Roberts); Audrey Totter (*Alice MacRoberts*); Regina Groves (*Joanne MacRoberts*); Ricky Kelman (*Tommy MacRoberts*); K.C. Butts (*Dinghy MacRoberts*).

6977 Our Miss Brooks. (Series; Comedy; CBS; 1952–1956). Constance ("Connie") Brooks is an English teacher at Madison High School in a small town of Madison. She lives at Mrs. Davis's boardinghouse on Carroll Avenue (Margaret Davis, the owner, has a cat named Minerva). After a hard day at school, Connie has what she calls "Schoolteacher's B & B" — bath and bed. Connie also has frequent dreams about her boyfriend, Philip Boynton, Madison's biology teacher. "As usual," Connie says about her dreams, "nothing happens."

Philip is shy, and Connie wishes he would take "brave shots." Connie started dating Philip in 1948 when he got his pet lab frog, McDougal. She says "that even though Philip is a biology teacher, there is a big difference between teaching it and learning it." Philip is just not romantic. He treats Connie with respect (too much, Connie believes). Despite the lack of affection (even kisses), Connie loves Philip and hopes to make a man out of him.

Osgood Conklin is Madison's always yelling, easily upset and stern principal. He was a major during World War II and spent four years as commander of Camp Fabrick in Ohio.

"He is a lame-brain dunce," says Osgood about Walter Denton, a student at the school. Walter is crazy in love with Osgood's daughter, Harriet, a student at Madison High. "Harriet is a wonderful girl," Walter says. "Walter's my life, my future, my all," exclaims Harriet; but if someone else should catch her fancy — "Who needs Walter," she says. Madison's star basketball player is Fabian ("Stretch") Snodgrass, a not too bright student who is the school's hope of winning the state championship.

The format changed in last season episodes: Madison High is demolished to make way for a highway. Connie acquires a job as an English teacher at Mrs. Nestor's Elementary School in California's San Fernando Valley. Philip and Connie's relationship is broken off when he secures employment as a biology teacher at an Arizona high school. Osgood acquires the job as principal at Mrs. Nestor's, and Mrs. Davis finds a new boardinghouse on Maple Street (where Connie again resides). Connie's new romantic interest is Gene Talbot, the school's handsome athletic director; Clint Albright is the gym instructor; Mrs. Nestor is the school's owner; Oliver Muncey is Mrs. Nestor's brother; and Benny Romero is the problem student.

Cast: Eve Arden (*Connie Brooks*); Robert Rockwell (*Philip Boynton*); Gale Gordon (*Osgood Conklin*); Richard Crenna (*Walter Denton*); Jane Morgan (*Margaret Davis*); Gloria McMillan (*Harriet Conklin*); Leonard Smith (*Fabian "Stretch" Snodgrass*); Gene Barry (*Gene Talbot*); William Ching (*Clint Albright*); Ricky Vera (*Benny Romero*); Nana Bryant (*Mrs. Nestor*); Virginia Gordon, Paula Winslow (*Martha Conklin*); Eddie Ryder (*Winston "Bones" Snodgrass*); Jesslyn Fax (*Angela*); Joseph Kearns (*Superintendent Stone*); Bob Sweeney (*Oliver Munsey*). **Announcer:** Bob Lemond.

6978 Our Native Land. (Experimental; Human Interest; DuMont; Sept. 19, 1945). A Lever Brothers-sponsored outing which, although experimental, was actually a pilot for a potential Wednesday night series. The basic format was to use travelogues, slides and narration to explore the various regions of the U.S. In the test, viewers are shown various sections of North Carolina, Alabama, Virginia and Kentucky. Skits were also used to dramatize incidents in the lives of the citizens of the states visited.

Cast: Casey Allen, Charles Lang, Helen Parrish, Jimsey Somers. **Vocals:** The Jubilaires. **Narrator:** Milton Bacon.

6979 Our Old School. (Pilot; Comedy; Syn.; Aug. 26 to 30,

1991). When students Andy and Brad, newly enrolled at Kramer College, find they have no place to live due to a mix up in dorm bookings, they find a home (Room 17) at Bonnie Meadows Gardens, House Number 502, a retirement hotel. Shortly after, two other students facing the same dilemma (Carly and Melanie) follow Andy and Brad and move into the only other available room (19) at the hotel. The five episode pilot (for a daily series) follows incidents in the lives of the four college students and the old timers who live at the hotel. Other regulars are the elders: Nate, Gracie, Meg, George and his wife, Maureen, and Eddie. Mort is Gracie's ex-husband.

Cast: Marc Riffon *(Andy Sullivan)*; Ivan Gueron *(Brad Cooper)*; Linda Larkin *(Carly Michael)*; Jill Novick *(Melanie Loren)*; Norman Fell *(Nate Campbell)*; Gloria DeHaven *(Gracie Tyler)*; Paddi Edwards *(Meg)*; Teddy Wilson *(George Wilson)*; Ruth Brown *(Maureen Wilson)*; Eric Christmas *(Eddie)*; Jacob Witkin *(Mort Tyler)*.

6980   *Our Place.* (Series; Variety; CBS; 1967). Comedians Jack Burns and Avery Schreiber oversee a lively program of music, songs and comedy that feature the singing group the Doodletown Pipers.

Program Open: "Welcome to *Our Place* starring the Doodletown Pipers, Jack Burns and Avery Schreiber and Rolph [Muppet dog] with tonight's special guest, Woody Allen. Brought to you by Polaroid, makers of the 1967 economy model of the Polaroid color pack camera. For color pictures in 60 seconds; black and white in 15 seconds."

Host: Jack Burns, Avery Schreiber. **Regulars:** The Doodletown Pipers. **Orchestra:** George Wilkins.

6981   *Our Planet Tonight.* (Pilot; Satire; NBC; April 22, 1987). A satirical spoof of newsmagazine series that reports on outrageous news stories (for example, teaching children in the womb; seeing eye cats; Japanese leisure wear; and Monkercise — Monks performing aerobics).

Hosts: Morgan Fairchild, John Houseman. **Correspondents:** Rich Hall, Mitchell Laurance, Jay Leno, Martha Quinn, Father Guido Sarducci, Jim Staahl.

6982   *Our Private World.* (Series; Drama; CBS; 1965). A prime-time version of the afternoon soap opera *As the World Turns* that, set in Chicago, relates incidents in the life of Lisa Hughes, a nurse in the admitting room of a hospital, as she struggles to rebuild her life after a painful divorce.

Cast: Eileen Fulton *(Lisa Hughes)*; Geraldine Fitzgerald *(Helen Eldridge)*; Nicholas Coster *(John Eldridge)*; Julienne Moore *(Eve Eldridge)*; Sam Groom *(Tom Eldridge)*; Robert Drivas *(Brad Robinson)*; Sandy Smith *(Dr. Tony Larson)*; Pamela Murphy *(Franny Martin)*; Sandra Scott *(Sandy Larson)*; Kenneth Tobey *(Dick)*.

6983   *Our Shining Moment.* (Pilot; Comedy-Drama; NBC; June 2, 1991). A bittersweet look at life in middle America in 1963 as seen through the experiences of the McGuire family: John, the manager of the Atlas Tire Company; his wife, Betty; their children, Maureen, Scooter and J.J. (John Jr.); and John's father, "Papa" McGuire. Wheels (William) is Scooter's friend.

Cast: Max Gail *(John McGuire)*; Cindy Pickett *(Betty McGuire)*; Don Ameche *(Papa McGuire)*; Louanne Ponce *(Maureen McGuire)*; Jonathan Brandis *(Scooter McGuire)*; Shawn Levy *(J.J. McGuire)*; Seth Green *(Wheels)*.

6984   *Our Song.* (Pilot; Comedy; Unaired; Produced for CBS in 1991). Judy Song is a liaison to Philip Harte, a politician whose district is San Francisco's Chinatown. Judy is also a nanny to Philip's young daughter, Spencer, and the proposal was to follow Judy as she struggles to balance her time between her two jobs.

Cast: George Hamilton *(Philip Harte)*; Lauren Tom *(Judy Song)*; Madeline Zima *(Spencer)*.

6985   *Our Street.* (Series; Serial; PBS; 1971–1974). Our Street is an any street in any city where families are caught in the echoes of slow-dying prejudice. The Robinsons, a poor African American family, are one such family and stories relate their search for dignity and respect. Mae and Bull are the parents; Slick, Tony and Kathy are their children; J.T. Robinson is Mae's half-brother.

Cast: Barbara Mealy *(Mae Robinson)*; Gene Cole, Clayton Corbin *(Bull Robinson)*; Curt Stewart *(Jet Robinson)*; Darryl F. Hill *(Slick Robinson)*; Tyrone James *(Tony Robinson)*; Saundra Sharp *(Kathy Robinson)*; Arthur French *(J.T. Robinson)*; Alfredine Parham *(Grandma Robinson)*; Janet League *(Cynthia)*; Frances Foster *(Emily)*; Birdie Hale *(Mrs. Ryder)*; Pat Perkins *(Perlina)*. **Music:** Don Schwartz.

6986   *Our Thirties.* (Pilot; Drama; Unaired; Produced for ABC in 2006). A look at the lives of a group of friends who are in their thirties and rethinking the way things are and how they should proceed.

Cast: Rachel Blanchard *(Jessica)*; Heather Stephens *(Alice)*; Dondre T. Whitfield *(Daniel)*; Rashida Jones *(Liz)*; Peter Serafinwicz *(Austin)*; Rashida Jones *(Liz)*; Sarah Lafleur *(Emily)*.

6987   *Our Time.* (Series; Variety; ABC; 1975). The music, TV shows, movies and world events of the 1960s are recalled with appropriate guests from the genre depicted.

Host: Karen Valentine. **Regular:** Harry Anderson. **Announcer:** M.G. Kelly. **Orchestra:** Lenny Stack.

6988   *Our World.* (Series; Documentary; ABC; 1986). The program recalls specific years in world events via film clips, music, objects and eyewitnesses.

Hosts: Linda Ellerbee, Ray Gandolf.

6989   *Out All Night.* (Series; Comedy; NBC; 1992-1993). Chelsea Paige is a former blues singer who now runs the trendy Club Chelsea in Los Angeles. Jeff Carswell, an NYU honors graduate, manages the club and stories follow Chelsea as she attempts to run the nightclub.

Chelsea is divorced and the mother of Charisse. Jeff was accepted into the Columbia School of Law but turned it down to pursue his music career in Los Angeles (he took the job as manager to make contacts. He is hoping to become a concert promoter then own his own business). Charisse is 25 years old and works as a fashion stylist for a company called Crane and Baxter. Other regulars are Vidal Thomas, Jeff's friend, a hopeful film maker who earns money by delivering pizzas; Angus McEwan, Jeff and Vidal's neighbor (Jeff and Vidal share an apartment in Chelsea's building); Shavon, the kid to whom Vidal is a Big Brother; and Otis, Jeff's father.

Cast: Patti LaBelle *(Chelsea Paige)*; Morris Chestnut *(Jeff Carswell)*; Duane Martin *(Vidal Thomas)*; Vivica A. Fox *(Charisse Chamberlain)*; Simon O'Brien *(Angus McEwan)*; Tahj Mowry *(Shavon)*; Bruce A. Young *(Otis Carswell)*. **Theme Vocal:** "Out All Night" by Patti LaBelle.

6990   *Out of Egypt.* (Series; Reality; Discovery Channel; 2009). Kara Cooney is a professor of Egyptian Art and Architecture at UCLA. She is young, attractive and out to uncover the common threads of ancient civilizations. Episodes relate her world travels as she explores the tombs and temples that may hold the secrets she is seeking.

6991   *Out of Jimmy's Head.* (Series; Comedy; Cartoon Network; 2007). The Cartoon Network's first live action-animated series. While enjoying himself at the Gollywood Theme Park, Jimmy Roberts is hit by the park's train ride. Jimmy is rushed to the hospital but with only one chance to save him, he is given a brain transplant — the frozen brain of Milt Appleby, a famous cartoonist. Jimmy survives the operation but he suffers from an unusual side effect — he can see and speak to cartoon characters that were created by Milt. Stories follow Jimmy's misadventures as he struggles to live a normal life while encountering the antics of Milt's creations (such as Tux the Penguin, Dolly Gopher, Crocco the Alligator and Golly Gopher). Based on the movie *Re-Animated*. Craig Wheeler is Jimmy's best friend; Robin is Craig's sister (who has a crush on Jimmy); Yancy is Jimmy's 16-year-old sister. She is a green alien and was adopted by Jimmy's mother, Louise, an astronaut, during one of her space flights; Jimmy's father, Ken, is a counselor at Jimmy's school (Greater Burbank Middle School). Sonny Appleby is Milt's deranged son. He is seeking to reclaim his father's brain (to extract the cartoons and become famous) and travels with a bag of money he calls Mittens.

Cast: Dominic Janes *(Jimmy Roberts)*; Jonathan Ethridge *(Craig Wheeler)*; Tinashe Kachringwe *(Robin Wheeler)*; Rhea Lando *(Yancy)*; Matt Knudsen *(Sonny Appleby)*; Bill Dwyer *(Ken Roberts)*; Rachel Quintana *(Louise Roberts)*; Tom Kenny *(Voice of Tux)*; Ellen Greene *(Voice of Dolly)*; Brian Posehn *(Voice of Crocco)*; Carlos Alazraqui *(Voice of Golly)*.

6992   *Out of Order*. (Series; Drama; Showtime; 2003). Mark Colm is a successful screenwriter with a dilemma: he is torn between his love for his clinically depressed wife, Lorna, who is also his writing partner, and Danni, a beautiful young woman who fulfills his fantasies and provides him with the attention Lorna cannot. Mark and Danni eventually have a passionate affair and stories, described as "a look at modern marriage," follow Mark as he tries to be the family man to Lorna and their son, Mark, but also enjoy a second, secret life with Danni.

Cast: Eric Stoltz *(Mark Colm)*; Felicity Huffman *(Lorna Colm)*; Kim Dickens *(Danni)*; Eric Stolz *(Mark Colm)*; Justine Bateman *(Annie)*; Adam Harrington *(Brock)*.

6993   *Out of Our Minds*. (Pilot; Comedy; Syn.; Dec. 1984). Comedy sketches based on odd but documented facts.

Hosts: Sherry Miller, David Steinberg. **Regulars:** Maggie Butterfield, Eugene Clark, Ben Gordon, Robert Hannah, John Hemphill, Sean Hewitt, Don Lake, Kathy Lasky, Debra McGrath, Carrie Shearstone, Max Smith, Nerene Virgin, Roy Wordsworth.

6994   *Out of Practice*. (Series; Comedy; CBS; 2005-2006). Benjamin Barnes is the youngest member of a family of doctors. Although he is a psychologist his family does not consider him to be a "real" doctor. His father, Stewart, is a gastroenterologist. Stewart is divorced from Lydia, a prominent cardiologist, and dating his ditzy receptionist, Crystal. Benjamin's older brother, Oliver, is a renowned plastic surgeon (breast implants have made him wealthy); and his sister, Regina, is an ER surgeon who is also a lesbian. Stories, which are set away from the hospital, focus on the problems that arise when the family gathers to discuss aspects of their lives.

Cast: Stockard Channing *(Lydia Barnes)*; Henry Winkler *(Stewart Barnes)*; Paula Marshall *(Regina Barnes)*; Christopher Gorham *(Benjamin Barnes)*; Ty Burrell *(Oliver Barnes)*; Jennifer Tilly *(Crystal)*.

6995   *Out of the Blue*. (Pilot; Comedy; CBS; Aug. 12, 1968). Hoping to make a study of the planet Earth, four aliens from the planet Kurzon, secretly land on Earth and visit the home of Josh Enders, a physics professor living in Hollywood. When Josh learns of their plan, he agrees to help them and keep their secret. The proposal

was to depict the adventures of four aliens (Dr. Aphrodite, Claude, Ethel and Solly) as they attempt to learn about life on Earth.

Cast: Shirley Jones *(Dr. Aphrodite)*; John McMartin *(Josh Enders)*; Carl Ballantine *(Claude)*; Marvin Kaplan *(Ethel)*; Barry Dennen *(Solly)*.

6996   *Out of the Blue*. (Series; Comedy; ABC; 1979). The Richards children, Chris (age 16), Laura (13), Stacey (10) and twins Jason and Shane (10) are orphans (their parents killed in a plane crash) who are cared for by their aunt, Marion MacNelmor. But celestial powers believe Marion can not handle the job alone.

On orders from her superior, Boss Angel assigns a Class Three Angel named Random to help Marion watch over the kids; but he is prohibited from using any of his heavenly powers to solve their problems.

Shortly after, Random arrives at the Richards home (217 Southampton Street in Chicago), seeking a basement apartment they have for rent. He quickly wins over the family, even Marion, who finds it strange that he has only one name ("I just have one name, Random, like Rambo and Cher"). Although Random is supposed to keep his true identity a secret, he reveals it to the children ("I'm an angel from heaven"), who vow to keep his secret. To be in a better position to help the children Random becomes a science teacher at the local high school (he teaches in Room 203, but the school is not named). Although angels are not permitted to interfere in human destiny (Non-involvement Act, Subsection B), Random uses magic "to help matters along."

Cast: Dixie Carter *(Marion MacNelmor)*; James Brogan *(Random)*; Olivia Barash *(Laura Richards)*; Tammy Lauren *(Stacey Richards)*; Clark Brandon *(Chris Richards)*; Jason Keller *(Jason Richards)*; Shane Keller *(Shane Richards)*; Eileen Heckart *(Boss Angel)*; Hannah Dean *(Gladys; the housekeeper)*.

6997   *Out of the Blue*. (Series; Comedy; Syn.; 1995). An unusual outdoor comedy (with dubbed in audience laughter) about six teenagers who work together at a marine life park (similar to Sea World) in Florida. Ed, Veronica, Charlie, Max, Timmy and Jose are the teens; Maria is the dolphin trainer (who is so interested in her work that she doesn't realize boys are giving her the eye). Peg, on the other hand, realizes she is gorgeous and dresses to please the opposite sex. Veronica is a dancer in the Big Splash Bash Show at the Nautilus Theater. Jose is the bilingual tour guide; Max and Charlie do various jobs around the park.

Cast: Brooke Burns *(Peg)*; Maria Arnedo *(Maria)*; Veronica Blume *(Veronica)*; Carlos Conde *(Charlie)*; Paulo Bernedetti *(Max)*; Jose Capote *(Jose)*; Timothy Martin *(Timmy)*.

6998   *Out of the Box*. (Series; Cartoon; Disney; 1998–2004). A playhouse made entirely of cardboard boxes is "home" to Tony and Vivian, the show's hosts, who relay learning messages to children via crafts, songs, music and skits.

Stars: Tony James, Vivian Bayubay *(a.k.a. Vivian McLaughlin)*.

6999   *Out of the Inkwell*. (Series; Cartoon; Syn.; 1961). Adventures of Koko the Clown, his girlfriend Kokete, his dog Kokonut and their antagonist Mean Moe. A made for television version of the silent theatrical cartoons made between 1915 and 1929. The title refers to Koko, who comes to life from an artist's inkwell ("From out of the inkwell comes Koko the Clown...").

Voice Cast: Larry Storch *(Koko/Kokete/Mean Moe)*.

7000   *Out of This World*. (Series; Comedy; Syn.; 1987–1991). It is 1972. Donna Froelich is young woman working as a waitress at Natural Norman's Organic Ice Cream Parlor. In another part of the galaxy, Troy Ethel Garland, a being from the planet Arteries, begins a mission to acquire help from his neighboring planets to defeat the warring Frigians (from the planet Frigid) who have attacked his world. During his mission, Troy's mortal enemy, Krangle the Skull Basher (Richard Moll), shoots at Troy and disables his ship. Troy crash-lands on Earth. Sometime after (not specified), Troy wanders into Natural Norman's and orders a Raspberry Radish Rocket Ship. It was love at first sight when Donna and Troy saw each other. They dated and married on July 27, 1974 (at the Our Lady of the Strip Wedding Chapel in Las Vegas) and blended life forms. Shortly after, Donna gives birth to a girl they named Eve ("Evie") Ethel Garland. Troy repairs his ship, completes his mission and returns to Arteries. Stories, which begin when Evie is 13 years old, relate events in her life.

Evie, half Earthling and half Anterien, possesses several powers: freezing and unfreezing time, "gleeping" (the ability to rearrange molecules by concentrating) and tele-transportation. Evie first attends the Marlowe School for Gifted Children, then Marlowe High School (both in Marlowe, California). She communicates with her father via a generic-link crystal cube that allows voice transmission (Troy calls her his "Earth Angel").

Evie lives with Donna in a spacious house at 17 Medvale Road in Marlowe, California. She explains her father's absence to her friends by saying that he is in the CIA.

Donna ran the Marlowe School for Gifted Children (1987-88), then became owner of the catering service Donna Delights Planning and Catering (1988–90) and finally the mayor of Marlowe (1990-91).

Evie's Uncle Beano (Donna's brother) is the overweight owner of the Waist-a-Weigh Diet Clinic (later changed to Beano's Health Club). Kyle X. Applegate, a former Hollywood film and television star, was the original mayor of Marlowe (1987–90). He lost in an election to Donna by one vote (500 to 501) and now serves as the police chief. In first season episodes, Kyle was the star of two former television series, *The Floridian* and *Mosquito Man*. During the second season, Kyle was a movie performer and the star of "Cowboy Kyle" feature films (titles include *The Good, the Bad and the Unattractive* and *Gunfight at the Pretty Good Corral*). Third season episodes find Kyle the star of a former television series called *Cowboy Kyle*. (He had a horse named Myron, and Sheldon Moskowitz, the frontier dentist, was his sidekick. Kyle was the marshal of Laramie Heights and wore fancy shirts with ruffles. Off the set he was called "The Ruffleman." Charlie Brill played Sheldon.)

Lindsey Selkirk is Evie's boy-crazy girlfriend. Chris Marian Fuller is Evie's on-and-off boyfriend. Like Lindsey, he too attended Marlowe High School (although he was a year ahead of Evie). He worked as the assistant manager of Chicken in a Basket and attends Marlowe Community College (1990-91).

Troy (who is never seen) is also called Troy of Arteries. Arteries is three billion miles from Earth ("just left of the moon"), and Anteriens resemble humans. When Evie asks, "Will I ever see you?" Troy responds with, "I'm working on it very hard" (Arteries is still at war and Troy is needed).

Cast: Donna Pescow (*Donna Garland*); Maureen Flannigan (*Evie Garland*); Doug McClure (*Kyle Applegate*); Joe Alaskey (*Beano Froelich*); Christina Nigra (*Lindsay Selkirk*); Stephen Burton (*Chris Fuller*); Burt Reynolds (*Voice of Troy*).

7001   *Out of Time.* (Pilot; Comedy-Drama; NBC; July 17, 1988). When Channing Taylor, a cop in Los Angeles in the year 2088, botches the capture of a mega criminal, he uses a time machine and tracks him to the year 1988. There he finds his great grandfather, Max Taylor, a rookie cop who will eventually transform the L.A.P.D. into an ultra-modern police force. Channing disposes of the criminal he was seeking but becomes trapped in 1988 when he discovers his

time machine is out of fuel. Channing and Max form a unique friendship and team to solve crimes — with a little help from future technology.

Cast: Bruce Abbott (*Channing Taylor*); Bill Maher (*Max Taylor*).

7002   *Out There.* (Series; Anthology; CBS; 1951-1952). Chilling science fiction presentations culled from original stories and pulp magazines. One of the first series to integrate filmed special effects in a live story. Donald Davis is the producer.

7003   *The Outcasts.* (Series; Western; ABC; 1968-1969). The post-Civil War West is the setting. Bound to an alliance of survival, two outcasts, Earl Corey, an uprooted Virginian aristocrat, and Jemal David, an ex-slave freed by the Proclamation, team and become bounty hunters. Stories depict their exploits, distrustful of each other because of their respected backgrounds, but standing together in times of duress. The overall series underlines the general feeling of prejudice and animosity toward blacks in the 1860s.

Cast: Don Murray (*Earl Corey*); Otis Young (*Jemal David*).

7004   *The Outer Limits.* (Series; Anthology; ABC; 1963–1965). A television screen is seen and The Control Voice opens the show: "There is nothing wrong with your television set. Do not attempt to adjust the picture. We are controlling transmission. We will control the horizontal. We will control the vertical. We can change the focus from a soft blur or sharpen it to crystal clarity. For the next hour sit quietly and we will control all that you see and hear. You are about to participate in a great adventure. You are about to experience the awe and mystery which reaches from the inner mind to *The Outer Limits*." Science fiction presentations that explore mysteries of the mind, universe and humanity.

The Control Voice: Vic Perrin.

7005   *The Outer Limits.* (Series; Anthology; USA; 1995–2002). A revised version of the 1963 ABC series that goes a bit beyond the concept of the original program to present not only science fiction tales, but of the paranormal.

The Control Voice opens the show: "There is nothing wrong with your television. Do not attempt to adjust the picture, we are controlling the transmission. We control the horizontal and the vertical. We can deluge you with a thousands channels or expand one single image to crystal clarity and beyond. We can shape your vision to anything our imagination can conceive. For the next hour we will control all that you see and hear. You are about to experience the awe and mystery which reaches from the deepest inner mind to *The Outer Limits*. Please stand by."

The Control Voice: Kevin Conway.

7006   *Outer Space Astronauts.* (Series; Comedy; Syfy; 2009-2010). Computer animated characters are combined with live action elements to relate the voyages of the *S.S. Oklahoma*, a futuristic space ship on a mission to "seek knowledge, adventure and whatever else they can come up with." Bruce Ripley is the always bored, uninteresting and untidy captain (who, despite his "attributes," manages to get the job done). Commander Dick Amos is the man who should be in charge (he has the most credentials) but his inability to command prevents him from doing so. Sunny Hunkle is a lieutenant with a disposition to match her name (she is also having a secret affair with Dick). Jimmy Peck is the seemingly simple-minded intern who assists Bruce; Johnny Boothe is the ship's reckless pilot; Andy Matheson is the chief weapons officer (Chad Brimley assists her); Ka'ak is the red-skinned alien ally; Pinto is the chief mechanic; Donna Kennedy is the operations officer (who fears technology); Kyle 14 is the ship's android.

Cast: Russell Barrett (*Bruce Ripley*); Adam Clinton (*Dick Amos*); Stephanie Clinton (*Sunny Hunkle*); Peter Burns (*Jimmy Peck*); Benjamin Nurick (*Johnny Boothe*); Laura Valdiva (*Andy Matheson*); Tony Bravo (*Chad Brimley*); Dana Kirk (*Donna Kennedy*); Jacey Margolis (*Ka'ak*); Jay Wendorff (*Kyle 14*); Steve Millunzi (*Pinto*).

7007   Outlaw. (Series; Drama; NBC; 2010). Cyrus Garza is a Supreme Court Justice who has become disenchanted with the system. Cyrus adheres to a strict interpretation of the law but when he finds he is unable to achieve the results that the Supreme Court was meant to do, he quits what he feels is a flawed system and establishes a private practice dedicated to help average citizens facing insurmountable odds. Cyrus is no angel himself— he is a playboy and gambler, but dedicated to upholding the law. Stories follow Cyrus and his team and they go to where they are needed to resolve legal issues. Al, Cyrus's childhood friend, is a defense attorney who assists him; Mereta is Cyrus's law clerk; Lucinda is Cyrus's unorthodox investigator (she uses her sex appeal to get information); Eddie is Cyrus's ambitious, Yale-educated law clerk.

Cast: Jimmy Smits (*Cyrus Garza*); David Ramsey (*Al Druzinsky*); Ellen Woglom (*Mereta Stockman*); Jesse Bradford (*Eddie Franks*); Carly Pope (*Lucinda Pearl*).

7008   Outlaw Star. (Series; Cartoon; Adult Swim; 2001). Sentinel III is a backward planet where Gene Starwind and his young associate, James Hawking, own Starwind and Hawking Enterprises, a company that tackles any job. After accepting a case wherein they are hired to safeguard an outlaw named "Hot Ice" Hilda, they become involved in a plot that nets them the XPG15A-II, nicknamed *Outlaw Star*, a highly advanced prototype space ship, and the caretakers of Melfina, a bio android who is the only one who can interface with the ship. Other members of the crew are Twilight Suzuka and Aisha Clanclan. Hilda had stolen the ship to find the Galactic Leyline, a mysterious land shrouded in myth and superstition but containing great treasures. Stories follow the ship's journey and the mishaps encountered by the crew, as they seek the forbidding land. Gilliam II is the ship's artificial intelligence system; Fred Luo is the arms merchant; Clyde is the bar owner on Sentinel III; Iris is the bar waitress.

Voice Cast: Bob Buchholz (*Gene Starwind*); Brianne Siddall (*James Hawking*); Emilie Brown (*Melfina*); Lenore Zann (*Aisha Clanclan*); Wendee Lee (*Twilight Suzuka*); Mary Elizabeth McGlynn ("*Hot Ice*" *Hilda*); Peter Spellos (*Gilliam II*); Ezra Weisz (*Fred Luo*); Richard Plantagenet (*Clyde*); Rebecca Forstadt (*Iris*).

7009   Outlaws. (Series; Western; NBC; 1960–1962). Stillwater, Oklahoma during the 1860s provides the setting. A look at the events surrounding the apprehension of outlaws as seen through the eyes of the outlaw being sought (first season) with second season episodes detailing their capture as seen through the eyes of Frank Caine, a tough, no-nonsense U.S. Marshal.

Cast: Barton MacLane (*Marshal Frank Caine*); Jack Gaynor (*Deputy Heck Martin*); Don Collier (*Deputy Will Foreman*); Bruce Yarnell (*Deputy Chalk Breeson*); Judy Lewis (*Constance Masters; Will's girlfriend*); Slim Pickens (*Slim; a citizen*).

7010   The Outlaws. (Pilot; Comedy; ABC; July 9, 1983). A few minutes after Stanley Flynn, a wacky inventor, and his partner, Eugene Griswold, enter a restaurant, their car is stolen by two inept jewel thieves. Following a high-speed car chase with police, the thieves return the car to where it was originally stolen and split. Unaware as to what has happened, Stanley and Eugene return to their car. Within seconds they are surrounded by police, mistaken as the jewel thieves, and arrested. Unable to prove their innocence, they are tried, convicted and sentenced to five years in prison. Determined to prove their innocence, Stanley and Eugene escape from prison with the help of Cindy Dawson, a TV reporter (for Channel 6 "Action News") interested in their plight. The unsold series was to follow their adventures as they struggle to find the real jewel thieves and avoid Captain Stryker, the prison guard who is determined to recapture his escaped prisoners.

Cast: Chris Lemmon (*Eugene Griswold*); Charles Rocket (*Stanley Flynn*); Joan Sweeney (*Cindy Dawson*); Charles Napier (*Captain Stryker*).

7011   Outlaws. (Series; Adventure; CBS; 1986-1987). Four bank-robbing outlaws (Harland, Wolf, Billy and Isaiah) are being pursued by a sheriff (Grail) in 1899 Houston, Texas, when they are struck by a mysterious bolt of lightning and transported to 1986 Houston. Soon the five men reconcile their differences and learn to survive in their new world. With their stolen gold coins (now worth a fortune) they purchase a ranch. Later, their neighbor, Maggie Randall, the local law enforcer, helps them establish the Double Eagle Ranch Detective Agency — their attempt to bring law and order to their new world. Stories relate their exploits as they dispense their own brand of justice to modern day outlaws. Harland is the leader of the infamous Pike Gang; Billy is his hot-headed brother; Isaiah, called "Ice," is a legendary gunfighter; and Wolf claims to be half Comanche and half Texan.

Cast: Rod Taylor (*John Grail*); Christine Belford (*Maggie Randall*); William Lucking (*Harland Pike*); Richard Roundtree (*Isaiah "Ice" McAdams*); Charles Napier (*Wolfson "Wolf" Lucas*); Patrick Houser (*Billy Pike*).

7012   Outnumbered. (Pilot; Comedy; Unaired. Produced for Fox in 2008). Greg and Jenna Embry are the parents of 12-year-old Kyle, seven-year-old Jack and six-year-old Lily. Greg and Jenna had an easy time of things until now. Their children are little monsters and their parents appear to be outnumbered as they struggle to cope with the numerous problems they now face. Kyle, a pre-teen, is anxious to become a teenager; Jack is an expert liar; Lily "has the diva act down pat." It's three against two and the proposal relates what happens when Greg and Jenna seek to gain control of their kids. Tanya is Jenna's slightly wacky spiritual healing sister; Eddie is Greg's scheming salesman brother.

Cast: Ken Marino (*Greg Embry*); Brooke Bloom (*Jenna Embry*); Ridge Canipe (*Kyle Embry*); Alina Foley (*Lily Embry*); Aidan Potter (*Jack Kiley*); Beth Dover (*Tanya*); Bill English (*Eddie Embry*).

7013   Outpost. (Pilot; Western; NBC; Mar. 22, 1962). A proposed spin off from *The Outlaws* (aired as the episode "Charge") about three bickering cavalry scouts (Ben, Frank and Myles) in the West of the 1890s. Chief White Tongue is their friend.

Cast: Claude Akins (*Sgt. Ben Thompson*); Jay Lanin (*Sgt. Frank Burling*); Christopher King (*Sgt. Myles Reece*); Frank DeKova (*Chief White Tongue*).

7014   Outpost. (Pilot; Science Fiction; CBS; Aug. 22, 1989). Icarus is a planet with volatile inhabitants, ecological dangers and disreputable outsiders who prey on the peaceful citizens. When Tom Morgan, the Marshal of Icarus, is killed, his daughter Rachel pins on his badge to continue his dream of upholding the peace in her human colony. Other regulars are Kelly, Rachel's sister; Drew, Rachel's brother; Cray, Rachel's android; Kazu, the mechanic; Doc Holmes and Captain Brian Stockwell.

Cast: Joanna Going (*Rachel Morgan*); Marissa Dunlop (*Kelly Morgan*); Ben Marley (*Drew Morgan*); Jeremy Flynn (*Cray*); Eiji Kusuhara (*Kazu*); Joseph Marcell (*Doc Holmes*); David Robb (*Brian Stockwell*).

7015 Outrageous Opinions. (Series; Discussion; Syn.; 1967). Helen Gurley Brown hosts a program wherein celebrity guests discuss various topical issues.

7016 The Outrider. (Pilot; Western; CBS; Mar. 28, 1959). In Ellsworth, Kansas, in the 1880s stood the Outrider House, a combination saloon, hotel and gambling hall owned by Megan Francis. The proposal was to relate Megan's efforts to maintain an honest business in an era of lawlessness. Aired as a segment of *Wanted: Dead or Alive.*

Cast: Jean Willes (*Megan Francis*).

7017 The Outside Man. (Pilot; Crime Drama; CBS; April 8, 1977). Richie Martinelli is "The Outside Man," a street-wise federal agent who goes undercover to apprehend dangerous criminals. He is assisted by Shaker Thompson and the proposal was to relate their case assignments.

Cast: Ron Leibman (*Richie Martinelli*); Woody Strode (*Shaker Thompson*).

7018 The Outsider. (Series; Crime Drama; NBC; 1968-1969). David Ross is an embittered ex-con who now works as a private detective in Los Angeles. He lives in a moderately furnished apartment at 36841 Braxton. There is a refrigerator but no food (he seems to survive on the one bottle of milk in it). He drives a rather beat up sedan and makes "less than $10,000 a year." While he should look like a disheveled detective, to match the rest of his life-style, he is just the opposite: well dressed, charming and polite — or rugged and two fisted, depending on the situation. Darren McGavin provides the narration as Ross strives to solve crimes. Pete Rugolo composed the theme.

Cast: Darren McGavin (*David Ross*).

7019 The Outsiders. (Series; Drama; Fox; 1990). An unusual concept that focuses on the events that befall the members of two youth gangs: the Greasers and the Socks. It is set in a small town in 1986 and focuses in particular on Pony Boy Curtis, head of the Greasers, and Cherry Valone, leader of the Socks. Soda Pop and Darrel (Pony Boy's brothers) and Tim, Two-Bit, Steve and Belinda are members of the Greasers. Randy, Marsha, Gregg, Buck, Barbara and Maria are the other members of the Socks. Based on characters from the novel *The Outsiders* by S.E. Hinton.

Cast: Jay R. Ferguson (*Pony Boy Curtis*); Kim Walker (*Cherry Valone*); Rodney Harvey (*Soda Pop Curtis*); Boyd Kestner (*Darrel Curtis*); Robert Rusher (*Tim Shepherd*); David Arquette (*Two-Bit Matthews*); Harold Pruett (*Steve Randle*); Heather McComb (*Belinda "Scout" Jenkins*); Scott Coffey (*Randy Adderson*); Jennifer McComb (*Marsha*); Sean Kanan (*Gregg*); Billy Bob Thornton (*Buck Merrill*); W. Scott Caldwell (*Barbara Richards*); Jenny Agutter (*Maria Rogers*).

7020 Outsider's Inn. (Series; Reality; CMT; 2008). Former *Brady Bunch* star Maureen McCormick (Marcia) takes on the challenge to run a bed and breakfast in rural East Tennessee. Episodes relate her progress (a lack of it in some cases) as she and her show business friends, Bobby Brown and Carnie Wilson, struggle to succeed.

7021 Outsourced. (Series; Comedy; NBC; 2010-2011). Mid America Novelties is a catalogue company known for its gag items (like the foam finger, whoopee cushions and the two beer helmet). All is progressing well for employee Todd Dempsey until he is assigned to India to oversee the company's outsourced call center. With little knowledge about India's culture Todd finds himself in the awkward position of not only having to adapt to a foreign land, but

teach his disbelieving employees how "to think, breathe and sell American." Charles is a fellow American in India who befriends Todd; Rajiv is the office head; Madhuri is the barely audible telephone operator; Tonya is the Australian expatriate with an eye for Todd; Asha is the gorgeous employee Todd seeks to impress.

Cast: Ben Rappaport (*Todd Dempsey*); Diedrich Bader (*Charlie Davies*); Pippa Black (*Tonya*); Rebecca Hazelwood (*Asha*); Rizwan Manji (*Rajiv Gidwant*); Anisha Nagarjan (*Madhuri*); Sacha Dhawan (*Manmeet*).

7022 Over and Out. (Pilot; Comedy; NBC; Aug. 11, 1976). The South Pacific during World War II is the setting. While traveling to Australia, five female communications officers (Betty, Cookie, Paula, Lizard and Alice) become stranded on an all-male army base when their plane crash lands on the island. The proposal was to relate the women's efforts to make their island their home (until they can be rescued) despite the objections of Paddy Patterson, an army captain who believes that war is a man's game and women are nothing but a jinx.

Cast: Michele Lee (*Capt. Betty Jack Daniels*); Susan Lanier (*Sgt. Cookie Dobson*); Pat Finley (*Lt. Paula Rabinowitz*); Alice Playten (*Sgt. Lizard Gossamer*); Mary Jo Catlett (*Sgt. Alice Pierson*); Ken Berry (*Capt. Paddy Patterson*); Stewart Moss (*Sgt. Travis Shelby III*); Dean Santoro (*Lt. Samuel Launius*).

7023 Over My Dead Body. (Series; Crime Drama; CBS; 1990-1991). Maxwell Beckett and Nikki Page are an unlikely pair of crime solvers: Maxwell is a former Scotland Yard Inspector turned mystery story writer; Nikki is a newspaper obituary writer seeking a position as a crime reporter.

Maxwell actually pretends to be a retired Scotland Yard inspector to give credibility to his books. He has written six books, one of which is titled *Over My Dead Body* and his publisher feels his books are losing sales because they have no grit.

Maxwell was called "Beckett of the Yard," or so he has led his readers to believe, and "The Catcher of Uncatchable Thieves, the Solver of Unsolvable Crimes." Maxwell also wrote a series of children's books — *M Mongoose* — under the pen name A.J. Edison. Diane is Maxwell's ex-wife.

Nikki is a pretty, brash, street-smart young woman in her late twenties who aspires to bigger and better things. While she does write the obit column for the San Francisco *Union*, her actual job is a journalist trainee. It was her fascination with Maxwell Beckett stories that enabled her to become an amateur sleuth. One night while nursing a cold, Nikki saw a man strangle a woman in the apartment across from hers. When no evidence of a crime could be found, the police dismissed the case. Nikki knows what she saw and believes a great sleuth like Maxwell Beckett is the man she needs. When Beckett dismisses Nikki as a flake, she prints his obituary in the paper. The prank almost costs Nikki her job, but it accomplishes her goal: she is able to convince her hero that a murder occurred and together set out to prove it; a political figure killed a prostitute to prevent his affair becoming a matter of public record.

The investigation stirs Maxwell's creative juices; Nikki feels she is acquiring the experience she needs to become a reporter. The two find they need each other and remain a team. Stories follow their efforts to solve crimes.

Cast: Edward Woodward (*Maxwell Beckett*); Jessica Lundy (*Nikki Page*); Carolyn Seymour (*Diane Beckett*).

7024 Over 17 Not Admitted. (Pilot; Magazine; Fox; April 24, 1988). A proposed weekly magazine directed at teenagers with reports on lifestyles, trends, fashions and previews of movie and TV shows.

Hosts: Mijin Hong, Andreas Kokino, Becky LeGrande, Brad Rubin, Tony Russell, Jr. **Announcer:** Jim Barton.

7025   *The Over-the-Hill Gang.* (Pilot; Western; ABC; Oct. 7, 1969). Shortly after retiring from the Texas Rangers, Captain Oren Hayes teams with three aged friends and former rangers (Nash Crawford, Gentleman George and Jason Fitch) to continue doing what they do best — keeping the peace as they roam throughout the Old West. A second pilot, *The Over-the-Hill Gang Rides Again* aired on Nov. 17, 1970, that dropped the Oren Hayes character and replaced him with an aging Texas Ranger called The Baltimore Kid.

Cast: Pat O'Brien (*Oren Hayes*); Walter Brennan (*Nash Crawford*); Chill Wills (*Gentleman George Agnew*); Edgar Buchanan (*Jason Fitch*); Fred Astaire (*The Baltimore Kid*).

7026   *Over the Top.* (Series; Comedy; ABC; 1997). Simon Ferguson is a famed actor (of stage, screen and television) who was married to a woman named Hadley Martin for 12 days 20 years ago. Hadley is now the manager of the Metropolitan Hotel in New York City; Simon has since faded from popularity and recently worked on the daytime TV soap opera *Days to Remember* (where he played Dr. Milo Lang Ingham and his brother, Ted Lang Ingham); National Television Studios produced the show. Hadley, who is the divorced mother of Gwen and Daniel, was also an actress, but her only claim to fame was a regional popcorn commercial. Now, unemployed, Simon pleads with Hadley for a job — and finds himself co-managing the hotel with Hadley. Stories relate Simon's efforts to function in a world apart from show business. Other regulars are Rose, Hadley's assistant; Yorgo, the Greek chef; and Robert, the hotel's chief investor.

Cast: Tim Curry (*Simon Ferguson*); Annie Potts (*Hadley Martin*); Marla Sokoloff (*Gwen Martin*); Luke Tarsitano (*Daniel Martin*); Liz Torres (*Rose*); John O'Hurley (*Robert McSwain*); Steve Carrell (*Yorgo Galfanikos*).

7027   *Overland Trail.* (Series; Western; Syn.; 1960). It is the mid-1860s. The Civil War has just ended and founders of the Overland Stage Coach Lines are seeking to establish a route from Missouri to California. They hire Frederick "Fred" Thomas Kelly, a former Union Army engineer, and his partner, Frank "Flip" Flippen, an adventurer who was raised by Indians after his parents were killed in a wagon train massacre, to oversee the project. Stories relate their experiences as they attempt to start and maintain the new stage coach route in a lawless era.

Cast: William Bendix (*Fred Thomas Kelly*); Doug McClure (*Frank "Flip" Flippen*).

7028   *Overseas Adventures.* (Series; Adventure; Syn.; 1953-1954). The syndicated title for *Foreign Intrigue* with James Daly as the star. See *Foreign Intrigue* for information.

7029   *Owen Marshall, Counselor at Law.* (Series; Crime Drama; ABC; 1971–1974). Owen Marshall is a brilliant criminal attorney based in Santa Barbara, California. He is shrewd, cunning and totally dedicated to defending his clients within the limits of the law. He is persistent and relentless and will not rest until he uncovers all the facts needed to win his case. Jess Brandon is Owen's assistant. He is a bit impetuous and, although he has great respect for Owen, he feels bending the rules is sometimes a necessary evil to accomplish a goal. Stories relate their case investigations and courtroom defenses. Melissa Marshall is Owen's daughter (Owen is a widower); Frieda Krause is Owen's secretary; Danny Paterno and Ted Warrick are Owen's colleagues.

Cast: Arthur Hill (*Owen Marshall*); Christine Matchett (*Melissa Marshall*); Lee Majors (*Jess Brandon*); Joan Darling (*Frieda Krause*); Reni Santoni (*Danny Paterno*); David Soul (*Ted Warrick*); Russell Johnson (*D.A. Grant*); Pat Harrington, Jr. (*Assistant D.A. Charlie Giannetta*); Henry Beckman (*Sgt. Roy Kessler*); Lindsay Workman (*Judge*); Bill Quinn (*Judge*); John Zaremba (*Judge*).

7030   *The Owl.* (Pilot Crime Drama; CBS; Aug. 3, 1991). Alex Leibet can't sleep. He has to do something with his time and if you have the money, he is there to help you. He can see in the dark and carries an arsenal of weapons with him. He uses an air dart gun (to knock out his enemies) and possesses amazing powers. He is also on a personal vendetta: to destroy a man named Hutchins — the man who killed his family in a car bombing that was meant for him. How Alex obtained his powers is a mystery and no one knows anything about him. The proposal was to relate Alex's exploits as the Owl, an around-the-clock vigilante who dispenses his own brand of justice. Other regulars are Alex's friends, Danny (a police officer) and Norbert (a bartender), people whose lives he saved and now help him when needed.

Cast: Adrian Paul (*Alex Leibet*); Patricia Charbonneau (*Danny Sontare*); Brian Thompson (*Norbert*).

7031   *The Owl and the Pussycat.* (Pilot; Comedy; NBC; Dec. 29, 1975). Felix Sherman is a hopeful writer who constantly gets rejections. Doris is a not-too-bright model and actress (she appeared in two television commercials and a newspaper ad) who will sometimes sell her body for money (although she detests being called a hooker). She is between last names (looking for the right one) and lives upstairs from Sherman. They meet one rainy night and form an unusual love-hate relationship and the proposal, based on the feature film of the same title, was to follow their romantic ups and downs.

Cast: Buck Henry (*Felix Sherman*); Bernadette Peters (*Doris*).

7032   *The Owners.* (Pilot; Comedy; Unaired; Produced for ABC in 2007). Events in the lives of young adults who are connected to each other through their pets is the premise of the unsold proposal.

Cast: Andrea Savage (*Sarah*); Christine Lakin (*Lynette*); Bryan Cuprill (*Jay*); Corri English (*Penny*); Frantz Latten (*Will*); Kevin Christy (*Roger*).

7033   *Oz.* (Series; Drama; HBO; 1997–2003). Oswald State Penitentiary, called Oz on the street, is a men's prison that houses the most notorious criminals to come before the justice system. Because of the disturbing nature of their crimes (from murder to cannibalism) these men have been placed in Oz. It is the wheelchair bound prisoner, Augustus Hill, who guides viewers through a section of Oz called Emerald City, an experimental rehabilitation unit established by Tim McManus. Stories, which are quite realistic and gritty, depict events in the lives of the prisoners.

Cast: Terry Kinney (*Tim McManus*); Harold Perrineau, Jr. (*Augustus Hill*); Ernie Hudson (*Warden Leo Glynn*); Robert Clohessy (*Officer Sean Murphy*); Edie Falco (*Officer Diane Whittlesey*); Zeljiko Ivanek (*Governor James Devlin*); Rita Moreno (*Sister Peter Marie Reimondo*); Lauren Velez (*Dr. Gloria Nathan*); B.D. Wong (*Father Ray Mukada*); Kirk Acevedo (*Miguel Alvarez*); Chuck Zito (*Chucky "The Enforcer" Pancamo*); Granville Adams (*Jerome Van Dyke; a.k.a. Zahir Arif*); Rob Bogue (*Jason Cramer*); David Zayas (*Enrique Morales*); Rob Bogue (*Jason Cramer*); Charles Busch (*Natalie "Nat" Ginsburg*); Sean Dugan (*Timmy Kirk*); Anthony Chisholm (*Burr Redding*); Kathryn Erbe (*Shirley Bellinger*); Stephen Gevedon (*Scott Ross*); Luis Guzman (*Raoul Hernandez; a.k.a. El Cid*); Christopher Meloni (*Chris Keller*); George Morfogen (*Bob Rebadow*); Blake Robbins (*Dave Bass*); Kristin Rohde (*Claire Howell*); Evan Seinfeld (*Jaz Hoyt*); Michael

Wright *(Omar White)*; Steven Wishnoff *(Tony Masters)*; Scott William Winters *(Cyril O'Reilly)*; J.D. Williams *(Kenny Wangler; a.k.a. Bricks)*; Sean Whitesell *(Donald Groves)*; Lee Tergesen *(Tobias Beecher)*; J.K. Simmons *(Vernon Schillinger)*.

7034   The Oz Kids. (Series; Cartoon; Syn.; 1995-1996). When the film *The Wizard of Oz* ended, Dorothy returned to Kansas and the Tin Woodman, Cowardly Lion and Scarecrow remained behind in the Land of Oz. Over time, these characters had children and have reunited in the magical Land of Oz. Stories relate incidents in the lives of Dot and Nettie, the children of Dorothy; Bela and Boris, the cubs of the Cowardly Lion; Tin Boy, son of the Tin Woodman; Scarecrow Jr., son of the Scarecrow; Andrea, the daughter of Glinda, the Good Witch; and Frank, the son of the Wizard of Oz.

Voice Cast: Julianne Michelle *(Dot)*; Shay Astar *(Andrea)*; Benjamin Salisbury *(Tin Boy)*; Bradley Pierce *(Boris)*; Jonathan Taylor Thomas *(Scarecrow Jr.)*; Steve Stoliar *(Tin Woodman)*.

7035   Ozmoe. (Series; Children; ABC; 1951). Studio Z is a storeroom in the sub-sub basement of the ABC television center. It is here that the antics of a group of electronically-operated marionettes are depicted: Ozmoe, a lighthearted monkey; Roderick Dhon't, the leprechaun; Horatio, the caterpillar; Misty Waters, a curvaceous mermaid; Poe the Crow; Sam the Clam; and Throckmorton, the sea serpent.

Voices: Bradley Bolke, Jack Urbant, Elinor Russell, Alan Stapleton, Jan Kindler.

7036   Ozzie and Harriet. (Series; Comedy; ABC; 1952–1966). The shortened *TV Guide* title for *The Adventures of Ozzie and Harriet*. See this title for information.

7037   Ozzie's Girls. (Series; Comedy; Syn.; 1973-1974). An update of *The Adventures of Ozzie and Harriet*. Ozzie Nelson, a retired band leader, and his wife, Harriet, live at 1822 Sycamore Street in the town of Hilldale. They are the parents of David and Ricky, who are now married and living on their own. To fill the void of not having children, Ozzie and Harriet rent their sons' former room to college co-eds Susan Hamilton and Jennifer MacKenzie (later to become Brenda MacKenzie). The girls pay rent based on what it now costs the Nelsons to run the house as opposed to them not living there. The school Brenda and Susan attend is called the "Campus" or the "College." Brenda is an Aquarius, sophisticated and neat. Susan is a hippie type and disorganized. She is a Pisces and plays the guitar. Lenore and her daughter, Alice, are Ozzie's neighbors; Gaye, Mike and Tom are Brenda and Susan's friends.

Cast: Ozzie Nelson *(Himself)*; Harriet Nelson *(Herself)*; Susan Sennett *(Susan Hamilton)*; Brenda Sykes *(Brenda MacKenzie)*; Lenore Stevens *(Lenore Morrison)*; Joie Guerico *(Alice Morrison)*; David Doyle *(Professor McCutcheon)*; Jim Begg *(Mailman)*; Gaye Nelson *(Gaye)*; Mike Wagner *(Mike)*; Mark Harmon *(Tom)*.

7038   Ozzy and Drix. (Series; Cartoon; Kids WB; 2002–2004). Adaptation of the feature film *Osmosis Jones* that takes place inside the body of a 13-year-old boy named Hector. Ozzy is a white blood cell cop and Drix is his partner, a cold pill and stories follow their efforts to save the City of Hector (the boy) from whatever he experiences from the outside world that affect his inner workings.

Voice Cast: Paul LaMarr *(Osmosis "Ozzy" Jones)*; Jeff Bennett *(Drix)*; Justin Cowden *(Hector Cruz)*; Jim Cummings *(Police Chief Cluteus)*; Alanna Ubach *(Mayor Spryman)*; Tasia Valenza *(Maria Amino)*.

7039   P. Diddy's Star Maker. (Series; Reality; MTV; 2009). Fourteen contestants (seven men and seven women) compete for a contract with Sean "P. Diddy" Combs' record label, Bad Boy Records. The program is billed as "an innovative performance elimination show" that has aspects of *American Idol* (singing challenges) combined with those of *America's Next Top Model* (contestants facing hands-on-experience, here in the music business). Each hopeful is judged by his or her abilities with the weakest performers facing elimination. The one singer who proves to be the best wins the contract. Kimberly Caldwell hosts.

7040   Pac-Man. (Series; Cartoon; ABC; 1983-1984). Adaptation of the video arcade game that follows Pac-Man, his wife Pepper, and their child, Baby Pac, as they battle Mezmaron, an evil being who seeks the location of the Power Forest (which supplies Pac-Man with his power) so he can become the ruler of Pac Land. Chomp Chomp is Pac-Man's dog; Sour Puss is his cat. Sue Monster, Inky Monster, Blinky Monster, Pinky Monster and Clyde Monster assist Mezmaron.

Voice Cast: Marty Ingels *(Pac-Man)*; Barbara Minkus *(Pepper)*; Russi Taylor *(Baby Pac)*; Frank Welker *(Chomp Chomp)*; Peter Cullen *(Sour Puss)*; Alan Lurie *(Mezmaron)*; Susan Silo *(Sue Monster)*; Barry Gordon *(Inky Monster)*; Chuck McCann *(Blinky Monster/Pinky Monster)*; Neilson Ross *(Clyde Monster)*.

7041   Pacific Blue. (Series; Crime Drama; USA; 1996–1999). Santa Monica, California, provides the backdrop for a look at the lives of the officers of the Santa Monica Bike Beach Patrol. Lieutenant T.C. Callaway heads the unit. He is an avid surfer and his hobby is restoring classic cars from the late 1960s and 70s. He is married to Officer Chris Kelly (who uses her maiden name). Officer Cory McNamara is a by-the-books cop who takes her job very seriously (but still has a sense of humor). Russ Granger is a rookie, newly graduated from the police academy. He is thrilled to be carrying a gun but has a bad attitude problem — and is addicted to gambling. He is so attached to his Harley (the brand of motorcycles the team uses) that he keeps it in the house he shares with Officer Jamie Strickland. Jamie is intelligent but she is new to the streets and often makes mistakes (but is very careful to cover her tracks).

Monika Harper is a cop with ambitions to become the police chief. She previously worked as an undercover cop for the Santa Monica P.D. Bobby Cruz is a former L.A.P.D. officer who works for a college campus security force. He is also caring for his 15-year-old sister, Teresa (their parents were killed in a car accident).

Anthony Palermo is a lieutenant and the original head of the unit. He has a positive attitude and believes situations can be resolved peacefully. Officer Chris Kelly worked in the public relations department before becoming a biker cop. Officer Victor Del Toro is the son of South American immigrants and grew up among the beaches of Santa Monica and Venice.

Cast: Jim Davidson *(T.C. Calloway)*; Paula Trickey *(Cory McNamara)*; Jeff Stearns *(Russ Granger)*; Shanna Moakler *(Monica Harper)*; Amy Hunter-Cornelius *(Jamie Strickland)*; Mario Lopez *(Bobby Cruz)*; Darlene Vogel *(Chris Kelly)*; Rick Rossovich *(Anthony Palermo)*; Marcos Ferraez *(Victor Del Toro)*.

7042   Pacific Palisades. (Series; Drama; Fox; 1997).The lives of a group of young professionals who live in Pacific Palisades, a large community in California. The principal characters are Robert Russo, the owner of the Pacific Palisades Realty Company (he is married to Kate but is having an affair with his secretary, Jessica Mitchell); Cory Robbins, a plastic surgeon, and his girlfriend, Ashley MacInally; Max Dunning and his accomplice, Laura Sinclair, two con artists.

Cast: Greg Evigan *(Robert Russo)*; Finola Hughes *(Kate Russo)*; Jocelyn Seagrave *(Jessica Mitchell)*; Lucky Vanous *(Matt Dunning)*;

Dylan Neal, J.J. Wyman (*Cory Robbins*); Natalia Cigliuti (*Rachel Whitaker*); Michelle Stafford (*Joanna Hadley*); Joan Collins (*Christina Hobson*); Brittney Powell (*Beth Hooper*); Jarrod Emick (*Nicholas Hadley*); Kimberly Davies (*Laura Sinclair*); J. Trevor Edmond (*Michael Kerris*); Jennifer Banko (*Ashley MacInally*); Paul Satterfield (*John Graham*).

7043   Pacific Station. (Series; Comedy; NBC; 1991). Robert "Bob" Ballard, Richard Capparelli, Sandy Calloway and Al Burkhardt are police detectives based at Pacific Station in Venice, California (Room 112 is their headquarters). Bob has been a detective for 20 years and had six partners; he has a dog named Arsenio. Richard, a health food advocate, is now Bob's partner. Richard was called "Donut" in high school and drives a 1962 Cadillac convertible. Al is partners with Sandy. Ken Epstein is the captain. He worked previously as the mayor's press secretary and has a degree in journalism and criminology.

Grace Ballard is Bob's wife and Dawn and Keith are their children. Judy Epstein is Kenny's wife and Cassandra is Richard's daughter (Richard had an affair at Woodstock in 1969 and didn't know he had a daughter—until she looked him up). Stories follow the events that spark the lives of these police officers and their families. Hank Bishop is the Deputy Police Commissioner.

Cast: Robert Guillaume (*Robert Ballard*); Richard Libertini (*Richard Caparelli*); John Hancock (*Hank Bishop*); Joel Murray (*Ken Epstein*); Ron Leibman (*Al Burkhardt*); Megan Gallagher (*Sandy Calloway*); Janet Carroll (*Judy Epstein*); Leroy Edwards III (*Keith Ballard*); Pam Grier (*Grace Ballard*); Monica Calhoun (*Dawn Ballard*); Meredith Scott Lynne (*Cassandra*).

7044   Paddington Bear. (Series; Cartoon; PBS; 1981). When his Aunt Lucy (a bear) retires and goes to the home for retired bears in Lima, Peru, her nephew stows away on a ship bound for England. He is later adopted by Mr. and Mrs. Brown, a couple who find him and name him Paddington (after the train station at which he has arrived). Stories depict Paddington's adventures as he learns about various aspects of life. Based on the children's books by Michael Bond.

Host: Joel Grey. **Voice of Paddington Bear:** Michael Hordern.

7045   Pageant Place. (Series; Reality; MTV; 2007). Documentary-like presentation that takes viewers behind the scenes of a beauty pageant to focus on the activities that occur as contestants for Miss Teen USA, Miss USA and Miss Universe become housemates as they await their chance to compete in the various competitions. Katie Blair, Tara Elizabeth Conner, Hilary Cruz, Riyo Mori, Rachel Smith are the stars.

7046   Painkiller Jane. (Pilot; Science Fiction; Syfy; Dec. 10, 2005). Jane Browning is a captain with the U.S. Army's Special Operations Forces. On an assignment in Russia to destroy what they believe is a heroin lab, Jane and her squad (codename: Painkiller) are exposed to an unknown biological agent. Almost immediately, the squad is affected and, as they exit the building, are gunned down by unknown soldiers in hazmet uniforms. Only one operative manages to survive—Jane (exactly who the assassins are is not explained).

Jane awakens in an army medical center in Virginia. Her wounds have healed themselves and she now possesses a metabolic rate 20 times that of a normal person—"She is unlike any woman on earth." Jane also possesses a number of developing super abilities (strength, speed and sight beyond normal vision) but she is also the military's top priority as they seek to discover what combination of chemicals have turned her into a superwoman.

Jane is cooperating with the military until she learns that she is

being transferred to "a secure location in Alaska." With one driving ambition—to find the person who changed her life "and kill him," Jane escapes and begins her quest—helping people along the way while eluding capture by the military—who want their secret weapon back.

Cast: Emmanuelle Vaugier (*Jane Browning*).

7047   Painkiller Jane. (Series; Science Fiction; Syfy; 2007). In a futuristic time there exists a group of genetically engineered people called Neurons, people with superhuman neurological powers who can perform telekinetic feats but who suffer from telepathic induced hallucinations over which they have no control. Because the Neurons cannot control their powers, they pose a threat to the country. Battling them is a secret government agency that operates from an abandoned subway platform. Their mission is to contain or, if necessary, neutralize the Neurons. The agency is also struggling to keep the presence of the Neurons a secret and avoid a public panic. The agency's chief agent is Jane Vasco, a former DEA agent with incredible regenerative powers. As a child Jane's father called her "Painkiller Jane" for her ability to mentally push through even the most painful situations. Although Jane cannot be killed, she does feel the pain of an injury before it miraculously heals.

Working with Jane are Andre McBride, the head of the agency; Conner King, the know-it-all agent; Riley Jensen, the computer whiz in charge of communications and surveillance; Seth Carpenter, the team's doctor; Maureen Bowers, Jane's former partner with the DEA (and best friend); and Joe Waterman, the subway's caretaker. Based on the comic book by Jimmy Palmotti and Joe Quesada and the 2005 Syfy Channel pilot of the same name (which see).

Cast: Kristanna Loken (*Jane Vasko*); Rob Stewart (*Andre McBride*); Noah Danby (*Connor King*); Alaina Huffman (*Maureen Bowers*); Sean Owen Roberts (*Riley Jensen*); Stephen Lobo (*Dr. Seth Carpenter*); Nathaniel Deveaux (*Joe Waterman*).

7048   Painting with Elke Sommer. (Series; Instruction; Syn.; 1985). Actress Elke Sommer offers painting instruction to viewers (in addition to being an accomplished actress, Elke's talents include beautiful art work).

7049   Pair of Kings. (Series; Comedy; Disney XD; 2010–). Brady and Boomer are 16-year-old fraternal twins whose life in Chicago suddenly changes when Mason, the royal advisor to the throne of Kinkow, a small American island that is part of Polynesia, discovers they are the heirs to the king's throne and must assume their roles as joint rulers. Kinkow is a land rich in odd customs and superstitions and Brady and Boomer are anything but familiar with the ways of their island nation. Stories follow the twin kings as they assume their positions as rulers, trying their best not to cause problems by their traditional American upbringing. Mikayla, Mason's teenage daughter assists them, while Lanny, a disgruntled cousin, seeks the throne by plotting to sabotage King Brady and King Boomer. Brady and Boomer are the children of a white father and black mother. Brady inherited his father's skin complexion while Boomer takes after his mother. Brady is rather lazy and uses his experiences being bullied in school as a means by which to solve problems. Boomer is more carefree, a bit reckless and enjoys Beyonce music and making jokes. Nancy and Bill are the twins aunt and uncle (who raised them after their parents death); Hibachi is the bully who owns Shredder Beach; Oogie is the lizard person who befriends Brady and Boomer; Aerosol is an evil mermaid who seeks to overthrow the kings and steal the castle; Amazonia is Aerosol's friend, a tall, dumb blonde mermaid.

Cast: Mitchel Musso (*King Brady*); Doc Shaw (*King Boomer*); Ryan Ochoa (*Lanny*); Geno Segers; (*Mason Makoola*); Kelsey Chow (*Mikayla*

Makoola); Martin Klebba (*Hibachi*); Tichina Arnold (*Aunt Nancy*); John Eric Bentley (*Uncle Bill*); Leslie Anne Huff (*Aerosol*); Madison Riley (*Amazonia*); Doug Brochu (*Oogie*).

7050 *The Palace.* (Series; Variety; Syn.; 1979). Celebrity guests perform against the background of the Hamilton Palace in Toronto, Canada.

Program Open: "Welcome to *The Palace Presents* with your host Jack Jones, And tonight, Jack's special guests, Marty Allen, Foster Brooks, Arlene Duggan, Chita Rivera, Doc Severenson. And now, ladies and gentlemen, the host of *The Palace*, Jack Jones."

Host: Jack Jones. **Orchestra:** Tommy Banks.

7051 *Palace Guard.* (Series; Crime Drama; CBS; 1991). The cops say, "The guy is harder to find than a virgin in Vegas." The "guy" is Thomas ("Tommy") Logan, a sophisticated thief whose specialty is robbing Palace Hotels all over the world. He is caught, however, robbing the New York Palace Hotel and sent to prison (Attica) for three years. After his release, Logan is approached by Arturo Taft, the Palace Hotel chain owner. Taft hires Logan as his security chief— "Who better knows the hotel's weaknesses than a master thief." (Arturo attended Saint Martin's Academy. He is actually Tom's father, but Tom doesn't know it. Arturo learned about Tom two years ago from his first wife, who left him before she knew she was pregnant.)

Tom is officially the special head of security for the Palace Corporation (when there is a problem at any hotel, Logan is sent to resolve it). The hotel caters to the wealthiest and classiest people in the world. Assisting Logan is Christine ("Christy") Cooper, the vice president of publicity and public relations. She is a former actress (she starred in the film *Broken Arrows and Fool's Paradise*). Christy left the movie business because "I hated cattle calls and sleaze balls hitting on me all day." Melissa is Arturo's 15-year-old daughter; Marshall is Christy's ex-husband. Mike Post composed the "Palace Guard Theme."

Cast: D.W. Moffett (*Thomas Logan*); Tony LoBianco (*Arturo Taft*); Marcy Walker (*Christine Cooper*); Noelle Parker (*Melissa Taft*); Dennis Boutsikaris (*Marshall Lyons*).

7052 *Pale Force.* (Series; Cartoon; Internet; 2007). Comedian Jim Gaffigan and talk show host Conan O'Brien are seen in animated form as crime fighters Jim and Conan, super heroes who are members of the Legion of Pale (an organization through which its members fight evil with the power of paleness). Stories follow Jim, the heroic, muscular hero, and his somewhat wimpy sidekick as they battle to protect the city from evil (most notably Lady Bronze and Philip Seymour Hoffman, a criminal who resembles Jim but never gets the glory he feels he deserves; he has now set his goal to bring Jim down).

Voice Cast: Jim Gaffigan (*Jim/Conan/Philip Seymour Hoffman*); Eartha Kitt (*Lady Bronze*).

7053 *Pall Mall Playhouse.* (Series; Anthology; ABC; 1955). Pall Mall cigarettes sponsored program of dramas that originally aired on other filmed anthology programs.

7054 *Palmerstown, U.S.A.* (Series; Drama; CBS; 1980–1981). Palmerstown, Tennessee, in 1935, is the setting for a view of life in a small town where whites and blacks co-exist for economic survival, as seen through the eyes of two boys: David Hall (white) and Booker T. Freeman (black), friends who struggle to remain friends in a world that does not approve of their relationship. Other regulars are W.D. Hall (a grocer) and Coralee, David's parents; Willie Joe, David's brother; Luther (a blacksmith) and Bessie Freeman, Booker's parents; Diana, Booker's sister; Willy, the town barber; the Sheriff and the following townspeople: Auntie Calpurnia, Mrs. Miller, Mailman

Jackson, Banker Hodges, Widder Brown, Major, the Reverend Teasdale, Roscoe, Hattie Lou, Jed, Noah, Charlie, Agnes, Deacon Shaw, Deacon Lewis. Originally titled *King of the Hill*. Also titled *Palmerstown*.

Cast: Beeson Carroll (*W.D. Hall*); Janis St. John (*Coralee Hall*); Brian G. Wilson (*David Hall*); Michael J. Fox (*Willie Jo Hall*); Bill Duke (*Luther Freeman*); Jonelle Allen (*Bessie Freeman*); Jermain H. Johnson (*Booker T. Freeman*); Star-Shemah Bobatoon (*Diana Freeman*); Kenneth White (*Sheriff*); Claudia McNeil (*Auntie Calpurnia*); Sarina Grant (*Mrs. Miller*); Morgan Freeman (*Mailman Jackson*); John Carter (*Banker Hodges*); Iris Kern (*Widder Brown*); Arthur Malet (*Major*); Davis Roberts (*the Rev. Teasdale*); John Hancock (*Roscoe*); Susan Battson (*Hattie Lou*); Kenneth White (*Jed*); Ted Gehring (*Noah*); Vernon Weddle (*Charlie*); Miriam Byrd-Nethery (*Agnes Peterson*); Fred Pinkard (*Deacon Shaw*); Stack Pierce (*Deacon Lewis*); Michael Greene (*Willy*).

7055 *Palmetto Pointe.* (Series; Drama; I; 2005). The first original series aired by the I (Independent) broadcast network. The small town of Palmetto Pointe is the setting for a look at the lives of a group of teenagers (and friends) who are heading off to college. The short-lived (seven episodes) program failed to really establish any situations but did tackle some controversial issues (such as teenage pregnancy and date rape); it ran from Aug. 28 to Oct. 16, 2005.

Cast: Sarah Edwards (*Millison Avery*); Timothy Woodward, Jr. (*Triston Sutton*); Nina Repeta (*Melinda Gale*); Madison Weidberg (*Lacey Timberline*); Brent Lovell (*Logan Jones*); Will Tiplett (*Josh Davidson*); Josh Holland (*Jason Sutton*); Amanda Baker (*Callah*); John Wesley Shipp (*Michael Jones*); Gabrielle Carteris (*Elizabeth Jones*); Jarrod Bruce (*Murphy Collins*).

7056 *Palms Precinct.* (Pilot; Crime Drama; NBC; Jan. 8, 1982). Inspector Alexandra Brewster is single; Inspector Carmine Monaco is divorced. They are opposite in character and work together as partners for the Palms City, California, Police Department. The proposal was to relate their efforts to solve the crimes that plague their small city. Other regulars are Captain Edward Hammersman, their superior; and Jeanine, Carmine's ex-wife.

Cast: Sharon Gless (*Alexandra Brewster*); Steve Ryan (*Carmine Monaco*); James Gallery (*Edward Hammersman*); Tricia O'Neil (*Jeanine Monaco*).

7057 *Pals.* (Pilot; Comedy; NBC; July 31, 1981). Frank Greene, an impetuous investment counselor, and Harry Miller, a stolid mortgage broker for the Mercantile Bank of California, are pals who are also brothers-in-law: Frank married Beverly and Harry married her sister, Shirley. The proposal was to focus on the mishaps that befall the couples.

Cast: Tony LoBianco (*Frank Greene*); Jeffrey Tambor (*Harry Miller*); Linda Carlson (*Shirley Miller*); Margaret Willock (*Beverly Greene*).

7058 *Pam: Girl on the Loose.* (Series; Reality; E!; 2008). An uncensored, in-depth profile of the vivacious Pamela Anderson as an actress, mother, business woman and animal activist.

Star: Pamela Anderson.

7059 *Pandemonium.* (Series; Cartoon; CBS; 1982–1983). When Mongragoor, the most evil being in the universe, attempts to steal the Pyramid of Power (the most sought after object since before time began), it falls from his hands and explodes, scattering pieces all over the Earth. One piece falls in Tibet where three Panda Bears (Chesty, Alganon and Timothy) find it. Meanwhile, in America, Peter Darrow, a young scientist, witnesses the mysterious explosion. Curious to discover more about the explosion, he and his sister, Peggy, rent a plane and head for Tibet. En-route their plane develops engine trouble and they crash land in a jungle where they meet and befriend the three talking Panda Bears. Seconds later the image of Mongragoor appears, seeking the piece possessed by the bears. Through Mongragoor, it is learned that each piece of the pyramid will lead its finder to the next piece and so on, until the pyramid is completed; its finder will then be granted enormous power. Stories depict Peter, Peggy and the bears' search to find the pyramid pieces before Mangragoor — who seeks the complete pyramid to control the universe.

Voices : Julie McWhirter, Jesse White, Cliff Norton, Walker Edmiston, Katie Leigh, Neilson Ross, William Woodson, Rick Dees, Alan Dinehart, David Banks.

7060   *Pandora and Friend.* (Pilot; Comedy; CBS; Mar 16, 1961). A proposed spin off from *The Ann Sothern Show* about an ever efficient secretary (Pandora) to a world-famous movie star (Anthony Bardot). Gabby is Pandora's friend (hence the title).

Cast: Pat Carroll (*Pandora*); Guy Mitchell (*Anthony Bardot*); Luke Anthony (*Gabby*).

7061   *Panhandle Pete and Jennifer.* (Series; Children; NBC; 1950-1951). Yarns told by Johnny Coons and presented in a cartoon-like format about a young woman, Jennifer Holt, and her life-size dummy, Panhandle Pete, the residents of a community called Chickamoochie Country.

Hosts: Jennifer Holt, Johnny Coons. **Organist:** Adele Scott.

7062   *Panic!* (Series; Anthology; NBC; 1957). Suspense dramas that depict the plight of people confronted with sudden, unexpected and perilous situations.

Program Open: "You are going to live through a moment of panic in a man's life. A moment so incredible that you may not believe it, yet its premise is true. This is the man [from the episode "Nightmare"]. All you need to know about him you will now in exactly one minute and forty-eight seconds. And then *Panic!*"

Host-Narrator: Westbrook Van Voorhis.

7063   *Pantomime Quiz.* (Series; Game; CBS; NBC; DuMont; ABC; 1947–1959). Two teams, each composed of four members, compete. The host gives one member of one team a charade. The player has to perform the charade within two minutes. The amount of time accumulated before the charade is identified is calculated. All remaining players compete in the same manner. Teams who accumulate the least amount of overall time are the winners. Home viewers, who submit charades, receive merchandise prizes if the team fails to identify their charades. See also *Stump the Stars*, the series that evolved from *Pantomime Quiz*. The program began locally in Los Angeles in 1947 with some episodes seen on kinescope in New York only (on WCBS-TV). It aired on CBS (1950-51; 1952-53; 1954; 1955–57), NBC (1952), DuMont (1953-54) and ABC (1955; 1959).

Host: Mike Stokey. **Regulars:** Dorothy Hart, Angela Lansbury, Rocky Graziano, Carol Haney, Hans Conried, Robert Clary, Jackie Coogan, Milt Kamen, Carol Burnett, Howard Morris, Denise Darcell, Stubby Kaye, Tom Poston, Vincent Price, Coleen Gray, Robert Stack, Sandra Spence, Dave Willock, Fred Clark, George O'Brien, George Macready, Frank DeVol, Beverly Tyler, Virginia Field. **Announcer:** Ken Niles, Art Fleming, Ed Reimers. **Music:** Frank DeVol.

7064   *Papa Cellini.* (Series; Comedy; ABC; 1952). Mama and Papa Cellini are the parents of Nita and Antonio. They live in New York City and stories relate the mishaps that befall the individual family members.

Cast: Tito Virolo, Carlo DeAngelo (*Papa Cellini*); Ada Ruggeri (*Mama Cellini*); Carol Sinclair (*Nita Cellini*); Aristide Sigismondi (*Antonio Cellini*).

7065   *Papa G.I.* (Pilot; Comedy; CBS; June 29, 1964). While performing in Korea, a U.S. Army entertainer (Sergeant Mike Parker), crosses the path of Kim Chi and Quang Duc, a homeless sister and brother who attach themselves to him. When Mike discovers they are orphans, he takes them under his wing and makes them part of his act. The proposal was to relate Mike's efforts to care for his new found family.

Cast: Dan Dailey (*Mike Parker*); Cherylene Lee (*Kim Chi*); Douglas Moe (*Quang Duc*).

7066   *Papa Romani.* (Pilot; Comedy; CBS; Jan. 19, 1950). A look at life in an Italian-American household as seen through the eyes of Papa Romani, his wife Mama (Josephine) and their children, Lucy and Mickey, who live at Number 8 Bleecker Street in New York City. Mrs. Greenstreet, is their neighbor.

Cast: Chico Marx (*Papa Romani*); Argentina Brunetti (*Mama Romani*); Alice Ann Kelley (*Lucy Romani*); Jeff Silver (*Mickey Romani*); Margaret Hamilton (*Mrs. Greenstreet*).

7067   *Papa Said No.* (Pilot; Comedy; CBS; April 4, 1958). Suzanne Stacey is young, beautiful, marriage minded and in search of the ideal husband. The proposal was to follow Suzanne's efforts to find that man of her dreams — and one that pleases her father, who seems to disapprove of all the boys Suzanne dates. John and Gabrielle are Suzanne's parents; aired as a segment of *Schlitz Playhouse of Stars*.

Cast: Yvonne Craig (*Suzanne Stacey*); Patric Knowles (*John Stacey*); Jeanne Manet (*Gabrielle Stacey*).

7068   *The Paper.* (Series; Reality; MTV; 2008). The daily activities of a group of teenagers at Cyprus Bay High School in Weston, Florida, who put out the school newspaper, *The Circuit*. All the newspaper office activities are seen through the eyes of Amanda Lorber, the editor who believes being bossy means getting the job done. Rhonda Weiss is the advisor.

7069   *The Paper Chase.* (Series; Drama; CBS; 1978-1979). An unidentified, prestigious northeastern university, is the setting for a look at the joys and frustrations of first-year law students. Especially featured is James Hart, an earnest Minnesota farm boy on a "paper chase" (a quest for a diploma that says he graduated from law school). The program also focuses on the relationship between James and Professor Charles Kingsfield, Jr., a brilliant contract law instructor who, feared for his classroom tyranny, either makes or breaks students. Based on the feature film of the same title. See also *The Paper Chase: The Second Year*, *The Paper Chase: The Third Year* and *The Paper Chase: The Graduation*.

Other regulars are students Elizabeth Logan, Franklin Ford, Willis Bell, Thomas Anderson, Jonathan Brooks, Linda O'Connor and Gregarian; Ashley Brooks, Jonathan's wife; Laura Nottingham, Kingsfield's secretary; Ernie, the owner of Ernie's Tavern (where James works); Susu, Ernie's waitress (first episode); Carol, Ernie's waitress (series); Dean Rutherford, head of the university; Susan Fields, Kingsfield's daughter; Lisa Bell, Willis's sister.

Program Open (Professor Kingsfield addressing his class): "The study of law is something new and unfamiliar to most of you — unlike any other schooling that you've ever known before. You teach yourselves the law but I train your minds. You come in here with a skull full of mush and if you survive, you leave thinking like a lawyer."

Cast: John Houseman (*Prof. Charles Kingsfield, Jr.*); James Stephens

(*James T. Hart*); Francine Tacker (*Elizabeth Logan*); Tom Fitzsimmons (*Franklin Ford*); James Keane (*Willis Bell*); Robert Ginty (*Thomas Anderson*); Jonathan Segal (*Jonathan Brooks*); Katherine Dunfee (*Linda O'Connor*); Stanley DeSantis (*Gregarian*); Deka Beaudine (*Ashley Brooks*); Betty Harford (*Laura Nottingham*); Charles Hallahan (*Ernie*); Marilu Henner (*Susu*); Carole Goldman (*Carol*); Jack Manning (*Dean Rutherford*); Susan Howard (*Susan Fields*); Wendy Rastatter (*Lisa Bell*). **Theme Vocal:** "The First Years" by Seals and Crofts.

7070   *The Paper Chase: The Graduation.* (Series; Drama; Showtime; 1986). The final installment in *The Paper Chase Series*. It began on CBS in 1978 as *The Paper Chase*. It moved to cable in 1983 as *The Paper Chase: The Second Year*. It then became *The Paper Chase: The Third Year*. *The Paper Chase: The Graduation* presents the final experiences of the original CBS students, James T. Hart, Franklin Ford and Willis Bell, as they graduate and begin their law careers. Other students are Rita Harriman, Laura, Rose Samuels, Tom Ford (Franklin's brother), Vivian and Gerald Golden. Professor Charles Kingsfield is the tough contract law instructor; Laura Nottingham is his loyal secretary and Martha Tyler is the professor friendly with Charles.

Cast: John Houseman (*Prof. Charles Kingsfield, Jr.*); James Stephens (*James T. Hart*); Tom Fitzsimmons (*Franklin Ford*); James Keane (*Willis Bell*); Betty Harford (*Laura Nottingham*); Diana Douglas (*Prof. Martha Tyler*); Clare Kirkconnell (*Rita Harriman*); Andra Millian (*Laura*); Michael Tucci (*Gerald Gordon*); Peter Nelson (*Tom Ford*); Penny Johnson (*Vivian*).

7071   *The Paper Chase: The Second Year.* (Series; Drama; Showtime; 1983-1984). A continuation of the CBS series *The Paper Chase* that continues to follow events in the life of James Hart, now a second year law student (who attends Professor Charles Kingsfield's contract law classes) and a researcher-writer for *The Law Review*, the school newspaper. Other students are Franklin Ford, Willis Bell, Connie Lehman (a first year law student and James's girlfriend); Gerald Golden, editor of *The Law Review*, Morrison, Vivian, Laura (first year law student), Rita Harriman and Zeiss. Laura Nottingham is Professor Kingsfield's secretary. *The Paper Chase: The Second Year* is the first dramatic series to make the transition from commercial to pay television. See also *The Paper Chase: The Third Year* and *The Paper Chase: The Graduation*.

Cast: John Houseman (*Prof. Charles Kingsfield, Jr.*); James Stephens (*James T. Hart*); Tom Fitzsimmons (*Franklin Ford*); James Keane (*Willis Bell*); Jane Kaczmarek (*Connie Lehman*); Michael Tucci (*Gerald Gordon*); Betty Harford (*Laura Nottingham*); Michael Shannon (*Morrison*); Penny Johnson (*Vivian*); Andra Millian (*Laura*); Clare Kirkconnell (*Rita Harriman*); Wortham Krimmer (*Zeiss*).

7072   *The Paper Chase: The Third Year.* (Series; Drama; Showtime; 1985). A second series spin off from *The Paper Chase* (see also *The Paper Chase: The Second Year* and *The Paper Chase: The Graduation*). The third year experiences of James T. Hart, Franklin Ford and Willis Bell (the students from the original CBS series), law students at a prestigious northeastern university. Other students are Rita Harriman, Laura, Tom Ford and Rose Samuels (a woman who fulfills a life-long dream by starting law school after her husband leaves her); Professor Charles Kingsfield, Jr., is the tough contract law instructor; Laura Nottingham is his loyal secretary; Martha Tyler is a professor. James has moved from a researcher-writer on *The Law Review* (the school newspaper) to its president.

Cast: John Houseman (*Prof. Charles Kingsfield, Jr.*); James Stephens (*James T. Hart*); Tom Fitzsimmons (*Franklin Ford*); James Keane (*Willis Bell*); Betty Harford (*Laura Nottingham*); Clare Kirk-

connell (*Rita Harriman*); Andra Millian (*Laura*); Peter Nelson (*Tom Ford*); Lainie Kazan (*Rose Samuels*); Diana Douglas (*Prof. Martha Tyler*).

7073   *Paper Dolls.* (Series; Drama; ABC; 1984). A behind-the-scenes look at the world of modeling as seen through the experiences of two beautiful teenage high fashion models (called "paper dolls"), Taryn Blake and Laurie Caswell. Dinah Caswell is Laurie's overprotective mother, and Julia Blake is Taryn's ambitious and scheming mother.

The beautiful Racine, a former fashion model, now runs the Racine Model Agency. She is in direct competition with Grant Harper, the devious owner of the Harper World Wide Modeling Agency. Also vying for a piece of the money to be made are Colette Ferrier, the owner of Ferrier Cosmetics; Mark Bailey, a fashion reporter for *Newsbeat Magazine*; and David Fenton, the owner of Tempus Sportswear. Michael Caswell is Dinah's husband; Wesley Harper is Grant's son; Blair Fenton is David's wife. Other regulars are Sara Frank, Blair's friend; Sandy, Racine's assistant; John Waite, the rock singer; Grayson Carr, the fashion reviewer; Larry Pennell, the loan shark; Don, a model; and Sammy, the photographer. In the television movie pilot, *Paper Dolls* (ABC, May 4, 1983), Joan Collins was Racine; Darryl Hannah was Taryn; Alexandra Paul played Laurie; and Joan Hackett was Taryn's mother, Julia Blake.

Cast: Nicollette Sheridan (*Taryn Blake*); Terry Farrell (*Laurie Caswell*); Jennifer Warren (*Dinah Caswell*); Brenda Vaccaro (*Julia Blake*); Morgan Fairchild (*Racine*); Lloyd Bridges (*Grant Harper*); Lauren Hutton (*Colette Ferrier*); Roscoe Born (*Mark Bailey*); Richard Beymer (*David Fenton*); John Bennett Perry (*Michael Caswell*); Dack Rambo (*Wesley Harper*); Mimi Rogers (*Blair Fenton*); Anne Schedeen (*Sara Frank*); Jonathan Frakes (*Sandy Parris*); John Waite (*Himself*); Larry Linville (*Grayson Carr*); Edward Power (*Larry Pennell*); Christopher York (*Don Bowren*); Mark Schneider (*Sammy*).

7074   *Paper Moon.* (Series; Comedy; ABC; 1974-1975). Adelaide ("Addie") Loggins is an 11-year-old girl who was raised by her mother, Essie Mae Loggins (not seen). Essie and Addie lived at 47 Bridge Corner in Ophelia, Kansas. Addie was born on November 19, 1922; Essie Mae was born in Oak View, Kansas. Addie is unaware of who her father is (Essie says only that he deserted her when Addie was born), but Addie suspects it is Moses ("Moze") Pray, a man "who met my mother in a barroom." In 1933 Essie Mae is killed in a car accident. Moses reads about Essie's death and decides to pay his last respects. At the funeral service, Addie sees Moses and immediately believes that he is her father — "I look like you," she tells him, but Moses insists, "I don't look like you. I'm not your father." Addie's nearest living relative is her Aunt Billie in St. Joseph. When Essie's friend learns that Moses is headed for Missouri, she asks him to take Addie to her aunt. Though reluctant, Moses agrees. Addie is also reluctant to live with an aunt who doesn't want her when she can be with her father.

Moses is a con artist; en route, he pulls a con selling Bibles which involves Addie. The two work well as a team. Moses soon realizes that he can't get rid of Addie, for she is determined to stay with him. "I make all the decisions," he tells her. "You just have to look like a pretty little girl" (her part in scams). Stories follow their adventures as they travel throughout the Midwest during the Great Depression.

Moses is a salesman for the Dixie Bible Company, and he drives a 1931 Roadster and his favorite scam is the "Widow Business." (Moses reads the obituary columns to find grieving widows. He attempts to sell the wife a Bible supposedly ordered by her late husband for her. The widow feels obligated and buys the Bible.) Addie keeps her "treasures" in an old cigar box and cares for their finances. Addie also calls herself Addie Pray. Based on the feature film of the same title (Moses was a salesman for the Kansas Bible Company here and Addie was nine years old).

Cast: Jodie Foster *(Addie Loggins)*; Christopher Connelly *(Moses Pray)*.

7075   *Paradise.* (Series; Western; CBS; 1988–1991). The original title (1988–1990) for what would later become *Guns of Paradise.* See this title for information.

7076   *Paradise Bay.* (Series; Drama; NBC; 1965-1966). Paradise Bay, a small coastal community in California, is the setting for a look at the impact of new world standards as experienced by the Morgan family: Jeff, a radio station manager, his wife, Mary, and their teenage daughter, Kitty.

Cast: Keith Andes *(Jeff Morgan)*; Marion Ross *(Mary Morgan)*; Heather North *(Kitty Morgan)*; Dennis Cole *(Duke Spaulding)*; Stephen Mines *(Fred Morgan)*; Walter Brooke *(Walter Montgomery)*; Mona Burns *(Judge Ellis)*; Jaclyn Carmichael *(Dianne)*; Paulle Clark *(Charlotte Baxter)*; Susan Crane *(June Hudson)*; Craig Curtis *(Chuck Lucas)*; June Dayton *(Lucy Spaulding)*; Brioni Farrell *(Rosita)*.

7077   *Paradise City.* (Series; Reality; MTV; 2007). Six young adults in their twenties are brought together and placed in Las Vegas where each attempts to fulfill their dreams of making it big. Each episode is a personal and professional profile as each goes about his separate way to make dramatic changes in their lives. Molly Sullivan, Destiny Davis, April Rawlings, Jack LaFleur, J.J. Jones and Greta Jewel are the stars.

7078   *Paradise Falls.* (Series; Drama; Here!; 2001–2008). Paradise Falls is a small resort in a lakeside town that appears to be a quiet vacation resort. Its roadside sign reads "Welcome to Paradise Falls Where It's Hot and Steamy All Year Round." It is also unusual in that it caters to gays and lesbians. Stories relate events in the lives of the people who find romance, intrigue and lust at the exclusive resort. The specialized series airs on the gay network Here! and contains explicit gay and lesbian love scenes.

Cast: Art Hindle *(Mayor Peter Braga)*; Chantal Quesnel *(Yvonne Bernini)*; Tammy Isbell *(Rose Bernini)*; Victoria Snow *(Francis Hunter)*; Cameron Graham *(Nick Braga)*; Dixie Seatle *(Bea Sutton)*; Michelle Latimer *(Trish Simpkin)*; Kim Poirier *(Roxy Hunter)*; Kim Schraner *(Jessica Lansing)*; Jim Thorburn *(Michael Mansfield)*; Robert Seeliger *(Jeff Bradshaw)*; Andrew Gillies *(Stanley Mansfield)*; Marni Thompson *(Valerie Hunter)*; Joshua Peace *(Samuel Sutton)*; Steve Cumyn *(Tony Beroni)*; Cherilee Taylor *(Pamela Harman)*; Allen Altman *(Billy Hunter)*; Alan Van Sprang *(Johnny Brice)*; Kate Trotter *(Anne Sutton)*; Mike Realba *(Ben Santos)*; Danielle Hampton *(Charlene Piercy)*; Sean Bell *(Travis Piercy)*; Raven Dauda *(Kelly Fairview)*; Frank Pellegrino *(Thomas Martinelli)*; Martin Roach *(Ravenhart)*; Debra McGrath *(Shirley Armstrong)*; Gary Hudson *(Brick Madison)*; Carla Collins *(Rusty Sinclair)*; Salvatore Antonio *(Sacha Martinelli)*; Wesley Morgan *(Ethan Banning)*; Meredith McGeachie *(Cate Banning)*; Kerry Lai Fatt *(Julie Cordry)*; Stephen Huszar *(Tucker Hardwood)*; Amanda Brugel *(Lynnie Jordan)*.

7079   *Paradise Hotel.* (Series; Reality; My Network TV; 2008). Paradise Hotel is a luxurious, secluded beachside resort. Here eleven singles are brought together in the hope of sparking a romance. The singles are urged to pair up or be replaced by a new single. The singles that are not compatible are eliminated. The object is for each single to stay as long as they can (the only rule is to find a mate or go home). Cameras follow the activities of the singles as they become intimate with each other. Amanda Byram hosts.

7080   *Paradise Lost.* (Series; Reality; Investigation Discovery; 2010). Many people dream of an exotic locale, sunny skies and a new life to escape to when their ordinary lives become mundane. For some, that dream comes true; but for others it becomes a real nightmare when their fantasized paradise becomes a nightmare. Each episode explores, through the actual people involved, those who sought their paradise but found only a horrible, sometimes life-threatening experience (for example, in the episode "Baby Snatcher," a trip to Mexico becomes a nightmare for a young mother when her newborn is kidnapped. In "High Stakes Bonanza," a married couple exploring the Nicaraguan Rain Forest face a life and death situation when the husband is kidnapped and held for a $2 million ransom. "Nightmare in Kenya" tells the story of a woman who moves to East Africa to follow her dream of opening a nightclub but finds her sanity being affected by voodoo). Victor Restis is the producer.

7081   *The Paradise Steamship Company.* (Pilot; Reality; Syn.; May 1987). Visits to places of interest around the world.

Hosts: Bob Chandler, Melody Rogers.

7082   *Paranoia.* (Series; Game; Fox Family; 2000). A live game show wherein one studio based contestant faces competition from players all over the country (picked up in various cities by satellite). A question is read and the first player to buzz in receives a chance to answer. If the studio player answers correctly, money is added to his score; if a remote player is correct, the money his deducted from his score. The object is for the studio player to eliminate the remote players by answering more questions correctly (satellite players can also be eliminated if they answer three questions incorrectly). If the studio player achieved his goal (eliminating the city players) he plays the bonus round where he can win ten times his winnings by answering nine questions in a row; then increase that amount by 100 times by answering a tenth question correctly.

Host: Peter Tomarken.

7083   *The Paranormal Borderline.* (Series; Reality; UPN; 1996). Unexplained phenomena is explored through the accounts of the people who claim to have experienced them.

Host: Jonathan Frakes.

7084   *Paranormal Cops.* (Series; Reality; A&E; 2010). Chicago Paranormal Detectives are "police officers by day and paranormal cops by night." The officers, who have had supernatural experiences, investigate cases of people who claim they are haunted. Each episode follows the team as they incorporate the latest scientific gizmos to uncover the truth. Thomas Froelich, Ron Fabiani, Brian Jones, Moriah Rhame, Pete Schleich, Austin Weinstock and Scott Ziarko are the cops.

7085   *Paranormal Court.* (Pilot; Reality; TLC; Mar. 27, 2010). Robert Hansen is a renowned psychic medium who has taken it upon himself to help families with unexplained questions concerning the death of a loved one. When a dispute erupts between two parties, Robert steps in and, through contact with the deceased one, provides the solution to resolve the problem. Participants who agree to the "court séances" are bound by "the ruling enlisted from the other side."

Host: Robert Hansen.

7086   *Paranormal State.* (Series; Reality; A&E; 2007). The Penn State Paranormal Research Society is a group of Penn State college students who investigate paranormal happenings. Ryan Buell formed it in 2001 when he claimed to have an unnatural connection with unusual phenomenon. While at Penn State he formed the group and now, accompanied by current students, the group investigates reports of ghostly happenings (with cameras capturing what they see — and don't see).

7087   *The Parent Game.* (Series; Game; Syn.; 1972). Three married couples compete in a game that compares their ideas about raising children with those of a child psychologist. The host asks a question relating to children and reveals four possible answers. Each couple chooses the answer they believe is correct. The correct answer is revealed and points are awarded accordingly (round one, five points per correct choice; round two, ten points; round three, fifteen points; round four, thirty points). The highest scoring couple wins a specially selected prize.

Host: Clark Race. **Announcer:** Johnny Jacobs.

7088   *The Parent Trap.* (Pilot; Comedy; NBC; Nov. 19 and 26, 1989). The Theatrical film *The Parent Trap* (1961) and its 1986 (July 26) Disney Channel TV movie sequel, *The Parent Trap II*, told the story of Sharon and Susan (Hayley Mills), twins separated at birth who find each other at a summer camp. The girls are now grown. Susan, an architect, is married to a writer (Jeffrey Wyatt) and is the step-mother to his three beautiful teenage daughters, triplets Lisa, Jesse and Megan. Sharon is single and still best friends with Susan. Lisa, Jesse and Megan are as mischievous as Sharon and Susan when they were young and the proposal was to relate events in their lives.

Cast: Hayley Mills (*Susan Wyatt/Sharon Evers*); Barry Bostwick (*Jeffrey Wyatt*); Leanna Creel (*Lisa Wyatt*); Monica Creel (*Jesse Wyatt*); Joy Creel (*Megan Wyatt*).

7089   *Parental Control.* (Series; Reality; MTV; 2006). A daily program that is a twist on the normal dating shows (like *The Dating Game*) that have been broadcast over the years. Here the parents get to choose whom their son or daughter will date. Each of the teens that appear has a date that is unacceptable to their parents (anything from looks to a lack of ambition to personality). Each parent of a chosen subject (son or daughter) is presented with a group of boys or girls who meet the standards of what they feel are acceptable dates for their children. When each parent makes a selection, they are brought face to face with their child and present their choices. The child can select either one (the one chosen by the father or mother) or keep the date he or she currently has. Michael Canter is the producer.

7090   *Parenthood.* (Series; Comedy; NBC; 1990). Four generations of one family living under the same roof and the chaos that results. Gil Buckman is an investment counselor. He is married to Karen and they are the parents of Kevin (age 10), Justin (nine) and Taylor (seven). Frank Buckman is Gil's father. He is married to Marilyn. Gil's older sister, Helen Lamkin is divorced. She is the mother of Julie and Gary. Julie is married to Todd. Susan, Gil's younger sister, a schoolteacher, is married to Nathan. They are the parents of Patty. Also adding chaos to the picture is Marilyn's mother, Great Grandma Greenwall.

Cast: Ed Begley, Jr. (*Gil Buckman*); Jayne Atkinson (*Karen Buckman*); Max Elliott Slade (*Kevin Buckman*); Zachary La Voy (*Justin Buckman*); Thora Birch (*Taylor Buckman*); William Windom (*Frank Buckman*); Sheila MacRae (*Marilyn Buckman*); Maryedith Burrell (*Helen Lamkin*); Bess Meyer (*Julie Lamkin*); Susan Norman (*Susan*); Ken Ober (*Nathan*); Ivyann Schwan (*Patty*); David Arquette (*Todd*); Leonardo Di Caprio (*Gary*); Mary Jackson (*Great Grandma Greenwall*).

7091   *The Parent'Hood.* (Series; Comedy; WB; 1997–1999). The Manhattan brownstone at 721 West 72nd Street in New York City is home to Robert Peterson, his wife, Geri and their children, Zaria, Nicholas and Ce Ce. Robert and Geri met in high school, were married at City Hall and first lived at 103rd and Amsterdam Avenue. Robert is a professor at New York University. Geri is a lawyer and says " the closest I've ever been to a trial was watching *Matlock* (she sits behind a desk under a stack of papers). She does volunteer work for the Women's Legal Society. In some episodes she appears to be a law clerk while in others she has her own practice (Geri Peterson — Attorney-at-Law).

Zaria, the eldest child, attends Hudson High School (as did her parents). She is a cheerleader and hosts the advice show, *Keep It Real* on the school radio station (WHBD). She won the Meritorious Student of the Year Award in her senior year (1999) and a college scholarship. Nicholas, who envisions himself as a great magician (Nicholas the Great), attends the William Sherman Grammar School. Also living with the Petersons is T. K. Anderson, a troubled street teen Geri took under her wing. T.K., a "D" student, attends Hudson High and works at Pookie's Pizza Galaxy. Stories relate events that befall the Peterson family.

Cast: Robert Townsend (*Robert Peterson*); Suzanne Douglas (*Geri Peterson*); Reagan Gomez-Preston (*Zaria Peterson*); Curtis Williams (*Nicholas Peterson*); Ashli Amari Adams (*Ce Ce Peterson*); Tyrone Dorzell Burton (*T.K. Anderson*).

7092   *Parenthood.* (Series; Drama; NBC; 2010–). Sarah Braverman appears to be a happily married, well adjusted woman. She is married to Seth Holt, the mother of Amber and Drew and works as a bartender. She lives in Fresno, California and all is progressing well until she turns 38. Her kids, especially Amber, have become rebellious and Seth, "a tortured musician with a drug problem," is absent from their lives (road trips) causing he and Sarah to divorce. Now, financially strapped, Sarah, Amber and Drew are forced to move to Berkeley and into the home of her parents (Zeek and Camille). Sarah's siblings and their children also become a part of their lives: Julia, her corporate lawyer sister (and her husband Joel and daughter Sydney). Adam, the eldest sibling, is married to Kristina and the father of Haddie and Max (who suffers from a form of autism called Asperser's Syndrome). Crosby, Sarah's brother, is living with a woman named Katie, but afraid to make a commitment to start a family. Conflict enters his life when a former girlfriend (Jasmine) returns, claiming that he is the father of her son (Jabbar). Stories, based on the 1989 feature film, relate the daily happenings in the lives of the Braverman family. Amber, Drew and Haddie attend Roosevelt High School; Adam sells Welsh Shoes from his home via the Internet. Maura Tierney was originally cast as Sarah but had to withdraw from the project when she was diagnosed with breast cancer.

Cast: Lauren Graham (*Sarah Braverman*); Mae Whitman (*Amber Holt*); Miles Heizer (*Drew Holt*); Craig T. Nelson (*Zeek Braverman*); Bonnie Bedelia (*Camille Braverman*); Erika Christensen (*Julia Braverman-Graham*); Sam Jaeger (*Joel Graham*); Peter Krause (*Adam Braverman*); Monica Potter (*Kristina Braverman*); Sarah Ramos (*Haddie Braverman*); Max Burkholder (*Max Braverman*); Dax Shepard (*Crosby Braverman*); Marguerite Moreau (*Katie*); Joy Bryant (*Jasmine*); Darin Heames (*Seth Holt*); William Baldwin (*Gordon Flint*); Savannah Paige Rae (*Sydney Graham*); Joy Bryant (*Jasmine Trussell*); Tyree Brown (*Jabbar Trussell*); Minka Kelly (*Gaby*); Michael B. Jordan (*Alex*).

7093   *Paris.* (Series; Crime Drama; CBS; 1979–1980). Woodrow Paris, called Woody, is a captain with the Metro Squad, a special detective unit of the Los Angeles Police Department (14th Precinct). He is also a college professor who teaches criminology on the side. Stories follow Woody as he attempts to practice what he teaches — good law enforcement and careful attention to the facts to bring criminals to justice. Woody is married to Barbara; Chief Jerome Bench is his superior.

Cast: James Earl Jones *(Woodrow "Woody" Paris)*; Lee Chamberlain *(Barbara Paris)*; Hank Garrett *(Jerome Bench)*; Cecilia Hart *(Sgt. Stacey Erickson)*; Jake Mitchell *(Sgt. Charlie Bogart)*; Frank Ramirez *(Sgt. Ernie Villas)*; Michael Warren *(Sgt. Willie Miller)*.

7094 *Paris Cavalcade of Fashion.* (Series; Women; NBC; 1948–1949). Faye Emerson and Julie Gibson co-host and narrate a program that features films of the latest Paris fashions.

7095 *Paris Hilton: My New BFF.* (Series; Reality; MTV; 2008–2009). Paris Hilton, called "America's Number One It Girl," seems to gain popularity wherever she goes and whatever she does. Paris is a party girl and loves to shop. Her inner circle are normally A-list celebrities but, for a change, Paris has decided to seek a non-show business figure to join her entourage. In the first cycle (2008) Fourteen "tabloid ready" women and two "flamboyant guys" compete for the honor of becoming Paris's new best friend. Paris oversees the competition and puts each potential friend through a series of challenges that test their loyalty, smarts, party skills and hotness. The one who is deemed the most worthy by Paris becomes her new best friend forever. Brittany Flickinger was chosen. A second cycle aired in 2009 with Paris seeking a new best friend when fame went to Brittany's head and the two became incompatible. Here 13 girls and one lone guy seek to fill Brittany's shoes. Stephen Hampton won the second cycle competition.

Host: Paris Hilton.

7096 *Paris Precinct.* (Series; Crime Drama; ABC; 1955). Inspectors Bolbec and Beaumont are attached to the Surete (The Paris, France, Police Department). They are not men who just sit behind a desk and direct operations; they get into the field and use their expertise to investigate crimes and track down criminals. Stories relate their case investigations, many of which take them away from their home base. Also known as *World Crime Hunt.*

Cast: Claude Dauphin *(Inspector Bolbec)*; Louis Jourdan *(Inspector Beaumont)*.

7097 *Paris 7000.* (Series; Mystery; ABC; 1970). Paris 7000 is the telephone number of the U.S. Consulate in France. It is here that Jack Brennan, an American troubleshooter, is based. Jack is handsome, two-fisted and has an eye for the ladies. He has also been assigned to help American tourists in need of help. Stories follow Jack as he does what it takes (including bending the rules) to insure the safety of tourists. Robert Stevens assists Jack; Jules Maurois is the French Suerte police chief Jack always seems to involve in his cases.

Cast: George Hamilton *(Jack Brennan)*; Jacques Aubuchon *(Jules Maurios)*; Gene Raymond *(Robert Stevens)*. **Theme Music:** "Paris 7000" by Michel Colombier.

7098 *Park Place.* (Series; Comedy; CBS; 1981). David Ross is the senior attorney at the Legal Assistance Bureau, a free legal-aid clinic on Park Place in New York City. He is assisted by several over-eager young attorneys (Jo, Jeff, Howie, Ernie, Mac and Brad) and stories relate their comical efforts to defend clients. Frances is David's secretary.

Cast: Harold Gould *(David Ross)*; Mary Elaine Monti *(Joel "Jo" Keene)*; David Clennon *(Jeff O'Neal)*; Don Calfa *(Howard "Howie" Beech)*; Cal Gibson *(Ernie Rice)*; Lionel Smith *(Aaron "Mac" MacRae)*; James Widdoes *(Brad Lincoln)*; Alice Drummond *(Frances Heine)*.

7099 *The Parker Family.* (Experimental; Comedy; NBC; May 9, 1941). A video adaptation of the radio series of the same title about

incidents in the lives of the Parkers, a not-so-typical American family.

Cast: Taylor Holmes *(Mark Parker)*; Violet Henning *(Mrs. Parker)*; Leon Janney *(Richard Parker; their son)*; Mitzi Gould *(Nancy Parker; their daughter)*; Helen Claire *(Mrs. Jennings)*; William Lynn *(Dr. Dennison)*.

7100 *Parker Kane.* (Pilot; Crime Drama; Unaired; Produced in 1990). A proposal about Parker Kane, a former cop (with the Long Beach, California Police Department) turned private detective.

Cast: Jeff Fahey *(Parker Kane)*; Drew Snyder *(Lt. Dunbar Fisk)*; Richard Zobel *(Det. Jack Hunter)*.

7101 *Parker Lewis Can't Lose.* (Series; Comedy; Fox; 1990–1992). Life at Santo Domingo High School in California as seen through the eyes of three "best buds," Parker Lewis, Mikey Randall and Jerry Steiner. Parker Lloyd Lewis is an enterprising student who simply can't lose — no matter what happens to him, he always comes out on top. He is the "cool" kid and has an ingenious plan for every situation; he resists authority and lives by his own rules. Parker, a sophomore, dreams of attending college and is a master of self-promotion.

Parker's parents, Judy and Martin Lewis, own Mondo Video, a video rental store. Asking them for advice, Parker says "is like looking for gasoline with a match — you're lucky to get out alive."

Michael Patrick ("Mikey") Randall, a sophomore, and Gerald ("Jerry") Steiner, a freshman, have been Parker's friends since childhood. Jerry works in the mall at Dog on a Stick as a counter boy.

Jerry, the youngest of the best buds, calls Parker and Mikey "Sirs" and Mr. Lewis and Mr. Randall. He collects "Star Trek" figurines and possesses "The Musso Excuse File" (a listing of excuses Parker uses to get out of jams).

Grace Musso, called Ms. Musso, is the stern, authoritarian principal who is out to get Parker. All Grace asks for "is a cup of coffee and a little peace and quiet in the morning" before she faces her nightmares — the students at Santo Domingo High. Parker calls Grace "more than a principal — a psychopath with tenure." Grace is feared by everyone and demands respect (her parents believe that a hunting lodge and rifle range is a good place for her to meet men).

Shelly Ann Lewis is Parker's 13-year-old sister. She is a freshman at Santo Domingo High and is following in the footsteps of her idol, Grace Musso (Shelly lives for the day when she can get the goods on Parker). Parker calls Shelly "Santo Domingo's hell cat" and is sure she is adopted (his nickname for her is "Shelly Belly"). Shelly is Grace's "pretty two-faced sugar plum freshman obedience trainee." Shelly is also a member of the snobbish Vogues, an all-girl club that is the terror of the school. (Called the "Glamour Girls of the Campus," they are selective in their associates and their signal to each other is air kisses. The rich and spoiled Melinda Harris is the chapter president.)

He believes that nine and a half years is almost a century and has been a junior at Santo Domingo for seven years. Lawrence ("Larry") Francis Kubiac is 20 years old, big (270 pounds, six feet seven inches tall), mean and "the most dangerous force ever to squeeze into a high school football uniform." Larry lives to eat and is very protective of his lunch (which he carries in a large paper bag with "Lary's Lunch" printed on it; Larry can't spell well). His catchphrase is "Eat now?" Frank Lemmer is Grace's special guidance counselor (she summons him with a silent dog whistle) and performs most of her dirty work.

Cast: Corin Nemec *(Parker Lewis)*; Maia Brewton *(Shelly Lewis)*; Anne Bloom, Mary Ellen Trainor *(Judy Lewis)*; Timothy Stack *(Martin Lewis)*; William Jayne *(Mikey Randall)*; Troy Slaten *(Jerry Steiner)*; Melanie Chartoff *(Grace Musso)*; Abraham Benrubi *(Larry*

Kubiac); Taj Johnson *(Frank Lemmer)*; Brooke Theiss *(Melinda Harris)*.

7102   The Parkers. (Series; Comedy; UPN; 1999–2004). A spin off from *Moesha*. Nikki and Kim Parker are not only mother and daughter but also best friends. They dress alike and think alike. Nikki is a cool mom. She attended one class at Crestridge High School to complete her education (sharing the same class with Kim) and enrolled at Santa Monica Junior College to get her education — at the same college as Kim — a situation that was made awkward at first but became acceptable to Kim in due time.

Nikki is 36 years old; Kim is 18. When Nikki became pregnant in high school at 16 she dropped out. She and Mel Parker married but divorced soon after (both were too young to make a marriage work). Stories relate the experiences of a mother and daughter as they attend college together. Nikki and Kim took jobs as phone psychics for the Karma Connection; Nikki sells Lady Egyptian Cosmetics. Other regulars are Stanley Oglevee, the professor on whom Nikki has a relentless crush (he has a dog named Bruno); Stevie, Chandra, T and Andell, are Kim's friends (Kim, Stevie and Chandra pledged Triple A — the Alpha Alpha Alpha Sorority).

Cast: Mo'Nique *(Nicole Parker)*; Countess Vaughn *(Kimberly "Kim" Parker)*; Jenna von Oy *(Stevie Van Lowe)*; Dorien Wilson *(Prof. Stanley Oglevee)*; Thomas Mikal Ford *(Mel Parker)*; Ken L *(T)*; Lark Voorhies *(Chandra Carrington)*; Yvette Wilson *(Andell Wilkerson)*.

7103   Parks and Recreation. (Series; Comedy; NBC; 2009–). Leslie Knope is the deputy director of the Parks and Recreation Department in Pawnee, Indiana. She is 34 years old, pretty, somewhat naïve, always cheery and out to change the world (or, at least, as she says, what she can do for her community in her current position). "People need help and it feels good to be needed," Leslie says about her job. Stories follow the idealistic Leslie as she sets out to do what is best, but almost always finds her efforts faltering due to the red tape of the bureaucratic system. Tom Haverford is Leslie's superior; Mark, Ann, April and Ron are Leslie's co-workers.

Cast: Amy Poehler *(Leslie Knope)*; Rashida Jones *(Ann Perkins)*; Paul Schneider *(Mark Brendanawicz)*; Aziz Ansari *(Tom Haverford)*; Nick Offerman *(Ron Swanson)*; Aubrey Plaza *(April Ludgate)*; Rob Lowe *(Chris Traeger)*; Adam Scott *(Ben Wyatt)*; Chris Pratt *(Andy Dwyer)*; Jama Williamson *(Wendy Haverford)*; Jim O'Heir *(Jerry Gergich)*.

7104   Parole. (Pilot; Drama; CBS; April 20, 1982). The day-to-day activities of a caring, street-wise Boston parole officer named Andrew "Andy" Driscoll. Suzanne is his wife; Mrs. Sawyer is the parole board officer. Sting performs the theme, "I Shall Be Released."

Cast: James Naughton *(Andy Driscoll)*; Lori Cardille *(Suzanne Driscoll)*; Barbara Meek *(Mrs. Sawyer)*.

7105   Parole Chief. (Pilot; Drama; NBC; July 31, 1956). A proposal about Patrick "Pat" Duggan, a parole chief who makes it his goal to rehabilitate young parolees just out of prison.

Cast: Pat O'Brien *(Pat Duggan)*.

7106   The Partners. (Series; Comedy; NBC; 1971-1972). During the Korean War a bumbling private named Lennie Crooke and a level-headed private named George Robinson became friends. A situation that would complicate their lives in later years — Lennie's knack for fouling everything up — began on the battlefields of Korea. While it is not made clear exactly what happened after the war, at some point they joined the Los Angeles Police Department. Lennie and George are detectives with the 33rd Precinct. Lennie lives at 21 Ridge Canyon Road; George resides at 1103 West 4th Street, Apart-

ment 302. "They make a lot of mistakes" says their captain, Aaron William Andrews. "But they've been together a long time, and they always get the job done."

What Andrews, who has been captain of the 33rd Precinct for ten years, doesn't know is that it is George who saves the day by covering for Lennie. Despite the fact that Lennie is plagued by misfortune and doesn't always follow standard police procedure (he forgets), his foul-ups always seem to work for them (Lennie has a tendency to lose his gun, frisk furniture for concealed weapons, and arrest people without reading them their rights). Other regulars are Sergeant Nelson Higgenbottom, and Freddie Butler, the man who confesses to every crime. Lalo Schifrin composed the theme.

Cast: Don Adams *(Lennie Crooke)*; Rupert Crosse *(George Robinson)*; John Doucette *(Aaron William Andrews)*; Dick Van Patten *(Nelson Higgenbottom)*; Robert Karvelas *(Freddie Butler)*.

7107   Partners. (Pilot; Drama; ABC; May 27, 1993). Davidson, Avery and Matheson is a medical practice owned by Dr. Harlan Davidson, an aging physician. He is about to retire and sell his practice to three young doctors (Andi, Eric and Ben). Just prior to the sale, Harlan has second thoughts, feeling the new generation doesn't know how to become part of the community like he has; he also feels that once he retires he will have nothing to do (he has been a widower for five years). Instead of retiring, Harlan sells his practice but retains his position as the senior partner. The doctors work in association with St. Anne's Hospital and the unsold series was to relate their efforts to save lives.

Cast: Jack Warden *(Dr. Harlan Davidson)*; Carol Huston *(Dr. Andi St. Clair)*; Dan Gauthier *(Dr. Eric Parker)*; Jeff Yagher *(Dr. Ben Michaels)*.

7108   Partners. (Series; Comedy; Fox; 1995–1996). Alicia, Owen and Bob are three best friends who share each other's joys and sorrows. Alicia is a lawyer with the firm of White, Corwin and Saxonhouse in San Francisco. When she became a full partner (two months after the series started) she called the firm "White, Corwin, Saxonhouse and the One with the Breasts." Owen and Bob are architects with the firm of Levitt and Associates. Owen is Alicia's fiancé; Bob worked at Candy World before his present job. Heather, the law office receptionist, was born in Alaska where she had two dogs named Scamp and Pixie. Emilio's, a bar-restaurant is the hangout.

Cast: Maria Pitillo *(Alicia)*; Tate Donovan *(Owen)*; Jon Cryer *(Bob)*; Catherine Lloyd Burns *(Heather)*.

7109   The Partners. (Pilot; Crime Drama; Unaired; Produced for ABC in 2003). After a drug bust goes wrong and millions of dollars in contraband goes missing, Christine Ryder, a detective with the L.A.P.D., who was in charge of the case, is reprimanded but not suspended. Instead, she is teamed with Holly Flynn, a by-the-books detective whom the department hopes will reform the rule-breaking, tough Christine. The proposal was to follow Christine and Holly, undercover narcotics cops as different as night and day, as they investigate cases.

Cast: Liz Vassey *(Det. Christine Ryder)*; Mary Catherine Garrison *(Det. Holly Flynn)*; Rick Hoffman *(Captain Terlesky)*; Richard Gunn *(Lt. Jones)*.

7110   Partners in Crime. (Pilot; Crime Drama; NBC; Mar. 24, 1973). Meredith Leland is a retired judge who is still eager to see that justice is served. Sam Hatch is an ex-con who has gone straight after being sentenced to jail by the judge. He holds no remorse and has teamed with Meredith to help her in her quest. The proposal was to relate their efforts to solve crimes. Other regulars are Judge

Charles Leland, Meredith's father; and police Lieutenant Fred Hartnett.

Cast: Lee Grant *(Meredith Leland)*; Lou Antonio *(Sam Hatch)*; John Randolph *(Charles Leland)*; Charles Drake *(Fred Hartnett)*.

7111   *Partners in Crime.* (Series; Crime Drama; NBC; 1984). Carole Stanwyck and Sydney Kovack are beautiful, amateur private investigators who run their late husband's company, the Caulfield Detective Agency in San Francisco. The company is also called the Raymond Dashill Caulfield Detective Agency. Both women married Raymond Caulfield and both women divorced him. Carole, Ray's first wife (1972–1975) was owed $62,000 in back alimony. Sydney, Ray's second wife (1976–1978) was owed $56,000 in back alimony. When Ray is killed during a case assignment, Carole and Sydney meet for the first time at the funeral. They inherit his company, a mutual mother-in-law (Jeanine), a housekeeper (Harvey) and a heavily mortgaged mansion. They became "Partners in Crime" after solving Ray's murder and deciding to remain a team.

Carole, a former New York debutante and teabag company heiress, lost her money through bad investments. She is a brunette and works as a freelance photographer. She lives at 654 Verona Drive and sometimes worries that she wears the wrong outfits for undercover assignments. Carole despises wearing an electronic bug on an assignment, which she places in her bra; sometimes in her pants pocket

Sydney is a stunning, street-wise blonde who grew up in the Mission District of San Francisco where she learned all the tricks of the trade — from lock picking to picking pockets. As a kid, she ran numbers for her father and had a mean left hook; she sent three school bullies to the dentist. She is now an aspiring but struggling musician — bass fiddle — who hopes to one day play with the San Francisco Symphony Orchestra. Sydney has been studying the bass for 20 years and lives at 921 Hayworth Street, Apartment 3C. Sydney can hot wire a car, carries lock picks with her at all times and only plays tennis because she feels she looks fabulous in a tennis outfit.

"We're not exactly Sherlock Holmes and Dr. Watson," says Carole, "but we get the job done." Sydney adds, "We call the cops a lot."

Jeanine Caulfield, Carole and Sydney's mutual mother-in-law, is the unpublished author of 57 books. She owns the Partners in Crime Book Store, later called Jeanine's Book Store, and lives with Carole and Sydney at the mansion. Harvey Shain cares for the mansion.

Program Open [Carole]: "This tall brunette (Carole), born with a silver spoon in her mouth, was private eye Raymond Caulfield's first wife. This street-wise blonde (Sydney) and I have two things in common — we were both married to the same man and we both divorced him. We met for the first time at his funeral. Are you ready for this? He left us his mansion, mortgaged to the hilt, and the Caulfield Detective Agency. And how do we manage? We call the cops a lot."

Cast: Lynda Carter *(Carole Stanwyck)*; Loni Anderson *(Sydney Kovack)*; Eileen Heckart *(Jeannie Caulfield)*; Walter Olkewicz *(Harvey Shain)*; Cameron Mitchell *(Duke Kovak; Sydney's father)*.

7112   *Partners in Crime.* (Series; Mystery; Syn.; 1985). When Tuppence and Tommy Beresford, a wealthy British couple discover that a detective agency is for sale, they purchase it with the hope of finding the same type of adventure they find as avid readers of detective novels. Stories, spiced with light humor, are set in London and relate their lighthearted exploits as the owner-operators of Blunt's International Detective Agency. Based on characters created by Agatha Christie.

Cast: Francesca Annis *(Tuppence Beresford)*; James Warwick *(Tommy Beresford)*; Arthur Cox *(Police Inspector Marriott)*.

7113   *Partners in Life.* (Pilot; Comedy; CBS; Aug. 31, 1990).

While tearing down the Max King Film Studios in California, workers uncovered 144 1930s and '40s theatrical comedy shorts starring the comedy team of Morton and Hayes — films that were thought lost forever. Each week one of these lost films was to be seen (hosted by Max King III). See also *Morton and Hayes*.

Cast: Rob Reiner *(Max King III)*; Kevin Pollak *(Chick Morton)*; Joe Guzaldo *(Eddie Hayes)*.

7114   *The Partridge Family.* (Series; Comedy; ABC; 1970–1974). A psychedelically painted 1957 Chevrolet school bus is the on-the-road home to a family of singers as they tour the country. Shirley Partridge is the mother, and with her children, Keith, Laurie, Danny, Chris and Tracy, they form the Partridge Family, "America's newest singing sensation." When not traveling, the family lives at 698 Sycamore Road in San Pueblo, California (address also given as the 700 block on Vassario Road).

Shirley, maiden name Renfrew, is a widow. She worked at the Bank of San Pueblo before joining the family as a singer. It was ten-year-old Danny who borrowed recording equipment from his school, made a tape of them singing and convinced agent Reuben Kincaid to take a chance on them. They first performed the song "Together" at Caesar's Palace in Las Vegas (in a show headlined by Johnny Cash). This led to a recording contract and success (their first album, "The Partridge Family," had a picture of a partridge on it). The family also has a dog named Simone.

"Most mothers have to worry about drugs and violence with their sons, but all your ding-a-ling son does is think about girls" says Laurie about her brother Keith. Keith is the eldest child and writes the songs for his family (he also plays guitar). Keith first attended San Pueblo High School and then San Pueblo Junior College. Laurie believes Keith only dates dumb girls because "they believe all the corny pickup lines he uses."

Laurie attends San Pueblo High School and reads *Liberal Outlook* magazine. While very pretty, Laurie never faced the problems of popularity with boys. She is a teenage women's libber, plays the keyboard, and sometimes objects to Keith's lyrics (which she feels are degrading to women; Keith writes love songs).

Danny is the schemer of the family and always out to make a dollar ("He usually comes up with six to eight schemes a week," says Reuben, who believes "he is a 40-year-old midget in a kid outfit"). Danny plays bass guitar and has one share of stock in A.T.&T. preferred (his most cherished possession).

Tracy, who plays tambourine, and Chris, who plays drums, are the youngest members of the family. In third-season episodes, Shirley (a widow) used her maiden name to enroll in college to complete her courses in psychology. Walter and Amanda are Shirley's parents; Doris Stevens and her children, Ricky and Donna are Shirley's neighbors; Bonnie is Reuben's girlfriend; Punky and Gloria are Danny's friends; Snake is a friend of the family. "When We're Singing" is the first season theme; "Come on Get Happy" is the theme for the remainder of the series.

Cast: Shirley Jones *(Shirley Partridge)*; David Cassidy *(Keith Partridge)*; Susan Dey *(Laurie Partridge)*; Danny Bonaduce *(Danny Partridge)*; Suzanne Crough *(Tracy Partridge)*; Jeremy Gelbwaks, Brian Forster *(Chris Partridge)*; Dave Madden *(Reuben Kincaid)*; Rosemary DeCamp *(Amanda Renfrew)*; Ray Bolger, Jackie Coogan *(Walter Renfrew)*; Nita Talbot *(Doris Stevens)*; Ricky Segal *(Ricky Stevens)*; Ronne Troup *(Donna Stevens)*; Patti Cohoon *(Gloria Hickey)*; Elaine Giftos *(Bonnie Kleinschmitt)*; Gary Dubin *(Punky Lazaar)*; Rob Reiner, Stuart Margolin *(Snake)*.

7115   *Partridge Family: 2200 A.D.* (Series; Cartoon; CBS; 1974-1975). A spin off from *The Partridge Family* that is set in the future (in the year A.D. 2200) and follows the family singing group as they tour the various planets. Shirley is the mother, a widow; Keith, Laurie, Danny, Tracy and Chris are her children; Reuben Kincaid is their manager; and Marion and Beannie are Keith's friends.

Voice Cast: Sherry Alberoni (*Shirley Partridge*); Susan Dey (*Laurie Partridge*); Danny Bonaduce (*Danny Partridge*); Chuck McLennan (*Keith Partridge*); Suzanne Crough (*Tracy Partridge*); Brian Forster (*Chris Partridge*); Dave Madden (*Reuben Kincaid*); Julie McWhirter (*Marion*); Allan Melvin (*Beannie*).

7116 Party at the Palms. (Series; Reality; E!; 2005–2006). Gorgeous *Playboy* magazine centerfold Jenny McCarthy offers viewers a behind-the-scenes look at "the wildest hot spot" in Las Vegas—the Palms Casino Hotel. The glitzy program follows Jenny as she meets celebrities, visits the various "hot spots" (like the poolside Skin Lounge and the rooftop Ghost Bar) and acquaints viewers with the ins and outs of partying at the casino.

Hostess: Jenny McCarthy.

7117 Party Down. (Series; Comedy; Starz; 2009–2010). In the 1980s Ann Jillian led a group of Los Angeles waitresses on ABC's *It's a Living.* In 2009, *Party Down* follows the antics of a group of Los Angeles waiters as they tackle various catering jobs (from Sweet 16 parties to weddings to a senior citizens gathering). Each affair is seen through the eyes of Henry Pollard, an actor waiting for his big break, as he and his crew do what they do best—wreck havoc. Casey, Constance, Kyle and Romano work with Henry; Ron is their boss at Party Down Catering; Lydia is the divorcee with a 13-year-old daughter (Escapade) who is pursuing stardom.

Cast: Adam Scott (*Henry Pollard*); Lizzy Caplan (*Casey Klein*); Jane Lynch (*Constance Carmell*); Ken Marino (*Ron Donald*); Ryan Hansen (*Kyle Bradway*); Martin Starr (*Romano DeBeers*); Megan Mullally (*Lydia Dunfree*); Kaitlyn Dever (*Escapade Dunfree*).

7118 Party Girl. (Series; Comedy; Fox; 1996). Mary is a young woman who is cared for by her godmother, Judy (her parents have passed away). Mary works with Judy at the New York Public Library. At night Mary is a party girl—the toast of the Manhattan clubs and parties. Judy feels Mary is a fun-loving girl who lacks responsibility. Mary, although vivacious and full of enthusiasm, feels she is responsible (she did take a job) and sets out to prove it. Stories follow Mary as she tries to settle into a job she dislikes and curtail her partying ways (which always get her into trouble—but she always comes out a winner). Wanda is Mary's co-worker; Oneal is her gay friend.

Cast: Christine Taylor (*Mary*); Swoosie Kurtz (*Judy Burkhard*); Merrin Dungey (*Wanda*); Matt Bollenghi (*Oneal*).

7119 Party Line. (Series; Game; NBC; 1947). An early quiz program wherein the host telephones a viewer (via post card selection) and asks him a question in return for a prize (money).

Host: Bert Parks.

7120 The Party Machine with Nia Peeples. (Series; Variety; Syn.; 1991). Singer-actress Nia Peeples oversees a night club–like party wherein celebrity guests dance, perform and mingle with other party goers.

Host: Nia Peeples. **Co-Host:** Sheena Easton. **Music:** Chris Cavrozzi.

7121 Party of Five. (Series; Drama; Fox; 1994–2000). The house at 3324 Broadway in San Francisco is home to the Salinger family: parents Nicholas and Diana and their children, Charlie, Julia, Bailey, Claudia and infant Owen.

Nicholas and Diana own Salinger's, a family restaurant on Filbert Street (their slogan is "Salinger's 'Cause You Gotta Eat"). One night in March of 1994 (six months before the series begins), tragedy strikes the family: a drunken driver kills Nicholas and Diana and the children are left to fend for themselves. Charlie, the oldest, takes on the responsibility of caring for his siblings and uses, in part, the $15,000 he receives every four months as part of his parent's estate. The family has an English bulldog named Thurber.

Stories follow events in the lives of the Salinger children as they struggle to remain a family despite the hard times that face them. Charlie is a womanizer and irresponsible. He is 24 years old. Julia is 15 years old and a sophomore at Grant High School. She is a straight "A" student and hopes to become a journalist. Bailey is 16 years old and a junior at Grant High School. He is more responsible than Charlie and helps care for his younger siblings. Eleven-year-old Claudia is in the fifth grade. She is very sweet but also a very private person. She hopes to become a concert violinist (like her mother). She feels it is her duty to keep the family together and solve the problems that arise. See also *The Time of Your Life*, the spin off series.

Cast: Matthew Fox (*Charlie Salinger*); Neve Campbell (*Julia Salinger*); Scott Wolf (*Bailey Salinger*); Lacey Chabert (*Claudia Salinger*); Paula Devicq (*Kirsten Bennett*); Tom Mason (*Joe Mangus*); Tamara Taylor (*Grace Wilcox*); Michael Goorgian (*Justin Thompson*); Alexandra Lee (*Callie Martel*); Marla Sokoloff (*Jody*); Jennifer Love Hewitt (*Sarah Reeves*); Carroll O'Connor (*Jacob Gordon*); Scott Grimes (*Will McCorkle*); Brandon and Taylor Porter (*Owen Salinger*); Steven and Andrew Cavarno (*Owen Salinger*).

7122 Party Time at Club Roma. (Series; Variety; NBC; 1950–1951). Ben Alexander hosts a Roma Wines sponsored program, filmed in San Francisco (the home of Roma Wines) that features audience participation, stunt contests, quizzes and performances by aspiring talent.

7123 Pasadena. (Series; Drama; Fox; 2001). Lily Greeley McAllister is a teenage girl who has lived a life of luxury as the daughter of Beth and Robert Greeley, a powerful family who run a publishing empire based in Pasadena, California. Life changes for Lily when a murder occurs in the family mansion and the police investigation threatens to expose buried family secrets. Serial-like stories follow Lily as she becomes involved in the mystery and intrigue of a family she really never knew.

Cast: Alison Lohman (*Lily Greeley McAllister*); Dana Delany (*Catherine McAllister*); Martin Donovan (*Will McAllister*); Natasha Gregson Wagner (*Beth Greeley*); Bathazar Getty (*Nate Greeley*); Mark Valley (*Robert Greeley*); Christopher Marquette (*Mason McAllister*); Nicole Paggi (*Jeanne Bradbury*); Alan Simpson (*Henry Bellow*).

7124 Pass the Buck. (Series; Game; NBC; 1978). A category topic is stated (for example, "A type of pie") and each of the four competing players must name an item that relates to the subject. Prize money starts at $100 and increases $25 each time an acceptable answer is given. When a player gives an incorrect response, he is defeated and a new topic is played. The game continues in this manner until one player remains; that player becomes the champion and wins the pot.

Host: Bill Cullen. **Announcer:** Bob Clayton.

7125 Passion. (Pilot; Comedy; CBS; Aug. 17, 1991). Amanda Brooks wrote the books *Naughty Nurses, Naughty Nurses Go to Hawaii* and *Naughty Nurses Go to Jail* for Low Rent Publishing. She wrote for *Vanity Fair* and worked as an editor for two magazines (*Urban Woman* and *City Style*). Jack Keenan is a sports magazine mogul whose only non-sports publication, *Ladies' Day* magazine, has hit rock bottom. In an attempt to save the magazine, Jack hires Amanda and gives her free reign to do what it takes to boost circulation. Amanda begins by changing the name of the magazine to *Passion* and the unsold series was to relate Amanda's attempts to save the magazine. Other regulars are Maryedith, the assistant editor (she has a passion for cats and has one named Mr. Fluffernutter); Veronica, the celebrity interviewer; and Kenneth, Jack's assistant.

Cast: Jane Seymour (*Amanda Brooks*); John Terry (*Jack Keenan*); Nancy Lenehan (*Maryedith Sweetzer*); Cristine Rose (*Veronica Andrews*); Josh Mostel (*Kenneth*).

7126   *Passion Cove.* (Series; Erotica; Cinemax; 2001–2005). Passion Cove is an exotic and secluded seaside resort that caters to gorgeous women and handsome men. While many (or all) come for only one thing (sex) how they achieved what they wanted (by unexpected reasons or circumstances) is the focal point of the soft-core pornography series. Casts differ with each episode. John Quinn is the producer and adult film stars, Kira Reed and Chloe Nichol are featured performers.

7127   *Passions.* NBC serial. May 15, 1999 to Aug. 7, 2008. See *Soap Operas*.

7128   *Passport to Danger.* (Series; Adventure; Syn.; 1954). Steve McQuinn is a diplomatic courier for the United States government. He is also the unwitting decoy of the Hungarian Secret Police. Stories, set in the trouble spots of the world, follow Steve as he attempts to carry out assignments for the government.

Cast: Cesar Romero (*Steve McQuinn*).

7129   *Password.* (Series; Game; CBS; NBC; ABC; 1961–2008). Two teams, each composed of a celebrity captain and a non-celebrity contestant, compete. A player receives a password (e.g., book) and through one word clues must convey its meaning to his partner. Word values begin at ten points and diminish by one point for each unsuccessful clue. The highest scoring team is the winner and the contestant receives a cash prize. Six versions appeared:

1. Password (CBS, 1961–67). **Host:** Allen Ludden. **Substitute Host:** Jack Clark. **Announcer:** Bern Bennett, Lee Vines. **Substitute Announcer:** Bob Kennedy, Gene Wood.

2. Password (ABC, 1971–74). **Host:** Allen Ludden. **Announcer:** John Harlan.

3. Password All Stars (ABC, 1974-75). **Host:** Allen Ludden. **Announcer:** John Harlan. Celebrities play for charity.

4. Password Plus (NBC, 1979–82). **Host:** Allen Ludden, Tom Kennedy. **Substitute Host:** Bill Cullen. **Announcer:** Gene Wood, Bob Hilton, Rich Jeffries.

5. Super Password (NBC, 1984–89). **Host:** Bert Convy. **Announcer:** Gene Wood. **Substitute Announcer:** Rich Jeffries.

6. Million Dollar Password (CBS, 2008-09). **Host:** Regis Philbin. **Announcer:** Jack Dennis. Adds a segment wherein players can win from $10,000 to $1 million by guessing from five out of ten passwords (for $5,000) to ten out of ten passwords (for $1 million) within ninety seconds.

7130   *Past Imperfect.* (Pilot; Comedy; Unaired; Produced for ABC in 1989). A video scrapbook is used to recount events in the life of a 30-year-old man (Ted) whose reminisces about imperfect occurrences of his past are seen in flashbacks by the home audience.

Cast: Howie Mandel (*Ted*); Talia Balsam (*Jill*); Sharon Spelman (*Ruth*); John Astin (*Sam*).

7131   *Past Life.* (Series; Drama; Fox; 2010). Dr. Kate McGinn is a psychologist with the Talmadge Center for Behavioral Sciences in New York City, a world-renowned institute dedicated to the study of the science of the soul. Kate, however, is not a typical psychologist: she is a firm believer in reincarnation and says, "It's not who you are, it's who you were." Several years earlier, Kate experienced a past life regression that confirmed her suspicion that people have lived before but the brain conceals these past lives until some action triggers it and the subject begins to have uncontrollable memories of what he or she was. Using regression therapy coupled with her own natural gift for reading people, Kate attempts to solve the mysteries of people who suffer from present day problems caused by past life traumas. Kate, however, cannot successfully treat patients alone. She needs the help of a detective and hires Price Whatley, a cynical, pragmatic former N.Y.P.D. homicide detective whose grief over the accidental death of his wife cost him his job when emotional problems interfered with his work (while on vacation in Mexico, Price urged his wife, Lauren, to dive off a cliff into the water below. Although afraid she did and was killed when she struck her head on rocks below the water).

Price simply does not believe in reincarnation and is often perplexed by the cases he investigates. Kate assures him — "The clues are there — you just have to know where to look."

Quick cut flashback sequences are used to recall a subject's past life as Kate and Price begin their investigation — "If a person has a regression, we are here to find out why," says Kate (who calls herself and Price "Past Life Specialists"). Dr. Malachi Talmadge is the founder and head of the institute; Dr. Rishi Karna is the institute's cognitive research scientist (he is from Calcutta , loves bad American TV programs, Cuban jazz "and driving everyone crazy"), Laney is Kate's mother (with whom she lives). Based on the book *The Reincarnation* by M.J. Rose.

Cast: Kelli Giddish (*Kate McGinn*); Nicholas Bishop (*Price Whatley*); Richard Schiff (*Malachi Talmadge*); Ravi Patel (*Rishi Karna*); Judith Ivey (*Laney McGinn*).

7132   *The Pat Boone Show.* (Series; Variety; ABC; NBC; Syn.; 1957–1969). Singer Pat Boone hosts a program of music and songs. Pat's 1966 and 1969 programs also feature celebrity interviews. Three versions appeared.

1. The Pat Boone Show (ABC, 1957–59; also known as *The Pat Boone Chevy Show*). **Host:** Pat Boone. **Regulars:** Louise O'Brien, The Artie Malvin Chorus, The McGuire Sisters, The Jada Quartet. **Orchestra:** Mort Lindsey.

2. The Pat Boone Show (NBC, 1966-67). **Host:** Pat Boone. **Orchestra:** Paul Smith.

3. Pat Boone in Hollywood (Syn., 1969). **Host:** Pat Boone. **Announcer:** Jay Stewart. **Orchestra:** Paul Smith.

7133   *Pat Paulsen's Half a Comedy Hour.* (Series; Comedy; ABC; 1970). Comedian Pat Paulsen hosts a half-hour program in which he appears in skits (with guests and regulars) that satirize the contemporary scene.

Program Open: "*Pat Paulsen's Half a Comedy Hour* with Mr. Hubert H. Humphrey, Daffy Duck and special guest star Debbie Reynolds, We will return for the fun right after these messages."

Host: Pat Paulsen. **Regulars:** Jean Byron, Sherry Miles, Bob Einstein, Pepe Brown, Vanetta Rogers, Pedro Regas. **Announcer:** Billy Sands.

7134   *The Pat Sajak Show.* (Series; Talk; CBS; 1989). A late night talk Program of celebrity interviews, monologues and musical numbers with *Wheel of Fortune* host Pat Sajak. The CBS series, which failed to put a dent in the ratings of *The Tonight Show Starring Johnny Carson*, was cancelled a year later.

Host: Pat Sajak. **Announcer:** Dan Miller.

7135   *The Patrice Munsel Show.* (Series; Variety; ABC; 1957-1958). A live program that showcases the musical talents of Metropolitan Opera soprano Patrice Munsel.
   Host: Patrice Munsel. **Regulars:** The Martins Quartet. **Orchestra:** Charles Sanford.

7136   *The Patricia Bowan Show.* (Series; Variety; ABC; 1951). A live program that showcases the dancing abilities of ballerina Patricia Bowan and her musical guest stars.
   Host: Patricia Bowan. **Regulars:** Maureen Cannon, Paul Shelly, The Pastels. **Music:** The Norman Paris Trio.

7137   *Patrick Stone.* (Pilot; Comedy; CBS; July 16, 1975). As far back as he can remember, Patrick Stone wanted to be a private detective. Despite the fact that he is mishap prone, Patrick follows that dream and opens his own office. The proposal was to follow Patrick as he attempts to help people and accomplishes success simply by accident.
   Cast: Jeff Davis (*Patrick Stone*).

7138   *Patrol Car.* (Series; Crime Drama; Syn.; 1955). The syndicated title (after its initial run) for *Inspector Fabian of Scotland Yard*. See this title for information.

7139   *The Patti Page Show.* (Series; Variety; Syn., NBC, CBS, ABC; 1955–1959). Singer Patti Page hosts a program of music, songs and light comedy. Four versions appeared:
   1. The Patti Page Show (Syn., 1955). **Host:** Patti Page. **Regulars:** The Page Five Singers. **Orchestra:** Jack Rael.
   2. The Patti Page Show (NBC, 1956). **Host:** Patti Page. **Regulars:** The Spellbinders, The Frank Lewis Dancers. **Orchestra:** Carl Hoff.
   3. The Patti Page Show (CBS, 1957). **Host:** Patti Page. **Regulars:** The Matt Mattox Dancers. **Orchestra:** Vic Schoen.
   4. The Patti Page Show (ABC, 1958-1959). **Host:** Patti Page. **Regulars:** Rocky Cole, The Jerry Packer Singers, The Matt Mattox Dancers. **Orchestra:** Vic Schoen.

7140   *Pattie Poole and Family.* (Pilot; Comedy; NBC; Jan. 18, 1988). Pattie Poole is the annoying, slightly wacky housewife to the Hogan family (from the series *The Hogan Family*). She is married to Peter (whom she calls "The Mister") and lives with her overbearing mother, Mother Poole. Events in the lives of a family who live to meddle in other people's lives is the focal point the proposal.
   Cast: Edie McClurg (*Pattie Poole*); Willard Scott (*Peter Poole*); Kathleen Freeman (*Mother Poole*).

7141   *The Patty Duke Show.* (Series; Comedy; ABC; 1963–1966). The home at 8 Remsen Drive (also given as 5 Remsen Street) in Brooklyn Heights, New York, is the residence of Martin Lane, his wife, Natalie, and their children Patty and Ross. Also living with them is Cathy Lane, Patty's sophisticated look-alike cousin. The family dog is named Tiger.
   Patricia ("Patty") Lane is a whirlwind of energy. She is enthusiastic, fun to be with, an average student at Brooklyn Heights High School and a bit prone to mishaps. She always tries to do the right thing (what she thinks is right) but those good intentions most often backfire and land her in trouble. Patty held a job as a waitress and singer at the Pink Percolator coffeehouse (where she worked under the name "Pittsburgh Patty"). She was also editor of her high school newspaper, the *Bugle* and has a steady boyfriend (Richard Harrison).
   Catherine ("Cathy") Margaret Rollin Lane lived previously in Glasgow, Scotland. Her father is Kenneth Lane, a foreign correspondent for the New York *Chronicle*. Kenneth's assignments constantly uproot Cathy. To enable her to get her high school education, Kenneth arranged with his brother, Martin, to let Cathy live with him in Brooklyn.
   Cathy attended Mrs. Tuttles of Mountain Briar private school (where she was the debate champion) before coming to America. Her father calls her "Kit Kat," and she has a built-in lie detector: she gets the hiccups when she lies or tries to. Cathy is a sophisticated teenage girl whose European background makes it difficult (at first) for her to adjust to Patty's American way of life. She is more addicted to schoolwork than Patty and sensitive to the fact that she is a bit different than other girls her age. Cathy also had a program (of classical music) on the school radio station, BHBH ("The Voice of Brooklyn Heights"). She and Patty enjoy sodas at the Shake Shop (later called Leslie's Ice Cream Parlor) after school.
   Patty Duke also played Betsy Lane, Patty's look-alike cousin from Atlanta, a Southern bombshell who took the boys of Brooklyn Heights by storm. While Patty called her a "Confederate Cleopatra," Betsy was, in reality, a lonely girl who desperately tried to get Cathy to leave so that she could stay with the Lanes (Betsy was ignored by her parents, who shipped her off to boarding schools, so they could devote full time to building up their business). Betsy's "security blanket" was her doll, Sara Jane.
   Martin Lane is the managing editor of the New York *Chronicle*. He was captain of his college football team and married Natalie when she was 17 years old. They honeymooned at Lake George and have been married for 20 years (according to first season episodes).
   Sue Ellen Turner is Patty's nemesis; Gloria is Patty's rival for Richard; Monica, Alice, Rosalind and Alfred are Patty's friends; Nikki Lee is Ross's friend; Sammy is the Shake Shop owner; Louie is the waiter; J.R. Castle (then T.J. Blodgett) is the publisher of the *Chronicle*; Miss Gordon is J.R.'s secretary; Jonathan Harris is Richard's father (owner of the Harrison Construction Company); Mrs. MacDonald is the Lane's housekeeper; and Kenneth Lane is Cathy's father; Ted is Cathy's boyfriend. Mark Miller played Martin Lane in the unaired pilot version of the series (clips of which are seen in the episode "Cousins," wherein Patty and Cathy meet for the first time).
   Cast: Patty Duke (*Patty Lane and Cathy Lane*); William Schallert (*Martin Lane and Kenneth Lane*); Jean Byron (*Natalie Lane*); Paul O'Keefe (*Ross Lane*); Eddie Applegate (*Richard Harrison*); Kitty Sullivan (*Sue Ellen Turner*); Skip Hinnant (*Ted Brownley*); Kelly Wood (*Gloria*); John McGiver (*J.R. Castle*); Susan Melvin (*Nikki Lee Blake*); Charles White (*Principal Brewster*); Sammy Smith (*Sammy*); David Doyle (*Jonathan Harris*); Amzie Strickland (*Richard's mother*); Alan Bruce, Robert Carson (*T.J. Blodgett; later*); Phyllis Coates (*Miss Gordon*); Bobby Diamond (*Louie*); Laura Barton, Kathy Garver (*Monica Robinson*); Margaret Hamilton (*Mrs. MacDonald*); Alice Rawlings (*Alice*); Robyn Millan (*Rosalind*); Jeff Siggins (*Alfred*).

7142   *The Paul Anka Show.* (Series; Variety; Syn.; 1983). Music, songs and celebrity interviews with singer Paul Anka as the host.

7143   *The Paul Arnold Show.* (Series; Variety; CBS; 1949-1950). Singer Paul Arnold hosts a program of music and songs that also spotlights the talents of guest artists.

7144   *Paul Bernard — Psychiatrist.* (Series; Drama; Syn.; 1972). Sessions between psychiatrist Dr. Paul Bernard and his patients (all female) are dramatized. The patient relates her elements of distress and in the final moments of the program, Dr. Bernard analyzes her seemingly uncomplicated and innocent thoughts. Produced with the cooperation of the Canadian Mental Heath Association.
   Cast: Chris Wiggins (*Dr. Paul Bernard*).

7145   *The Paul Dixon Show.* (Series; Variety; ABC; DuMont; 1951–1955). Singer Paul Dixon oversees a program of music and songs that also features the talents of Dotty Mack and Wanda Lewis. Aired on ABC (Aug. 8, 1951 to Sept. 4, 1952) and DuMont (Sept. 29, 1952 to April 8, 1955).

7146   *The Paul Hartman Show.* (Series; Comedy; CBS; 1953-1954). The alternate title for *Pride of the Family.* See this title for information.

7147   *The Paul Hogan Show.* (Series; Comedy; Syn.; 1981). Australian-produced program of adult oriented comedy sketches with actor Paul Hogan.

Host: Paul Hogan. **Regulars:** Delvene Delaney, Roger Stevens, John Blackman, Karin Pini, Sue McIntosh, Glenn Shorock, Marion Edward, Graham Matrick, Andrew Harwood.

7148   *The Paul Lynde Show.* (Series; Comedy; ABC; 1972-1973). Paul Simms is an attorney with the firm of McNish and Simms in Ocean Grove, California. He lives with his wife, Martha, at 3 Prescott Drive and has a double martini when he comes home from work. He is easily exasperated and believes he is in a rat race "and the rats are winning." His eldest daughter, Barbara, is married to Howie Dickerson, a genius she met at college (he was going through the dictionary looking for mistakes). Paul dislikes the annoying Howie, who works as a caddy, and feels he may be the reason why he is headed for a nervous breakdown. Howie has been around the world three times, charts the stock market for fun, is a walking encyclopedia and a connoisseur of fine wine. Paul's younger daughter, Sally, is fascinated by Howie and believes he is the smartest person she knows. Sally attends Ocean Grove Junior High School. Barney and Grace are Howie's parents; Alice is Paul's secretary; J.T. McNish is Paul's boss; Jimmy is Sally's friend.

Cast: Paul Lynde *(Paul Simms)*; Elizabeth Allen *(Martha Simms)*; Jane Actman *(Barbara Dickerson)*; John Calvin *(Howie Dickerson)*; Pamelyn Ferdin *(Sally Simms)*; Herb Voland *(J.T. McNish)*; Jerry Stiller *(Barney Dickerson)*; Anne Meara *(Grace Dickerson)*; Allison McKay *(Alice)*; Anson Williams, Stuart Getz *(Jimmy Lyons)*.

7149   *Paul Sand in Friends and Lovers.* (Series; Comedy; CBS; 1974-1975). The life, fantasies and romantic misadventures of Robert Dreyfuss, a young bachelor and bass violinist with the Boston Symphony Orchestra. Other regulars are Charlie Dreyfuss, Robert's brother; Janis, Charlie's wife; Fred Myerback, Robert's friend; Jack Reardon, the orchestra manager; Mason Woodruff, the orchestra conductor; Ben and Marge, Robert's parents; Estelle Milner, an orchestra member; Doris Myerback, Fred's wife and Susan, Robert's girlfriend.

Cast: Paul Sand *(Robert Dreyfuss)*; Michael Pataki *(Charlie Dreyfuss)*; Penny Marshall *(Janis Dreyfuss)*; Steve Landesberg *(Fred Myerback)*; Dick Wesson *(Jack Reardon)*; Craig Richard Nelson *(Mason Woodruff)*; Jack Gilford *(Ben Dreyfuss)*; Jan Miner *(Marge Dreyfuss)*; Sharon Spelman *(Susan)*; Dena Dietrich *(Estelle Milner)*; Karen Morrow *(Doris Myerback)*.

7150   *Paul Whiteman's Saturday Night Revue.* (Series; Variety; ABC; 1949–1952). Bandleader Paul Whiteman hosts a program of music and songs.

Host: Paul Whiteman. **Regulars:** Lina Romay, Earl Wrightson, Eric Viola, Joe Young, Duffy Otel, Maureen Cannon. **Orchestra:** Paul Whiteman.

7151   *Paul Whiteman's TV Teen Club.* (Series; Variety; ABC; 1949–1954). Performances by teenage talent discoveries. The winners, judged first by studio audience applause, then by celebrity guests, receive professional coaching and a chance to return at a later date for a chance at possible discovery.

Host: Paul Whiteman. **Co-Host:** Margo Whiteman, Nancy Lewis. **Regulars:** Andrea McLaughlin, Nancy Lewis, June Keegan, Maureen Cannon, The Ray Porter Singers. **Orchestra:** Paul Whiteman.

7152   *The Paul Williams Show.* (Pilot; Comedy; NBC; June 27, 1979). Paul Hamilton is an aspiring television personality who plays Marvin the Martian, the host of a kid show on KFAP in Denver, Colorado. He is loved by thousands of children, but longs for better things (his efforts to achieve those goals is the focal point of the unsold series). Other regulars are Victoria, the program director; Barbara, Paul's girlfriend; Deborah, Paul's neighbor; and Denny, Paul's agent.

Cast: Paul Williams *(Paul Hamilton)*; Amanda McBroom *(Victoria Woodbridge)*; Sandra Kerns *(Barbara)*; Dana Hill *(Deborah)*; Rick Podell *(Denny Morton)*.

7153   *The Paul Winchell Show.* (Series; Variety; NBC; 1950–1956). A potpourri of music, songs, comedy skits and quizzes with ventriloquist Paul Winchell and his dummy assistants, Jerry Mahoney and Knucklehead Smiff. The quiz segment, titled "What's My Name?" calls for players to identify the name of a famous person through clues provided by Paul and his dummies as they dramatize an incident in the subject's life. War Bonds are awarded to the winners. Irene Manning appears as the spokeswoman for Cheer dishwashing liquid.

Program Open: "Cheer, the new blue Cheer, the only suds with the new blue magic whitener, presents *The Paul Winchell Show,* starring Jerry Mahoney and Knucklehead Smiff."

Host: Paul Winchell. **Regulars:** Dorothy Claire, Ken Spaulding, Mary Ellen Terry, Margaret Hamilton, Patricia Bright, Jimmy Blaine, Sid Raymond, Hilda Vaughn, Maybin Hugh. **Music:** Milton DeLugg, John Gart.

7154   *The Paul Winchell Show.* (Series; Children; ABC; 1957–1961). A program of music and comedy featuring the antics of Jerry Mahoney and Knucklehead Smiff, the dummies of ventriloquist Paul Winchell.

Host: Paul Winchell. **Music:** Milton DeLugg.

7155   *The Paula Poundstone Show.* (Series; Variety; ABC; 1993). Comedienne Paula Poundstone is best when she responds to suggestions and basis a performance on that. Transferring her comedy club act to television and trying to sustain it for sixty minutes proved to be a difficult task and the series was cancelled after two episodes (Oct. 30 to Nov. 6, 1993).

Host: Paula Poundstone. **Announcer:** Ed Hall.

7156   *Paula Stone's Toy Shop.* (Series; Children; ABC; 1955). The setting is a toy shop where music, comedy and fantasy are presented by Paula and her friend, Freddie Fun.

Cast: Paula Stone *(Paula)*; Tim Herbert *(Freddie Fun)*.

7157   *Pauly.* (Series; Comedy; Fox; 1998). Edward Sherman is a wealthy real estate magnate. He is a widower and the father of Pauly, a slacker with no trace of ambition. Dawn Delaney is a gorgeous young aerobics instructor — a woman who has just become engaged to Edward. Pauly not only feels his carefree life style is in jeopardy, but Dawn is much too young for his father. While the main focus is on Pauly's (fruitless) efforts to break up his father and Dawn (and protect his freeloading existence), flashback and fantasy sequences are also used to show Pauly at a younger age and in situations that will arise if a wedding occurs. Burger is Pauly's friend (the owner of a video store); Zachary is Dawn's ten-year-old son; Sumi is Edward's housekeeper.

Cast: Pauly Shore (*Pauly Sherman*); David Dukes (*Edward Sherman*); Charlotte Ross (*Dawn Delaney*); Amy Hill (*Sumi*); Kevin Weisman (*Burger*); Theo Greenly (*Zachary Delaney*).

7158　The Paw Paws. (Series; Cartoon; Syn.; 1985). The Paw Paws are a group of magical bears That help good defeat evil. Stories focus in particular on the good Princess Paw Paw and her efforts to prevent the evil Dark Paw from seizing her kingdom.

Voices: Susan Blu, Ruth Buzzi, Scatman Crothers, Jerry Dexter, Pat Fraley, Billie Hayes, Mitzi McCall, Howard Morris, Robert Ridgley, Neilson Ross, Marilyn Schreffler, Frank Welker.

7159　Pawn Queens. (Series; Reality; TLC; 2010–). Minda Grabiec and Nikki Ruehl are close friends who are part owners (with Tom and Greg) of a pawn shop, geared toward female clients, called Napperville Jewelry and Loan. Like their male counterparts on *Pawn Stars*, Minda and Nikki appraise items brought into their shop outside of Chicago and viewers are given an insight into their value and rareness.

7160　Pawn Stars. (Series; Reality; History; 2009–). The Gold and Silver Pawn Shop is a real pawn shop in Las Vegas, Nevada. It is a family owned business, founded by Richard Harrison (called "The Old Man") and his son, Rick. Corey, Rick's son, assists him as does Corey's friend, Austin "Chumlee" Russell. Episodes basically deal with people entering the shop to either sell or pawn and item with the viewer being given facts about the items being seen (usually through Rick's narration).

Program Open: "I'm Rick Harrison and this is my pawn shop. I work here with the Old Man and my son, Big Hoss. If there is one thing I learned after 25 years is that you'll never know what comes through that door."

7161　Pay Cards. (Series; Game; Syn.; 1968-1969). Three contestants compete in a game of poker. Twenty cards, which contain singles, pairs and three and four of a kind, are displayed face down on an electronic board. By selecting the numbered cards (one to twenty), players have to build a five-card hand better than their opponents. Players begin by selecting three cards, then two on their next turn. The player with the best hand is the winner and receives a cash prize: $10 for a pair; $30 for three of a kind or a full house; $100 for four of a kind.

Program Open: "You're the king and queen when you play television's first card game, *Pay Cards*. And here's the ace up our sleeve, the host who pays, Art James."

Host: Art James. **Announcer:** Fred Collins.

7162　Pay It Off. (Series; Game; BET; 2009). A program that tries to help people in debt relieve some of their financial headaches by competing against each other for a chance to win up to $25,000. Although billed as "the first game show of its kind specifically aimed at helping individuals defray their bills and debts," several other shows (like *Balance Your Budget* and *Queen for a Day*) aired similar formats. Players state their dilemmas then compete in question-and-answer rounds of increasing difficulty to win money. Actress Kim Coles is the first African-American female to host a prime time network game show (Adam Wade was the first African-American male to host a daytime game show, *Musical Chairs*, in 1974 on CBS).

Host: Kim Coles.

7163　Pay the Piper. (Pilot; Crime Drama; NBC; May 18, 1966). Frederick Piper is playboy who enjoys the good life. He is a ladies'

man, an avid tennis player and spends his spare time working as an insurance investigator. The proposal, a spin off from *The Bob Hope Chrysler Theater* was to follow Piper as he investigates cases of probable insurance fraud.

Cast: Jack Kelly (*Frederick Piper*).

7164　Payne. (Series; Comedy; CBS; 1999). American version of the British series *Fawlty Towers* (about a bumbling innkeeper named Basil Fawlty). Here, the innkeeper is Royal Payne, a henpecked man whose wife, Constance, rules not only him but also the entire inn. Breeze O'Rourke is the housekeeper; and Mo is the befuddled, foreign bellboy. Stories follow Royal as he struggles to cope with the numerous staff and guest problems he encounters. The first episode follows the original format of the British version. However, when the producers chose to Americanize the program and alter the concept, it was cancelled three episodes later.

Cast: John Larroquette (*Royal Payne*); JoBeth Williams (*Constance Payne*); Julie Benz (*Breeze O'Rourke*); Rick Basalla (*Mo*).

7165　PB & J Otter. (Series; Cartoon; Disney; 1998). A house boat on the shore of Lake Hoohaw provides the setting for a look at a family of otters (Peanut, Jelly and Baby Butter Otter) as they struggle to cope with the world in which they live.

Voice Cast: Adam Rose (*Peanut Otter*); Brook Jenell Slack (*Jelly Otter*); Gina Marie Tortorici (*Baby Butter Otter*).

7166　P.D.Q. (Series; Game; Syn.; 1965–1970). Two teams compete, each composed of two members. One member of each team is placed in a soundproof isolation booth. The sound and light are turned off in one booth, allowing the other team to compete. The outside player stands before a phrase that is spelled out in large plastic letters and not visible to his booth partner. The object is for the booth player to identify the phrase from key letters his partner removes from one wall and places on another that is visible to him. Once the phrase is identified, the letters are removed from the wall and the opposing team competes in the same manner with the same phrase. The team who use the fewest letters to make an identification is the winner of the round. A two-out-of-three game competition is played with merchandise prizes awarded to the winners.

Program Open: "Mickey Manners ... Ruta Lee ... Paul Winchell on the game of quick thinking P.D.Q. starring Dennis James."

Host: Dennis James. **Announcer:** Kenny Williams. **Music:** Mort Garson.

7167　Peabody's Improbable History. (Series; Cartoon; ABC; 1959). A segment of *Rocky and His Friends*. See this title for information.

7168　Peaceable Kingdom. (Series; Drama; CBS; 1989). Rebecca Cafferty is the widowed mother of three children: Courtney, Sam and Dean. She lives in New York City (at 101 Park Avenue) but accepts a job in California to become the director of the Los Angeles County Zoo. Her dream is to turn the zoo into a model for promoting animal survival. Rebecca is assisted by her brother, Dr. Jed McFadden, the curator of mammals.

The Caffertys live in a special home that is located in the zoo and reserved for its director. Courtney and Dean attend Liberty High School (in New York, they were enrolled in the Marquis private school). Sam has a pet seal named Rover. Rebecca and Jed attended Madison High School. In the unaired pilot version of the series, Jed was Rebecca's love interest, not her brother.

"The Peaceable Kingdom Theme" was composed by David McHugh.

Cast: Lindsay Wagner (*Rebecca Cafferty*); Melissa Clayton (*Courtney*

Cafferty); Victor DiMattia *(Sam Cafferty)*; Michael Manasseri *(Dean Cafferty)*; Tom Wopat *(Dr. Jed McFadden)*.

7169   The Peanut Is a Serious Guy. (Experimental; Educational; DuMont; June 6, 1944). An institutional program put on by the National Peanut Council to promote the nutritional values of the peanut. The story finds Mr. Peanut (a double-jointed peanut puppet on strings created by Tom Jewett and Maria Gambarelli) asking the host to revise his image so people will not think of him as ballgame and circus snacks. Two recipes are given (for a peanut milk shake and a peanut cake) to show some of the many uses for peanuts.
Host: Maria Gambarelli. **Theme:** I'm a Serious Guy" by Carley Mills.

7170   Pearl. (Series; Comedy; CBS; 1996-1997). Pearl Caraldo is the widow of a longshoreman. After being deprived of a college education (she married right out of high school), Pearl applies for a student loan, writes an essay and is accepted into Swindon University (which is 4.2 miles from her home). All is progressing well for Pearl until she enrolls in the most prestigious class in the school — Humanities (the human condition) taught by the school's toughest teacher — Stephen Pynchon, a stickler for the rules who accepts no nonsense from his students (the failure rate in his class is 67.3 percent — the highest in the nation. If a student needs help he will only speak to them between 3:05 and 3:12 P.M. on Wednesday). Pearl, however, is as stubborn and abrasive as Stephen and a romantic relationship begins to develop. Stories follow Pearl as she begins a new life — and a new love with Stephen (who is not all that thrilled with a serious relationship; at least not yet). Other regulars are Anne, Pearl's friend; Joey, Pearl's son; and students Amy Lee, Margaret and Frankie.
Cast: Rhea Perlman *(Pearl Caraldo)*; Malcolm McDowell *(Stephen Pynchon)*; Carol Kane *(Annie Carmen)*; Lucy Liu *(Amy Lee)*; Nikki Cox *(Margaret Woodrow)*; Kevin Corrigan *(Frankie Spivak)*; Dash Milhok *(Joey Caraldo)*.

7171   The Pearl Bailey Show. (Series; Variety; ABC; 1971). Singer Pearl Bailey hosts a lively program of music and songs that also spotlights performances by her celebrity guests.
Host: Pearl Bailey. **Announcer:** Roger Carroll. **Orchestra:** Louis Bellson.

7172   Pearlie. (Series; Cartoon; Qubo; 2009). Fairy Land is a magical world inhabited by moth-like fairies. It is here that Pearlie, a pretty, perky, long-haired blonde fairy attempts to maintain the tranquility of her domain (especially Jubilee Park). Opposing Pearlie's disgusting goodness is her cousin Saphira, who yearns to control Fairyland. Stories follow Pearlie as she attempts to keep Fairyland a happy place despite Saphira's efforts to defeat her.
Voice Cast: Marieve Herington *(Pearlie)*; Michelle Monteith *(Saphira)*; Helene Joy *(Opal)*; Neil Crone *(Mr. Flea)*; Christian Potenza *(Scrag)*; Fiona Reid *(Great Aunt Gamet)*; Jonathan Wilson *(Ludwig)*. **Theme Vocal:** Louise Anton.

7173   Pebbles and Bamm Bamm. (Series; Cartoon; CBS; 1971-1972). A spin off from *The Flintstones* that relates events in the lives of Pebbles Flintstone, the teenage daughter of Fred and Wilma Flintstone, and Bamm Bamm Rubble, the adopted son of Barney and Betty Rubble as they begin their life at Bedrock High School. Moonrock, Fabian, Penny, Cindy and Wiggy are their friends.
Voice Cast Sally Struthers *(Pebbles Flintstone)*; Jay North *(Bamm Bamm Rubble)*; Lennie Weinrib *(Moonrock)*; Carl Esser *(Fabian)*; Mitzi McCall *(Penny)*; Gay Hartwig *(Cindy/Wiggy)*.

7174   Peck's Bad Girl. (Series; Comedy; CBS; 1959). Torey Peck is a very pretty 12-year-old girl who lives in a small American town. She is the daughter of Steve, a research scientist, and Jennifer Peck and has not yet developed an interest in "girlie things." She prefers "guy stuff" (like sports) and loves her life as a tomboy. Torey is also a bit mischievous and stories relate the events that spark Torey's life as she enjoys doing what she does, but deep down knowing that, like her equally pretty girlfriend, Francesca, she will one day abandon her boyish ways for dresses and dates with boys. Roger is Torey's brother.
Cast: Patricia McCormack *(Torey Peck)*; Wendell Corey *(Steve Peck)*; Marsha Hunt *(Jennifer Peck)*; Roy Ferrell *(Roger Peck)*; Reba Waters *(Francesca)*.

7175   The Pee Wee King Show. (Series; Variety; ABC; 1955). Music and songs featuring country and western entertainers with orchestra leader Pee Wee King as the host. Also known as *Pee Wee King's Flying Ranch*.
Host: Pee Wee King. **Regulars:** Ellen Long, Chuck Wiggins, Neal Burris, Redd Stuart, Bonnie Sloan, The Golden West Cowboys, The Cleveland Jamboree, The Teddy Raymond Quartet. **Music:** Pee Wee King.

7176   Pee Wee's Playhouse. (Series; Children; CBS; 1986–1991). A live (and expensive) Saturday morning program that features comedian Pee Wee Herman in zany skits set against a dazzling magical playhouse (also the apparent home of Pee Wee). Visitors to the playhouse include Miss Yvonne (called Miss Y-vonne by Pee Wee); Captain Carl, Cowboy Curtis, the Housewife (who lives next door), the King of Cartoons (who introduces an animated short), Opal, Conky Knucklehead, Dixie and Dirty Dog. Pee Wee also has his own genie, Jambi, that grants his wishes — that, in the end, teach him (and the children of the viewing audience) responsible lessons.
Cast: Paul Reubens *(Pee Wee Herman)*; Phil Hartman *(Captain Carl)*; Natasha Lyonne *(Opal)*; Gilbert Lewis *(King of Cartoons)*; Joann Carlo *(Dixie)*; Laurence Fishburne *(Cowboy Curtis)*; Wayne White *(Dirty Dog/Randy)*; John Paragon *(Jambi)*; Lynne Stewart *(Miss Yvonne)*; Gregory Harrison *(Conky Knucklehead)*; Alison Mark *(Housewife)*.

7177   Peep in the Big Wide World. (Series; Cartoon; PBS; 2006). Peep is a young yellow bird that is anxious to learn about life. As he travels throughout the forest he encounters the various animals that inhabit it. Stories, which relate learning aspects to children, follow Peep as he discovers the wonders of nature.
Voice Cast: Scott Beaudin *(Peep)*; Joan Cusack *(Narrator)*.

7178   Peep Show. (Pilot; Comedy; Unaired; Produced for Fox in 2005). Mark and Jeremy are roommates but also as different as night and day. Mark is neat and tidy; Jeremy is untidy and the Odd Couple–like proposal was to relate their efforts to live together.
Cast: Johnny Galecki *(Mark)*; Josh Meyers *(Jeremy)*; Alexandra Holden *(Sophie)*; Margaret Easley *(Erin)*; Rachel Boston *(Marsha)*.

7179   Peeping Times. (Pilot; Comedy; NBC; Jan. 25, 1978). Spoofs of television newsmagazine series with correspondents Miles Rathbourne and Dan Cochran.
Cast: Alan Oppenheimer *(Miles Rathbourne)*; David Letterman *(Dan Cochran)*. **Regulars:** Sharon Spelman, Ron Carey, Michael Fairman, Lee Delano, J.J. Barry, Murphy Dunne.

7180   Peer Pressure. (Series; Game; Syn.; 1997). A game show for teenagers. Three teens begin the game by standing at the starting position of a stage-sized game board. The object is answer questions and reach the finish line. Correctly answered questions move players closer to the finish line — but it also offers them a choice (the reason why it is called *Peer Pressure*): accept a prize and move back two spaces or stay where you are to get closer to the finish line and the grand prize. The first player to reach that finish line is the winner.

Host: Nick Spano. **Co-Host:** Valarie Rae Miller.

7181   *Peggy Fleming's Ice Stories.* (Pilot; Talk; Syn.; Jan. 14, 1995). One-on-one interviews with figure skating champions, past and present. The program is an attempt to cash in on the new popularity of figure skating and also features clips of subjects in action as well as information concerning their personal lives.

Host: Peggy Fleming. **Guests:** Michelle Kwan, Oksana Baiul, Kristi Yamaguchi, Elvis Stajko.

7182   *Pelswick.* (Series; Cartoon; CBS; 2002–2003). Pelswick Eggert is a 13-year-old boy who yearns to live a normal life despite the fact that he is wheelchair bound (how he came to be disabled is not revealed). Pelswick feels degraded when people take pity on him and stories follow his efforts to live as normal a life as possible despite his handicap. Ace and Goon are Pelswick's friends; Julie is the girl on whom Pelswick has a crush; Kate and Bobby are Pelswick's siblings; Quentin is Pelswick's father (his mother, Marilyn is mentioned but does not appear); Gram Gram is Pelswick's grandmother; Boyd is the school bully.

Voice Cast: Robert Tinkler *(Pelswick Eggert)*; Phil Guerrero *(Ace Nakamra)*; Peter Oldring *(Goon Gunderson)*; Julie Lemieux *(Julie Smockford)*; Kim Kuhteubl *(Sandra Scottle)*; Tracey Moore *(Kate Eggert)*; Tony Rosato *(Quentin Pelswick)*; Ellen Ray Hennessy *(Gram Gram Priscilla)*; Chuck Campbell *(Boyd Scolarzo)*.

7183   *Pen 'n' Inc.* (Pilot; Comedy; CBS; Aug. 15, 1981). Alan Ozley is an artist for the Essex, Connecticut, *Register*, a conservative small-town newspaper, who dreams of becoming the political cartoonist. The imaginative program combines live action with animation as Alan's thoughts and fantasies come to vivid life for him (and the viewer) through the use of animation. Other regulars are Debbie, T.W.'s daughter; Gretchen, Alan's landlady; Raymond, the layout editor; and Dexter, the copy editor.

Cast: Matt McCoy *(Alan Ozley)*; Brianne Leary *(Debbie Winson)*; Peter Hobbs *(T.W. Winson)*; Andra Akers *(Gretchen Vanderwyck)*; Charles Thomas Murphy *(Raymond Babbitt)*; Doug Cox *(Dexter Budd)*.

7184   *The Pendulum.* (Series; Anthology; Syn.; 1956). John Bentley hosts the syndicated series title for sixty-five episodes of *The Vise.*

7185   *Penelope Beware!* (Pilot; Comedy; Unaired; Produced for CBS in 1966). Fidos Porter was a "kind" man (he would kick the dog each morning before his coffee and look forward to thunderstorms hoping to see a bird get hit by lightning). His servants (Lucretia, the housekeeper; Boris, the cook; Fellini, the chauffeur; and Igor, the butler) are even more despicable; the four worst people he has ever known — but people he has promised everything to in his will. Following Mr. Porter's death, a will instructs that all of Porter's assets be given to "the sweetest, most kind person on earth" — an orphan he found named Penelope Brown. However, to inherit the money, Penelope must live in the house (the Old Porter Mansion) with the servants for five years. If, however, Penelope should die under normal circumstances before the five years are up, the servants will inherit the Porter fortune. The proposal was to follow a rather naive Penelope's efforts to distribute the Porter money to the needy — against the wishes of the servants — who seek a way to kill her naturally so they can inherit the fortune. Janet is Penelope's guardian.

Cast: Ann Elder *(Penelope Brown)*; Nina Foch *(Lucretia)*; Iggie Wolfington *(Boris)*; Severn Darden *(Igor)*; Johnny Haymer *(Fellini)*; Emmaline Henry *(Janet Peabody)*.

7186   *The Penguins of Madagascar.* (Series; Cartoon; Nick; 2008–2009). Skipper, Kowalski, Private and Rico are four penguins that reside at the Central Park Zoo in New York City. The penguins are secret agents and perform undercover missions to battle evil. While living at the zoo provides them with the perfect cover, they find their secret threatened by Julian, the self-proclaimed king of the Lemurs, as he seeks to become the ruler of the zoo animals (Maurice and Mort assist him). Stories follow the penguins as they not only perform missions but seek to stop Julian from becoming the zoo's supreme leader. Adapted from the films *The Penguins of Madagascar* and *Madagascar: Escape to Africa.*

Voice Cast: Tom McGrath *(Skipper)*; Jeff Bennett *(Kowalski)*; James Patrick Stuart *(Private)*; John Di Maggio *(Rico)*; Danny Jacobs *(Julian)*; Kevin Michael Richardson *(Maurice)*; Andy Richter *(Mort)*.

7187   *Penn and Teller: BS.* (Series; Reality; Showtime; 2003–). Magicians Penn and Teller take to the airwaves to expose services, products or ideas that are just foolish but sucker people into them. Each program is devoted to a specific topic, and using humor Penn and Teller try to expose the reasons why some things are just, in polite terms, hogwash.

7188   *Pennies from Heaven.* (Series; Fantasy; PBS; 1979). England during the 1930s is the setting. Dramatic action is combined with period songs to chronicle the travels of Arthur Parker, a sheet-music salesman who fantasizes about the songs he sells. Janet is his wife; Eileen is his mistress.

Cast: Bob Hoskins *(Arthur Parker)*; Gemma Craven *(Janet Parker)*; Cheryl Campbell *(Eileen)*; Kenneth Colley *(The Accordion Man)*.

7189   *Penny to a Million.* (Series; Game; ABC; 1955). Two teams compete, each composed of five members. Through a series of general-knowledge question and answer rounds, eight of the ten players are eliminated (by an incorrect response). The remaining two players compete in a spelling bee wherein they receive one penny doubled to a possible million ($10,000) for each word they spell correctly. The surviving player receives what money he has won, returns the following week, competes again in the question-and-answer session, and if successful again, competes in the spelling bee to increase the money he has already won.

Host: Bill Goodwin.

7190   *Pensacola: Wings of Gold.* (Series; Drama; Syn.; 1997–2000). The Sea Dragons is a four-person unit of jet fighter pilots. In season one, William Kelly, a lieutenant colonel, headed the group. He was divorced and was struggling to reestablish ties with his estranged teenage daughter, Janine. His team consisted of Wendell "Cypher" McCray, Annalisa "Stinger" Lindstrom, Robert "Chaser" Griffin and A.J. "Buddha" Conaway. Colonel Rebecca Hodges was Williams's superior.

In the second season, Janine was sent off to college and William became the head of a unit that trains fighter pilots. The students were Tucker "Spoon" Henry III, Alexandra "Ice" Jensen and Kate Anderson. Major McArthur "Hammer" Lewis, Jr., was William's superior. Abigail "Mad Dog" Holley (a student) joined the cast in the final season.

Cast: James Brolin *(Lt. Col. William Kelly)*; Kristanna Loken *(Janine Kelly)*; Rodney Van Johnson *(Lt. Wendell McCray)*; Kathryn

Morris (*Lt. Annalisa Lindstrom*); Rodney Rowland (*Lt. Robert Griffin*); Salvatore Xuereb (*Lt. A.J. Conaway*); Kenny Johnson (*Lt. Butch Barnes*); Sandra Hess (*Alexandra Jensen*); Barbara Niven (*Kate Anderson*); Brynn Thayer (*Col. Rebecca Hodges*); Michael Trucco (*Tucker Henry III*); Bobby Hosea (*Maj. McArthur Lewis, Jr.*); Felicity Waterman (*Abigail Holley*).

7191   *Pentagon U.S.A.* (Series; Drama; CBS; 1953). Factual dramatizations based on the files of the United States Army, Criminal Investigation Division. Premiered as *Pentagon Confidential* but changed to *Pentagon U.S.A.* on its second telecast.

Cast: Addison Richards (*Criminal Investigation Division Colonel*); Gene Lyons (*Police Detective*); Edward Binns (*Army Investigator*); Larry Fletcher (*Army Investigator*).

7192   *Penthouse Sonata.* (Series; Variety; ABC; 1949). Singer June Browne, backed by the Fine Arts Quartet, host and performs in a short lived (two episode) program deigned to bring light classical music to television. Aired on June 19 and 26, 1949.

7193   *People.* (Pilot; Reality; ABC; Dec. 15, 1957). Interviews with the people "The Man" (host) meets while walking on the street (in Los Angeles in the pilot).

Host: Ben Alexander.

7194   *People.* (Series; Variety; CBS; 1978). An adaptation of *People* magazine to television: celebrity profiles and interviews.

Host: Phyllis George. **Music:** Tony Romeo.

7195   *People Are Funny.* (Series; Game; NBC; 1946–1984). A television adaptation of the radio program wherein various members of the studio audience perform stunts for cash and/or merchandise prizes. Three versions appeared:

1. *People Are Funny* (NBC Pilot, June 11, 1946). **Host:** Art Linkletter. **Announcer:** Ed Herlihy.
2. *People Are Funny* (NBC, 1954–1961). **Host:** Art Linkletter. **Announcer:** Pat McGeehan.
3. *People Are Funny* (NBC, 1984). **Host:** Flip Wilson. **Announcer:** Dick Tufeld.

7196   *People Do the Craziest Things.* (Series; Reality; ABC; 1984). The program, which borrows its format from *Candid Camera* and *People Are Funny*, challenges people to perform outlandish stunts in return for cash. Cancelled after two episodes.

Host: Bert Convy.

7197   *People Like Us.* (Pilot; Drama; NBC; April 19, 1976). Events in the day-to-day lives of the Allmans, a contemporary American family, and their struggles to retain their close ties amid economic instability and a changing moral climate. The regulars are: Davy, the father, a steelworker; Irene, his wife; Sharon and Lennie, their children; and Anna, Davy's mother.

Cast: Eugene Roche (*Davy Allman*); Katherine Helmond (*Irene Allman*); Eileen McDonough (*Sharon Allman*); Grant Goodeve (*Lennie Allman*); Irene Tedrow (*Anna Allman*).

7198   *People Magazine on TV.* (Pilot; Magazine; CBS; Aug. 4 and Nov. 14, 1988; Jan. 27, 1989). A three pilot attempt at a video edition of the weekly magazine that was to report on people in all walks of life.

Hosts: Sandy Hill (*First Pilot*); Jane Wallace (*Pilots 2 and 3*). **Correspondents:** David Andelman, Mike Marley, Martha Quinn.

7199   *The People Next Door.* (Series; Comedy; CBS; 1989).

Walter Kellogg is a cartoonist with a unique ability to make things appear just by imagining them. He lives in the town of Covington (whose major industry is eggs) and is married to Abigail MacIntyre, his second wife, a psychologist. Walter is also the father of Aurora and Matthew, the children he had with his late first wife. Walter is the creator of the comic strip "The People Next Door." As Walter draws his strips, the audience sees his ideas come to life. Other regulars are Sissy, Abigail's neurotic sister (the owner of a beauty shop called Sissy's Hot Rollers) and Truman Phipps, the mailman.

Cast: Jeffrey Jones (*Walter Kellogg*); Mary Gross (*Abigail MacIntyre*); Jaclyn Bernstein (*Aurora Kellogg*); Chance Quinn (*Matthew Kellogg*); Christina Pickles (*Sissy MacIntyre*); Leslie Jordan (*Truman Phipps*).

7200   *People to People.* (Pilot; Interview; ABC; Jan. 9 to 13, 1984). A five-part proposal for a daily series of interviews with people from all walks of life.

Host: Rona Barrett.

7201   *People Will Talk.* (Series; Game; NBC; 1963). A yes or no type of question is read to fifteen selected members of the studio audience. Each member locks in their choice. Each of the two contestants who compete chooses a player and has to predict how that person answered the question. Each correct guess awards the player one point. The player with the highest score is the winner and receives merchandise prizes.

Host: Dennis James.

7202   *The People's Choice.* (Series; Comedy; CBS; 1955–1958). New City, California, is a city built in a hurry. It is famous for its lettuce crops, and it is near Los Angeles. Some people have streetlights, some have no sewers, some have terrible roads. Socrates ("Sock") Miller and his aunt, Augusta "Gus" Bennett, live in a trailer camp in New City's Paradise Park. Sock, who graduated from Cornell University (Phi Beta Kappa), was raised by his aunt following his parents' deaths when he was three years old. He served a hitch in Korea (as a marine sergeant) and is now an ornithologist for the government's Bureau of Fish and Wildlife. His job is to "follow the birds" (he files reports on migratory birds, as their flights foretell climatic conditions and aid farmers when planting crops). When he was first introduced, Sock's assignment was to track the Yellow Necked Nuthatch. There is one other resident living with Sock—his basset hound, Cleo. Cleo was six months old when Sock, a corporal at the time, won her in a crap game. Cleo, whose thoughts can be heard by voice over dubbing, is glad that Sock can't talk for her—"If he could, I'd be off the show."

One day Sock befriends Amanda ("Mandy") Peoples, the pretty daughter of New City's mayor, John Peoples, when she becomes stranded on a country road and he stops to fix her flat tire. It's a love at first sight. When Mandy discovers that Sock is being transferred to Ohio (to find out why the Rose Breasted Grosbeak is laying smaller eggs this season), she devises a plan to keep him in town (and with her).

Mandy feels that Sock is the right man to fill a city council vacancy and encourages him to run. Sock does and is elected 5th District councilman (Sock received special permission from the Department of Fish and Wildlife, Western Division, to remain in New City until his term of office is completed.)

Two marriages resulted. Aunt Gus married Mayor Peoples and Sock married Mandy in 1957. Shortly after his marriage, Sock applies for a position as a lawyer with Barker Amalgamated in New York City. They hire Sock—but as the sales manager for Barkerville, a housing development with 294 houses for sale "20 miles from nowhere." Houses sell for $15,995, and Sock and Mandy live rent free in the model house (number 119).

Hexley ("Hex") Rollo is a friend of Sock's from childhood who now resides in New City.

Pierre Quincy is Sock's friend, an eccentric painter. Sock calls him the "Michelangelo of Paradise Trailer Park."

Cast: Jackie Cooper (*Sock Miller*); Patricia Breslin (*Mandy Peoples*); Margaret Irving (*Gus Bennett*); Paul Maxey (*John Peoples*); Dick Wesson (*Rollo*); Leonid Kinsley (*Pierre*); Mary Jane Croft (*Voice of Cleo*).

7203   The People's Court. (Series; Reality; Syn.; 1981–1993; 1997–). Real people fighting real legal battles before a real judge in a California Municipal Court. Plaintiffs and defendants are seen presenting their legal issues from plea to final verdict. The program, with Judge Joseph Wapner was based in California. When the series was revised for syndication (1997) with former New York Mayor Ed Koch as the judge, it was videotaped in New York City and switched from a 30-minute to a 60-minute format.

Judges: Joseph A. Wapner, Ed Koch, Jerry Sheindlin, Marilyn Milian. **Bailiff:** Rusty Burrell, Joseph Ann Longobardi, Douglas MacIntosh. **Interviewer:** Curt Chaplin, Doug Llewellyn. **Host:** Harvey Levin. **Studio Anchor:** Carol Martin.

7204   The People's Court of Small Claims. (Series; Drama; Syn.; 1958). The program features reenactments of actual small-claims court hearings.

Judge: Orrin B. Evans.

7205   Pepper Ann. (Series; Cartoon; ABC; 1997–2000). Pepper Ann Pearson, a twelve-year-old girl who has just started middle school in the town of Hazelnut, yearns to be cool. Unfortunately, Pepper Ann is awkward and somewhat of a nerd — and her seemingly strange behavior makes her being cool highly unlikely. But that does not discourage our heroine and stories follow Pepper Ann as she strives to become one of the cool kids in school. Nicky Little and Milo Kamalani are Pepper Ann's best friends. Nicky is a perfectionist (or tries to be) and Milo appears to be weird as his hobby (art) reflects his philosophical approach to life. Craig is a year older than Pepper Ann and the coolest kid at Hazelnut Middle School. Trinket is the spoiled, rich girl at school. Other characters are twins Tessa and Vanessa (the editor's of the school's newspaper, *Hazel Nuts 'n' Bolts*); Lydia is Pepper Ann's single mother; Moose (real name Margaret Rose) has a boy's nickname but is actually Pepper Ann's tomboy sister. Dieter (who is German and constantly eats), Stuart (the class geek) and Gwen (the blonde on whom Milo has a crush) are other students.

Voice Cast: Kathleen Wilhoite (*Pepper Ann Pearson*); Clea Lewis (*Nicky Little*); Danny Cooksey (*Milo Kamalini*); April Winchell (*Lydia Pearson*); Pamela Adlon (*Moose Pearson*); Jenna Von Oy (*Trinket St. Blaire*); Kimmy Robertson (*Gwen Mezzrow*); Jeff Bennett (*Dieter Liederhosen*); Luke Perry (*Stuart Walldinger*); Don Adams (*Principal Herbert Hickey*); April Winchell (*Grandma Pearson*); Jeff Bennett (*Craig Bean*).

7206   Pepper Dennis. (Series; Comedy-Drama; WB; 2006). Pepper Dennis, an on-the-air reporter for WEIE-TV, Channel 4 in Chicago, is called "WEIE's Number One Reporter." She is sweet and provocative and looking for a man who is her intellectual equal.

Pepper's real name is Patricia "Patty" Dinkle. From as early as she can remember, Patty wanted to become a newscaster. This became a strong ambition after she met her hero, Walter Cronkite, as a teenager. She attended Northwestern University and upon graduation changed her name to the more broadcast friendly Pepper Dennis. Pepper got her first big break when she substituted for a reporter who took a week off to get a chin implant. Pepper learned the business

from the show's producer, Jack Bell. Even when Pepper is off from work, she is on duty; she can't resist a story.

Pepper lives with her divorced sister, Kathy (the receptionist at WEIE). Stories follow Pepper's life — at home and at work where she is somewhat mishap prone as she goes about gathering and reporting stories hoping to one day become the evening news program anchor. Kimmy is Pepper's friend, a makeup artist; Chick is her in-the-field cameraman; Charlie Babcock is the news anchorman; Blanca Martinez is the weathergirl (who also hosts *Get Up Chicago*, a morning show); Garfield is Pepper's sound man.

When Jack Bell resigns to enjoy a carefree life in the Caribbean, he is replaced by Les Gay, the news director who wants sensationalized stories (as opposed to Jack's hard news stories).

Cast: Rebecca Romijn (*Pepper Dennis*); Brooke Burns (*Kathy Dinkle-Williams*); Josh Hopkins (*Charlie Babcock*); Brett Cullen (*Jack Bell*); Lindsay Price (*Kimmy*); Alexandra Barreto (*Blanca Martinez*); Rider Strong (*Chick Durka*); Frederick Koehler (*Les Gay*); Pooch Hall (*Garfield*).

7207   Peppermint Rose. (Pilot; Cartoon; Fox; Nov. 26, 1992). In the mystical land of Peppermint Rose all beauty comes from a magical flower called the Peppermint Rose. One day a family of monsters (Tubber, Hubber and Blubber) from the gloomy kingdom of Bugoona, steal the Peppermint Rose as a gift for their queen, Betalia "an incredibly ugly beetle who intends to eat it." While searching the world for a special helper, the good wizard of Peppermint Rose, Diminutive, finds Rose Richards and her friends, Daisy, Lilly and Violet — all named after flowers and all kind-hearted. The girls are magically transported to Peppermint Rose and asked to help. With the assistance of Peddle Puff, Diminutive's helper, the girls save Peppermint Rose from Betalia, but make a bitter enemy of her as she is determined to get back the rose. Acting on orders from the Wisdom of Lunar Light, the source of all wizards wisdom, Diminutive bestows upon the girls the names Peppermint Rose, Vanilla Daisy, Lemondrop Lilly and Merrymint Violet and appoints them as guardians of the special rose. The proposal was to relate the girls' efforts to protect Peppermint Rose from the evil Betalia.

Voices: Beau Berdahl, John Greenshaw, Carl Hammond, Larry Kenny, Michael Mulhern, Romeo Muller, Eden Riegel, Donna Vivino, Wendy Yondorf.

7208   Pepsi-Cola Playhouse. (Series; Anthology; ABC; 1953–1955). Pepsi-Cola sponsored program of live and filmed dramas featuring such stars as Jean Byron, Nancy Gates, Marguerite Chapman, Craig Stevens, Lloyd Corrigan, Jack Kelly, Carolyn Jones, Claude Akins, Karen Sharpe, Rick Jason, Sally Brophy, Lee Marvin, Brian Keith, Hayden Rorke and John Hoyt.

Host: Arlene Dahl, Anita Colby, Polly Bergen.

7209   Perfect Hair Forever. (Series; Cartoon; Adult Swim; 2005). A spoof of Japanese animated series (Anime) as seen through the adventures of Gerald, a young boy who, for unknown reasons, is starting to lose his hair. With the help of Rod, the Anime God and his mentor, Uncle Grandfather, Gerald begins a quest to find a cure called Perfect Hair Forever.

Voice Cast: Kim Manning (*Gerald*); Dave Willis (*Uncle Grandfather*); H. Jon Benjamin (*Twisty*); Dave Willis (*Coffio*).

7210   A Perfect Life. (Pilot; Comedy; UPN; Dec. 26, 1995). Dylan Forrester is a twenty something yuppie enjoying the perfect life. He works in the new products division of a computer software company and buys what he wants. Suddenly his company is dissolved and he is left out of work. Dylan bought his own apartment, a new car and various other luxury items and now must find a way to pay for them. The job he wants is not out there and he must take whatever comes along. Other regulars are Timber Lake, his neighbor, a lawyer with the firm of Benton, Batten and Counter (she hates her life, her job and her co-workers); and Jonas and Steve, Dylan's friends.

Cast: Tim Conlon *(Dylan Forrester)*; Jensen Daggett *(Timber Lake)*; Saverio Guerra *(Jonas)*; Lenny Venito *(Steve)*.

7211   The Perfect Match. (Series; Game; Syn.; 1967). Two three-member teams, the men vs. the women, compete in a game wherein the women must discover which male a computer has matched her with and vice versa. Three rounds are played in which the six players question each other about romantic situations and problems. At the end of the third round, each female secretly chooses the male she feels is best suited for her and vice versa. Players who match each other receive $50. The computer choices, which are validated by the Computer Match Company, are revealed. Couples who paired themselves as did the computer have a perfect match and each receive $200.

Program Open: "These three young men have been matched by a computer with these three young ladies. Are you able to tell who has been matched with whom. Welcome to *The Perfect Match*, the game where contestants attempt to discover who the IBM 360 computer has selected as their perfect match. And now here's the perfect man to help us all find the perfect match, Dick Enberg."

Host: Dick Enberg.

7212   Perfect Match: New York. (Series; Reality; ABC; 2003). Matchmaking program in which two people, believed to be the perfect match for each other are put to the test in a series of challenges to see if they are truly a perfect couple.

Host: Bob Goen. **Announcer:** Randy West.

7213   Perfect Strangers. (Series; Comedy; ABC; 1986–1992). In the Mediterranean there exists a small sheep herding island called Mypos. When Balki Bartokomous discovers that he has an American cousin named Larry Appleton who is one-sixty-fourth Myposian, he sets out to find him. His search ends in Chicago when he finds Larry Appleton, a clerk at the Ritz Discount Store. Cousin Larry, as Balki calls him, allows Balki to live with him (the Caldwell Hotel at 627 Lincoln Boulevard) and stories relate Balki's efforts to adjust to the American way of life.

Donald ("Twinkie") Twinkacetti is the gruff owner of the Ritz Discount Store. Edwina is his wife; Marie and Donnie are their children.

Second season episodes find Larry and Balki working for a newspaper (the Chicago *Chronicle*); Larry as an assistant editor; Balki as a mailroom clerk. Larry now has a girlfriend named Jennifer Lyons, and Balki dates her roommate, Mary Anne Spencer. Lydia Markham, a columnist ("Dear Lydia"), also hosts the television series *Lydia Live*. Harriette is a security guard at the paper (her character was spun off into the series *Family Matters*).

Larry and Jennifer married in the episode of Sept. 27, 1991, and set up housekeeping on Elm Street — in a home they find they cannot afford. With three bedrooms and two and one half baths, they solve their money problems by renting the other bedrooms to Balki and Mary Anne. On April 18, 1992, Balki and Mary Anne married. Balki also draws the comic "Dimitri's World" (about a cuddly little sheep) for the *Chronicle*. In the unaired pilot version, Louie Anderson played Cousin Larry.

Jennifer and Mary Anne have been friends since they were eight years old. They are both stewardesses for an unnamed airline. Mary Anne thinks that living with Jennifer is like living with a Barbie doll (she is too neat and perfect). Jennifer feels that Mary Anne is sloppy

and hates it when she hogs the bathroom ("It takes her three hours to put on her makeup"). David Pomerantz sings the theme, "Nothing's Gonna Stop Me Now."

Cast: Mark Linn-Baker *(Larry Appleton)*; Bronson Pinchot *(Balki Bartokomous)*; Melanie Wilson *(Jennifer Lyons)*; Rebeca Arthur *(Mary Anne Spencer)*; Ernie Sabella *(Donald "Twinkie" Twinkacetti)*; Jo Marie Payton *(Harriette Baines Winslow)*; Belita Moreno *(Edwina Twinkacetti)*; Erica Gayle *(Marie Twinkacetti)*; Matthew Licht *(Donnie Twinkacetti)*; Belita Moreno *(Lydia Markham)*.

7214   Performing As…. (Series; Reality; Fox; 2003). Ordinary people who idolize a famous singer receive a makeover to appear as that person. They perform (as their idol) and are judged by how they look, sound and move. The one "singer" who has all the attributes of the person he or she is impersonating wins. Todd Newton hosts; Damon Elliot and Karen Glauber are the judges.

7215   The Perils of Pauline. (Pilot; Comedy; Unaired; Produced in 1967). George is one of the world's wealthiest men. Pauline is a beautiful orphan he met as a child in an orphanage and fell in love with her promising one day to come back for her when he made his millions. The years past and George made his money, but the unforeseen happened — Pauline was adopted and her whereabouts unknown. A distressed George begins a world wide search to find his Pauline and the unsold series was to chart his efforts, most of which are foiled by Stan Martin, a love-starved great white hunter, who also wants Pauline, a damsel who is always in perpetual danger, for himself. When a series could not be sold to television, additional footage was shot and it was released theatrically. Pat Bone sings the theme, "Where Are You My Pretty Pauline?"

Cast: Pamela Austin *(Pauline)*; Pat Boone *(George)*; Hamilton Camp *(Thorpe; George's aide)*; Terry-Thomas *(Stan Martin)*.

7216   The Perils of Penelope Pitstop. (Series; Cartoon; CBS; 1969–1971). Becoming the legal guardian of Penelope Pitstop, a young and vulnerable female racecar driver, Sylvester Sneekly dons the guise of the Hooded Claw and intends to acquire her wealth by killing her. Traveling around the world in her car, *The Compact Pussycat*, Penelope and her protectors, the Ant Hill Mob, struggle to foil the Hooded Claw's sinister efforts.

After Penelope is seen yelling, "Help! Help!" and announcer opens the show: "*The Perils of Penelope Pitstop* starring the Ant Hill Mob, their car Chugaboom and that hated villain, the Hooded Claw. Penelope Pitstop, heiress to a vast fortune, is in perpetual peril from her fortune-seeking guardian, Sylvester Sneekley. But unknown to her, he is really the Hooded Claw. Foiling his fiendish plots are Penelope's protectors, the Ant Hill Mob."

Voice Cast: Janet Waldo *(Penelope Pitstop)*; Paul Lynde *(Sylvester Sneekly)*; Paul Winchell *(Claude/Softy)*; Don Messick *(Zippy/Pockets/Dum Dum/Snoozy)*; **Announcer:** Gary Owens.

7217   The Perkins Family. (Series; Drama; PBS; 1986). Incidents in the daily lives of the Perkins, an American family of five. All roles are played by children and are ad-libbed.

Cast: Betsy Bleil *(Elaine Perkins)*; Stapp Beaton *(Jonathan Perkins)*; Chandra Wilson *(Tracy Perkins)*; Veronica Rosas *(Chris Perkins)*; Wiley Wiggins *(Alex Perkins)*.

7218   The Perry Como Show. (Series; Variety; CBS; NBC; 1950; 1955). Singer Perry Como hosts an informal program of music and songs. See also *The Chesterfield Supper Club*. Two versions appeared:

1. The Perry Como Show (CBS, 1950–55). **Host:** Perry Como. **Regulars:** Geri Fontaine, Margie Fontaine, Bea Fontaine, The Ray

Charles Singers. **Announcer:** Joel Aldred, Durward Kirby, Dick Stark. **Orchestra:** Mitchell Ayres.

2. *The Perry Como Show* (NBC, 1955–59). **Host:** Perry Como. **Regulars:** Geri Fontaine, Margie Fontaine, Bea Fontaine, Mindy Carson, Don Adams, Joey Heatherton, Kaye Ballard, Milt Kamen, Sandy Stewart, The Ray Charles Singers, The Louis Da Pron Dancers. **Announcer:** Ed Herlihy, Frank Gallop. **Orchestra:** Mitchell Ayres.

7219   *Perry Mason.* (Series; Crime Drama; CBS; 1957–1966). Perry Mason is a brilliant criminal attorney working out of Los Angeles. His retainer fees range from $1,000 to $5,000 and he works by the books — even when the odds are stacked up against his client. Perry refuses to plea bargain because he believes risking the life of his client is better than ruining it with a suspicious way out or a reduced sentence. While Perry is also competent as a detective, it is in the courtroom where his abilities become evident. He is shrewd and never lets it be known that at times he did not have sufficient evidence to defend a client (he always waits for that last minute piece of evidence to free a client).

Della Street is Perry's efficient, loyal secretary. She occasionally assists Perry in the field (often helps by donning various disguises). Paul Drake is Perry's investigator; Hamilton Burger is the prosecuting attorney; Gertie Lade is Perry's receptionist; Margo is Drake's secretary; David Gideon is Perry's associate (later episodes) and Perry works with the following police officials: Lt. Arthur Tragg, Lt. Steve Drumm; Sergeant Brice and Lt. Andy Anderson. Based on characters created by Erle Stanley Gardner; 245 episodes were filmed (the last one in color).

Cast: Raymond Burr *(Perry Mason)*; Barbara Hale *(Della Street)*; William Hopper *(Paul Drake)*; Ray Collins *(Lt. Arthur Tragg)*; William Talman *(Hamilton Burger)*; Richard Anderson *(Lt. Steve Drumm)*; Connie Cezon *(Gertie Lade)*; Paul Courtland *(Margo)*; Karl Held *(David Gideon)*; Lee Miller *(Sgt. Brice)*; Wesley Lau *(Lt. Andy Anderson)*.

7220   *Perry Presents.* (Series; Variety; NBC; 1959). Singers Jaye P. Morgan, Teresa Brewer and Tony Bennett host a program of music and songs that replaced *The Perry Como Show* for the summer of 1959.

Host: Jaye P. Morgan, Teresa Brewer, Tony Bennett. **Regulars:** Hans Conried, The Four Lads, The Modernaires, The Louis Da Pron Dancers, The Mel Pahl Chorus. **Announcer:** Ed Herlihy. **Orchestra:** Mitchell Ayres, Jimmy Lytell.

7221   *Person to Person.* (Series; Interview; CBS; 1953–1961). The host, seated in a studio, interviews prominent people from their homes via remote pickup. Aired from Oct. 2, 1953 to July 2, 1959; and June 23, 1961 to Sept. 16, 1961.

Host: Edward R. Murrow (1953–59), Charles Collingwood (1961). **Announcer:** Bob Dixon.

7222   *Personal and Confidential.* (Pilot; Magazine; NBC; July 1 to 5, 1983). A five-part proposal for a daily program of celebrity interviews, gossip, beauty advice and health tips.

Hosts: Christine Belford, Ruth Batchelor, Steve Edwards, Kathy Cronkite.

7223   *Personal and Confidential.* (Pilot; Drama; Unaired; Produced in 1988). Cyndy Garvey oversees a program of dramatizations based on letters written by people seeking help with their problems.

7224   *Personal Appearance.* (Series; Anthology; CBS; 1958).

Summer program of dramas that were originally broadcast on other filmed anthology series.

7225   *Personal Appearance Theater.* (Series; Anthology; ABC; 1951-1952). Weekly, half-hour program that combines comedy, mystery and drama presentations.

7226   *Personality.* (Series; Game; NBC; 1967–1969). Three celebrities compete in a game wherein they have to determine how well they know each other, as well as themselves. Three rounds are played which tests each celebrity's knowledge of himself and his colleagues (basically through a series of questions and answers). When a celebrity scores a correct answer he wins $25, which is awarded to the home viewer he represents (chosen via a post card selection).

Program Open: "Today, Corbett Monica, Mimi Hines and Phil Ford play *Personality* with our special guest star Glen Ford. And now here is our host, Larry Blyden."

Host: Larry Blyden. **Announcer:** Jack Clark.

7227   *Personality Puzzle.* (Series; Game; ABC; 1953). The object calls for players to guess the identities of celebrity guests via an examination of tools of the guest's trade and a series of indirect question-and-answer rounds. The player (four compete) with the most correct identifications is the winner and receives merchandise prizes.

Host: John Conte, Robert Alda. **Regular:** Lisa Ferraday.

7228   *Personals.* (Series; Game; CBS; 1991). The program brings people together to arrange dates and compatibility. A man or woman, placed in a chair on stage, is interviewed and asked a series of personal questions. Prior to the broadcast personal ads were placed in newspapers to acquire candidates. Video tapes were made and are screened to find three people who match the interviewed person's wants. These three people are introduced and also interviewed. The questions previously asked of the stage player are read for the three mates with two possible responses. Each possible mate must guess what the subject said. One point is scored per correct response. When one of the three possible mates acquires three points the match is made and the two are given an all-expenses paid date.

Host: Mike Dubelko. **Announcer:** Jennifer Martin. **Music:** Stormy Stacks.

7229   *Persons Unknown.* (Series; Mystery; NBC; 2010). Downtown Hotel in an apparently deserted town concealed in a mountainous area. A diverse group of strangers have been mysteriously taken from their ordinary lives and assembled here. Where they are is unknown. Escape is impossible (an invisible force field surrounds the town and prevents anyone from entering or leaving) and there appears to be no apparent connection between any of the prisoners. What each has, however, is a desire to escape and return to their everyday lives. The prisoners are constantly monitored by security cameras (although they have no idea who is watching them) and constantly threatened physically, emotionally and psychologically. The only option they have is to rely on each other for survival. The interesting but rather vague series (more questions than answers) follows the prisoners as they seek the identity of their captors, the reason for their abduction and a way out of town. The main prisoners are Janet, a young mother who runs a daycare center; Graham, a marine sergeant; Charlie, a banker, Moria, a teacher's counselor; Victoria, a party girl; and Joe, a man with a mysterious and unknown past. Their only outside hope appears to be Mark Renbe, a San Francisco investigative reporter who begins looking into Janet's disappearance but becomes mystified by strange, baffling clues that make his job all that more difficult.

Cast: Daisy Betts *(Janet Cooper)*; Tina Holmes *(Moria Doherty)*;

Alan Ruck (*Charlie Morse*); Chadwick Boseman (*Graham McNair*); Kate Lang Johnson (*Tori Fairchild*); Jason Wiles (*Joe Tucker*); Sean O'Bryan (*Bill Blackman*); Kandyse McClure (*Erika Taylor*); Gerald Kyd (*Mark Renbe*); Lola Glaudini (*Kat Damatto*).

7230   *Perspective on Greatness.* (Series; Documentary; Syn.; 1961). Film clips and interviews are used to recall incidents in the lives of celebrated individuals.

Host-Narrator: Pat O'Brien, Celeste Holm, Joan Fontaine.

7231   *The Persuaders.* (Series; Adventure; ABC; 1971–1972). Judge Fulton is a man dedicated to upholding the law. He was a judge for 15 years, and during that time he did his best to defend the innocent and punish the guilty: "The guilty ones that came to court, that is. One of the anomalies of the law is that in protecting the innocent, the guilty go free too. Since my retirement, I've done my best to redress that in my small private way. Now I have time to think, to study, to search for loopholes others might have overlooked." He needs someone to champion his cause. His choice: Brett Sinclair and Danny Wilde, a titled British Lord, and an American millionaire. Brett and Danny met at a bar in France and were arrested for fighting when they disagreed on how many olives a drink (a Creole Scream) should have. The judge learned of their arrest and offered them a choice: three months in jail or help him. "You are men with immense quality and potential and you fight—you fight over an olive. You are both docile and foolish and a useless waste of humanity. But you like to fight. All right, I'll give you a fight. I'll either make use of you or see that you are put away for three months." When playboys Danny and Brett realize that it also means 90 nights, they agree to help the judge. Stories relate the globe-trotting exploits of Brett and Danny as they use their unique skills to help Judge Fulton bring criminals to justice.

Lord Brett Sinclair was "born with a silver spoon in his mouth and all he does is lick the jam from it." Sinclair was once a proud and noble name that stood for justice and defended freedom—but that was before immense wealth changed it. Brett is a first class athlete, a connoisseur of the arts and a gourmet with a lusty taste in wine and women.

Danny Wilde is a multimillionaire who made and lost several fortunes. Making money has become so easy for him that he doesn't really bother anymore. But that wasn't always the case. He was born in the Bronx and lived in one of its poorest sections. His optimism, courage and a sense of humor pushed him to the top of the financial heap. He has a remarkable talent, but he just wastes it. "You just drift around the world gambling and womanizing. You were a nothing who became something. You are a nothing again," says Fulton. The judge compares Brett and Danny to chemicals: "Take two relatively harmless compounds like nitro and glycerin. Mix them together and you have a very potent combination. Handle it carelessly and it can blow your head off. Nitro and glycerin—and I light the fuse."

Cast: Roger Moore (*Brett Sinclair*); Tony Curtis (*Danny Wilde*); Laurence Naismith (*Judge Fulton*); George Merritt (*Chivers; Brett's butler*).

7232   *Pet Alien.* (Series; Cartoon; Cartoon Network; 2005). Tommy Cadle is a 13-year-old boy with five very unusual companions: aliens from the planet Conforma who have crash landed on Earth (in the town of DeSpray Bay) and taken refuge in the local lighthouse. Stories follow Tommy and the mishaps he encounters with his alien friends (Dinko, Gumpers, Swanky, Flip and Scruffy). The aliens do not wear disguises and it is only Tommy who recognizes them as such (other humans apparently can't tell). Gabby is the girl who fancies Tommy (although he des not feel the same way); Granville DeSpray is a descendant of the town founders; Clinton Jefferson III is the boy

who enjoys annoying Tommy; Melba Manners is the girl who, due to her shrill and loud voice, gets Tommy to do her bidding; Cap'm Spangley runs the local taffy shop.

Voice Cast: Charlie Schlatter (*Tommy/Clinton*); Charles Adler (*Dinko/Flip*); Candi Milo (*Gabby/Melba*); Jess Hamell (*Gumpers and Swanky*).

7233   *The Pet Set.* (Series; Discussion; Syn.; 1971). A program of pet care, ecology and wildlife preservation with actress Betty White as the host.

Hostess: Betty White. **Regulars:** Ralph Helfer, Dare Miller. **Announcer:** Allen Ludden.

7234   *Pete and Gladys.* (Series; Comedy; CBS; 1960–1962). Peter Porter, a salesman for the Springer, Slocum and Klever Insurance Company in Los Angeles, and Gladys Hooper, a scatterbrained secretary, fell in love, eloped and married nine years earlier (1951) in the small town of Colbyville; they later set up housekeeping in Westwood, California.

Gladys is very pretty, but never uses her looks to achieve something. She doesn't mean to cause problems for Pete, but things just happen and, rather than asking for Pete's help, she tries to solve problems on her own. Naturally, what can go wrong does and Pete eventually becomes involved and most often resolves the situation. Pete puts up with all of Gladys's harebrained antics because "I've gotten used to her; I'm addicted to her."

"When strange things are looking to happen, somebody gives them Gladys's address," says Janet Colton, Gladys's friend and neighbor. Gladys is the entertainment chair of the Junior Matron's League of the Children's Hospital and is a member of the Westwood Bowling League with friends Janet and Hilda Crocker.

Barry Slocum is Pete's boss; Laura is his wife; Bruce is Gladys's nephew; Peggy and Ernie Briggs are the Porter's friends; George is Janet's husband; Paul is Peter's uncle. A spin off from *December Bride*, in which Gladys was never seen but was often talked about.

Program Open: "Yes, it's *Pete and Gladys*... starring Harry Morgan and Cara Williams.... Brought to you by Carnation Evaporated Milk, the milk from contented cows and by Carnation Instant Non Fat Dry Milk, the magic crystals instant."

Cast: Harry Morgan (*Peter Porter*); Cara Williams (*Gladys Porter*); Verna Felton (*Hilda Crocker*); Bill Hinnant (*Bruce*); Barry Kelly (*Barry Slocum*); Helen Kleeb (*Laura Slocum*); Mina Kolb (*Peggy Briggs*); Joe Mantell (*Ernie Briggs*); Alvy Moore (*Howie*); Barbara Stuart (*Alice*); Peter Leeds (*George Colton*); Shirley Mitchell (*Janet Colton*); Gale Gordon (*Paul Porter*).

7235   *Pete Kelly's Blues.* (Series; Crime Drama; NBC; 1959). "The period was called the Roaring Twenties," says Pete Kelly, a cornet player and leader of a jazz band called the Big Seven. "It was an age of jazz music, speakeasies, rum running, bathtub gin, murder, reprisal and organized disorder."

For Pete Kelly, it began in Chicago. As a kid he became fascinated with the cornet and set his goal on becoming a musician. In one episode, Pete mentions that musician Gus Trudeaux taught him how to play the cornet. They became friends but when Gus became involved with the mob, Pete left Chicago and headed for Kansas City, Missouri, the series setting. Later, Pete mentions he was a struggling musician who befriended Gus at a union meeting. However, he also befriended a piano player named Augie and he and Augie drifted to Kansas City where Pete later formed the Big Seven.

Pete lives in a small room on Grand Avenue near Washington Square. Pete would like to do nothing else then play the cornet, but that was not meant to be as trouble seems to find him no matter where he goes. While not an official private detective, Pete becomes a somewhat unofficial source of law and order when he risks his life to help people in trouble.

Pete and the Big Seven play regularly at Lupo's, a brownstone turned funeral parlor turned speakeasy at 17 Cherry Street. "It's a standard speakeasy," says Pete. "The booze is cut but the prices aren't. The beer is good and the whiskey is aged — if you get there later in the day. We play here from 10 PM to 4 AM, with a pizza break at midnight. The hours are bad, but the music suits us. There's one other thing about 17 Cherry Street and that's trouble. You can get it by the yard, the pound, wholesale and retail."

George Lupo owns the speakeasy. Savannah Brown is Pete's friend, a singer at Fat Annie's, a speakeasy on the Kansas side; Johnny Cassiano is an officer with the Kansas City Police Department. Dick Cathcart is the off screen cornet player for Pete; the Matty Matlock Combo provides music for the club scenes. Connee Boswell sings the theme "Pete Kelly's Blues." Based on the radio program of the same title.

Cast: William Reynolds (*Pete Kelly*); Phil Gordon (*George Lupo*); Connee Boswell (*Savannah Brown*); Anthony Eisley (*Johnny Cassiano*) **Band Members:** Johnny Silver, Than Wyenn, Fred Beems, Ricky Allen, Dick Cathcart.

7236   *Pete 'n' Tillie.* (Pilot; Comedy; CBS; Mar. 28, 1974). Pete is a 43-year-old school teacher; Tillie is a 39-year-old social worker who has a tendency to become involved in the personal lives of her welfare clients. After years of living alone, Pete and Tillie decide to marry and set up housekeeping in San Francisco. The proposal was to relate their efforts to adjust to marriage. Norma Jean is their housekeeper.

Cast: Cloris Leachman (*Tillie Schaefer*); Carmine Caridi (*Pete Schaefer*); Mabel Albertson (*Norma Jean Ryerson*).

7237   *The Peter and Mary Show.* (Series; Comedy; NBC; 1950-1951). The experiences of Peter and Mary, a husband and wife show business couple who entertain celebrity guests in their New Rochelle (New York) home. Claude is their friend; Mary is their house keeper.

Cast: Peter Lind Hayes (*Peter*); Mary Healy (*Mary*); Claude Stroud (*Claude*); Mary Wickes (*Mary*).

7238   *Peter Gunn.* (Series; Crime Drama; NBC, 1958–1960; ABC, 1960-1961). Peter Gunn is a former cop turned private detective who operates out of Los Angeles, California. He resides at 351 Ellis Park Road. His company, known as both Gunn Investigations and Peter Gunn's Private Detective Agency, was established on July 5, 1957.

Peter Gunn is a sophisticated, well-dressed, debonair detective. He speaks respectfully, frequents a classy hangout (Mother's, a waterfront nightclub) but, despite all his class, he has a flare for violence — whether it was with his fists or gunplay. Edie Hart, Gunn's romantic interest, is the glamorous and sophisticated singer at Mother's. In later episodes, Edie takes over the club from Mother and changes the name to Edie's. Edie resides at the Bartell Hotel (owned by a Mr. Bartell). Lieutenant Jacoby of the 13th Precinct of the L.A.P.D. Homicide Squad, is Gunn's police department contact. Babby is one of Gunn's snitches, a diminutive pool hustler; he often tells Peter to "think tall." Emmett plays the piano at Mother's; Leslie is the Edie's Club Maitre d'; Wilbur is the owner of Cooky's Coffee House, a less-desirable shop frequented by Gunn for information. Henry Mancini composed the series jazz score and theme "Peter Gunn."

In 1967, Craig Stevens recreated his role as Peter Gunn in a theatrical film called *Gunn.* Laura Devon was Edie; Edward Asner, Lieutenant Jacoby; and M.T. Marshall, Mother. On April 23, 1989,

ABC aired the TV movie *Peter Gunn.* Peter Strauss was Peter Gunn; Barbara Williams was Edie; Peter Jurasik was Lieutenant Jacoby (given the first name of Herschel); Pearl Bailey was mother; and David Rappaport played Spec, Gunn's diminutive snitch.

Cast: Craig Stevens (*Peter Gunn*); Lola Albright (*Edie Hart*); Herschel Bernardi (*Lt. Jacoby*); Hope Emerson (*Mother*); Billy Barty (*Babby*); Morris Erby (*Sgt. Lee Davis*); James Lanphier (*Leslie*); Herb Ellis (*Wilbur*); Peter Mamakos (*Lieutenant Vasquez*); Joseph Kearns (*Mr. Bartell*).

7239   *Peter Hunter, Private Eye.* (Pilot; Crime Drama; Syn.; 1948). Peter Hunter is a rugged private detective based in New York City. He is molded after feature film private detectives and the proposal was to relate his violent approach to achieving justice for his clients.

Cast: Frank Albertson (*Peter Hunter*).

7240   *The Peter Lind Hayes Show.* (Series; Variety; ABC; 1958-1959). Music and songs with singers Peter Lind Hayes and his wife Mary Healy as the hosts

Host: Peter Lind Hayes, Mary Healy. **Regulars:** Don Cherry, John Bubbles, The Four Voices, The Malagon Sisters. **Orchestra:** Bert Farber.

7241   *Peter Loves Mary.* (Series; Comedy; NBC; 1960-1961). After 20 years on the road and living out of trunks, Peter Lindsey and his wife, Mary, decide to give up show business and settle down. Peter, a comedian, singer and dancer, and Mary, a singer and dancer, and their children, Leslie and Steve, move to 130 Maple Street in a small Connecticut town called Oakdale.

Peter and Mary performed in air force shows in the South Pacific during World War II, assisted Bob Hope with his USO tours, and appeared before royalty the world over. They always exited stage left, and the Porter Theatrical Agency represented them. Now, they seek only to settle down and enjoy life with their children (who attend the Oakdale School).

Mary is now a member of the P.T.A., the Garden Club and the Book Club. Peter, who has show business in his blood, performs at the Imperial Room in Manhattan but prefers "the living room circuit" (performing for their friends when Mary gives a party, which she does on a weekly basis). Wilma is their housekeeper; Charlie is her boyfriend; Happy is Peter's agent.

Cast: Peter Lind Hayes (*Peter Lindsey*); Mary Healy (*Mary Lindsey*); Merry Martin (*Leslie Lindsey*); Gil Smith (*Steve Lindsey*); Bea Benaderet (*Wilma*); Alan Reed (*Happy Richman*); Arch Johnson (*Charlie*).

7242   *The Peter Marshall Variety Show.* (Series; Variety; Syn.; 1976). Peter Marshall, best known as the host of *The Hollywood Squares*, hosts a program of music, song and celebrity interviews.

Host: Peter Marshall. **Regulars:** Denny Evans, Rod Gist, Chapter 5. **Orchestra:** Alan Copeland.

7243   *Peter Pan and the Pirates.* (Series; Cartoon; Fox; 1990). Peter Pan is the fun-loving boy who never grows up. One day he befriends the Darling children (Wendy John, Michael and Tootles) and with the help of his fairy companion, Tinkerbell, gives them the ability to fly and whisks them off to his home in Never Land. Here the evil pirate Captain James T. Hook and his dastardly crew have been terrorizing the land. Stories follow Peter Pan, Tinkerbell and the Darling children as they battle the evils of Captain Hook.

Voice Cast: Jason Marsden (*Peter Pan*); Tim Curry (*Captain James T. Hook*); Christina Lange (*Wendy Darling*); Whitby Hertford (*Michael Darling*); Jack Lynch (*John Darling*); Chris Allport (*Tootles Darling*); Debi Derryberry (*Tinkerbell*); Jack Angel (*Cookson*); Adam

Carl *(Nibs)*; Ed Gilbert *(Smee)*; Tony Jay *(Alf Mason)*; Scott Menville *(Slightly)*; Cree Summer *(Tiger Lily)*; Michael Wise *(Big Chief Little Panther)*.

7244   *The Peter Potamus Show.* (Series; Cartoon; Syn.; 1964). The overall title for three cartoon segments.

1. Peter Potamus. Peter Potamus, a purple hippo, and his friend So So the Monkey, find adventure traveling around the world.

2. Yippie, Yappie and Yahooey. Three mischievous dogs attempt to guard their king.

3. Breezly and Sneezly. Breezly the Polar Bear and his friend Sneezly the seal seek warmth in the barracks of an Army post called Camp Frostbite in the North Pole.

Voice Cast: Daws Butler *(Peter Potamus)*; Don Messick *(So So)*; Hal Smith *(Yippie)*; Daws Butler *(Yappie)*; Daws Butler *(Yahooey)*; Hal Smith *(The King)*; Howard Morris *(Breezly)*; Mel Blanc *(Sneezly)*; John Stephenson *(Army Colonel)*.

7245   *Peter Potter's Juke Box Jury.* (Series; Discussion; ABC; 1953-1954). Guest Hollywood personalities judge and discuss the merits of just and/or pre-released recordings.

Program Open: "Will it be a hit (sound of a Bong!) or a miss (sound of a Clunk!)? Yes, it's *The Peter Potter Show*, direct from Hollywood, with your host, radio personality Peter Potter and brought to you by Hazel Bishop. Hazel Bishop, makers of Hazel Bishop long-lasting lipstick; Hazel Bishop's long-lasting complexion glow and Hazel Bishop's new long-lasting nail polish. And now, join our Juke Box Jury and your host Peter Potter...."

Host: Peter Potter.

7246   *Petrocelli.* (Series; Crime Drama; NBC; 1974–1976). Anthony Petrocelli, called Tony, is a Harvard-educated, Italian-American attorney working out of San Remo, a southwestern cattle town with its share of crime and corruption (more than would be expected from such an area). Tony is married to Maggie and Pete Toley works as his investigator although Tony also investigates client's cases to gather additional information. He and Pete often work with Frank Kaiser, the assistant District Attorney and John Clifford, a lieutenant with the San Remo Police Department. Stories follow Tony as he uses what tactics he can, but staying within the limits of the law to defend his clients. The pilot film, *Night Games* aired on Mar. 16, 1974.

Cast: Barry Newman *(Tony Petrocelli)*; Susan Howard *(Maggie Petrocelli)*; Albert Salmi *(Pete Toley)*; Michael Bell *(Frank Kaiser)*; David Huddleston *(Lt. John Clifford)*.

7247   *Petticoat Fever.* (Experimental; Stage Play; NBC; Nov. 25, 1945). A three-act play, first produced on Broadway in 1935, that tells of the boredom felt by Bascom Dinsmore, a radio operator in the Labrador wilds who hasn't seen a beautiful woman in two years. The comedy begins when a Canadian Mounted Policeman and his gorgeous fiancée (Ethel) are forced to share Dinsmore's hut when their plane runs out of gas.

Cast: John McQuade *(Bascom Dinsmore)*; Ann Burr *(Ethel)*; Philip Tonge *(Canadian Mountie)*.

7248   *Petticoat Junction.* (Series; Comedy; CBS; 1963-1970). Kate Bradley is a widow and the mother of three beautiful daughters: Billie Jo, Bobbie Jo and Betty Jo. She owns the Shady Rest Hotel in Hooterville, a small farming community of 72 farms. Kate is assisted by her uncle, Joe Carson, the town's fire chief (when there is work to be done, Uncle Joe fakes an attack of lumbago; his favorite place at the hotel is the rocking chair on the front porch).

Billie Jo, the oldest and most flirtatious of the Bradley girls, attends class at the Pixley Secretarial School; her first job was secretary to

Oliver Fenton, an author whose books have been banned in Hooterville. Bobbie Jo, the studious sister, and Betty Jo, the tomboy, attend Hooterville High School. Betty Jo married Steve Elliott in fourth season episodes and they later became the parents of Kathy Jo. Steve was born in Seattle and became a crop duster when he was discharged from the air force. He crashed his plane in Hooterville when he saw the girls swimming in the water tower that feeds the local train, the Cannonball Express, and paid more attention to them than to where he was flying. He later became partners with Uncle Joe and formed the Carson-Elliott Crop Dusting Company. Prior to his role as Steve, Mike Minor played Don Plout, the son of Kate's archenemy, Selma Plout.

Kate was replaced as the mother figure on the show in 1968 by Dr. Janet Craig; Bea Benaderet's death that year ended the Kate Bradley character. During Kate's illness, her Cousin Mae and Aunt Helen cared for the family. Boy is the Bradley family dog (actually owned by Betty Jo, whom he followed home from school one day; press releases refer to Boy as the "Shady Rest Dog," played by Higgins).

Communities neighboring Hooterville are Pixley and Crabtree Corners. The Cannonball Express, an 1890s steam engine, coal car and combination mail/baggage/coach car, is owned by the C.F.&W. Railroad. (Railroad vice president Homer Bedloe is the valley's nemesis, as he seeks to scrap the ancient Cannonball.) Charley Pratt is the engineer, and Floyd Smoot is the conductor. Betty Jo's biggest thrill is driving the Cannonball.

Sam Drucker is the owner of the general store; Norman Curtis is the railroad president; Fred Ziffel and his wife Doris are pig farmers; Ben Miller and Newt Kiley are farmers; Barton Stuart is the valley doctor (before Janet); Wendell Gibbs, the Cannonball engineer (later); Orrin Pike is the game warden; Henrietta Plout is Selma's daughter; Herby Bates is a friend of the Bradley girls.

The show's title refers to the Cannonball's watering stop at the Shady Rest Hotel. The Bradley girls swim in the tank on hot days — and their petticoats can be seen hanging over the top rim. In the original, unaired pilot version, Sharon Tate played Billie Jo (she was dropped by the producers of the family oriented show when they learned she had posed for a *Playboy* layout).

Cast: Bea Benaderet *(Kate Bradley)*; Edgar Buchanan *(Joe Carson)*; Jeannine Riley, Gunilla Hutton, Meredith MacRae *(Billie Jo Bradley)*; Pat Woodell, Lori Saunders *(Bobbie Jo Bradley)*; Linda Kaye Henning *(Betty Jo Bradley)*; Frank Cady *(Sam Drucker)*; Charles Lane *(Homer Bedloe)*; Roy Roberts *(Norman Curtis)*; Hank Patterson *(Fred Ziffel)*; Barbara Pepper *(Doris Ziffel)*; Byron Foulger *(Wendell Gibbs)*; Jonathan Daly *(Orrin Pike)*; Regis Toomey *(Dr. Barton Stuart)*; June Lockhart *(Dr. Janet Craig)*; Elvia Allman *(Selma Plout)*; Lynette Winter *(Henrietta Plout)*; Don Washbrook *(Herby Bates)*; Elaine and Danielle Hubbel *(Kathy Jo Elliott)*; Tom Fadden *(Ben Miller)*; Kay E. Kuter *(Newt Kiley)*; Mike Minor *(Steve Elliott)*.

7249   *Peyton Place.* (Series; Drama; ABC; 1964–1969). Dramatic incidents in the lives of the people of Peyton Place, a small New England town. Based on the novel by Grace Metalious. See also *Return to Peyton Place*.

Program Open: "This is the continuing story of *Peyton Place* starring Dorothy Malone as Constance MacKenzie ... Ed Nelson as Michael Rossi ... Ryan O'Neal as Rodney Harrington ... Barbara Parkins as Betty Anderson ... Tom O'Connor as Elliott Carson ... Christopher Connelly as Norman Harrington ... Patricia Morrow as Rita Harrington ... James Douglas as Steven Cord."

Principal Cast: Dorothy Malone, Lola Albright *(Constance MacKenzie Carson)*; Tim O'Connor *(Elliott Carson)*; Ed Nelson *(Michael Rossi)*; Mia Farrow *(Alison MacKenzie)*; Ryan O'Neal *(Rodney Harrington)*; Frank Ferguson *(Eli Carson)*; Christopher Connelly *(Norman Harrington)*; Barbara Parkins *(Betty Anderson Harrington)*;

Patricia Morrow (*Rita Jacks Harrington*); Paul Langton (*Leslie Harrington*); Evelyn Scott (*Ada Jacks*); James Douglas (*Stephen Cord*); George Macready (*Martin Peyton*); Ruth Warrick (*Hannah Cord*); Warner Anderson (*Matthew Swain*); Patricia Breslin (*Laura Brooks*); Mariette Hartley (*Claire Morton*); Diana Hyland (*Susan Winter*); Percy Rodrigues (*Dr. Harry Miles*); Barbara Rush (*Marsha Russell*); Glynn Turman (*Lew Miles*); Ruby Dee (*Alma Miles*); Jeanne Buckley (*Joanne Walker*); Carolyn Russell (*Elizabeth Walker*); Myrna Fahey (*Jennifer Ivers*); Lee Grant (*Stella Chernak*); Gena Rowlands (*Adrienne Van Leyden*); Joan Blackman (*Marian Fowler*); Leslie Nielsen (*Vincent Markham*); Michael Christian (*Joe Rossi*). **Announcer:** Dick Tufeld.

7250   *Peyton Place: The Next Generation.* (Pilot; Drama; NBC; May 13, 1985). An unrealized update of *Peyton Place* that continues to relate events in the lives of the people of the small New England town with many hidden secrets.

Cast: Dorothy Malone (*Constance MacKenzie Carson*); Tim O'Connor (*Elliot Carson*); Barbara Parkins (*Betty Harrington Cord*); Ed Nelson (*Dr. Michael Rossi*); Patricia Morrow (*Rita Jacks Harrington*); Evelyn Scott (*Ada Jacks*); Ruth Warwick (*Hannah Cord*); James Douglas (*Steven Cord*); Christopher Connelly (*Norman Harrington*); Marguerite Hickey (*Megan MacKenzie*); Deborah Goodrich (*Kelly Carson*); Bruce Greenwood (*Dana Harrington*); Tony Quinn (*Joey Harrington*); John Beck (*Dorian Blake*).

7251   *PG Porn.* (Series; Comedy; Internet; 2008-2009). The Triple X (and even single X) rating is removed from adult films to present a PG version of what goes on behind the scenes of pornographic films. The "sexy hot chick" and the "handsome dude" are present and episodes begin like a real skin flick — but it's not the expected that happens but the unexpected — from bad acting to awful camera angles to atrocious lighting.

Cast: James Gunn, Brian Gunn, Sean Gunn, Tiffany Shepis, MacKenzie Firgens, Lee Kirk, Belladonna.

7252   *The Phantom.* (Pilot; Adventure; Unaired; Produced in 1961). The Phantom is a mysterious figure for justice in Africa. There is no background information on him. He, along with the rest of the story, is just thrown at the viewer (had it aired) with no explanation as to who he is or why he protects Africa from evil. In the pilot episode, titled "No Escape," the Phantom goes undercover as a worker on the plantation of a Mrs. Harris (Paulette Goddard) to find out who is responsible for the deaths of several workers. Other regulars are R.G. Mallory, the Commissioner (whom the Phantom helps); and Devil, the Phantom's German Shepherd.

Cast: Roger Creed (*The Phantom*); Reginald Denny (*R.G. Mallory*).

7253   *The Phantom.* (Pilot; Adventure; Syfy; June 20, 2010). Kit Walker appears to be a somewhat ordinary young man, a twenty-something college student (at Columbia School of Law in New York City) and an exceptional athlete. He is also the twenty-second generation Phantom, a mysterious figure who battles for good in the jungles of the fictional country of Bengalie. The legend of The Phantom began more than 400 years ago when Kit's ancestor first donned a costume that earned him the name The Phantom for his ability to appear when needed than vanish just as mysteriously. As the legend grew over the years it also appeared that The Phantom was immortal and also became known as "The Ghost Who Walks." In reality, The Phantom legacy has been handed down from generation to generation making it appear that The Phantom never dies. Adapting this basic 1936 newspaper strip by Lee Falk, Syfy's version updates the superhero to the 21st century. The original Phantom wore a costume but possessed no superpowers. He used his wit, strength and

agility to fight evil. The 2010 Phantom is given a costume like no Phantom before him: a bulletproof suit that acts as an exo-skeleton that gives him incredible strength and speed. The pilot, originally produced as a two-part TV movie (but reworked to run as a four-hour program) pits Kit against the Singh Brotherhood, a ruthless syndicate of pirates (as old as the original Phantom himself) whose chief (mad) scientist, Bella Lithia, has developed a means by which to control people's minds through cable TV. The Phantom is assisted by the sultry Guran and Abel Vandermaark, his trainer; Renee is Kit's love interest.

Cast: Ryan Carnes (*Kit Walker*); Sandrine Holt (*Guran*); Jean Marchand (*Abel Vandermaark*); Isabella Rossellini (*Dr. Bella Lithia*); Cameron Goodman (*Renee Davidson*); Cas Anvar (*Rhatib Singh*).

7254   *Phantom 2040.* (Series; Cartoon; Syn.; 1984-1985). An adaptation of the comic book of the same title. It is the year 2040, a time when plant and animal life is disappearing and New Brazil is one of the few places in the world where jungles still exist. One man, Kit Walker, Jr., loves nature, but can only get it through the video game "Virtual Reality Battleworld"; he hopes to one day leave the city and become an ecological engineer and work in the jungles of New Brazil. Kit is an orphan and the son of a father he never really knew — a man who was the Phantom, a mysterious figure who has protected Africa for over 500 years. It was a secret known only by his father's sister, Eloise (with whom Kit now lives). One day, Kit stumbles upon a secret vault in the house and finds a mysterious skull ring. He then follows a dark hallway and is led to a secret chamber that houses Guran, his late father's aide. Through Guran Kit learns that in the year 1566 a sailing ship was attacked by pirates from the Bay of Bangala. All the passengers perished, except for one young boy, who was rescued by a native from an African tribe called the Bandai. The boy was raised by the tribe and taught their secret ways. He swore an oath on the skull of his father's killer to fight injustice wherever he finds it as the Phantom. For twenty-three generations a Walker has become the Phantom so the world would believe there is only one man — a man who cannot die — the Phantom. "You are your father's son," Guran tells young Kit, "and now it's your turn." Guran presents Kit with his costume (the Phase Suit) so he too can continue the legend of the Phantom and fight for injustice. The pilot episode, titled "Generation Unto Generation," relates the history of the Phantom and establishes his battle against Rebecca Madison, the owner of Maximum, Inc., who wants to control the world.

Max is Rebecca's evil son; Graft is Rebecca's aide; and Jenna and Tran are Kit's friends (who are unaware of his secret identity).

Voices: Scott Valentine (*Kit/Phantom*); Margot Kidder (*Rebecca Madison*); J.D. Hall (*Guran*); Ron Perlman (*Graft*); Jeff Bennett (*Maxwell Madison*); Kath Soucie (*Jenna*); Dustin Nguyen (*Tran*); Carrie Snodgress (*Aunt Eloise*).

7255   *Phenom.* (Series; Comedy; ABC; 1993-1994). Angela Doolan is the phenomenon of the title, a natural at tennis, "a child blessed by the hand of God; something that comes along once in a lifetime," says her coach Lou Della Rose. Angela, 15, lives at 1728 Avalon Drive in Agora, California, with her mother Dianne, sister Mary Margaret and brother Brian.

Angela won the Sixteen and Under championship of Southern California and is struggling to cope with the demands of potential stardom while at the same time be a normal teenage girl. Angela attends Miraculous Medal High School, practices tennis 35 hours a week and her most embarrassing moment occurred during a tournament match when her halter top slipped and exposed her left breast. Her dream is to win Wimbledon.

Dianne is 42 years old, divorced from Jack and works as a certified shorthand reporter (transcribes notes from tape). Jack, who calls Dianne "Sharkey," is a former minor league ball player turned beer salesman.

Mary Margaret attends third grade at Miraculous Medal Elementary School. Angela likes to talk with Mary Margaret "because she listens, never interrupts and doesn't understand a word I say."

Brian, a hopeful art student, attends the Tim Pacaso Art Academy. He works at Hector's Tacos and previously held a job as the front-gate security guard at the Leisure Time Retirement Home. His girl-friend is Roanne.

Lou lives at 3079 Los Costas and owns the Lou Della Rose Tennis Academy in La Hoya. When someone asks "Who's Lou Della Rose," he responds, "Just the best damned tennis coach in history." He first saw Angela at the Southern California Championships and offered her a full scholarship (she trains there on weekends).

Cast: Angela Goethals *(Angela Doolan)*; Judith Light *(Dianne Doolan)*; Ashley Johnson *(Mary Margaret Doolan)*; William Devane *(Lou Della Rose)*; Todd Louiso *(Brian Doolan)*; Jennifer Lien *(Roanne)*; John Getz *(Jack)*.

7256   *Phenomenon.* (Series; Reality; NBC; 2007). A search for America's most talented psychic. The program, described as "a journey into the world of the unexplained," pits ten extra-ordinary people (each claiming to possess unique psychic abilities) against each other with viewers determining the fate of each one. Two world famous psychics judge each psychic's performance. Each performer is given a special toll free telephone number and viewers' votes determine who goes (lowest votes) and who stays. The one psychic who receives the highest vote score on the next to last episode (revealed on the final episode) wins $250,000 and the title "Phenomenon." Tim Vincent hosts. Criss Angel and Uri Geller are the judges.

7257   *The Phil Donahue Show.* (Series; Discussion; Syn.; 1967). A pioneering talk-discussion program that set the president for all such series that followed. The program began as discussions on the contemporary issues that affect people in their daily lives. As the times changed, it progressed into a forum where vital issues took center stage and viewers were given all the facts — no matter how brutal — with the people involved in the issues.

Host: Phil Donahue.

7258   *Phil of the Future.* (Series; Comedy; Disney; 2004–2007). Parents Lloyd and Barbara Diffy and their teenage children, Phil and Pim, are a normal family of the future (in the year 2121). Lloyd is a positron engineer for the Wizard Corporation; Barbara is a housewife (whose job is made easier by electronic helpers) and Phil and Pim are typical kids of the future — spoiled by the numerous electronic advances that have made education simple.

For their annual vacation, the Diffy's decide to explore various eras in time. Lloyd rents a time machine from Marty's Used Time Machines and Water Slides. During their return trip to the year 2121, the time machine malfunctions and strands them in America in a town called Pickford in the year 2004. Lloyd is unable to repair the time machine and the Diffy's are forced to make the past their home. Also joining them is Curtis, a caveman who stowed away on the time machine when the Diffy's visited the prehistoric era. Stories follow events in the lives of the Diffy's as they struggle to adjust to and fit in the primitive 21st century.

Phil and Pim attend the Herbert G. Wells High School. Phil is friends with Keely Teslow, a girl of our time to whom he reveals his secret (and who becomes involved with all the wacky predicaments futuristic technology involves Phil with). Lloyd disguised the time machine as an RV but is unable to find the parts needed to fix it (not yet invented). Phil is a whiz in math and tries to be the good guy

and help people in need. Pim has "shimmering blue lagoon eyes" and loves to play practical jokes; she also has a mean streak and will get even with anyone who crosses her. Keely yearns to be a reporter and hosts the school's daily TV newscast. Debbie Berwick is the all-too perfect girl at school who drives Pim batty; Joel Messerschmidt is a stern teacher; and Principal Hackett oversees the school.

Cast: Ricky Ullman *(Phil Diffy)*; Amy Bruckner *(Pim Diffy)*; Alyson Michalka *(Keely Teslow)*; Lise Simms *(Barbara Diffy)*; Craig Anton *(Lloyd Diffy)*; J.P. Manoux *(Curtis/Principal Hackett)*; Kay Panabaker *(Debbie Berwick)*; Joel Brooks *(Joel Messerschmidt)*.

7259   *The Phil Silvers Arrow Show.* (Series; Variety; NBC; 1948-1949). Arrow Shirts sponsored program of music, songs and comedy hosted by actor-comedian Phil Silvers.

Host: Phil Silvers. **Regulars:** Jack Gilford, Connie Sawyer, Jerry Hausner, Len Hale, Herbert Coleman, The Mack Triplets. **Orchestra:** Harry Salter.

7260   *The Phil Silvers Show.* (Series; Comedy; CBS; 1955–1959). Master Sergeant Ernest Bilko is stationed at the Camp Freemont army base at Fort Baxter in Kansas (later episodes are set in Grove City, California). There, he is in charge of the 3rd Platoon of the Company B Motor Pool (24th Division), and he is totally dedicated to acquiring money by manipulating the U.S. Army for his own personal benefit.

Bilko, a master con artist, began his "career" during World War II. At that time he was with the 38th Division and stationed on New Guinea; he supplied the USO girls with something they desperately needed but were unable to get — nylons, at five dollars a pair. After the war, Bilko, a master at pool and cards, was transferred to Fort Baxter where he now commands Company B: Privates Duane Doberman, Dino Paparelli, Sam Fender, Fielding Zimmerman, and Corporal Henshaw. The base cook, Rupert Ritzik, is Bilko's main patsy.

John T. ("Jack") Hall is the commanding officer. Other soldiers are: Corporal Rocco Barbella, Sergeant Francis Grover, Private Mullin, Private Lester Mendelsohn, Private Greg Chickeriny and Sergeant Stanley Sowicki.

WAC Master Sergeant Joan Hogan is Bilko's girlfriend; "Stacked" Stacy is the waitress at the local diner; Emma is Rupert's nagging wife; Nell is John's wife; Edna is John's secretary. Originally titled *You'll Never Get Rich* and also known as *Sergeant Bilko.*

Cast: Phil Silvers *(Ernest Bilko)*; Paul Ford *(John Hall)*; Maurice Gosfield *(Duane Doberman)*; Billy Sands *(Dino Paparelli)*; Herbie Faye *(Sam Fender)*; Mickey Freeman *(Fielding Zimmerman)*; Allan Melvin *(Corporal Henshaw)*; Joe E. Ross *(Rupert Ritzik)*; Elisabeth Fraser *(Joan Hogan)*; Harvey Lembeck *(Rocco Barbella)*; Jimmy Little *(Francis Grover)*; Jack Healy *(Private Mullin)*; Gerald Hiken *(Lester Mendelsohn)*; Bruce Kirby *(Greg Chickeriny)*; Harry Clark *(Stanley Sowicki)*; Hope Sansberry *(Nell Hall)*; Nelson Olmstead *(Captain Hodges)*; Barbara Barrie *(Edna; a nurse)*; Beatrice Pons *(Emma Ritzik)*; Nicholas Saunders *(Captain Barker)*; Julie Newmar *("Stacked" Stacy)*; Skippy Colby *(Edna; Hall's secretary)*; George Kennedy *(Various M.P. roles)*. **Announcer:** Bern Bennett.

7261   *The Philanthropist.* (Series; Drama; NBC; 2009). Teddy Rist is a billionaire (the 99th richest man in the world) who is also the co-CEO (with Philip Maidstone) of the New York–based Maidstone-Rist, Inc., a conglomerate that purchases and sells natural resources. Teddy (as he likes to be called) was married (to Julia) and the father of a young son (Bobby). His life changed when Bobby died. He divorced and "my normal life didn't seem normal anymore. I had to do something else, something more." But what?

During a business trip to Nigeria, Teddy rescues a young African boy abandoned during a fierce hurricane — "I'm not the heroic type. Reckless, yes; Superman hardly. In an odd way, the kid saved me."

With a new found goal in life, Teddy uses his business sense and money-making skills to help people who are unable to help themselves. Stories follow Teddy as he travels the world and uses every dirty trick in the book to achieve his goal. Olivia, Philip's wife, runs the company's non-profit organization; Dax is Teddy's bodyguard; AJ is Teddy's assistant.

Cast: James Purefoy *(Teddy Rist)*; Jesse L. Martin *(Philip Maidstone)*; Neve Campbell *(Olivia Maidstone)*; Michael Kenneth Williams *(Dax Vaughn)*; Lindy Booth *(AJ Butterfield)*; Amanda Douge *(Julia Rist)*.

7262 *Philbert.* (Pilot; Comedy; Unaired; Produced for ABC in 1962). A *Philbert* comic book sells for twenty cents. It is drawn by a man named Griff and it is about a talkative, know-it-all little man. One day Philbert comes to life (in animated form) to help guide Griff's life. The proposal was to relate the mishaps that befall Griff as he struggles to cope with a diminutive man he can't control (Philbert lives on Griff's drawing board; Griff's dog, Hap, can also see him). Angela is Griff's girlfriend.

Cast: William Schallert *(Griff)*; Joanna Barnes *(Angela)*; Turstin Howard *(Philbert's Voice)*.

7263 *Philbin's People.* (Series; Talk; Syn.; 1969-1970). A late night talk program (12:30 A.M. to 2:00 A.M.) wherein host Regis Philbin conducts a roundtable discussion on current topics of interest with five guest panelists.

7264 *Philby.* (Pilot; Comedy; ABC; July 21, 1989). *The Betty Randall Show* is a talk program hosted by Betty Randall, a beautiful woman with a knack for bringing out the worst in her guests. To protect her, the station hires Philip "Philby" Arenzo, an obnoxious bodyguard. The proposal was to relate Philby's experiences with the cast, crew and guests of Betty's show. Other regulars are Mickey, Betty's manager; Don, the producer.

Cast: Terrence Mann *(Philip "Philby" Arenzo)*; Finola Hughes *(Betty Randall)*; Ken Lerner *(Mickey)*; Peter White *(Don)*.

7265 *The Philco Television Playhouse.* (Series; Anthology; NBC; 1948–1956). Equity-Philco Company sponsored program of quality dramas that features such performers as Rod Steiger, Walter Matthau, Burgess Meredith, Cara Williams, Eva Marie Saint, Bing Crosby, Ralph Bellamy, Lillian Gish, Dorothy Gish, E.G. Marshall, Leslie Nielsen, Phyllis Kirk, Jose Ferrer, Cameron Mitchell and Margaret Hayes.

Program Open: "Philco, famous for quality the world over, the world's largest manufacturer of super-powered radios; the first high fidelity television sets built for the American public; full fidelity radio phonographs. Philco, famous for advanced design in refrigerators, in home freezers, in home ranges and air conditioning for home and industry presents *Philco Television Playhouse.* Tonight's play, "Ernie Barger is 50," starring Ed Begley, Carmen Mathews, Howard St. John and John Carradine."

Host: Bert Lytell (1948-49).

7266 *Philip Marlowe.* (Series; Crime Drama; ABC; 1959-1960). Philip Marlowe is a rugged private detective who wanders from state to state to track down criminals and solve crimes. Stories follow his case investigations as he not only dishes out the rough stuff, but often becomes a recipient of rough treatment from those he is pursuing. Based on the character created by Raymond Chandler.

Cast: Philip Carey *(Philip Marlowe)*.

7267 *Philip Marlowe, Private Eye.* (Series; Crime Drama; HBO; 1983). Los Angeles during its turbulent era of criminal unrest, the 1930s, is the setting. Philip Marlowe is a hard-boiled private detective struggling to make a living amid the turmoil that exists. He is as tough as nails and feels this is the only way he can survive doing what he does. He believes a private eye's profession is not an easy one and bending the law to suit his own purpose is the only way to stay one step ahead of the felons he is seeking. He has an uneasy alliance with the police (especially Lieutenant Magee) who feel that Marlowe's breaking the law to achieve results makes him as guilty as the felons he is chasing. Annie Riorden, Marlowe's lovely girlfriend, often fears for Philip's life, and often becomes a part of the dangerous cases he investigates. The series, originally titled *Chandlertown* relates Marlowe's unorthodox investigations into cases that start off simply but escalate into baffling crimes that, despite what the police believe, are glad when Marlowe solves them. Based on characters created by Raymond Chandler. Moe Kaufman composed "Marlowe's Theme."

Cast: Powers Boothe *(Philip Marlowe)*; Kathryn Leigh Scott *(Annie Riorden)*; William Kearns *(Lieutenant Magee)*.

7268 *Philip Morris Playhouse.* (Series; Anthology; CBS; 1953-1954). Philip Morris cigarettes sponsored program of live dramatic presentations.

Host: Charles Martin, Kent Smith. **Announcer:** Joe King.

7269 *Phillip and Barbara.* (Pilot; Comedy; NBC; Aug. 31, 1976). Philip and Barbara Logan are a married couple who also work as television script writers. Their marriage works well, especially at home, where they respect each other; at work, however, they do not always see eye to eye. The proposal was to follow the conflicts that arise at work as they bicker over the contents of what they are assigned to write. Shirley and George are co-workers; Edna is Barbara's mother.

Cast: John Astin *(Phillip Logan)*; Patty Duke *(Barbara Logan)*; Rosemary DeCamp *(Edna)*; Ann Prentiss *(Shirley)*; Leonard Frey *(George)*; Alex Henteloff *(Roger)*; Patti Jerome *(Secretary)*.

7270 *Philly.* (Series; Drama; ABC; 2001-2002). Kathleen Maguire is a young woman with one powerful ambition: the pursuit of justice. She is a criminal lawyer in a small Philadelphia firm who devotes all her energies to defending clients. Kathleen is divorced (from Daniel Cavanaugh, the District Attorney) and is the mother of 10-year-old Patrick. Kathleen is raising Patrick as a single mother and economic necessity forcers her to represent just about anybody with a legit claim.

Patrick has been shattered by the divorce. He is a bright child and has a knack for playing one parent against the other. Daniel always seizes upon the opportunity to make Kathleen look bad in front of Patrick. Other regulars are Will Froman, Kathleen's partner; Terry Loomis, the Assistant D.A.; and Patricia, Kathleen's receptionist.

Cast: Kim Delaney *(Kathleen Maguire)*; Kyle Secor *(Daniel Cavanaugh)*; Scotty Leavenworth *(Patrick Cavanaugh)*; Tom Everett *(Will Froman)*; Rick Hoffman *(Terry Loomis)*; Diana Maria-Riva *(Patricia)*; Veronica Hamel *(Judge Marjorie Brennan)*; Dena Dietrich *(Judge Ellen Armstrong)*; Ron Canada *(Judge Henry Griffin)*.

7271 *Philly Heat.* (Pilot; Drama; ABC; July 1, 1995). Battalion 6 of Engine Company 31, Ladder 7, is the busiest fire house in Philadelphia. Stan Kelly is the newly appointed chief and through his eyes the work of firefighters is depicted.

Cast: Peter Boyle *(Stan Kelly)*; Mary Mara *(Laura Walker)*; Tate Donovan *(Kevin Gaffney)*; Ving Rhames *(DeWitt Wardlaw)*; Adam Trese *(John Kennedy Faletta)*.

7272 *Phineas and Ferb.* (Series; Cartoon; Disney; 2008). Phineas Flynn and Ferb Fletcher are stepbrothers who actually like each other (not to mention get along with each other). It is summer vacation and Phineas and Ferb have 104 days off from school. But what to do with all that free time? Their answer — whatever they can to enjoy their freedom. Putting a damper on their outrageous activities is Candace, Phineas's obnoxious, trouble-making older sister who seeks only to tattle (to their mother) and get them in hot water. Perry, Phineas and Ferb's pet platypus, is also there to experience his masters' idiotic adventure. In reality, however, Perry is a secret agent who, when everyone around him is preoccupied, becomes a secret agent, battling Dr. Doofenshmirtz, a crazed professor seeking to dominate the world.

Voice Cast: Vincent Martella (*Phineas Flynn*); Thomas Sangster (*Ferb Fletcher*); Ashley Tisdale (*Candace Flynn*); Dee Bradley Baker (*Perry the Platypus*); Dan Povenmire (*Dr. Doofenshmirtz*); Caroline Rhea (*Linda Flynn-Fletcher*); Richard O'Brien (*Lawrence Fletcher*).

7273 *The Phoenix.* (Series; Fantasy; ABC; 1982). During an archaeological expedition in Peru, Dr. Ward Frazier discovers a gold sarcophagus that bears the seal of the Phoenix (the ancient symbol of rebirth). The sarcophagus is brought to Los Angeles where tests reveal that it contains a well-preserved humanoid that is linked with ancient Egypt. When the sarcophagus's seal is broken, an extraterrestrial being named Bennu is awakened and emerges into a hostile twentieth century. Possessed of superhuman powers (which he derives from the sun), Bennu, who is actually an ancient astronaut awakened before his time, escapes from the center for Astro Archaeology.

Now free, Bennu begins a search to find Mira, his partner from the planet El DeBrande. Mira, it is learned, is the woman who knows Bennu's earthly mission, which is to affect the earth's future. Stories depict Bennu's search for Mira, whom he believes is entombed in Indian burial grounds north of the 30th parallel, and his attempts to escape from Preminger, the man who believes Bennu is an ancient astronaut and seeks to capture him. The pilot film aired on April 26, 1981.

Program Open: "Long ago in a remote corner of the world, ancient astronauts landed from a distant planet with a gift for mankind — the Phoenix. For a thousand years he has waited, suspended in time and now he has awakened to complete his mission. He searches for his partner, Mira, for only she knows his ultimate assignment on Earth. Dependent upon the sun for his strength and survival, endowed with superior intelligence, he has developed the powers of the human mind. Though relentlessly pursued by those who seek to control him, he must stay free."

Cast: Judson Scott (*Bennu of the Golden Light*); Richard Lynch (*Preminger*); E.G. Marshall (*Dr. Ward Frazier*); Sheila Frazier (*Mira*).

7274 *The Phone.* (Series; Reality; MTV; 2009). Participants must solve a "terrifying" mystery to win money. Prior to the show's debut, a number of people signed up to become contestants on a new reality series. For each program, four of the applicants receive an unexpected phone call and are told to go to a specific location. Here, they are to wait for further instructions. Unknown to the participants, a pre-arranged situation has been set up (for example, in the first episode, a car explosion in front of them). After the mysterious incident, each of the gamers (as they are called) receives a call on their cell phones from "The Operator." The Operator starts the game by instructing the gamers in their quest: find, in this instance, the mad bomber. The Operator presents the gamers with a series of clues that require both physical and mental skills to accomplish. Players who are unable to complete a challenge are eliminated. The one player who manages to survive the barrage of clues and solve the mystery wins. Emmett J. Scanlan is the Operator.

7275 *Photocrime.* (Pilot; Crime Drama; CBS; Oct. 2, 1945). Dramatizations based on the "Photocrime" feature of *Look magazine.* The pilot story, "Death Comes to Broadway," tells of a penniless, wanted criminal (Sidney Blackmer), his dim-witted wife (Mary Orr) and their involvement with a New York hood (Robert Emhardt).

7276 *Photocrime.* (Series; Crime Drama; ABC; 1949). Hannibal Cobb is an easy-going inspector with the New York City Police Department. He is a rather gentle person who takes life one step at a time. He is persistent when it comes to investigating crimes but prefers the least violent means to solve them. Hannibal is also a man who thrives on crime scene photographs to stir his deductive abilities. He believes that photographs often possess clues that are often overlooked when crime scenes are first inspected for evidence. Hannibal's efforts to solve crimes, usually murders, are the focal point of stories.

Cast: Chuck Webster (*Inspector Hannibal Cobb*).

7277 *Photon.* (Series; Science Fiction; Syn.; 1986). Before the beginning of time there existed Photon, the source of all power in the universe. For unknown reasons, Photon exploded and divided itself into two separate universes — one good, the other evil, with both seeking to control all the power of the Photon.

In an attempt to help good defeat evil (in particular the Warlord of Arr), a group of aliens (Tivia, Lord Beathan, Uncle Pike, Parcival and Leon) ban together to fight the Warlord. Seeking additional help, the aliens recruit Christopher Jarvis (alias Bhodi Li), an exceptional earthling who agrees to help them. Stories relate the Photon Warriors efforts to defeat the Warlord and protect the cosmos from his evil attempts to rule it.

Cast: Christopher Lockwood (*Bhodi Li*); Loretta Haywood (*Tivia*); Graham Ravey (*Lord Beathan*); Eros Rivers (*Parcival*); Akiyoshi Ono (*Leon*); Kazuhisa Kahamaru (*Uncle Pike*); David Anthony (*Mandaar*); Techchi Igarashi (*Docaar*); Yoshito Nagatsuka (*Destructaar*).

7278 *Phyl and Mikhy.* (Series; Comedy; CBS; 1980). Phyllis Wilson, called Phyl, is a very pretty student at Pacific Western University. It is here that she is the star of the track team and that her father, Max, is the team coach. Mikhail "Mikhy" Orlov is a Russian track star that has come to the U.S. for a track meet at Pacific Western. Phyl and Mikhy meet, fall in love and marry, thus enabling Mikhy to live with Phyl in California. Phyl and Mikhy move in with her father at 11 Evergreen Place; the Soviet Union, who had high hopes of Mikhy competing in the Olympics, has assigned Vladimir Gimenko to keep an eye on Mikhy and convince him to return to the Mother Land. Stories follow events in the lives of two young adults from different worlds as they attempt to make their marriage work. Gwyn is Max's (a widower) romantic interest; Eugene "Truck" Morley is Max's friend, the alumni president.

Cast: Murphy Cross (*Phyllis Wilson Orlov*); Rick Lohman (*Mikhy Orlov*); Larry Haines (*Max Wilson*); Michael Pataki (*Vladimir Gimenko*); Jack Dodson (*Edgar Morley*); Rae Allen (*Gwyn Bates*); Deborah Pratt (*Connie*); Valerie Landsburg (*Beth*); Karen Werner (*Karen*); Debbie Kelman (*Debbie*); Sammy Jones (*TV Announcer*).

7279 *Phyllis.* (Series; Comedy; CBS; 1975–1977). A spin off from *The Mary Tyler Moore Show* wherein the character of Phyllis Lindstrom was depicted as Mary Richards friend and landlord. After the death of her never-seen husband, Lars, Phyllis and her daughter Bess move from Minneapolis to San Francisco to begin new lives. They acquire a home at 4482 Bayview Drive and in first season episodes Phyllis works as the assistant to Julie Erskine, the owner of Erskine's Commercial Photography Studio. Second season episodes dropped the photography studio storyline and found Phyllis employed as the administrative assistant to Dan Valenti, an executive for the San Francisco Board of Supervision. Stories, in both formats, relate Phyllis's mishaps as she attempts to adjust to the business world.

Other regulars are Leo Heatherton, Julie's photographer; Audrey Dexter, Phyllis's mother-in-law; Jonathan Dexter, Audrey's husband; Sally Dexter, Jonathan's mother; Leonard Marsh, Dan's associate; Harriet Hastings, Leonard's assistant; Mark Valenti, Dan's nephew; Arthur Lanson, Sally's boyfriend; and Van Horn, the park wino who befriends Phyllis.

Cast: Cloris Leachman (*Phyllis Lindstrom*); Lisa Gerritsen (*Bess Lindstrom*); Barbara Colby, Liz Torres (*Julie Erskine*); Richard Schaal (*Leo Heatherton*); Jane Rose (*Audrey Dexter*); Henry Jones (*Jonathan Dexter*); Judith Lowry (*Sally Dexter*); Carmine Caridi (*Dan Valenti*); John Lawlor (*Leonard Marsh*); Garn Stephens (*Harriet Hastings*); Craig Wasson (*Mark Valenti*); Burt Mustin (*Arthur Lanson*); Jack Elam (*Van Horn*); Penny Santon (*Dan's Mother*).

7280 The Phyllis Diller Show. (Series; Comedy; ABC; 1966-1967). The mid-season title for *The Pruitts of Southampton*. See this title for information.

7281 The P.I. (Pilot; Crime Drama; CBS; Mar. 28, 1976). A proposed spin off from *Bronk* about Frank Carey a former gun-shy secret service agent turned roughneck private investigator.

Cast: Vic Morrow (*Frank Carey*).

7282 The P.I. (Pilot; Crime Drama; ABC; Mar. 3, 1994). Jessica "Jessie" Morgan is young and beautiful and eager to strike out on her own as an artist. She leaves Atlanta for Los Angeles, where she hopes to enroll in the Art Institute. When Jessie arrives in L.A., she moves in with a girlfriend (Michelle) but soon finds she has no place to live when her friend steals her money and skips town. With no other choice, Jessie decides to look up her father, Max Morgan, who deserted the family when she was just a kid. Max is rather untidy, loves to gamble, is always broke and runs a two-bit private detective agency called Morgan Investigations. Max agrees to let Jessie stay with him until she finds a job. When Max needs help investigating a case he enlists Jessie's help. When they resolve the case Max asks Jessie to stay with him so he can make things up to her. Jessie feels they work well together—and they become a team. The proposal, a spin off from *Matlock* was to relate the investigations of a father and daughter team of private investigators. Allison Darnell is a detective with the L.A.P.D.

Cast: George Peppard (*Max Morgan*); Tracy Nelson (*Jessie Morgan*); Elyssa Davalos (*Allison Darnell*).

7283 Piccadilly Palace. (Series; Variety; ABC; 1967). Actress Millicent Martin hosts a program of celebrity performances from London's Piccadilly Palace.

Program Open: "*Piccadilly Palace* ... starring Eric Morecombe and Ernie Wise, Millicent Martin, George Fame and the Fame Group ... and Bobby Vinton.... From London, in color, *Piccadilly Palace.*"

Host: Millicent Martin. **Regulars:** Eric Morecambe, Ernie Wise, The Michael Sammes Singers, The Paddy Stone Dancers. **Orchestra:** Jack Parnell.

7284 Pick and Pat. (Series; Variety; ABC; 1949). Blackface comedians Pick and Pat host a program of minstrel acts, making it a television first, but also short lived (Jan. 20 to Mar. 17, 1949).

Hosts: Pick Padgett, Pat Malone. **Regulars:** Jack Carter, Mary Small.

7285 The Pick-Up Artist. (Series; Reality; VH-1; 2007). Eight men who lack certain social skills, are brought together and taught the art of picking up girls by Mystery, a best-selling author ("A social misfit turned seducer extraordinaire"). With the help of his coaches, Matador and J Dog, Mystery seeks one man to become a woman seducer called "Master Pick-Up Artist." Master V hosts.

7286 Pick Your Brain. (Series; Game; Syn.; 1993). Children between the ages of 11 and 15 compete in a question and answer session for a chance to win a $100 college savings bond. There are no special production values here or fancy graphics and no difficult rules to follow. The host poses a question. The first player to sound a buzzer signal receives a chance to answer. A correct response scores the player a point; the player with the highest point score is the winner and receives the savings bond.

Host: Marc Summers. **Co-Host:** Meredith Summers.

7287 Picket Fences. (Series; Crime Drama; CBS; 1992–1996). Rome, Wisconsin, is a small town characterized by strange citizens and unusual crimes. There is Peter Breck (Michael Jeter), a man fascinated by frogs and called "The Frogman." K.C. McDonald (Jessica Tuck), called "The Snake Lady," collects snakes and carries a boa with her at all times. Frank Tucker (David Provall) is a man obsessed with potatoes and carries a five pound bag of Idaho potatoes with him wherever he goes; he has earned the nickname "Frank the Potato Man." There is the mysterious and unknown "Serial Bather," a man who breaks into people's homes when they are out to take a bath; and Louise Talbot (Natalija Nagulich), the town's transsexual schoolteacher; before her sex change, she was Walter Souder. Dealing justice to anyone who breaks the law is Jimmy Brock, the local sheriff, and his deputies, Maxine Stewart and Kenny Locas. Jimmy is married to Jill and the father of three children: Kimberly, Matthew and Zachary. The Brocks reside at 211 Willow Road.

Jimmy, the son of criminal attorney Walter Brock (James Coburn), was previously married to a woman named Lydia (Cristine Rose), who is Kimberly's birth mother. A year after divorcing Lydia, Jimmy married Jill and moved to Rome because it was safe. Jill is a private practice doctor who is also on call at Norwood Hospital, later said to be Thayer Hospital.

Kimberly, 16 years old, attends Rome High School, and has aspirations of becoming a singer (changed in later episodes when she became a clerk to the town's legal eagle, Douglas Wambaugh, and set her sights on becoming a lawyer). The series took a bold step forward in the episode of April 29, 1993, "Sugar and Spice," when Kimberly begins to question her sexuality. She is talking to her girlfriend, Lisa Fenn (Alexandra Lee), when Lisa brings up the prospect of what it would be like to kiss a girl. Kimberly is reluctant to try it until Lisa tells her how erotic she read it was. They become curious and kiss, possibly the first such erotic kiss on TV. Both appear to like it, but Kimberly has a serious side effect: is she a lesbian or is she straight. The series ended without really resolving Kimberly's dilemma.

Matthew and Zachary attend the Fisher Elementary School. Matthew envisions himself as a detective while Zachary shows promise of becoming a musician (he plays trombone). The Sheriff's department is located in the Rome City Hall Building in Hogan County. Maxine, called Max, is famous for ending the murdering careers of "The Green Bay Chopper" and "The Cupid Killer." Kenny was born in Illinois and was a former Golden Gloves Boxer.

Douglas Wambaugh is the town's outspoken Jewish attorney. He will take any case "because Wambaugh is on the side of principle" and requires two things: The truth and a $1,000 retainer. Myriam is his nagging wife. Carter Pike is the town's medical examiner or "Chief Pathologist" as he calls himself. He yearns to become a detective but finds he is unable due to his uncontrollable urge to perform autopsies. Rachel Harris is the town's ultra-sexy mayor. Henry Bone is the tough, no nonsense judge who rules from the Hogan County Court House.

Cast: Tom Skerritt *(Jimmy Brock)*; Kathy Baker *(Jill Brock)*; Holly Marie Combs *(Kimberly Brock)*; Justin Shenkarow *(Matthew Brock)*; Adam Wylie *(Zachary Brock)*; Lauren Holly *(Maxine Stewart)*; Costas Mandylor *(Kenny Locas)*; Fyvush Finkel *(Douglas Wambaugh)*; Kelly Connell *(Carter Pike)*; Leigh-Taylor Young *(Rachel Harris)*; Erica Yohn *(Myriam Wambaugh)*; Ray Walston *(Henry Bone)*.

7288 *Pictionary.* (Series; Game; Syn.; 1989). Two three-member teams of children compete. In Round One, the Relay Round, two categories are shown. One team picks the category; the other team must play. Each member of the team at play receives 20 seconds with which to draw pictures associated with the category topic. While one player draws, the teammates must identify the picture. Each correct identification scores one point. The opposing team competes in the same manner. In Round Two, the Puzzle Round, each team picks one player to sketch pictures that will identify a specific topic. Each correct guess wins the team 10 points. In the third round, one member of each team is selected to draw. Players draw in turn — but any team can guess by pressing a buzzer signal. If correct, that team scores points; if not, the opposing team receives a chance. The team with the highest score is the winner and is awarded prizes.

Host: Brian Robbins. **Score Keeper:** Julie Friedman. **Judge:** Kirk Zumwalt. **Announcer:** Harry Stevens.

7289 *Pictionary.* (Series; Game; Syn.; 1997). Two teams, each composed of two celebrities and one non-celebrity contestant, compete. Round one finds one player attempting to convey a phrase that shares a common word (for example, fire truck, fire house) to his teammate. Each correct identification awards the team $100. Round two ups the time from 45 seconds to three minutes to give each member of each team a turn at guessing and giving clues. One hundred dollars is again awarded for each correct response. The team with the highest cash score wins the game and plays the bonus round. Here, one member is chosen to be the artist and must draw items that relate one word to the next (for example, if the key word is chair, then the related words are table, seat, legs, etc.). The team has 90 seconds. Each word guessed by the teammate scores money ($100 for the first four words; $300 for words five to seven; $1,000 for each additional word).

Host: Alan Thicke. **Announcer:** Joe Cipriano.

7290 *Picture This.* (Series; Game; CBS; 1963). Two teams compete, each composed of two members. One member of each team is given a phrase that is concealed from his partner. The player with the phrase then directs his partner by telling him what clues to draw to identify it. The "artist" who is first to identify the phrase wins the round and scores points. The game is played so as to allow all players to share equally on directing and drawing. The team with the highest point score is the winner and receives a cash prize.

Host: Jerry Van Dyke. **Announcer:** Lee Vines

7291 *Picture Window.* (Pilot; Comedy; NBC; Sept. 8, 1961). Amy and Joe Saxton are a happily married couple with a young son (Peter). They live in the suburbs and are barely able to make ends meet. Amy wants to break into the community's society circle; Joe is forever seeking ways to raise extra money. The proposal was to focus on Amy and Joe as they attempt to cope with the daily problems that confront them.

Cast: Mary LaRoche *(Amy Saxton)*; Charles Stewart *(Joe Saxton)*; Peter Oliphant *(Peter Saxton)*.

7292 *A Piece of Cake.* (Pilot; Comedy; CBS; Aug. 15, 1990).

Wally and Lionel are brothers-in-law (Wally is married to Doreen and Lionel to her sister, Tanya) and co-owners of Wally's Bakery Shop. The proposal was to relate their misadventures at home and at work.

Cast: Cleavant Derricks *(Wally)*; T.K. Carter *(Lionel)*; Vanessa Bell Calloway *(Doreen)*; Tonya Williams *(Tanya)*.

7293 *Pig Sty.* (Series; Comedy; UPN; 1995). Randy Fitzgerald is a struggling writer who earns what money he can as a bartender. He is often frustrated by the fact that he can't find a girl and is single. He shares a somewhat untidy apartment with four friends (Johnny, Cal, P.J. and Joe) and stories relate the events that spark their lives. Johnny is a young district attorney; Cal is an unscrupulous advertising executive; P.J. is a hopeful songwriter; and Joe is a doctor just beginning his residency at a New York hospital. Tess, a struggling actress, is the building's superintendent.

Cast: Brian McNamara *(Randy Fitzgerald)*; Matthew Bortenghi *(Johnny Barzano)*; David Arnott *(Cal Evans)*; Timothy Fall *(P.J. Morris)*; Sean O'Bryan *(Joe Dantley)*; Liz Vassey *(Tess Gallaway)*.

7294 *The Pigeon.* (Pilot; Crime Drama; ABC; Nov. 4, 1969). Larry Miller is a private detective working out of Los Angeles. He is assisted by Dave Williams and they often help Lieutenant Frank Miller when their cases also become police matters. Larry is aggressive; Dave is laid back and the proposal was to relate their case investigations.

Cast: Sammy Davis, Jr. *(Larry Miller)*; Roy Glenn, Sr. *(Frank Miller)*; Pat Boone *(Dave Williams)*.

7295 *The Pillars of Earth.* (Series; Drama; Starz; 2010). Melodrama, illicit sex, incest, rape, fierce bloody battles, revenge, passion, greed and treachery all combine to present the staggering adaptation of the novel by Ken Follett that details the building of a cathedral in the fictional town of Kingsbridge in 12th century England. Principal characters: Waleran Bigod is the evil clergyman (later to become a Bishop) who will stop at nothing to achieve his goal of absolute power. Tom Builder is the master mason contracted to construct the great cathedral. Maud, the legitimate daughter of King Henry VIII, and her illegitimate brother, Glouchester, team to battle the current king (Stephen) over her rightful claim to the throne (Maud is hindered by the fact that she is a woman and many nobles are unwilling to support her). Bartholomew, the prior Earl of Shiring, is a staunch supporter of Maud's right to the throne (his attempts to help Maud ultimately cause his downfall). Percy Hamleigh is a gentleman farmer who owns valuable land in the Earldom of Shiring. He is married to Regan, a megalomaniac who possesses a dream to climb the kingdom's social ladder. William Hamleigh, Percy and Regan's son, is Regan's pawn in her quest for power. Aliena, Bartholomew's daughter, is the object of William's obsession, and a woman determined to reestablish her family's position in the kingdom by helping her younger brother, Richard, win back what was wrongfully taken from him — the title of Earl of Shiring. Jack is Tom's protégé and a vital part in building the cathedral. Ellen is Jack's mother, a healer who uses her instincts and education to help Jack achieve his goals. Elizabeth is the 10-year-old daughter of an Earl in Maud's court. To gain political leverage, Regan arranges her marriage to her 24-year-old son, William.

Cast: Ian McShane *(Waleran Bigod)*; Rufus Sewell *(Tom Builder)*; Alison Pill *(Maud)*; Hayley Atwell *(Aliena)*; David Oakes *(William Hamleigh)*; Sarah Parish *(Regan Hamleigh)*; Robert Bathurst *(Percy Hamleigh)*; Natalia Woerner *(Ellen)*; Eddie Redmayne *(Jack)*; Tony Curran *(King Stephen)*; Sam Claflin *(Richard)*; Skye Lourie *(Elizabeth)*; Matthew Macfadyen *(Prior Philip)*; Donald Sutherland *(Bartholomew)*; Matt Devere *(Glouchester)*.

7296   *Pine Lake Lodge.* (Pilot; Comedy; Syn.; June 1961). Bill Baxter is the owner of Pine Lake Lodge, a resort just outside of Los Angeles. While Bill may be the owner, it is actually Martha, his assistant who keeps the business afloat. Bill is like a big kid and forever finding trouble—situations that could mean the end of the lodge. The proposal, a spin off from *Mister Ed* was to focus on Bill's efforts to do what he thinks is best for the lodge. Ann is Bill's niece; Cindy is Ann's daughter; Milo is the handyman. Originally produced as *The Bill Bendix Show*.

Cast: William Bendix (*Bill Parker*); Nancy Kulp (*Martha*); Coleen Gray (*Ann*); Marlene DeLamater (*Cindy*); John Quaylen (*Milo Simmons*).

7297   *Pink Collar.* (Pilot; Drama; Unaired; Produced for ABC in 2006). The American Accident Insurance Agency is a prestigious organization that is staffed mostly by women, Hayden, Claire and Alix being the principal employees. Hayden and Claire are best friends, but both are competing for a job as vice president. Hayden is a hard worker, but she tends to make minor mistakes that make her look bad to her supervisors; Claire, the ultimate competitor, has been sidetracked when she discovers a one night stand has left her pregnant and she now must decide between a career and motherhood. Alix, the newest employee, has everything going for her—beauty, an MBA degree and minority status. The proposal was to follow the women as compassion and competition clash, all of which is designed to show that the work place is also a woman's world.

Cast: Alicia Silverstone (*Hayden Flynn*); Hedy Burress (*Claire Shoop*); Ryan Michelle Bathe (*Alix*); Kristin Bauer (*Eve*); Matt Malloy (*Marcel*); Reggie Austin (*Steve*).

7298   *The Pink House.* (Pilot; Comedy; Unaired; Produced for NBC in 2010). Jamie, Emily, Fitz and Rob are friends and recent college graduates who are exploring the next phase of their lives. The proposal was to relate the mishaps that occur.

Cast: Katharine McPhee (*Emily*); Ashley Madekwe (*Jamie*); Michael Cassidy (*John "Fitz" Fitzgerald*); Zach Cregger (*Rob Burnett*).

7299   *Pink Lady.* (Series; Variety; NBC; 1980). Pink Lady, Japan's top-rated singers, team with American comic Jeff Altman for a program of music, song and comedy that is also known as *Pink Lady and Jeff*.

Host: Jeff Altman. **Co-Host:** Pink Lady (*Mei and Kei*). **Regulars:** Sid Caesar (as *Mei and Kei's father*); Sherry Eiken, Anna Mathias, Jim Varney, The Peacock Dancers. **Announcer:** Donald Rickles. **Orchestra:** Matthew McCauley.

7300   *The Pink Panther.* (Series; Cartoon; NBC; 1969–1979). The Pink Panther, the a non-talking and non discouraging animal that evolved from "The Pink Panther Theme" by Henry Mancini, is seen in various stories that find him attempting to cope with life despite the problems he counters from the Little Man. Also titled *The Pink Panther Laugh & Half Hour and a Half Show*. Other segments are *Inspector Clouseau* (the bumbling French detective), *The Ant and the Aardvark* (an ant attempts to avoid a hungry Aardvark); *Texas Toads* and *Mister Jaw* (mischievous shark).

Host: Lennie Schlutz. **Voices:** John Byner, Dave Barry, Paul Frees, Rich Little, Mel Blanc, Marvin Miller, Athena Ford, June Foray, Arte Johnson, Joan Gerber, Pat Harrington, Jr., Paul Winchell, Hal Smith, Larry Storch, Frank Welker.

7301   *Pink Panther and Pals.* (Series; Cartoon; Cartoon Network; 2010–). Modern adaptations of the 1960s theatrical animated shorts *The Pink Panther* and *The Ant and the Aardvark*. The Pink Panther segment has remained basically the same as it was originally conceived with the main exception being that The Pink Panther has been made younger (a teenager). He is still non-speaking and still encounters a problem with every thing he does. Hoarse is Panther's friend; Big Nose (originally The Little Man) is Panther's nemesis; Dog is the evil canine of Big Nose. *The Ant and the Aardvark* segment also remains basically the same with the Ant seeking to avoid being eaten by the Aardvark.

Voice Cast: Alex Nussbaum (*Pink Panther Vocal Effects*); Eddie Garvar (*Aardvark*); Kel Mitchell (*Ant*).

7302   *Pink Panther and Sons.* (Series; Cartoon; NBC; 1984–1985). A spin off from *The Pink Panther* that relates the antics of Pinky and Panky, the mischievous offspring of movie land's Pink Panther (from the song of the same name by Henry Mancini).

Voice Cast: Billy Bowles (*Pinky*); B.J. Ward (*Panky/Punkin*); Sherry Lynn (*Chatta*); Jeannie Elias (*Anney/Lione*); Frank Welker (*Finko/Rocko*).

7303   *Pinky and Company.* (Experimental; Comedy; NBC; July 28, 1939). Vaudeville comic Pinky Lee and two unidentified assistants (a man and a woman) perform various comedy sketches.

7304   *Pinky and the Brain.* (Series; Cartoon; WB; 1995–1998). Pinky is a dim-witted mouse and his friend, the Brian, a genius, are genetically engineered white mice who live in a cage at Acme Labs. The Brain has only one never-ending goal: to conquer the world. He comes up with seemingly ingenious plans and each night, when the lab closes, Pinky and the Brain escape from their cage and attempt to do the impossible—take over the world. Unfortunately, Pinky accompanies Brain and more often than not, manages to throw a monkey wrench into the works and foul up Brain's plan. But don't fret—there is always tomorrow night and a new plan to take over the world. A spin off from *Animaniacs* where short *Pinky and the Bain* segments occasionally aired. After its initial run, it returned for a short-lived 1998 spin off called *Pinky, Elmyra and the Brain* (which see).

Voice Cast: Maurice LaMarche (*The Brain*); Rob Paulsen (*Pinky*).

7305   *Pinky, Elmyra and the Brain.* (Series; Cartoon; WB; 1998-1999). A spin off from *Pinky and the Brain*. Pinky and the Brain are two genetically engineered white mice that live in a cage at Acme Labs. Brain has plans to take over the world and each night he and Pinky escape from their cages to set one such plan in motion (always foiled by Pinky's blundering). When Acme Labs closes, the lab mice find themselves being adopted by Elmyra Duff, a little girl who loves animals so much (too much) that they can't wait to escape from her bedroom and live anywhere else. Now, living in a cage in Elmyra's bedroom, the Brain still plots to take over the world, but this time, he must keep the secret from Elmyra, avoid her and Pinky's continual antics, and deal with Rudy Mookich, the neighborhood bully.

Voice Cast: Rob Paulsen (*Pinky*); Maurice LaMarche (*The Brain*); Cree Summer (*Elmyra Duff*); Nancy Cartwright (*Rudy Mookich*).

7306   *The Pinky Lee Show.* (Series; Comedy; NBC; 1950–1956). Music, songs, circus variety acts and burlesque like comedy routines with vaudeville comedian Pinky Lee as the host.

Host: Pinky Lee. **Regulars:** Betty Jane Howarth (as *Lily Chrysanthemum*); Roberta Shore, Mel Knootz, Jimmy Brown. **Announcer:** Ken Mayer, Jerry Lawrence. **Music:** The Charlie Couch Trio.

7307   *Pinwheel.* (Series; Children; Nick; 1979–1989). Live action hosts Jake and Kim and their puppet friends present various entertainment for children. Puppets include Luigi O'Brien, who could talk to vegetables; Silas the Snail, whose slow means of moving made him late for everything; Molly, the elderly mole; Ebenezer T. Squint, a mean green creature; hobo bugs Plus and Minus; and Orelia the fortune teller. Assisting Jake and Kim are human co-hosts Smitty and Sal, the local newspaper reporters. Began locally in Columbus, Ohio, on the Pinwheel Channel in 1979. A year later Pinwheel became Nickelodeon and the program ran for an additional nine years.

Cast: George James (*Jake*); Arline Miyazaki (*Kim*); Betty Rozek (*Sal*); Dale Engel (*Smitty*).

7308   *Pioneer Spirit.* (Pilot; Comedy; NBC; July 21, 1969). Dissatisfied with city life, Jeff Wilson, a route map maker for the Los Angeles Automobile Club, convinces his wife (Cherry) and his friends (Harvey and Carl) to move to Nome, Alaska, where they can get 1600 acres of land free if they homestead it. The proposal was to relate their adventures as homesteaders. Other regulars are Ada, Harvey's wife; and Jenny, Carl's wife. Roy Clark performs the theme, "Pioneer Spirit."

Cast: Rich Little (*Jeff Wilson*); Marcia Rodd (*Cherry Wilson*); Roy Clark (*Harvey*); Donna Jean Young (*Ada*); Craig Huebing (*Carl*); Francine York (*Jenny*).

7309   *Pioneer Woman.* (Pilot; Western; ABC; Dec. 19, 1973). Following the death of her husband (John), a courageous young woman (Margaret Sergeant) decides to begin a new life with her children (Sarah and Jeremy) as homesteaders in the rugged Wyoming territory of 1867. The proposal was to relate Margaret's efforts to make a life for herself and her children.

Cast: Joanna Pettet (*Margaret Sergeant*); Helen Hunt (*Sarah Sergeant*); Russell Baer (*Jeremy Sergeant*).

7310   *The Pioneers.* (Series; Anthology; Syn.; 1964). The syndicated title for 104 selected episodes of *Death Valley Days* hosted by Will Rogers, Jr.

7311   *Pip the Piper.* (Series; Children; ABC; NBC; 1961-1962). Pipertown is a magical and musical city in the clouds. It is here that the fantasy-like adventures of Pip the Piper and his friends Miss Merrynote and Mr. Leader, the buffoon are depicted . Aired on ABC (Jan. 1 to May 28, 1961) and NBC (June 24, 1961 to Sept. 22, 1962).

Cast: Jack Spear (*Pip the Piper*); Phyllis Spear (*Miss Merrynote*); Lucien Kaminsky (*Mr. Leader*).

7312   *Piper's Pets.* (Pilot; Comedy; NBC; May 31, 1973). Dr. Donald Piper is a competent veterinarian with a noticeable flaw: he is very nervous and easily excitable. He is assisted by Lester, a not-too-bright vet who has a knack for upsetting him and the proposal was to focus on Dr. Piper as he tries to maintain his composure amid the numerous aggravations that plague him. Maggie is Lester's wife; and Thelma is Donald's receptionist.

Cast: Don Knotts (*Donald Piper*); Peter Isacksen (*Lester*); Maggie Roswell (*Maggie*); Jacque Lynn Colton (*Thelma*).

7313   *Pippi Longstocking.* (Pilot; Fantasy; ABC; Jan. 8, 1961). Susan is a pretty but lonely young girl whose dreams of a magical girl come to life for her and the viewer as Pippilotta "Pippy" Longstocking, a brilliant girl whose father is a cannibal king and who lives in a strange house with a horse and a monkey. Aired on *The Shirley Temple Theater* and based on the stories by Astrid Lindgren.

Cast: Gina Gillespie (*Susan/Pippi Longstocking*); Willard Waterman (*Papa Efriam*); Barbara Eiler (*Mrs. Scholfield*); Renie Raino (*Miss Lindquist*).

7314   *Pippi Longstocking.* (Pilot; Fantasy; ABC; Nov. 2 and 9, 1985). Pippilotta Delicatessa Windowshade Mackrelmint Efriam Longstocking, commonly known as Pippi Longstocking, is a feisty red-haired young girl who lives without adults, spins tall tales and enjoys exciting adventures. The proposal was to relate Pippi's various adventures with her best friends Annika and Tommy. Pippi's father, Captain Efriam Longstocking, is a pirate at sea and she says, "My mother is an angel in heaven." She lives with a monkey named Mr. Nilsson and a horse called Horse.

Cast: Carrie Heim (*Pippi Longstocking*); Alyson Court (*Annika*); Eric Hebert (*Tommy*); David Waldern (*Efriam Longstocking*).

7315   *Pippi Longstocking.* (Series; Cartoon; Qubo; 2009). Pippilotta Longstocking (Pippi for short) is the daughter of Ephriam Longstocking, a sea captain (who, after being shipwrecked, became a cannibal king) and lives in a home (Villa Villekula) with a monkey (Mr. Nilsson) and a horse (Horse). Her best friends are her neighbors, Tommy and Annika Settergren (a brother and sister). Pippi was raised by her father and is very intelligent despite the lack of a formal education. She is very strong, distrusts adults and possesses two treasures: a suitcase filled with gold coins and a large chest of drawers that contain items of interest to her. Stories follow Pippi as she goes about leading a life children can only dream of. Based on the books by Astrid Lindgren and produced in England. Kling and Klang are the police officers who aide Pippi; Bloom and Thunder Carlson are the crooks seeking Pippi's gold.

Voice Cast: Melissa Altro (*Pippi Longstocking*); Olivia Garrett (*Annika*); Noah Reid (*Tommy*); Richard Binsky (*Mr. Nilsson*); Ben Campbell (*Captain Longstocking*); Karen Bernstein (*Mrs. Settergen*); Ray Landry (*Mr. Settergren*); Rick Jones (*Officer Kling*); Philip Williams (*Officer Klang*); Wayne Robson (*Bloom*); Ken Carlson (*Thunder Carlson*).

7316   *Pirate Islands.* (Series; Adventure; Fox; 2003). Kate Redding is a teenage girl fascinated by video games. Being the daughter of a video game developer, she gets to test the latest games before they are marketed. Her father's latest creation is "Pirate Islands," wherein the player must beat an 18th century pirate to a hidden treasure. Kate has two younger siblings, Sarah and Nicholas, who are also testing the game with her. When Sarah sees that a scanner is attached to the game, she tests it by scanning a hat into the game. As she is doing this, a thunderstorm is beginning to develop. When a bolt of lightning flashes, it causes a power surge that charges the scanner and engulfs the children in its power. Kate, Sarah and Nicholas are transported inside the game console and onto Pirate Island, where the pirates of the evil Captain Blackheart immediately capture them. From out of nowhere comes Mars, a character in the game, who rescues them, and takes them to his secret island (Castaway Island), where he and a group of young children live (they are cared for by Mars and Carmen, the only other teenagers on the island beside Kate). Mars and Carmen have chosen Castaway Island as their hideaway to avoid capture by Blackheart, who is seeking them and the other castaways.

Kate believes she is in a game but what is happening can't be happening. She feels that if she can find the scanner (which was lost in the transfer) and turn it on, she can reverse the process and return home. But in the meantime, she Sarah and Nicholas have to avoid capture by the pirates. Kate, Sarah and Nicholas quickly adapt to their new environment and set up a base in a tree house their father programmed into the game. Each of the islands has an icon (a symbol in the computer game to indicate a doorway) that enables travel from one island to another through its magic portal. Carmen believes Kate's appearance will mean capture for them by Captain Blackheart. The series, produced in Australia, aired Saturday morning on Fox; a concluding episode was never shown (the episodes shown here left Sarah, Kate and Nicholas stranded in the video game and seeking ways to outsmart Blackheart and retrieve the scanner).

Cast: Brooke Harmon (*Kate Redding*); Eliza Taylor-Cotter (*Sarah Redding*); Nicholas Donaldson (*Nicholas Redding*); Oliver Ackland (*Mars*); Lucia Smyrk (*Carmen*); Colin Moody (*Captain Blackheart*); Andy McPhee (*Cutthroat Jack*); Darcy Bonser (*Perry*); Madeleine Jay (*Lizard*); Jim Daly (*Dugal*); Jasper Bagg (*Darcy the Dandy*); Franklyn Ajaye (*Five Spice*); Russell Allan (*Ugly Sam*); Graham Jahne (*Ned Crow*).

7317   Pirate Master. (Series; Reality; CBS; 2007). Sixteen "modern day pirates" attempt to find $1 million in hidden treasure. The pirates, all who have knowledge of sailing, are housed aboard *Picton Castle*, a 179-foot square-rigger ship. Each pirate must pull his (or her) own weight or face elimination. The first episode divides the players into two equal teams: the Red and the Black. It also begins the first treasure hunt as each team is given a map and a compass. The ship is docked in the Caribbean off the island of Dominica. The pirates use the map (as well as their wits) to find the treasure hidden on the rather rough terrain island. The first team to find the treasure chest (which is well hidden) wins its contents (gold coins) and the money is split. Players who fail to meet the expectations of the other pirates are placed in a lifeboat, "cut" lose and set adrift. The one pirate who acquires the largest booty on the last episode wins and becomes "The Pirate Master." Cameron Daddo hosts.

7318   The Pirates of Dark Water. (Series; Cartoon; ABC; 1991). Mer (also called Octopon) is a distant planet of water that is being threatened with extinction by Dark Water, a carnivorous form of water that devours everything it crosses. Ren is a young hero on a quest to save his planet. Ren is the son of a lighthouse keeper. One day, after rescuing a man from the sea, Ren learns from the man, who once served with Ren's true father, that he is the son of the king of Octopon. To claim his rightful heritage, Ren must find the Thirteen Treasures of Rule. The treasures will also save the planet by stopping the Dark Water. Ren receives a magic compass from the man as well as three assistants: Ioz, the pirate, Tula, a young girl, and Niddler the Monkey Bird. Stories relate Ren's journey—made more dangerous by Bloth, an evil pirate who has learned of the treasure and now seeks it for himself.

Voice Cast: George Newbern (*Ren*); Roddy McDowall (*Niddler*); Jodi Benson (*Tula*); Hector Elizondo (*Ioz*); Brock Peters (*Bloth*).

7319   The Pirates of Flounder Bay. (Pilot; Comedy; ABC; Aug. 26, 1966). The small town of Flounder Bay in the 1880s is the setting. The town's most notable resident is Barnaby Kidd, a pirate captain who has an infamous grandfather—the notorious Captain Kidd. Barnaby, however, is nothing like his grandfather, who was mean and evil; he is kind-hearted and trouble-prone and the unsold series was to relate Barnaby's bumbling efforts to become as famous as his grandfather. Other regulars are The Governor; Captain Jack Slash, the rival pirate; Abner Bunker, the mayor; Molly Bunker, Abner's daughter (and Barnaby's romantic interest); and Barnaby's crew of misfits: Sidney, Taggert, Flint, Wimple, Chips and Lookout.

Cast: William Cort (*Barnaby Kidd*); Basil Rathbone (*Governor*); Keenan Wynn (*Jack Slash*); Harold Peary (*Abner Bunker*); Bridget Hanley (*Molly Bunker*); Jack Soo (*Sidney*); Charles Dierkop (*Taggert*); Burt Mustin (*Flint*); Jim Connell (*Wimple*); Peter Bonerz (*Chips*); Jim Begg (*Lookout*).

7320   Pistols 'n' Petticoats. (Series; Comedy; CBS; 1966-1967). Wretched, Colorado, 1871, is a wild and woolly town plagued by outlaws, greedy land barons and constant Indian uprisings. Harold Sikes is the deputy sheriff. Unfortunately, he is clumsy, unable to shoot straight and plagued by guns that get stuck in his holster (making him slow on the draw). He trips a lot and has a white horse that

he can't exactly ride (the horse always stops short and throws him off).

Coming to Harold's rescue (and the actual keepers of the peace) are the gun-toting Hanks family (ranchers). Henrietta, nicknamed "Hank," is an attractive widow "who could fire a gun with one hand milking a goat and hit a coyote on the run." Andrew, called "Grandpa," is Henrietta's father. He is a former Union Army private and is hopeless without his glasses (he can't see or shoot straight without them). He carries his former army rifle with him at all times; "he kept his gun in trim—nobody messed around with him."

Andrew's wife (name not mentioned; called "Honey" by Andrew) is a sweet looking elderly lady who "was best at shootin' buttons off a rustler's vest." Lucy, Henrietta's beautiful daughter, is very feminine and is in love with Harold. Although she rarely uses a gun, she is an expert shot and conceals one in a lacy garter she wears on her right thigh. Lucy has faith in Harold but can't convince her mother that "Harold can rescue people in distress and things like that." "Lucy, dear," responds Henrietta, "that's woman's work." As the theme says, "Chasing bandits to them was fun ... every outlaw in the West would run from Pistols and Petticoats."

Bernard Courtney is the land baron seeking to obtain the Hanks' ranch; Jed Timmins is the crooked lawyer; Eagle Shadow is chief of the Kiowa Indians; Gray Hawk is Eagle Shadow's son; Great Bear is chief of the Atona Indians; Little Bear is Great Bear's son; Cyrus Breech is the gun smuggler. There is also the unnamed town drunk and the unnamed W.C. Fields type of character who hangs out at the Wretched saloon.

In the original, unaired pilot film (produced in 1966), Chris Noel played Lucy Hanks and Joel D. McCrea was Sheriff Eric (the same type of role that later became Harold Sykes).

Cast: Ann Sheridan (*Henrietta Hanks*); Carole Wells (*Lucy Hanks*); Douglas V. Fowley (*Andrew Hanks*); Ruth McDevitt (*Grandma Hanks*); Gary Vinson (*Harold Sikes*); Robert Lowery (*Bernard Courtney*); Morgan Woodward (*Mark Hangman*); Stanley Adams (*Jed Timmins*); Lon Chaney, Jr. (*Eagle Shadow*); Marc Cavell (*Gray Hawk*); Jay Silverheels (*Great Bear*); Alex Henteloff (*Little Bear*); Eleanor Audley (*Mrs. Tinsley*); Leo Gordon (*Cyrus Breech*); Gil Lamb (*Town drunk*); Bill Oberlin (*W.C. Fields–like citizen*).

7321   Pitching Horseshoes. (Series; Anthology; NBC; 1950-1951). The alternate title for *Billy Rose's Playbill*. See this title for information.

7322   Pitfall. (Series; Anthology; Syn.; 1955). Dramas that revolve around people caught in a web of concealed danger. Gale Storm, Richard Denning, Bonita Granville, Lynn Bari, Patric Knowles, Robert Hutton, Suzanne Dabert and Elizabeth Patterson were among the stars that appeared.

7323   Pitfall. (Series; Game; Syn.; 1981). Two players compete. A five-point or a five-minute game (which ever happens first) is played. The host reads a question to which four answers appear on a board. Each member of the studio audience selects one answer by pressing a button that corresponds to one of the answers. Each player selects one answer. The studio audience votes are tabulated and the highest percentage answer is revealed. The player whose answer matches the studio audience response receives one point. The winner, the player with the highest score, receives no money; instead he gets two pit passes. The winner now faces a large bridge that contains eight sections (six sections are safe; two are pitfalls). Before entering the top level of the bridge, the player receives his two pit passes. The player begins on section one. A question is read. If the player answers correctly, he receives $100 and advances to the next section. The object is for the player to get from section one to section eight within

100 seconds. If a player feels that the section he will be entering is a pitfall, he uses one of his pit passes and avoids that particular section. If a player enters a pitfall, that section lowers one level and the player remains there until he answers a question correctly. The player earns what money he has accumulated ($100 per section per correct answer) plus a new car if he manages to get through all eight sections within the time limit.

Host: Alex Trebek. **Announcer:** John Barton.

7324   The Pitts. (Series; Comedy; Fox; 2003). Mail Boxes and Mail More is a store owned by marrieds Bob and Liz Pitts. They are the parents of Faith and Pete and 555-5555 is their phone number. They live in Nevada in a house located at the bottom of a mountain with a very large boulder perched at the top edge of the mountain and apparently ready to fall.

Faith is 16 years old and attends Stateville High School. She believes her family is cursed — "Life is a bowl of cherries — but you can' have the cherries without the pits." Bob has been struck by lightning; Pete has been possessed and exorcised; Faith has a haunted violin, has been struck in the head by a pipe (when their hot water heater exploded) and believes boys are afraid of her because her family has bad luck. No matter what the Pitts do, extremely bad luck accompanies them. The only lucky thing they have is their dog — Lucky. Stories follow the Pitts as they go about living a life that is the pits.

Liz wears Jaclyn Smith original dresses (available at K-Mart); Pete likes hanging out at the dump and go to health clubs "to laugh at the fat guys" and to go to the back of Korean restaurants "to look for cat parts." The series was quite unusual and entertaining but lasted only four episodes.

Cast: Dylan Baker *(Bob Pitts)*; Kellie Waymire *(Liz Pitts)*; Lizzy Caplan *(Faith Pitts)*; David Henrie *(Pete Pitts)*.

7325   The Pitts. (Pilot; Cartoon; Unaired; Produced for Fox in 2008). An animated version of the short-lived 2003 live action series about the world's unluckiest family, the Pitts: parents Bob and Liz and their children Faith and Petey.

Voice Cast: Allison Janney *(Liz Pitt)*; Dylan Baker *(Bob Pitt)*; Lizzy Caplan *(Faith Pitt)*; Andy Milonakis *(Petey Pitt)*.

7326   Pixanne. (Series; Children; Syn.; 1978). Pixanne is a very pretty fairy who lives in a magical forest. She loves to sing, dance and tell stories and through her activities, educational information is related to children.

Program Open: "Hi, I'm Pixanne. Fly with me through my magic forest and we'll have lots of fun and adventure together. Don't go away."

Cast: Jane Norman *(Pixanne)*; The Addid Williams Puppets *(Regulars)*.

7327   P.J. Sparkles. (Pilot; Cartoon; Fox; Nov. 26, 1992). P.J. is a young girl who wishes for love on full moons. All P.J. has ever known is Mrs. O'Malley's Orphanage. Every time she makes a friend, they are adopted and she is alone again. One night P.J., accompanied by her horse, Blaze, makes a wish upon a star. The night is cloudy, but as the clouds roll by, a bright star shines on P.J. and in a flash of light, she and Blaze are magically transported to Twinkle Town. There P.J. learns from the Wishing Star that for untold times the children of Twinkle Town have wished upon the Wishing Star for someone to come here and love them. (Twinkle Town was magically created by all the lights of all the stars ever wished upon by children. The land exists because of the children's dreams and love.) P.J. was brought here to lead them and love them. Because she now sparkles, P.J. takes the last name of Sparkles. P.J.'s love makes the children of Twinkle

Town happy, so much so that the Wishing Star asks her to help other children. P.J. appoints three children (Glimmer, Sparks and Glowee) as her assistants to rule Twinkle Town in her absence. However, trouble enters the picture when the Cloak, the Master of the Dark, and his evil wife, Betty, turn Twinkle Town into a gloom town. The proposal was to relate P.J.'s efforts to defeat the Cloak and restore beauty to Twinkle Town.

Voice Cast: Jodi Benson *(P.J. Sparkles)*; Robby Benson *(Blaze)*; Oliver Muirhead *(The Cloak)*; Roger Hess *(Betty)*; Olivia Hack *(Glowee)*; Janna Michaels *(Glimmer)*; Dana Goetz *(Sparks)*; Samantha Eggar *(Wishing Star)*.

7328   The PJ's. (Series; Comedy; Fox, 1999-2000; WB, 2000-2001). Thurgood Stubbs is the maintenance engineer, called "Supa" by the tenants, of the 13-story Hilton Jacobs Building in the Projects. Thurgood is married to Muriel and they share a basement apartment. Thurgood is 48 years old "but looks 60." Hoping to provide a place for the tenants to relax, Thurgood purchased the abandoned movie theater on Al Sharpton Boulevard from HUD (Housing and Urban Development) for one dollar; it soon became the Thurgood Stubbs Neighborhood Theater. For Thurgood, rent day is as much fun as eviction day.

Muriel, most always seen in a pink blouse with "Paris" on it, is president of Women United to Save Our Projects. She is totally devoted to Thurgood and keeps a daily record of her activities in her journal.

Regular tenants are Juicy Hudson, the overweight boy who idolizes Thurgood and wears a sign that reads "Do Not Feed"; the elderly Mrs. Avery, whom Thurgood calls "a dried-up old gargoyle," is forever hitting him with her cane; Mambo Garcelle is the voodoo priestess Thurgood calls "Haiti Lady" or "Voodoo Queen"; Calvin is Juicy's friend; and Sanchez is the once-promising opera star whose passion for cigarettes now forces him to speak with a throat microphone. Filmed in a puppet-animation process called Fomation; Phil Morris provided Thurgood's voice in two episodes.

Voice Cast: Eddie Murphy *(Thurgood Stubbs)*; Loretta Devine *(Muriel Stubbs)*; Ja'net DuBois *(Mrs. Avery)*; Cheryl Frances Harrington *(Mambo Garcelle)*; Pepe Serna *(Sanchez)*; Crystal Scales *(Calvin)*.

7329   Place the Face. (Series; Game; CBS; NBC; 1953–1955). Specially selected contestants are placed opposite someone from their past. Through a series of clues that are provided by the host, the players have to associate each other's faces. The first player to make the association is the winner and receives merchandise prizes. Aired on CBS (July 2, 1953 to Aug. 26, 1954) and NBC (Sept. 25 to Dec. 25, 1954; and June 28 to Sept. 13, 1955).

Host: Jack Smith (1953), Jack Paar (1954), Bill Cullen (1955).

7330   Places Please. (Series; Variety; CBS; 1948-1949). Barry Wood oversees a program that is set in the backstage of a television studio and presents performances by bit players (new talent discoveries) and cronies from Broadway shows and nightclubs.

7331   Plain Jane. (Series; Reality; CW; 2010). Billed as "a new life-changing reality series" wherein a plain Jane receives a complete makeover (by fashion expert and host Louise Roe) in the hope that it will help build her self-confidence and give her a new outlook on life.

7332   The Plainclothesman. (Series; Crime Drama; DuMont; 1949–1954). The subjective camera method is used to detail the investigations of a never-seen lieutenant with the New York City Police Department. By use of the subjective camera, which enacts emotion and becomes the eyes of the lieutenant, the viewer hears the actor's voice and experiences situations as if he were actually present.

Cast: Ken Lynch (*The Unseen Lieutenant*); Jack Orrinson (*Sergeant Brady*).

7333 *Plan B.* (Pilot; Comedy; Unaired; Produced for ABC in 2003). As a teenager Caroline planned her future—where she would be by the time she was thirty. That time has arrived and Caroline has not achieved her goals. She has no man in her life, a mother (Lydia) with plenty of advice, an advising, always pregnant kid sister (Amy) and a difficult time resisting snack foods. The proposal was to relate Caroline's efforts to reexamine her life and achieve those long sought goals.

Cast: Caroline Rhea (*Caroline*); Millicent Martin (*Lydia*); Kali Rocha (*Amy*).

7334 *Planet Earth.* (Pilot; Science Fiction; ABC; April 23, 1974). A sequel to *Genesis II* about Dylan Hunt, a scientist who was lost in 1979 during a suspended animation accident and found 154 years later (A.D. 2133) by the people of a civilization called Pax (peace), the one area on Earth that escaped a nuclear war in the twentieth century. The revised proposal was to depict Dylan's exploits, as the leader of a Pax science team, as he seeks to rebuild the Earth into a newer and wiser civilization. Harper-Smythe is Dylan's assistant; Peter is a Pax leader; Isaiah is a featured Pax.

Cast: John Saxon (*Dylan Hunt*); Janet Margolin (*Harper-Smythe*); Ted Cassidy (*Isaiah*); Rai Tasco (*Peter Kimbridge*).

7335 *Planet of the Apes.* (Series; Science Fiction; CBS; 1974). A U.S. space capsule, launched in 1988, is approaching Alpha Centauri when it penetrates a radioactive turbulence area. The ship is propelled to Earth in the year 3881—a time when intelligent apes are ruling what is left of a world devastated by a holocaust sometime in the year 2000.

Two of the three astronauts aboard the ship — Colonel Alan Virdon and Captain Peter ("Pete") Burke — are captured by the ape leader Urko and imprisoned (the third astronaut, identified only as Jonesy, was killed on impact). The apes believe that simians have always ruled the world. There are humans in this time, but they are servants, laborers and farmers. Ape Prefect Zaius believes that Pete and Alan are a threat to their species because they have greater knowledge and abilities than the other humans; if it were known that there are intelligent humans, it would cause the apes' humans to revolt. Urko thinks that Pete and Alan should be killed before their presence becomes known. Zaius orders that the astronauts be kept alive, however, so their knowledge can be learned by the ape leaders. Urko disapproves.

Zaius's assistant, Galen, becomes intrigued by the astronauts' intelligence, and in seeking to learn more about them, he becomes their friend. One night, after Alan and Pete are fed, their cell door is left unlocked. As Pete and Alan emerge from their cell, Galen sees that Urko has set a trap to kill them. Galen yells, "Watch out!" to Pete and Alan; a fight ensues, and one of Urko's lieutenants is killed. Pete and Alan manage to escape, but Galen is caught and imprisoned—despite the fact that he accuses Urko of setting a trap. When Pete and Alan learn of Galen's imprisonment, they rescue him, and soon the three become fugitives from the state. Stories relate the trio's adventures as they seek a way to return to the Earth of the 1980s. Adapted from the feature film series of the same title.

Alan believes that their only hope of returning home is to use the ship's magnetic disk (which recorded the flight), find a computer and reverse the process. Their major problem: finding a computer and human intelligence enough to build a ship.

Pete and Alan crash-landed in California. The apes have renamed this area Central City, and it is ruled by the High Council. Where he is not known, Galen pretends to be Protus; Pete and Alan pose as his servants.

Cast: Roddy McDowall (*Galen*); Ron Harper (*Alan Virdon*); James Naughton (*Peter Burke*); Mark Leonard (*Urko*); Booth Coleman (*Zaius*); Woodrow Patfrey (*Veska*).

7336 *Planet Patrol.* (Series; Adventure; Syn.; 1963). The work of the agents for the Galasphere Patrol, an 21st century interplanetary police force that has been established to protect the planets of a united solar system. Marionette characters include Colonel Raeburn, the Galasphere leader; Captain Larry Dart; Husky, the Martian; Slim the Venusian; and Berridge, the enemy. Also known as *Space Patrol*.

Voice Cast: Dick Vosburgh (*Captain Larry Dart*); Murray Kash (*Colonel Raeburn*); Ysanne Churchron (*Marla*); Libby Morris (*Marla*); Ysanne Churchron, Libby Morris (*Cassiopeia*); Libby Morris (*Gabbler*).

7337 *Planet Sheen.* (Series; Cartoon; Nick; 2010–). A spin off from *The Adventures of Jimmy Neutron: Boy Genius*. Sheen Estevez, Jimmy Neutron's friend, sneaks into Jimmy's lab and finds a top secret rocket ship Jimmy constructed. While fiddling with the controls, Sheen launches the rocket and himself into outer space. He crash lands on the planet Zeenu, where he angers Dorkus, an evil being whose home was destroyed by the rocket ship. When Sheen learns his ship has been disabled by the crash, he finds that he is marooned on Zeenu, a planet of purple aliens. As Sheen makes friends, especially with Doppy and Nesmith (the talking chimp) and attempts to adjust to a new life, he also finds himself being threatened by Dorkus, who plans to get even with Sheen for what he did to him.

Voice Cast: Jeff Garcia (*Sheen Estevez*); Rob Paulsen (*Doppy*); Bob Jones (*Nesmith*); Soleil Moon Frye (*Aseefa*); Jeff Bennett (*Dorkus*); Candi Milo (*Princess Oomlout I*); Morgan Murphy (*Princess Oomlout II*); Fred Tatasciore (*Emperor*).

7338 *The Plant Family.* (Pilot; Comedy; CBS; Sept. 2, 1978). Lyla and Augie Plant own a run-down house in a borderline neighborhood in southern California. They have a married daughter (Ava) and a maid (Geneva) and the proposal was to follow the mishaps that occur as all family members ban together to devise various schemes to get rich quick. Other regulars are Art, Ava's husband; and Homer Jay, Geneva's son.

Cast: Joyce Van Patten (*Lyla Plant*); Norman Alden (*Augie Plant*); Kay Heberle (*Ava*); Larry Hankin (*Art*); Jo Marie Payton (*Geneva*); DeWayne Hessie (*Homer Jay*).

7339 *The Plasticman Comedy/Adventure Show.* (Series; Cartoon; ABC; 1979–1981). The overall title for four cartoon series.

1. Plasticman. Plasticman (who can stretch his skin) is an agent for the National Bureau of Investigation. Penny, his girlfriend, and Hoola Hoola assist him as they carry out assignments.

2. Mightyman and Yukk. Mightyman, the world's smallest superhero, and Yukk, the world's ugliest dog, battle the sinister forces of evil.

3. Rickety Rocket. Rickety Rocket, a talking space ship, and its human assistants, Cosgrove, Venus, Splashdown and Sunstroke, battle interplanetary evil.

4. Fangface and Fangpuss. Sherman "Fang" Fangsworth is a teenager who changes into a werewolf under the moon and reverts to normal at sunup. Together with his friends Kim, Buff and Puggsy, Fang fights the forces of evil—more often than not as a werewolf. Fangpuss is Sherman's cousin.

Voice Cast: Michael Bell (*Plasticman*); Melendy Britt (*Penny*); Joe

Baker (*Hoola Hoola*); Peter Cullen (*Mightyman*); Frank Welker (*Yukk*); Al Fann (*Rickety Rocket*); Bobby Ellerbee (*Cosgrove*); Dee Timberlake (*Venus*); Johnny Brown (*Splashdown*); John Anthony Bailey (*Sunstroke*); Jerry Dexter (*Fangface/Fangpuss/Biff*); Susan Blu (*Kim*); Bart Braverman (*Puggsy*).

7340   *Platinum*. (Series; Drama; UPN; 2003). Grady and Jackson Rhames are brothers who have built the now successful Platinum Records from the ground up. The company, based in New York, caters to rap and hip-hop performers and stories follow the brothers as they struggle to maintain their enterprise. Jade is their younger sister; Monica is Jackson's wife; David Ross is their friend and chief counsel.

Cast: Sticky Fingaz (*Grady Rhames*); Jason George (*Jackson Rhames*); Davetta Sherwood (*Jade Rhames*); Lalanya Masters (*Monica Rhames*); Steven Pasquale (*David Ross*); Sarah Manninen (*Olivia Ross*).

7341   *Platinum Babies*. (Series; Reality; WE; 2009). Jessica Denay and Natalie Klein of the Hot Moms Club are profiled as they work with wealthy parents as they throw expensive baby showers in anticipation of their new arrival. Also featured is Kimberlee Mitchell, who helps outfit nurseries and baby proofs homes.

7342   *Platinum Weddings*. (Series; Reality; WE; 2006). Just how much should a wedding cost? If you are rich it doesn't matter and *Platinum Weddings* caters to such people. Each episode is a look at a highly extravagant wedding — not so much the ceremony itself, but the preparations and expenses that go into the making of such affairs — from exorbitant meals ($1,500 a head) to lavish wedding gowns ($50,000 and up). Julie Pryor and Larry Flachs host.

7343   *Platonically Incorrect*. (Pilot; Comedy; Unaired; Produced for ABC in 2003). Ever since college, when Darlene and Scott became fast friends, it was like fate had intended them to be together forever. Their friends and family can see this and believe they should marry, but Darlene and Scott consider each other just best friends and made a solemn pact that falling in love with each other is off limits. Darlene and Scott are the co-hosts of a local TV talk show where their on-air presence also dictates that they should be a married couple (despite the fact that she's neurotic but adorable; and he's immature but lovable). The proposal was to follow Darlene and Scott as they share each other's joys and sorrows with friends hoping they will see the light and realize they are the perfect couple.

Cast: A.J. Langer (*Darlene*); Tom Everett Scott (*Scott*); Kali Rocha (*Katie*); Brian Scolaro (*Bob*).

7344   *Platypus Man*. (Series; Comedy; UPN; 1995). Richard Jeni considers himself a "Platypus Man" (a solitary male, like the male platypus). He is a chef and hosts *Cooking with the Platypus Man*, "a TV cooking show for guys." Lou is the show's executive producer; Paige is Richard's neighbor, a sportswriter and Tommy is Richard's brother, a bartender. Stories relate events in the personal and working life of Richard as he struggles to cope with the numerous problems that confront him.

Cast: Richard Jeni (*Himself*); Denise Miller (*Paige McAllister*); David Dundara (*Tommy Jeni*); Ron Orbach (*Lou Golembiewski*).

7345   *Play Nice*. (Pilot; Comedy; Unaired; Produced for CBS in 2006). Sarah and Scott are the offspring of Roger and Barbara Buntz, the owners of the Buntz Toy Company. Roger and Barbara believe the time has come for them to step aside and let their children take over the business. Sarah is responsible; Scott is just the opposite and the proposal was to follow their efforts to run the family business.

Cast: Fred Willard (*Roger*); Swoosie Kurtz (*Barbara*); Sara Rue (*Sarah*); Timm Sharp (*Scott*).

7346   *Play or Be Played*. (Pilot; Drama; Unaired; Produced for NBC in 2007). Unethical attorneys in a prestigious New York are the subjects of a proposal that depicts them doing whatever it takes to win their high profile cases, including out maneuvering each other.

Cast: Kurtwood Smith (*Gene Whitacre*); Christina Vidal (*Gail*); Alan Tudyk (*Charlie*); Andrew Lincoln (*Joe*); Frankie Faison (*Lyle*); Megan Dodds (*Hannah*).

7347   *Play the Game*. (Pilot; Game; ABC; Jan. 30, 1946). Selected studio audience members compete in a game of charades in return for prizes. Twenty such games were played and songs by Ireene Wicker and Vic Hammer were interspersed between the games.

Cast: Charlotte Adams, Alan Chedzcy, Vic Hammer, Willard Mullen, Ireene Wicker, Harvey Zourbough.

7348   *Play the Percentages*. (Series; Game; Syn.; 1980). Two teams compete, each composed of two members. A question, based on a survey of 300 people, is read. One member of each team predicts the percentage of people surveyed who were able to answer the question. The actual percentage is revealed and the player who comes closest wins the percentage value in points. The first team to score 300 points is the winner and receives $300.

Host: Geoff Edwards. **Announcer:** Jay Stewart. **Music:** Hal Hidey.

7349   *Play Your Hunch*. (Series; Game; CBS; ABC; NBC; 1958–1963). Two husband-and-wife couples compete in a game based on solving problems by instinct. Three sets that pertain to one subject are displayed. The couples have to determine the factor that distinguishes one from the others. The first couple to score three correct identifications is the winner and receives merchandise prizes. Aired on CBS (1958-59), ABC (1959), and NBC (1959–63).

Host: Richard Hayes, Gene Rayburn, Merv Griffin, Robert Q. Lewis. **Assistant:** Liz Gardner.

7350   *Playboy After Dark*. (Series; Variety; Syn.; 1969). Music and conversation with *Playboy* magazine publisher Hugh Hefner as the host (and surrounded by the Playboy Bunnies).

Host: Hugh Hefner. **Bunny Hostess:** Barbi Benton. **Music:** Tommy Oliver.

7351   *The Playboy Radio Show*. (Series; Erotica; Playboy Channel; 2010). A behind-the-scenes visual look at the "naughty" happenings that occur at the real life SIRIUS radio station, Playboy Radio. Supposedly based on "tons of requests from fans and subscribers to put cameras in the studio," the sexual shenanigans that could only once be heard are taped and edited to present a weekly 30-minute recap of "everything you love about Playboy Radio taken to a whole other level."

Stars: Christy Canyon (host of *Night Calls*); Tiffany Granath (host of *Afternoon Advice*); Andrea Lowell (host of *The Playboy Morning Show*); and Nicki Hunter (host of *Private Calls*).

7352   *Playboy Shootout*. (Series; Reality; Playboy; 2010). Ten beautiful female models and ten talented photographers compete for the opportunity to appear in and shoot a *Playboy* magazine layout. Each week the models and photographers are paired for challenges that test their ability to model and capture the essence of what it takes to appear in an issue of *Playboy*. Each photo shoot is judged by a celebrity panel "and only the photos that live up to Playboy's highest class of sex appeal and style" assure that these models and photographers continue onto the next stage of the competition. The one team that meets all the requirements set by Playboy head Hugh Hefner wins the competition.

Host: Brande Roderick *(2001 Playmate of the Year)*. **Judges:** Cara Zavaleta *(Playboy Playmate)*; Stephen Wayada *(Playboy photographer)*; plus a celebrity guest.

7353 *Playboy's Beach House.* (Series; Erotica; Playboy; 2010). A home in the hills of Malibu Beach, California, is outfitted with cameras to capture the activities of the guests who attend the wild parties thrown by the Playboy Channel ("May we remind you that this is Playboy TV, so bikinis are purely optional"). Music guests perform and girls, familiar to the Playboy audience, guest host (including Andrea Lowell, Vikki Ikki and Colleen Shannon).

7354 *Playboy's Penthouse.* (Series; Variety; Syn.; 1959–1960). The Chicago penthouse of *Playboy* magazine publisher Hugh Hefner is the setting for a casual program of conversation and entertainment wherein guests mingle with the Playboy Bunnies.

Host: Hugh Hefner. **Music:** The Marty Robertson Trio.

7355 *Played By Fame.* (Series; Comedy; BET; 2009). Average people with a desire to spend a dream day with their favorite celebrity are the subjects. Once such a person is selected and introduced to his or her favorite star, the tables are turned on the subject as the celebrity pulls a series of pranks designed to drive the fan crazy (and have him wondering "Why is my favorite celebrity buggin' out on me?").

Host: Al Shearer. **Regulars:** Dana Hanna, Arthur Richardson, Candice Marie Flournoy, Matt Duffett, Jayne Entwistle.

7356 *Players.* (Series; Crime Drama; NBC; 1997–1998). In an attempt to capture criminals who prove to be clever and continually avoid apprehension, the FBI recruits three prisoners, who are released on parole, to assist agent Christine Kowalski: Charlie O'Bannon, a skilled computer hacker; Isaac "Ice" Gregory, a street hustler; and Alphonse Royo, a skilled con artist. Stories, which also focus on the personal lives of each team member, relates their efforts to bring criminals to justice.

Cast: Mia Korf *(Christine Kowalski)*; Costas Mandylor *(Alphonse Royo)*; Ice T *(Isaac "Ice" Gregory)*; Frank John Hughes *(Charlie O'Bannon)*.

7357 *Players.* (Series; Comedy; Spike; 2010). Bruce and Ken Fitzgerald are mismatched brothers who own the Players Sports Bar and Grill. Bruce is a free spirit, irresponsible and sees the bar as a way to drink for free, bet on sports games and date the waitresses. Ken is uptight and more responsible and has only one goal: focus on making a profit, keeping the bar open, avoid lawsuits and correct the establishments numerous code violations. Stories follow the brothers as each tries to get the other to think his way and the calamity that results. Krista is the bar's promiscuous waitress (prefers married men and B-list athletes); Barb is the neurotic and insecure waitress; Hickey is a retired cop who works as a bartender; Calvin is the dim-witted bar keep who hopes to become a sports model.

Cast: Matt Walsh *(Bruce Fitzgerald)*; Ian Roberts *(Ken Fitzgerald)*; Danielle Schneider *(Krista DiMarco)*; June Diane Raphael *(Barb Tolan)*; Jack McGee *(Hickey)*; D. James Pumphrey *(Calvin Trout)*.

7358 *Playhouse 90.* (Series; Anthology; CBS; 1956–1960). Quality ninety-minute dramatic presentations featuring such top name performers as Fay Wray, Charles Bronson, George C. Scott, Angela Lansbury, Claire Bloom, Patrick Macnee, Margaret O'Brien, Edward G. Robinson, Joan Blondell, Mickey Rooney, Joanne Woodward, Roddy McDowall, Rita Moreno, Jack Lemmon, William Bendix, Boris Karloff, Paul Newman, Elizabeth Montgomery, Phyllis Kirk and Claudette Colbert. Martin Manulis, John Houseman, Russell Stoneman, Fred Coe, Arthur Penn and Hubbell Robinson are the producers.

Program Open: "January 22, 1959. Live from Television City in Hollywood. Art Carney, Leslie Nielsen, Katharine Bard, Jack Klugman, Bonita Granville ... starring tonight on *Playhouse 90*. Brought to you by Kimberly Clark, world leader in quality products from home and industry" (from the episode "The Velvet Alley").

7359 *Playhouse of Mystery.* (Series; Anthology; CBS; 1957). Rebroadcasts of mystery dramas that originally aired on *Schlitz Playhouse of Stars.*

7360 *Playhouse of Stars.* (Series; Anthology; CBS; 1952). Actress Irene Dunne hosts a summer program of dramatic presentations that ran from May 30 to Sept. 10, 1952.

7361 *Playhouse of Stars.* (Series; Anthology; NBC; 1960). A summer program of dramas that aired on other filmed anthology series.

7362 *Playhouse Thirty.* (Pilot; Comedy; Unaired; Produced for Fox in 1992). Comedy skits that were to involve the host, guest stars and the studio audience.

Host: Jon Lovitz.

7363 *Playing It Straight.* (Series; Reality; Fox; 2007). Can a straight, pretty girl pick a gay male from a group of straight and gay men? Jackie Thomas is the girl. She is introduced to 14 handsome men, some of whom are gay, but by looks it is impossible to tell whom. As Jackie gets to know each of the men she must determine (without asking) which men are gay and which men are straight. Each week she eliminates two of the men she believes are gay (on the first episode she eliminated two straight men). Stereotypes that usually depict gays are not in play here and if Jackie can choose a straight guy in the final episode, they split $1 million; if she chooses a gay, he gets all the money. Daphne Brogdon hosts.

7364 *Playmate Show and Tell.* (Series; Reality; Internet; 2008). Gorgeous Playboy Playmates appear to offer advice—"You get the goods right from the source that matters—beautiful, sophisticated women." The advice given by the girls (anything from buying lingerie to dating to better love making) is coupled with comedy bits from the troupe Summer of Tears.

Hosts: Sara Jean Underwood *(2007 Playmate of the Year)*, Jayde Nicole *(2008 Playmate of the Year)*. **Regulars:** Alison Waite *(May 2006 Playmate of the Month)*; Lauren Michelle Hill *(Feb. 2001 Playmate of the Month)*.

7365 *Playwrights '56.* (Series; Anthology; NBC; 1955–1956). Quality dramatic productions broadcast on a rotating basis with *The Armstrong Circle Theater, The United States Steel Hour* and *The 20th Century-Fox Hour.* The series, produced by Fred Coe, ran from Oct. 4, 1955 to June 19, 1956 and featured such stars as Phyllis Kirk, E.G. Marshall, Paul Newman, Kim Stanley, Janice Rule, Ethel Waters, Sylvia Sidney, Lee Grant, Dina Merrill, Jane Wyatt and Franchot Tone.

7366 *Pleading Guilty.* (Pilot; Drama; Unaired; Produced for TNT in 2010). Mack Malloy is an ex-cop and recovering alcoholic who finds employment as an investigator for a prestigious corporate law firm — a law firm with partners as dishonest as the some of the clients they represent. The proposal was to follow Mack's investigations as he uncovers the evidence his superiors need to clear their clients.

Cast: Jason Isaacs (*Mack Malloy*); Isabelle Fuhrman (*Carrie Malloy*); John Larroquette (*Martin Gold*); Melinda McGraw (*Elsie Malloy*); Madchen Amick (*Amelia Briccia*).

7367   *Please Don't Eat the Daisies.* (Series; Comedy; NBC; 1965–1967). At Ridgemont College in Ridgemont City, James ("Jim") Nash, a teaching assistant, and Joan Holliday, a journalism student, meet and fall in love. The time is 1952 and shortly after, Jim and Joan marry. They set up housekeeping in a small apartment on Second Street. It was a struggle to make ends meet, and Jim was contemplating giving up teaching for a better paying job until Joan convinced him to follow his dream and become a professor.

On their tenth month anniversary, Jim surprises Joan with a puppy they name Lad. Jim holds the dog and speaks for it: "Your husband informed me that I was to keep you company while he is away educating the youth of America. He has just been promoted to the position of instructor." It is at this time that Joan tells Jim she is pregnant (a baby they name Kyle is born seven months later).

When the series actually begins, Joan and Jim and their children, Kyle, Joel and twins Trevor and Tracy live at 228 Circle Avenue in Ridgemont City. Jim is now an English professor at Ridgemont College and Joan, who works out of their home, is a freelance magazine writer who pens articles under the name Joan Holliday. Joel, Trevor and Tracy attend Ridgemont Grammar School, while 12-year-old Kyle is enrolled at Ridgemont Junior High. Stories relate events in the lives of the Nash family. Herb and Marge Thornton are their neighbors; J. Pat O'Malley appeared as Joan's world-traveling father, Mr. Holliday. Based on the book by Jean Kerr.

Cast: Mark Miller (*Jim Nash*); Patricia Crowley (*Joan Nash*); Kim Tyler (*Kyle Nash*); Brian Nash (*Joel Nash*); Jeff Fithian (*Trevor Nash*); Joe Fithian (*Tracy Nash*); King Donovan (*Herb Thornton*); Shirley Mitchell (*Marge Thornton*).

7368   *Please Stand By.* (Series; Comedy; Syn.; 1978). Frank Lambert is a family man who runs KRDA, Channel 4, a TV station from his garage in DeQueen, New Mexico. He is married to Carol and is the father of Susan, David and Rocky. Stories follow the family's mishaps as they attempt to run the station that is off the air more than it is on. Vicki James, Dennis "Crash" Lopez and Sam assist them.

Cast: Richard Schaal (*Frank Lambert*); Elinor Donahue (*Carol Lambert*); Darian Mathias (*Susan Lambert*); Stephen M. Schwartz (*David Lambert*); Bryan Scott (*Rocky Lambert*); Marcie Barkin (*Vicki James*); Danny Mora (*Dennis Lopez*); Gary Oakes (*Sam*). **Theme Vocal:** "Please Stand By" by Stephen M. Schwartz.

7369   *Pleasure Cove.* (Pilot; Comedy-Drama; NBC; Jan. 3, 1979). Pleasure Cove is a posh resort that is operated as part of the Xavier Hotel chain. Brief incidents in the lives of its guests, presented as a series of vignettes, is the focal point of the unsold project. The regulars are Henry, the manager; Julie, the reservations clerk; Kim, the assistant manager; Osaki, the desk clerk; and Chip, the local gambler.

Cast: James Murtaugh (*Henry Sinclair*); Melody Anderson (*Julie*); Constance Forslund (*Kim Parker*); Ernest Harada (*Osaki*); Jerry Lacy (*Chip Garvey*).

7370   *The Pleasure Zone.* (Series; Erotica; Cinemax; 1999). The Pleasure Zone is an Internet website run by a gorgeous woman named Serena. When one logs onto her site, they type in their password and are introduced to a dating service like no other in the history of television. Serena is also like no other matchmaker ever to appear on TV. She knows who is right for whom and once a match is made, a story follows to relate what happens (mostly soft core sex and female nudity). Casts vary with each episode.

Cast: Eden Svendahl (*Serena*).

7371   *Plymouth.* (Pilot; Science Fiction; Unaired; Produced for ABC in 1990). An proposal about a close-knit community of people who are offered the challenge of establishing the first settlement and mining operation on the moon.

Cast: Cindy Pickett (*Addy Mathewson*); Dale Midkiff (*Gil*); Richard Hamilton (*Wendell*).

7372   *Poetry and Music.* (Pilot; Variety; DuMont; Nov. 1, 1946). Vera Massey hosts a proposed program that was to present music, songs and poetry readings.

7373   *Point Pleasant.* (Series; Drama; Fox; 2005). A young woman named Christina Nickson is celebrating the end of the school year on a cruise ship when a storm suddenly erupts and Christina is plunged into the sea. She is rescued by a lifeguard (Jesse Parker) and brought to the home of Ben Kramer, the local doctor in Point Pleasant, a small New Jersey shore town. Ben discovers that Christina is suffering from amnesia and invites her to stay with his family (his wife, Meg, and their daughter, Judy) until she regains her memory.

Christina's presence can change people. She is actually a Child of Darkness and under the protection of the Devil. She is also the daughter of a woman of God and evil and good forces will soon come face to face for Christina.

Christina can concentrate and control events, even what people dream. She also has an unusual birthmark — a circle with three curves indicating the Devil's number of 666.

Ancient texts name Point Pleasant as the greatest coming of evil since the angels fell from the heavens. Christina's mother was named Ann and she has her mother's pure heart. But the Devil seduced Ann and Christina also possesses evil.

As Christina begins to regain her memory she realizes that she has been brought to Point Pleasant for a very specific reason — to learn her true identity: the offspring of a mortal woman and the Devil and to become part of the ultimate fight for her soul. Will she become good or evil?

Stories detail Christina's interactions with the people of Point Pleasant, how she discovers who she really is (through records at St. Mark's Church. Christina is from New York; her mother was born in Point Pleasant); her struggles to control the demon inside her (and the powers that come with it); and, if shown (the series ended without a conclusion), the battle of good vs. evil.

Paula is Jesse's girlfriend; Amber is Paula's mother; Sarah is the God-ferrying woman of the town; and Thomas Boyd is the mysterious man who attaches himself to Christina.

Cast: Elisabeth Harnois (*Christina Nickson*); Sam Page (*Jesse Parker*); Richard Burgi (*Ben Kramer*); Susan Walters (*Meg Kramer*); Aubrey Dollar (*Judy Kramer*); Brent Weber (*Jesse Parker*); Cameron Richardson (*Paula*); Dina Meyer (*Amber*); Alex Carter (*Captain Logan*); Grant Show (*Thomas Boyd*).

7374   *Pointman.* (Series; Crime Drama; Syn.; 1995). Constantine Harper, called Connie, is the owner of Spanish Pete's, a beach resort on the Florida Coast. Although Connie is bitter (an investment counselor who was framed and imprisoned, but later exonerated) he is willing to help people in trouble who have nowhere else to turn. When asked for help, Connie usually poses as someone else to resolve the situation. If the situation becomes too difficult to handle alone, he calls on his former prison buddies for help. Stories follow Connie as he tries to prevent what happened to him to happening to other innocent people.

Cast: Jack Scalia (*Constantine "Connie" Harper*).

7375   *Pokemon.* (Series; Cartoon; Cartoon Network; 1998–2004). A Pokemon is a pocket monster and there are 150 such Pokemon in the world. Ash Ketchum is a ten-year-old boy who has just received his first Pokemon, Pikachu, from Professor Oak. A Pokemon, once captured, can be trained. Ash aspires to be the greatest Pokemon trainer in the world. But to so he must search the world and capture all 150 Pokemon. Misty, Max, Tracey, Brock and Hikari, Ash's friends, join him on his journey. Stories relate their adventures as they search surreal lands for the various Pokemon.

Voice Cast: Veronica Taylor (*Ash*); Veronica Taylor (*May*); Eric Stuart (*Brock*); Ted Lewis (*Tracey*); Rachel Lillis (*Misty*); Amy Birnbaum (*Max*); Ken Gates, Mike Pollock (*Narrator*).

7376   *Poker After Dark.* (Series; Game; NBC; 2007–). The backroom of a casino in Las Vegas provides the setting for a look at a poker game where professionals vie for a winner-take-all pot of $120,000.

Host: Shana Hiatt (*2007*); Marianele Pereya (*2008*); Leeann Tweeden (*2008– *). **Announcer;** Oliver "Ali" Nejad.

7377   *Pole Position.* (Series; Cartoon; CBS; 1984-1985). When a mysterious accident claims the lives of their parents, the Darret children (Dan, Tess and Daisy) follow in their footsteps and become agents for Pole Position, a secret organization that battles crime and corruption. Stories relate their exploits as they enlist two high-tech vehicles of justice (Wheels, a clever Mustang, and Roadie, a sharp racer) to battle evildoers. Based on the video arcade game.

Voice Cast: Lisa Lindgren (*Tess*); Kaleena Kiff (*Daisy*); David Coburn (*Dan*); Jack Angel (*Dr. Zachary*); Marilyn Schreffler (*Kuma*); Mel Franklin (*Wheels*); Darryl Hickman (*Roadie*).

7378   *Police Academy: The Series.* (Series; Comedy; Syn.; 1997). A television adaptation of the *Police Academy* movies that relate the mishaps of a group of aspiring but screw-up rookies at the Police Academy. While learning they do solve crimes — mostly by stupidity — and half the time do not even realize there is a crime to solve.

Cast: Joe Flaherty (*Comdr. Stuart Hefilfinger*); Michael Winslow (*Sgt. Larvell Jones*); Tony Longo (*Luke Kackley*); P.J. Ochlan (*Lester Shane*); Christine Gonzales (*Alicia Conchita Montoya Cervantes*); Heather Campbell (*Annie Medford*); Jeremiah Birkett (*Dean Tackleberry*); Matt Borlenghi (*Richard Casey*); Rod Crawford (*Rusty Ledbetter*); Toby Proctor (*Dirk Tackleberry*).

7379   *Police Call.* (Series; Anthology; Syn.; 1955). Dramatizations based on the files of various law enforcement agencies throughout the country.

7380   *Police File.* (Pilot; Crime Drama; ABC; June 25, 1994). Police Detective Isabella Vargas is young, intelligent, well-educated and sensitive. Her partner, Detective Jim Stone is street smart and tough. They are attached to a precinct called the Two-Five, which is representative of any police precinct in any city. Jack O'Leary, representing a typical police lieutenant, is their squad room commander and it is through his eyes that the viewer sees police work in action.

Cast: Sean McCann (*Jack O'Leary*); Jacqueline Samuda (*Isabella Vargas*); Eugene Glazer (*Jim Stone*).

7381   *Police Squad!* (Series; Comedy; ABC; 1982). An unidentified city, called "The Tuba Capital of the World," is home to Frank

Drebin, a detective lieutenant with an unnamed special unit of what is called the Police Department, headquartered, as Frank says, "at the Police Station." Frank has an office in the squad room and is also referred to as Captain Drebin. Frank cares about people. He believes it is necessary to break the law to help people threatened by evil. Although he does his best to follow the rules, he is plagued by an uncanny presence that dulls his sense of reality and makes him somewhat of a buffoon when justice calls. Frank appears to be a 24-hour-a-day cop; he rarely relaxes and seems to have made the squad room his second home. He lives at 14 Cherry Street at Galena Avenue next to the Military Millinery Store. Frank appears to have only one snitch — a man named Johnny who works as a shoeshine "boy." Johnny knows everything about everything and will tell what he knows for $20.

Frank's superior is Captain Ed Hocken. Officer Norberg of the Undercover Unit assists Frank. Ted Olson is the sleazy police chemist who appears to enjoy performing hazardous experiments on children but is never given the chance; he is always interrupted by Frank. Only six episodes were filmed and each features a special guest star (Lorne Greene, Georg Stanford Brown, Florence Henderson, William Shatner, Robert Goulet and William Conrad) that are killed off in the opening theme. Rex Hamilton as Abraham Lincoln is announced as a regular in the opening theme but never appears in the show. Based on the comedy style of the movie *Airplane* that just didn't work on TV, although the series did spawn two theatrical films: *The Naked Gun* and *The Naked Gun 2½: The Smell of Fear.*

Cast: Leslie Nielsen (*Frank Drebin*); Alan North (*Ed Hocken*); Ed Williams (*Ted Olson*); Peter Lupus (*Officer Norberg*); William Duell (*Johnny*).

7382   *Police Station.* (Series; Crime Drama; Syn.; 1959). The day-to-day operations of a police station (Precinct 11) of a big city. Real cases are dramatized and followed from the crime to the arrest to the conviction.

Cast: Baynes Barron (*Sgt. White*); Henry Beckman (*Sgt. Stan Albertson*); Roy Wright (*Det. Pat Green*); Larry Kerr (*Det. Chuck Mitchell*).

7383   *Police Story.* (Series; Anthology; CBS; 1952). Norman Rose hosts dramas, based on the files of various police departments, that are broadcast live from New York City.

7384   *Police Story.* (Pilot; Crime Drama; NBC; Sept. 8, 1967). Police work in action as seen through the eyes of James Paige, the captain of a metropolitan police force.

Cast: Steve Ihnat (*Capt. James Paige*); Rafer Johnson (*Lt. Roy Haggerty*); Grace Lee Witney (*Sgt. Lily Monroe*).

7385   *Police Story.* (Series; Anthology; NBC; 1973–1980). The day-to-day struggles of police officers are dramatized in stories based on the official files of various law enforcement agencies throughout the country. Notable performers include Larry Hagman, David Birney, Angie Dickinson, Lloyd Bridges, Pernell Roberts, Tina Louise, Scott Brady, Jackie Cooper, Vic Morrow, Paul Burke, Hari Rhodes, Elaine Joyce, Anne Jeffreys, Chuck Connors, Anjanette Comer, Elinor Donahue and Howard Duff. Produced by Stanley Kallis and David Gerber.

7386   *Police Surgeon.* (Series; Crime Drama; Syn.; 1972). A spin off from *Dr. Simon Locke.* Feeling that he can best use his skills as a physician to help the police solve crimes, Dr. Simon Locke leaves his practice in Dixon Mills, Canada, and becomes a surgeon with the Emergency Medical Unit of the Metropolitan Police Department in Toronto. Simon is not only a brilliant surgeon, but he also has the mind of a detective and stories relate his attempts to not only save lives but track down and arrest those responsible for taking them.

Cast: Sam Groom (*Dr. Simon Locke*); Len Birman (*Lt. Jack Gordon*); Larry D. Mann (*Lt. Jack Gordon*); Marc Hebet (*Tony; Simon's driver*); Nerene Virgin (*Police Radio Dispatcher*).

7387   Police Woman. (Series; Crime Drama; NBC; 1974–1978). Pepper Anderson is an attractive police woman with the Criminal Conspiracy Division of the Los Angeles Police Department. Pepper's real name is Lee Ann, also given as Suzanne, but likes to be called Pepper "because it's my nickname." Pepper lives at 102 Crestview Drive and rarely talks about her family; it is only known that she has a much younger sister named Cheryl. Cheryl is autistic and attends the Austin School for Learning Disabilities; Pepper mentioned that she was caring for Cheryl. Pepper was a high fashion model who quit her glamorous job when she became bored with it. She attended the Los Angeles Police Academy and first worked in vice before her promotion to her current position as a sergeant.

Pepper is the only woman on a squad that includes her superior, Sergeant William "Bill" Crowley, and investigators Joe Stiles and Pete Royster. Pepper seems to attract seedy characters while working on a case and often acts as bait. While Pepper is careful not to reveal too much cleavage, an inside joke said Pepper needed a pair of forty-fives to protect her thirty-eights. Although Pepper gets shot at, hit, punched and often finds her clothes getting ripped, she takes it all in stride—"It comes with the territory." Bill is a career cop and still in love with his ex-wife, Jackie. Joe was a former medic during the Vietnam War.

The original pilot episode, titled "The Gamble," aired on *Police Story* (NBC, Mar. 26, 1974). Here Angie Dickinson played Lisa Beaumont, a vice squad detective with the L.A.P.D. Bert Convy was Sergeant Bill Crowley and Ed Bernard and Charles Dierkop played the roles of Detectives Styles and Royster. The story finds Lisa posing as a prostitute to expose the leader of a gambling syndicate.

Cast: Angie Dickinson (*Pepper Anderson*); Earl Holliman (*Bill Crowley*); Ed Bernard (*Joe Stiles*); Charles Dierkop (*Pete Royster*); Nicole Kallis (*Cheryl Anderson*); Kandi Keith (*Harriet Styles; Joe's wife*).

7388   Police Women of Broward County. (Series; Reality; TLC; 2009). A female version of Fox's *Cops* that looks at a group of police women attached to the Broward County, Florida, Police Department as they patrol and investigate various crimes (from petty thefts to prostitution and drugs). To distinguish itself from *Cops*, the program also focuses on the personal lives of the featured deputies. The deputies are Julie Bower, Shelunda Cooper, Ana Murillo, Andrea Penoyer.

7389   Police Women of Maricopa County. (Series; Reality; TLC; 2010). Maricopa County, comprised of Phoenix, Arizona and the surrounding 9200 square miles, is considered one of the toughest (and largest) counties in the U.S. Joe Arpaio, known as "America's Toughest Sheriff," oversees the Maricopa County Sheriff's Office. Deborah Moyer, Lindsey Smith, Kelly Bocard and Amie Duong are the female detectives assigned to the unit and episodes relate aspects of their tours of duty as they deal with lawbreakers.

7390   Police Women of Memphis. (Series; Reality; TLC; 2010). A look at the often dangerous work of a group of police women attached to the Memphis, Tennessee, Police Department as thy battle crime in one of the nation's most dangerous cities. The deputies are Aubrey Olson, Arica Logan, Joy Jefferson and Virginia Awkward.

7391   Politically Incorrect. (Series; Comedy; Comedy Central; ABC; 1993–2002). *Indecision '96* is a fictional television show where guests with political ambitions get a chance to sound off. Such people as well as special interest groups are placed opposite a panel of outrageous comedians to debate the issues in a satirical way to defuse the notion that all such debates must be serious. Aired on Comedy Central (1993–96) and ABC (1996–2002).

Cast: Al Franken, Travis Davis, Kevin Meaney, Chris Rock, Jeffrey Selwyn, Barbara Olson.

7392   Polka-Go-Round. (Series; Variety; ABC; 1958-1959). Carolyn DeZurik, Jimmy Hutchinson, Rusty Gill, Jack Cordaro, Lou Druss, John Hunt, Tom Fouts, The Polka Rounders and The Singing Waiters join host Bob Lewandowski for a program of polka music and songs.

7393   Polka Party. (Series; Variety; Syn.; 1958). Stan Jaworski and Al Siszeski provide the music for a program of polka music and songs hosted by Eddie Gronet and Dolores Ann Duda.

7394   Polka Time. (Series; Variety; ABC; 1956). A weekly program of polka music and songs.

Host: Bruno Junior Zienlisnki. **Regulars:** Carolyn DeZurik, The Polka Chips, The Kenal Siodmy Folk Dancers. **Music:** Stan Wolowic.

7395   The Polly Bergen Show. (Series; Variety; NBC; 1957-1958). Actress-singer Polly Bergen hosts a lively program of music, songs and light comedy.

Host: Polly Bergen. **Regulars:** Bill Bergen, The Peter Gennero Dancers. **Orchestra:** Luther Henderson, Jr.

7396   Poltergeist: The Legacy. (Series; Drama; Showtime; Syfy; Syn.; 1996–2001). Poltergeist: The Legacy is a journal that chronicles the secret work of a society called the Legacy, people with special abilities that battle the evils that inhabit the shadows of the night. Derek Rayne, Rachel Corrigan, Alex Moreau, Nick Boyle and Kristen Adams are members of the San Francisco Legacy. Members have not asked for their special abilities; they accept them and are devoted to understanding and containing paranormal phenomena, often at the risk of their own lives.

Derek is the House Leader. He is 44 years old and says, "I was born into the fight against evil." His father, Winston Rayne, was head of the San Francisco house until he was killed by a demon. Derek, embittered and torn between his own desires and his destiny with the Legacy, spent years tracking down and destroying that demon. He was then chosen to head the Legacy. Derek possesses doctorates in theology and biological anthropology. He has psychic abilities and an extensive knowledge of science, mythology and a history of the Legacy itself.

Rachel is the Legacy's psychological specialist. She is a firm believer in science and brings her medical expertise, skepticism and open mind to the mysteries that face the Legacy. She is very dedicated to her daughter, Katherine, a ten-year-old who shows promise of extraordinary psychic abilities. Rachel would like to keep Katherine, whom she calls Kat, away from the work of the Legacy, but Kat's touch of second sight draws her into the evils that haunt the Legacy.

Alexandra, called Alex, holds the position of researcher. She is a brilliant student of anthropology who possesses innate curiosity and psychic abilities (which drew her to Derek's attention). She has a natural gift for the paranormal which she acquired from her grandmother, a Creole woman deeply involved in the occult. Alex possesses a university education in science and a highly developed social conscience as well as an outstanding talent for difficult research.

Nick is 38 years old and while his position is researcher, he often finds himself in physical battles with demons. Nick is an adventurer and spent time as a Navy S.E.A.L. While he would like to react with a quick punch, experience has taught him that the forces of darkness can be dangerous and his keen sense of intelligence curbs his tendency to act first and think later.

Kristen Adams was born in Boston, Massachusetts, where she was a member of the Boston Legacy House (she is on loan to the San Francisco House). Kristen is an anthropologist and graduated after three years at Harvard with an Honors degree. Her father, Justin Adams, is a noted professor in New England who served as a consultant to the Legacy on a number of occasions. Several years ago he mysteriously disappeared while working on a Legacy dig site in Istanbul. It is because of this that Kristen has joined the Legacy — to help defeat evil and find her missing father. Aired on Showtime (1996–1998); Syfy (1999) and Syndication (repeats, 1999–2001).

Cast: Derek DeLint (*Derek Rayne*); Helen Shaver (*Rachel Corrigan*); Robbi Chong (*Alex Moreau*); Martin Cummins (*Nick Boyle*); Kristin Lehman (*Kristen Adams*); Alexandra Purvis (*Katherine Corrigan*).

7397   *Ponch's Angels.* (Pilot; Crime Drama; NBC; Feb. 28 and Mar. 1, 1981). Melanie Mitchell and Paula Woods are officers with the L.A.P.D. Both girls are proficient at riding motorcycles and are teamed to become an experimental project of female motorcycle patrol officers. Ponch (Erik Estrada) and Jon (Larry Wilcox) from the series *CHiPs* are assigned to train them and the proposal was to relate Melanie and Paula's experiences as motorcycle officers.

Cast: Trisha Townsend (*Melanie Mitchell*); Barbara Stock (*Paula Wood*).

7398   *Ponderosa.* (Series; Western; PAX; 2001-2002). A prequel to the 1959–1973 NBC series *Bonanza* that is set in 1849 at a time when Ben Cartwright had to yet establish his Ponderosa Ranch near Virginia City, Nevada. The first episode shows the Cartwright's arriving in Nevada. Ben and his wife, Marie, are the parents of Little Joe (a pre-teen here). Ben's other sons, from former wives, are Adam (from Elizabeth) and Eric, called Hoss (from Inga). It is also establishes Ben and his family living in the town of Eagle Station (Virginia City has apparently not yet been established. The town is dreary and Ben and Marie are working at the local trading post). One day Marie is killed in an explosion while working. Ben had made a promise to Marie to begin a ranch. That dream begins when Eli, the elderly owner of the trading post, gives Ben a deed to 160 acres of land in Lake Tahoe — land that would later become the Ponderosa Ranch. It is Hoss who suggests calling the ranch the Ponderosa after the Ponderosa tress that inhabit the land. This totally changes the original concept of the original series. In it Ben had already established the ranch. It was on a trip to New Orleans that he met and married Marie. She helped design the ranch house but died from a fall from a horse. Stories chart the Cartwright's progress as they carve an empire. Ben, Adam and Hoss believe in justice and will risk their lives to maintain the peace.

Other regulars are Hop Sing, Ben's cook; Jack Wolf, owner of the Eagle Station Livery Stable (as well as a hotel and bar); Carlos, Ben's foreman (a former Mexican soldier whom he befriended in Eagle Station); Maggie Green and her daughter, Tess, ranchers; Shelby, the rival saloon owner; Frenchy, the gunsmith.

Cast: Daniel Hugh-Kelly (*Ben Cartwright*); Matt Carmody (*Adam Cartwright*); Drew Powell (*Eric "Hoss" Cartwright*); Jared Daperis (*Little Joe Cartwright*); Jim Knobeloch (*Jack Wolf*); Gareth Yuen (*Hop Sing*); Nicky Wendt (*Shelby Sterrett*); Josephine Byrnes (*Maggie Green*); Lisa Baumuol (*Marie Cartwright*); Bruce Dickinson (*Big Dan Larson*); Sara Gleeson (*Tess Green*); Abbe Holmes (*Ruth Orowitz*); Brad Dourif (*Maurice "Frenchy" Devereaux*); Marcella Toro (*Isabella Maria Rivera De Vega*); Fernando Carrillo (*Carlos Rivera De Vega*).

7399   *The Pontiac Show.* (Pilot; Variety; CBS; Jan. 21, 1949). A proposed program of variety performances under the sponsorship of Pontiac Automotive Dealers. The program, which promoted the new 1949 Pontiac, featured songs by Dick Haymes and Dorothy Shay; comedy by Gene Sheldon; and dancing by Fred and Susan Barry and the Silver Streaks (three male and female dancers). Ed Herlihy did the announcing.

7400   *Pony Express.* (Series; Western; Syn.; 1960). The Central Overland Express, better known as the Pony Express, was established in the 1860s as a means of delivering the mail faster than as by stagecoach. Brett Clark is its chief troubleshooter and stories relate his experiences as he protects the express riders from the various dangers that exist (from outlaws to renegade Indians) and insure the safe delivery of the mail. Tom Clyde assists Brett.

Cast: Grant Sullivan (*Brett Clark*); Bill Cord (*Tom Clyde*); Don Dorell (*Donovan*).

7401   *Poochinski.* (Pilot; Comedy; NBC; July 9, 1990). While investigating a case, Detective Stanley Poochinski is killed. Shortly after, he gets a new lease on life when he is reincarnated in the body of an English bulldog — the pet of his former partner, Detective Robert McKay. The proposal was to follow McKay's efforts to solve crimes with the help of his former partner, a dog who speaks only to him.

Cast: Peter Boyle (*Stanley Poochinski*); George Newbern (*Robert McKay*).

7402   *Poor Devil.* (Pilot; Comedy; NBC; Feb. 14, 1973). After 1400 years of failure, Sammy, a bumbling, soft-touch disciple from Hell, is given a chance to redeem himself by securing souls for Satan. The proposal was to relate Sammy's misadventures when he becomes personally involved with his targets and tends to save them rather than condemn them. Mr. Bligh is Lucifer's aide.

Cast: Sammy Davis, Jr. (*Sammy*); Christopher Lee (*Lucifer*); Gino Conforti (*Mr. Bligh*).

7403   *Poor Mr. Campbell.* (Pilot; Comedy; CBS; Aug. 7, 1962). Harley Campbell is a composed, quiet man who relishes his privacy. Unfortunately, Harley is married to Adrice, a nag who makes life miserable for him. Harley often envisions how enjoyable life would be without Adrice and the proposal was to follow Harley as he seeks ways to enjoy life despite the way he actually lives. Grindl is their maid; Priscilla is Adrice's friend, a beautician.

Cast: Edward Andrews (*Harley Campbell*); Agnes Moorehead (*Adrice Campbell*); Ruta Lee (*Priscilla Edwards*); Mary Grace Canfield (*Grindl*).

7404   *Poor Richard.* (Pilot; Comedy; CBS; Jan. 21, 1984). After losing his money to gambling, the once wealthy Richard Manning III poses as a butler to remain in his former Beverly Hills mansion, now owned by Ruby Hopper, an Iowa country bumpkin who became a millionaire by inventing a pig feed supplement. The proposal was to follow Richard's misadventures as he tries to regain his wealth and the complications that ensue when his urge to gamble destroys his dreams. Other regulars are Terry, the cook; and Jimmy, the gardener.

Cast: George Hamilton (*Richard Manning III*); Geoffrey Lewis (*Ruby Hopper*); Alley Mills (*Terry Robinson*); John Hunsaker (*Jimmy*).

7405   *P.O.P.* (Pilot; Comedy; NBC; Aug. 29, 1984). After deserting his family twenty years ago, a lovable con artist named P. Oliver Prendergast decides to give up his life of roaming and return to his estranged family (his wife, Rosalyn, the publisher of a magazine called *Personality Plus*, and his now grown sons, Johnny and Russell).

The proposal was to relate Oliver's efforts to become a father and husband to a family he really doesn't know. Other regulars are Maggie, Dana, Frank and Marc, employees of Rosalyn.

Cast: Charles Durning *(P. Oliver Prendergast)*; Bea Arthur *(Rosalyn Gordon)*; Todd Graff *(Johnny Prendergast)*; James Lashly *(Russell Prendergast)*; Fran Drescher *(Maggie Newton)*; Jane Anderson *(Dana McNeil)*; Antonio Fargas *(Frank Wilkey)*; Anthony Holland *(Marc Alderman)*.

7406 *Pop! Goes the Country.* (Series; Variety; Syn.; 1974). Country and western entertainers perform in a program hosted by Ralph Emery. The Statler Brothers perform the theme, "Pop Goes the Country" with Jim Malloy and Jerry Whitehurst providing the backup music.

7407 *The Pop 'n' Rocker Game.* (Series; Game; Syn.; 1983). Three contestants compete. In Round One (the Visual Round), the host reads a music-oriented question that is accompanied by a visual aid. The player who is first to buzz in receives a chance to answer. If correct, $50 is awarded. Several such rounds are played. In the second round, a sixty-second rapid-fire question-and-answer session is held with questions beginning at $50 and increasing by $10 for each additional question. The player with the highest cash score at the end of round two is the winner.

Host: Jon Bauman.

7408 *The Popcorn Kid.* (Series; Comedy; CBS; 1987). At 2222 Algonquin Parkway in Kansas City stands a movie palace called the Majestic Theater. Lynne, Scott, Gwen and Willie are four teenagers who operate the popcorn concession. Their misadventures as they attempt to operate the stand are the focal point of stories. Leonard is the manager; Marlon is the projectionist.

Cast: Faith Ford *(Lynne Holly Brickhouse)*; Bruce Norris *(Scott Creasman)*; Penelope Ann Miler *(Gwen Stuttlemeyer)*; Jeffrey Joseph *(Willie Dawson)*; Raye Birk *(Leonard Brown)*; John Christopher Jones *(Marlon Bond)*.

7409 *Popeye and Son.* (Series; Cartoon; CBS; 1987). An updated version of the 1930s theatrical cartoon *Popeye the Sailor.* After decades of bickering and fighting for the affections of Olive Oyl (a skinny, fickle woman), sailors Popeye and Bluto decide to end their battle, settle down and start a family. Popeye marries Olive (who becomes Olive Oyl-Popeye) and they have a son, Popeye Jr. Bluto also marries (Mrs. Bluto) and he has a son, Tank. The series begins nine years later. Popeye Jr. is not like his father — he hates spinach (which gave Popeye incredible strength); Tank is like his father — a bully (and Popeye Jr. is his number one target). Wimpy, Popeye's friend from the movie series (who loved hamburgers) has opened a chain of hamburger stands; and Jeep, the magical animal is also a part of the revision. The series sets the stage for the once settled feud to continue as Popeye Jr. comes to the aid of those threatened by the evil Tank. Dee Dee, Rad, Polly and Woody are friends of Popeye Jr.

Voice Cast: Maurice LaMarche *(Popeye)*; Allan Melvin *(Bluto)*; Marilyn Schreffler *(Olive Oyl-Popeye)*; Josh Rodine *(Popeye Jr.)*; David Marks *(Tank Bluto)*; Allan Melvin *(Wimpy)*; Kaleena Kiff *(Dee Dee)*; Penina Segall *(Polly)*; B.J. Ward *(Rad)*; Don Messick *(Eugene the Jeep)*; Nancy Cartwright *(Woody)*.

7410 *Popeye Doyle.* (Pilot; Crime Drama; NBC; Sept. 7, 1986). Popeye Doyle is a tough, rumpled and dedicated detective with the N.Y.P.D. The character first appeared in the feature film *The French Connection* and the proposal was to follow Popeye's relentless pursuit of criminals, usually those guilty of murder. Other regulars are Detective Tony Parese; Lieutenant Gregory Paulus; and Connie, Tony's wife.

Cast: Ed O'Neill *(Popeye Doyle)*; Matthew Laurance *(Tony Parese)*; James Handy *(Gregory Paulus)*; Joanna Perica *(Connie Parese)*.

7411 *Popeye the Sailor.* (Series; Cartoon; Syn.; 1956). The endless battle between love-hungry sailors Popeye and Bluto over the long-sought affections of Olive Oyl, a skinny, fickle woman. Stories relate the battle for good over evil as Popeye uses spinach to achieve incredible strength and fight the forces of injustice. Comprised of theatrical cartoons produced from 1933 to 1954.

Voice Cast: Det Poppen, Floyd Buckley, Jack Mercer *(Popeye)*; Jackson Beck *(Bluto)*; Olive LaMoy, Mae Questel *(Olive Oyl)*; Charles Lawrence *(Wimpy)*; Mae Questel *(Swee'pea)*; Arnold Stang *(Shorty)*; Jack Mercer *(Pupeye/Peepeye/Poopeye/Pipeye/Poopdeck Pappy)*.

7412 *Popeye the Sailor.* (Series; Cartoon; Syn.; 1962). A made-for-television version of the theatrical series (see prior title) about Popeye, a sailor who uses the incredible strength he derives from spinach to help good defeat evil. Brutus (not Bluto) is Popeye's nemesis; Olive Oyl is Popeye's girlfriend; Poopdeck Pappy is Popeye's father; Swee'pee is Olive's nephew.

Voice Cast: Jack Mercer *(Popeye)*; Mae Questel *(Olive Oyl)*; Jackson Beck *(Brutus)*; Mae Questel *(Evil Sea Hag)*; Mae Questel *(Swee'pea)*; Jack Mercer *(Poopdeck Pappy)*.

7413 *Popi.* (Series; Comedy; CBS; 1976). New York City is the setting for a story about Abraham Rodriquez, the Puerto Rican father of two children, as he struggles to hold down two jobs and raise his two mischievous sons, Abraham Jr. and Luis. Abraham is a widower. Lupe is his romantic interest; Angelo is Abraham's friend; Mr. Diaz is Abraham's employer. In the pilot film, Liz Torres played Lupe.

Cast: Hector Elizondo *(Abraham Rodriquez)*; Anthony Perez *(Abraham Rodriquez, Jr.)*; Dennis Vasquez *(Luis Rodriquez)*; Edith Diaz *(Lupe)*; Lou Criscuolo *(Angelo Maggio)*; Frank Lugo *(Mr. Diaz)*.

7414 *Popples.* (Series; Cartoon; Syn.; 1986). While exploring the treasures of their attic, a young sister and brother (Bonnie and Billy) discover an old box of toys and a group of friendly creatures that inhabit it called Popples. Stories relate the misadventures that occur as Bonnie and Billy strive to keep secret the existence of the very mischievous Popples.

Voice Cast: Valri Bromfield *(Bonnie/Mike)*; Jackie Berger *(Billy)*; Donna Christie *(Potato Chip)*; Jeannie Elias *(Penny)*; Louise Vallance *(Party/Punkity/Prize/Puffball)*; Sharon Noble *(Pancake)*; Severine Morisot *(Bonnie)*; Danny Mann *(Punkster/Putter)*; Maurice LaMarche *(Puzzle)*; Hadley Kay *(P.C. Popple)*.

7415 *Popstars: USA.* (Series; Reality; WB; 2001-2002). An attempt to create new musical groups. In the first incarnation (2001) five women were chosen from thousands (at open auditions) to form the group Eden's Crush. The program chronicles the process that goes into making a group — from the auditions to the final result (with all the pressures, traumas and truly hard work that goes into the making of a recording group). The second incarnation (2002) chronicles the forming of the group Scene 23 (which was composed of both men and women). Both groups flourished for a while after being created but have since vanished from the scene.

Ana Marin Lombo, Maile Misajon, Nicole Scherzinger, Ivette Sosa, Rosanna Tavarez are Eden's Crush. Monika Christian, Laurie Gidosh, Donavan Green, Josh Henderson, Dorothy Szamborska are Scene 23.

7416 *Popular.* (Series; Drama; WB; 1999-2000). A look at the popular and not so popular students at John F. Kennedy High School in Los Angeles. Samantha McPherson, called Sam, is a reporter for the school newspaper, *The Zapruder Reporter*. She, Lilly Esposito and Carmen Ferrara are the "unpopular" girls. Brooke McQueen, the head cheerleader (of the Glamazons), Nicole Julian and Mary Cherry are the popular girls.

Samantha attended Ocean Park Elementary School. She believes she is pretty "but I will never be a *17* magazine girl because they don't airbrush in real life." She is also on the yearbook committee at school (*The Camelot*) and wishes she had a more developed bust line.

Lily loves to show cleavage and has doubts about her sexuality (she kissed Carmen in a moment of indecision). Lily's teachers believe she is a troublemaker because she stands up for what she believes is wrong (like dissecting frogs for a biology class). She wants to save the world and works as a waitress at Mr. Cluck's Family Restaurant.

Carmen is slightly overweight and desperately wants to be thin to become a cheerleader, although she also says "I like being a little flawed. It's me." No matter what obstacles life throws at Carmen, she always manages to overcome them.

With her blonde hair and slim figure, Brooke appears to be perfect "But I'm not. I wish I had breasts that bounce and I have a bad habit of starring at myself in the mirror" (thinks she is fat). When Brooke was eight years old her mother abandoned her and her father. Brooke talks in her sleep, is a member of the Honors Society and was a Homecoming Queen.

Mary Cherry is a very beautiful 16-year-old blonde. She is the daughter of Cheri Cherry, a fabulously wealthy businesswoman (owner of the Cheri Cherry Corporation). Mary is a member of the cheerleading team, the Glamazons. She idolizes her mother and wants to be the star of her life (her mother knows Mary is not very smart but claims "She's as loyal as a Rockweiller").

Other students are Sugar Daddy, John Ford and Harrison John. Sugar Daddy is a white teen that has immersed himself in his notion of black youth culture. His real name is Michael Bernadino and he is somewhat heavy set but he doesn't let that bother him. Josh is the school's star football player. Harrison lives with his lesbian mother, Robin (who works as a pharmacist) and the situation causes stress in his life; he has a crush on Lily whom he believes "has a nice ass and porn star hair." Roberta "Bobbi" Glass is the school's tough gym teacher.

Cast: Carly Pope (*Samantha McPherson*); Leslie Bibb (*Brooke McQueen*); Tammy Lynn Michaels (*Nicole Julian*); Leslie Grossman (*Mary Cherry*); Tamara Mello (*Lily Esposito*); Sara Rue (*Carmen Ferrara*); Ron Lester (*Sugar Daddy*); Christopher Gorman (*Harrison John*); Bryce Johnson (*Josh Ford*); Diane Delano (*Bobbi Glass*); Alley Mills (*Robin John*); Delta Burke (*Cheri Cherry*); Lisa Darr (*Jane McPherson; Samantha's mother*).

7417   Popzilla. (Series; Cartoon; MTV; 2009). A rapid-fire animated sketch show that spoofs current events, celebrities and pop culture.

Voices: Phil LaMarr, Catherine Reitman, James Adomian, Eliza Schneider, Sam Riegel, Patrick Walsh, Edi Patterson, Michael David Cassidy, Billy Merritt, Amanda Philipson, Sean Clements, Allan McLeod, Freddy Lockhart, Jared Miller, Kevin Pederson, Rachael Dillon, Marlene Maginot, R.J. Fried, Tim Hedrick.

7418   Porky Pig and Friends. (Series; Cartoon; ABC; 1964–1967). A packaged series of Warner Bros. theatrical cartoons, produced from 1948–1965, that relates the misadventures of the stuttering Porky Pig. Additional segments include *Daffy Duck, Bugs Bunny, Sylvester and Tweety* and *Foghorn Leghorn*.

Voice Characterizations: Mel Blanc.

7419   Port Charles. ABC serial. June 1, 1997 to Oct. 3, 2003. See *Soap Operas*.

7420   The Porter Wagoner Show. (Series; Variety; Syn.; 1960). Singer Porter Wagoner hosts a program of performances by country and western entertainers.

Host: Porter Wagoner. **Regulars:** Dolly Parton, Barbara Lee, Bruce Osborne, Spec Rose. **Announcer:** Don Housner. **Music:** The Wagon Masters.

7421   Portia Faces Life. (Series; Drama; CBS; 1954-1955). The dramatic story of Portia Manning, an attorney and mother, as she struggles to divide her time between the demands of work and the necessities of a home and family. Walter is Portia's husband; Shirley and Dick are their children; Carl is Walter's brother.

Cast: Fran Carlon, Frances Reid (*Portia Manning*); Karl Swenson, Donald Woods (*Walter Manning*); Ginger McManus, Renne Jarrett (*Shirley Manning*); Charles Taylor (*Dick Manning*); Patrick O'Neal (*Carl Manning*); Joan Chambers (*Bea*).

7422   Portrait of a Legend. (Series; Tribute; Syn.; 1981). Tributes to great legends of music. Film clips and current-day interviews recall a subject's career.

Host: James Darren. **Music:** John D'Andrea, David Wheatley.

7423   The Possessed. (Pilot; Drama; NBC; May 1, 1977). Kevin Leahy is an ex-minister fallen from the grace of God and expelled from the Catholic church. After a fatal automobile accident, Leahy is brought back to life. To gain salvation, he is ordered to seek out and destroy evil. The proposal was to follow Leahy as he helps people threatened by the unknown (usually demonic forces).

Cast: James Farentino (*Kevin Leahy*).

7424   Postman Pat. (Series; Cartoon; NBC; 2007). Pat is a friendly postman in Greendale, a British town where everyone knows everyone else. In addition to delivering the mail, Pat involves himself in the lives of the people he meets and stories follow the incidents that occur in their lives. Produced in England.

Voices: Ken Bersie, Carole Boyd, Archie Panjobi, Kulvinder Gehr, Janet James.

7425   Potatoes and Dragons. (Series; Cartoon; This TV; 2010). King Hugo III is the stern ruler of the Land of Potatoes, a kingdom patterned after Camelot, that also has a piece-loving, fire-breathing dragon that disapproves of Hugo's iron hand rule. Hugo is equally upset with Dragon as Dragon threatens to compromise his rule. To resolve the problem, Hugo has put a bounty out on Dragon and a segment of each episode finds a new knight coming to the Land of Potatoes to defeat Dragon, but only to find himself being defeated and running for his life. Princess Melodine is Hugo's daughter. She loves Dragon and helps him defeat the knights sent by her father. Harry is Hugo's absent-minded right-hand man; Riri is the court jester; Merlin is Hugo's magician; Juju is the young girl who lives in the castle and assists Melodine.

Voice Cast: Carrie Finlay (*Melodine*); Mark Camacho (*Dragon*); Mike Tsar (*Hugo/Harry*); Mark Hauser (*Riri*); Anne Bovaird (*Juju*); Helen Kin (*Big Mama*).

7426   Pottsville. (Pilot; Comedy; CBS; Feb. 27, 1980). Bulldog O'Halloran is an harassed labor leader and the president of Local 605 of the National Factory Workers Union in Pottsville, a small manufacturing town. The proposal was to relate Bulldog's efforts to solve the constant barrage of problems that befall him and his company, the Farraday Sandpaper Corporation. Other regulars are Grace, his wife; Tinker, their son; Bill, Bulldog's union assistant; Holden, the company owner (Farraday Sandpaper); Gardy, Holden's wife; Ted, Holden's son; Randy, Pippa, Helen and Sue, the office girls; and Snell, Holden's aide.

Cast: Forrest Tucker *(Bulldog O'Halloran)*; Jan Miner *(Grace O'Halloran)*; George O'Hanlon, Jr. *(Tinker O'Halloran)*; Richard Brestoff *(Bill Gentry)*; John Lawlor *(Holden Farraday)*; Nina Foch *(Gardy Farraday)*; Jimmy Samuels *(Ted Farraday)*; Hamilton Camp *(Snell)*; Jane Daly *(Randy)*; Heidi Gold *(Pippa)*; Edie McClurg *(Helen)*; Lynne Thigpen *(Sue)*.

7427   *Pound Puppies.* (Series; Cartoon; ABC; 1986). Looker, Howler, Whooper, Catgut and Nose Marie are puppies (called Pound Puppies) who live in a pound but can escape at night through a secret tunnel to explore (and find misadventure) in the outside world. Holly is the puppies human friend who shares in their adventures; Katrina Stoneheart is Holly's guardian; Brattina is Katrina's spoiled daughter.

Voice Cast: Ami Foster *(Holly)*; Adrienne Alexander *(Brattina)*; Pat Carroll *(Katrina Stoneheart)*; Ruth Buzzi *(Nose Marie)*; Nancy Cartwright *(Brighteyes)*; Dan Gilvezan *(Cooler)*; Robert Morse *(Howler)*; B.J. Ward *(Whopper)*; Frank Welker *(Catgut)*.

7428   *The Powder Room.* (Pilot; Comedy; NBC; Aug. 26, 1971). Life as seen through the eyes of women. The proposal presented three vignettes: "The Militant." Joey Heatherton as a co-ed who is determined to seduce her professor (Jack Cassidy); "The Affair." An over-thirty housewife (Jeanine Burnier) attempts to revive her husband's (Jack Cassidy) romantic appetite; "The Mourner." Elaine Stritch as an over-forty widow seeking a new mate (Jack Cassidy).

Host: Jack Cassidy.

7429   *Power Girls.* (Series; Reality; MTV; 2005). Lizzie Grubman is the owner of Lizzie Grubman's, a presitigious PR firm in New York City. Rachel, Millie, Kelli and Allie are her Power Girls, agents who plan everything from nightclub openings to album launches to wrangling the paparazzi. Episodes follow the Power Girls as they drum up the publicity for their clients.

7430   *Power of Attorney.* (Series; Reality; Syn.; 2000). A small claims court is the setting. The plaintiff and defendants are real and the cases are real. But here, instead of the litigants arguing their cases, court appointed attorneys do the arguing. The judge then delivers a decision that is binding and cannot be appealed.

Judge: Andrew P. Napolitano. **Court Reporter:** Francine McGwire. **Bailiff:** Joe Catalano, Jr.

7431   *The Power of 10.* (Series; Game; CBS; 2007). Two players compete for the opportunity to win $10 million. The players stand opposite each other in the Elimination Round (where one player must defeat the other). All questions are based on a national poll as to how Americans responded to specific questions asked of them. The game begins when the host asks the first question (for example, "What percentage of American women consider themselves feminists?"). Each player has ten seconds in which to lock in their guess (from zero to one hundred percent). The correct answer is revealed and the player who has come closest to the result survey scores one point. Five such questions are played and the first player to score three points is the winner. This player now competes for the grand prize.

Five questions are played and each money amount is increased by the power of ten. Question one is worth $1,000 and the player has a 40-point range (higher or lower) to help him. Question two, worth $10,000, gives the player a 30-point range. Question three is worth

$100,000 but the player's point range is now 20 points higher or lower than the actual answer. The fourth question gives the player a 10-point range and $1 million is at stake. If the player is correct on this question, the answer is not given (the actual survey percentage). To win $10 million the player has no point range help and must give the actual survey percentage number (in the question used above, 29 percent was the answer. If that were the question here, the player would have to respond with 29 to win). The player can quit at any time and leave with the money he has won. An incorrect answer defeats a player and his winnings are decreased by the power of ten (if the player is at the $10,000 level and misses, he wins $1,000).

Host: Drew Carey.

7432   *The Power Rangers.* (Series; Science Fiction; Fox; ABC; Nick; 1998–2011). Twelve program spin off from *The Mighty Morphin Power Rangers.*

1. Power Rangers Turbo (Fox, 1998-99). Tommy, Kat, Ashley, Tanya, T.J., Justin, Adam, Cassie and Carlos are the Power Rangers, teenagers with extraordinary abilities who protect Angel City from the evils of outer space. The Rangers use high tech, transformable cars (that become awesome fighting machines) to assist them in their seeming endless battles. **Cast:** Jason David Frank *(Tommy)*, Catherine Sutherland *(Kat)*, Tracy Lynn Cruz *(Ashley)*, Nakia Burrise *(Tanya)*, Selwyn Ward *(T.J.)*, Blake Foster *(Justin)*, Johnny Yong Bosch *(Adam)*, Patricia Jaa Lee *(Cassie)*, Roger Velasco *(Carlos)*.

2. Power Rangers in Space (Fox, 1999-2000). The Power Rangers, who protect Angel Grove City from evil space invaders, are guided by Alpha and incorporate the U.S. space shuttle to battle the evil Rita Repulsa and her cohorts Divatox and Astronomus, the Princess of Evil. The Power Rangers are Ashley, Cassie, Carlos and T.J. Lord Zedd, an enemy from the parent series, returns to wreck havoc on Angel Grove City. **Cast:** Tracy Lynn Cruz *(Ashley)*, Patricia Jaa Lee *(Cassie)*, Roger Velasco *(Carlos)*, Selwyn Ward *(T.J.)*, Donene Kistler *(Alpha)*, Barbara Goodson *(Rita Repulsa)*, Hilary Shephard Turner *(Divatox)*, Melody Perkins *(Astronomus)*, Robert Axelrod *(Lord Zedd)*.

3. Power Rangers Time Force (Fox, 2000-01). The Power Rangers, the protectors of Angel Grove City, are Time Force Officers and live together in the town's Clock Tower. The Rangers are able to travel through time to battle the evils of Ransik and Nadria, evil beings bent on destroying the Earth. Wes, Katie, Jen, Lucas and Trip are the Power Rangers. Circuit, the mechanical owl, is their computer link to the future; Wes's father, Mr. Collins, runs Bio-Lab; Eric is the lab's head of security. **Cast:** Jason Faunt *(Wes)*, Deborah Estelle Phillips *(Katie)*, Erin Cahill *(Jen)*, Michael Copon *(Lucas)*, Kevin Kleinberg *(Trip)*, Edward Albert *(Mr. Collins)*, Vernon Wells *(Ransik)*, Kate Sheldon *(Nadria)*, Daniel Southworth *(Eric)*.

4. Power Rangers Ninja Storm (ABC, 2001-02). Shane, Tori and Dustin are members of the Wind Ninja Academy, a secret society whose members use the art of the Ninja to battle evil (here, Lothar, a renegade Ninja who seeks to conquer the earth). Each of the Power Rangers are special. Dustin, Child of the Earth, has the power of the Yellow Wind Ranger. Tori, fluid and graceful like water, is the Blue Wind Ranger. Shane, reaching for the stars, commands the power of the Red Wind Ranger. Together they become the Wind Power Rangers, protectors of the Earth. Their master is Sensel, a Ninja master who was transformed into a guinea pig (puppet) when his good forces met Lothar's bad forces. His son, Cam, assists him. Kapri and Marah, Lothar's evil nieces, assist him. **Cast:** Pva Maagasiva *(Shane)*, Sally Martin *(Tori)*, Glenn McMillan *(Dustin)*, Jason Chan *(Cam)*, Grant McFarland *(Lothar/Sensel's Voice)*, Katrina Browne *(Kapri)*, Katrina Devine *(Marah)*.

5. Power Rangers World Force (Fox, 2002-03). Animaria was a land where the people and creatures of Earth lived in harmony. Master

Org, a great evil, and his assistant, Toxica, caused destruction by polluting the land. One being, Princess Shayla escaped the destruction when her warrior protectors took her to the Temple in the Valley of the Swords. There she entered a long, suspended sleep, waiting for a time when the world would need her help. In a fierce battle, the ancient warriors defeated Master Org, Toxica and their soldiers and imprisoned them in stone. As the centuries passed, man has allowed the Earth to become polluted again. The pollution weakened the stone cells of Master Org and his army and caused them to rise again, seeking to once again control the Earth. The pollution also causes Princess Shayla and her power animals (protectors) to awake. To help her defeat Master Org and Toxica, Shayla recruits five teenagers to help her: Cole, Taylor, Alyssa, Max and Danny. The teens become the new Power Rangers and their battle to defeat Master Org is depicted. **Cast:** Marie Crouch *(Princess Shayla)*, Ricardo Medina, Jr. *(Cole)*, Alyson Kipperman *(Taylor)*, Jessica Ray *(Alyssa)*, Philip Jeanmarie *(Max)*, Jack Guzman *(Danny)*, Ilia Volok *(Master Org)*, Sin Wong *(Toxica)*.

6. Power Rangers Dino Thunder (ABC, 2004-05). Dr. Thomas Oliver is a science teacher at Reefside High School in Angel City. One day on a field trip to find prehistoric fossils, Kira, Ethan and Connor, three of Professor Oliver's students, find a mysterious cave and three crystals. The crystals are from an asteroid that crashed into the Earth millions of years ago and killed the dinosaurs. When Thomas, one of the original Power Rangers (from the series *The Mighty Morphin Power Rangers*), learns of his student's discovery, he uses dinosaur DNA to transform them into the Power Rangers Dino Thunder to battle Anton Mercer, an evil scientist who seeks the crystals and uses his evil bio zords to wreck havoc on the Earth. **Cast:** Jason David Frank *(Tommy Oliver)*, James Napier *(Conner McKnight)*, Kevin Duhney *(Ethan James)*, Emma Lahana *(Kira Ford)*, Katrina Devine *(Cassidy Cornell)*, Mirama Smith *(Elsa)*, Tom Hern *(Cassidy)*, Lathan Gaines *(Dr. Anton Mercer)*.

7. Power Rangers S.P.D. (ABC, 2005-06). The Power Rangers (Sydney, Bridge, Elizabeth, Schuyler and Jack), trained at the Ranger Academy (a futuristic police force) by Commander Anubis "Doggie" Cruger, battle Emperor Grumm, an evil alien who is threatening to destroy the earth. **Cast:** Brandon Jay McLaren *(Jack Landors)*, Chris Violette *(Schuyler "Sky" Tate)*, Matt Austin *(Bridge Carson)*, Monica May *(Elizabeth "Z" Delgado)*, Alycia Purrott *(Sydney "Syd" Drew)*, John Tui *(Commander Anubis "Doggie" Cruger)*, Olivia James-Baird *(Mora)*, Michelle Langstone *(Dr. Katherine "Kat" Manx)*, Rene Naufahu *(Emperor Graumm)*.

8. Power Rangers Mystic Force (ABC, 2006-07). Six teenagers (Nick, Vida, Xander, Madison, Chip and Daggeron), residents of Briarwood City, use their magical abilities as Power Rangers to battle the dark forces of evil (especially the unseen Imperius) who rules from the dark regions of space. Uldonna is the sorceress who endowed the teenagers with their magic; she is assisted by Clare. **Cast:** Firass Dirani *(Nick Russell)*, Angie Diaz *(Vida)*, Richard Bran Catisano *(Xander)*, Melanie Vallejo *(Madison)*, Nic Sampson *(Chip Thorn)*, John Cui *(Daggeron)*, Peta Rutter *(Udonna)*, Antonia Prebble *(Clare)*, Stuart Devenie *(Voice of Imperius)*.

9. Power Rangers: Operation Overdrive (ABC, 2007-08). After ten years of searching, archeologist Andrew Radford finds the Corona Aurora, a fabulous crown of jewels that contains great power. Upon touching the crown, Radford unleashes a great evil — Norg and Flurious, aliens seeking the crown for the power it will afford them. To battle the evil he has unleashed, Radford gathers four teenagers (Ronny, Will, Rose and Dax) and presents them with special suits he has created that transforms them into Power Rangers. Mark, Andrew's son, joins them and stories relate their efforts to defeat Norg and Flurious. **Cast:** Caitlin Murphy *(Ronny)*, James Maclurcan *(Mark)*, Rhoda Montemayor *(Rose)*, Samuel Yuen *(Dax)*, Samuel

Benta *(Will)*, Rod Lousich *(Andrew Radford)*, Rod Weatherly *(Spencer; the butler)*, Kelson Henderson *(Norg)*, Gerald Urquhart *(Flurious)*.

10. Power Rangers Jungle Fury (ABC, 2008-09). Ten thousand years ago an evil being named Dai Shi believed animals should rule the planet and humans eliminated. As Dai Shi put his plan into effect, warriors called the Order of Pai Zhug (The Order of the Claw), defeated him and imprisoned his spirit in a magical box that has been guarded by the Pai Zhug ever since. At a Pai Zhug training temple in modern times, three students, Casey, Theo and Lily are being trained by Master Mao in the martial arts and as the future protectors of the Pai Zhug. When a renegade student (Jarrod) steals the box containing Dai Shi's spirit and unleashes it, the students set out on a quest to recapture Dai Shi before he can carry out his plans of domination. Camille (short for Chameleon), a beautiful woman who can change her form, and the Army of Fear (mutants) assist Dai Shi. **Cast:** Anna Hutchison *(Lily)*, Aljin Abella *(Theo)*, Jason Smith *(Casey)*, Holly Shanahan *(Camille)*, David de Lautour *(R.J.)*, Bede Skinner *(Dai Shi/Jarrod)*, Sarah Thomson *(Fran)*, Nathaniel Lees *(Master Mao)*.

11. Power Rangers R.P.M. (ABC, 2009-10). In a futuristic era, a computer virus called Venjix takes control of the world's computers and creates an army of robotic soldiers in an effort to control mankind. Humans have retreated to the domed city of Cornith, the last refuge for safety. To protect Cornith City, a group of young people (Dillon, Summer, Flynn, Scott and Ziggy) have become Power Rangers, mankind's last hope. The Power Rangers are controlled by a computer named Dr. K and stories relate their efforts to safeguard Cornith City by destroying the monstrous computer viruses Venjix sends to eliminate his enemies. Colonel Mason Truman is the military leader of Cornith City; Tenaya 7 is the human-looking woman created by Venjix to infiltrate Cornith City. **Cast:** Dan Ewing *(Dillon)*, Rosie McIver *(Summer Landsdown)*, Ari Boyland *(Flynn McAllister)*, Eka Darville *(Scott Truman)*, Milo Cawthorne *(Ziggy Grover)*, Adeliade Kane *(Tenaya 7)*, James Gaylyne *(Col. Mason Truman)*, Andrew Laing *(Voice of Venjix)*.

12. Power Rangers Samurai (Nick, 2011). Jayden, Kevin, Mia, Emily and Mike are the reborn Power Rangers who harness the mystical Samurai Symbols of Power to battle evil with their elements of Fire, Water, Sky, Forest and Earth. They are each assisted by a Zord, a special spirit animal, that gives them extra strength when needed. Jayden, the Red Ranger, has the element of Fire and the Lion Zord. Blue Ranger Kevin has the Water element and the Dragon is his Zord. Mia, the Pink Ranger has the Turtle Zord and Sky is her element. Green Ranger Mike has the Bear Zord and the element of the Forest. Emily, element Earth, is the Yellow Ranger and the Ape is her Zord. **Cast:** Alex Hamilton *(Jayden)*, Erika Fong *(Mia)*, Brittany Pirtie *(Emily)*, Najee De-Tiege *(Kevin)*, Hector David, Jr. *(Mike)*.

7433   *The Power Team.* (Pilot; Cartoon; Fox; Nov. 25, 1994). Johnny is a teenage boy fascinated by video games. One day, while playing a game called "The Power Team," five of its heroes (Max Force, Quick, Tyrone, Zerous and their car, Bigfoot) come to life when Johnny pushes the joystick on his control box. The team has been assigned to Johnny to battle crime, particularly the evils of Mr. Big, an overweight, diminutive hood, and his assistants, Joe and Spike, who plan to take over the city.

Voices: Mike Donovan, Terry Klassen, Lee Jeffrey, Jason Michaels, Richard Newman, John Novak, Dale Wilson.

7434   *The Power Within.* (Pilot; Adventure; ABC; May 11, 1979). During an electrical storm, Chris Darrow, a young daredevil pilot, is struck by lightning. The lightning transforms Chris into a virtual human dynamo — energy he uses to battle evil. (It is explained that before his birth, Chris's mother had been exposed to an accidental overdose of radiation, which had been absorbed by Chris, and years later saved his life when struck by the lightning.) Originally titled *Power Man*. Other regulars are Bill, Chris's mechanic; and General Tom Darrow, Chris's father.

Cast: Art Hindle *(Chris Darrow)*; Joe Rossulo *(Bill Carmalie)*; Edward Binns *(Tom Darrow)*.

7435   *Powerhouse*. (Series; Drama; PBS; 1982-1983). Jennifer, Pepper, Kevin, Lolo, Thelma, Bobby and Tony are members of the Powerhouse, a community home run by Brenda Gaines. Stories, aimed at teenagers and designed to instill lessons in living and good health habits, relate the teens efforts to help each other as well as others seeking guidance.

Cast: Sandra Bowie *(Brenda Gaines)*; Domenica Galati *(Jennifer)*; Jessica Prentice *(Pepper)*; Michael Mack *(Kevin)*; Jason Kravits *(Lolo)*; David Labrosa *(Bobby)*; Anne Helms-Irons *(Thelma)*; Michael Wikes *(Tony)*.

7436   *The Powerpuff Girls*. (Series; Cartoon; Syn.; 1998). Blossom, Bubbles and Buttercup are three young sisters who possess super powers. The girls live in Townsville and stories relate their efforts to battle evil.

Blossom is the leader. She is the most intelligent of the girls and comes up with their plan of attack. Bubbles is sweet and kind and very sensitive. Buttercup is tough and lives for the confrontations she encounters. Other characters are Professor Utonium, the creator of the Powerpuff Girls; Mojo Jojo, a villain who was originally Utonium's assistant (the chemical [Chemical X] that created the Powerpuff Girls adversely affected him); Ms. Keane, the girls' teacher at Pokey Oaks Kindergarten; and the Mayor, the leader of Townsville who uses a hotline to contact the Powerpuff Girls when the need arises.

Voice Cast: Tara Strong *(Bubbles)*; Cathy Cavadini *(Blossom)*; Elizabeth Daily *(Buttercup)*; Tom Kenny *(Mayor/Utonium)*; Jennifer Hale *(Ms. Keane)*; Roger L. Jackson *(Mojo Jojo)*. **Narrator:** Ernie Anderson, Tom Kenny.

7437   *The Powers of Matthew Star*. (Series; Science Fiction; NBC; 1982-1983). When the planet Quandris is invaded by aliens, its young prince, Ehawk, is sent to Earth to develop his powers until they become strong enough for him to return to Quandris and battle its enemies. Ehawk and his guardian, Dehay, settle in a California town called Crestridge, where Ehawk assumes the role of Matthew Star, a high school student, and Dehay assumes the identity of Walt Shepherd, a science teacher at Crestridge High School (Matthew and Walt are awaiting a special ship to take them back to Quandris — in their year 8312, at which time Matthew's powers will have been developed). Stories depict Matthew's efforts to develop his powers, live a free life and battle the enemies of Quandris who have come to Earth to kill him. Originally titled *Knight Star* then *Star Prince, The Powers of David Star* and *The Powers of Daniel Star*. In the original pilot film (broadcast on April 5, 1983) Peter Barton is referred to as David Star and his guardian is Max, played by Gerald S. O'Loughlin.

Other regulars are Pam Elliott, Matthew's friend; General Fredrick Tucker, the Air Force commander who enlists Matthew's aid (he was replaced by Mr. Wymore); Mr. Curtis, the coach at Crestridge High School; Mr. Heller, the principal; Queen Nadra, Matthew's mother; Bob, a student.

Cast: Peter Barton *(Matthew Star)*; Louis Gossett, Jr. *(Walt Shepherd)*; Amy Steele *(Pam Elliott)*; John Crawford *(Gen. Frederick Tucker)*; James Karen *(Mr. Wymore)*; Barry Van Dyke *(Mr. Curtis)*; Chip Frye *(Bob)*; Tricia O'Neil *(Queen Nadra)*; Michael Fairman *(Mr. Heller)*. **Theme Song:** "The Powers of Matthew Star" by Michel Rubini, Denny Jaeger.

7438   *Powers Play*. (Pilot; Drama; CBS; Aug. 30, 1986). Following the death of the father she never knew, Rowena Powers inherits BPI (Ben Powers International), a powerful world-wide conglomerate based in Arizona. The proposal was to relate Rowena's struggles to protect her interests in the company. Other regulars are Lucas Cord, the company president (Rowena is Chairman of the Board); and Harry, Rowena's grandfather.

Cast: Sheree J. Wilson *(Rowena Powers)*; David Birney *(Lucas Cord)*; Noah Beery, Jr. *(Harry)*.

7439   *The Powers That Be*. (Series; Comedy; NBC; 1992-1993). Washington, D.C., is the setting for a comical look at the Powers, a dysfunctional political family: Senator William ("Bill") Franklin Powers, his wife, Margaret, their married daughter, Caitlin Van Horne and Sophie Lipkin, Bill's illegitimate daughter from a wartime romance (she now works for her father as a political aide).

Bill, a liberal Democrat, is 65 years old and has been a senator for 26 years. He and Margaret live at 2292 Applewood Drive. Margaret is yearning to become a First Lady and is grooming Bill for the Oval Office. She is younger than Bill and is actively involved in the political arena (she will join any charity to further Bill's political career).

Caitlin is very pretty, but also petty, self-serving and vain. She is married to the wimpy congressman Theodore Van Horne, who is unable to stand up to or overcome her dominance over him (he says simply, "Yes, dear," to everything she asks, and he appears to be on the brink of suicide). Caitlin and Theodore are the parents of young Pierce. Caitlin loves to wear pink and calls Margaret "Mummy."

Jordan Miller is Bill's legislative assistant (or press agent in some episodes) and Bill's mistress; she calls Bill "Button" (they have a secret rendezvous every Sunday morning; Margaret thinks Bill is at church). Bradley Grist is Bill's P.R. man, and Charlotte is the Powers' maid. She is famous for her crab cakes but is constantly belittled by Margaret and seems to live in fear of her. Charlotte and Theodore have a secret crush on each other (possibly the only thing that is keeping Theodore from killing himself). Stephen Bishop sings the theme, "The Powers That Be."

Cast: John Forsythe *(Bill Franklin)*; Holland Taylor *(Margaret Franklin)*; Valerie Mahaffey *(Caitlin Van Horne)*; Robin Bartlett *(Sophie Lipkin)*; David Hyde Pierce *(Theodore Van Horne)*; Joseph Gordon-Levitt *(Pierce Van Horne)*; Eve Gordon *(Jordan Miller)*; Peter MacNichol *(Bradley Grist)*.

7440   *The Practice*. (Series; Comedy; NBC; 1976-1977). Dr. Jules Bedford is a gruff but lovable doctor who practices on the Lower East Side of New York City. David Bedford, Jules' son, is an uptown physician with one goal in mind: convince his father to give up his shabby practice and join him on Park Avenue. Stories follow a father and son's efforts to treat their patients in the manner to which they have become accustomed and Jules' on-going battle to stay where he is. Other regulars are Jenny Bedford, David's wife; Molly Gibbons, Jules' nurse; Helen, Jules's receptionist; Paul and Tony, David's sons; Dr. Roland Caine, David's partner; Nate, the hospital restaurant waiter; Lenny, the intern; Dr. Byron Fisk, David's friend; and Harry Bedford, Jules's brother.

Cast: Danny Thomas *(Jules Bedford)*; David Spielberg *(David Bedford)*; Shelley Fabares *(Jenny Bedford)*; Dena Dietrich *(Molly Gibbons)*; Didi Conn *(Helen)*; Allen Price *(Paul Bedford)*; Damon Raskin *(Tony Bedford)*; John Byner *(Roland Caine)*; Sam Laws *(Nate)*; Barry Gordon *(Byron Fisk)*; Mike Evans *(Lenny)*; Jan Murray *(Harry Bedford)*.

7441   *The Practice*. (Series; Drama; ABC; 1997–2004). Donnell, Young, Berluti and Frutt is a Boston-based law firm that considers every client important and worth what ever battle it takes to win their case. The lawyers of the firm are compassionate and are experts at legal maneuvers (all done within the limits of the law). Robert Donnell is the senior defense attorney and the firm's founder. Jimmy Berluti, Ellenor Frutt, Eugene Young and Lindsay Dole are junior partners. Jessica Capshaw is a paralegal and a third year law student; Tara Wilson is the ethically challenged lawyer; Jamie Stringer is the newest member of the firm, a recent law school graduate.

Cast: Dylan McDermott *(Robert Donnell)*; Steve Harris *(Eugene Young)*; Camryn Manheim *(Ellenor Frutt)*; Michael Badalucco *(Jimmy Berluti)*; Jessica Capshaw *(Jamie Stringer)*; Rhona Mitra *(Tara Wilson)*; James Spader *(Alan Shore)*; Kelli Williams *(Lindsay Dole)*; Lisa Gay Hamilton *(Rebecca Washington)*; Lara Flynn Boyle *(Helen Gamble)*; Marla Sokoloff *(Lucy Hatcher)*; Bill Smitrovich *(ADA Ken Walsh)*; Ron Livingston *(ADA Alan Lowe)*; Jason Kravits *(ADA Richard Bay)*.

7442　*Prairie Home Companion with Garrison Keillor.* (Series; Variety; Disney; 1985). A television adaptation of the radio program in which host Garrison Keillor relates stories about life in the small town of Lake Woebegone in Mist County, Minnesota. Name guests, mostly country and western singers, appear on each episode.

Host: Garrison Keillor.

7443　*Pranked.* (Series; Comedy; MTV; 2009). A clip program that presents "the best pranks ever captured on camera and posted online."

Amir Blumenfeld and Streeter Seidell host.

7444　*Prehistoric Planet.* (Series; Children; Discovery Kids; 2002). A rather realistic look at the way dinosaurs lived and flourished on earth millions of years ago (seen via computer animation). Each program is devoted to a specific subject (like predators) of a specific breed of dinosaur.

Program Open: "You're traveling back in time — millions of years flash by in seconds. You're going face-to-face with the wildest creatures that ever walked the earth. You're about to explore *Prehistoric Planet.*"

Narrator: Ben Stiller, Christopher Slater.

7445　*Premiere.* (Experimental; Variety; CBS; June 25, 1951). An historic CBS event: its first attempt at commercial color broadcasting to a five city cable hookup (New York, Baltimore, Philadelphia, Washington, D.C., and Boston). The program featured the performances of top CBS personalities and showed the potential of color television (even though there were, for example, only 30 color sets in New York City). Although the CBS color wheel system was the one favored by the FCC, it never caught on. The system showed brilliant color but played havoc with faces and hair, giving a two-tone look. The show was also a great plug for the sponsors who backed it: General Mills, Wrigley's Gum, Pepsi-Cola, Toni Home Permanent, Proctor and Gamble, Standard Brands, Aunt Jemima Pancake Flour, Ivory Soap, Tender Leaf Tea, Chase and Sanborn Coffee, Ford Lincoln and Mercury Cars and Revlon Lipstick.

Performers: Robert Alda, Isabel Bigley, The Bil and Cora Baird Marionettes, Faye Emerson, Arthur Godfrey, Durward Kirby, Sam Levinson, Garry Moore, The New City Ballet Company, Ed Sullivan. **Miss CBS Color:** Patty Painter. **CBS Guests:** William S. Paley *(chairman)*; Frank Stanton *(president)*; Wayne Coy *(FCC Chairman)*. **Orchestra:** Archie Bleyer.

7446　*Premiere.* (Pilot; CBS; 1968). The overall title for eight pilot films: *Call to Danger; Crisis; Higher and Higher, Attorneys at Law; Lassiter; Operation: Greasepaint; Out of the Blue; The Search* and *A Walk in the Night.*

7447　*Presenting Susan Anton.* (Series; Variety; NBC; 1979). A program of music, songs and comedy that highlights the talents of actress Susan Anton.

Program Open: "*Presenting Susan Anton.* Susan's guests tonight are Norman Fell, Johnny Mathis and 'Mr. Whipple,' Dick Wilson (from Charmin bathroom tissue commercials). Ladies and gentlemen, Miss Susan Anton."

Host: Susan Anton. **Regulars:** Barbara Brownell, Jack Fletcher, Jack Knight, Terry McGovern, Jimmy Martinez, Buddy Powell, Donovan Scott, Marcie Vosburgh, Dick Wilson, The Walter Painter Dancers. **Orchestra:** Ian Bernard, Larry White.

7448　*Presidio Med.* (Series; Drama; CBS; 2002–2003). Presidio Medical Group is a prestigious hospital in San Francisco. Stories relate events in the lives of the mostly female doctors in residence as they put the patient above everything else in an attempt to treat the disease and find the needed treatments for a patient's full recovery.

Cast: Dana Delany *(Dr. Rae Brennan)*; Blythe Danner *(Dr. Harriet Lanning)*; Julianne Nicholson *(Dr. Jules Keating)*; Sasha Alexander *(Dr. Jackie Collette)*; Paul Black Thorne *(Dr. Matt Slingerland)*; Anna Deavere Smith *(Dr. Letty Jordan)*; Oded Fehr *(Dr. Nicholas Kokoris)*; Jennifer Siebel *(Cyndy Lloyd)*; David Kaufman *(Norman Drum)*.

7449　*Press Your Luck.* (Series; Game; CBS; 1983). A question is read to three contestants. The first player to buzz in receives a chance to answer. His answer, plus two additional answers, are revealed to the other players. The remaining two players have the opportunity to select one answer. Points (called spins) are awarded thus: three spins for the player who buzzed in first if he has the correct answer; if he is wrong, the other player can receive one spin if he chose the correct answer. Four such rounds are played. Players then receive the opportunity to use their spins on a large electronic game board. The board is divided into 20 squares, each of which revolves rapidly. Squares contains cash amounts, merchandise prizes and Whammies. The object is for a player to accumulate as much cash and merchandise as possible within his allotted amount of time without hitting a Whammy (which automatically wipes out all his earnings). The player with the overall highest cash/merchandise score is the winner.

Host: Peter Tomarken. **Announcer:** Rod Roddy.

7450　*Pressure Point.* (Pilot; Game; Unaired; Produced for CBS in 1990). Three contestants compete. A question is read followed by the initials to the answer. The first player to buzz in receives a chance to answer. If he is correct he scores points. The highest point scorer is the winner.

Host: Clint Holmes. **Announcer:** Jim McKrell.

7451　*The Preston Episodes.* (Series; Comedy; Fox; 1995). David Preston is a college professor (teaches Shakespeare) who, after his divorce, decides on a career change and acquires a job as a writer for a celebrity magazine called *Stuff.* Incidents in David's life as he goes about acquiring stories for the magazine are the focal point of stories (only two of which aired). Larry Dunhill is the paper's editor; Kelly Freeman, Adam Green, Harlow, Larry Dunhill and Derek Clooney are David's co-workers.

Cast: David Alan Grier *(David Preston)*; Judith Scott *(Kelly Freeman)*; Clive Revill *(Larry Dunhill)*; Matthew Walker *(Adam Green)*; Jeff Horny *(Ned)*; Tommy Hinkley *(Derek Clooney)*; Brent Hinkley *(Harlow)*.

7452   The Pretender. (Series; Drama; NBC; 1996–2000). The Center is a mysterious organization that seeks and trains specially endowed human beings. Such a person is a man known only as Jarod. Jarod possesses a very high I.Q. and has the ability to impersonate people. He was taken from his family as a child and raised on the goals of the center.

Jarod's abilities are tested through various simulations. As Jarod grew up he also wised up and realized these simulations were not being used to help people. Fearing they may be planning to use him for sinister purposes, Jarod escapes from the Center and sets out to find his real family—and use the abilities he learned at the Center to help people in trouble he finds along the way by becoming anyone he wants to be.

Jarod, however, is not as free as he thinks. The Center wants him back and assigns Sydney, Jarod's father figure, to retrieve him. Also pursuing Jarod are Catherine Parker, Jarod's childhood friend (her father runs the Center) and Broots, a computer whiz who obeys his superiors no matter what he may asked to do. After its NBC run, TNT produced two TV movies based on the series: *The Pretender 2001* (Jan. 22, 2001) and *The Pretender: Island of the Haunted* (Dec. 10, 2001).

Cast: Michael T. Weiss (*Jarod*); Andrea Parker (*Catherine Parker*); Jon Gries (*Broots*); Patrick Bauchau (*Sydney*); Ryan Merriman (*Young Jarod; flashbacks*).

7453   The Pretenders. (Pilot; Adventure; CBS; July 5, 1988). Nick Stuart was a dashing U.S. government undercover agent who was killed during an assignment. Nick's long-estranged twin brother, Jack, is found by the government and asked to masquerade as his brother. Jack is the direct opposite of Nick—an irreverent, anti-authoritarian, down-on-his-luck disc jockey who was fired from his last nine jobs. But Jack needs the money and agrees to become his brother. He is teamed with Nick's beautiful and sophisticated partner, Alexandra Greer, and the proposal was to relate their collision of classes and attitudes as Jack struggles to play the part of his brother in the midst of dangerous crime-fighting missions. Sam Everett is their superior.

Cast: Amanda Pays (*Alexandra Greer*); Roger Wilson (*Jack Stuart*); Mitchell Laurance (*Sam Everett*).

7454   Pretty Little Liars. (Series; Mystery; ABC Family; 2010–2011). Alison DiLaurentis, Aria Montgomery, Hanna Marin, Emily Fields and Spencer Hastings are 15-year-old girls who attend Rosewood High School in Rosewood, Pennsylvania. Alison is the Queen Bee of the group. She is manipulative, vindictive and knows the secrets of all her friends. Aria is a gorgeous free spirit; Emily is the school's star athlete. She is also confused by her sexuality as she finds herself being drawn to Maya, a new girl in town. Spencer is the overachiever. She s a straight *A* student and is under constant pressure to do her best. Hanna is the school's "It Girl" and is an expert at creating a facade for the perfect life. She goes after what she wants; the more forbidding it is the better for her (for example, shoplifting).

One stormy night during an unsupervised camping trip, the girls become drunk and when they awaken the next morning, Alison has mysteriously disappeared. The story immediately progresses one year later. Alison is still missing and is presumed dead. Aria, Spencer, Hanna and Emily have drifted apart but on the anniversary of Alison's disappearance, they are suddenly brought together again when they each receive a text message from a mysterious stranger identified as "A." The text messages reveal information that only Alison would know and the girls suspect that Alison is still alive. A short time later a body is found that is identified as Alison's. The text messages keep coming, however, and a vague figure that resembles Alison is occa-

sionally seen by the remaining friends. On the night of Alison's disappearance the girls swore not to talk about what happened. Their secret has now bonded them together—but has Alison come from beyond the grave (to seek revenge?) and destroy their lives by revealing their deepest, darkest secrets? The police have begun an investigation into Alison's death and stories follow the girls as they seek to protect their secrets and uncover the identity of "A." Ellen is Aria's mother, a woman who prides herself on respecting her children and trusting her family. Byron, Aria's father, is a college professor who is having a secret affair with one of his students. Ashley, Hanna's mother, will do anything for her daughter (Ashley's husband abandoned the family and left them with nothing). This created an impenetrable bond between mother and daughter. Ezra Fitz is Rosewood High's new English teacher; Mona Vanderwall is a popular girl at school who is also friends with Hanna.

Cast: Lucy Hale (*Aria Montgomery*); Ashley Benson (*Hanna Marin*); Troian Bellisario (*Spencer Hastings*); Shay Mitchell (*Emily Fields*); Sasha Pieterse (*Alison DiLaurentis*); Bianca Lawson (*Maya St. Germain*); Holly Marie Combs (*Ella Montgomery*); Chad Lowe (*Byron Montgomery*); Ian Harding (*Ezra Fitz*); Laura Leighton (*Ashley Marin*); Janel Parrish (*Mona Vanderwall*); Tammin Sursok (*Jenna Cavanaugh*); Keegan Allen (*Toby Cavanaugh*); Carlson Young (*Amber*); Bryce Johnson (*Detective Wilden*).

7455   Pretty Wicked. (Series; Reality; Oxygen; 2009). Program host CariDee English (winner of the seventh cycle of *America's Next Top Model*) says, "I meet ... many beautiful people all the time, but when they open their mouths and say something rude or ... ignorant—you don't see their beauty anymore. All you see is an ugly person." Ten women who fit this description, are chosen to embrace their inner beauty and not rely on their looks. Each of the women compete in a series of challenges that test their ability to have the right attitude—not how to apply makeup or dress for an occasion. Kyle Cease (self-help comedian), Dr. Jenn Berman (psycho therapist), Mia Tyler (model) are the judges.

7456   Pretty Wild. (Series; Reality; E!; 2010). Tess Neiers (age 19), Alexis Neiers (18) and Gabrielle Neiers (15) are the daughters of Andrea Arlington, a 1980s former Playboy Playmate. The sisters are gorgeous and have had an unstructured upbringing. Andrea manages her daughters modeling careers and episodes relate incidents in their lives as they live each day to the fullest.

7457   Preview Theater. (Pilot; NBC; 1961). A summer series of pilot films produced for the 1961-62 season. See: *Five's a Family, Happily Ever After, Harry's Business, Heave Ho Harrigan, I Married a Dog, Innocent Jones, Miss Bishop, Picture Window* and *Shore Leave.*

7458   Preview Tonight. (Pilot; ABC; 1966). "Each year many of the new shows developed for television fail to make the networks schedules even though they are entertaining and well produced. Tonight's pilot film is one of these. We invite you behind the scenes to see what you think of *Pursue and Destroy* on *Preview Tonight.*" The overall title for pilot films produced for the 1966-67 season. See: *The Cliff Dwellers, Great Bible Adventures, Pursue and Destroy, Roaring Camp, Somewhere in Italy ... Company B.*

7459   Prey. (Series; Science Fiction; Syfy; 1998). As the Earth progressed over the centuries, many species have come and gone. Man has survived, but a new species of humanoids has evolved from Global Warming—evil beings with only one driving ambition: annihilate the human race and take over the world. Dr. Sloan Parker, a leading bio anthropologist, has uncovered their existence and now heads a team of scientists dedicated to uncovering ways to stop them.

Humans are now the prey and stories follow mankind's battle for survival.

Cast: Debra Messing *(Dr. Sloan Parker)*; Vincent Ventresca *(Dr. Edward Tate)*; Larry Drake *(Dr. Walter Atwood)*; Frankie Faison *(Ray Peterson)*; Adam Storke *(Tom Daniels)*.

7460   The Price Is Right. (Series; Game; NBC; ABC; Syn. CBS; 1956–). The game varies greatly in presentation but the basic format calls for contestants to guess the manufacturer's suggested retail price for various merchandise. Players who surpass the retail price forfeit their chance to win that particular item; the player whose bid comes closest to the selling price receives the item.

Bill Cullen Program Open: "Tonight these four people meet to compete for the prizes of a lifetime on *The Price Is Right*, brought to you by Spiedel, America's first name in watch bands ... and now, your host on *The Price Is Right*, Bill Cullen."

Bob Barker Program Open: "Here it comes! Television's most exciting hour of fantastic prizes. The fabulous 60 minute *Price Is Right*. Zane Burch — come on down! Mark Becker — come on down! Lori Stone — come on down! Sandra Obrist — come on down! You are the first four contestants on *The Price Is Right*. And now here is the star of *The Price Is Right*, Bob Barker." Six versions appeared.

1. The Price Is Right (NBC, 1956–63; ABC, 1963–65). **Host:** Bill Cullen. **Substitute Hosts Include:** Jack Clark, Johnny Gilbert, Bob Kennedy, Sonny Fox, Sam Levenson, Jack Narz, Robert Q. Lewis, Don Pardo, Arlene Francis. **Models:** Carolyn Stroupe, Beverly Bentley, Toni Wallace, June Ferguson, Gail Sheldon. **NBC Announcer:** Don Pardo. **ABC Announcer:** Johnny Gilbert. **NBC Substitute Announcers Include:** Dick Dudley, Roger Tuttle, Vic Roby. **ABC Substitute Announcer:** Ed Jordan.

2. The Price Is Right (CBS, 1972–). **Daytime Host:** Bob Barker (1972–2007); Drew Carey (2007–). **Syndicated Host:** Dennis James (1972–76), Bob Barker (1976–79). **Models Include:** Anitra Ford, Holly Hallstrom, Janice Pennington, Dian Parkinson, Kathleen Bradley, Lanisha Cole, Brandi Sherwood, Phire Dawson, Gabrielle Tuiten, Nicki Schlieler Ziering, Heather Kozar, Claudia Jordan. **Announcer:** Johnny Olson, Gene Wood, Rod Roddy, Rich Fields, J.D. Roberto, Jeff Davis, Brad Sherwood, David Lawrence, Steve White, George Gray. **Models: (2009–2011):** Gwendolyn Osborn, Lanisha Cole, Rachel Reynolds, Amber Lancaster, Tiffany Cole. Originally titled *The New Price Is Right* (1972–75).

3. The Price Is Right (Syn., 1985-86). **Host:** Tom Kennedy. **Models:** Holly Hallstrom, Janice Pennington, Dian Parkinson. **Announcer:** Johnny Olson, Rod Roddy.

4. The Price Is Right Special (CBS, 1986). **Host:** Bob Barker. **Models:** Dian Parkinson, Holly Hallstrom. **Announcer:** Rod Roddy.

5. The Price Is Right (Syn., 1994-95). **Host:** Doug Davidson. **Models:** Julie Cialini, Lisa Stahl, Ferrari Ferris. **Announcer:** Burton Richardson.

6. The Price Is Right Million Dollar Spectacular (CBS, 2008). **Host:** Drew Carey. **Models:** Brandi Sherwood, Rachel Reynolds, Gabrielle Tuite. **Announcer:** Rich Fields.

7461   The Price of Beauty. (Series; Reality; VH-1; 2010). A sincere effort to explore the meaning of true beauty in different cultures. Reality TV star and singer Jessica Simpson, who has battled weight problems, and her two best friends, CaCee Kobb and Ken Paves, travel around the world to meet everyday women and examine their traditions, practices and opinions on beauty.

7462   Pride and Joy. (Series; Comedy; NBC; 1995). Amy and Greg Sherman are the parents of an infant (Mel). Their best friends and neighbors, Carol and Nathan, are also the parents of a newborn son (Mitchell). The wives work as ad agency partners; the husbands stay at home — Greg because he is a free-lance writer; Nathan because he is unemployed (recently laid off from his job on Wall Street). Episodes relate their efforts to overcome the everyday problems in coping with life in New York City.

Cast: Julie Warner *(Amy Sherman)*; Craig Bierko *(Greg Sherman)*; Caroline Rhea *(Carol Greene)*; Jeremy Piven *(Nathan Greene)*.

7463   Pride of the Family. (Series; Comedy; ABC; 1953-1954). Albie Morrison is the advertising head of the *Chronicle*, a small town newspaper. He is married to Catherine and they are the parents of Ann and Albie Jr. Albie is a kind-hearted man who asks very little from life: a productive day at work, a good home-cooked dinner and obedient children. The children are quite good and cause few problems. Catherine is not only a good cook, but an attractive and caring mother. Work is another story as acquiring accounts and dealing with numerous work-related problems tend to make Albie a bit grumpy and his efforts to resolve the problems at home and at work are the focal point of stories. Also known as *The Phil Hartman Show*.

Cast: Paul Hartman *(Albie Morrison)*; Fay Wray *(Catherine Morrison)*; Natalie Wood *(Ann Morrison)*; Bobby Hyatt *(Albie Morrison, Jr.)*.

7464   The Primary English Class. (Pilot; Comedy; ABC; Aug. 15, 1977). Sandy Lambert teaches English to foreign-born adults new to the U.S. Her classes are held in a California night school and the proposal was to relate Sandy's efforts to help her students in class and out. Other regulars are Hal, the auto shop teacher; and Sandy's students: Yosef, Lupe, Sergio, Wilhelm, Yoko and Chuma.

Cast: Valerie Curtin *(Sandy Lambert)*; Murphy Dunne *(Hal)*; Harvey Jason *(Yosef Ari)*; Maria O'Brien *(Lupe)*; Joe Bennett *(Sergio)*; Bob Holt *(Wilhelm Ritterman)*; Suesie Elene *(Yoko)*; Freeman King *(Chuma)*.

7465   The Prime of Miss Jean Brodie. (Series; Drama; PBS; 1979). Edinburgh, Scotland, in 1930 is the setting for a look at the life of Jean Brodie, a vain and eccentric teacher employed at the Marcia Blaine School for Girls. Other teachers are Mrs. MacDonald, Miss Gaunt, Mr. Lawson and Ted Lloyd. Students are Sandy, Giulia, Jenny, Rose and Mary. Based on the 1961 novel by Muriel Spark and produced by Scottish TV.

Cast: Geraldine McEwan *(Jean Brodie)*; Madeleine Christie *(Mrs. MacDonald)*; Georgine Anderson *(Miss Gaunt)*; Lynsey Baxter *(Sandy)*; Romana Kaye *(Giulia)*; Amanda Kirby *(Jenny Gray)*; Tracey Childs *(Rose Stanley)*; Jean McKinley *(Mary)*; George Cormack *(Mr. Lawson)*; John Castle *(Ted Lloyd)*. **Hostess:** Julie Harris.

7466   Prime Times. (Pilot; Comedy; NBC; April 4, 1983). Spoofs of television — its past, present and imagined future via inter cutting clips from old series with new sketches.

Host: Leslie Nielsen. **Regulars:** Lewis Arquette, Thom Bray, Hamilton Camp, Jan Hooks, Julie Payne, Deborah Pratt.

7467   Primetime Glick. (Series; Comedy; Comedy Central; 2001–2003). A comical spoof of talk shows featuring Jiminy Glick, a host with an absurd history, interviewing (but often forgetting their names) top show business personalities. Jiminy is comically grotesque (obese) as the result of swallowing a Tonka truck as a child that lodged in his stomach. He is the son of Omar and Isabella and, as a result of the Tonka incident, was a sickly child. He graduated from Gale Gordon High School (named after Lucille Ball's long-time sidekick) and, with acting in his blood, ventured off to Hollywood where he acquired his first role: the kleptomaniac nephew of detective *Barnaby Jones* on CBS. He later worked as the personal assistant to Charles Bronson and in 19991, after meeting *Rowan and Martin's Laugh-In* producer George Schlatter, was offered the role of host for the talk show *La La Wood*. He then acquired his current series, *Primetime Glick*. Jiminy is married to Dixie and is the father of Mason, Matthew and Modine.

Cast: Martin Short (*Jiminy Glick*); Lex Lang (*Announcer*); Michael McKean (*Adrien Van Vorhees*); Jan Hooks (*Dixie Glick*); Alex Baker (*Guitarist*); David Lee McLain (*Zoltan*); Brett Gilbert (*Ladislof*).

7468   *Primeval*. (Series; Science Fiction; BBC America; 2008). Nick Cutter is a professor of Paleontology at the Center Metropolitan University in London. He is called an "evolutionary zoologist" and investigates gaps in the evolutionary record. Eight years earlier, Nick's wife, Helen (his assistant), mysteriously disappeared in a time-ripping anomaly. Then, suddenly she reappeared in the present day — as do prehistoric creatures who cross the corridors of time via the unexplained anomalies. Helen holds the key to the riddle of the anomalies and stories follow Nick and his team as they struggle to protect society from the past as it threatens not only the present, but the future. Stephen is Nick's assistant; Abby is the reptile expert; Connor is the college intern with an interest in dinosaurs; Claudia is the government's (Ministry of Science and Technology) agent who oversees Nick's investigations; James is the government official who seeks to keep the public in the dark about what is happening.

Cast: Douglas Henshall (*Nick Cutter*); Juliet Aubrey (*Helen Cutter*); Andrew Lee Potts (*Conner Temple*); Lucy Brown (*Claudia Brown*); James Murray (*Stephen Hart*); Hannah Spearritt (*Abby Maitland*); Ben Miller (*James Lester*).

7469   *Primus*. (Series; Adventure; Syn.; 1971). Carter Primus is an ex-Navy frogman turned troubleshooter who operates Primus, Inc., a Nassau-based company that tackles dangerous underwater assignments. Toni Hayden, a beautiful girl who loves to wear bikinis, is his partner; Charles Kingman is his rugged assistant. Tegtight is Carter's operational base in Nassau. *Dagat* is "the Mother Ship" (where he stores most of his underwater equipment); the *Orka* is his patrol boat (for surface surveillance); the *Pegasus* is his underwater exploratory vehicle; and *Big Kate* is his underwater robot. Leonard Rosenman composed the theme.

Cast: Robert Brown (*Carter Primus*); Eva Renzi (*Toni Hyden*); Will Kuluva (*Charlie Kingman*). **Narrator:** Robert Brown.

7470   *The Prince of Motor City*. (Pilot; Drama; Unaired; Produced for ABC in 2008). When a mysterious accident claims the life of James Hamilton III, the founder and owner of Hamilton Motors, Detroit's fourth largest auto plant, his son, Jamie Hamilton, a philosophy lecturer, inherits the business. Paul Riley, the company CEO is unhappy that he did not inherit the company and Jaime is not sure he wants the power and wealth the company can give him. There is a mystery surrounding James's death and Jamie is suddenly being haunted by a moody Elvis song that was his father's favorite. To further complicate Jamie's life are mysterious, meaningful messages from complete strangers, voices from inanimate objects and the appearance of his father's ghost, which tells him "I want revenge." The proposal, which sounds like a comedy, is actually intended to be a suspenseful journey for Jamie as he takes over the company and seeks to uncover the truth about his father's death.

Cast: Warren Christie (*Jamie Hamilton*); John Carroll Lynch (*Paul Riley*); Piper Perabo (*Meg Riley*); Andie MacDowell (*Gertrude Hamilton*); Aunjanue Ellis (*Cora Neel*).

7471   *The Prince of Tennis*. (Series; Cartoon; Cartoon Network; 2001). Ryoma Echizen is a 12-year-old boy and tennis prodigy. He is known for his "twist serve" and is a member of the Seishun Gakuen Middle School Tennis Team. The Japanese produced program is a coming-of-age story that follows Ryoma, called "The Prince of Tennis," as he trains and competes in tournaments.

Voice Cast: David Neil Black (*Ryoma Echizen*); Jack Butler (*Sadoharu Inui*); Kirk Thornton (*Kunimitsu Tezuka*); Barbara Goodson (*Sumire Ryazaki*); Doug Ertholtz (*Takeshi*).

7472   *Prince Planet*. (Series; Cartoon; Syn.; 1966). Prince Planet is a alien being who poses as a boy named Bobby on Earth. He is a member of the Universal Peace Corps of the planet Radion. His mission is to determine if Earth qualifies for membership in the Galactic Union of Worlds. While Bobby makes his evaluation (he lives in New Meropolis), he battles the forces of evil that threaten the planet.

Diana Worthy and her father, Pop Worthy, are Bobby's friends. Dan Dynamo is his wrestler friend; Aji Baba is a magician; Warlock (a Martian) and Krag (from the planet Kragmire) are Bobby's enemies. By the use of his magic pendant, Bobby can transform himself into Prince Planet, a daring crusader for justice. Produced in Japan and also known as *The Prince of Planets*.

Voice Cast: Catherine Byers (*Prince Planet/Bobby*); Carl Banas (*Dan Dynamo*); Sandy Warshaw (*Diana Worthy*); Jeff Gillen (*Pop Worthy*); Kurt Nagel (*Aji Baba*); Frank Schuller (*Krag*); Arnie Warren (*Warlock*).

7473   *Prince Street*. (Series; Crime Drama; NBC; 1997). A print shop on the south side section of Manhattan on Prince Street is the front for a secret unit of the N.Y.P.D. The unit, headed by Lieutenant Tom Warner, has been assigned the dangerous task of infiltrating gangs, bust drug kingpins and go and do whatever is necessary to put criminals behind bars. Nina Echeverria, Alex Gage, James Tasio, Donny Hanson, Anthony Libretti and Diane Hoffman are Tom's agents and stories (only two of which aired) relate their undercover assignments.

Cast: Joe Morton (*Lt. Tom Warner*); Mariska Hargitay (*Det. Nina Echeverria*); Lawrence Monoson (*Det. James Tasio*); Vincent Spano (*Det. Alex Gage*); Steven Martin (*Det. Anthony Libretti*); Dana Eskelson (*Det. Diane Hoffman*); Sam Rockwell (*Det. Donny Hanson*).

7474   *Prince Valiant*. (Series; Cartoon; Family Channel; 1994). England in the 11th century is the setting. Valiant, the Prince of Thule, awakens from a dream in which he envisioned himself being surrounded by King Arthur to become a Knight of his Round Table. Prince Valiant begins a quest to follow that dream. On the way to Camelot he meets Rowenne, a blacksmith's daughter, and Arn, a peasant, who join him in his quest. Stories follow Prince Valiant, Rowenne and Arn as they find Camelot then train to become knights.

Voice Cast: Robby Benson (*Prince Valiant*); Noelle North (*Rowenne*); Michael Horton (*Arn*); Efrem Zimbalist, Jr. (*King Arthur*); Samantha Eggar (*Queen Guinevere*); James Avery (*Sir Bryant*); Tim Curry (*Sir Gawain*); Patty Duke (*Lady Morgana*).

7475   *The Princes of Malibu*. (Series; Reality; Fox; 2005). The "princes" of the title are Brandon and Brody Jenner, the spoiled stepsons of Olympic decathlete Bruce Jenner and his ex-wife Linda Thompson (now married to music producer David Foster). Brody and Brandon do not work, are not ambitious and have a knack for getting into trouble. They live off David's money and David is desperately trying to get them to stand on their own two feet. Stories follow Brandon and Brody as they do what they want no matter what attempts are made to change them.

7476   *Princess Gwenevere and the Jewel Riders*. (Series; Cartoon; Syn.; 1995-1996). Avalon (also called New Camelot) is a magical kingdom whose crown jewels maintain a stable link to allow magic to co-exist with its inhabitants. When Merlin, a powerful wizard is thrust into this magic (called Wild Magic) to acquire the jewels for the evil Lady Kale, he foils her by scattering the jewels all across Avalon. The magic has become unstable and now threatens to destroy Avalon. Three heroes come to the rescue: Princess Gwenevere and her best friends, Tamara and Falen. The girls each possess a jewel that gives them a special link to the crown jewels. Assisted by Academes, Merlin's faithful owl, Princess Gwenevere, Tamara and Falen begin a trek to not only recover the scattered jewels and restore harmony, but also find Merlin (who is lost in the dark regions of Wild Magic) and stop Lady Kale from becoming ruler of Avalon. In later episodes, the jewels are called Wizard's Jewels and Lady Kale acquires an assistant — the evil witch Morgana.

Princess Gwenevere is heiress to the throne. As the leader of the Jewel Riders, she acquires power from her Sunstone and rides a unicorn named Sunstar. Tamara cares about people and animals and receives her power through her Heart Stone; her unicorn is Moon Dance. Falen is a free spirit and the Moonstone endows her with power; Shadow Song is her unicorn. Lady Kale is Gwenevere's aunt, She is bitter for not being chosen as a Jewel Rider in her youth and was corrupted by evil in the form of the Dark Stone (which is later learned to have been created by Morgana when she tried to take over Avalon but was exiled to the Wild Magic by Merlin. She has now escaped and has returned to finish what she started).

Voice Cast: Kerry Butler, Jean Louisa Kelly *(Princess Gwenevere)*; Corinne Orr *(Lady Kale)*; Deborah Allison, Laura Dean, John Beach, Bob Kaliban, Henry Mandell.

7477   *Princess Natasha.* (Series; Cartoon; Cartoon Network; 2004). Natasha is Princess of the country of Zoraia. She is secretly an agent who defends her homeland from evil, especially her uncle, Lubek, who is plotting to take over Zoraia. Natasha is currently an exchange student and living in America with her host family, the O'Briens (who are unaware of her secrets). Natasha is adjusting to Fountain Park, Illinois, plays varsity basketball on the school team and has just experienced her first crush — on Greg, the elder O'Brien son. Stories chronicle her adventures as a student and secret agent. Oleg, her friend, assists her in her battle against Uncle Lubek (who has now set her sights on Fountain Park).

Voice Cast: Amy Casanova *(Princess Natasha)*; Steve Moverly *(Announcer)*; Dan Green *(King Carl/The General)*; Megan Hollingshead *(Mrs. O'Brien)*.

7478   *Princess Tenko and the Guardians of Magic.* (Series; Cartoon; Syn.; 1995). Tenko is a beautiful magical princess who, as the head of a magic school, not only teaches children, but uses her abilities to entertain audiences from the stage. Tenko's experiences with her students, the Guardians (Bolt, Speed, Ali and Hawk) are explored as they use their combined abilities to destroy evil (especially the chaos caused by her former students Jana and Jason, evil twin magicians, who are seeking to increase their abilities by finding a power source called the Starfire Gems). Based on the real Princess Tenko, the stage name of Mariko Itakura, a former singer turned magician. At the end of each episode, the real Princess Tenko appears to perform an illusion or teach children a magic trick. Produced in Japan.

Cast: Mariko Itakura *(Princess Tenko)*.

7479   *Princesses.* (Series; Comedy; CBS; 1991). A luxurious apartment at 4107 5th Avenue in Manhattan is the rent-free residence of Princess Georgina ("Georgy") De La Rue, Tracy Dillon and Melissa ("Mel") Kirshner — three working girls who all dream of marrying wealthy men.

Tracy and Melissa met in college. Tracy planned to become a writer; Melissa sought to own her own cosmetics business. They vowed that when they reached age 28, they would meet handsome twins, get married and live next door to each other in Connecticut. They would each have two kids and maintain their careers. "What a pathetic illusion that was," says Mel, as they now share a small apartment in New York City and are struggling to make ends meet, Tracy as a creative writing teacher for adults at Manhattan College (she is later said to be teaching adult remedial English) and Mel as a cosmetics saleswoman at Macy's.

At this same time, but in another part of the world, the title of princess of Scilly (a small group of islands off the southwest coast of England) is bestowed upon 18-year-old Georgina De La Rue when she marries the elder Prince Frederick. Some years later, after Frederick's death, Georgy inherits his money, but his family contests the will and Gerogy, not born of royal blood, is left penniless. Luck appears to be on her side when a friend offers to let her stay in his 5th Avenue New York apartment for one year while he is in Europe. Unknown to Georgy, her friend has also given the apartment as a wedding gift to Michael DeCrow (James Read), the man Tracy plans to marry.

At the apartment, Tracy and Mel meet Georgy. When Georgy learns that Michael was given the apartment first, she makes plans to leave. However, before she does, Tracy discovers that Michael has two ex-wives and cancels the wedding. Georgy receives the apartment and extends an invitation to Tracy and Mel: "Since I'm all alone with no friends and no family, how would you feel about moving in here and becoming my mates?" Tracy and Mel accept the offer.

Georgy was a British stage performer before she became a princess. She was tap dancing in the play *No, No, Prime Minister* when Frederick spotted her. He came backstage, they fell in love and married. Now, being an unemployed princess, Georgy seeks to become a dancer on Broadway, but can't seem to find anything — "If I wasn't meant to be a performer, why did God give me the talent to sing and dance a little? ... I'm just a simple princess looking for work." Stories relate incidents in their lives as they seek the perfect mates.

Cast: Twiggy Lawson *(Georgy De La Rue)*; Julie Hagerty *(Tracy Dillon)*; Fran Drescher *(Melissa Kirshner)*.

7480   *Prison Break.* (Series; Drama; Fox; 2005–2009). As the series begins, Lincoln Burrows has been arrested and found guilty of killing the brother of the Vice President of the United States. He is actually innocent (later learned that he was framed) and is sent to the Fox River State Penitentiary. Lincoln's brother, Michael Scofield, a structural engineer, believes Lincoln is innocent and in what appears to be a foolish, if not dangerous plan to free Lincoln, gets himself arrested (by attempting to rob a bank) and sent to Fox River. Suspenseful stories relate the brothers planning and eventual escape from Fox River. Now, as fugitives (second season) Michael and Lincoln try to stay one step ahead of the authorities who are seeking to recapture them. Subtle hints during this time reveal that an evil and secret organization called The Company has infiltrated the government and were actually responsible for Lincoln's plight (The Company is also seeking to kill the brothers). Michael and Lincoln flee to Panama (season three) just as it is revealed that Lincoln's case was reviewed and he was found to be innocent. The brothers, however, are not really safe — The Company's hired killers are still seeking them. From this point on, the series becomes complex and difficult to follow for all the twists and turns the writers present to keep a one season show on the air for longer than anticipated; in short, when the action switches to Los Angeles (fourth season), it is basically Michael and Lincoln's efforts to bring down The Company with the help of Homeland Security agent Don Self.

Cast: Dominic Purcell *(Lincoln Burrows)*; Wentworth Miller

(Michael Scofield); Sarah Wayne Callies *(Dr. Sara Tancredi)*; Amaury Nolasco *(Fernando Sucre)*; Robert Knepper *(Theodore "T-Bag" Bagwell)*; Wade Williams *(Bradley Bellick)*; William Fichtner *(Alexander Mahone)*; Paul Adelstein *(Paul Kellerman)*; , Marshall Allman *(L.J. Burrows)*; Rockmond Dunbar *(Benjamin Miles "C-Note" Franklin)*; Jodi Lyn O'Keefe *(Gretchen Morgan)*; Robin Tunney *(Veronica Donovan)*; Stacy Keach *(Warden Henry Pope)*; Leon Russom *(Gen. Jonathan Katz)*; Philip Edward Van Lear *(Louis Patterson)*; Peter Stormare *(John Abruzzi)*; Muse Watson *(Charles Westmoreland)*; Frank Grillo *(Nick Savrinn)*; Jason Davis *(Agent Wheeler)*; Patricia Wettig *(Vice Pres. Caroline Reynolds)*; Barbara Eve Harris *(FBI Agent Lang)*; Michael Rapaport *(Donald Self)*; Reggie Lee *(Bill Kim)*; Matt DeCaro *(Roy Geary)*; Chris Vance *(James Whistler)*; Danay Garcia *(Sofia Lugo)*; Lane Garrison *(David "Tweener" Apolsksi)*; DuShon Monique Brown *(Nurse Katie Welch)*; Silas Weir Mitchell *(Charles "Haywire" Patoshik)*.

7481   Prison Wives. (Series; Reality; Investigation Discovery; 2010). Real stories of love with a twist — men and women who have fallen in love and remain devoted to each other despite the fact that the wives are serving time in prison. Interviews are presented with each spouse, family members and friends to show viewers how such couples remain devoted to each other. The wives are Jane Bailey, Georgia Benson, Pam Booker, Juli Cummings, Grace Dark Horse, Cheryl Engelke, Latoya Marion, Elli Panitz, Annika Powell, Gail Sullivan, Debra Wilmont and Tanya Windham.

7482   The Prisoner. (Series; Fantasy; CBS; 1968). John Drake, a secret agent for the Ministry in England, allows a scientist he was ordered to find to defect when he discovers that the scientist is being sought for a deadly mind-transference device that he invented. When Drake returns to the Ministry, he is reprimanded for his actions. Believing that what he did was right, Drake resigns — "It is a matter of principle."

Principle or not, someone else (assumed to be the Ministry) believes differently. At his home, Drake is packing his bags to leave London when an unknown man, dressed in black, places a nozzle in the keyhole of the front door. A gas is released and Drake is knocked unconscious. Soon afterward, Drake awakens to find himself in a strange room. He discovers that he is no longer a man, but a number — Number 6 — and the prisoner of a self-contained community known as the Village.

Soon afterward, Number 6 enters the Green Dome and meets one of the Village leaders, Number 2. Although he is unable to discover who his captors are or where the Village is, Number 6 learns the reason for his abduction: "It is a question of your resignation. A lot of people are curious about why you suddenly left. The information in your head is priceless. A man like you is worth a great deal on the open market. It is my job to check your motives."

Stories relate Number 6's efforts to discover who his captors are and his desperate attempts to escape from the Village. "We want information." "You won't get it." "By hook or crook we will." "Who is Number 1?" "You are Number 6." "I am not a number, I am a free man!"

The Village is a fantasy-like area bounded by mountains and ocean. It is a place from which there is no escape. The Village leaders have instructions "not to damage Number 6, but to get all he knows. He must be won over, not broken." The Silent Butler is Number 6's only friend.

Number 6 is assumed to be John Drake, although his name is never revealed (*The Prisoner* is a continuation of the last episode of the series *Secret Agent* in which Patrick McGoohan played British intelligence agent John Drake).

Cast: Patrick McGoohan *(Number 6)*; Angelo Muscat *(The Silent Butler)*; Colin Gordon, Clifford Evans, Mary Morris, John Sharpe,

Peter Wyngarde, Guy Doleman, Leo McKern *(Number 2)*; Kenneth Griffith *(Village president)*.

7483   The Prisoner. (Adventure; Fantasy; AMC; 2009). A remake of the prior title. The Village is a mysterious prison from which there is no escape ("There is only in — and no out"). A man, an employee of a shadowy data company (Summakor) is feared to be a threat to its secrets and kidnapped. He is given a number (Six) and placed in the Village for only one reason: break his spirit and discover the truth. Six, however, is a strong-willed man ("I am not a number") who insists that he did nothing wrong and is fiercely resistant to the numerous attempts to break him. Number Two is the man who oversees Village operations for an unknown superior. Like the original series, Number Two's job is to defeat Number Six. Also, as before, characters are only identified by numbers. M-2 is Number Two's wife (who is kept in a comatose state); Number 11-12 is their gay son (Number 909 is his lover). There are also two women in Number Six's life (Dr. 4-15 and 313), but nothing is really made clear (do they love him or are they a ploy by Number Two to achieve his goal). Number 147 is the cab driver who, like the Silent Butler in the original series, appears to be on Number Six's side. Produced in England and filmed in Nambia, South Africa.

Cast: Jim Caviezel *(Number Six)*; Ian McKellen *(Number Two)*; Rachel Blake *(M-2)*; Hayley Atwell *(Number 4-15)*; Ruth Wilson *(Number 313)*; Jamie Campbell Bower *(Number 11-12)*; Vincent Regan *(Number 909)*; Lennie James *(Number 147)*; Jessica Haines *(Number 554)*; Jeffrey R. Smith *(Number 16)*.

7484   Prisoner: Cell Block H. (Series; Drama; Syn.; 1980). A harsh view of life in a women's prison (the Wentworth Detention Center) in Melbourne, Australia as seen through the experiences of principal prisoners Karen Travers, Lynnette Warner, Bea Smith, Frieda "Franky" Doyle, Doreen Anderson, Marilyn Mason, Jeannie "Mum" Brooks and Elizabeth Birdsworth.

Karen, a schoolteacher, was convicted of killing her brutal husband (she offered no defense at her trial, other than to claim she is innocent; she was given life). Lynnette is naïve country girl who was falsely convicted of kidnapping and attempting to murder her employer's child. She received a ten year sentence when she was unable to prove she was framed. Lynnette is single and was a professional nanny.

Bea is a qualified hairdresser and was convicted, initially, of murdering a co-worker. She was released on parole after serving ten years but was later recommitted for killing her husband. She is the toughest of the women and the undisputed leader of the prison society.

Franky was sentenced to life for armed robbery and murder. She is also a lesbian with an unrequited passion for Karen. Doreen was a battered child and is easily led into crime. She has many petty convictions, but was sentenced to four years for breaking and entering.

Marilyn, a fashion model, was sentenced to 12 years for soliciting. She has many such prior convictions and is known to have worked in a porno movie. Jeannie was sentenced to life for killing her husband. Elizabeth is the oldest of the inmates and was given life for mass murder (she accidentally killed four sheep shearers by poisoning their food "to teach them a lesson"). She is obsessed with escaping.

Meg Jackson is the sympathetic prison guard, and has a happy relationship with her husband, prison psychologist Bill Jackson. Vera Bennett is the cruel and harsh prison guard who hopes her rule of iron will get her the prison governorship. Vera is single and lives at home with her invalid mother. She has no social life and lives for her job at the prison. Erica Davidson is the prison governor. She is capable of running the prison, but her approach keeps her remote and she fails to understand the frustrations of the prisoners. Lynne Hamilton sings the theme, "On the Inside."

Cast: Peita Toppano *(Karen Travers)*; Kerry Armstrong *(Lynnette Warner)*; Carol Burns *(Franky Doyle)*; Val Lehman *(Bea Smith)*; Margaret Laurence *(Marilyn Anne Mason)*; Colette Mann *(Doreen Anderson)*; Mary Ward *(Jeannie Brooks)*; Sheila Florance *(Elizabeth Birdsworth)*; Patsy King *(Erica Davidson)*; Elspeth Ballantyne *(Meg Jackson)*; Fiona Spence *(Vera Bennett)*; Don Baker *(Bill Jackson)*; Amanda Muggleton *(Chrissy Latham)*; Sally Cahill *(Barbara Davidson)*; Leslie Baker *(Monica Ferguson)*; Penny Stewart *(Kathleen Leach)*; Sigrid Thornton *(Roselyn Colson)*; Margot Knight *(Sharon Gilmour)*.

7485   *Prisoners of the Lost Universe.* (Pilot; Science Fiction; Showtime; Aug. 15, 1983). While interviewing Dr. Hartman, a physicist who has invented a device to transport objects into another dimension, Carrie Madison, host of the Los Angeles television show, *The Weird and the Wacky*, Dan Roebuck, an electrician for Dynacall Electro Maintenance, and the doctor are transported to another world when they are toppled into the beam of the machine by earthquake tremors. They materialize in a strange world of wizards and warriors and ally themselves to three strange creatures (The Greenman, who can speak to any creature; Malachi, a diminutive thief; and the Manbeast, a giant who can only grunt). The proposal was to relate their adventures in various worlds as they seek to find a way back to their own world.

Cast: Kay Lenz *(Carrie Madison)*; Richard Hatch *(Dan Roebuck)*; Ray Charleson *(The Greenman)*; Peter O'Farrell *(Malachi)*; Philip Van Der Byl *(Kahar, the Manbeast)*; Kenneth Hendel *(Dr. B. Hartman)*.

7486   *Private Benjamin.* (Series; Comedy; CBS; 1981). Judith ("Judy") Benjamin is the beautiful, spoiled daughter of a wealthy family. When her life-style becomes boring to her, she joins the army to find more excitement. She soon finds herself totally out of place when she discovers that the system does not exactly fulfill her needs. Judy's attempts to get the army to do things her way — and the army's efforts to turn her into a real soldier — are the focal point of stories.

Judy was first stationed at Fort Trams then Fort Bradley in Hobart, California ("The shoelace capital of the Northeast"). There, as part of the 2nd Platoon, B Company, Judy was a soldier in training for possible combat. When Judy graduated from boot camp (Jan. 25, 1982), she was assigned to the Public Affairs Office as the administrative assistant to Captain Doreen Lewis (later promoted to inspector general of Fort Bradley; Judy's primary job is to issue press releases.)

Colonel Lawrence ("Ironman") Fielding is the commanding officer; Sergeant Lucien C. Ross is Doreen's second in command.

Maria Gianelli, Rayleen White, Carol Winter, Lu Ann Hubble, Jackie Simms and Stacy Kouchalakas are the other privates attached to Judy's company. (Jackie worked in the motor pool; Stacy works with Judy in the office.) Major Amanda Allen replaced Captain Lewis in the last two episodes. Based on the Goldie Hawn film of the same name.

Cast: Lorna Patterson *(Pvt. Judy Benjamin)*; Eileen Brennan *(Capt. Doreen Lewis)*; Hal Williams *(Sgt. Lucien C. Ross)*; Robert Mandan *(Col. Lawrence Fielding)*; Lisa Raggio *(Pvt. Maria Gianelli)*; Joyce Little *(Pvt. Rayleen White)*; Ann Ryerson *(Pvt. Carol Winter)*; Joan Roberts *(Pvt. Barbara Ann Glass)*; Lucy Webb *(Pvt. Lu Anne Hubble)*; Francesca P. Roberts *(Pvt. Harriet Dorsey)*; Damita Jo Freeman *(Pvt. Jackie Sims)*; Wendie Jo Sperber *(Pvt. Stacy Kouchalakas)*; Polly Holliday *(Major Amanda Allen)*; Joel Brooks *(Lt. Billy Dean)*; Rebecca Field-Holden *(Pvt. Vicky Saunders)*; Barbara Barrie, K Callan *(Harriet Benjamin)*; William Daniels *(Ted Benjamin)*; Jordan Charney *(Capt. Bill Hookstraton)*; Stephanie Faracy *(Pvt. Sherry Stern)*.

7487   *Private Eye.* (Series; Crime Drama; NBC; 1987–1988). Los Angeles in 1956 is the setting. Jack Cleary is an officer with the L.A.P.D. His brother, Nick is a private detective (owner of The Nick Cleary Agency). To cover up a scandal, high-ranking officers frame Jack for taking bribes and he is dismissed from the force. Shortly after, Nick is killed while investigating a case. Jack inherits his brother's agency — and Johnny Betts, a street musician who had assisted Nick. Stories follow Jack's activities as he sets out to solve client's problems and prove he was framed.

Other regulars are Dottie, the agency's secretary; and Charlie Fontana, Jack's friend on the force.

Cast: Michael Woods *(Jack Cleary)*; Josh Brolin *(Johnny Betts)*; Bill Sadler *(Det. Charlie Fontana)*; Lisa Jane Persky *(Dottie)*; Jay O. Saunders *(Nick Cleary; pilot only)*.

7488   *Private Practice.* (Series; Drama; ABC; 2007–). *Grey's Anatomy* spin off that focuses on Addison Forbes Montgomery, a doctor at Seattle Grace Hospital who leaves Seattle after her marriage breaks up to begin a practice in California at the Oceanside Wellness Center in Santa Monica. Here, she joins with Naomi and Sam Bennett, her friends from medical school (Naomi is a fertility and hormone specialist; Sam is an internist and medical book author; they are divorced but co-exist for the sake of their teenage daughter, Maya). Dr. Cooper Freedman is the center's resident physician; Dr. Violet Turner is the unit's psychiatrist; Dr. Peter Wilder is the alternative medicine specialist; William Dell Parker is the co-op receptionist; Charlotte King is the chief of staff at the nearby hospital.

Cast: Kate Walsh *(Addison Forbes Montgomery)*; Amy Brenneman *(Violet Turner)*; Tim Daly *(Peter Wilder)*; Audra McDonald *(Naomi Bennett)*; Paul Adelstein *(Cooper Freedman)*; KaDee Strickland *(Charlotte King)*; Chris Lowell *(William Dell Parker)*; Taye Diggs *(Sam Bennett)*; Michael Patrick Thornton *(Dr. Fife)*; James Morrison *(William White, the clinic owner)*.

7489   *Private Secretary.* (Series; Comedy; CBS; 1953–1957). International Artists, Inc. is a theatrical agency located on the twenty-second floor (Suite 2201) of a building at 10 East 56th Street in New York City. Peter Sands is its founder; Susan ("Susie") Camille McNamara is his private secretary; and Violet ("Vi") Praskins is the agency's receptionist/switchboard operator.

Susie began working for Peter in 1945 (she previously served three years as a WAVE). She types 65 words a minute and takes 125 words per minute by shorthand. Susie lives at the Brockhurst Apartments (Apt. H) on East 92nd Street in Manhattan.

Peter was in the air force for four years before he established International Artists (in an early episode he referred to "a remarkable talent he discovered: Harriet Lake"—Ann Sothern's real name). He calls Susie "the most faithful and loyal secretary I ever had."

Vi began working for Peter in 1949. She is interested in horoscopes and Susie believes Vi is an old maid, but Vi feels she is not: "I'm still looking for Mr. Right." Mickey Calhoun, called "Cagey," is Peter's scheming rival, the owner of the M.C. Calhoun Agency (he calls Susie "Foxy"). Also known as *Susie*.

Cast: Ann Sothern *(Susie McNamara)*; Don Porter *(Peter Sands)*; Ann Tyrrell *(Vi Praskins)*; Jesse White *(Cagey Calhoun)*; Joan Banks *(Sylvia; Susie's friend)*.

7490   *Private Sessions.* (Pilot; Drama; NBC; Mar. 15, 1985). Joseph Braeden and Elizabeth Bolger are doctors who share adjoining offices in Manhattan. Joseph is a psychotherapist, Elizabeth a psychoanalyst, and the proposal was to focus on their experiences as they deal with various patient problems. Other regulars are Angie, their secretary; Millie, Joseph's daughter; Claire, Joseph's ex-wife; and Ramone, the doorman at Joe's Apartment house.

Cast: Mike Farrell (*Joseph Braeden*); Maureen Stapleton (*Elizabeth Bolger*); Denise Miller (*Angie*); Mary Tanner (*Millie Braeden*); Kathryn Walker (*Claire Braeden*); David LaBoisa (*Ramone*).

7491   *Private Sessions.* (Series; Reality; A&E; 2007). Personal profiles of contemporary musicians (from pop to country and western). Each program is devoted to one performer and features in-depth interviews and exclusive performances.

Host: Lynn Hoffman.

7492   *Privileged.* (Series; Drama; CW; 2008–2009). Megan Smith is a college graduate with a journalism degree from Yale University. She wants to write about people that matter, people who make a difference, but is instead working for a New York tabloid magazine. Through a connection with her editor, Megan receives a chance to fulfill that dream. She moves to Palm Beach, Florida, and meets with Laurel Limoges, a widow who turned a small company (Limoges Cosmetics) into a mega enterprise. She is also the guardian of Laurel's two beautiful, 16-year-old twin granddaughters, Sage and Rose (orphaned when their parents were killed in a plane crash).

Sage and Rose are rich and spoiled. Laurel wants them to attend Duke University, but the girls, who attend Cielo Prep, have little interest in school work (Megan receives $1500 a week and if she can succeed, Laurel will pay off her student loans). As Megan begins she finds Rose is interested in attending Duke but Sage, a free spirit, sees Megan as a threat. Rose means a great deal to Sage and she feels Megan is trying to steal her away — something she means to see not happen. Stories follow Megan as she struggles to fulfill Laurel's wishes. Lily is Megan's sister; Marco is Laurel's gourmet chef; Will is Laurel's neighbor; Artie is Megan's father, who runs Captain Artie's Boat Tours.

Cast: JoAnna Garcia (*Megan Smith*); Anne Archer (*Laurel Limoges*); Lucy Kate Hale (*Rose Baker*); Ashley Newbrough (*Sage Baker*); Kristina Apgar (*Lily Smith*); Allan Louis (*Marco Giordello*); Brian Hallisay (*Will Phillips*); David Giuntoli (*Jacob Cassidy*); John Allen Nelson (*Artie*).

7493   *Prize Performance.* (Series; Variety; CBS; 1950). Arlene Francis and Peter Donald oversee a program in which amateur, but talented singers and dancers perform with the hope of being discovered.

7494   *Pro Stars.* (Series; Cartoon; NBC; 1991). Super athletes Bo Jackson, Wayne Gretzky and Michael Jordan are seen in both live action segments and in animated form as they join forces to use their combined prowess to right wrongs wherever they find them. The live segments are wraparounds with the sports stars relating aspects of the episode to children.

Cast: Michael Jackson (*Himself*); Dorian Harewood (*Michael Jackson; voice*); Wayne Gretzky (*Himself*); Townsend Coleman (*Wayne Gretzky; voice*); Bo Jackson (*Himself*); Dave Fennoy (*Bo Jackson; voice*); Susan Silo (*Mama*); Diana Barrows (*Denise*); Tara Strong (*Laura*).

7495   *Probe.* (Series; Adventure; ABC; 1988). Austin James, "the greatest scientific mind of the century," has established Serendip, a high tech research development company to help benefit mankind. Austin, however, soon tires of Serendip, and retreats to "The Batcave," an old warehouse where he lives and also conducts experiments "in the cause of justice." Austin also has an eccentric obsession about crime and, with the assist of his pretty but ditsy secretary, Michele Castle (whom Austin calls Mickey) stories relate their efforts to solve crimes Austin reads about in the newspapers. Austin thinks while he sleeps, has a photographic memory and can recall information faster than a computer. His pet spider, Steve, has free reign in "The Batcave." Mickey has a bad memory and left her last employer "because my boss said I could do the job better in the nude." Howard Millhouse is the man who runs Serendip for Austin while he pursues criminals.

Cast: Parker Stevenson (*Austin James*); Ashley Crow (*Michele Castle*); Jon Cypher (*Howard Millhouse*).

7496   *Problem Child.* (Series; Cartoon; USA; 1993). Adaptation of the feature film of the same title about a very mischievous young boy (Junior Healy) and the havoc he wrecks on all those around him: his policeman father, Ben Healy, Jr., his grandfather, "Big Ben" Healy, the owner of a sporting goods store, his mother, Flo, his siblings, Betsy and Ross, his friends, Cyndi and Spencer and his school principal (at Toe Valley Elementary), Mr. Peabody.

Voice Cast: Ben Diskin (*Junior Healy*); Jonathan Harris (*"Big Ben" Healy*); Mark Taylor (*Ben Healy, Jr.*); Nancy Cartwright (*Betsy and Ross*); Gilbert Gottfried (*Mr. Peabody*); Elizabeth Daily (*Cyndi*); Cree Summer (*Spencer*).

7497   *Producer's Choice.* (Series; Anthology; NBC; 1960). Rebroadcasts of selected episodes of *G.E. Theater*, *Lux Playhouse* and *Schlitz Playhouse of Stars*.

7498   *Professional Father.* (Series; Comedy; CBS; 1955). Dr. Thomas Wilson is a child psychologist who says that "Patience is the key to all problems." But he has little patience himself when it comes to his family and their problems. Steve lives at 11 Van Nest Lane with his wife, Helen, and children Kathryn and Thomas Jr. Kathryn, called Kit by Helen and Kitten by Thomas, has a tendency to trip over things (Thomas says "She's just clumsy"); Kit responds with "no damage" after such incidents. Thomas Jr., called Twig, is a member of the Beavers baseball team; both children attend Sweeter Elementary School. Thomas enjoys fly fishing at the "Lake" and when he is faced with a troubled boy at work, he gives him a broken clock to fix (he has a closet full of clocks and uses them as a form of therapy). Twig says "holy haystack" when something excites him; Helen feels that her motherly instincts are all that are needed to solve her family's problems. Nora is their housekeeper; Fred and Marge are their neighbors; Mr. Briggs is the mailman.

Cast: Steve Dunne (*Dr. Thomas Wilson*); Barbara Billingsley (*Helen Wilson*); Beverly Washburn (*Kathryn Wilson*); Ted Marc (*Tommy Wilson*); Ann O'Neil (*Nora*); Joseph Kearns (*Fred*); Phyllis Coates (*Madge*); Arthur Q. Brian (*Mr. Briggs*).

7499   *Profiler.* (Series; Crime Drama; NBC; 1996–2000). Samantha Waters is a profiler, a forensic psychologist with a unique ability to feel for the victims of crime and understand the criminal mind. She is not a psychic. Her highly developed intuition allows her to think in pictures and visualize the frame of mind of both the killer and the victim. Samantha looks beyond the obvious and rarely takes a guess. She is part of the V.C.T.F. (Violent Crimes Task Force), a special unit of the FBI that attempts to solve the baffling and bizarre crimes of any police department in the nation.

Samantha, a widow, lives with her daughter Chloe in a converted firehouse station (Engine 23 Trucking Company) at 501 Almada. Her close friend, Angel Brown, a young artist who makes a living as a sculptor, lives with her and Chloe.

As a child, Samantha and her mother enjoyed solving puzzles. It made Samantha feel alive. Now, for Samantha, trying to find a killer is like trying to solve a puzzle. In 1993, Samantha came close to uncovering the identity of a killer the FBI called Jack of All Trades. To distract her, Jack killed her husband. A devastated Samantha resigned from the FBI and moved to the country with Chloe to live an anonymous life. In 1996, when a rash of serial killings stumps the FBI, Bailey Monroe, head of the V.C.T.F. in Atlanta, Georgia, coaxes Samantha out of her self-imposed retirement to come and work for him. Samantha agrees, but under two conditions: her personal life remains confidential and "I get what I want when I need it."

Jack of All Trades is perhaps the most clever and diabolical criminal ever to appear as a regular on a television series. Jack killed to draw Samantha close to him. Jack's real name is Albert Neurquary (Dennis Christopher) and was originally called Jack by the V.C.T.F. because his real name was not known (in early episodes that feature Jack, his screen credit reads only "and Jack"). When Jack tried to turn Chloe against Samantha, he made his fatal mistake. Samantha tracked him, faced him, and in an extremely tense and unexpected moment, shot him dead at point blank range. Although unethical, but justified, Samantha's nightmare was over; but so was her job. On Oct. 21, 1999, Samantha resigned "to do what I need, what Chloe needs — each other." She is replaced by Rachel Burke, a former profiler in Seattle, then Houston, who joined Bailey's team. Like Samantha, Rachel can see into the criminal mind and explain the unexplained. Rachel, however, need not be present at a crime scene to receive images — "I could be brushing my teeth or grinding coffee when they come." Rachel has an 88 percent accuracy rate — "But it's that other 12 percent that bothers me." Rachel was a prosecuting attorney (1996), then an instructor for special agents at the Virginia FBI training center. She became an FBI agent "because I was sick of seeing criminals beat the system. They should be behind bars." When Rachel was ten years old, the girl who lived next door disappeared. A week before she vanished, the girl told Rachel her parents didn't want children and felt her life was empty (she was being raised by a nanny). Seven days later the girl was found, dead, at the bottom of a well. Rachel felt the girl had lived her life in the dark. It was this incident that led Rachel to believe she had the gift to see what others could not when she envisioned the girl in the well.

Bailey, head of the V.C.T.F., has complete authority. He is in the office 14 to 16 hours a day and is struggling to raise his troublesome 17-year-old daughter, Frances. Frances is rebellious and feels her father treats her like a marine in boot camp — "He commands and doesn't listen." Like Samantha (and Rachel) Bailey is totally dedicated to work and has little time for a social or private life. In the pilot episode, Bailey was said to head the FBI Investigative Support Unit.

Other members of the V.C.T.F. are John Grant, Grace Alvarez, Nathan Brubaker and George Findley. John, a cynical agent, often questions Samantha's approaches to solving crimes. He was a former cop with the Atlanta Police Department. Grace is the team's gifted forensics expert (she has a knack for finding evidence other medical examiners overlook). Nathan, an ex-attorney turned FBI agent, often questions Bailey's authority as to the legal issues of an order. George, the team's computer whiz, is a former world class hacker who uses his skills to help the FBI. Angelo Badalmonti composed the original "Profiler Theme" (with Ally Walker); Jeff Rona, the new "Profiler Theme" (with Jamie Luner).

Cast: Ally Walker (*Samantha Waters*); Robert Davi (*Bailey Monroe*); Erica Gimpel (*Angel Brown*); Caitlin Wachs, Evan Rachel Wood (*Chloe Waters*); Jamie Luner (*Rachel Burke*); Julian McMahon (*John Grant*); Roma Maffia (*Grace Alvarez*); Michael Whaley (*Nathan Brubaker*); Peter Frechette (*George Findley*).

**7500	*Profiles.*** (Pilot; Drama; ABC; June 6, 1994). *Profiles* is a television talk show hosted by Billie Baker Baer that tackles the hot issues. The proposal was to profile a different group of people who are grilled by Billy (while they are talking, flashbacks are used to reveal more than they are willing to express on the air).

Cast: Suzanne Pleshette (*Billie Baker Baer*); John Apicella (*Her*

producer); Sip Culler (*Stage manager*); Richard Israel (*Production assistant*).

**7501	*Profiles in Courage.*** (Series; Anthology; NBC; 1964-1965). Dramas, based on the book *Profiles in Courage* by John F. Kennedy, that stress the valor of political figures who risked their lives to tackle unpopular causes. Notable performers include Carroll O'Connor, Barbara Feldon, Tom Bosley, Arthur Franz, George Grizzard, Barry Morse, Simon Oakland, Herschel Bernardi, Albert Salmi, Rosemary Harris, Brian Keith, Edward Asner, J.D. Cannon, Peggy McCay, Betsy Jones-Moreland, Andrew Prine, Sue Randall, Peter Lawford, Burgess Meredith, Janice Rule, Walter Matthau and David McCallum.

**7502	*Profit.*** (Series; Drama; Fox; 1996). Jim Profit is a man with no redeeming qualities. This may be reflected by his childhood, when he was an abused child (he spent much time in a cardboard box with a hole cut in the side to allow him to watch a TV that was never turned off). His horrific upbringing most likely accounts for some of his actions as an adult: Having sex with (then blackmailing) his heroin-addicted stepmother, Bobbi; setting his father on fire; illegal wire tapping; computer fraud; being intimate with the boss's wife; kidnapping the sick mother of a secretary then seeking ransom; creating false charges and complex schemes to destroy his competitors to rise within his company.

Jim Profit is, despite what he has done, an executive at Gracen and Gracen, an international conglomerate. His wheeling and dealings to destroy his competition to get ahead is the focal point of stories that features a rather unethical character as not only the protagonist but the narrator.

Other regulars are Joanne Meltzer, the chief of security at Gracen; Gail Koner, Jim's secretary and co-conspirator; Peter Gracen, the company head; Chaz, Peter's older brother and co–CEO.

Cast: Adrian Pasdar (*Jim Profit*); Lisa Zane (*Joanne Meltzer*); Lisa Blount (*Bobbi Stankowski*); Jack Gwaltney (*Peter Gracen*); Keith Szarabajka (*Charles Henry "Chaz" Gracen*); Allison Hossack (*Nora Gracen*); Lisa Darr (*Gail Koner*).

**7503	*Program Playhouse.*** (Pilot; DuMont; 1949). Half-hour pilot films (then called test films) for the DuMont Network. See: *Federal Agent, Hands of Murder, Roscoe Karns and Inky Poo, The Timid Soul,* and *Trouble, Inc.*

**7504	*Project G.E.E.K.E.R.*** (Series; Cartoon; CBS; 1996). In a futuristic era, a mega corporation known as Moloch Industries controls most of the planet Earth (as well as several other planets). Mister Moloch, who is on a quest to become the ruler of the world, initiates Project GKR (Geno-Kinetic Research) and hires a brilliant (but insane) Doctor (Maston) to create an android with awesome powers to do his bidding. Maston creates just what Moloch desires — Geeker, an artificial human. However, before Moloch can use him for his diabolical plan to suppress anyone who opposes him, Geeker is stolen by a thief (Lady MacBeth) and her intelligent dinosaur, Noah. Lady MacBeth had planned to sell her latest acquisition on the black market — but when she discovers what she actually has, she changes her mind (Geeker has not been fully programmed and is actually a child with awesome powers he is not capable of comprehending). Lady MacBeth and Noah soon learn that Moloch has discovered they are the culprits and has begun a search to find them. Stories follow Lady MacBeth (called Becky by Geeker) as she and Noah struggle to protect Geeker from Moloch and stop his conquest of the world.

Voice Cast: Cree Summer (*Becky*); Billy West (*Geeker*); Charles Adler (*Dr. Maston*); Jim Cummings (*Moloch*); Brad Garrett (*Noah*).

7505   *Project Greenlight.* (Series; Reality; HBO; 2001). A program, created by actors Matt Damon and Ben Affleck, and film producer Chris Moore, that spotlights the scripts of hopeful Hollywood directors. Applicants submit their scripts to the creators' production company, Live Planet. Each is read and evaluated and the winner receives the opportunity of a lifetime — turn his script into a Miramax film. Here, the winner, Peter Jones, gets to direct his script, *Stolen Summer.* The cameras follow Peter as he goes about directing his film. The concluding episode shows the premiere of *Stolen Summer* at the Sundance Film Festival.

Cast: Ben Affleck, Matt Damon, Brian Dennehy, Marie Frick, Jonathan Gordon, Bonnie Hunt, Peter Jones, Chris Moore, Brendan Murphy, Kevin Pollak, Meryl Poster, Aidan Quinn.

7506   *Project Runway.* (Series; Reality; Bravo, 2004–2008; Lifetime, 2009–). Following on the heels of *America's Next Top Model*, *Project Runway*, created by model Heidi Klum (in association with Elle magazine), focuses on the fashion designing end of the business. Up and coming fashion designers compete against each other for a coveted spot in the New York Fashion Show (a monthly event that is held in the fall and in the spring). Each contestant competes in a weekly challenge and is seen preparing his models and the problems he encounters as the big day approaches. The designer with the best presentation is the winner. Heidi Klum and Tim Gunn host.

7507   *Project Tin Man.* (Pilot; Science Fiction; ABC; July 30, 1990). At the government lab Linotech, Dr. Robert Craig, head of a secret project called Tin Man, creates a mechanical man the military hopes to turn into the ultimate soldier. When an attempt is made to turn Tin Man into what the military believes is the perfect fighting machine, the robot's built-in moral program rejects killing. It is decided to terminate Tin Man by denying it the solar energy it needs to survive. However, before its battery life is depleted, Tin Man (who calls himself Daniel) manages to escape and revive himself. The proposal was to relate Daniel's efforts to avoid capture by the military (who seek to retrieve him) and find his creator to discover his true purpose. Daniel is assisted by Dr. Naomi Fisher, woman who helps him escape capture then agrees to help him with his quest.

Cast: Hunt Block (*Daniel*); Catherine Mary Stewart (*Dr. Naomi Fisher*).

7508   *Project UFO.* (Series; Drama; NBC; 1978-1979). Dramatizations of UFO (Unidentified Flying Objects) incidents as seen through the investigations of United States Air Force Major Jake Gatlin and his assistant Harry Fitz. Based on the official records of the U.S. Air Force's Project Blue Book, the federal government's record of UFO reports and investigations. Libby is their secretary; Ben Ryan is their captain.

Cast: William Jordan (*Jake Gatlin*); Caskey Swaim (*Harry Fitz*); Aldine King (*Libby*); Edward Winter (*Ben Ryan*). **Narrator:** Jack Webb.

7509   *Projection Room.* (Series; Anthology; ABC; 1952). Short-lived (two episode) program (Mar. 19 to Mar. 25, 1952) of live mystery presentations hosted by actress Ruth Gilbert.

7510   *Prom Queen.* (Series; Drama; Internet; 2007). A look at the senior class of Edward Adams High School — a class whose students are preparing for the prom but during which time secrets threaten to destroy friendships and have adverse effects on the five girls who are competing for prom queen.

Cast: Katy Stoll (*Sadie*); Sean Hankinson (*Ben*); Laura Howard (*Danica*); Alexandra French (*Nikki*); Haley Mancini (*Lauren*); David Loren (*Chad*); Jake Shideler (*Josh*); Andre Boyer (*Brett*); Sheila Vand

(*Courtney*); John Shires (*Nolan*); Mills Allison (*Curtis*); Amy Kay Raymond (*Jill*); Kateland Carr (*Michele*).

7511   *Prom Queen: Summer Heat.* (Series; Drama; Internet; 2007). A spin-off from *Prom Queen* that follows students from Edward Adams High School as they seek to escape the mysteries that haunted them in high school by retreating to Mexico for their summer vacation.

Cast: Katy Stoll (*Sadie*); Sean Hankinson (*Ben*); Laura Howard (*Danica*); Alexandra French (*Nikki*); Angela Arimento (*Marisol*); Jake Shideler (*Josh*).

7512   *Promised Land.* (Series; Drama; CBS; 1996–1999). After losing his job, Russell Greene decides to follow a long sought dream: travel across the country in search of adventure. Russell is married to Claire and they are the parents of Dinah and Josh. They begin their journey in an old suburban trailer and stories relate their adventures as they discover the country's wonders and help people in trouble along the way. Also joining them are Hattie, Russell's mother and Nathaniel, his nephew. A spin off from *Touched by an Angel.*

Cast: Gerald McRaney (*Russell Greene*); Wendy Phillips (*Claire Greene*); Celeste Holm (*Hattie Greene*); Sarah Schaub (*Dinah Greene*); Austin O'Brien (*Josh Greene*); Eddie Karr (*Nathaniel Greene*); Ossie Davis (*Eeasmus Jones*); Kathryne Dora (*Shamaya Taggert*); Richard Thomas (*Joe Greene*); Ashleigh Norman (*Margaret Noteworthy*); Eugene Byrd (*Lawrence Taggert*).

7513   *Proof Positive: Evidence of the Paranormal.* (Series; Reality; Syfy; 2000). Cutting edge technology is used to explore the fine line between science fiction and fact (for example, ghostly occurrences, demonic possession, alien encounters). Amanda Tapping hosts.

7514   *Pros and Cons.* (Pilot; Crime Drama; ABC; Jan. 26, 1986). The Fraud and Bunco Squad is a special division of the Los Angeles County's Sheriff's Office that investigates the bilking schemes of confidence men. The proposal was to relate the cases of its team (Bernie, Patty, Audrey, Christie, Val and Dolly) as they attempt to beat the cons at their own games. Lu Leonard's character is called "Dolly" in the show, but is credited as "Lou" on press material.

Cast: Bernie Casey (*Lt. Bernie Rollins*); Carol Potter (*Patty Finley*); Wendy Cutler (*Audrey*); Jennifer Runyon (*Christie*); Sheryl Lee Ralph (*Val*); Lu Leonard (*Dolly*).

7515   *Pros and Cons.* (Series; Crime Drama; ABC; 1991-1992). The Bird and O'Hannon Agency at 1122 North Plaza in Los Angeles is a private detective organization owned by Gabriel Bird and Mitch O'Hannon. The character of Gabriel Bird was originally featured on the series *Gabriel's Fire* (ABC, 1990-91, which see for background information).

Gabriel worked as an investigator for Victoria Heller. When Victoria leaves her practice to become a judge; Gabriel opens his own agency, Gabriel Bird Investigations. On his first case, Gabriel is hired by a woman to follow her husband whom she believes is having an affair. The suspect is actually a hit man who has been hired to kill Los Angeles private detective Mitch O'Hannon. In Los Angeles, Gabriel saves Mitch's life when he prevents the hit from taking place. The two join forces (and eventually become partners) to solve the case. It is learned that Mitch's secretary used information to blackmail a client; the client thought Mitch was the blackmailer and hired the hit man.

Gabriel loves gardening and owns a house at 808 Magnolia Drive. Josephine, his romantic interest from *Gabriel's Fire* relocates to Los Angeles when Gabriel asks her to marry him. The wedding occurs in the episode of Oct. 10, 1991 and Josephine acquires a job as the manager of a restaurant called the Angel Grill.

Gabriel goes to extremes to get the job done and keeps a diary of everything he does. Mitch served in Korea and was with the 40th Sunburst Unit; Gabriel was with the 24th Infantry. Gabriel thinks Mitch is too careless and calls him "a lunatic; he acts like a teenager." Mitch feels that acting on impulse is the best way to get the job done. Mitch was previously partners in a firm called Pryor and O'Hannon. The series was originally titled *Bird and Katt* and featured James Earl Jones and Richard Crenna as squabbling private detectives named Gabriel Bird and Peter Katt.

Cast: James Earl Jones (*Gabriel Bird*); Richard Crenna (*Mitch O'Hannon*); Laila Robins (*Victoria Heller*); Madge Sinclair (*Josephine Austin*).

7516   Pros and Cons. (Pilot; Drama; Unaired; Produced for ABC in 2004). Jack Fallon is a slick con artist, considered the best in the game by police, who knows "the angles between the angles." Jack has been so confident that he eventually lets his guard down and is caught red-handed in a scheme. Jack, however, is not imprisoned. He is recruited by the FBI to assemble a crack team of criminals to expose fraud from the inside out. The proposal was to follow Jack and his principle recruits, Charlie (his ex-girlfriend) and Eddie (his nephew) as they work with federal agent Chris Van Horn to break the law to uphold the law.

Cast: Paul Blackthorne (*Jack Fallon*); Natasha Henstridge (*Charlie*); William Baldwin (*Chris Van Horn*); Dorian Missick (*Eddie*); Eric Bogosian (*Murph*).

7517   Protect and Serve. (Pilot; Crime Drama; Unaired; Produced for CBS in 2006). Life on the street as cops patrol and protect the suburbs of Los Angeles.

Cast: Dean Cain (*Mike Borelli*); Eric Balfour (*Paul Grogan*); Jessica Pare (*Hope Cook*); Monica Potter (*Lizzie Borelli*); Victoria Cartagena (*Anita Esparza*); Thad Luckinbill (*Tim Cook*); Tamala Jones (*Sharon Harvey*).

7518   Protect and Surf. (Pilot; Crime Drama; ABC; Aug. 6, 1989). Surf House is a beach residence in Santa Monica, California, that is home to Mike, Dwight, Jodi, Bob, Jesse and Dan, officers with the Westside Police Department. The proposal was to relate their assignments as they patrol and protect the city. The above information is based on viewing. Press information lists David Oliver's character as "Mike Duggan" and Tasia Valenza as Tasia Valenz.

Cast: David Oliver (*Mike Deegan*); Tasia Valenza (*Jodi Lampert*); Phill Lewis (*Bob Bailey*); Randy Vasquez (*Jesse Gomez*); Justin Williams (*Dan Mikolay*).

7519   The Protectors. (Series; Adventure; Syn.; 1972). The Protectors is an international organization that unites the finest investigators in the world to battle crime in the capitals of Europe. Harry Rule is the featured American member of the team; Contessa Caroline de Contini is the British representative and Paul Buchet is the French agent.

Harry is a strategist and carefully plans the course of action the team will take on assignments. Caroline is a gorgeous woman, used by Harry for distraction, who is a master of deductive reasoning, an expert shot, and quite capable of defending herself in adverse situations. Paul is the suave ladies' man who is also a skilled investigator, but somewhat too quick to use his fists. Stories relate their efforts to solve cases that often find them incorporating means as underhanded as the criminals they are pursuing. Suki is Harry's housekeeper (in London) and he has a dog named Gus.

Cast: Robert Vaughn (*Harry Rule*); Nyree Dawn Porter (*Caroline de Contini*); Tony Anholt (*Paul Buchet*); Yasuko Nagazumi (*Suki*); Anthony Chinn (*Chino; a Protector*). **Theme Vocal:** "Avenues and Alleyways" by Tony Christie.

7520   Proud Earth. (Pilot; Drama; NBC; May 23, 1960). The Idaho Territory of the late 1860s is the setting for a proposal about a homesteader (Isaiah Macabee) and his efforts to carve a new life for himself and his family (wife Rebecca and their son Adam). Mr. March is the powerful ranch owner who wants Isaiah's land; Gwen is his wife; Roan is his son. Aired as a segment of *The Alcoa/Goodyear Theater.*

Cast: John Larch (*Isaiah Macabee*); Vivi Janiss (*Rebecca Macabee*); Joe Gallison (*Adam Macabee*); William Meigs (*Mr. March*); Jay Strong (*Roan March*); Karin Dicker (*Gwen March*).

7521   The Proud Family. (Series; Cartoon; Disney; 2001–2005). Incidents in the life of 14-year-old Penny Proud are depicted as she struggles to cope with the world around her. Penny is the daughter of Oscar and Trudy and she lives with her twin sisters Bee Bee and Cee Cee and her grandmother, Suga Mama. Her experiences with her friends are also depicted: Zoey, Dijonay, LaCienega and Sticky. Also complicating Penny's life are the bullying Gross sisters.

Voice Cast: Kyla Pratt (*Penny Proud*); Tommy Davidson (*Oscar Proud*); Paula Jai Parker (*Trudy Proud*); Tara Strong (*Bebe Proud*); Jo Marie Payton (*Suga Mama*); Cedric the Entertainer (*Bobby Proud*); Karen Malina White (*Dijonay Jones*); Soleil Moon Frye (*Zoey*); Alisa Reyes (*LaCienega*); Orlando Brown (*Sticky Wenn*); Lydia Look (*The Chang Triplets*).

7522   Providence. (Series; Drama; NBC; 1999–2002). Providence, Rhode Island, provides the setting for incidents in the life of Dr. Sydney Hansen, a successful plastic surgeon who leaves her practice in California after the sudden death of her mother, to help guide her dysfunctional family — her father, Jim, a veterinarian, her sister, Joanie, and her younger brother, Robbie. Sydney has established herself as a doctor with the local free clinic and she receives help in dealing with her family from her mother, Lynda, who appears to her in her dreams.

Cast: Melina Kanakaredes (*Dr. Sydney Hansen*); Mike Farrell (*Dr. Thomas Hansen*); Concetta Tomei (*Lynda Hansen*); Paula Cale (*Joanie Hansen*); Seth Peterson (*Robbie Hansen*); Leslie Silva (*Dr. Helen Reynolds*); Sarah Spiegel (*Young Sydney; flashbacks*); Samaria Graham (*Izzy Munez*); Toni DeRose (*Patrice*); Maria Pitillo (*Tina Calcatera*); Tessa Allen (*Hannah Hansen*).

7523   Prudence and the Chief. (Pilot; Comedy; ABC; Aug. 26, 1970). On behalf of the United Council of Churches, Prudence MacKenzie, a widow and the mother of two children (Gavin and Fergus) accepts an assignment to establish a school on a Cheyenne Indian reservation. The proposal was to follow Prudence, a missionary and school teacher, as she attempts to teach the Indian children. Snow Eagle is the Chief of the Cheyenne; Leticia is Prudence's mother.

Cast: Sally Ann Howes (*Prudence MacKenzie*); Rick Jason (*Chief Snow Eagle*); Kathryn Givney (*Leticia MacKenzie*); Teddy Quinn (*Gavin MacKenzie*); Johnny Lee (*Fergus MacKenzie*).

7524   Prudential Family Playhouse. (Series; Anthology; CBS; 1950-1951). A live program of dramatic productions sponsored by the Prudential Life Prudential Life Insurance. Notable performers include Peggy Ann Garner, Gertrude Lawrence, Kevin McCarthy, Carol Channing, Bethel Leslie, Helen Hayes, Gene Lockhart, Haila Stoddard, Carole Stone, Jessica Tandy, Grace Kelly, Richard Greene, Cyril Ritchard, June Lockhart and Dorothy Gish.

7525   The Pruitts of Southampton. (Series; Comedy; ABC; 1966-1967). "The Pruitts of Southampton live like the richest folks, but what the folks don't know is that the Pruitts are flat broke...."

When an Internal Revenue investigation discloses that she owes ten million dollars in back taxes, society matron Phyllis Pruitt, who has never worked a day in her life, is forced to sell her valuables and drastically reduce her living style. Stories, set in Southampton (on Long Island in New York) relate Phyllis's efforts to maintain the appearance of wealth and social status in an eight-room home with one car and a butler. In mid season, the program's format changed (as did it's title to *The Phyllis Diller Show*) to depict Phyllis's adventures as a landlady when she begins an elegant boarding house in an attempt to pay off her debt. Other regulars are Stephanie Pruitt, Phyllis's daughter; Ned Pruitt, Phyllis's uncle; Sturgis, the butler; Regina Wentworth, Phyllis's social rival; Suzy Wentworth, Regina's daughter; Baldwin, the IRS Agent; General Cannon, Phyllis's friend; Norman Krump and Vernon Bradley, boarders in the Pruitt home; Rudy, Phyllis's cousin; and Harvey, Phyllis's brother.

Cast: Phyllis Diller *(Phyllis Pruitt)*; Pamela Freeman *(Stephanie Pruitt)*; Reginald Gardner *(Ned Pruitt)*; Grady Sutton *(Sturgis)*; Gypsy Rose Lee *(Regina Wentworth)*; Lisa Loring *(Suzy Wentworth)*; Richard Deacon *(Agent Baldwin)*; John McGiver *(General Cannon)*; Marty Ingels *(Norman Krump)*; Billy DeWolfe *(Vernon Bradley)*; John Astin *(Rudy)*; Paul Lynde *(Harvey)*. **Theme Vocal:** "The Pruitts of Southampton" by Phyllis Diller.

7526   *Pryor's Place.* (Series; Children; CBS; 1984-1985). Pryor's Place is a special, magical neighborhood populated by children. It is here that the younger set learn lessons about life through the cast of regulars and the various celebrities who visit. Comedian Richard Pryor appears as the host who introduces his young audience to a world where children rule and adults take second place.

Little Richie and Wally are the main children. Miss Stern is the schoolteacher; Meatrack is the neighborhood bully. Rita is Richie's cousin; Solly is the adult friend of the host. The Sid and Marty Krofft Puppets also play various characters that live in the neighborhood.

Cast: Richard Pryor *(Host)*; Akili Prince *(Little Richie)*; Cliffy Magee *(Wally)*; Marla Gibbs *(Miss Stern)*; Keland Love *(Meatrack)*; Milt Kogan *(Solly)*; Kim Fields *(Rita)*. **Theme Vocal:** "Pryor's Place" by Ray Parker, Jr.

7527   *P.S. I Luv U.* (Series; Crime Drama; CBS; 1991-1992). Cody and Dani Powell are an unusual pair of private detectives. They are in the Federal Witness Protection Program, pretend to be married and operate P.S.I. (Palm Springs Investigations), a small security firm in Palm Springs, California, as a cover to protect their real identities.

Dani is actually Wanda Talbert, a beautiful con artist who moves from town to town pulling scams. Cody is really Joey Paciorek, a detective with the N.Y.P.D. When a con by Wanda goes wrong and she is captured by Joey, he offers her a chance to avoid jail by helping him expose a drug lord. During the assignment, Wanda is exposed as an undercover agent. The drug lord escapes but Wanda is now in jeopardy: if the mobster is caught, Wanda's testimony can convict him. To protect Wanda, it is decided to give her a new identity. Matthew Durning, a former Justice Department federal marshal, arranges for their new life style. He reassigns Joey as Dani's bodyguard and "husband."

Dani originally worked as the receptionist for P.S.I. She is later a case worker when she helps Cody apprehend a big time mobster. Dani was born in the Bronx and grew up on the streets. She learned at an early age how to con people but was taught how to perfect her craft by her uncle, Ray Barkley (Patrick Macnee), an international rogue and confidence man. Cons have given Dani the life she loves, and spending money is her favorite hobby. Dani is not only an expert at relieving people of their money, but is capable of opening safes

and picking locks. She carries a lock pick with her at all times; "It's in my bra. It's the safest place I know."

Cody, born in New York City, was a street cop for 12 years before becoming a plainclothes detective. He was an honest cop and did virtually everything by the book; he objects, at times, to Dani's habit of pulling cons to get the job done. Cody comes from a long line of police officers and would like to return to the force one day with a clean record.

JoJo is the P.S.I. radio dispatcher; Sonny Bono appeared as himself, the mayor of Palm Springs. Greg Evigan and Suzanne Fountain sing the theme "P.S., I Love You."

Cast: Greg Evigan *(Cody Powell)*; Connie Sellecca *(Dani Powell)*; Earl Holliman *(Matthew Durning)*; Jayne Frazer *(JoJo)*.

7528   *PSI Factor: Chronicles of the Paranormal.* (Series; Anthology; Syn.; 1996). Recreations of documented facts on the paranormal. Actor Dan Aykroyd, the program's host, is also deeply interested in the subject matter and convinced a psychic think tank (the Office of Scientific Investigation and Research) to allow him access to their files (what the program is based on). Dan says, "I'm the fourth generation in my family with psychic interests" and his hosting chores resemble those of Rod Serling (*The Twilight Zone*) and Robert Stack (*Unexplained Mysteries*). Although the program is called an anthology (which usually means no regular casts) *PSI Factor* incorporates regulars associated with the Office of Scientific Investigation: Lindsay Donner (data analyst), Peter Axon (physicist), Ray Donahue (security director), Frank Elsinger (operations director), doctors Curtis Rollins and Claire Davison; and professors Connor Doyle and Anton Hendricks.

Cast: Dan Aykroyd *(Host)*; Nancy Anne Sakovich *(Lindsay Donner)*; Colin Fox *(Anton Hendricks)*; Matt Frewer *(Matt Prager)*; Soo Garay *(Claire Davison)*; Barclay Hope *(Peter Axon)*; Peter MacNeill *(Ray Donahue)*; Nigel Bennett *(Frank Elsinger)*; Paul Miller *(Connor Doyle)*; Peter Blais *(Lennox "L.Q." Cooper)*.

7529   *Psych.* (Series; Crime Drama; USA; 2006–2010). Shawn Spencer is a man with phenomenal powers of observation. As early as he can remember, Shawn was taught how to act, think and observe like a detective. Rather than put his talents to use in a productive way, like becoming a police officer (like his father, Henry), Shawn becomes somewhat of a slacker, taking random jobs to get by.

Shawn is fascinated by crimes scenes and studies such scenes by reading the newspaper and watching TV. When he realizes he has found something that was overlooked, he calls the police with a tip because nothing escapes his razor sharp mind. One tip, however, backfires and Shawn is arrested as the prime suspect. Although he does not possess any actual clairvoyant abilities, Shawn convinces the police he is a psychic and is exonerated. Impressed by his "abilities," the police department hires Shawn as a consultant to help them solve difficult cases (he also opens an agency called Psych to help people). Assisting Shawn is his friend Burton "Gus" Guster, a pharmaceutical salesman (for Center Coast Pharmaceuticals) who finds keeping Shawn out of trouble to be his biggest challenge.

Cast: James Roday *(Shawn Spencer)*; Dule Hill *(Burton "Gus" Guster)*; Corbin Bernsen *(Henry Spencer)*; Kristen Nelson *(Chief Vick)*; Timothy Omundson *(Detective Lassiter)*; Maggie Lawson *(Juliet)*.

7530   *The Psychiatrist.* (Series; Drama; NBC; 1971). James Whitman is a young psychiatrist based in Los Angeles. He believes in the new but sometimes controversial techniques of modern medical therapy. He is partners with Bernard Altman, an older (and wiser) psychiatrist who believes in time honored methods but is not adverse to the progress that the medical field has accomplished. Stories, which are character studies of people with psychiatric problems, relate the doctors' experiences as they treat each patient with the methods they feel will give them the best results. Aired as a segment of *Four-in-One*.

Cast: Roy Thinnes *(Dr. James Whitman)*; Luther Adler *(Dr. Bernard Altman)*.

7531   Psychic Hollywood: The Search for Truth. (Series; Reality; E!; 2009). Psychics help celebrity guests find answers to their personal problems. Carla Baron, James Van Praagh and Shaman Durek are the hosts.

7532   Psychic Kids: Children of the Paranormal. (Series; Reality; A&E; 2008–2010). Children, aged eight to twelve (and who live in remote sections of the country) are profiled as they use their psychic abilities to communicate with the spirits of deceased children. The children meet with professional psychologists (to help them understand what is happening) but credibility is questioned by bad camera work (extreme close-ups of the children's eyes) and eerie music to suggest something is happening when nothing is. Lisa Miller and Chip Coffey host.

7533   Public Defender. (Series; Drama; CBS; 1954-1955). Bart Andrews is a public defender of indigent people. He is dedicated to uncovering the facts behind each case and does not prejudge his clients; just because they do not have money for an attorney is no reason why they should not receive a fair chance in court.

Program Open: "A Public Defender is an attorney employed by the community and responsible for giving legal aid without cost to any person who seeks it and is financially unable to employ private counsel. It is also his duty to defend those accused of crime until the issue is decided in a court of law. The first public defenders office in the United States was opened in January 1913. Over the years other offices have opened and today their handful has grown to a network of lawyers dedicated to protecting the rights of our clients."

Cast: Reed Hadley *(Bart Matthews)*.

7534   The Public Life of Cliff Norton. (Series; Comedy; NBC; 1952). Capsule skits that depict one man's approaches and solutions to everyday problems.

Host: Cliff Norton.

7535   Public Morals. (Series; Comedy; CBS; 1996). Lieutenant Neil Fogerty is the head of a Vice Squad unit of the N.Y.P.D. and stories were set to relate his team's investigations into assigned cases. Raunchy language, however, caused the show's cancellation the same night it premiered (Oct. 30, 1996). Other regulars are Valerie, Neil's assistant; Corinne, a gorgeous blonde detective; Mickey, a hard-nosed street cop; Darnell, a by-the-books detective; Ken, a not-too-bright detective; and Richie Biondi, the gay civilian aid.

Cast: Peter Gerety *(Lt. Neil Fogerty)*; Bill Brochtrup *(Det. John Irvin)*; Julianne Christie *(Det. Corinne O'Boyle)*; Donal Logue *(Det. Ken Schuler)*; Jana Marie Hupp *(Det. Valerie Vandergroot)*; Larry Romano *(Richie Biondi)*; Joseph Latimore *(Darnell Ruggs)*; Doris Belack *(Gabrielle Biondi)*.

7536   Public Prosecutor. (Series; Mystery-Game; Syn.; DuMont; 1947–1952). The original concept (Syn., 1947-48), was that of short mystery programs designed to be used, with commercials, in twenty-minute spots. In 1951 (to 1952), when the DuMont network acquired the program, it became a mystery game in which a panel of three detective-fiction experts would view a fifteen-minute mystery that was stopped prior to the denouncement. Players, at this point, were asked to identify the culprit. The film was then played to reveal the answer. Also known as *Crawford Mystery Theater*.

Cast: John Howard *(Prosecuting Attorney)*; Anne Gwynne *(His Assistant)*; Walter Sande *(Police Lieutenant)*.

7537   Publicity Girl. (Pilot; Comedy; Unaired; Produced in 1956). Jan Sterling as a public relations employee at a public relations firm in Southern California. Jack Chertok is the producer.

7538   Pucca. (Series; Cartoon; Disney XD; 2009). Pucca, the sweet and adorable daughter of the owner of the Ja Jang Chinese Restaurant, has, for one so young, only one true love: Garu, a dedicated Ninja student. Unfortunately for Pucca, Garu has no interest in her. Geared to children six to eleven years of age and combining 3D and Flash animation, stories relate Pucca's trials and tribulations as she pursues her one true love.

Voice Cast: Tabitha St. Germaine *(Pucca)*; Brian Drummond *(Garu)*; Michael Dobson *(Ho)*; Shannon Chan-Kent *(Chief)*; Lee Tockar *(Dada)*; Dale Wilson *(Linguini)*.

7539   Pud's Prize Party. (Series; Variety; ABC; 1952). Todd Russell oversees a talent competition in which non-professional children compete for the title "The Most Talented Child of the Week" and its award: merchandise prizes.

7540   Pulitzer Prize Playhouse. (Series; Anthology; ABC; 1950–1952). Adaptations of Pulitzer Prize-winning plays, stories and novels hosted and narrated by Elmer Davis. Notable performers include John Forsythe, James Dunn, Mildred Natwick, Nina Foch, Polly Rowles, Wright King, Helen Hayes, Kent Smith, Biff McGuire, Jonathan Harris, Elizabeth Patterson, Otto Kruger and Murvyn Vye.

7541   Pulling. (Series; Comedy; Sundance; 2008). Donna and her fiancé Karl have been a couple for many years (they are in their late twenties). Donna has lived a life that was basically carefree. As the big day approaches it dawns on Donna that what she has been doing will soon end. Impulsively she calls off their wedding days before the event to continue living a life she loves. She moves in with her friends Karen (a party girl) and the man-hungry Louise, and stories follow events in the lives of the three women. Produced in England.

Cast: Sharon Horgan *(Donna)*; Tanya Franks *(Karen)*; Rebekah Staton *(Louise)*; Cavan Clerkin *(Karl)*.

7542   Pumpboys and Dinettes on Television. (Pilot; Musical Variety; NBC; Aug. 15, 1983). The L&M Gas Station along Highway 57 in Frog Level, North Carolina, is the setting for a look at the singing and dancing abilities of four pumpboys (Jim, L.M., Jackson and Eddie) who work the local L&M Gas Station, and two sisters, Rhetta and Prudie Cupp, who own and operate the nearby Double Cupp Diner. Based on the Broadway play of the same title.

Cast: Jim Wann *(Jim)*; Mark Hardwick *(L.M.)*; John Foley *(Jackson)*; John Schimmel *(Eddie)*; Cass Morgan *(Rhetta Cupp)*; Debra Monk *(Prudie Cupp)*. **Orchestra:** George Wyle.

7543   Punch and Jody. (Pilot; Drama; NBC; Nov. 26, 1974). Life in the circus world as seen through the experiences of Peter "Punch" Travers, a jack-of-all-trades performer with Charny's Great American Circus, and his teenage daughter, Jody, the child he never knew he had who suddenly becomes his responsibility (when his ex-wife, Helen, dies in a car accident, Peter learns that Helen had kept Jody secret because of his roustabout way of life). Other regulars are Lil, the circus owner; Dan, the booking agent; Aurora, Punch's assistant in his knife throwing act; Woody, the travel coordinator; Delbart, the tiger tamer; Ben, a juggler; and Mr. and Mrs. Stilts, performers.

Cast: Glenn Ford (*Peter Travers*); Pam Griffin (*Jody Travers*); Ruth Roman (*Lillian "Lil" Charny*); Parley Baer (*Dan Baxter*); Pat Morita (*Ben*); Cynthia Hayward (*Aurora*); Mel Stewart (*Woody*); Donald Barry (*Delbart Clyde Butz*); Billy Barty (*Mr. Stilts*); Patty Maloney (*Mrs. Stilts*).

7544   *Punk'd*. (Series; Reality; MTV; 2003). Ashton Kutcher, famous for pulling pranks on ordinary people as well as celebrities, does what he does best again, this time on celebrities who have become too big (in their own minds) and need to be brought back down to earth. Ashton Kutcher hosts and is assisted in pranks by Julia Lea Wolov, Michael O'Hara, Johanna Black, Sharon Houston, Ryan Pinkston, Jill Bartlett, Minnie Goode, Chris Tarantino, Sabrina Machado, Sean Lewis, Allan Havey, Chris Ellwood, Jill Wagner and Whitney Cummings.

7545   *Punky Brewster*. (Series; Comedy; NBC, 1984–1986; Syn., 1986–1988). When her husband walks out on her, and a young mother (Susan Brewster) feels no longer able to care for her seven-year-old daughter, she abandons the child and her dog, Brandon, in a Chicago shopping mall. The girl, Penelope ("Punky") Brewster, manages to find a place to live — an empty apartment (2D) in a building managed by Henry Warnimont, a 60-year-old gruff widower.

One day the adorable orphan is discovered by Henry. Punky takes an instant liking to Henry ("Well, Brandon," she says, "we gotta trust somebody sometime") and tells Henry what has happened, concluding with, "Maybe my mother just forgot about me; but one day she'll come back and we'll live happily ever after."

Henry hires a private detective to find Punky's mother. The days pass and Punky feels she has found a home — until Henry tells her the detective was unable to find her mother and that he is sending her to the Department of Children and Family Services. Feeling abandoned again, Punky packs her suitcase. "I must be a terrible person," she tells Henry. "First my father walks out on me, then my mother ditches me, then you try and get rid of me. Nobody wants me around. Well, that's okay, I don't need anybody. I can take care of myself." She leaves. Henry then realizes that his life has changed for the better since he met Punky and that he needs her as much as she needs him. He files a petition to adopt her and later becomes Punky's guardian. "I'm not nobody anymore," exclaims Punky. "I'm Punky Brewster!"

On her first Christmas with Henry, Punky wished that Santa would reunite her with her mother. For Christmas, Punky gave Henry a homemade pipe; Henry gave Punky roller skates. While Punky did not get her wish (Henry made every attempt to grant it), Santa did leave her something: her mother's musical jewelry box; the gift Punky made for her mother, earrings, were gone. Was it a miracle? Punky thinks so, because "all you have to do is believe." Henry too had a dream that one day he would have a child; it came true when Punky came into his life (Henry was married many years ago to a woman named Claudia; she died a year after they were married).

Henry and Punky live in Apartment 2A at 2520 Michigan Avenue in Chicago. Henry is a photographer who owns the Warnimont Studios. Punky loves to wear miniskirts and believes that everything will be all right no matter how bad things look — "That's Punky power!"

Cherie Johnson is Punky's best friend. She lives in Apartment 3A with her grandmother, Betty Johnson, a nurse at Cook County Hospital (Betty raised Cherie after her parents' deaths).

"I even look gorgeous when I'm nervous," says Margaux Kramer, Punky's very rich and very spoiled girlfriend. She lives on Oak Lane and takes lessons from her mother on how to fire servants. The closest Margaux ever comes to poverty is when she visits Punky at home (she considers it "the poverty pit"). Gary Portnoy sings the theme, "Everytime You Turn Around."

Cast: Soleil Moon Frye (*Punky Brewster*); George Gaynes (*Henry Warnimont*); Cherie Johnson (*Cherie Johnson*); Ami Foster (*Margaux Kramer*); Susie Garrett (*Betty Johnson*); Robyn Lively (*Lisa; Punky's friend*); Loyita Chapel (*Margaux's mother*); Ernie Sabella (*Margaux's father*); Casey Ellison (*Allen Anderson; Punky's friend*).

7546   *Punky Brewster*. (Series; Cartoon; NBC; 1985-1986). Continued events in the life of Penelope "Punky" Brewster, a mischievous little girl who is the adopted daughter of a gruff photographer (Henry). Margaux, Cherie and Allen are Punky's friends.

Voice Cast: Soleil Moon Frye (*Punky Brewster*); George Gaynes (*Henry Warnimont*); Ami Foster (*Margaux Kramer*); Cherie Johnson (*Cherie Johnson*); Casey Ellinson (*Allen Anderson*).

7547   *A Pup Named Scooby-Doo*. (Series; Cartoon; ABC; 1998). A prequel to *Scooby-Doo, Where Are You?* that presents the cast as youngsters. Shaggy, Velma, Daphne and Freddy are kids who are interested in the paranormal. As teenagers (the original series) they ran a company called Mystery, Inc.; here, with the cowardly puppy, Scooby-Doo, they have begun The Scooby-Doo Detective Agency. Stories follow their efforts (all hindered by Scooby-Doo) to solve mysteries.

Voice Cast: Don Messick (*Scooby-Doo*); Kellie Martin (*Daphne Blake*); Christina Lange (*Velma Dinkley*); Casey Kasem (*Norville "Shaggy" Rogers*); Carl Stevens (*Freddy Jones*).

7548   *Puppetman*. (Pilot; Comedy; CBS; July 3, 1987). Gary (no last name given) is a single father and the head puppeteer on *Dragon Time*, a local kids show on WGRF-TV in Madison, Wisconsin. The proposal was to relate Gary's efforts to divide his time between work and raising his six-year-old son, Zack. Other regulars are Rita, the show's hostess; Bud, the producer; Del and Holly, puppeteers; Bud Jr., Bud's son; and Mitchell, the station head.

Cast: Fred Newman (*Gary*); Julie Payne (*Rita*); Michael Carter (*Zack*); Jack Burns (*Bud Stone*); Steve Levitt (*Bud Stone, Jr.*); Richard Hunt (*Del*); Lisa Waltz (*Holly*); Ron Fassler (*Mitchell*).

7549   *Pure Insanity*. (Pilot; Game; Fox; Aug. 11, 1990). Eight contestants compete in a series of crazy and outlandish events with the object being to outperform one another. Winners receive a grand prize of $15,000 ($2500 of which they must donate to a local hometown charity).

Hosts: David Alan Grier, Alan Hunter.

7550   *The Purex Special for Women*. (Series; Anthology; NBC; 1960-1961). Sympathetic dramatizations based on the problems faced by women. Following the drama, a brief discussion is held with a guest doctor or psychiatrist. Sponsored by Purex and also knows as *Special for Women*.

Host: Pauline Fredericks.

7551   *Pursue and Destroy*. (Pilot; Drama; ABC; Aug. 14, 1966). The South Pacific during World War II is the setting for a proposal about the officers and crew of a U.S. Naval submarine commanded by Russ Enright.

Cast: Van Williams (*Cmdr. Russ Enright*); Paul Comi (*Lt. Barney Redesko*); David Thorpe (*Lt. James Ford*); Ward Wood (*Chief Alex Jacobs*); Dee Pollack (*Chip Malloy*).

7552   *Pursuit*. (Series; Anthology; CBS; 1958-1959). Tense dramas that depict the plight of people being pursued by others. The pilot film, "The Lady Died at Midnight," aired on Feb. 23, 1958 and told the tale of a convicted murderer (Earl Holliman) who vows to break out of prison and get even with those responsible for his capture.

7553 The Pursuit of Happiness. (Series; Comedy; ABC; 1988). John Marshall University in Philadelphia is a prestigious college where the world-renowned history professor, Roland G. Duncan teaches. David Hanley is a footloose idealist. After years of traveling across the U.S. David decides to settle down in Philadelphia. David has a teaching degree in history but never really pursued a career. Now, with time on his hands, David applies for the position of assistant professor to the distinguished Roland Duncan. Stories follow David as he tries to implement aspects of his travels into his classes — and change Roland from a stuff shirt to a free spirit (or as much of a free spirit he can instill in a man who is positively set in his ways). Other regulars are Sara Duncan, Roland's daughter; Margaret Callahan, an assistant history professor; Ms. Lopez, Roland's secretary; Veronica Morris, David's friend; and Professors Gruber and Stevens.

Cast: Brian Keith (*Roland G. Duncan*); Paul Provenza (*David Hanley*); Judie Aronson (*Sara Duncan*); Wendel Meldrum (*Margaret Callahan*); Wesley Thompson (*Vernon Morris*); Mary Farrell (*Professor Gruber*); John Petlock (*Professor Stevens*); Wanda DeJesus (*Ms. Lopez*).
Theme Vocal: "The Pursuit of Happiness" by Mendy Lee.

7554 The Pursuit of Happiness. (Series; Comedy; NBC; 1995). Steve Rutledge and Alex Chosek are partners in the Chicago-based law firm of Rutledge and Chosek. The partners have divided the work — Steve handles innocent people; Alex "handles everything else." Steve also teaches physics at Roosevelt University and feels he was born under a ladder or that a black cat crossed his path because bad luck seems to follow him around like a shadow. Alex thinks it's all in Steve's head but Steve can't shake his unfortunate streak and stories focus in particular on Steve as he struggles to cope with life despite the constant mishaps that plague him. Other regulars are Mackenzie, Steve's wife; Jean, the office secretary; Larry, Mackenzie's brother; and Steve's Grandmother.

Cast: Tom Amandes (*Steve Rutledge*); Melinda McGraw (*Mackenzie Rutledge*); Brad Garrett (*Alex Chosek*); Meredith Scott Lynn (*Jean Mathias*); Larry Miller (*Larry*); Maxine Stuart (*Steve's Grandmother*).

7555 Push, Nevada. (Series; Mystery; ABC; 2002). Push is a small Nevada gambling town. It has only 1,000 residents but pays out the biggest jackpots in the state. It is also filled with corruption — namely casino boss Silas.

In Washington, D.C., IRS agent Jim Prufrock receives a fax (perhaps by mistake), which is a spreadsheet for a skimming scam. Was the fax a mistake? Was it intended? A mystery begins and also involves the viewing audience. The series is interactive (as long as you have a computer) and presents clues to the whereabouts of the missing million dollars. As Jim arrives in Push, he begins his investigation. Clues will lead Jim — and viewers to the whereabouts of the million dollars. The program, however, is so complex that it requires watching every second of every episode. The idea sounds good but the slow moving story coupled with difficult to follow clues led ABC to cancel it after seven episodes (it was scheduled to run 13 episodes with the viewer who solved the puzzle winning the missing money). Mary Sloman is the mysterious woman Jim meets at a dance bar called Slomans; Darlene Prufrock is Jim's wife.

Cast: Derek Cecil (*Jim Prufrock*); Jon Polito (*Silas*); Scarlett Chorvat (*Mary Sloman*); Abby Brammell (*Darlene Prufrock*).

7556 Pushed. (Series; Drama; Internet; 2009). London is a successful model and appears to have the ideal life. She is married to Kurt (who appears very loving) and has an equally "loving" sister, Sasha. London is also very wealthy as she inherited her mother's estate when she became of age. London, however, is not as innocent as she appears. As a kid, she appears to have killed her mother (pushed her off a hiking trail) but was never convicted. The incident still proves troubling for London and she is seeing a psychiatrist (Dr. Rosen). Unknown to London, Kurt has secretly bugged their home to watch her every move. Sasha is more deceitful than she appears and both are seeking to acquire London's wealth. Although short (about three minutes each) episodes relate in soap opera–like fashion, London's efforts to overcome the inner demons that are threatening to destroy her life.

Cast: Veronica Taylor (*London*); Mark Matkevich (*Kurt*); Holland Roden (*Sasha*); Catherine Hicks (*Dr. Rosen*); Scott Seymour (*Zip*); Kimberly Horner (*Jennifer*); Molly Culver (*Katherine*).

7557 Pushing Daisies. (Series; Drama; ABC; 2007–2009). As a youngster growing up in Cour Couers, Ned lived a mostly carefree life. He enjoyed running in the fields with his dog Digby and, at the age of nine, he had a crush on his next-door neighbor, eight-year-old Charlotte Charles, whom he called "Chuck."

One day, when Digby is hit by a truck, Ned's life changes forever. He touches the dog and, to his surprise, brings him back to life. But his special gift — which Ned has no way of explaining, also has a serious side effect. A second touch will return the deceased back to being dead. And, if Ned keeps a deceased alive for longer than sixty seconds, someone else must die to take his or her place.

As Ned grows, he becomes fearful of his "gift" and becomes somewhat of a loner. He eventually becomes a baker and establishes his own business — The Pie Hole.

One night, while chasing a suspect, private detective Emerson Cod witness Ned's gift when the suspect falls off a building roof, dies and returns to life when Ned touches him. When Ned sees Cod pursuing the culprit, he touches the culprit and returns him to being dead. Cod finds Ned very useful and the two form a business partnership — Ned can touch a victim, bring him back to life, ask him who killed him, touch him again then solve the case. All is progressing well for Ned until he hears a news bulletin about a young woman being killed aboard a cruise ship and being dumped into the ocean. When authorities recover her body and her name is revealed — Charlotte Charles, Chuck makes it his business to restore her life to find out who killed her. But Ned violates his own rule and lets Chuck live — a situation that finds Ned, who still loves Chuck, never able to touch her and she never able to touch him. With Cod's help, Ned and Chuck find Chuck's killer (someone who mistook her for a diamond smuggler). The three become a team to solve murders by asking the victims to identify their killers. Lily and Vivian are Chuck's aunts.

Cast: Lee Pace (*Ned*); Anna Friel (*Charlotte "Chuck" Charles*); Chi McBride (*Emerson Cod*); Swoosie Kurtz (*Chuck's Aunt Lily*); Ellen Greene (*Chuck's Aunt Vivian*); Kristin Chenoweth (*Olive Snook*); Jim Dale (*Narrator*); Field Carter (*Young Ned*).

7558 Pushing Twilight. (Series; Drama; Internet; 2008). Reality-like program in which a group of disenchanted young people dare each other to complete a series of tasks that cause them to go places and accomplish feats they never thought they were capable of doing.

Cast: D.C. Douglas (*Host*); Adam Edgar (*Mason Marks*); Jamie Anderson (*Layla Marks*); Jonathan Beran (*Dominic Moss*); Daniel Robaine (*Jacob Wright*); Eric Emmanuel (*Cole Edwards*); Jackie Seldan (*Avery Ward*); Lacy Phillips (*Madison Price*); Makinna Ridgeway (*Paige Gray*).

7559 The Pussycat Dolls Present Girlicious. (Series; Reality; CW; 2008). A spin-off from *The Pussycat Dolls Present the Search for the Next Doll* that finds Pussycat Dolls creator Robin Antin seeking three special girls for a new group to be called Girlicious. Girlicious is similar to the Pussycat Dolls — sexy singers and dancers "but with their own funky style; a sense of girl power with a twist." Fifteen talented girls, chosen from open auditions, are brought to Los Angeles where they not only live together but compete against each other for the top three spots. Each week the girls compete in specific song and dance numbers (either in groups or solos) with the weakest performers being eliminated by Robin and her team of judges. The three girls who prove themselves in song, dance, movement and personality become Girlicious. The final episode changed the concept that had originally been established when the judges, faced with four very talented girls (Natalie Mejia, Tiffanie Anderson, Nichole Cordova and Chrystina Sayers) in the final elimination chose to make Girlicious a four girl group instead of the original three. Girlicious performed a song from their first album "Like Me" to close out the series.

Host: Mark McGrath. **Judges:** Robin Antin, Kimberly "Lil Kim" Jones, Ron Fair.

7560   *The Pussycat Dolls Present: The Search for the Next Doll.* (Series; Reality; CW; 2007). Pussycat Dolls are a successful all-girl singing group whose premiere album, "PCD," sold over five million copies. It also produced five hit singles. The six-girl group (originally scantily clad) sang at a Los Angeles club before recording their first album. The group, created by Robin Antin, is now seeking a seventh girl — and the program gives one girl the chance of a lifetime — to become a Pussycat Doll. Nine finalists, chosen from open auditions all over the country, compete on a weekly basis by performing songs and/or dances (together or alone). One girl is eliminated each week with three remaining hopefuls appearing on the last show. Two of these girls are eliminated and the remaining girl becomes a Pussycat Doll. The girls are judged by a panel of three: Robin Antin, Ron Fair (chairman of Geffen Records) and lead Pussycat singer Nicole Scherzinger. Asia, Chelsea and Melissa R (as identified) were the three finalists. Asia was selected as the new Pussycat Doll.

Host: Mark McGrath. **Judges:** Robin Antin, Ron Fair, Nicole Scherzinger.

7561   *Puttin' on the Hits.* (Series; Contest; Syn.; 1984). The program spotlights ordinary people as they mimic their favorite performers. Prizes are awarded to the best performers on each show.

Host: Alan Fawcett. **Theme Music:** "Puttin' on the Hits" by David Russo.

7562   *Putting on the Kids.* (Series; Contest; Syn.; 1986). A juvenile version of *Putting on the Hits* in which kids (aged 6 to 12) pantomime recordings of famous songs. Acts, judged on originality, lip-sync and performances are scored from 1 to 100 with the highest scoring performer receiving a $500 savings bond.

Host: Michael Young.

7563   *The Puzzle Game.* (Pilot; Game; Unaired; Produced for CBS in 1989). Two teams of related people (for example, husband and wife, cousins) compete. The object calls for each team to identify video puzzles in return for cash (with the highest scoring team winning).

Host: Jim Lange.

7564   *Puzzle Quest.* (Series; Children; Nick; 1994–1996). Hosts Julie Woo and Skye Nakaiye host a program wherein puppets of different ethnic backgrounds meet at the Puzzle Place to play games, tell stories, learn how to get along, communicate and just hang out to have a good time.

Cast: Alice Dinnean, Dionne Quon (*Julie Woo*); Peter Linz , Candi Milo (*Skye Nakaiye*); Noel MacNeal, Alanna Ubach (*Leon MacNeal*);

Jim Martin, Jason Marsden (*Ben Olafson*); Alison Mork, Dee Bradley Baker (*Jody Silver*); Carmen Osbahr, Carlos Alazraqui (*Kiki Flores*).

7565   *Pyramid.* (Series; Game; Syn.; 2002–2004). A revised version of what originally began as *The $10,000 Pyramid* (but was also revised as *The $20,000 Pyramid*, *The $25,000 Pyramid* and *The $100,000 Pyramid*). A pyramid with six subject categories is displayed on stage. Two teams compete. One member of one team selects a category and a topic is revealed (for example, "As Time Goes By"). The host reads the question associated with it ("Describe these things associate with time") and the player must relate one word clues to each of the six words contained in the category. Three such rounds are played with the highest scoring team receiving a chance to play the Pyramid. Six subjects are displayed (each worth a different money amount). The player facing the pyramid relates one-word clues to the identity of each subject to his partner. If all six are guessed, the non-celebrity player wins $10,000 and a chance to compete again and again face the pyramid (this time for and additional $15,000) by guessing all six categories. If not, the player wins what money is represented by the categories he identifies.

Host: Donny Osmond. **Announcer:** John Cramer.

7566   *Q.E.D.* (Series; Game; ABC; 1951). The object calls for a celebrity panel to solve mystery stories that are submitted by members of the viewing audience. The host relays the facts, and panelists each receive one guess. If the mystery remains unsolved, the sender receives a merchandise prize. Also known as *Mystery File*.

Host: Fred Uttal, Doug Browning. **Regular Panelists:** Nina Foch, Hy Brown.

7567   *Q.E.D.* (Series; Adventure; CBS; 1982). Constantly mocked as a fool for his ingenious inventions, Quentin E. Deverill, an American science professor at Harvard, resigns in mid-semester to pursue his own private research. Stories, set in London, England in 1912, relate Deverill's exploits as an amateur sleuth and slightly eccentric inventor. Other regulars are Betsy, his assistant; Charlie, the reporter for the International Wireless Telegraph Service; Phipps, Quentin's right hand man; Jenny, Quentin's secretary; and Dr. Stephen Kilkiss, the evil German scientist bent on destroying the world.

Cast: Sam Waterson (*Quentin E. Deverill*); Sarah Berger (*Betsy Stevens*); A.C. Weary (*Charlie Andrews*); George Innes (*Phipps*); Carolyn Langrishe (*Jenny Martin*); Julian Glover (*Dr. Stephen Kilkiss*).

7568   *Q.T. Hush.* (Series; Cartoon; Syn.; 1960). Q.T. Hush is a fumbling private detective who solves crimes purely by accident. He is assisted by Shamus, his dog, and Quincy, his shadow, who can operate independently of him.

Voice Cast: Dallas McKennon (*Q.T. Hush*).

7569   *Quack Pack.* (Series; Cartoon; ABC; 1996-1997). An update of the series *Duck Tales* that presents the nephews of Donald Duck, Huey, Dewey and Louie as teenagers who do what teenagers do best — causing countless headaches for their uncle with their antics (and the easily exasperated Donald's efforts to cope with them). Donald's girlfriend, Daisy Duck, is seen here as a TV reporter (for a show called *What in the World*).

Voice Cast: Tony Anselmo (*Donald Duck*); Kath Soucie, April Winchell (*Daisy Duck*); Jeannie Elias (*Huey Duck*); Pamela Adlon (*Dewey Duck*); Elizabeth Daily (*Louie Duck*); Tim Curry (*Moltoc*); Pat Fraley (*Gwumpki*).

7570   *Quadrangle.* (Series; Variety; CBS; 1949). A college campus is the setting for a twice weekly program of music and songs that is also known as *Campus Corner*.

Host: Beverly Fite. **Regulars:** Frank Stevens, Burt Taylor, Dean Campbell, Bob Burkhardt, Claire Granville, Ray Kirschner.

7571   *Quail Lake.* (Pilot; Drama; NBC; May 18, 1977). William Stone, the widowed father of two children (Margaret and Michael) is a fire captain who transfers from the city to the wilds of Pine Canyon, California, as the operator of a one-man fire rescue station on Quail Lake to enable him to be with his kids during the day while at work and at night. The proposal, also known as *Pine Canyon Is Burning* was to relate Stone's experiences. Anne is the school teacher and William's romantic interest; Ed is a retired fire captain who also lives in the canyon.

Cast: Kent McCord (*William Stone*); Megan McCord (*Margaret Stone*); Shane Sinutko (*Michael Stone*); Brit Lind (*Anne Walker*); Andrew Duggan (*Ed Wilson*).

7572   *Quantum Leap.* (Series; Science Fiction; NBC; 1989–1993). Quantum Leap is a secret government project concerned with time travel (it is hidden in the desert 30 miles outside the town of Destiny County, New Mexico). When the government threatens to cut off its funding, quantum physics professor Dr. Samuel ("Sam") Beckett takes matters into his own hands and attempts to prove that a man can be sent into time. Sam steps into the unit's acceleration chamber and vanishes. He is sent back into time and can travel (leap) only within 30 years of his own lifetime, beginning in 1953 (when he was born); however, a system malfunction traps Sam in time — where he is destined to remain until he can be retrieved. Through brainwave transmissions, Sam receives the holographic assistance of Al Calavicci, an admiral who is a project observer (and who can be seen and heard only by Sam).

While bouncing around in time, Sam assumes the identities of people he never knew to correct a mistake they made and set history straight (that is, according to what a computer named Ziggy deems it should be). The audience sees Sam in the various roles — but other people see the person Sam has become (when Sam looks into a mirror, he sees the person whose identity he has assumed; this person is transported to the "Waiting Room" at the Quantum Leap complex). When a mission has been completed, Sam is propelled (leaps) into another time period and the person — man or woman — is restored to his or her normal self. (Dogs, certain children and mentally unstable people can also see Al.)

Al, who carries a slightly defective miniature Ziggy (his hand link to the computer), has known Sam for many years. Al was born on June 15, 1945, and grew up in an orphanage. He ran away from the orphanage to join a circus and later enlisted in the navy. In 1969 Al married a girl named Beth (Susan Diol), the only girl, he says, he really loved. Al was next sent to Vietnam (at which time he began smoking cigars). He was later reported as missing in action and was assumed dead. When he was found in 1973 Beth had remarried, and Al never returned to her.

Sam was born and raised on a farm in Elkridge, Indiana. He built Ziggy as a parallel hybrid computer to run Quantum Leap. Sam gave Ziggy, which has a billion gigabyte capacity, Barbra Streisand's ego ("In my lab, Ziggy has a female voice"). Al's hologram is sent through time via the Imaging Chamber. Sam's romantic interest was a girl named Donna Alisi (Teri Hatcher and Mimi Kuzyk), a fellow scientist he worked with on the Star Bright Project in 1972. Sam's catchphrase is "Oh, boy" (which he says when he discovers who he has become or something goes wrong).

Program Open: "Dr. Sam Beckett stepped into the Quantum Leap accelerator. He finds himself trapped in the past, facing mirror images of his own self and driven by an unknown force to make history for the better. His only guide on this journey is Al, an observer from his own time in the form of a hologram that only Sam can see

and hear. And so Dr. Beckett finds himself leaping from life to life striving to make right what once was wrong, hoping that each time he leaps he will be the last."

Cast: Scott Bakula (*Sam Beckett*); Dean Stockwell (*Al Calavicci*).

7573   *Quark.* (Series; Comedy; NBC; 1978). It is A.D. 2226 and the voyages of a U.G.S.P. (United Galaxy Sanitation Patrol) garbage ship as it patrols the deep regions of space picking up the trash of the planets of the United Galaxies are depicted.

Adam Quark is the ship's commander. "I myself am just an ordinary human, descended from planet Earth.... My ancestors were members of a subgroup called Americans."

Betty I and Betty II hold the joint position of second in command. "One of them is a clone," Adam says, "an artificial, laboratory created identical twin of the other. I'm extremely fond of Betty — if I only knew which Betty it is that I am extremely fond of." Both Bettys, blonde bombshells, are also in love with Adam, and each says she is the real Betty (the clone Betty was made from a cell taken from under the fingernail of the real Betty). In the pilot episode, the twins playing the role were credited as Tricia and Cibbie Barnett (the same actresses as in the series, only with shorter hair in the pilot).

Jean/Gene is the ship's chief engineer. She/he is a transmute and possesses a full set of female and male chromosomes. Jean/Gene unpredictably switches genders (via voice and actions; she/he always appears physically as a male), depending on the situations the ship encounters.

Ficus Panderato is the chief science officer. He is a plant in human form from the planet Vegeton. He has a logical mind and finds humor against his nature.

Andy is a cowardly Servo Mechanical Android that Adam built and is still trying to perfect. Andy is primitively designed (a square Plexiglass head and a rectangular metal body), and the Load Control Box is his "girlfriend." In the pilot episode, Andy was created by O.B. Mudd (Douglas V. Fowley), an eminent scientist who was the ship's research and equipment specialist.

Dr. Otto Robert Palindrome is the always harassed superintendent and chief of Perma Base One, the base of the U.G.S.P. The Head, distinguished by a very large forehead and apparently no body, is commander-in-chief of U.G.S.P. and "wrote a book on headaches."

Interface is a beautiful four handed girl who serves as an intergalactic telephone operator (one must contact Interface in order to speak to the Head). The pilot aired on May 7, 1977.

Cast: Richard Benjamin (*Adam Quark*); Tricia Barnstable (*Betty I*); Cyb Barnstable (*Betty II*); Tim Thomerson (*Jean/Gene*); Richard Kelton (*Ficus*); Conrad Janis (*Otto Palindrome*); Alan Caillou (*The Head*); Bobby Porter (*Andy*); Misty Rowe (*Interface*).

7574   *Quarterlife.* (Series; Drama; Internet; 2007). Dylan Krieger is an editor who not only works for a magazine but produces an Internet video blog called *quarterlife.com* — a site through which she presents insightful incidents in the lives of her friends (most notably Danny, Lisa, Debra and Andy). Web stories relate those posted incidents. Quarterlife.com is also a real web site that is a social networking service that allows members of the creative community to express their talents. See also the following title.

Cast: Bitsie Tulloch (*Dylan Krieger*); Maite Schwartz (*Lisa*); David Walton (*Danny*); Michelle Lombardo (*Debra*); Kevin Christy (*Andy*); Lolita Davidovich (*Mindy Krieger*); Barrett Swatek (*Brittany*); Barbara Williams (*Maggie*); Jill E. Alexander (*Mary*); Bree Turner (*Carly*).

7575   *Quarterlife.* (Series; Drama; NBC; 2008). A network adaptation of the Internet series (prior title) that focuses on the lives of a group of friends who are in their twenties. Principal focus is on Dylan Krieger, a writer for *Attitude* magazine who relates her feelings about herself and her friends on the Internet blog site *Quarterlife*.

Dylan feels she is cursed — "I can see what people are thinking, what they want to say but can't." These thoughts are seen by the viewer through Dylan's blogs. Lisa, Ted, Danny, Debra and Andy are Dylan's friends.

Lisa, a bartender, "has party girl syndrome," says Dylan. Lisa is also hoping to become an actress but her acting teacher feels she lacks talent (or, as he says, "She thinks her beauty can get her anything"). Danny and Jed are TV commercial producers; Debra is Danny's girlfriend (although Jed is secretly in love with her); Brittany works with Dylan.

The program was cancelled the same night it premiered (Feb. 26, 2008). Had it continued (six episodes were produced) serial-like stories would have followed the young adults as they faced the daily challenges of life.

Cast: Bitsie Tulloch (*Dylan Krieger*); Maite Schwartz (*Lisa*); Scott Michael Foster (*Jed Burlin*); David Walton (*Danny Franklin*); Michelle Lombardo (*Debra*); Kevin Christy (*Andy*); Barrett Swatek (*Brittany*).

7576   The Queen and I. (Series; Comedy; CBS; 1969). Duffy is the first mate of *The Amsterdam Queen*, an old and decrepit ocean liner (docked at New York Harbor). The ship has seen better times and its owners have decided to send her to the scrap yards. Duffy is a master schemes and sees the ship as a paradise for his money-making ventures. His efforts to save the ship are the focal point of stories. Oliver Nelson is the first officer; Wilma Winslow is Duffy's love interest; the ship's captain is Washburn; Commodore Dodds owns the ship; and members of Duffy's crew are Becker, Ozzie, Max and Barney.

Cast: Larry Storch (*Duffy*); Billy DeWolfe (*Oliver Nelson*); Liam Dunn (*Captain Washburn*); Reginald Owen (*Commodore Dodds*); Barbara Stuart (*Wilma Winslow*); Carl Ballantine (*Becker*); Dave Willock (*Ozzie*); Dave Morick (*Max Kowalski*); Pat Morita (*Barney*).

7577   Queen Bees. (Series; Reality; Nick; 2008). Teenage girls who epitomize meanness are brought together in an attempt to change their attitudes and become nice to others. Each of the girls competes in a series of challenges and the one girl who changes for the best wins $25,000 for her school. Dr. Michelle R. Callahan hosts. Gisabelle Castillo, Yoanna House, Kiana Jenkins, Shavon Jovi, Brittany Keiffer, Camille Lopez, Michelle Madonna and Stassi Schroeder are the Queen Bees.

7578   Queen for a Day. (Series; Contest; NBC; ABC; Syn.; 1956; 1970). Four women appear on stage and bare their souls to the studio audience, stating their single most needed object. Through electronic voting machines, the audience selects the one woman they feel is the most needy. The woman is crowned "Queen for a Day" and receives, in addition to the sought article, various merchandise prizes.

1957 Program Open: "Once again from Hollywood's great Moulin Rogue Theater Restaurant, Hartz Mountain, the pet products for happier, healthier pets, proudly presents *Queen for a Day*, the Cinderella show starring the king of Queen for a Day, Mr. Jack Bailey." Two versions appeared:

1. Queen for a Day (NBC, 1956–60; ABC, 1960–64). **Host:** Jack Bailey. **Assistant:** Jeanne Cagney. **Announcer:** Gene Baker (NBC), John Harlan (ABC).

2. Queen for a Day (Syn., 1970). **Host:** Dick Curtis. **Assistant:** Nancy Myers. **Announcer:** Carl King.

7579   Queen of Clubs. (Series; Erotica; Playboy; 2004). A striptease competition in which gorgeous women bare all and compete

for the title of "Queen of Clubs." Contestants chosen for their obvious attributes, participate in various challenges (mostly how to be alluring and sexy while disrobing) with the one girl showing how to take it off and maintain an aura of sexuality that does not become vulgar, winning the competition. The hosts are joined by celebrity guests to judge the competition.

Hosts: Crystal Knight, Gloria Velez.

7580   The Queen of Swords. (Series; Adventure; Syn.; 2000–2001). Santa Helena is a small town in Old California (1817) that is ruled by Luise Rivera Montoya, a corrupt and evil military colonel who is seeking to become the law of the land. Dona Maria Teresa Alvarado is a young woman living in Madrid, Spain, when she receives word that her father, Don Alvarado, has been killed in a fall from a horse (in actuality, he has been shot by the soldiers of Montoya for resisting arrest).

A short time later, Dona Maria Teresa, called Tessa, and her servant, Marta arrive in Santa Helena to find the once glorious Alvarado mansion in shambles and about to be repossessed by Montoya for unpaid back taxes. Unable to pay the taxes and not believing her father, an expert horseman, died accidentally, Tessa decides to remain and avenge his death. The answer as to how comes one night when Tessa receives a ghostly visit from her father. He tells her that his "Avenging Angel will make things right." As they speak, Don Alvarado tells Tessa to find the Santa Rita, a rare bottle of wine in the cellar. As Tessa searches, she finds the bottle of wine and pulls it from the rack. A secret door opens to reveal gold and other treasures her father hid from Montoya. Tessa also finds a sword ("My father was saving it for a son he never had") and devises a way to avenge her father's death. She dons a lacy black mask, tight black blouse and pants (with a red scarf around her waist) and a calling card — the Queen of Swords (taken from the tarot deck of cards). Although Tessa battles the evils of Montoya, she is branded a villain.

The town's padre believes the Queen is "a miracle of God for all the good she does." Colonel Montoya calls the Queen "an evil spirit who threatens the very destiny of the whole public." He also believes that the Queen is no ordinary woman. "She has a good heart. And when I catch her I'll keep it in a jar on my desk." Tessa's dual identity is known only to Marta. When not helping the people of Santa Helena as the Queen, Tessa appears as an aristocrat who has returned to her homeland to take over the family estate (which she does when she pays Montoya the back taxes). As the Queen, Tessa rides a brown horse she calls Chico.

Montoya's captain, Marcus Grisham is the man who killed Tessa's father, but Tessa cannot prove it. Grisham was apparently in the U.S. Army and dishonorably discharged (he is wanted for murder and fraud). He somehow hooked up with Montoya and has been his right hand man ever since. Montoya has made it Grisham's job "to get the Queen of Swords or I'll have your head instead of hers." Marta, who looks out for Tessa, is a psychic and reads Tarot cards. Jose Feliciano sings the theme, "Behind the Mask."

Cast: Tessie Santiago (*Tessa Alvarado*); Valentine Pelka (*Luise Rivera Montoya*); Anthony Lemke (*Marcus Grisham*); Paulina Galvez (*Marta*).

7581   The Queen Was in the Kitchen. (Experimental; Comedy-Drama; DuMont; Jan. 30, 1945). The American Central Manufacturing Company (makers of American Kitchens) sponsored a program designed to show housewives what kitchens will look like in the future (following World War II). Skits, narration and film shorts were used to convey the message that the kitchen is the busiest place in the house.

Host-Narrator: Allen Prescott. **Cast:** David Kerman, Abby Lewis, Dick Monahan, Woody Parker, Amy Sidell, Leonard Sherer, Arnold Stang.

7582   Queens Supreme. (Series; Drama; CBS; 2003). Jack Moran is a Judge at the Queens Supreme Court in New York. He is described as smart, clever, a problem solver "and he's a 12-year-old kid at times." Jack is not your normal judge. He does what he wants, does not follow the rules (he does, however, just manage to stay within the limits of the law) and eavesdrops on his juries (through the vent system). He carries a gun in a shoulder holster and will do outrageous things in his courtroom to prove his point. The unique but short-lived program (three episodes) allows viewers to eavesdrop on Jack's rather unpredictable courtroom proceedings.

Jack is married to Maude (maiden name McPherson). They have been together for 11 years and she is seeking a divorce. Maude is a lawyer, designs clothes (she has her own clothing line) and lives apart from Jack in a loft in SoHo. Cameron is Jack's law assistant (she knows law cases by heart and can recite any case asked of her). Mike is Jack's law clerk.

Cast: Oliver Platt (*Judge Jack Moran*); Robert Loggia (*Judge Thomas O'Neill*); Annabella Sciorra (*Judge Kim Vicidomini*); L. Scott Caldwell (*Judge Rose Barnes*); James Madio (*Mike Powell*); Mary Harrill (*Cameron Hull*); Kristen Johnston (*Maude Moran*).

7583   Queer as Folk. (Series; Drama; Showtime; 2000–2005). The lives of a group of gay men (Brian, Justin, Ted, Michael, Blake and Emmett) and lesbians (Deborah, Lindsay, Daphne and Jennifer) living in Pittsburgh, Pennsylvania. Stories, based on the British series of the same title, relate the problems each encounters and how they overcome their difficulties.

Cast: Dean Armstrong (*Blake Wyzecki*); Gale Harold (*Brian Kinney*); Randy Harrison (*Justin Taylor*); Scott Lowell (*Theodore "Ted" Schmidt*); Peter Paige (*Emmett Honeycutt*); Thea Gill (*Lindsay "Linz" Peterson*); Sharon Gless (*Deborah Jane Grassi Novotny*); Sherry Miller (*Jennifer Taylor*); Makyla Smith (*Daphne Chanders*); Harris Allan (*James Montgomery*); Robert Gant (*Ben Bruckner-Novotny*); Chris Potter (*Dr. David Cameron*); Jack Wetherall (*Vic Grassi*).

7584   Queer Eye for the Straight Girl. (Series; Reality; Bravo; 2005). A spin off from *Queer Eye for the Straight Guy.* Here a team of four gay men, all stylists, take ordinary Los Angeles women and give them a complete makeover "to impress and inspire." The stylists are Honey Labrador, Robbie Loughlin, Damon Pease and Danny Teeson.

7585   Queer Eye for the Straight Guy. (Series; Reality; Bravo; 2003). Five men, each of whom is gay, and each with a special talent, set out to do complete makeovers on straight men. Carson Kressley is a fashion expert; Jai Rodriquez is a "culture vulture"; Ted Allen is a food and wine connoisseur; Kyan Douglas is a grooming professional; and Thomas Filicia is a "design doctor." See also *Queer Eye for the Straight Girl.*

7586   The Quest. (Series; Western; NBC; 1976). A wagon train traveling across the prairie is attacked by Cheyenne Indians. Young Morgan Baudine and his sister are captured and taken by separate tribes. Eight years later, the Army frees Morgan, who has the Indian name Two Persons. Learning that his sister is still reputed to be living with the Cheyenne, Morgan begins a search to find her. By chance he meets Quentin, his long-lost brother (who was raised by an aunt in San Francisco), who has also begun a search to find Patricia. Reunited by a common goal, they begin a hazardous quest to find their sister. Stories concern their adventures as they travel throughout the rugged west of the last quarter of the 19th century.

Program Open: "The legend of the Baudine brothers. This is their story. This is *The Quest.*"

Cast: Kurt Russell (*Morgan Baudine*); Tim Matheson (*Quentin Baudine*).

7587   The Quest. (Series; Adventure; ABC; 1982). When it is realized that Charles Phillipe, the aging king of Glendora, a small European monarchy, is the last of his line, and that the kingdom, now under British domain, will revert back to French rule, a special search is begun to find an heir. Four Americans are summoned to the mythical Glendora: Dan Underwood, a photojournalist; Carrie Welby, a New York department store shoe buyer; Art Henley, a retired, young-at-heart cop from Wilko, Kansas; and Cody Johnson, a confidence man. Each is found to possess royal blood and to be a descendant from Glendora's royal family. In a last-ditch attempt to save Glendora from becoming a French possession, a special quest is enacted to find a new king — or queen — to the throne.

Based on a 13th century tradition, the quest is a race that is held to find the most worthy, noble and valorous person to become ruler. Jeopardizing their quest is Louie Dardinay, an exiled Glendora Count who seeks to regain his title by making sure no one is crowned and Glendora reverts back to the French. Stories relate the adventures of Dan, Carrie, Art and Cody as they reluctantly work as a team — to complete the quest and defeat Dardinay. The series ran for 5 episodes with no conclusion. Sir Edward Vallier is the quest overseer.

Cast: Perry King (*Dan Underwood*); Karen Austin (*Caroline "Carrie" Welby*); Noah Beery, Jr. (*Art Henley*); Ray Vitte (*Cody Johnson*); Michael Billington (*Louie Dardinay*); John Rhys Davies (*Sir Edward Vallier*); Ralph Michael (*Charles Phillipe*). **Theme Vocal:** "Kings and Queens" by Lisa Lee.

7588   Quick and Quiet. (Pilot; Comedy; CBS; Aug. 18, 1981). Elliott Cooper is a gambler and ne'er-do-well who inherits Quick and Quiet, a Los Angeles–based detective agency owned by his late father, T.C. Cooper, a disreputable private eye. When Elliott begins ransacking the office looking for some sort of inheritance with which to pay off his gambling debts, T.C.'s ghost appears to Elliott on a mission to help him walk the straight and narrow and become a productive citizen. The proposal was to relate the investigations of a reluctant detective and his ghostly partner as they attempt to solve mysteries. Camille is Elliott's secretary.

Cast: William Windom (*T.C. Cooper*); Rick Lohman (*Elliott Cooper*); Millie Slavin (*Camille*).

7589   Quick As a Flash. (Series; Game; ABC; 1953-1954). Two teams compete, each composed of two members. A specially prepared film sequence that describes a person, place or event is played. The first player to identify himself through a flashing light signal (which is activated by pressing a button), receives a chance to answer. If he identifies the subject, he receives one point; if he fails, he and his partner are disqualified from that particular round. The opposing team then views the entire film and is allowed one free guess. The winners, the highest point scorers, receive merchandise prizes.

Host: Bobby Sherwood, Clayton "Bud" Collyer. **Regulars:** Jimmy Nelson, Faye Emerson.

7590   The Quick Draw McGraw Show. (Series; Cartoon; Syn.; 1959). The overall title for three animated segments:

1. Quick Draw McGraw. Quick Draw McGraw, a dim-witted horse, and his deputy Baba Looey, the burro, struggle to maintain law and order in New Mexico.

2. Snooper and Blabber. Snooper the cat and Blabber the mouse team to battle crime.

3. Augie Doggie and Doggie Daddy. A father's efforts to control his potentially juvenile delinquent son.

Voice Cast: Daws Butler (*Quick Draw McGraw/Baba Looey/Snooper/Blabber/Augie Doggie*); Doug Young (*Doggie Daddy*).

7591   *Quick on the Draw.* (Series; Game; DuMont; 1952). The object calls for contestants to identify phrases that are suggested by a series of cartoon drawings. Aired locally in New York (from 1950–1952) with Eloise McElhone as the host. The DuMont version ran from Jan. 8 to Dec. 9, 1952.

Hostess: Robin Chandler. **Artist:** Bob Dunn.

7592   *Quiller.* (Pilot; Adventure; ABC; 1975). Quiller, as he is known, is an intelligence officer (secret agent) for the British Government. He is assisted by a girl named Rosalind and their efforts to resolve complex international incidents were the focal point of the proposal. Angus Kinloch is their superior and two pilots were produced: *Quiller: Price of Violence* (Dec. 3, 1975, wherein they safeguard a doctor being sought by a killer) and *Quiller: Night of the Father* (Dec. 10, 1975, wherein Quiller and Rosalind probe the death of a fellow agent).

Cast: Michael Jayston (*Quiller*); Sinead Cusack (*Rosalind*); Moray Watson (*Angus Kinloch*).

7593   *Quincy, M.E.* (Series; Crime Drama; NBC; 1976–1983). Dr. Quincy is a medical examiner with the mind of a detective. He works for the Los Angeles County Coroner's Office and believes in investigating for himself the circumstances surrounding a victim of crime.

Quincy was a surgeon before becoming a pathologist; his specialty is now forensic pathology. He lives on a boat docked at the Marina Del Ray "which I'm thinking of selling and moving into the lab" where he spends a great deal of time. Quincy has no first name; people refer to him as Quincy or Dr. Quincy. A camera shot of his I.D. card revealed that his first name has the initial R. Quincy refuses police protection when working on a case. He is stubborn and will not back down. His 17 years experience as a medical examiner has made him confident in his findings "and I will risk my reputation on my findings."

When the series begins, Quincy is a widower. He and his first wife, Helen (Anita Gillette in flashbacks), honeymooned at Lake Tahoe. She called him Quince. Helen dreamed of having children — four boys and three girls — but Quincy, who had just started to practice, wanted to wait until they were more financially secure. He was afraid children would deny him his commitment to medicine. Helen died from a brain tumor before she could realize her dream. Quincy's second wife, Emily Hanover (Anita Gillette) was a doctor Quincy married in the episode of Feb. 23, 1983. There was no mention of the fact that Emily was a dead ringer for Helen and she too apparently never knew his first name as she called him Honey, Quince and Quincy. Helen appeared in the episode of Mar.1979 ("Promises to Keep"); Emily was introduced in the episode of Sept. 29, 1982 ("Rattlesnakes").

Robert Astin is Quincy's superior, the assistant deputy coroner. Dr. Sam Fugiyama assists Quincy. Danny Tovo owns the local bar hangout, Danny's Place. Frank Monihan is a lieutenant with the Homicide Division of the L.A.P.D. Lee Potter was Quincy's girlfriend in first season episodes. She is also the bikini-clad girl seen sharing a drink with Quincy on his boat in the opening theme. Robin is Astin's secretary; Johnny is a bartender at Danny's; Diane is a waitress; Ernie is the lab photographer.

Cast: Jack Klugman (*Dr. R. Quincy*); Lynnette Mettey (*Lee Potter*); Anita Gillette (*Dr. Emily Hanover/Helen Quincy*); John S. Ragin (*Dr. Robert Astin*); Robert Ito (*Dr. Sam Fugiyama*); Garry Walberg (*Lt. Frank Monihan*); Val Bisoglio (*Danny Tovo*); Joseph S. Roman (*Sergeant Brill*); Karen Philipp (*Robin*); Aimee Eccles (*Dr. Alice Ting*); Marc Scott Taylor (*Marc; a pathologist*); Diane Markoff (*Diane*); Johnny Nolan (*Johnny*); Eddie Garrett (*Eddie*); Diana Muldaur (*Dr. Janet Carlisle*).

7594   *Quintuplets.* (Series; Comedy; Fox; 2004). Bob and Carol Chase are a happily married couple who live at 3 Barrington Drive in Nutley, New Jersey. They are also the parents of 15-year-old quintuplets: Paige, Penny, Parker, Pearce and Patton. Bob and Carol received a lot of attention but it was Carol who became the neighborhood celebrity — "People waved at me and called me 'The Mom of the Quints.'"

Paige is a beautiful blonde who is also a bit dense. She (and her siblings) attend North Nutley High School. If Paige knew what a sexpot was she would be one. She dresses to be alluring but doesn't realize how much damage she does when boys see her. Her expertise seems to be applying makeup and claims: "I have great hair and personality."

Penny is very smart and says, "I accomplish things by science — it can't be explained." Penny is rather self-centered, loves to read, is shrewd, cunning and rather proud of herself when she manipulates someone to accomplish something. Her goal is to become a Broadway show director and is the only quint that wears glasses. She has an anger issue when she gets mad.

Pearce is the weird child. He has a high-pitched voice and seems to live in a world of his own (he functions in the real world but everything must make sense to him). He is opposed to violence of any kind and talking to Pearce "is like trying to nail Jell-O to a tree stump."

Parker considers himself to be a hunk and a ladies' man. He is on the school's basketball team and can't stand rejection.

Patton is the shortest of the siblings. He is constantly teased for this but tries not to let it bother him. He tries to hit on any girl he sees and honestly thinks he is "a cool dude."

Cast: Andy Richter (*Bob Chase*); Rebecca Creskoff (*Carol Chase*); Sara Wright (*Paige Chase*); April Matson (*Penny Chase*); Jake McDorman (*Parker Chase*); Johnny Lewis (*Pearce Chase*); Ryan Pinkston (*Patton Chase*).

7595   *The Quiz Kids.* (Series; Game; DuMont; NBC; Syn. CBS Cable; 1945–1980). The program, based on the radio series, is set in a schoolroom where the host, dressed in a cap and gown, asks some rather difficult questions of four very bright children. Four versions appeared:

1. The Quiz Kids (DuMont Pilot, Mar. 6, 1945). **Quizmaster:** Joe Kelly.

2. The Quiz Kids (NBC, 1949–52; CBS, 1953; 1956). **Quizmaster:** Joe Kelly, Clifton Fadiman.

3. The Quiz Kids (Syn., 1980). **Quizmaster:** Jim McKrell. **Announcer:** Michael Adams.

4. The Quiz Kids (CBS Cable, 1981). **Host:** Norman Lear.

7596   *Quiz Kids Challenge.* (Series; Game; Syn.; 1990). Two three-member teams compete: the kids vs. the adults. A board with several categories is revealed. One player selects a category and a question is read. The first team player to sound a bell signal receives a chance to answer. If the player is correct money is scored. The player with the last correct response chooses the next category. The game continues in this manner and the team with the highest score is the winner.

Host: Jonathan Prince. **Announcer:** Johnny Gilbert.

7597   *Quizzing the News.* (Series; Game; ABC; 1948-1949). The object calls for a panel to identify news events through a series of three cartoon drawings, which are presented to them one at a time.

Host: Allen Prescott. **Panelists:** Arthur Q. Bryan, Mary Hunter, Ray Joseph, Milton Caniff. **Artist:** Albee Treider.